HOWARD THE DUCK

THE COMPLETE COLLECTION VOL. 3

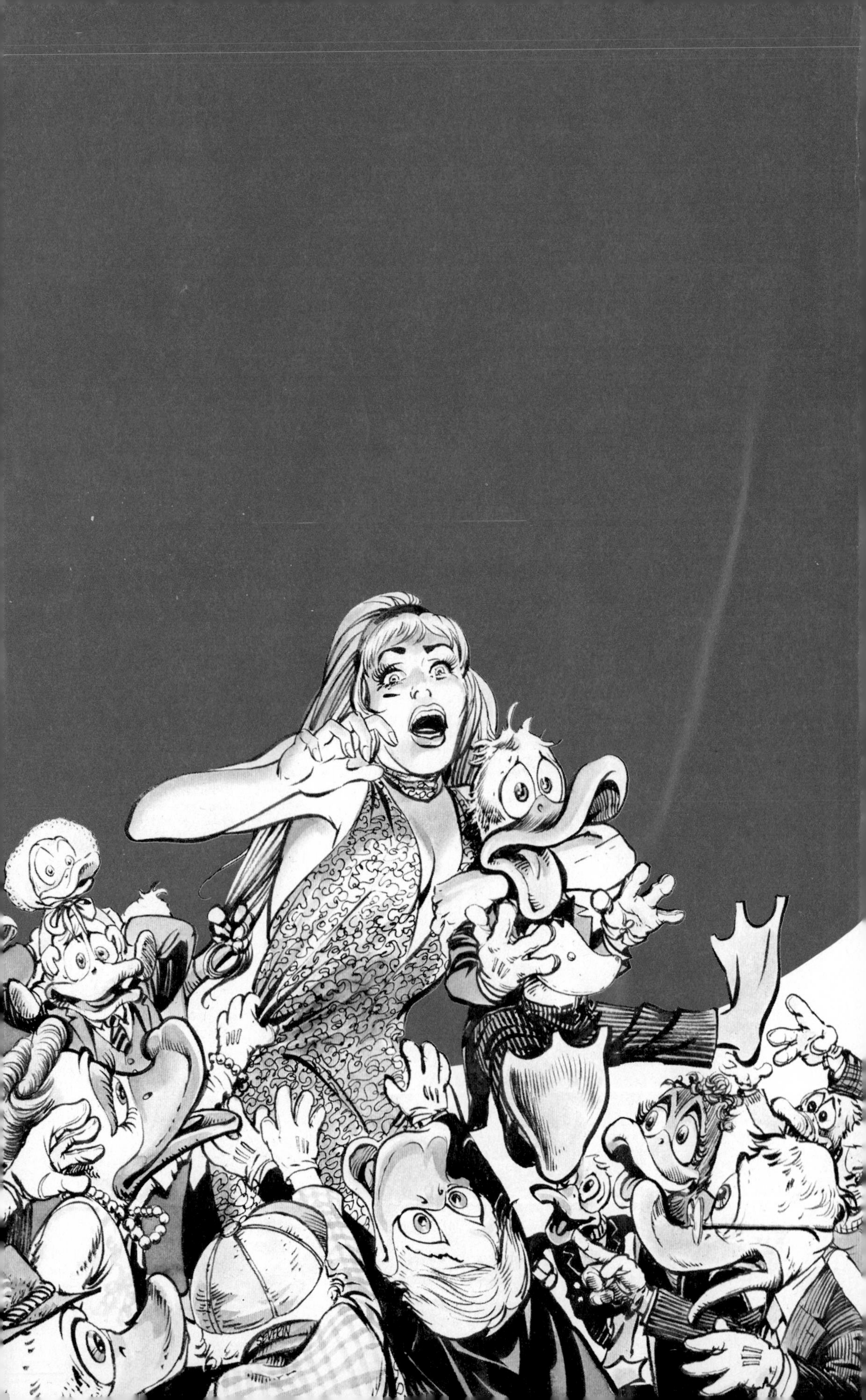

HOWARD THE DUCK

WRITERS:
Bill Mantlo with Mark Gruenwald,
Lynn Graeme, Michael Weiss & Roger Stern

PENCILERS:
Gene Colan, John Buscema & Michael Golden with Jerry Bingham,
Marie Severin, Ned Sonntag, Vicente Alcazar, Pat Broderick & co.

INKERS:
Klaus Janson, Dave Simons & Bob McLeod with Josef Rubinstein, Marie Severin,
Ned Sonntag, Alfredo Alcala, Tom Palmer, Vicente Alcazar, Armando Gil & co.

LETTERERS:
Irv Watanabe, Jim Novak,
Michael Higgins, Tom Orzechowski,
Joe Rosen & Mark Rogan with Ned Sonntag

ASSISTANT EDITOR:
Mark Gruenwald

ASSOCIATE EDITOR:
Ralph Macchio

CONSULTING EDITOR:
Roy Thomas

EDITORS:
Rick Marschall & Lynn Graeme

COVER ARTIST:
John Pound

Howard the Duck created by Steve Gerber & Val Mayerik

COLLECTION EDITOR: Mark D. Beazley
ASSOCIATE EDITOR: Sarah Brunstad
ASSOCIATE MANAGER, DIGITAL ASSETS: Joe Hochstein
ASSOCIATE MANAGING EDITOR: Alex Starbuck
EDITOR, SPECIAL PROJECTS: Jennifer Grünwald
VP, PRODUCTION & SPECIAL PROJECTS: Jeff Youngquist
RESEARCH: Mike Hansen
LAYOUT: Jeph York
PRODUCTION: ColorTek & Joe Frontirre
BOOK DESIGNER: Adam Del Re
SVP PRINT, SALES & MARKETING: David Gabriel

EDITOR IN CHIEF: Axel Alonso
CHIEF CREATIVE OFFICER: Joe Quesada
PUBLISHER: Dan Buckley
EXECUTIVE PRODUCER: Alan Fine

Special Thanks to Gary Henderson & Dana Perkins

HOWARD THE DUCK: THE COMPLETE COLLECTION VOL. 3. Contains material originally published in magazine form as HOWARD THE DUCK MAGAZINE #2-7. First printing 2016. ISBN# 978-1-302-90204-9. Published by MARVEL WORLDWIDE, INC., a subsidiary of MARVEL ENTERTAINMENT, LLC. OFFICE OF PUBLICATION: 135 West 50th Street, New York, NY 10020. Copyright © 2016 MARVEL No similarity between any of the names, characters, persons, and/or institutions in this magazine with those of any living or dead person or institution is intended, and any such similarity which may exist is purely coincidental. **Printed in the U.S.A.** ALAN FINE, President, Marvel Entertainment; DAN BUCKLEY, President, TV, Publishing & Brand Management; JOE QUESADA, Chief Creative Officer; TOM BREVOORT, SVP of Publishing; DAVID BOGART, SVP of Business Affairs & Operations, Publishing & Partnership; C.B. CEBULSKI, VP of Brand Management & Development, Asia; DAVID GABRIEL, SVP of Sales & Marketing, Publishing; JEFF YOUNGQUIST, VP of Production & Special Projects; DAN CARR, Executive Director of Publishing Technology; ALEX MORALES, Director of Publishing Operations; SUSAN CRESPI, Production Manager; STAN LEE, Chairman Emeritus. For information regarding advertising in Marvel Comics or on Marvel.com, please contact Vit DeBellis, Integrated Sales Manager, at vdebellis@marvel.com. For Marvel subscription inquiries, please call 888-511-5480. Manufactured between 5/20/2016 and 7/4/2016 by R.R. DONNELLEY, INC., SALEM, VA, USA.

10 9 8 7 6 5 4 3 2 1

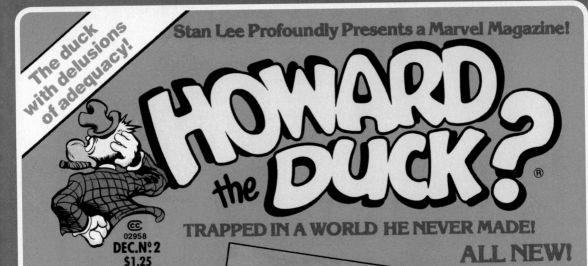

The duck with delusions of adequacy!

Stan Lee Profoundly Presents a Marvel Magazine!

HOWARD the DUCK? ®

TRAPPED IN A WORLD HE NEVER MADE!

ALL NEW!

02958
DEC. Nº 2
$1.25

See Howard battle the forces of evil thru the power of massive mediocrity!

*

A FIGHT TO THE FINISH-- OR AT LEAST THE HALF-WAY MARK--IN THE DREAD REALM OF THE DIGITAL DIMENSION!

*

ALSO:
A web-footed review of HOWARD's spotted past!

*

ALSO:
Putting the pants on HOWARD!

WARNING: THE SURGEON-GENERAL HAS DE-TERMINED THAT NOT BUYING THIS BOOK MAY BE DANGEROUS TO YOUR HEALTH.

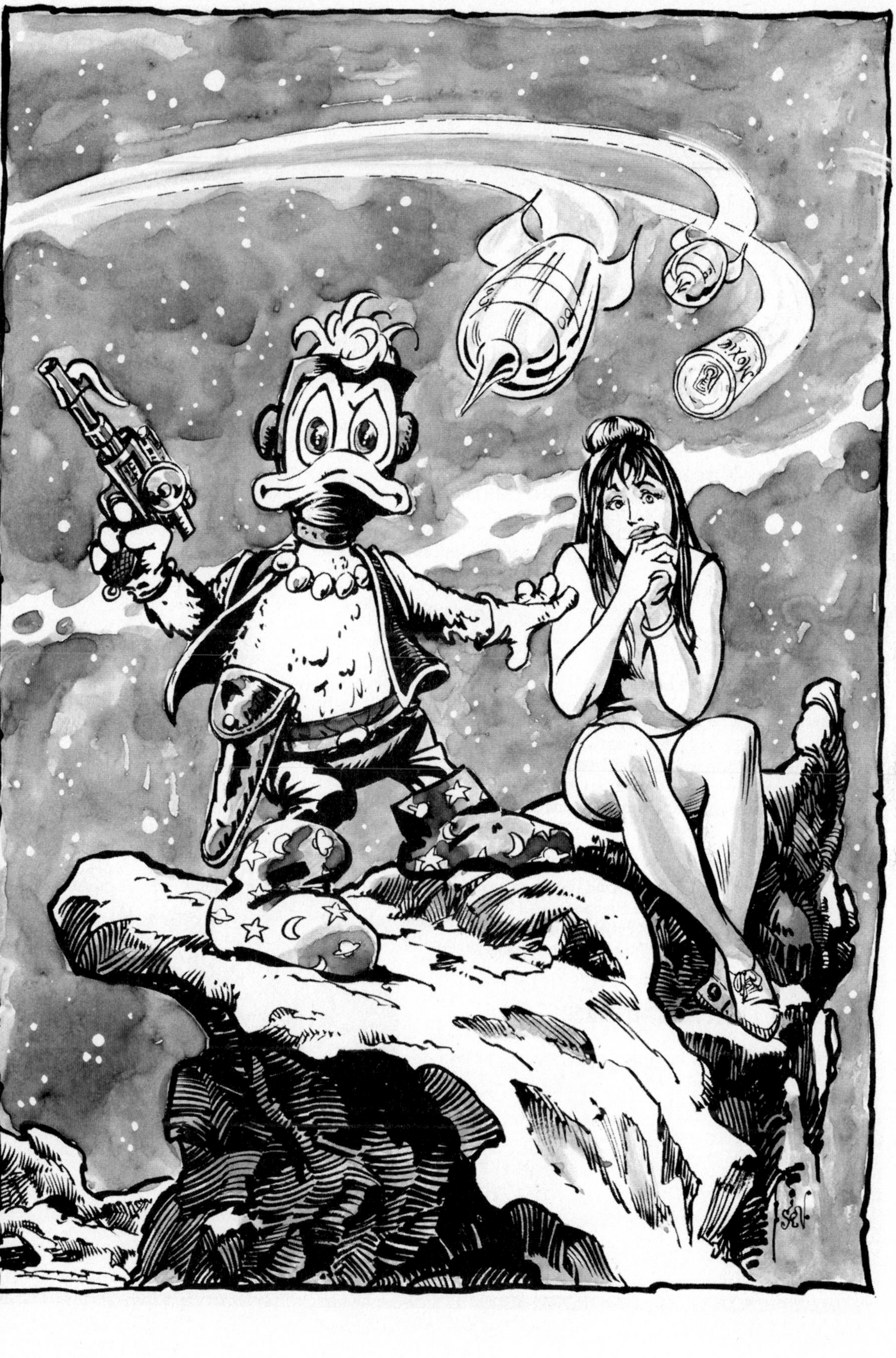

STAN LEE Presents:

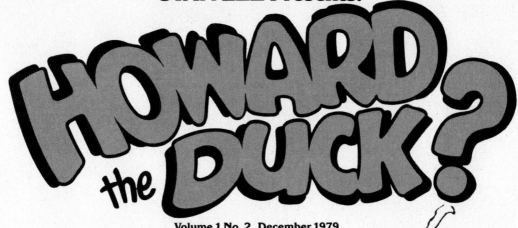

HOWARD the DUCK?

Volume 1 No. 2 December 1979

JIM SHOOTER Editor-in-Chief • **RICK MARSCHALL** Editor • **RALPH MACCHIO** Associate Editor
MARK GRUENWALD Insulting Editor • **ROY THOMAS** Consulting Editor • **MILT SCHIFFMAN** V.P. Production
NORA MACLIN Design Director • **IRV WATANABE, JIM NOVAK** Letterers
PETER LEDGER, DAVIDA LICHTER-DALE, ED NORTON, ELIOT BROWN Staff & Such • **MARIE SEVERIN**
Frontispiece • **VAL MAYERIK** Cover

CONTENTS

FEATURES

A far-out foray into fashion as we get a tailored glimpse at what the well-dressed duck will deign to be seen in next year. Updates to appear in Mallard's Quarterly. By **Bill Mantlo, Gene Colan,** and **Klaus Janson.**

In a mad financial universe beyond recession, Howard the Duck and his beloved Bev are swept into the deadly digital designs of the fiscal fiend—Pro Rata, Cosmic Accountant! By **Bill Mantlo, Gene Colan** and **Dave Simons.**

DEPARTMENTS

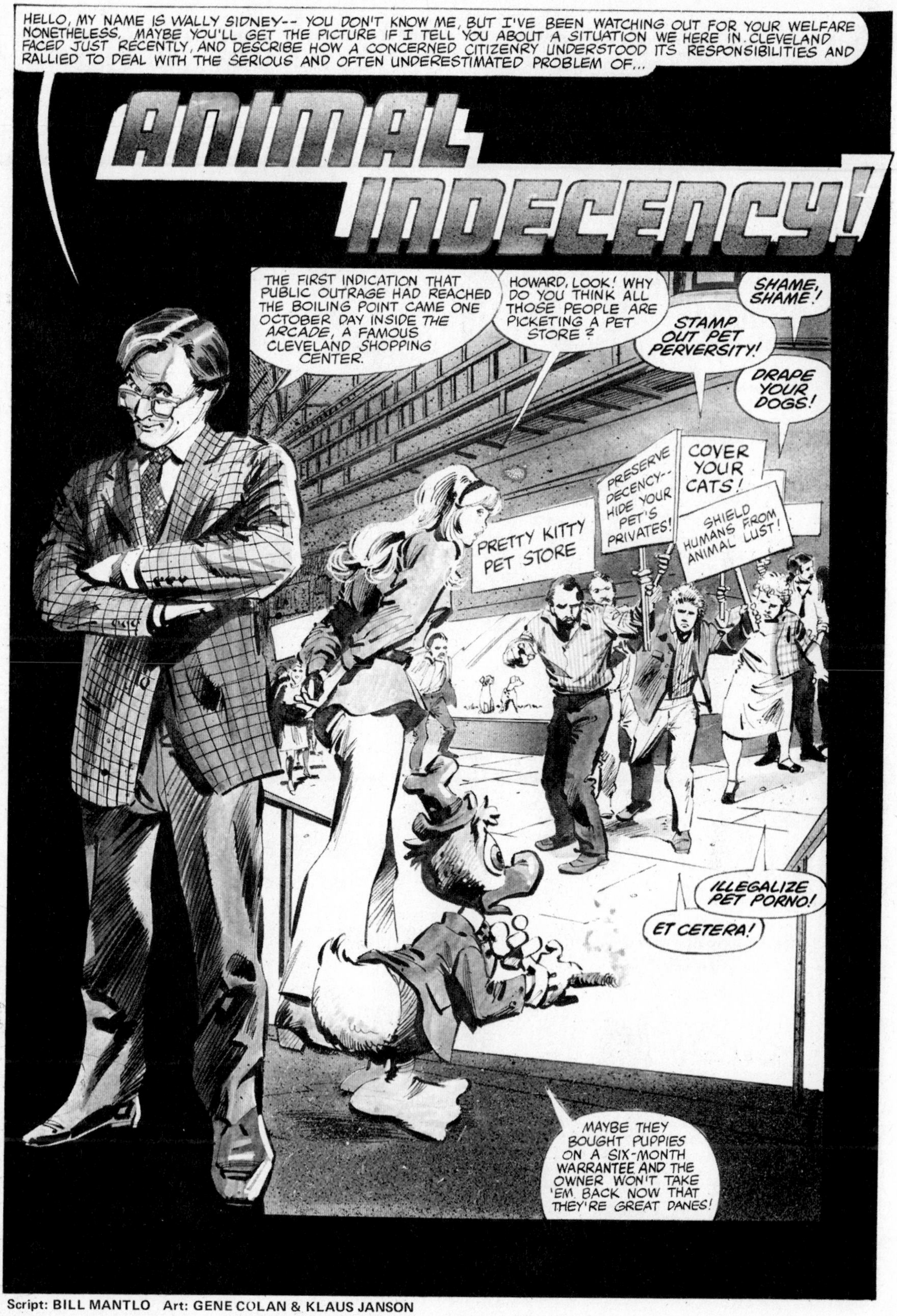
HELLO, MY NAME IS WALLY SIDNEY-- YOU DON'T KNOW ME, BUT I'VE BEEN WATCHING OUT FOR YOUR WELFARE NONETHELESS. MAYBE YOU'LL GET THE PICTURE IF I TELL YOU ABOUT A SITUATION WE HERE IN CLEVELAND FACED JUST RECENTLY, AND DESCRIBE HOW A CONCERNED CITIZENRY UNDERSTOOD ITS RESPONSIBILITIES AND RALLIED TO DEAL WITH THE SERIOUS AND OFTEN UNDERESTIMATED PROBLEM OF...
ANIMAL INDECENCY!
THE FIRST INDICATION THAT PUBLIC OUTRAGE HAD REACHED THE BOILING POINT CAME ONE OCTOBER DAY INSIDE THE ARCADE, A FAMOUS CLEVELAND SHOPPING CENTER.
HOWARD, LOOK! WHY DO YOU THINK ALL THOSE PEOPLE ARE PICKETING A PET STORE?
SHAME, SHAME!
STAMP OUT PET PERVERSITY!
DRAPE YOUR DOGS!
PRESERVE DECENCY-- HIDE YOUR PET'S PRIVATES!
COVER YOUR CATS!
SHIELD HUMANS FROM ANIMAL LUST!
PRETTY KITTY PET STORE
ILLEGALIZE PET PORNO!
ET CETERA!
MAYBE THEY BOUGHT PUPPIES ON A SIX-MONTH WARRANTEE AND THE OWNER WON'T TAKE 'EM BACK NOW THAT THEY'RE GREAT DANES!

Script: BILL MANTLO Art: GENE COLAN & KLAUS JANSON

"THE 'DEMONSTRATION FOR DECENCY' WAS WELL UNDERWAY BY THE TIME THE DUCK ARRIVED..."

HEY, LADY! WHAT GIVES? SOMEBODY FIND OUT THIS PET STORE KILLS WHALES ON THE SIDE?

INDEED NOT! WE ARE HERE TO PROTEST THE CONTINUED INDECENCY THAT ALLOWS ANIMALS TO APPEAR UNCLOTHED IN PUBLIC! WE--

--MY WORD! YOU-YOU'RE A DUCK, AREN'T YOU?

SHIRLEY'S FAINTED! WHAT'S GOING ON HERE?

A NAKED DUCK?!? EEEEEEEEE!

LOOK! A DUCK!

HOWARD, WHAT DID YOU DO?

UNDRAPED! SCANDALOUS! IT-IT TALKS!

SHORT OF EXISTING, TOOTS? SEARCH ME!

"THAT IS HOW I FIRST CAME TO SET EYES ON THE DUCK, THE SUDDEN SILENCE ON THE PART OF THE PROTESTERS DRAWING ME TO THE WINDOW OF MY CLOTHING STORE IN THE ARCADE."

AH! A TEST OF THE DECENCY COMMITTEE'S RESOLVE IF EVER THERE WAS ONE!

"I WAS NOT YET READY TO INTERVENE IN PERSON...SO I MERELY WATCHED...AND WAITED."

LET ME GET THIS STRAIGHT...

I'LL TELL YOU! THESE PEOPLE ARE SICK, BUT I CAN'T FIGHT THEM ANYMORE! THEIR BOYCOTT HAS HURT MY SALES! I-I'VE GOT TO GIVE IN!

PETS WITHOUT CLOTHES ARE LIKE RA...

GIVE IN TO THESE BOZOS? WHY, LADY? WHAT IS IT THEY WANT FROM YA?

SOB! DECENCY! THEIR WARPED IDEA OF IT, ANYWAY! YOU KNOW THEIR TYPE! FIRST THEY LEGISLATE THE KIND OF CLOTHING PEOPLE MUST WEAR...

...THEN THEY PASS LAWS, IN THE NAME OF THE PUBLIC DECENCY, DEMANDING THAT PETS BE PANOPLIED AS WELL!

AWNK

WHINE

MEEOW

ARE

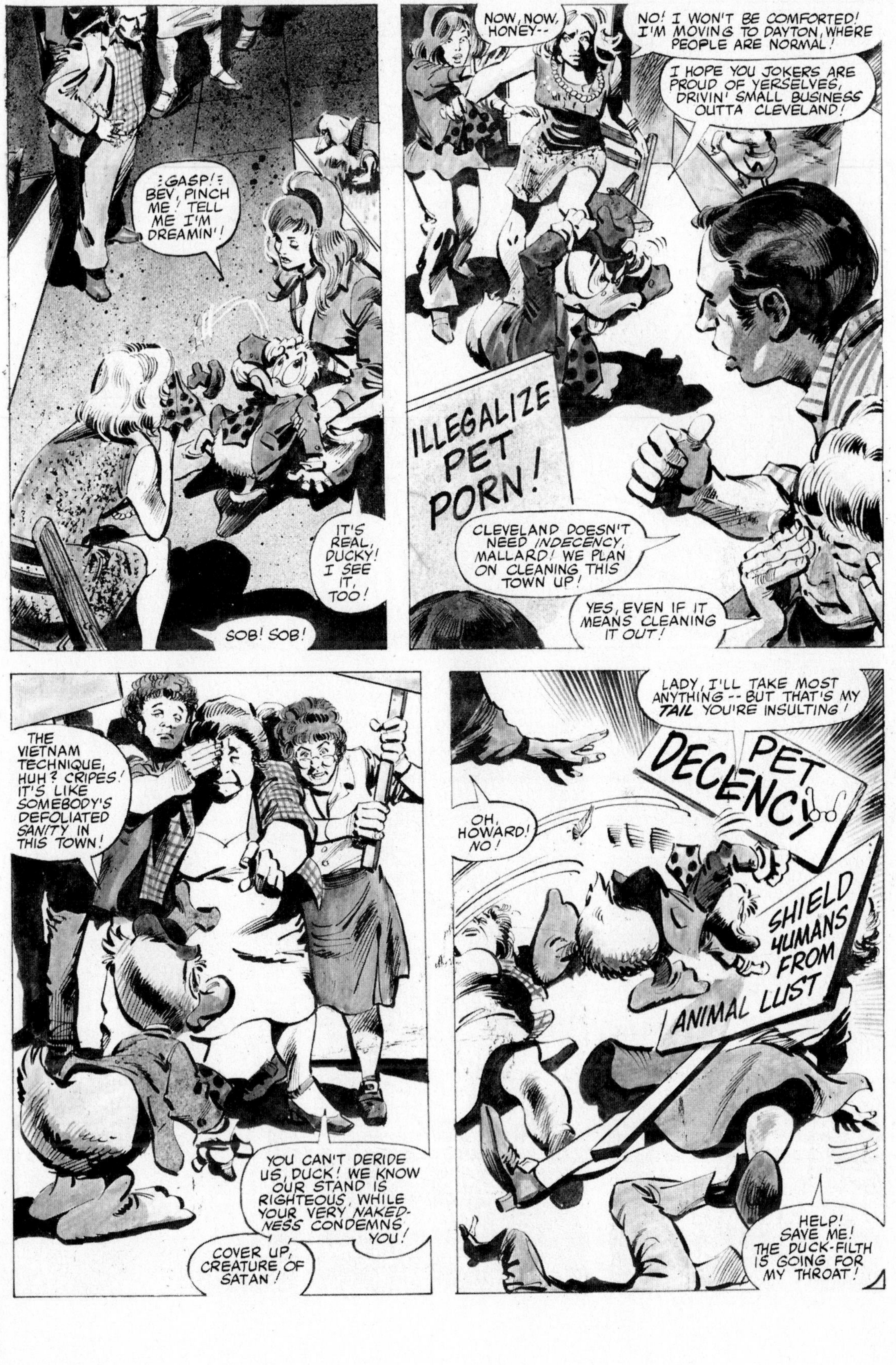

GASP! BEV, PINCH ME! TELL ME I'M DREAMIN'!
IT'S REAL, DUCKY! I SEE IT, TOO!
SOB! SOB!
NOW, NOW, HONEY--
NO! I WON'T BE COMFORTED! I'M MOVING TO DAYTON, WHERE PEOPLE ARE NORMAL!
I HOPE YOU JOKERS ARE PROUD OF YERSELVES, DRIVIN' SMALL BUSINESS OUTTA CLEVELAND!
ILLEGALIZE PET PORN!
CLEVELAND DOESN'T NEED INDECENCY, MALLARD! WE PLAN ON CLEANING THIS TOWN UP!
YES, EVEN IF IT MEANS CLEANING IT OUT!
THE VIETNAM TECHNIQUE, HUH? CRIPES! IT'S LIKE SOMEBODY'S DEFOLIATED SANITY IN THIS TOWN!
YOU CAN'T DERIDE US, DUCK! WE KNOW OUR STAND IS RIGHTEOUS, WHILE YOUR VERY NAKEDNESS CONDEMNS YOU!
COVER UP, CREATURE OF SATAN!
LADY, I'LL TAKE MOST ANYTHING -- BUT THAT'S MY TAIL YOU'RE INSULTING!
PET DECENCY!
OH, HOWARD! NO!
SHIELD HUMANS FROM ANIMAL LUST
HELP! SAVE ME! THE DUCK-FILTH IS GOING FOR MY THROAT!

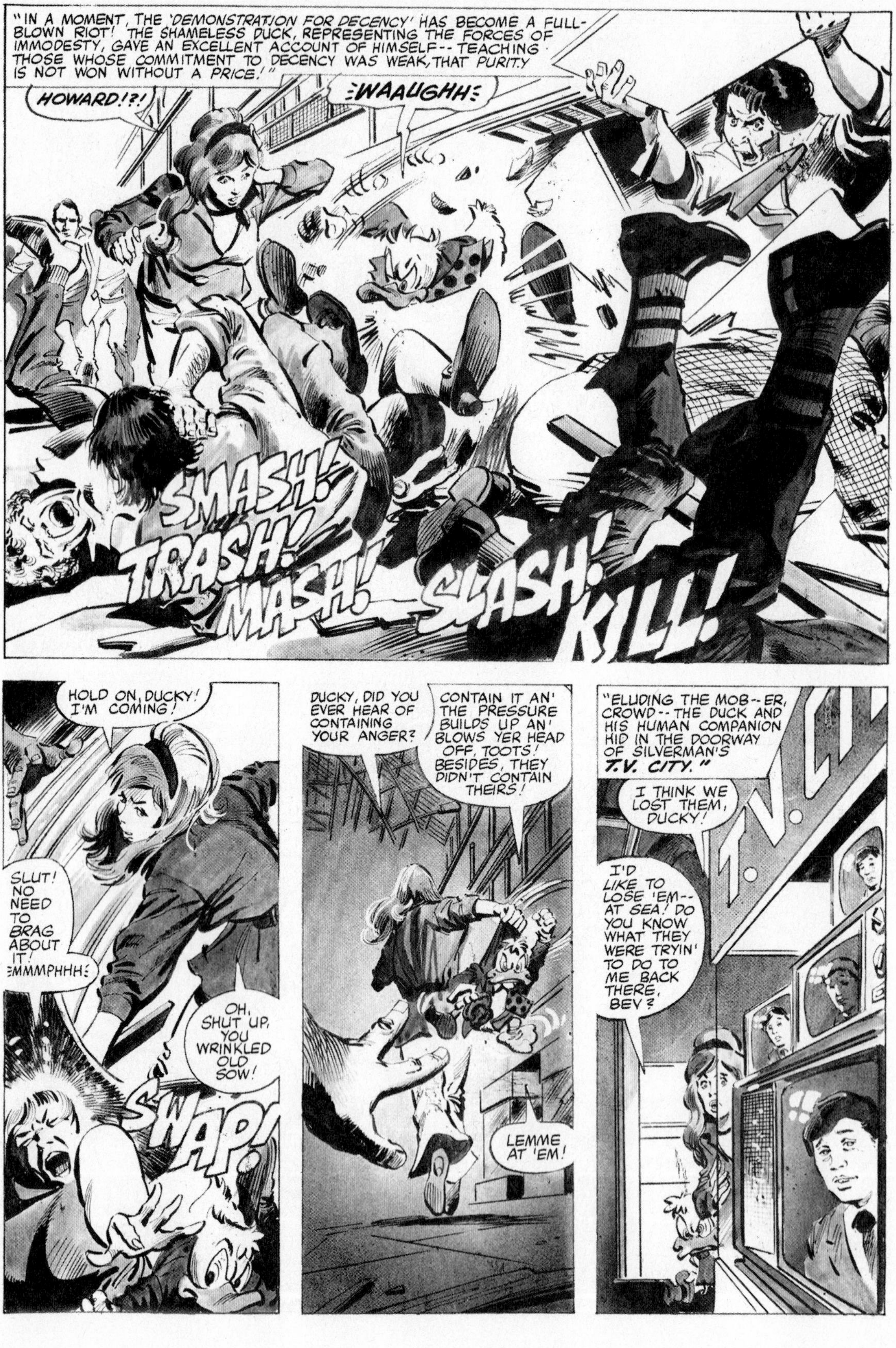
"IN A MOMENT, THE 'DEMONSTRATION FOR DECENCY' HAS BECOME A FULL-BLOWN RIOT! THE SHAMELESS DUCK, REPRESENTING THE FORCES OF IMMODESTY, GAVE AN EXCELLENT ACCOUNT OF HIMSELF -- TEACHING THOSE WHOSE COMMITMENT TO DECENCY WAS WEAK, THAT PURITY IS NOT WON WITHOUT A PRICE!"
HOWARD!?!
WAAUGHH
SMASH! TRASH! MASH! SLASH! KILL!
HOLD ON, DUCKY! I'M COMING!
SLUT! NO NEED TO BRAG ABOUT IT! EMMMPHHH!
OH, SHUT UP, YOU WRINKLED OLD SOW!
SWAP!
DUCKY, DID YOU EVER HEAR OF CONTAINING YOUR ANGER?
CONTAIN IT AN' THE PRESSURE BUILDS UP AN' BLOWS YER HEAD OFF, TOOTS! BESIDES, THEY DIDN'T CONTAIN THEIRS!
LEMME AT 'EM!
"ELUDING THE MOB -- ER, CROWD -- THE DUCK AND HIS HUMAN COMPANION HID IN THE DOORWAY OF SILVERMAN'S T.V. CITY."
I THINK WE LOST THEM, DUCKY!
I'D LIKE TO LOSE 'EM -- AT SEA! DO YOU KNOW WHAT THEY WERE TRYIN' TO DO TO ME BACK THERE, BEV?

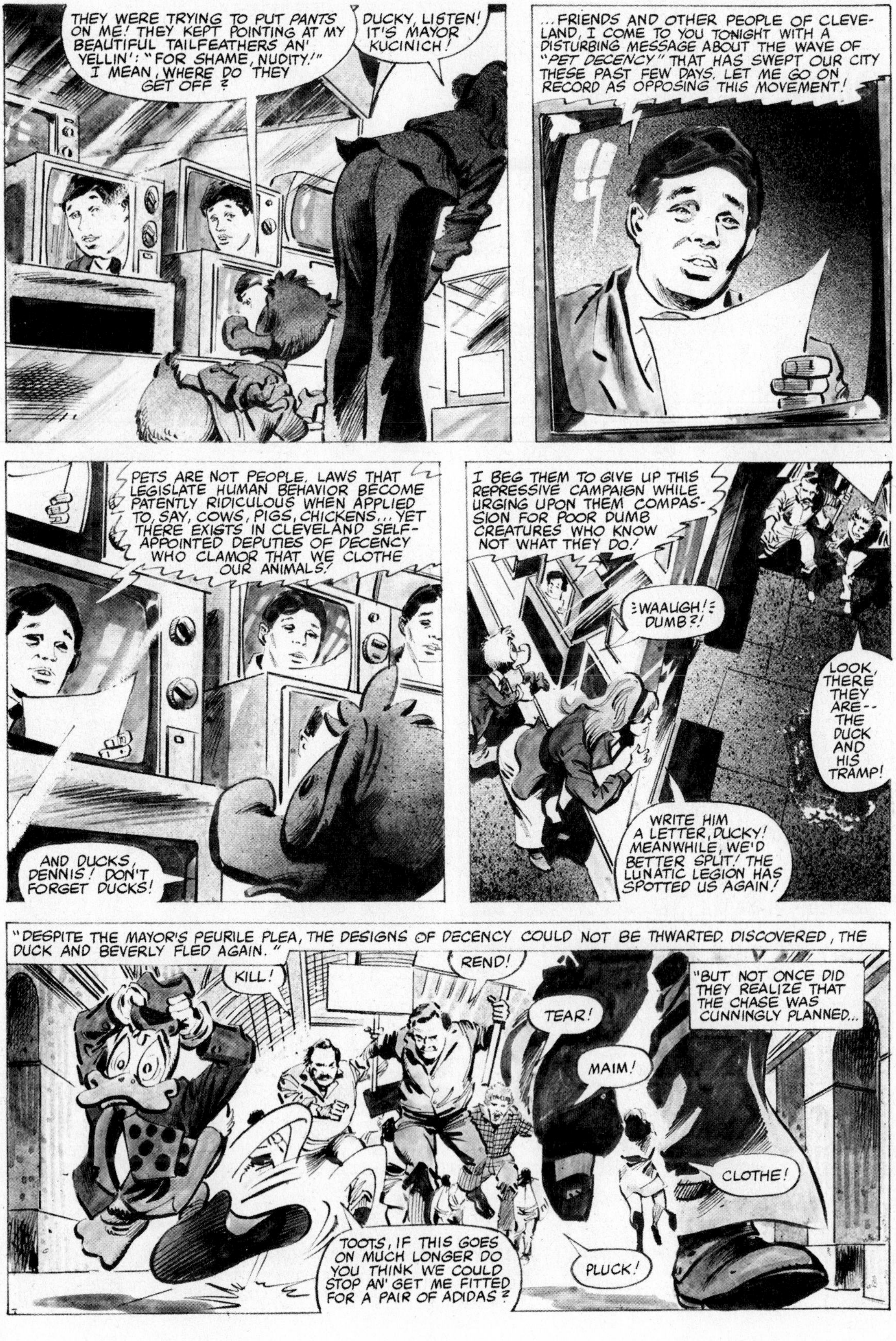
THEY WERE TRYING TO PUT PANTS ON ME! THEY KEPT POINTING AT MY BEAUTIFUL TAILFEATHERS AN' YELLIN': "FOR SHAME, NUDITY!" I MEAN, WHERE DO THEY GET OFF?
DUCKY, LISTEN! IT'S MAYOR KUCINICH!
...FRIENDS AND OTHER PEOPLE OF CLEVELAND, I COME TO YOU TONIGHT WITH A DISTURBING MESSAGE ABOUT THE WAVE OF "PET DECENCY" THAT HAS SWEPT OUR CITY THESE PAST FEW DAYS. LET ME GO ON RECORD AS OPPOSING THIS MOVEMENT!
PETS ARE NOT PEOPLE. LAWS THAT LEGISLATE HUMAN BEHAVIOR BECOME PATENTLY RIDICULOUS WHEN APPLIED TO, SAY, COWS, PIGS, CHICKENS... YET THERE EXISTS IN CLEVELAND SELF-APPOINTED DEPUTIES OF DECENCY WHO CLAMOR THAT WE CLOTHE OUR ANIMALS!
AND DUCKS, DENNIS! DON'T FORGET DUCKS!
I BEG THEM TO GIVE UP THIS REPRESSIVE CAMPAIGN WHILE URGING UPON THEM COMPASSION FOR POOR DUMB CREATURES WHO KNOW NOT WHAT THEY DO!
WAAUGH! DUMB?!
LOOK, THERE THEY ARE-- THE DUCK AND HIS TRAMP!
WRITE HIM A LETTER, DUCKY! MEANWHILE, WE'D BETTER SPLIT! THE LUNATIC LEGION HAS SPOTTED US AGAIN!
"DESPITE THE MAYOR'S PEURILE PLEA, THE DESIGNS OF DECENCY COULD NOT BE THWARTED. DISCOVERED, THE DUCK AND BEVERLY FLED AGAIN."
KILL!
REND!
"BUT NOT ONCE DID THEY REALIZE THAT THE CHASE WAS CUNNINGLY PLANNED...
TEAR!
MAIM!
CLOTHE!
TOOTS, IF THIS GOES ON MUCH LONGER DO YOU THINK WE COULD STOP AN' GET ME FITTED FOR A PAIR OF ADIDAS?
PLUCK!

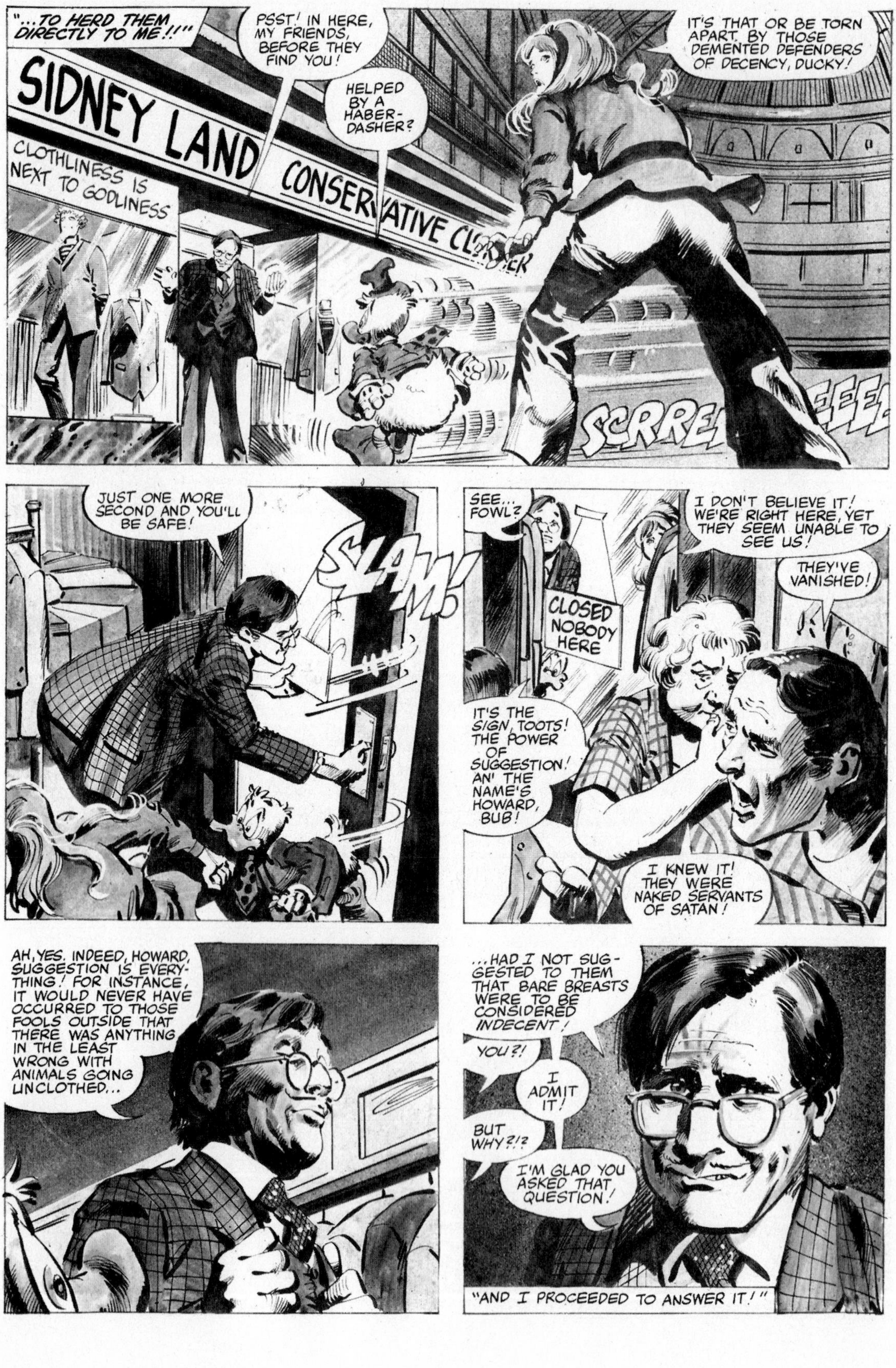
"...TO HERD THEM DIRECTLY TO ME!!"
PSST! IN HERE, MY FRIENDS, BEFORE THEY FIND YOU!
HELPED BY A HABER-DASHER?
IT'S THAT OR BE TORN APART, BY THOSE DEMENTED DEFENDERS OF DECENCY, DUCKY!
SIDNEY LAND
CONSERVATIVE CLOTHIER
CLOTHLINESS IS NEXT TO GODLINESS
SCRREEEEEL
JUST ONE MORE SECOND AND YOU'LL BE SAFE!
SLAM!
SEE... FOWL?
I DON'T BELIEVE IT! WE'RE RIGHT HERE, YET THEY SEEM UNABLE TO SEE US!
THEY'VE VANISHED!
CLOSED NOBODY HERE
IT'S THE SIGN, TOOTS! THE POWER OF SUGGESTION! AN' THE NAME'S HOWARD, BUB!
I KNEW IT! THEY WERE NAKED SERVANTS OF SATAN!
AH, YES. INDEED, HOWARD, SUGGESTION IS EVERYTHING! FOR INSTANCE, IT WOULD NEVER HAVE OCCURRED TO THOSE FOOLS OUTSIDE THAT THERE WAS ANYTHING IN THE LEAST WRONG WITH ANIMALS GOING UNCLOTHED...
...HAD I NOT SUGGESTED TO THEM THAT BARE BREASTS WERE TO BE CONSIDERED INDECENT!
YOU?!
I ADMIT IT!
BUT WHY?!?
I'M GLAD YOU ASKED THAT QUESTION!
"AND I PROCEEDED TO ANSWER IT!"

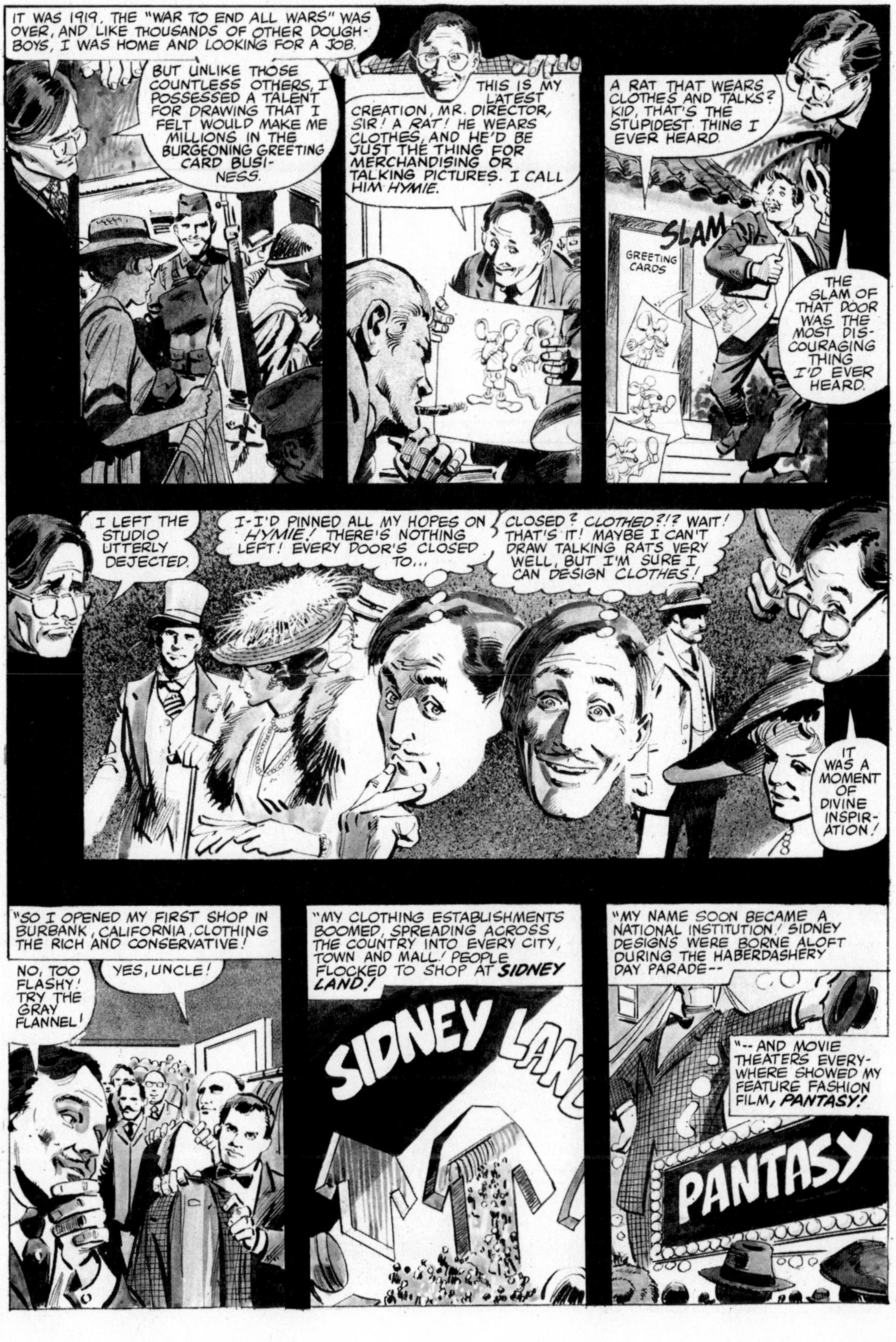
IT WAS 1919, THE "WAR TO END ALL WARS" WAS OVER, AND LIKE THOUSANDS OF OTHER DOUGH-BOYS, I WAS HOME AND LOOKING FOR A JOB.
BUT UNLIKE THOSE COUNTLESS OTHERS, I POSSESSED A TALENT FOR DRAWING THAT I FELT WOULD MAKE ME MILLIONS IN THE BURGEONING GREETING CARD BUSI-NESS.
THIS IS MY LATEST CREATION, MR. DIRECTOR, SIR! A RAT! HE WEARS CLOTHES, AND HE'D BE JUST THE THING FOR MERCHANDISING OR TALKING PICTURES. I CALL HIM HYMIE.
A RAT THAT WEARS CLOTHES AND TALKS? KID, THAT'S THE STUPIDEST THING I EVER HEARD.
SLAM
GREETING CARDS
THE SLAM OF THAT DOOR WAS THE MOST DIS-COURAGING THING I'D EVER HEARD.
I LEFT THE STUDIO UTTERLY DEJECTED.
I-I'D PINNED ALL MY HOPES ON HYMIE! THERE'S NOTHING LEFT! EVERY DOOR'S CLOSED TO...
CLOSED? CLOTHED?!? WAIT! THAT'S IT! MAYBE I CAN'T DRAW TALKING RATS VERY WELL, BUT I'M SURE I CAN DESIGN CLOTHES!
IT WAS A MOMENT OF DIVINE INSPIR-ATION!
"SO I OPENED MY FIRST SHOP IN BURBANK, CALIFORNIA, CLOTHING THE RICH AND CONSERVATIVE!
NO, TOO FLASHY! TRY THE GRAY FLANNEL!
YES, UNCLE!
"MY CLOTHING ESTABLISHMENTS BOOMED, SPREADING ACROSS THE COUNTRY INTO EVERY CITY, TOWN AND MALL! PEOPLE FLOCKED TO SHOP AT SIDNEY LAND!
SIDNEY LAND
"MY NAME SOON BECAME A NATIONAL INSTITUTION! SIDNEY DESIGNS WERE BORNE ALOFT DURING THE HABERDASHERY DAY PARADE--
"--AND MOVIE THEATERS EVERY-WHERE SHOWED MY FEATURE FASHION FILM, PANTASY!
PANTASY

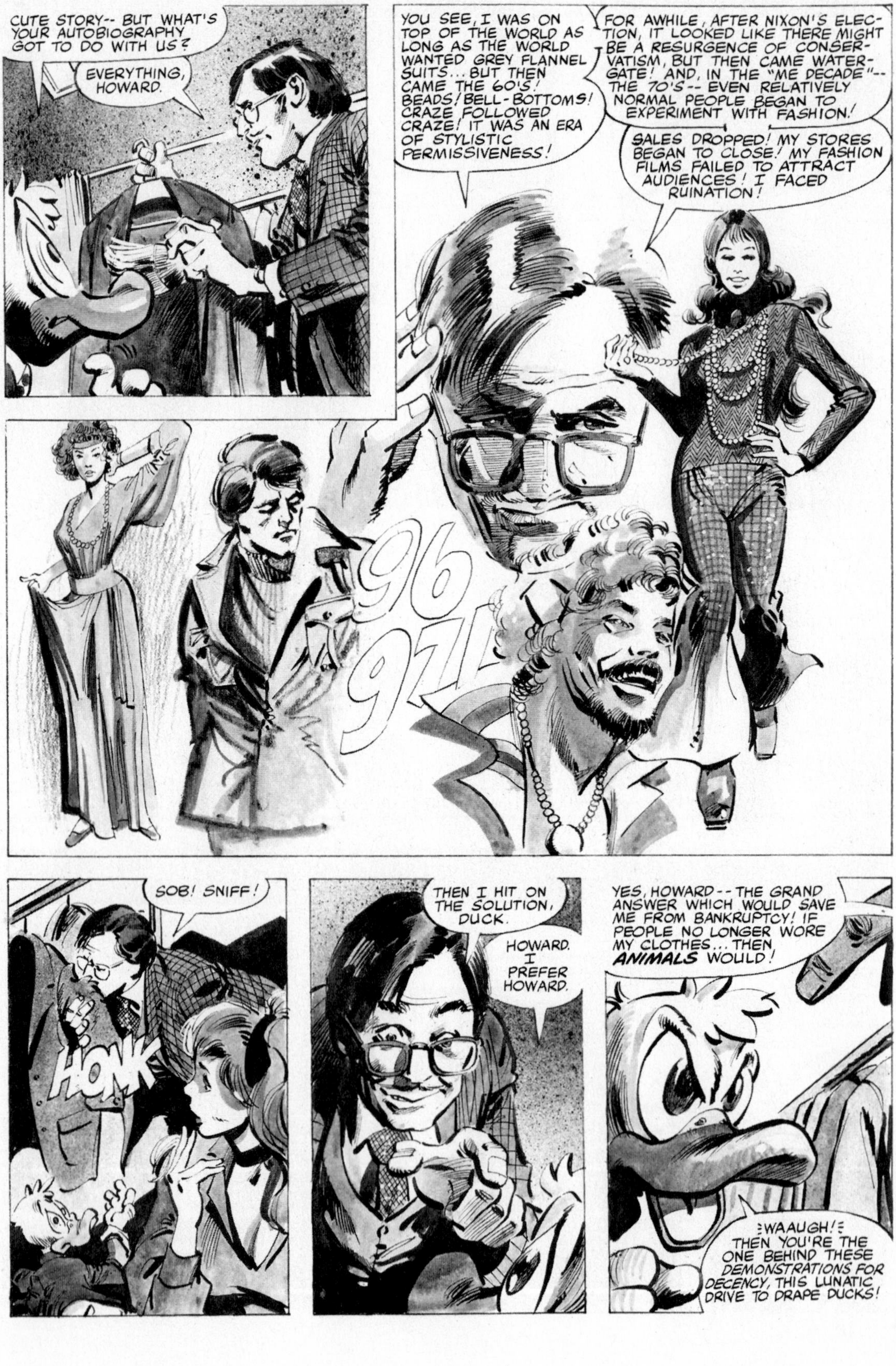
CUTE STORY-- BUT WHAT'S YOUR AUTOBIOGRAPHY GOT TO DO WITH US?
EVERYTHING, HOWARD.
YOU SEE, I WAS ON TOP OF THE WORLD AS LONG AS THE WORLD WANTED GREY FLANNEL SUITS... BUT THEN CAME THE 60'S! BEADS! BELL-BOTTOMS! CRAZE FOLLOWED CRAZE! IT WAS AN ERA OF STYLISTIC PERMISSIVENESS!
FOR AWHILE, AFTER NIXON'S ELECTION, IT LOOKED LIKE THERE MIGHT BE A RESURGENCE OF CONSERVATISM, BUT THEN CAME WATERGATE! AND, IN THE "ME DECADE"-- THE 70'S-- EVEN RELATIVELY NORMAL PEOPLE BEGAN TO EXPERIMENT WITH FASHION!
SALES DROPPED! MY STORES BEGAN TO CLOSE! MY FASHION FILMS FAILED TO ATTRACT AUDIENCES! I FACED RUINATION!
SOB! SNIFF!
HONK
THEN I HIT ON THE SOLUTION, DUCK.
HOWARD. I PREFER HOWARD.
YES, HOWARD-- THE GRAND ANSWER WHICH WOULD SAVE ME FROM BANKRUPTCY! IF PEOPLE NO LONGER WORE MY CLOTHES... THEN ANIMALS WOULD!
WAAUGH! THEN YOU'RE THE ONE BEHIND THESE DEMONSTRATIONS FOR DECENCY, THIS LUNATIC DRIVE TO DRAPE DUCKS!

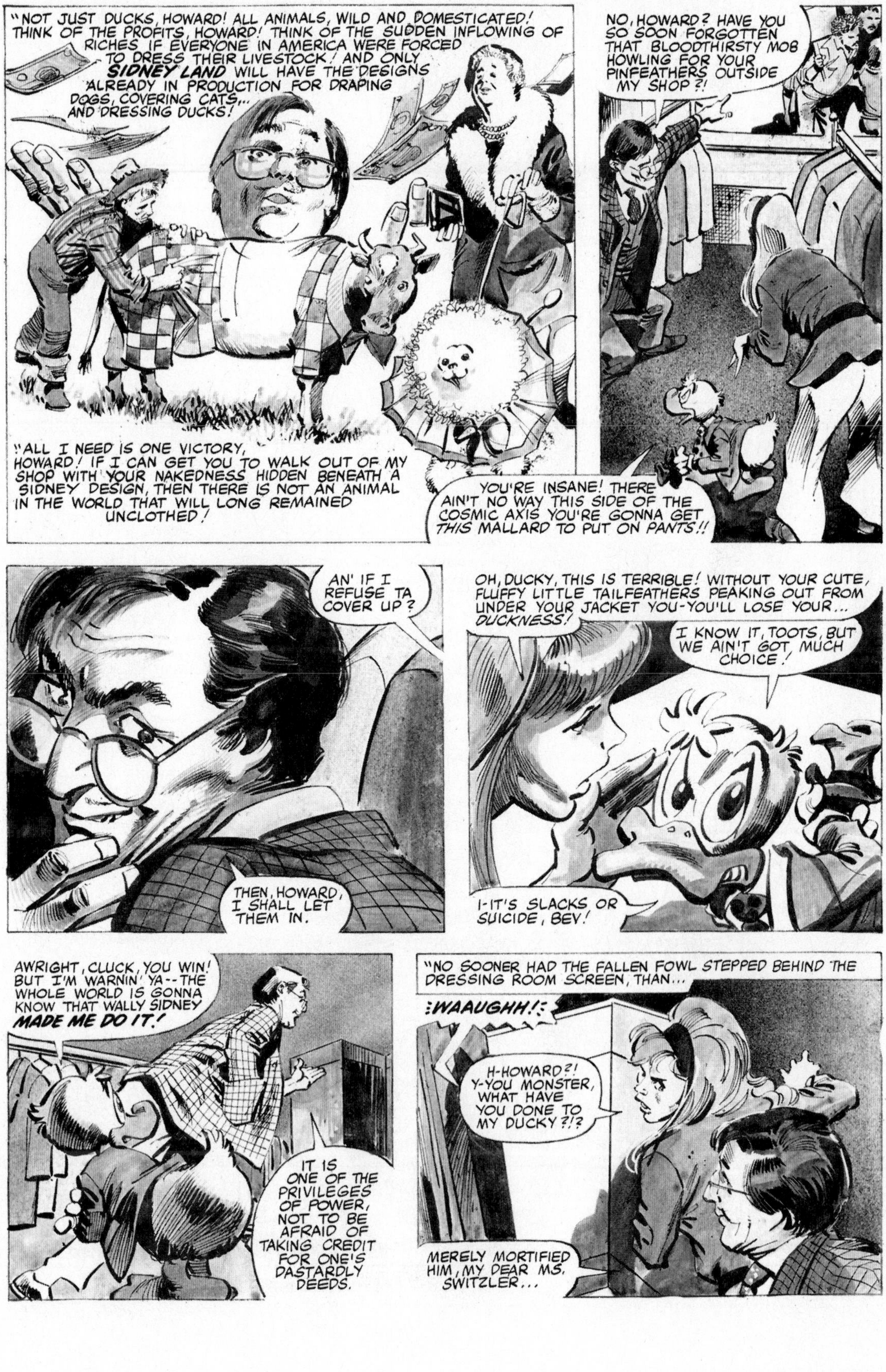
"NOT JUST DUCKS, HOWARD! ALL ANIMALS, WILD AND DOMESTICATED! THINK OF THE PROFITS, HOWARD! THINK OF THE SUDDEN INFLOWING OF RICHES IF EVERYONE IN AMERICA WERE FORCED TO DRESS THEIR LIVESTOCK! AND ONLY SIDNEY LAND WILL HAVE THE DESIGNS ALREADY IN PRODUCTION FOR DRAPING DOGS, COVERING CATS,... AND DRESSING DUCKS!
"ALL I NEED IS ONE VICTORY, HOWARD! IF I CAN GET YOU TO WALK OUT OF MY SHOP WITH YOUR NAKEDNESS HIDDEN BENEATH A SIDNEY DESIGN, THEN THERE IS NOT AN ANIMAL IN THE WORLD THAT WILL LONG REMAINED UNCLOTHED!
NO, HOWARD? HAVE YOU SO SOON FORGOTTEN THAT BLOODTHIRSTY MOB HOWLING FOR YOUR PINFEATHERS OUTSIDE MY SHOP?!
YOU'RE INSANE! THERE AIN'T NO WAY THIS SIDE OF THE COSMIC AXIS YOU'RE GONNA GET THIS MALLARD TO PUT ON PANTS!!
AN' IF I REFUSE TA COVER UP?
THEN, HOWARD, I SHALL LET THEM IN.
OH, DUCKY, THIS IS TERRIBLE! WITHOUT YOUR CUTE, FLUFFY LITTLE TAILFEATHERS PEAKING OUT FROM UNDER YOUR JACKET YOU-YOU'LL LOSE YOUR... DUCKNESS!
I KNOW IT, TOOTS, BUT WE AIN'T GOT MUCH CHOICE!
I-IT'S SLACKS OR SUICIDE, BEV!
AWRIGHT, CLUCK, YOU WIN! BUT I'M WARNIN' YA--THE WHOLE WORLD IS GONNA KNOW THAT WALLY SIDNEY MADE ME DO IT!
IT IS ONE OF THE PRIVILEGES OF POWER, NOT TO BE AFRAID OF TAKING CREDIT FOR ONE'S DASTARDLY DEEDS.
"NO SOONER HAD THE FALLEN FOWL STEPPED BEHIND THE DRESSING ROOM SCREEN, THAN...
WAAUGHH!
H-HOWARD?! Y-YOU MONSTER, WHAT HAVE YOU DONE TO MY DUCKY?!?
MERELY MORTIFIED HIM, MY DEAR MS. SWITZLER...

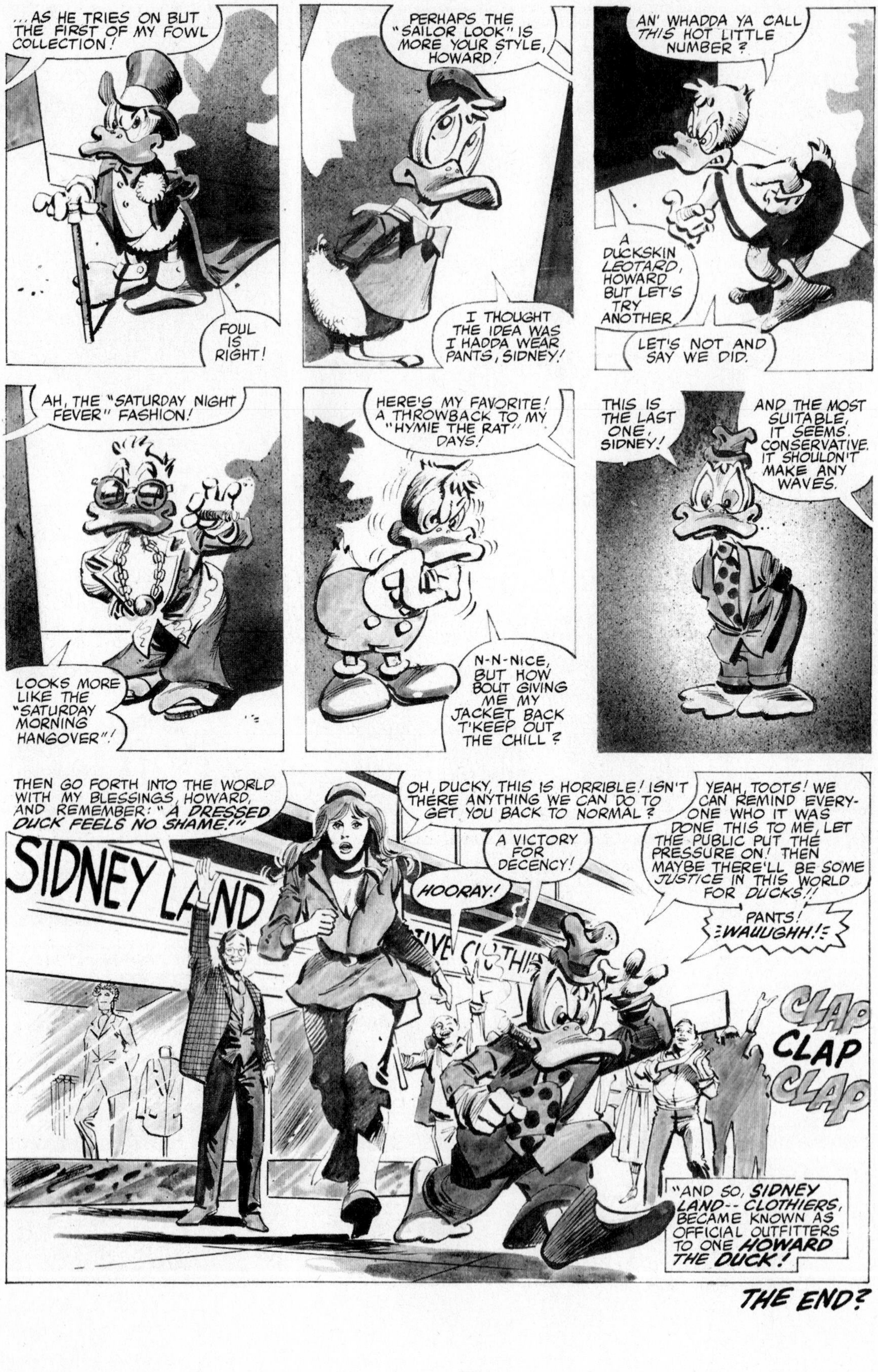
...AS HE TRIES ON BUT THE FIRST OF MY FOWL COLLECTION!
FOUL IS RIGHT!
PERHAPS THE "SAILOR LOOK" IS MORE YOUR STYLE, HOWARD!
I THOUGHT THE IDEA WAS I HADDA WEAR PANTS, SIDNEY!
AN' WHADDA YA CALL THIS HOT LITTLE NUMBER?
A DUCKSKIN LEOTARD, HOWARD BUT LET'S TRY ANOTHER.
LET'S NOT AND SAY WE DID.
AH, THE "SATURDAY NIGHT FEVER" FASHION!
LOOKS MORE LIKE THE "SATURDAY MORNING HANGOVER"!
HERE'S MY FAVORITE! A THROWBACK TO MY "HYMIE THE RAT" DAYS!
N-N-NICE, BUT HOW BOUT GIVING ME MY JACKET BACK T'KEEP OUT THE CHILL?
THIS IS THE LAST ONE, SIDNEY!
AND THE MOST SUITABLE, IT SEEMS. CONSERVATIVE. IT SHOULDN'T MAKE ANY WAVES.
THEN GO FORTH INTO THE WORLD WITH MY BLESSINGS, HOWARD, AND REMEMBER: "A DRESSED DUCK FEELS NO SHAME!"
SIDNEY LAND
OH, DUCKY, THIS IS HORRIBLE! ISN'T THERE ANYTHING WE CAN DO TO GET YOU BACK TO NORMAL?
A VICTORY FOR DECENCY!
HOORAY!
YEAH, TOOTS! WE CAN REMIND EVERY-ONE WHO IT WAS DONE THIS TO ME, LET THE PUBLIC PUT THE PRESSURE ON! THEN MAYBE THERE'LL BE SOME JUSTICE IN THIS WORLD FOR DUCKS!!
PANTS!
WAUUGHH!
CLAP
CLAP
CLAP
"AND SO, SIDNEY LAND-- CLOTHIERS, BECAME KNOWN AS OFFICIAL OUTFITTERS TO ONE HOWARD THE DUCK!
THE END?

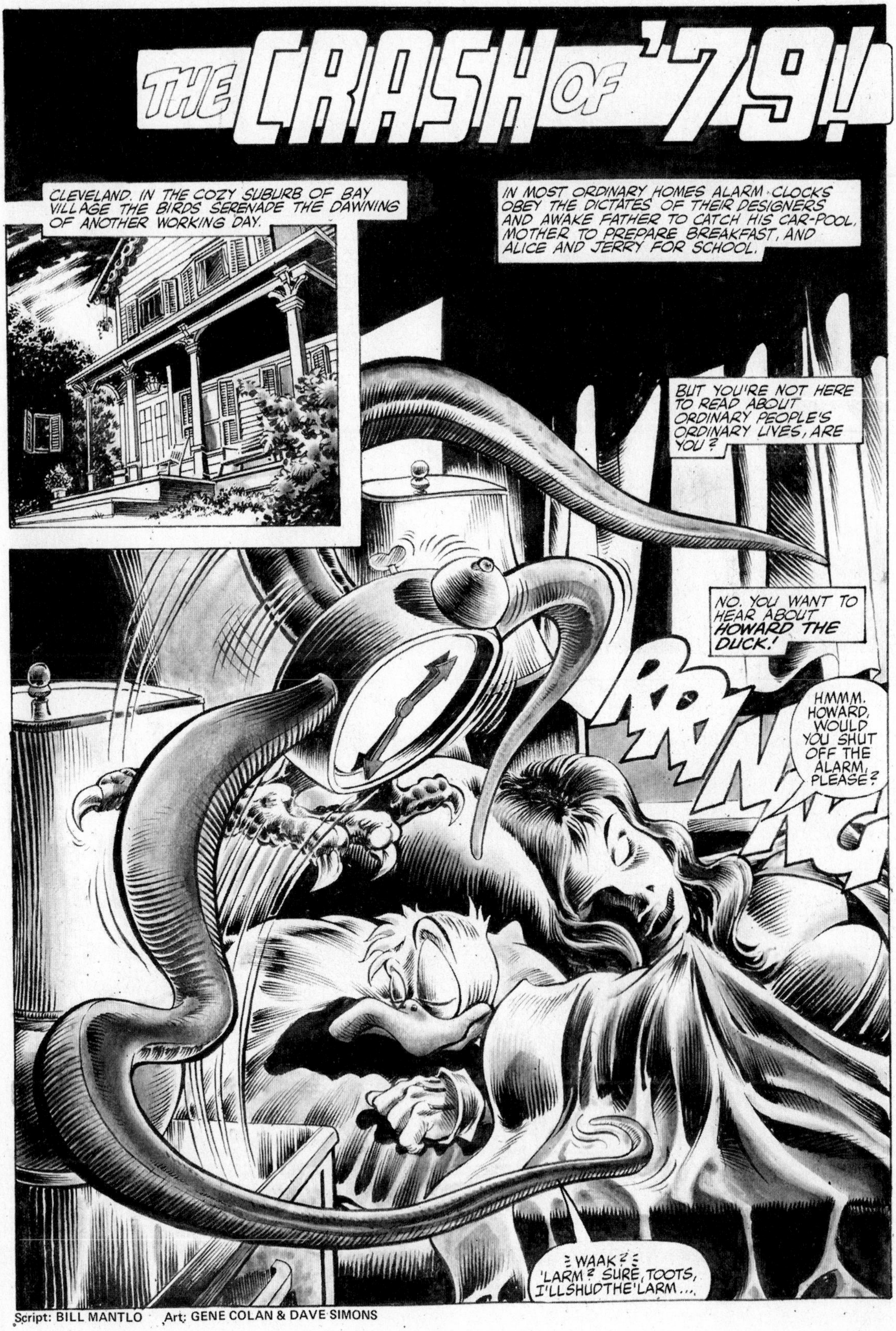
THE CRASH OF '79!
CLEVELAND. IN THE COZY SUBURB OF BAY VILLAGE THE BIRDS SERENADE THE DAWNING OF ANOTHER WORKING DAY.
IN MOST ORDINARY HOMES ALARM CLOCKS OBEY THE DICTATES OF THEIR DESIGNERS AND AWAKE FATHER TO CATCH HIS CAR-POOL, MOTHER TO PREPARE BREAKFAST, AND ALICE AND JERRY FOR SCHOOL.
BUT YOU'RE NOT HERE TO READ ABOUT ORDINARY PEOPLE'S ORDINARY LIVES, ARE YOU?
NO. YOU WANT TO HEAR ABOUT HOWARD THE DUCK!
RRRANNNG!
HMMM. HOWARD, WOULD YOU SHUT OFF THE ALARM, PLEASE?
WAAK? 'LARM? SURE, TOOTS, I'LL SHUT THE 'LARM...

Script: BILL MANTLO Art: GENE COLAN & DAVE SIMONS

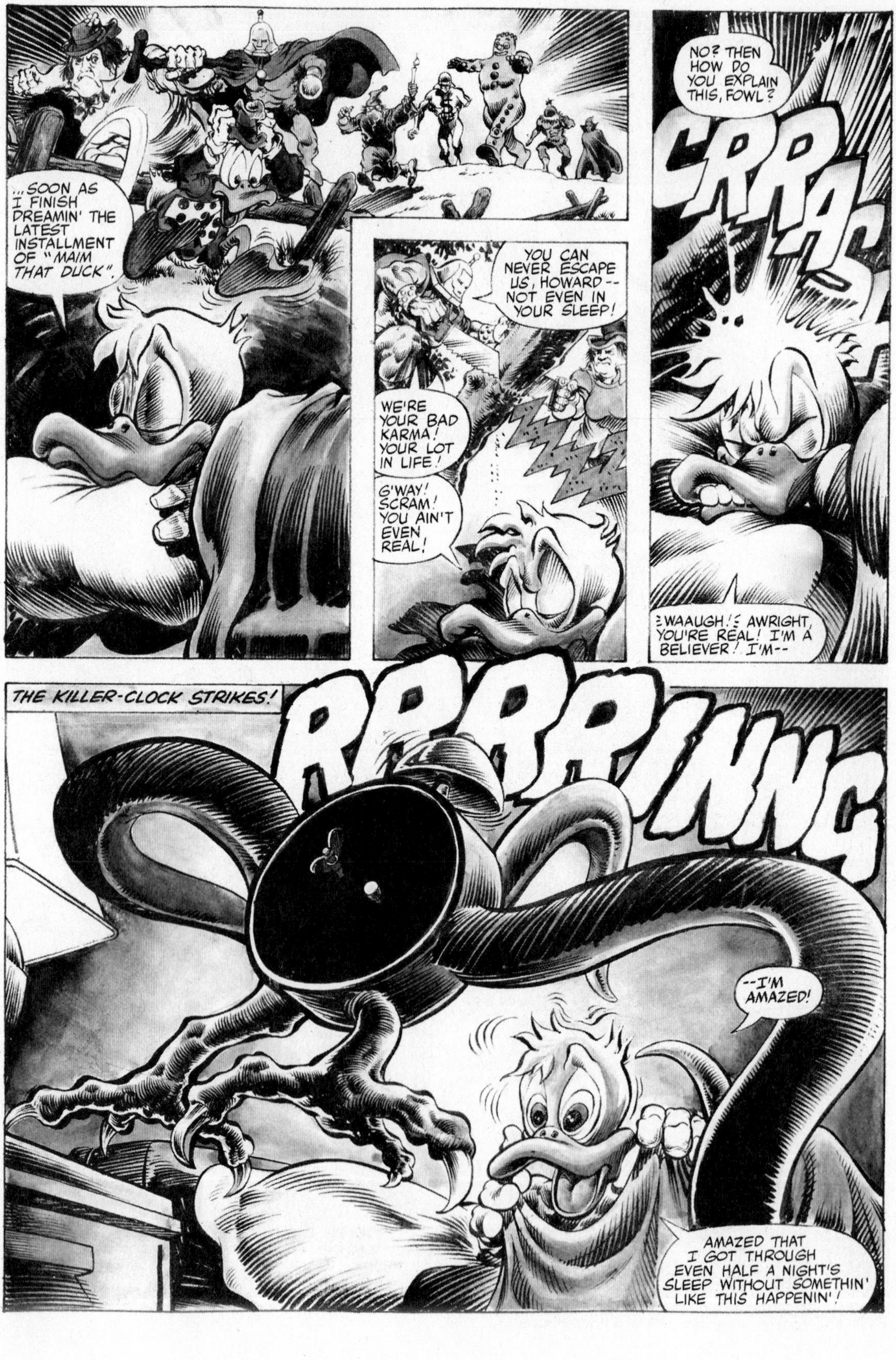
...SOON AS I FINISH DREAMIN' THE LATEST INSTALLMENT OF "MAIM THAT DUCK".
YOU CAN NEVER ESCAPE US, HOWARD-- NOT EVEN IN YOUR SLEEP!
WE'RE YOUR BAD KARMA! YOUR LOT IN LIFE!
G'WAY! SCRAM! YOU AIN'T EVEN REAL!
NO? THEN HOW DO YOU EXPLAIN THIS, FOWL?
CRRAC
WAAUGH! AWRIGHT, YOU'RE REAL! I'M A BELIEVER! I'M--
THE KILLER-CLOCK STRIKES!
RRRRINNG
--I'M AMAZED!
AMAZED THAT I GOT THROUGH EVEN HALF A NIGHT'S SLEEP WITHOUT SOMETHIN' LIKE THIS HAPPENIN'!

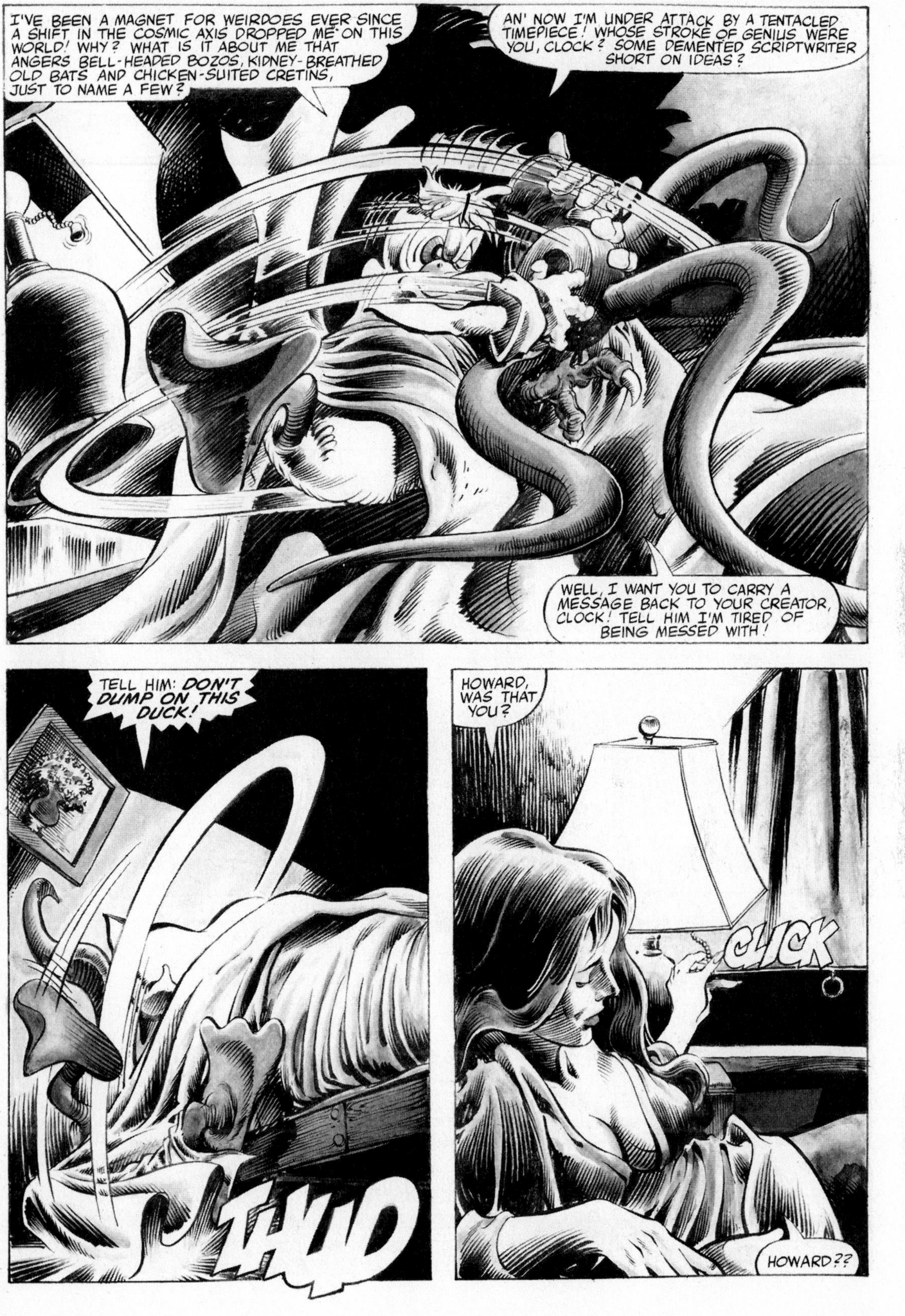

I'VE BEEN A MAGNET FOR WEIRDOES EVER SINCE A SHIFT IN THE COSMIC AXIS DROPPED ME ON THIS WORLD! WHY? WHAT IS IT ABOUT ME THAT ANGERS BELL-HEADED BOZOS, KIDNEY-BREATHED OLD BATS AND CHICKEN-SUITED CRETINS, JUST TO NAME A FEW?
AN' NOW I'M UNDER ATTACK BY A TENTACLED TIMEPIECE! WHOSE STROKE OF GENIUS WERE YOU, CLOCK? SOME DEMENTED SCRIPTWRITER SHORT ON IDEAS?
WELL, I WANT YOU TO CARRY A MESSAGE BACK TO YOUR CREATOR, CLOCK! TELL HIM I'M TIRED OF BEING MESSED WITH!
TELL HIM: DON'T DUMP ON THIS DUCK!
THUD
HOWARD, WAS THAT YOU?
CLICK
HOWARD??

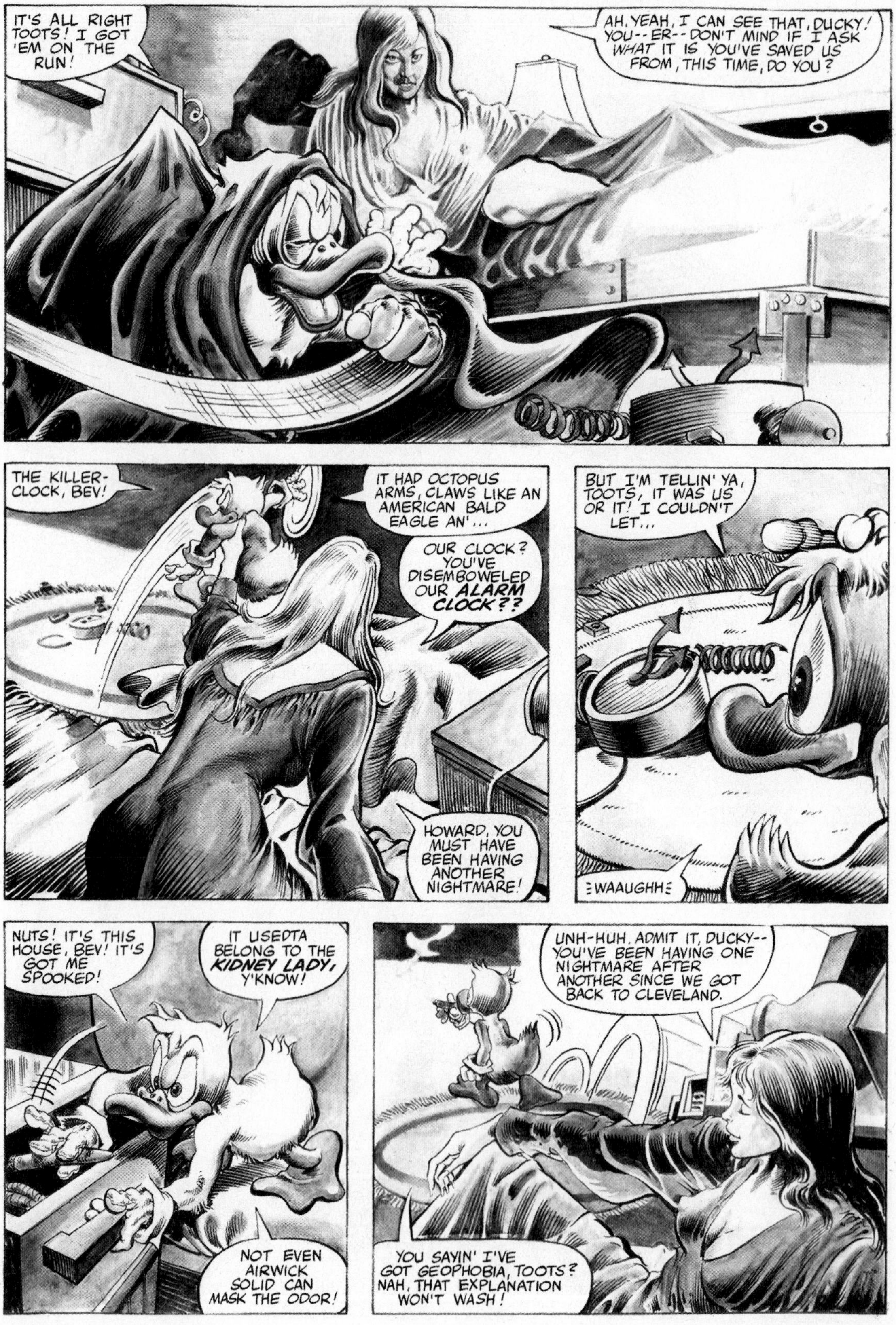

IT'S ALL RIGHT TOOTS! I GOT 'EM ON THE RUN!
AH, YEAH, I CAN SEE THAT, DUCKY! YOU--ER--DON'T MIND IF I ASK WHAT IT IS YOU'VE SAVED US FROM, THIS TIME, DO YOU?
THE KILLER-CLOCK, BEV!
IT HAD OCTOPUS ARMS, CLAWS LIKE AN AMERICAN BALD EAGLE AN'...
OUR CLOCK? YOU'VE DISEMBOWELED OUR ALARM CLOCK??
HOWARD, YOU MUST HAVE BEEN HAVING ANOTHER NIGHTMARE!
BUT I'M TELLIN' YA, TOOTS, IT WAS US OR IT! I COULDN'T LET...
WAAUGHH
NUTS! IT'S THIS HOUSE, BEV! IT'S GOT ME SPOOKED!
IT USEDTA BELONG TO THE KIDNEY LADY, Y'KNOW!
NOT EVEN AIRWICK SOLID CAN MASK THE ODOR!
UNH-HUH. ADMIT IT, DUCKY--YOU'VE BEEN HAVING ONE NIGHTMARE AFTER ANOTHER SINCE WE GOT BACK TO CLEVELAND.
YOU SAYIN' I'VE GOT GEOPHOBIA, TOOTS? NAH, THAT EXPLANATION WON'T WASH!

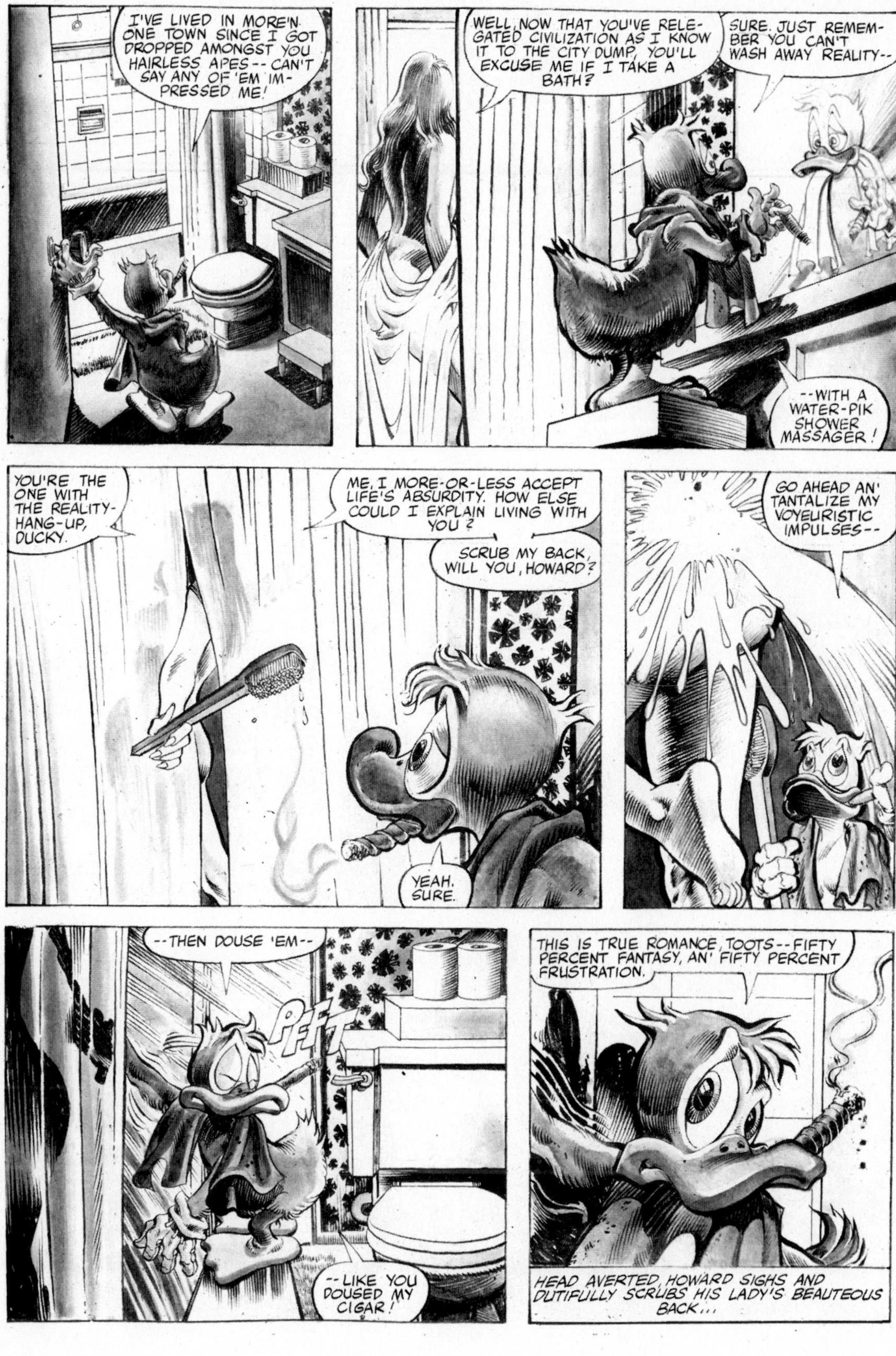
I'VE LIVED IN MORE'N ONE TOWN SINCE I GOT DROPPED AMONGST YOU HAIRLESS APES-- CAN'T SAY ANY OF 'EM IMPRESSED ME!
WELL, NOW THAT YOU'VE RELEGATED CIVILIZATION AS I KNOW IT TO THE CITY DUMP, YOU'LL EXCUSE ME IF I TAKE A BATH?
SURE. JUST REMEMBER YOU CAN'T WASH AWAY REALITY--
--WITH A WATER-PIK SHOWER MASSAGER!
YOU'RE THE ONE WITH THE REALITY-HANG-UP, DUCKY.
ME, I MORE-OR-LESS ACCEPT LIFE'S ABSURDITY. HOW ELSE COULD I EXPLAIN LIVING WITH YOU?
SCRUB MY BACK, WILL YOU, HOWARD?
YEAH. SURE.
GO AHEAD AN' TANTALIZE MY VOYEURISTIC IMPULSES--
--THEN DOUSE 'EM--
PFFT
--LIKE YOU DOUSED MY CIGAR!
THIS IS TRUE ROMANCE, TOOTS--FIFTY PERCENT FANTASY, AN' FIFTY PERCENT FRUSTRATION.
HEAD AVERTED, HOWARD SIGHS AND DUTIFULLY SCRUBS HIS LADY'S BEAUTEOUS BACK...

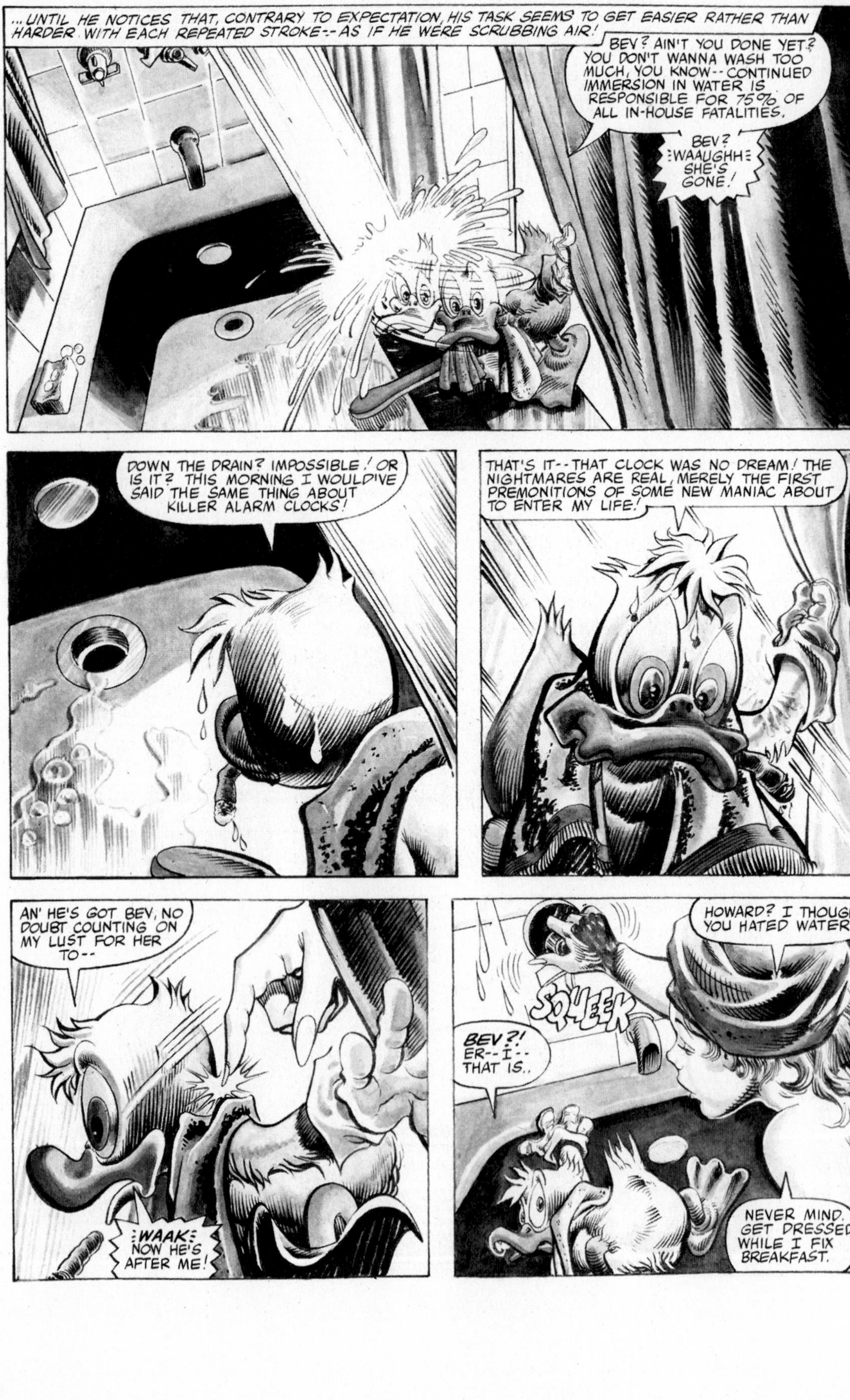
...UNTIL HE NOTICES THAT, CONTRARY TO EXPECTATION, HIS TASK SEEMS TO GET EASIER RATHER THAN HARDER WITH EACH REPEATED STROKE--AS IF HE WERE SCRUBBING AIR!
BEV? AIN'T YOU DONE YET? YOU DON'T WANNA WASH TOO MUCH, YOU KNOW--CONTINUED IMMERSION IN WATER IS RESPONSIBLE FOR 75% OF ALL IN-HOUSE FATALITIES.
BEV? WAAUGHH SHE'S GONE!
DOWN THE DRAIN? IMPOSSIBLE! OR IS IT? THIS MORNING I WOULD'VE SAID THE SAME THING ABOUT KILLER ALARM CLOCKS!
THAT'S IT--THAT CLOCK WAS NO DREAM! THE NIGHTMARES ARE REAL, MERELY THE FIRST PREMONITIONS OF SOME NEW MANIAC ABOUT TO ENTER MY LIFE!
AN' HE'S GOT BEV, NO DOUBT COUNTING ON MY LUST FOR HER TO--
WAAK! NOW HE'S AFTER ME!
HOWARD? I THOUGHT YOU HATED WATER!
SQUEEK
BEV?! ER--I--THAT IS..
NEVER MIND. GET DRESSED WHILE I FIX BREAKFAST.

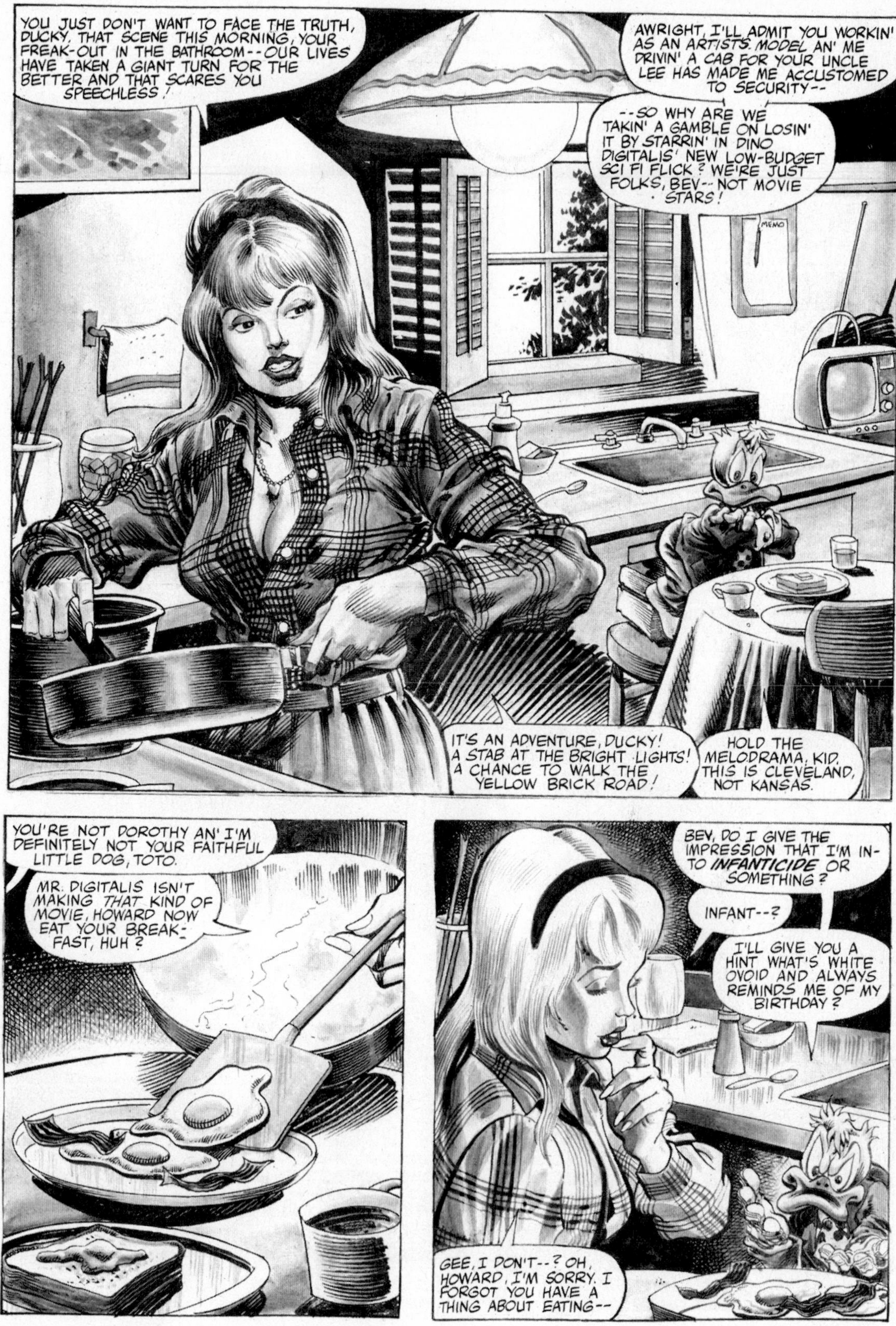
YOU JUST DON'T WANT TO FACE THE TRUTH, DUCKY. THAT SCENE THIS MORNING, YOUR FREAK-OUT IN THE BATHROOM--OUR LIVES HAVE TAKEN A GIANT TURN FOR THE BETTER AND THAT SCARES YOU SPEECHLESS!
AWRIGHT, I'LL ADMIT YOU WORKIN' AS AN ARTISTS' MODEL AN' ME DRIVIN' A CAB FOR YOUR UNCLE LEE HAS MADE ME ACCUSTOMED TO SECURITY--
--SO WHY ARE WE TAKIN' A GAMBLE ON LOSIN' IT BY STARRIN' IN DINO DIGITALIS' NEW LOW-BUDGET SCI FI FLICK? WE'RE JUST FOLKS, BEV--NOT MOVIE STARS!
MEMO
IT'S AN ADVENTURE, DUCKY! A STAB AT THE BRIGHT LIGHTS! A CHANCE TO WALK THE YELLOW BRICK ROAD!
HOLD THE MELODRAMA, KID. THIS IS CLEVELAND, NOT KANSAS.
YOU'RE NOT DOROTHY AN' I'M DEFINITELY NOT YOUR FAITHFUL LITTLE DOG, TOTO.
MR. DIGITALIS ISN'T MAKING THAT KIND OF MOVIE, HOWARD. NOW EAT YOUR BREAKFAST, HUH?
BEV, DO I GIVE THE IMPRESSION THAT I'M INTO INFANTICIDE OR SOMETHING?
INFANT--?
I'LL GIVE YOU A HINT. WHAT'S WHITE, OVOID AND ALWAYS REMINDS ME OF MY BIRTHDAY?
GEE, I DON'T--? OH, HOWARD, I'M SORRY. I FORGOT YOU HAVE A THING ABOUT EATING--

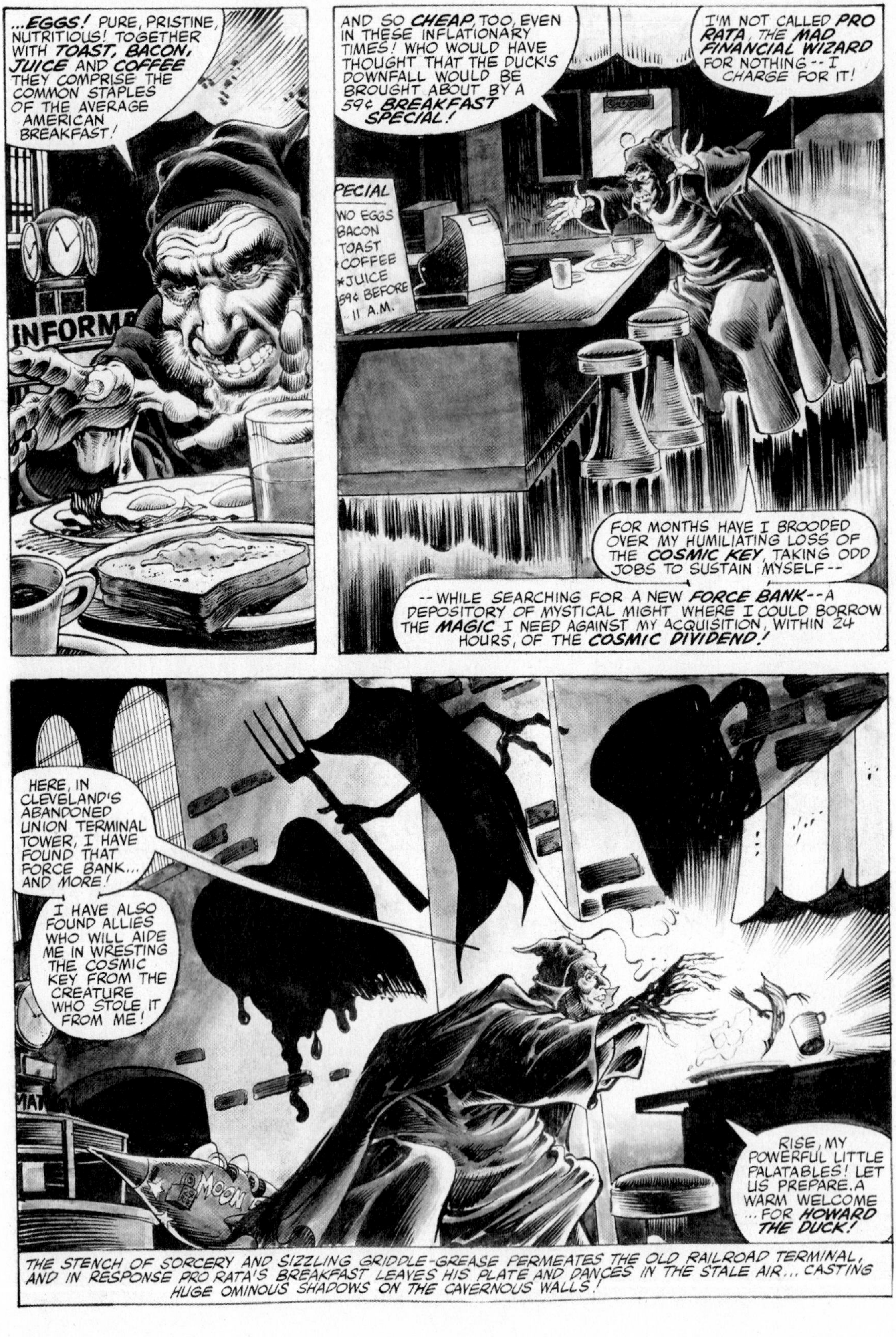

...EGGS! PURE, PRISTINE, NUTRITIOUS! TOGETHER WITH TOAST, BACON, JUICE AND COFFEE THEY COMPRISE THE COMMON STAPLES OF THE AVERAGE AMERICAN BREAKFAST!
INFORMA
AND SO CHEAP, TOO, EVEN IN THESE INFLATIONARY TIMES! WHO WOULD HAVE THOUGHT THAT THE DUCK'S DOWNFALL WOULD BE BROUGHT ABOUT BY A 59¢ BREAKFAST SPECIAL!
I'M NOT CALLED PRO RATA, THE MAD FINANCIAL WIZARD FOR NOTHING -- I CHARGE FOR IT!
PECIAL
WO EGGS
BACON
TOAST
COFFEE
JUICE
59¢ BEFORE
11 A.M.
FOR MONTHS HAVE I BROODED OVER MY HUMILIATING LOSS OF THE COSMIC KEY, TAKING ODD JOBS TO SUSTAIN MYSELF--
--WHILE SEARCHING FOR A NEW FORCE BANK--A DEPOSITORY OF MYSTICAL MIGHT WHERE I COULD BORROW THE MAGIC I NEED AGAINST MY ACQUISITION, WITHIN 24 HOURS, OF THE COSMIC DIVIDEND!
HERE, IN CLEVELAND'S ABANDONED UNION TERMINAL TOWER, I HAVE FOUND THAT FORCE BANK... AND MORE!
I HAVE ALSO FOUND ALLIES WHO WILL AIDE ME IN WRESTING THE COSMIC KEY FROM THE CREATURE WHO STOLE IT FROM ME!
MOON
RISE, MY POWERFUL LITTLE PALATABLES! LET US PREPARE A WARM WELCOME ...FOR HOWARD THE DUCK!
THE STENCH OF SORCERY AND SIZZLING GRIDDLE-GREASE PERMEATES THE OLD RAILROAD TERMINAL, AND IN RESPONSE PRO RATA'S BREAKFAST LEAVES HIS PLATE AND DANCES IN THE STALE AIR... CASTING HUGE OMINOUS SHADOWS ON THE CAVERNOUS WALLS!

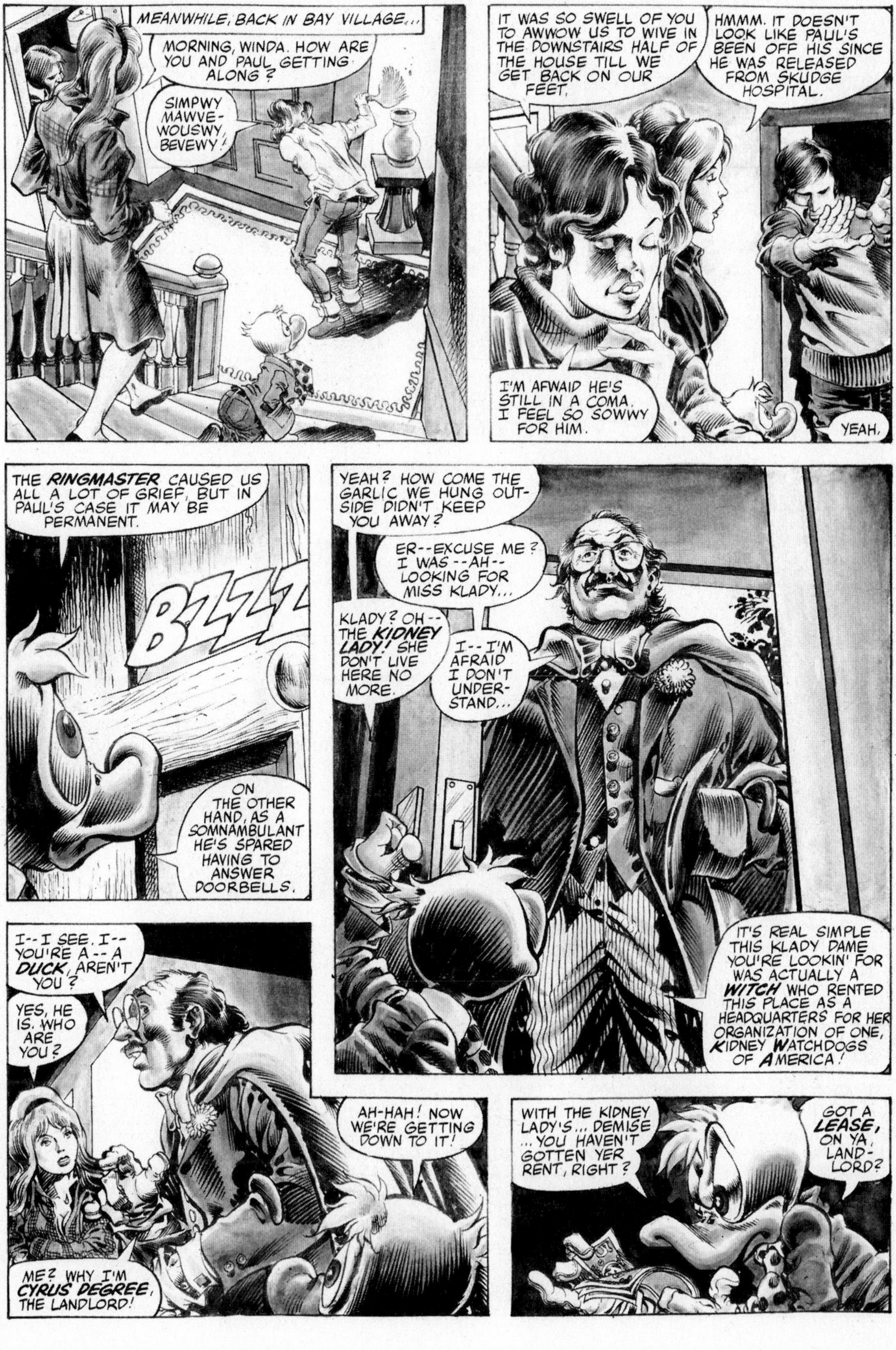
MEANWHILE, BACK IN BAY VILLAGE...
MORNING, WINDA. HOW ARE YOU AND PAUL GETTING ALONG?
SIMPWY MAWVE-WOUSWY, BEVEWY!
IT WAS SO SWELL OF YOU TO AWWOW US TO WIVE IN THE DOWNSTAIRS HALF OF THE HOUSE TILL WE GET BACK ON OUR FEET.
HMMM. IT DOESN'T LOOK LIKE PAUL'S BEEN OFF HIS SINCE HE WAS RELEASED FROM SKUDGE HOSPITAL.
I'M AFWAID HE'S STILL IN A COMA. I FEEL SO SOWWY FOR HIM.
YEAH.
THE RINGMASTER CAUSED US ALL A LOT OF GRIEF, BUT IN PAUL'S CASE IT MAY BE PERMANENT.
BZZZ
ON THE OTHER HAND, AS A SOMNAMBULANT HE'S SPARED HAVING TO ANSWER DOORBELLS.
YEAH? HOW COME THE GARLIC WE HUNG OUTSIDE DIDN'T KEEP YOU AWAY?
ER--EXCUSE ME? I WAS--AH--LOOKING FOR MISS KLADY...
KLADY? OH--THE KIDNEY LADY! SHE DON'T LIVE HERE NO MORE.
I--I'M AFRAID I DON'T UNDERSTAND...
IT'S REAL SIMPLE THIS KLADY DAME YOU'RE LOOKIN' FOR WAS ACTUALLY A WITCH WHO RENTED THIS PLACE AS A HEADQUARTERS FOR HER ORGANIZATION OF ONE, KIDNEY WATCHDOGS OF AMERICA!
I--I SEE. I--YOU'RE A--A DUCK, AREN'T YOU?
YES, HE IS. WHO ARE YOU?
ME? WHY I'M CYRUS DEGREE, THE LANDLORD!
AH-HAH! NOW WE'RE GETTING DOWN TO IT!
WITH THE KIDNEY LADY'S... DEMISE ...YOU HAVEN'T GOTTEN YER RENT, RIGHT?
GOT A LEASE, ON YA, LANDLORD?

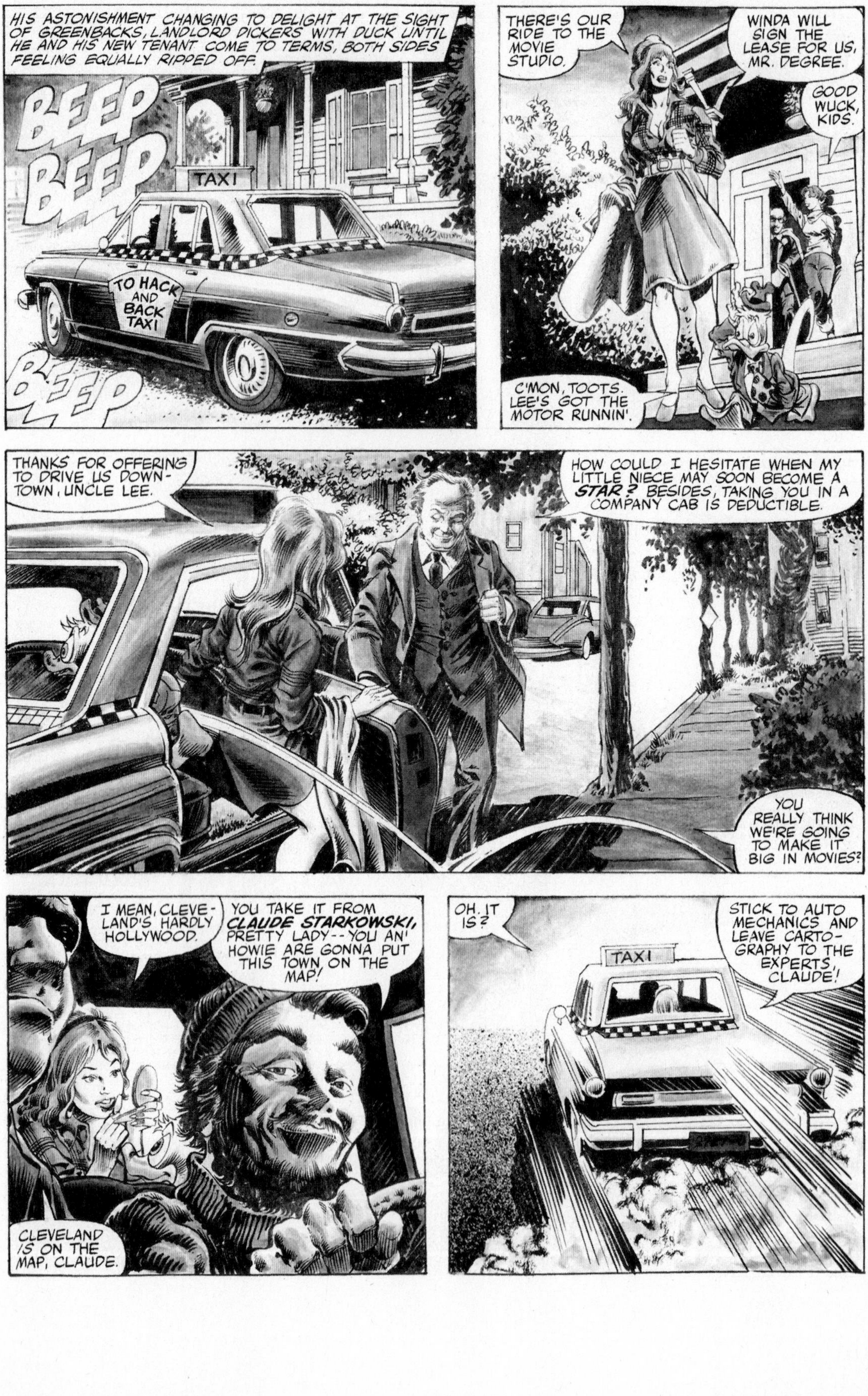
HIS ASTONISHMENT CHANGING TO DELIGHT AT THE SIGHT OF GREENBACKS, LANDLORD DICKERS WITH DUCK UNTIL HE AND HIS NEW TENANT COME TO TERMS, BOTH SIDES FEELING EQUALLY RIPPED OFF.
BEEP BEEP
TAXI
TO HACK AND BACK TAXI
BEEP
THERE'S OUR RIDE TO THE MOVIE STUDIO.
WINDA WILL SIGN THE LEASE FOR US, MR. DEGREE.
GOOD WUCK, KIDS.
C'MON, TOOTS. LEE'S GOT THE MOTOR RUNNIN'.
THANKS FOR OFFERING TO DRIVE US DOWN-TOWN, UNCLE LEE.
HOW COULD I HESITATE WHEN MY LITTLE NIECE MAY SOON BECOME A STAR? BESIDES, TAKING YOU IN A COMPANY CAB IS DEDUCTIBLE.
YOU REALLY THINK WE'RE GOING TO MAKE IT BIG IN MOVIES?
I MEAN, CLEVE-LAND'S HARDLY HOLLYWOOD.
YOU TAKE IT FROM CLAUDE STARKOWSKI, PRETTY LADY-- YOU AN' HOWIE ARE GONNA PUT THIS TOWN ON THE MAP!
CLEVELAND IS ON THE MAP, CLAUDE.
OH, IT IS?
STICK TO AUTO MECHANICS AND LEAVE CARTO-GRAPHY TO THE EXPERTS, CLAUDE!
TAXI

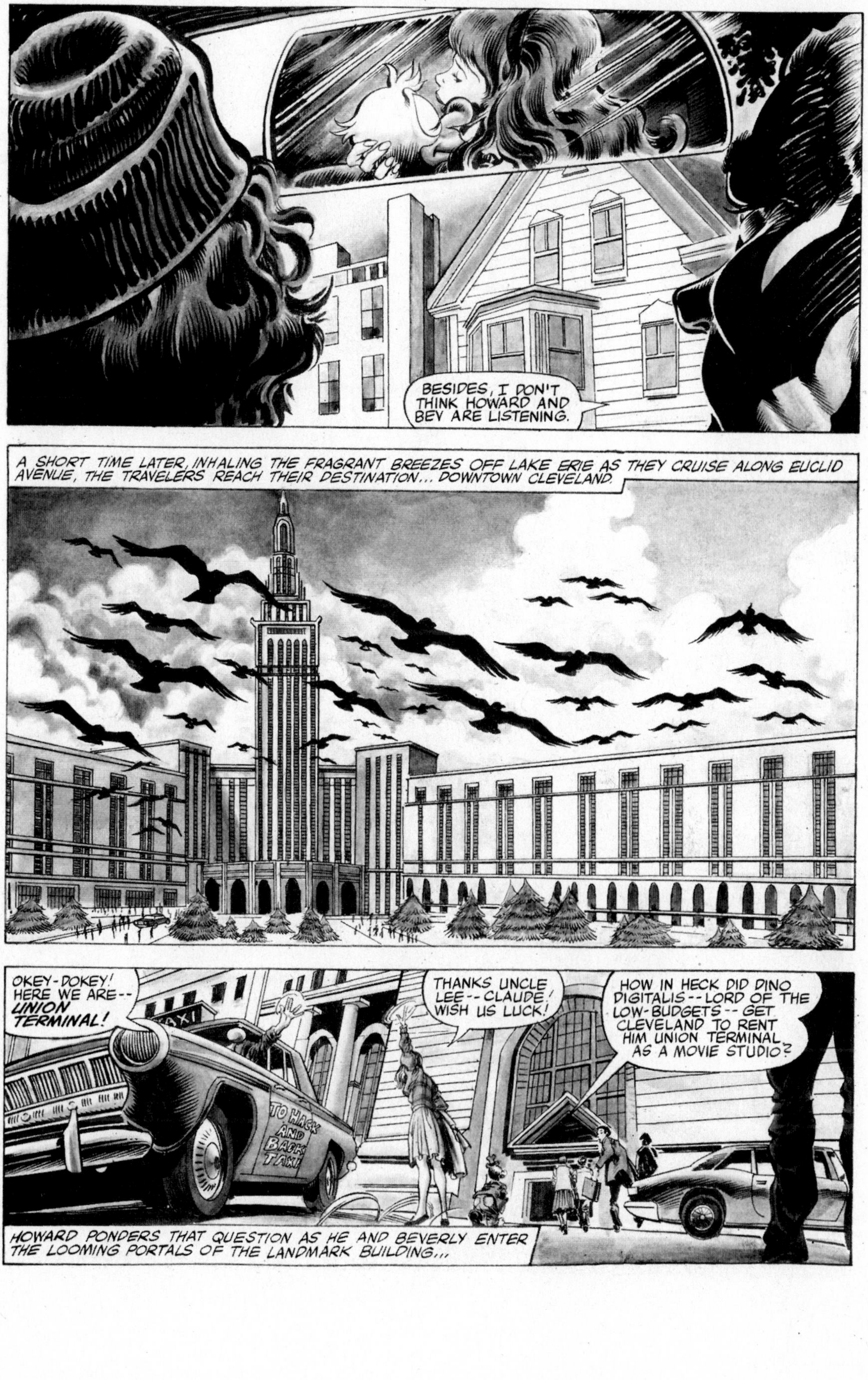
BESIDES, I DON'T THINK HOWARD AND BEV ARE LISTENING.
A SHORT TIME LATER, INHALING THE FRAGRANT BREEZES OFF LAKE ERIE AS THEY CRUISE ALONG EUCLID AVENUE, THE TRAVELERS REACH THEIR DESTINATION... DOWNTOWN CLEVELAND.
OKEY-DOKEY! HERE WE ARE-- UNION TERMINAL!
TAXI
TO HACK AND BACK TAXI
THANKS UNCLE LEE-- CLAUDE! WISH US LUCK!
HOW IN HECK DID DINO DIGITALIS--LORD OF THE LOW-BUDGETS--GET CLEVELAND TO RENT HIM UNION TERMINAL AS A MOVIE STUDIO?
HOWARD PONDERS THAT QUESTION AS HE AND BEVERLY ENTER THE LOOMING PORTALS OF THE LANDMARK BUILDING...

...UNTIL THEY STAND STARING AWESTRUCK AT THE GLAMOROUS GLITTERING *TRANS-FORMATION* THE ONCE-UTILITARIAN TERMINAL HAS UNDERGONE.

HOWARD, I--I DON'T BELIEVE IT! IT'S HOLLYWOOD, RIGHT HERE IN CLEVE-LAND!

MAYBE L.A. SUNK AND THEY HAD TO TRANSPLANT IT FAST!

BUT, DESPITE HIS GRUFF DEMEANOR, HOWARD IS IMPRESSED--AND SCARED. NOTHING DINO DIGITALIS HAD TOLD THEM PREPARED HIM FOR THE OVERWHELMING SCHMALTZ OF THE "HOLLY-WOOD EXPERIENCE".

HE WAS HOPING HE WOULDN'T HAVE TO FULFILL YESTERDAY'S FOOLISH AGREEMENT TO ACT IN DIGITALIS' NEW FILM. NOW IT LOOKS INEVITABLE.

INFORMATION
INFORMATION INCOMING TRAINS INFORMAT

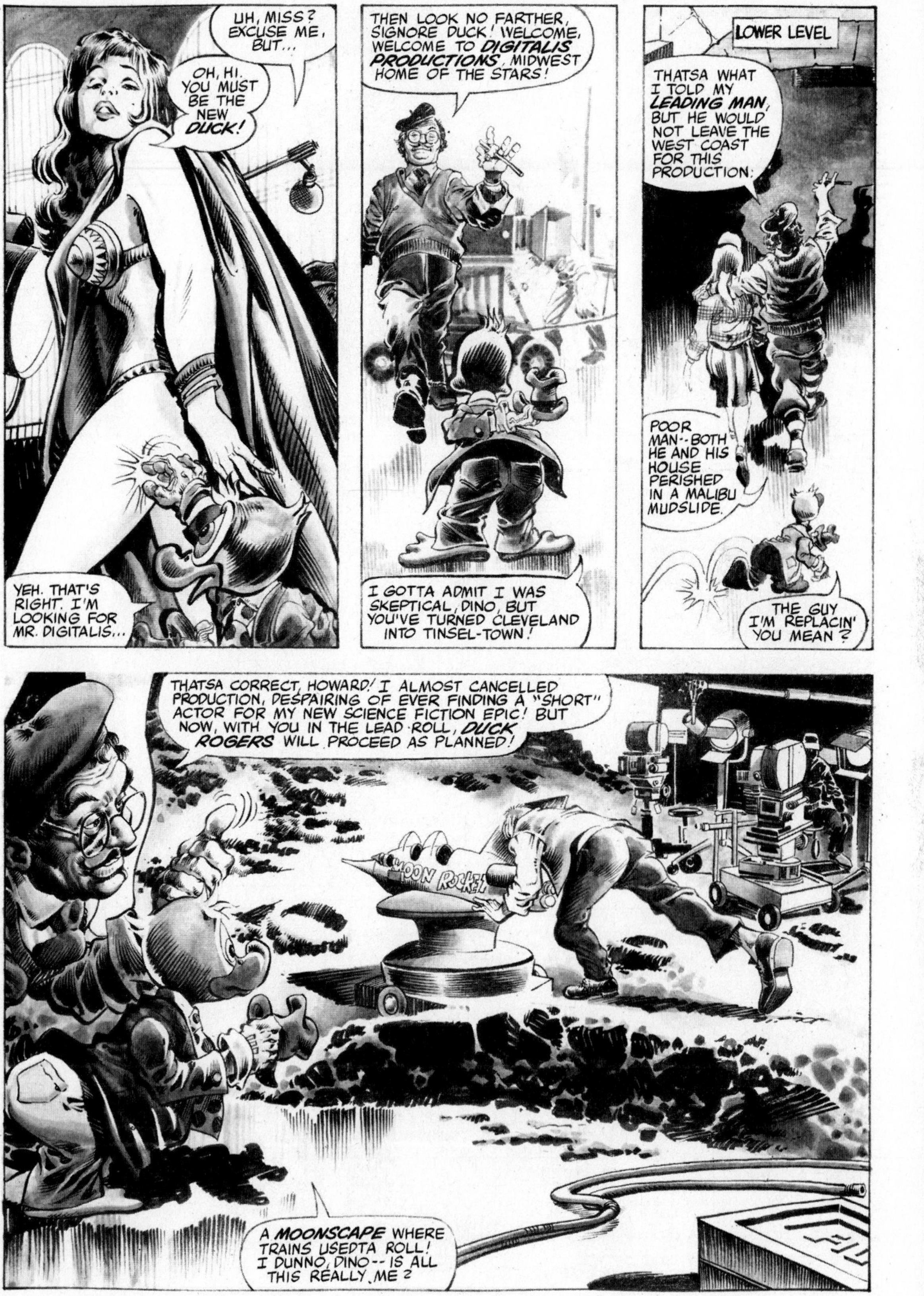
UH, MISS? EXCUSE ME, BUT...
OH, HI. YOU MUST BE THE NEW DUCK!
YEH. THAT'S RIGHT. I'M LOOKING FOR MR. DIGITALIS...
THEN LOOK NO FARTHER, SIGNORE DUCK! WELCOME, WELCOME TO DIGITALIS PRODUCTIONS, MIDWEST HOME OF THE STARS!
I GOTTA ADMIT I WAS SKEPTICAL, DINO, BUT YOU'VE TURNED CLEVELAND INTO TINSEL-TOWN!
LOWER LEVEL
THATSA WHAT I TOLD MY LEADING MAN, BUT HE WOULD NOT LEAVE THE WEST COAST FOR THIS PRODUCTION;
POOR MAN--BOTH HE AND HIS HOUSE PERISHED IN A MALIBU MUDSLIDE.
THE GUY I'M REPLACIN' YOU MEAN?
THATSA CORRECT, HOWARD! I ALMOST CANCELLED PRODUCTION, DESPAIRING OF EVER FINDING A "SHORT" ACTOR FOR MY NEW SCIENCE FICTION EPIC! BUT NOW, WITH YOU IN THE LEAD ROLL, DUCK ROGERS WILL PROCEED AS PLANNED!
MOON ROCKET
A MOONSCAPE WHERE TRAINS USEDTA ROLL! I DUNNO, DINO--IS ALL THIS REALLY ME?

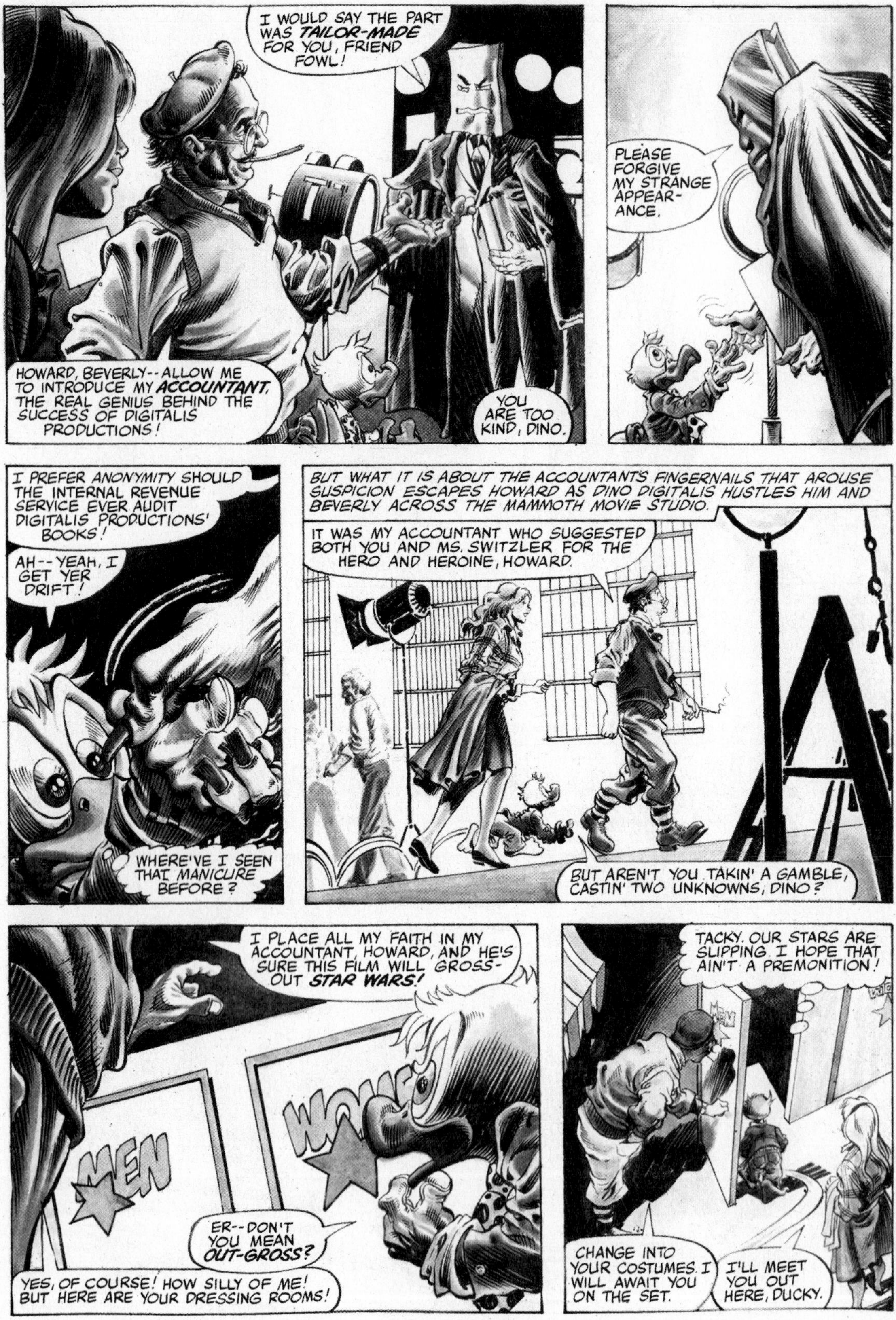
I WOULD SAY THE PART WAS TAILOR-MADE FOR YOU, FRIEND FOWL!
HOWARD, BEVERLY--ALLOW ME TO INTRODUCE MY ACCOUNTANT, THE REAL GENIUS BEHIND THE SUCCESS OF DIGITALIS PRODUCTIONS!
YOU ARE TOO KIND, DINO.
PLEASE FORGIVE MY STRANGE APPEAR-ANCE.
I PREFER ANONYMITY SHOULD THE INTERNAL REVENUE SERVICE EVER AUDIT DIGITALIS PRODUCTIONS' BOOKS!
AH--YEAH, I GET YER DRIFT!
WHERE'VE I SEEN THAT MANICURE BEFORE?
BUT WHAT IT IS ABOUT THE ACCOUNTANT'S FINGERNAILS THAT AROUSE SUSPICION ESCAPES HOWARD AS DINO DIGITALIS HUSTLES HIM AND BEVERLY ACROSS THE MAMMOTH MOVIE STUDIO.
IT WAS MY ACCOUNTANT WHO SUGGESTED BOTH YOU AND MS. SWITZLER FOR THE HERO AND HEROINE, HOWARD.
BUT AREN'T YOU TAKIN' A GAMBLE, CASTIN' TWO UNKNOWNS, DINO?
I PLACE ALL MY FAITH IN MY ACCOUNTANT, HOWARD, AND HE'S SURE THIS FILM WILL GROSS-OUT STAR WARS!
MEN
ER--DON'T YOU MEAN OUT-GROSS?
YES, OF COURSE! HOW SILLY OF ME! BUT HERE ARE YOUR DRESSING ROOMS!
TACKY. OUR STARS ARE SLIPPING. I HOPE THAT AIN'T A PREMONITION!
MEN
CHANGE INTO YOUR COSTUMES. I WILL AWAIT YOU ON THE SET.
I'LL MEET YOU OUT HERE, DUCKY.

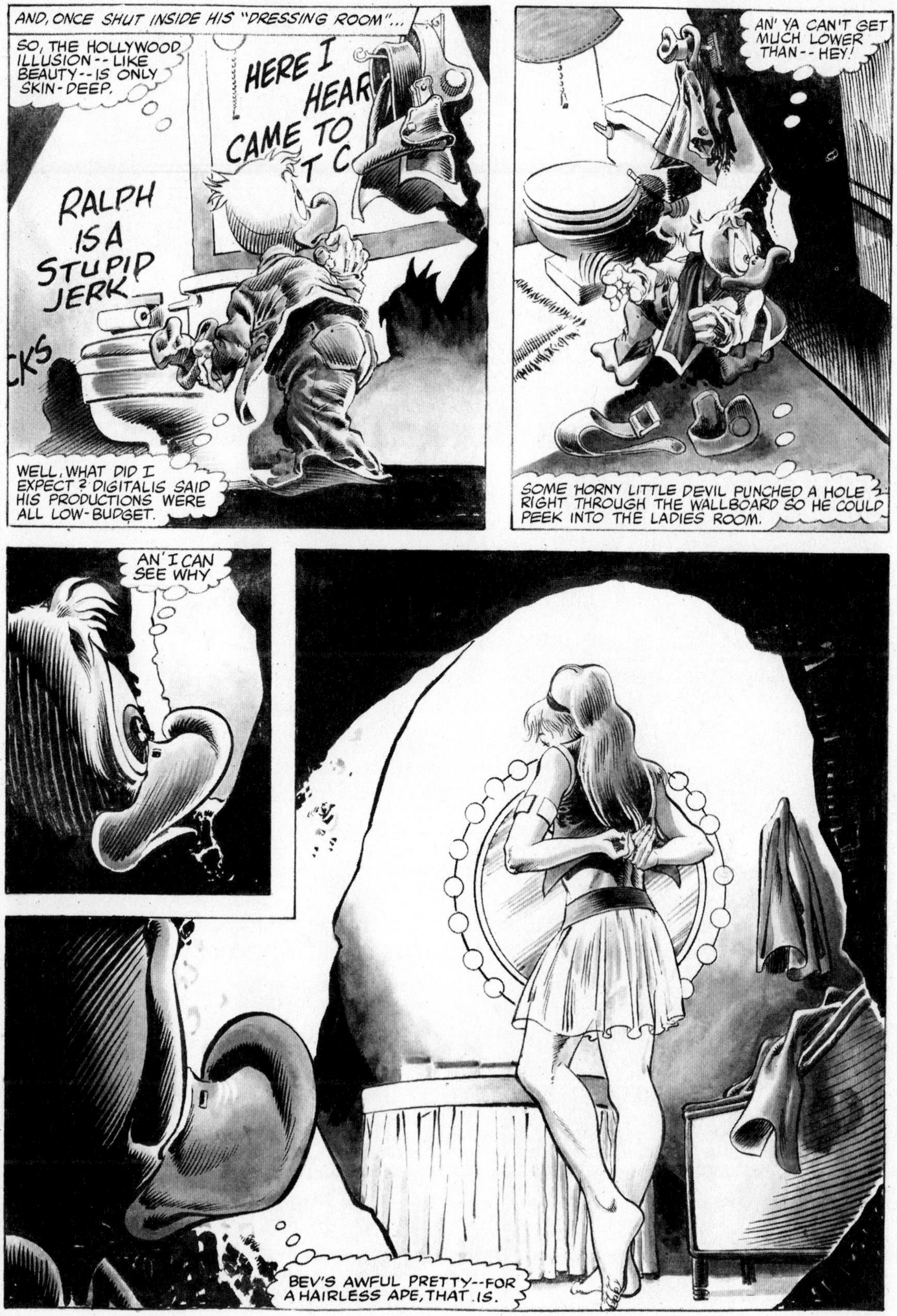
AND, ONCE SHUT INSIDE HIS "DRESSING ROOM"...
SO, THE HOLLYWOOD ILLUSION--LIKE BEAUTY--IS ONLY SKIN-DEEP.
HERE I HEAR CAME TO T C
RALPH IS A STUPID JERK
WELL, WHAT DID I EXPECT? DIGITALIS SAID HIS PRODUCTIONS WERE ALL LOW-BUDGET.
AN' YA CAN'T GET MUCH LOWER THAN--HEY!
SOME HORNY LITTLE DEVIL PUNCHED A HOLE RIGHT THROUGH THE WALLBOARD SO HE COULD PEEK INTO THE LADIES ROOM.
AN' I CAN SEE WHY
BEV'S AWFUL PRETTY--FOR A HAIRLESS APE, THAT IS.

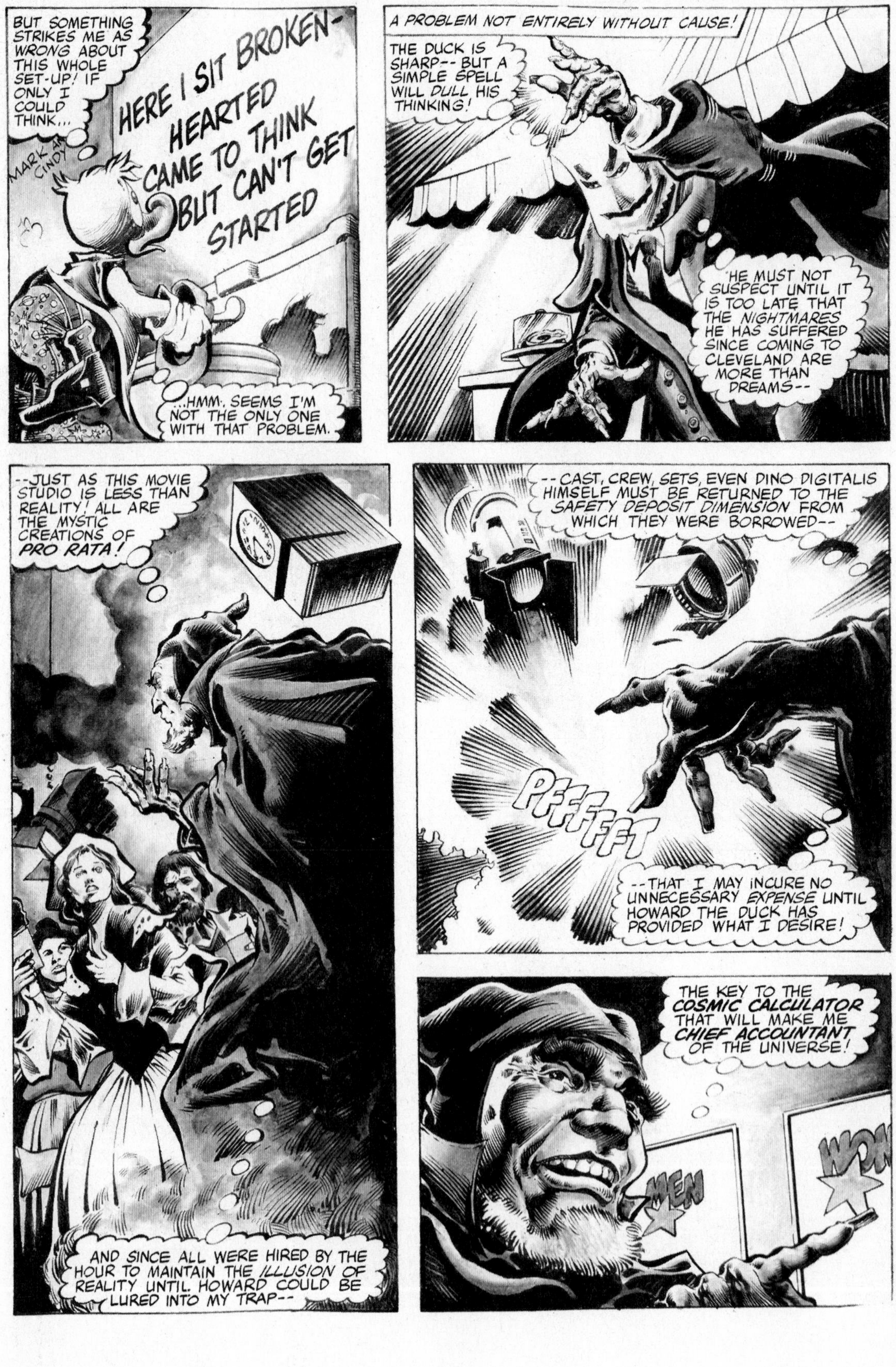

BUT SOMETHING STRIKES ME AS WRONG ABOUT THIS WHOLE SET-UP! IF ONLY I COULD THINK...
HERE I SIT BROKEN-HEARTED CAME TO THINK BUT CAN'T GET STARTED
...HMM. SEEMS I'M NOT THE ONLY ONE WITH THAT PROBLEM.
A PROBLEM NOT ENTIRELY WITHOUT CAUSE!
THE DUCK IS SHARP-- BUT A SIMPLE SPELL WILL DULL HIS THINKING!
HE MUST NOT SUSPECT UNTIL IT IS TOO LATE THAT THE NIGHTMARES HE HAS SUFFERED SINCE COMING TO CLEVELAND ARE MORE THAN DREAMS--
--JUST AS THIS MOVIE STUDIO IS LESS THAN REALITY! ALL ARE THE MYSTIC CREATIONS OF PRO RATA!
AND SINCE ALL WERE HIRED BY THE HOUR TO MAINTAIN THE ILLUSION OF REALITY UNTIL HOWARD COULD BE LURED INTO MY TRAP--
--CAST, CREW, SETS, EVEN DINO DIGITALIS HIMSELF MUST BE RETURNED TO THE SAFETY DEPOSIT DIMENSION FROM WHICH THEY WERE BORROWED--
PFFFFFT
--THAT I MAY INCURE NO UNNECESSARY EXPENSE UNTIL HOWARD THE DUCK HAS PROVIDED WHAT I DESIRE!
THE KEY TO THE COSMIC CALCULATOR THAT WILL MAKE ME CHIEF ACCOUNTANT OF THE UNIVERSE!
MEN

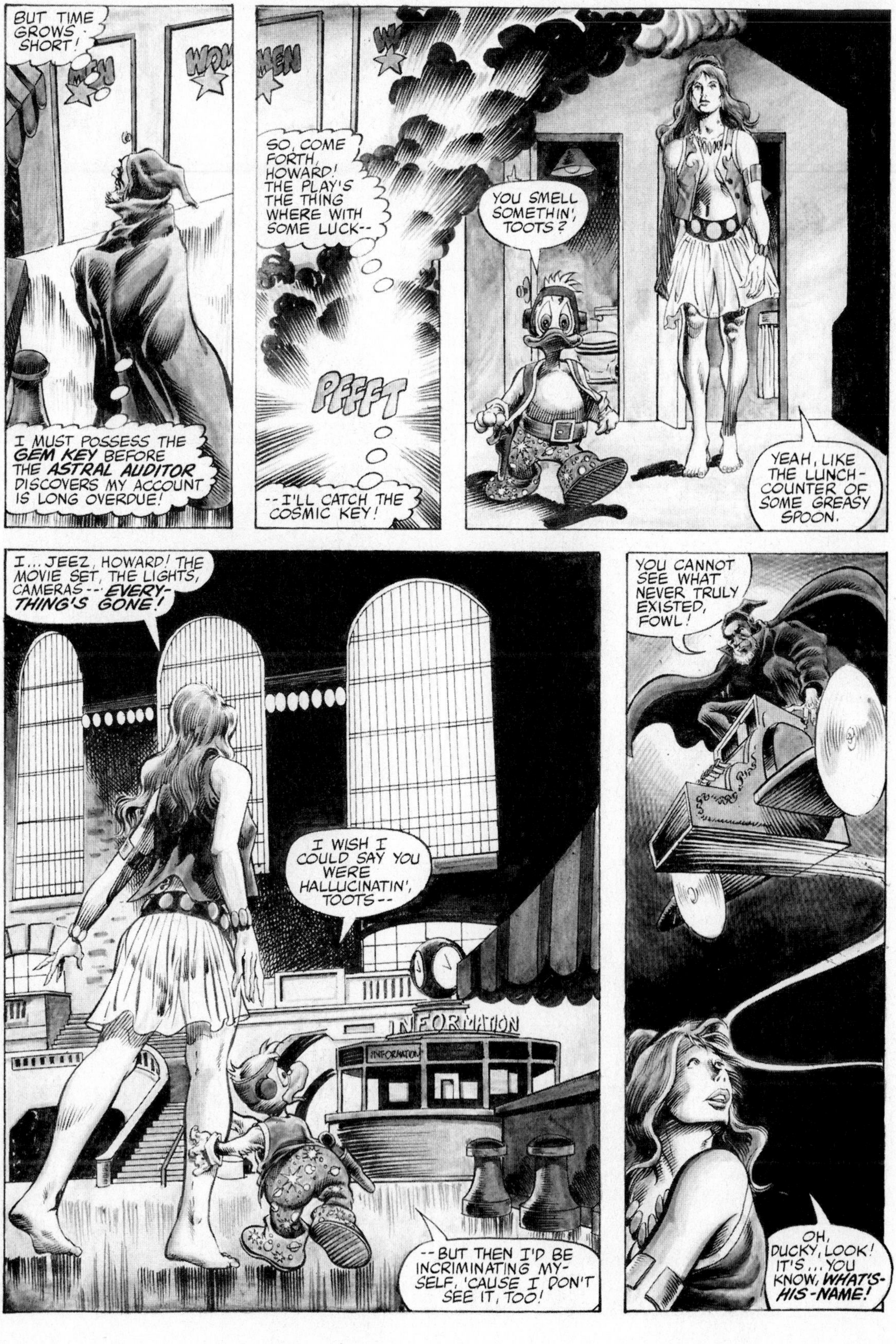
BUT TIME GROWS SHORT!
MEN
WOMEN
I MUST POSSESS THE GEM KEY BEFORE THE ASTRAL AUDITOR DISCOVERS MY ACCOUNT IS LONG OVERDUE!
SO, COME FORTH, HOWARD! THE PLAY'S THE THING WHERE WITH SOME LUCK--
PFFFT
--I'LL CATCH THE COSMIC KEY!
YOU SMELL SOMETHIN', TOOTS?
YEAH, LIKE THE LUNCH-COUNTER OF SOME GREASY SPOON.
I... JEEZ, HOWARD! THE MOVIE SET, THE LIGHTS, CAMERAS-- EVERY-THING'S GONE!
I WISH I COULD SAY YOU WERE HALLUCINATIN', TOOTS--
INFORMATION
--BUT THEN I'D BE INCRIMINATING MY-SELF, 'CAUSE I DON'T SEE IT, TOO!
YOU CANNOT SEE WHAT NEVER TRULY EXISTED, FOWL!
OH, DUCKY, LOOK! IT'S... YOU KNOW, WHAT'S-HIS-NAME!

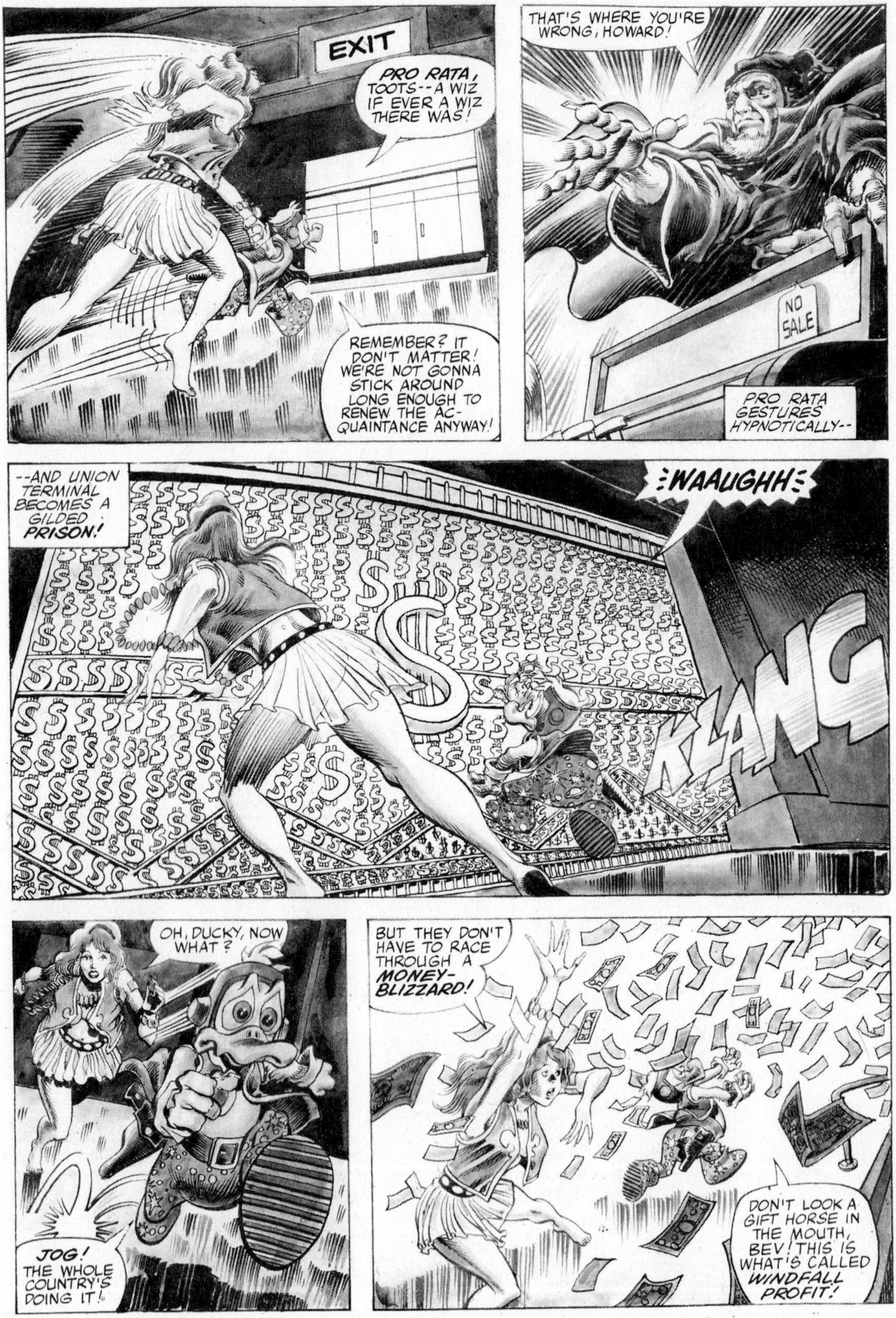
EXIT
PRO RATA, TOOTS--A WIZ IF EVER A WIZ THERE WAS!
REMEMBER? IT DON'T MATTER! WE'RE NOT GONNA STICK AROUND LONG ENOUGH TO RENEW THE AC-QUAINTANCE ANYWAY!
THAT'S WHERE YOU'RE WRONG, HOWARD!
NO SALE
PRO RATA GESTURES HYPNOTICALLY--
--AND UNION TERMINAL BECOMES A GILDED PRISON!
WAAUGHH
KLANG
OH, DUCKY, NOW WHAT?
JOG! THE WHOLE COUNTRY'S DOING IT!
BUT THEY DON'T HAVE TO RACE THROUGH A MONEY-BLIZZARD!
DON'T LOOK A GIFT HORSE IN THE MOUTH, BEV! THIS IS WHAT'S CALLED WINDFALL PROFIT!

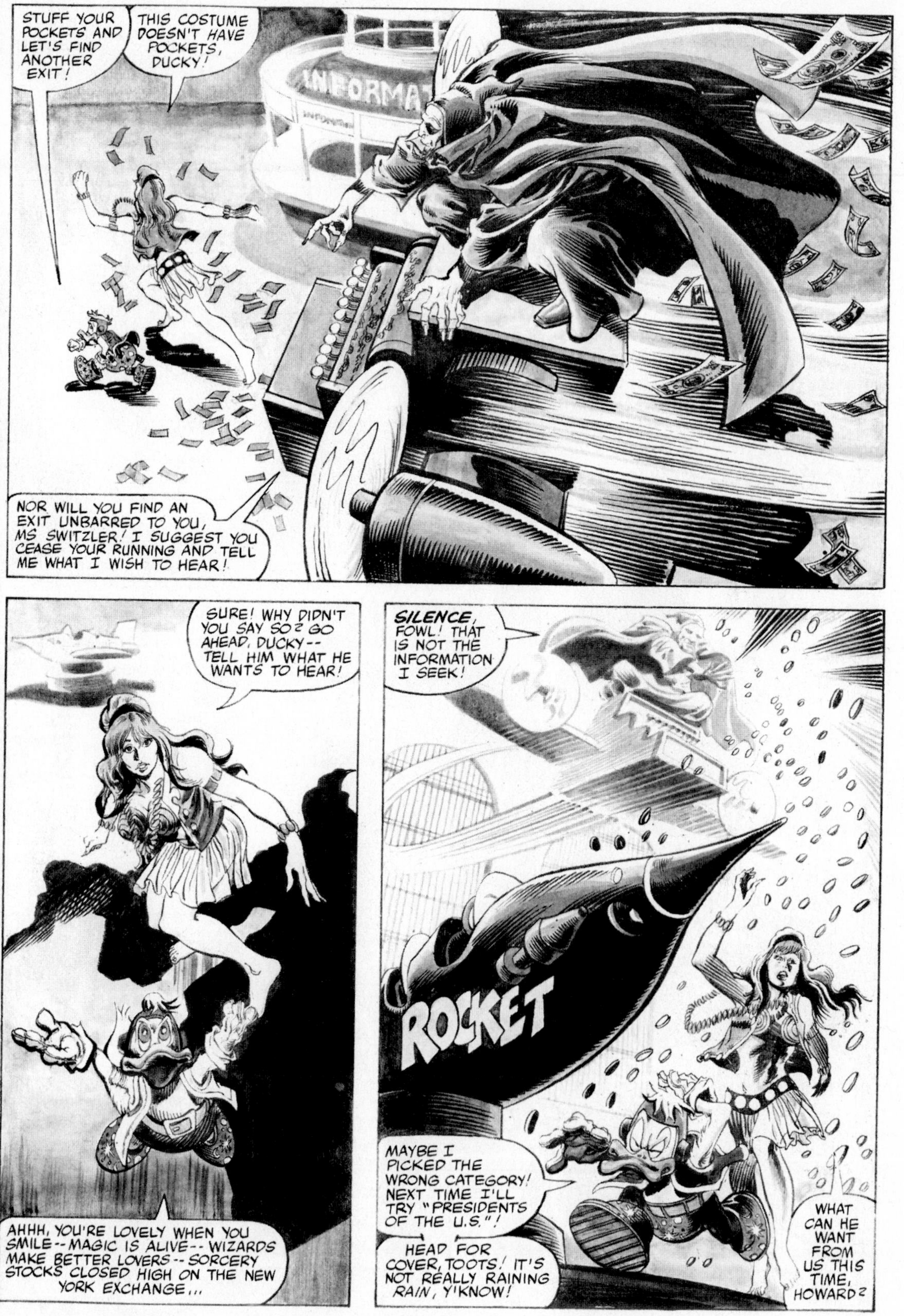
STUFF YOUR POCKETS AND LET'S FIND ANOTHER EXIT!
THIS COSTUME DOESN'T *HAVE* POCKETS, DUCKY!
INFORMAT
NOR WILL YOU FIND AN EXIT UNBARRED TO YOU, MS SWITZLER! I SUGGEST YOU CEASE YOUR RUNNING AND TELL ME WHAT I WISH TO HEAR!
SURE! WHY DIDN'T YOU SAY SO? GO AHEAD, DUCKY-- TELL HIM WHAT HE WANTS TO HEAR!
AHHH, YOU'RE LOVELY WHEN YOU SMILE--MAGIC IS ALIVE--WIZARDS MAKE BETTER LOVERS--SORCERY STOCKS CLOSED HIGH ON THE NEW YORK EXCHANGE...
SILENCE, FOWL! THAT IS NOT THE INFORMATION I SEEK!
ROCKET
MAYBE I PICKED THE WRONG CATEGORY! NEXT TIME I'LL TRY "PRESIDENTS OF THE U.S."!
HEAD FOR COVER, TOOTS! IT'S NOT REALLY RAINING *RAIN*, Y'KNOW!
WHAT CAN HE WANT FROM US THIS TIME, HOWARD?

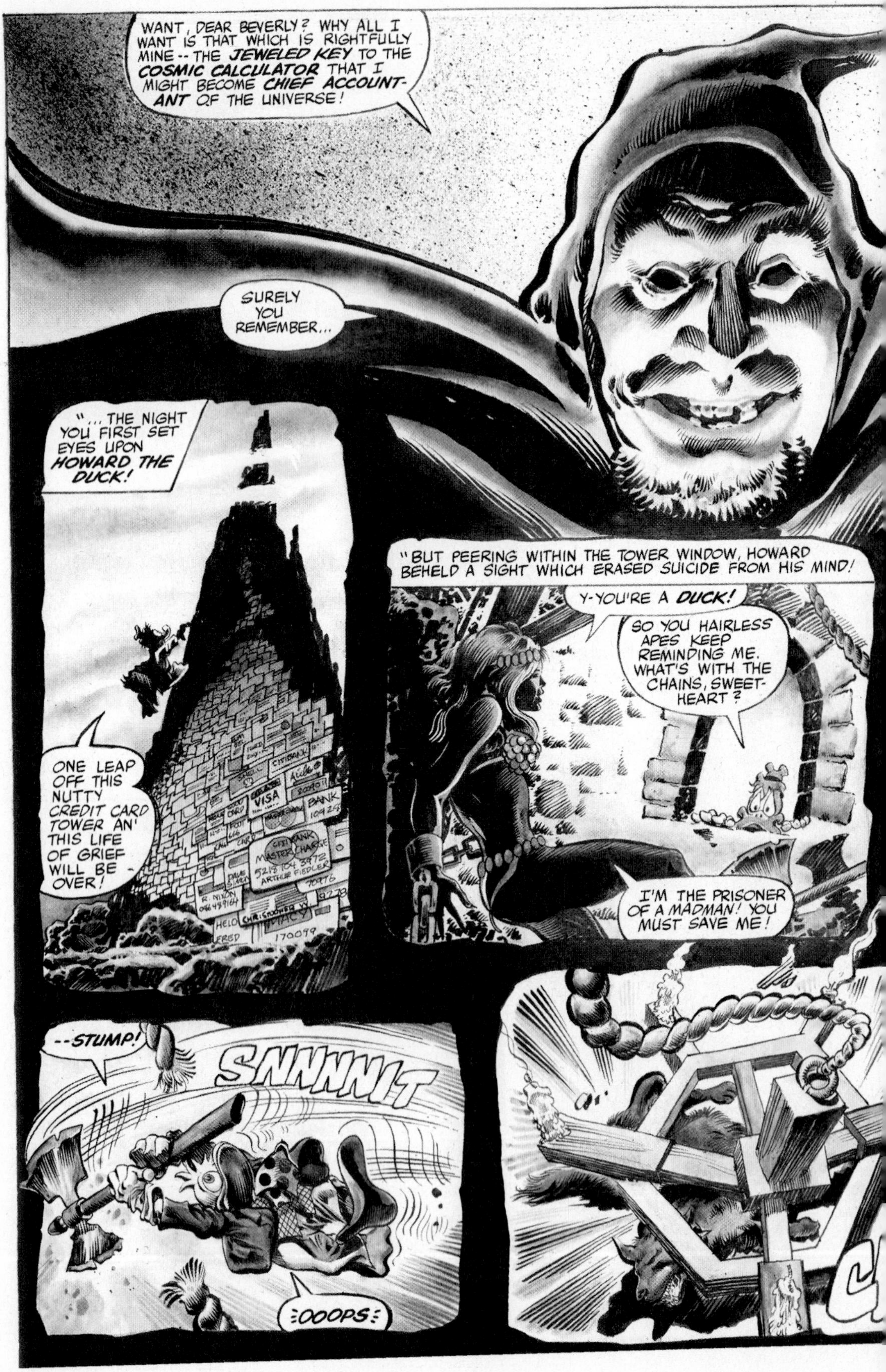
WANT, DEAR BEVERLY? WHY ALL I WANT IS THAT WHICH IS RIGHTFULLY MINE -- THE JEWELED KEY TO THE COSMIC CALCULATOR THAT I MIGHT BECOME CHIEF ACCOUNTANT OF THE UNIVERSE!
SURELY YOU REMEMBER...
"...THE NIGHT YOU FIRST SET EYES UPON HOWARD THE DUCK!
ONE LEAP OFF THIS NUTTY CREDIT CARD TOWER AN' THIS LIFE OF GRIEF WILL BE OVER!
VISA
BANK
CITIBANK MASTER CHARGE
ARTHUR FIEDLER
R. NIXON
"BUT PEERING WITHIN THE TOWER WINDOW, HOWARD BEHELD A SIGHT WHICH ERASED SUICIDE FROM HIS MIND!
Y-YOU'RE A DUCK!
SO YOU HAIRLESS APES KEEP REMINDING ME. WHAT'S WITH THE CHAINS, SWEETHEART?
I'M THE PRISONER OF A MADMAN! YOU MUST SAVE ME!
--STUMP!
SNNNNIT
OOOPS

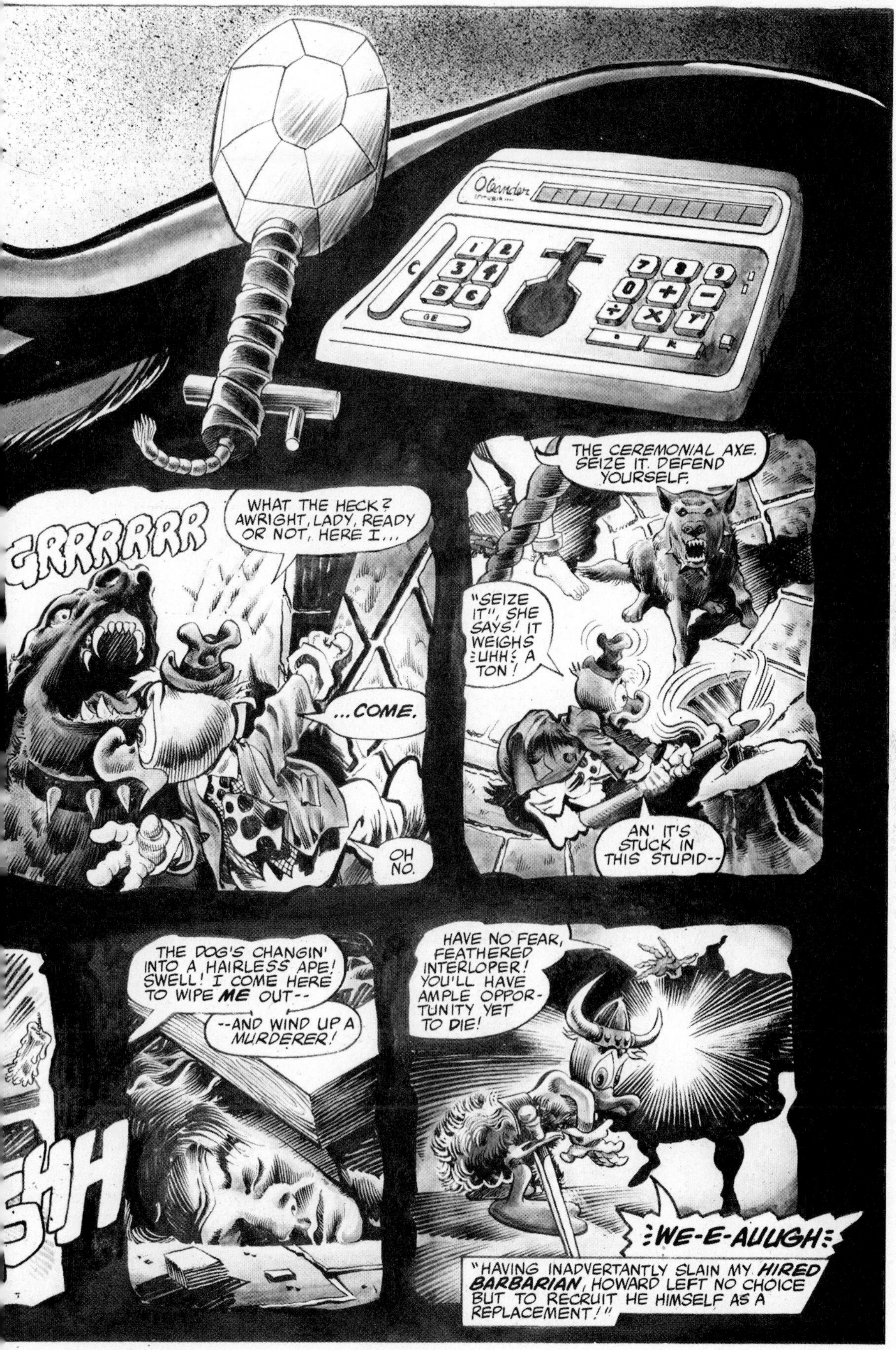
Oleander
GE
GRRRRRR
WHAT THE HECK? AWRIGHT, LADY, READY OR NOT, HERE I...
...COME.
OH NO.
THE CEREMONIAL AXE. SEIZE IT. DEFEND YOURSELF.
"SEIZE IT", SHE SAYS! IT WEIGHS UHH A TON!
AN' IT'S STUCK IN THIS STUPID--
SHH
THE DOG'S CHANGIN' INTO A HAIRLESS APE! SWELL! I COME HERE TO WIPE ME OUT--
--AND WIND UP A MURDERER!
HAVE NO FEAR, FEATHERED INTERLOPER! YOU'LL HAVE AMPLE OPPORTUNITY YET TO DIE!
WE-E-AUUGH
"HAVING INADVERTANTLY SLAIN MY HIRED BARBARIAN, HOWARD LEFT NO CHOICE BUT TO RECRUIT HE HIMSELF AS A REPLACEMENT!"

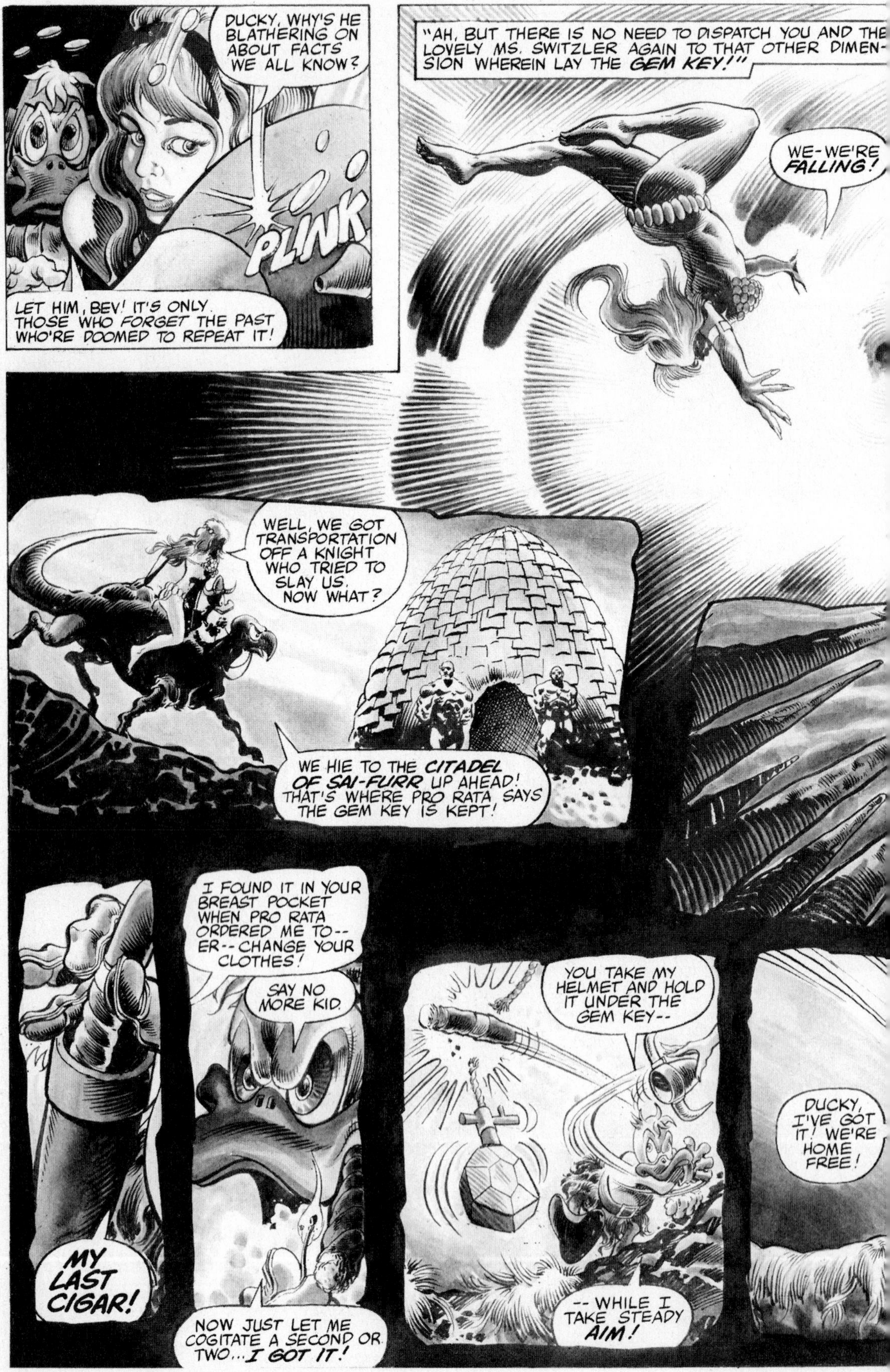
DUCKY, WHY'S HE BLATHERING ON ABOUT FACTS WE ALL KNOW?
PLINK
LET HIM, BEV! IT'S ONLY THOSE WHO FORGET THE PAST WHO'RE DOOMED TO REPEAT IT!
"AH, BUT THERE IS NO NEED TO DISPATCH YOU AND THE LOVELY MS. SWITZLER AGAIN TO THAT OTHER DIMENSION WHEREIN LAY THE GEM KEY!"
WE-WE'RE FALLING!
WELL, WE GOT TRANSPORTATION OFF A KNIGHT WHO TRIED TO SLAY US. NOW WHAT?
WE HIE TO THE CITADEL OF SAI-FURR UP AHEAD! THAT'S WHERE PRO RATA SAYS THE GEM KEY IS KEPT!
MY LAST CIGAR!
I FOUND IT IN YOUR BREAST POCKET WHEN PRO RATA ORDERED ME TO-- ER--CHANGE YOUR CLOTHES!
SAY NO MORE KID.
NOW JUST LET ME COGITATE A SECOND OR TWO... I GOT IT!
YOU TAKE MY HELMET AND HOLD IT UNDER THE GEM KEY--
--WHILE I TAKE STEADY AIM!
DUCKY, I'VE GOT IT! WE'RE HOME FREE!

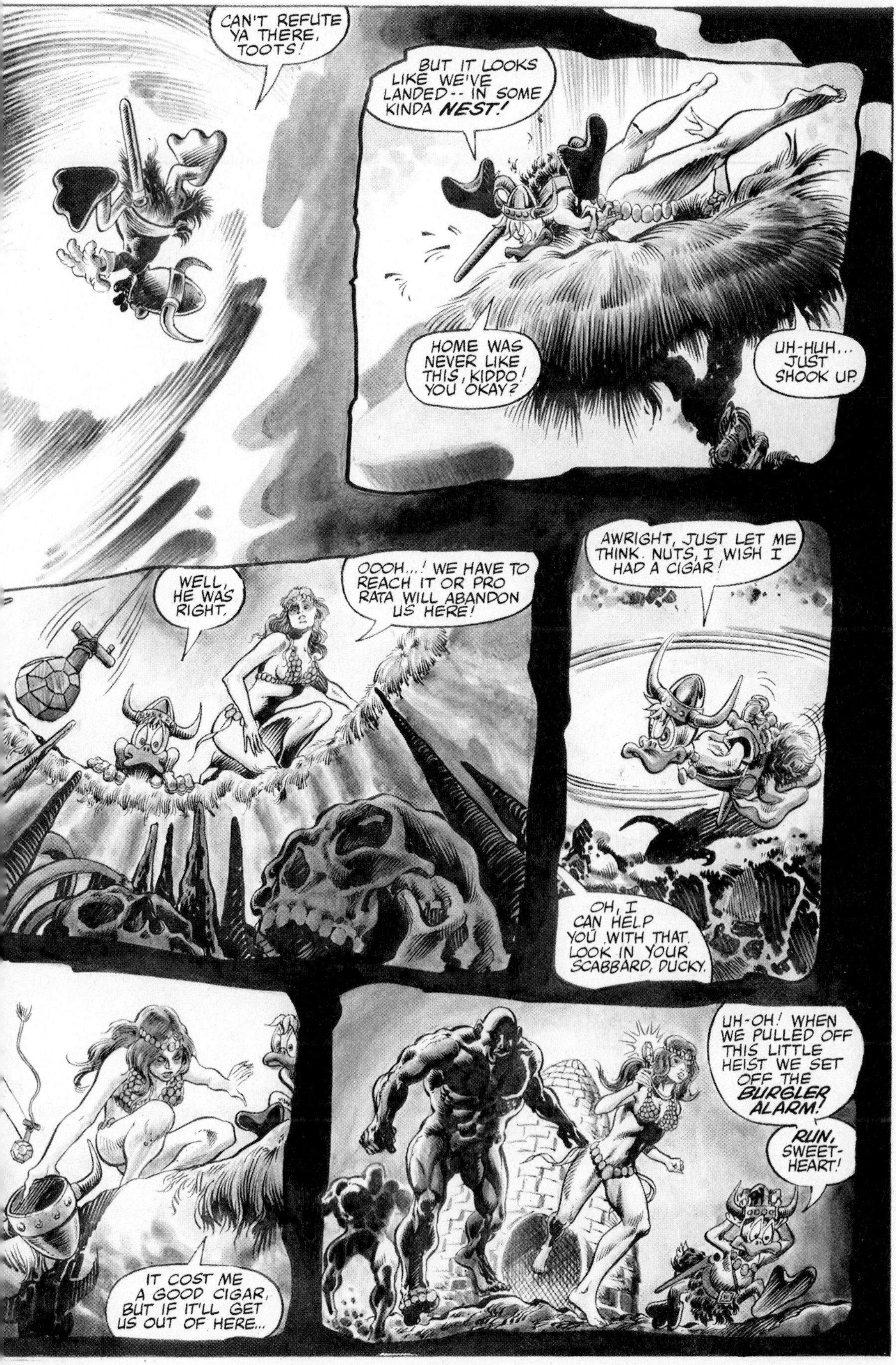
CAN'T REFUTE YA THERE, TOOTS!
BUT IT LOOKS LIKE WE'VE LANDED-- IN SOME KINDA NEST!
HOME WAS NEVER LIKE THIS, KIDDO! YOU OKAY?
UH-HUH... JUST SHOOK UP.
WELL, HE WAS RIGHT.
OOOH...! WE HAVE TO REACH IT OR PRO RATA WILL ABANDON US HERE!
AWRIGHT, JUST LET ME THINK. NUTS, I WISH I HAD A CIGAR!
OH, I CAN HELP YOU WITH THAT. LOOK IN YOUR SCABBARD, DUCKY.
IT COST ME A GOOD CIGAR, BUT IF IT'LL GET US OUT OF HERE...
UH-OH! WHEN WE PULLED OFF THIS LITTLE HEIST WE SET OFF THE BURGLER ALARM!
RUN, SWEET-HEART!

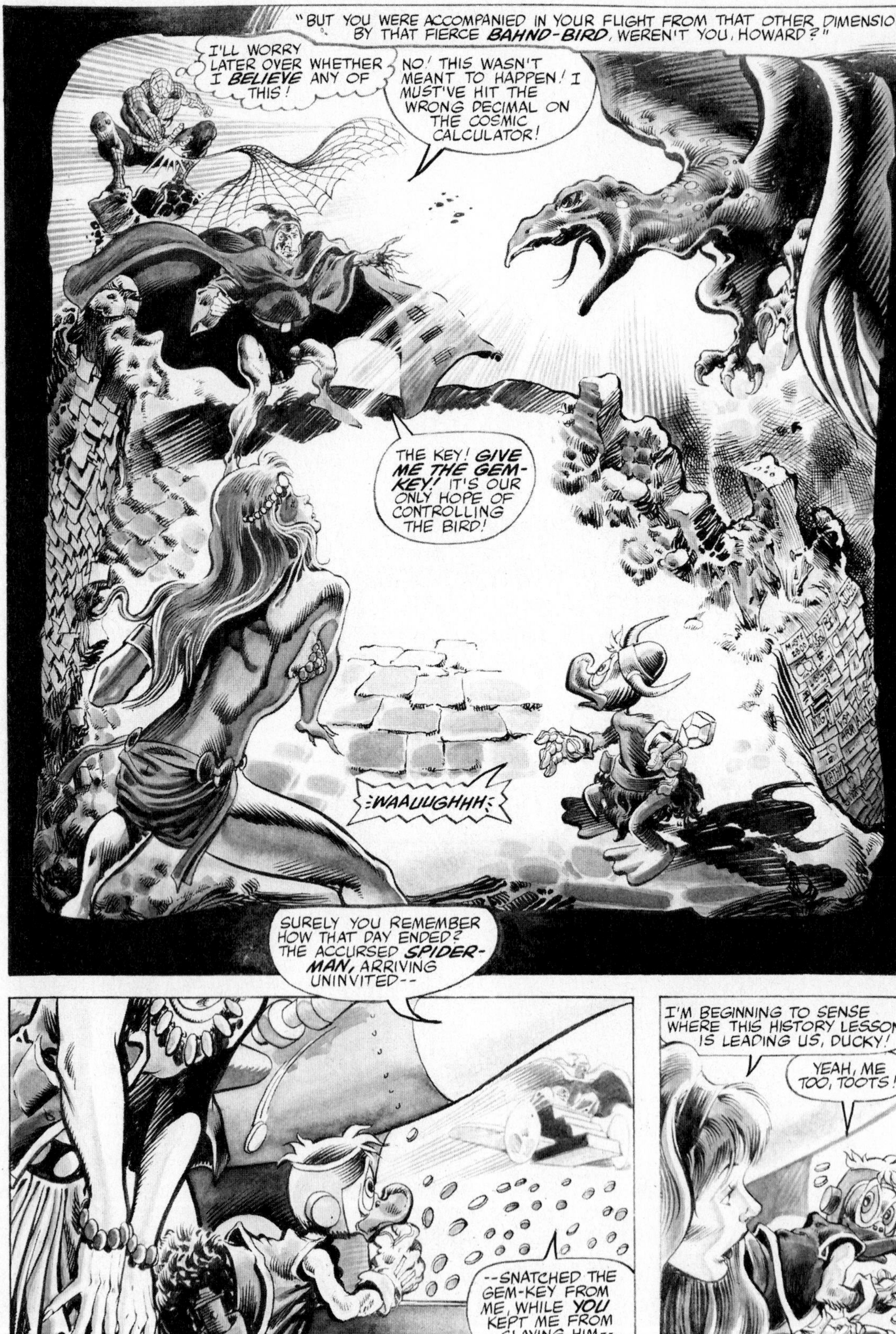
"BUT YOU WERE ACCOMPANIED IN YOUR FLIGHT FROM THAT OTHER DIMENSION BY THAT FIERCE BAHND-BIRD, WEREN'T YOU, HOWARD?"
I'LL WORRY LATER OVER WHETHER I BELIEVE ANY OF THIS!
NO! THIS WASN'T MEANT TO HAPPEN! I MUST'VE HIT THE WRONG DECIMAL ON THE COSMIC CALCULATOR!
THE KEY! GIVE ME THE GEM-KEY! IT'S OUR ONLY HOPE OF CONTROLLING THE BIRD!
WAAUUGHHH
SURELY YOU REMEMBER HOW THAT DAY ENDED? THE ACCURSED SPIDER-MAN, ARRIVING UNINVITED--
--SNATCHED THE GEM-KEY FROM ME, WHILE YOU KEPT ME FROM SLAYING HIM--
I'M BEGINNING TO SENSE WHERE THIS HISTORY LESSON IS LEADING US, DUCKY!
YEAH, ME TOO, TOOTS!

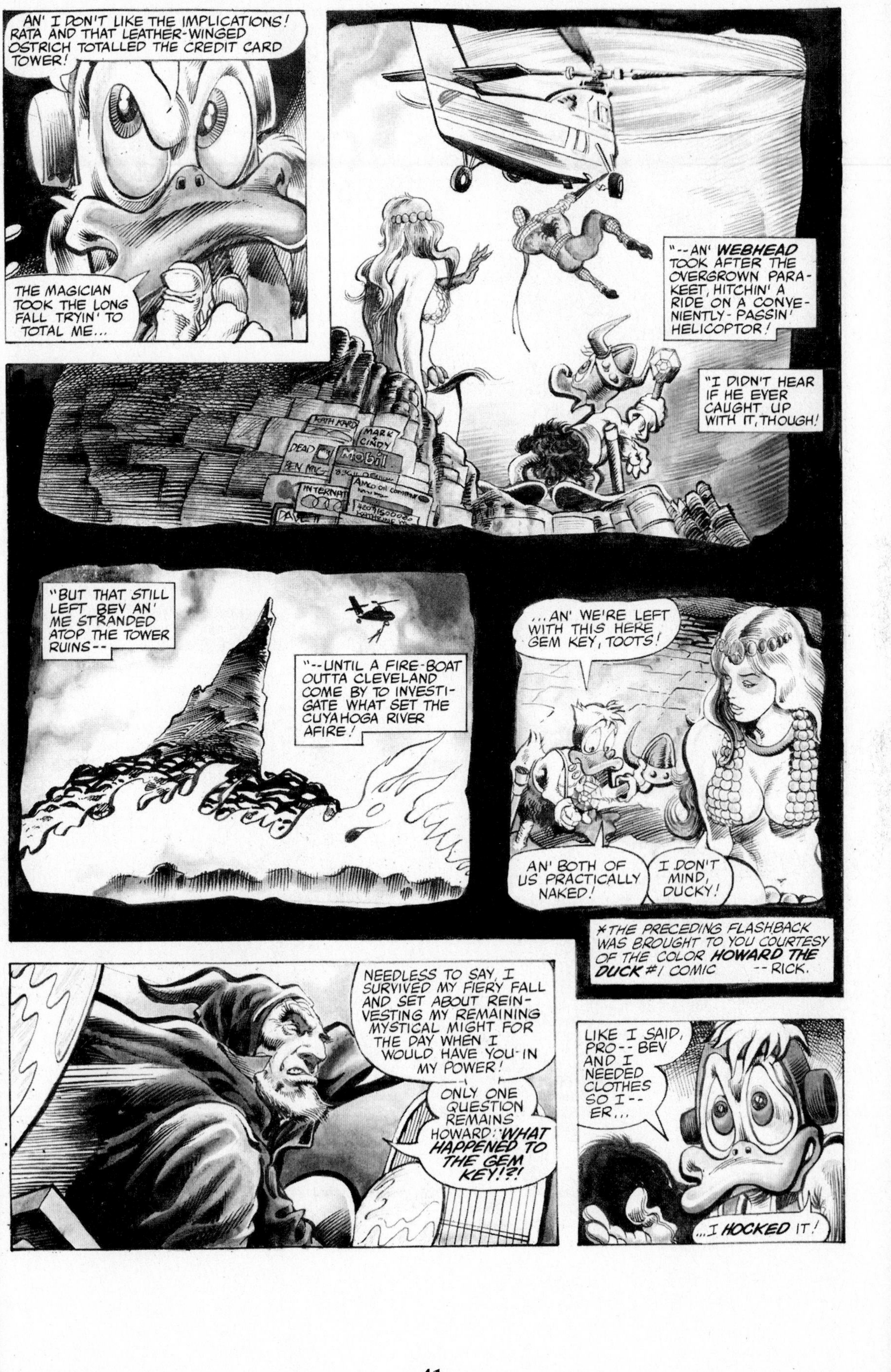

AN' I DON'T LIKE THE IMPLICATIONS! RATA AND THAT LEATHER-WINGED OSTRICH TOTALLED THE CREDIT CARD TOWER!
THE MAGICIAN TOOK THE LONG FALL TRYIN' TO TOTAL ME...
"--AN' WEBHEAD TOOK AFTER THE OVERGROWN PARA-KEET, HITCHIN' A RIDE ON A CONVE-NIENTLY-PASSIN' HELICOPTOR!
"I DIDN'T HEAR IF HE EVER CAUGHT UP WITH IT, THOUGH!
"BUT THAT STILL LEFT BEV AN' ME STRANDED ATOP THE TOWER RUINS--
"--UNTIL A FIRE-BOAT OUTTA CLEVELAND COME BY TO INVESTI-GATE WHAT SET THE CUYAHOGA RIVER AFIRE!
...AN' WE'RE LEFT WITH THIS HERE GEM KEY, TOOTS!
AN' BOTH OF US PRACTICALLY NAKED!
I DON'T MIND, DUCKY!
*THE PRECEDING FLASHBACK WAS BROUGHT TO YOU COURTESY OF THE COLOR HOWARD THE DUCK #1 COMIC --RICK.
NEEDLESS TO SAY, I SURVIVED MY FIERY FALL AND SET ABOUT REIN-VESTING MY REMAINING MYSTICAL MIGHT FOR THE DAY WHEN I WOULD HAVE YOU-IN MY POWER!
ONLY ONE QUESTION REMAINS HOWARD: "WHAT HAPPENED TO THE GEM KEY!?!
LIKE I SAID, PRO--BEV AND I NEEDED CLOTHES SO I--ER...
...I HOCKED IT!

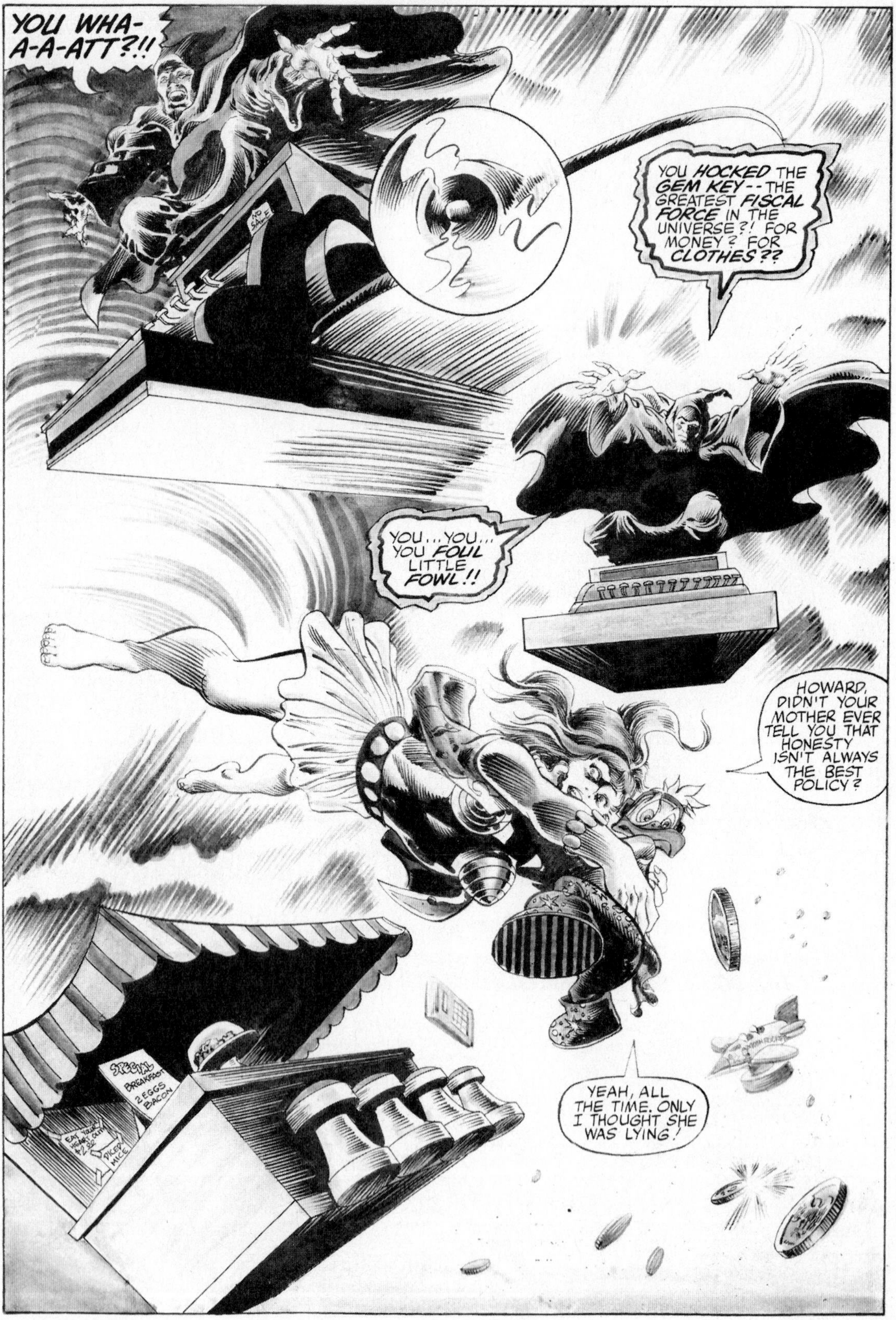
YOU WHA-A-A-ATT?!!
YOU HOCKED THE GEM KEY--THE GREATEST FISCAL FORCE IN THE UNIVERSE?! FOR MONEY? FOR CLOTHES??
YOU... YOU... YOU FOUL LITTLE FOWL!!
HOWARD, DIDN'T YOUR MOTHER EVER TELL YOU THAT HONESTY ISN'T ALWAYS THE BEST POLICY?
YEAH, ALL THE TIME. ONLY I THOUGHT SHE WAS LYING!
SPECIAL BREAKFAST 2 EGGS BACON

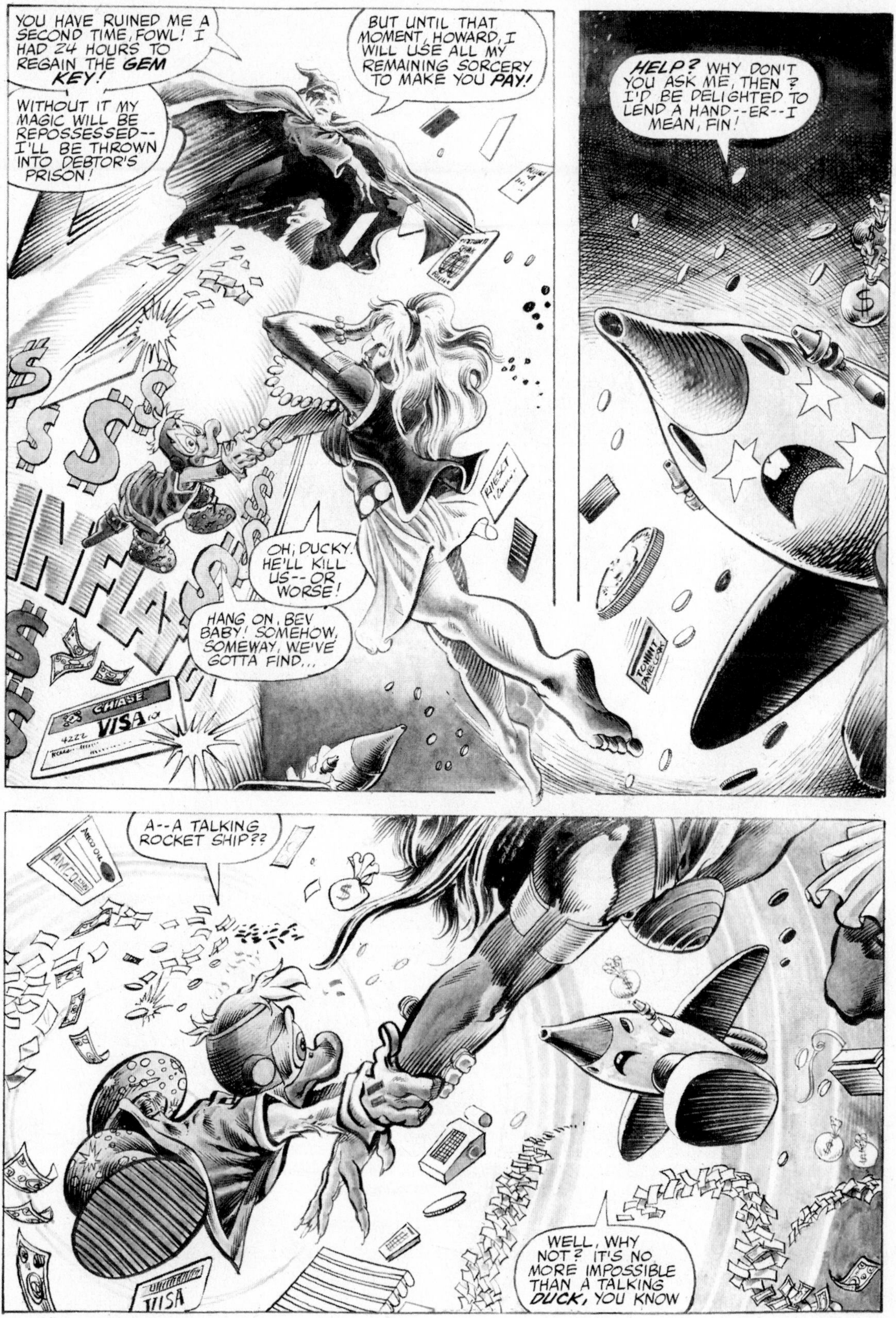
YOU HAVE RUINED ME A SECOND TIME, FOWL! I HAD 24 HOURS TO REGAIN THE GEM KEY!
WITHOUT IT MY MAGIC WILL BE REPOSSESSED-- I'LL BE THROWN INTO DEBTOR'S PRISON!
BUT UNTIL THAT MOMENT, HOWARD, I WILL USE ALL MY REMAINING SORCERY TO MAKE YOU PAY!
OH, DUCKY! HE'LL KILL US--OR WORSE!
HANG ON, BEV BABY! SOMEHOW, SOMEWAY, WE'VE GOTTA FIND...
CHASE
VISA
HELP? WHY DON'T YOU ASK ME, THEN? I'D BE DELIGHTED TO LEND A HAND--ER--I MEAN, FIN!
A--A TALKING ROCKET SHIP??
WELL, WHY NOT? IT'S NO MORE IMPOSSIBLE THAN A TALKING DUCK, YOU KNOW
VISA

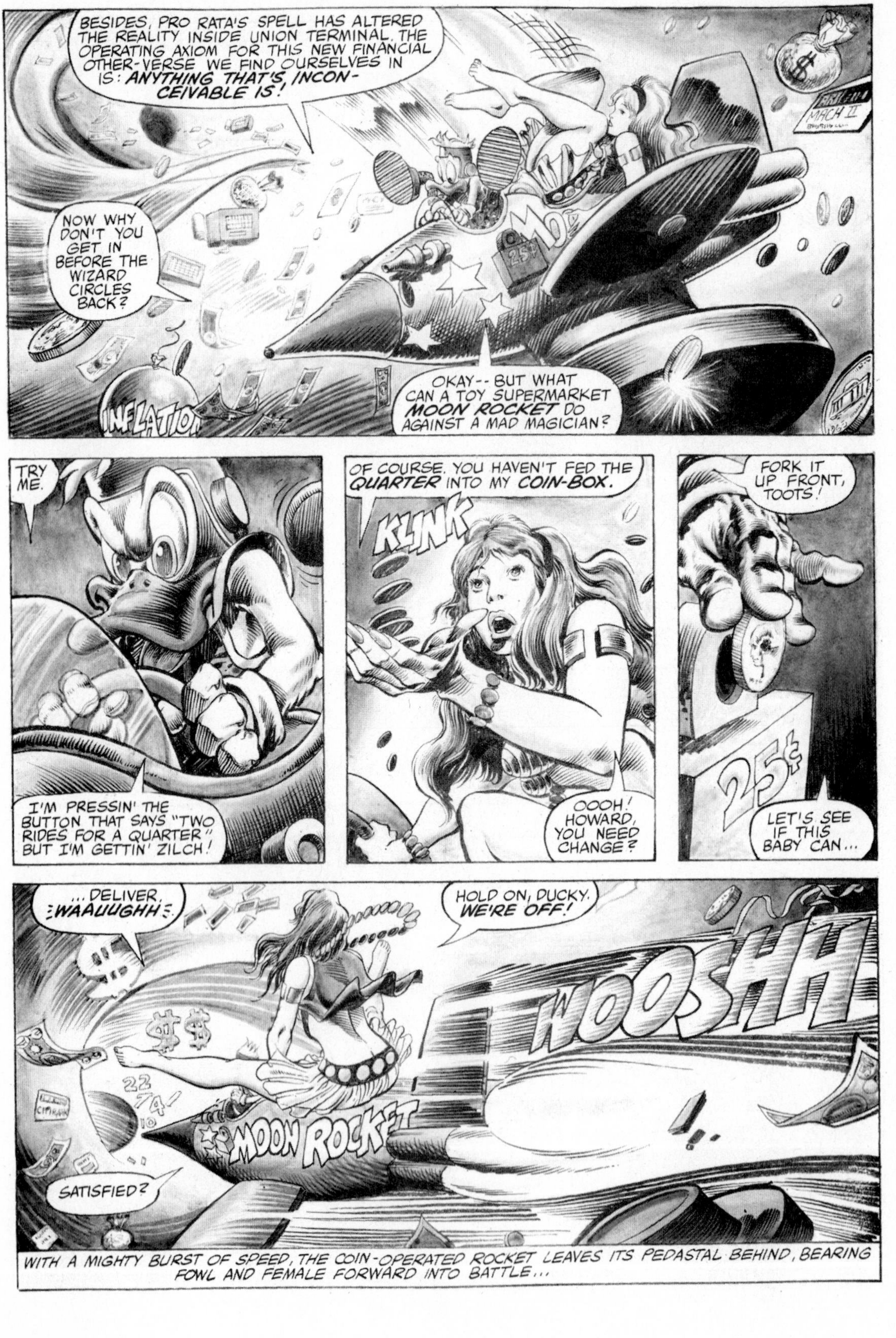
BESIDES, PRO RATA'S SPELL HAS ALTERED THE REALITY INSIDE UNION TERMINAL. THE OPERATING AXIOM FOR THIS NEW FINANCIAL OTHER-VERSE WE FIND OURSELVES IN IS: ANYTHING THAT'S INCONCEIVABLE IS!
NOW WHY DON'T YOU GET IN BEFORE THE WIZARD CIRCLES BACK?
OKAY-- BUT WHAT CAN A TOY SUPERMARKET MOON ROCKET DO AGAINST A MAD MAGICIAN?
INFLATION
25¢
TRY ME.
I'M PRESSIN' THE BUTTON THAT SAYS "TWO RIDES FOR A QUARTER" BUT I'M GETTIN' ZILCH!
OF COURSE. YOU HAVEN'T FED THE QUARTER INTO MY COIN-BOX.
KLINK
OOOH! HOWARD, YOU NEED CHANGE?
FORK IT UP FRONT, TOOTS!
25¢
LET'S SEE IF THIS BABY CAN...
...DELIVER. WAAUUGHH
HOLD ON, DUCKY. WE'RE OFF!
WOOSHH
MOON ROCKET
SATISFIED?
WITH A MIGHTY BURST OF SPEED, THE COIN-OPERATED ROCKET LEAVES ITS PEDASTAL BEHIND, BEARING FOWL AND FEMALE FORWARD INTO BATTLE...

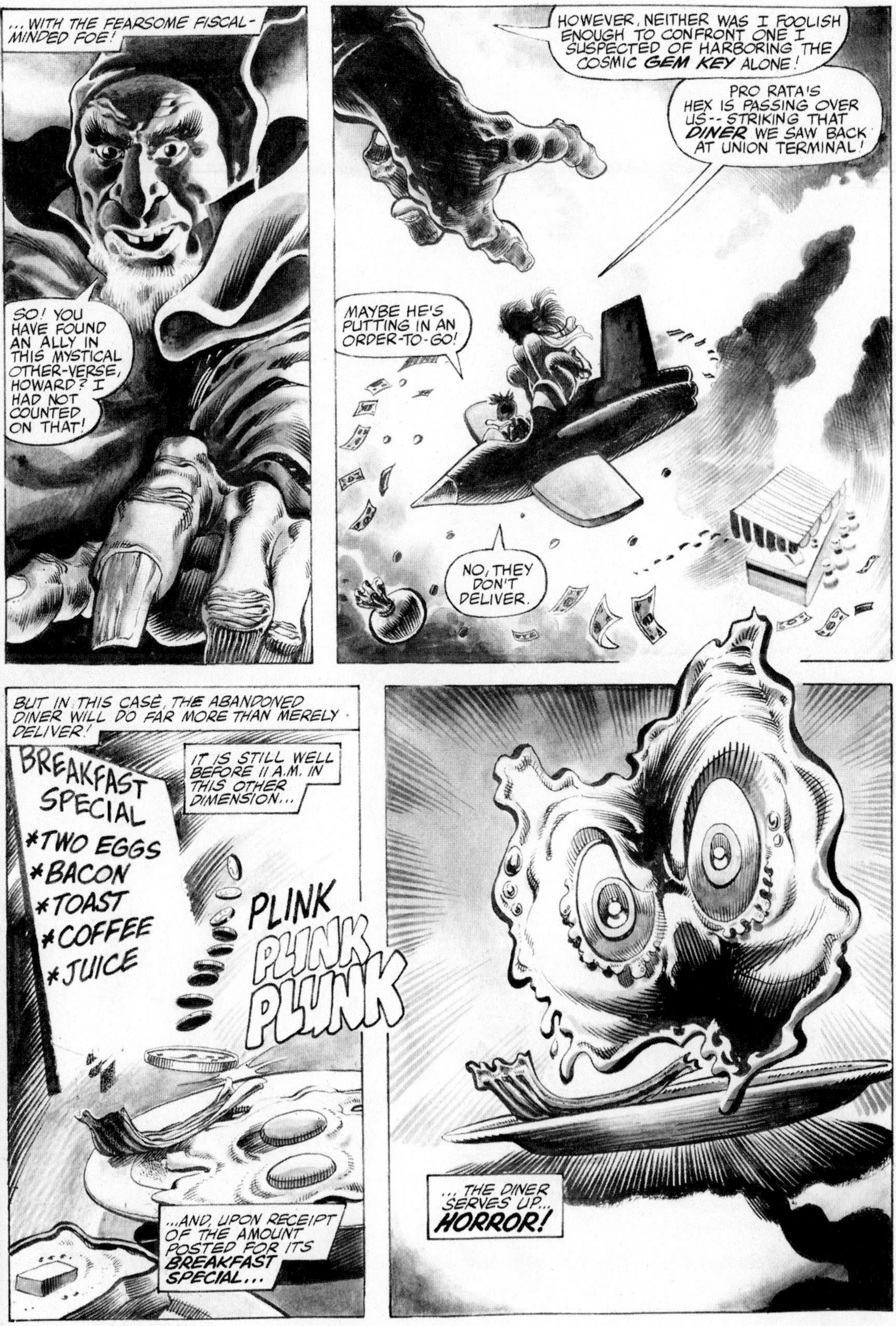

...WITH THE FEARSOME FISCAL-MINDED FOE!
SO! YOU HAVE FOUND AN ALLY IN THIS MYSTICAL OTHER-VERSE, HOWARD? I HAD NOT COUNTED ON THAT!
HOWEVER, NEITHER WAS I FOOLISH ENOUGH TO CONFRONT ONE I SUSPECTED OF HARBORING THE COSMIC GEM KEY ALONE!
PRO RATA'S HEX IS PASSING OVER US-- STRIKING THAT DINER WE SAW BACK AT UNION TERMINAL!
MAYBE HE'S PUTTING IN AN ORDER-TO-GO!
NO, THEY DON'T DELIVER.
BUT IN THIS CASE, THE ABANDONED DINER WILL DO FAR MORE THAN MERELY DELIVER!
IT IS STILL WELL BEFORE 11 A.M. IN THIS OTHER DIMENSION...
BREAKFAST SPECIAL
*TWO EGGS
*BACON
*TOAST
*COFFEE
*JUICE
PLINK
PLINK
PLUNK
...AND, UPON RECEIPT OF THE AMOUNT POSTED FOR ITS BREAKFAST SPECIAL...
...THE DINER SERVES UP... HORROR!

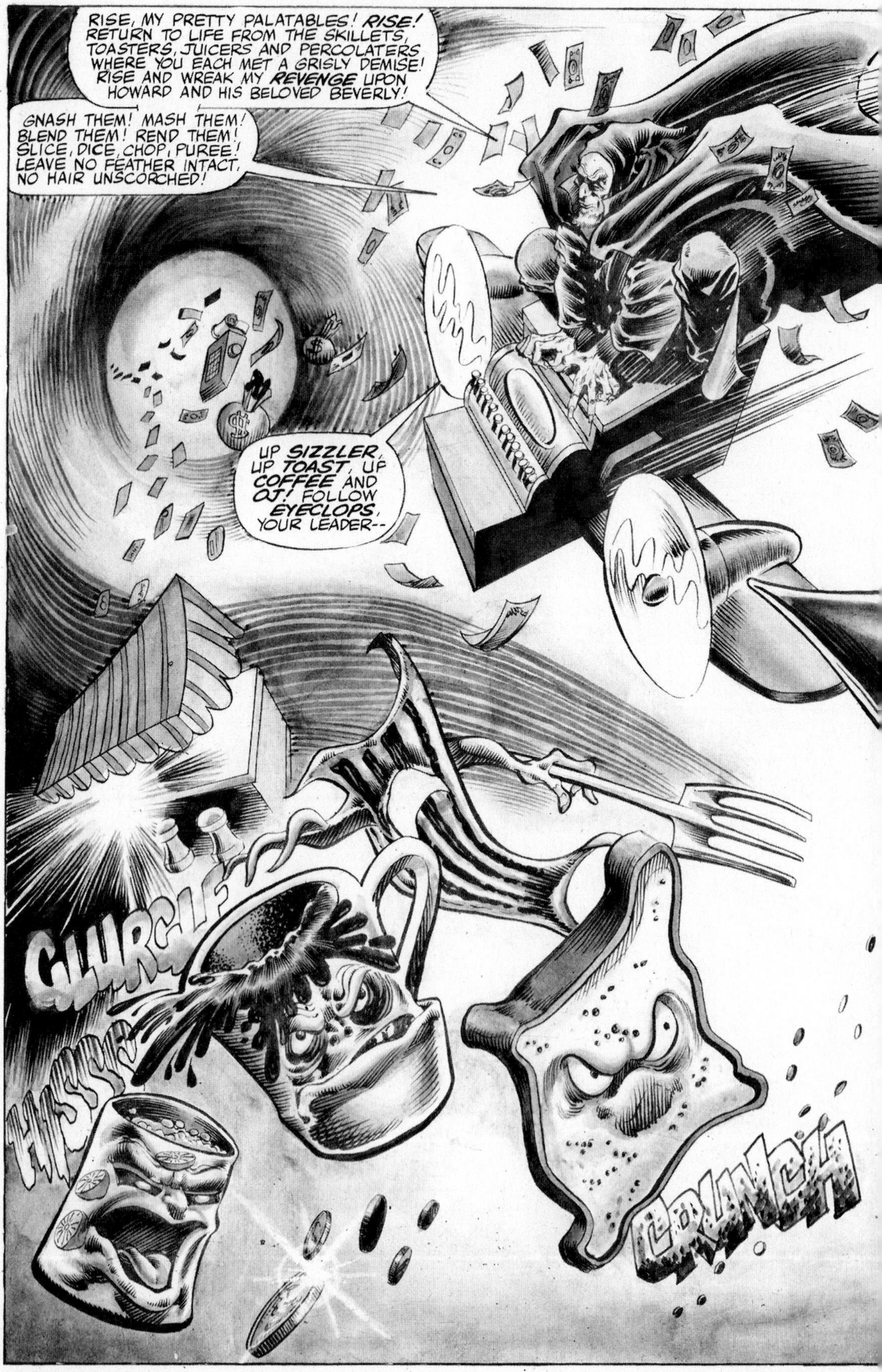
RISE, MY PRETTY PALATABLES! RISE! RETURN TO LIFE FROM THE SKILLETS, TOASTERS, JUICERS AND PERCOLATERS WHERE YOU EACH MET A GRISLY DEMISE! RISE AND WREAK MY REVENGE UPON HOWARD AND HIS BELOVED BEVERLY!
GNASH THEM! MASH THEM! BLEND THEM! REND THEM! SLICE, DICE, CHOP, PUREE! LEAVE NO FEATHER INTACT, NO HAIR UNSCORCHED!
UP SIZZLER, UP TOAST, UP COFFEE AND OJ! FOLLOW EYECLOPS, YOUR LEADER--
GLURGLE
HISSSS
CRUNCH

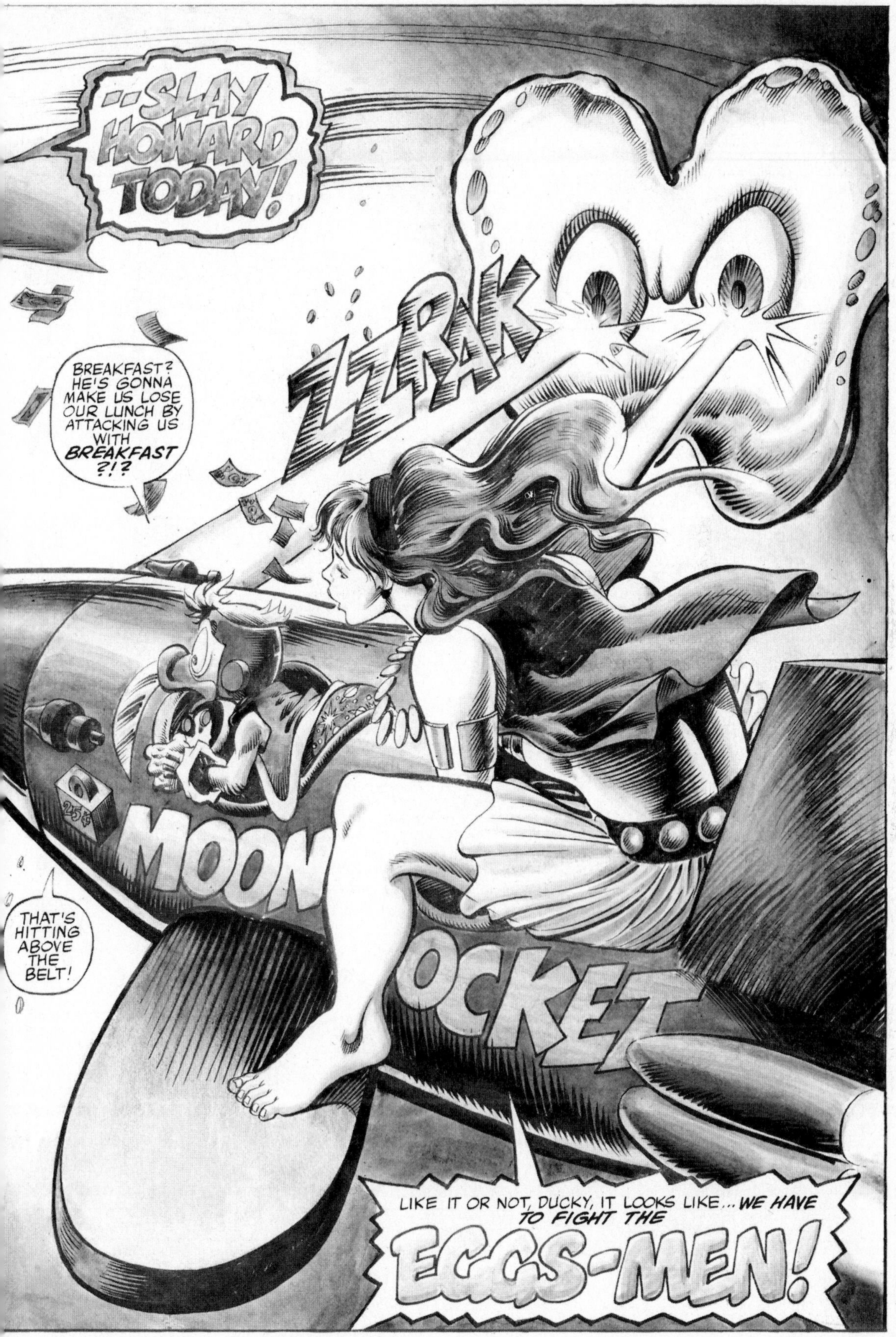
--SLAY HOWARD TODAY!
BREAKFAST? HE'S GONNA MAKE US LOSE OUR LUNCH BY ATTACKING US WITH BREAKFAST?!?
ZZRAK
MOON ROCKET
THAT'S HITTING ABOVE THE BELT!
LIKE IT OR NOT, DUCKY, IT LOOKS LIKE... WE HAVE TO FIGHT THE EGGS-MEN!

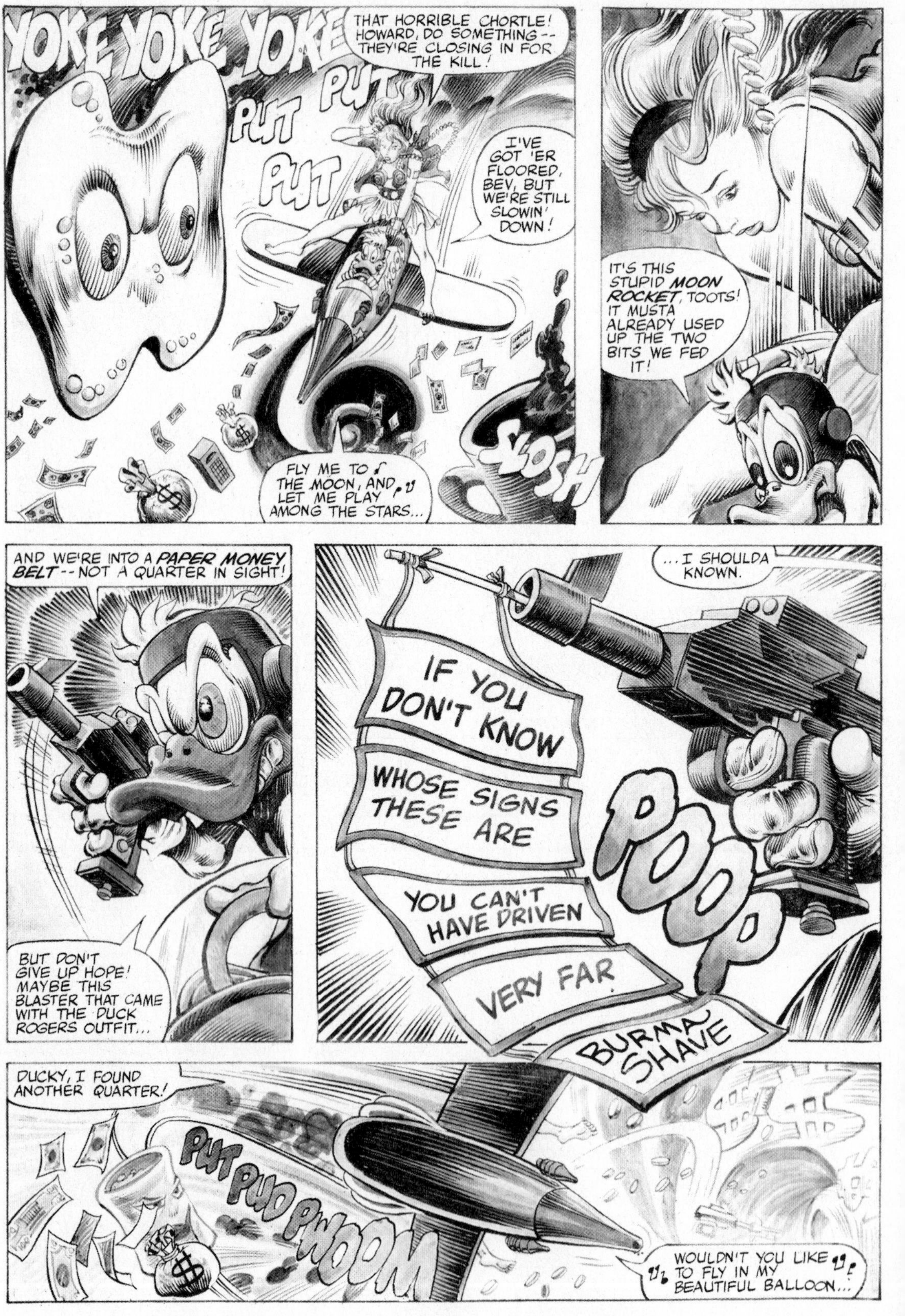
YOKE YOKE YOKE
THAT HORRIBLE CHORTLE! HOWARD, DO SOMETHING -- THEY'RE CLOSING IN FOR THE KILL!
PUT PUT
PUT
I'VE GOT 'ER FLOORED, BEV, BUT WE'RE STILL SLOWIN' DOWN!
FLY ME TO THE MOON, AND LET ME PLAY AMONG THE STARS...
SLOSH
IT'S THIS STUPID *MOON ROCKET*, TOOTS! IT MUSTA ALREADY USED UP THE TWO BITS WE FED IT!
AND WE'RE INTO A *PAPER MONEY BELT* -- NOT A QUARTER IN SIGHT!
BUT DON'T GIVE UP HOPE! MAYBE THIS BLASTER THAT CAME WITH THE DUCK ROGERS OUTFIT...
...I SHOULDA KNOWN.
IF YOU DON'T KNOW
WHOSE SIGNS THESE ARE
YOU CAN'T HAVE DRIVEN
VERY FAR
BURMA SHAVE
POOP
DUCKY, I FOUND ANOTHER QUARTER!
PUT PUD PWOOM
WOULDN'T YOU LIKE TO FLY IN MY BEAUTIFUL BALLOON...

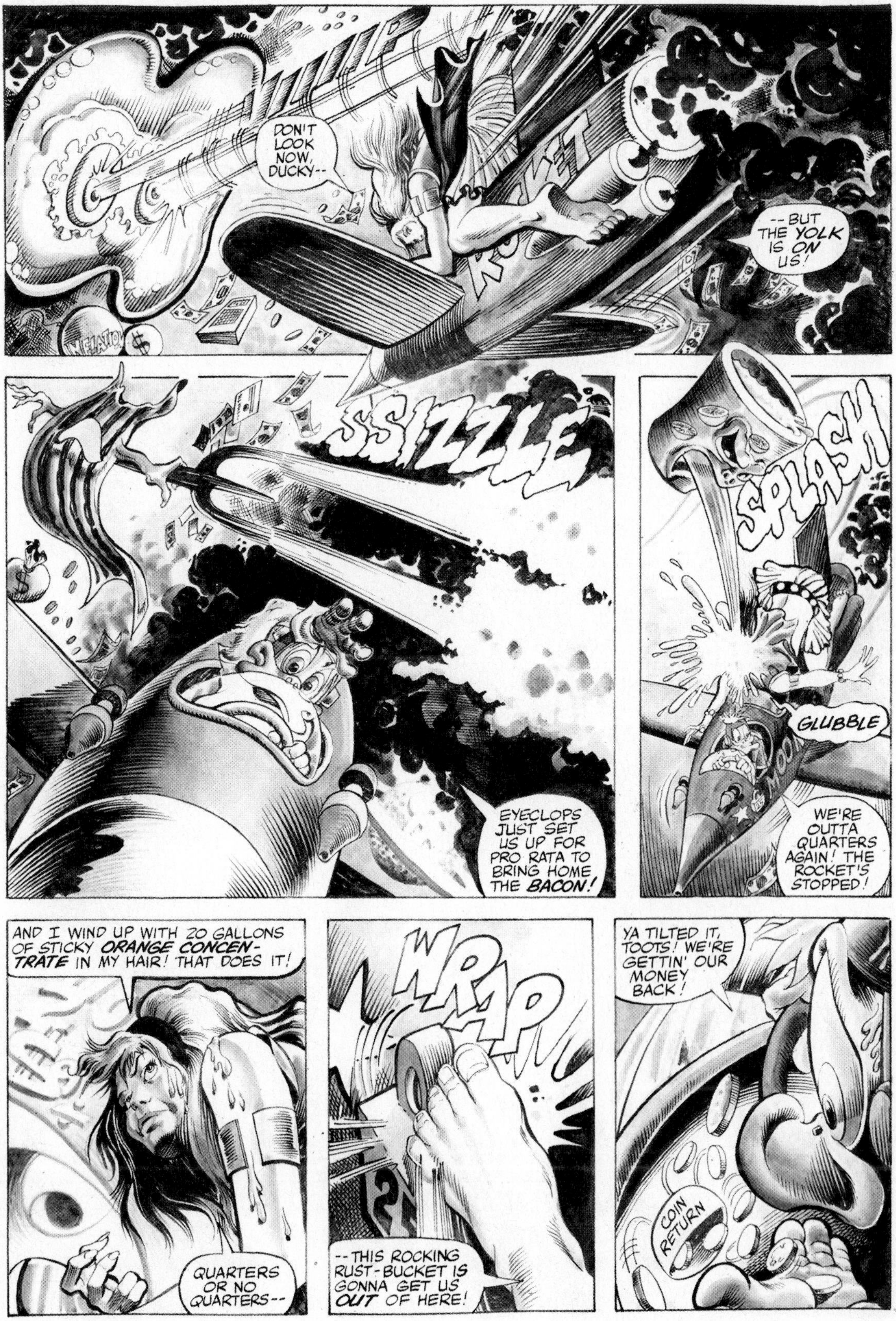
DON'T LOOK NOW, DUCKY--
--BUT THE YOLK IS ON US!
INFLATION
SSIZZLE
EYECLOPS JUST SET US UP FOR PRO RATA TO BRING HOME THE BACON!
SPLASH
GLUBBLE
WE'RE OUTTA QUARTERS AGAIN! THE ROCKET'S STOPPED!
AND I WIND UP WITH 20 GALLONS OF STICKY ORANGE CONCENTRATE IN MY HAIR! THAT DOES IT!
QUARTERS OR NO QUARTERS--
WRAP
--THIS ROCKING RUST-BUCKET IS GONNA GET US OUT OF HERE!
YA TILTED IT, TOOTS! WE'RE GETTIN' OUR MONEY BACK!
COIN RETURN

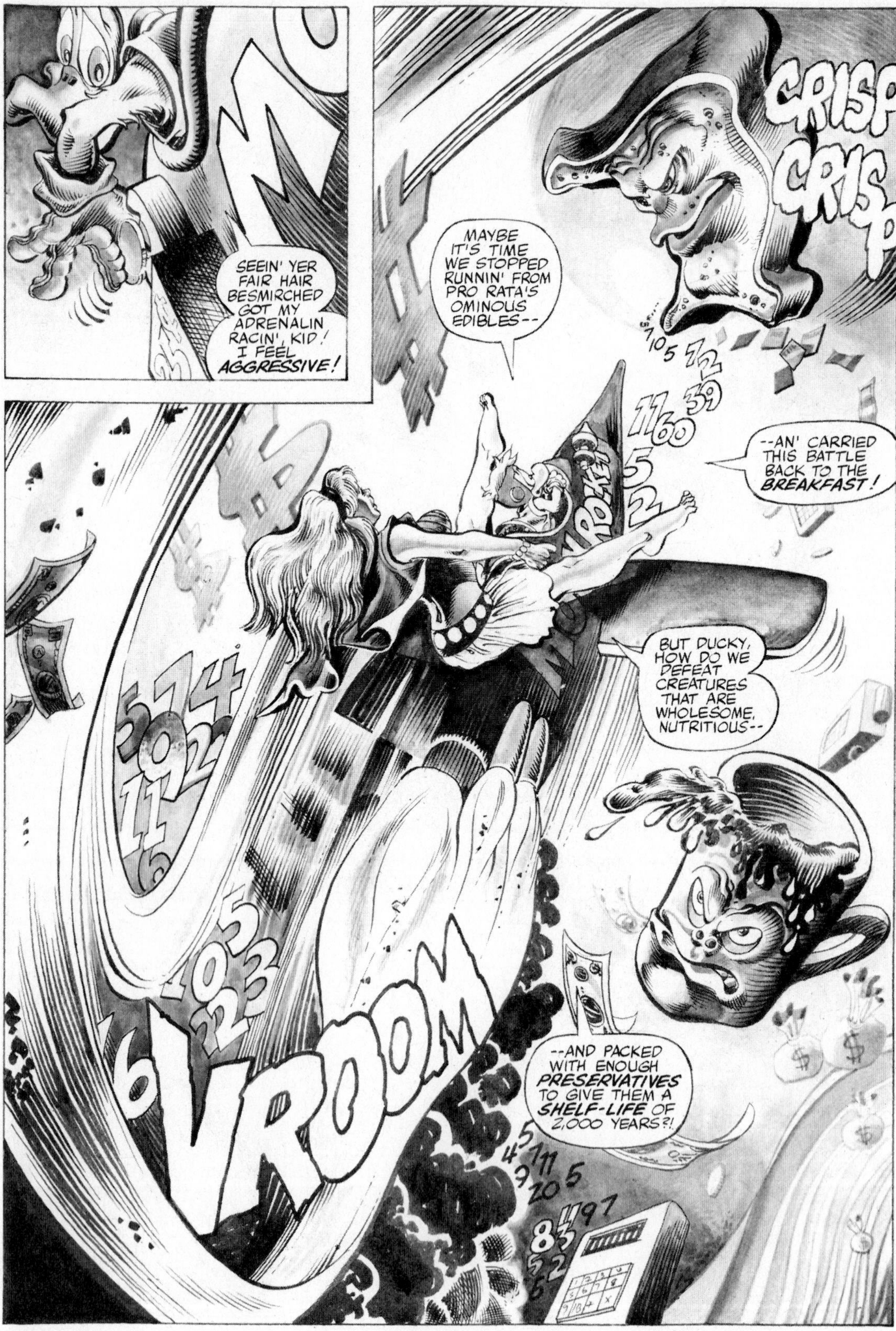
SEEIN' YER FAIR HAIR BESMIRCHED GOT MY ADRENALIN RACIN', KID! I FEEL *AGGRESSIVE*!
CRISP
CRISP
MAYBE IT'S TIME WE STOPPED RUNNIN' FROM PRO RATA'S OMINOUS EDIBLES--
--AN' CARRIED THIS BATTLE BACK TO THE *BREAKFAST*!
BUT DUCKY, HOW DO WE DEFEAT CREATURES THAT ARE WHOLESOME, NUTRITIOUS--
--AND PACKED WITH ENOUGH *PRESERVATIVES* TO GIVE THEM A *SHELF-LIFE* OF 2,000 YEARS?!
VROOM

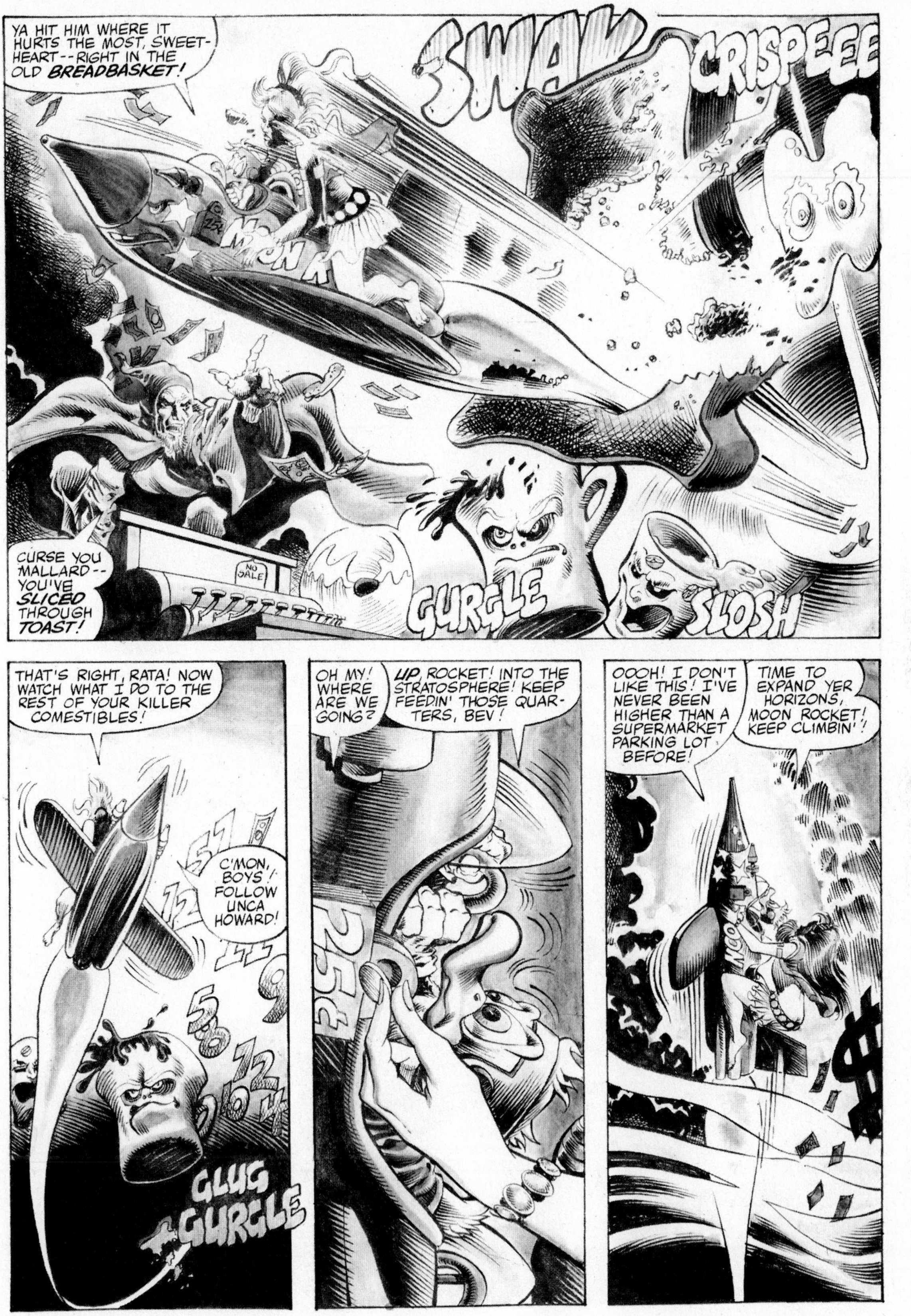
YA HIT HIM WHERE IT HURTS THE MOST, SWEET-HEART--RIGHT IN THE OLD BREADBASKET!
SWAK
CRISPEEE
CURSE YOU MALLARD-- YOU'VE SLICED THROUGH TOAST!
NO SALE
GURGLE
SLOSH
THAT'S RIGHT, RATA! NOW WATCH WHAT I DO TO THE REST OF YOUR KILLER COMESTIBLES!
C'MON, BOYS! FOLLOW UNCA HOWARD!
GLUG
GURGLE
OH MY! WHERE ARE WE GOING?
UP, ROCKET! INTO THE STRATOSPHERE! KEEP FEEDIN' THOSE QUARTERS, BEV!
OOOH! I DON'T LIKE THIS! I'VE NEVER BEEN HIGHER THAN A SUPERMARKET PARKING LOT BEFORE!
TIME TO EXPAND YER HORIZONS, MOON ROCKET! KEEP CLIMBIN'!

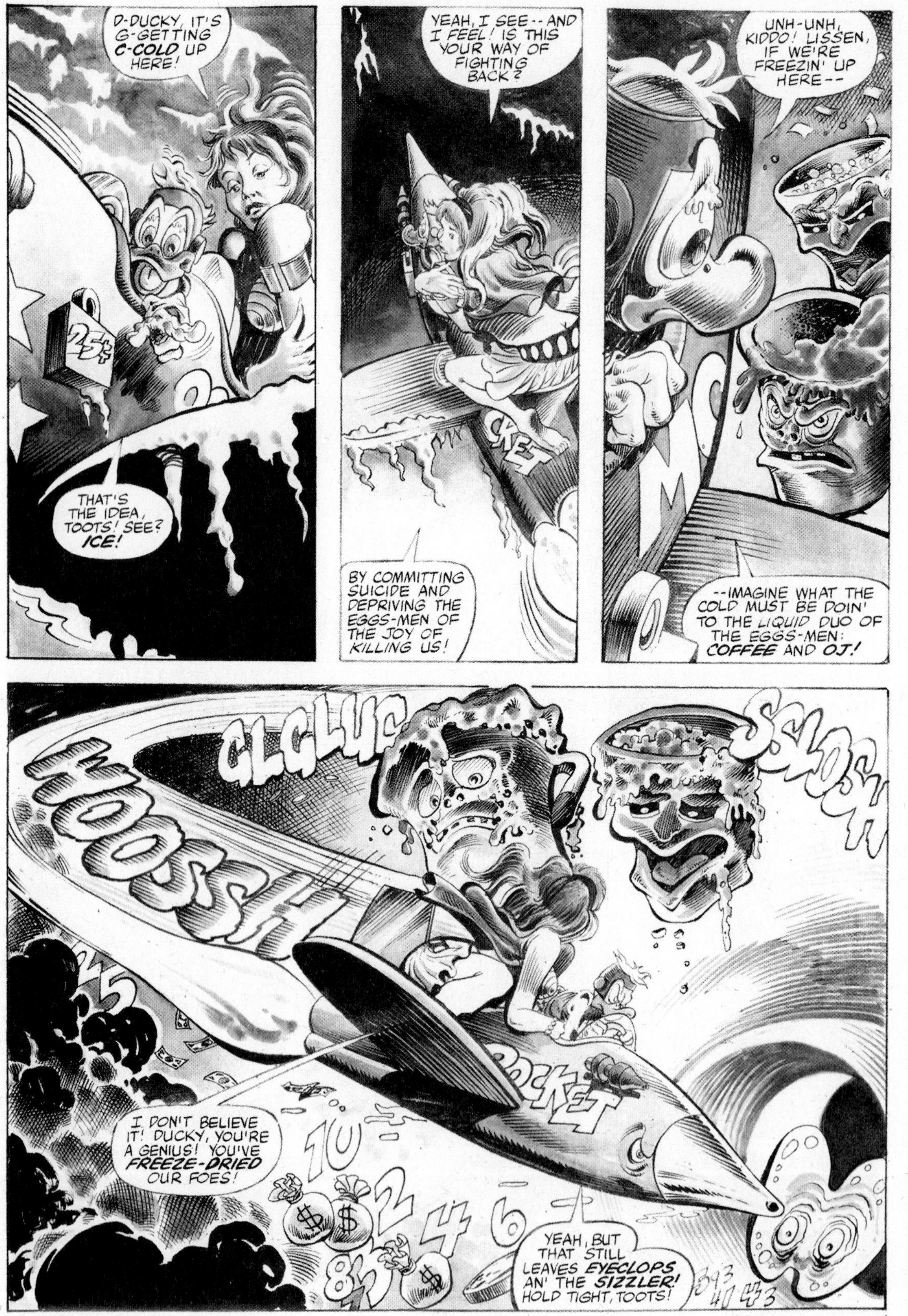

D-DUCKY, IT'S G-GETTING C-COLD UP HERE!
THAT'S THE IDEA, TOOTS! SEE? ICE!
YEAH, I SEE--AND I FEEL! IS THIS YOUR WAY OF FIGHTING BACK?
BY COMMITTING SUICIDE AND DEPRIVING THE EGGS-MEN OF THE JOY OF KILLING US!
UNH-UNH, KIDDO! LISSEN, IF WE'RE FREEZIN' UP HERE--
--IMAGINE WHAT THE COLD MUST BE DOIN' TO THE LIQUID DUO OF THE EGGS-MEN: COFFEE AND OJ!
I DON'T BELIEVE IT! DUCKY, YOU'RE A GENIUS! YOU'VE FREEZE-DRIED OUR FOES!
YEAH, BUT THAT STILL LEAVES EYECLOPS AN' THE SIZZLER! HOLD TIGHT, TOOTS!

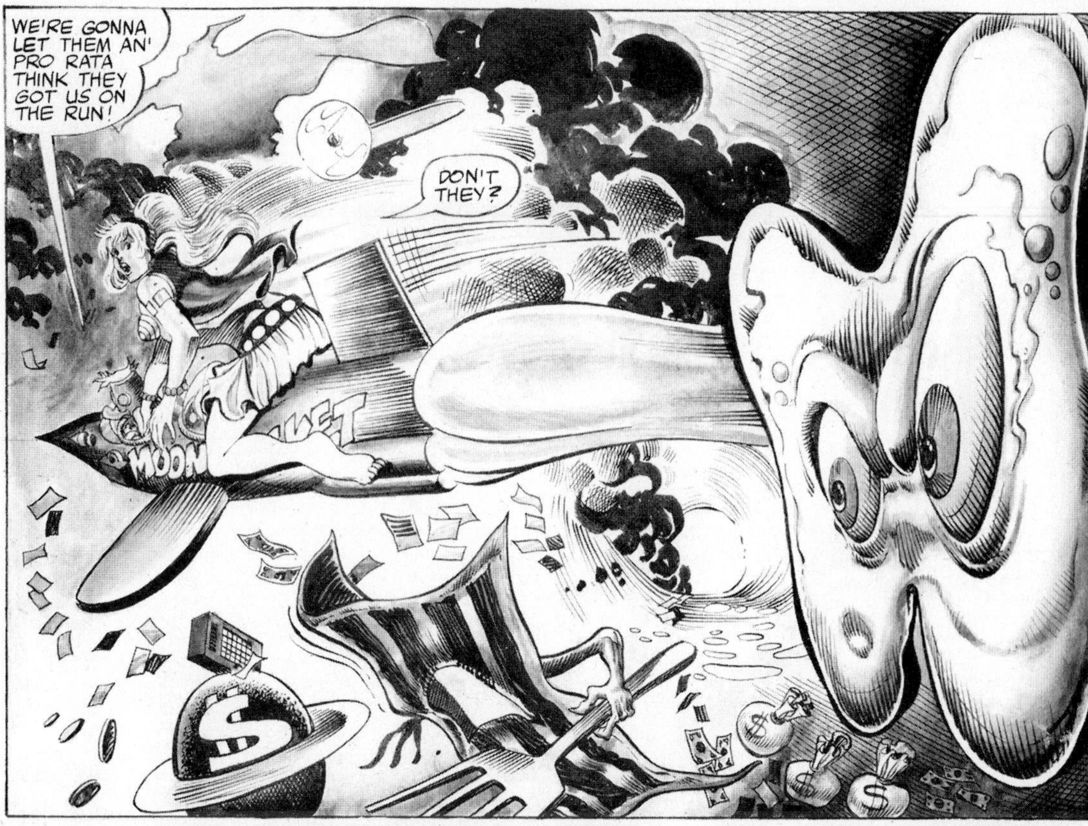
WE'RE GONNA LET THEM AN' PRO RATA THINK THEY GOT US ON THE RUN!
DON'T THEY?
MOON

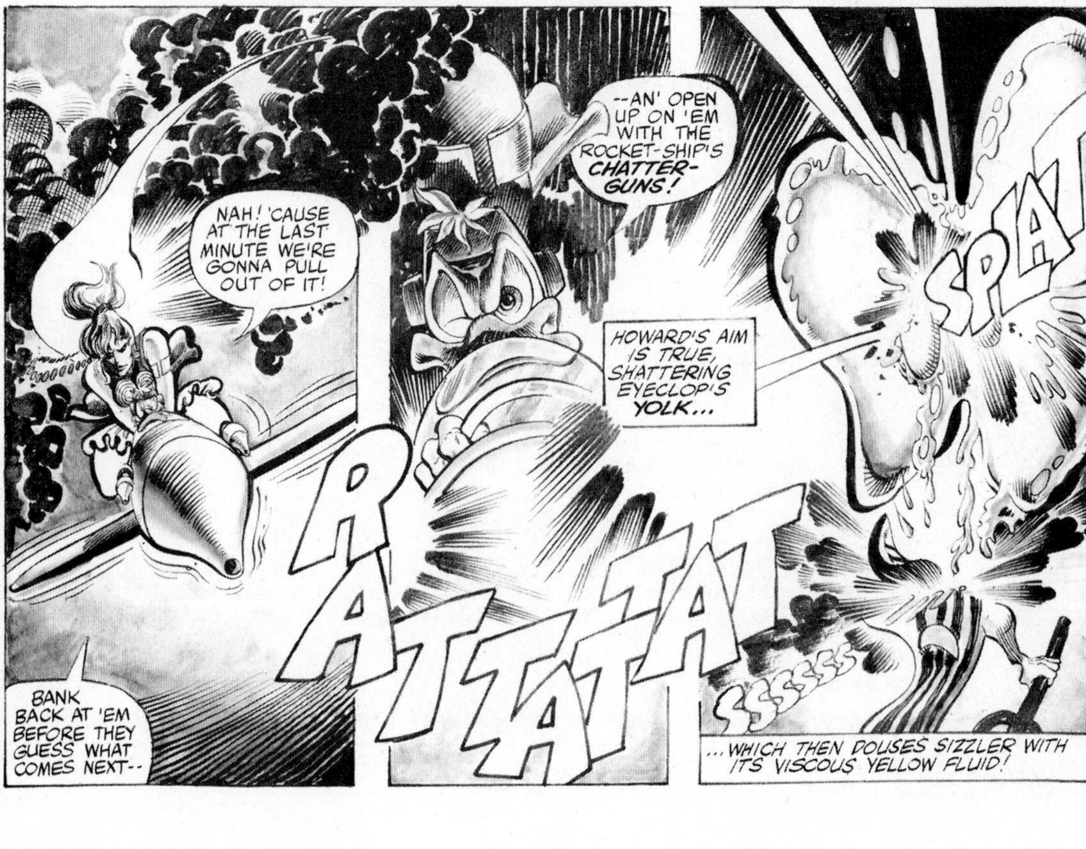
NAH! 'CAUSE AT THE LAST MINUTE WE'RE GONNA PULL OUT OF IT!
BANK BACK AT 'EM BEFORE THEY GUESS WHAT COMES NEXT--
--AN' OPEN UP ON 'EM WITH THE ROCKET-SHIP'S CHATTER-GUNS!
RATTATTATTAT
HOWARD'S AIM IS TRUE, SHATTERING EYECLOP'S YOLK...
SPLAT
SSSSSS
...WHICH THEN DOUSES SIZZLER WITH ITS VISCOUS YELLOW FLUID!

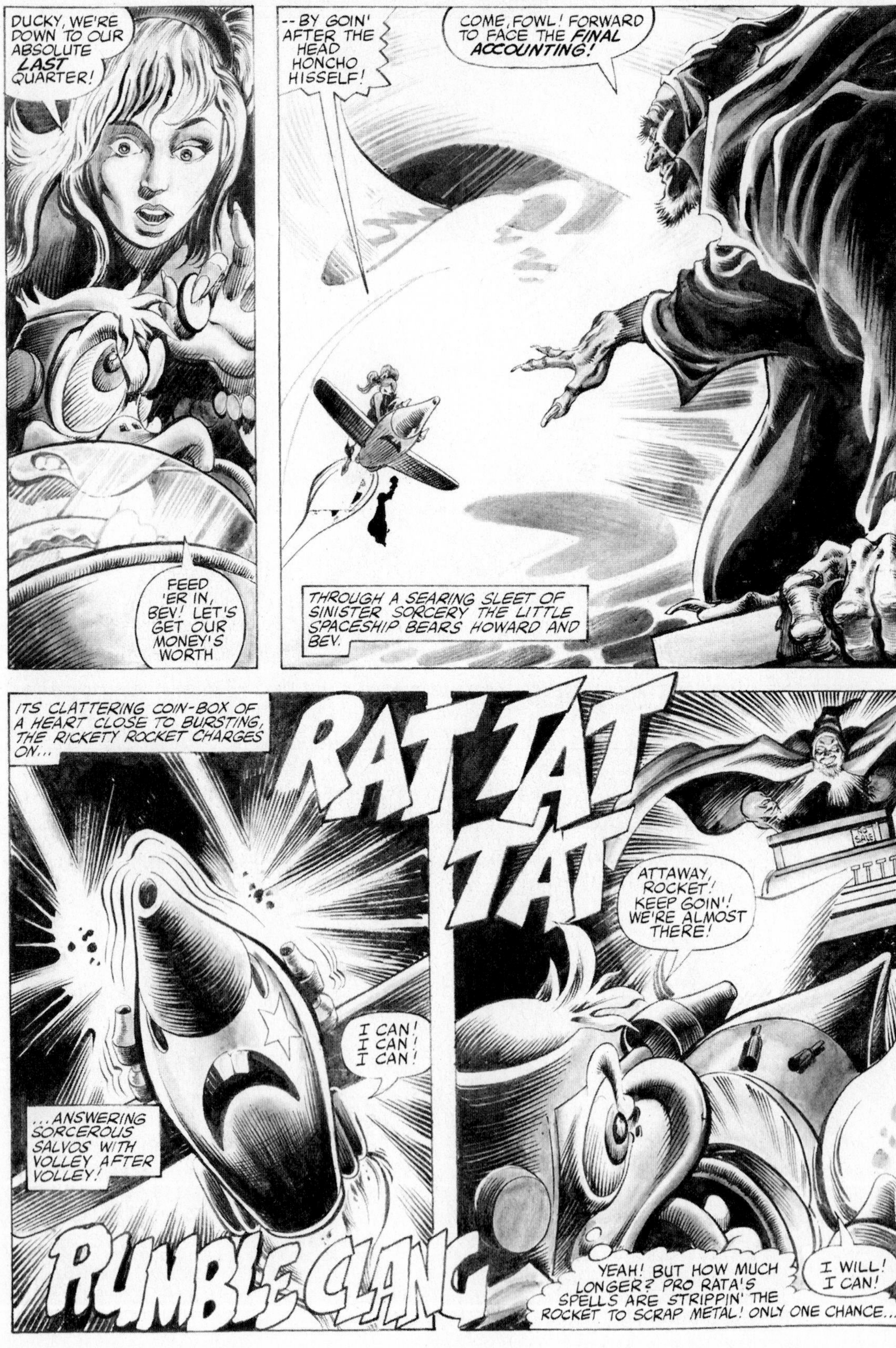
DUCKY, WE'RE DOWN TO OUR ABSOLUTE LAST QUARTER!
FEED 'ER IN, BEV! LET'S GET OUR MONEY'S WORTH
--BY GOIN' AFTER THE HEAD HONCHO HISSELF!
COME, FOWL! FORWARD TO FACE THE FINAL ACCOUNTING!
THROUGH A SEARING SLEET OF SINISTER SORCERY THE LITTLE SPACESHIP BEARS HOWARD AND BEV.
ITS CLATTERING COIN-BOX OF A HEART CLOSE TO BURSTING, THE RICKETY ROCKET CHARGES ON...
RAT TAT TAT TAT
ATTAWAY, ROCKET! KEEP GOIN'! WE'RE ALMOST THERE!
I CAN! I CAN! I CAN!
...ANSWERING SORCEROUS SALVOS WITH VOLLEY AFTER VOLLEY!
RUMBLE CLANG
YEAH! BUT HOW MUCH LONGER? PRO RATA'S SPELLS ARE STRIPPIN' THE ROCKET TO SCRAP METAL! ONLY ONE CHANCE...
I WILL! I CAN!

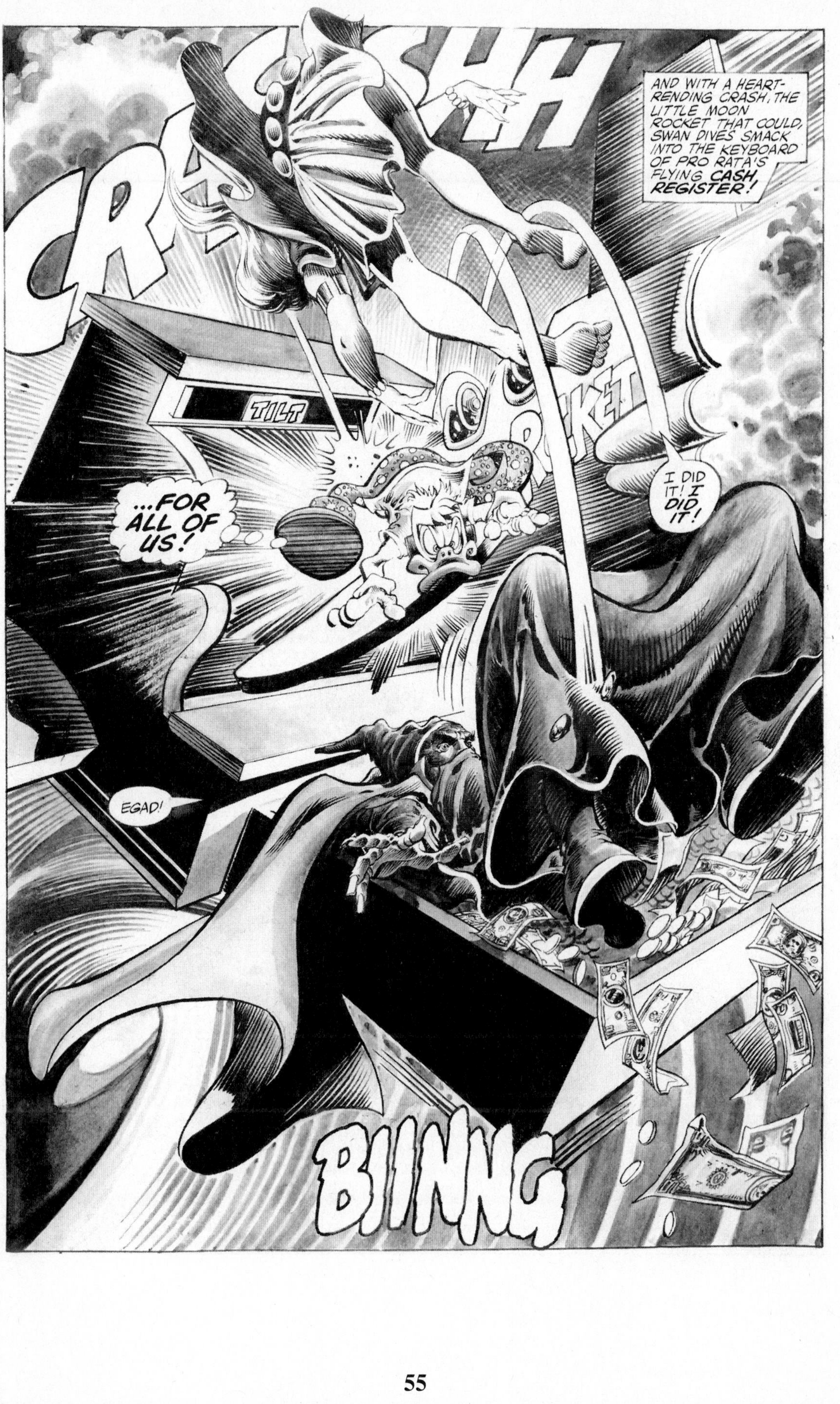
CRASHH
AND WITH A HEART-RENDING CRASH, THE LITTLE MOON ROCKET THAT COULD, SWAN DIVES SMACK INTO THE KEYBOARD OF PRO RATA'S FLYING CASH REGISTER!
TILT
ROCKET
I DID IT! I DID IT!
...FOR ALL OF US!
EGAD!
BIINNG

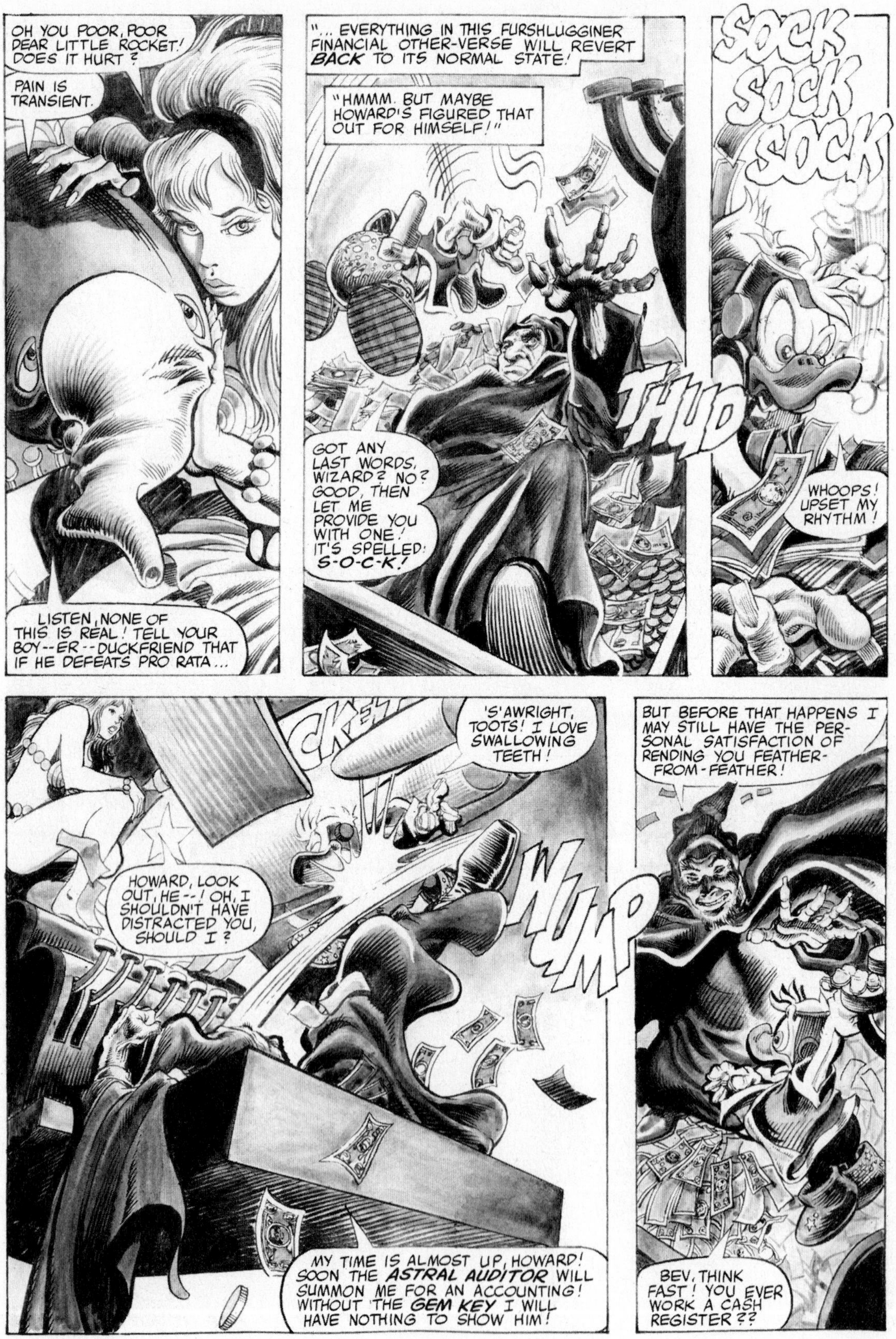

OH YOU POOR, POOR DEAR LITTLE ROCKET! DOES IT HURT?
PAIN IS TRANSIENT.
LISTEN, NONE OF THIS IS REAL! TELL YOUR BOY--ER--DUCKFRIEND THAT IF HE DEFEATS PRO RATA...
"... EVERYTHING IN THIS FURSHLUGGINER FINANCIAL OTHER-VERSE WILL REVERT BACK TO ITS NORMAL STATE!
"HMMM. BUT MAYBE HOWARD'S FIGURED THAT OUT FOR HIMSELF!"
GOT ANY LAST WORDS, WIZARD? NO? GOOD, THEN LET ME PROVIDE YOU WITH ONE! IT'S SPELLED: S-O-C-K!
THUD
SOCK
SOCK
SOCK
WHOOPS! UPSET MY RHYTHM!
'S'AWRIGHT, TOOTS! I LOVE SWALLOWING TEETH!
HOWARD, LOOK OUT, HE--! OH, I SHOULDN'T HAVE DISTRACTED YOU, SHOULD I?
WUMP
MY TIME IS ALMOST UP, HOWARD! SOON THE ASTRAL AUDITOR WILL SUMMON ME FOR AN ACCOUNTING! WITHOUT THE GEM KEY I WILL HAVE NOTHING TO SHOW HIM!
BUT BEFORE THAT HAPPENS I MAY STILL HAVE THE PERSONAL SATISFACTION OF RENDING YOU FEATHER-FROM-FEATHER!
BEV, THINK FAST! YOU EVER WORK A CASH REGISTER??

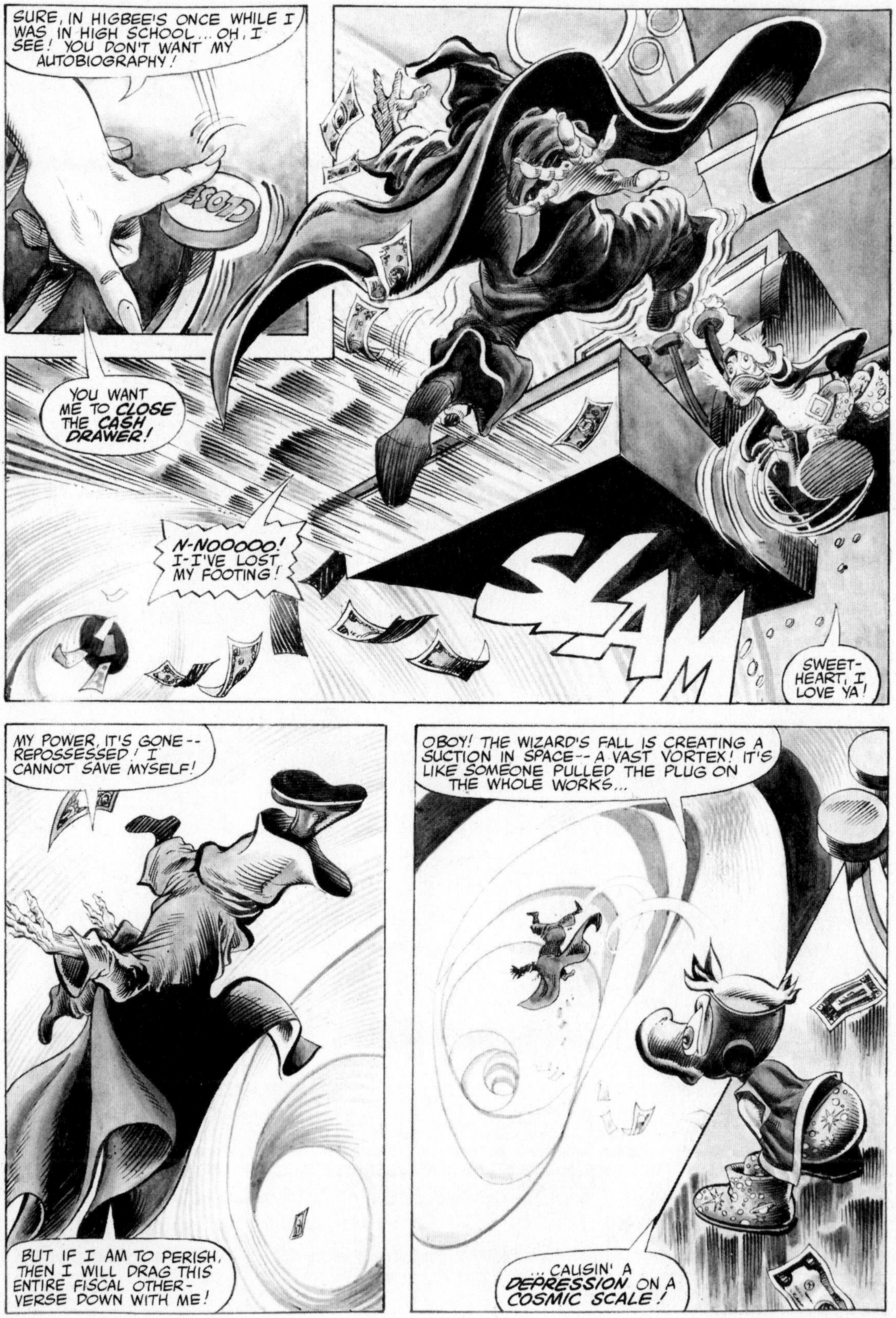
SURE, IN HIGBEE'S ONCE WHILE I WAS IN HIGH SCHOOL... OH, I SEE! YOU DON'T WANT MY AUTOBIOGRAPHY!
CLOSE
YOU WANT ME TO CLOSE THE CASH DRAWER!
N-NOOOOO! I-I'VE LOST MY FOOTING!
SLAM
SWEET-HEART, I LOVE YA!
MY POWER, IT'S GONE-- REPOSSESSED! I CANNOT SAVE MYSELF!
BUT IF I AM TO PERISH, THEN I WILL DRAG THIS ENTIRE FISCAL OTHER-VERSE DOWN WITH ME!
OBOY! THE WIZARD'S FALL IS CREATING A SUCTION IN SPACE-- A VAST VORTEX! IT'S LIKE SOMEONE PULLED THE PLUG ON THE WHOLE WORKS...
...CAUSIN' A DEPRESSION ON A COSMIC SCALE!

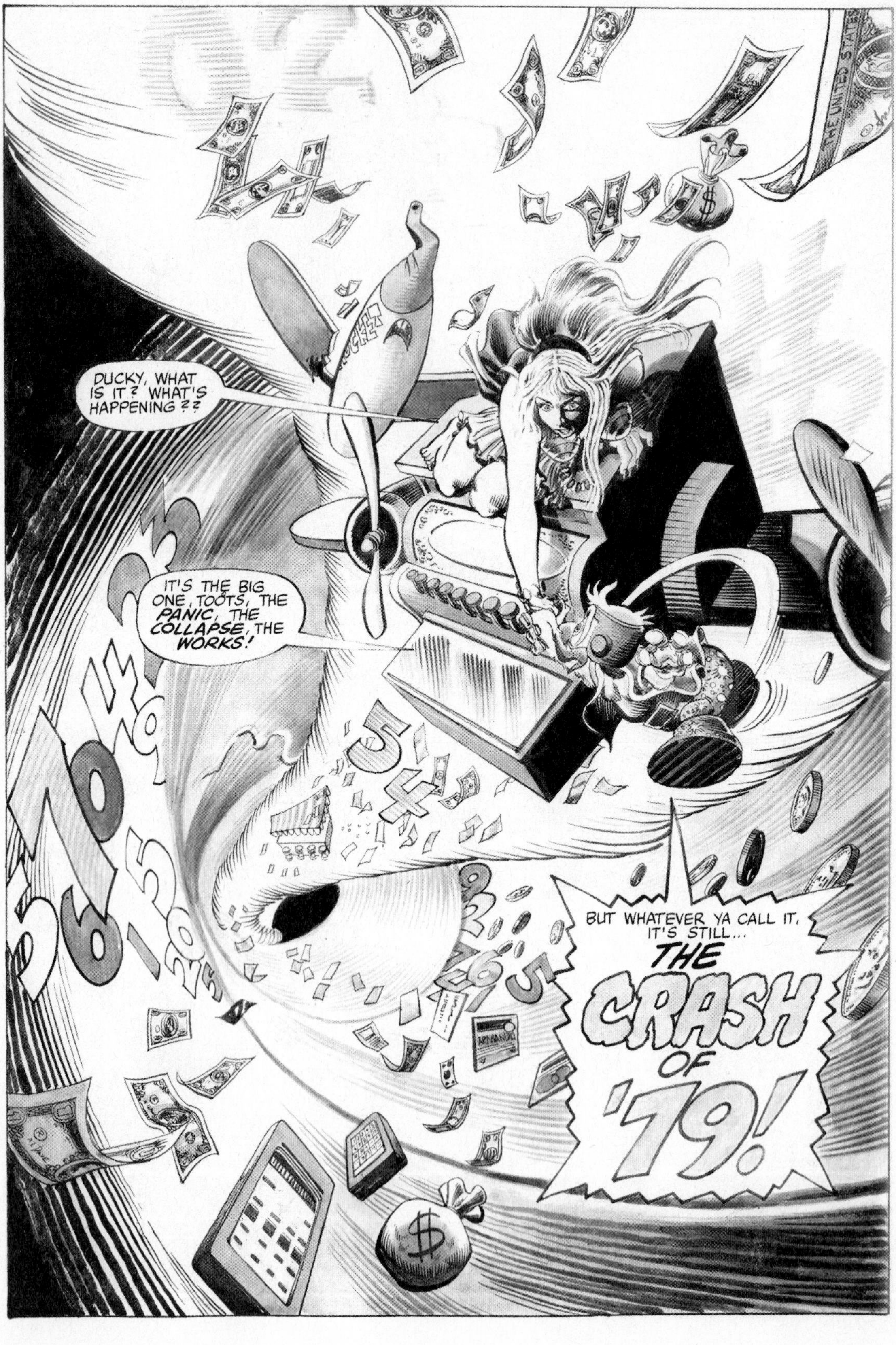
DUCKY, WHAT IS IT? WHAT'S HAPPENING??
IT'S THE BIG ONE, TOOTS, THE PANIC, THE COLLAPSE, THE WORKS!
BUT WHATEVER YA CALL IT, IT'S STILL... THE CRASH OF '79!

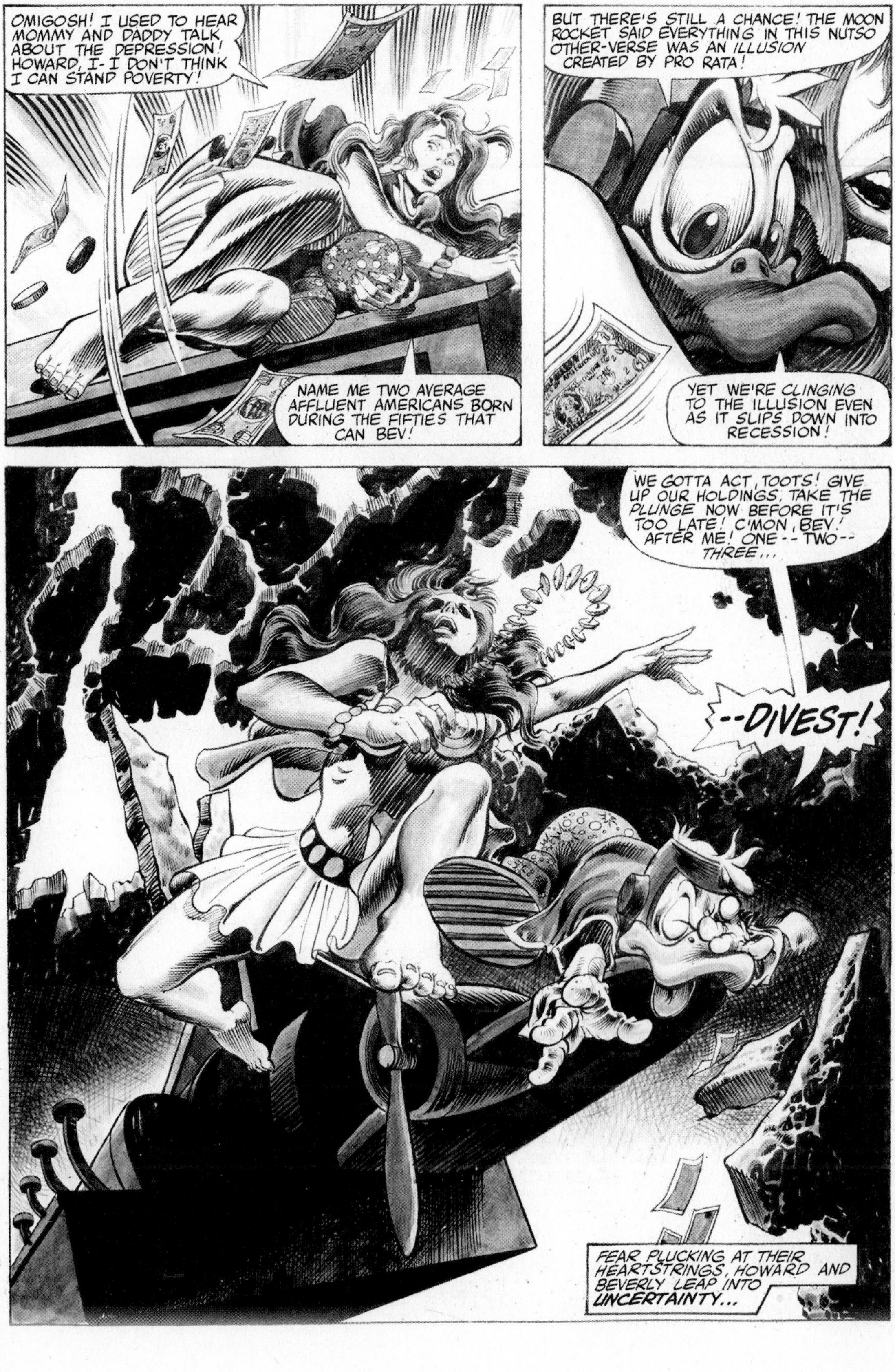
OMIGOSH! I USED TO HEAR MOMMY AND DADDY TALK ABOUT THE DEPRESSION! HOWARD, I- I DON'T THINK I CAN STAND POVERTY!
NAME ME TWO AVERAGE AFFLUENT AMERICANS BORN DURING THE FIFTIES THAT CAN BEV!
BUT THERE'S STILL A CHANCE! THE MOON ROCKET SAID EVERYTHING IN THIS NUTSO OTHER-VERSE WAS AN ILLUSION CREATED BY PRO RATA!
YET WE'RE CLINGING TO THE ILLUSION EVEN AS IT SLIPS DOWN INTO RECESSION!
WE GOTTA ACT, TOOTS! GIVE UP OUR HOLDINGS, TAKE THE PLUNGE NOW BEFORE IT'S TOO LATE! C'MON, BEV! AFTER ME! ONE--TWO--THREE...
--DIVEST!
FEAR PLUCKING AT THEIR HEARTSTRINGS, HOWARD AND BEVERLY LEAP INTO UNCERTAINTY...

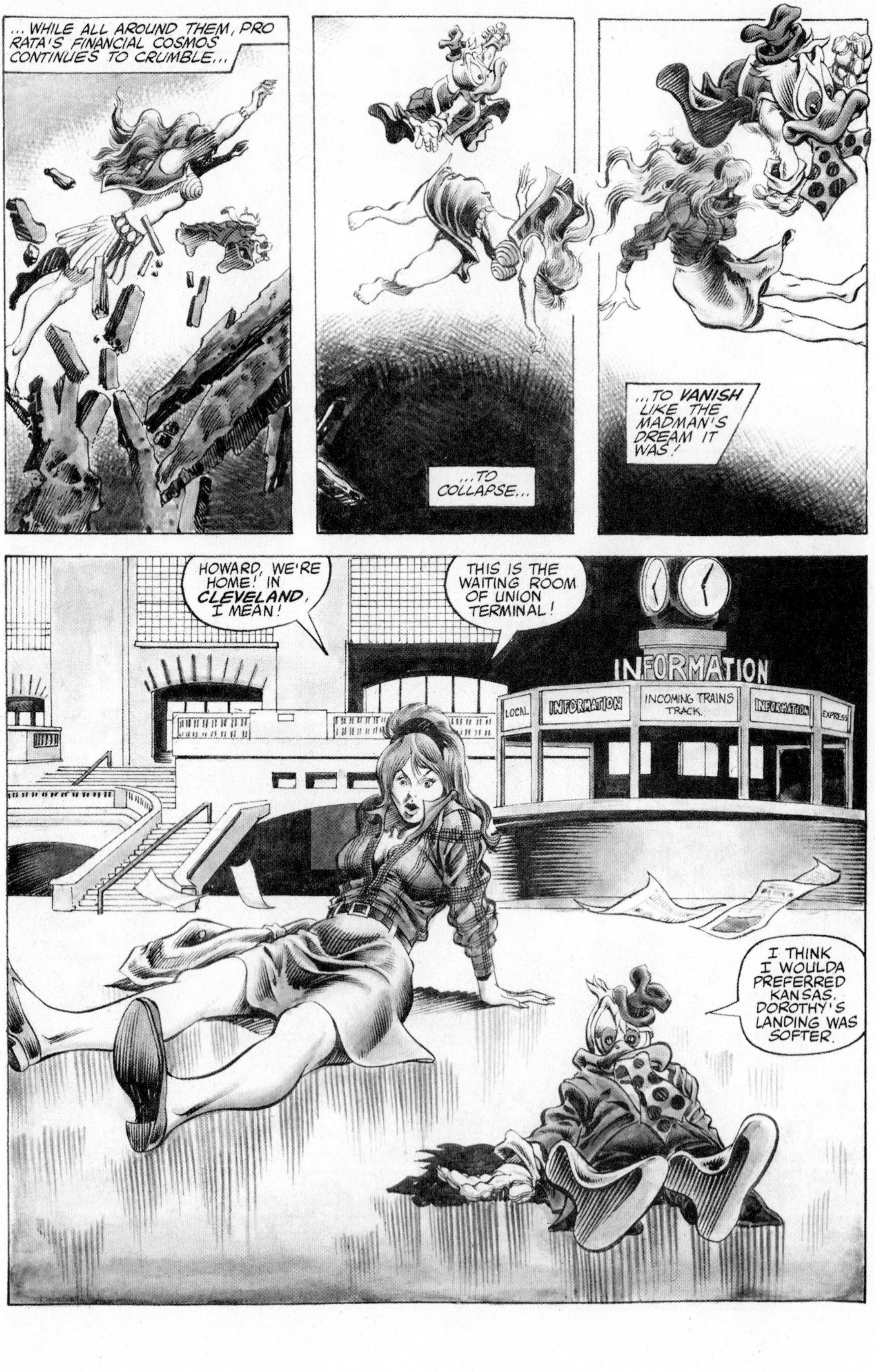
...WHILE ALL AROUND THEM, PRO RATA'S FINANCIAL COSMOS CONTINUES TO CRUMBLE...
...TO COLLAPSE...
...TO VANISH LIKE THE MADMAN'S DREAM IT WAS!
HOWARD, WE'RE HOME! IN CLEVELAND, I MEAN!
THIS IS THE WAITING ROOM OF UNION TERMINAL!
INFORMATION
LOCAL
INFORMATION
INCOMING TRAINS TRACK.
INFORMATION
EXPRESS
I THINK I WOULDA PREFERRED KANSAS. DOROTHY'S LANDING WAS SOFTER.

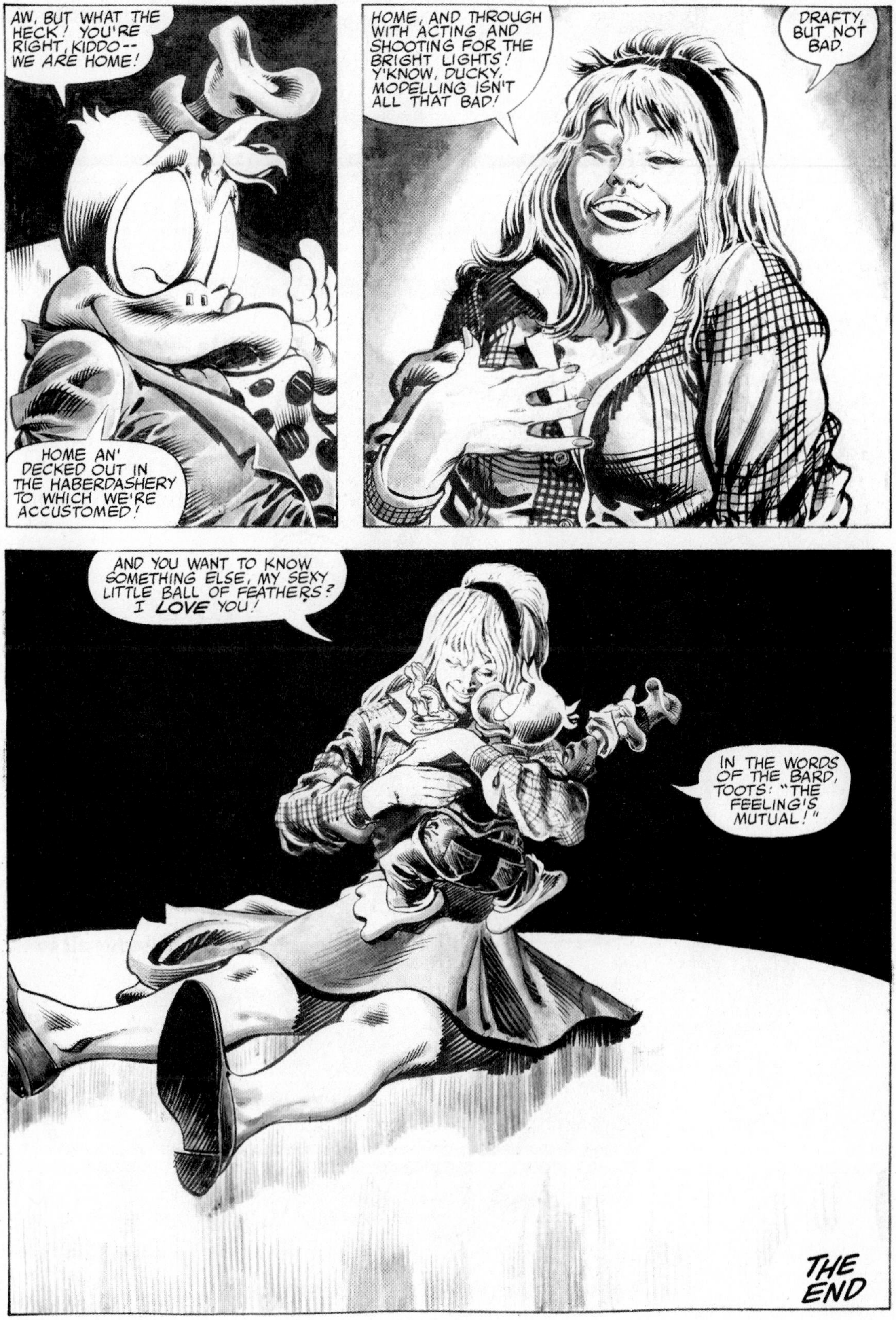
AW, BUT WHAT THE HECK! YOU'RE RIGHT, KIDDO-- WE ARE HOME!
HOME AN' DECKED OUT IN THE HABERDASHERY TO WHICH WE'RE ACCUSTOMED!
HOME, AND THROUGH WITH ACTING AND SHOOTING FOR THE BRIGHT LIGHTS! Y'KNOW, DUCKY, MODELLING ISN'T ALL THAT BAD!
DRAFTY, BUT NOT BAD.
AND YOU WANT TO KNOW SOMETHING ELSE, MY SEXY LITTLE BALL OF FEATHERS? I LOVE YOU!
IN THE WORDS OF THE BARD, TOOTS: "THE FEELING'S MUTUAL!"
THE END

NEXT ISSUE

Tis the season to be jolly with
an Xmas extravaganza direct from Cleveland!

"A Christmas for Carol"

Plus:
A fabulous feature
on the life
and times of our
disoriented Duck!

It's a gaggle of yuletide yuks all in

HOWARD the DUCK? #3

Wauughing your way in mid-December!

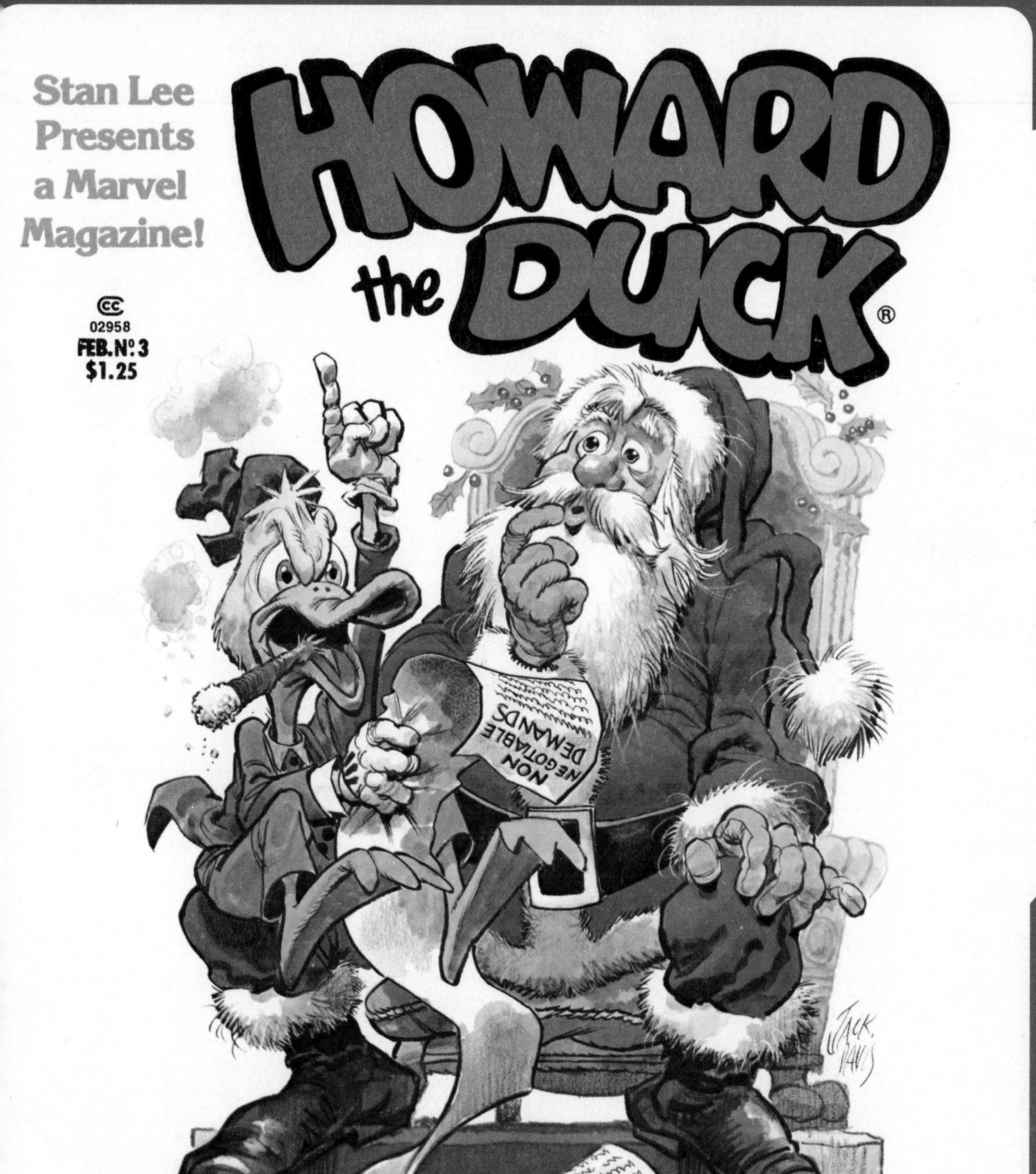
Stan Lee Presents a Marvel Magazine!
HOWARD the DUCK®
CC
02958
FEB. №3
$1.25
NON NEGOTABLE DEMANDS
JACK DAVIS
Special Christmas Issue!

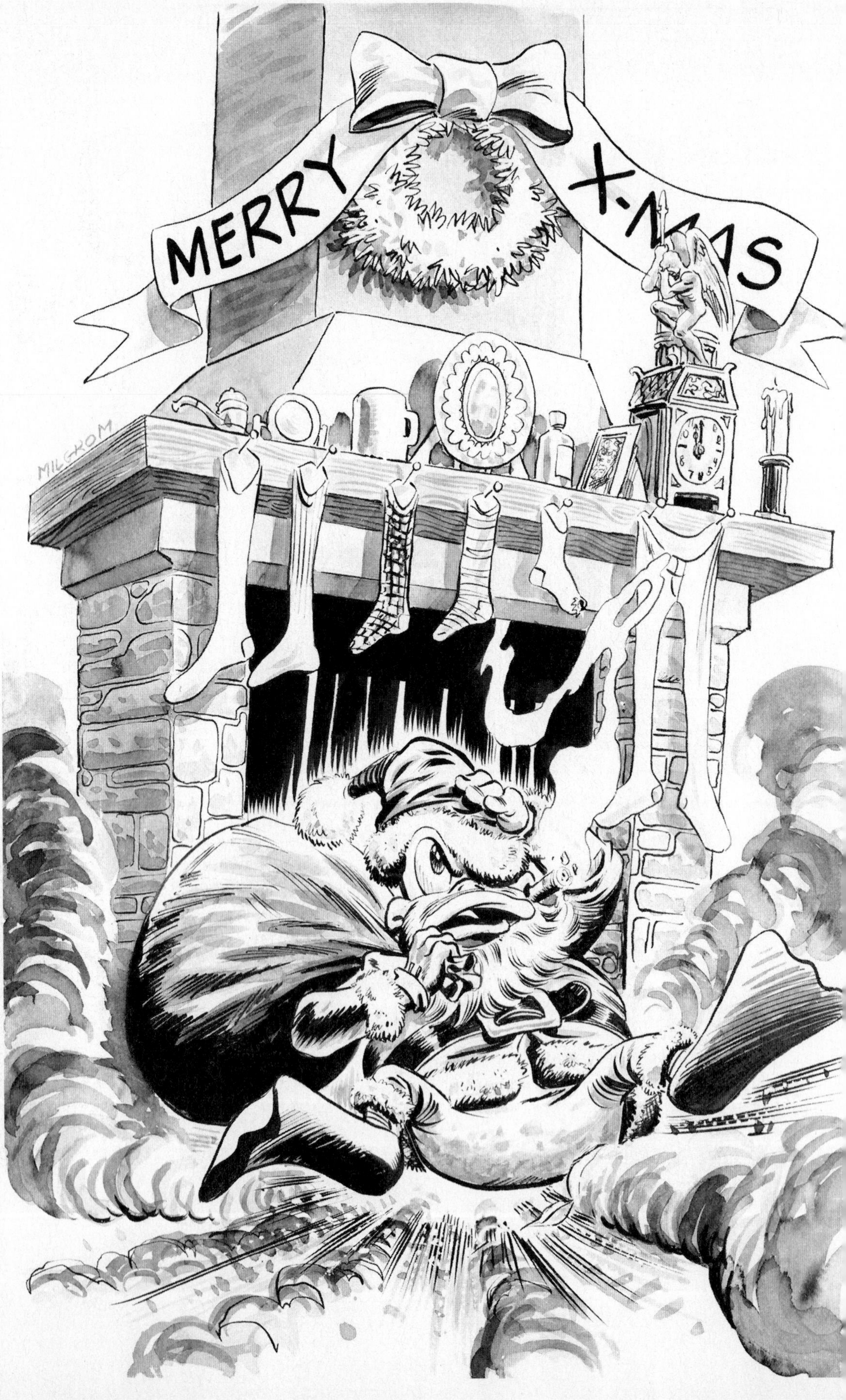
MERRY X-MAS
MILGROM

STAN LEE Presents:

HOWARD the DUCK

Volume 1 No. 3 February 1980

JIM SHOOTER Editor-In-Chief • **LYNN GRAEME** Editor • **RALPH MACCHIO** Associate Editor
MARK GRUENWALD Insulting Editor • **ROY THOMAS** Consulting Editor • **MILT SCHIFFMAN** V.P. Production
NORA MACLIN Design Director • **MIKE HIGGINS, TOM ORZ** Letterers
DAVIDA LICHTER-DALE, ED NORTON, ELIOT BROWN , JOE ALBELO, MARK ROGAN Staff & Such
Frontispiece **AL MILGROM** · **JACK DAVIS** Cover
＊Special Thanks to **RICK MARSCHALL** ＊

CONTENTS

FEATURES

Can Howard rekindle hope in the heart of an embittered little girl? Can Mr. and Mrs. Santa Claus find a nice condominium in Florida? Will Greedy Killerwatt and his horde of North Pole mutants increase their gross national products? Can the Howard the Duck staff get away with making fun of Christmas? Find out the answers to these and many other questions you didn't ask in this toe-chilling and heart-warming story! By **BILL MANTLO, GENE COLAN**, and **DAVE SIMONS.**

The saga of Howard the Duck from swamp to Cleveland in this world of hairless apes! By **BILL MANTLO, JERRY BINGHAM**, and **JOE RUBINSTEIN.**

DEPARTMENTS

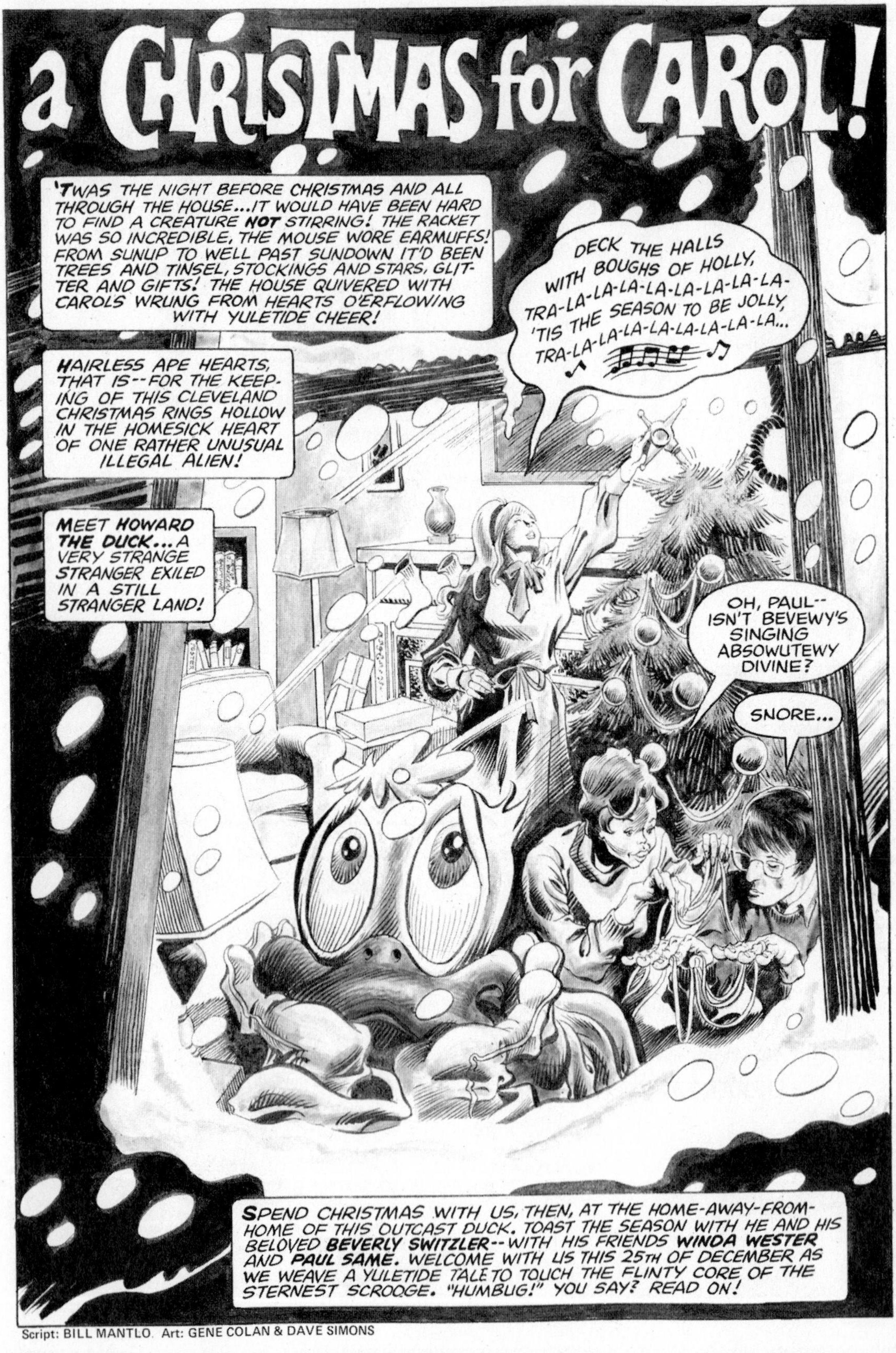
a CHRISTMAS for CAROL!
'TWAS THE NIGHT BEFORE CHRISTMAS AND ALL THROUGH THE HOUSE...IT WOULD HAVE BEEN HARD TO FIND A CREATURE NOT STIRRING! THE RACKET WAS SO INCREDIBLE, THE MOUSE WORE EARMUFFS! FROM SUNUP TO WELL PAST SUNDOWN IT'D BEEN TREES AND TINSEL, STOCKINGS AND STARS, GLITTER AND GIFTS! THE HOUSE QUIVERED WITH CAROLS WRUNG FROM HEARTS O'ERFLOWING WITH YULETIDE CHEER!
DECK THE HALLS WITH BOUGHS OF HOLLY, TRA-LA-LA-LA-LA-LA-LA-LA-LA- 'TIS THE SEASON TO BE JOLLY, TRA-LA-LA-LA-LA-LA-LA-LA-LA...
HAIRLESS APE HEARTS, THAT IS--FOR THE KEEPING OF THIS CLEVELAND CHRISTMAS RINGS HOLLOW IN THE HOMESICK HEART OF ONE RATHER UNUSUAL ILLEGAL ALIEN!
MEET HOWARD THE DUCK...A VERY STRANGE STRANGER EXILED IN A STILL STRANGER LAND!
OH, PAUL-- ISN'T BEVEWY'S SINGING ABSOWUTEWY DIVINE?
SNORE...
SPEND CHRISTMAS WITH US, THEN, AT THE HOME-AWAY-FROM-HOME OF THIS OUTCAST DUCK. TOAST THE SEASON WITH HE AND HIS BELOVED BEVERLY SWITZLER--WITH HIS FRIENDS WINDA WESTER AND PAUL SAME. WELCOME WITH US THIS 25TH OF DECEMBER AS WE WEAVE A YULETIDE TALE TO TOUCH THE FLINTY CORE OF THE STERNEST SCROOGE. "HUMBUG!" YOU SAY? READ ON!

Script: BILL MANTLO. Art: GENE COLAN & DAVE SIMONS

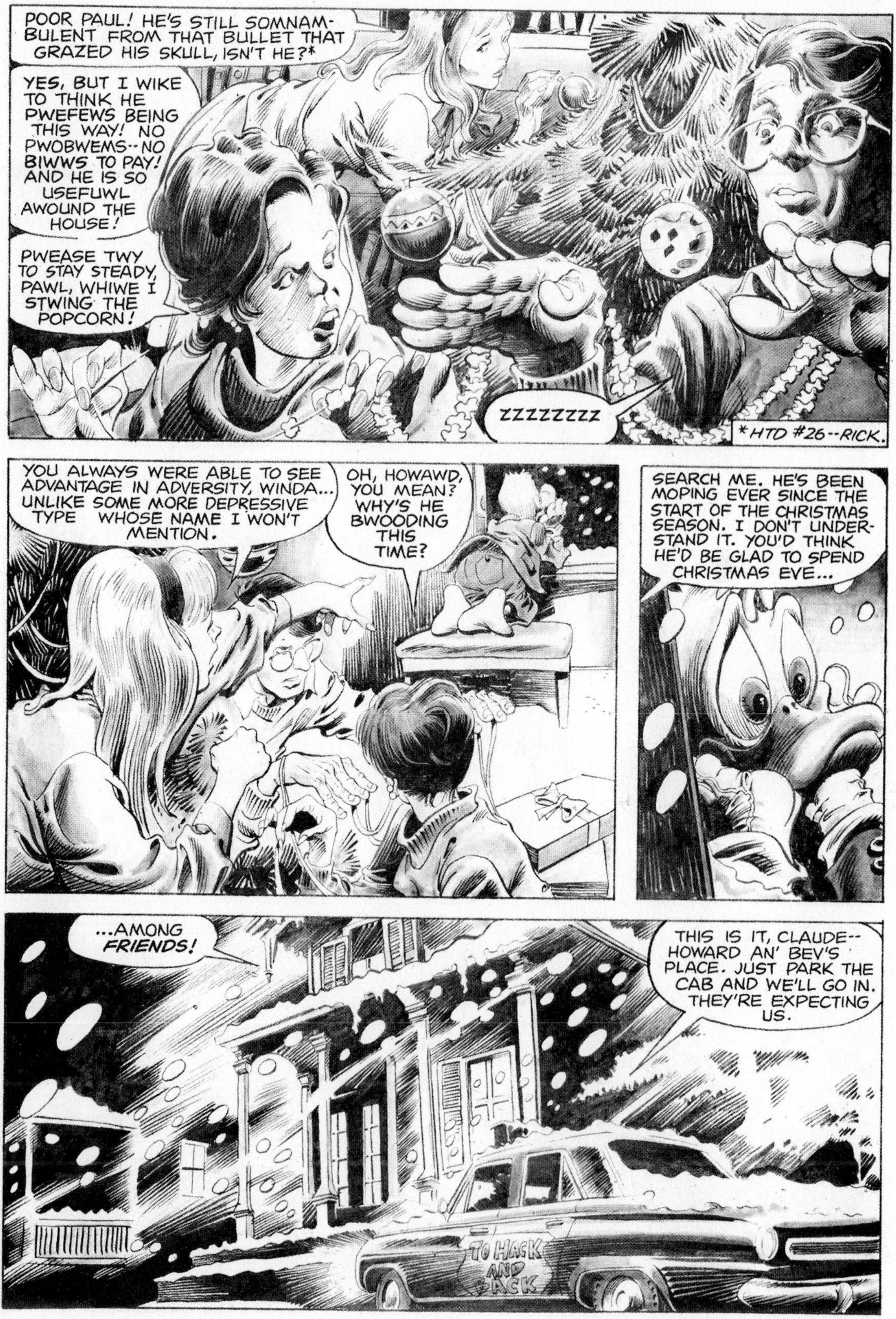
POOR PAUL! HE'S STILL SOMNAMBULENT FROM THAT BULLET THAT GRAZED HIS SKULL, ISN'T HE?*
YES, BUT I WIKE TO THINK HE PWEFEWS BEING THIS WAY! NO PWOBWEMS--NO BIWWS TO PAY! AND HE IS SO USEFUWL AWOUND THE HOUSE!
PWEASE TWY TO STAY STEADY, PAWL, WHIWE I STWING THE POPCORN!
ZZZZZZZZ
*HTD #26--RICK.
YOU ALWAYS WERE ABLE TO SEE ADVANTAGE IN ADVERSITY, WINDA... UNLIKE SOME MORE DEPRESSIVE TYPE WHOSE NAME I WON'T MENTION.
OH, HOWAWD, YOU MEAN? WHY'S HE BWOODING THIS TIME?
SEARCH ME. HE'S BEEN MOPING EVER SINCE THE START OF THE CHRISTMAS SEASON. I DON'T UNDERSTAND IT. YOU'D THINK HE'D BE GLAD TO SPEND CHRISTMAS EVE...
...AMONG FRIENDS!
THIS IS IT, CLAUDE-- HOWARD AN' BEV'S PLACE. JUST PARK THE CAB AND WE'LL GO IN. THEY'RE EXPECTING US.
TO HACK AND BACK

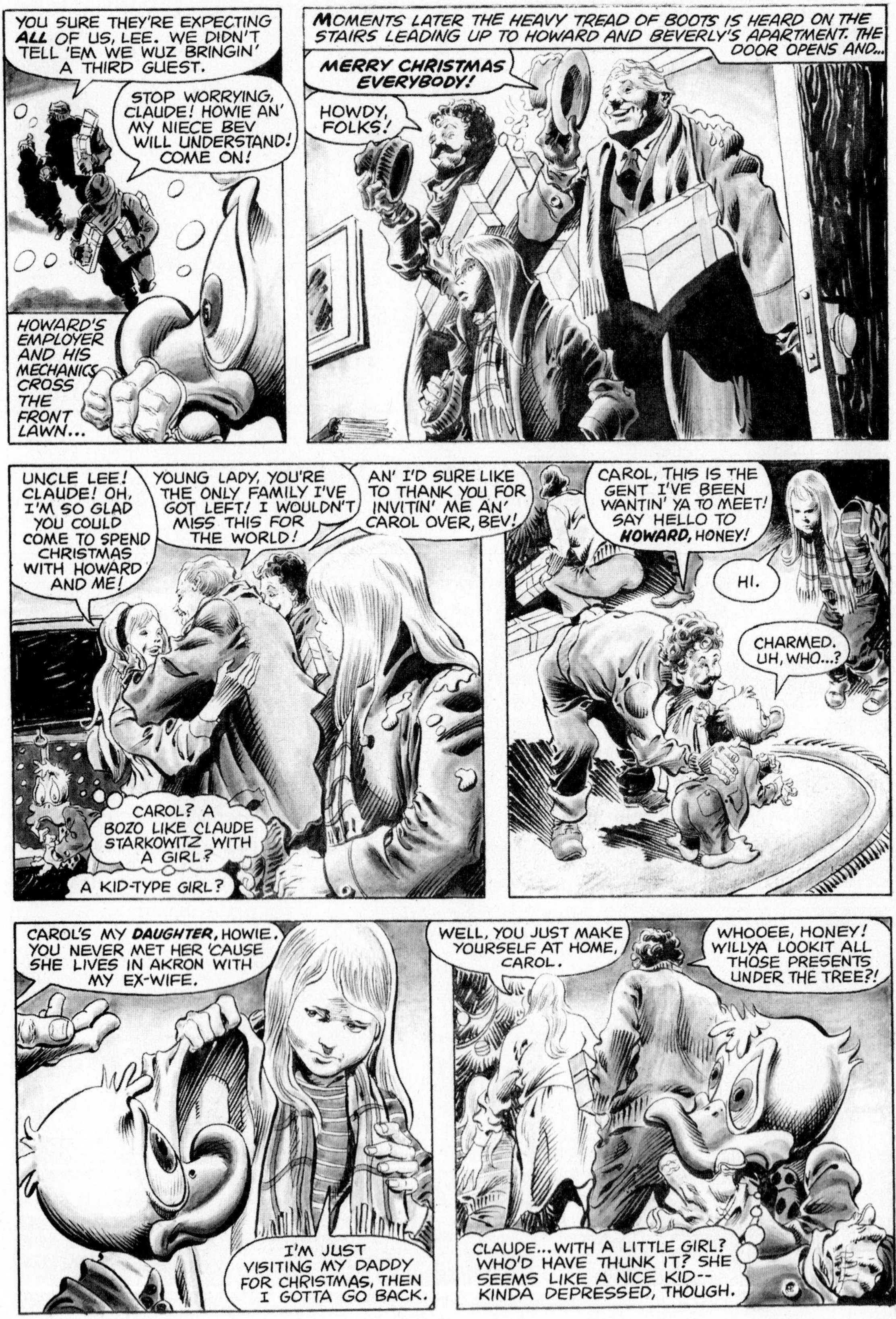

YOU SURE THEY'RE EXPECTING ALL OF US, LEE. WE DIDN'T TELL 'EM WE WUZ BRINGIN' A THIRD GUEST.
STOP WORRYING, CLAUDE! HOWIE AN' MY NIECE BEV WILL UNDERSTAND! COME ON!
HOWARD'S EMPLOYER AND HIS MECHANICS CROSS THE FRONT LAWN...
MOMENTS LATER THE HEAVY TREAD OF BOOTS IS HEARD ON THE STAIRS LEADING UP TO HOWARD AND BEVERLY'S APARTMENT. THE DOOR OPENS AND...
MERRY CHRISTMAS EVERYBODY!
HOWDY, FOLKS!
UNCLE LEE! CLAUDE! OH, I'M SO GLAD YOU COULD COME TO SPEND CHRISTMAS WITH HOWARD AND ME!
YOUNG LADY, YOU'RE THE ONLY FAMILY I'VE GOT LEFT! I WOULDN'T MISS THIS FOR THE WORLD!
AN' I'D SURE LIKE TO THANK YOU FOR INVITIN' ME AN' CAROL OVER, BEV!
CAROL? A BOZO LIKE CLAUDE STARKOWITZ WITH A GIRL?
A KID-TYPE GIRL?
CAROL, THIS IS THE GENT I'VE BEEN WANTIN' YA TO MEET! SAY HELLO TO HOWARD, HONEY!
HI.
CHARMED. UH, WHO...?
CAROL'S MY DAUGHTER, HOWIE. YOU NEVER MET HER 'CAUSE SHE LIVES IN AKRON WITH MY EX-WIFE.
I'M JUST VISITING MY DADDY FOR CHRISTMAS, THEN I GOTTA GO BACK.
WELL, YOU JUST MAKE YOURSELF AT HOME, CAROL.
WHOOEE, HONEY! WILLYA LOOKIT ALL THOSE PRESENTS UNDER THE TREE?!
CLAUDE... WITH A LITTLE GIRL? WHO'D HAVE THUNK IT? SHE SEEMS LIKE A NICE KID-- KINDA DEPRESSED, THOUGH.

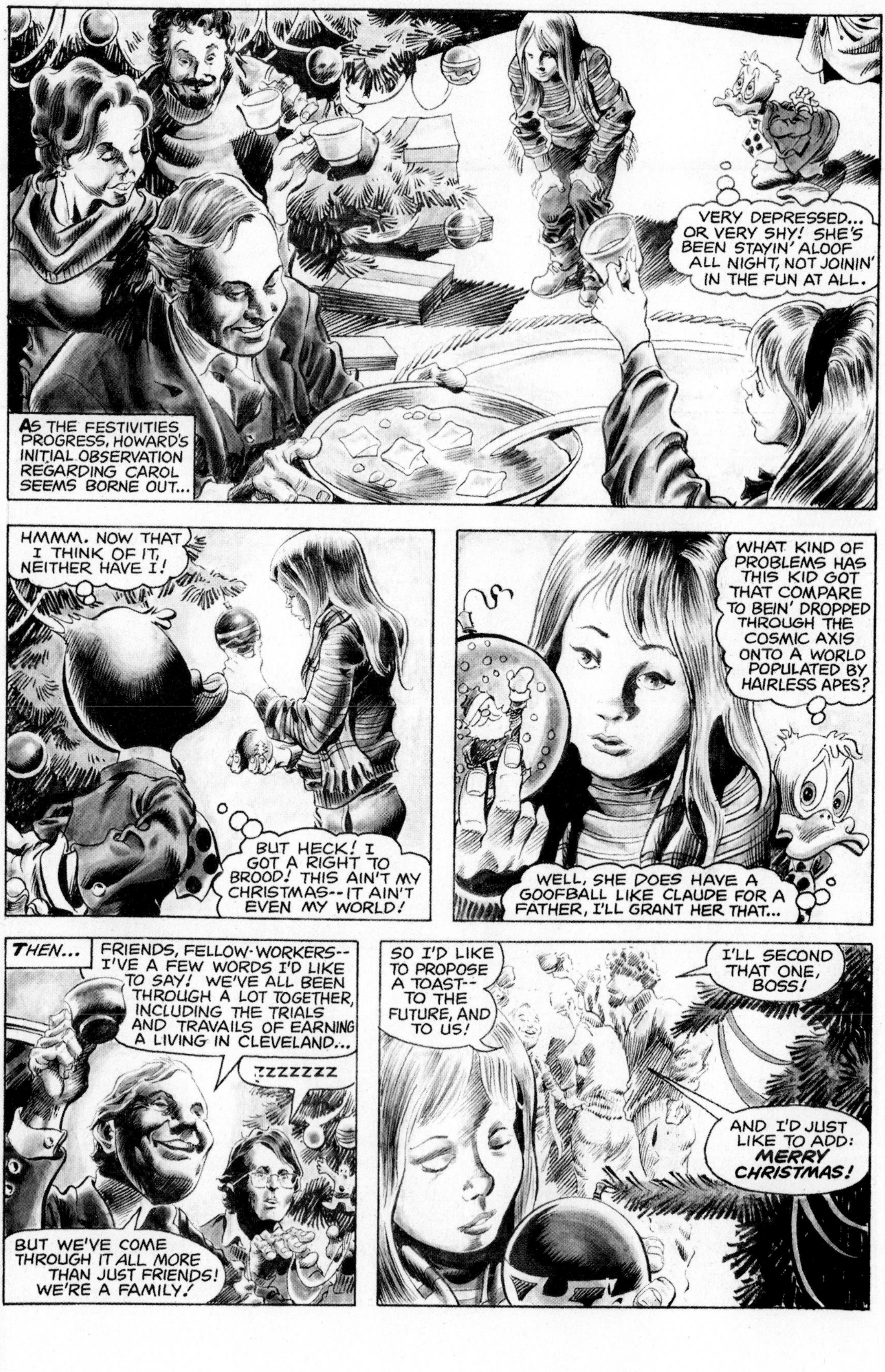
VERY DEPRESSED... OR VERY SHY! SHE'S BEEN STAYIN' ALOOF ALL NIGHT, NOT JOININ' IN THE FUN AT ALL.
AS THE FESTIVITIES PROGRESS, HOWARD'S INITIAL OBSERVATION REGARDING CAROL SEEMS BORNE OUT...
HMMM. NOW THAT I THINK OF IT, NEITHER HAVE I!
BUT HECK! I GOT A RIGHT TO BROOD! THIS AIN'T MY CHRISTMAS--IT AIN'T EVEN MY WORLD!
WHAT KIND OF PROBLEMS HAS THIS KID GOT THAT COMPARE TO BEIN' DROPPED THROUGH THE COSMIC AXIS ONTO A WORLD POPULATED BY HAIRLESS APES?
WELL, SHE DOES HAVE A GOOFBALL LIKE CLAUDE FOR A FATHER, I'LL GRANT HER THAT...
THEN...
FRIENDS, FELLOW-WORKERS--I'VE A FEW WORDS I'D LIKE TO SAY! WE'VE ALL BEEN THROUGH A LOT TOGETHER, INCLUDING THE TRIALS AND TRAVAILS OF EARNING A LIVING IN CLEVELAND...
ZZZZZZZ
BUT WE'VE COME THROUGH IT ALL MORE THAN JUST FRIENDS! WE'RE A FAMILY!
SO I'D LIKE TO PROPOSE A TOAST--TO THE FUTURE, AND TO US!
I'LL SECOND THAT ONE, BOSS!
AND I'D JUST LIKE TO ADD: MERRY CHRISTMAS!

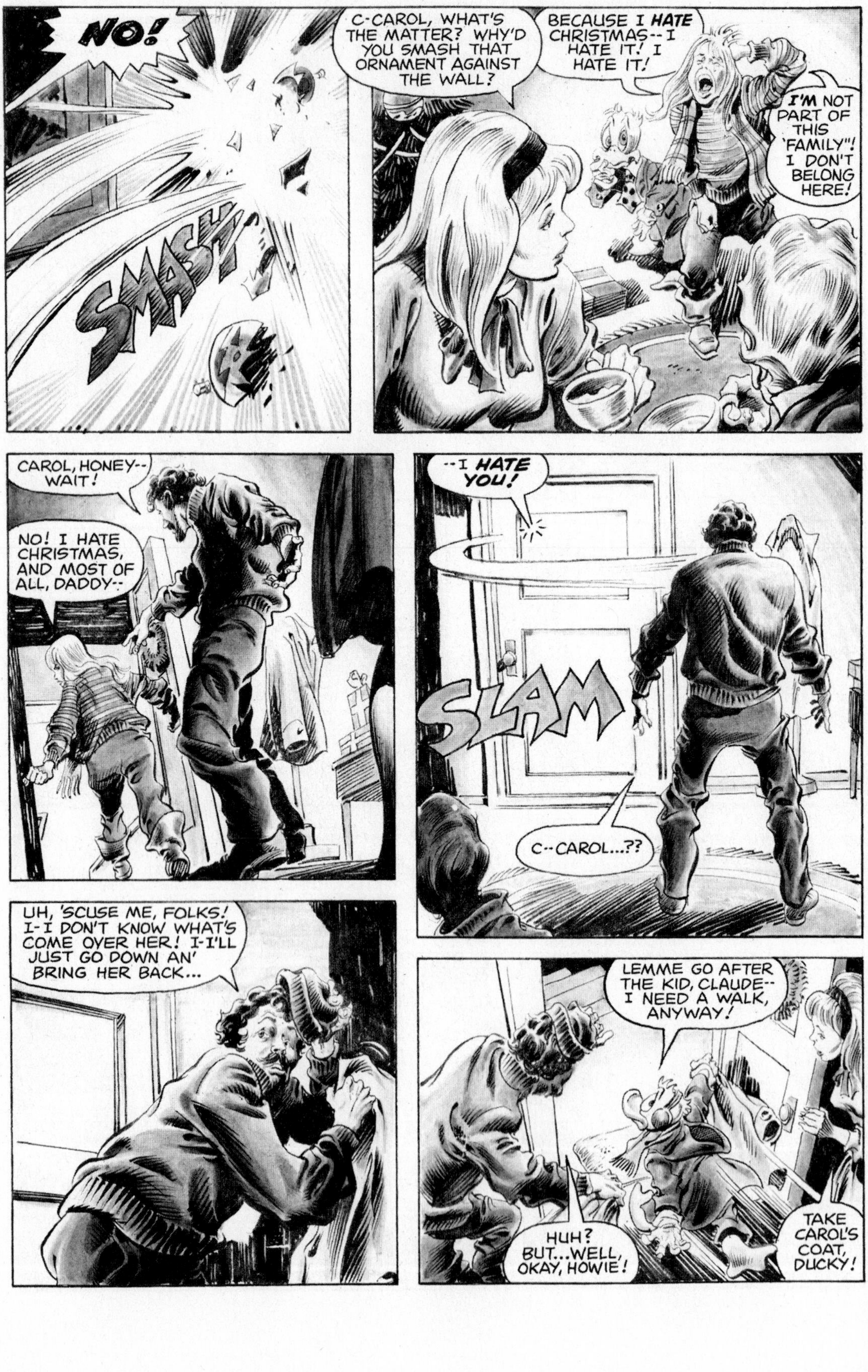
NO!
SMASH!
C-CAROL, WHAT'S THE MATTER? WHY'D YOU SMASH THAT ORNAMENT AGAINST THE WALL?
BECAUSE I HATE CHRISTMAS-- I HATE IT! I HATE IT!
I'M NOT PART OF THIS 'FAMILY"! I DON'T BELONG HERE!
CAROL, HONEY-- WAIT!
NO! I HATE CHRISTMAS, AND MOST OF ALL, DADDY--
--I HATE YOU!
SLAM
C--CAROL...??
UH, 'SCUSE ME, FOLKS! I-I DON'T KNOW WHAT'S COME OVER HER! I-I'LL JUST GO DOWN AN' BRING HER BACK...
LEMME GO AFTER THE KID, CLAUDE-- I NEED A WALK, ANYWAY!
HUH? BUT...WELL, OKAY, HOWIE!
TAKE CAROL'S COAT, DUCKY!

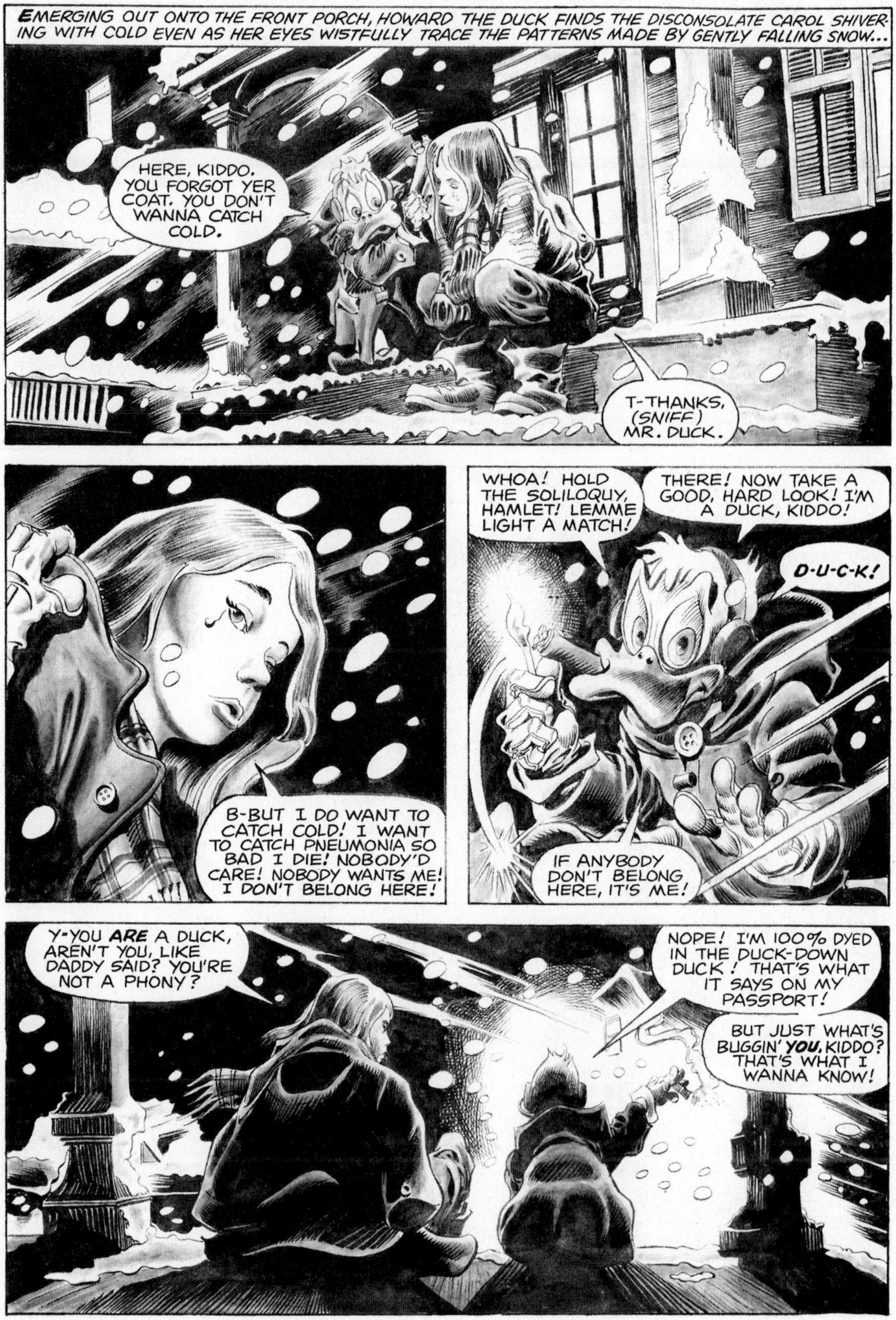
EMERGING OUT ONTO THE FRONT PORCH, HOWARD THE DUCK FINDS THE DISCONSOLATE CAROL SHIVERING WITH COLD EVEN AS HER EYES WISTFULLY TRACE THE PATTERNS MADE BY GENTLY FALLING SNOW...
HERE, KIDDO. YOU FORGOT YER COAT. YOU DON'T WANNA CATCH COLD.
T-THANKS, (SNIFF) MR. DUCK.
B-BUT I DO WANT TO CATCH COLD! I WANT TO CATCH PNEUMONIA SO BAD I DIE! NOBODY'D CARE! NOBODY WANTS ME! I DON'T BELONG HERE!
WHOA! HOLD THE SOLILOQUY, HAMLET! LEMME LIGHT A MATCH!
THERE! NOW TAKE A GOOD, HARD LOOK! I'M A DUCK, KIDDO!
D-U-C-K!
IF ANYBODY DON'T BELONG HERE, IT'S ME!
Y-YOU ARE A DUCK, AREN'T YOU, LIKE DADDY SAID? YOU'RE NOT A PHONY?
NOPE! I'M 100% DYED IN THE DUCK-DOWN DUCK! THAT'S WHAT IT SAYS ON MY PASSPORT!
BUT JUST WHAT'S BUGGIN' YOU, KIDDO? THAT'S WHAT I WANNA KNOW!

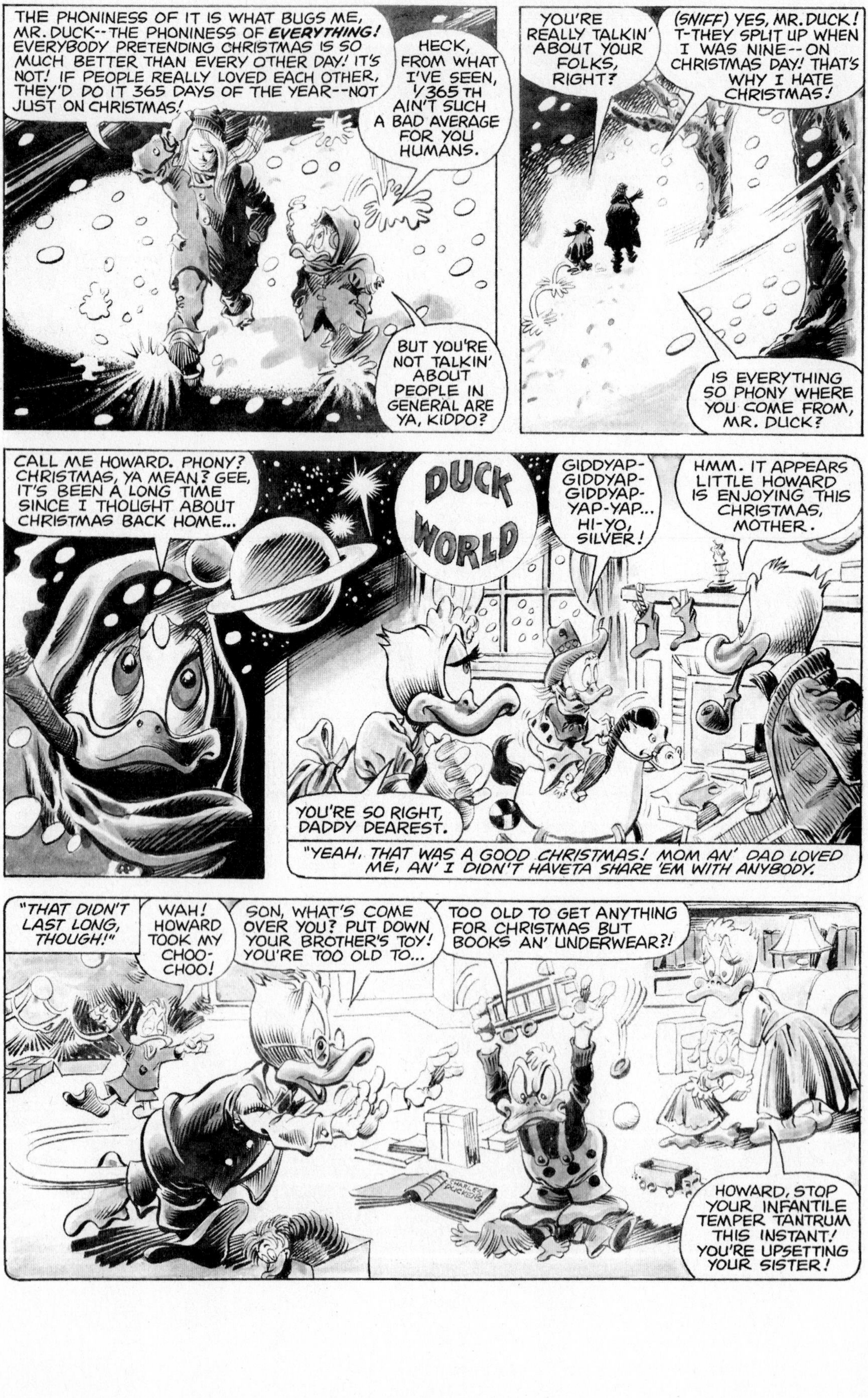
THE PHONINESS OF IT IS WHAT BUGS ME, MR. DUCK--THE PHONINESS OF *EVERYTHING!* EVERYBODY PRETENDING CHRISTMAS IS SO MUCH BETTER THAN EVERY OTHER DAY! IT'S NOT! IF PEOPLE REALLY LOVED EACH OTHER, THEY'D DO IT 365 DAYS OF THE YEAR--NOT JUST ON CHRISTMAS!
HECK, FROM WHAT I'VE SEEN, 1/365TH AIN'T SUCH A BAD AVERAGE FOR YOU HUMANS.
BUT YOU'RE NOT TALKIN' ABOUT PEOPLE IN GENERAL ARE YA, KIDDO?
YOU'RE REALLY TALKIN' ABOUT YOUR FOLKS, RIGHT?
(*SNIFF*) YES, MR. DUCK! T-THEY SPLIT UP WHEN I WAS NINE--ON CHRISTMAS DAY! THAT'S WHY I HATE CHRISTMAS!
IS EVERYTHING SO PHONY WHERE YOU COME FROM, MR. DUCK?
CALL ME HOWARD. PHONY? CHRISTMAS, YA MEAN? GEE, IT'S BEEN A LONG TIME SINCE I THOUGHT ABOUT CHRISTMAS BACK HOME...
DUCK WORLD
GIDDYAP-GIDDYAP-GIDDYAP-YAP-YAP... HI-YO, SILVER!
HMM. IT APPEARS LITTLE HOWARD IS ENJOYING THIS CHRISTMAS, MOTHER.
YOU'RE SO RIGHT, DADDY DEAREST.
"YEAH, THAT WAS A GOOD CHRISTMAS! MOM AN' DAD LOVED ME, AN' I DIDN'T HAVETA SHARE 'EM WITH ANYBODY.
"THAT DIDN'T LAST LONG, THOUGH!"
WAH! HOWARD TOOK MY CHOO-CHOO!
SON, WHAT'S COME OVER YOU? PUT DOWN YOUR BROTHER'S TOY! YOU'RE TOO OLD TO...
TOO OLD TO GET ANYTHING FOR CHRISTMAS BUT BOOKS AN' UNDERWEAR?!
CHARLES DUCKENS
HOWARD, STOP YOUR INFANTILE TEMPER TANTRUM THIS INSTANT! YOU'RE UPSETTING YOUR SISTER!

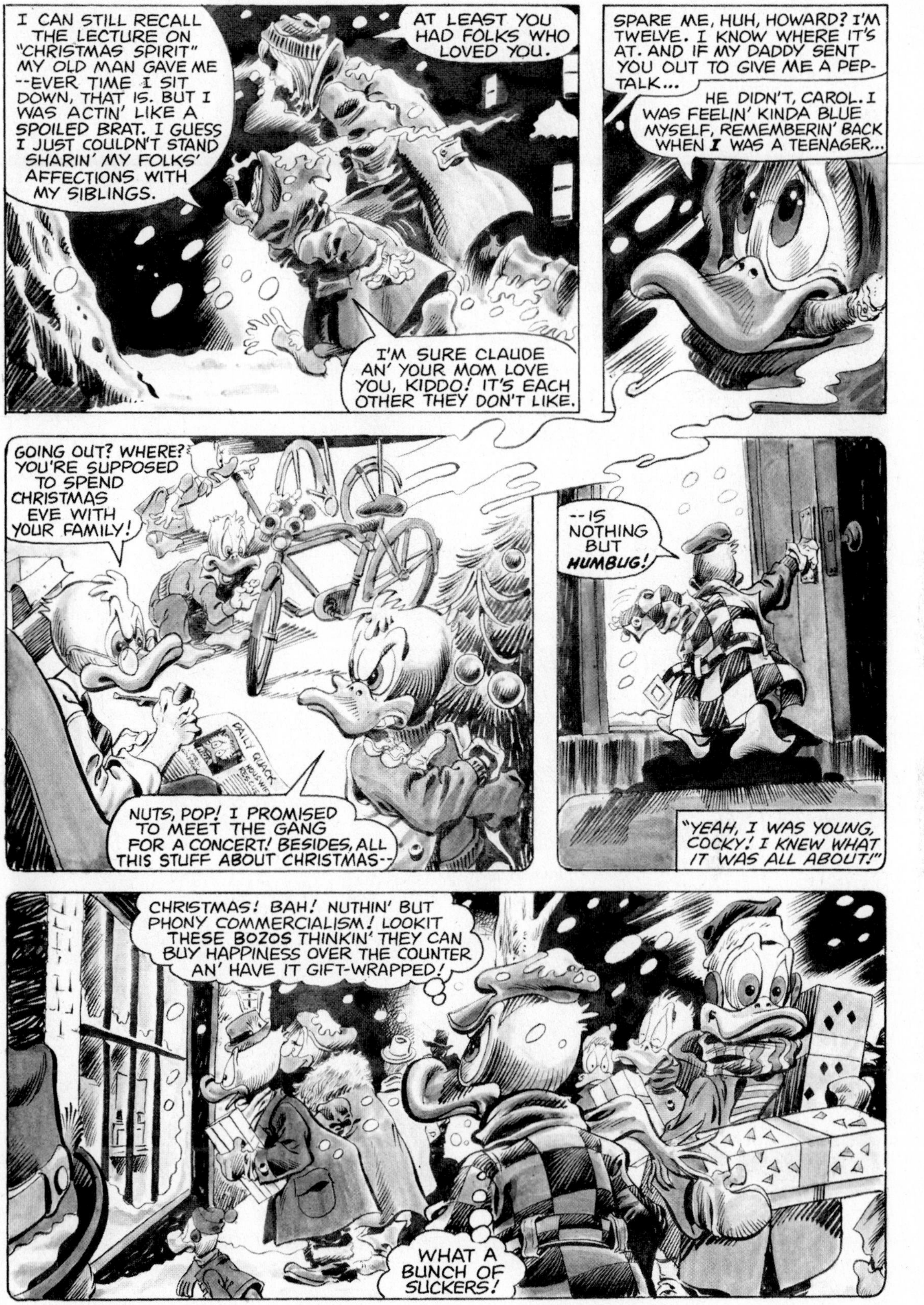
I CAN STILL RECALL THE LECTURE ON "CHRISTMAS SPIRIT" MY OLD MAN GAVE ME --EVER TIME I SIT DOWN, THAT IS. BUT I WAS ACTIN' LIKE A SPOILED BRAT. I GUESS I JUST COULDN'T STAND SHARIN' MY FOLKS' AFFECTIONS WITH MY SIBLINGS.
AT LEAST YOU HAD FOLKS WHO LOVED YOU.
I'M SURE CLAUDE AN' YOUR MOM LOVE YOU, KIDDO! IT'S EACH OTHER THEY DON'T LIKE.
SPARE ME, HUH, HOWARD? I'M TWELVE. I KNOW WHERE IT'S AT. AND IF MY DADDY SENT YOU OUT TO GIVE ME A PEP-TALK...
HE DIDN'T, CAROL. I WAS FEELIN' KINDA BLUE MYSELF, REMEMBERIN' BACK WHEN I WAS A TEENAGER...
GOING OUT? WHERE? YOU'RE SUPPOSED TO SPEND CHRISTMAS EVE WITH YOUR FAMILY!
DAILY QUACK
NUTS, POP! I PROMISED TO MEET THE GANG FOR A CONCERT! BESIDES, ALL THIS STUFF ABOUT CHRISTMAS--
--IS NOTHING BUT HUMBUG!
"YEAH, I WAS YOUNG, COCKY! I KNEW WHAT IT WAS ALL ABOUT!"
CHRISTMAS! BAH! NUTHIN' BUT PHONY COMMERCIALISM! LOOKIT THESE BOZOS THINKIN' THEY CAN BUY HAPPINESS OVER THE COUNTER AN' HAVE IT GIFT-WRAPPED!
WHAT A BUNCH OF SUCKERS!

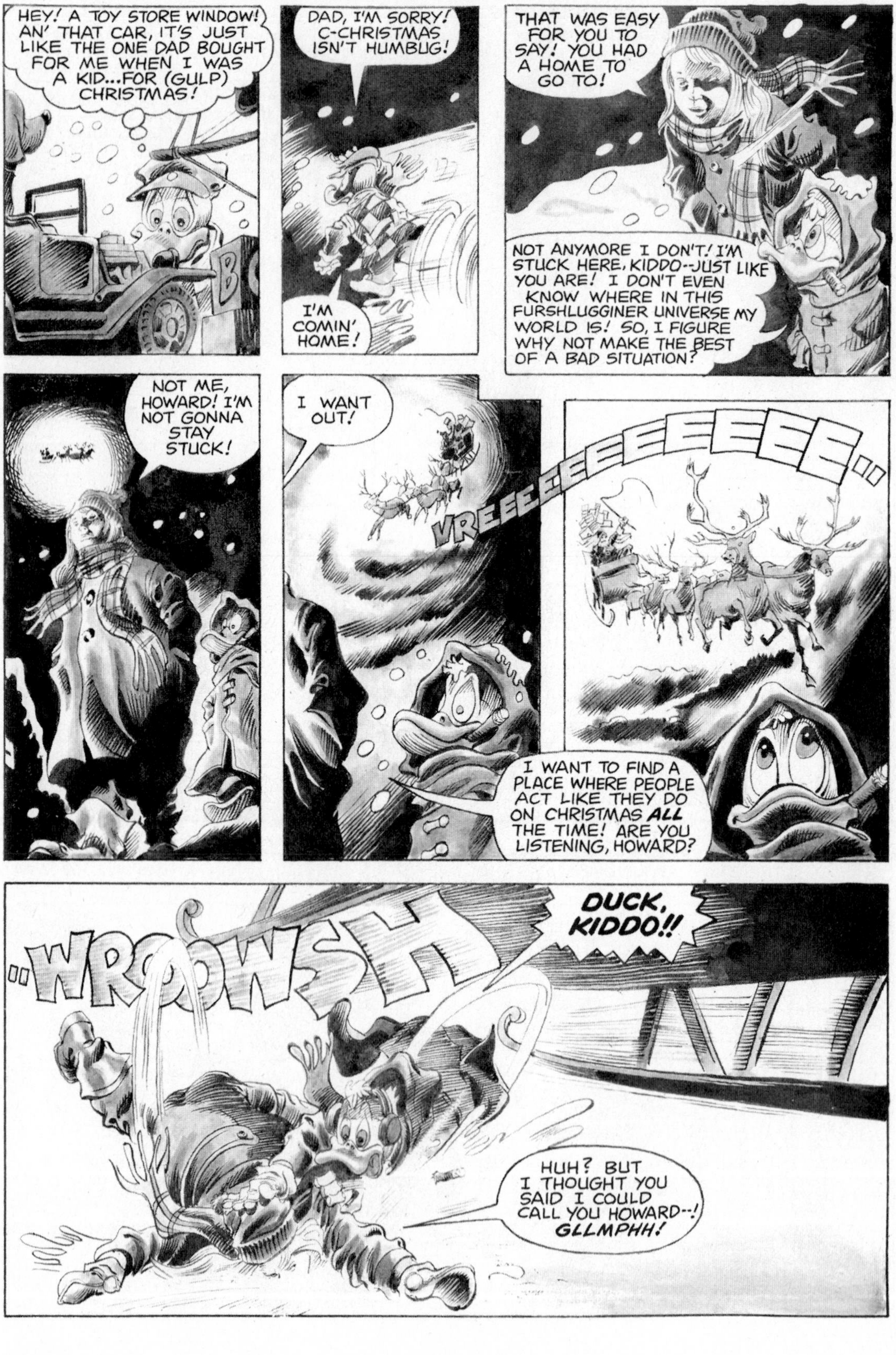
HEY! A TOY STORE WINDOW! AN' THAT CAR, IT'S JUST LIKE THE ONE DAD BOUGHT FOR ME WHEN I WAS A KID...FOR (GULP) CHRISTMAS!
DAD, I'M SORRY! C-CHRISTMAS ISN'T HUMBUG!
I'M COMIN' HOME!
THAT WAS EASY FOR YOU TO SAY! YOU HAD A HOME TO GO TO!
NOT ANYMORE I DON'T! I'M STUCK HERE, KIDDO--JUST LIKE YOU ARE! I DON'T EVEN KNOW WHERE IN THIS FURSHLUGGINER UNIVERSE MY WORLD IS! SO, I FIGURE WHY NOT MAKE THE BEST OF A BAD SITUATION?
NOT ME, HOWARD! I'M NOT GONNA STAY STUCK!
I WANT OUT!
VREEEEEEEEEEEEE..
I WANT TO FIND A PLACE WHERE PEOPLE ACT LIKE THEY DO ON CHRISTMAS ALL THE TIME! ARE YOU LISTENING, HOWARD?
..WROOWSH
DUCK, KIDDO!!
HUH? BUT I THOUGHT YOU SAID I COULD CALL YOU HOWARD--! GLLMPHH!

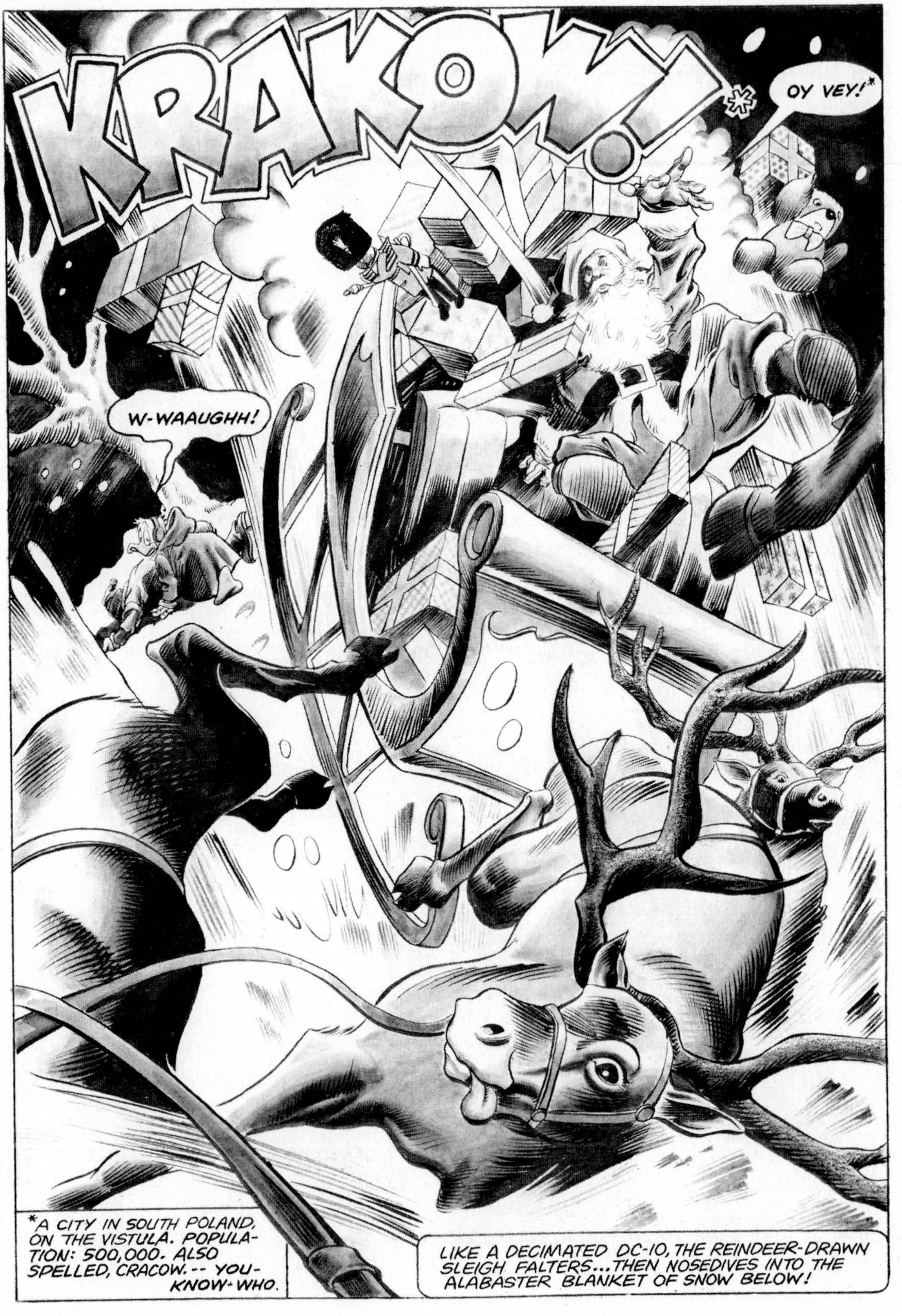
KRAKOW!*
OY VEY!*
W-WAAUGHH!
*A CITY IN SOUTH POLAND, ON THE VISTULA. POPULATION: 500,000. ALSO SPELLED, CRACOW.-- YOU-KNOW-WHO.
LIKE A DECIMATED DC-10, THE REINDEER-DRAWN SLEIGH FALTERS...THEN NOSEDIVES INTO THE ALABASTER BLANKET OF SNOW BELOW!

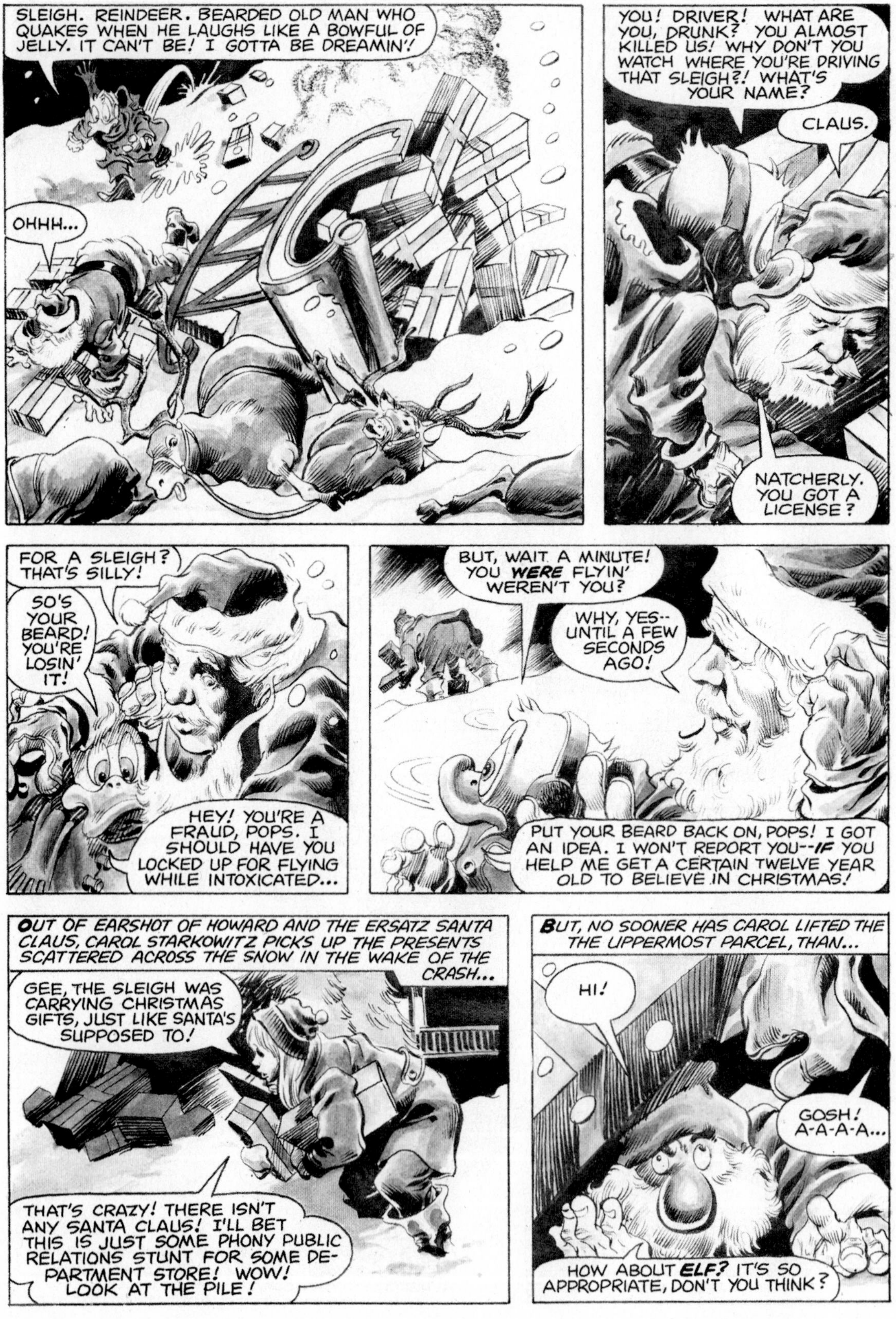
SLEIGH. REINDEER. BEARDED OLD MAN WHO QUAKES WHEN HE LAUGHS LIKE A BOWFUL OF JELLY. IT CAN'T BE! I GOTTA BE DREAMIN'!
OHHH...
YOU! DRIVER! WHAT ARE YOU, DRUNK? YOU ALMOST KILLED US! WHY DON'T YOU WATCH WHERE YOU'RE DRIVING THAT SLEIGH?! WHAT'S YOUR NAME?
CLAUS.
NATCHERLY. YOU GOT A LICENSE?
FOR A SLEIGH? THAT'S SILLY!
SO'S YOUR BEARD! YOU'RE LOSIN' IT!
HEY! YOU'RE A FRAUD, POPS. I SHOULD HAVE YOU LOCKED UP FOR FLYING WHILE INTOXICATED...
BUT, WAIT A MINUTE! YOU WERE FLYIN' WEREN'T YOU?
WHY, YES-- UNTIL A FEW SECONDS AGO!
PUT YOUR BEARD BACK ON, POPS! I GOT AN IDEA. I WON'T REPORT YOU--IF YOU HELP ME GET A CERTAIN TWELVE YEAR OLD TO BELIEVE IN CHRISTMAS!
OUT OF EARSHOT OF HOWARD AND THE ERSATZ SANTA CLAUS, CAROL STARKOWITZ PICKS UP THE PRESENTS SCATTERED ACROSS THE SNOW IN THE WAKE OF THE CRASH...
GEE, THE SLEIGH WAS CARRYING CHRISTMAS GIFTS, JUST LIKE SANTA'S SUPPOSED TO!
THAT'S CRAZY! THERE ISN'T ANY SANTA CLAUS! I'LL BET THIS IS JUST SOME PHONY PUBLIC RELATIONS STUNT FOR SOME DE-PARTMENT STORE! WOW! LOOK AT THE PILE!
BUT, NO SOONER HAS CAROL LIFTED THE THE UPPERMOST PARCEL, THAN...
HI!
GOSH! A-A-A-A...
HOW ABOUT ELF? IT'S SO APPROPRIATE, DON'T YOU THINK?

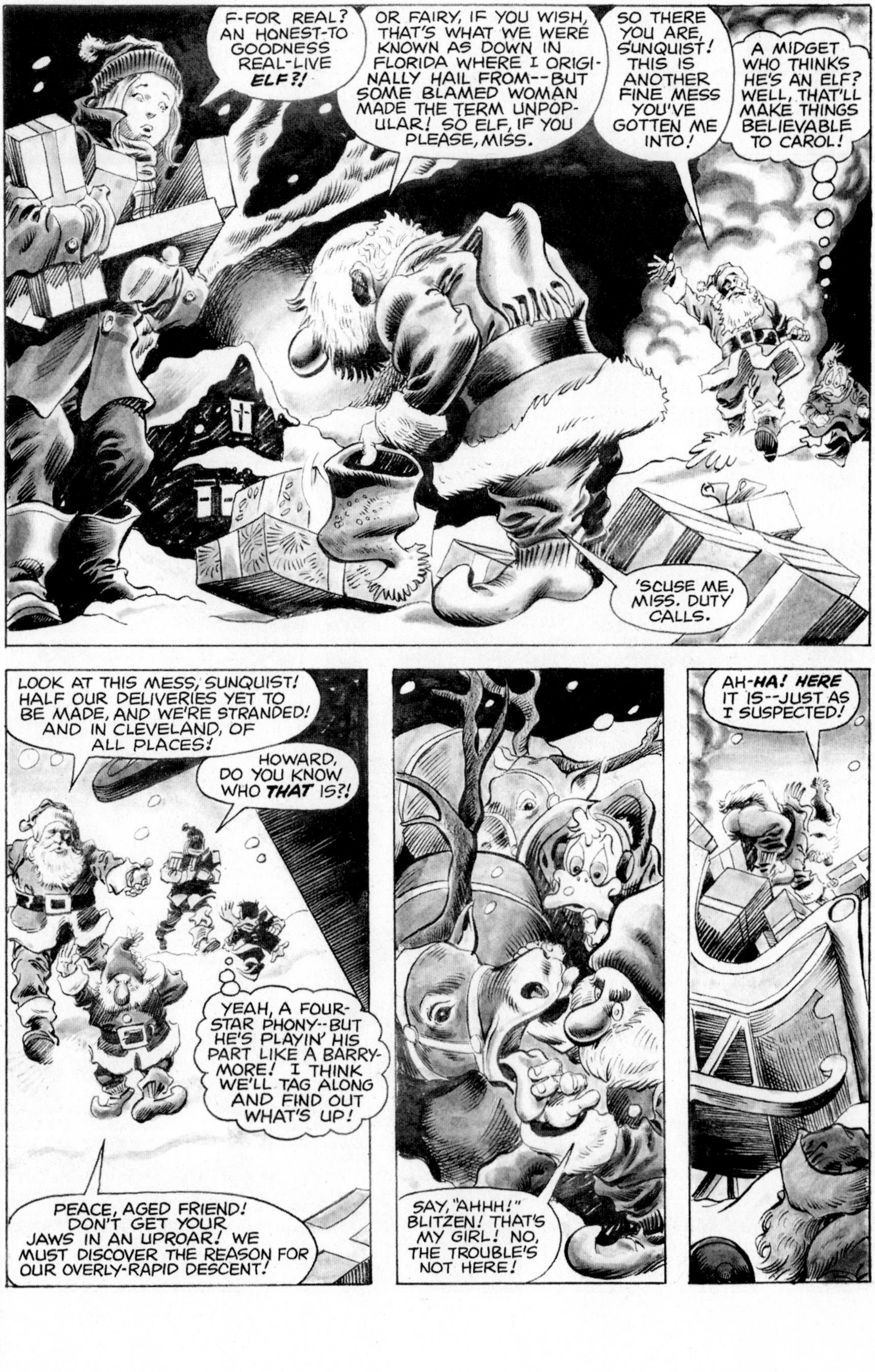
F-FOR REAL? AN HONEST-TO GOODNESS REAL-LIVE ELF?!
OR FAIRY, IF YOU WISH, THAT'S WHAT WE WERE KNOWN AS DOWN IN FLORIDA WHERE I ORIGINALLY HAIL FROM--BUT SOME BLAMED WOMAN MADE THE TERM UNPOPULAR! SO ELF, IF YOU PLEASE, MISS.
SO THERE YOU ARE, SUNQUIST! THIS IS ANOTHER FINE MESS YOU'VE GOTTEN ME INTO!
A MIDGET WHO THINKS HE'S AN ELF? WELL, THAT'LL MAKE THINGS BELIEVABLE TO CAROL!
'SCUSE ME, MISS. DUTY CALLS.
LOOK AT THIS MESS, SUNQUIST! HALF OUR DELIVERIES YET TO BE MADE, AND WE'RE STRANDED! AND IN CLEVELAND, OF ALL PLACES!
HOWARD, DO YOU KNOW WHO THAT IS?!
YEAH, A FOUR-STAR PHONY--BUT HE'S PLAYIN' HIS PART LIKE A BARRYMORE! I THINK WE'LL TAG ALONG AND FIND OUT WHAT'S UP!
PEACE, AGED FRIEND! DON'T GET YOUR JAWS IN AN UPROAR! WE MUST DISCOVER THE REASON FOR OUR OVERLY-RAPID DESCENT!
SAY, "AHHH!" BLITZEN! THAT'S MY GIRL! NO, THE TROUBLE'S NOT HERE!
AH-HA! HERE IT IS--JUST AS I SUSPECTED!

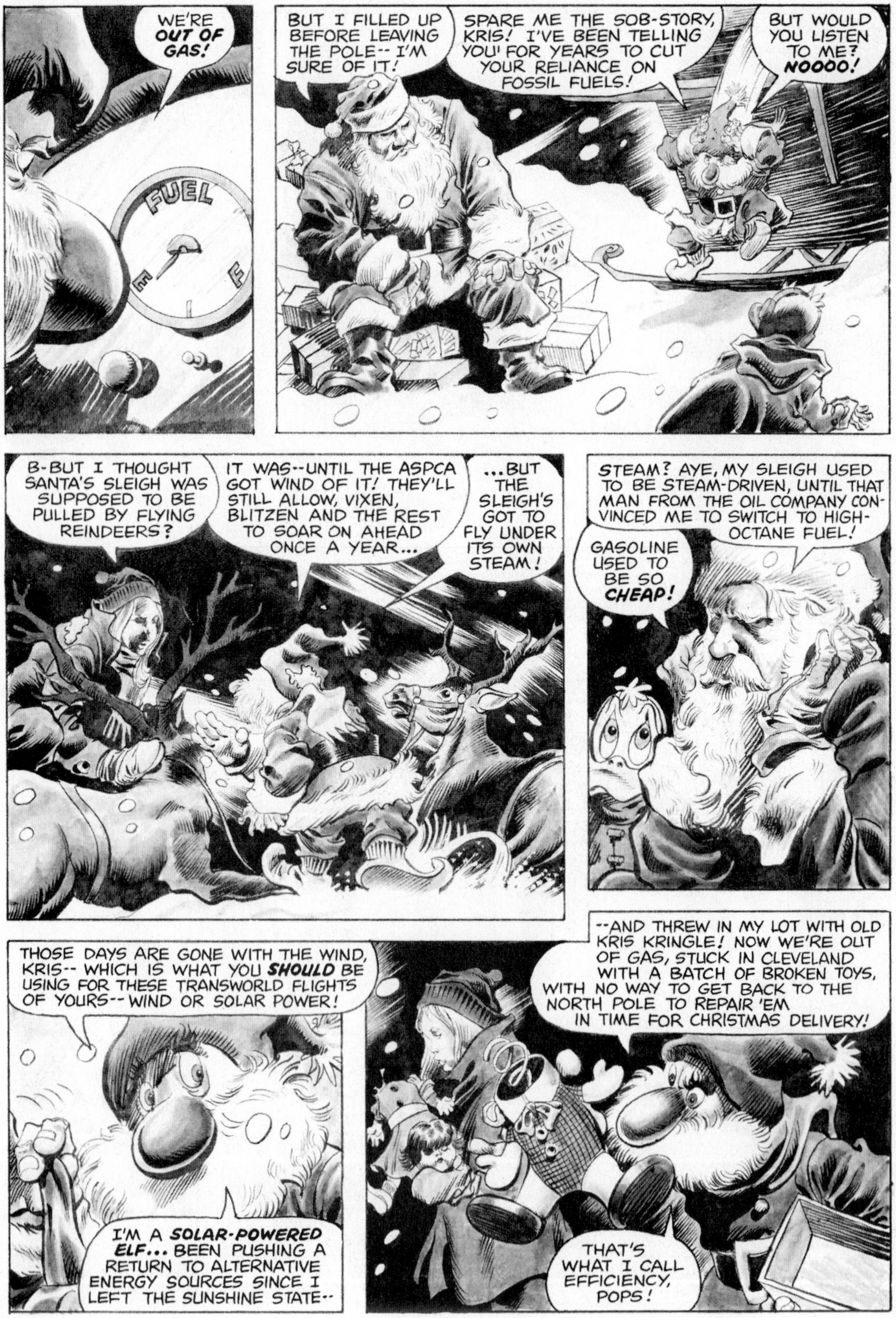
WE'RE **OUT OF GAS!**
FUEL
E F
BUT I FILLED UP BEFORE LEAVING THE POLE-- I'M SURE OF IT!
SPARE ME THE SOB-STORY, KRIS! I'VE BEEN TELLING YOU! FOR YEARS TO CUT YOUR RELIANCE ON FOSSIL FUELS!
BUT WOULD YOU LISTEN TO ME? **NOOOO!**
B-BUT I THOUGHT SANTA'S SLEIGH WAS SUPPOSED TO BE PULLED BY FLYING REINDEERS?
IT WAS--UNTIL THE ASPCA GOT WIND OF IT! THEY'LL STILL ALLOW, VIXEN, BLITZEN AND THE REST TO SOAR ON AHEAD ONCE A YEAR...
...BUT THE SLEIGH'S GOT TO FLY UNDER ITS OWN STEAM!
STEAM? AYE, MY SLEIGH USED TO BE STEAM-DRIVEN, UNTIL THAT MAN FROM THE OIL COMPANY CONVINCED ME TO SWITCH TO HIGH-OCTANE FUEL!
GASOLINE USED TO BE SO **CHEAP!**
THOSE DAYS ARE GONE WITH THE WIND, KRIS-- WHICH IS WHAT YOU **SHOULD** BE USING FOR THESE TRANSWORLD FLIGHTS OF YOURS-- WIND OR SOLAR POWER!
I'M A **SOLAR-POWERED ELF...** BEEN PUSHING A RETURN TO ALTERNATIVE ENERGY SOURCES SINCE I LEFT THE SUNSHINE STATE--
--AND THREW IN MY LOT WITH OLD KRIS KRINGLE! NOW WE'RE OUT OF GAS, STUCK IN CLEVELAND WITH A BATCH OF BROKEN TOYS, WITH NO WAY TO GET BACK TO THE NORTH POLE TO REPAIR 'EM IN TIME FOR CHRISTMAS DELIVERY!
THAT'S WHAT I CALL EFFICIENCY, POPS!

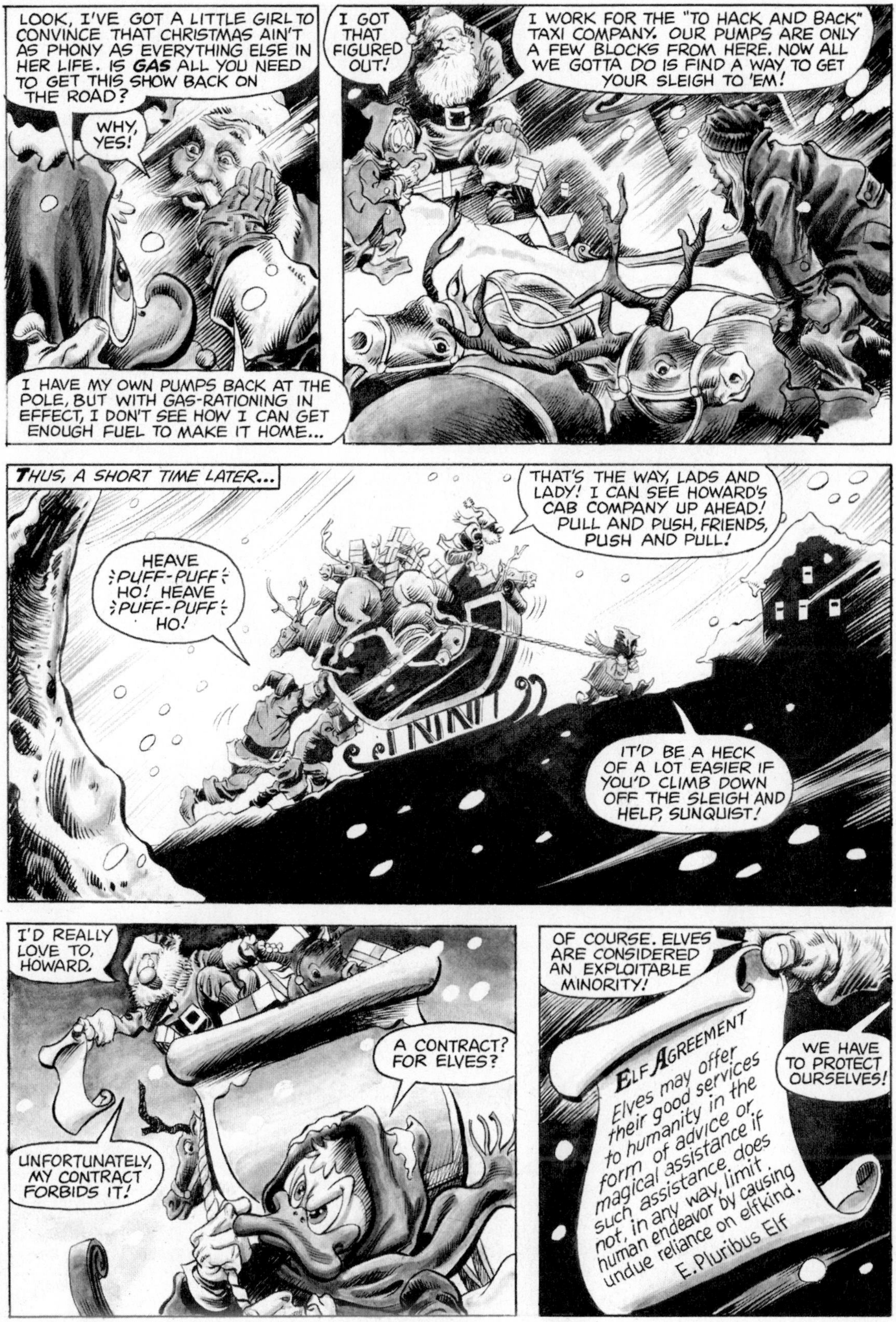
LOOK, I'VE GOT A LITTLE GIRL TO CONVINCE THAT CHRISTMAS AIN'T AS PHONY AS EVERYTHING ELSE IN HER LIFE. IS GAS ALL YOU NEED TO GET THIS SHOW BACK ON THE ROAD?
WHY, YES!
I HAVE MY OWN PUMPS BACK AT THE POLE, BUT WITH GAS-RATIONING IN EFFECT, I DON'T SEE HOW I CAN GET ENOUGH FUEL TO MAKE IT HOME...
I GOT THAT FIGURED OUT!
I WORK FOR THE "TO HACK AND BACK" TAXI COMPANY. OUR PUMPS ARE ONLY A FEW BLOCKS FROM HERE. NOW ALL WE GOTTA DO IS FIND A WAY TO GET YOUR SLEIGH TO 'EM!
THUS, A SHORT TIME LATER...
HEAVE PUFF-PUFF HO! HEAVE PUFF-PUFF HO!
THAT'S THE WAY, LADS AND LADY! I CAN SEE HOWARD'S CAB COMPANY UP AHEAD! PULL AND PUSH, FRIENDS, PUSH AND PULL!
IT'D BE A HECK OF A LOT EASIER IF YOU'D CLIMB DOWN OFF THE SLEIGH AND HELP, SUNQUIST!
I'D REALLY LOVE TO, HOWARD.
UNFORTUNATELY, MY CONTRACT FORBIDS IT!
A CONTRACT? FOR ELVES?
OF COURSE. ELVES ARE CONSIDERED AN EXPLOITABLE MINORITY!
ELF AGREEMENT
Elves may offer their good services to humanity in the form of advice or magical assistance if such assistance does not, in any way, limit human endeavor by causing undue reliance on elfkind.
E. Pluribus Elf
WE HAVE TO PROTECT OURSELVES!

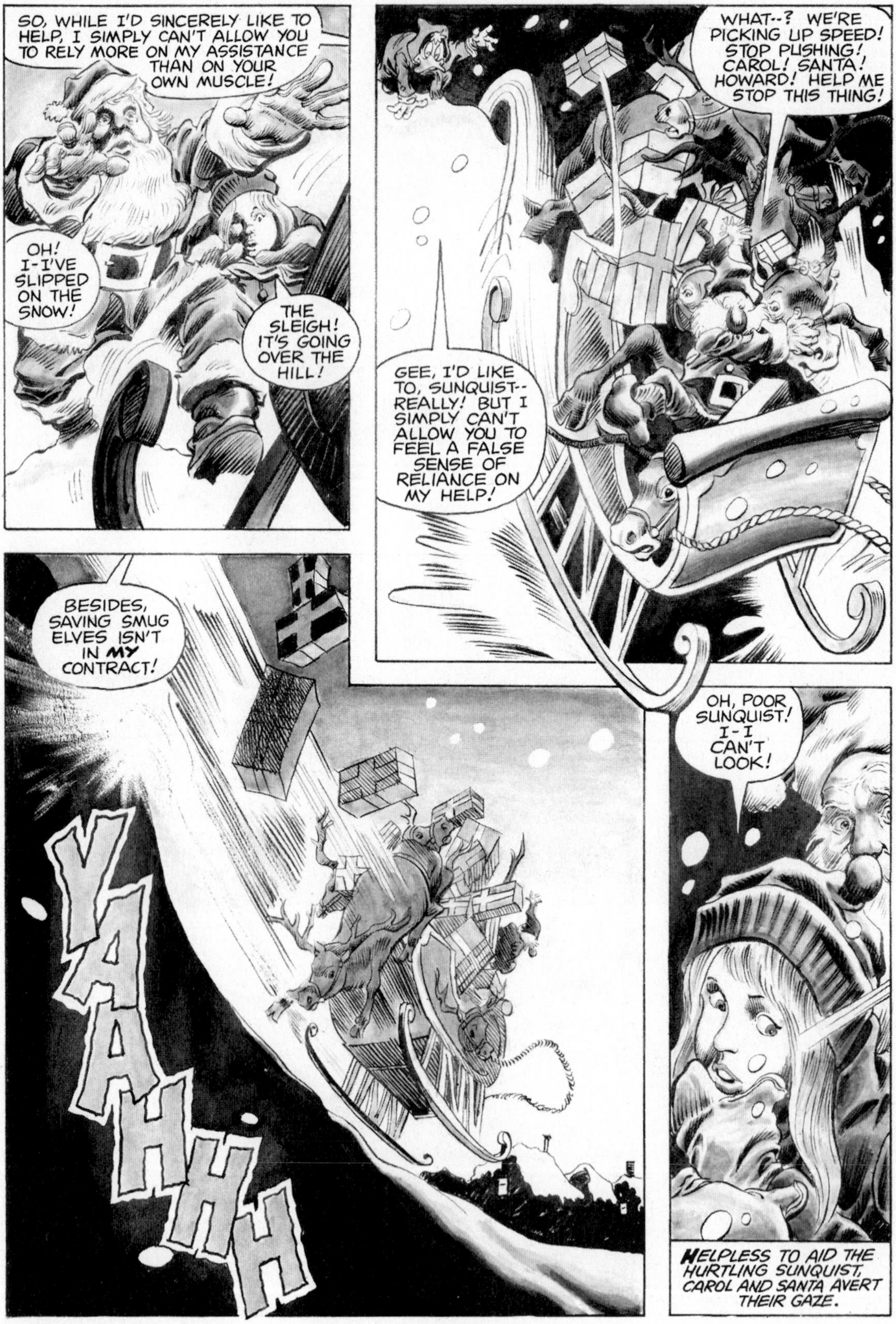
SO, WHILE I'D SINCERELY LIKE TO HELP, I SIMPLY CAN'T ALLOW YOU TO RELY MORE ON MY ASSISTANCE THAN ON YOUR OWN MUSCLE!
OH! I-I'VE SLIPPED ON THE SNOW!
THE SLEIGH! IT'S GOING OVER THE HILL!
WHAT--? WE'RE PICKING UP SPEED! STOP PUSHING! CAROL! SANTA! HOWARD! HELP ME STOP THIS THING!
GEE, I'D LIKE TO, SUNQUIST--REALLY! BUT I SIMPLY CAN'T ALLOW YOU TO FEEL A FALSE SENSE OF RELIANCE ON MY HELP!
BESIDES, SAVING SMUG ELVES ISN'T IN MY CONTRACT!
YAAHHHH
OH, POOR SUNQUIST! I-I CAN'T LOOK!
HELPLESS TO AID THE HURTLING SUNQUIST, CAROL AND SANTA AVERT THEIR GAZE.

BUT IT IS THEIR EARS THAT ARE ASSAULTED, BY THE RESULTANT RESOUNDING... AS THE SLEIGH COLLIDES WITH ITS DESTINATION...

CRASH...

OH, SUNQUIST TSK. --YOU'RE HURT!

BUT AT LEAST THE GAS PUMPS SURVIVED THE IMPACT.

NOW ALL WE GOTTA DO IS REFUEL SANTA'S SLEIGH...

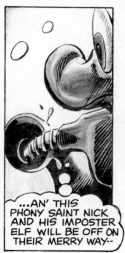

...AN' THIS PHONY SAINT NICK AND HIS IMPOSTER ELF WILL BE OFF ON THEIR MERRY WAY--

--LEAVIN' CAROL NONE THE WISER THAT SHE'S BEEN DECEIVED INTO BELIEVIN' IN CHRISTMAS BY A PAIR OF FRAUDS!

DING!

200.00

TOTAL SALE

≹WAAUGHH≹

IT COST TWO HUNDRED BUCKS TO FILL THE TANK ON THIS THING! I CAN'T LET THESE TWO BOZOES FLY OFF AND LEAVE LEE WITH THE FUEL BILL!

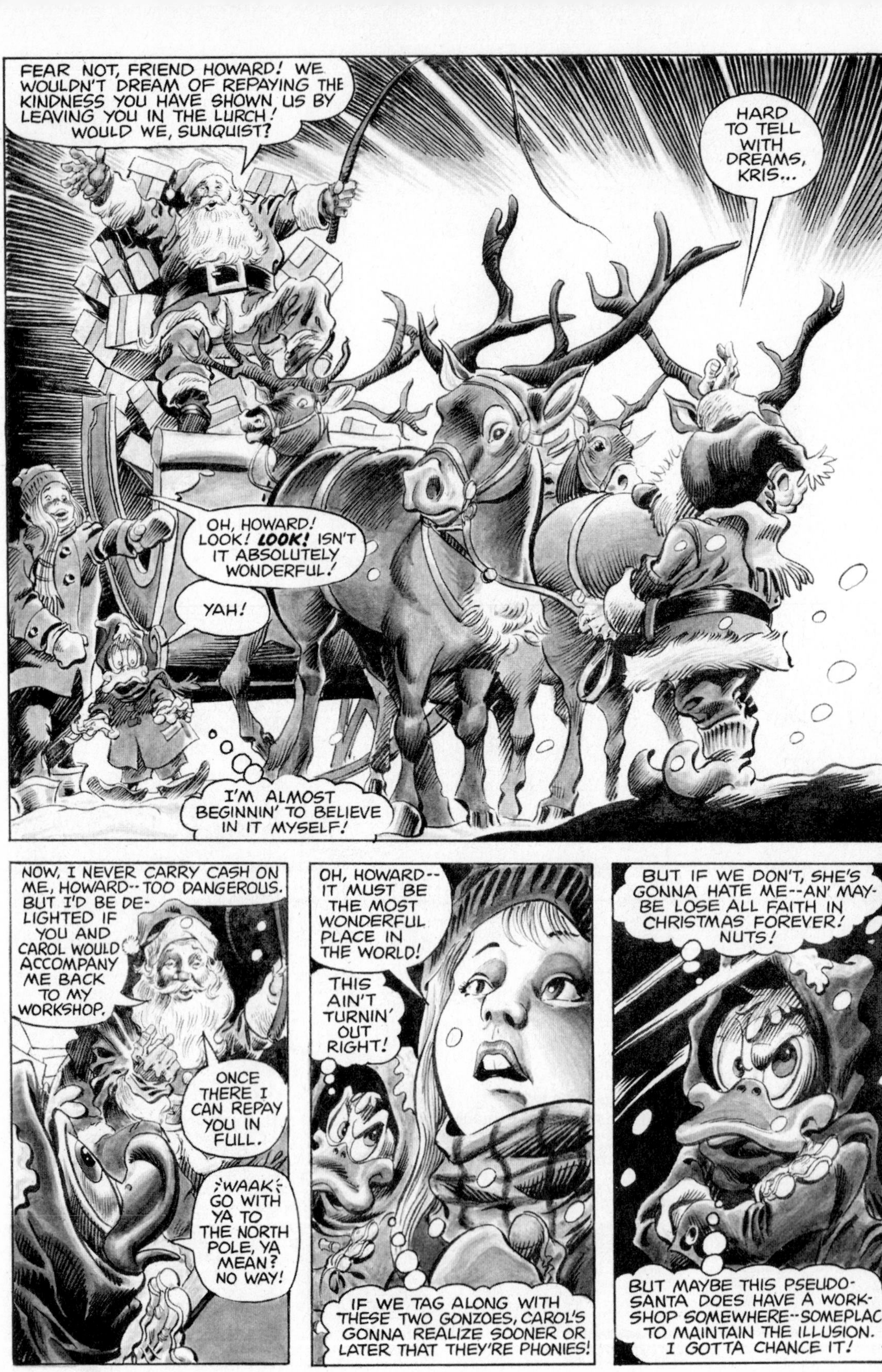
FEAR NOT, FRIEND HOWARD! WE WOULDN'T DREAM OF REPAYING THE KINDNESS YOU HAVE SHOWN US BY LEAVING YOU IN THE LURCH! WOULD WE, SUNQUIST?
HARD TO TELL WITH DREAMS, KRIS...
OH, HOWARD! LOOK! **LOOK!** ISN'T IT ABSOLUTELY WONDERFUL!
YAH!
I'M ALMOST BEGINNIN' TO BELIEVE IN IT MYSELF!
NOW, I NEVER CARRY CASH ON ME, HOWARD--TOO DANGEROUS. BUT I'D BE DE-LIGHTED IF YOU AND CAROL WOULD ACCOMPANY ME BACK TO MY WORKSHOP.
ONCE THERE I CAN REPAY YOU IN FULL.
WAAK GO WITH YA TO THE NORTH POLE, YA MEAN? NO WAY!
OH, HOWARD-- IT MUST BE THE MOST WONDERFUL PLACE IN THE WORLD!
THIS AIN'T TURNIN' OUT RIGHT!
IF WE TAG ALONG WITH THESE TWO GONZOES, CAROL'S GONNA REALIZE SOONER OR LATER THAT THEY'RE PHONIES!
BUT IF WE DON'T, SHE'S GONNA HATE ME--AN' MAY-BE LOSE ALL FAITH IN CHRISTMAS FOREVER! NUTS!
BUT MAYBE THIS PSEUDO-SANTA DOES HAVE A WORK-SHOP SOMEWHERE--SOMEPLACE TO MAINTAIN THE ILLUSION. I GOTTA CHANCE IT!

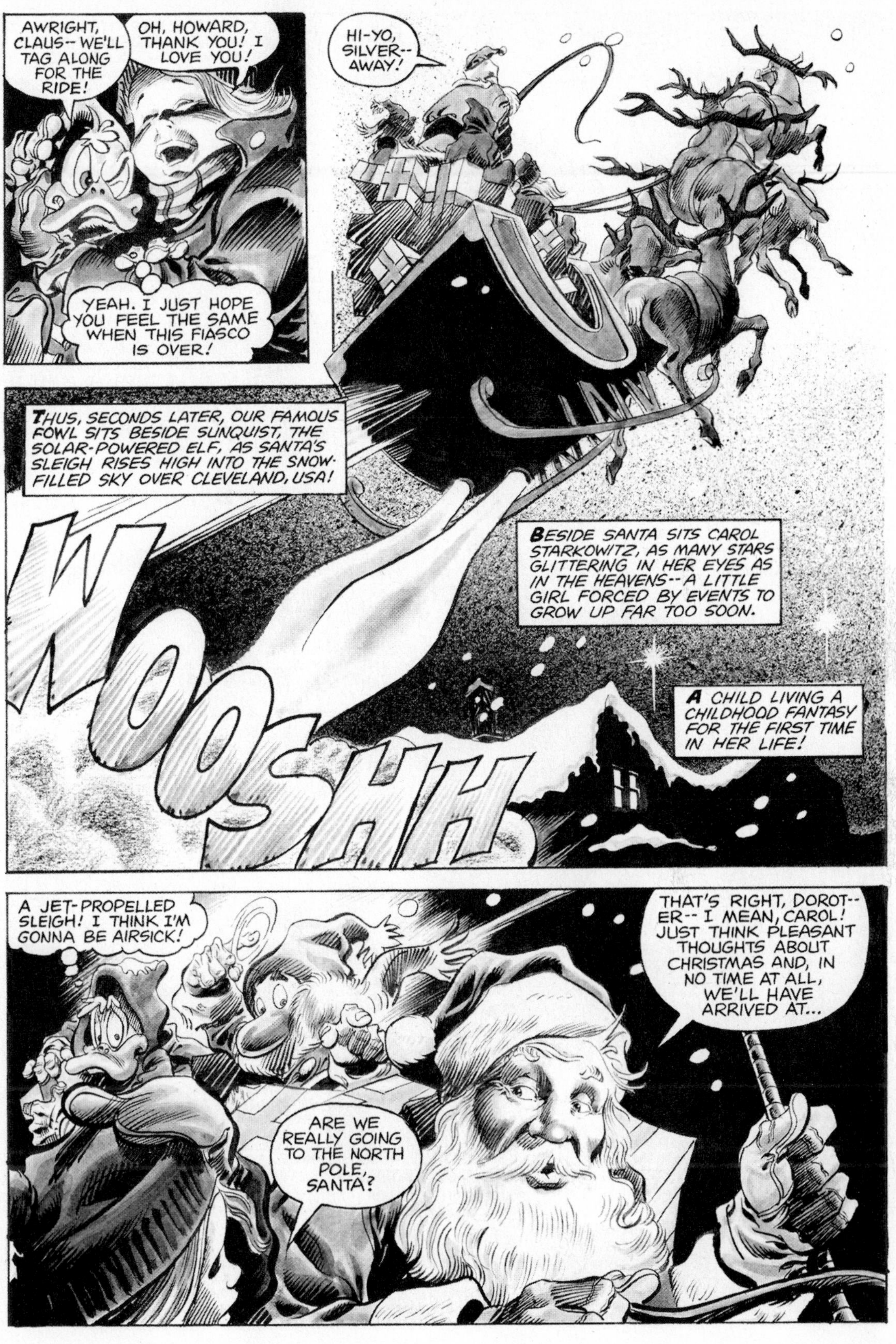
AWRIGHT, CLAUS-- WE'LL TAG ALONG FOR THE RIDE!
OH, HOWARD, THANK YOU! I LOVE YOU!
YEAH. I JUST HOPE YOU FEEL THE SAME WHEN THIS FIASCO IS OVER!
HI-YO, SILVER-- AWAY!
THUS, SECONDS LATER, OUR FAMOUS FOWL SITS BESIDE SUNQUIST, THE SOLAR-POWERED ELF, AS SANTA'S SLEIGH RISES HIGH INTO THE SNOW-FILLED SKY OVER CLEVELAND, USA!
WOOOSHH
BESIDE SANTA SITS CAROL STARKOWITZ, AS MANY STARS GLITTERING IN HER EYES AS IN THE HEAVENS-- A LITTLE GIRL FORCED BY EVENTS TO GROW UP FAR TOO SOON.
A CHILD LIVING A CHILDHOOD FANTASY FOR THE FIRST TIME IN HER LIFE!
A JET-PROPELLED SLEIGH! I THINK I'M GONNA BE AIRSICK!
THAT'S RIGHT, DOROTER-- ER-- I MEAN, CAROL! JUST THINK PLEASANT THOUGHTS ABOUT CHRISTMAS AND, IN NO TIME AT ALL, WE'LL HAVE ARRIVED AT...
ARE WE REALLY GOING TO THE NORTH POLE, SANTA?

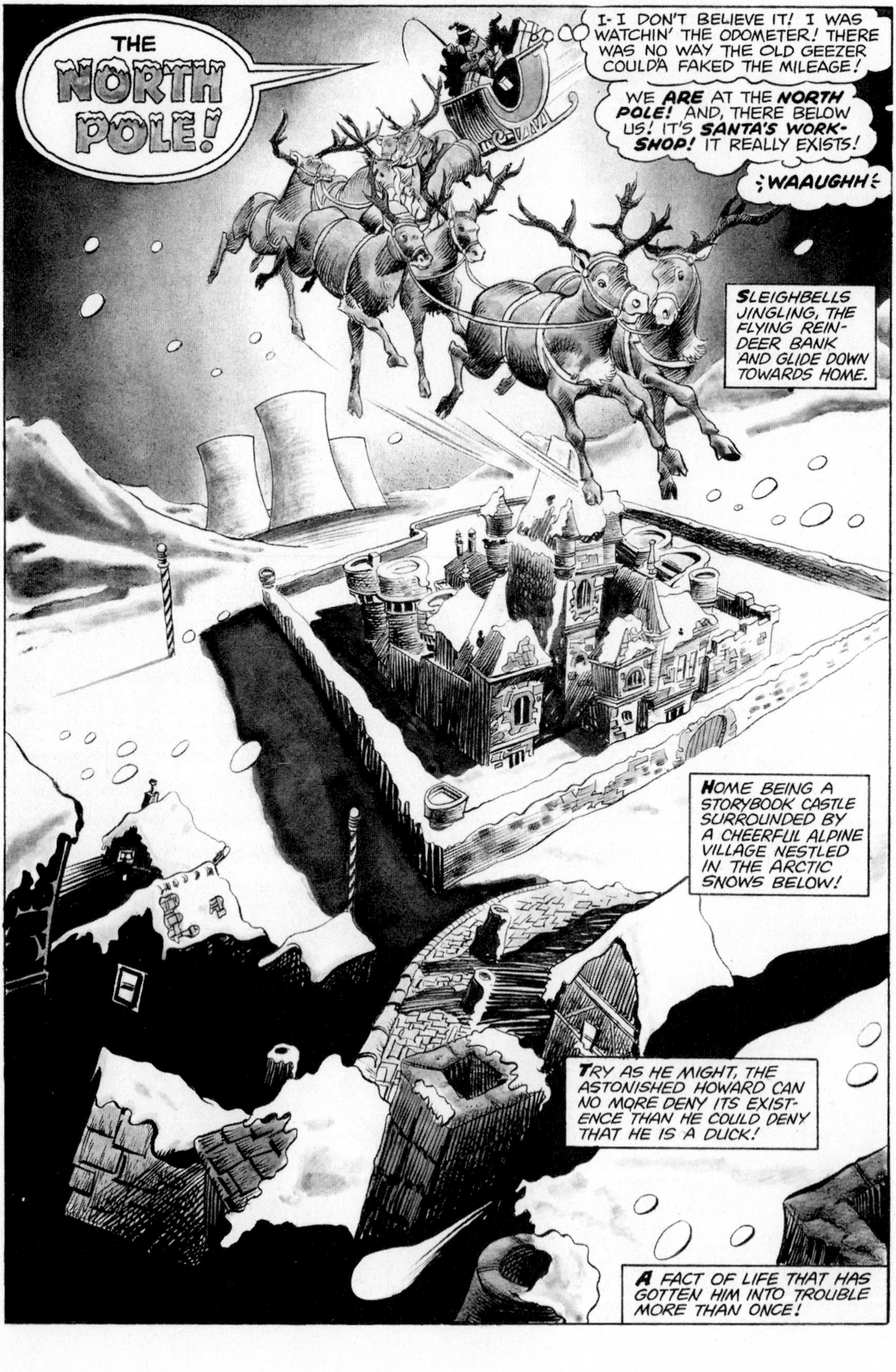
THE NORTH POLE!
I- I DON'T BELIEVE IT! I WAS WATCHIN' THE ODOMETER! THERE WAS NO WAY THE OLD GEEZER COULD'A FAKED THE MILEAGE!
WE ARE AT THE NORTH POLE! AND, THERE BELOW US! IT'S SANTA'S WORK-SHOP! IT REALLY EXISTS!
WAAUGHH
SLEIGHBELLS JINGLING, THE FLYING REIN-DEER BANK AND GLIDE DOWN TOWARDS HOME.
HOME BEING A STORYBOOK CASTLE SURROUNDED BY A CHEERFUL ALPINE VILLAGE NESTLED IN THE ARCTIC SNOWS BELOW!
TRY AS HE MIGHT, THE ASTONISHED HOWARD CAN NO MORE DENY ITS EXIST-ENCE THAN HE COULD DENY THAT HE IS A DUCK!
A FACT OF LIFE THAT HAS GOTTEN HIM INTO TROUBLE MORE THAN ONCE!

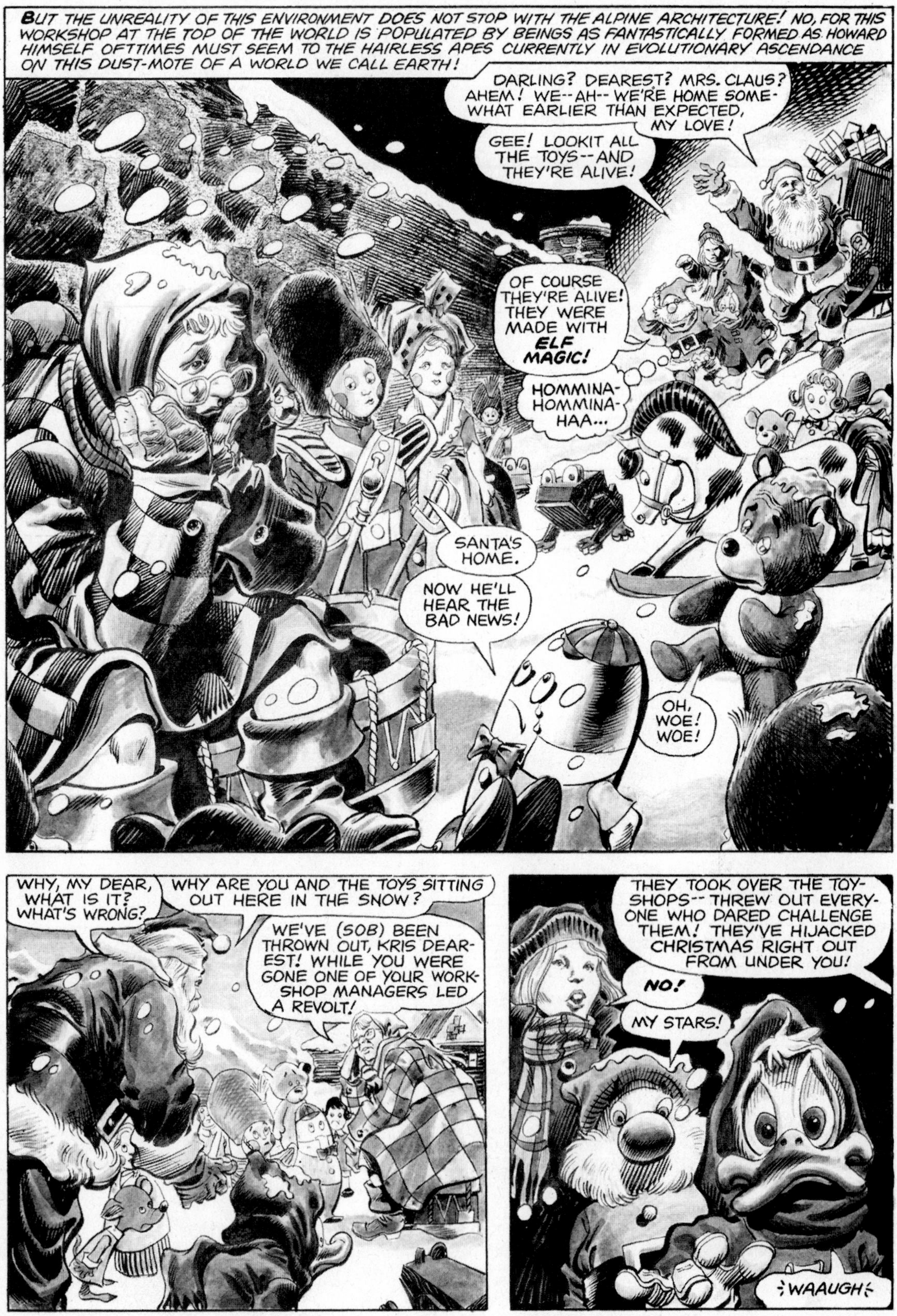

BUT THE UNREALITY OF THIS ENVIRONMENT DOES NOT STOP WITH THE ALPINE ARCHITECTURE! NO, FOR THIS WORKSHOP AT THE TOP OF THE WORLD IS POPULATED BY BEINGS AS FANTASTICALLY FORMED AS HOWARD HIMSELF OFTTIMES MUST SEEM TO THE HAIRLESS APES CURRENTLY IN EVOLUTIONARY ASCENDANCE ON THIS DUST-MOTE OF A WORLD WE CALL EARTH!
DARLING? DEAREST? MRS. CLAUS? AHEM! WE--AH--WE'RE HOME SOMEWHAT EARLIER THAN EXPECTED, MY LOVE!
GEE! LOOKIT ALL THE TOYS--AND THEY'RE ALIVE!
OF COURSE THEY'RE ALIVE! THEY WERE MADE WITH ELF MAGIC!
HOMMINA-HOMMINA-HAA...
SANTA'S HOME.
NOW HE'LL HEAR THE BAD NEWS!
OH, WOE! WOE!
WHY, MY DEAR, WHAT IS IT? WHAT'S WRONG?
WHY ARE YOU AND THE TOYS SITTING OUT HERE IN THE SNOW?
WE'VE (SOB) BEEN THROWN OUT, KRIS DEAREST! WHILE YOU WERE GONE ONE OF YOUR WORKSHOP MANAGERS LED A REVOLT!
THEY TOOK OVER THE TOYSHOPS--THREW OUT EVERYONE WHO DARED CHALLENGE THEM! THEY'VE HIJACKED CHRISTMAS RIGHT OUT FROM UNDER YOU!
NO!
MY STARS!
WAAUGH

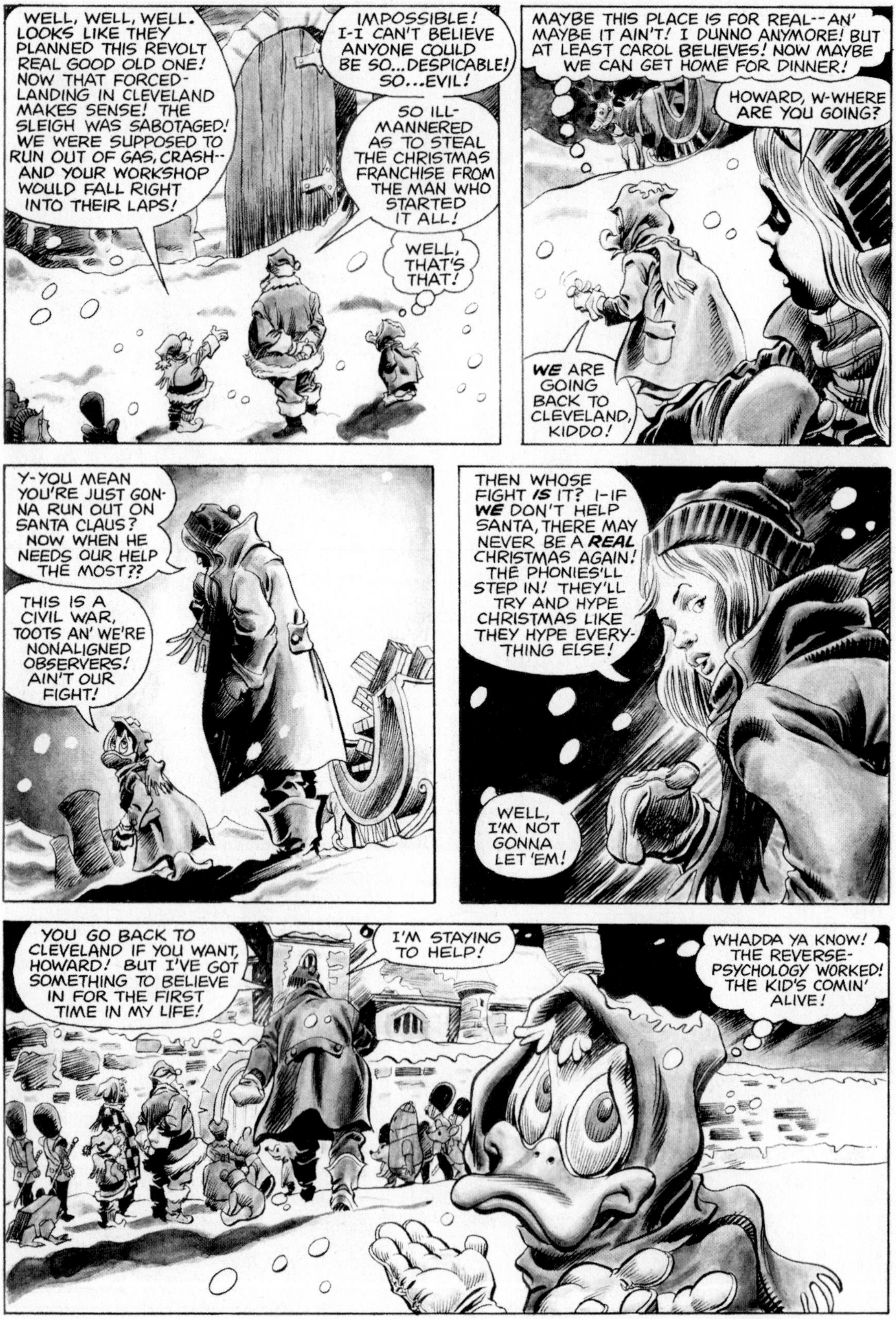
WELL, WELL, WELL. LOOKS LIKE THEY PLANNED THIS REVOLT REAL GOOD OLD ONE! NOW THAT FORCED-LANDING IN CLEVELAND MAKES SENSE! THE SLEIGH WAS SABOTAGED! WE WERE SUPPOSED TO RUN OUT OF GAS, CRASH-- AND YOUR WORKSHOP WOULD FALL RIGHT INTO THEIR LAPS!
IMPOSSIBLE! I-I CAN'T BELIEVE ANYONE COULD BE SO...DESPICABLE! SO...EVIL!
SO ILL-MANNERED AS TO STEAL THE CHRISTMAS FRANCHISE FROM THE MAN WHO STARTED IT ALL!
WELL, THAT'S THAT!
MAYBE THIS PLACE IS FOR REAL--AN' MAYBE IT AIN'T! I DUNNO ANYMORE! BUT AT LEAST CAROL BELIEVES! NOW MAYBE WE CAN GET HOME FOR DINNER!
HOWARD, W-WHERE ARE YOU GOING?
WE ARE GOING BACK TO CLEVELAND, KIDDO!
Y-YOU MEAN YOU'RE JUST GONNA RUN OUT ON SANTA CLAUS? NOW WHEN HE NEEDS OUR HELP THE MOST??
THIS IS A CIVIL WAR, TOOTS AN' WE'RE NONALIGNED OBSERVERS! AIN'T OUR FIGHT!
THEN WHOSE FIGHT IS IT? I-IF WE DON'T HELP SANTA, THERE MAY NEVER BE A REAL CHRISTMAS AGAIN! THE PHONIES'LL STEP IN! THEY'LL TRY AND HYPE CHRISTMAS LIKE THEY HYPE EVERYTHING ELSE!
WELL, I'M NOT GONNA LET 'EM!
YOU GO BACK TO CLEVELAND IF YOU WANT, HOWARD! BUT I'VE GOT SOMETHING TO BELIEVE IN FOR THE FIRST TIME IN MY LIFE!
I'M STAYING TO HELP!
WHADDA YA KNOW! THE REVERSE-PSYCHOLOGY WORKED! THE KID'S COMIN' ALIVE!

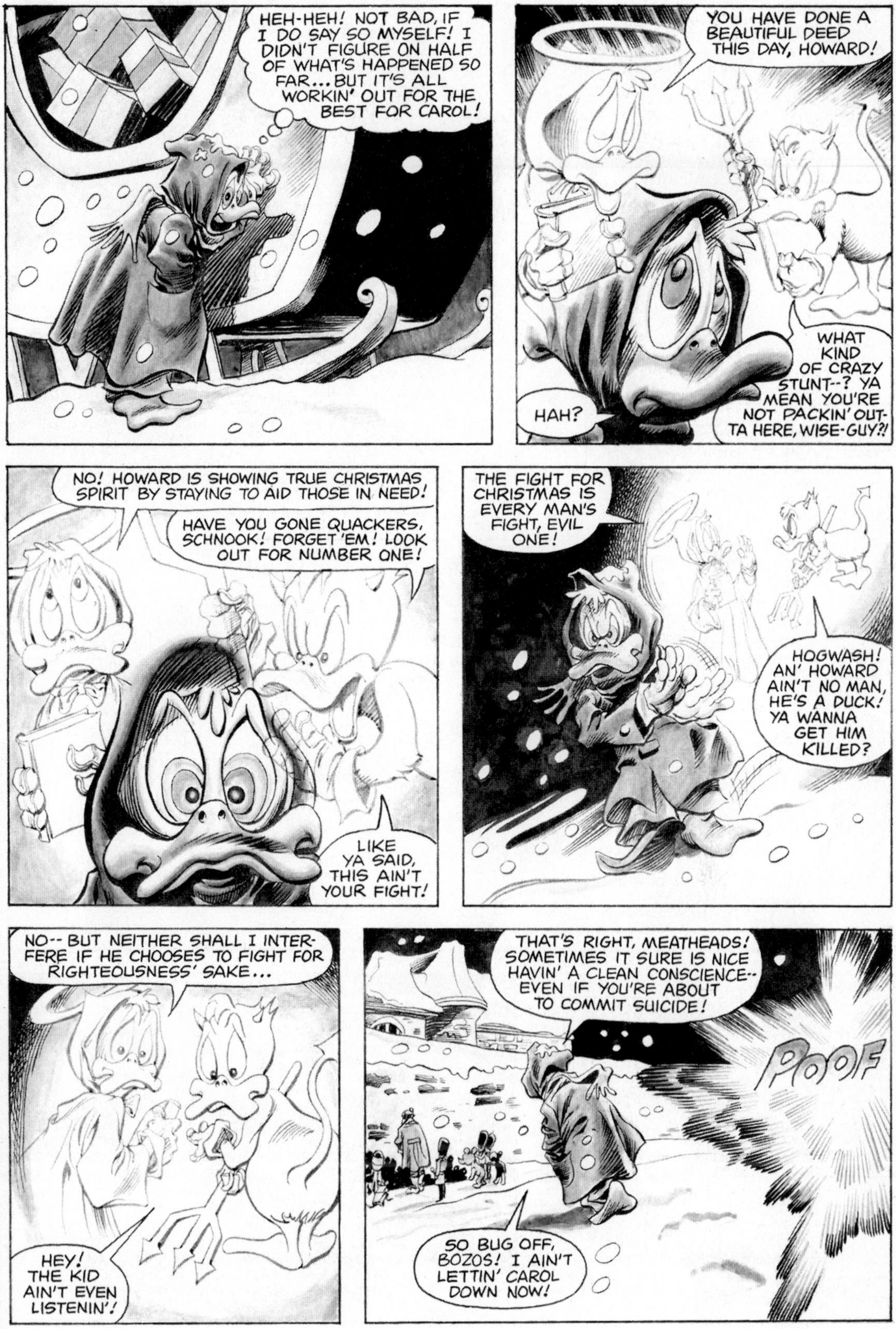
HEH-HEH! NOT BAD, IF I DO SAY SO MYSELF! I DIDN'T FIGURE ON HALF OF WHAT'S HAPPENED SO FAR... BUT IT'S ALL WORKIN' OUT FOR THE BEST FOR CAROL!
YOU HAVE DONE A BEAUTIFUL DEED THIS DAY, HOWARD!
HAH?
WHAT KIND OF CRAZY STUNT--? YA MEAN YOU'RE NOT PACKIN' OUTTA HERE, WISE-GUY?!
NO! HOWARD IS SHOWING TRUE CHRISTMAS SPIRIT BY STAYING TO AID THOSE IN NEED!
HAVE YOU GONE QUACKERS, SCHNOOK! FORGET 'EM! LOOK OUT FOR NUMBER ONE!
LIKE YA SAID, THIS AIN'T YOUR FIGHT!
THE FIGHT FOR CHRISTMAS IS EVERY MAN'S FIGHT, EVIL ONE!
HOGWASH! AN' HOWARD AIN'T NO MAN, HE'S A DUCK! YA WANNA GET HIM KILLED?
NO-- BUT NEITHER SHALL I INTERFERE IF HE CHOOSES TO FIGHT FOR RIGHTEOUSNESS' SAKE...
HEY! THE KID AIN'T EVEN LISTENIN'!
THAT'S RIGHT, MEATHEADS! SOMETIMES IT SURE IS NICE HAVIN' A CLEAN CONSCIENCE-- EVEN IF YOU'RE ABOUT TO COMMIT SUICIDE!
POOF
SO BUG OFF, BOZOS! I AIN'T LETTIN' CAROL DOWN NOW!

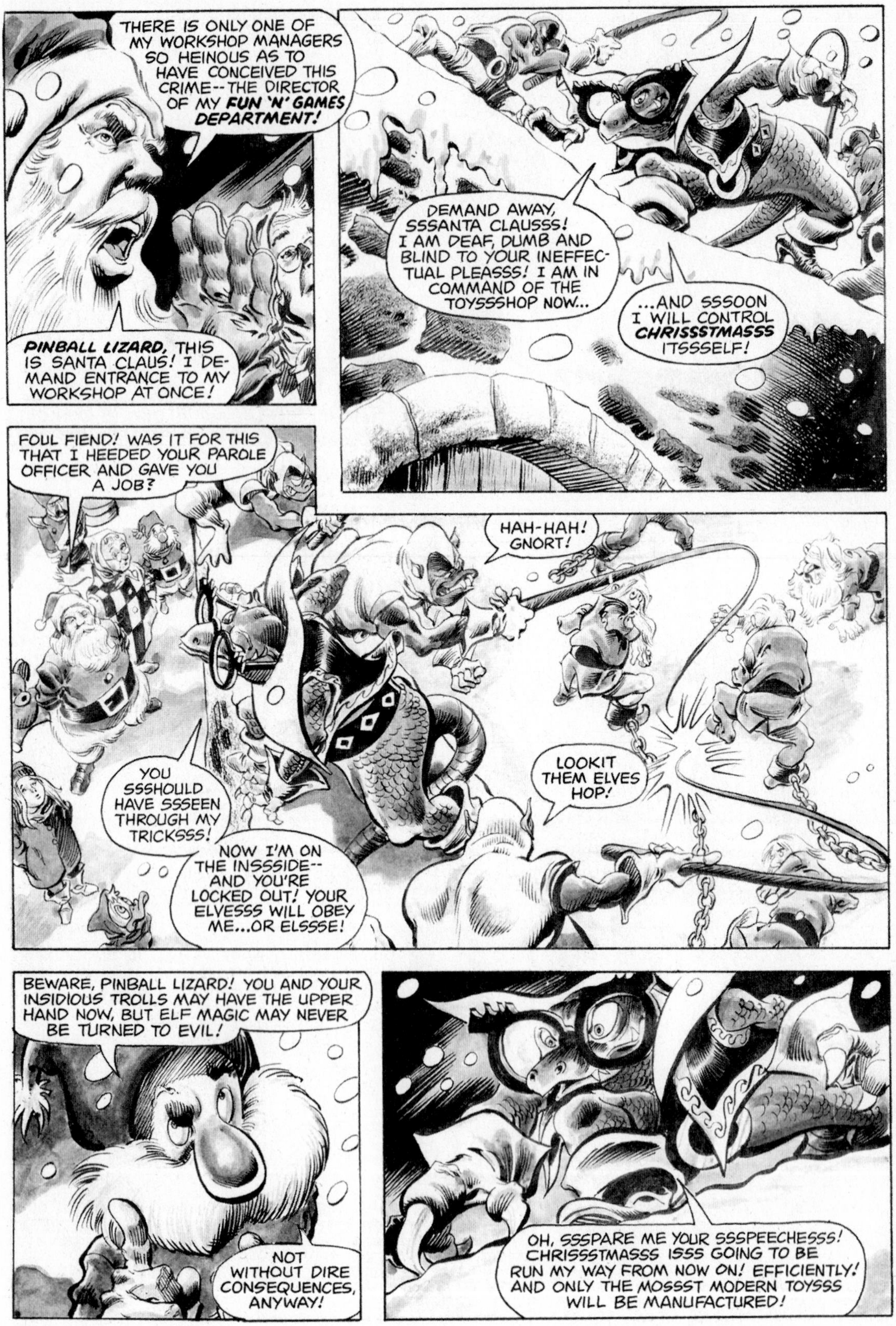
THERE IS ONLY ONE OF MY WORKSHOP MANAGERS SO HEINOUS AS TO HAVE CONCEIVED THIS CRIME--THE DIRECTOR OF MY FUN 'N' GAMES DEPARTMENT!
PINBALL LIZARD, THIS IS SANTA CLAUS! I DEMAND ENTRANCE TO MY WORKSHOP AT ONCE!
DEMAND AWAY, SSSANTA CLAUSSS! I AM DEAF, DUMB AND BLIND TO YOUR INEFFECTUAL PLEASSS! I AM IN COMMAND OF THE TOYSSSHOP NOW...
...AND SSSOON I WILL CONTROL CHRISSSTMASSS ITSSSELF!
FOUL FIEND! WAS IT FOR THIS THAT I HEEDED YOUR PAROLE OFFICER AND GAVE YOU A JOB?
HAH-HAH! GNORT!
YOU SSSHOULD HAVE SSSEEN THROUGH MY TRICKSSS!
NOW I'M ON THE INSSSIDE--AND YOU'RE LOCKED OUT! YOUR ELVESSS WILL OBEY ME...OR ELSSSE!
LOOKIT THEM ELVES HOP!
BEWARE, PINBALL LIZARD! YOU AND YOUR INSIDIOUS TROLLS MAY HAVE THE UPPER HAND NOW, BUT ELF MAGIC MAY NEVER BE TURNED TO EVIL!
NOT WITHOUT DIRE CONSEQUENCES, ANYWAY!
OH, SSSPARE ME YOUR SSSPEECHESSS! CHRISSSTMASSS ISSS GOING TO BE RUN MY WAY FROM NOW ON! EFFICIENTLY! AND ONLY THE MOSSST MODERN TOYSSS WILL BE MANUFACTURED!

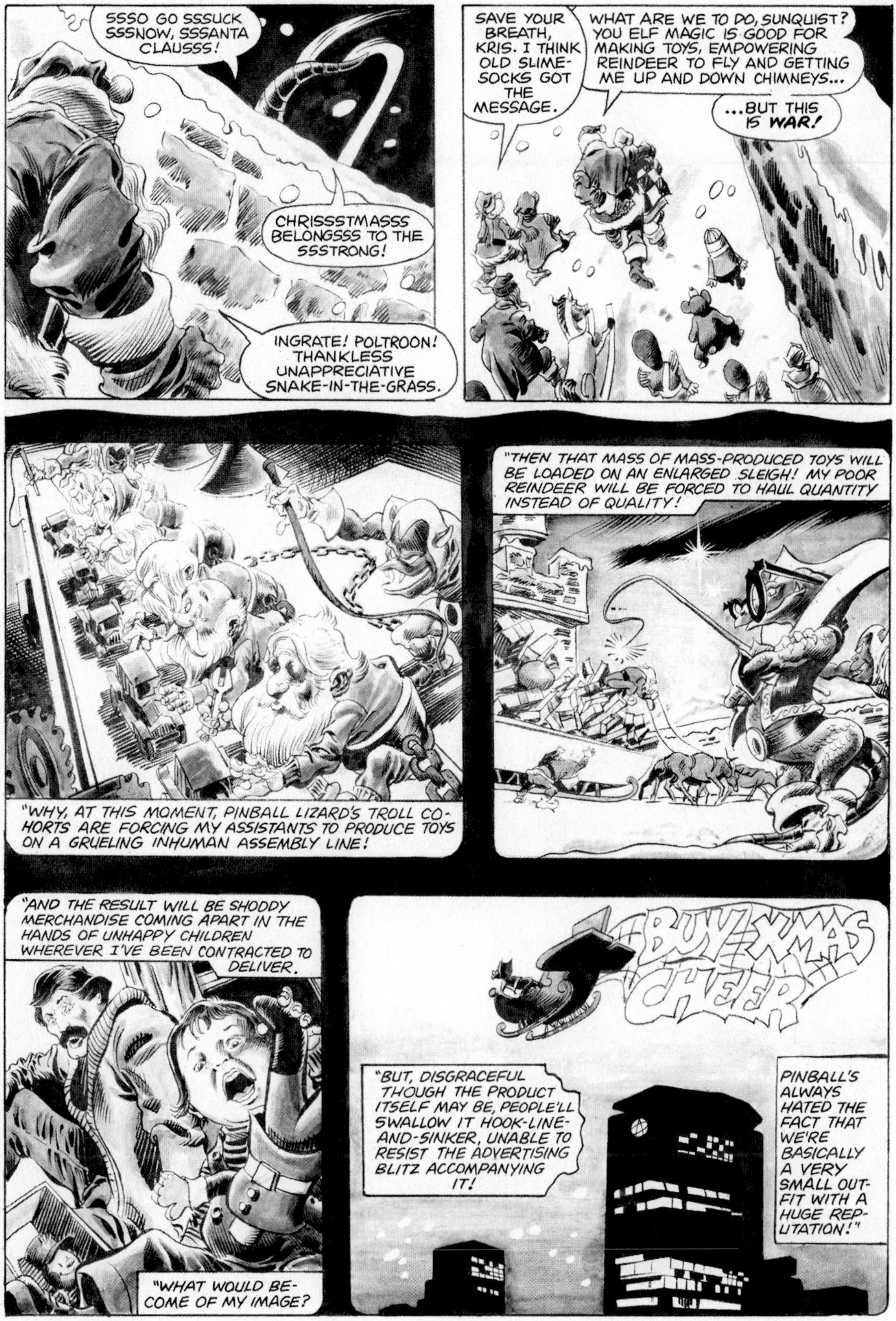
SSSO GO SSSUCK SSSNOW, SSSANTA CLAUSSS!
CHRISSSTMASSS BELONGSSS TO THE SSSTRONG!
INGRATE! POLTROON! THANKLESS UNAPPRECIATIVE SNAKE-IN-THE-GRASS.
SAVE YOUR BREATH, KRIS. I THINK OLD SLIME-SOCKS GOT THE MESSAGE.
WHAT ARE WE TO DO, SUNQUIST? YOU ELF MAGIC IS GOOD FOR MAKING TOYS, EMPOWERING REINDEER TO FLY AND GETTING ME UP AND DOWN CHIMNEYS...
...BUT THIS IS WAR!
"WHY, AT THIS MOMENT, PINBALL LIZARD'S TROLL CO-HORTS ARE FORCING MY ASSISTANTS TO PRODUCE TOYS ON A GRUELING INHUMAN ASSEMBLY LINE!
"THEN THAT MASS OF MASS-PRODUCED TOYS WILL BE LOADED ON AN ENLARGED SLEIGH! MY POOR REINDEER WILL BE FORCED TO HAUL QUANTITY INSTEAD OF QUALITY!
"AND THE RESULT WILL BE SHODDY MERCHANDISE COMING APART IN THE HANDS OF UNHAPPY CHILDREN WHEREVER I'VE BEEN CONTRACTED TO DELIVER.
"WHAT WOULD BE-COME OF MY IMAGE?
BUY XMAS CHEER
"BUT, DISGRACEFUL THOUGH THE PRODUCT ITSELF MAY BE, PEOPLE'LL SWALLOW IT HOOK-LINE-AND-SINKER, UNABLE TO RESIST THE ADVERTISING BLITZ ACCOMPANYING IT!
PINBALL'S ALWAYS HATED THE FACT THAT WE'RE BASICALLY A VERY SMALL OUT-FIT WITH A HUGE REP-UTATION!"

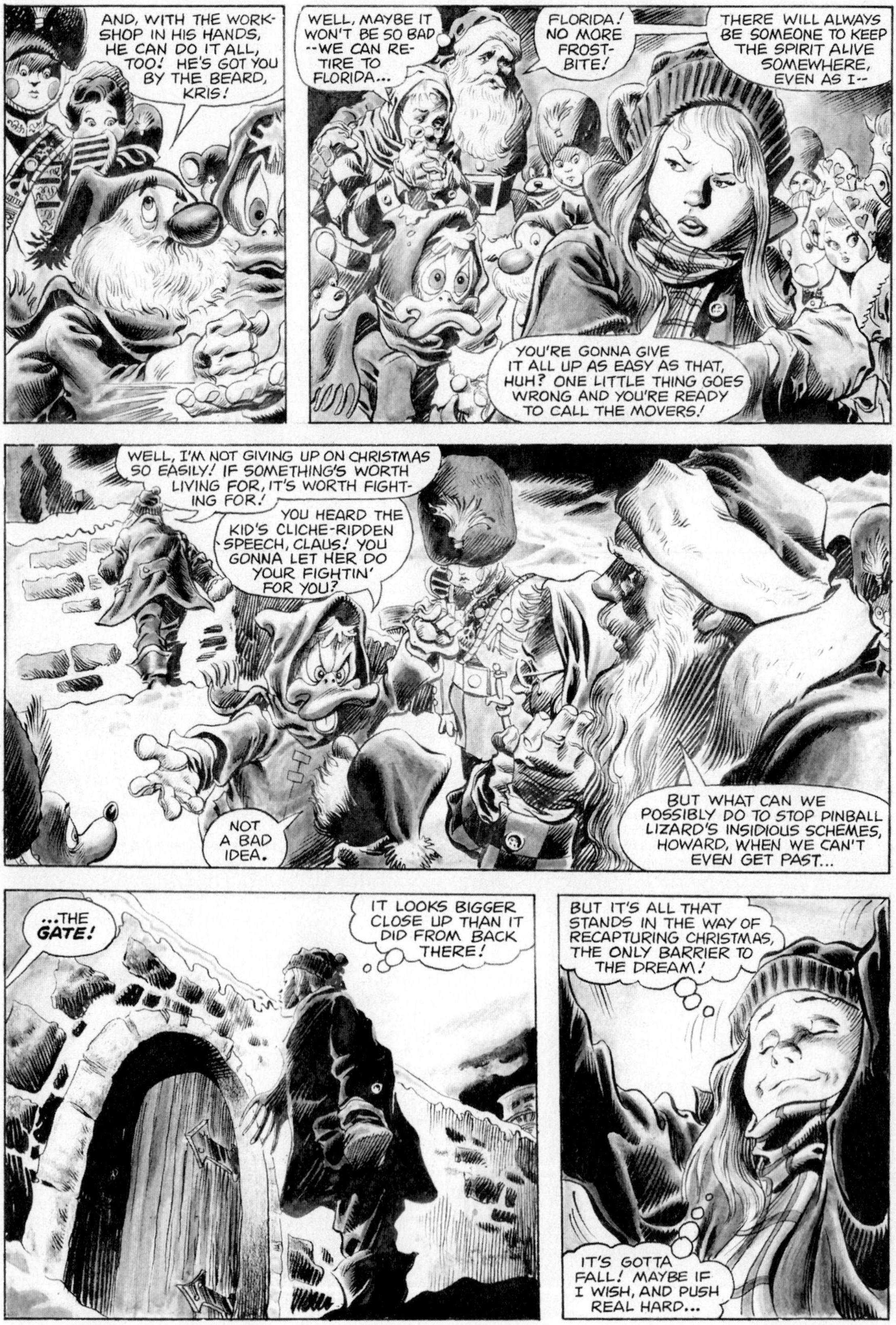
AND, WITH THE WORK-SHOP IN HIS HANDS, HE CAN DO IT ALL, TOO! HE'S GOT YOU BY THE BEARD, KRIS!
WELL, MAYBE IT WON'T BE SO BAD --WE CAN RE-TIRE TO FLORIDA...
FLORIDA! NO MORE FROST-BITE!
THERE WILL ALWAYS BE SOMEONE TO KEEP THE SPIRIT ALIVE SOMEWHERE, EVEN AS I--
YOU'RE GONNA GIVE IT ALL UP AS EASY AS THAT, HUH? ONE LITTLE THING GOES WRONG AND YOU'RE READY TO CALL THE MOVERS!
WELL, I'M NOT GIVING UP ON CHRISTMAS SO EASILY! IF SOMETHING'S WORTH LIVING FOR, IT'S WORTH FIGHT-ING FOR!
YOU HEARD THE KID'S CLICHE-RIDDEN SPEECH, CLAUS! YOU GONNA LET HER DO YOUR FIGHTIN' FOR YOU?
NOT A BAD IDEA.
BUT WHAT CAN WE POSSIBLY DO TO STOP PINBALL LIZARD'S INSIDIOUS SCHEMES, HOWARD, WHEN WE CAN'T EVEN GET PAST...
...THE GATE!
IT LOOKS BIGGER CLOSE UP THAN IT DID FROM BACK THERE!
BUT IT'S ALL THAT STANDS IN THE WAY OF RECAPTURING CHRISTMAS, THE ONLY BARRIER TO THE DREAM!
IT'S GOTTA FALL! MAYBE IF I WISH, AND PUSH REAL HARD...

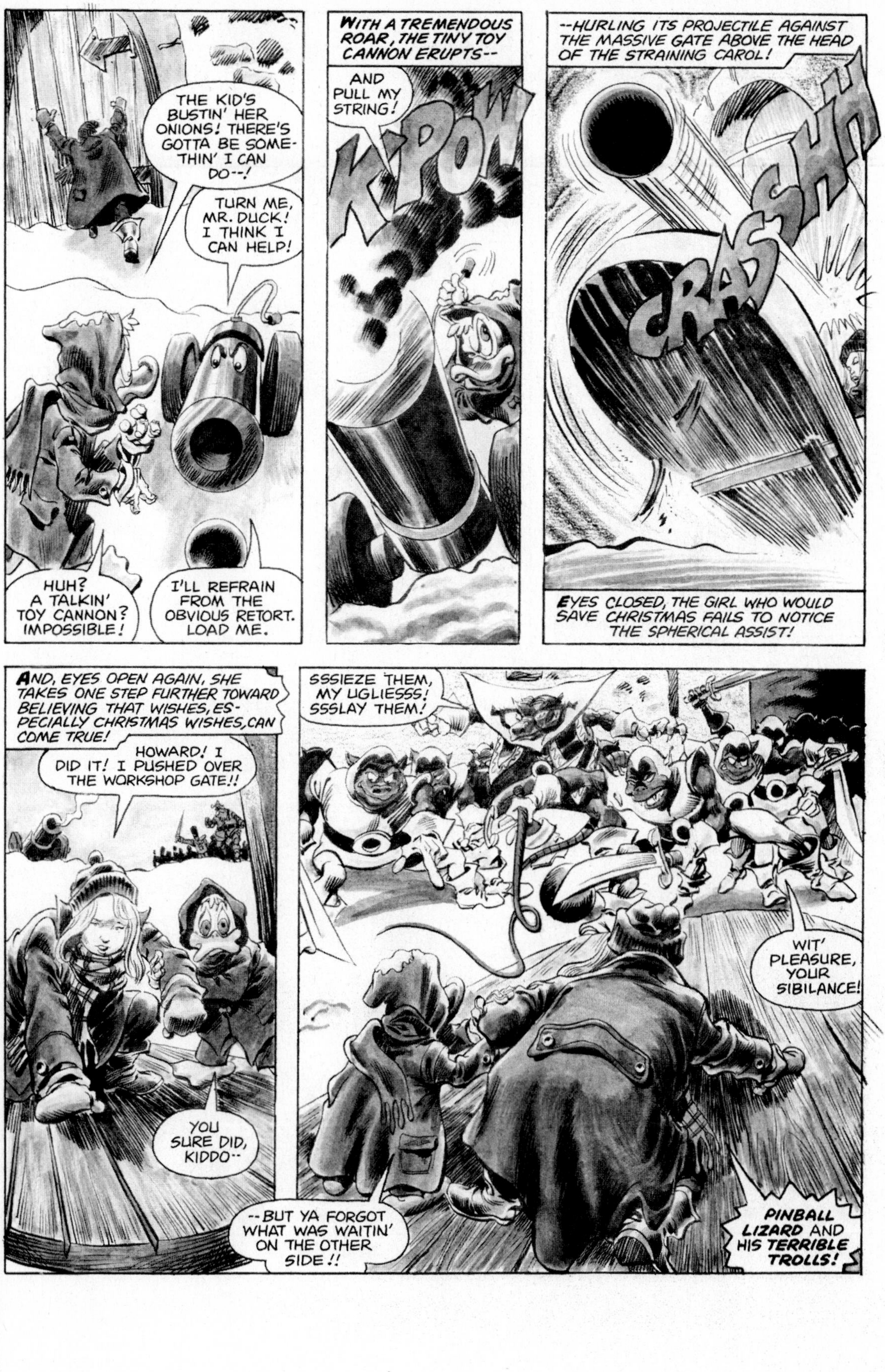
THE KID'S BUSTIN' HER ONIONS! THERE'S GOTTA BE SOMETHIN' I CAN DO--!
TURN ME, MR. DUCK! I THINK I CAN HELP!
HUH? A TALKIN' TOY CANNON? IMPOSSIBLE!
I'LL REFRAIN FROM THE OBVIOUS RETORT. LOAD ME.
WITH A TREMENDOUS ROAR, THE TINY TOY CANNON ERUPTS--
AND PULL MY STRING!
K-POW
--HURLING ITS PROJECTILE AGAINST THE MASSIVE GATE ABOVE THE HEAD OF THE STRAINING CAROL!
CRASSHH
EYES CLOSED, THE GIRL WHO WOULD SAVE CHRISTMAS FAILS TO NOTICE THE SPHERICAL ASSIST!
AND, EYES OPEN AGAIN, SHE TAKES ONE STEP FURTHER TOWARD BELIEVING THAT WISHES, ESPECIALLY CHRISTMAS WISHES, CAN COME TRUE!
HOWARD! I DID IT! I PUSHED OVER THE WORKSHOP GATE!!
YOU SURE DID, KIDDO--
SSSIEZE THEM, MY UGLIESSS! SSSLAY THEM!
WIT' PLEASURE, YOUR SIBILANCE!
--BUT YA FORGOT WHAT WAS WAITIN' ON THE OTHER SIDE!!
PINBALL LIZARD AND HIS TERRIBLE TROLLS!

BUT, EVEN AS THE ENEMY ADVANCES...
EH? SLINGS AN' ARROWS? WHAT OUTRAGEOUS FORTUNE!
SANTA'S COMIN' TO SAVE US, CAROL!
"THE TOYS ARE ATTACKING!"
Louisville Slugger
WOODEN SOLDIERS-- MARCH!

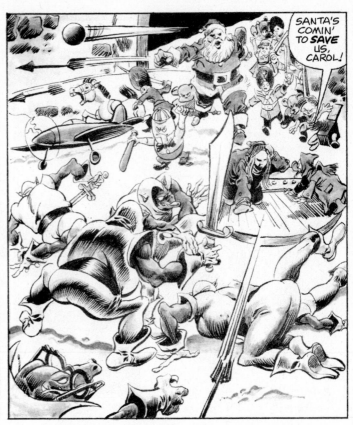

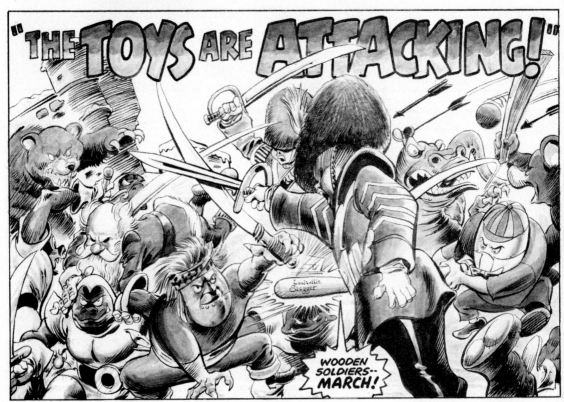

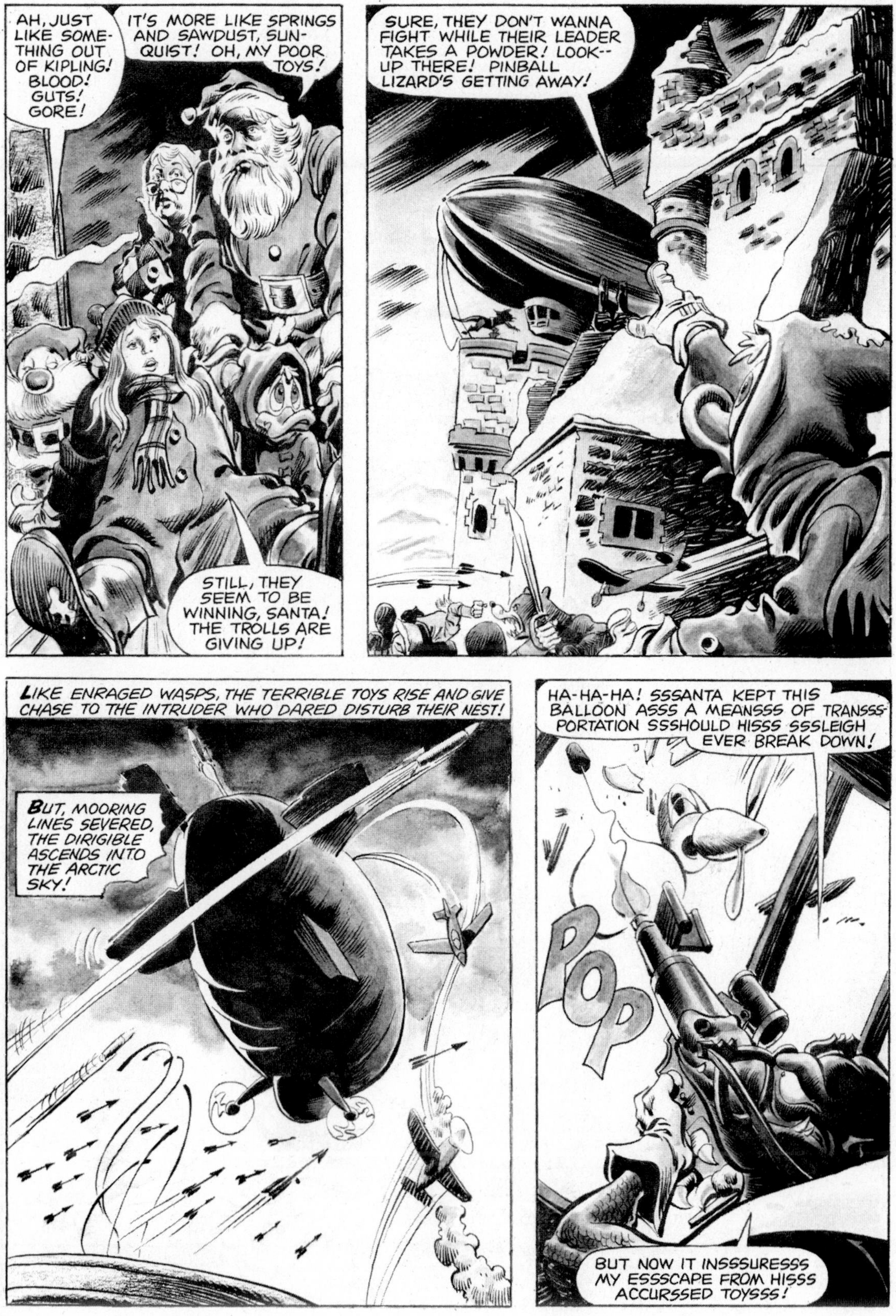
AH, JUST LIKE SOME-THING OUT OF KIPLING! BLOOD! GUTS! GORE!
IT'S MORE LIKE SPRINGS AND SAWDUST, SUN-QUIST! OH, MY POOR TOYS!
STILL, THEY SEEM TO BE WINNING, SANTA! THE TROLLS ARE GIVING UP!
SURE, THEY DON'T WANNA FIGHT WHILE THEIR LEADER TAKES A POWDER! LOOK-- UP THERE! PINBALL LIZARD'S GETTING AWAY!
LIKE ENRAGED WASPS, THE TERRIBLE TOYS RISE AND GIVE CHASE TO THE INTRUDER WHO DARED DISTURB THEIR NEST!
BUT, MOORING LINES SEVERED, THE DIRIGIBLE ASCENDS INTO THE ARCTIC SKY!
HA-HA-HA! SSSANTA KEPT THIS BALLOON ASSS A MEANSSS OF TRANSSS-PORTATION SSSHOULD HISSS SSSLEIGH EVER BREAK DOWN!
POP
BUT NOW IT INSSSURESSS MY ESSSCAPE FROM HISSS ACCURSSED TOYSSS!

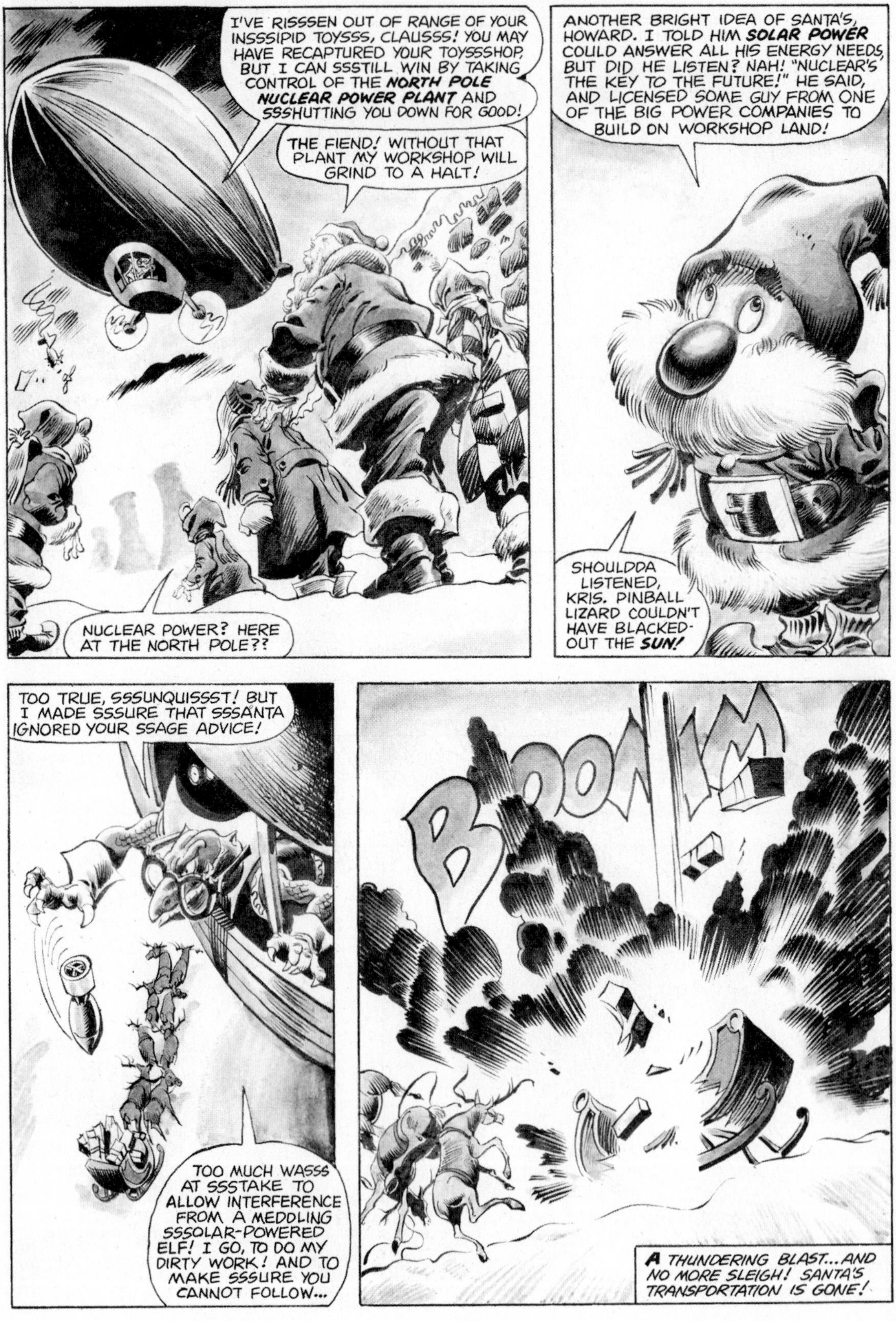
I'VE RISSSEN OUT OF RANGE OF YOUR INSSSIPID TOYSSS, CLAUSSS! YOU MAY HAVE RECAPTURED YOUR TOYSSSHOP, BUT I CAN SSSTILL WIN BY TAKING CONTROL OF THE NORTH POLE NUCLEAR POWER PLANT AND SSSHUTTING YOU DOWN FOR GOOD!
THE FIEND! WITHOUT THAT PLANT MY WORKSHOP WILL GRIND TO A HALT!
NUCLEAR POWER? HERE AT THE NORTH POLE??
ANOTHER BRIGHT IDEA OF SANTA'S, HOWARD. I TOLD HIM SOLAR POWER COULD ANSWER ALL HIS ENERGY NEEDS, BUT DID HE LISTEN? NAH! "NUCLEAR'S THE KEY TO THE FUTURE!" HE SAID, AND LICENSED SOME GUY FROM ONE OF THE BIG POWER COMPANIES TO BUILD ON WORKSHOP LAND!
SHOULDDA LISTENED, KRIS. PINBALL LIZARD COULDN'T HAVE BLACKED-OUT THE SUN!
TOO TRUE, SSSUNQUISSST! BUT I MADE SSSURE THAT SSSANTA IGNORED YOUR SSAGE ADVICE!
TOO MUCH WASSS AT SSSTAKE TO ALLOW INTERFERENCE FROM A MEDDLING SSSOLAR-POWERED ELF! I GO, TO DO MY DIRTY WORK! AND TO MAKE SSSURE YOU CANNOT FOLLOW...
BOOM
A THUNDERING BLAST...AND NO MORE SLEIGH! SANTA'S TRANSPORTATION IS GONE!

PINBALL LIZARD'S LEAVING...
OH, HOWARD, DO SOMETHING!
...TO PULL THE PLUG ON THE NORTH POLE!
WHO ME? I'M JUST VISITIN'!
TALK TO YOUR HOST-- IT'S HIS FAULT ALL THIS HAPPENED TO BEGIN WITH!
DON'T BLAME SANTA, HOWARD! HE PROBABLY DIDN'T KNOW NUCLEAR ENERGY WAS BAD!
NO, I KNEW IT MIGHT BE DANGEROUS, CAROL!
I-I GUESS I JUST THOUGHT THEY'D FIND SOME WAY TO MAKE IT SAFE, GIVEN TIME! AND THEN, I OWNED ALL THIS LAND UP HERE! EVEN IF SOMETHING WENT WRONG, I DIDN'T THINK ANYONE WOULD BE HURT!
BUT THEN I FOUND OUT ABOUT...THE ANTARCTICA SYNDROME!
THE (GASP!) ANTARCTICA SYNDROME!
GEE, WHAT'S THAT??
SOMETHING TERRIBLE, I'M AFRAID. LISTEN, AND I'LL EXPLAIN...

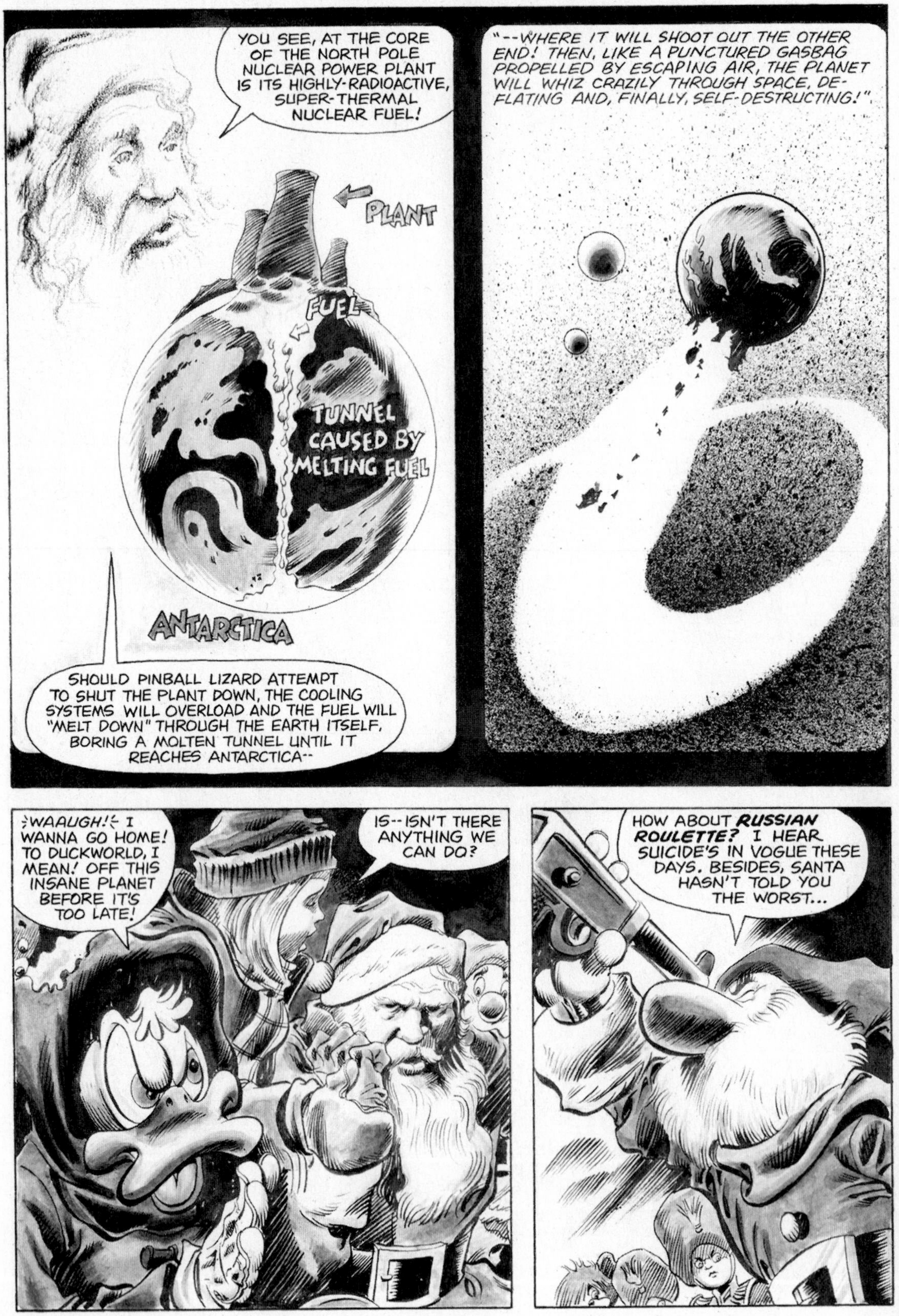
YOU SEE, AT THE CORE OF THE NORTH POLE NUCLEAR POWER PLANT IS ITS HIGHLY-RADIOACTIVE, SUPER-THERMAL NUCLEAR FUEL!
PLANT
FUEL
TUNNEL CAUSED BY MELTING FUEL
ANTARCTICA
SHOULD PINBALL LIZARD ATTEMPT TO SHUT THE PLANT DOWN, THE COOLING SYSTEMS WILL OVERLOAD AND THE FUEL WILL "MELT DOWN" THROUGH THE EARTH ITSELF, BORING A MOLTEN TUNNEL UNTIL IT REACHES ANTARCTICA--
"--WHERE IT WILL SHOOT OUT THE OTHER END! THEN, LIKE A PUNCTURED GASBAG PROPELLED BY ESCAPING AIR, THE PLANET WILL WHIZ CRAZILY THROUGH SPACE, DEFLATING AND, FINALLY, SELF-DESTRUCTING!"
WAAUGH! I WANNA GO HOME! TO DUCKWORLD, I MEAN! OFF THIS INSANE PLANET BEFORE IT'S TOO LATE!
IS--ISN'T THERE ANYTHING WE CAN DO?
HOW ABOUT RUSSIAN ROULETTE? I HEAR SUICIDE'S IN VOGUE THESE DAYS. BESIDES, SANTA HASN'T TOLD YOU THE WORST...

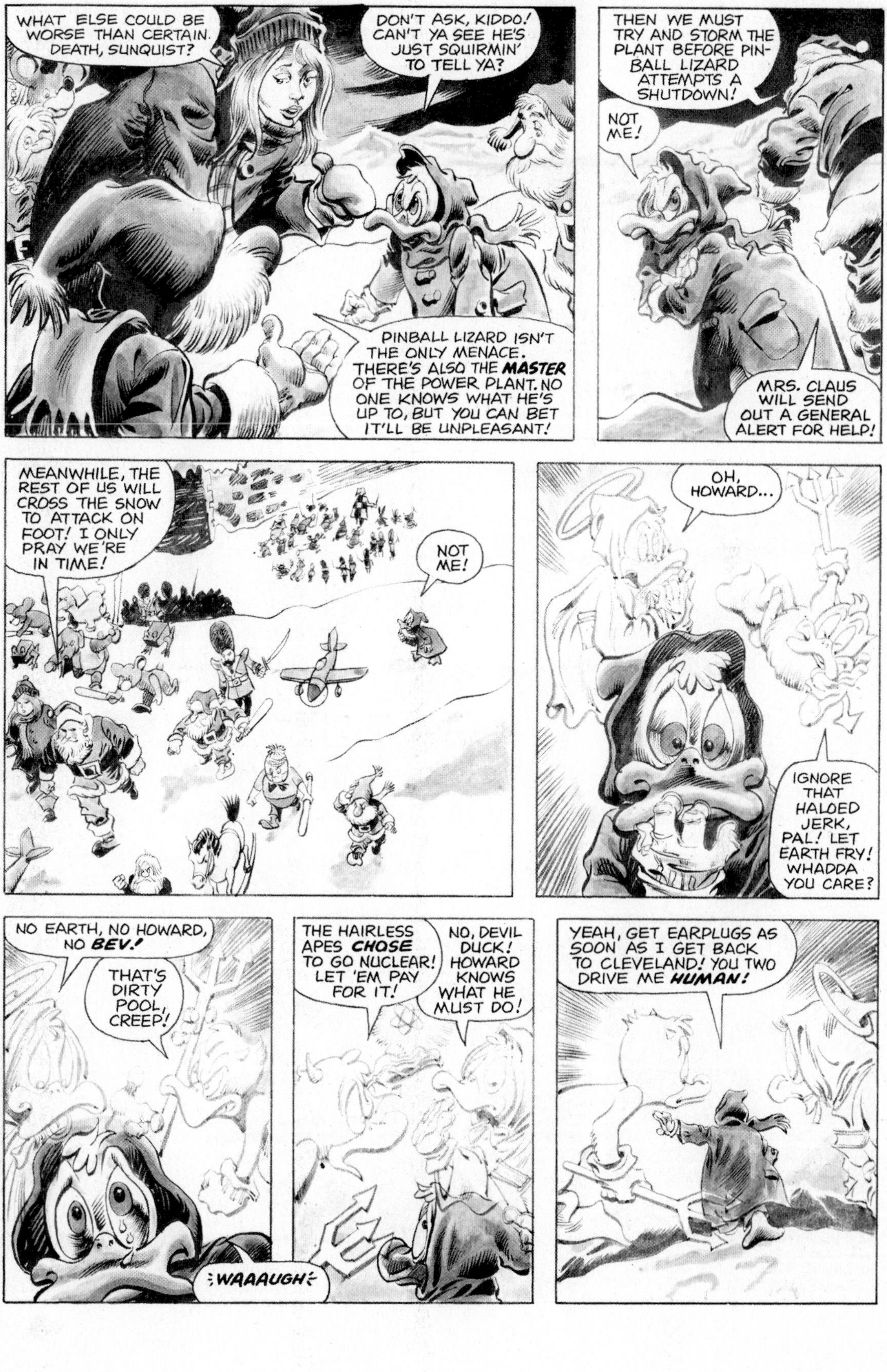
WHAT ELSE COULD BE WORSE THAN CERTAIN. DEATH, SUNQUIST?
DON'T ASK, KIDDO! CAN'T YA SEE HE'S JUST SQUIRMIN' TO TELL YA?
PINBALL LIZARD ISN'T THE ONLY MENACE. THERE'S ALSO THE **MASTER** OF THE POWER PLANT. NO ONE KNOWS WHAT HE'S UP TO, BUT YOU CAN BET IT'LL BE UNPLEASANT!
THEN WE MUST TRY AND STORM THE PLANT BEFORE PINBALL LIZARD ATTEMPTS A SHUTDOWN!
NOT ME!
MRS. CLAUS WILL SEND OUT A GENERAL ALERT FOR HELP!
MEANWHILE, THE REST OF US WILL CROSS THE SNOW TO ATTACK ON FOOT! I ONLY PRAY WE'RE IN TIME!
NOT ME!
OH, HOWARD...
IGNORE THAT HALOED JERK, PAL! LET EARTH FRY! WHADDA YOU CARE?
NO EARTH, NO HOWARD, NO **BEV!**
THAT'S DIRTY POOL, CREEP!
WAAAUGH
THE HAIRLESS APES **CHOSE** TO GO NUCLEAR! LET 'EM PAY FOR IT!
NO, DEVIL DUCK! HOWARD KNOWS WHAT HE MUST DO!
YEAH, GET EARPLUGS AS SOON AS I GET BACK TO CLEVELAND! YOU TWO DRIVE ME **HUMAN!**

THUS, JOINING IN THE RAG TAG ARMY TRUDGING ACROSS THE FROZEN WASTES TOWARD THE OMINOUSLY LOOMING TOWERS OF THE NORTH POLE NUCLEAR FACILITY, IS ONE HARRIED BUT HEADSTRONG **HOWARD THE DUCK!**

:WAAAUGH: WE'LL **NEVER** GET THERE AT THIS RATE!

FEAR NOT, HOWARD! THIS EXPERIENCE HAS TAUGHT ME TO RELY ON NATURAL MODES OF TRANSPORTATION...AND EVEN NOW MRS. CLAUS'S RADIO-ALERT IS HAVING THE DESIRED RESULTS! LOOK!

"HELP IS ON THE WAY!"

ARF! ARF!

WOOF! WOOF!

MUSH, YOU HUSKIES!

GREETINGS, OLD FRIEND. WE ARE GLAD YOU HAVE REGAINED YOUR SENSES!

YES, CHIEF OLLAKOOK! I SEE NOW THAT I WAS TOO **HASTY!**

INDEED! IT HAS LONG BEEN ESTABLISHED FACT THAT ESKIMOS RECEIVE MORE RADIATION FROM NUCLEAR FALLOUT THAN THOSE IN THE TEMPERATE ZONES WHO TRIGGER THE BOMBS AND BUILD THE PLANTS!

WE WILL HELP YOU DESTROY THIS DEVIL-PLANT, OLD ONE, BEFORE IT DESTROYS US ALL!

KIDDO, **LIE** TO ME! TELL ME THIS IS ALL A DREAM AN' I'LL WAKE UP BACK IN CLEVELAND!

ON SECOND THOUGHT, SKIP THE PART ABOUT CLEVELAND!

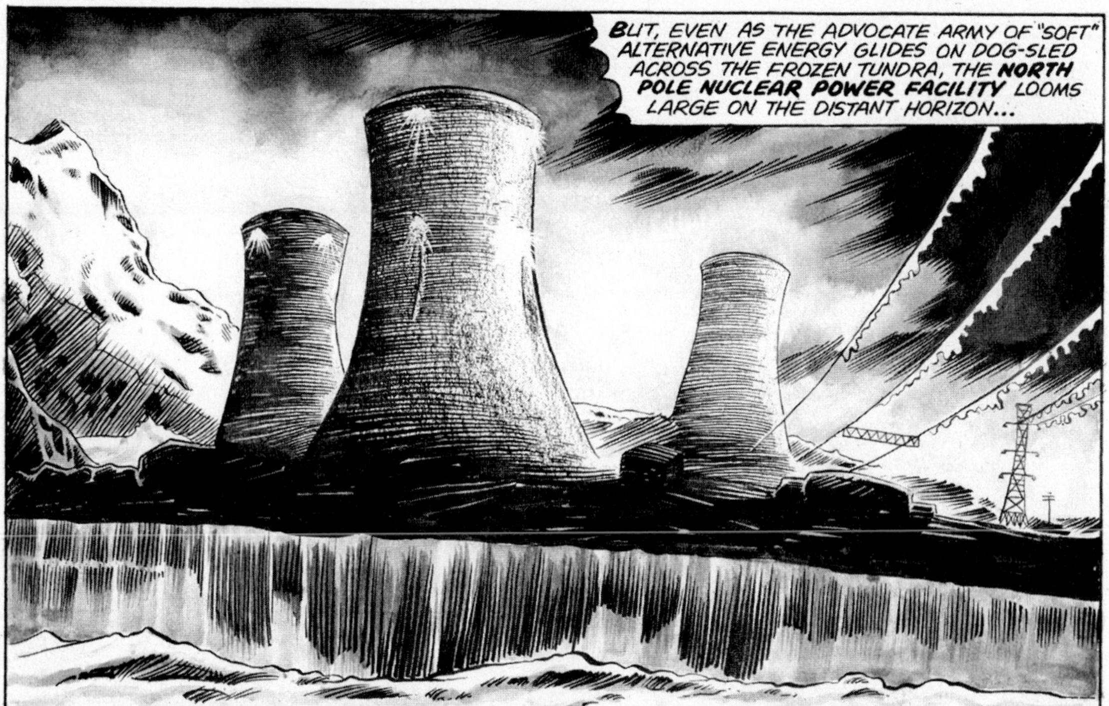
BUT, EVEN AS THE ADVOCATE ARMY OF "SOFT" ALTERNATIVE ENERGY GLIDES ON DOG-SLED ACROSS THE FROZEN TUNDRA, THE NORTH POLE NUCLEAR POWER FACILITY LOOMS LARGE ON THE DISTANT HORIZON...

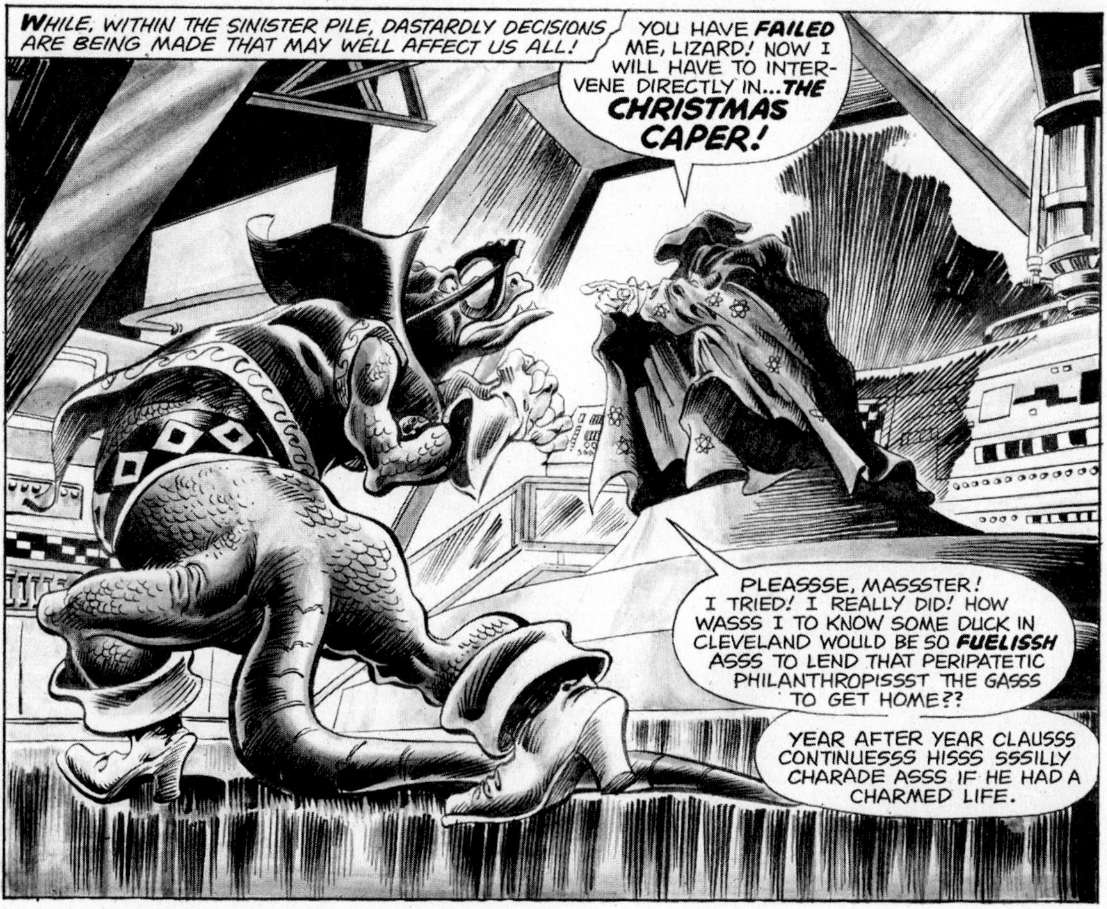
WHILE, WITHIN THE SINISTER PILE, DASTARDLY DECISIONS ARE BEING MADE THAT MAY WELL AFFECT US ALL!
YOU HAVE FAILED ME, LIZARD! NOW I WILL HAVE TO INTERVENE DIRECTLY IN...THE CHRISTMAS CAPER!
PLEASSSE, MASSSTER! I TRIED! I REALLY DID! HOW WASSS I TO KNOW SOME DUCK IN CLEVELAND WOULD BE SO FUELISSH ASSS TO LEND THAT PERIPATETIC PHILANTHROPISSST THE GASSS TO GET HOME??
YEAR AFTER YEAR CLAUSSS CONTINUESSS HISSS SSSILLY CHARADE ASSS IF HE HAD A CHARMED LIFE.

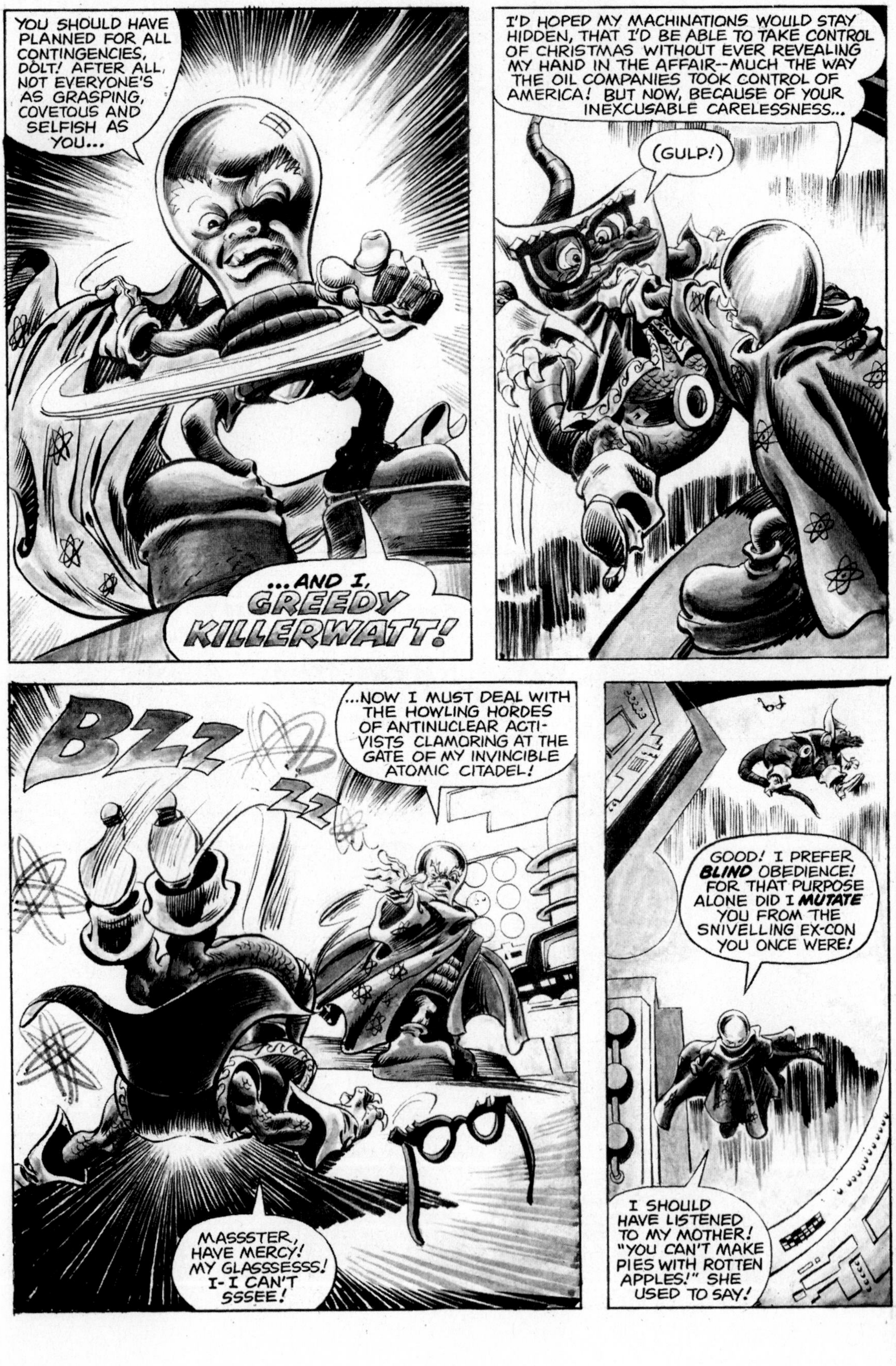
YOU SHOULD HAVE PLANNED FOR ALL CONTINGENCIES, DOLT! AFTER ALL, NOT EVERYONE'S AS GRASPING, COVETOUS AND SELFISH AS YOU...
...AND I, GREEDY KILLERWATT!
I'D HOPED MY MACHINATIONS WOULD STAY HIDDEN, THAT I'D BE ABLE TO TAKE CONTROL OF CHRISTMAS WITHOUT EVER REVEALING MY HAND IN THE AFFAIR--MUCH THE WAY THE OIL COMPANIES TOOK CONTROL OF AMERICA! BUT NOW, BECAUSE OF YOUR INEXCUSABLE CARELESSNESS...
(GULP!)
BZZZZZ
...NOW I MUST DEAL WITH THE HOWLING HORDES OF ANTINUCLEAR ACTIVISTS CLAMORING AT THE GATE OF MY INVINCIBLE ATOMIC CITADEL!
MASSSTER, HAVE MERCY! MY GLASSSESSS! I- I CAN'T SSSEE!
GOOD! I PREFER BLIND OBEDIENCE! FOR THAT PURPOSE ALONE DID I MUTATE YOU FROM THE SNIVELLING EX-CON YOU ONCE WERE!
I SHOULD HAVE LISTENED TO MY MOTHER! "YOU CAN'T MAKE PIES WITH ROTTEN APPLES!" SHE USED TO SAY!

"BUT, IF I'D LISTENED TO MOTHER, I NEVER WOULD HAVE TAKEN THAT JOB AT THREE MILE ISLAND NUCLEAR FACILITY AS A 'JUMPER'--A WORKER HIRED TO ENTER 'HOT' AREAS OF NUCLEAR PLANTS TO DO VARIOUS TASKS...

"...SUCH AS ABSORBING SECONDS MORE RADIATION THAN THE AVERAGE NUCLEAR WORKER ABSORBED IN THE COURSE OF A LIFETIME!

"THE PAY WAS GOOD--

"--BUT THE FRINGE BENEFITS WERE LOUSY!"

D-DIZZY! M-MAYBE I SHOULDN'T HAVE WORKED OVER-TIME TODAY!

"THAT WAS AN UNDERSTATEMENT! BY THE TIME THEY HAULED ME OUT OF THERE, I WAS GLOWING LIKE A LIGHTBULB!

"AN ANATOMICAL ANALOGY THAT MY BODY ITSELF WAS SOON TO MAKE!

AMAZING! THIS MAN IS MUTATING INTO A LIVING LIGHT-BULB!!

INCANDESCENT OR FLOURESCENT?

PERHAPS A MORE IMPORTANT QUESTION, IS--AC OR DC??

I DON'T FEEL SO GOOD!

"BUT, IN TIME, I FELT BETTER-- STRONGER THAN EVER BEFORE!

"YET, MY STRANGENESS MADE OTHERS SHUN ME!

MOMMY, THAT MAN WAS GLOWING!

HUSH! HE WAS JUST A LITTLE LIGHT-HEADED!

"THE FOOLS!"

"TAUNT ME, WOULD THEY? I'D STILL THEIR LAUGHTER, BY STEALING AWAY THAT WHICH THEY HELD MOST DEAR...

"CHRISTMAS!"

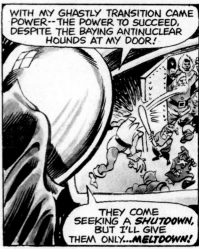

WITH MY GHASTLY TRANSITION CAME POWER--THE POWER TO SUCCEED, DESPITE THE BAYING ANTINUCLEAR HOUNDS AT MY DOOR!

THEY COME SEEKING A SHUTDOWN, BUT I'LL GIVE THEM ONLY...MELTDOWN!

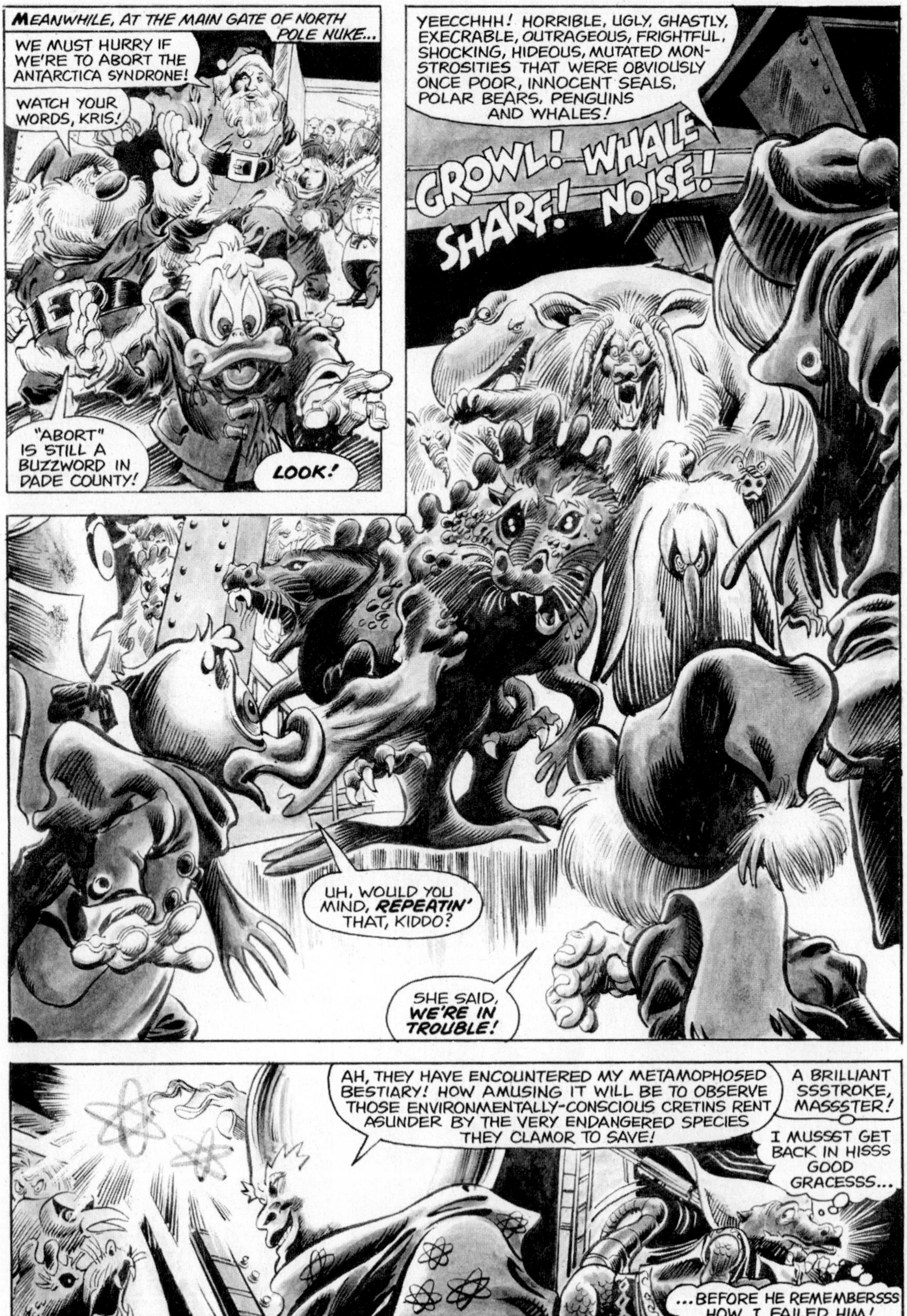
MEANWHILE, AT THE MAIN GATE OF NORTH POLE NUKE...
WE MUST HURRY IF WE'RE TO ABORT THE ANTARCTICA SYNDRONE!
WATCH YOUR WORDS, KRIS!
"ABORT" IS STILL A BUZZWORD IN DADE COUNTY!
LOOK!
YEECCHHH! HORRIBLE, UGLY, GHASTLY, EXECRABLE, OUTRAGEOUS, FRIGHTFUL, SHOCKING, HIDEOUS, MUTATED MONSTROSITIES THAT WERE OBVIOUSLY ONCE POOR, INNOCENT SEALS, POLAR BEARS, PENGUINS AND WHALES!
GROWL! WHALE
SHARF! NOISE!
UH, WOULD YOU MIND, REPEATIN' THAT, KIDDO?
SHE SAID, WE'RE IN TROUBLE!
AH, THEY HAVE ENCOUNTERED MY METAMOPHOSED BESTIARY! HOW AMUSING IT WILL BE TO OBSERVE THOSE ENVIRONMENTALLY-CONSCIOUS CRETINS RENT ASUNDER BY THE VERY ENDANGERED SPECIES THEY CLAMOR TO SAVE!
A BRILLIANT SSSTROKE, MASSSTER!
I MUSSST GET BACK IN HISSS GOOD GRACESSS...
...BEFORE HE REMEMBERSSS HOW I FAILED HIM!

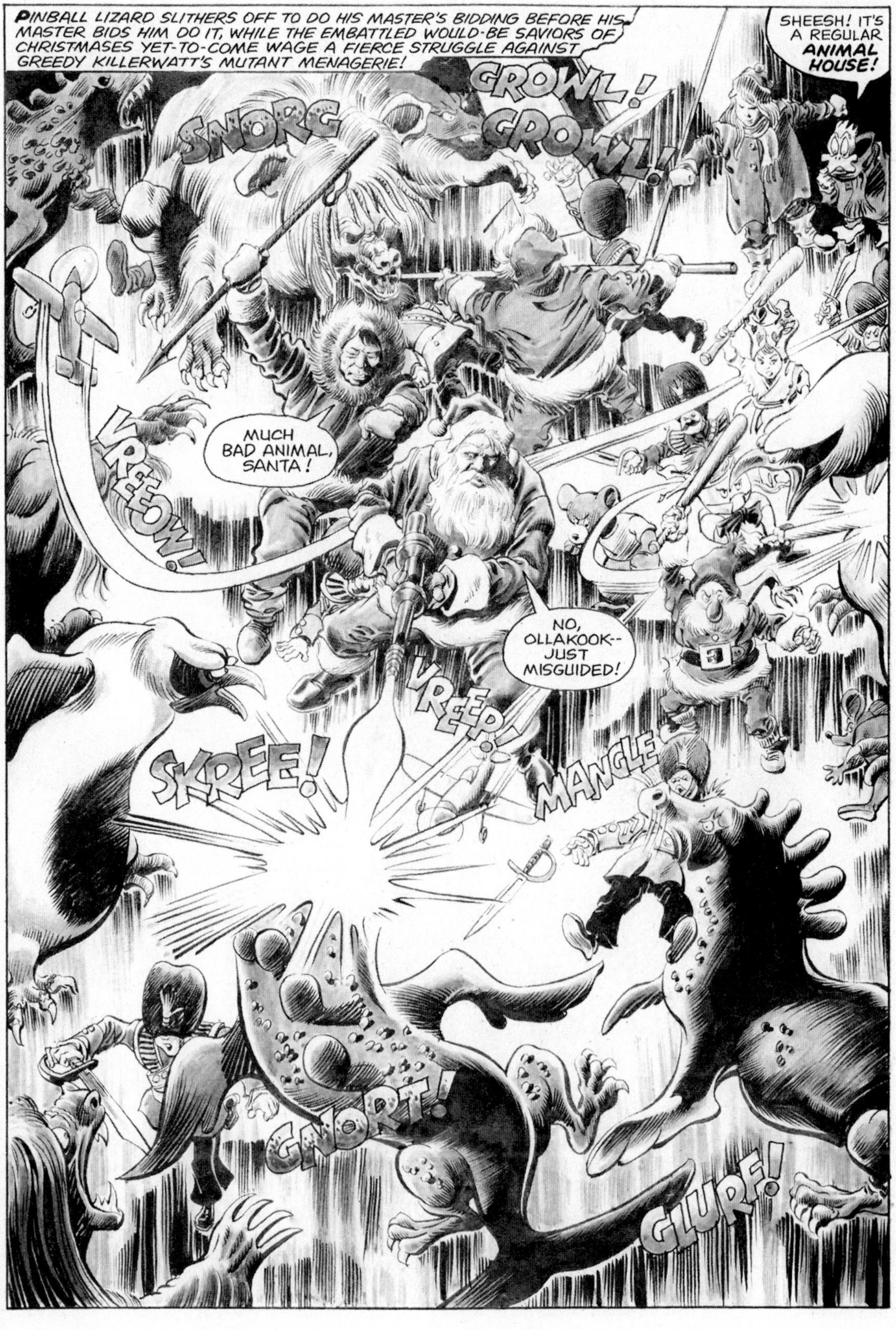
PINBALL LIZARD SLITHERS OFF TO DO HIS MASTER'S BIDDING BEFORE HIS MASTER BIDS HIM DO IT, WHILE THE EMBATTLED WOULD-BE SAVIORS OF CHRISTMASES YET-TO-COME WAGE A FIERCE STRUGGLE AGAINST GREEDY KILLERWATT'S MUTANT MENAGERIE!
SHEESH! IT'S A REGULAR ANIMAL HOUSE!
GROWL!
SNORG
GROWL!
VREEOW!
MUCH BAD ANIMAL, SANTA!
NO, OLLAKOOK-- JUST MISGUIDED!
VREEP!
SKREE!
MANGLE
GNORT!
GLURF!

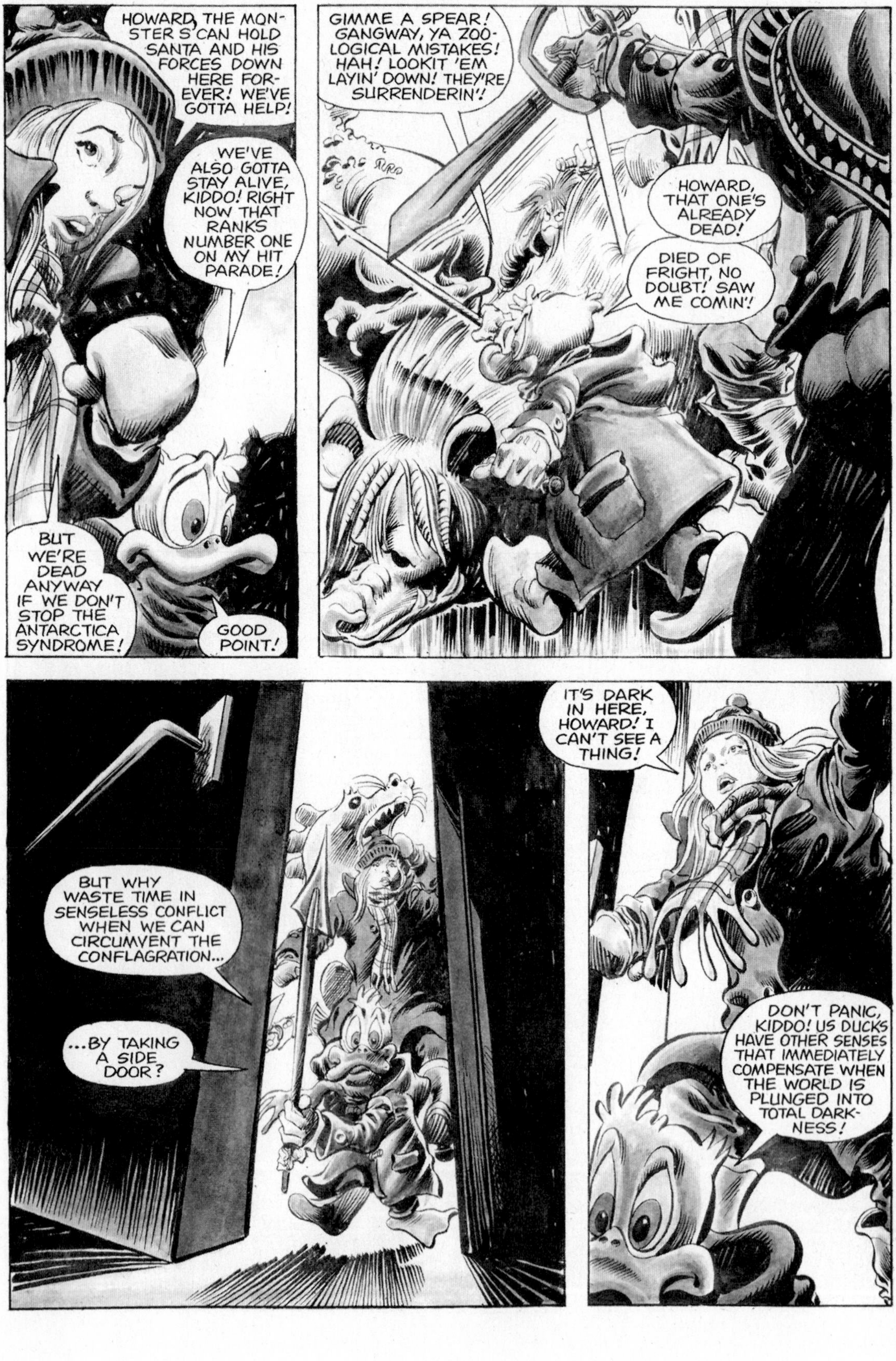
HOWARD, THE MONSTERS CAN HOLD SANTA AND HIS FORCES DOWN HERE FOREVER! WE'VE GOTTA HELP!
WE'VE ALSO GOTTA STAY ALIVE, KIDDO! RIGHT NOW THAT RANKS NUMBER ONE ON MY HIT PARADE!
BUT WE'RE DEAD ANYWAY IF WE DON'T STOP THE ANTARCTICA SYNDROME!
GOOD POINT!
GIMME A SPEAR! GANGWAY, YA ZOOLOGICAL MISTAKES! HAH! LOOKIT 'EM LAYIN' DOWN! THEY'RE SURRENDERIN'!
HOWARD, THAT ONE'S ALREADY DEAD!
DIED OF FRIGHT, NO DOUBT! SAW ME COMIN'!
BUT WHY WASTE TIME IN SENSELESS CONFLICT WHEN WE CAN CIRCUMVENT THE CONFLAGRATION...
...BY TAKING A SIDE DOOR?
IT'S DARK IN HERE, HOWARD! I CAN'T SEE A THING!
DON'T PANIC, KIDDO! US DUCKS HAVE OTHER SENSES THAT IMMEDIATELY COMPENSATE WHEN THE WORLD IS PLUNGED INTO TOTAL DARKNESS!

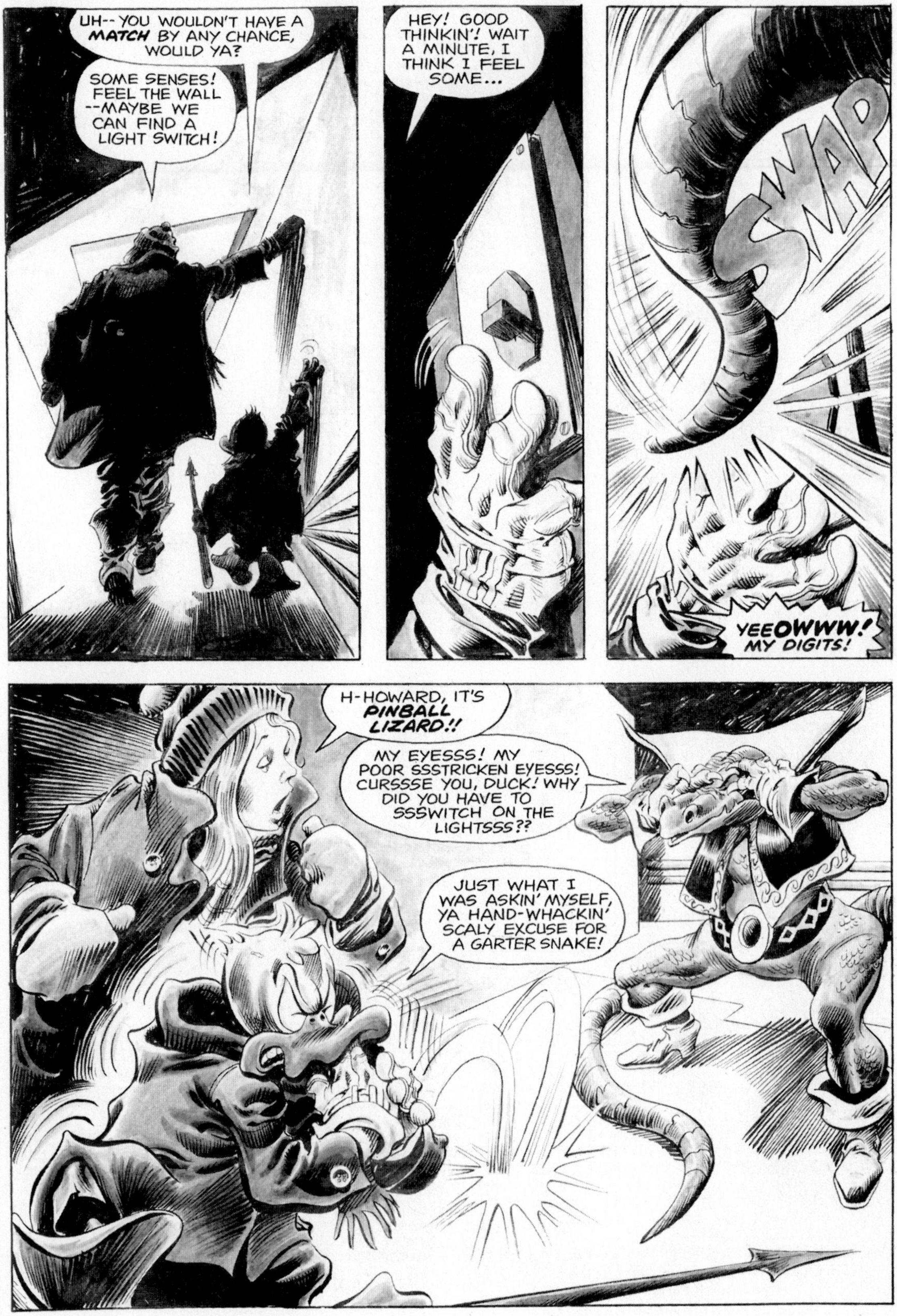
UH-- YOU WOULDN'T HAVE A MATCH BY ANY CHANCE, WOULD YA?
SOME SENSES! FEEL THE WALL --MAYBE WE CAN FIND A LIGHT SWITCH!
HEY! GOOD THINKIN'! WAIT A MINUTE, I THINK I FEEL SOME...
SWAP
YEEOWWW! MY DIGITS!
H-HOWARD, IT'S PINBALL LIZARD!!
MY EYESSS! MY POOR SSSTRICKEN EYESSS! CURSSSE YOU, DUCK! WHY DID YOU HAVE TO SSSWITCH ON THE LIGHTSSS??
JUST WHAT I WAS ASKIN' MYSELF, YA HAND-WHACKIN' SCALY EXCUSE FOR A GARTER SNAKE!

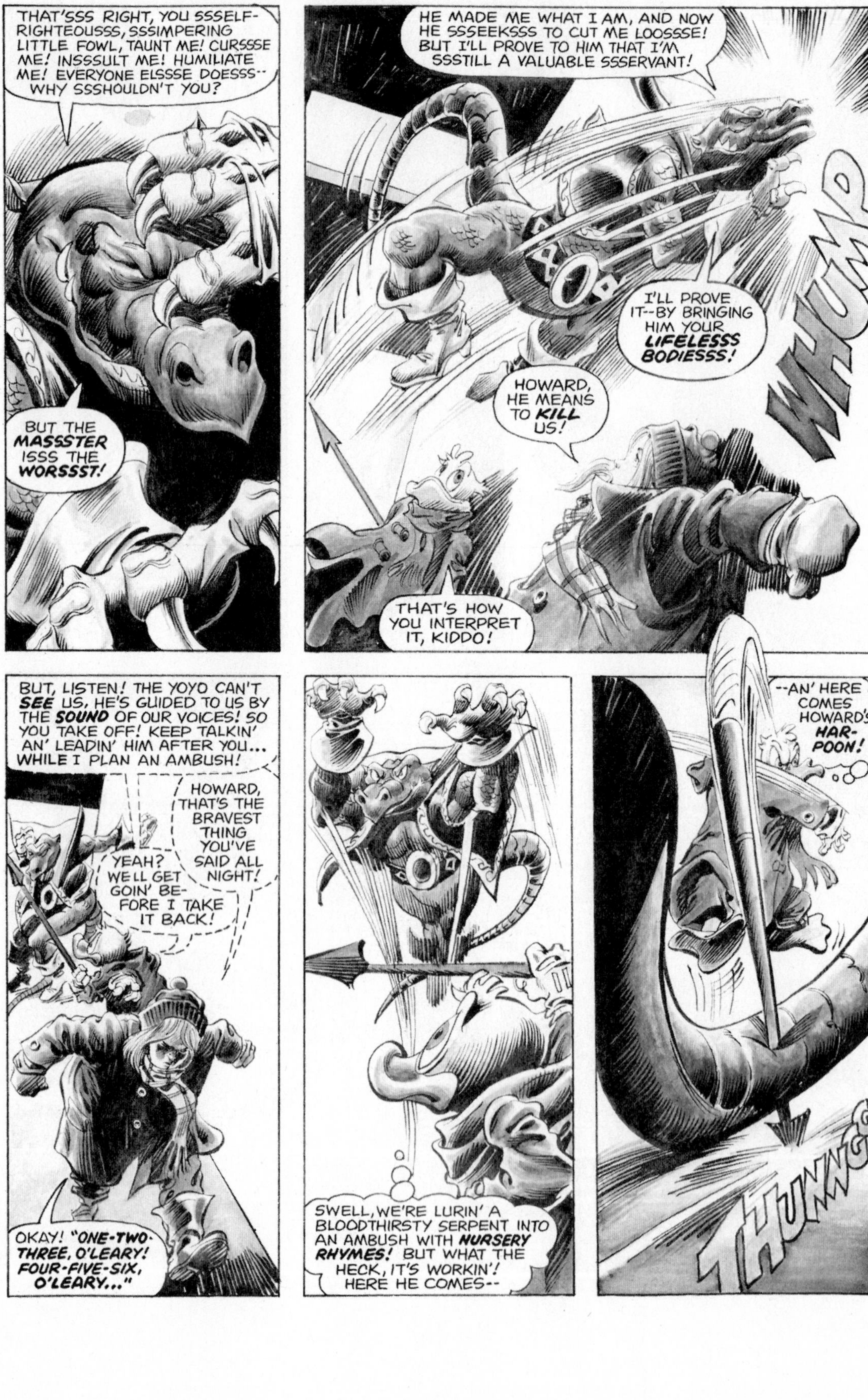
THAT'SSS RIGHT, YOU SSSELF-RIGHTEOUSSS, SSSIMPERING LITTLE FOWL, TAUNT ME! CURSSSE ME! INSSSULT ME! HUMILIATE ME! EVERYONE ELSSSE DOESSS-- WHY SSSHOULDN'T YOU?
BUT THE MASSSTER ISSS THE WORSSST!
HE MADE ME WHAT I AM, AND NOW HE SSSEEKSSS TO CUT ME LOOSSSE! BUT I'LL PROVE TO HIM THAT I'M SSSTILL A VALUABLE SSSERVANT!
I'LL PROVE IT--BY BRINGING HIM YOUR LIFELESSS BODIESSS!
WHUMP
HOWARD, HE MEANS TO KILL US!
THAT'S HOW YOU INTERPRET IT, KIDDO!
BUT, LISTEN! THE YOYO CAN'T SEE US, HE'S GUIDED TO US BY THE SOUND OF OUR VOICES! SO YOU TAKE OFF! KEEP TALKIN' AN' LEADIN' HIM AFTER YOU... WHILE I PLAN AN AMBUSH!
HOWARD, THAT'S THE BRAVEST THING YOU'VE SAID ALL NIGHT!
YEAH? WELL GET GOIN' BEFORE I TAKE IT BACK!
OKAY! "ONE-TWO-THREE, O'LEARY! FOUR-FIVE-SIX, O'LEARY..."
SWELL, WE'RE LURIN' A BLOODTHIRSTY SERPENT INTO AN AMBUSH WITH NURSERY RHYMES! BUT WHAT THE HECK, IT'S WORKIN'! HERE HE COMES--
--AN' HERE COMES HOWARD'S HAR-POON!
THUNNGG

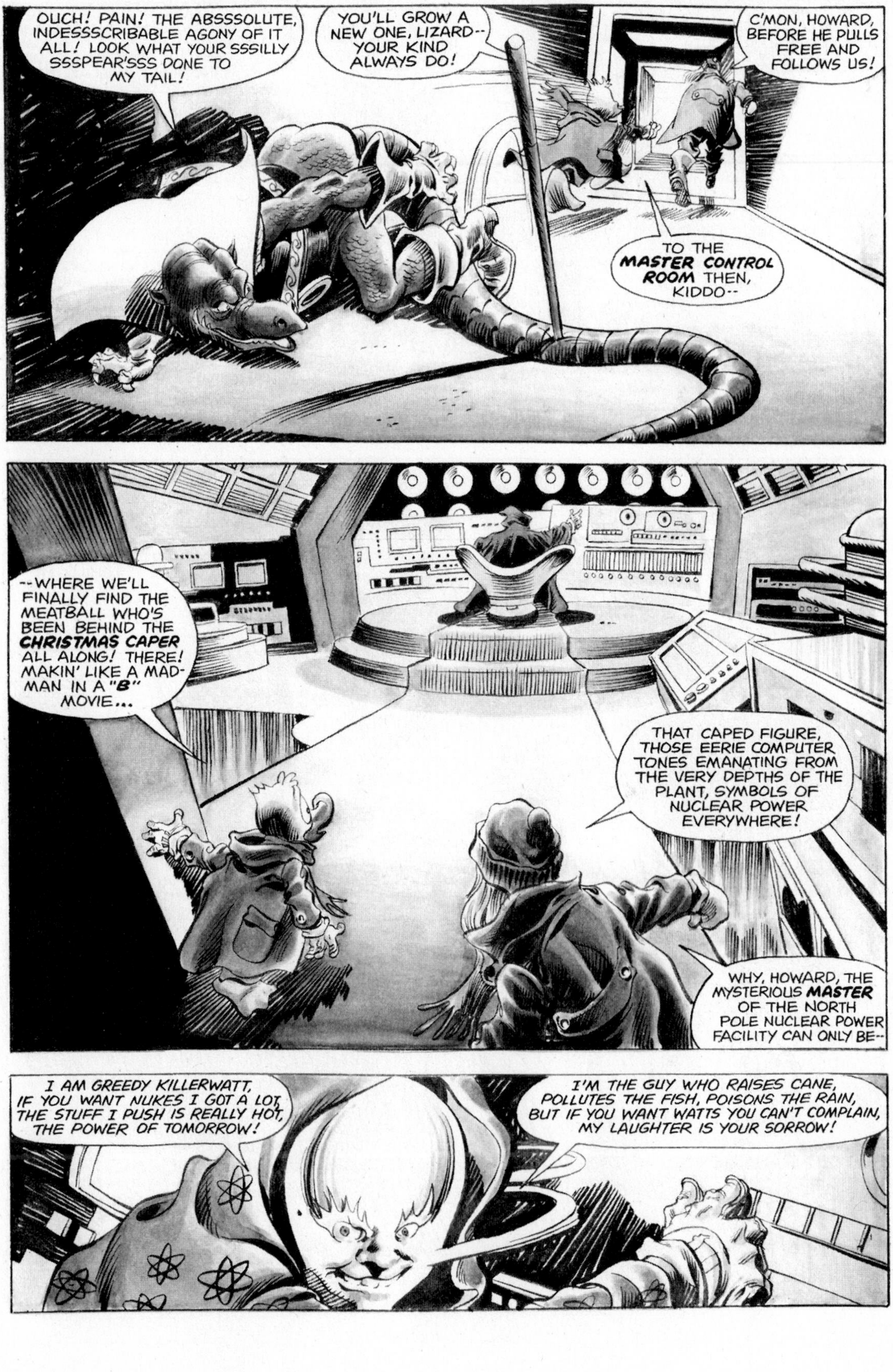
OUCH! PAIN! THE ABSSSOLUTE, INDESSSCRIBABLE AGONY OF IT ALL! LOOK WHAT YOUR SSSILLY SSSPEAR'SSS DONE TO MY TAIL!
YOU'LL GROW A NEW ONE, LIZARD-- YOUR KIND ALWAYS DO!
C'MON, HOWARD, BEFORE HE PULLS FREE AND FOLLOWS US!
TO THE MASTER CONTROL ROOM THEN, KIDDO--
--WHERE WE'LL FINALLY FIND THE MEATBALL WHO'S BEEN BEHIND THE CHRISTMAS CAPER ALL ALONG! THERE! MAKIN' LIKE A MADMAN IN A "B" MOVIE...
THAT CAPED FIGURE, THOSE EERIE COMPUTER TONES EMANATING FROM THE VERY DEPTHS OF THE PLANT, SYMBOLS OF NUCLEAR POWER EVERYWHERE!
WHY, HOWARD, THE MYSTERIOUS MASTER OF THE NORTH POLE NUCLEAR POWER FACILITY CAN ONLY BE--
I AM GREEDY KILLERWATT, IF YOU WANT NUKES I GOT A LOT, THE STUFF I PUSH IS REALLY HOT, THE POWER OF TOMORROW!
I'M THE GUY WHO RAISES CANE, POLLUTES THE FISH, POISONS THE RAIN, BUT IF YOU WANT WATTS YOU CAN'T COMPLAIN, MY LAUGHTER IS YOUR SORROW!

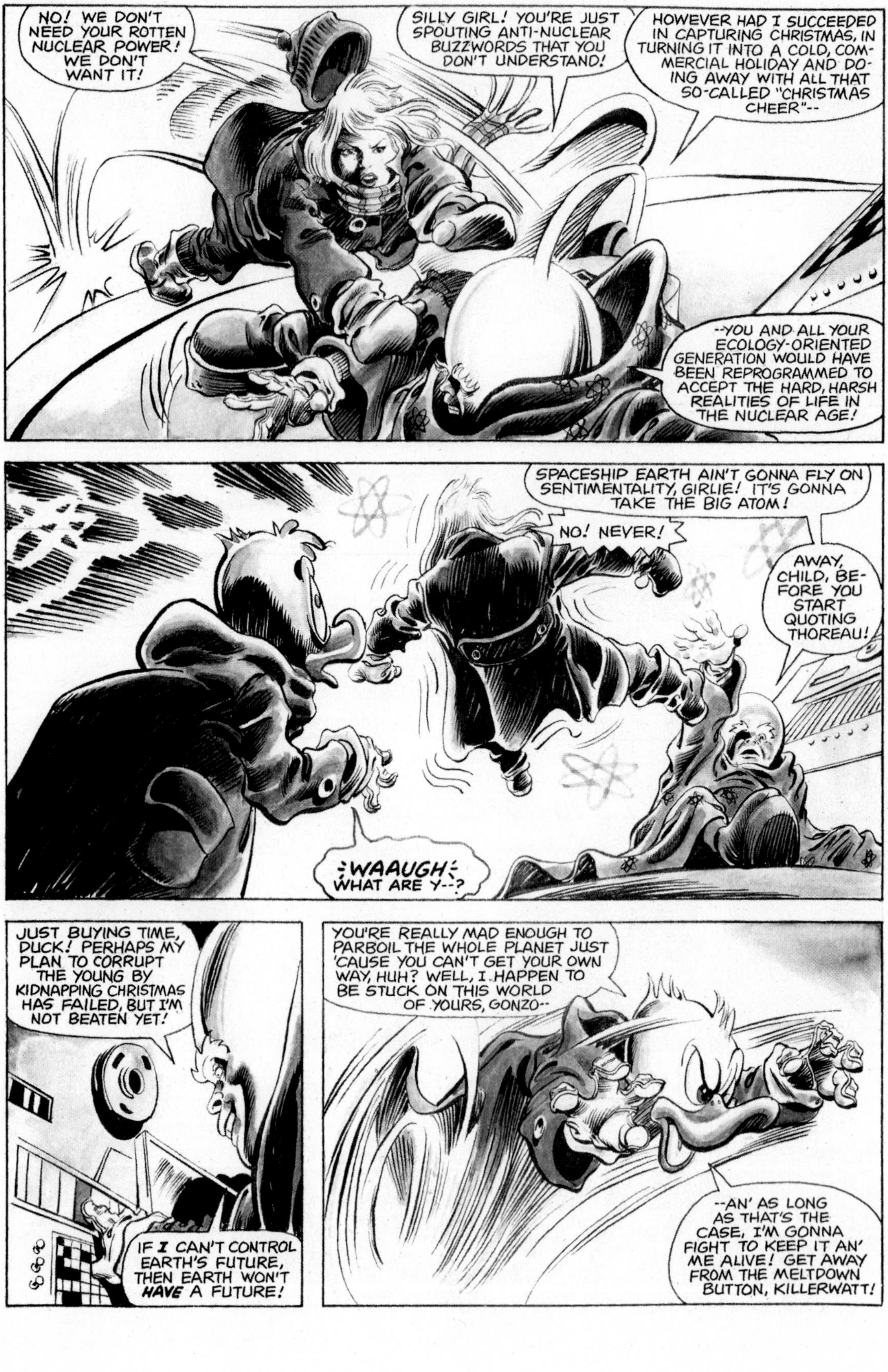
NO! WE DON'T NEED YOUR ROTTEN NUCLEAR POWER! WE DON'T WANT IT!
SILLY GIRL! YOU'RE JUST SPOUTING ANTI-NUCLEAR BUZZWORDS THAT YOU DON'T UNDERSTAND!
HOWEVER HAD I SUCCEEDED IN CAPTURING CHRISTMAS, IN TURNING IT INTO A COLD, COMMERCIAL HOLIDAY AND DOING AWAY WITH ALL THAT SO-CALLED "CHRISTMAS CHEER"--
--YOU AND ALL YOUR ECOLOGY-ORIENTED GENERATION WOULD HAVE BEEN REPROGRAMMED TO ACCEPT THE HARD, HARSH REALITIES OF LIFE IN THE NUCLEAR AGE!
SPACESHIP EARTH AIN'T GONNA FLY ON SENTIMENTALITY, GIRLIE! IT'S GONNA TAKE THE BIG ATOM!
NO! NEVER!
AWAY, CHILD, BEFORE YOU START QUOTING THOREAU!
WAAUGH WHAT ARE Y--?
JUST BUYING TIME, DUCK! PERHAPS MY PLAN TO CORRUPT THE YOUNG BY KIDNAPPING CHRISTMAS HAS FAILED, BUT I'M NOT BEATEN YET!
IF I CAN'T CONTROL EARTH'S FUTURE, THEN EARTH WON'T HAVE A FUTURE!
YOU'RE REALLY MAD ENOUGH TO PARBOIL THE WHOLE PLANET JUST 'CAUSE YOU CAN'T GET YOUR OWN WAY, HUH? WELL, I HAPPEN TO BE STUCK ON THIS WORLD OF YOURS, GONZO--
--AN' AS LONG AS THAT'S THE CASE, I'M GONNA FIGHT TO KEEP IT AN' ME ALIVE! GET AWAY FROM THE MELTDOWN BUTTON, KILLERWATT!

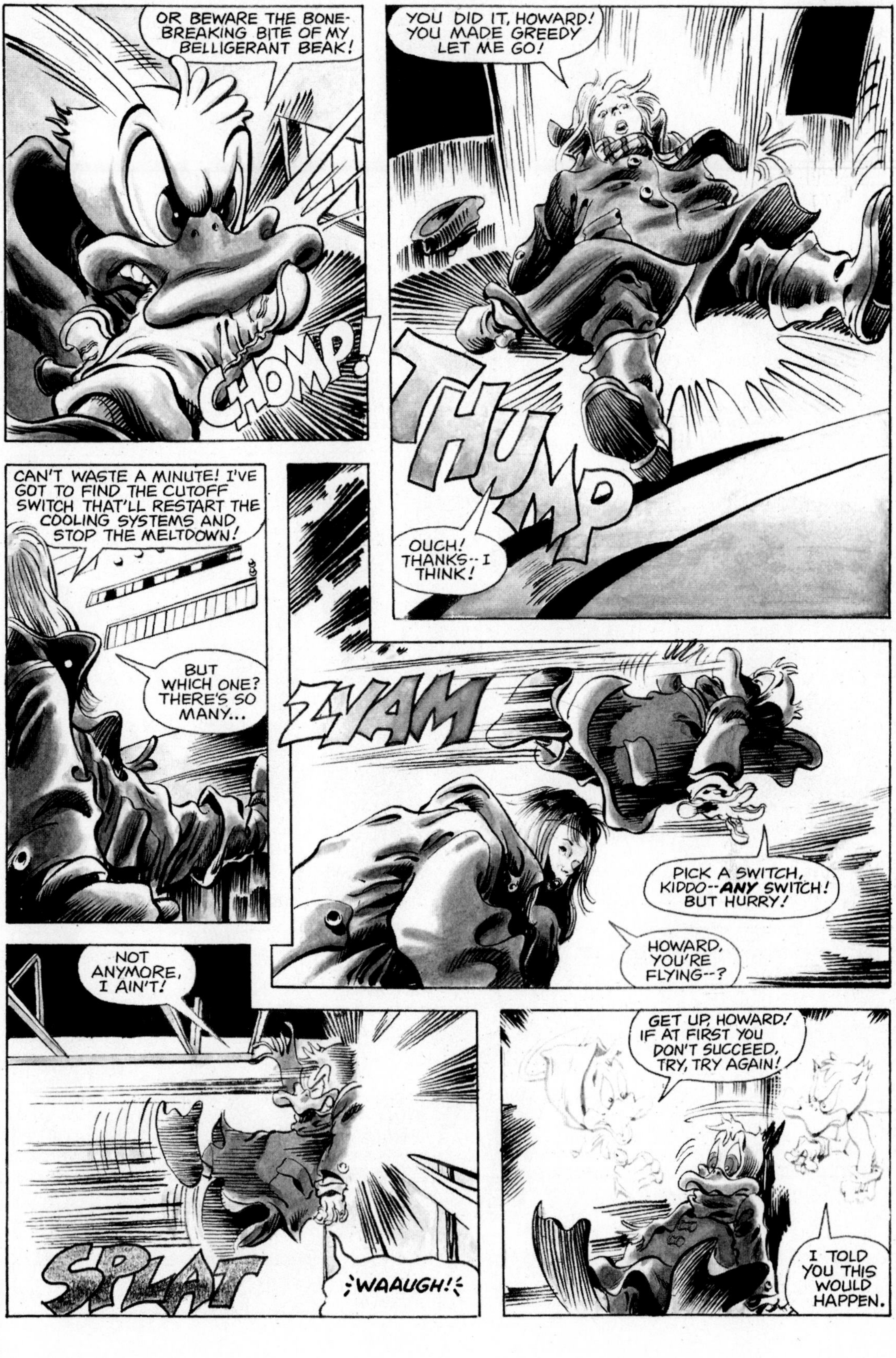

OR BEWARE THE BONE-BREAKING BITE OF MY BELLIGERANT BEAK!
CHOMP!
YOU DID IT, HOWARD! YOU MADE GREEDY LET ME GO!
THUMP
OUCH! THANKS-- I THINK!
CAN'T WASTE A MINUTE! I'VE GOT TO FIND THE CUTOFF SWITCH THAT'LL RESTART THE COOLING SYSTEMS AND STOP THE MELTDOWN!
BUT WHICH ONE? THERE'S SO MANY...
ZWAM
PICK A SWITCH, KIDDO--ANY SWITCH! BUT HURRY!
HOWARD, YOU'RE FLYING--?
NOT ANYMORE, I AIN'T!
SPLAT
WAAUGH!
GET UP, HOWARD! IF AT FIRST YOU DON'T SUCCEED, TRY, TRY AGAIN!
I TOLD YOU THIS WOULD HAPPEN.

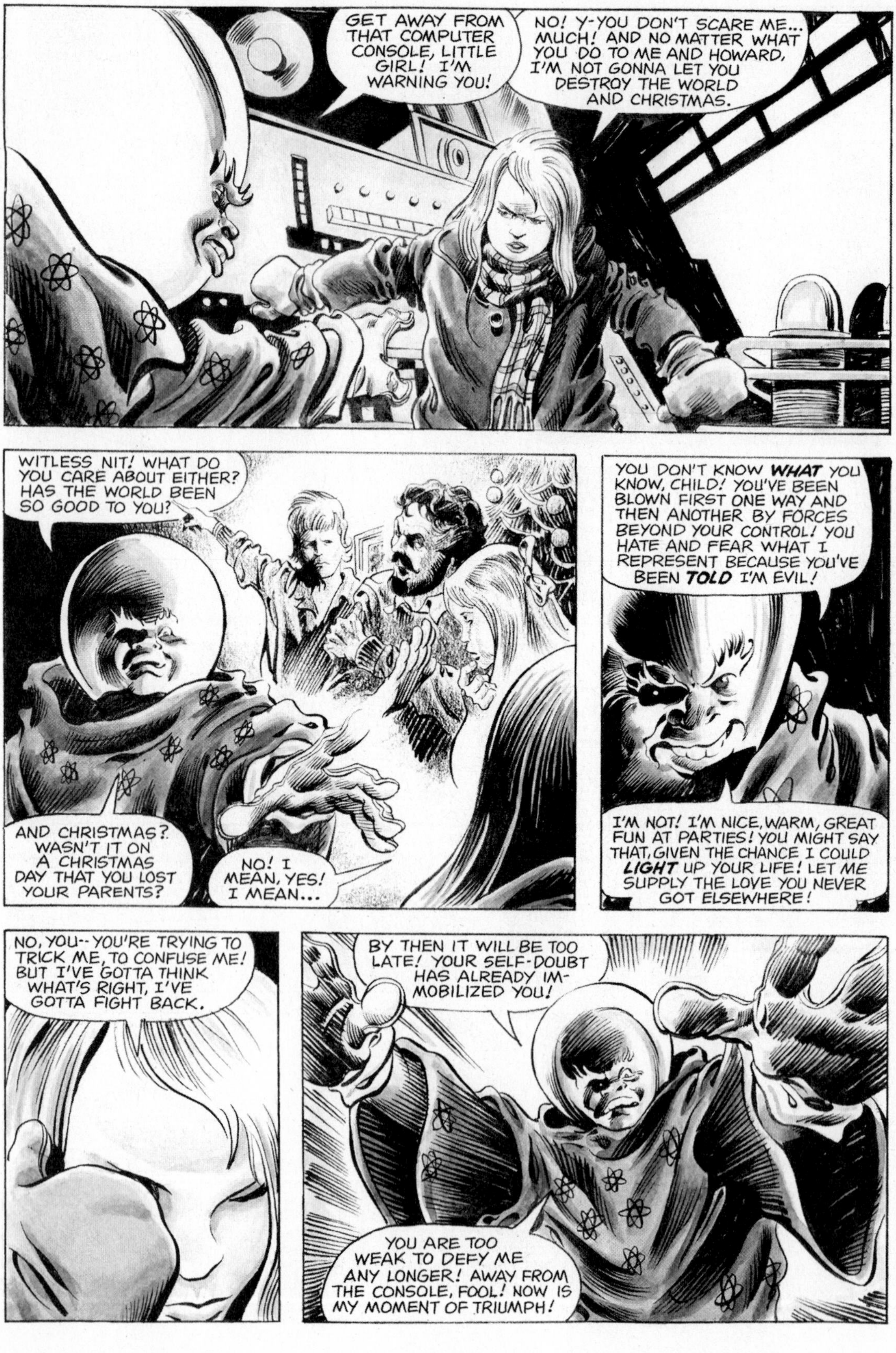
GET AWAY FROM THAT COMPUTER CONSOLE, LITTLE GIRL! I'M WARNING YOU!
NO! Y-YOU DON'T SCARE ME... MUCH! AND NO MATTER WHAT YOU DO TO ME AND HOWARD, I'M NOT GONNA LET YOU DESTROY THE WORLD AND CHRISTMAS.
WITLESS NIT! WHAT DO YOU CARE ABOUT EITHER? HAS THE WORLD BEEN SO GOOD TO YOU?
AND CHRISTMAS? WASN'T IT ON A CHRISTMAS DAY THAT YOU LOST YOUR PARENTS?
NO! I MEAN, YES! I MEAN...
YOU DON'T KNOW WHAT YOU KNOW, CHILD! YOU'VE BEEN BLOWN FIRST ONE WAY AND THEN ANOTHER BY FORCES BEYOND YOUR CONTROL! YOU HATE AND FEAR WHAT I REPRESENT BECAUSE YOU'VE BEEN TOLD I'M EVIL!
I'M NOT! I'M NICE, WARM, GREAT FUN AT PARTIES! YOU MIGHT SAY THAT, GIVEN THE CHANCE I COULD LIGHT UP YOUR LIFE! LET ME SUPPLY THE LOVE YOU NEVER GOT ELSEWHERE!
NO, YOU-- YOU'RE TRYING TO TRICK ME, TO CONFUSE ME! BUT I'VE GOTTA THINK WHAT'S RIGHT, I'VE GOTTA FIGHT BACK.
BY THEN IT WILL BE TOO LATE! YOUR SELF-DOUBT HAS ALREADY IMMOBILIZED YOU!
YOU ARE TOO WEAK TO DEFY ME ANY LONGER! AWAY FROM THE CONSOLE, FOOL! NOW IS MY MOMENT OF TRIUMPH!

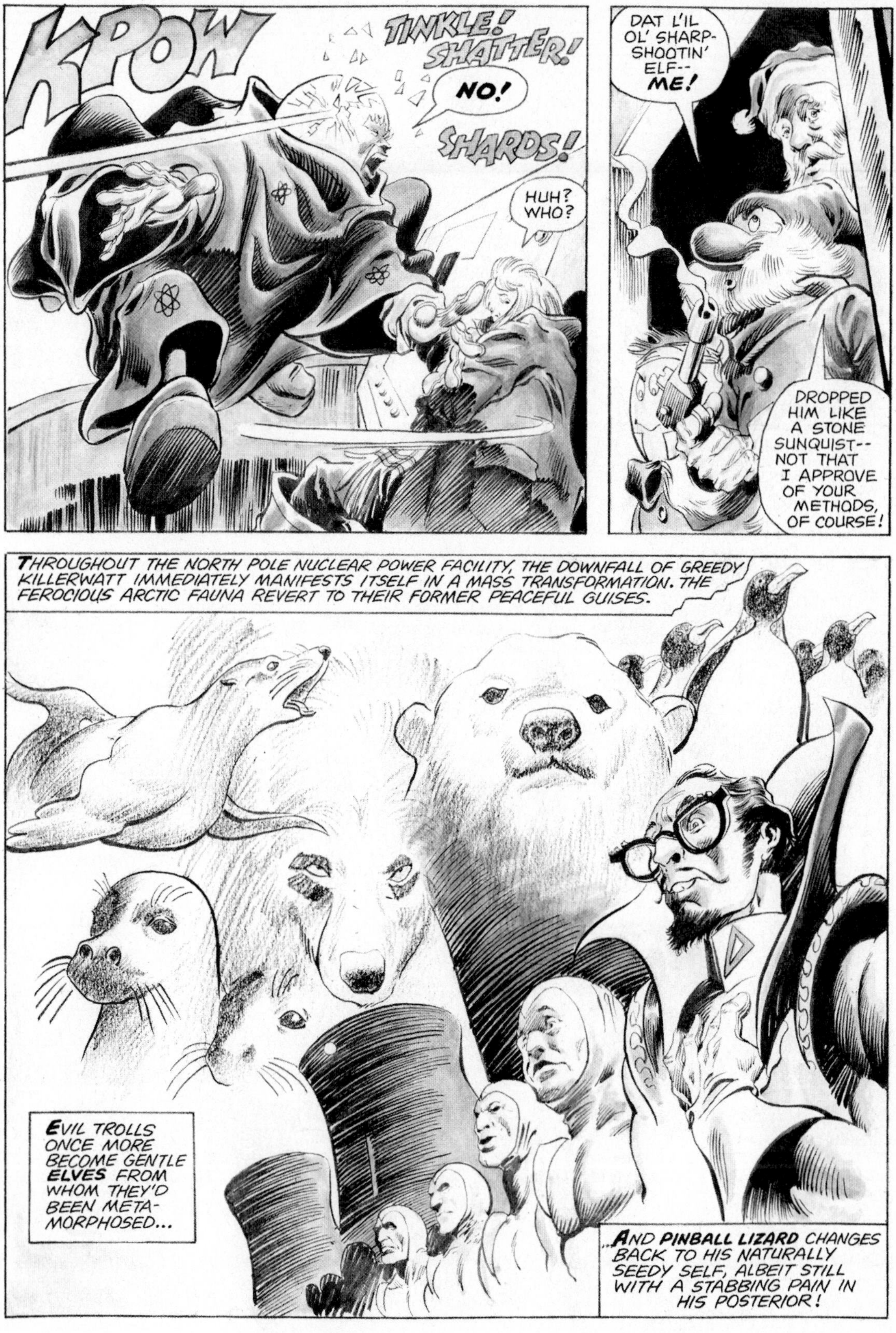
KPOW
TINKLE! SHATTER!
NO!
SHARDS!
HUH? WHO?
DAT L'IL OL' SHARP-SHOOTIN' ELF-- ME!
DROPPED HIM LIKE A STONE SUNQUIST-- NOT THAT I APPROVE OF YOUR METHODS, OF COURSE!
THROUGHOUT THE NORTH POLE NUCLEAR POWER FACILITY, THE DOWNFALL OF GREEDY KILLERWATT IMMEDIATELY MANIFESTS ITSELF IN A MASS TRANSFORMATION. THE FEROCIOUS ARCTIC FAUNA REVERT TO THEIR FORMER PEACEFUL GUISES.
EVIL TROLLS ONCE MORE BECOME GENTLE ELVES FROM WHOM THEY'D BEEN META-MORPHOSED...
...AND PINBALL LIZARD CHANGES BACK TO HIS NATURALLY SEEDY SELF, ALBEIT STILL WITH A STABBING PAIN IN HIS POSTERIOR!

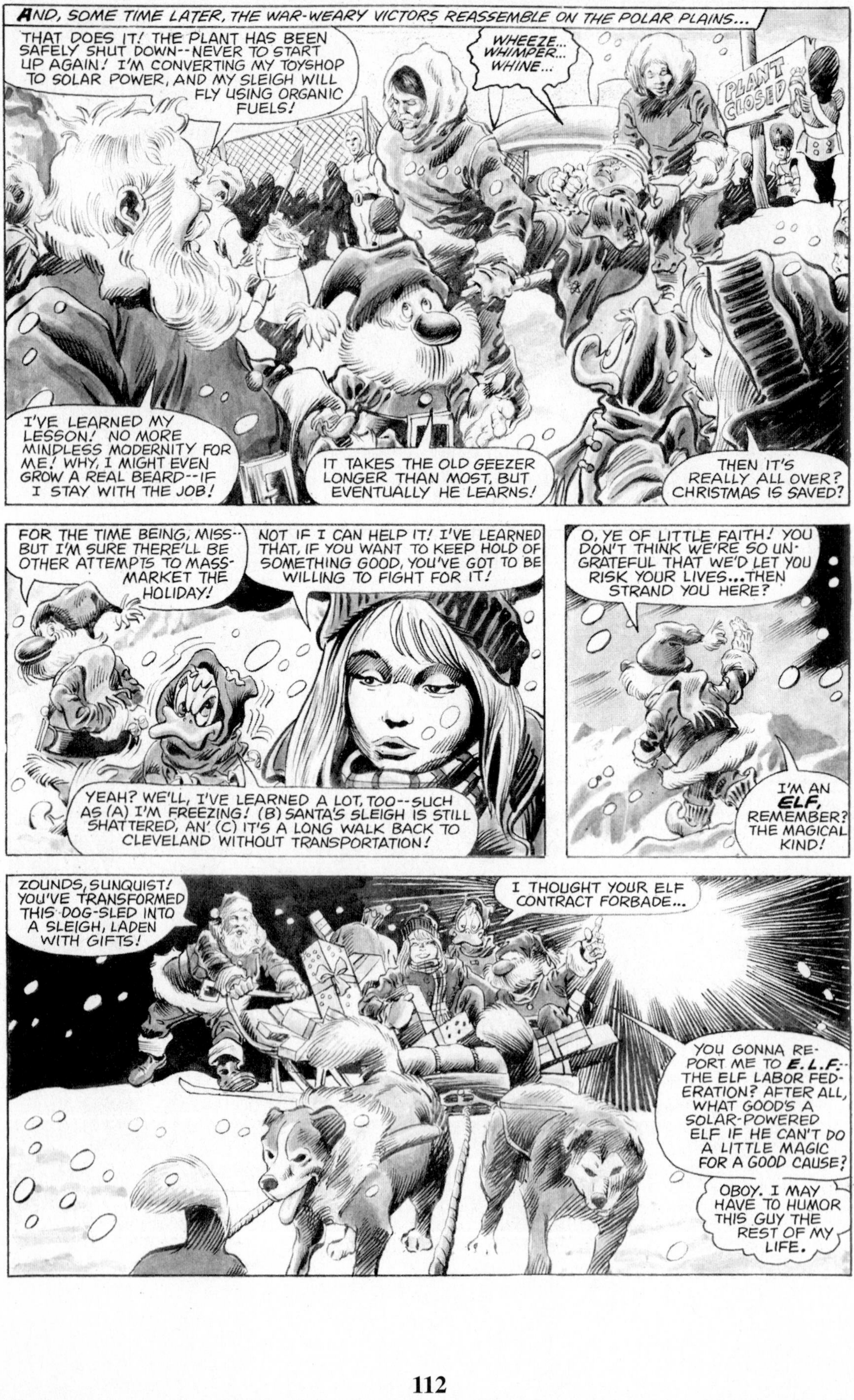
AND, SOME TIME LATER, THE WAR-WEARY VICTORS REASSEMBLE ON THE POLAR PLAINS...
THAT DOES IT! THE PLANT HAS BEEN SAFELY SHUT DOWN--NEVER TO START UP AGAIN! I'M CONVERTING MY TOYSHOP TO SOLAR POWER, AND MY SLEIGH WILL FLY USING ORGANIC FUELS!
WHEEZE... WHIMPER... WHINE...
PLANT CLOSED
I'VE LEARNED MY LESSON! NO MORE MINDLESS MODERNITY FOR ME! WHY, I MIGHT EVEN GROW A REAL BEARD--IF I STAY WITH THE JOB!
IT TAKES THE OLD GEEZER LONGER THAN MOST, BUT EVENTUALLY HE LEARNS!
THEN IT'S REALLY ALL OVER? CHRISTMAS IS SAVED?
FOR THE TIME BEING, MISS--BUT I'M SURE THERE'LL BE OTHER ATTEMPTS TO MASS-MARKET THE HOLIDAY!
NOT IF I CAN HELP IT! I'VE LEARNED THAT, IF YOU WANT TO KEEP HOLD OF SOMETHING GOOD, YOU'VE GOT TO BE WILLING TO FIGHT FOR IT!
YEAH? WE'LL, I'VE LEARNED A LOT, TOO--SUCH AS (A) I'M FREEZING! (B) SANTA'S SLEIGH IS STILL SHATTERED, AN' (C) IT'S A LONG WALK BACK TO CLEVELAND WITHOUT TRANSPORTATION!
O, YE OF LITTLE FAITH! YOU DON'T THINK WE'RE SO UNGRATEFUL THAT WE'D LET YOU RISK YOUR LIVES...THEN STRAND YOU HERE?
I'M AN ELF, REMEMBER? THE MAGICAL KIND!
ZOUNDS, SUNQUIST! YOU'VE TRANSFORMED THIS DOG-SLED INTO A SLEIGH, LADEN WITH GIFTS!
I THOUGHT YOUR ELF CONTRACT FORBADE...
YOU GONNA REPORT ME TO E.L.F.-- THE ELF LABOR FEDERATION? AFTER ALL, WHAT GOOD'S A SOLAR-POWERED ELF IF HE CAN'T DO A LITTLE MAGIC FOR A GOOD CAUSE?
OBOY. I MAY HAVE TO HUMOR THIS GUY THE REST OF MY LIFE.

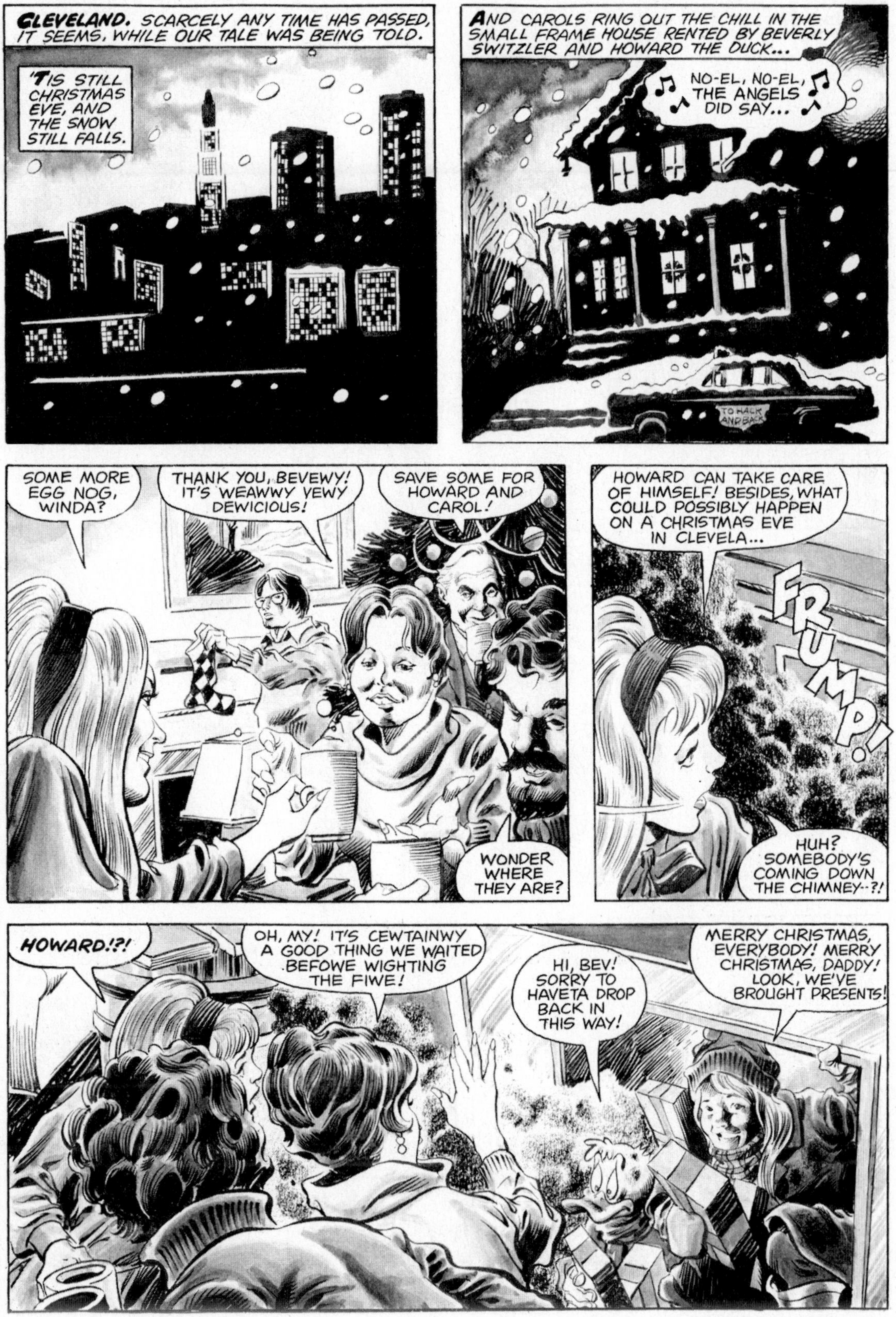

CLEVELAND. SCARCELY ANY TIME HAS PASSED, IT SEEMS, WHILE OUR TALE WAS BEING TOLD.
'TIS STILL CHRISTMAS EVE, AND THE SNOW STILL FALLS.
AND CAROLS RING OUT THE CHILL IN THE SMALL FRAME HOUSE RENTED BY BEVERLY SWITZLER AND HOWARD THE DUCK...
NO-EL, NO-EL, THE ANGELS DID SAY...
TO HACK AND BACK
SOME MORE EGG NOG, WINDA?
THANK YOU, BEVEWY! IT'S WEAWWY YEWY DEWICIOUS!
SAVE SOME FOR HOWARD AND CAROL!
WONDER WHERE THEY ARE?
HOWARD CAN TAKE CARE OF HIMSELF! BESIDES, WHAT COULD POSSIBLY HAPPEN ON A CHRISTMAS EVE IN CLEVELA...
FRUMP!
HUH? SOMEBODY'S COMING DOWN THE CHIMNEY--?!
HOWARD!?!
OH, MY! IT'S CEWTAINWY A GOOD THING WE WAITED BEFOWE WIGHTING THE FIWE!
HI, BEV! SORRY TO HAVETA DROP BACK IN THIS WAY!
MERRY CHRISTMAS, EVERYBODY! MERRY CHRISTMAS, DADDY! LOOK, WE'VE BROUGHT PRESENTS!

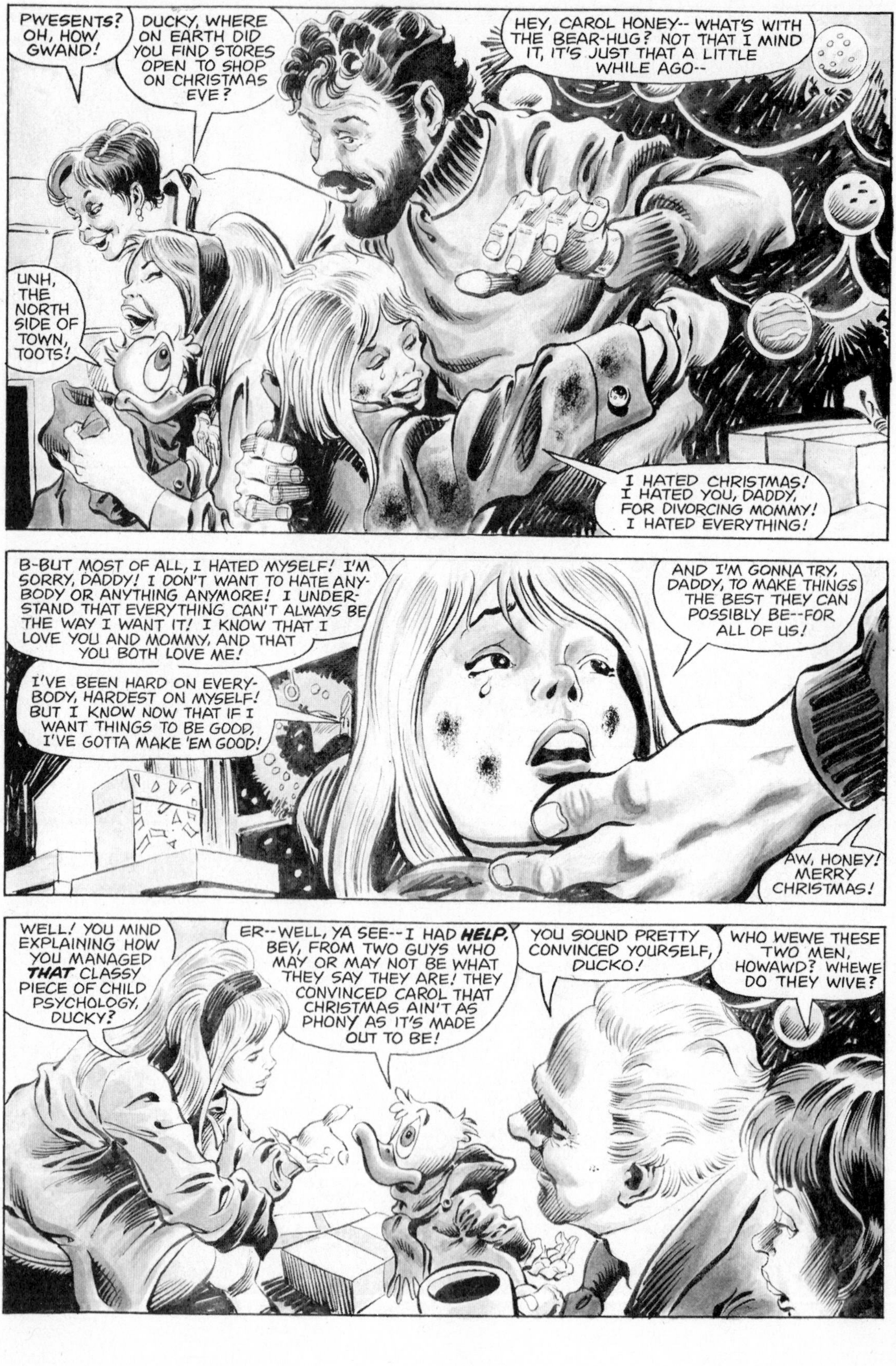
PWESENTS? OH, HOW GWAND!
DUCKY, WHERE ON EARTH DID YOU FIND STORES OPEN TO SHOP ON CHRISTMAS EVE?
HEY, CAROL HONEY-- WHAT'S WITH THE BEAR-HUG? NOT THAT I MIND IT, IT'S JUST THAT A LITTLE WHILE AGO--
UNH, THE NORTH SIDE OF TOWN, TOOTS!
I HATED CHRISTMAS! I HATED YOU, DADDY, FOR DIVORCING MOMMY! I HATED EVERYTHING!
B-BUT MOST OF ALL, I HATED MYSELF! I'M SORRY, DADDY! I DON'T WANT TO HATE ANYBODY OR ANYTHING ANYMORE! I UNDERSTAND THAT EVERYTHING CAN'T ALWAYS BE THE WAY I WANT IT! I KNOW THAT I LOVE YOU AND MOMMY, AND THAT YOU BOTH LOVE ME!
I'VE BEEN HARD ON EVERYBODY, HARDEST ON MYSELF! BUT I KNOW NOW THAT IF I WANT THINGS TO BE GOOD, I'VE GOTTA MAKE 'EM GOOD!
AND I'M GONNA TRY, DADDY, TO MAKE THINGS THE BEST THEY CAN POSSIBLY BE--FOR ALL OF US!
AW, HONEY! MERRY CHRISTMAS!
WELL! YOU MIND EXPLAINING HOW YOU MANAGED THAT CLASSY PIECE OF CHILD PSYCHOLOGY, DUCKY?
ER--WELL, YA SEE--I HAD HELP, BEV, FROM TWO GUYS WHO MAY OR MAY NOT BE WHAT THEY SAY THEY ARE! THEY CONVINCED CAROL THAT CHRISTMAS AIN'T AS PHONY AS IT'S MADE OUT TO BE!
YOU SOUND PRETTY CONVINCED YOURSELF, DUCKO!
WHO WEWE THESE TWO MEN, HOWAWD? WHEWE DO THEY WIVE?

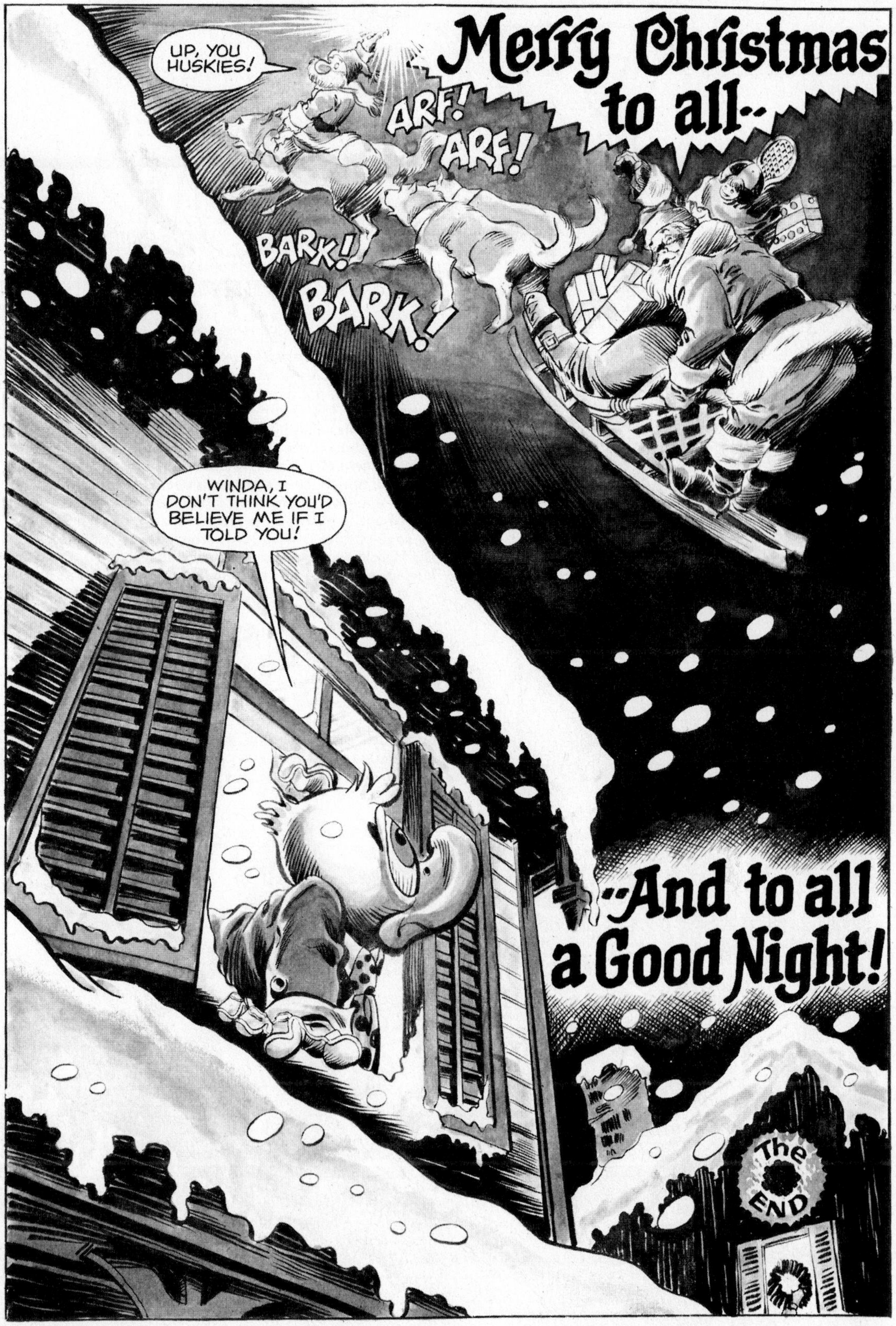
UP, YOU HUSKIES!
Merry Christmas to all..
ARF! ARF!
BARK! BARK!
WINDA, I DON'T THINK YOU'D BELIEVE ME IF I TOLD YOU!
..And to all a Good Night!
The END

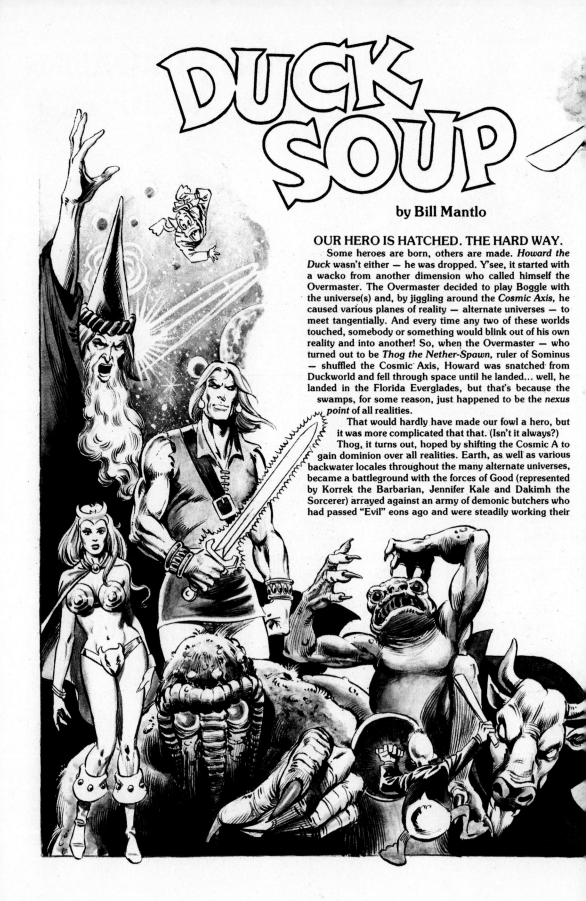

DUCK SOUP

by Bill Mantlo

OUR HERO IS HATCHED. THE HARD WAY.

Some heroes are born, others are made. *Howard the Duck* wasn't either — he was dropped. Y'see, it started with a wacko from another dimension who called himself the Overmaster. The Overmaster decided to play Boggle with the universe(s) and, by jiggling around the *Cosmic Axis,* he caused various planes of reality — alternate universes — to meet tangentially. And every time any two of these worlds touched, somebody or something would blink out of his own reality and into another! So, when the Overmaster — who turned out to be *Thog the Nether-Spawn,* ruler of Sominus — shuffled the Cosmic Axis, Howard was snatched from Duckworld and fell through space until he landed... well, he landed in the Florida Everglades, but that's because the swamps, for some reason, just happened to be the *nexus point* of all realities.

That would hardly have made our fowl a hero, but it was more complicated that that. (Isn't it always?)

Thog, it turns out, hoped by shifting the Cosmic A to gain dominion over all realities. Earth, as well as various backwater locales throughout the many alternate universes, became a battleground with the forces of Good (represented by Korrek the Barbarian, Jennifer Kale and Dakimh the Sorcerer) arrayed against an army of demonic butchers who had passed "Evil" eons ago and were steadily working their

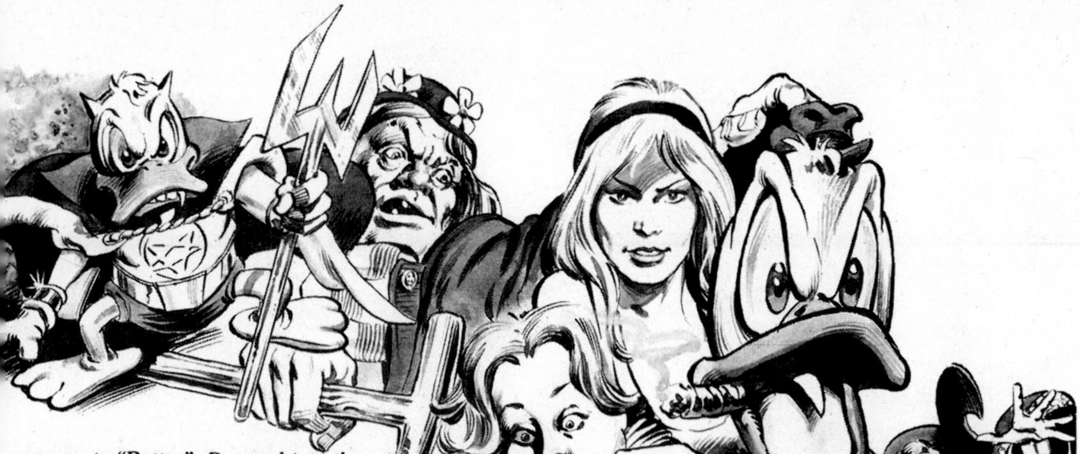

way up to "Rotten". Dropped into the midst of all this, our notably unheroic drake fought for his life even as he fought down his own hysteria, until Dakimh reappeared and bamfed the quartet to his sorcerous dimension where he explained (relatively) the whole mess, and enlisted their aid in the war against the Overmaster. They set out through a dimensional Nowhere — proceeded to a state of Un-ness — onto a ribbon that laced Nothing to Nullity — and onto the stepping-stones of Oblivion. There Howard misstepped... and fell to Earth.

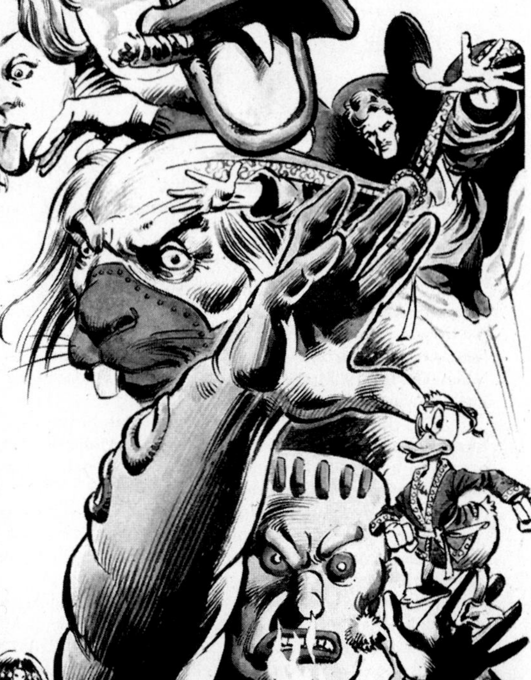

Earth. You've all heard of it. It's two turns to the right of Alpha Centauri — a big blue marble inhabited by animals, insects... and the ruling class, *hairless apes.* Us, Jack. You and me.

Imagine yourself two foot-seven, feathered, webbed feet, possessed of an argumentative personality, and you'll understand Howard's culture shock upon arriving on our ball of mud... with no way to get home. To him, we were a contradiction — hairless apes, animals. To us, he was — well, a talking duck! It was a concept we could accept in the movies, on TV, or filled with helium and floating thirty feet up during the Macy's Thanksgiving Day Parade, but it wasn't the kind of concept you liked to confront during the

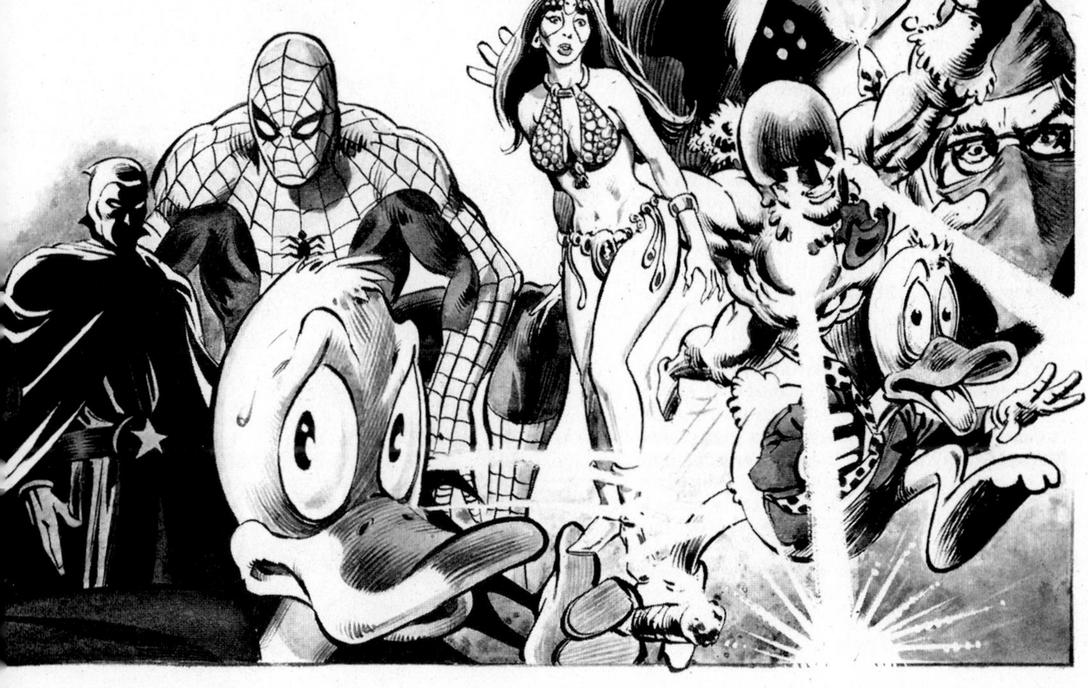

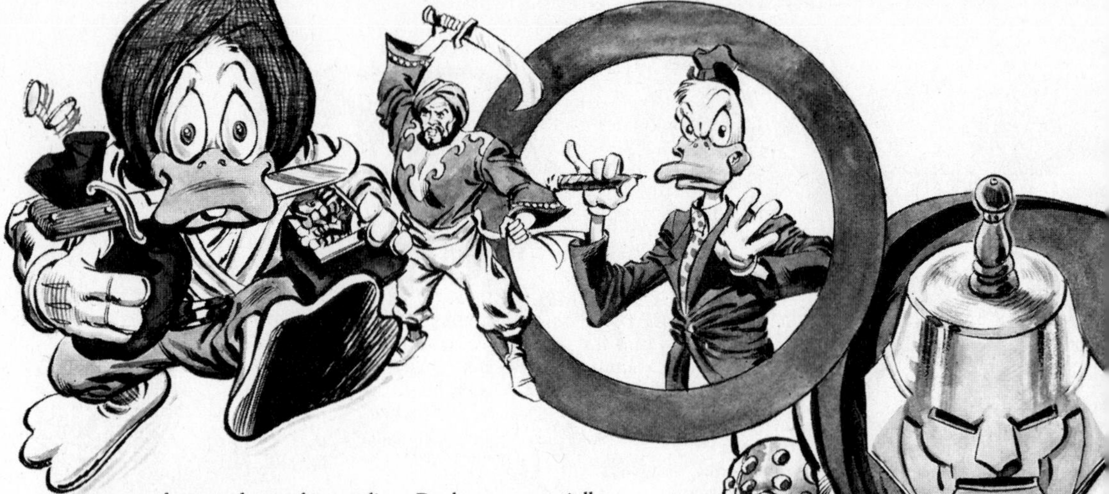

course of your day-to-day reality. Ducks — especially *talking* ducks — are not the status quo in Cleveland. No way in Cleveland!

BIRD IN AN UNGILDED CAGE.

But Howard wasn't the kind of mallard to give in to despair. Alright, so he was in exile! So what? He could cope — he was copesetic! He'd take what this world had to offer, and wrest his fortune from the very jaws of disaster. That's when *Garko the Man-Frog* leaped from a window-ledge and into Howard's life!

Like the man said, "Perhaps the time he had spent in the *Un-world* had made him too rash, too foolishly daring — or perhaps the sudden appearance of this *monster* had tapped a hitherto unknown reservoir of *courage* within him..." Whatever the case, Howard fought back against Garko with a savagery he's never known before, and found himself filled with a determination to *win,* to carve a place for himself in this world he never made!

He won — and got arrested for his trouble. But his interlude in Cleveland's jails was brief... lasting only as long ad it took Police Commissioner Gordonski to find that there was no zipper to Howard's duck suit. Despondent, thrown from jail, nothing but Duck-Bucks in his pocket in a town fiercely adverse to foreign currency, Howard decided the only course of salvation was in finding a job... with the police themselves! To that end he set out to ambush the notorious farm killer that was making headlines and, luring the fanged and caped *Hellcow* to its doom, Howard expected to be justly rewarded. But Cleveland didn't want to own up to talking ducks, be they heroes or not! The forces of law and order turned their blue backs on Howard, leaving him to face a dark and threatening world... all *alone!*

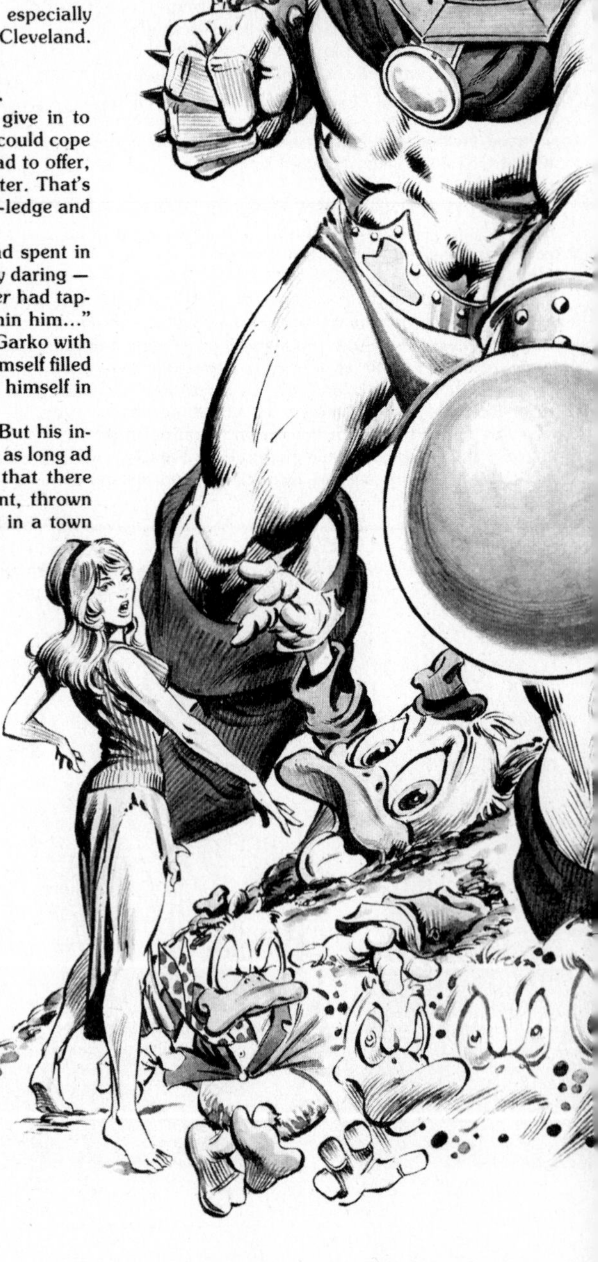

LAME DUCK FOR PRESIDENT!

Rather than that, Howard chose *suicide!* Paddling out over the Cuyahoga River, he approached an ominous tower from which he intended to hurl himself, thus ending his sojourn on Earth. But the tower turned out to be made of credit cards and, scaling its synthetic outer walls, Howard came upon a vision of loveliness held captive by the *Sorcerer Accountant Pro Rata.* He rescued *Beverly Switzler* from the mage's

clutches with the help of a certain friendly neighborhood *Spider-Man.*

It soon became obvious that Earth wasn't about to allow him to off himself and that maybe — just maybe — there was some reason why he, of all the ducks on Duckworld, was chosen to fall through the Cosmic Axis. Maybe Howard wasn't just *any* duck! Maybe he was *special!* He was certainly lucky — if you can call it luck — in facing down one bizarre situation after the other, from the *Deadly Space-Turnip,* to *Winky-Man,* to pretty *Patty* and her *Cookie Creature,* to his nomination for — gasp — *President of the United States!*

Forget the fact that he had no chance, that he wasn't a natural-born citizen — there were still those who chose to take his candidacy seriously enough to try to have him humiliated, controlled... or assassinated! Seeking a way out, Howard's subconscious led him to the Greenwich Village doorway of *Dr. Stephen Strange* — Master of the Mystic Arts — and mage in residence of the dynamic *Defenders!* Displaying a certain knack for that ol' Black — and White — Magic, Howard wielded Dr. Strange's sorcery against a host of mediocrities... and at the same time found his decision made for him. He would *stay* on Earth — for awhile, at any rate.

But the pressures of running for the Presidency, of dodging assassin's bullets and yellow press took its toll on our fowl. Clearing up his and Bev's reputation after a plot by *Le Beaver* to smear them both, Howard hopped a bus for Cleveland... and *crackup!* Yeah, like in lost marbles, the big *breakdown!* Between Kidney Ladies and demonic possession, he was the perfect candidate for *duck's-head soup* — the funny farm! He wasn't alone, either! Between lisping *Winda Wester* — a nice kid whose parents thought she was possessed by the devil — *Nurse Barbara,* the *Reverend Joon Moon Yuc* and Yuccies, and — well, he *looked* like Adolph Hitler — Howard couldn't tell the staff from the inmates. Possessed by the demonic second half of Daimon Helstrom, the *Son of Satan,* Howard fled the asylum (and a storyline which we promise soon to resolve!) and became reunited with Bev, Winda and Paul Same (Winky Man).

DUCK IN HOT WATER

Normalcy, right? Wrong. Seems even a simple shopping trip leads these days to flying carpets, magic lamps, and... well, *Bagmom* and an Arabian

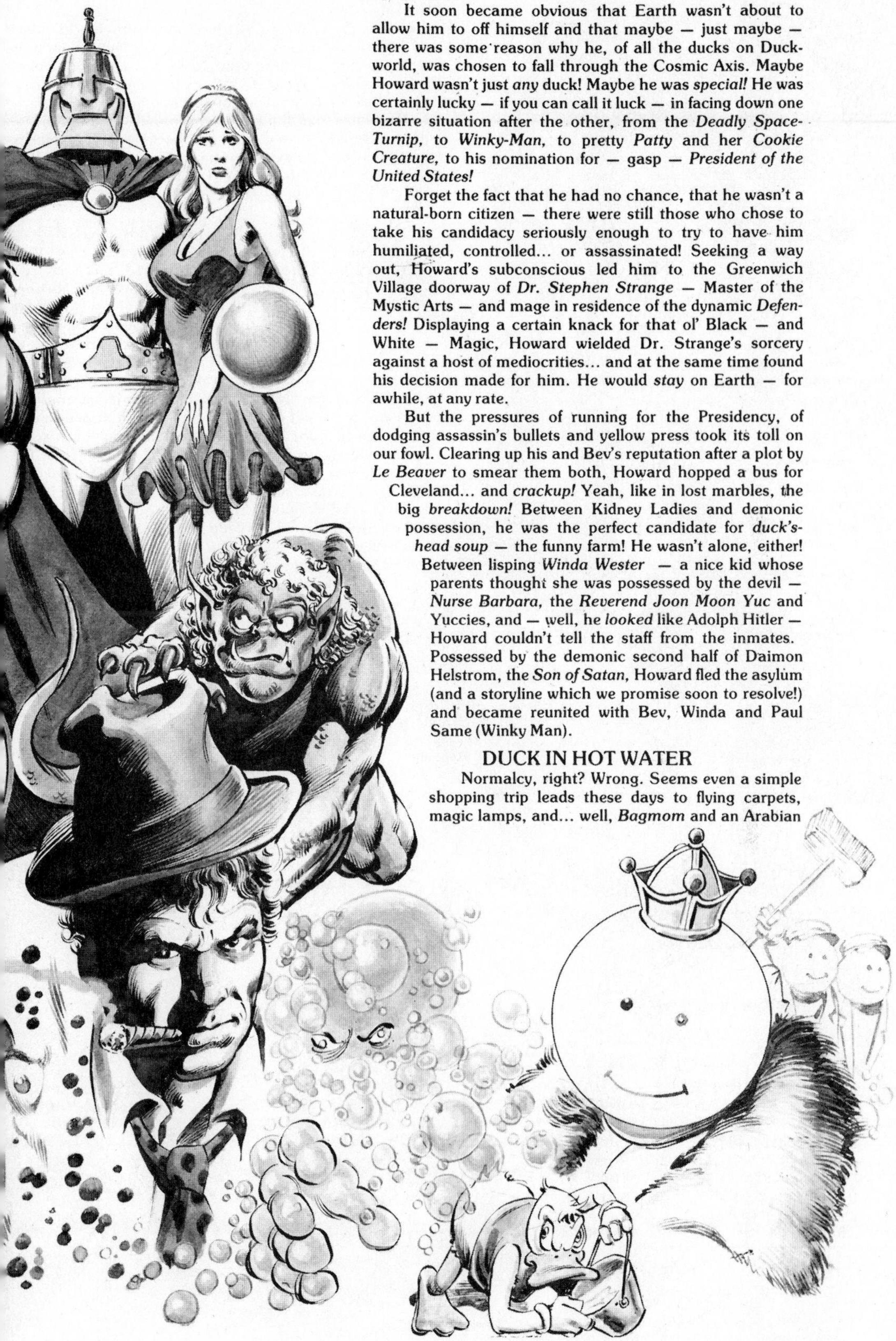

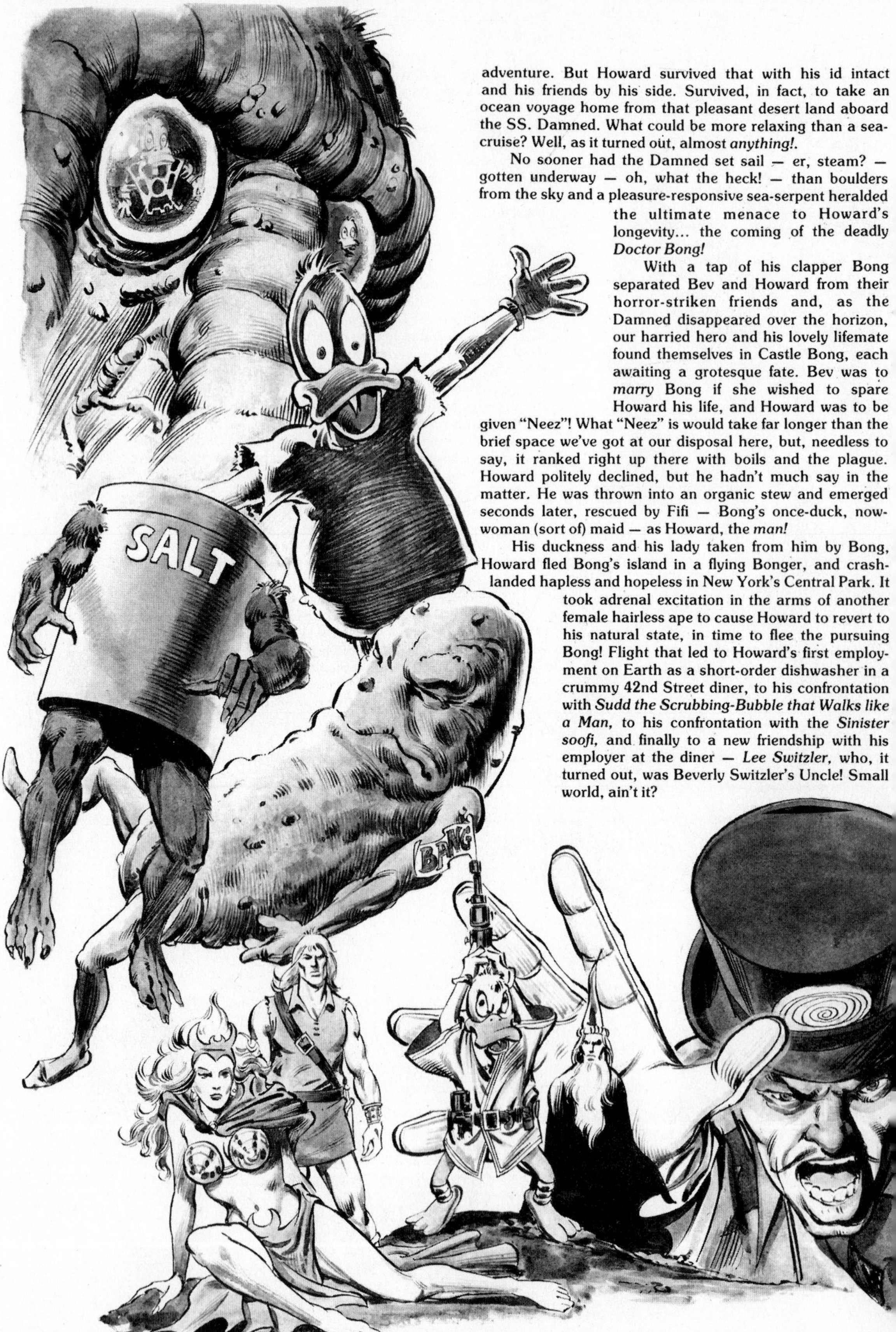
SALT
BANG

adventure. But Howard survived that with his id intact and his friends by his side. Survived, in fact, to take an ocean voyage home from that pleasant desert land aboard the SS. Damned. What could be more relaxing than a sea-cruise? Well, as it turned out, almost *anything!*.

No sooner had the Damned set sail — er, steam? — gotten underway — oh, what the heck! — than boulders from the sky and a pleasure-responsive sea-serpent heralded the ultimate menace to Howard's longevity... the coming of the deadly *Doctor Bong!*

With a tap of his clapper Bong separated Bev and Howard from their horror-striken friends and, as the Damned disappeared over the horizon, our harried hero and his lovely lifemate found themselves in Castle Bong, each awaiting a grotesque fate. Bev was to *marry* Bong if she wished to spare Howard his life, and Howard was to be given "Neez"! What "Neez" is would take far longer than the brief space we've got at our disposal here, but, needless to say, it ranked right up there with boils and the plague. Howard politely declined, but he hadn't much say in the matter. He was thrown into an organic stew and emerged seconds later, rescued by Fifi — Bong's once-duck, now-woman (sort of) maid — as Howard, the *man!*

His duckness and his lady taken from him by Bong, Howard fled Bong's island in a flying Bonger, and crash-landed hapless and hopeless in New York's Central Park. It took adrenal excitation in the arms of another female hairless ape to cause Howard to revert to his natural state, in time to flee the pursuing Bong! Flight that led to Howard's first employment on Earth as a short-order dishwasher in a crummy 42nd Street diner, to his confrontation with *Sudd the Scrubbing-Bubble that Walks like a Man,* to his confrontation with the *Sinister soofi,* and finally to a new friendship with his employer at the diner — *Lee Switzler,* who, it turned out, was Beverly Switzler's Uncle! Small world, ain't it?

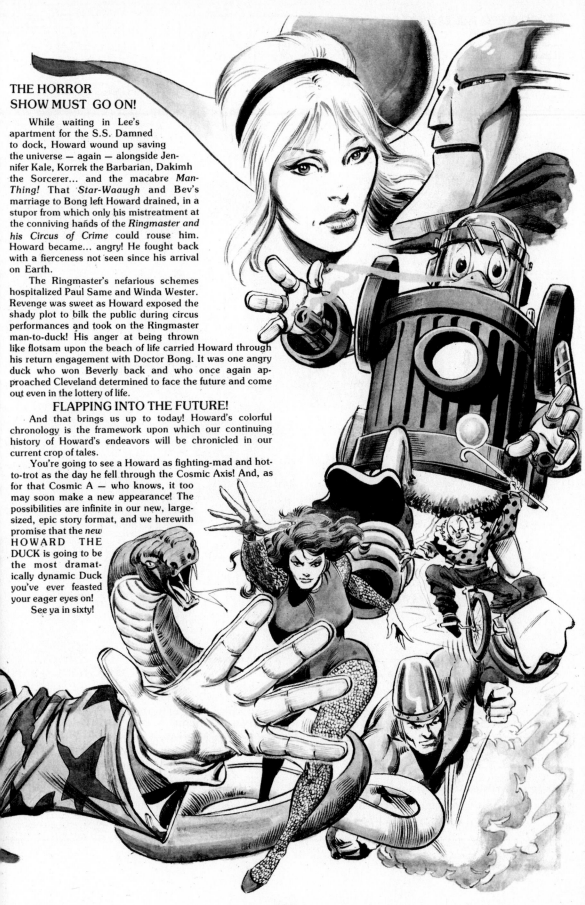

THE HORROR SHOW MUST GO ON!

While waiting in Lee's apartment for the S.S. Damned to dock, Howard wound up saving the universe — again — alongside Jennifer Kale, Korrek the Barbarian, Dakimh the Sorcerer... and the macabre *Man-Thing!* That *Star-Waaugh* and Bev's marriage to Bong left Howard drained, in a stupor from which only his mistreatment at the conniving hands of the *Ringmaster and his Circus of Crime* could rouse him. Howard became... angry! He fought back with a fierceness not seen since his arrival on Earth.

The Ringmaster's nefarious schemes hospitalized Paul Same and Winda Wester. Revenge was sweet as Howard exposed the shady plot to bilk the public during circus performances and took on the Ringmaster man-to-duck! His anger at being thrown like flotsam upon the beach of life carried Howard through his return engagement with Doctor Bong. It was one angry duck who won Beverly back and who once again approached Cleveland determined to face the future and come out even in the lottery of life.

FLAPPING INTO THE FUTURE!

And that brings us up to today! Howard's colorful chronology is the framework upon which our continuing history of Howard's endeavors will be chronicled in our current crop of tales.

You're going to see a Howard as fighting-mad and hot-to-trot as the day he fell through the Cosmic Axis! And, as for that Cosmic A — who knows, it too may soon make a new appearance! The possibilities are infinite in our new, large-sized, epic story format, and we herewith promise that the *new* HOWARD THE DUCK is going to be the most dramatically dynamic Duck you've ever feasted your eager eyes on!

See ya in sixty!

COMING AQUACKTIONS

PLAYDUCK featuring HOWARD THE DUCK

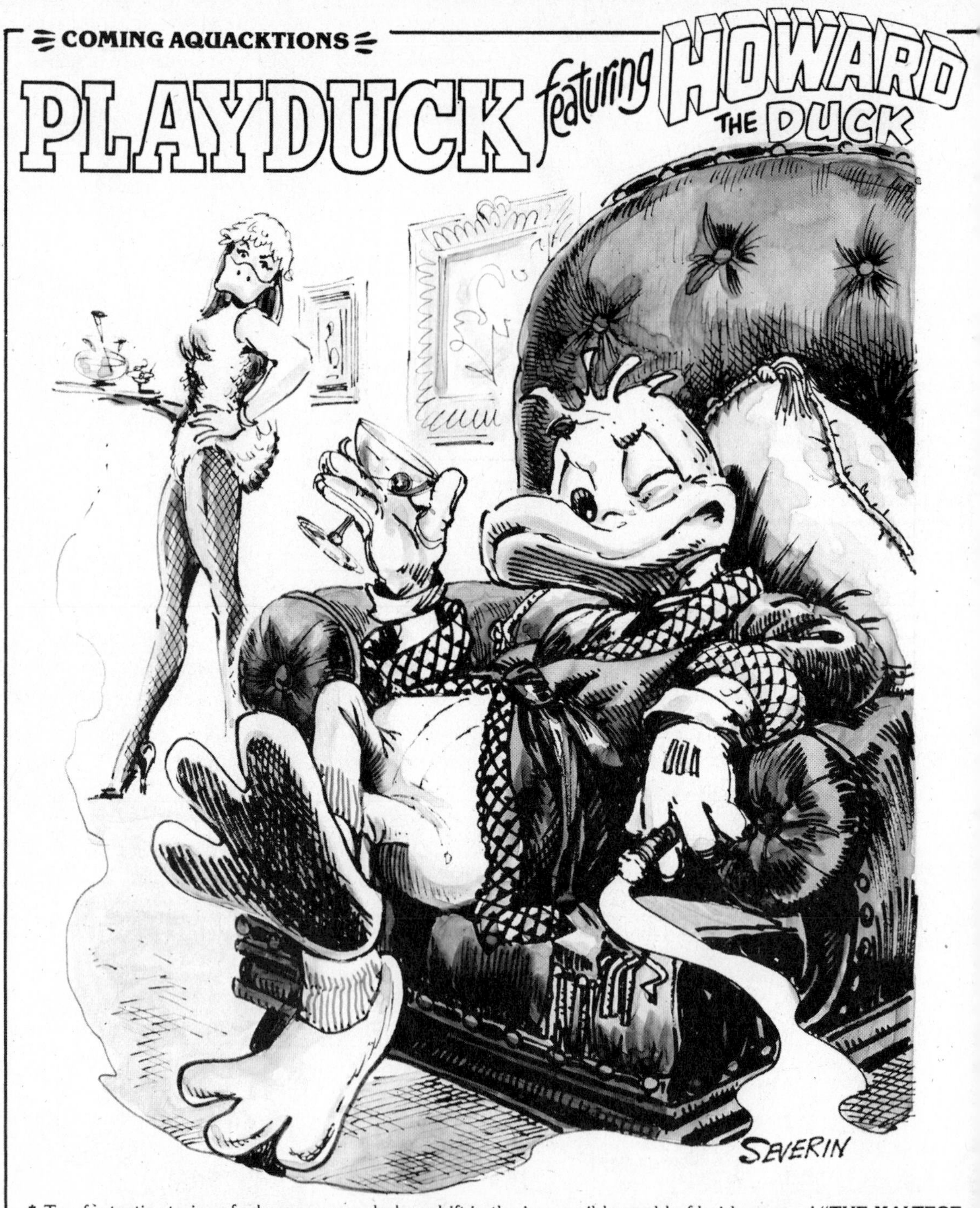
SEVERIN

* Two fantastic stories of a brave young drake adrift in the impossible world of hairless apes! **"THE MALTESE COCKROACH"** and **"THE DREADCLIFF CUCKOOS,"** both by **DUCKBILL MANTLO!**
* The **PLAYDUCK** interview with **TRUMAN CAPOULTRY,** author of the hard-hitting examination of the religious cult, the WACcies, and it's beginning in the disappearance of HOWARD X (last name unknown), **"DUCKING OUT: THE STRANGE DISAPPEARANCE OF THE DUCK NAMED HOWARD."** By **MARK GRUENWAUGH.**
* **"PRISONER OF DUCKS,"** the first installment of the shocker by **NORMAN MALLARD.**
* **DUCKMATE** of the MONTH, Ms **AMY QUACKTON!**
* And don't miss these regular **PLAYDUCK** features— **PLAYBILL** and **THE PLAYDUCK ADVISOR**

Issue #4 On Sale February 15th

WAUUGH

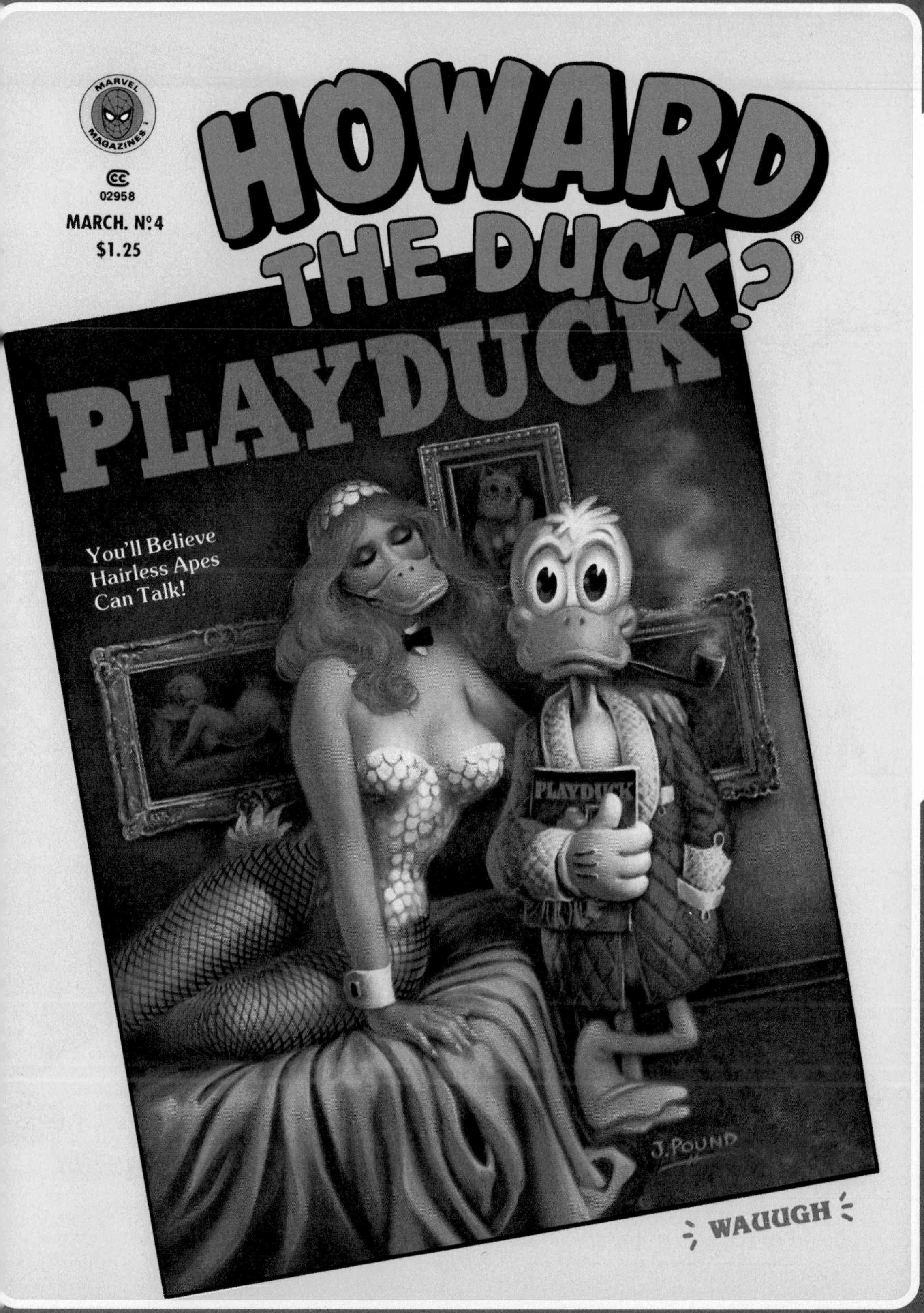
MARVEL MAGAZINES
CC
02958
MARCH. Nº4
$1.25
HOWARD THE DUCK?®
PLAYDUCK
You'll Believe Hairless Apes Can Talk!
PLAYDUCK
J. POUND
WAUUGH

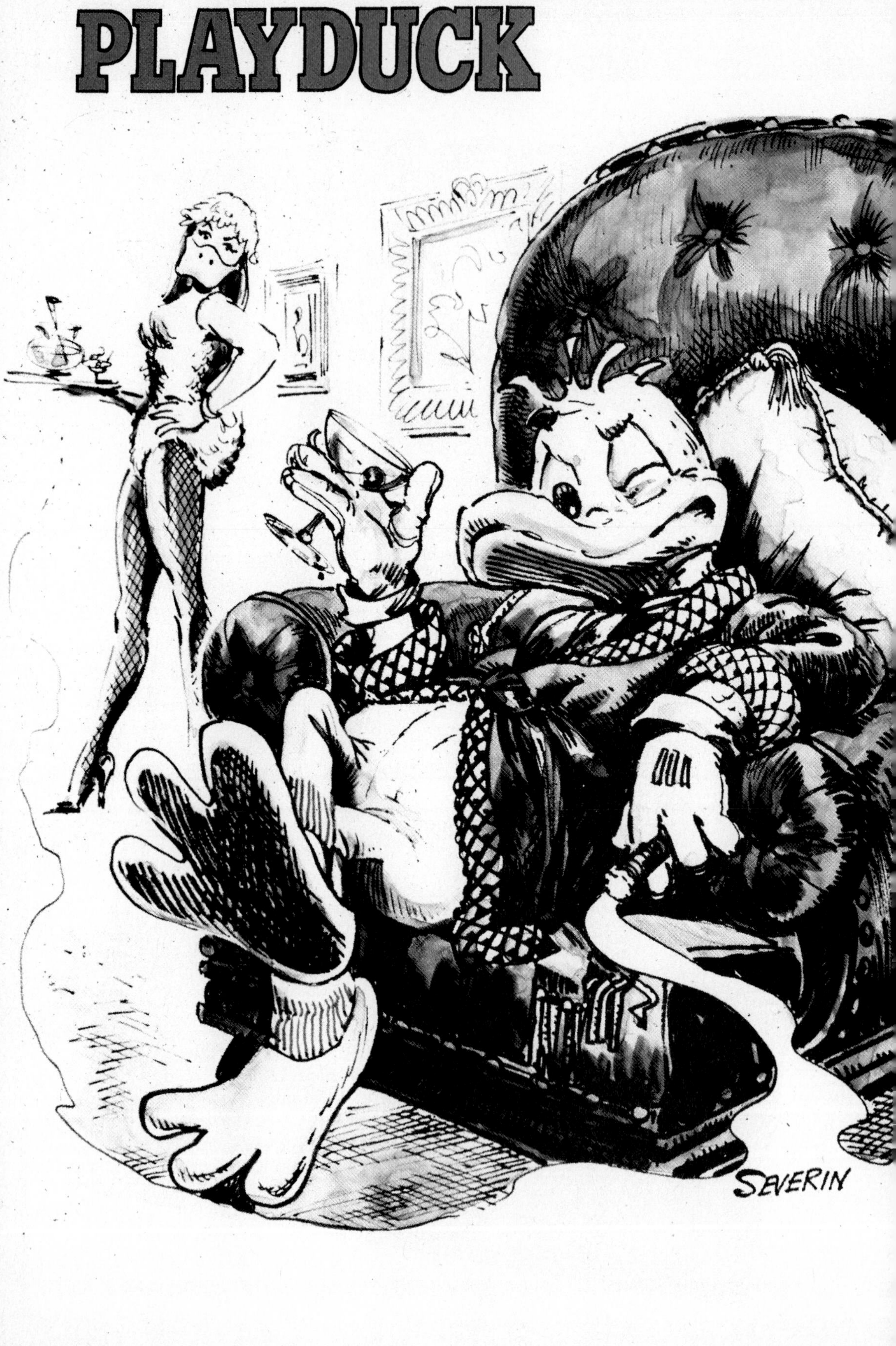
PLAYDUCK
SEVERIN

STAN LEE Presents:

HOWARD THE DUCK

Volume 1 No. 4   March. 1980

JIM SHOOTER Editor-in-Chief • LYNN GRAEME Editor • RALPH MACCHIO Associate Editor
MARK GRUENWALD Insulting Editor • ROY THOMAS Consulting Editor
MILTON SCHIFFMAN V.P. Production • NORA MACLIN Design Director
JOE ROSEN, MICHAEL HIGGINS, IRVING WATANABE Letterers
DAVIDA LICHTER-DALE, ELIOT BROWN, JOHN TARTAGLIONE, ROB CAROSELLA, ED NORTON,
ROGER STERN, CARL GAFFORD, DANNY CRESPI, MARIE SEVERIN, Staff & Such
Spot Illustrations: **NED SONNTAG & MARIE SEVERIN**
Frontispiece by MARIE SEVERIN Cover by JOHN POUND

CONTENTS

EDITORIAL

Dear Reader:

In this issue we examine the success of our sister magazine, HOWARD THE DUCK, which is based, as I'm sure you all know by now, on the disappearance of a fellow fowl, and the imaginative speculations about the subsequent whereabouts and activities (if any) of this enigmatic character.

From the inception of the HOWARD THE DUCK magazine public response has been enthusiastic and divided. Is the HOWARD cult, WAKKie, a sincere religion? An outrageous farce engaged in duping the dopes? Or is it just a fad that will quickly fade away? And what of Truman Capoultry's claims to "psychic" knowledge of the circumstances of Howard's current existence? Because of this and many other questions — and because we had to fill an issue up real fast — we decided to mount a serious inquiry into this matter. We leave it to you, the reader, to wade between fact and fable.

In addition to the HOWARD material we include your favorite PLAYDUCK features: the DUCKMATE, of course, without which no PLAYDUCK issue would be worthy of the name; the REVIEW; the ADVISER; and the WISE QUACKS letters column.

As winter begins drawing to the end of its cycle and molting season approaches it is, as always, a time for reflection.

Reflect well on the lessons to be learned from the HOWARD THE DUCK phenomenon. Perhaps we all are "trapped in a world we never made" because we have neglected to interact positively enough with our fellow creatures, neglected to take responsibility for our society.

Think on it.

Meanwhile, there's the next PLAYDUCK issue to look forward to, an issue that will reprint that always popular item, THE PLAYDUCK BILLOSOPHER!

WAUK

Graeme Quacker

ONLY "WHEEZATON" TURNS OUT CHAMPIONS LIKE THESE!

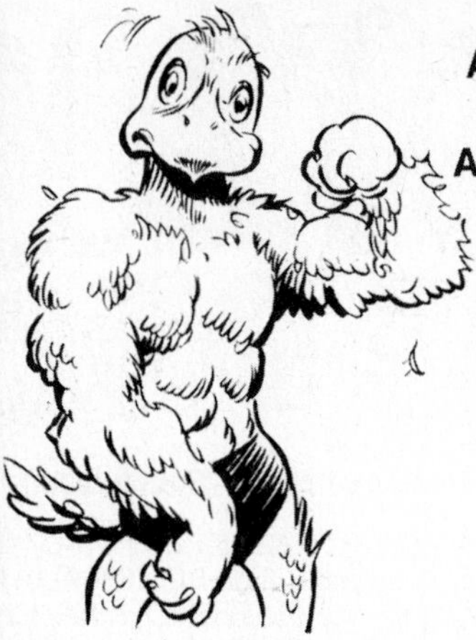

ADD 3 INCHES TO YOUR ARMS — — FAST!

ADD 5 INCHES TO YOUR CHEST — — FAST!

ADD 1 INCH TO YOUR BEAK — — FAST!

WITH *WHEEZATON!*

This is no antiquated system like the one offered by Lido — or the outdated course Celestial is trying to sell for $40!

Bill Web, '79:
"Mr. New Stork:"
"I never believed I could gain any real muscle because of my short size (1') — until I tried "WHEEZATON!"

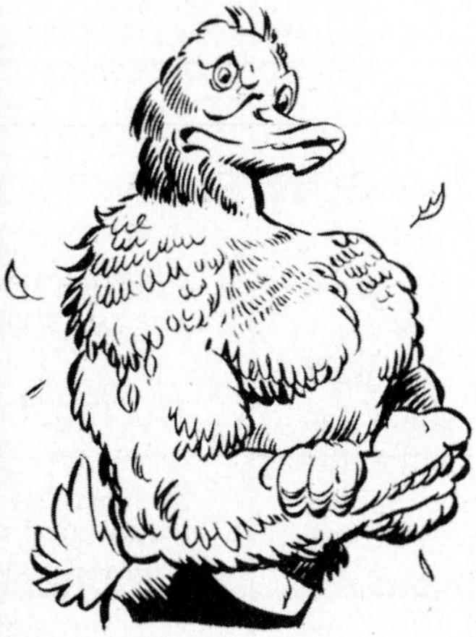

WHEEZATON is an amazing new system offering the most modern, fastest-working muscle building techniques ever discovered!
Just three seconds — yes, that's three seconds — a day and you can become the drake you've always wanted to be!

Qak Quill, '78 "Mr. Wow:"
"WHEEZATON" really persuades muscles to grow!"

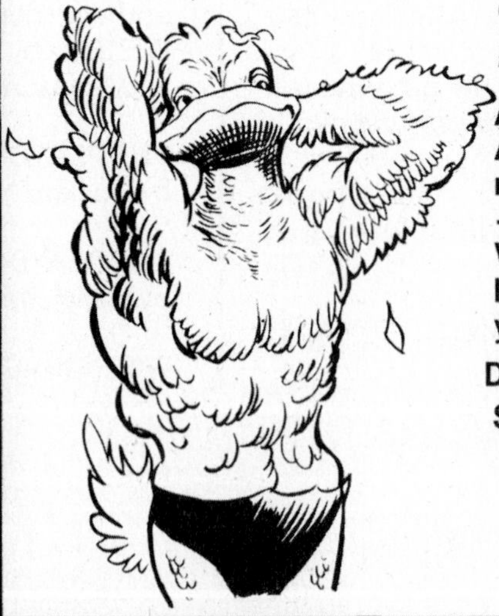

Are you fat? WHEEZATON turns that soft mushy flab into muscle —FAST! Are you skinny? WHEEZATON packs healthy, solid pounds on your frame — FAST!

DON'T WASTE ANY TIME! SEND FOR *WHEEZATON* TODAY!

Harold Brruk, '78 "Mr. New Stork:"
"Worth 100 times the price!"

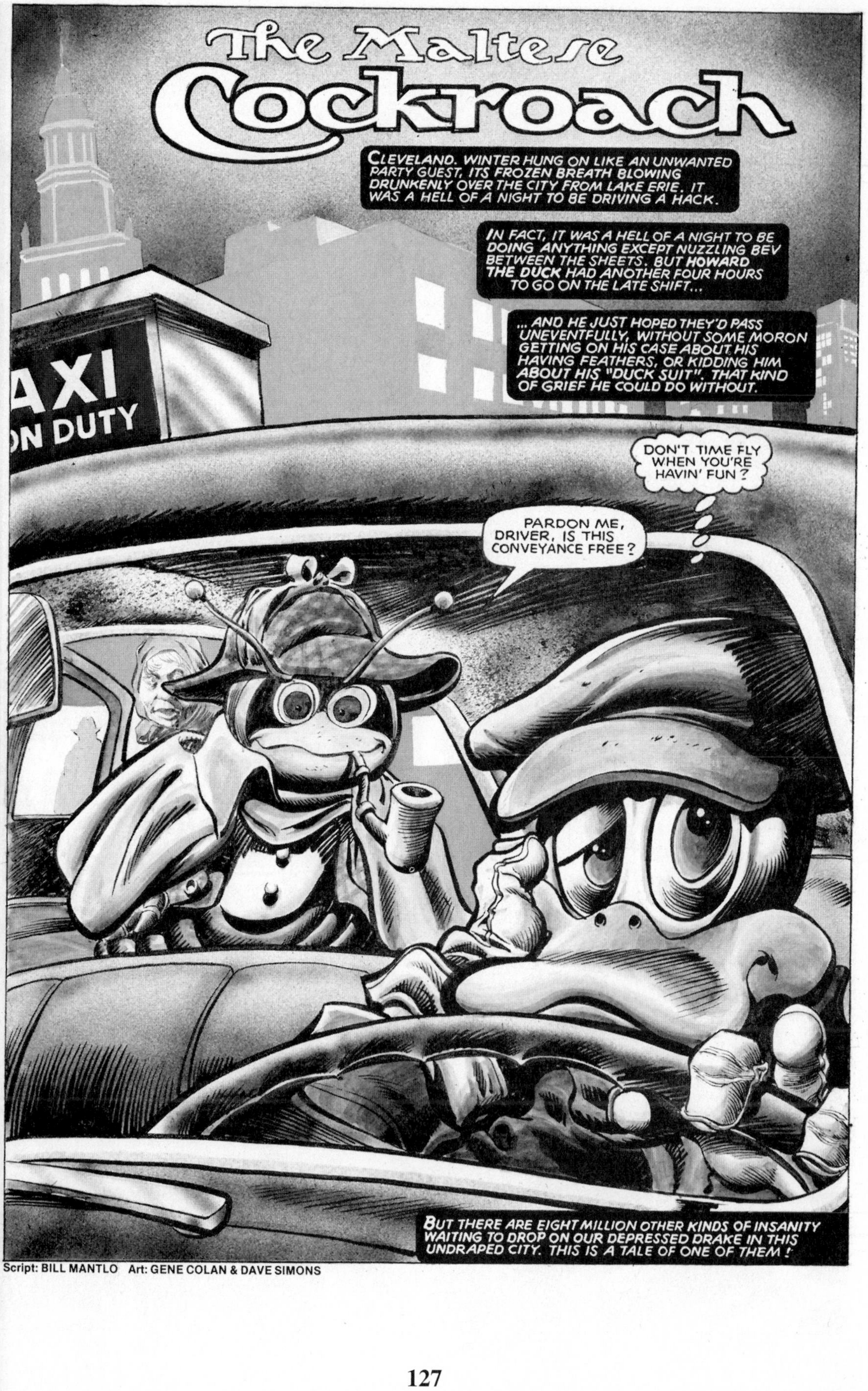
The Maltese Cockroach
CLEVELAND. WINTER HUNG ON LIKE AN UNWANTED PARTY GUEST, ITS FROZEN BREATH BLOWING DRUNKENLY OVER THE CITY FROM LAKE ERIE. IT WAS A HELL OF A NIGHT TO BE DRIVING A HACK.
IN FACT, IT WAS A HELL OF A NIGHT TO BE DOING ANYTHING EXCEPT NUZZLING BEV BETWEEN THE SHEETS. BUT HOWARD THE DUCK HAD ANOTHER FOUR HOURS TO GO ON THE LATE SHIFT...
... AND HE JUST HOPED THEY'D PASS UNEVENTFULLY, WITHOUT SOME MORON GETTING ON HIS CASE ABOUT HIS HAVING FEATHERS, OR KIDDING HIM ABOUT HIS "DUCK SUIT". THAT KIND OF GRIEF HE COULD DO WITHOUT.
AXI
ON DUTY
DON'T TIME FLY WHEN YOU'RE HAVIN' FUN?
PARDON ME, DRIVER, IS THIS CONVEYANCE FREE?
BUT THERE ARE EIGHT MILLION OTHER KINDS OF INSANITY WAITING TO DROP ON OUR DEPRESSED DRAKE IN THIS UNDRAPED CITY. THIS IS A TALE OF ONE OF THEM!
Script: BILL MANTLO Art: GENE COLAN & DAVE SIMONS

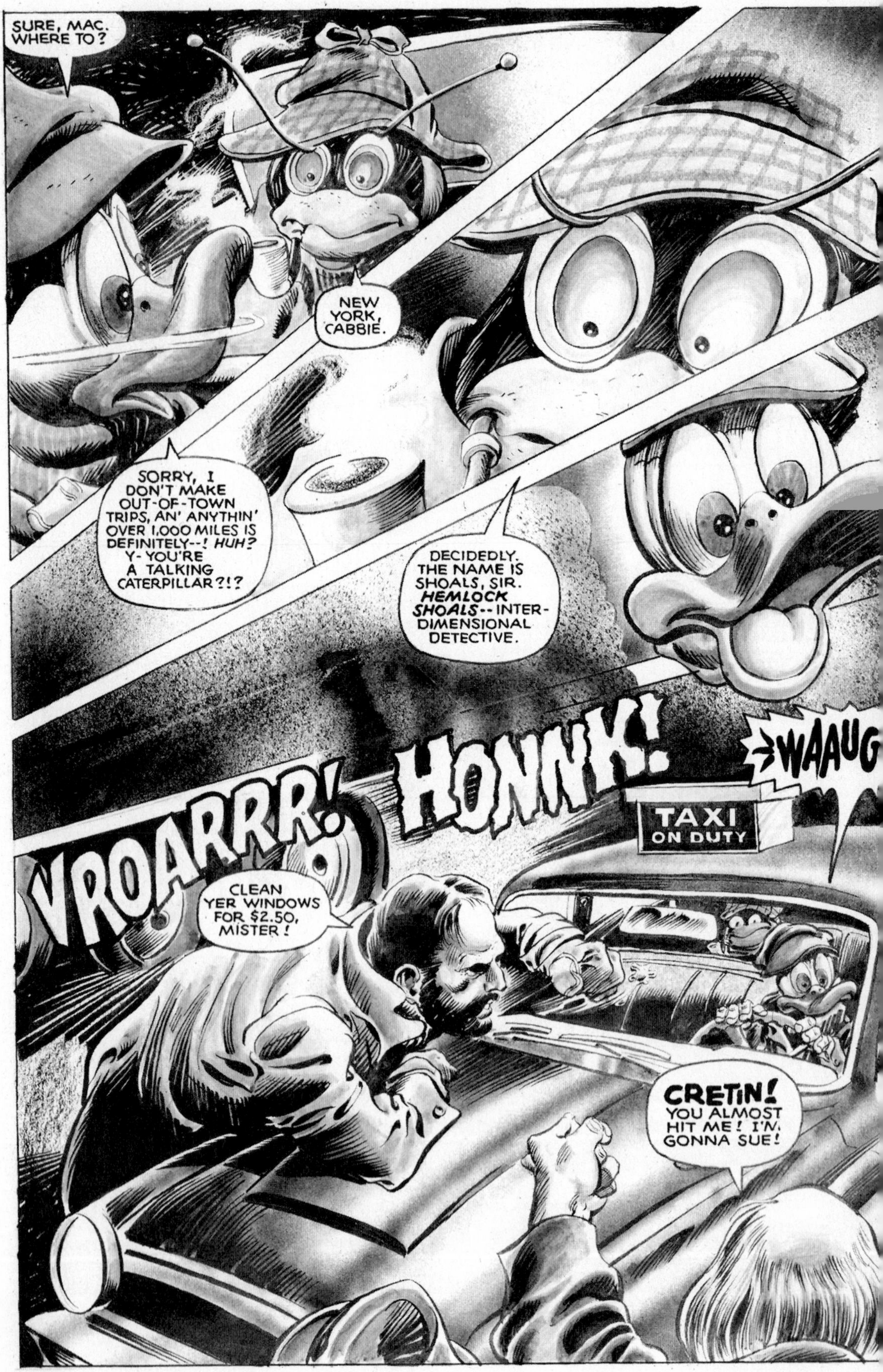
SURE, MAC. WHERE TO?
NEW YORK, CABBIE.
SORRY, I DON'T MAKE OUT-OF-TOWN TRIPS, AN' ANYTHIN' OVER 1,000 MILES IS DEFINITELY--! HUH? Y-YOU'RE A TALKING CATERPILLAR?!?
DECIDEDLY. THE NAME IS SHOALS, SIR. HEMLOCK SHOALS--INTER-DIMENSIONAL DETECTIVE.
VROARRR!
HONNK!
WAAUG
TAXI ON DUTY
CLEAN YER WINDOWS FOR $2.50, MISTER!
CRETIN! YOU ALMOST HIT ME! I'M GONNA SUE!

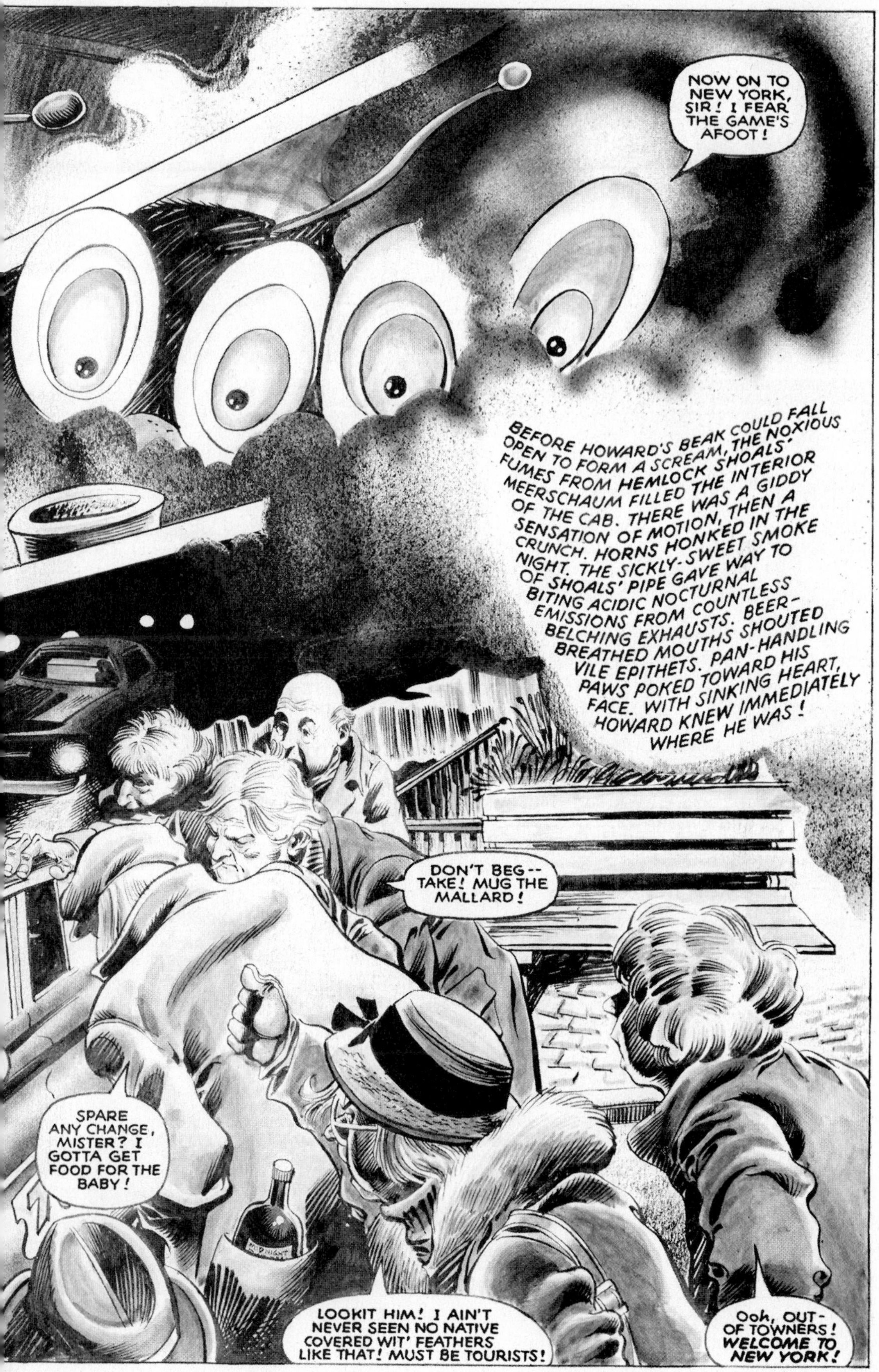
NOW ON TO NEW YORK, SIR! I FEAR THE GAME'S AFOOT!
BEFORE HOWARD'S BEAK COULD FALL OPEN TO FORM A SCREAM, THE NOXIOUS FUMES FROM HEMLOCK SHOALS' MEERSCHAUM FILLED THE INTERIOR OF THE CAB. THERE WAS A GIDDY SENSATION OF MOTION, THEN A CRUNCH. HORNS HONKED IN THE NIGHT. THE SICKLY-SWEET SMOKE OF SHOALS' PIPE GAVE WAY TO BITING ACIDIC NOCTURNAL EMISSIONS FROM COUNTLESS BELCHING EXHAUSTS. BEER-BREATHED MOUTHS SHOUTED VILE EPITHETS. PAN-HANDLING PAWS POKED TOWARD HIS FACE. WITH SINKING HEART, HOWARD KNEW IMMEDIATELY WHERE HE WAS!
DON'T BEG-- TAKE! MUG THE MALLARD!
SPARE ANY CHANGE, MISTER? I GOTTA GET FOOD FOR THE BABY!
LOOKIT HIM! I AIN'T NEVER SEEN NO NATIVE COVERED WIT' FEATHERS LIKE THAT! MUST BE TOURISTS!
Ooh, OUT-OF TOWNERS! WELCOME TO NEW YORK!

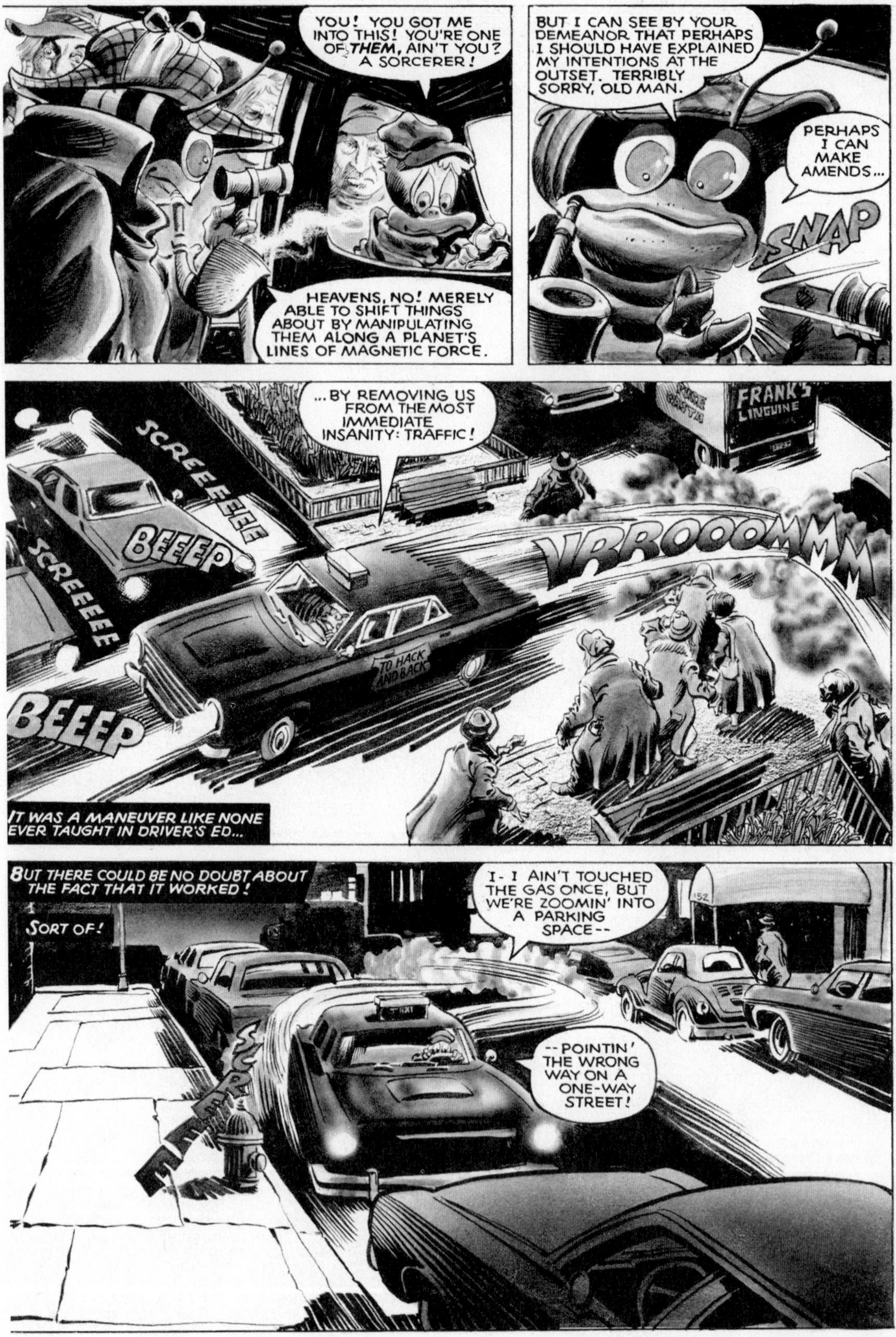
YOU! YOU GOT ME INTO THIS! YOU'RE ONE OF THEM, AIN'T YOU? A SORCERER!
HEAVENS, NO! MERELY ABLE TO SHIFT THINGS ABOUT BY MANIPULATING THEM ALONG A PLANET'S LINES OF MAGNETIC FORCE.
BUT I CAN SEE BY YOUR DEMEANOR THAT PERHAPS I SHOULD HAVE EXPLAINED MY INTENTIONS AT THE OUTSET. TERRIBLY SORRY, OLD MAN.
PERHAPS I CAN MAKE AMENDS...
SNAP
...BY REMOVING US FROM THE MOST IMMEDIATE INSANITY: TRAFFIC!
FRANK'S LINGUINE
SCREEEEEEE
BEEEP
SCREEEEEE
VRROOOOMMM
TO HACK AND BACK
BEEEP
IT WAS A MANEUVER LIKE NONE EVER TAUGHT IN DRIVER'S ED...
BUT THERE COULD BE NO DOUBT ABOUT THE FACT THAT IT WORKED!
SORT OF!
I- I AIN'T TOUCHED THE GAS ONCE, BUT WE'RE ZOOMIN' INTO A PARKING SPACE--
--POINTIN' THE WRONG WAY ON A ONE-WAY STREET!

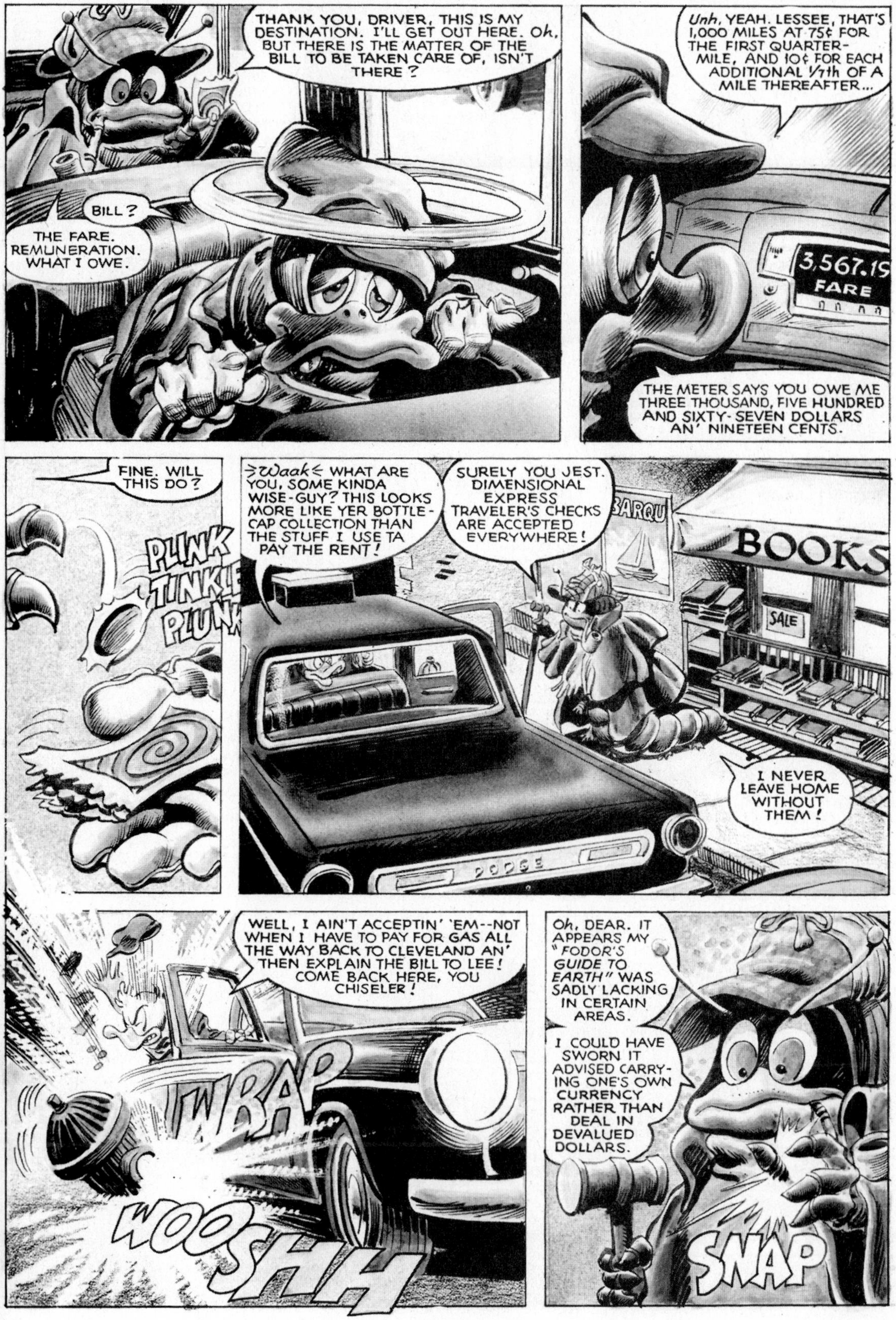
THANK YOU, DRIVER, THIS IS MY DESTINATION. I'LL GET OUT HERE. Oh, BUT THERE IS THE MATTER OF THE BILL TO BE TAKEN CARE OF, ISN'T THERE?
BILL?
THE FARE. REMUNERATION. WHAT I OWE.
Unh, YEAH. LESSEE, THAT'S 1,000 MILES AT 75¢ FOR THE FIRST QUARTER-MILE, AND 10¢ FOR EACH ADDITIONAL 1/7th OF A MILE THEREAFTER...
3,567.19
FARE
THE METER SAYS YOU OWE ME THREE THOUSAND, FIVE HUNDRED AND SIXTY-SEVEN DOLLARS AN' NINETEEN CENTS.
FINE. WILL THIS DO?
PLINK
TINKLE
PLUNK
>Waak< WHAT ARE YOU, SOME KINDA WISE-GUY? THIS LOOKS MORE LIKE YER BOTTLE-CAP COLLECTION THAN THE STUFF I USE TA PAY THE RENT!
SURELY YOU JEST. DIMENSIONAL EXPRESS TRAVELER'S CHECKS ARE ACCEPTED EVERYWHERE!
BARQU
BOOKS
SALE
I NEVER LEAVE HOME WITHOUT THEM!
DODGE
WELL, I AIN'T ACCEPTIN' 'EM--NOT WHEN I HAVE TO PAY FOR GAS ALL THE WAY BACK TO CLEVELAND AN' THEN EXPLAIN THE BILL TO LEE! COME BACK HERE, YOU CHISELER!
WRAP
WOOSHH
Oh, DEAR. IT APPEARS MY "FODOR'S GUIDE TO EARTH" WAS SADLY LACKING IN CERTAIN AREAS.
I COULD HAVE SWORN IT ADVISED CARRYING ONE'S OWN CURRENCY RATHER THAN DEAL IN DEVALUED DOLLARS.
SNAP

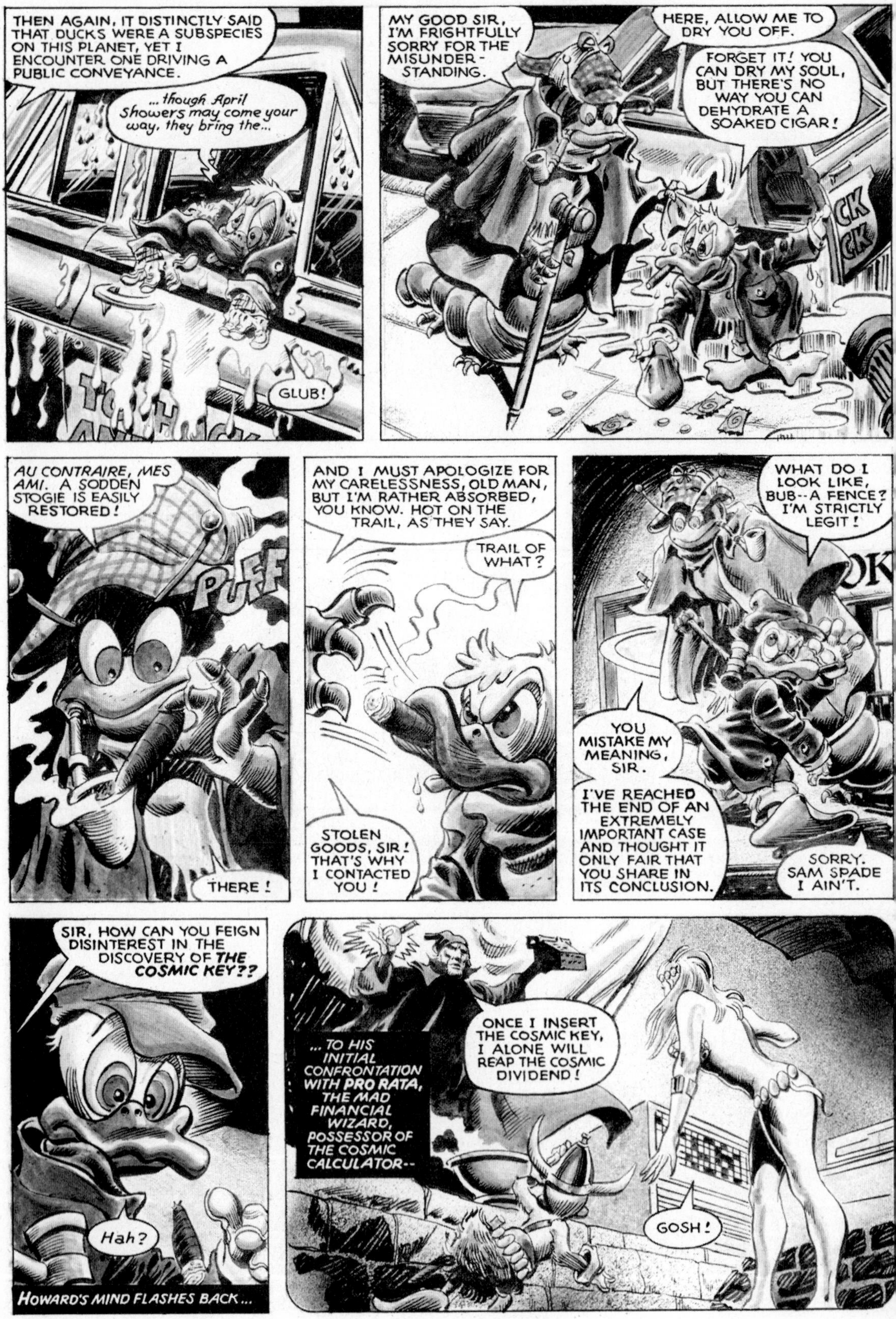
THEN AGAIN, IT DISTINCTLY SAID THAT DUCKS WERE A SUBSPECIES ON THIS PLANET, YET I ENCOUNTER ONE DRIVING A PUBLIC CONVEYANCE.
...though April Showers may come your way, they bring the...
GLUB!
MY GOOD SIR, I'M FRIGHTFULLY SORRY FOR THE MISUNDER-STANDING.
HERE, ALLOW ME TO DRY YOU OFF.
FORGET IT! YOU CAN DRY MY SOUL, BUT THERE'S NO WAY YOU CAN DEHYDRATE A SOAKED CIGAR!
AU CONTRAIRE, MES AMI. A SODDEN STOGIE IS EASILY RESTORED!
PUFF
THERE!
AND I MUST APOLOGIZE FOR MY CARELESSNESS, OLD MAN, BUT I'M RATHER ABSORBED, YOU KNOW. HOT ON THE TRAIL, AS THEY SAY.
TRAIL OF WHAT?
STOLEN GOODS, SIR! THAT'S WHY I CONTACTED YOU!
WHAT DO I LOOK LIKE, BUB--A FENCE? I'M STRICTLY LEGIT!
YOU MISTAKE MY MEANING, SIR.
I'VE REACHED THE END OF AN EXTREMELY IMPORTANT CASE AND THOUGHT IT ONLY FAIR THAT YOU SHARE IN ITS CONCLUSION.
SORRY. SAM SPADE I AIN'T.
SIR, HOW CAN YOU FEIGN DISINTEREST IN THE DISCOVERY OF THE COSMIC KEY??
Hah?
HOWARD'S MIND FLASHES BACK...
...TO HIS INITIAL CONFRONTATION WITH PRO RATA, THE MAD FINANCIAL WIZARD, POSSESSOR OF THE COSMIC CALCULATOR--
ONCE I INSERT THE COSMIC KEY, I ALONE WILL REAP THE COSMIC DIVIDEND!
GOSH!

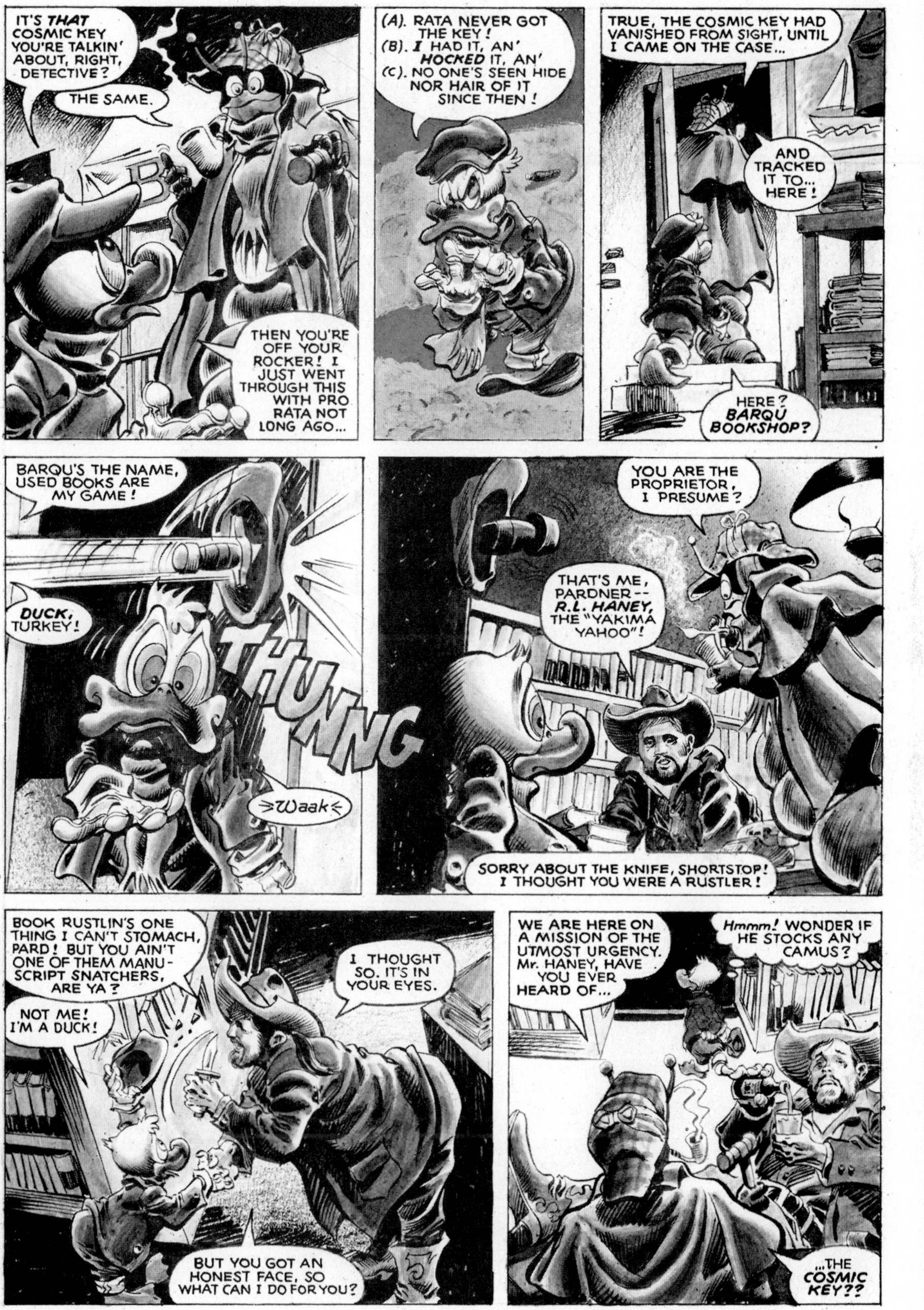
IT'S THAT COSMIC KEY YOU'RE TALKIN' ABOUT, RIGHT, DETECTIVE?
THE SAME.
THEN YOU'RE OFF YOUR ROCKER! I JUST WENT THROUGH THIS WITH PRO RATA NOT LONG AGO...
(A). RATA NEVER GOT THE KEY! (B). I HAD IT, AN' HOCKED IT, AN' (C). NO ONE'S SEEN HIDE NOR HAIR OF IT SINCE THEN!
TRUE, THE COSMIC KEY HAD VANISHED FROM SIGHT, UNTIL I CAME ON THE CASE...
AND TRACKED IT TO... HERE!
HERE? BARQU BOOKSHOP?
BARQU'S THE NAME, USED BOOKS ARE MY GAME!
DUCK, TURKEY!
THUNNG
WAAK
YOU ARE THE PROPRIETOR, I PRESUME?
THAT'S ME, PARDNER-- R.L. HANEY, THE "YAKIMA YAHOO"!
SORRY ABOUT THE KNIFE, SHORTSTOP! I THOUGHT YOU WERE A RUSTLER!
BOOK RUSTLIN'S ONE THING I CAN'T STOMACH, PARD! BUT YOU AIN'T ONE OF THEM MANU-SCRIPT SNATCHERS, ARE YA?
NOT ME! I'M A DUCK!
I THOUGHT SO. IT'S IN YOUR EYES.
BUT YOU GOT AN HONEST FACE, SO WHAT CAN I DO FOR YOU?
WE ARE HERE ON A MISSION OF THE UTMOST URGENCY. Mr. HANEY, HAVE YOU EVER HEARD OF...
Hmmm! WONDER IF HE STOCKS ANY CAMUS?
...THE COSMIC KEY??

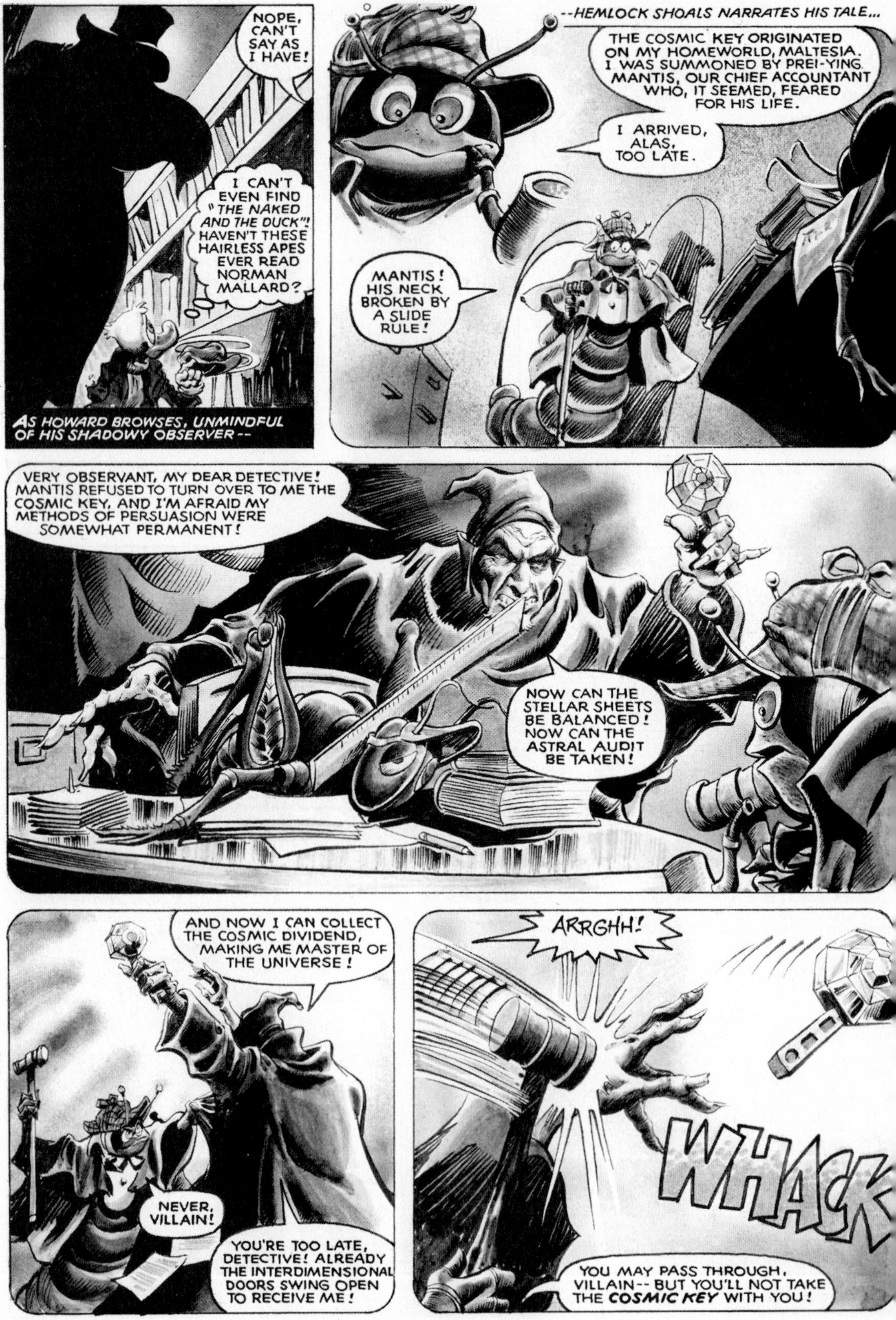
NOPE, CAN'T SAY AS I HAVE!
I CAN'T EVEN FIND "THE NAKED AND THE DUCK"! HAVEN'T THESE HAIRLESS APES EVER READ NORMAN MALLARD?
AS HOWARD BROWSES, UNMINDFUL OF HIS SHADOWY OBSERVER--
--HEMLOCK SHOALS NARRATES HIS TALE...
THE COSMIC KEY ORIGINATED ON MY HOMEWORLD, MALTESIA. I WAS SUMMONED BY PREI-YING MANTIS, OUR CHIEF ACCOUNTANT WHO, IT SEEMED, FEARED FOR HIS LIFE.
I ARRIVED, ALAS, TOO LATE.
MANTIS! HIS NECK BROKEN BY A SLIDE RULE!
VERY OBSERVANT, MY DEAR DETECTIVE! MANTIS REFUSED TO TURN OVER TO ME THE COSMIC KEY, AND I'M AFRAID MY METHODS OF PERSUASION WERE SOMEWHAT PERMANENT!
NOW CAN THE STELLAR SHEETS BE BALANCED! NOW CAN THE ASTRAL AUDIT BE TAKEN!
AND NOW I CAN COLLECT THE COSMIC DIVIDEND, MAKING ME MASTER OF THE UNIVERSE!
NEVER, VILLAIN!
YOU'RE TOO LATE, DETECTIVE! ALREADY THE INTERDIMENSIONAL DOORS SWING OPEN TO RECEIVE ME!
ARRGHH!
WHACK
YOU MAY PASS THROUGH, VILLAIN-- BUT YOU'LL NOT TAKE THE COSMIC KEY WITH YOU!

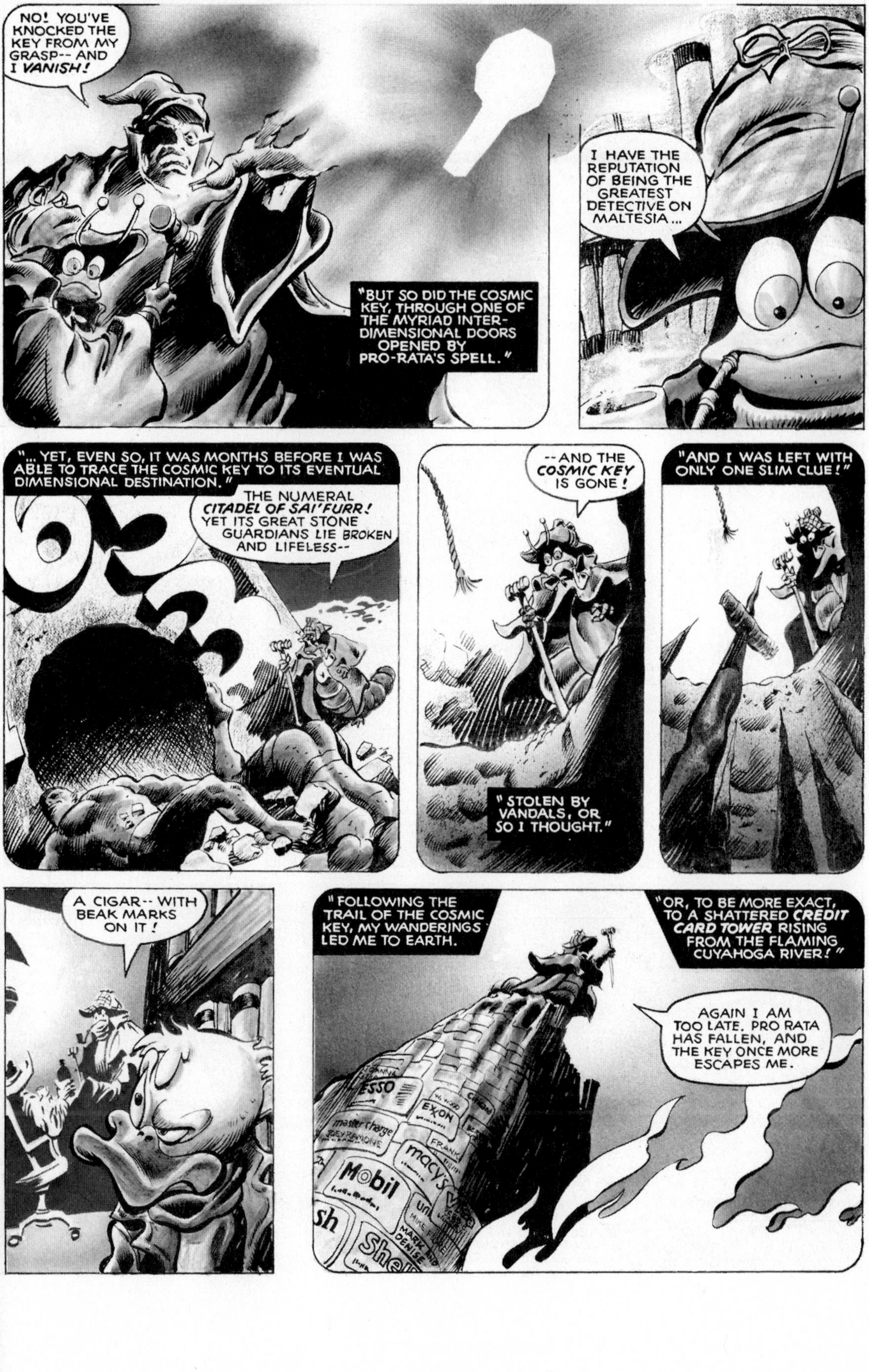
NO! YOU'VE KNOCKED THE KEY FROM MY GRASP-- AND I VANISH!
"BUT SO DID THE COSMIC KEY, THROUGH ONE OF THE MYRIAD INTER-DIMENSIONAL DOORS OPENED BY PRO-RATA'S SPELL."
I HAVE THE REPUTATION OF BEING THE GREATEST DETECTIVE ON MALTESIA...
"...YET, EVEN SO, IT WAS MONTHS BEFORE I WAS ABLE TO TRACE THE COSMIC KEY TO ITS EVENTUAL DIMENSIONAL DESTINATION."
THE NUMERAL CITADEL OF SAI'FURR! YET ITS GREAT STONE GUARDIANS LIE BROKEN AND LIFELESS--
--AND THE COSMIC KEY IS GONE!
"STOLEN BY VANDALS, OR SO I THOUGHT."
"AND I WAS LEFT WITH ONLY ONE SLIM CLUE!"
A CIGAR-- WITH BEAK MARKS ON IT!
"FOLLOWING THE TRAIL OF THE COSMIC KEY, MY WANDERINGS LED ME TO EARTH.
"OR, TO BE MORE EXACT, TO A SHATTERED CREDIT CARD TOWER RISING FROM THE FLAMING CUYAHOGA RIVER!"
AGAIN I AM TOO LATE. PRO RATA HAS FALLEN, AND THE KEY ONCE MORE ESCAPES ME.
ESSO
EXXON
master charge
JOEY RAMONE
macy's
Mobil

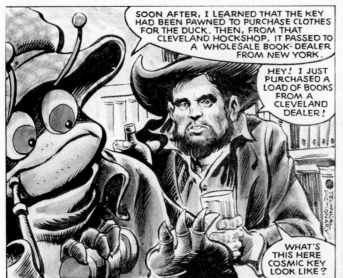

SOON AFTER, I LEARNED THAT THE KEY HAD BEEN PAWNED TO PURCHASE CLOTHES FOR THE DUCK. THEN, FROM THAT CLEVELAND HOCKSHOP, IT PASSED TO A WHOLESALE BOOK-DEALER FROM NEW YORK.

HEY! I JUST PURCHASED A LOAD OF BOOKS FROM A CLEVELAND DEALER!

WHAT'S THIS HERE COSMIC KEY LOOK LIKE?

Oh, SOMETHING LIKE--

SNAP

--THIS!

YEAH, RIGHT! KINDA MULTI-FACETED, WITH A HANDLE!

SHINES LIKE A RAINBOW, THOUGH!

WHILE THE ONE I GOT HERE IN MY DESK IS AS BLACK AS NIGHT!

'COURSE, THAT DON'T MEAN ANYTHING. PEOPLE HAVE TRIED TO DISGUISE THEIR VALUABLES WITH A COAT OF PAINT BEFORE THIS!

SNIK SNIK SNIK!

BUT WHAT GOES ON CAN BE SCRAPED OFF...

EUREKA! IT'S YOUR JEWELLED COSMIC KEY ALL RIGHT, SHOALS!

Huh? IT'S THE GUY WHO WAS LOOKIN' AT BOOKS IN THE BACK ROOM?!

AND IT IS MINE, HUMAN! MINE!

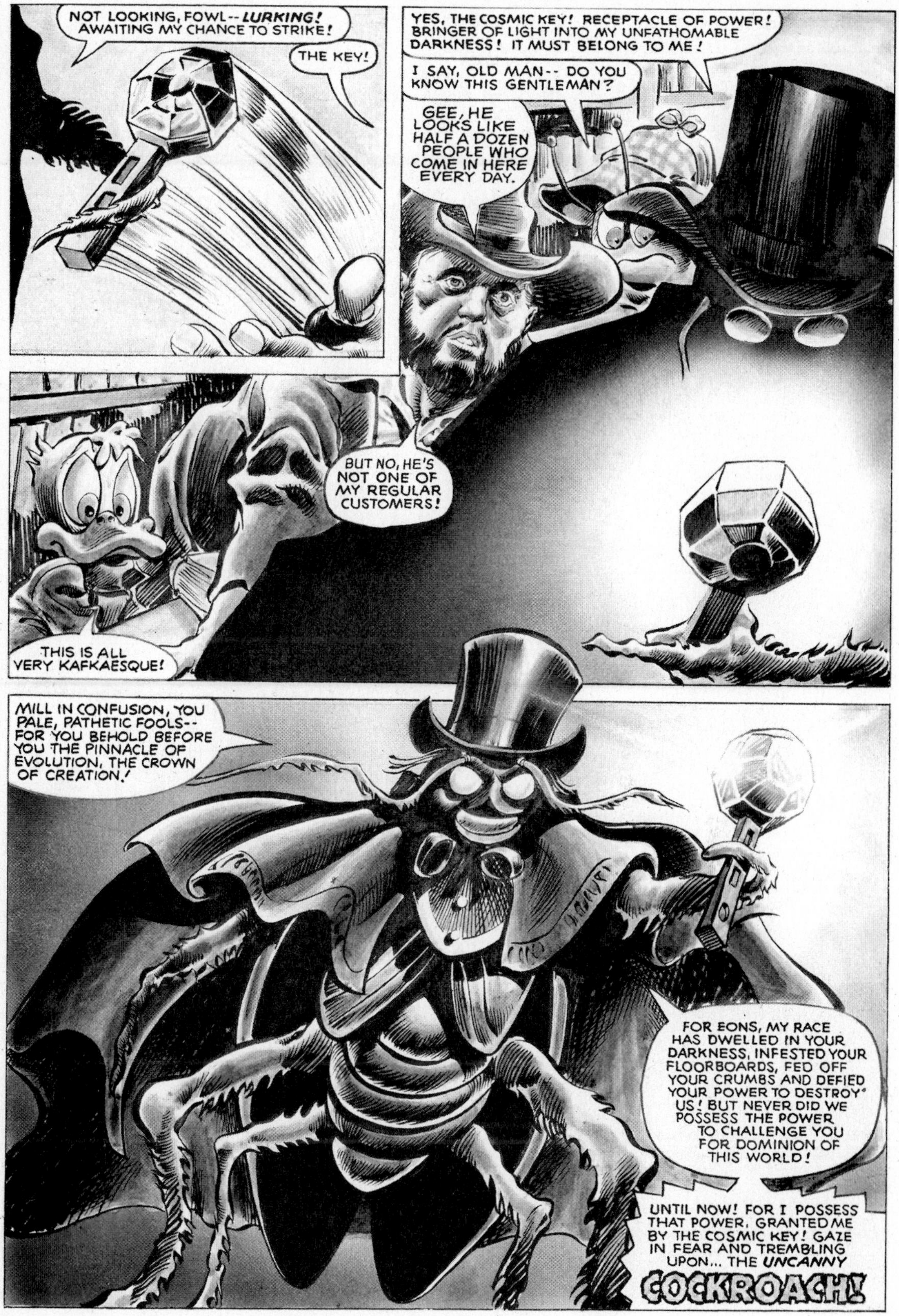
NOT LOOKING, FOWL-- LURKING! AWAITING MY CHANCE TO STRIKE!
THE KEY!
YES, THE COSMIC KEY! RECEPTACLE OF POWER! BRINGER OF LIGHT INTO MY UNFATHOMABLE DARKNESS! IT MUST BELONG TO ME!
I SAY, OLD MAN-- DO YOU KNOW THIS GENTLEMAN?
GEE, HE LOOKS LIKE HALF A DOZEN PEOPLE WHO COME IN HERE EVERY DAY.
BUT NO, HE'S NOT ONE OF MY REGULAR CUSTOMERS!
THIS IS ALL VERY KAFKAESQUE!
MILL IN CONFUSION, YOU PALE, PATHETIC FOOLS-- FOR YOU BEHOLD BEFORE YOU THE PINNACLE OF EVOLUTION, THE CROWN OF CREATION!
FOR EONS, MY RACE HAS DWELLED IN YOUR DARKNESS, INFESTED YOUR FLOORBOARDS, FED OFF YOUR CRUMBS AND DEFIED YOUR POWER TO DESTROY US! BUT NEVER DID WE POSSESS THE POWER TO CHALLENGE YOU FOR DOMINION OF THIS WORLD!
UNTIL NOW! FOR I POSSESS THAT POWER, GRANTED ME BY THE COSMIC KEY! GAZE IN FEAR AND TREMBLING UPON... THE UNCANNY
COCKROACH!

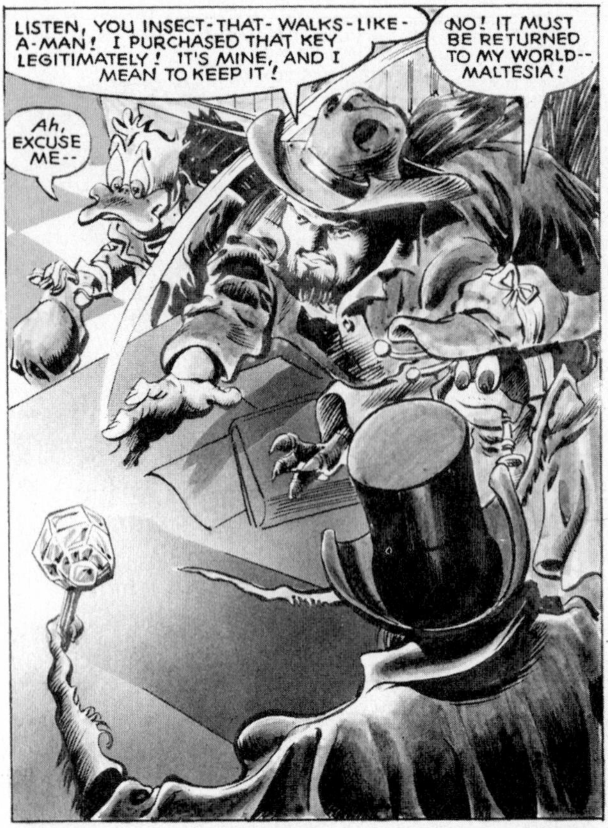
LISTEN, YOU INSECT-THAT-WALKS-LIKE-A-MAN! I PURCHASED THAT KEY LEGITIMATELY! IT'S MINE, AND I MEAN TO KEEP IT!
NO! IT MUST BE RETURNED TO MY WORLD-- MALTESIA!
Ah, EXCUSE ME--

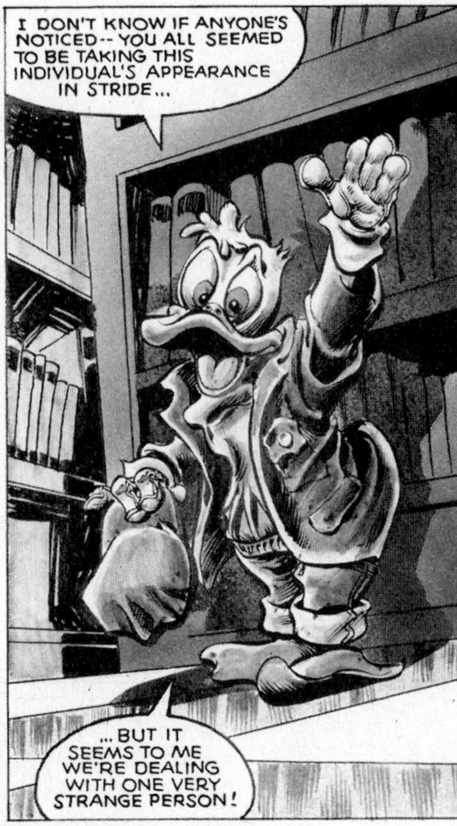
I DON'T KNOW IF ANYONE'S NOTICED-- YOU ALL SEEMED TO BE TAKING THIS INDIVIDUAL'S APPEARANCE IN STRIDE...
...BUT IT SEEMS TO ME WE'RE DEALING WITH ONE VERY STRANGE PERSON!

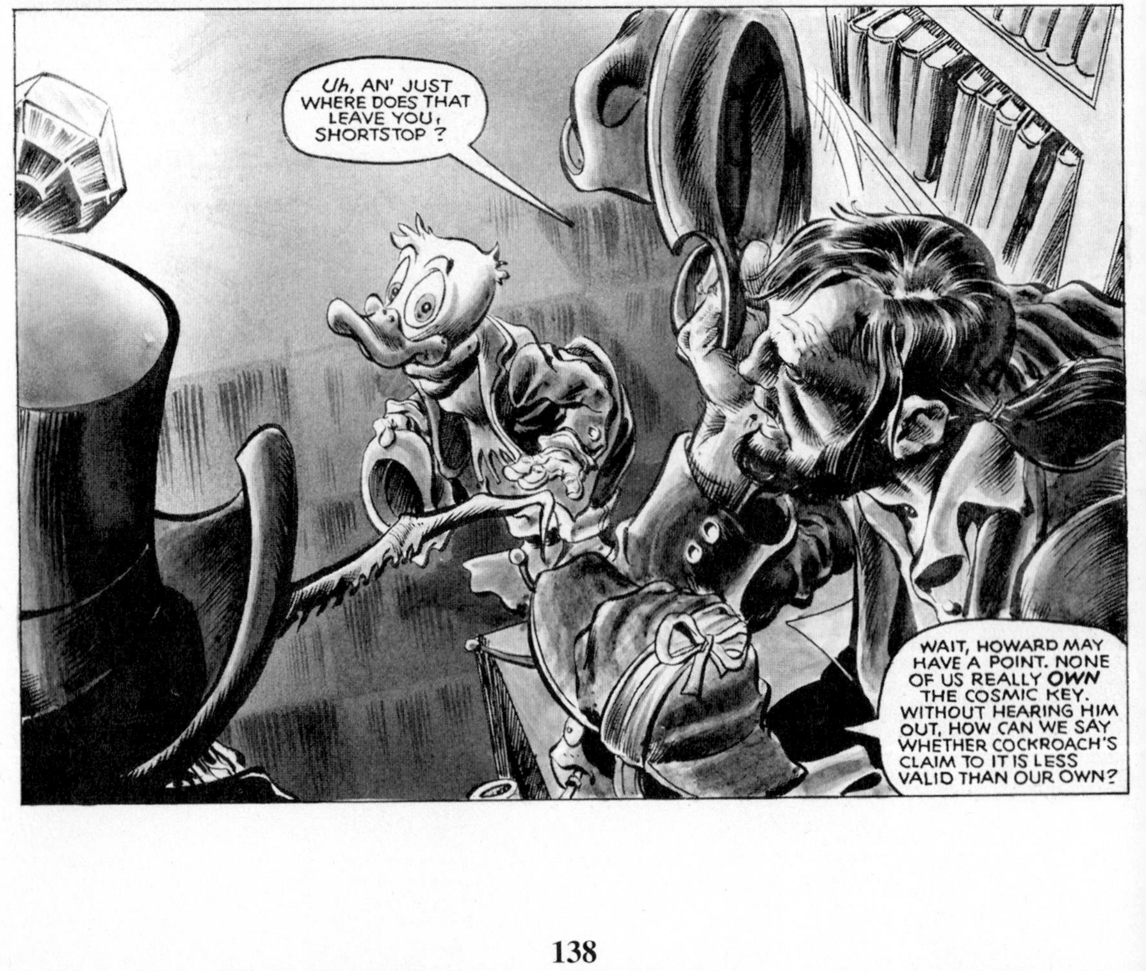
Uh, AN' JUST WHERE DOES THAT LEAVE YOU, SHORTSTOP?
WAIT, HOWARD MAY HAVE A POINT. NONE OF US REALLY OWN THE COSMIC KEY. WITHOUT HEARING HIM OUT, HOW CAN WE SAY WHETHER COCKROACH'S CLAIM TO IT IS LESS VALID THAN OUR OWN?

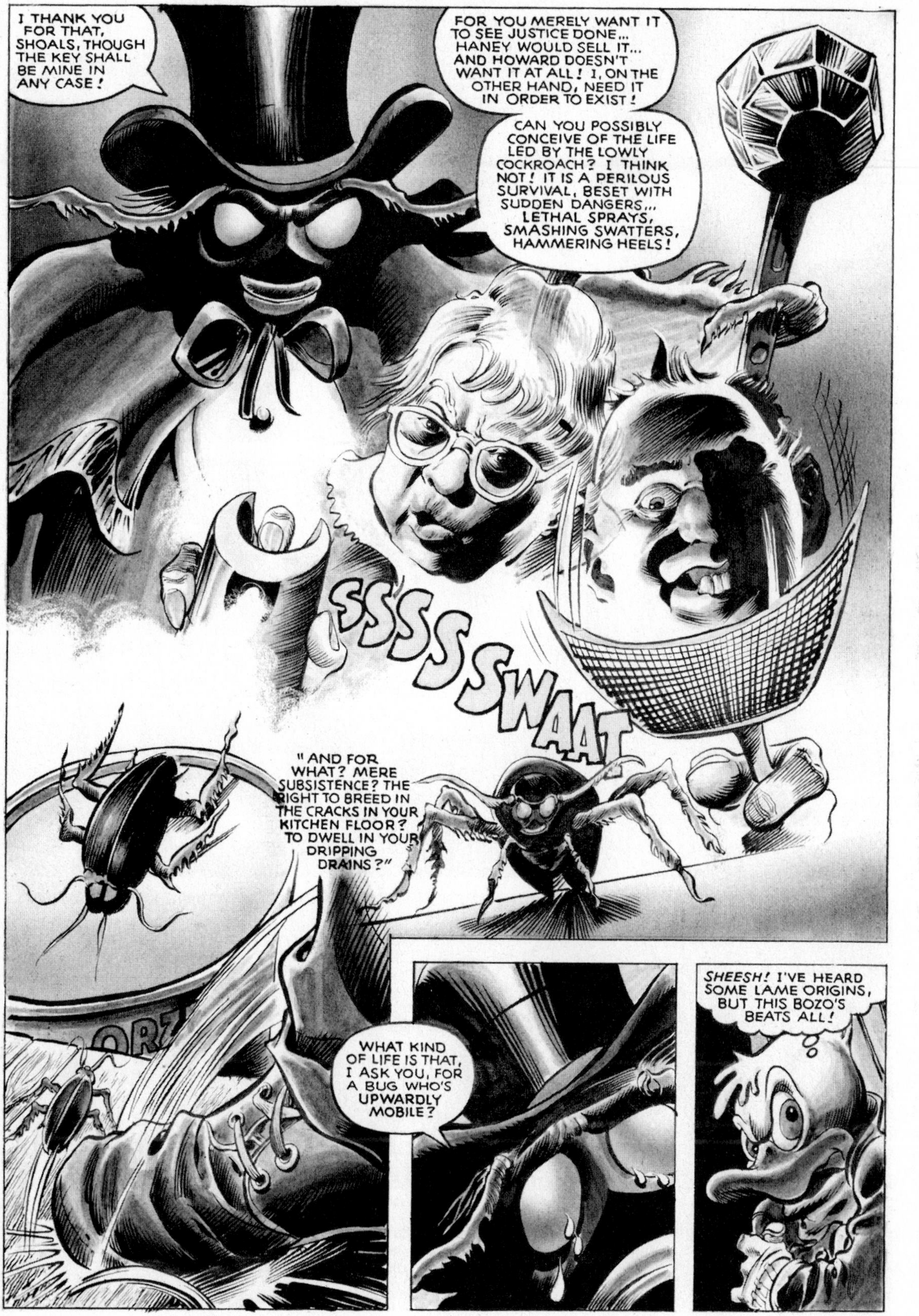
I THANK YOU FOR THAT, SHOALS, THOUGH THE KEY SHALL BE MINE IN ANY CASE!
FOR YOU MERELY WANT IT TO SEE JUSTICE DONE... HANEY WOULD SELL IT... AND HOWARD DOESN'T WANT IT AT ALL! I, ON THE OTHER HAND, NEED IT IN ORDER TO EXIST!
CAN YOU POSSIBLY CONCEIVE OF THE LIFE LED BY THE LOWLY COCKROACH? I THINK NOT! IT IS A PERILOUS SURVIVAL, BESET WITH SUDDEN DANGERS,... LETHAL SPRAYS, SMASHING SWATTERS, HAMMERING HEELS!
SSSSSWAAT
"AND FOR WHAT? MERE SUBSISTENCE? THE RIGHT TO BREED IN THE CRACKS IN YOUR KITCHEN FLOOR? TO DWELL IN YOUR DRIPPING DRAINS?"
WHAT KIND OF LIFE IS THAT, I ASK YOU, FOR A BUG WHO'S UPWARDLY MOBILE?
SHEESH! I'VE HEARD SOME LAME ORIGINS, BUT THIS BOZO'S BEATS ALL!

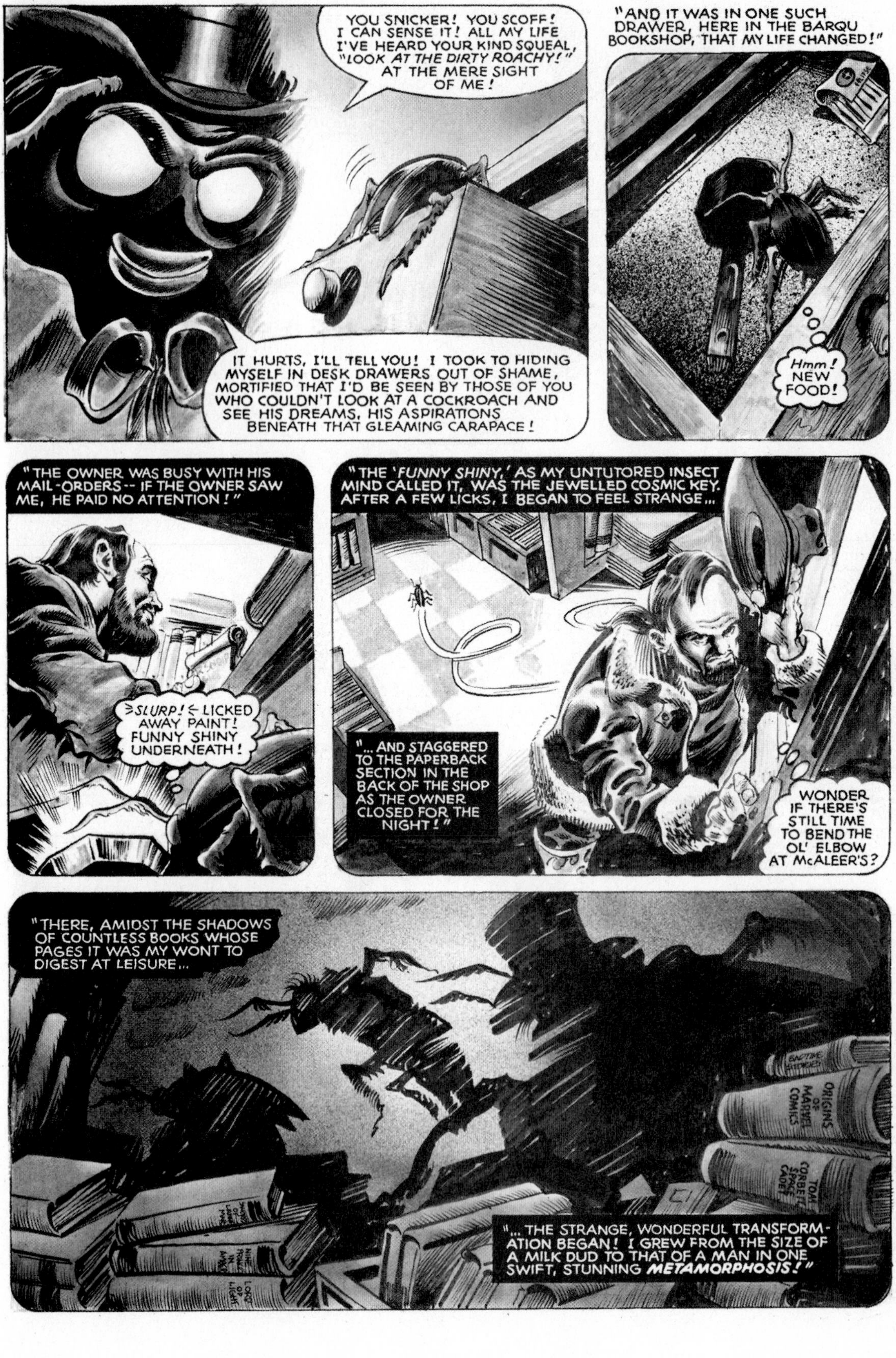
YOU SNICKER! YOU SCOFF! I CAN SENSE IT! ALL MY LIFE I'VE HEARD YOUR KIND SQUEAL, "LOOK AT THE DIRTY ROACHY!" AT THE MERE SIGHT OF ME!
IT HURTS, I'LL TELL YOU! I TOOK TO HIDING MYSELF IN DESK DRAWERS OUT OF SHAME, MORTIFIED THAT I'D BE SEEN BY THOSE OF YOU WHO COULDN'T LOOK AT A COCKROACH AND SEE HIS DREAMS, HIS ASPIRATIONS BENEATH THAT GLEAMING CARAPACE!
"AND IT WAS IN ONE SUCH DRAWER, HERE IN THE BARQU BOOKSHOP, THAT MY LIFE CHANGED!"
Hmm! NEW FOOD!
"THE OWNER WAS BUSY WITH HIS MAIL-ORDERS -- IF THE OWNER SAW ME, HE PAID NO ATTENTION!"
⋝SLURP!⋜ LICKED AWAY PAINT! FUNNY SHINY UNDERNEATH!
"THE 'FUNNY SHINY,' AS MY UNTUTORED INSECT MIND CALLED IT, WAS THE JEWELLED COSMIC KEY. AFTER A FEW LICKS, I BEGAN TO FEEL STRANGE...
"... AND STAGGERED TO THE PAPERBACK SECTION IN THE BACK OF THE SHOP AS THE OWNER CLOSED FOR THE NIGHT!"
WONDER IF THERE'S STILL TIME TO BEND THE OL' ELBOW AT McALEER'S?
"THERE, AMIDST THE SHADOWS OF COUNTLESS BOOKS WHOSE PAGES IT WAS MY WONT TO DIGEST AT LEISURE...
ORIGINS OF MARVEL COMICS
TOM CORBETT SPACE CADET
LORD OF LIGHT
"... THE STRANGE, WONDERFUL TRANSFORMATION BEGAN! I GREW FROM THE SIZE OF A MILK DUD TO THAT OF A MAN IN ONE SWIFT, STUNNING METAMORPHOSIS!"

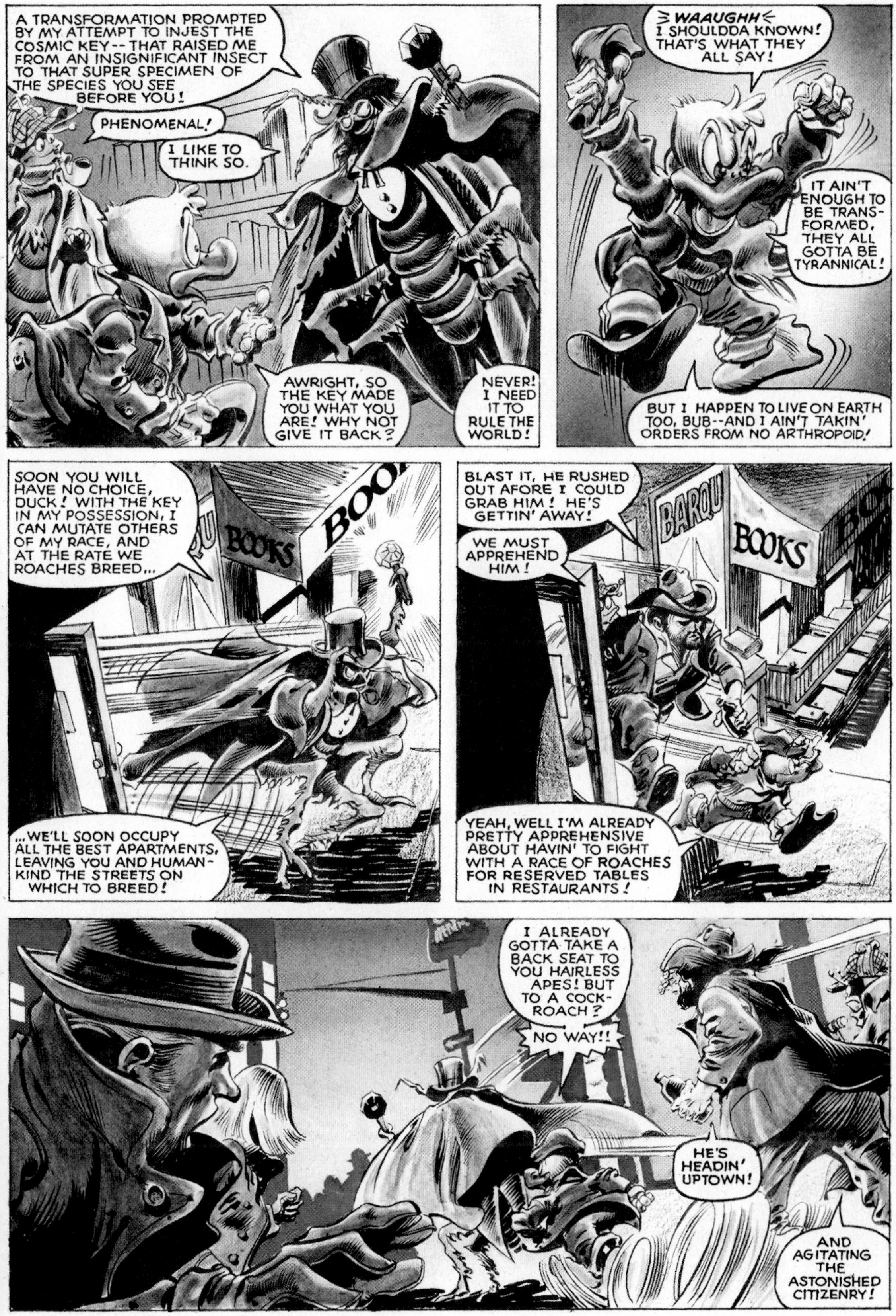
A TRANSFORMATION PROMPTED BY MY ATTEMPT TO INJEST THE COSMIC KEY -- THAT RAISED ME FROM AN INSIGNIFICANT INSECT TO THAT SUPER SPECIMEN OF THE SPECIES YOU SEE BEFORE YOU!
PHENOMENAL!
I LIKE TO THINK SO.
AWRIGHT, SO THE KEY MADE YOU WHAT YOU ARE! WHY NOT GIVE IT BACK?
NEVER! I NEED IT TO RULE THE WORLD!
WAAUGHH I SHOULDDA KNOWN! THAT'S WHAT THEY ALL SAY!
IT AIN'T ENOUGH TO BE TRANS-FORMED, THEY ALL GOTTA BE TYRANNICAL!
BUT I HAPPEN TO LIVE ON EARTH TOO, BUB--AND I AIN'T TAKIN' ORDERS FROM NO ARTHROPOID!
SOON YOU WILL HAVE NO CHOICE, DUCK! WITH THE KEY IN MY POSSESSION, I CAN MUTATE OTHERS OF MY RACE, AND AT THE RATE WE ROACHES BREED...
BOOKS
...WE'LL SOON OCCUPY ALL THE BEST APARTMENTS, LEAVING YOU AND HUMAN-KIND THE STREETS ON WHICH TO BREED!
BLAST IT, HE RUSHED OUT AFORE I COULD GRAB HIM! HE'S GETTIN' AWAY!
WE MUST APPREHEND HIM!
BARQU
BOOKS
YEAH, WELL I'M ALREADY PRETTY APPREHENSIVE ABOUT HAVIN' TO FIGHT WITH A RACE OF ROACHES FOR RESERVED TABLES IN RESTAURANTS!
I ALREADY GOTTA TAKE A BACK SEAT TO YOU HAIRLESS APES! BUT TO A COCK-ROACH?
NO WAY!!
HE'S HEADIN' UPTOWN!
AND AGITATING THE ASTONISHED CITIZENRY!

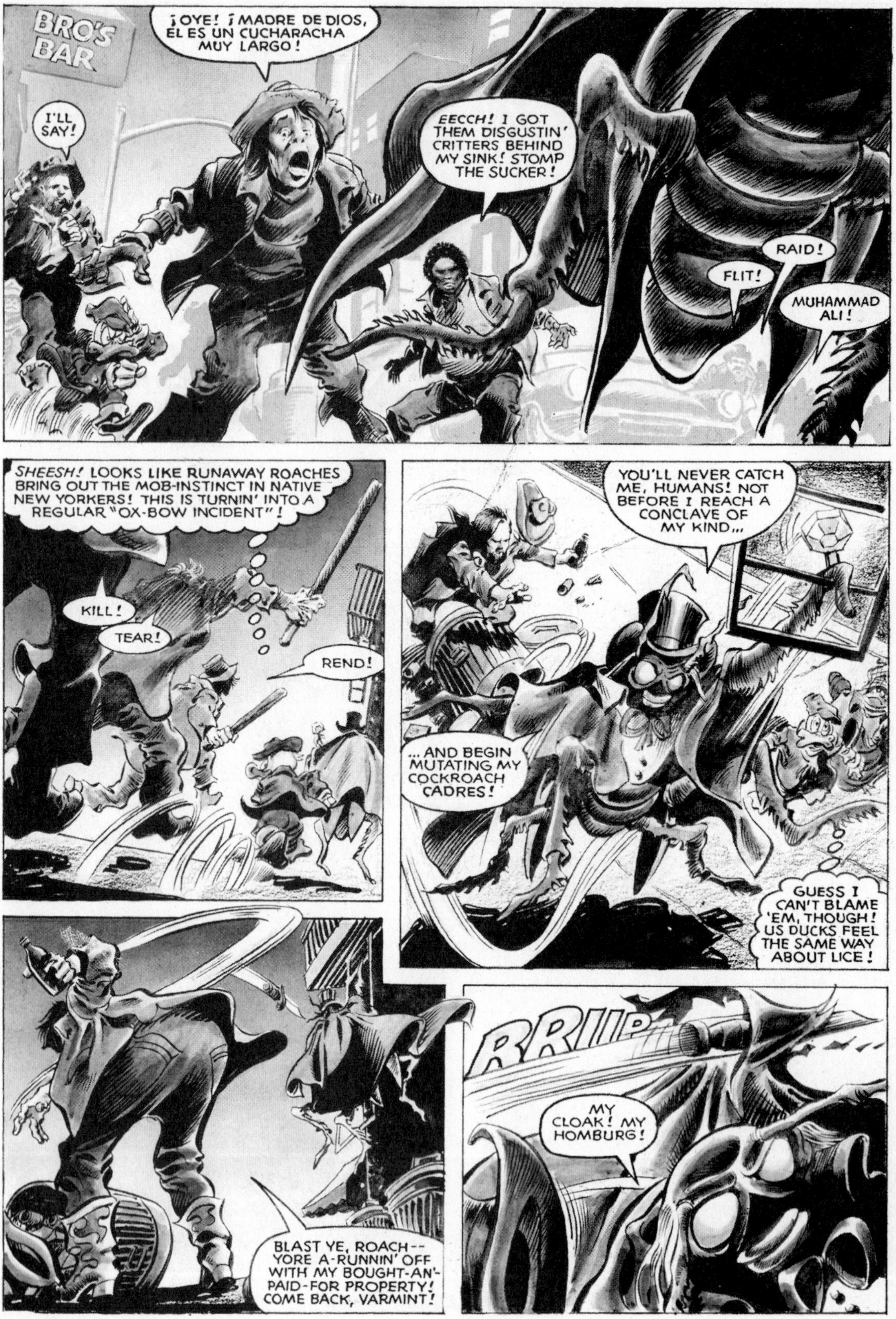
BRO'S BAR
¡OYE! ¡MADRE DE DIOS, EL ES UN CUCHARACHA MUY LARGO!
I'LL SAY!
EECCH! I GOT THEM DISGUSTIN' CRITTERS BEHIND MY SINK! STOMP THE SUCKER!
RAID!
FLIT!
MUHAMMAD ALI!
SHEESH! LOOKS LIKE RUNAWAY ROACHES BRING OUT THE MOB-INSTINCT IN NATIVE NEW YORKERS! THIS IS TURNIN' INTO A REGULAR "OX-BOW INCIDENT"!
KILL!
TEAR!
REND!
YOU'LL NEVER CATCH ME, HUMANS! NOT BEFORE I REACH A CONCLAVE OF MY KIND...
...AND BEGIN MUTATING MY COCKROACH CADRES!
GUESS I CAN'T BLAME 'EM, THOUGH! US DUCKS FEEL THE SAME WAY ABOUT LICE!
BLAST YE, ROACH-- YORE A-RUNNIN' OFF WITH MY BOUGHT-AN'-PAID-FOR PROPERTY! COME BACK, VARMINT!
RRIIP
MY CLOAK! MY HOMBURG!

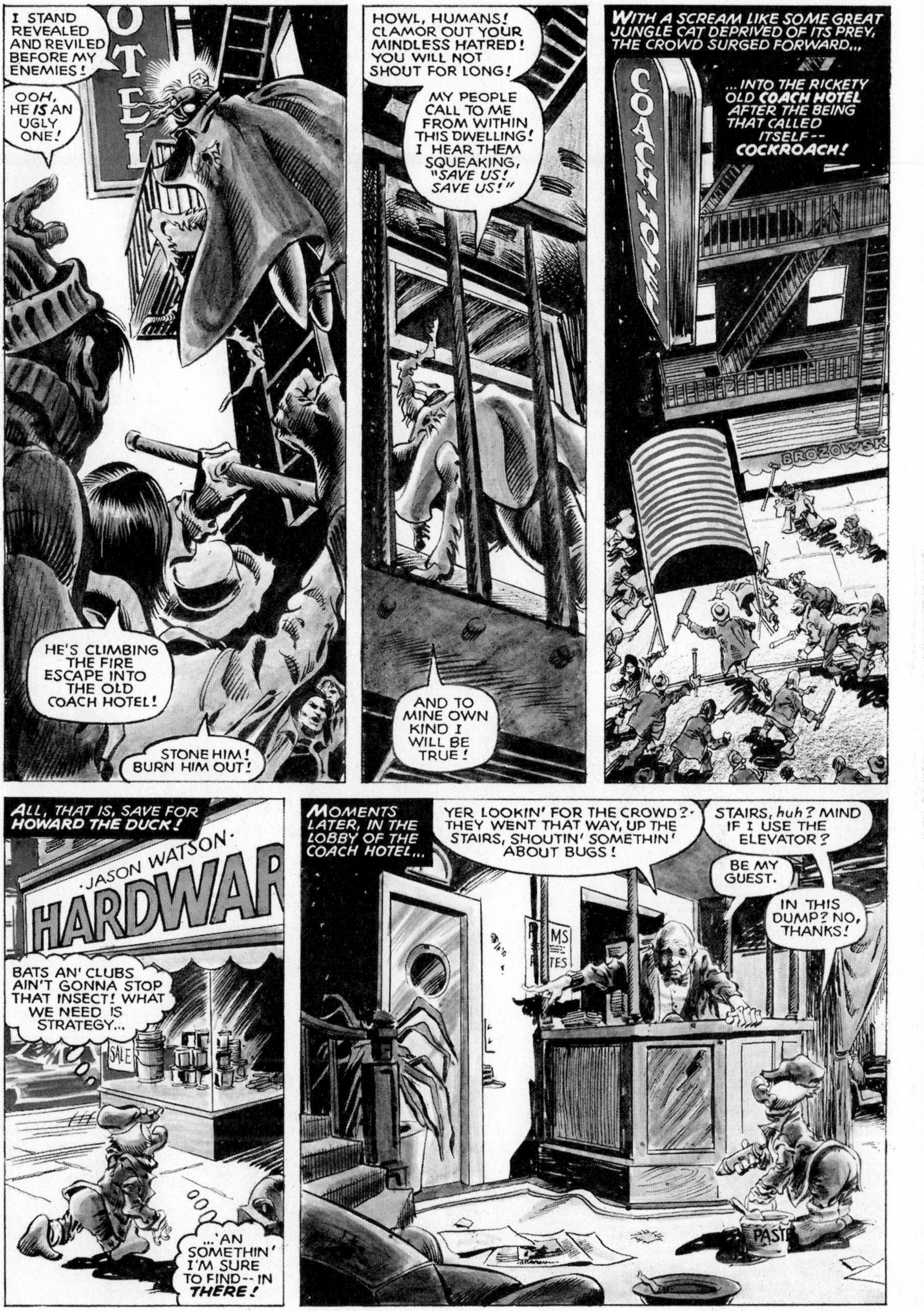
I STAND REVEALED AND REVILED BEFORE MY ENEMIES!
OOH, HE *IS* AN UGLY ONE!
HE'S CLIMBING THE FIRE ESCAPE INTO THE OLD COACH HOTEL!
STONE HIM! BURN HIM OUT!
HOWL, HUMANS! CLAMOR OUT YOUR MINDLESS HATRED! YOU WILL NOT SHOUT FOR LONG!
MY PEOPLE CALL TO ME FROM WITHIN THIS DWELLING! I HEAR THEM SQUEAKING, "SAVE US! SAVE US!"
AND TO MINE OWN KIND I WILL BE TRUE!
WITH A SCREAM LIKE SOME GREAT JUNGLE CAT DEPRIVED OF ITS PREY, THE CROWD SURGED FORWARD...
COACH HOTEL
...INTO THE RICKETY OLD COACH HOTEL AFTER THE BEING THAT CALLED ITSELF-- COCKROACH!
BROZOWSK
ALL, THAT IS, SAVE FOR HOWARD THE DUCK!
·JASON WATSON·
HARDWAR
BATS AN' CLUBS AIN'T GONNA STOP THAT INSECT! WHAT WE NEED IS STRATEGY...
SALE
...'AN SOMETHIN' I'M SURE TO FIND-- IN *THERE!*
MOMENTS LATER, IN THE LOBBY OF THE COACH HOTEL...
YER LOOKIN' FOR THE CROWD? THEY WENT THAT WAY, UP THE STAIRS, SHOUTIN' SOMETHIN' ABOUT BUGS!
STAIRS, *huh?* MIND IF I USE THE ELEVATOR?
BE MY GUEST.
IN THIS DUMP? NO, THANKS!
PASTE

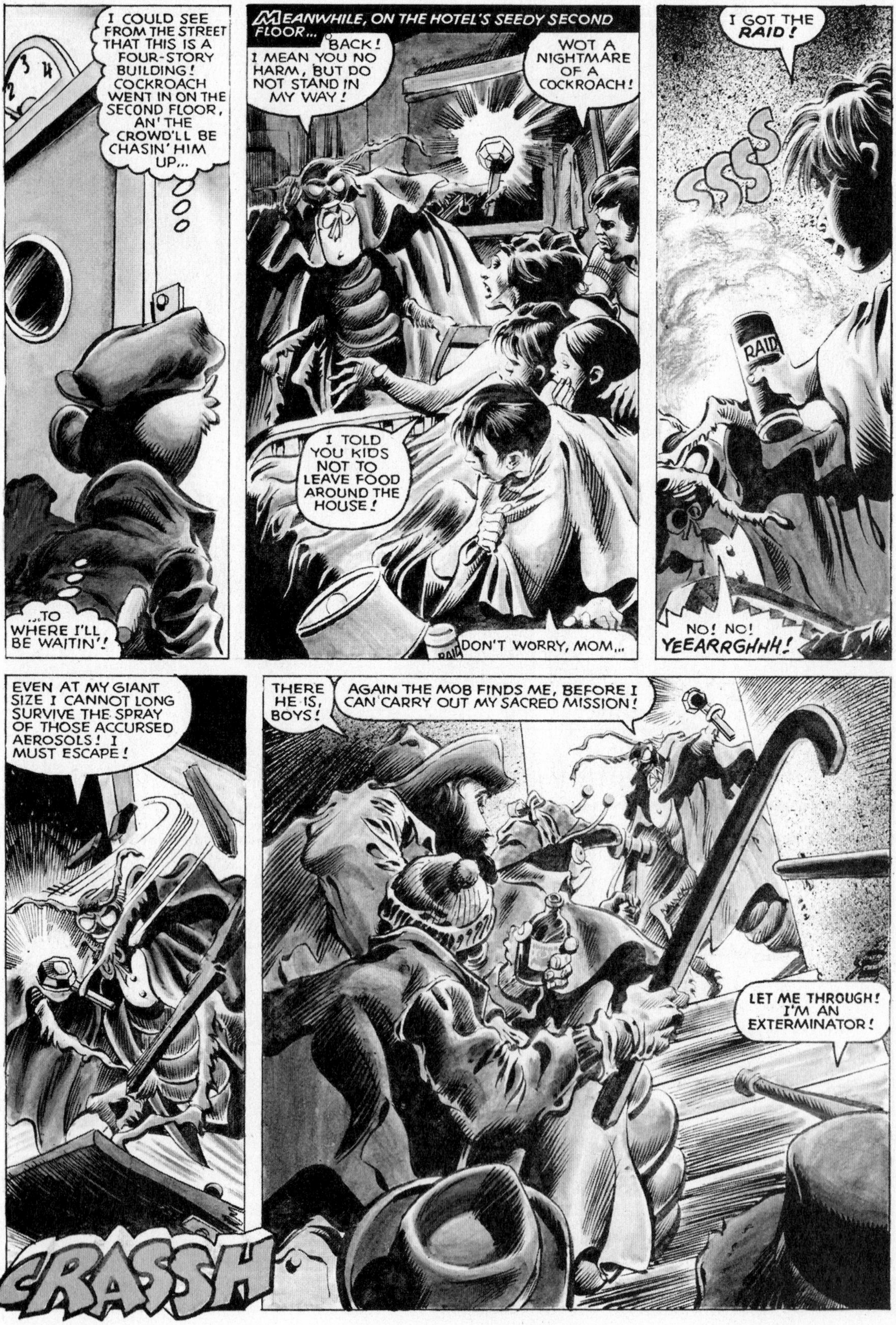
I COULD SEE FROM THE STREET THAT THIS IS A FOUR-STORY BUILDING! COCKROACH WENT IN ON THE SECOND FLOOR, AN' THE CROWD'LL BE CHASIN' HIM UP...
...TO WHERE I'LL BE WAITIN'!
MEANWHILE, ON THE HOTEL'S SEEDY SECOND FLOOR...
BACK! I MEAN YOU NO HARM, BUT DO NOT STAND IN MY WAY!
WOT A NIGHTMARE OF A COCKROACH!
I TOLD YOU KIDS NOT TO LEAVE FOOD AROUND THE HOUSE!
DON'T WORRY, MOM...
RAID
I GOT THE RAID!
SSSS
RAID
NO! NO! YEEARRGHHH!
EVEN AT MY GIANT SIZE I CANNOT LONG SURVIVE THE SPRAY OF THOSE ACCURSED AEROSOLS! I MUST ESCAPE!
CRASSH
THERE HE IS, BOYS!
AGAIN THE MOB FINDS ME, BEFORE I CAN CARRY OUT MY SACRED MISSION!
LET ME THROUGH! I'M AN EXTERMINATOR!

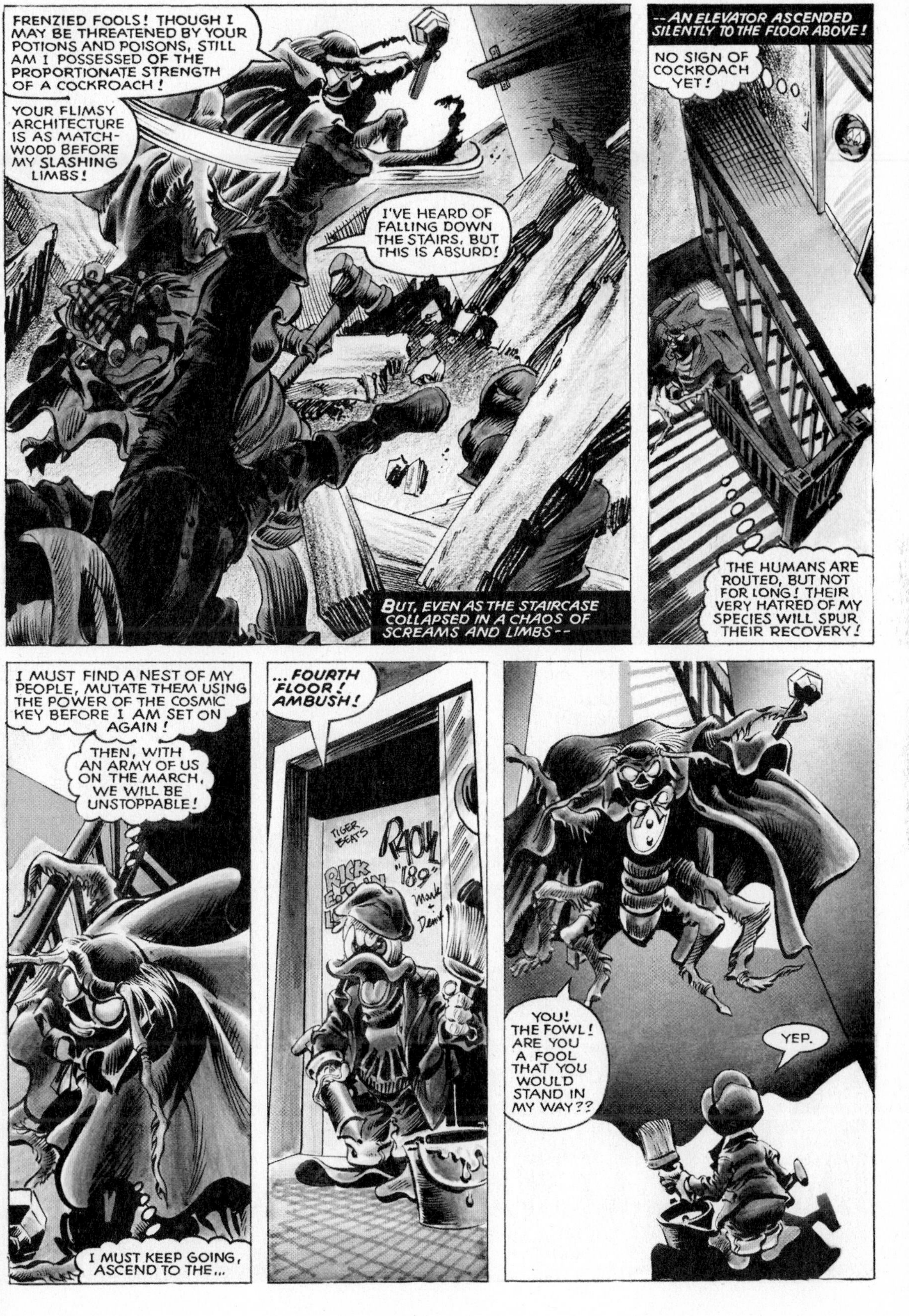
FRENZIED FOOLS! THOUGH I MAY BE THREATENED BY YOUR POTIONS AND POISONS, STILL AM I POSSESSED OF THE PROPORTIONATE STRENGTH OF A COCKROACH!
YOUR FLIMSY ARCHITECTURE IS AS MATCH-WOOD BEFORE MY SLASHING LIMBS!
I'VE HEARD OF FALLING DOWN THE STAIRS, BUT THIS IS ABSURD!
BUT, EVEN AS THE STAIRCASE COLLAPSED IN A CHAOS OF SCREAMS AND LIMBS--
--AN ELEVATOR ASCENDED SILENTLY TO THE FLOOR ABOVE!
NO SIGN OF COCKROACH YET!
THE HUMANS ARE ROUTED, BUT NOT FOR LONG! THEIR VERY HATRED OF MY SPECIES WILL SPUR THEIR RECOVERY!
I MUST FIND A NEST OF MY PEOPLE, MUTATE THEM USING THE POWER OF THE COSMIC KEY BEFORE I AM SET ON AGAIN!
THEN, WITH AN ARMY OF US ON THE MARCH, WE WILL BE UNSTOPPABLE!
I MUST KEEP GOING, ASCEND TO THE...
...FOURTH FLOOR! AMBUSH!
TIGER BEATS
RAOUL
"189"
YOU! THE FOWL! ARE YOU A FOOL THAT YOU WOULD STAND IN MY WAY??
YEP.

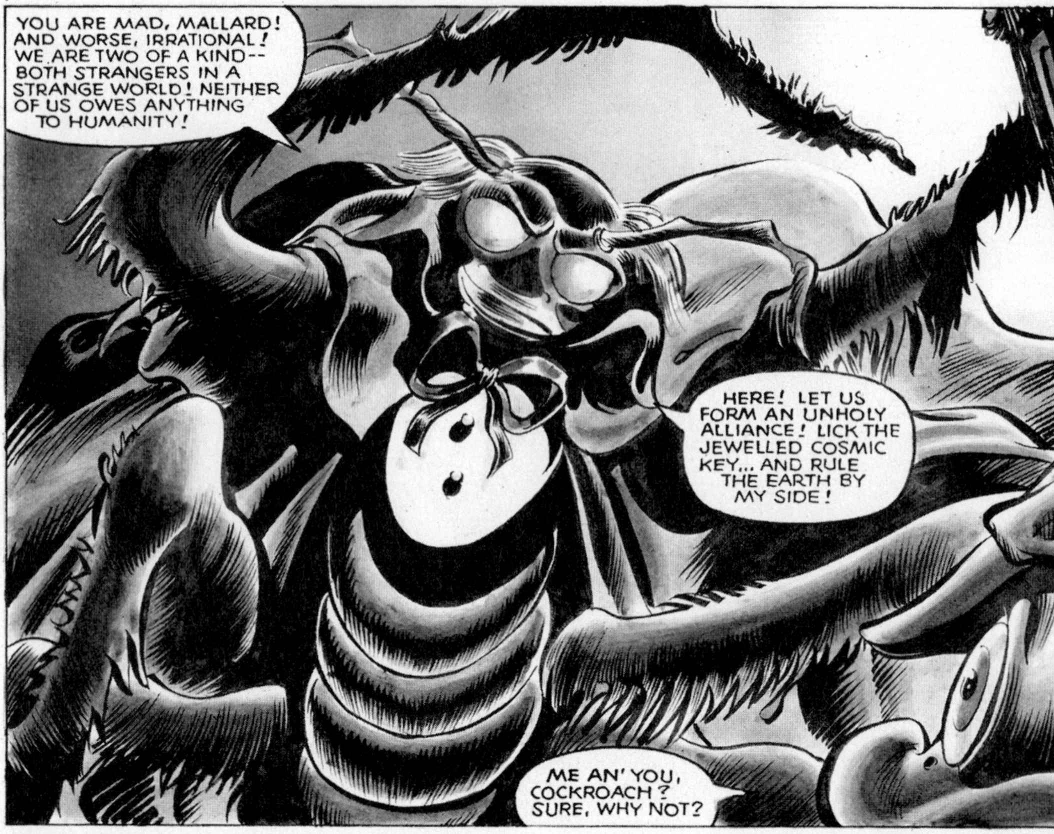

YOU ARE MAD, MALLARD! AND WORSE, IRRATIONAL! WE ARE TWO OF A KIND-- BOTH STRANGERS IN A STRANGE WORLD! NEITHER OF US OWES ANYTHING TO HUMANITY!
HERE! LET US FORM AN UNHOLY ALLIANCE! LICK THE JEWELLED COSMIC KEY... AND RULE THE EARTH BY MY SIDE!
ME AN' YOU, COCKROACH? SURE, WHY NOT?

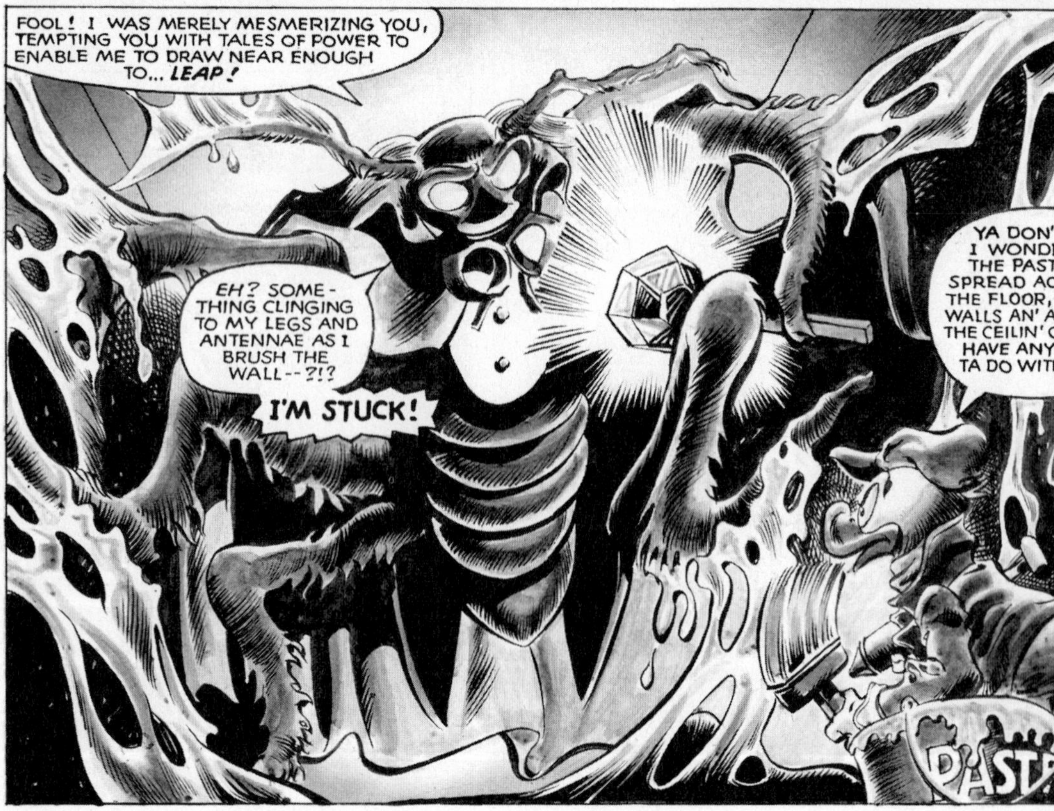

FOOL! I WAS MERELY MESMERIZING YOU, TEMPTING YOU WITH TALES OF POWER TO ENABLE ME TO DRAW NEAR ENOUGH TO... LEAP!
EH? SOME-THING CLINGING TO MY LEGS AND ANTENNAE AS I BRUSH THE WALL--?!?
I'M STUCK!
YA DON'T SAY? I WONDER IF THE PASTE I SPREAD ACROSS THE FLOOR, UP THE WALLS AN' ALONG THE CEILIN' COULD HAVE ANYTHIN' TA DO WITH IT?

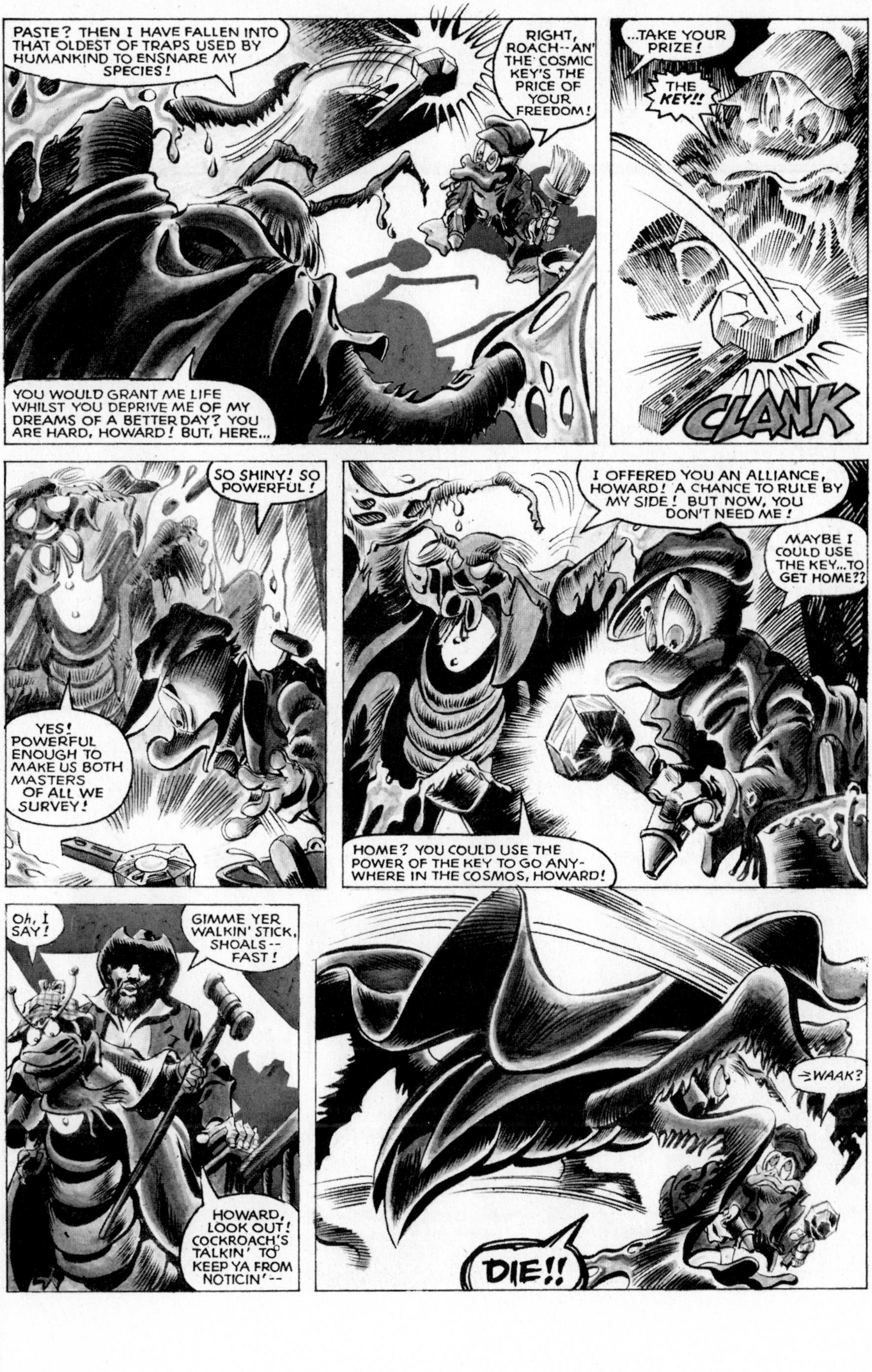
PASTE? THEN I HAVE FALLEN INTO THAT OLDEST OF TRAPS USED BY HUMANKIND TO ENSNARE MY SPECIES!
RIGHT, ROACH--AN' THE COSMIC KEY'S THE PRICE OF YOUR FREEDOM!
YOU WOULD GRANT ME LIFE WHILST YOU DEPRIVE ME OF MY DREAMS OF A BETTER DAY? YOU ARE HARD, HOWARD! BUT, HERE...
...TAKE YOUR PRIZE!
THE KEY!!
CLANK
SO SHINY! SO POWERFUL!
YES! POWERFUL ENOUGH TO MAKE US BOTH MASTERS OF ALL WE SURVEY!
I OFFERED YOU AN ALLIANCE, HOWARD! A CHANCE TO RULE BY MY SIDE! BUT NOW, YOU DON'T NEED ME!
MAYBE I COULD USE THE KEY...TO GET HOME??
HOME? YOU COULD USE THE POWER OF THE KEY TO GO ANYWHERE IN THE COSMOS, HOWARD!
Oh, I SAY!
GIMME YER WALKIN' STICK, SHOALS--FAST!
HOWARD, LOOK OUT! COCKROACH'S TALKIN' TO KEEP YA FROM NOTICIN'--
WAAK?
DIE!!

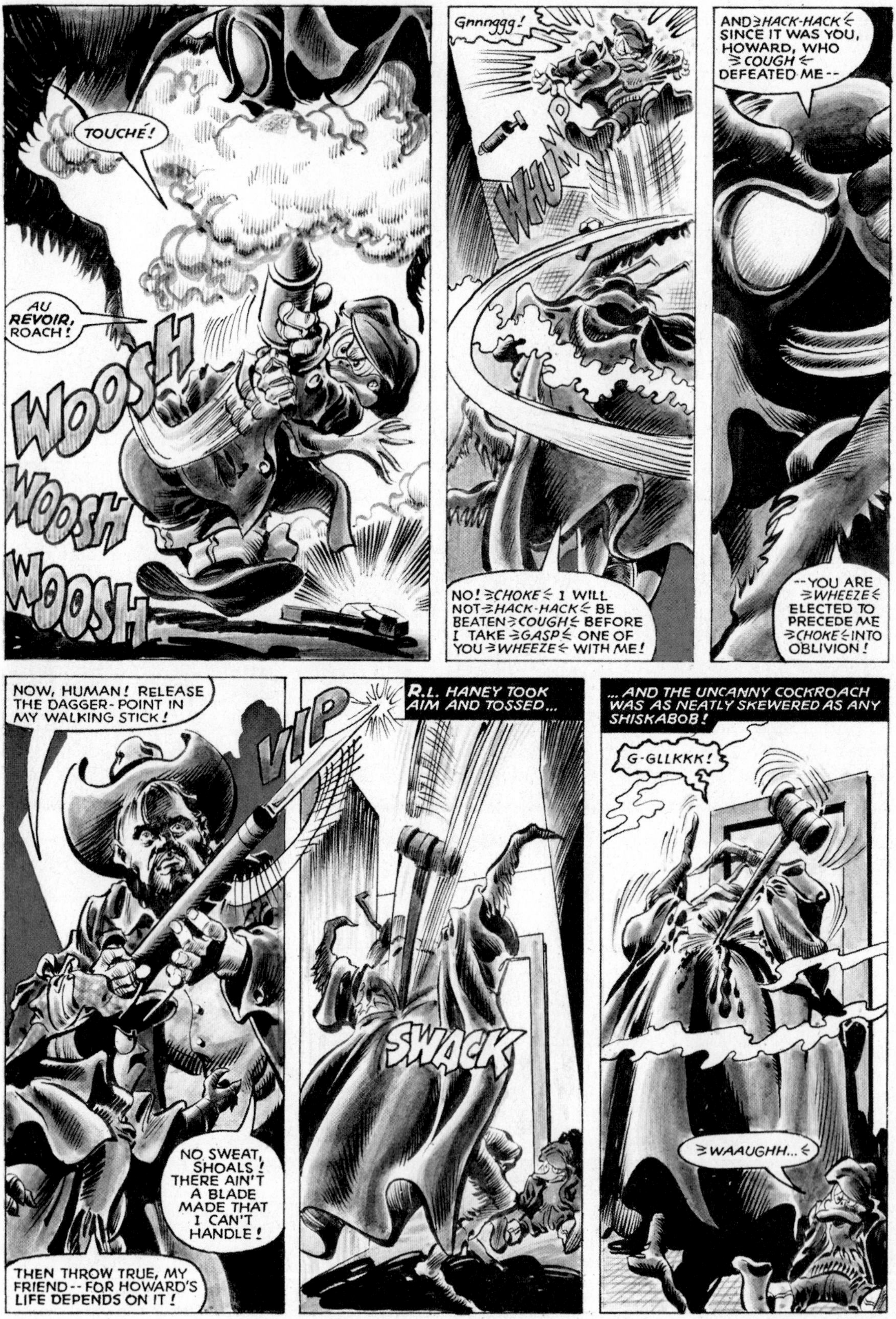
TOUCHÉ!
AU REVOIR, ROACH!
WOOSH
WOOSH
WOOSH
Gnnnggg!
WHUMP
NO! ≥CHOKE≤ I WILL NOT ≥HACK-HACK≤ BE BEATEN ≥COUGH≤ BEFORE I TAKE ≥GASP≤ ONE OF YOU ≥WHEEZE≤ WITH ME!
AND ≥HACK-HACK≤ SINCE IT WAS YOU, HOWARD, WHO ≥COUGH≤ DEFEATED ME--
--YOU ARE ≥WHEEZE≤ ELECTED TO PRECEDE ME ≥CHOKE≤ INTO OBLIVION!
NOW, HUMAN! RELEASE THE DAGGER-POINT IN MY WALKING STICK!
VIP
NO SWEAT, SHOALS! THERE AIN'T A BLADE MADE THAT I CAN'T HANDLE!
THEN THROW TRUE, MY FRIEND-- FOR HOWARD'S LIFE DEPENDS ON IT!
R.L. HANEY TOOK AIM AND TOSSED...
SWACK
...AND THE UNCANNY COCKROACH WAS AS NEATLY SKEWERED AS ANY SHISKABOB!
G-GLLKKK!
≥WAAUGHH...≤

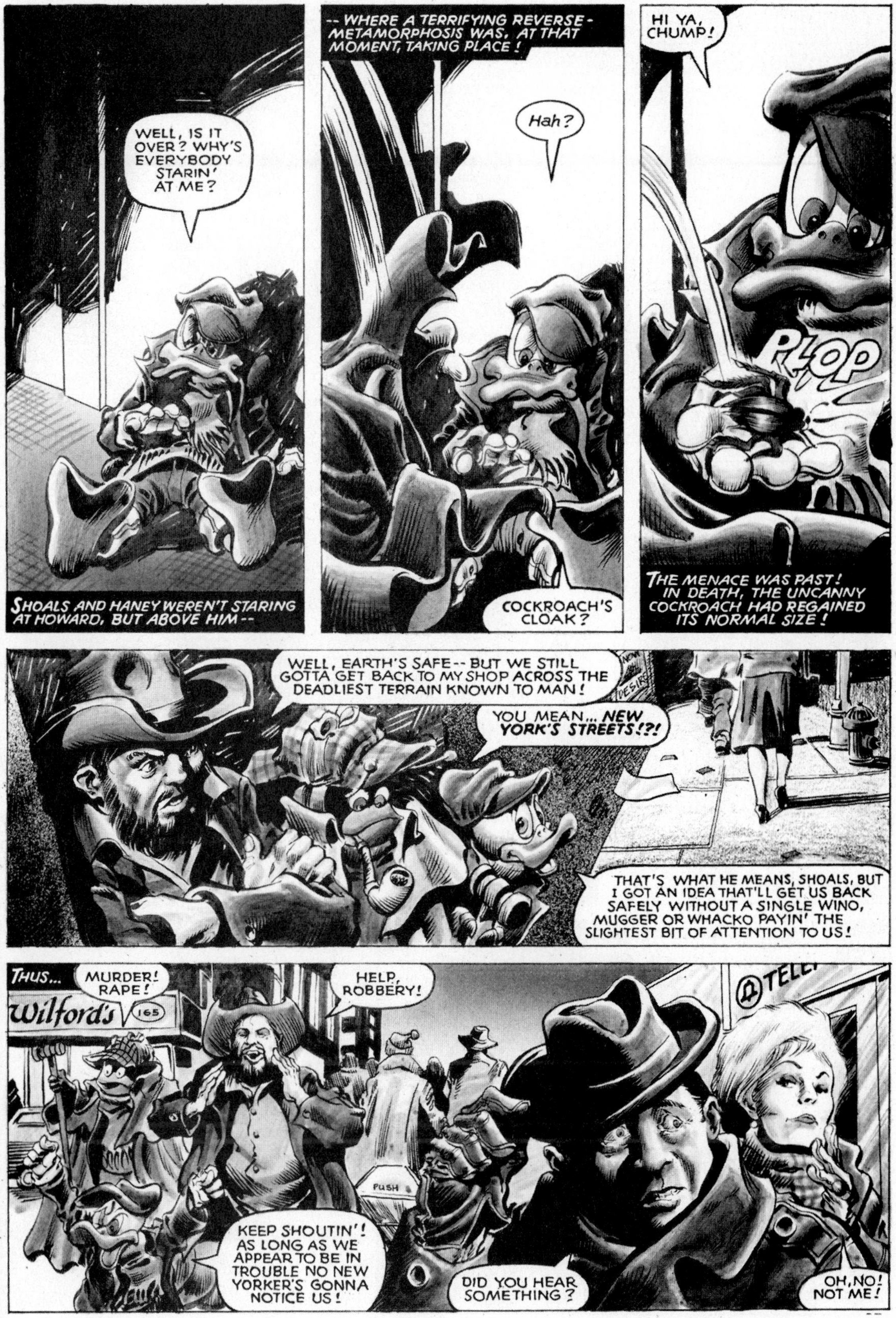
WELL, IS IT OVER? WHY'S EVERYBODY STARIN' AT ME?
SHOALS AND HANEY WEREN'T STARING AT HOWARD, BUT ABOVE HIM--
-- WHERE A TERRIFYING REVERSE-METAMORPHOSIS WAS, AT THAT MOMENT, TAKING PLACE!
Hah?
COCKROACH'S CLOAK?
HI YA, CHUMP!
PLOP
THE MENACE WAS PAST! IN DEATH, THE UNCANNY COCKROACH HAD REGAINED ITS NORMAL SIZE!
WELL, EARTH'S SAFE-- BUT WE STILL GOTTA GET BACK TO MY SHOP ACROSS THE DEADLIEST TERRAIN KNOWN TO MAN!
YOU MEAN... NEW YORK'S STREETS!?!
THAT'S WHAT HE MEANS, SHOALS, BUT I GOT AN IDEA THAT'LL GET US BACK SAFELY WITHOUT A SINGLE WINO, MUGGER OR WHACKO PAYIN' THE SLIGHTEST BIT OF ATTENTION TO US!
THUS...
MURDER! RAPE!
Wilford's 165
HELP, ROBBERY!
PUSH
KEEP SHOUTIN'! AS LONG AS WE APPEAR TO BE IN TROUBLE NO NEW YORKER'S GONNA NOTICE US!
DID YOU HEAR SOMETHING?
OH, NO! NOT ME!

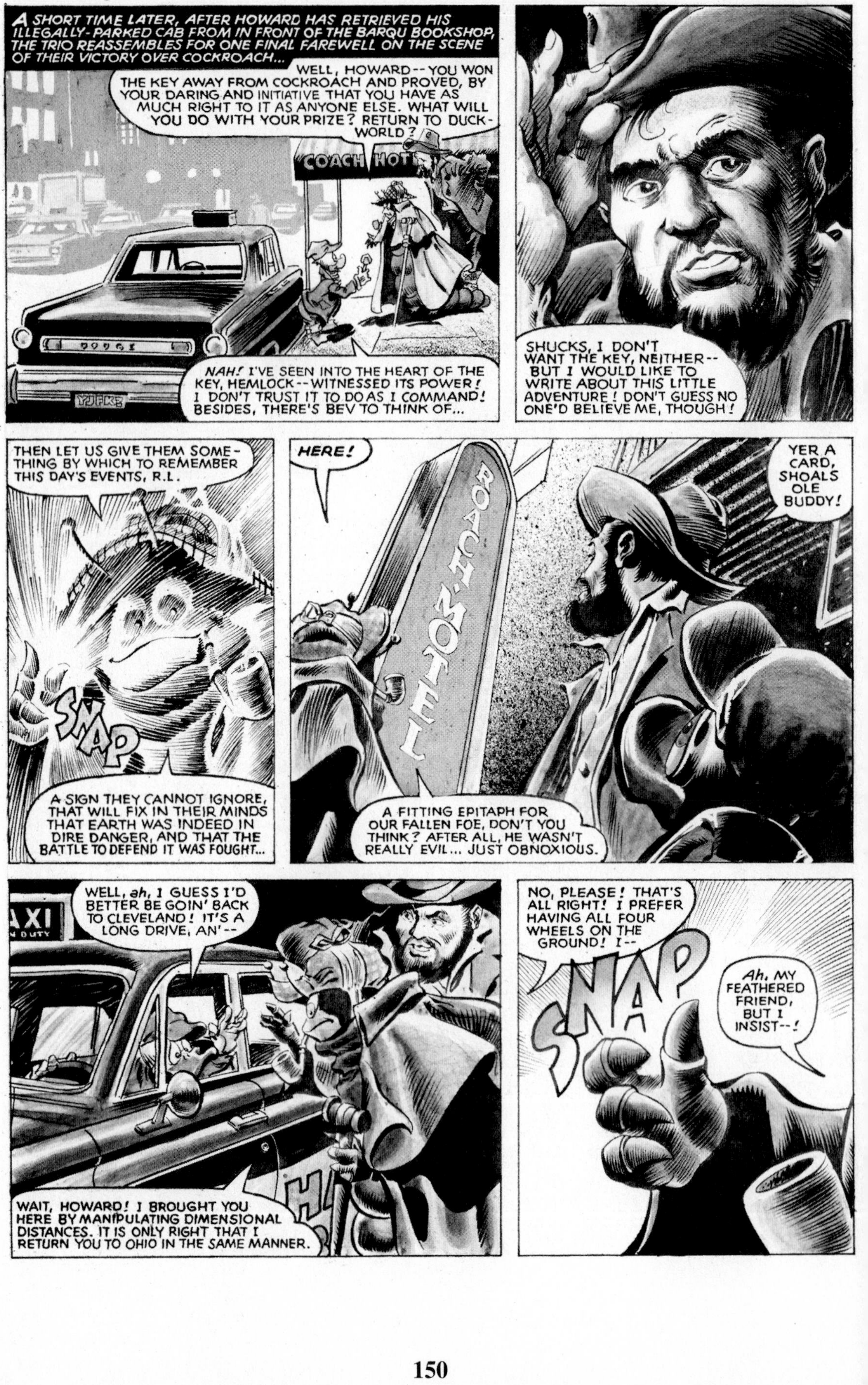
A SHORT TIME LATER, AFTER HOWARD HAS RETRIEVED HIS ILLEGALLY-PARKED CAB FROM IN FRONT OF THE BARQU BOOKSHOP, THE TRIO REASSEMBLES FOR ONE FINAL FAREWELL ON THE SCENE OF THEIR VICTORY OVER COCKROACH...
WELL, HOWARD -- YOU WON THE KEY AWAY FROM COCKROACH AND PROVED, BY YOUR DARING AND INITIATIVE THAT YOU HAVE AS MUCH RIGHT TO IT AS ANYONE ELSE. WHAT WILL YOU DO WITH YOUR PRIZE? RETURN TO DUCK-WORLD?
COACH HOT
NAH! I'VE SEEN INTO THE HEART OF THE KEY, HEMLOCK -- WITNESSED ITS POWER! I DON'T TRUST IT TO DO AS I COMMAND! BESIDES, THERE'S BEV TO THINK OF...
SHUCKS, I DON'T WANT THE KEY, NEITHER -- BUT I WOULD LIKE TO WRITE ABOUT THIS LITTLE ADVENTURE! DON'T GUESS NO ONE'D BELIEVE ME, THOUGH!
THEN LET US GIVE THEM SOME-THING BY WHICH TO REMEMBER THIS DAY'S EVENTS, R.L.
SNAP
A SIGN THEY CANNOT IGNORE, THAT WILL FIX IN THEIR MINDS THAT EARTH WAS INDEED IN DIRE DANGER, AND THAT THE BATTLE TO DEFEND IT WAS FOUGHT...
HERE!
ROACH-MOTEL
A FITTING EPITAPH FOR OUR FALLEN FOE, DON'T YOU THINK? AFTER ALL, HE WASN'T REALLY EVIL... JUST OBNOXIOUS.
YER A CARD, SHOALS OLE BUDDY!
WELL, ah, I GUESS I'D BETTER BE GOIN' BACK TO CLEVELAND! IT'S A LONG DRIVE, AN'--
WAIT, HOWARD! I BROUGHT YOU HERE BY MANIPULATING DIMENSIONAL DISTANCES. IT IS ONLY RIGHT THAT I RETURN YOU TO OHIO IN THE SAME MANNER.
NO, PLEASE! THAT'S ALL RIGHT! I PREFER HAVING ALL FOUR WHEELS ON THE GROUND! I--
SNAP
Ah, MY FEATHERED FRIEND, BUT I INSIST--!

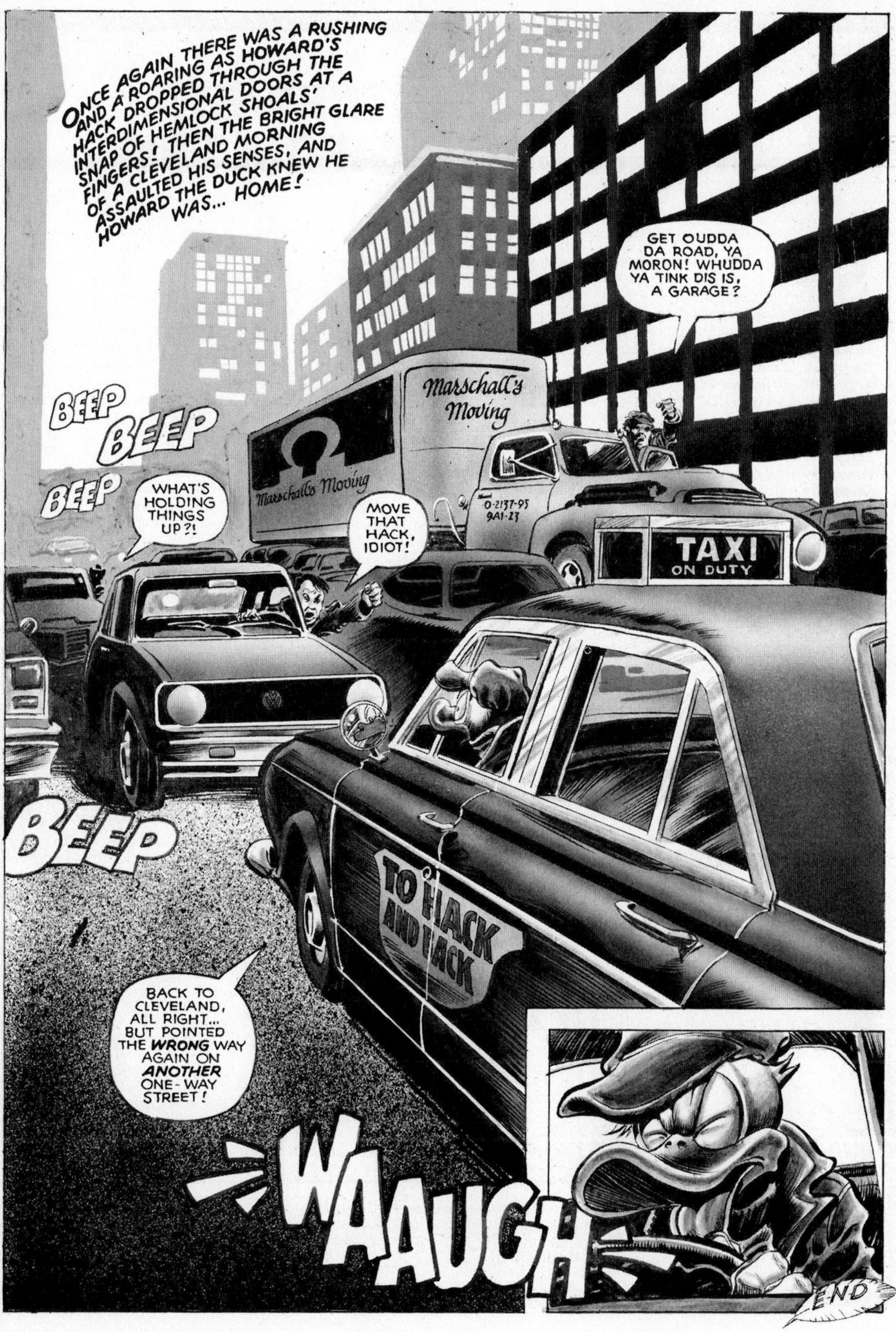
ONCE AGAIN THERE WAS A RUSHING AND A ROARING AS HOWARD'S HACK DROPPED THROUGH THE INTERDIMENSIONAL DOORS AT A SNAP OF HEMLOCK SHOALS' FINGERS! THEN THE BRIGHT GLARE OF A CLEVELAND MORNING ASSAULTED HIS SENSES, AND HOWARD THE DUCK KNEW HE WAS... HOME!
GET OUDDA DA ROAD, YA MORON! WHUDDA YA TINK DIS IS, A GARAGE?
Marschall's Moving
Marschall's Moving
BEEP
BEEP
BEEP
WHAT'S HOLDING THINGS UP?!
MOVE THAT HACK, IDIOT!
TAXI
ON DUTY
BEEP
BACK TO CLEVELAND, ALL RIGHT... BUT POINTED THE WRONG WAY AGAIN ON ANOTHER ONE-WAY STREET!
WAAUGH
END

PLAYDUCK INTERVIEW
with TRUMAN CAPOULTRY

Scarcely five years ago, an incident occurred that had a profound effect on the national psyche, as well as on the mind and career of one of the nation's most provocative authors. The incident was the strange disappearence of the drake known as "Howard Blank" before a live audience at a presidential speech in Wackington DC. Truman Capoultry, already renowned for such prose ducumentaries as "In Cold Water" and "Breakfast at Tuffany's," saw the now-famous footage shot by QBC news-hen Webb McGroober and was captivated by it. Here was perhaps the most astounding occurrence ever recorded by camera in front of hundreds of witnesses: the vanishing of a duck into thin air. Capoultry saw the raw material here for his next major fictional ducumentary. Over the next three and a half years, he set forth ex-

haustively researching the incident, interviewing eyewitnesses to the event, and every person who owned up to knowing "Howard Blank." The information, once compiled, took a year to distill into novelized form. The result was *DUCKING OUT*: THE STRANGE DISAPPEARANCE OF A DUCK NAMED HOWARD, a spellbinding account of the last twenty-four hours of Howard's life on Earth, the circumstances of his disappearance, and his current whereabouts. In past months, the editors of PLAYDUCK have been honored to serialize this controversial ducu-novel to be released in paperback by Quacmillan Books in April. In conjunction with this final installment of **DUCKING OUT,** we have sent freelance interviewer Mark Gruenwaugh to conduct the first major interview with Capoultry since his 1971 best-seller,

"The Gay Drake." Gruenwaugh describes the sessions:

"I knew in advance that Truman would be a tough quacker to interview. His reclusive but flamboyant lifestyle, his aversion to anonymity and fame, and his unabiding contempt for the press all gave me good reason to be apprehensive. Yet when I met Truman at his Duckhattan apartment, he seemed a changed drake —something in the course of writing his latest work had had a profound effect on him, even as the incident he wrote about had on many of the eye-witnesses. In fact, I had even suspected that Truman had become a WACkie (Witness of the Ascension Cult), a gaggle of fanatic believers in Howard's secular sacrifice. I began my interview with this topic . . ."

PLAYDUCK: *DUCKING OUT* promises

"I've grown to identify with Howard. I see his plight as a parable of modern duckkind."

"I do not believe that duckkind is the only intelligent lifeform in the universe, nor that ours is the only universe in existence."

"Everyone should take note: Don't lose your grip on reality or it may lose its grip on you."

to be your most popular work to date. How has it changed you?

CAPOULTRY: Well, after spending four years living and breathing a single subject, one becomes very involved in it. The search for Howard was one of the most challenging assignments I ever set out for myself. It began as a magazine article for *The New Yolker* and blossomed into . . . an obsession. I've grown to identify with Howard. I see his plight as a parable of modern duckkind.

PLAYDUCK: There is hardly a drake in the U.S. who has not seen the famous footage of his disappearance. Some seem to be traumatized by it; the WACkies have made him into a martyr. How similar is their viewpoint to yours?

CAPOULTRY: While they may have gotten a bit carried away with some of their acts of fanaticism, the WACkies are championing a valid point that I agree with: society is causing the individual to vanish.

PLAYDUCK: Is this what Howard meant to represent?

CAPOULTRY: Not consciously.

PLAYDUCK: What do we really know about this nebbish of a duck?

CAPOULTRY: Precious little that distinguishes him from the run-of-the-pond drake. In fact, my research indicated that it was his very unremarkableness that distinguishes him. All those who claim to have known him told me the same thing: he was the most extraordinary nebbish they've ever known.

PLAYDUCK: I'm not sure I understand. How can he be extraordinary if there's nothing that distinguishes him from your average drake?

CAPOULTRY: I did not mean to imply that he was average. He was very unaverage. He didn't fit into any category, least of all the common one. Because his rugged individualism was so potentially threatening and disruptive, Howard created a blind for himself, an appearance of blending in. I am convinced that he spent years trying to attain absolute anonymity for himself, the way others spend years trying to become famous. Somehow he managed to destroy or alter virtually all government records of himself, in an attempt to become a nonentity. He seemed obsessed with it, as if it were a reaction to his out-of-placedness. It was like a bid for non-existence.

PLAYDUCK: If Howard managed to go to such lengths to remain unknown—to the extent that we are not really even sure of his last name—how did you find out so much about him?

CAPOULTRY: Well, for one thing I gained access to the President's Warden Report. Since Howard disappeared in front of the president during a televised speech, it became a subject of official in-

quiry. The leading theory had been that Howard accidentally stumbled into some sort of disintegration ray intended for the President. My book, of course, thoroughly discredits this notion.

PLAYDUCK: Before we go into that, mind giving us your views on what Howard was doing at a political rally? If he was so neurotic about his privacy, why would he make such a public appearance?

CAPOULTRY: As I explained in my novel which you obviously have not read, I am convinced that it was a fluke he was even there at all. From most reports, he was on his way to the drugstore to buy some cigars when he was swept up in the crowd of demonstrators denouncing President Duxon's domestical policy. Before he knew it, he was at front of the crowd, in front of all the cameras. And then—poof, he was gone.

PLAYDUCK: The cosmic axis shifted on him, as the bookjacket says.

CAPOULTRY: Right.

PLAYDUCK: Probably the aspect of *DUCKING OUT* that has created the fervor—at least among our readers—is your speculations as to Howard's fate.

CAPOULTRY: The are not speculations, Mr. Gruenwaugh. They are insights.

PLAYDUCK: Alright then, insights. Would you mind explaining where you got the notion that Howard simply popped out of reality and ended up on some fantastical alternate world?

CAPOULTRY: Your skepticism is not very well disguised. Anyway, about a year ago, as I was in the midst of writing my duckuscript, I began having these very odd vivid dreams. They were about Howard. At first I squawked it up to overwork. Yet never before have I had such vivid dreams. They began with the sensation of falling through space—not black space, as we know it, but a strange sort of grey space. Drifting, without sensation, in absence of natural law. For about a week I had the same dream. Then one night I dreamt Howard arrived somewhere. It was a strange world inhabited by creatures unlike anything here on Earth. They were bipedal like ourselves, but giants two or three times our size, much like apes in the zoo except that they were hairless but for the tops of their heads and the interface of their limbs and torso. These creatures were almost as intelligent as ourselves, and even had a society that parodies our own in major respects. They called their kind "humans."

PLAYDUCK: These "humans" have become quite a topic of controversy if we can believe the letters in our PLAYDUCK FORUM [*Editor's note: We can.*] Some have called your ideas heretical, some pass it off as a fad like Von Danikwak's

Ponds of the Gods stir a few years ago. Can you in all conscience say you believe in these humans?

CAPOULTRY: Emphatically yes. I do not believe that duckkind is the only intelligent lifeform in the universe, nor that ours is the only universe in existence. I believe there are all sorts of baroque variations on our species on other worlds, places where the dominant lifeform may be mice, dogs, cats, woodpeckers, magpies, even creatures that have no counterpart here on Earth—like the hairless apes.

PLAYDUCK: How is it that Howard happened upon the world of hairless apes rather than any of these others?

CAPOULTRY: I don't wish to get into the metaphysics. But the point is: despite his being born in our world, Howard didn't belong here—he didn't fit in—and somehow some cosmic power saw that and took him away.

PLAYDUCK: To a place where he would fit in better?

CAPOULTRY: Not really. Certainly a place where he fit in as well as here. I don't think Howard would fit in anywhere —he's a singularity, an anomaly—wherever he goes, he's out of place. And because of that, he is fated to never find a place to belong—a home. And that, to me, is Howard's significance to us: we all are to a certain degree out of place. One of Howard's last recorded words were—

PLAYDUCK: "I don't belong here. I'm trapped in a world I never made." It's become a litany among the WACkies these days.

CAPOULTRY: Yes it has. While all of us feel that way sometimes, for some of us it may be true all the time.

PLAYDUCK: You're saying that there are other potential Howards who may one day just duck out of sight?

CAPOULTRY: Probably others who already have. Howard simply had the fortune of being recorded on film as having done so. Check your missing person bureau.

PLAYDUCK: Do you think Howard is happy where he is?

CAPOULTRY: About as happy as he'd be had he remained here. The paradoxical thing is that he is adept at adaptibility while being unassimilateable. I think he may even get to the point where he will lose touch with the reality he is in, and duck out of that world, too. Everyone should take note: Don't lose your grip on reality or it may lose its grip on you.

PLAYDUCK: Metaphysics aren't that interesting to our readers. How about telling us your ideas on how a female hairless ape can get down with a drake?

CAPOULTRY: In my view, its a matter
(CONTINUED ON PAGE 88)

153

THE OLD DRAKE'S TALE

Long, long ago, in the time before the great flood, there lived in the land of Anastis a wizened old drake by the name of Widgeon. Now Widgeon was a drake of great wealth and power, having plyed the rivers of Anastis for over half a century (as we now tell the passing of time), and in that time he had built a mighty empire of shipping and trading. His wealth had grown and grown until it rivalled that of the fabled Emperor Penguin himself! The gold in his coffers equalled not merely twenty times Widgeon's weight, but twenty times twenty! Precious gems and pearls as large as a young gosling spilled from the many chests in his counting house. And, in all the lands around, none save royalty lived as well as widgeon.

Yet, for all his wealth and power, Widgeon was not loved. He had, you see, come into his wealth through the basest of business dealings... undercutting his competitors and doublecrossing anyone foolish enough to enter a partnership with him. And so, while Widgeon's fortunes grew, the good ducks of the land came to curse his name beneath their breath.

"No one appreciates a successful business-duck," groused Widgeon one day. "The towns-ducks all hate me.. they can't wait for me to die." It was then that a sudden realization struck the old drake.

"Why... one day I *shall* die! And then, this beautiful estate, my businesses, all that I have worked and connived for will fall into other hands! But my riches must not go to those who hate me! I must have an heir... I must have a son!" So saying, the old drake waddled off to contract a marriage broker — for such was the custom in those days — and that very evening, the broker delivered to Widgeon the most beautiful young duck the island kingdoms had ever seen.

Barely more than a duckling, her name was Mareca, and her beauty was like the lily floating on a still pond. From the tip of her bill to the webbing 'twixt her toes, she was a vision of feathery pulchritude. But all her beauty was wasted on Widgeon, for he was a duck of many years, nearly into his dotage, and knew nothing of the arts of love and loving. And, though he was a good provider, he never laid so much as a feather on Mareca's fair form.

So it was that after a year had passed and Mareca had laid no egg, Widgeon began to worry. "Oh, woe! Still I have no heir!" wheezed the old drake. "Surely, I have fallen under some curse." And, thinking his problems to be of supernatural causes, he sent his servants out in search of a learned duck who might show him how to break his curse.

Now, that very day, there happened to pass through the marketplace a young, wandering sorcerer by the name of Merganser. A handsome drake was Merganser, and his bright eyes gleamed beneath his hood as he heard Widgeon's servants make their inquiries in the town. "I can help your master!" he boldly declared, and the towns-ducks all jeered, for their hatred of Widgeon was as great as the cat's dislike of water. Nevertheless, the old drake's servants conducted the sorcerer to their master, for they were fearful of what might befall them, were they to return empty-winged.

Brought before the business-duck, the crafty Merganser bowed deeply and spake: "Great Widgeon, though I am but half your age, I have traveled far and learned much... and I guarantee that I can lift this curse that keeps you childless."

Hearing this, the old drake's heart leapt with joy. "If you can insure that I have a son, sorcerer, a third of my riches shall be yours!"

"Agreed!" cried Merganser. "I shall begin at once! The first thing I must do is examine your wife."

So honey-tongued was the young drake, so subtle his magicks, that old Widgeon had his wife brought before them at once... and that was nearly Merganser's undoing. For, the moment he beheld Mareca, he was caught up in a spell as powerful as any he had ever woven. Her beauty was such that it entranced the sorcerer. And, in truth, she was not unaffected by his presence, for she was a vibrant young duck in the bloom of youth, and she did pine for affection.

"If you would leave us...?" quacked Merganser. "My magicks could take a while, and I am sure your businesses cry for your attention." And with little more prodding than that, the old fool left them in his study.

154

from The Anatidian Chronicles... as translated by Sir James Mallardy

Once alone, the sorcerer took Mareca in his wings and comforted her, as she began to cry. "Oh, handsome sir, do not teach that old scoundrel what it means to be a husband. He has not touched me in all the twelvemonth of our marriage, and I would leave it stay that way."

A gentle smile ran across Merganser's bill, and he began to sqawk with glee. "Fear not, fair-feathered one. I have no intention of aiding your master in that way... I know him for what he is! Still and all, I think we can provide him with an heir!" That evening, when Widgeon returned to his study, he was met by a grim-faced Merganser and a sobbing Mareca. "Gracious sire," the sorcerer began, "I fear it is not you who are cursed, but your wife. She shall never bear you an heir."

A look of anger rolled over the old drake's bill. "Wretched hen!" he puffed, turning on his young bride, "I'll make you wish you'd never been hatched!"

"No, sire!" cried Merganser, clutching at the old one's wing. "To attack Mareca would only transfer the curse to you! Besides, there is yet a way in which you yourself could have a son!"

"But I am a drake," croaked the wheezing fowl. "I cannot lay an egg!"

'Even so," assured the sorcerer, "my magicks can create an egg which will bring you forth a son... a son nearly full-grown! Come!" And, leading the shaken Widgeon into the great hall of his estate, Merganser began to order the servants about — having them move a huge cauldron into the room's center and assemble a mighty kiln in the great fireplace.

In the kiln he formed a gigantic egg, an egg so perfectly formed in two halves, that those halves fit together showing nary a seam. Then, Merganser turned his attention to preparing two draughts... one to be poured into the egg, the other to be poured into Widgeon. The first was a smelly brew, containing some of the old drake's tail feathers, as well as scrapings from his bill and webbed toes. But the second was a pleasanter liquid, made from certain herbs and strong spirits.

Finally, with the skill of a brewer, Merganser decanted the smelly fluid into the egg and sealed it tight. Then he built a hasty nest around it and beckoned Widgeon near. "Now comes the most important step!" he warned the old drake. "You must climb atop the egg and hatch it!"

"Hatch it?!" cried the drake. "But that will take..."

"But a night!" assured the sorcerer. "Here, drink this potion! It will attune you to the rhythms of the egg. Then, with but a night of sitting, you shall have your son!"

"Very well," said Widgeon. And, draining the cup, he climbed atop the egg. In moments, the potion took effect, and he fell sound asleep.

No sooner did his snoring fill the room, than a door opened and Mareca entered, pulling her young brother after her. Directing the two ducks to the egg, Merganser slid old Widgeon off its surface and carefully drained every drop of the smelly solution into the cesspool... replacing the liquid with Mareca's brother!

"Be very still now," whispered Merganser to the young duck. "I have left just enough of an opening for you to take breath. When you hear the old drake begin to stir, then you can stir, too." And, bidding the future heir farewell, Mareca and Merganser loaded a wagon with a third of Widgeon's treasury and stole off into the night.

When dawn finally broke, Widgeon felt wakefulness creep back over his bones. And then he felt something... different. He looked beneath him and saw the egg, and then he remembered! And, as he remembered, the egg suddenly shook violently... once... twice... and it was asunder, spilling the blinking young duckling out of the nest.

"My son!" cried Widgeon, clutching the duckling to his breast.

"Mother?" mumbled the duckling.

"Yes... YES!" quacked Widgeon joyously. "I am your father... but I am also your mother!" And, still holding the duckling to him, the old fool of a drake ran out into the marketplace, laughing and quacking and shouting at the top of his lungs:

"I'm a mother! Do you hear? I'm a mother!"

And all the ducks of the town had to agree.

155

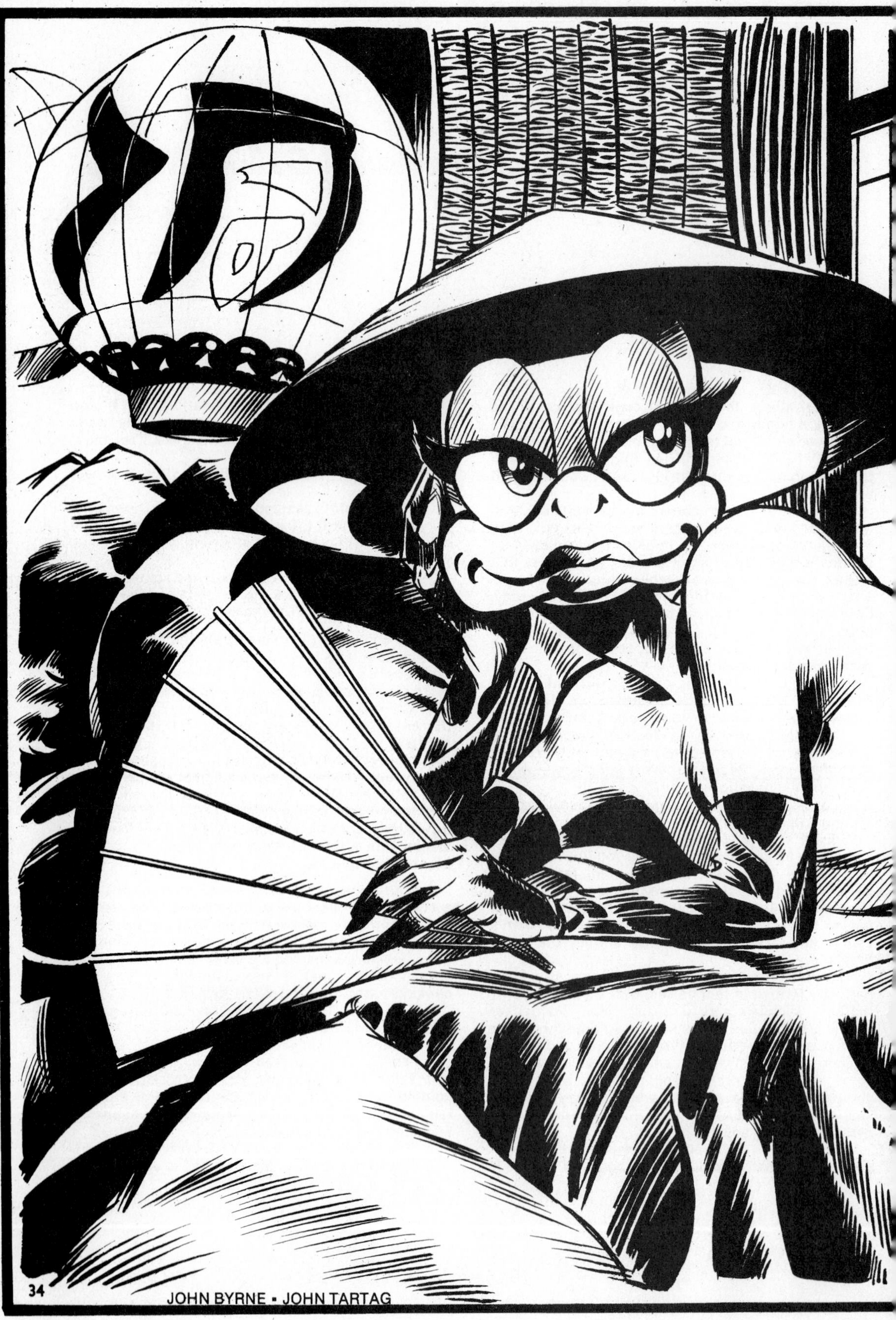
34
JOHN BYRNE • JOHN TARTAG

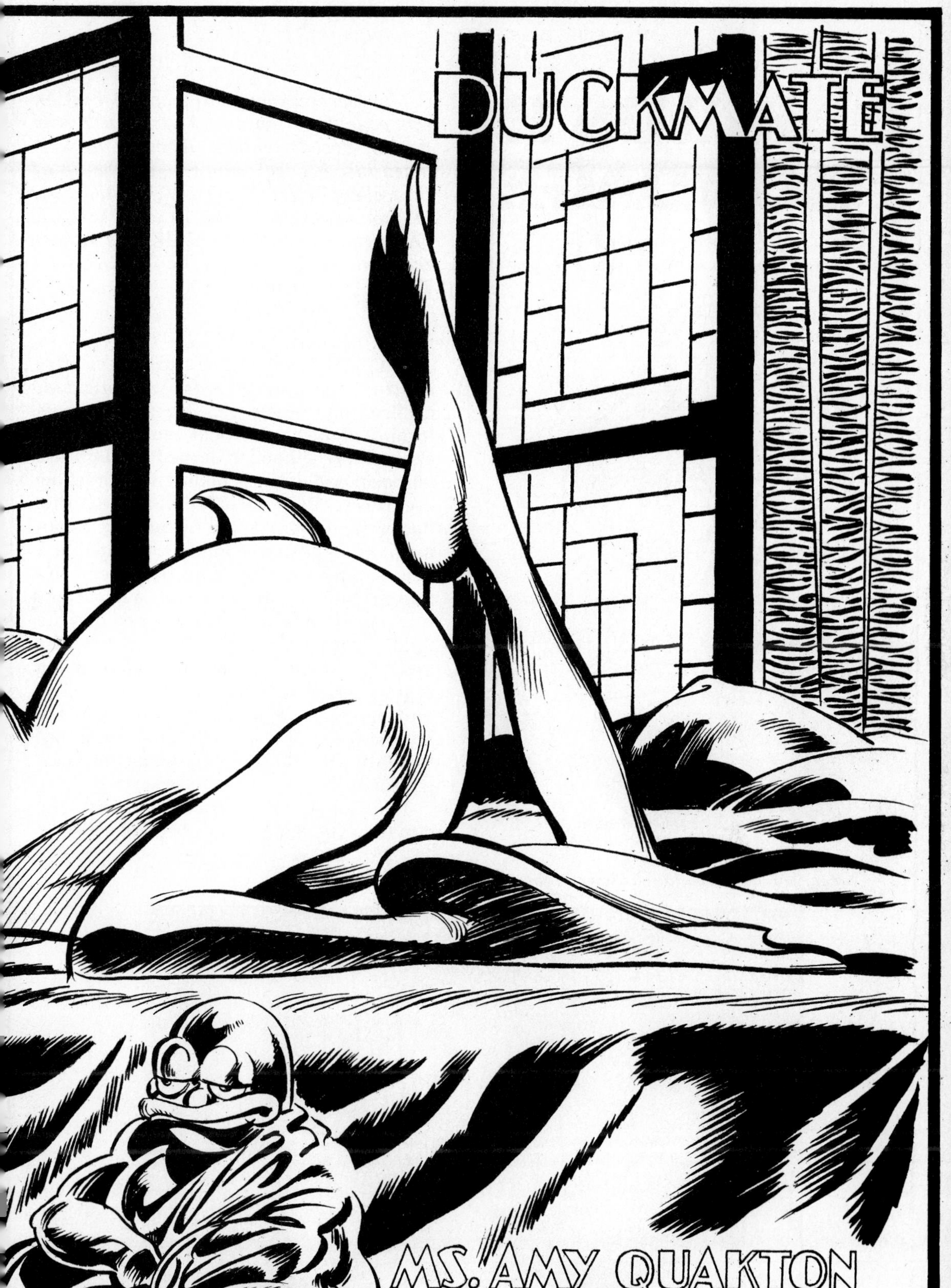
DUCKMATE
MS. AMY QUAKTON
35

BIRDS IN BONDAGE!

A PLAYDUCK Expose

After Attending Bhagduck Charm School....

The hearbreaking photograph you see on this page is not an outtake from a movie: not a posed fantasy from a drake's magazine. It's real, and it is just the tip of the iceberg of poultry slavery that still exists in our world! Read on as PLAYDUCK investigative reporter Baak Waaker reveals the truth of the wide traffic in BIRDS IN BONDAGE!

At first the mind refuses to believe. But it's true. Here, in the most sophisticated, civilized city in America exists a gang of foreign fiends and local lechers whose shameful livelihood is earned through the innocent and helpless bodies of their fellow creatures. PLAYDUCK infiltrated this dastardly organization by posing as an agent of an eastern country interested in a new supply for hens for the potentate's harem. It took only the greasing of various feathered hands and I was ushered into the dank, close basement within which the beauties pictured on this page were caged together in hopeless misery. Too shocked and terrified to quack or cluck, these victims of drake lust huddled, shaking, beneath the threatening whips of their captors!

Truthfully, this reporter found the situation shocking almost beyond belief!

The Prisoner Of Ducks

By Norman Mallard

A stunning foray into the embattled relationships between modern drakes and ducks. Have the proponents of Ducky Lib so twisted the reality of these relations as to imply the subjugation of duck by drake when exactly the opposite is true?

S ometimes the Prisoner thought ducks had begun to withdraw respect from drakes when egg-laying lost its danger. For once Duktor Beakwaak discovered the cause of nest fever the duck began to be insulated from the dramatic possibilitiy of the loss of feathers. When feather-loss was a real, potent possibility the duck looked at her drake with eyes of love or hate, but as *important* — the creature that could bring to her bliss or sorrow, a full flock of feathers or none. Now the drake is, it seems, no more than a surrogate duck, taking courses in how to sit on eggs, waaking in fear at the thought of upsetting the brooding, snappish duck.

Technology, then, by increasing duckdom's power over nature, reduced the drake before the duck.

Unhappily, the Prisoner is given to opening up more subjects than he's able to close. Ducks and drakes molt each other in the years of their love if it's a half-love, or a love drenched with hate, or a love bleak as the resigned air of mates who have become friends... The mass of drakes and ducks molt each other slowly in the years of their nesting together, or pass the molting on to their eggs. It's worth the reminder that becoming more masculine doesn't involve simple "imprinting."

Still he had not answered the question with which he began.

Continued on Page 112

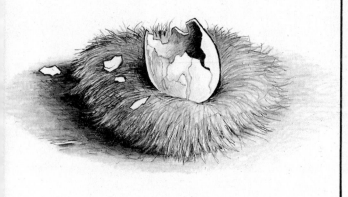

ASHAMED? DESPONDENT? LOSING FEATHERS?

Don't let pathological molting ruin *your* life!

Turn to FEATHERMORE! This fantastic new method brings quick replacement of feathers lost through injury, illness, or sordid activities.

Don't let this happen to you!

Send for your FEATHERMORE by August 1st and receive a watch that grinds, whips, and performs brain surgery!

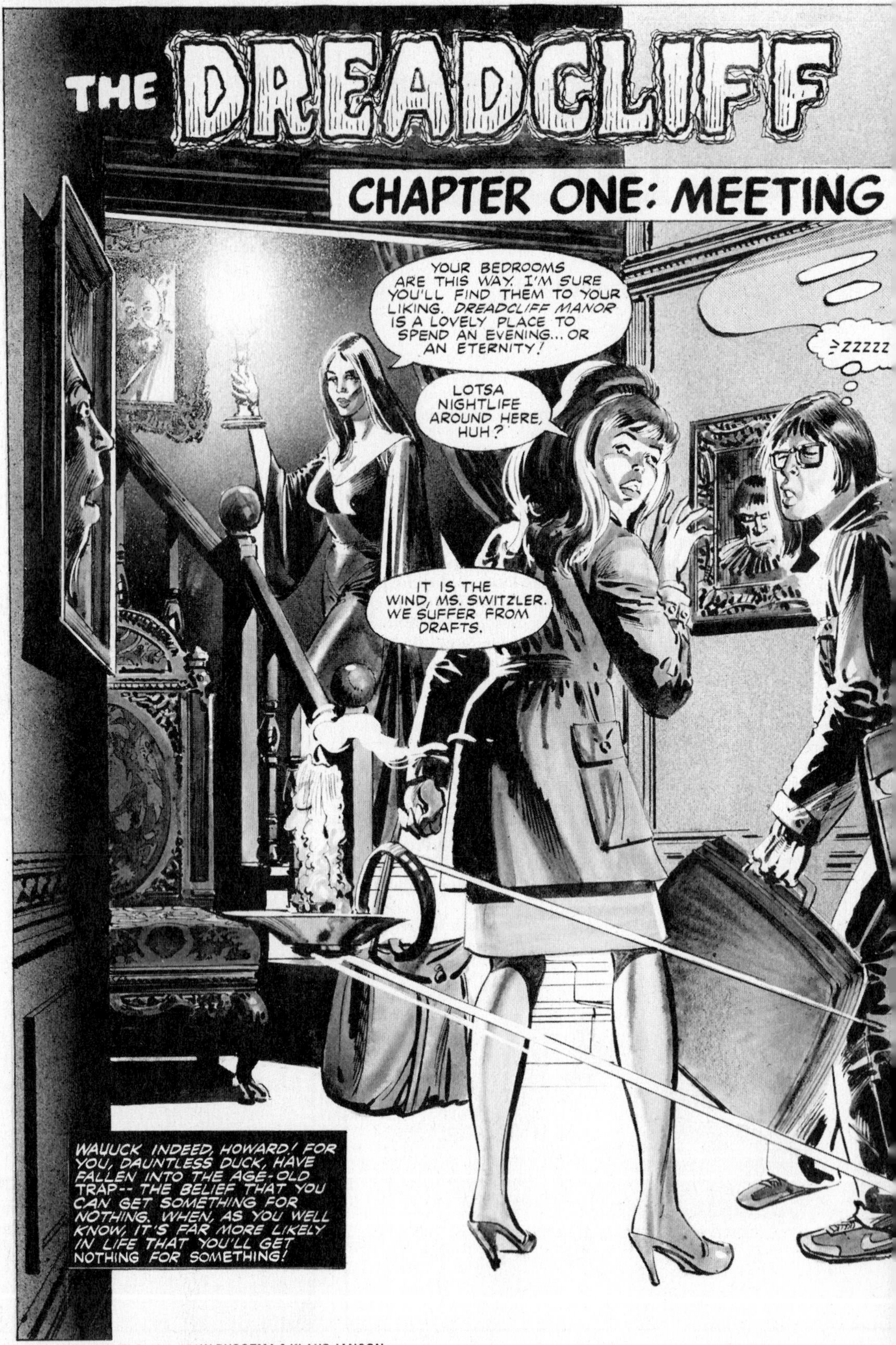
THE DREADCLIFF
CHAPTER ONE: MEETING
YOUR BEDROOMS ARE THIS WAY. I'M SURE YOU'LL FIND THEM TO YOUR LIKING. DREADCLIFF MANOR IS A LOVELY PLACE TO SPEND AN EVENING... OR AN ETERNITY!
ƷZZZZZ
LOTSA NIGHTLIFE AROUND HERE, HUH?
IT IS THE WIND, MS. SWITZLER. WE SUFFER FROM DRAFTS.
WAUUCK INDEED, HOWARD! FOR YOU, DAUNTLESS DUCK, HAVE FALLEN INTO THE AGE-OLD TRAP-- THE BELIEF THAT YOU CAN GET SOMETHING FOR NOTHING. WHEN, AS YOU WELL KNOW, IT'S FAR MORE LIKELY IN LIFE THAT YOU'LL GET NOTHING FOR SOMETHING!

Script: BILL MANTLO Art: JOHN BUSCEMA & KLAUS JANSON

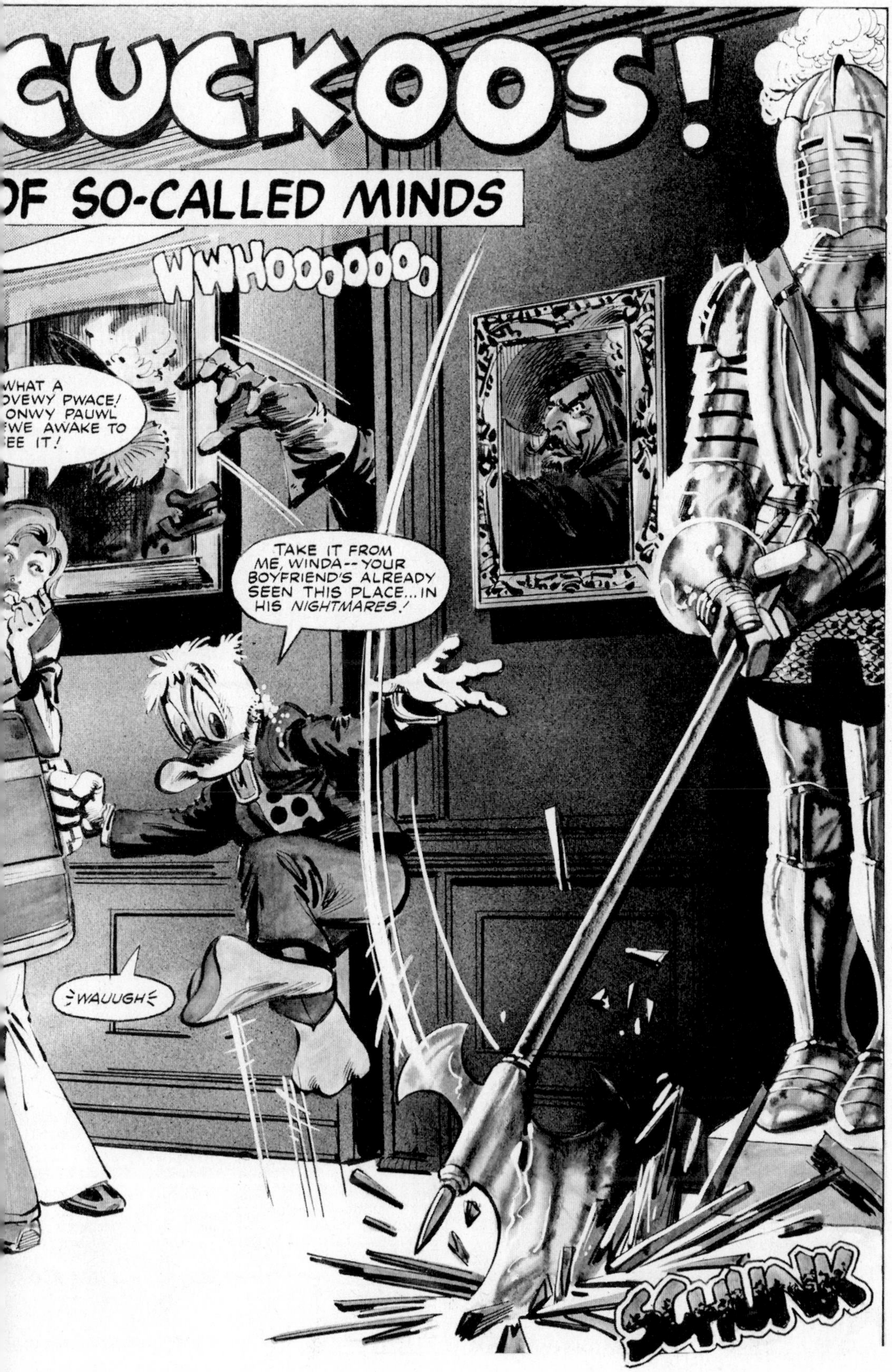
CUCKOOS!
OF SO-CALLED MINDS
WWHOOOOOOO
WHAT A OVEWY PWACE! ONWY PAUWL WE AWAKE TO EE IT!
TAKE IT FROM ME, WINDA--YOUR BOYFRIEND'S ALREADY SEEN THIS PLACE...IN HIS NIGHTMARES!
WAUUGH

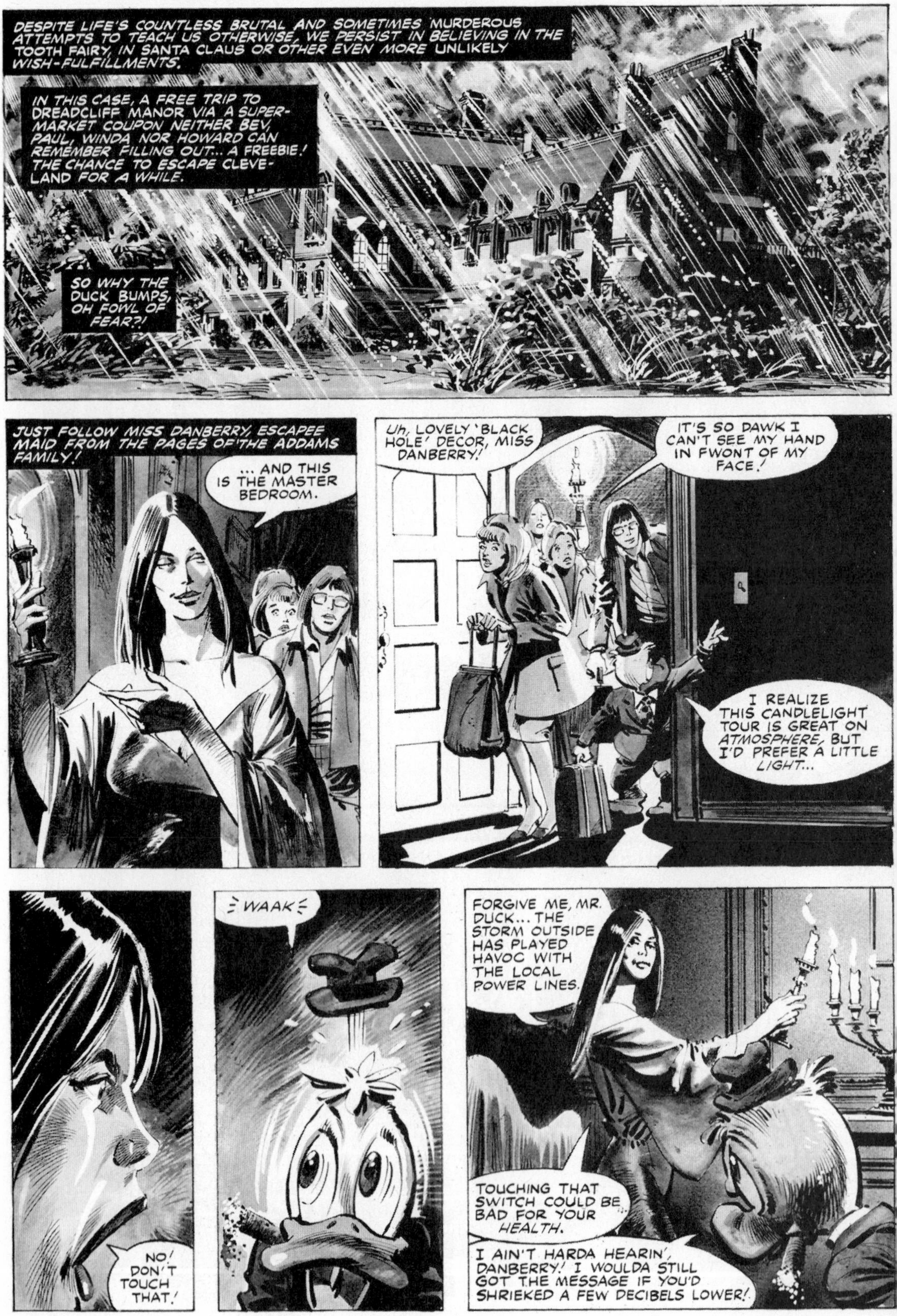
DESPITE LIFE'S COUNTLESS BRUTAL AND SOMETIMES MURDEROUS ATTEMPTS TO TEACH US OTHERWISE, WE PERSIST IN BELIEVING IN THE TOOTH FAIRY, IN SANTA CLAUS OR OTHER EVEN MORE UNLIKELY WISH-FULFILLMENTS.
IN THIS CASE, A FREE TRIP TO DREADCLIFF MANOR VIA A SUPER-MARKET COUPON NEITHER BEV, PAUL, WINDA NOR HOWARD CAN REMEMBER FILLING OUT... A FREEBIE! THE CHANCE TO ESCAPE CLEVE-LAND FOR A WHILE.
SO WHY THE DUCK BUMPS, OH FOWL OF FEAR?!
JUST FOLLOW MISS DANBERRY, ESCAPEE MAID FROM THE PAGES OF THE ADDAMS FAMILY!
... AND THIS IS THE MASTER BEDROOM.
Uh, LOVELY 'BLACK HOLE' DECOR, MISS DANBERRY!
IT'S SO DAWK I CAN'T SEE MY HAND IN FWONT OF MY FACE!
I REALIZE THIS CANDLELIGHT TOUR IS GREAT ON ATMOSPHERE, BUT I'D PREFER A LITTLE LIGHT...
NO! DON'T TOUCH THAT!
WAAK
FORGIVE ME, MR. DUCK... THE STORM OUTSIDE HAS PLAYED HAVOC WITH THE LOCAL POWER LINES.
TOUCHING THAT SWITCH COULD BE BAD FOR YOUR HEALTH.
I AIN'T HARDA HEARIN', DANBERRY! I WOULDA STILL GOT THE MESSAGE IF YOU'D SHRIEKED A FEW DECIBELS LOWER!

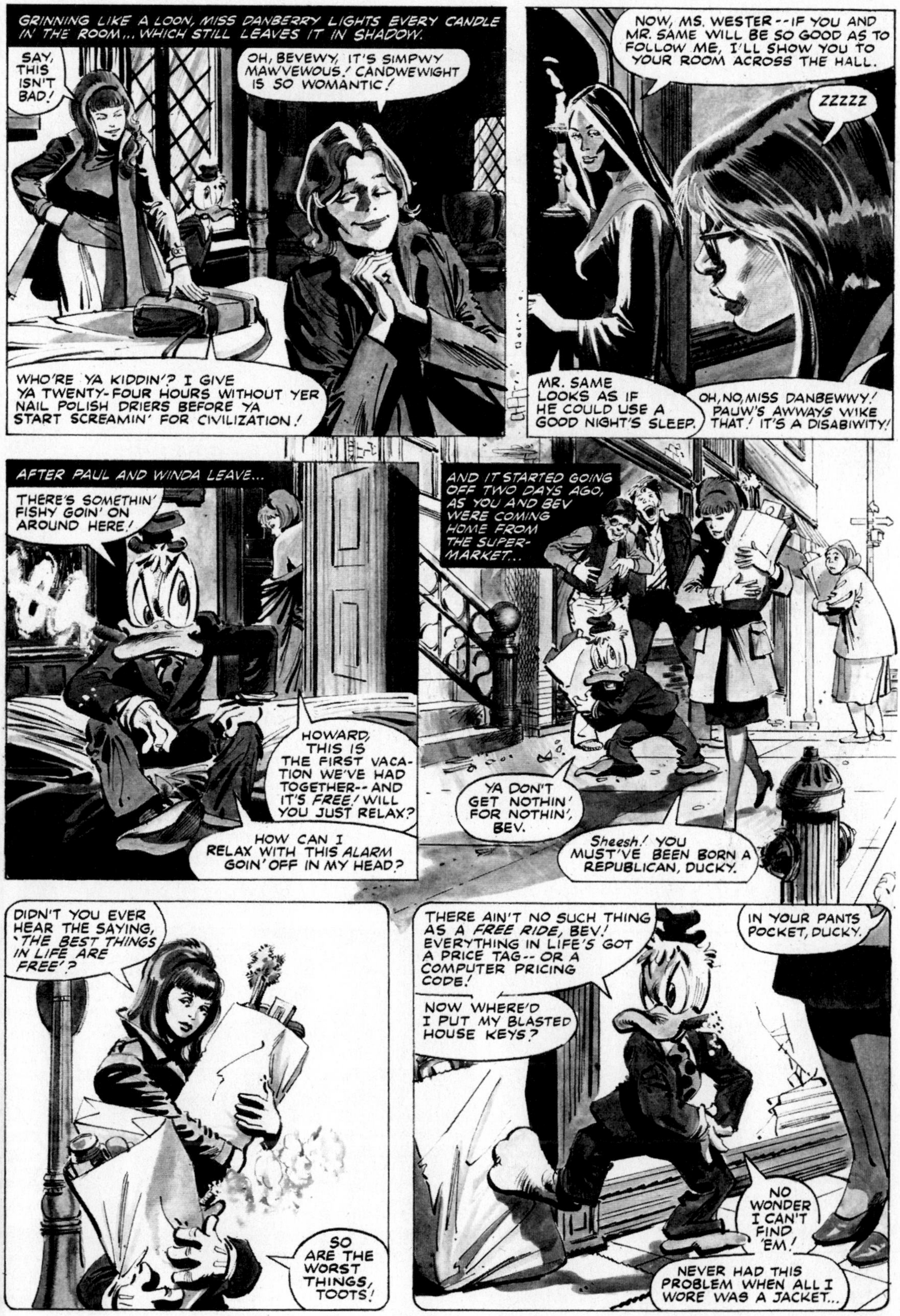
GRINNING LIKE A LOON, MISS DANBERRY LIGHTS EVERY CANDLE IN THE ROOM... WHICH STILL LEAVES IT IN SHADOW.
SAY, THIS ISN'T BAD!
OH, BEVEWY, IT'S SIMPWY MAWVEWOUS! CANDWEWIGHT IS SO WOMANTIC!
WHO'RE YA KIDDIN'? I GIVE YA TWENTY-FOUR HOURS WITHOUT YER NAIL POLISH DRIERS BEFORE YA START SCREAMIN' FOR CIVILIZATION!
NOW, MS. WESTER--IF YOU AND MR. SAME WILL BE SO GOOD AS TO FOLLOW ME, I'LL SHOW YOU TO YOUR ROOM ACROSS THE HALL.
ZZZZZ
MR. SAME LOOKS AS IF HE COULD USE A GOOD NIGHT'S SLEEP.
OH, NO, MISS DANBEWWY! PAUW'S AWWAYS WIKE THAT! IT'S A DISABIWITY!
AFTER PAUL AND WINDA LEAVE...
THERE'S SOMETHIN' FISHY GOIN' ON AROUND HERE!
HOWARD, THIS IS THE FIRST VACATION WE'VE HAD TOGETHER--AND IT'S FREE! WILL YOU JUST RELAX?
HOW CAN I RELAX WITH THIS ALARM GOIN' OFF IN MY HEAD?
AND IT STARTED GOING OFF TWO DAYS AGO, AS YOU AND BEV WERE COMING HOME FROM THE SUPER-MARKET...
YA DON'T GET NOTHIN' FOR NOTHIN', BEV.
Sheesh! YOU MUST'VE BEEN BORN A REPUBLICAN, DUCKY.
DIDN'T YOU EVER HEAR THE SAYING, 'THE BEST THINGS IN LIFE ARE FREE'?
SO ARE THE WORST THINGS, TOOTS!
THERE AIN'T NO SUCH THING AS A FREE RIDE, BEV! EVERYTHING IN LIFE'S GOT A PRICE TAG--OR A COMPUTER PRICING CODE!
NOW WHERE'D I PUT MY BLASTED HOUSE KEYS?
IN YOUR PANTS POCKET, DUCKY.
NO WONDER I CAN'T FIND 'EM!
NEVER HAD THIS PROBLEM WHEN ALL I WORE WAS A JACKET...

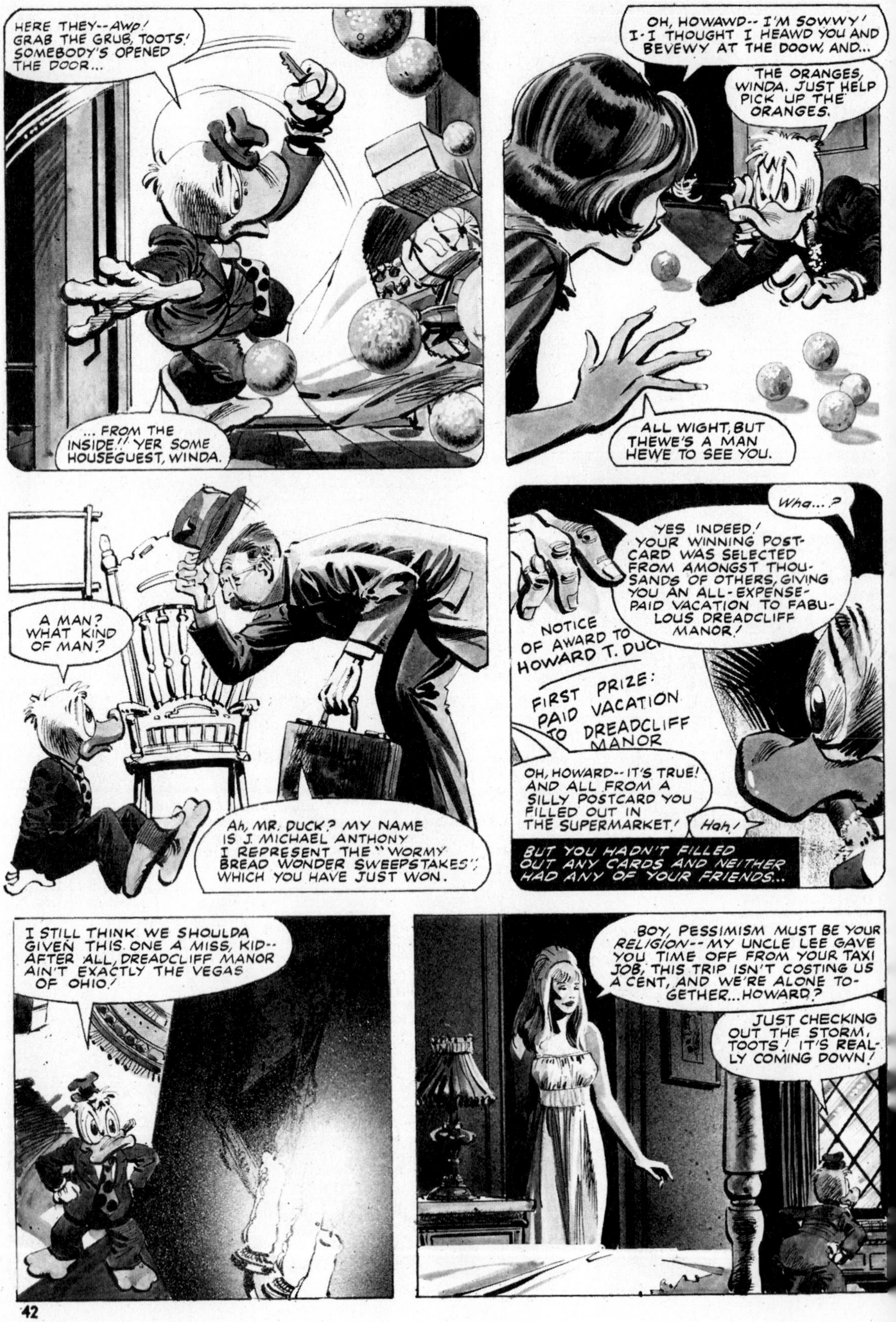
HERE THEY--Awp! GRAB THE GRUB, TOOTS! SOMEBODY'S OPENED THE DOOR...
... FROM THE INSIDE!! YER SOME HOUSEGUEST, WINDA.
OH, HOWAWD-- I'M SOWWY! I-I THOUGHT I HEAWD YOU AND BEVEWY AT THE DOOW, AND...
THE ORANGES, WINDA. JUST HELP PICK UP THE ORANGES.
ALL WIGHT, BUT THEWE'S A MAN HEWE TO SEE YOU.
A MAN? WHAT KIND OF MAN?
Ah, MR. DUCK? MY NAME IS J. MICHAEL ANTHONY I REPRESENT THE "WORMY BREAD WONDER SWEEPSTAKES", WHICH YOU HAVE JUST WON.
Wha...?
YES INDEED! YOUR WINNING POST-CARD WAS SELECTED FROM AMONGST THOU-SANDS OF OTHERS, GIVING YOU AN ALL-EXPENSE-PAID VACATION TO FABU-LOUS DREADCLIFF MANOR!
NOTICE OF AWARD TO HOWARD T. DUCK
FIRST PRIZE: PAID VACATION TO DREADCLIFF MANOR
OH, HOWARD-- IT'S TRUE! AND ALL FROM A SILLY POSTCARD YOU FILLED OUT IN THE SUPERMARKET!
Hah!
BUT YOU HADN'T FILLED OUT ANY CARDS AND NEITHER HAD ANY OF YOUR FRIENDS...
I STILL THINK WE SHOULDA GIVEN THIS ONE A MISS, KID-- AFTER ALL, DREADCLIFF MANOR AIN'T EXACTLY THE VEGAS OF OHIO!
BOY, PESSIMISM MUST BE YOUR RELIGION-- MY UNCLE LEE GAVE YOU TIME OFF FROM YOUR TAXI JOB, THIS TRIP ISN'T COSTING US A CENT, AND WE'RE ALONE TO-GETHER... HOWARD?
JUST CHECKING OUT THE STORM, TOOTS! IT'S REAL-LY COMING DOWN!
42

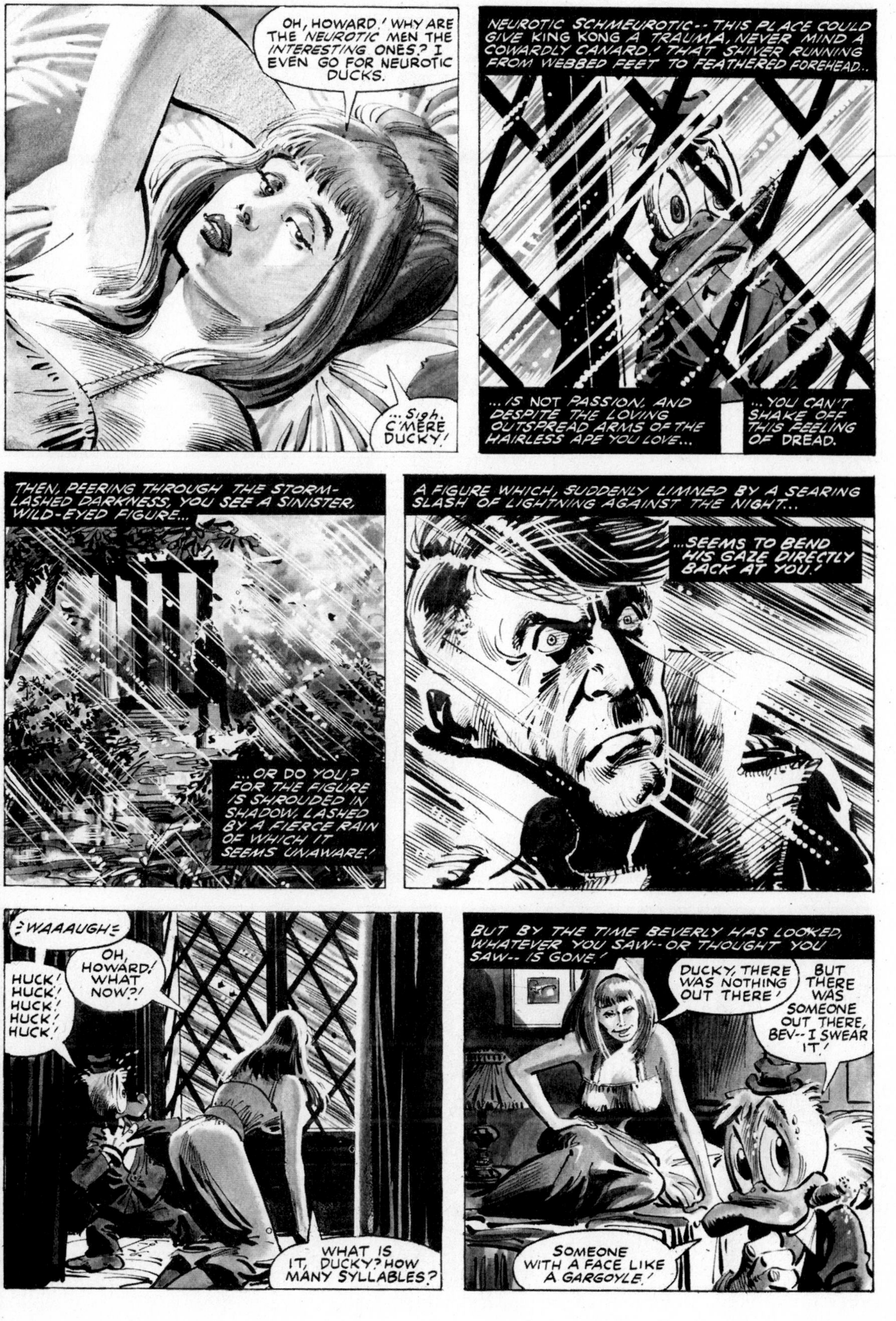
OH, HOWARD! WHY ARE THE NEUROTIC MEN THE INTERESTING ONES? I EVEN GO FOR NEUROTIC DUCKS.
...Sigh. C'MERE DUCKY!
NEUROTIC SCHMEUROTIC-- THIS PLACE COULD GIVE KING KONG A TRAUMA, NEVER MIND A COWARDLY CANARD! THAT SHIVER RUNNING FROM WEBBED FEET TO FEATHERED FOREHEAD...
...IS NOT PASSION. AND DESPITE THE LOVING OUTSPREAD ARMS OF THE HAIRLESS APE YOU LOVE...
...YOU CAN'T SHAKE OFF THIS FEELING OF DREAD.
THEN, PEERING THROUGH THE STORM-LASHED DARKNESS, YOU SEE A SINISTER, WILD-EYED FIGURE...
...OR DO YOU? FOR THE FIGURE IS SHROUDED IN SHADOW, LASHED BY A FIERCE RAIN OF WHICH IT SEEMS UNAWARE!
A FIGURE WHICH, SUDDENLY LIMNED BY A SEARING SLASH OF LIGHTNING AGAINST THE NIGHT...
...SEEMS TO BEND HIS GAZE DIRECTLY BACK AT YOU!
WAAAUGH
OH, HOWARD! WHAT NOW?!
HUCK! HUCK! HUCK! HUCK! HUCK!
WHAT IS IT, DUCKY? HOW MANY SYLLABLES?
BUT BY THE TIME BEVERLY HAS LOOKED, WHATEVER YOU SAW--OR THOUGHT YOU SAW-- IS GONE!
DUCKY, THERE WAS NOTHING OUT THERE!
BUT THERE WAS SOMEONE OUT THERE, BEV-- I SWEAR IT!
SOMEONE WITH A FACE LIKE A GARGOYLE!

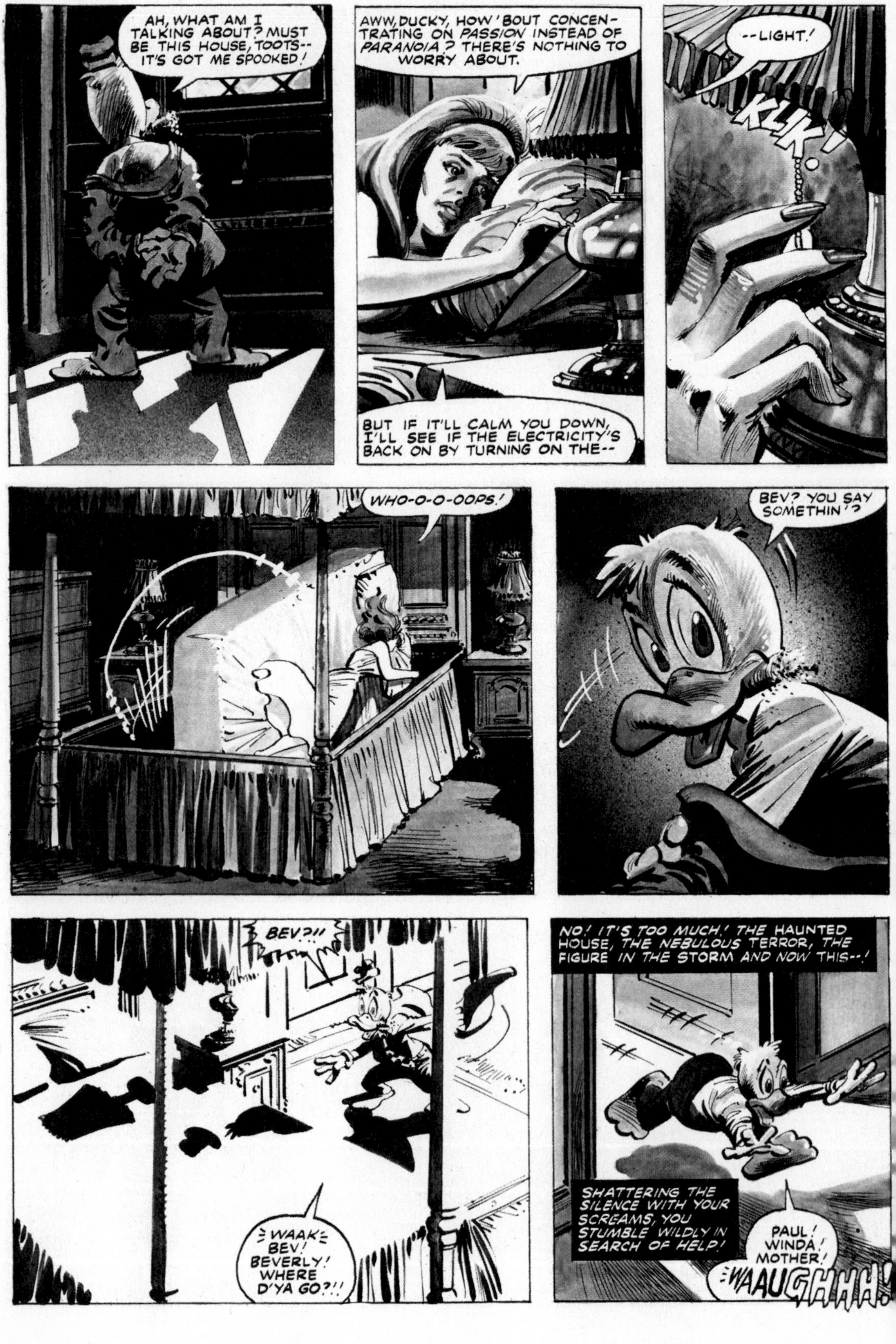

AH, WHAT AM I TALKING ABOUT? MUST BE THIS HOUSE, TOOTS-- IT'S GOT ME SPOOKED!
AWW, DUCKY, HOW 'BOUT CONCENTRATING ON PASSION INSTEAD OF PARANOIA? THERE'S NOTHING TO WORRY ABOUT.
BUT IF IT'LL CALM YOU DOWN, I'LL SEE IF THE ELECTRICITY'S BACK ON BY TURNING ON THE--
--LIGHT!
KLIK!
WHO-O-O-OOPS!
BEV? YOU SAY SOMETHIN'?
BEV?!!
WAAK BEV! BEVERLY! WHERE D'YA GO?!!
NO! IT'S TOO MUCH! THE HAUNTED HOUSE, THE NEBULOUS TERROR, THE FIGURE IN THE STORM AND NOW THIS--!
SHATTERING THE SILENCE WITH YOUR SCREAMS, YOU STUMBLE WILDLY IN SEARCH OF HELP!
PAUL! WINDA! MOTHER!
WAAUGHHH!

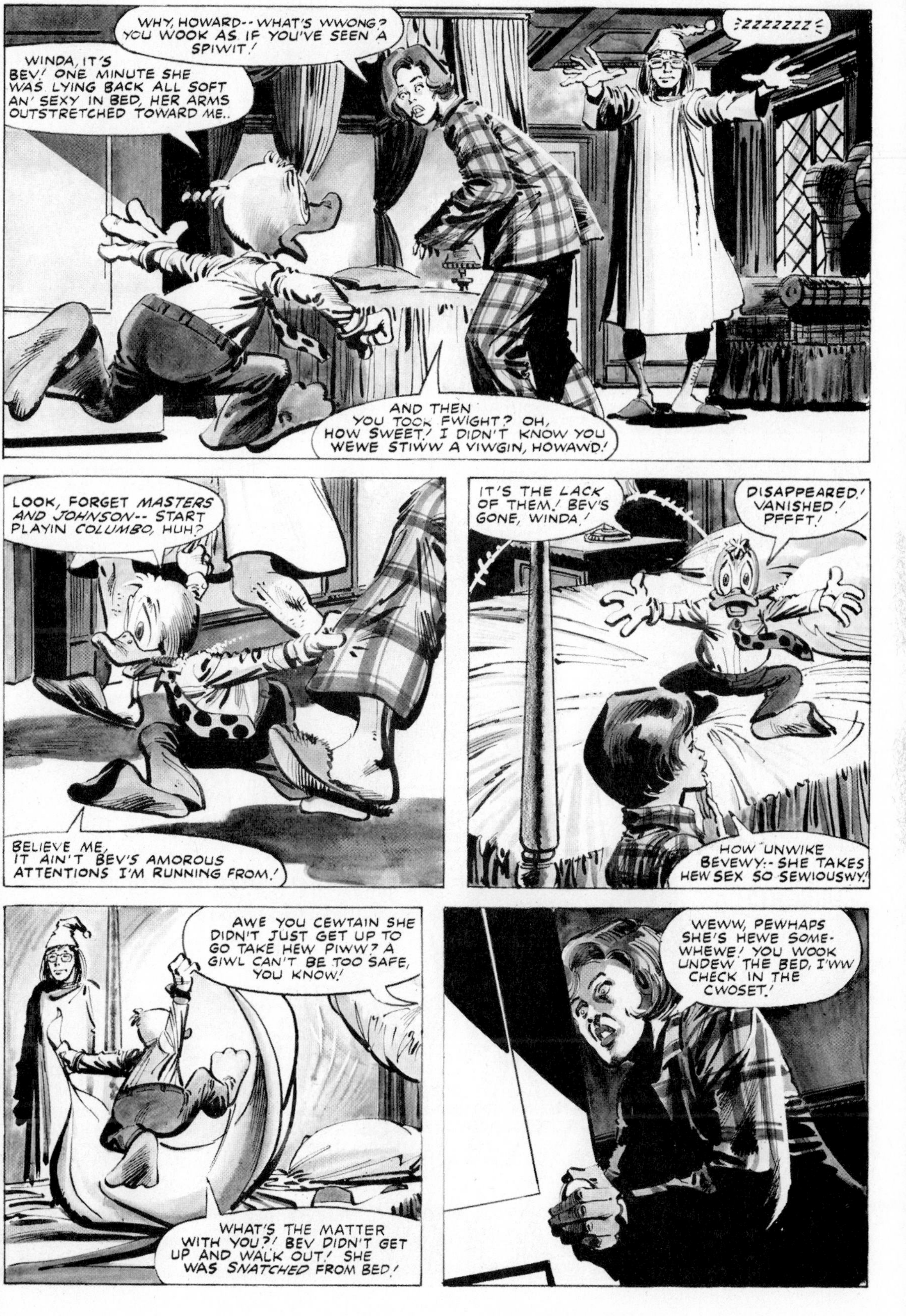
WHY, HOWARD--WHAT'S WWONG? YOU WOOK AS IF YOU'VE SEEN A SPIWIT!
WINDA, IT'S BEV! ONE MINUTE SHE WAS LYING BACK ALL SOFT AN' SEXY IN BED, HER ARMS OUTSTRETCHED TOWARD ME..
ZZZZZZZ
AND THEN YOU TOOK FWIGHT? OH, HOW SWEET! I DIDN'T KNOW YOU WEWE STIWW A VIWGIN, HOWAWD!
LOOK, FORGET MASTERS AND JOHNSON-- START PLAYIN COLUMBO, HUH?
BELIEVE ME, IT AIN'T BEV'S AMOROUS ATTENTIONS I'M RUNNING FROM!
IT'S THE LACK OF THEM! BEV'S GONE, WINDA!
DISAPPEARED! VANISHED! PFFFT!
HOW UNWIKE BEVEWY:- SHE TAKES HEW SEX SO SEWIOUSWY!
AWE YOU CEWTAIN SHE DIDN'T JUST GET UP TO GO TAKE HEW PIWW? A GIWL CAN'T BE TOO SAFE, YOU KNOW!
WHAT'S THE MATTER WITH YOU?! BEV DIDN'T GET UP AND WALK OUT! SHE WAS SNATCHED FROM BED!
WEWW, PEWHAPS SHE'S HEWE SOME-WHEWE! YOU WOOK UNDEW THE BED, I'WW CHECK IN THE CWOSET!

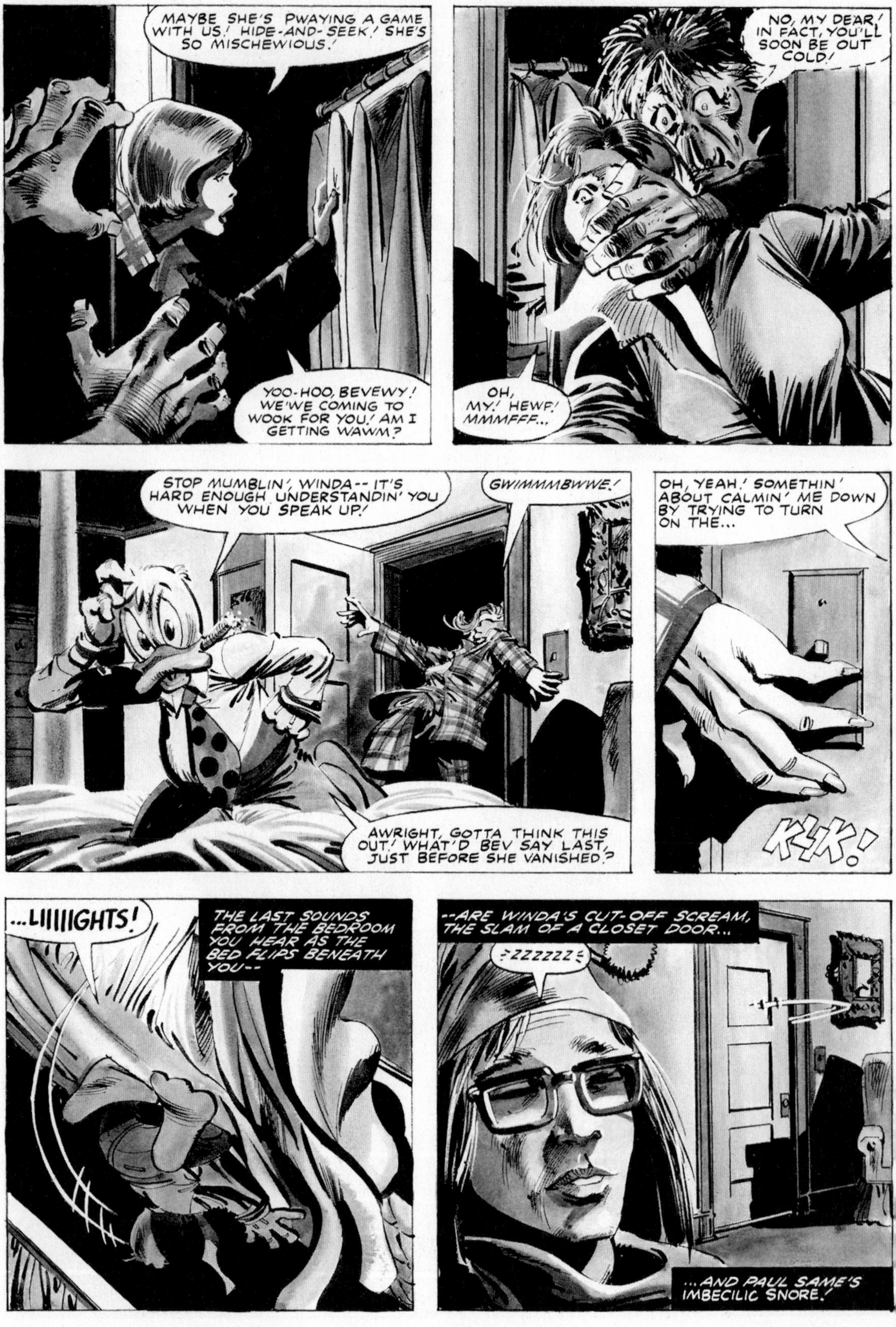

MAYBE SHE'S PWAYING A GAME WITH US! HIDE-AND-SEEK! SHE'S SO MISCHEWIOUS!
YOO-HOO, BEVEWY! WE'WE COMING TO WOOK FOR YOU! AM I GETTING WAWM?
NO, MY DEAR! IN FACT, YOU'LL SOON BE OUT COLD!
OH, MY! HEWP! MMMFFF...
STOP MUMBLIN', WINDA-- IT'S HARD ENOUGH UNDERSTANDIN' YOU WHEN YOU SPEAK UP!
GWIMMMBWWE!
AWRIGHT, GOTTA THINK THIS OUT! WHAT'D BEV SAY LAST, JUST BEFORE SHE VANISHED?
OH, YEAH! SOMETHIN' ABOUT CALMIN' ME DOWN BY TRYING TO TURN ON THE...
KLIK!
...LIIIIIGHTS!
THE LAST SOUNDS FROM THE BEDROOM YOU HEAR AS THE BED FLIPS BENEATH YOU--
--ARE WINDA'S CUT-OFF SCREAM, THE SLAM OF A CLOSET DOOR...
ZZZZZZ
...AND PAUL SAME'S IMBECILIC SNORE!

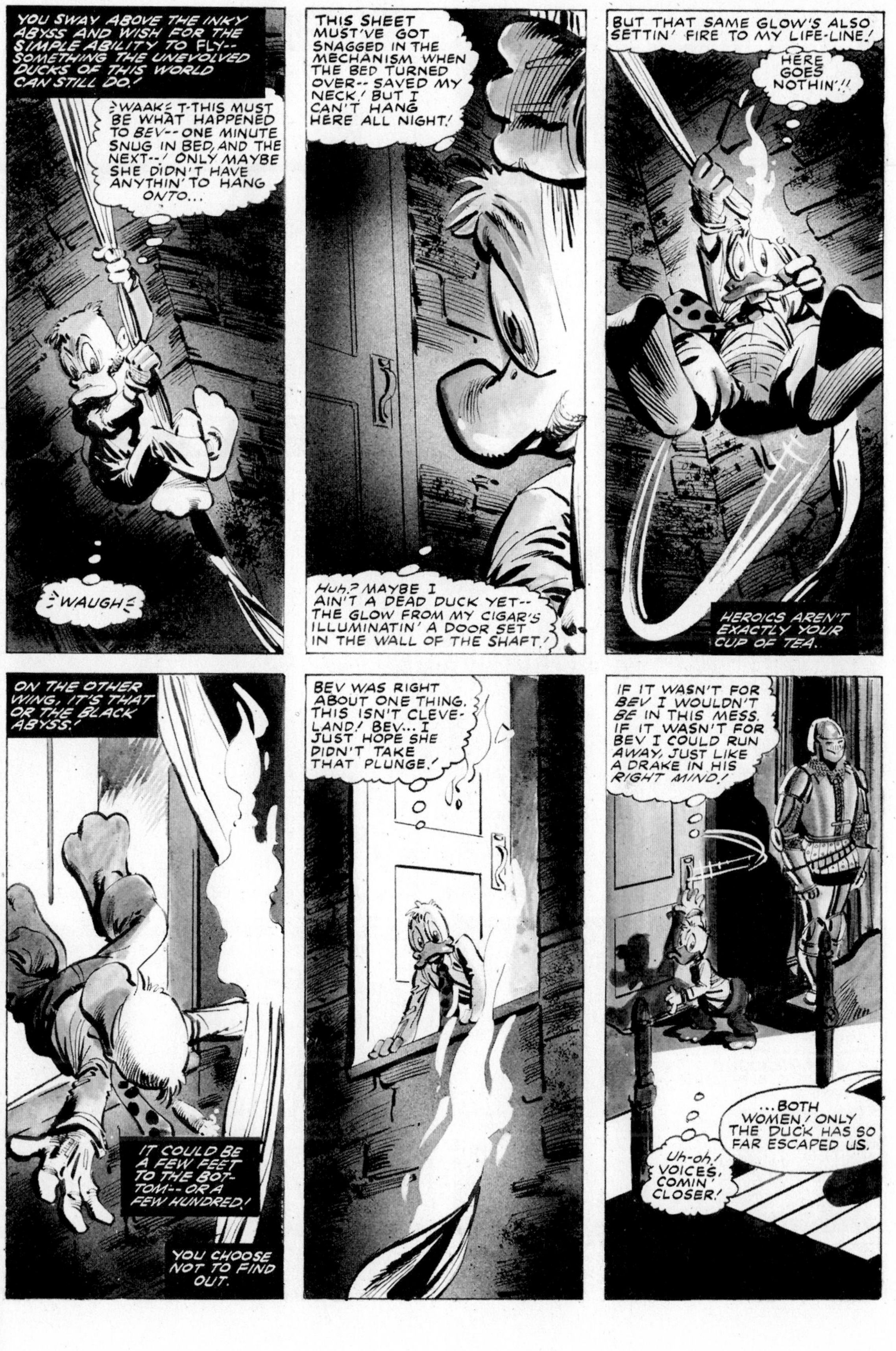
YOU SWAY ABOVE THE INKY ABYSS AND WISH FOR THE SIMPLE ABILITY TO FLY-- SOMETHING THE UNEVOLVED DUCKS OF THIS WORLD CAN STILL DO.!
WAAK! T-THIS MUST BE WHAT HAPPENED TO BEV-- ONE MINUTE SNUG IN BED, AND THE NEXT--! ONLY MAYBE SHE DIDN'T HAVE ANYTHIN' TO HANG ONTO...
WAUGH
THIS SHEET MUST'VE GOT SNAGGED IN THE MECHANISM WHEN THE BED TURNED OVER-- SAVED MY NECK! BUT I CAN'T HANG HERE ALL NIGHT!
HUH? MAYBE I AIN'T A DEAD DUCK YET-- THE GLOW FROM MY CIGAR'S ILLUMINATIN' A DOOR SET IN THE WALL OF THE SHAFT!
BUT THAT SAME GLOW'S ALSO SETTIN' FIRE TO MY LIFE-LINE!
HERE GOES NOTHIN'!!
HEROICS AREN'T EXACTLY YOUR CUP OF TEA.
ON THE OTHER WING, IT'S THAT OR THE BLACK ABYSS!
IT COULD BE A FEW FEET TO THE BOTTOM-- OR A FEW HUNDRED!
YOU CHOOSE NOT TO FIND OUT.
BEV WAS RIGHT ABOUT ONE THING. THIS ISN'T CLEVELAND! BEV... I JUST HOPE SHE DIDN'T TAKE THAT PLUNGE!
IF IT WASN'T FOR BEV I WOULDN'T BE IN THIS MESS. IF IT WASN'T FOR BEV I COULD RUN AWAY, JUST LIKE A DRAKE IN HIS RIGHT MIND!
...BOTH WOMEN! ONLY THE DUCK HAS SO FAR ESCAPED US.
UH-OH! VOICES, COMIN' CLOSER!

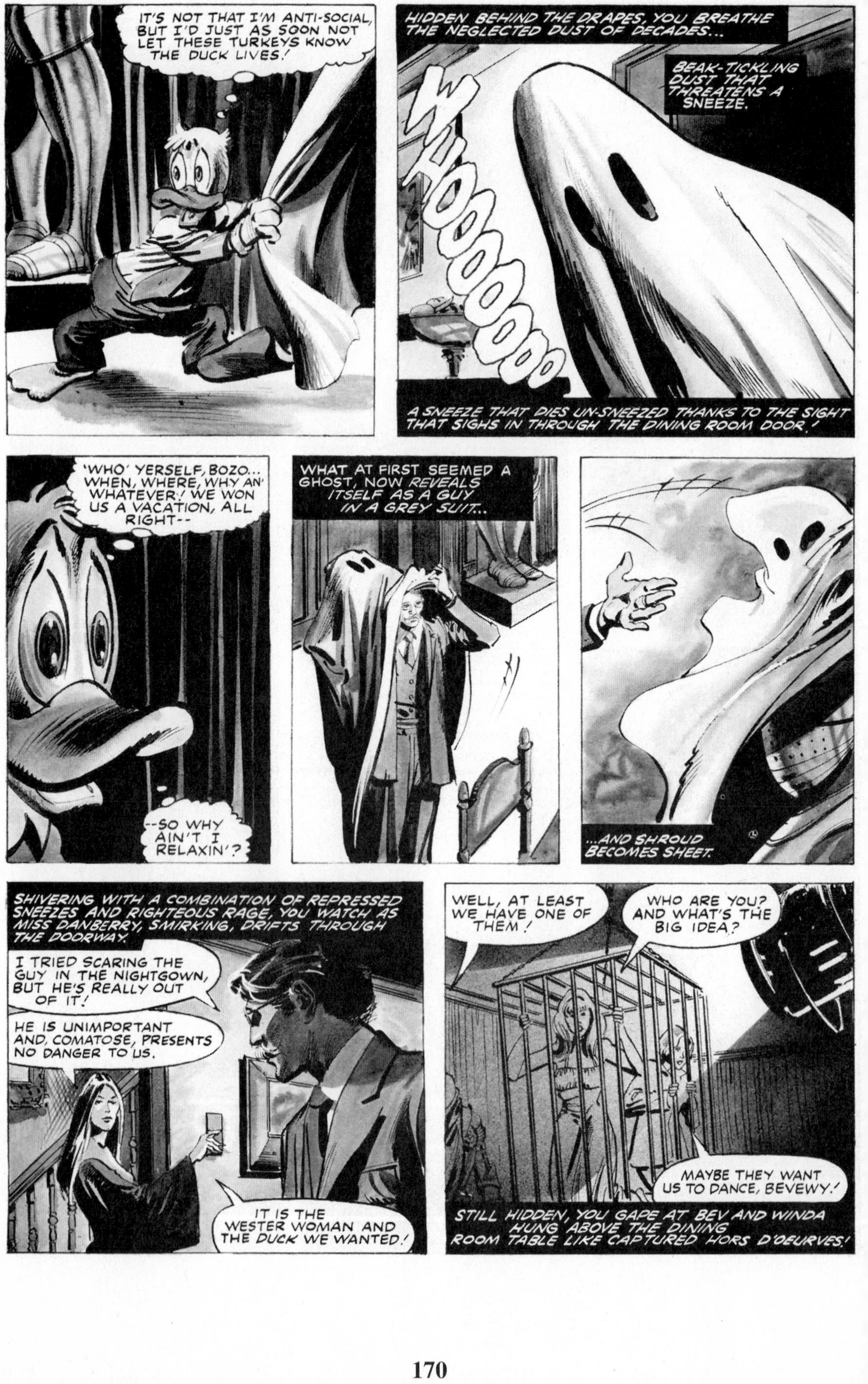
IT'S NOT THAT I'M ANTI-SOCIAL, BUT I'D JUST AS SOON NOT LET THESE TURKEYS KNOW THE DUCK LIVES!
HIDDEN BEHIND THE DRAPES, YOU BREATHE THE NEGLECTED DUST OF DECADES...
BEAK-TICKLING DUST THAT THREATENS A SNEEZE.
WHOOOOOOOOO
A SNEEZE THAT DIES UN-SNEEZED THANKS TO THE SIGHT THAT SIGHS IN THROUGH THE DINING ROOM DOOR!
'WHO' YERSELF, BOZO... WHEN, WHERE, WHY AN' WHATEVER! WE WON US A VACATION, ALL RIGHT--
--SO WHY AIN'T I RELAXIN'?
WHAT AT FIRST SEEMED A GHOST, NOW REVEALS ITSELF AS A GUY IN A GREY SUIT...
...AND SHROUD BECOMES SHEET.
SHIVERING WITH A COMBINATION OF REPRESSED SNEEZES AND RIGHTEOUS RAGE, YOU WATCH AS MISS DANBERRY, SMIRKING, DRIFTS THROUGH THE DOORWAY.
I TRIED SCARING THE GUY IN THE NIGHTGOWN, BUT HE'S REALLY OUT OF IT!
HE IS UNIMPORTANT AND, COMATOSE, PRESENTS NO DANGER TO US.
IT IS THE WESTER WOMAN AND THE DUCK WE WANTED!
WELL, AT LEAST WE HAVE ONE OF THEM!
WHO ARE YOU? AND WHAT'S THE BIG IDEA?
MAYBE THEY WANT US TO DANCE, BEVEWY!
STILL HIDDEN, YOU GAPE AT BEV AND WINDA HUNG ABOVE THE DINING ROOM TABLE LIKE CAPTURED HORS D'OEURVES!

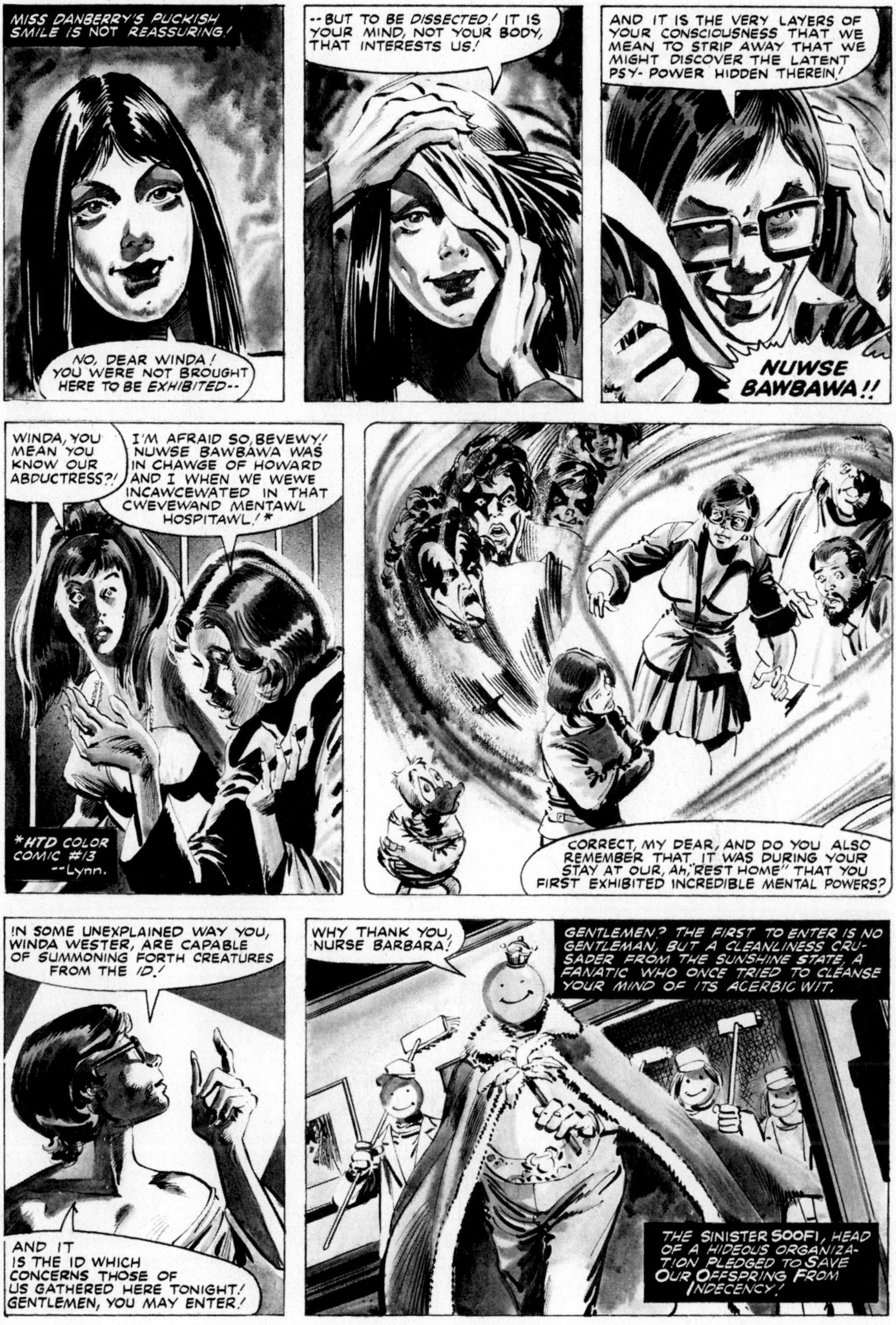

MISS DANBERRY'S PUCKISH SMILE IS NOT REASSURING!
NO, DEAR WINDA! YOU WERE NOT BROUGHT HERE TO BE EXHIBITED--
--BUT TO BE DISSECTED! IT IS YOUR MIND, NOT YOUR BODY, THAT INTERESTS US!
AND IT IS THE VERY LAYERS OF YOUR CONSCIOUSNESS THAT WE MEAN TO STRIP AWAY THAT WE MIGHT DISCOVER THE LATENT PSY-POWER HIDDEN THEREIN!
NUWSE BAWBAWA!!
WINDA, YOU MEAN YOU KNOW OUR ABDUCTRESS?!
I'M AFRAID SO, BEVEWY! NUWSE BAWBAWA WAS IN CHAWGE OF HOWARD AND I WHEN WE WEWE INCAWCEWATED IN THAT CWEVEWAND MENTAWL HOSPITAWL!*
*HTD COLOR COMIC #13 --Lynn.
CORRECT, MY DEAR, AND DO YOU ALSO REMEMBER THAT IT WAS DURING YOUR STAY AT OUR, Ah, "REST HOME" THAT YOU FIRST EXHIBITED INCREDIBLE MENTAL POWERS?
IN SOME UNEXPLAINED WAY YOU, WINDA WESTER, ARE CAPABLE OF SUMMONING FORTH CREATURES FROM THE ID!
AND IT IS THE ID WHICH CONCERNS THOSE OF US GATHERED HERE TONIGHT! GENTLEMEN, YOU MAY ENTER!
WHY THANK YOU, NURSE BARBARA!
GENTLEMEN? THE FIRST TO ENTER IS NO GENTLEMAN, BUT A CLEANLINESS CRUSADER FROM THE SUNSHINE STATE, A FANATIC WHO ONCE TRIED TO CLEANSE YOUR MIND OF ITS ACERBIC WIT.
THE SINISTER SOOFI, HEAD OF A HIDEOUS ORGANIZATION PLEDGED TO SAVE OUR OFFSPRING FROM INDECENCY!

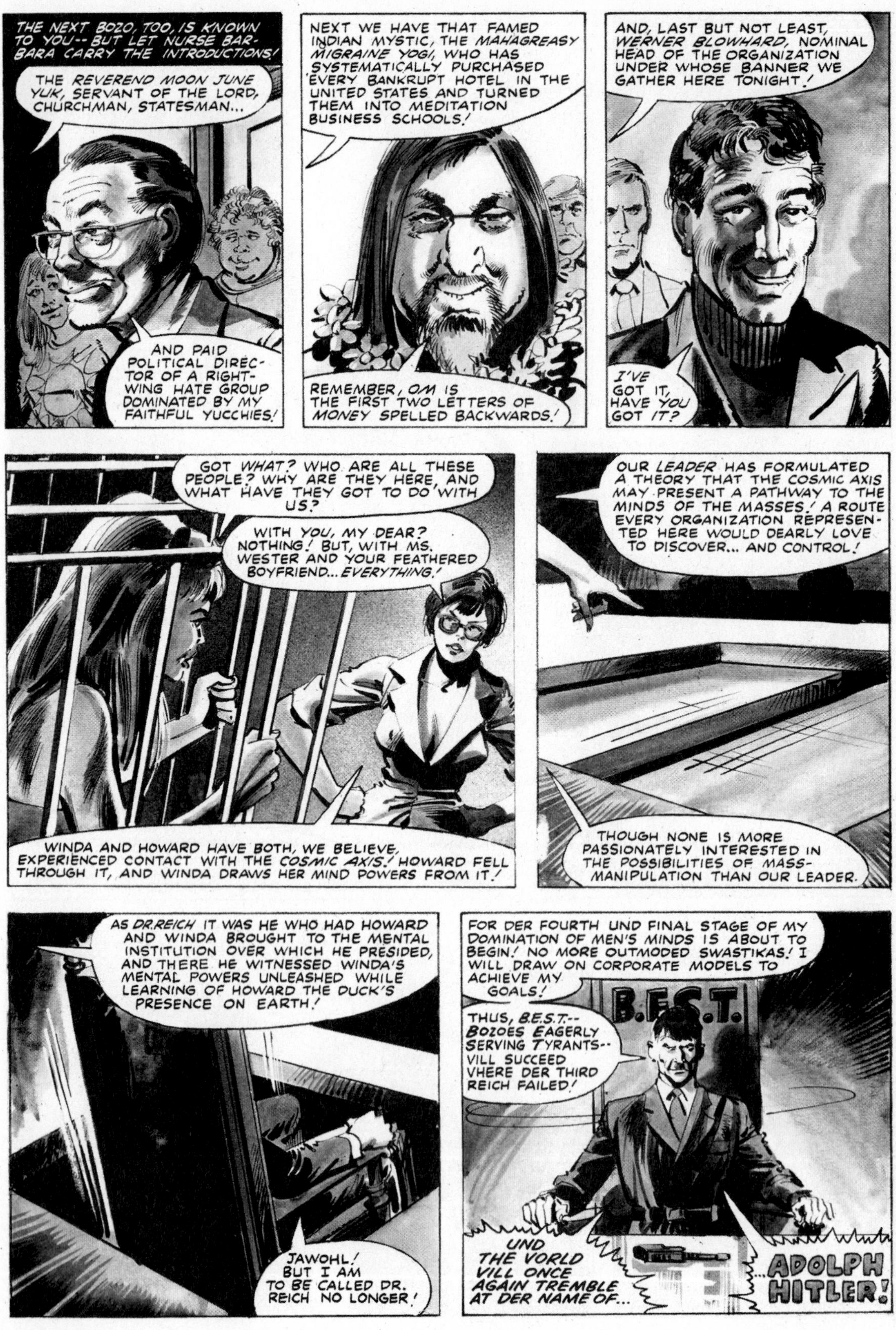
THE NEXT BOZO, TOO, IS KNOWN TO YOU-- BUT LET NURSE BARBARA CARRY THE INTRODUCTIONS!
THE REVEREND MOON JUNE YUK, SERVANT OF THE LORD, CHURCHMAN, STATESMAN...
AND PAID POLITICAL DIRECTOR OF A RIGHT-WING HATE GROUP DOMINATED BY MY FAITHFUL YUCCHIES!
NEXT WE HAVE THAT FAMED INDIAN MYSTIC, THE MAHAGREASY MIGRAINE YOGI, WHO HAS SYSTEMATICALLY PURCHASED EVERY BANKRUPT HOTEL IN THE UNITED STATES AND TURNED THEM INTO MEDITATION BUSINESS SCHOOLS!
REMEMBER, OM IS THE FIRST TWO LETTERS OF MONEY SPELLED BACKWARDS!
AND, LAST BUT NOT LEAST, WERNER BLOWHARD, NOMINAL HEAD OF THE ORGANIZATION UNDER WHOSE BANNER WE GATHER HERE TONIGHT!
I'VE GOT IT, HAVE YOU GOT IT?
GOT WHAT? WHO ARE ALL THESE PEOPLE? WHY ARE THEY HERE, AND WHAT HAVE THEY GOT TO DO WITH US?
WITH YOU, MY DEAR? NOTHING! BUT, WITH MS. WESTER AND YOUR FEATHERED BOYFRIEND... EVERYTHING!
WINDA AND HOWARD HAVE BOTH, WE BELIEVE, EXPERIENCED CONTACT WITH THE COSMIC AXIS! HOWARD FELL THROUGH IT, AND WINDA DRAWS HER MIND POWERS FROM IT!
OUR LEADER HAS FORMULATED A THEORY THAT THE COSMIC AXIS MAY PRESENT A PATHWAY TO THE MINDS OF THE MASSES! A ROUTE EVERY ORGANIZATION REPRESENTED HERE WOULD DEARLY LOVE TO DISCOVER... AND CONTROL!
THOUGH NONE IS MORE PASSIONATELY INTERESTED IN THE POSSIBILITIES OF MASS-MANIPULATION THAN OUR LEADER.
AS DR. REICH IT WAS HE WHO HAD HOWARD AND WINDA BROUGHT TO THE MENTAL INSTITUTION OVER WHICH HE PRESIDED, AND THERE HE WITNESSED WINDA'S MENTAL POWERS UNLEASHED WHILE LEARNING OF HOWARD THE DUCK'S PRESENCE ON EARTH!
JAWOHL! BUT I AM TO BE CALLED DR. REICH NO LONGER!
FOR DER FOURTH UND FINAL STAGE OF MY DOMINATION OF MEN'S MINDS IS ABOUT TO BEGIN! NO MORE OUTMODED SWASTIKAS! I WILL DRAW ON CORPORATE MODELS TO ACHIEVE MY GOALS!
B.E.S.T.
THUS, B.E.S.T.-- BOZOES EAGERLY SERVING TYRANTS-- VILL SUCCEED VHERE DER THIRD REICH FAILED!
UND THE VORLD VILL ONCE AGAIN TREMBLE AT DER NAME OF...
...ADOLPH HITLER!

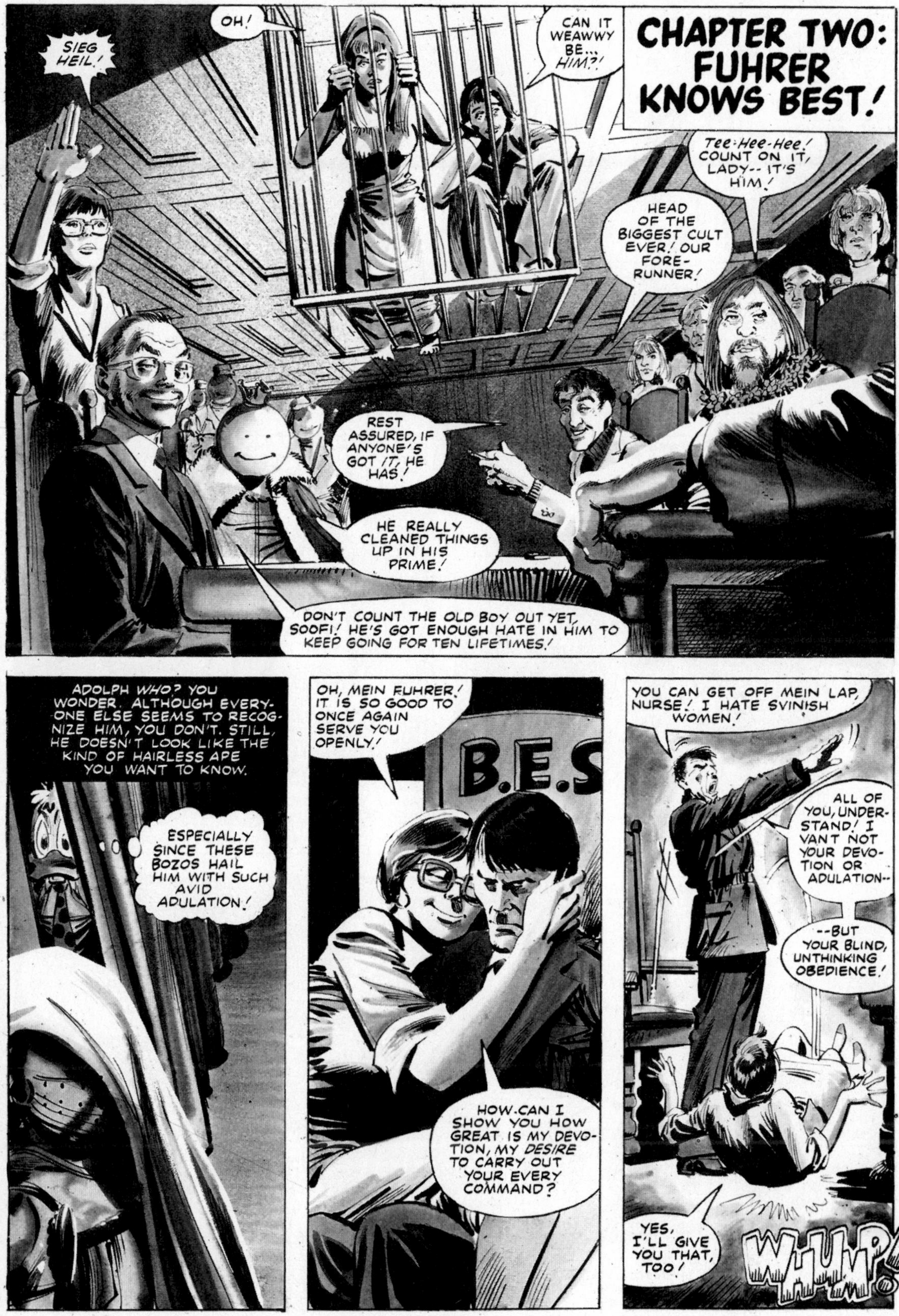
CHAPTER TWO: FUHRER KNOWS BEST!
SIEG HEIL!
OH!
CAN IT WEAWWY BE... HIM?!
TEE-HEE-HEE! COUNT ON IT, LADY-- IT'S HIM!
HEAD OF THE BIGGEST CULT EVER! OUR FORE-RUNNER!
REST ASSURED, IF ANYONE'S GOT IT, HE HAS!
HE REALLY CLEANED THINGS UP IN HIS PRIME!
DON'T COUNT THE OLD BOY OUT YET, SOOFI! HE'S GOT ENOUGH HATE IN HIM TO KEEP GOING FOR TEN LIFETIMES!
ADOLPH WHO? YOU WONDER. ALTHOUGH EVERY-ONE ELSE SEEMS TO RECOG-NIZE HIM, YOU DON'T. STILL, HE DOESN'T LOOK LIKE THE KIND OF HAIRLESS APE YOU WANT TO KNOW.
ESPECIALLY SINCE THESE BOZOS HAIL HIM WITH SUCH AVID ADULATION!
OH, MEIN FUHRER! IT IS SO GOOD TO ONCE AGAIN SERVE YOU OPENLY!
B.E.S
HOW CAN I SHOW YOU HOW GREAT IS MY DEVO-TION, MY DESIRE TO CARRY OUT YOUR EVERY COMMAND?
YOU CAN GET OFF MEIN LAP, NURSE! I HATE SVINISH WOMEN!
ALL OF YOU, UNDER-STAND! I VANT NOT YOUR DEVO-TION OR ADULATION--
--BUT YOUR BLIND, UNTHINKING OBEDIENCE!
YES, I'LL GIVE YOU THAT, TOO!
WHUMP!

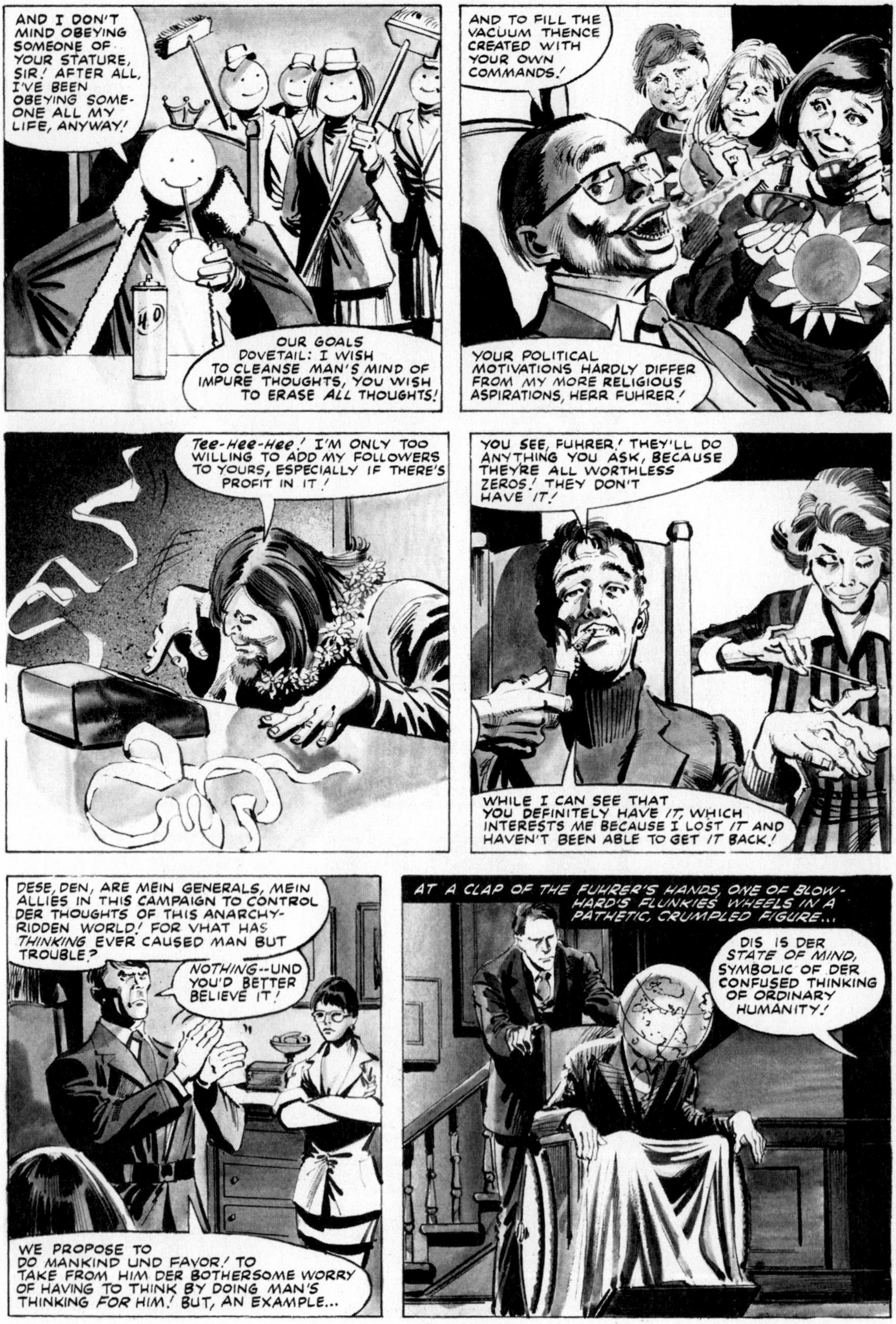
AND I DON'T MIND OBEYING SOMEONE OF YOUR STATURE, SIR! AFTER ALL, I'VE BEEN OBEYING SOME-ONE ALL MY LIFE, ANYWAY!
OUR GOALS DOVETAIL: I WISH TO CLEANSE MAN'S MIND OF IMPURE THOUGHTS, YOU WISH TO ERASE *ALL* THOUGHTS!
AND TO FILL THE VACUUM THENCE CREATED WITH YOUR OWN COMMANDS!
YOUR POLITICAL MOTIVATIONS HARDLY DIFFER FROM MY MORE RELIGIOUS ASPIRATIONS, HERR FUHRER!
Tee-Hee-Hee! I'M ONLY TOO WILLING TO ADD MY FOLLOWERS TO YOURS, ESPECIALLY IF THERE'S PROFIT IN IT!
YOU SEE, FUHRER! THEY'LL DO ANYTHING YOU ASK, BECAUSE THEY'RE ALL WORTHLESS ZEROS! THEY DON'T HAVE *IT*!
WHILE I CAN SEE THAT YOU DEFINITELY HAVE *IT*, WHICH INTERESTS ME BECAUSE I LOST *IT* AND HAVEN'T BEEN ABLE TO GET *IT* BACK!
DESE, DEN, ARE MEIN GENERALS, MEIN ALLIES IN THIS CAMPAIGN TO CONTROL DER THOUGHTS OF THIS ANARCHY-RIDDEN WORLD! FOR VHAT HAS *THINKING* EVER CAUSED MAN BUT TROUBLE?
NOTHING--UND YOU'D BETTER BELIEVE IT!
WE PROPOSE TO DO MANKIND UND FAVOR! TO TAKE FROM HIM DER BOTHERSOME WORRY OF HAVING TO THINK BY DOING MAN'S THINKING *FOR* HIM! BUT, AN EXAMPLE...
AT A CLAP OF THE FUHRER'S HANDS, ONE OF BLOW-HARD'S FLUNKIES WHEELS IN A PATHETIC, CRUMPLED FIGURE...
DIS IS DER *STATE OF MIND*, SYMBOLIC OF DER CONFUSED THINKING OF ORDINARY HUMANITY!

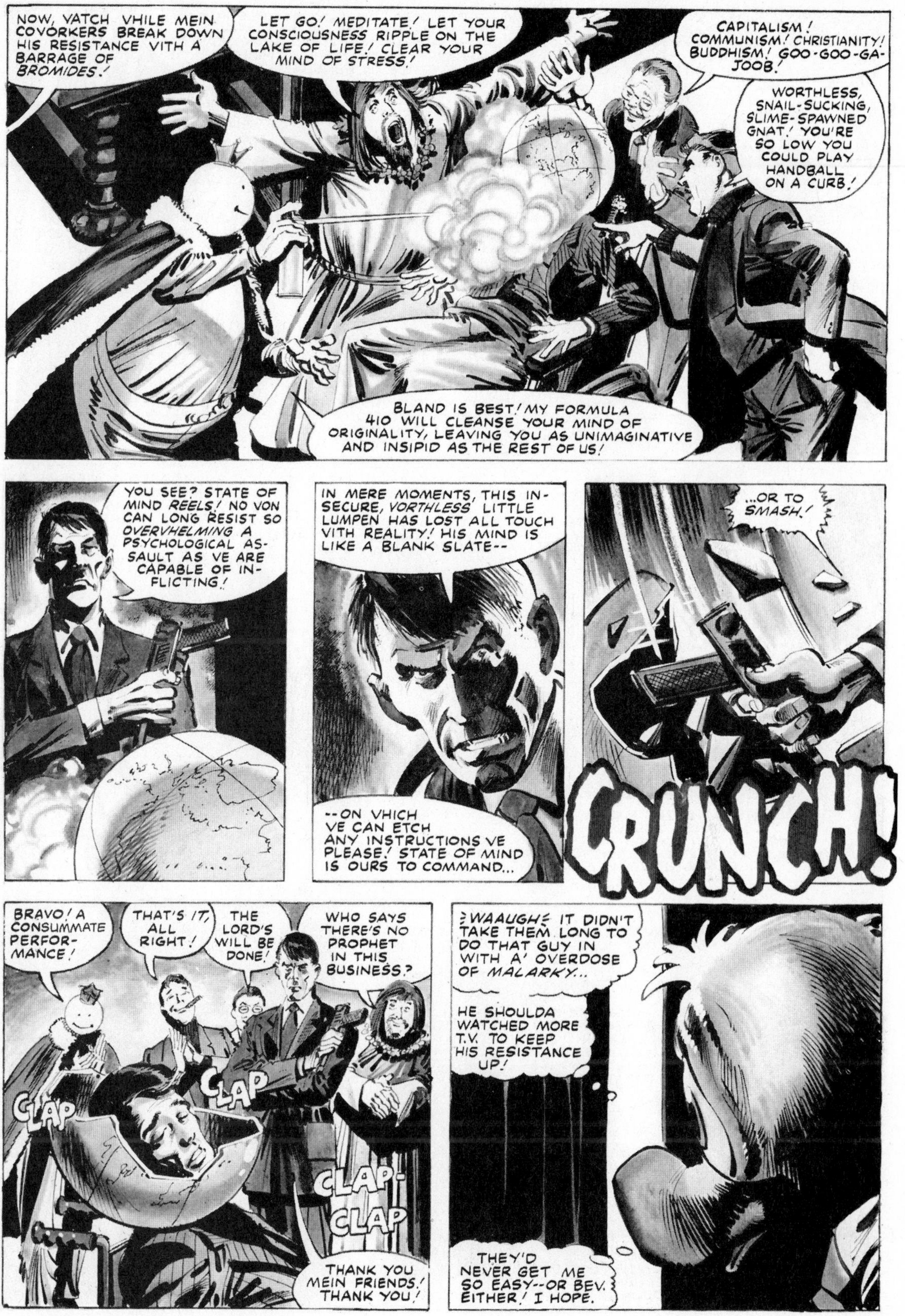
NOW, VATCH VHILE MEIN COVORKERS BREAK DOWN HIS RESISTANCE VITH A BARRAGE OF BROMIDES!
LET GO! MEDITATE! LET YOUR CONSCIOUSNESS RIPPLE ON THE LAKE OF LIFE! CLEAR YOUR MIND OF STRESS!
CAPITALISM! COMMUNISM! CHRISTIANITY! BUDDHISM! GOO-GOO-GA-JOOB!
WORTHLESS, SNAIL-SUCKING, SLIME-SPAWNED GNAT! YOU'RE SO LOW YOU COULD PLAY HANDBALL ON A CURB!
BLAND IS BEST! MY FORMULA 410 WILL CLEANSE YOUR MIND OF ORIGINALITY, LEAVING YOU AS UNIMAGINATIVE AND INSIPID AS THE REST OF US!
YOU SEE? STATE OF MIND REELS! NO VON CAN LONG RESIST SO OVERVHELMING A PSYCHOLOGICAL ASSAULT AS VE ARE CAPABLE OF INFLICTING!
IN MERE MOMENTS, THIS INSECURE, VORTHLESS LITTLE LUMPEN HAS LOST ALL TOUCH VITH REALITY! HIS MIND IS LIKE A BLANK SLATE--
--ON VHICH VE CAN ETCH ANY INSTRUCTIONS VE PLEASE! STATE OF MIND IS OURS TO COMMAND...
...OR TO SMASH!
CRUNCH!
BRAVO! A CONSUMMATE PERFORMANCE!
THAT'S IT, ALL RIGHT!
THE LORD'S WILL BE DONE!
WHO SAYS THERE'S NO PROPHET IN THIS BUSINESS?
CLAP
CLAP
CLAP-CLAP
THANK YOU MEIN FRIENDS! THANK YOU!
WAAUGH! IT DIDN'T TAKE THEM LONG TO DO THAT GUY IN WITH A' OVERDOSE OF MALARKY...
HE SHOULDA WATCHED MORE T.V. TO KEEP HIS RESISTANCE UP!
THEY'D NEVER GET ME SO EASY--OR BEV. EITHER! I HOPE.

YOUR FAVORITE HAIRLESS APE FEELS THE SAME!

BIG DEAL! SO YOU CAN BRAINWASH ONE OF YOUR OWN DISCIPLES!

HOWARD AND WINDA ARE STRONG ENOUGH INDIVIDUALS TO RESIST YOUR MIND MANIPULATIONS!

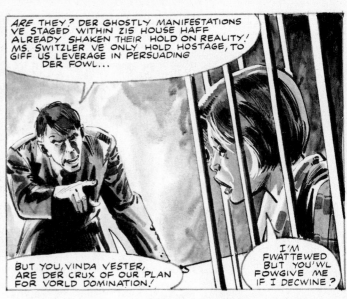

ARE THEY? DER GHOSTLY MANIFESTATIONS VE STAGED WITHIN ZIS HOUSE HAFF ALREADY SHAKEN THEIR HOLD ON REALITY! MS. SWITZLER VE ONLY HOLD HOSTAGE, TO GIFF US LEVERAGE IN PERSUADING DER FOWL...

BUT YOU, VINDA VESTER, ARE DER CRUX OF OUR PLAN FOR VORLD DOMINATION!

I'M FWATTEWED BUT YOU'WL FOWGIVE ME IF I DECWINE?

NEIN! WINDA!

OH, HEWP ME, BEVEWY! HEWP ME!

YOU HAVE NOTHING TO FEAR, MY DEAR! THIS IS A FAMILY SHOW!

APPROVED BY MY CHURCH!

VINDA VESTER HAS REVEALED VAST PSYCHIC POWERS-- UND, USING HER MIND TO GAIN ACCESS TO DER COSMIC AXIS, VE CAN BEGIN TO PROJECT OUR CONTROL ONTO DER CONFUSED BLANK-SLATE MINDS OF THE ENTIRE WORLD!

BUT BEFORE ENDANGERING MEIN ALLIES, DER COSMIC AXIS MUST BE TESTED... BY VON WHO HAS PASSED THROUGH IT BEFORE! NURSE BARBARA, BRING IN DER DUCK!

B-BUT, MEIN FUHRER, I-I THOUGHT YOU WERE COORDINATING THE DUCK'S CAPTURE?

VAT?! YOU MEAN DER VERDAMMT DUCK IS NOT YET IN OUR CLUTCHES?!?

INCOMPETENTS! BUNGLERS! CAN I NEVER FIND UNDERLINGS CAPABLE OF DOING AN HONEST DAY'S DESTRUCTION!

OUT! ALL OF YOU! UND DO NOT RETURN UNTIL DER DUCK IS CAUGHT!

COWED AND SHEEPISH, THE DISCIPLES SHAMBLE OUT IN SEARCH OF THE TALKING DUCK WHO MIGHT HOLD THE SECRET OF THE COSMIC AXIS-- YOU!

SINCE YOU HADN'T BEEN FOUND AT THE BOTTOM OF THE SHAFT, THEY ASSUMED YOU'D BEEN TAKEN UPSTAIRS.

176

BUT, EVEN AS THE DISCIPLES DEPART, ANOTHER, UNHEEDED FIGURE DESCENDS THE STAIRS!

PAUL! SLEEPWALKIN' AS USUAL. NO ONE'S PAYIN' ANY ATTENTION TO HIM-- THE STORY OF HIS LIFE.

SAY, HE'S GIVIN' ME AN IDEA THAT JUST MAY GET US OUTTA THIS MESS! BUT FIRST I GOTTA BORROW THIS DISCARDED "GHOST" SHEET...

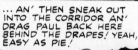

... AN' THEN SNEAK OUT INTO THE CORRIDOR AN' DRAG PAUL BACK HERE BEHIND THE DRAPES! YEAH, EASY AS PIE!

ALL I GOTTA DO IS AVOID BEIN' SPOTTED BY THE CREEP QUINTET.

THIS PROVED EVEN EASIER THAN YOU'D HOPED, SINCE THOSE NASTIES WERE ABSORBED AT THE MOMENT IN PERSECUTIN' POOR WINDA!

Tee-Hee-Hee! RELAX, DEAR CHILD! YOU ARE TENSE, FULL OF STRESS!

LET YOURSELF GO WITH THE FLOW-- AND TELL US WHAT YOU WANT TO KNOW!

SPLOOSH!

YOU FAT SWOB!

NOW, NOW, MY DEAR! THAT'S NO WAY TO SPEAK TO THE MAHA-GREASY! HE'S ONLY DOING THE LORD'S WORK, AS ARE WE ALL!

OF COURSE, THE DIVINE WILL DOES NEED IN-TERPRETING!

WAP

BY THE WAY, WINDA-- YOUR RELATIONSHIP WITH A SOMNAM-BULANT ISN'T QUITE STRAIGHT, YOU KNOW? ARE YOU KINKY?

THAT'S NONE OF YOUW BUSINESS! PAUWL AND I HAVE A PEWFECTWY SOUND WEWATIONSHIP!

YOU'RE WORTHLESS, STUPID AND SICK!

UP YOUW'S! I'M NOT AFWAID OF YOU! YOU CAN AWW GO TO HEWW!

THAT'S PRECISELY WHERE THEY WILL BE GOING, MY DEAR!

WHOOOOOO

177

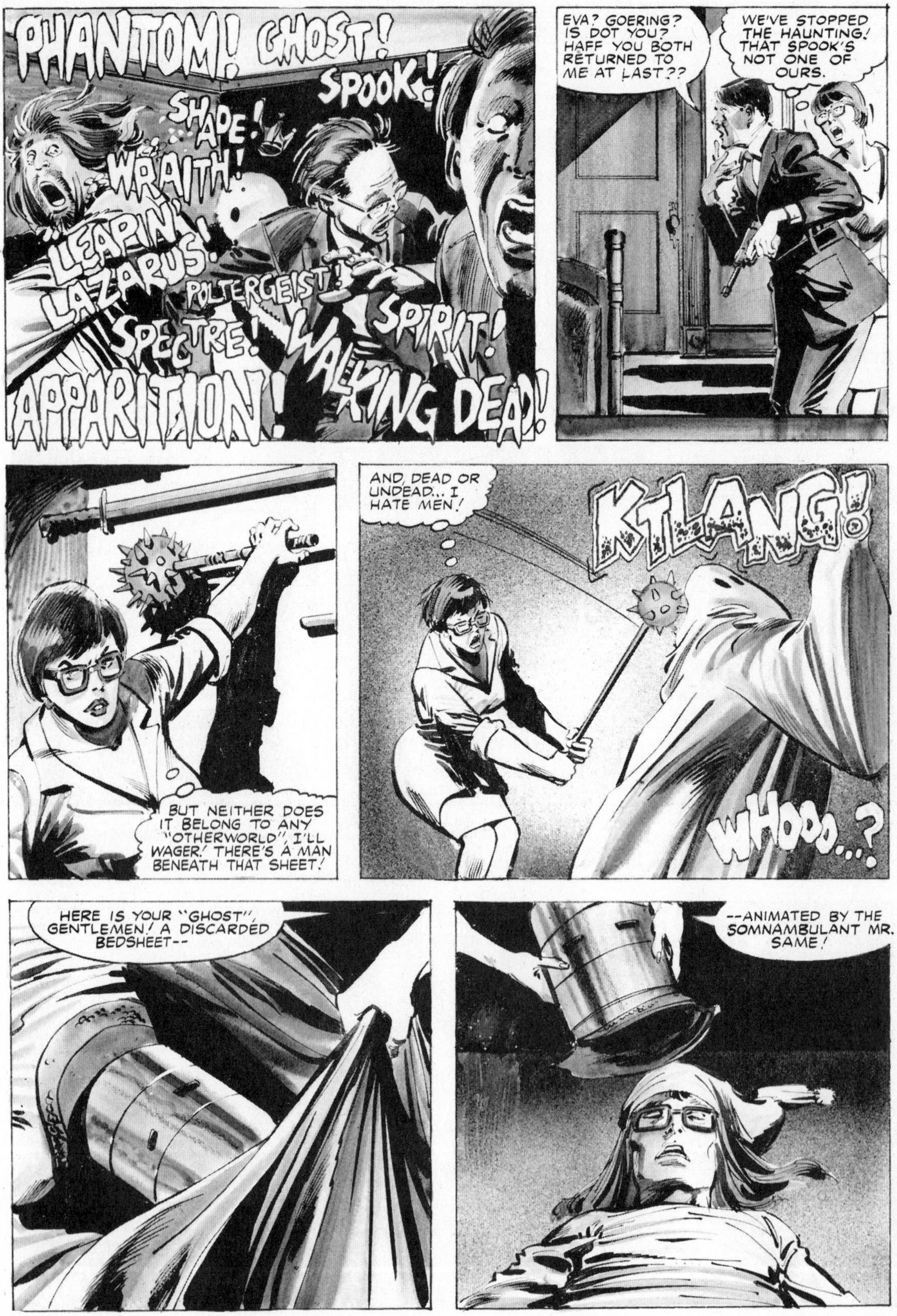
PHANTOM! GHOST!
SPOOK!
SHADE!
WRAITH!
LEAPIN' LAZARUS!
POLTERGEIST!
SPECTRE!
SPIRIT!
APPARITION!
WALKING DEAD!
EVA? GOERING? IS DOT YOU? HAFF YOU BOTH RETURNED TO ME AT LAST??
WE'VE STOPPED THE HAUNTING! THAT SPOOK'S NOT ONE OF OURS.
BUT NEITHER DOES IT BELONG TO ANY "OTHERWORLD", I'LL WAGER! THERE'S A MAN BENEATH THAT SHEET!
AND, DEAD OR UNDEAD... I HATE MEN!
KTLANG!
WHOOO...?
HERE IS YOUR "GHOST", GENTLEMEN! A DISCARDED BEDSHEET--
--ANIMATED BY THE SOMNAMBULANT MR. SAME!

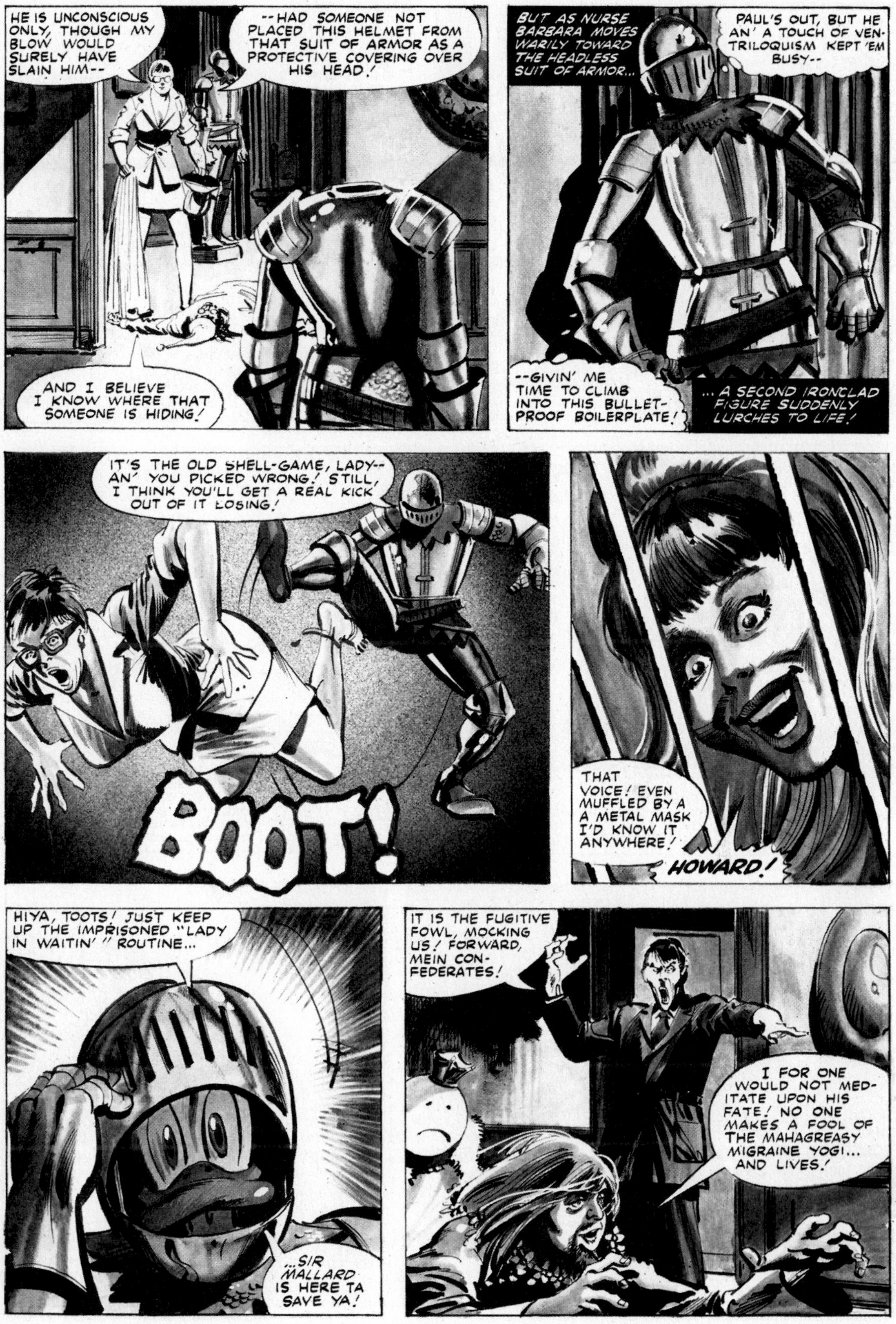
HE IS UNCONSCIOUS ONLY, THOUGH MY BLOW WOULD SURELY HAVE SLAIN HIM--
--HAD SOMEONE NOT PLACED THIS HELMET FROM THAT SUIT OF ARMOR AS A PROTECTIVE COVERING OVER HIS HEAD!
AND I BELIEVE I KNOW WHERE THAT SOMEONE IS HIDING!
BUT AS NURSE BARBARA MOVES WARILY TOWARD THE HEADLESS SUIT OF ARMOR...
PAUL'S OUT, BUT HE AN' A TOUCH OF VENTRILOQUISM KEPT 'EM BUSY--
--GIVIN' ME TIME TO CLIMB INTO THIS BULLET-PROOF BOILERPLATE!
...A SECOND IRONCLAD FIGURE SUDDENLY LURCHES TO LIFE!
IT'S THE OLD SHELL-GAME, LADY-- AN' YOU PICKED WRONG! STILL, I THINK YOU'LL GET A REAL KICK OUT OF IT LOSING!
BOOT!
THAT VOICE! EVEN MUFFLED BY A A METAL MASK I'D KNOW IT ANYWHERE!
HOWARD!
HIYA, TOOTS! JUST KEEP UP THE IMPRISONED "LADY IN WAITIN'" ROUTINE...
...SIR MALLARD IS HERE TA SAVE YA!
IT IS THE FUGITIVE FOWL, MOCKING US! FORWARD, MEIN CONFEDERATES!
I FOR ONE WOULD NOT MEDITATE UPON HIS FATE! NO ONE MAKES A FOOL OF THE MAHAGREASY MIGRAINE YOGI... AND LIVES!

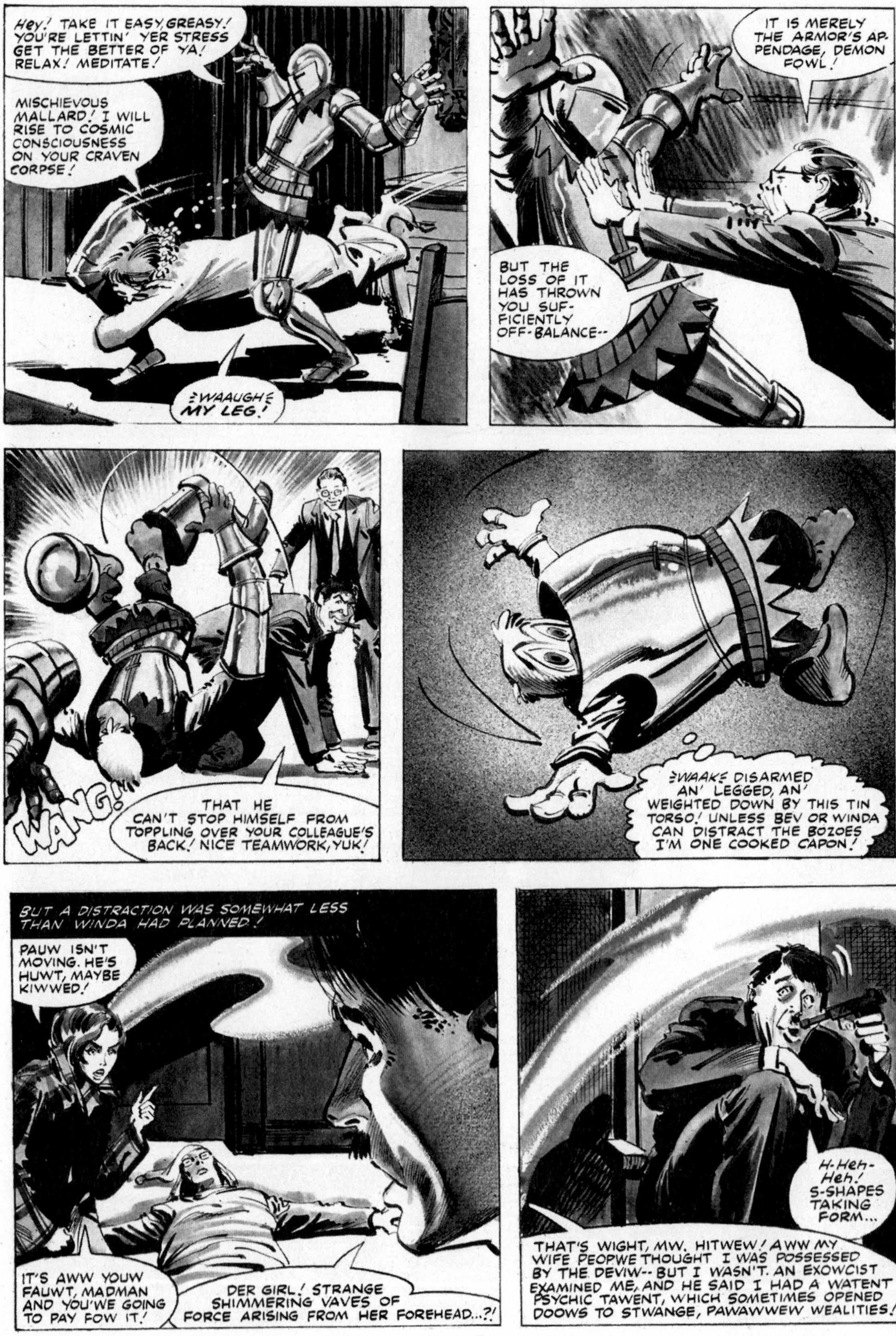

Hey! TAKE IT EASY, GREASY! YOU'RE LETTIN' YER STRESS GET THE BETTER OF YA! RELAX! MEDITATE!
MISCHIEVOUS MALLARD! I WILL RISE TO COSMIC CONSCIOUSNESS ON YOUR CRAVEN CORPSE!
WAAUGH MY LEG!
IT IS MERELY THE ARMOR'S APPENDAGE, DEMON FOWL!
BUT THE LOSS OF IT HAS THROWN YOU SUFFICIENTLY OFF-BALANCE--
WANG!
THAT HE CAN'T STOP HIMSELF FROM TOPPLING OVER YOUR COLLEAGUE'S BACK! NICE TEAMWORK, YUK!
WAAK DISARMED AN' LEGGED, AN' WEIGHTED DOWN BY THIS TIN TORSO! UNLESS BEV OR WINDA CAN DISTRACT THE BOZOES I'M ONE COOKED CAPON!
BUT A DISTRACTION WAS SOMEWHAT LESS THAN WINDA HAD PLANNED!
PAUW ISN'T MOVING. HE'S HUWT, MAYBE KIWWED!
IT'S AWW YOUW FAUWT, MADMAN AND YOU'WE GOING TO PAY FOW IT!
DER GIRL! STRANGE SHIMMERING VAVES OF FORCE ARISING FROM HER FOREHEAD...?!
H-HEH-HEH! S-SHAPES TAKING FORM...
THAT'S WIGHT, MW. HITWEW! AWW MY WIFE PEOPWE THOUGHT I WAS POSSESSED BY THE DEVIW-- BUT I WASN'T. AN EXOWCIST EXAMINED ME, AND HE SAID I HAD A WATENT PSYCHIC TAWENT, WHICH SOMETIMES OPENED DOOWS TO STWANGE, PAWAWWEW WEALITIES!

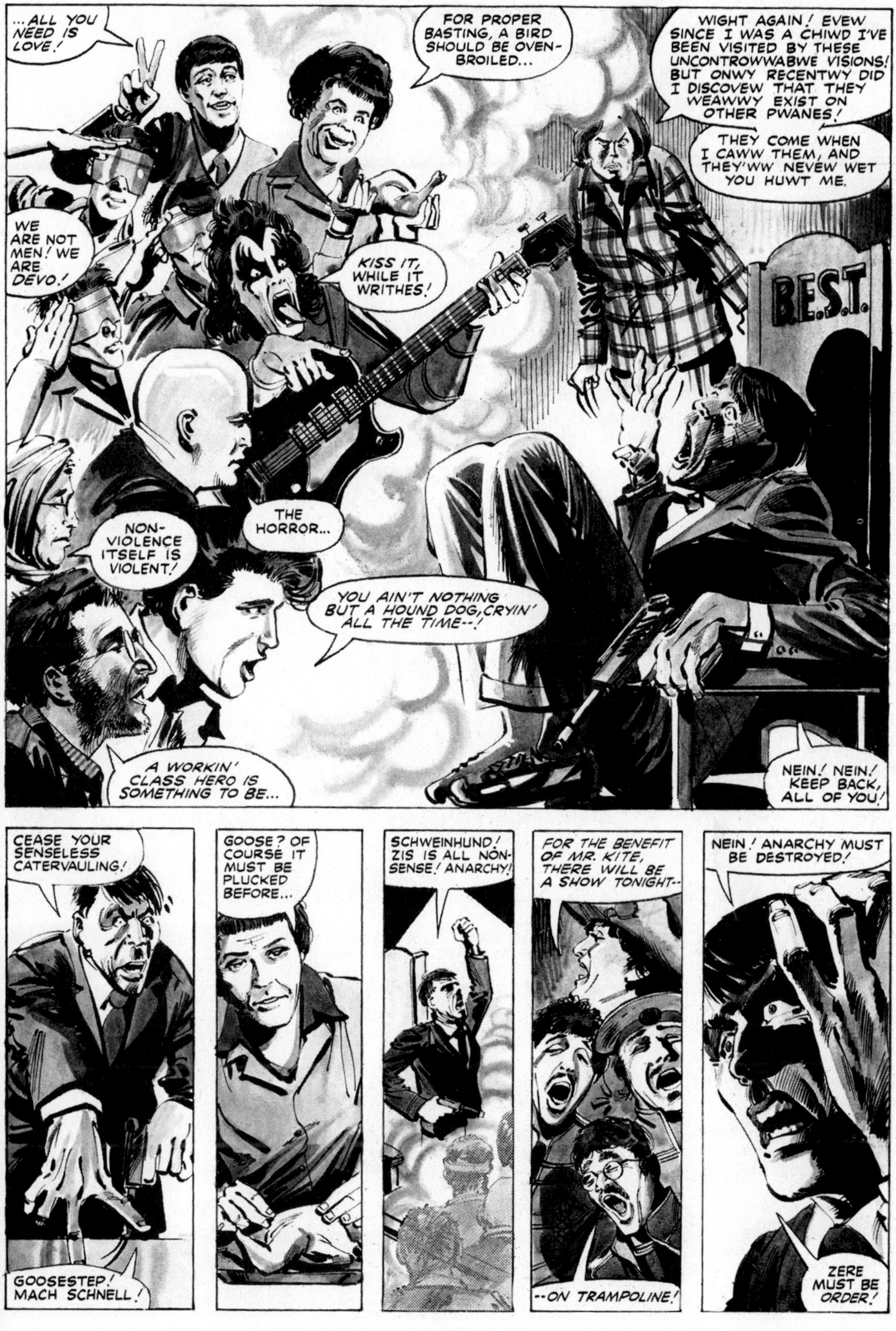
...ALL YOU NEED IS LOVE!
FOR PROPER BASTING, A BIRD SHOULD BE OVEN-BROILED...
WIGHT AGAIN! EVEW SINCE I WAS A CHIWD I'VE BEEN VISITED BY THESE UNCONTROWWABWE VISIONS! BUT ONWY RECENTWY DID I DISCOVEW THAT THEY WEAWWY EXIST ON OTHER PWANES!
THEY COME WHEN I CAWW THEM, AND THEY'WW NEVEW WET YOU HUWT ME.
WE ARE NOT MEN! WE ARE DEVO!
KISS IT, WHILE IT WRITHES!
B.E.S.T.
THE HORROR...
NON-VIOLENCE ITSELF IS VIOLENT!
YOU AIN'T NOTHING BUT A HOUND DOG, CRYIN' ALL THE TIME--!
A WORKIN' CLASS HERO IS SOMETHING TO BE...
NEIN! NEIN! KEEP BACK, ALL OF YOU!
CEASE YOUR SENSELESS CATERVAULING!
GOOSESTEP! MACH SCHNELL!
GOOSE? OF COURSE IT MUST BE PLUCKED BEFORE...
SCHWEINHUND! ZIS IS ALL NON-SENSE! ANARCHY!
FOR THE BENEFIT OF MR. KITE, THERE WILL BE A SHOW TONIGHT--
--ON TRAMPOLINE!
NEIN! ANARCHY MUST BE DESTROYED!
ZERE MUST BE ORDER!

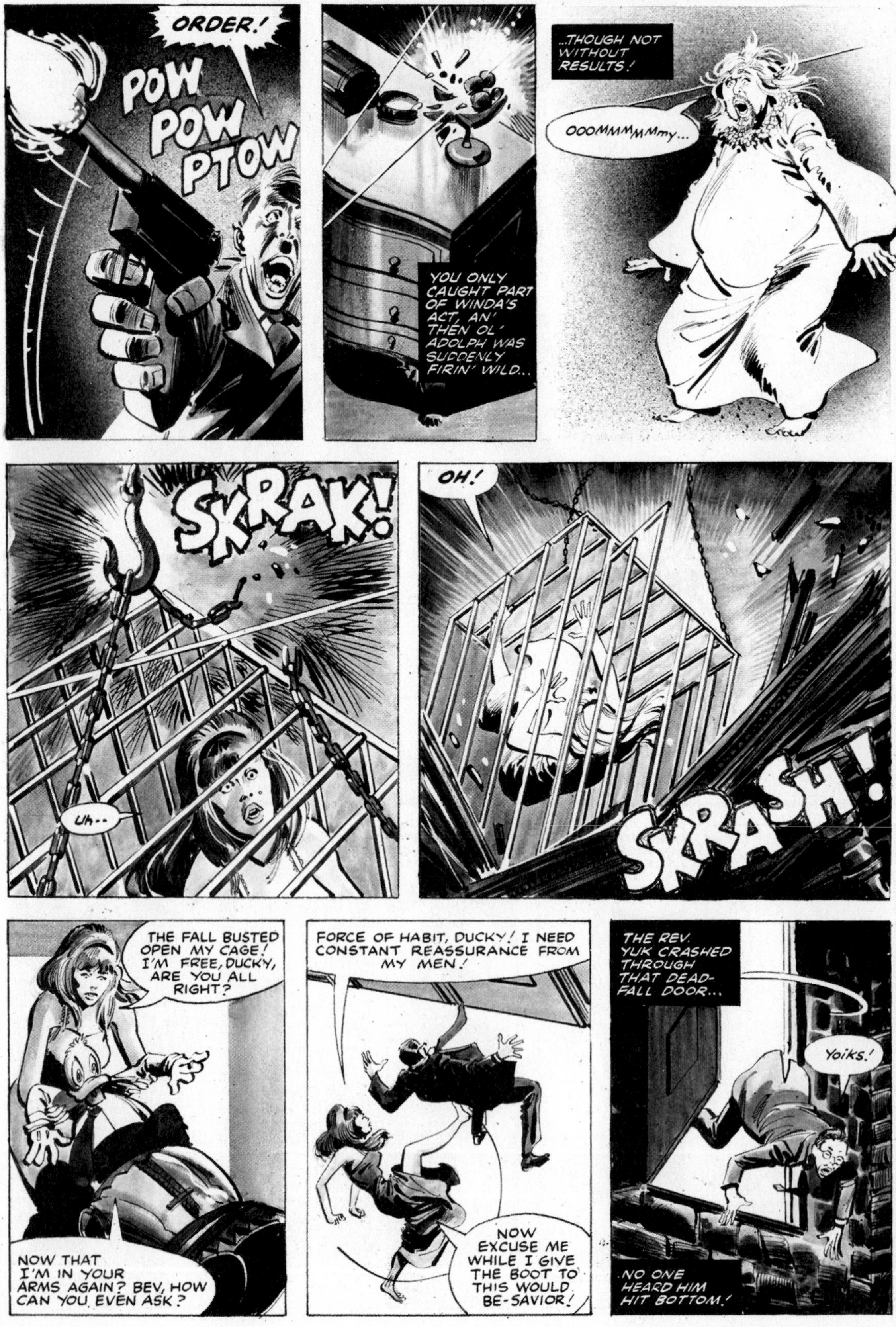
ORDER!
POW
POW
PTOW
YOU ONLY CAUGHT PART OF WINDA'S ACT, AN' THEN OL' ADOLPH WAS SUDDENLY FIRIN' WILD...
...THOUGH NOT WITHOUT RESULTS!
OOOMMMMMmy...
SKRAK!
Uh...
OH!
SKRASH!
THE FALL BUSTED OPEN MY CAGE! I'M FREE, DUCKY, ARE YOU ALL RIGHT?
NOW THAT I'M IN YOUR ARMS AGAIN? BEV, HOW CAN YOU EVEN ASK?
FORCE OF HABIT, DUCKY! I NEED CONSTANT REASSURANCE FROM MY MEN!
NOW EXCUSE ME WHILE I GIVE THE BOOT TO THIS WOULD BE-SAVIOR!
THE REV. YUK CRASHED THROUGH THAT DEAD-FALL DOOR...
Yoiks!
NO ONE HEARD HIM HIT BOTTOM!

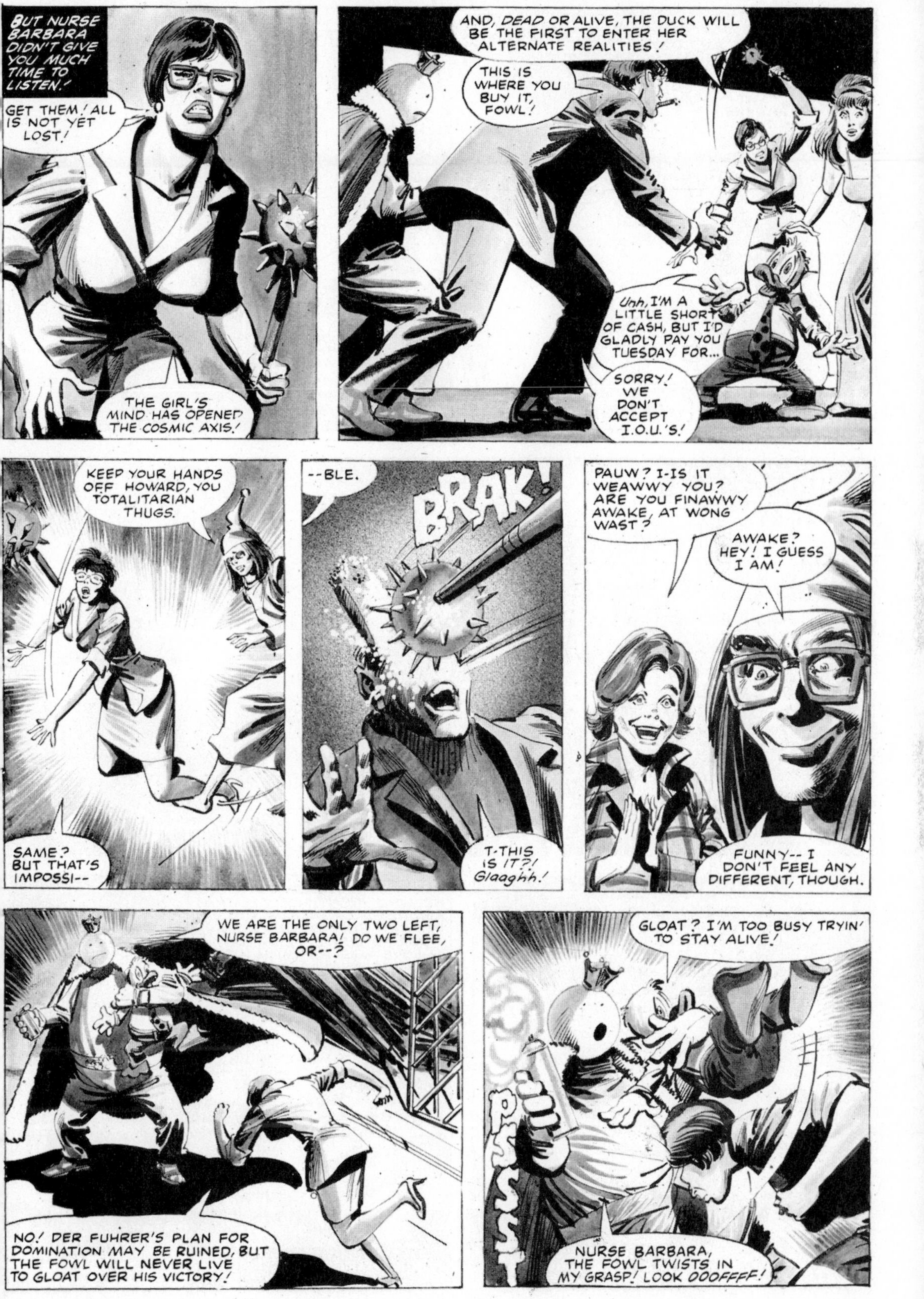
BUT NURSE BARBARA DIDN'T GIVE YOU MUCH TIME TO LISTEN!
GET THEM! ALL IS NOT YET LOST!
THE GIRL'S MIND HAS OPENED THE COSMIC AXIS!
AND, DEAD OR ALIVE, THE DUCK WILL BE THE FIRST TO ENTER HER ALTERNATE REALITIES!
THIS IS WHERE YOU BUY IT, FOWL!
Unh, I'M A LITTLE SHORT OF CASH, BUT I'D GLADLY PAY YOU TUESDAY FOR...
SORRY! WE DON'T ACCEPT I.O.U.'S!
KEEP YOUR HANDS OFF HOWARD, YOU TOTALITARIAN THUGS.
SAME? BUT THAT'S IMPOSSI--
--BLE.
BRAK!
T-THIS IS IT?! Glaaghh!
PAUW? I-IS IT WEAWWY YOU? ARE YOU FINAWWY AWAKE, AT WONG WAST?
AWAKE? HEY! I GUESS I AM!
FUNNY-- I DON'T FEEL ANY DIFFERENT, THOUGH.
WE ARE THE ONLY TWO LEFT, NURSE BARBARA! DO WE FLEE, OR--?
NO! DER FUHRER'S PLAN FOR DOMINATION MAY BE RUINED, BUT THE FOWL WILL NEVER LIVE TO GLOAT OVER HIS VICTORY!
GLOAT? I'M TOO BUSY TRYIN' TO STAY ALIVE!
PSSST
NURSE BARBARA, THE FOWL TWISTS IN MY GRASP! LOOK OOOFFFF!

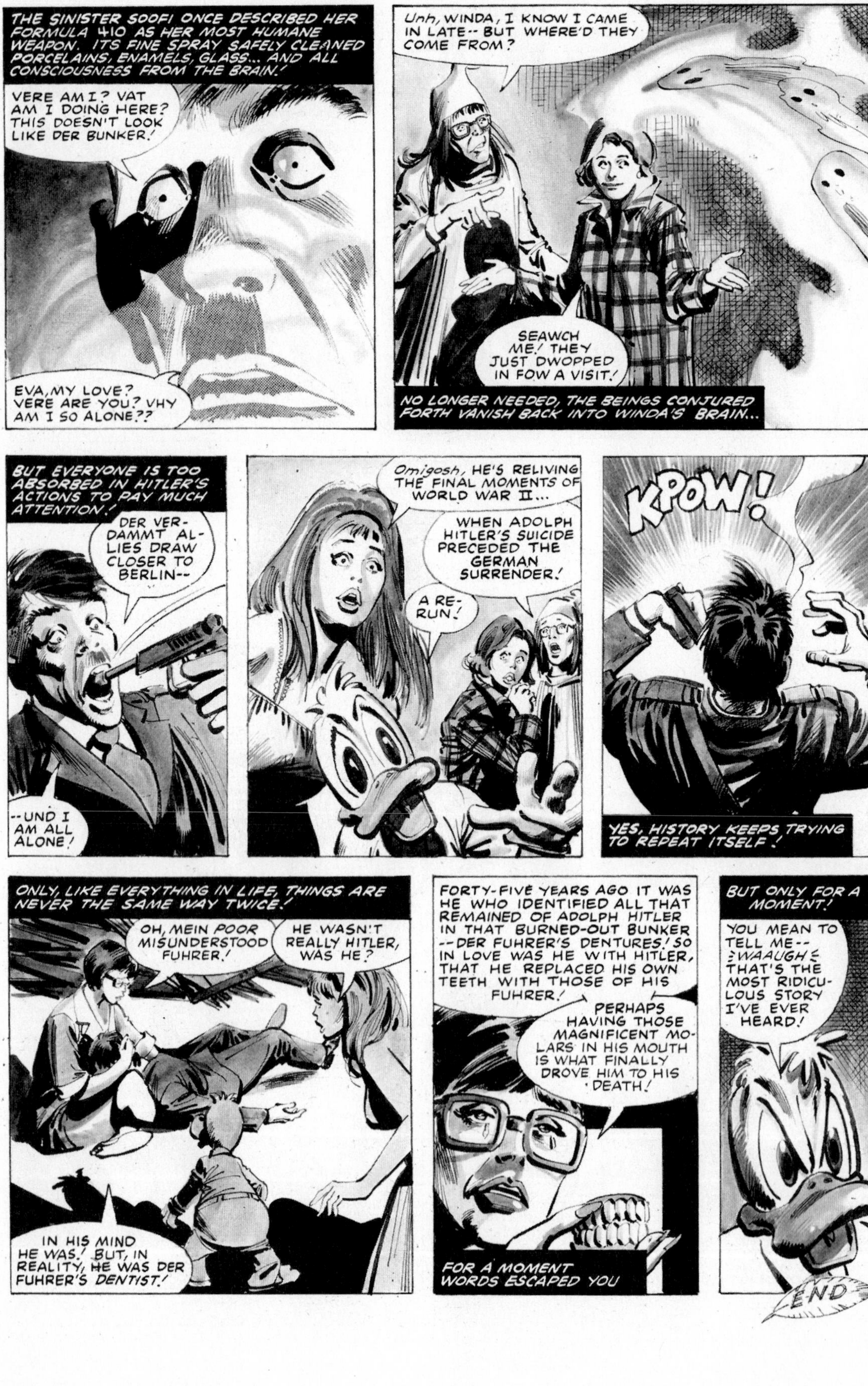
THE SINISTER SOOFI ONCE DESCRIBED HER FORMULA 410 AS HER MOST HUMANE WEAPON. ITS FINE SPRAY SAFELY CLEANED PORCELAINS, ENAMELS, GLASS... AND ALL CONSCIOUSNESS FROM THE BRAIN!
VERE AM I? VAT AM I DOING HERE? THIS DOESN'T LOOK LIKE DER BUNKER!
EVA, MY LOVE? VERE ARE YOU? VHY AM I SO ALONE??
Unh, WINDA, I KNOW I CAME IN LATE-- BUT WHERE'D THEY COME FROM?
SEAWCH ME! THEY JUST DWOPPED IN FOW A VISIT!
NO LONGER NEEDED, THE BEINGS CONJURED FORTH VANISH BACK INTO WINDA'S BRAIN...
BUT EVERYONE IS TOO ABSORBED IN HITLER'S ACTIONS TO PAY MUCH ATTENTION!
DER VER-DAMMT AL-LIES DRAW CLOSER TO BERLIN--
--UND I AM ALL ALONE!
Omigosh, HE'S RELIVING THE FINAL MOMENTS OF WORLD WAR II...
WHEN ADOLPH HITLER'S SUICIDE PRECEDED THE GERMAN SURRENDER!
A RE-RUN!
KPOW!
YES, HISTORY KEEPS TRYING TO REPEAT ITSELF!
ONLY, LIKE EVERYTHING IN LIFE, THINGS ARE NEVER THE SAME WAY TWICE!
OH, MEIN POOR MISUNDERSTOOD FUHRER!
HE WASN'T REALLY HITLER, WAS HE?
IN HIS MIND HE WAS! BUT, IN REALITY, HE WAS DER FUHRER'S DENTIST!
FORTY-FIVE YEARS AGO IT WAS HE WHO IDENTIFIED ALL THAT REMAINED OF ADOLPH HITLER IN THAT BURNED-OUT BUNKER --DER FUHRER'S DENTURES! SO IN LOVE WAS HE WITH HITLER, THAT HE REPLACED HIS OWN TEETH WITH THOSE OF HIS FUHRER!
PERHAPS HAVING THOSE MAGNIFICENT MO-LARS IN HIS MOUTH IS WHAT FINALLY DROVE HIM TO HIS DEATH!
FOR A MOMENT WORDS ESCAPED YOU
BUT ONLY FOR A MOMENT!
YOU MEAN TO TELL ME-- WAAUGH THAT'S THE MOST RIDICU-LOUS STORY I'VE EVER HEARD!
END

PLAYDUCK REVIEWS

By Duckbill Mantlo

Kurt Vonneduck's DUCK'S CRADLE is a mature, imaginative novel — perhaps the best he has ever written. One of the most daring and irreverent drakes of our time, Vonneduck has here concocted a delicious and irreverent fantasy about the end of Duckworld — replete with atomic scientists, ugly ducklings, fowl play and a brand new method of hatching eggs. Possibly the best political satire since Pierre Fouwlle's PLANET OF THE PEOPLE.

THE WEB AND THE WOK is Thomas Wolf's story of a struggling young restauranteur recounting his youth in a southern pond, his college days mastering the fine art of haute cuisine, his impassioned affair with Dinah Duck, his debutante heartthrob, and his eventual recognition as one of the finest chefs in the eggistential style. Wolf (despite his duckophomorphic nom de plume) is a passionate drake who handles his character with the sensitivity of an artist walking on eggs.

Mario Duckzo has created an extraordinary novel in THE DUCKFATHER. It pulsates with dramatic and evil incident, brute rage, and the naked terror of the infamous underworld. Duckzo takes us inside the violence-infested domain of East Ductroit during the savage days of prohibition. He shows us trial by gunfire and torture as heavily-accented Sicilian ducks torment their captives by applying hot feathers to their webbed feet. THE DUCKFATHER is essentially the story of one drake and his power... Muffia leader Vito Sergioleone, a benevolent duckspot who stops at nothing to gain and hold the pond from which he rose to power. Read it — and weep!

HEART OF DUCKNESS is one of the most terrifying journeys into the soul of duckkind ever penned by the webbed hand. Joseph Duckrad guides us up-pond after the sinister Mr. Klutz, into the aboriginal horror of primeval night. HEART OF DUCKNESS has also served as the model for Francis Ford Duckola's multi-million dollar motion picture, ADUCKECLIPSE NOW! Years in the making, this story of a dedicated young drake astronomer's search for the meaning of life in the Black Holes of outer space incorporates all the mystery of Duckrad's novel with all the glitter that is Duckywood.

For fifteen years ducklings too young to remember their first album have been clamoring for the reunion of that almost-mythical rock group, the BEAKLES. Now, at long last, it looks as if Paw, Gorge, Gone and Ducko have finally decided to give their youthful fans what they want. Soon to be released, SGT. BEAKLES LONELY TARTS CLUB BAND follows the musical styles of those lovable Duckerpool lads from their first rockaducky days of MEET THE BEAKLES, through their movie careers and hits such as A HARD DUCK'S NIGHT, and on past even the current Ducksco craze. Having outlasted their most prominent imitators, the ROLLING CLONES, the BEAKLES are back in stride with this 2—LP set, reaffirming that it's better late than never. And no. Paw isn't dead!

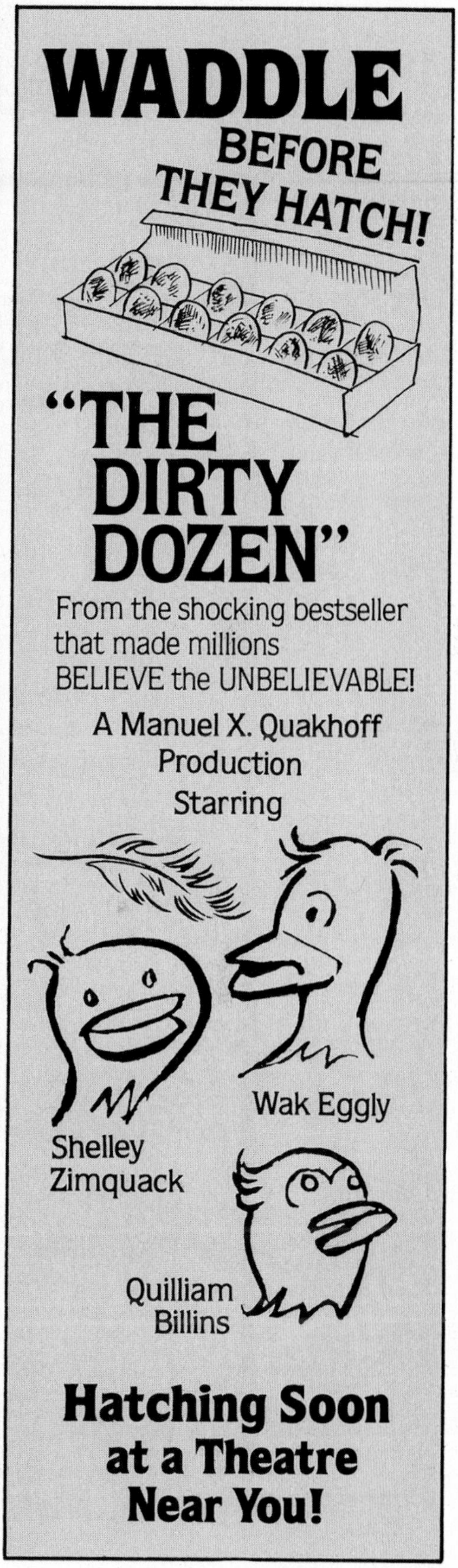
WADDLE
BEFORE THEY HATCH!
"THE DIRTY DOZEN"
From the shocking bestseller that made millions BELIEVE the UNBELIEVABLE!
A Manuel X. Quakhoff Production
Starring
Wak Eggly
Shelley Zimquack
Quilliam Billins
Hatching Soon at a Theatre Near You!

PLAYDUCK ADVISOR

Several months ago I became engaged to this duck I have known for several years. Our relationship up until now has been very satisfying. But then, just the other night, she said she wanted to try something new. While I'm about as adventurous as the next drake when it comes to nestmaking techniques, what she had in mind was, to say the least, shocking. She filled up her tub with this black, sticky substance and plopped herself down on it, inviting me to join her. I tried it, but I can't say it did anything for me. She called me a fluffy-duffy and said it was one of the current rages in nestmaking. Is this true?

——P.S., Beakston, Mass.

Tar-and-feathers (or T/F as it is called by aficianados) is indeed one of the up and coming kinky techniques practiced by trendier couples these days. While many drakes like yourself have an aversion to dirty deeds, some of us wallow in them. In New Stork City there are a number of T/F specialty clubs open for business. We recommend that you give it another try before you let your fiance's preference come between you.

*   *   *   *

I have become hopelessly involved with a woman of another race. She is everything I've ever wanted in another person and I couldn't imagine giving her up. Yet I can tell my community is not ready for a relationship between a duck and a chicken. Are there any liberal cities in the U.S. where interracial marriages are accepted?

——E.V., Flock, Ark.

To tell you the truth, E.V., your best bet would be to find a farm somewhere for the two of you. Although many communities have gotten more liberal these days, you will still find rampant chickenism almost anywhere.

*   *   *   *

My boyfriend has this annoying habit of saying "Get down!" every time he wants to become intimate with me. I find this expression rude and a real turn off. What can I do?

Ms. M.C., Philaduffia, Penn.

Tell your boyfriend how you feel about his slang, and if he still insists on using it, tell him to pluck off.

*   *   *   *

I just saw "Duck Throat" for the fifth time and I've just got to know: were the special effects real or faked?

——K.T., Stamford, Conn.

Quite real, friend. Some ducks have phenomenal bills.

*   *   *   *

Is it true that the length of one's tailfeathers determines one's

(continued on p. 324)

WISE QUACKS

Dear Ms. Quacker:

I just completed reading the long-awaited debut of Howard the Duck in magazine format. Artsy fartsy. I, for one, could have lived forever without seeing Howard crawl into bed with a nude hairless ape. I mean, it's bad enough that they're *hairless* and *featherless,* and that a young drake is supposed to be having a physical relationship with one — did you have to show all that disgusting featherless flesh? What the _____ is wrong with your imagination? My imagination is one _____ of a lot better than your _____ graphics and more enjoyable — not to mention being a lot less _____. Why the _____ did you have to take a perfectly enjoyable bunch of loonies and misfits and turn them into characters that are rejects from an "Open Season" reader's dream?

And since when is Bev a 44D? Will _____ and _____ make her a more interesting character? Shame on you for making Howard the Duck a _____ with the morals of a _____ and introducing bestiality via a _____ with a nude hairless ape! Take all this _____ and _____ out or cancel my subscription immediately!

_________,
Quacken Billbone

Gee, Ms. Billbone, we're sorry if we offended... It's just that Beverly has become such a believable, *real* person to us that we've begun taking her hairless apeness for granted. Furthermore, PLAYDUCK prides itself on always being on the forefront of Poultry Rights and cannot in all conscience ignore the moral question involved in *any* king of bigotry — even that against apes, hairless or not. Perhaps, Ms. Billbone, you'd better examine your own soul before making judgments.

Dear Ms. Quacker,

I'm writing to ask you a few questions about Howard the Duck's survival on Peopleworld. First of allo though it makes a nice scary point, the idea that *duck* would be considered a delicious *food* is disgusting. Cannibalism is going too far. I mean, it just isn't funny. On the other wing, the idea that a drake could actually be physically attracted to a hairless ape is *hilarious!* It also makes some good points about racism: Howard loves Bev because, hairless ape or not, she has a good soul. Even though he probably finds her revolting, he never lets it show. We could all, ducks and drakes alike, learn from such highmindedness.

One thing I have trouble accepting, though, is that Howard could walk around and even have a job as a cab driver without hairless apes going berserk. Why, if I were to call a cab and a hairless ape was driving it I'd be sure to notice and so would all my friends if it happened to them. If a hairless ape appeared on our streets it would be sure to cause a panic. Now, though a duck on peopleworld isn't as ridiculous as a hairless ape on earth, it does seem to me that there'd be more of a fuss. So I think you should show Howard fighting off the hairless apes with their terrible square teeth and long funny looking fingers and toes and the yicky long stringy hair on their heads and faces.

Waauck,
Feather Quackstein

P.S. I like it when startled hairless apes yell "yipes" or some such funny hairless ape sound. Keep up the good work.

Well, Mr. Quackstein, our feeling is that Howard is possessed of so much natural dignity that he fits in virtually anywhere — even on the impossible world of hairless apes!

Dear Playduck:

I must protest against the denial of the fundamental assumption of our religious doctrine inherent in your Howard the Duck magazine. To even conjecture about the existence of other species which have evolved into intelligence negates the basic premise that God created Duckkind in His image. The evolution of intelligence in wild and domestic animals such as mice or dogs or apes is absurd. You would do the world a great service by ceasing publication of this subversive and scabrous magazine. Until you see fit to do so, I feel that all books about Howard should be banned from our libraries.

Rev. Q. Coffeather

Well, Reverend, we must sadly disagree. There is more to Howard than meets the eye, as evidence, take note of the extraordinary WACKie movement. For more on this angle, see the Truman Capoultry interview in this issue.

Continued on Page 73

AND YOU WANT TO KNOW SOMETHING ELSE, MY SEXY LITTLE BALL OF FEATHERS? I LOVE YOU!
IN THE WORDS OF THE BARD, TOOTS: "THE FEELING'S MUTUAL!"

HOWARD THE DUCK

COMING AQUACKTIONS

Howard flees from the madness in the Heart of America through the Cosmic Axis in "CAPTAIN AMERICANA"

By Bill Mantlo, Gene Colan & Dave Simons

Plus!

Howard the Duck meets Dracula in "DRAKULA"

By Bill Mantlo & Michael Golden

AND The most controversial Marvel cover yet !

You'll love it or
You'll hate it.
But you *can't* ignore
'Drakula,' the astounding depiction by Larry Fredericks

On Sale Late March

WAUUGH

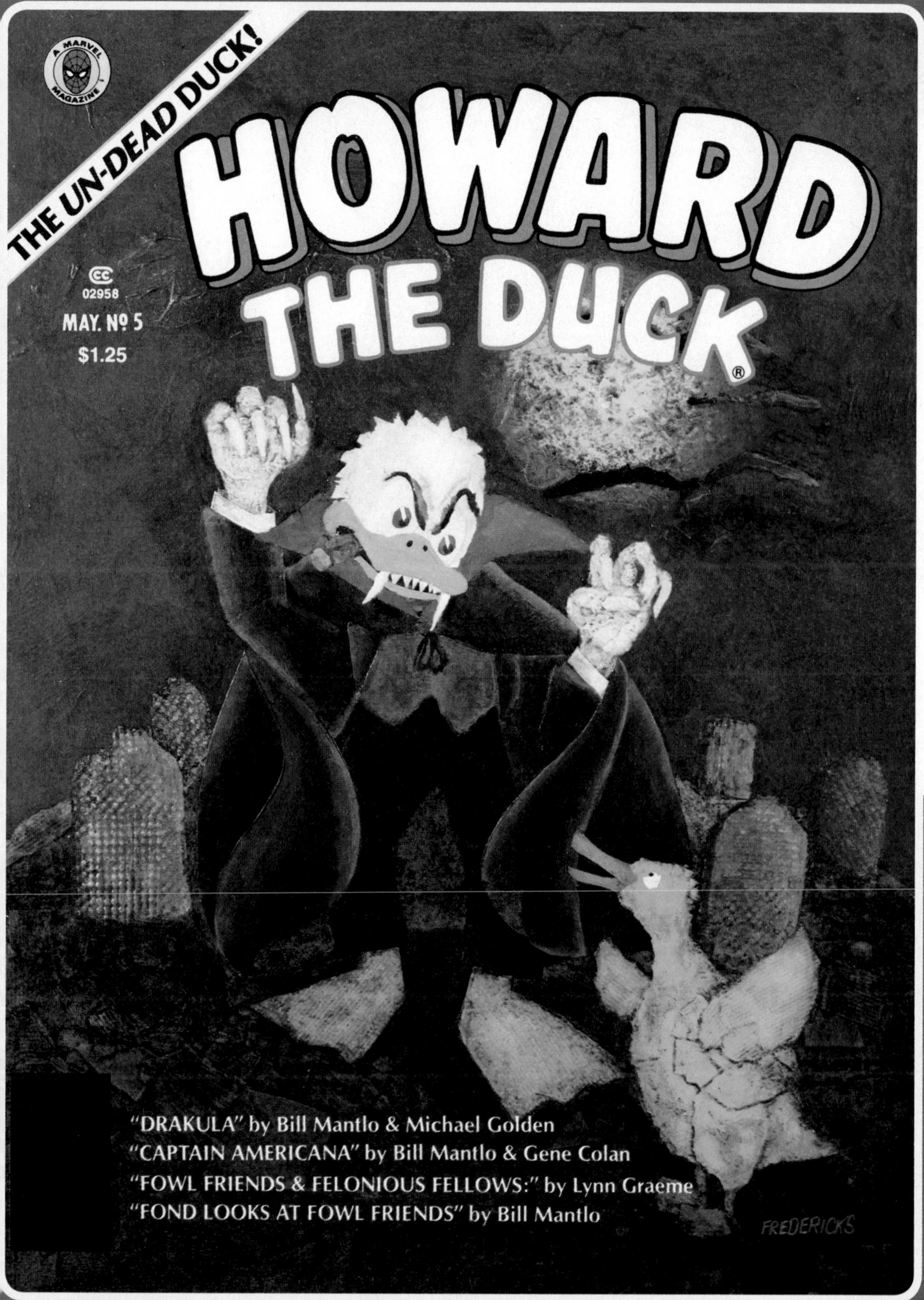

A MARVEL MAGAZINE
THE UN-DEAD DUCK!
HOWARD THE DUCK®
02958
MAY. Nº 5
$1.25
"DRAKULA" by Bill Mantlo & Michael Golden
"CAPTAIN AMERICANA" by Bill Mantlo & Gene Colan
"FOWL FRIENDS & FELONIOUS FELLOWS:" by Lynn Graeme
"FOND LOOKS AT FOWL FRIENDS" by Bill Mantlo
FREDERICKS

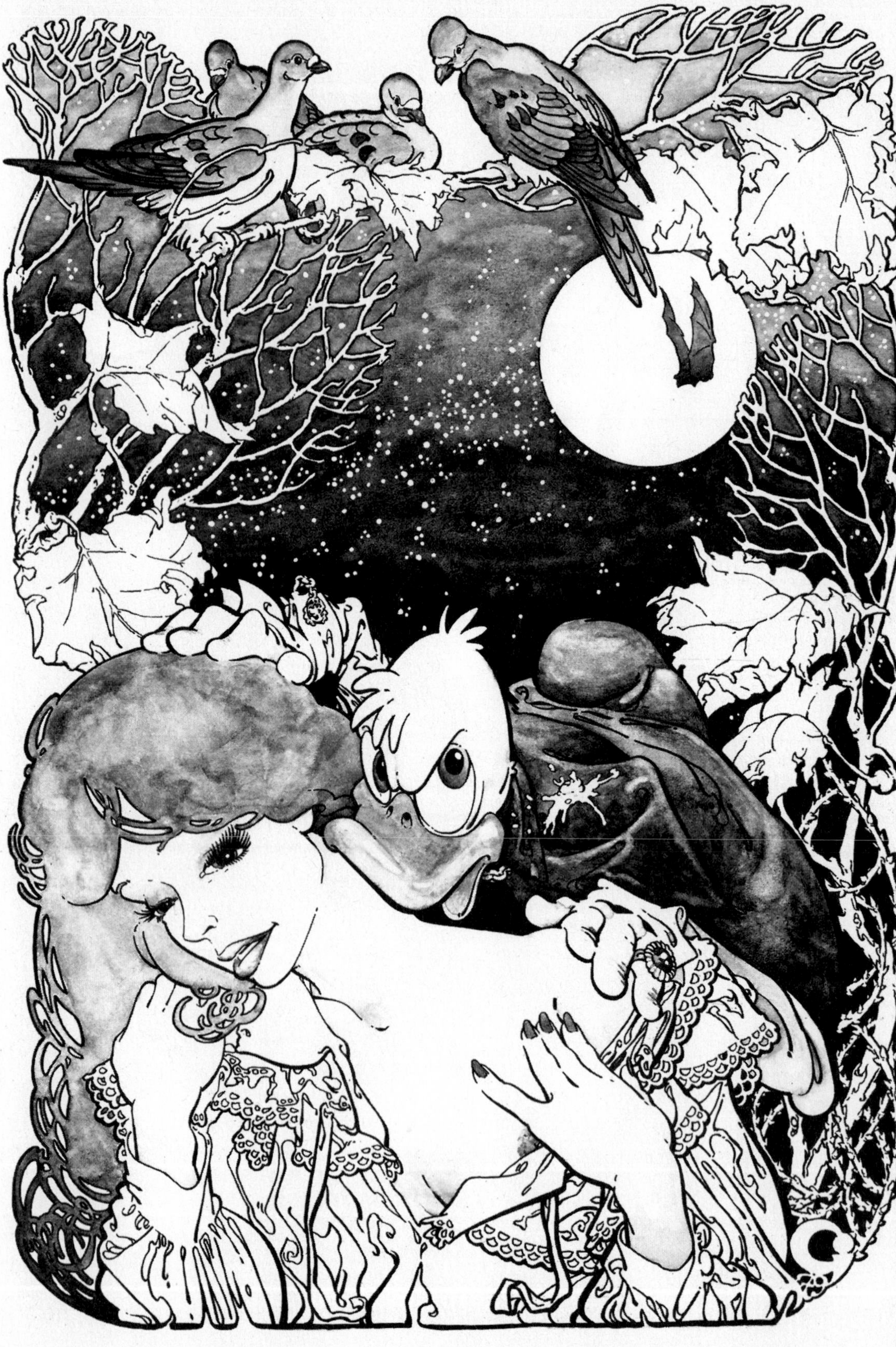

STAN LEE Presents:
HOWARD THE DUCK

Volume 1 No. 5   **May 1980**

JIM SHOOTER Editor-in-Chief • **LYNN GRAEME** Editor • **RALPH MACCHIO** Associate Editor
MARK GRUENWALD Insulting Editor • **MILT SCHIFFMAN** V.P. Production • **NORA MACLIN** Design Director
JIM NOVACK, JOE ROSEN Letterers
**DAVIDA LICHTER-DALE, DANNY CRESPI, JOHN TARTAGLIONE, ROB CAROSELLA,
MIKE HIGGINS, ELIOT BROWN, ED NORTON, HELLEN KATZ, LINDA FLORIO** Sensational Staff
MICHAEL GOLDEN Frontispiece **LARRY FREDERICKS** Cover Collage

CONTENTS

Save This Editor!

Hey, there!

Welcome to the Howard the Duck School of Fine Arts!

You hold in your hands an example of Marvel's willingness to take chances. Upon the positive or negative reaction of you, the reader, rests the head and heart of this editor as well as a hefty bet or two. Because, hard though it is for *me* to understand, some people did not like this cover when they first saw it. But before getting into the heavy drama, terror, delirium, and such, let me give you some background:

Once upon a time in faraway Spain there lived one of the greatest artists humankind has yet produced. His name was Pablo Picasso. Now while you and I might sweat and struggle over a piece of writing or art, this was not Picasso's way. He had come so far through the kiln of creativity (the blasting heat of which burns out or diminishes all but the most talented) that to him art was returned to what it had originally been. Play. (All art, visual and otherwise, is, in essence, play of a very serious kind.)

At any rate, Picasso, while playing one day, began to add objects to his oil canvas. And paint over them, and glaze, and add more objects. Pablo Picasso had created *collage.* The art of collage represents one of the most radical changes in art history, and you would be amazed to find out how few real changes there have been from cave artist to our present generation.

All the above I've learned since commissioning the cover you see on this magazine. Nonetheless, the playful, inventive quality of the medium has always attracted me. So when I met Larry Fredericks, a commercial and graphic artist whose chief love is collage, I thought he would be perfect as the artist of the "Drakula" issue of HOWARD THE DUCK.

Let me tell you a little about how Larry created "Drakula."

He began by sketching the layout of the picture. Larry then drew shapes on both textured and flat papers and either cut or ripped them out. The resulting pieces of paper were applied to a heavy board that had been painted with glue, and another layer of glue was painted over them. The picture, which now existed as shapes and areas of dark and light, was painted in several layers with mixed oils, turpentine and a painting medium to give a glazed effect. Finally, the entire collage was given a thin coat of varnish. This resulted in a satiny texture.

Listen, I've got money bet on this painting. *I* say that Howard the Duck readers are attracted to the book in the first place because of Howard's daring, individuality and chutzpah.

I say that you are gonna *love* this painting, and buy this issue of the magazine like crazy.

But if you don't like it, you don't like it.

It's really up to you... Will this editor win lotsa neat bets? Will Stan Lee and Jim Shooter be rewarded for their faith in me? Let us know how you feel, and whether you'd like to see more risk taking with this magazine!

Write on!

Lynn

192

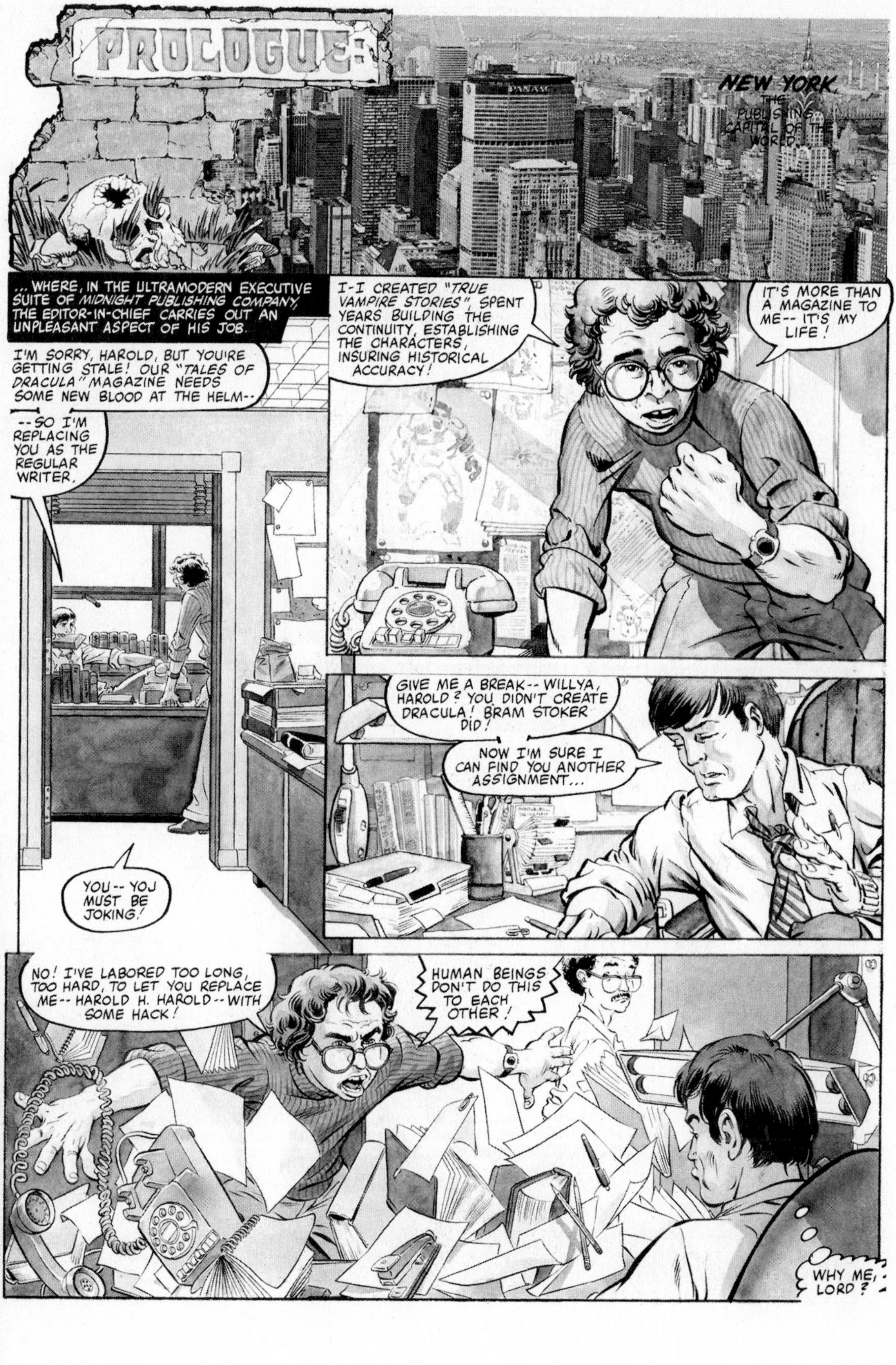
PROLOGUE:
NEW YORK
THE PUBLISHING CAPITAL OF THE WORLD.
... WHERE, IN THE ULTRAMODERN EXECUTIVE SUITE OF MIDNIGHT PUBLISHING COMPANY, THE EDITOR-IN-CHIEF CARRIES OUT AN UNPLEASANT ASPECT OF HIS JOB.
I'M SORRY, HAROLD, BUT YOU'RE GETTING STALE! OUR "TALES OF DRACULA" MAGAZINE NEEDS SOME NEW BLOOD AT THE HELM--
--SO I'M REPLACING YOU AS THE REGULAR WRITER.
YOU -- YOU MUST BE JOKING!
I-I CREATED "TRUE VAMPIRE STORIES", SPENT YEARS BUILDING THE CONTINUITY, ESTABLISHING THE CHARACTERS, INSURING HISTORICAL ACCURACY!
IT'S MORE THAN A MAGAZINE TO ME-- IT'S MY LIFE!
GIVE ME A BREAK-- WILLYA, HAROLD? YOU DIDN'T CREATE DRACULA! BRAM STOKER DID!
NOW I'M SURE I CAN FIND YOU ANOTHER ASSIGNMENT...
NO! I'VE LABORED TOO LONG, TOO HARD, TO LET YOU REPLACE ME-- HAROLD H. HAROLD-- WITH SOME HACK!
HUMAN BEINGS DON'T DO THIS TO EACH OTHER!
WHY ME, LORD?

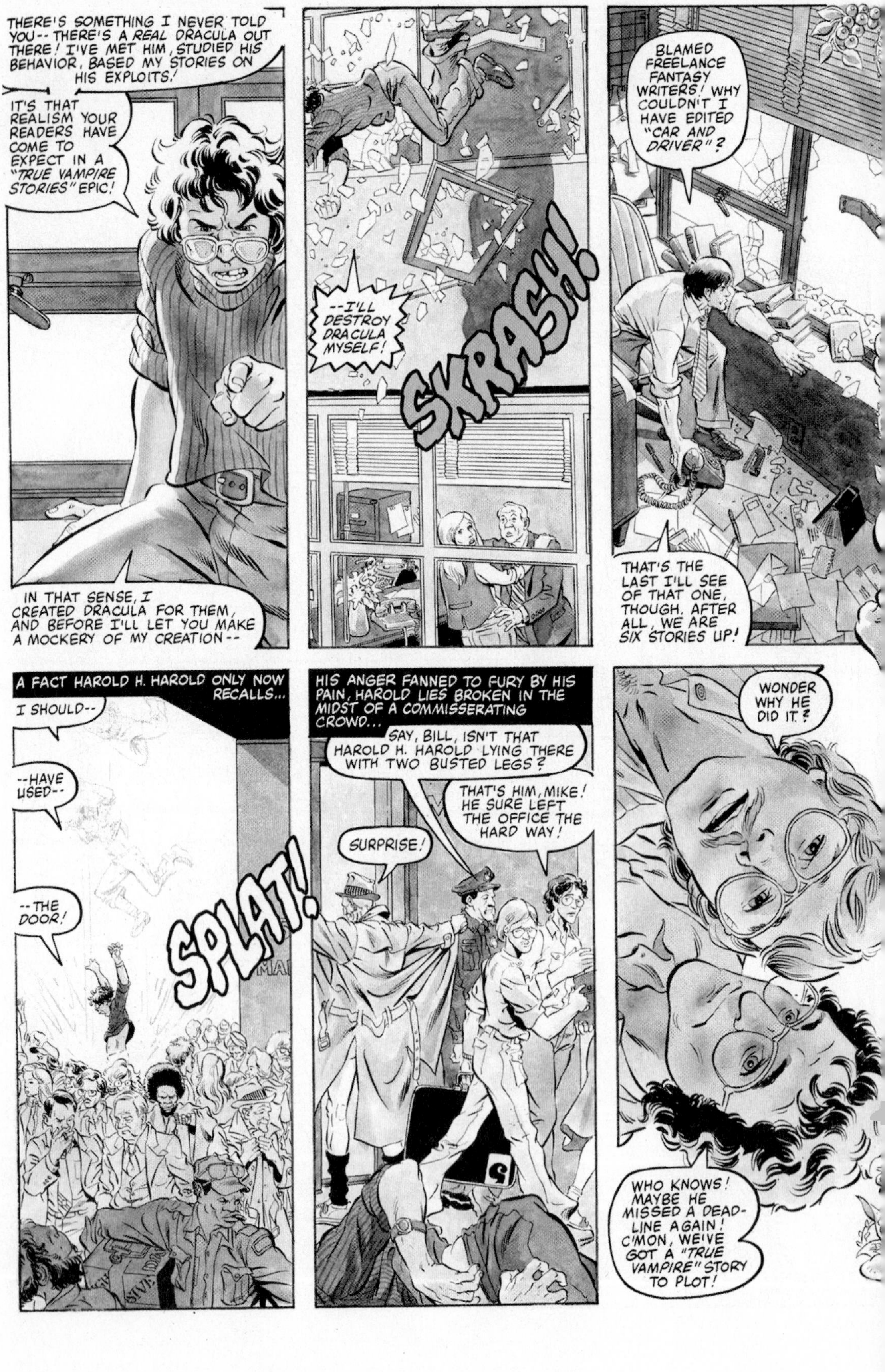
THERE'S SOMETHING I NEVER TOLD YOU-- THERE'S A REAL DRACULA OUT THERE! I'VE MET HIM, STUDIED HIS BEHAVIOR, BASED MY STORIES ON HIS EXPLOITS!
IT'S THAT REALISM YOUR READERS HAVE COME TO EXPECT IN A "TRUE VAMPIRE STORIES" EPIC!
IN THAT SENSE, I CREATED DRACULA FOR THEM, AND BEFORE I'LL LET YOU MAKE A MOCKERY OF MY CREATION--
--I'LL DESTROY DRACULA MYSELF!
SKRASH!
BLAMED FREELANCE FANTASY WRITERS! WHY COULDN'T I HAVE EDITED "CAR AND DRIVER"?
THAT'S THE LAST I'LL SEE OF THAT ONE, THOUGH. AFTER ALL, WE ARE SIX STORIES UP!
A FACT HAROLD H. HAROLD ONLY NOW RECALLS...
I SHOULD--
--HAVE USED--
--THE DOOR!
SPLAT!
HIS ANGER FANNED TO FURY BY HIS PAIN, HAROLD LIES BROKEN IN THE MIDST OF A COMMISSERATING CROWD...
SAY, BILL, ISN'T THAT HAROLD H. HAROLD LYING THERE WITH TWO BUSTED LEGS?
THAT'S HIM, MIKE! HE SURE LEFT THE OFFICE THE HARD WAY!
SURPRISE!
WONDER WHY HE DID IT?
WHO KNOWS! MAYBE HE MISSED A DEAD-LINE AGAIN! C'MON, WE'VE GOT A "TRUE VAMPIRE" STORY TO PLOT!

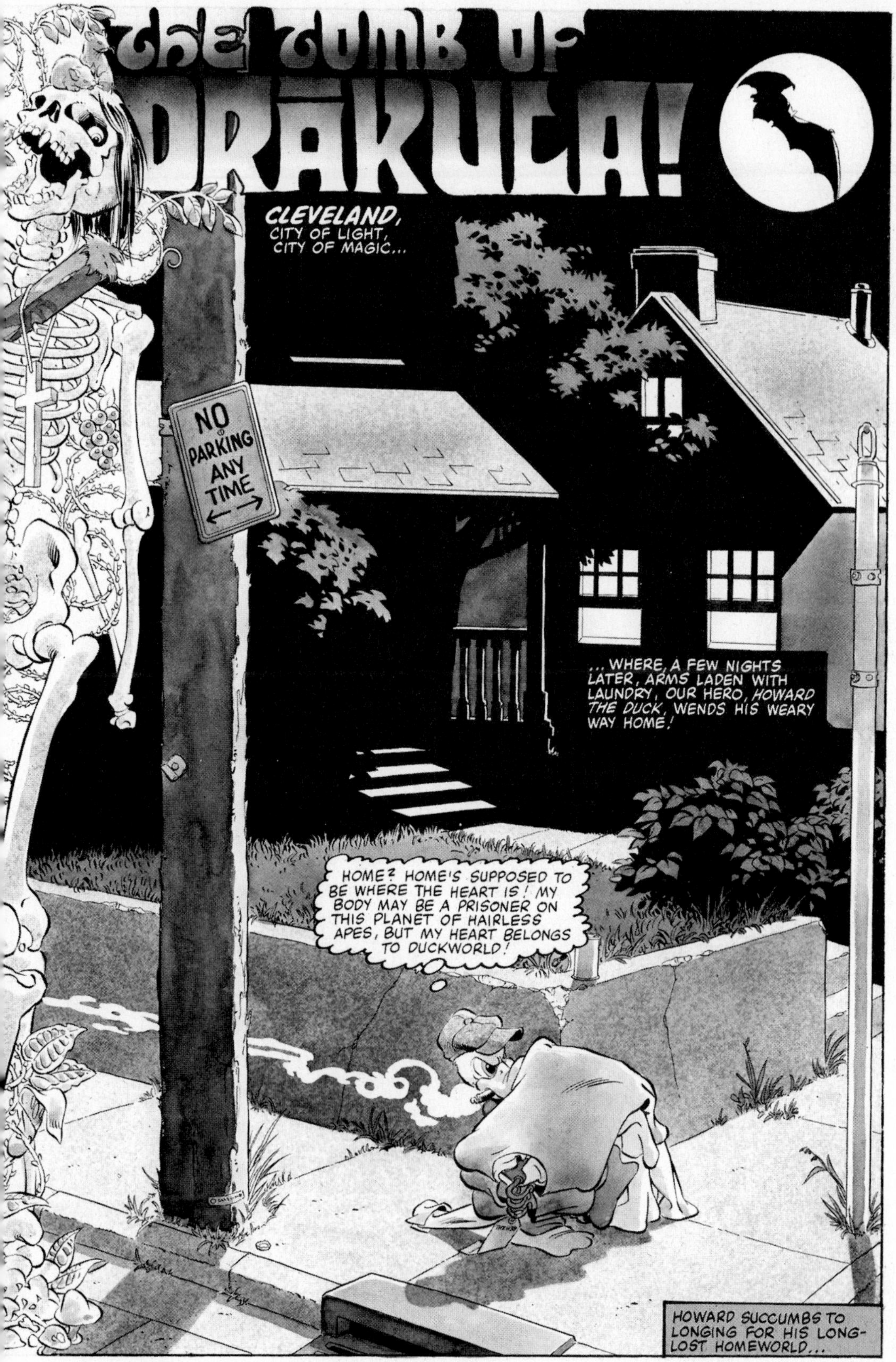
THE TOMB OF DRAKULA!
CLEVELAND, CITY OF LIGHT, CITY OF MAGIC...
NO PARKING ANY TIME
... WHERE, A FEW NIGHTS LATER, ARMS LADEN WITH LAUNDRY, OUR HERO, HOWARD THE DUCK, WENDS HIS WEARY WAY HOME!
HOME? HOME'S SUPPOSED TO BE WHERE THE HEART IS! MY BODY MAY BE A PRISONER ON THIS PLANET OF HAIRLESS APES, BUT MY HEART BELONGS TO DUCKWORLD!
HOWARD SUCCUMBS TO LONGING FOR HIS LONG-LOST HOMEWORLD...

Script: BILL MANTLO Art: MICHAEL GOLDEN & BOB McLEOD

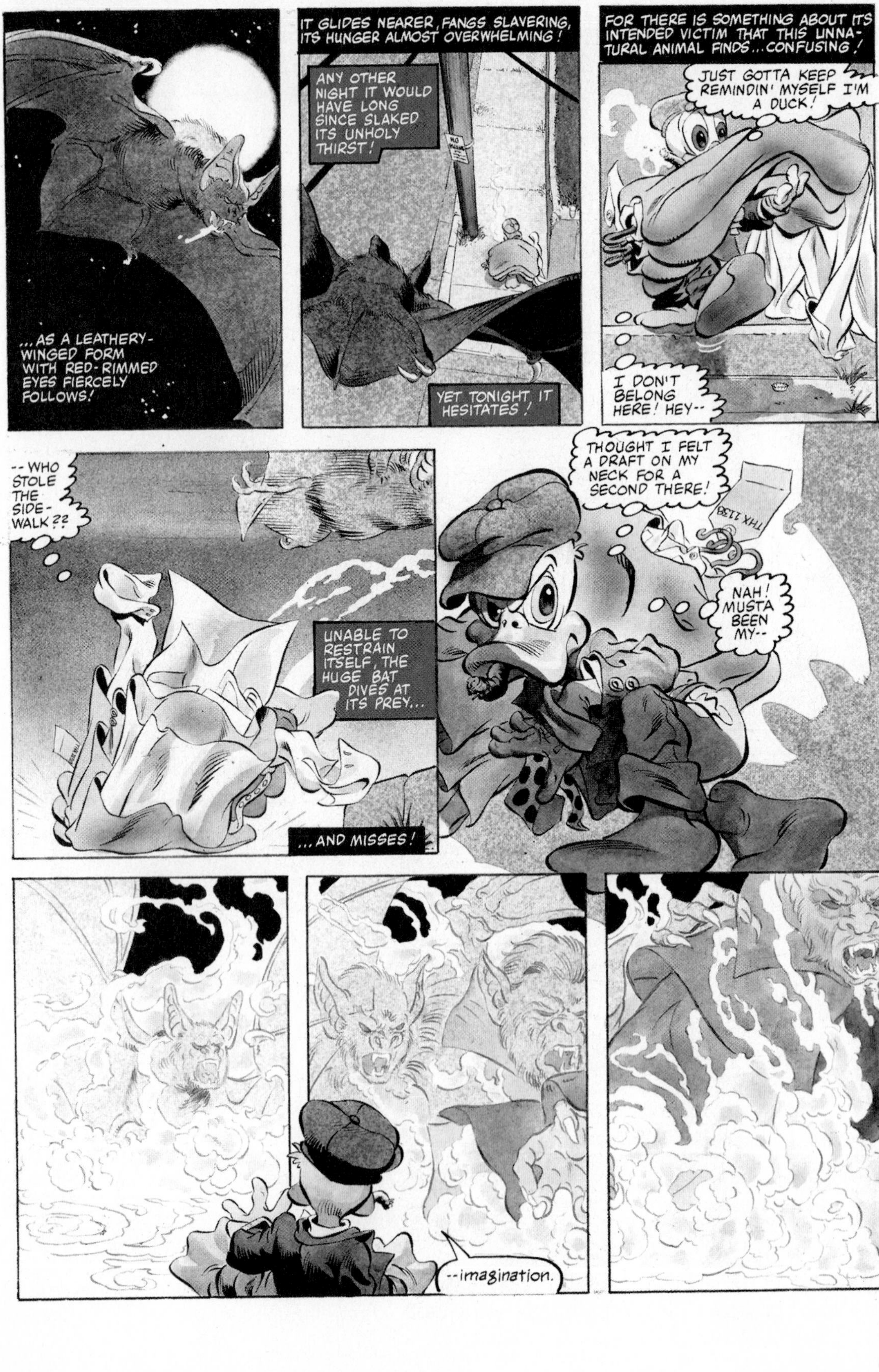
...AS A LEATHERY-WINGED FORM WITH RED-RIMMED EYES FIERCELY FOLLOWS!
IT GLIDES NEARER, FANGS SLAVERING, ITS HUNGER ALMOST OVERWHELMING!
ANY OTHER NIGHT IT WOULD HAVE LONG SINCE SLAKED ITS UNHOLY THIRST!
YET TONIGHT, IT HESITATES!
FOR THERE IS SOMETHING ABOUT ITS INTENDED VICTIM THAT THIS UNNATURAL ANIMAL FINDS...CONFUSING!
JUST GOTTA KEEP REMINDIN' MYSELF I'M A DUCK!
I DON'T BELONG HERE! HEY--
--WHO STOLE THE SIDEWALK??
UNABLE TO RESTRAIN ITSELF, THE HUGE BAT DIVES AT ITS PREY...
...AND MISSES!
THOUGHT I FELT A DRAFT ON MY NECK FOR A SECOND THERE!
THX 1138
NAH! MUSTA BEEN MY--
--imagination.

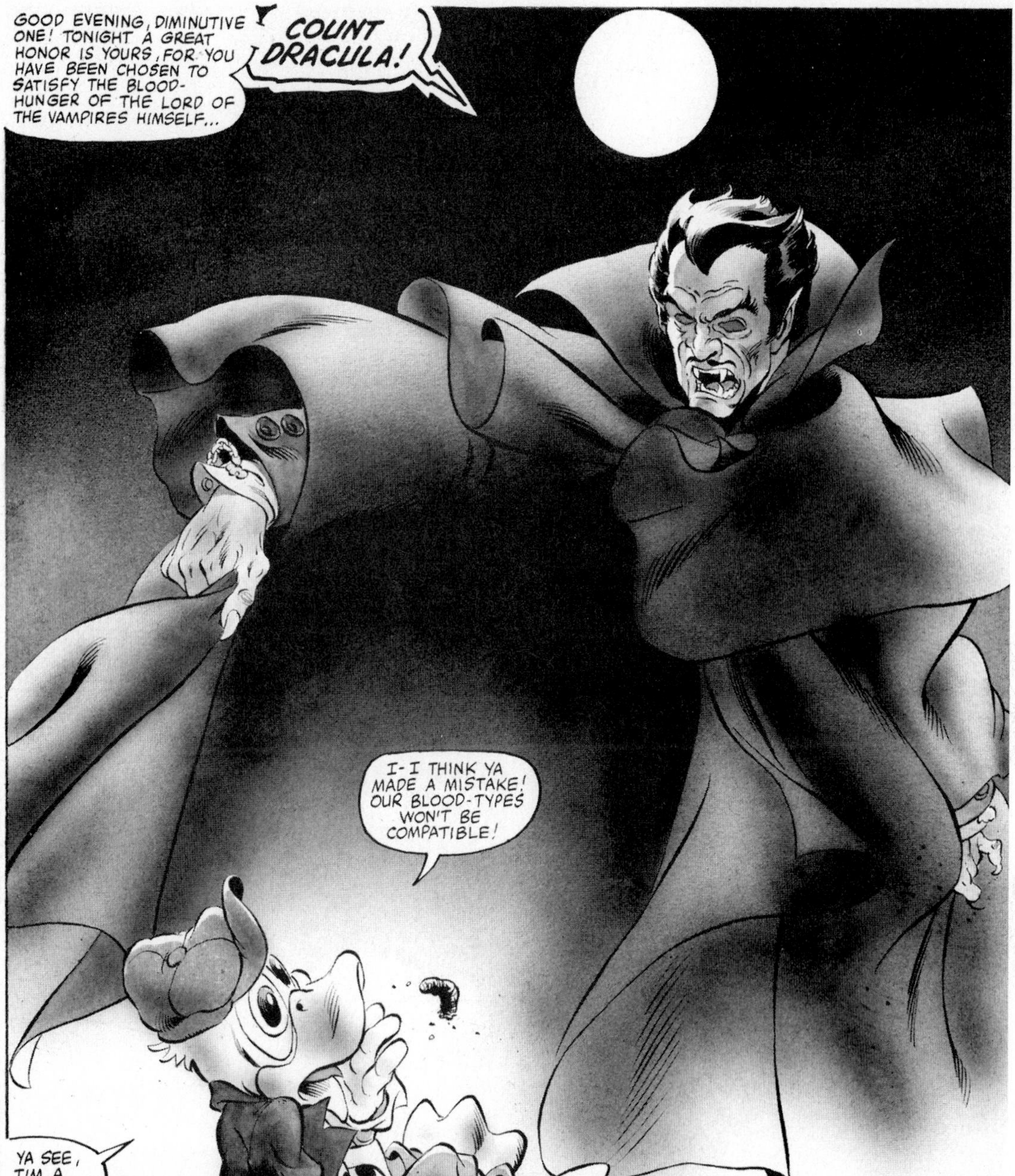
GOOD EVENING, DIMINUTIVE ONE! TONIGHT A GREAT HONOR IS YOURS, FOR YOU HAVE BEEN CHOSEN TO SATISFY THE BLOOD-HUNGER OF THE LORD OF THE VAMPIRES HIMSELF...
COUNT DRACULA!
I-I THINK YA MADE A MISTAKE! OUR BLOOD-TYPES WON'T BE COMPATIBLE!
YA SEE, I'M A D-D-DU...

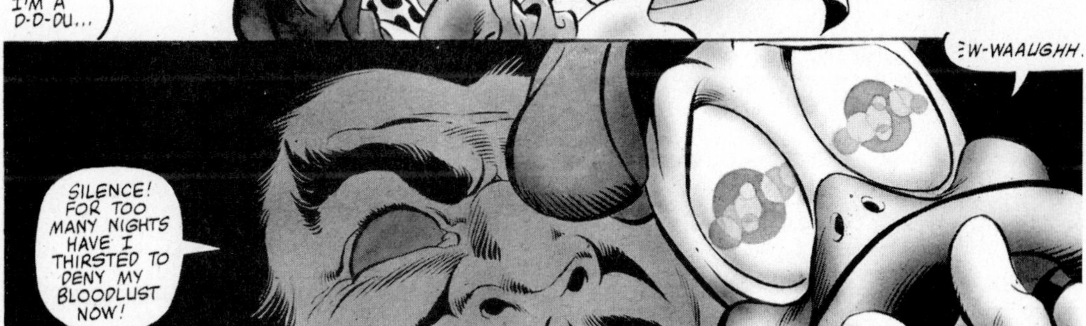
EW-WAAUGHH!
SILENCE! FOR TOO MANY NIGHTS HAVE I THIRSTED TO DENY MY BLOODLUST NOW!

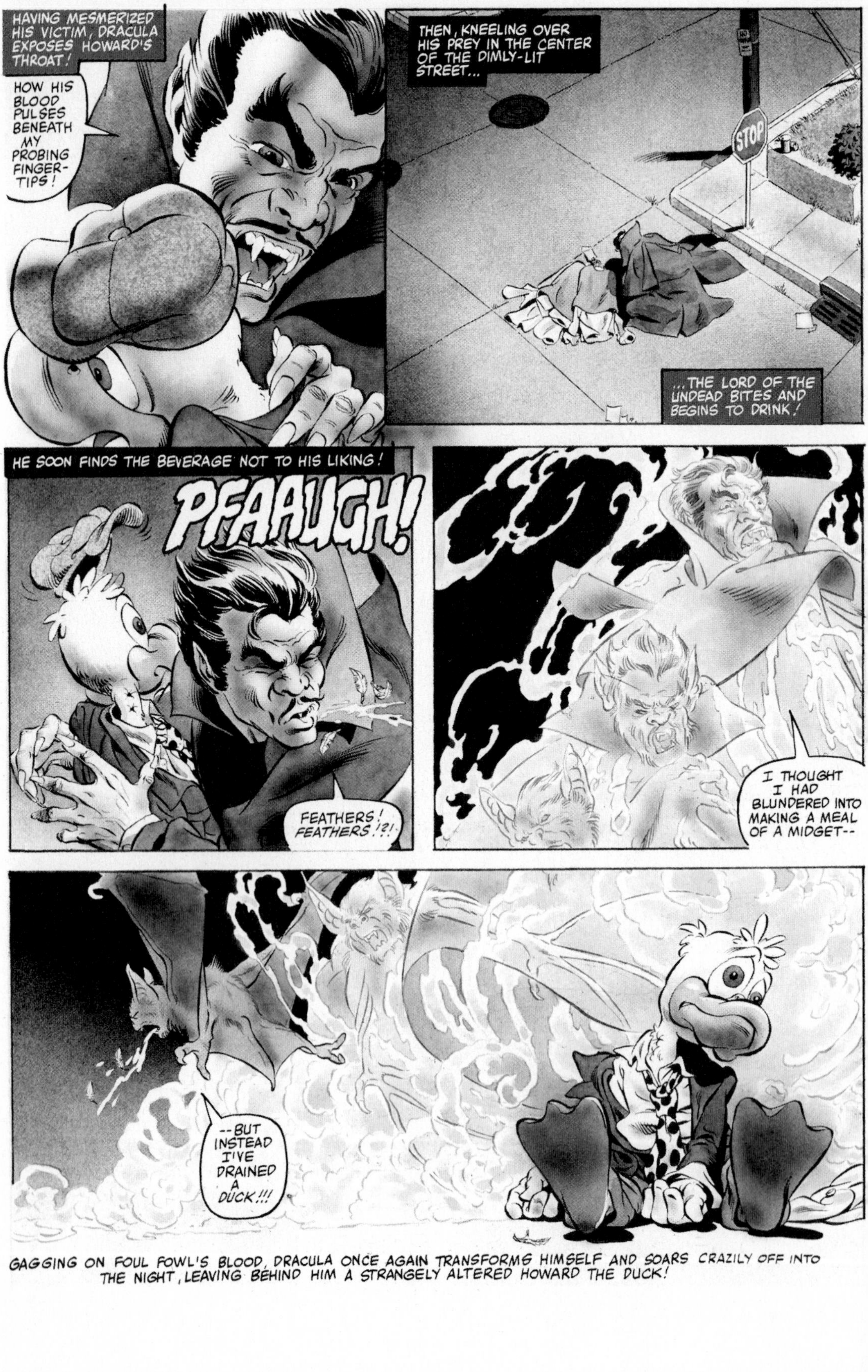
HAVING MESMERIZED HIS VICTIM, DRACULA EXPOSES HOWARD'S THROAT!
HOW HIS BLOOD PULSES BENEATH MY PROBING FINGER-TIPS!
THEN, KNEELING OVER HIS PREY IN THE CENTER OF THE DIMLY-LIT STREET...
STOP
...THE LORD OF THE UNDEAD BITES AND BEGINS TO DRINK!
HE SOON FINDS THE BEVERAGE NOT TO HIS LIKING!
PFAAUGH!
FEATHERS! FEATHERS!?!
I THOUGHT I HAD BLUNDERED INTO MAKING A MEAL OF A MIDGET--
--BUT INSTEAD I'VE DRAINED A DUCK!!!
GAGGING ON FOUL FOWL'S BLOOD, DRACULA ONCE AGAIN TRANSFORMS HIMSELF AND SOARS CRAZILY OFF INTO THE NIGHT, LEAVING BEHIND HIM A STRANGELY ALTERED HOWARD THE DUCK!

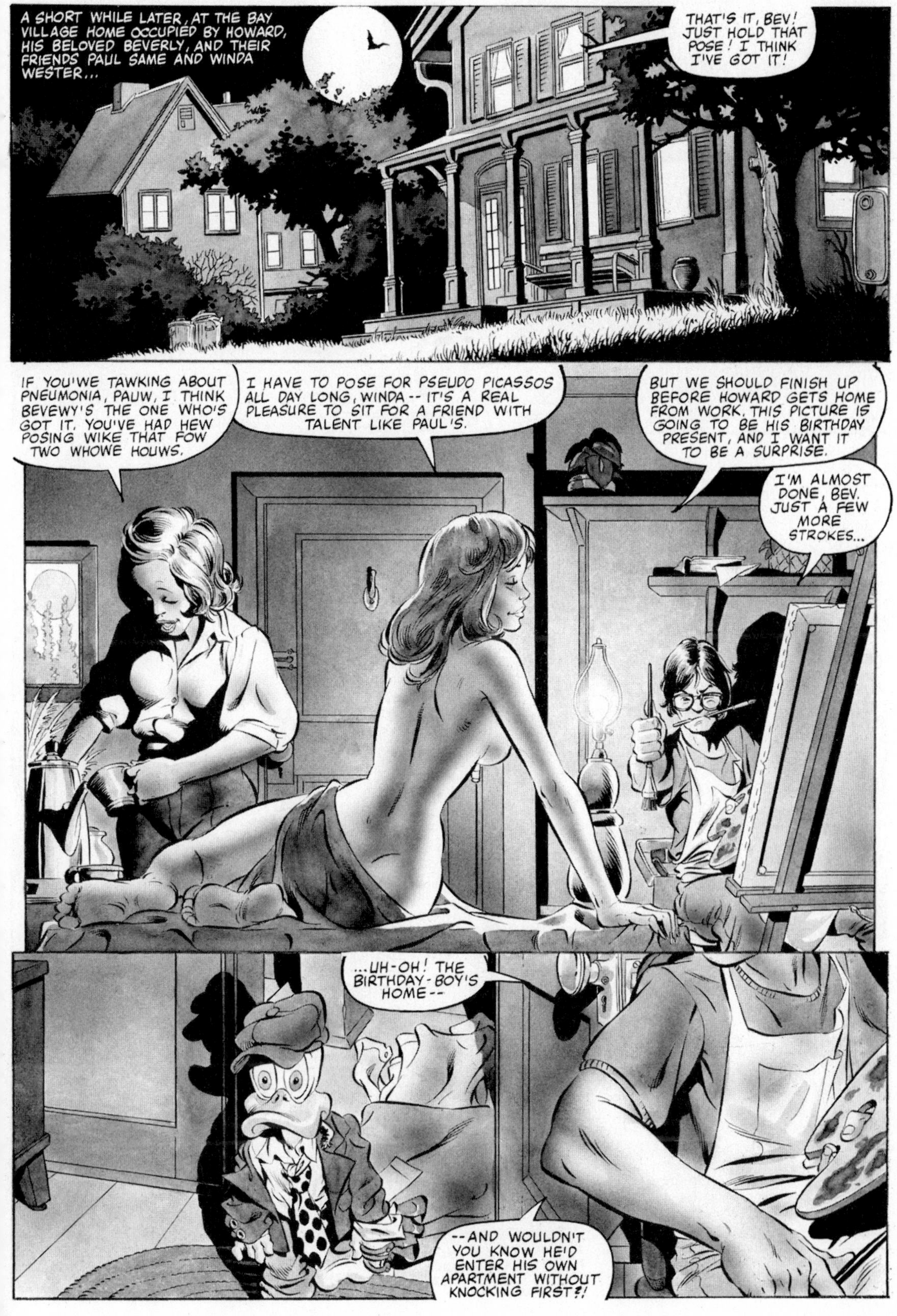

A SHORT WHILE LATER, AT THE BAY VILLAGE HOME OCCUPIED BY HOWARD, HIS BELOVED BEVERLY, AND THEIR FRIENDS PAUL SAME AND WINDA WESTER...
THAT'S IT, BEV! JUST HOLD THAT POSE! I THINK I'VE GOT IT!
IF YOU'WE TAWKING ABOUT PNEUMONIA, PAUW, I THINK BEVEWY'S THE ONE WHO'S GOT IT. YOU'VE HAD HEW POSING WIKE THAT FOW TWO WHOWE HOUWS.
I HAVE TO POSE FOR PSEUDO PICASSOS ALL DAY LONG, WINDA -- IT'S A REAL PLEASURE TO SIT FOR A FRIEND WITH TALENT LIKE PAUL'S.
BUT WE SHOULD FINISH UP BEFORE HOWARD GETS HOME FROM WORK. THIS PICTURE IS GOING TO BE HIS BIRTHDAY PRESENT, AND I WANT IT TO BE A SURPRISE.
I'M ALMOST DONE, BEV. JUST A FEW MORE STROKES...
...UH-OH! THE BIRTHDAY-BOY'S HOME --
--AND WOULDN'T YOU KNOW HE'D ENTER HIS OWN APARTMENT WITHOUT KNOCKING FIRST?!

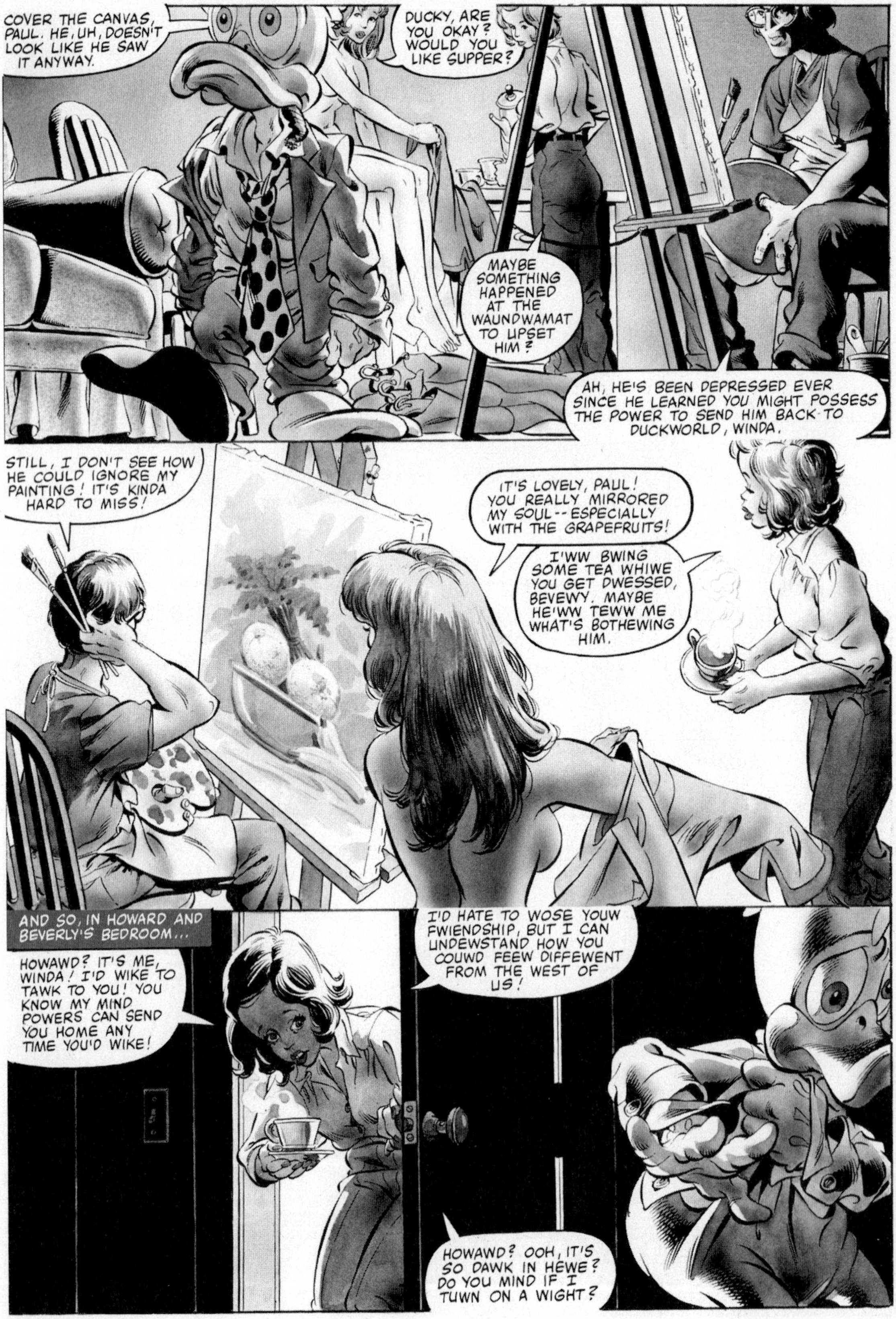
COVER THE CANVAS, PAUL. HE, UH, DOESN'T LOOK LIKE HE SAW IT ANYWAY.
DUCKY, ARE YOU OKAY? WOULD YOU LIKE SUPPER?
MAYBE SOMETHING HAPPENED AT THE WAUNDWAMAT TO UPSET HIM?
AH, HE'S BEEN DEPRESSED EVER SINCE HE LEARNED YOU MIGHT POSSESS THE POWER TO SEND HIM BACK TO DUCKWORLD, WINDA.
STILL, I DON'T SEE HOW HE COULD IGNORE MY PAINTING! IT'S KINDA HARD TO MISS!
IT'S LOVELY, PAUL! YOU REALLY MIRRORED MY SOUL--ESPECIALLY WITH THE GRAPEFRUITS!
I'WW BWING SOME TEA WHIWE YOU GET DWESSED, BEVEWY. MAYBE HE'WW TEWW ME WHAT'S BOTHEWING HIM.
AND SO, IN HOWARD AND BEVERLY'S BEDROOM...
HOWAWD? IT'S ME, WINDA! I'D WIKE TO TAWK TO YOU! YOU KNOW MY MIND POWERS CAN SEND YOU HOME ANY TIME YOU'D WIKE!
I'D HATE TO WOSE YOUW FWIENDSHIP, BUT I CAN UNDEWSTAND HOW YOU COUWD FEEW DIFFEWENT FROM THE WEST OF US!
HOWAWD? OOH, IT'S SO DAWK IN HEWE? DO YOU MIND IF I TUWN ON A WIGHT?

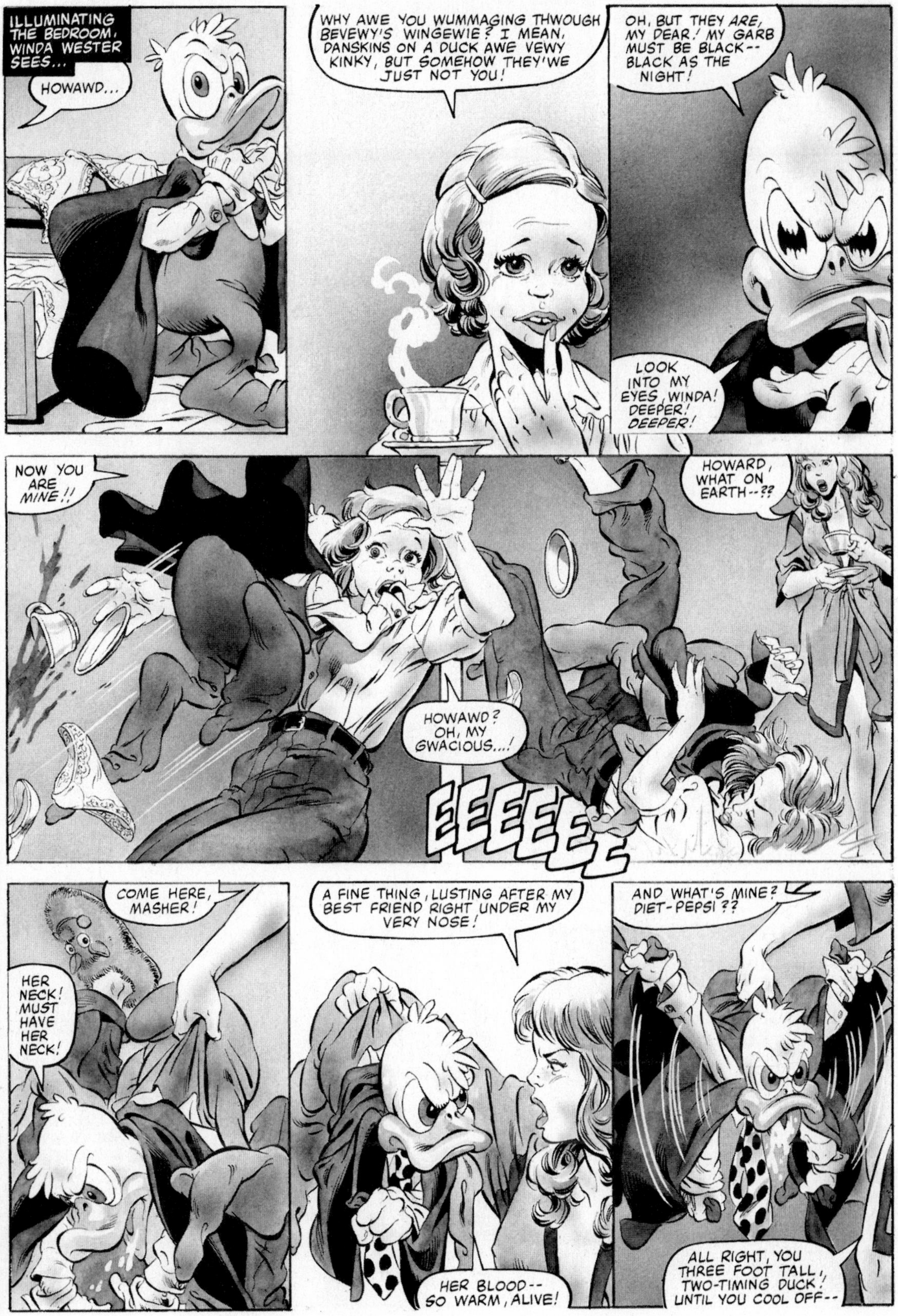
ILLUMINATING THE BEDROOM, WINDA WESTER SEES...
HOWAWD...
WHY AWE YOU WUMMAGING THWOUGH BEVEWY'S WINGEWIE? I MEAN, DANSKINS ON A DUCK AWE VEWY KINKY, BUT SOMEHOW THEY'WE JUST NOT YOU!
OH, BUT THEY ARE, MY DEAR! MY GARB MUST BE BLACK-- BLACK AS THE NIGHT!
LOOK INTO MY EYES, WINDA! DEEPER! DEEPER!
NOW YOU ARE MINE!!
HOWARD, WHAT ON EARTH--??
HOWAWD? OH, MY GWACIOUS...!
EEEEEEE
COME HERE, MASHER!
HER NECK! MUST HAVE HER NECK!
A FINE THING, LUSTING AFTER MY BEST FRIEND RIGHT UNDER MY VERY NOSE!
HER BLOOD-- SO WARM, ALIVE!
AND WHAT'S MINE? DIET-PEPSI??
ALL RIGHT, YOU THREE FOOT TALL, TWO-TIMING DUCK! UNTIL YOU COOL OFF--

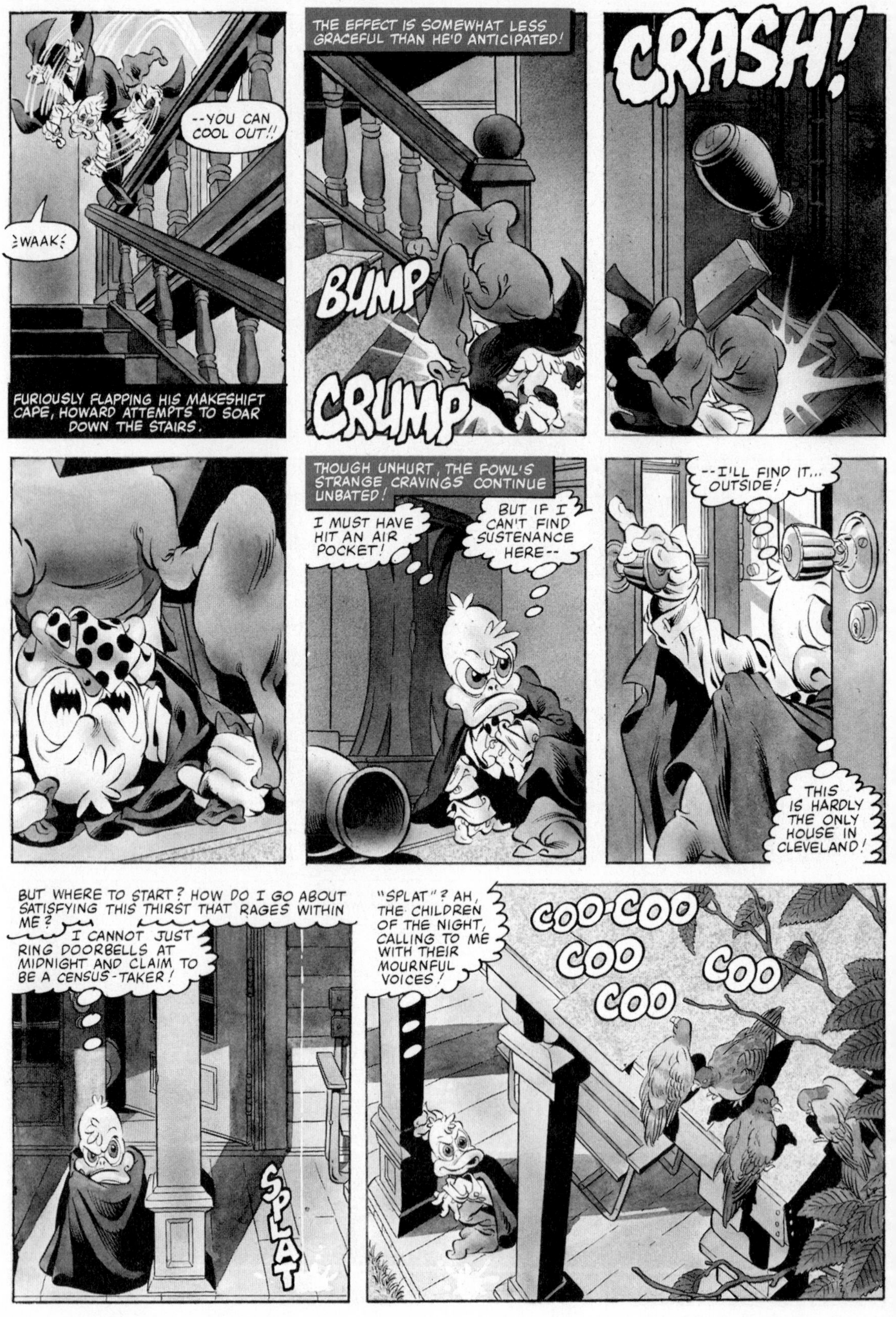
--YOU CAN COOL OUT!!
WAAK
FURIOUSLY FLAPPING HIS MAKESHIFT CAPE, HOWARD ATTEMPTS TO SOAR DOWN THE STAIRS.
THE EFFECT IS SOMEWHAT LESS GRACEFUL THAN HE'D ANTICIPATED!
BUMP
CRUMP
CRASH!
THOUGH UNHURT, THE FOWL'S STRANGE CRAVINGS CONTINUE UNBATED!
I MUST HAVE HIT AN AIR POCKET!
BUT IF I CAN'T FIND SUSTENANCE HERE--
--I'LL FIND IT... OUTSIDE!
THIS IS HARDLY THE ONLY HOUSE IN CLEVELAND!
BUT WHERE TO START? HOW DO I GO ABOUT SATISFYING THIS THIRST THAT RAGES WITHIN ME?
I CANNOT JUST RING DOORBELLS AT MIDNIGHT AND CLAIM TO BE A CENSUS-TAKER!
SPLAT
"SPLAT"? AH, THE CHILDREN OF THE NIGHT, CALLING TO ME WITH THEIR MOURNFUL VOICES!
COO-COO
COO
COO
COO

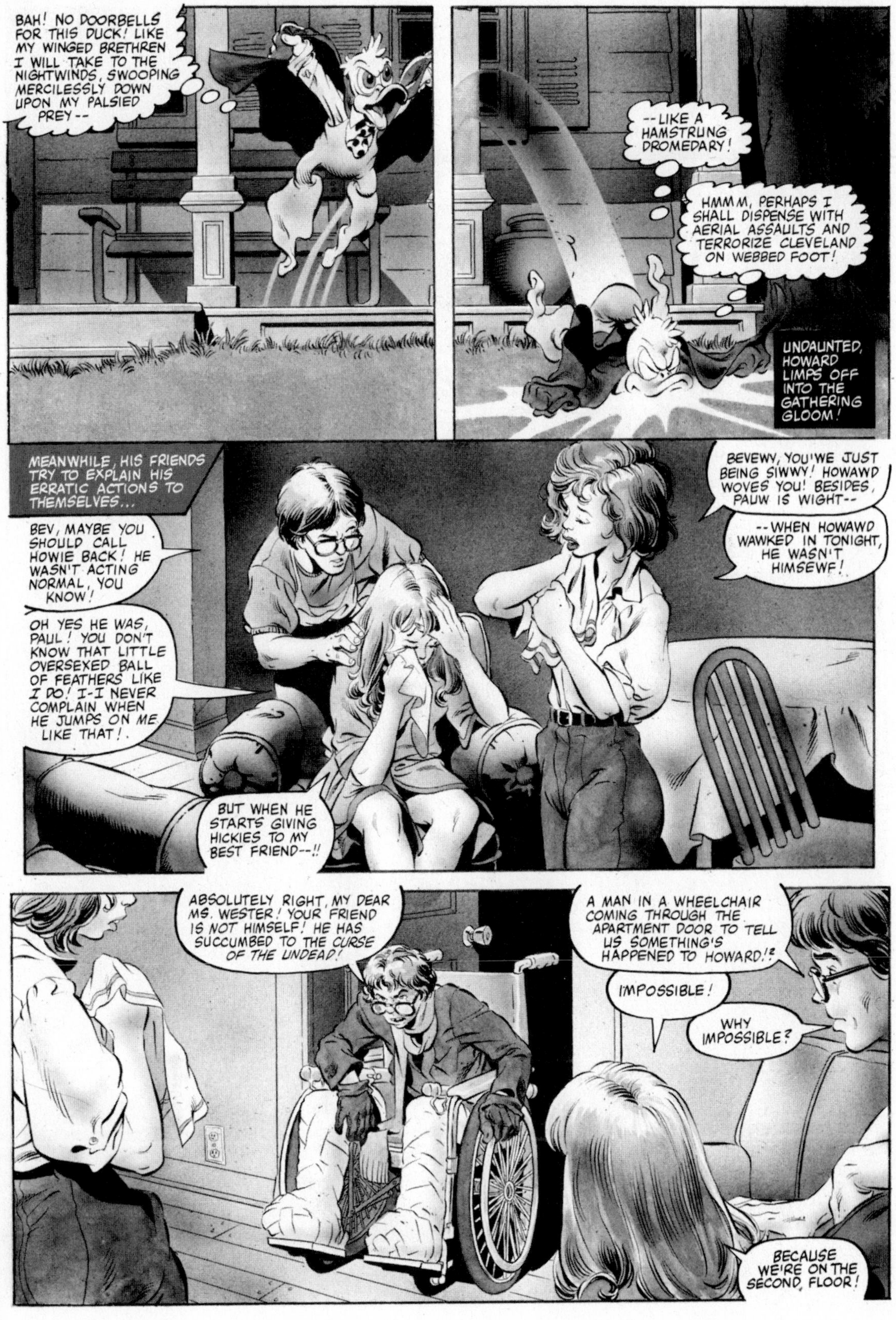
BAH! NO DOORBELLS FOR THIS DUCK! LIKE MY WINGED BRETHREN I WILL TAKE TO THE NIGHTWINDS, SWOOPING MERCILESSLY DOWN UPON MY PALSIED PREY--
--LIKE A HAMSTRUNG DROMEDARY!
HMMM, PERHAPS I SHALL DISPENSE WITH AERIAL ASSAULTS AND TERRORIZE CLEVELAND ON WEBBED FOOT!
UNDAUNTED, HOWARD LIMPS OFF INTO THE GATHERING GLOOM!
MEANWHILE, HIS FRIENDS TRY TO EXPLAIN HIS ERRATIC ACTIONS TO THEMSELVES...
BEV, MAYBE YOU SHOULD CALL HOWIE BACK! HE WASN'T ACTING NORMAL, YOU KNOW!
OH YES HE WAS, PAUL! YOU DON'T KNOW THAT LITTLE OVERSEXED BALL OF FEATHERS LIKE I DO! I-I NEVER COMPLAIN WHEN HE JUMPS ON ME LIKE THAT!
BUT WHEN HE STARTS GIVING HICKIES TO MY BEST FRIEND--!!
BEVEWY, YOU'WE JUST BEING SIWWY! HOWAWD WOVES YOU! BESIDES, PAUW IS WIGHT--
--WHEN HOWAWD WAWKED IN TONIGHT, HE WASN'T HIMSEWF!
ABSOLUTELY RIGHT, MY DEAR MS. WESTER! YOUR FRIEND IS NOT HIMSELF! HE HAS SUCCUMBED TO THE CURSE OF THE UNDEAD!
A MAN IN A WHEELCHAIR COMING THROUGH THE APARTMENT DOOR TO TELL US SOMETHING'S HAPPENED TO HOWARD!?
IMPOSSIBLE!
WHY IMPOSSIBLE?
BECAUSE WE'RE ON THE SECOND FLOOR!

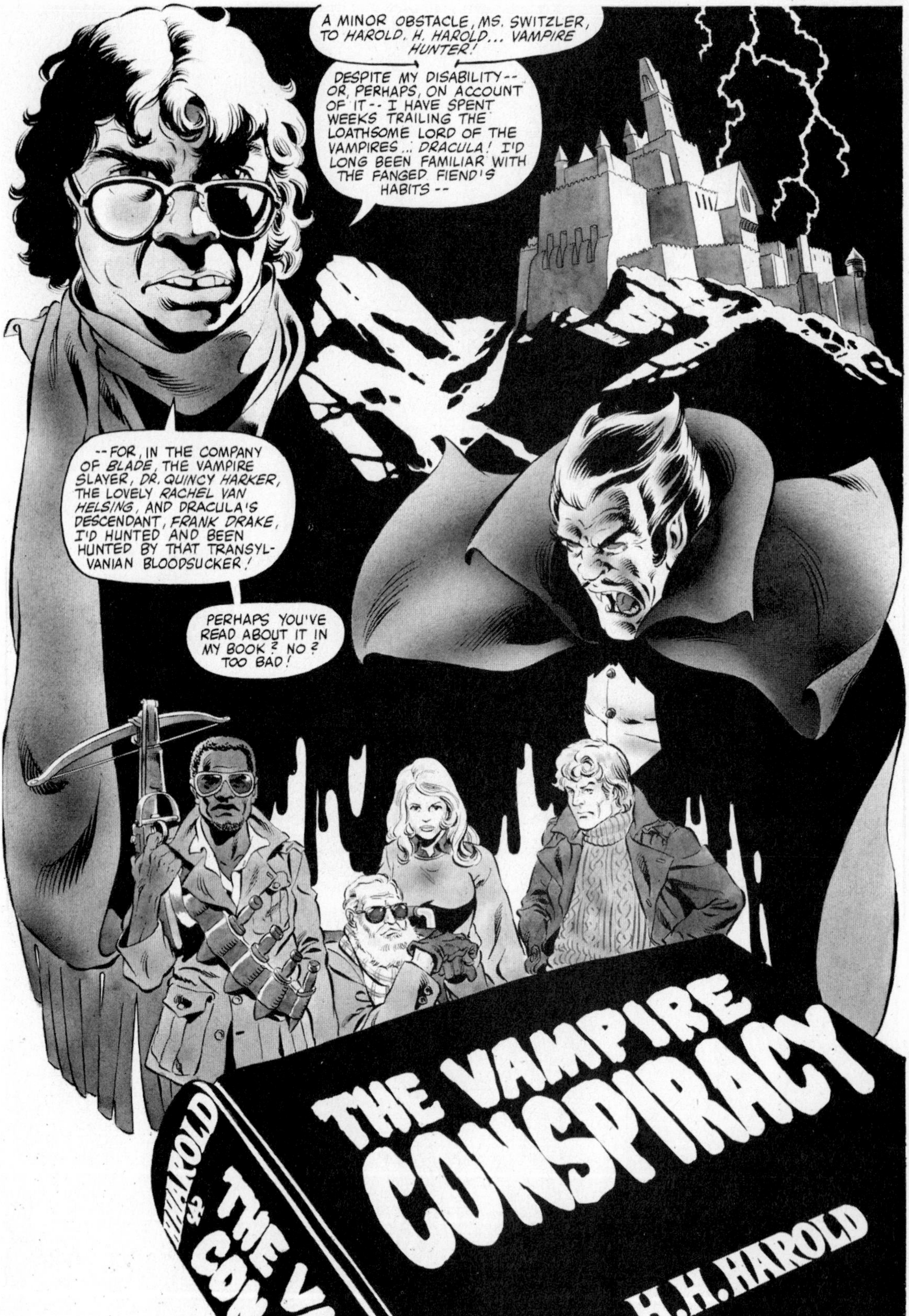
A MINOR OBSTACLE, MS. SWITZLER, TO HAROLD. H. HAROLD... VAMPIRE HUNTER!
DESPITE MY DISABILITY-- OR, PERHAPS, ON ACCOUNT OF IT-- I HAVE SPENT WEEKS TRAILING THE LOATHSOME LORD OF THE VAMPIRES... DRACULA! I'D LONG BEEN FAMILIAR WITH THE FANGED FIEND'S HABITS --
--FOR, IN THE COMPANY OF BLADE, THE VAMPIRE SLAYER, DR. QUINCY HARKER, THE LOVELY RACHEL VAN HELSING, AND DRACULA'S DESCENDANT, FRANK DRAKE, I'D HUNTED AND BEEN HUNTED BY THAT TRANSYLVANIAN BLOODSUCKER!
PERHAPS YOU'VE READ ABOUT IT IN MY BOOK? NO? TOO BAD!
THE VAMPIRE CONSPIRACY
H.H.HAROLD
H.H.HAROLD
THE V
CON

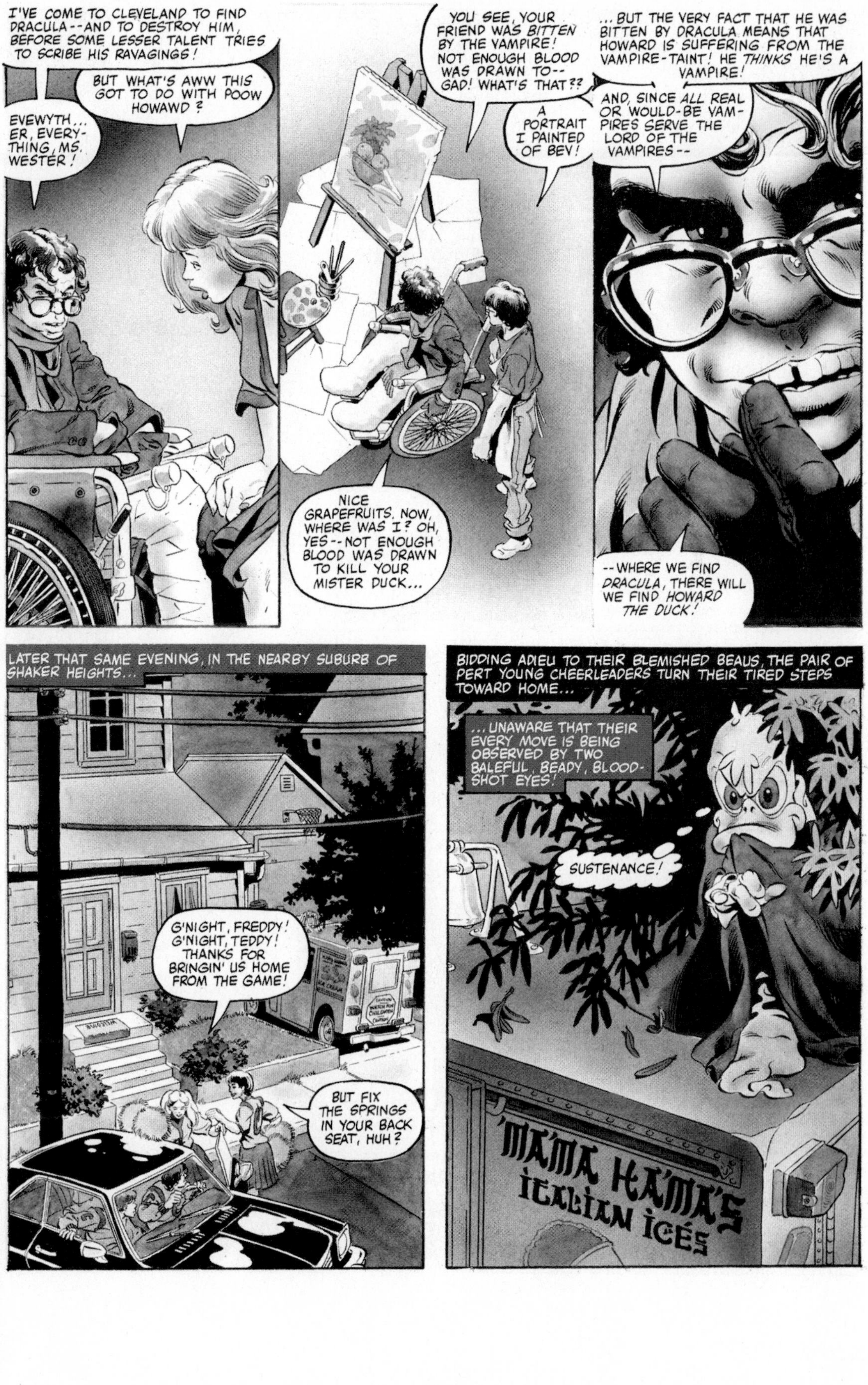
I'VE COME TO CLEVELAND TO FIND DRACULA--AND TO DESTROY HIM, BEFORE SOME LESSER TALENT TRIES TO SCRIBE HIS RAVAGINGS!
BUT WHAT'S AWW THIS GOT TO DO WITH POOW HOWAWD?
EVEWYTH... ER, EVERYTHING, MS. WESTER!
YOU SEE, YOUR FRIEND WAS BITTEN BY THE VAMPIRE! NOT ENOUGH BLOOD WAS DRAWN TO-- GAD! WHAT'S THAT??
A PORTRAIT I PAINTED OF BEV!
NICE GRAPEFRUITS. NOW, WHERE WAS I? OH, YES--NOT ENOUGH BLOOD WAS DRAWN TO KILL YOUR MISTER DUCK...
... BUT THE VERY FACT THAT HE WAS BITTEN BY DRACULA MEANS THAT HOWARD IS SUFFERING FROM THE VAMPIRE-TAINT! HE THINKS HE'S A VAMPIRE!
AND, SINCE ALL REAL OR WOULD-BE VAMPIRES SERVE THE LORD OF THE VAMPIRES--
--WHERE WE FIND DRACULA, THERE WILL WE FIND HOWARD THE DUCK!
LATER THAT SAME EVENING, IN THE NEARBY SUBURB OF SHAKER HEIGHTS...
G'NIGHT, FREDDY! G'NIGHT, TEDDY! THANKS FOR BRINGIN' US HOME FROM THE GAME!
BUT FIX THE SPRINGS IN YOUR BACK SEAT, HUH?
BIDDING ADIEU TO THEIR BLEMISHED BEAUS, THE PAIR OF PERT YOUNG CHEERLEADERS TURN THEIR TIRED STEPS TOWARD HOME...
... UNAWARE THAT THEIR EVERY MOVE IS BEING OBSERVED BY TWO BALEFUL, BEADY, BLOOD-SHOT EYES!
SUSTENANCE!
MAMA HAMA'S
ITALIAN ICES

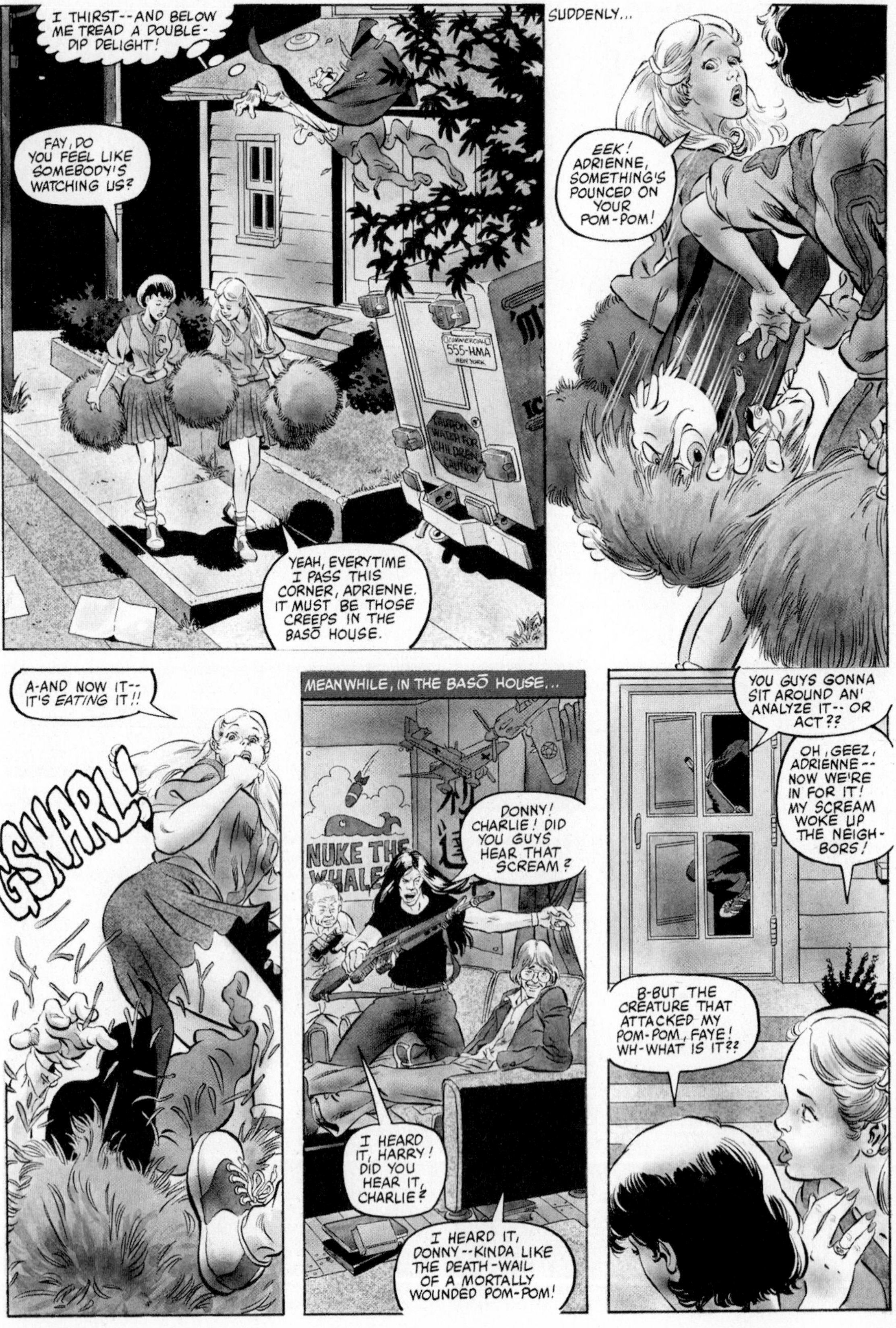
I THIRST--AND BELOW ME TREAD A DOUBLE-DIP DELIGHT!
FAY, DO YOU FEEL LIKE SOMEBODY'S WATCHING US?
555-HMA
NEW YORK
CAUTION WATCH FOR CHILDREN CAUTION
YEAH, EVERYTIME I PASS THIS CORNER, ADRIENNE. IT MUST BE THOSE CREEPS IN THE BASŌ HOUSE.
SUDDENLY...
EEK! ADRIENNE, SOMETHING'S POUNCED ON YOUR POM-POM!
A-AND NOW IT--IT'S EATING IT!!
GSNARL!
MEANWHILE, IN THE BASŌ HOUSE...
NUKE THE WHALE
DONNY! CHARLIE! DID YOU GUYS HEAR THAT SCREAM?
I HEARD IT, HARRY! DID YOU HEAR IT, CHARLIE?
I HEARD IT, DONNY--KINDA LIKE THE DEATH-WAIL OF A MORTALLY WOUNDED POM-POM!
YOU GUYS GONNA SIT AROUND AN' ANALYZE IT--OR ACT??
OH, GEEZ, ADRIENNE--NOW WE'RE IN FOR IT! MY SCREAM WOKE UP THE NEIGHBORS!
B-BUT THE CREATURE THAT ATTACKED MY POM-POM, FAYE! WH-WHAT IS IT??

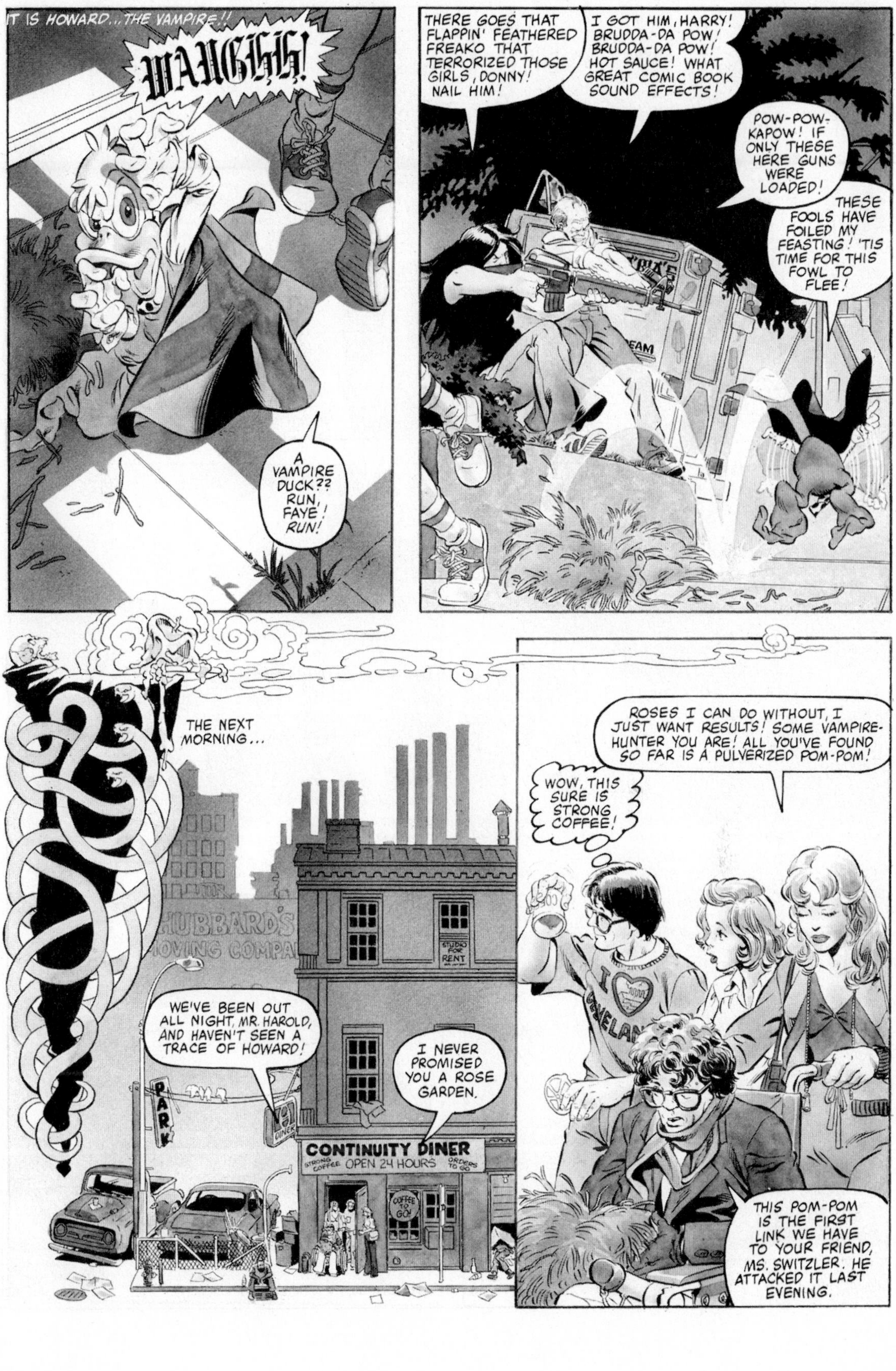

IT IS HOWARD...THE VAMPIRE!!
WAUGHH!
A VAMPIRE DUCK?? RUN, FAYE! RUN!
THERE GOES THAT FLAPPIN' FEATHERED FREAKO THAT TERRORIZED THOSE GIRLS, DONNY! NAIL HIM!
I GOT HIM, HARRY! BRUDDA-DA POW! BRUDDA-DA POW! HOT SAUCE! WHAT GREAT COMIC BOOK SOUND EFFECTS!
POW-POW-KAPOW! IF ONLY THESE HERE GUNS WERE LOADED!
THESE FOOLS HAVE FOILED MY FEASTING! 'TIS TIME FOR THIS FOWL TO FLEE!
THE NEXT MORNING...
HUBBARD'S MOVING COMPA
STUDIO FOR RENT
WE'VE BEEN OUT ALL NIGHT, MR. HAROLD, AND HAVEN'T SEEN A TRACE OF HOWARD!
I NEVER PROMISED YOU A ROSE GARDEN.
PARK
DINER
CONTINUITY DINER
STRONG COFFEE OPEN 24 HOURS ORDERS TO GO
COFFEE TO GO!
ROSES I CAN DO WITHOUT, I JUST WANT RESULTS! SOME VAMPIRE-HUNTER YOU ARE! ALL YOU'VE FOUND SO FAR IS A PULVERIZED POM-POM!
WOW, THIS SURE IS STRONG COFFEE!
THIS POM-POM IS THE FIRST LINK WE HAVE TO YOUR FRIEND, MS. SWITZLER. HE ATTACKED IT LAST EVENING.

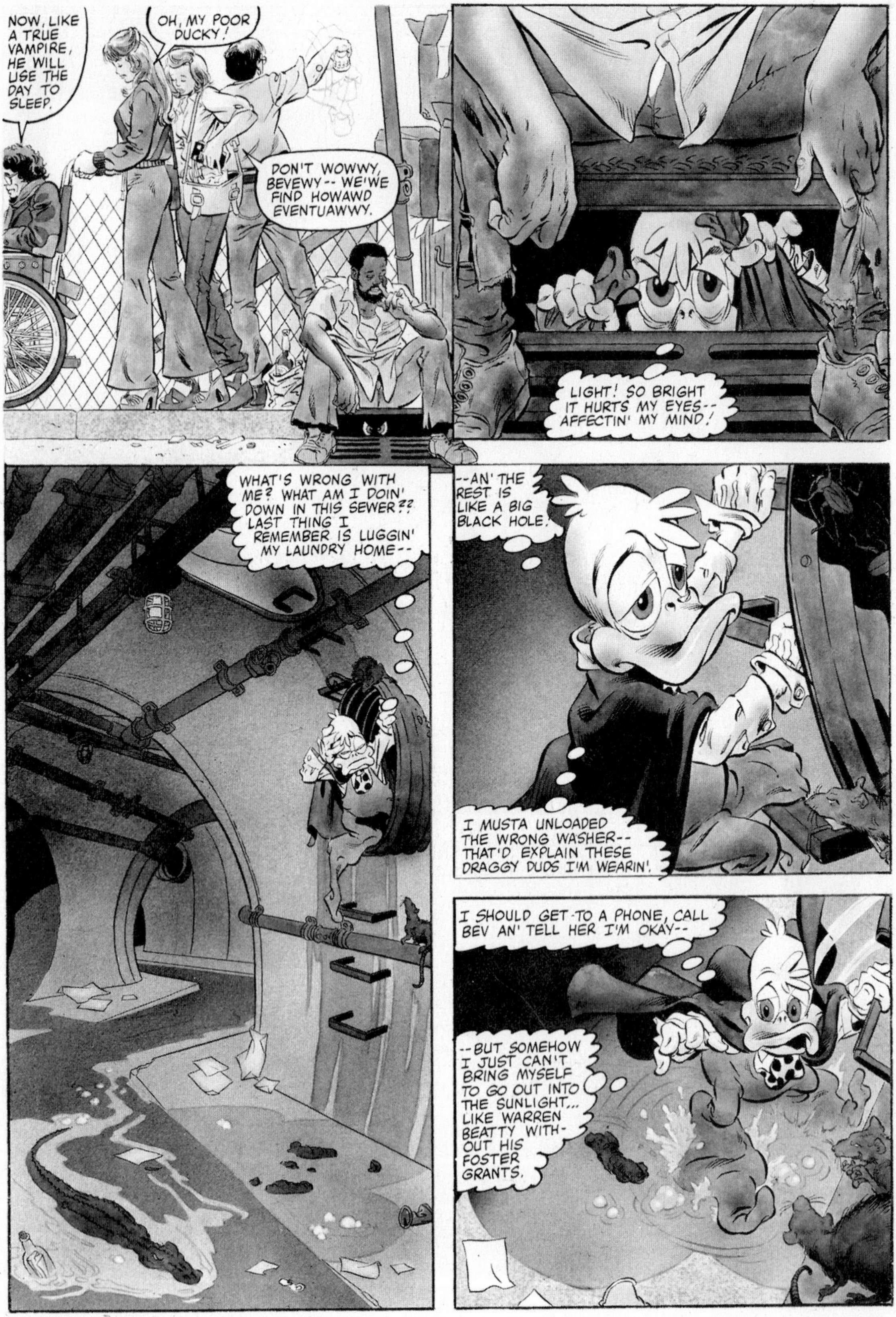
NOW, LIKE A TRUE VAMPIRE, HE WILL USE THE DAY TO SLEEP.
OH, MY POOR DUCKY!
DON'T WOWWY, BEVEWY-- WE'WE FIND HOWAWD EVENTUAWWY.
LIGHT! SO BRIGHT IT HURTS MY EYES-- AFFECTIN' MY MIND!
WHAT'S WRONG WITH ME? WHAT AM I DOIN' DOWN IN THIS SEWER?? LAST THING I REMEMBER IS LUGGIN' MY LAUNDRY HOME--
--AN' THE REST IS LIKE A BIG BLACK HOLE.
I MUSTA UNLOADED THE WRONG WASHER-- THAT'D EXPLAIN THESE DRAGGY DUDS I'M WEARIN'.
I SHOULD GET TO A PHONE, CALL BEV AN' TELL HER I'M OKAY--
--BUT SOMEHOW I JUST CAN'T BRING MYSELF TO GO OUT INTO THE SUNLIGHT... LIKE WARREN BEATTY WITHOUT HIS FOSTER GRANTS.

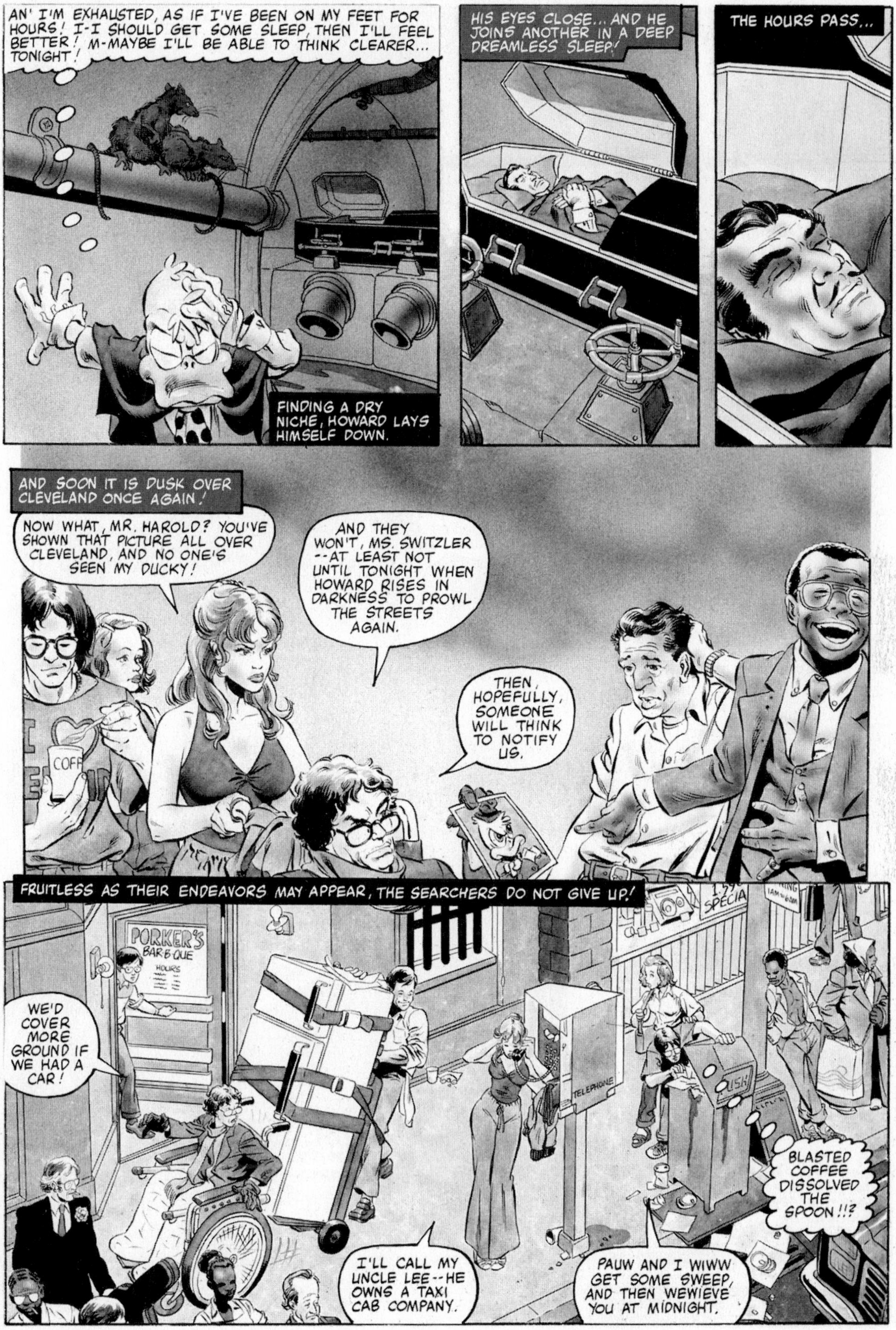

AN' I'M EXHAUSTED, AS IF I'VE BEEN ON MY FEET FOR HOURS! I-I SHOULD GET SOME SLEEP, THEN I'LL FEEL BETTER! M-MAYBE I'LL BE ABLE TO THINK CLEARER... TONIGHT!
FINDING A DRY NICHE, HOWARD LAYS HIMSELF DOWN.
HIS EYES CLOSE... AND HE JOINS ANOTHER IN A DEEP DREAMLESS SLEEP!
THE HOURS PASS...
AND SOON IT IS DUSK OVER CLEVELAND ONCE AGAIN!
NOW WHAT, MR. HAROLD? YOU'VE SHOWN THAT PICTURE ALL OVER CLEVELAND, AND NO ONE'S SEEN MY DUCKY!
AND THEY WON'T, MS. SWITZLER --AT LEAST NOT UNTIL TONIGHT WHEN HOWARD RISES IN DARKNESS TO PROWL THE STREETS AGAIN.
THEN, HOPEFULLY, SOMEONE WILL THINK TO NOTIFY US.
FRUITLESS AS THEIR ENDEAVORS MAY APPEAR, THE SEARCHERS DO NOT GIVE UP!
PORKER'S BAR-B-QUE
HOURS
WE'D COVER MORE GROUND IF WE HAD A CAR!
TELEPHONE
BLASTED COFFEE DISSOLVED THE SPOON!!?
I'LL CALL MY UNCLE LEE--HE OWNS A TAXI CAB COMPANY.
PAUW AND I WIWW GET SOME SWEEP, AND THEN WEWIEVE YOU AT MIDNIGHT.

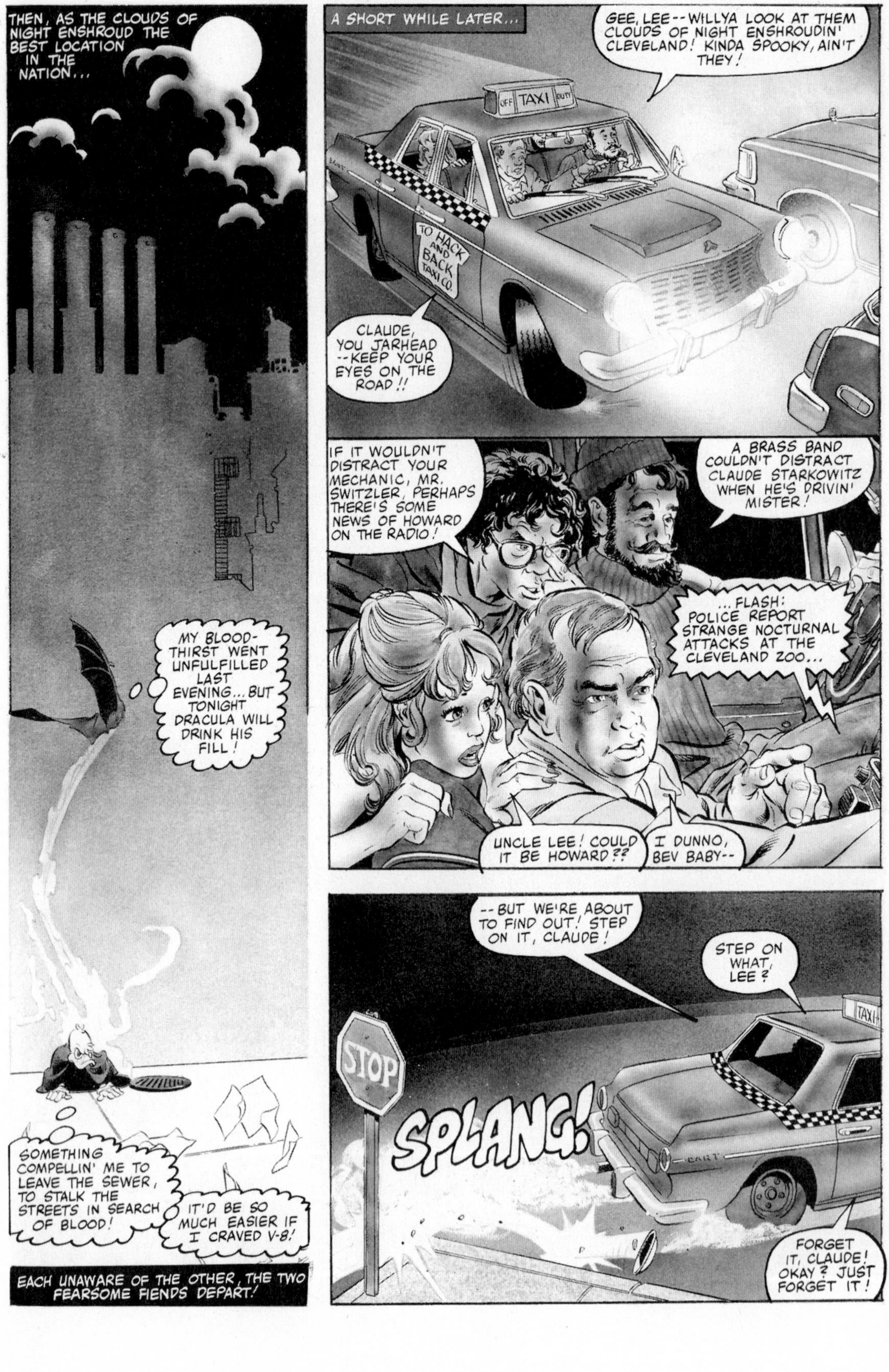
THEN, AS THE CLOUDS OF NIGHT ENSHROUD THE BEST LOCATION IN THE NATION...
MY BLOOD-THIRST WENT UNFULFILLED LAST EVENING... BUT TONIGHT DRACULA WILL DRINK HIS FILL!
SOMETHING COMPELLIN' ME TO LEAVE THE SEWER, TO STALK THE STREETS IN SEARCH OF BLOOD!
IT'D BE SO MUCH EASIER IF I CRAVED V-8!
EACH UNAWARE OF THE OTHER, THE TWO FEARSOME FIENDS DEPART!
A SHORT WHILE LATER...
GEE, LEE--WILLYA LOOK AT THEM CLOUDS OF NIGHT ENSHROUDIN' CLEVELAND! KINDA SPOOKY, AIN'T THEY!
OFF TAXI DUTY
TO HACK AND BACK TAXI CO.
CLAUDE, YOU JARHEAD --KEEP YOUR EYES ON THE ROAD!!
IF IT WOULDN'T DISTRACT YOUR MECHANIC, MR. SWITZLER, PERHAPS THERE'S SOME NEWS OF HOWARD ON THE RADIO!
A BRASS BAND COULDN'T DISTRACT CLAUDE STARKOWITZ WHEN HE'S DRIVIN' MISTER!
...FLASH: POLICE REPORT STRANGE NOCTURNAL ATTACKS AT THE CLEVELAND ZOO...
UNCLE LEE! COULD IT BE HOWARD??
I DUNNO, BEV BABY--
--BUT WE'RE ABOUT TO FIND OUT! STEP ON IT, CLAUDE!
STEP ON WHAT, LEE?
STOP
SPLANG!
FORGET IT, CLAUDE! OKAY? JUST FORGET IT!

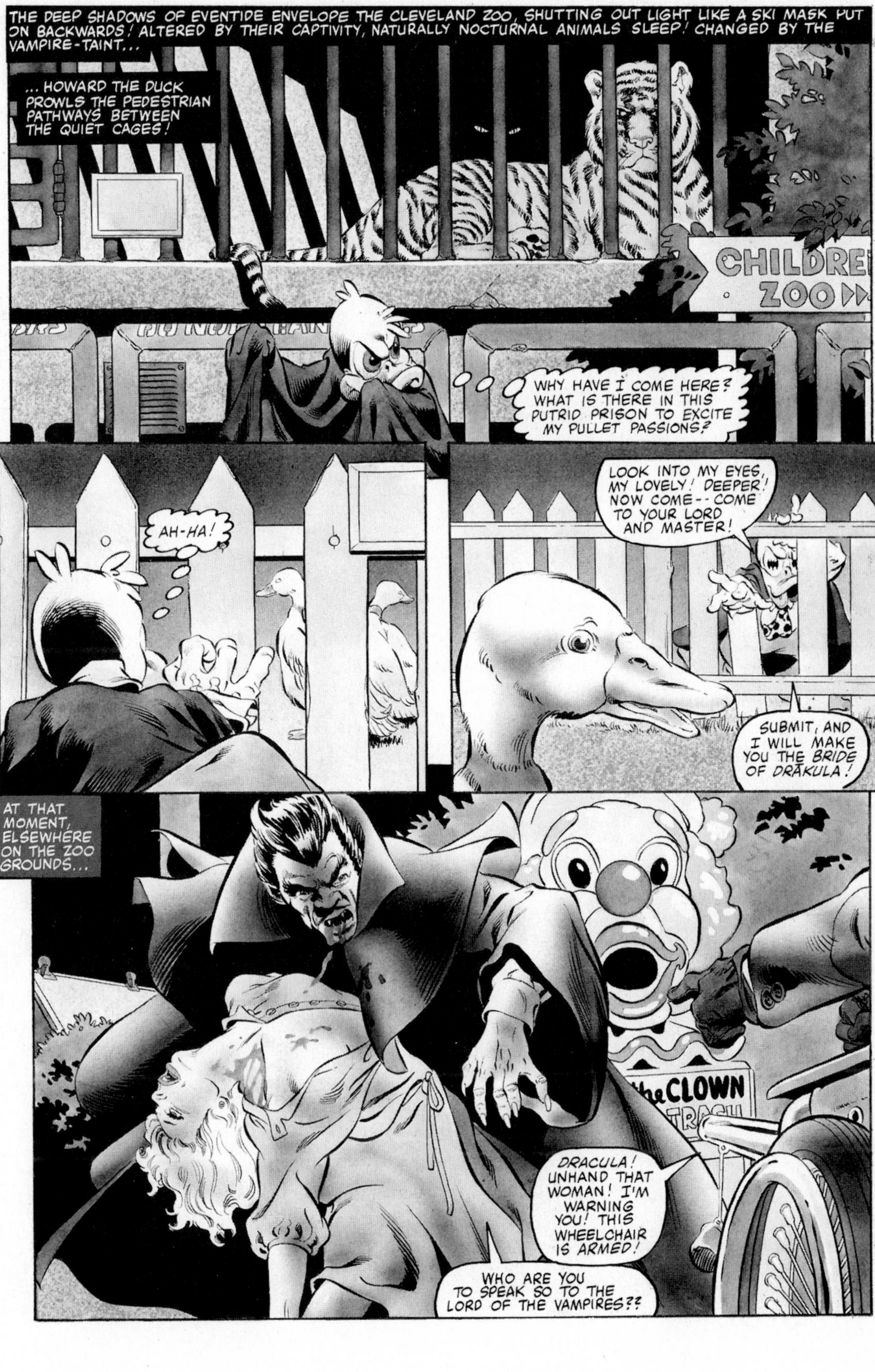
THE DEEP SHADOWS OF EVENTIDE ENVELOPE THE CLEVELAND ZOO, SHUTTING OUT LIGHT LIKE A SKI MASK PUT ON BACKWARDS! ALTERED BY THEIR CAPTIVITY, NATURALLY NOCTURNAL ANIMALS SLEEP! CHANGED BY THE VAMPIRE-TAINT...
... HOWARD THE DUCK PROWLS THE PEDESTRIAN PATHWAYS BETWEEN THE QUIET CAGES!
CHILDRE
ZOO
WHY HAVE I COME HERE? WHAT IS THERE IN THIS PUTRID PRISON TO EXCITE MY PULLET PASSIONS?
AH-HA!
LOOK INTO MY EYES, MY LOVELY! DEEPER! NOW COME-- COME TO YOUR LORD AND MASTER!
SUBMIT, AND I WILL MAKE YOU THE BRIDE OF DRAKULA!
AT THAT MOMENT, ELSEWHERE ON THE ZOO GROUNDS...
the CLOWN
DRACULA! UNHAND THAT WOMAN! I'M WARNING YOU! THIS WHEELCHAIR IS ARMED!
WHO ARE YOU TO SPEAK SO TO THE LORD OF THE VAMPIRES??

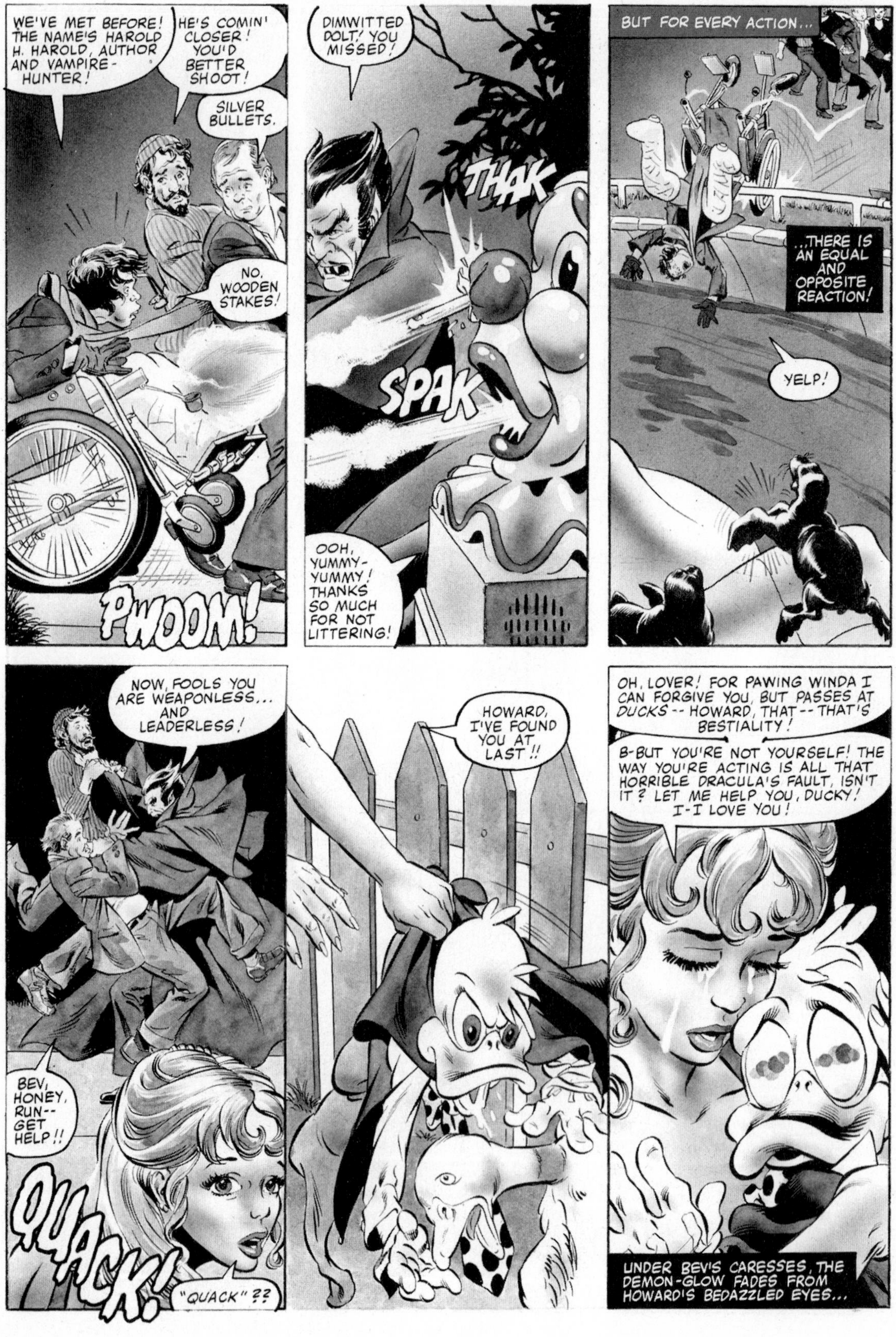

WE'VE MET BEFORE! THE NAME'S HAROLD H. HAROLD, AUTHOR AND VAMPIRE-HUNTER!
HE'S COMIN' CLOSER! YOU'D BETTER SHOOT!
SILVER BULLETS.
NO, WOODEN STAKES!
PWOOM!
DIMWITTED DOLT! YOU MISSED!
THAK
SPAK
OOH, YUMMY-YUMMY! THANKS SO MUCH FOR NOT LITTERING!
BUT FOR EVERY ACTION...
...THERE IS AN EQUAL AND OPPOSITE REACTION!
YELP!
NOW, FOOLS YOU ARE WEAPONLESS,... AND LEADERLESS!
BEV, HONEY, RUN-- GET HELP!!
QUACK!
"QUACK"??
HOWARD, I'VE FOUND YOU AT LAST!!
OH, LOVER! FOR PAWING WINDA I CAN FORGIVE YOU, BUT PASSES AT DUCKS -- HOWARD, THAT -- THAT'S BESTIALITY!
B-BUT YOU'RE NOT YOURSELF! THE WAY YOU'RE ACTING IS ALL THAT HORRIBLE DRACULA'S FAULT, ISN'T IT? LET ME HELP YOU, DUCKY! I-I LOVE YOU!
UNDER BEV'S CARESSES, THE DEMON-GLOW FADES FROM HOWARD'S BEDAZZLED EYES...

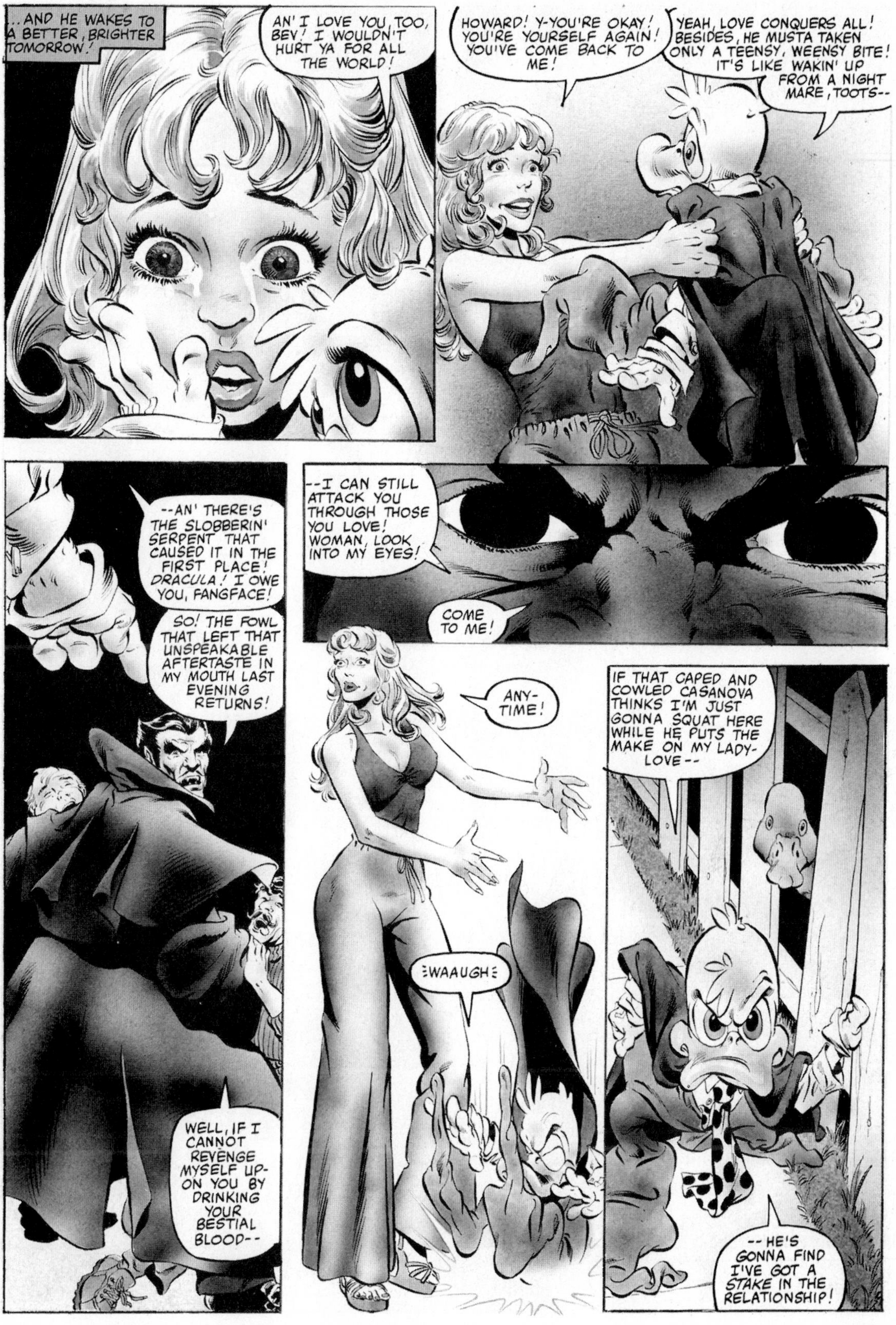
..AND HE WAKES TO A BETTER, BRIGHTER TOMORROW!
AN' I LOVE YOU, TOO, BEV! I WOULDN'T HURT YA FOR ALL THE WORLD!
HOWARD! Y-YOU'RE OKAY! YOU'RE YOURSELF AGAIN! YOU'VE COME BACK TO ME!
YEAH, LOVE CONQUERS ALL! BESIDES, HE MUSTA TAKEN ONLY A TEENSY, WEENSY BITE! IT'S LIKE WAKIN' UP FROM A NIGHT MARE, TOOTS--
--AN' THERE'S THE SLOBBERIN' SERPENT THAT CAUSED IT IN THE FIRST PLACE! DRACULA! I OWE YOU, FANGFACE!
SO! THE FOWL THAT LEFT THAT UNSPEAKABLE AFTERTASTE IN MY MOUTH LAST EVENING RETURNS!
WELL, IF I CANNOT REVENGE MYSELF UP-ON YOU BY DRINKING YOUR BESTIAL BLOOD--
--I CAN STILL ATTACK YOU THROUGH THOSE YOU LOVE! WOMAN, LOOK INTO MY EYES!
COME TO ME!
ANY-TIME!
WAAUGH
IF THAT CAPED AND COWLED CASANOVA THINKS I'M JUST GONNA SQUAT HERE WHILE HE PUTS THE MAKE ON MY LADY-LOVE--
--HE'S GONNA FIND I'VE GOT A STAKE IN THE RELATIONSHIP!

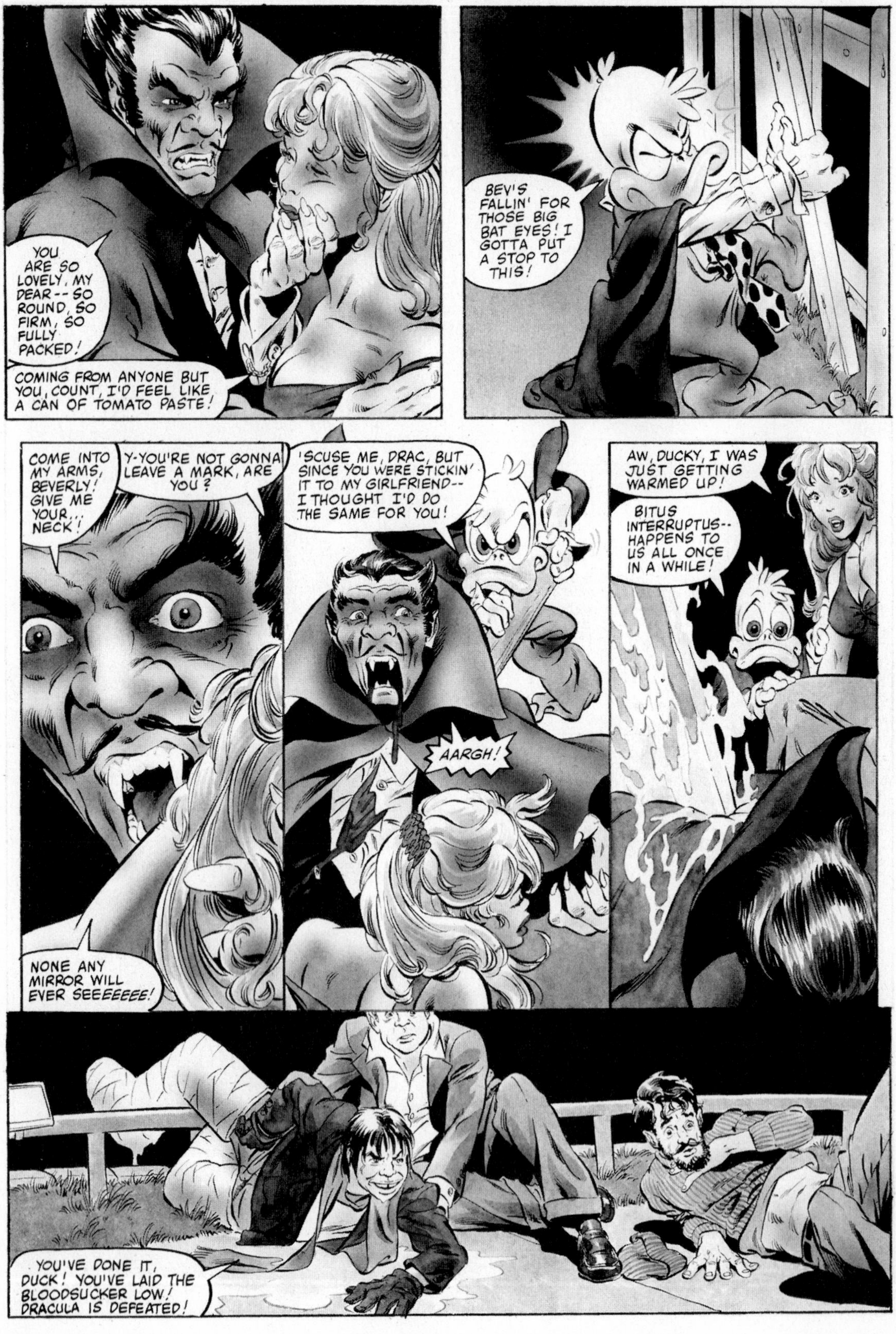
YOU ARE SO LOVELY, MY DEAR -- SO ROUND, SO FIRM, SO FULLY PACKED!
COMING FROM ANYONE BUT YOU, COUNT, I'D FEEL LIKE A CAN OF TOMATO PASTE!
BEV'S FALLIN' FOR THOSE BIG BAT EYES! I GOTTA PUT A STOP TO THIS!
COME INTO MY ARMS, BEVERLY! GIVE ME YOUR... NECK!
Y-YOU'RE NOT GONNA LEAVE A MARK, ARE YOU?
NONE ANY MIRROR WILL EVER SEEEEEEE!
'SCUSE ME, DRAC, BUT SINCE YOU WERE STICKIN' IT TO MY GIRLFRIEND-- I THOUGHT I'D DO THE SAME FOR YOU!
AARGH!
AW, DUCKY, I WAS JUST GETTING WARMED UP!
BITUS INTERRUPTUS-- HAPPENS TO US ALL ONCE IN A WHILE!
YOU'VE DONE IT, DUCK! YOU'VE LAID THE BLOODSUCKER LOW! DRACULA IS DEFEATED!

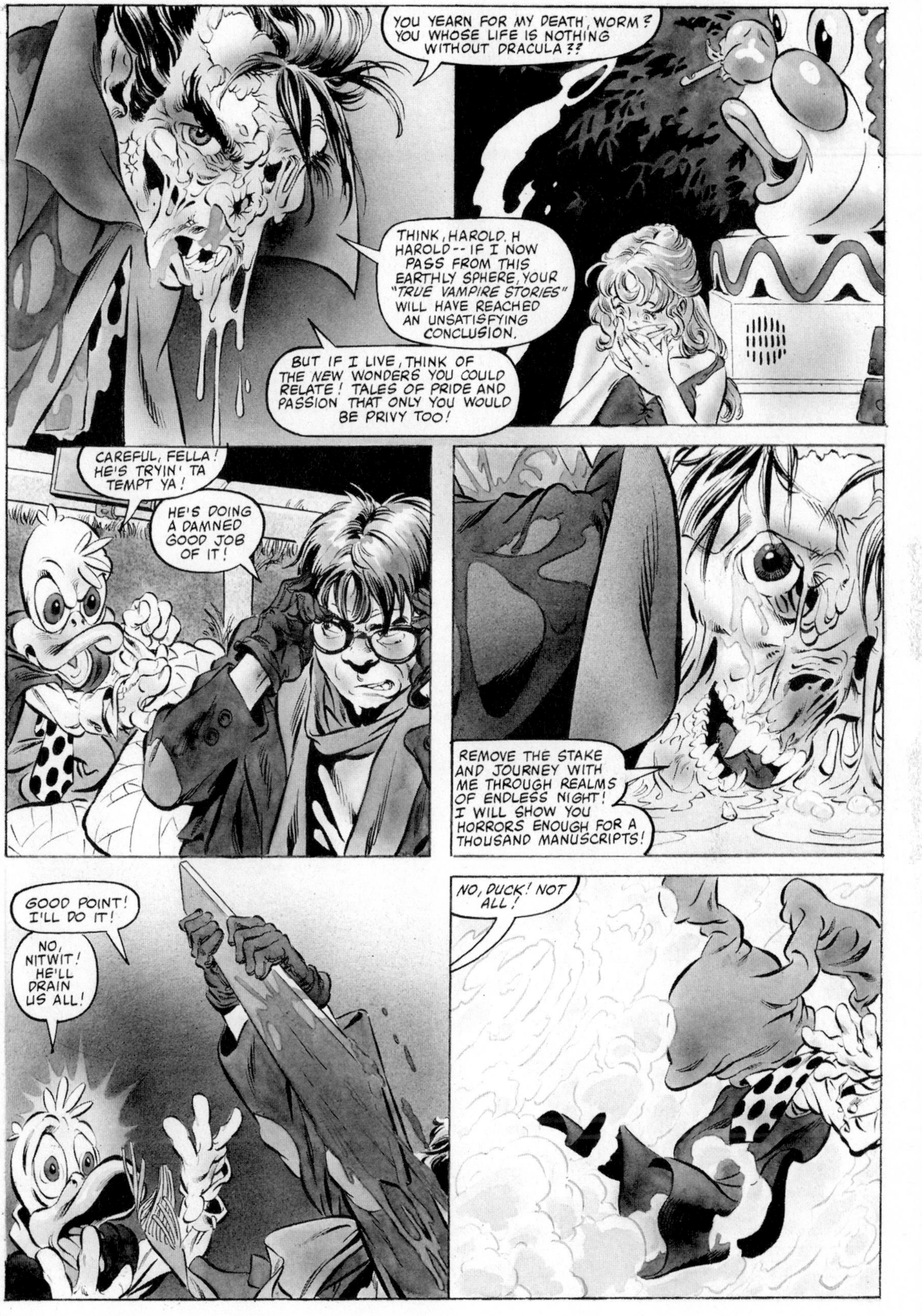
YOU YEARN FOR MY DEATH, WORM? YOU WHOSE LIFE IS NOTHING WITHOUT DRACULA??
THINK, HAROLD H. HAROLD-- IF I NOW PASS FROM THIS EARTHLY SPHERE, YOUR "TRUE VAMPIRE STORIES" WILL HAVE REACHED AN UNSATISFYING CONCLUSION.
BUT IF I LIVE, THINK OF THE NEW WONDERS YOU COULD RELATE! TALES OF PRIDE AND PASSION THAT ONLY YOU WOULD BE PRIVY TOO!
CAREFUL, FELLA! HE'S TRYIN' TA TEMPT YA!
HE'S DOING A DAMNED GOOD JOB OF IT!
REMOVE THE STAKE AND JOURNEY WITH ME THROUGH REALMS OF ENDLESS NIGHT! I WILL SHOW YOU HORRORS ENOUGH FOR A THOUSAND MANUSCRIPTS!
GOOD POINT! I'LL DO IT!
NO, NITWIT! HE'LL DRAIN US ALL!
NO, DUCK! NOT ALL!

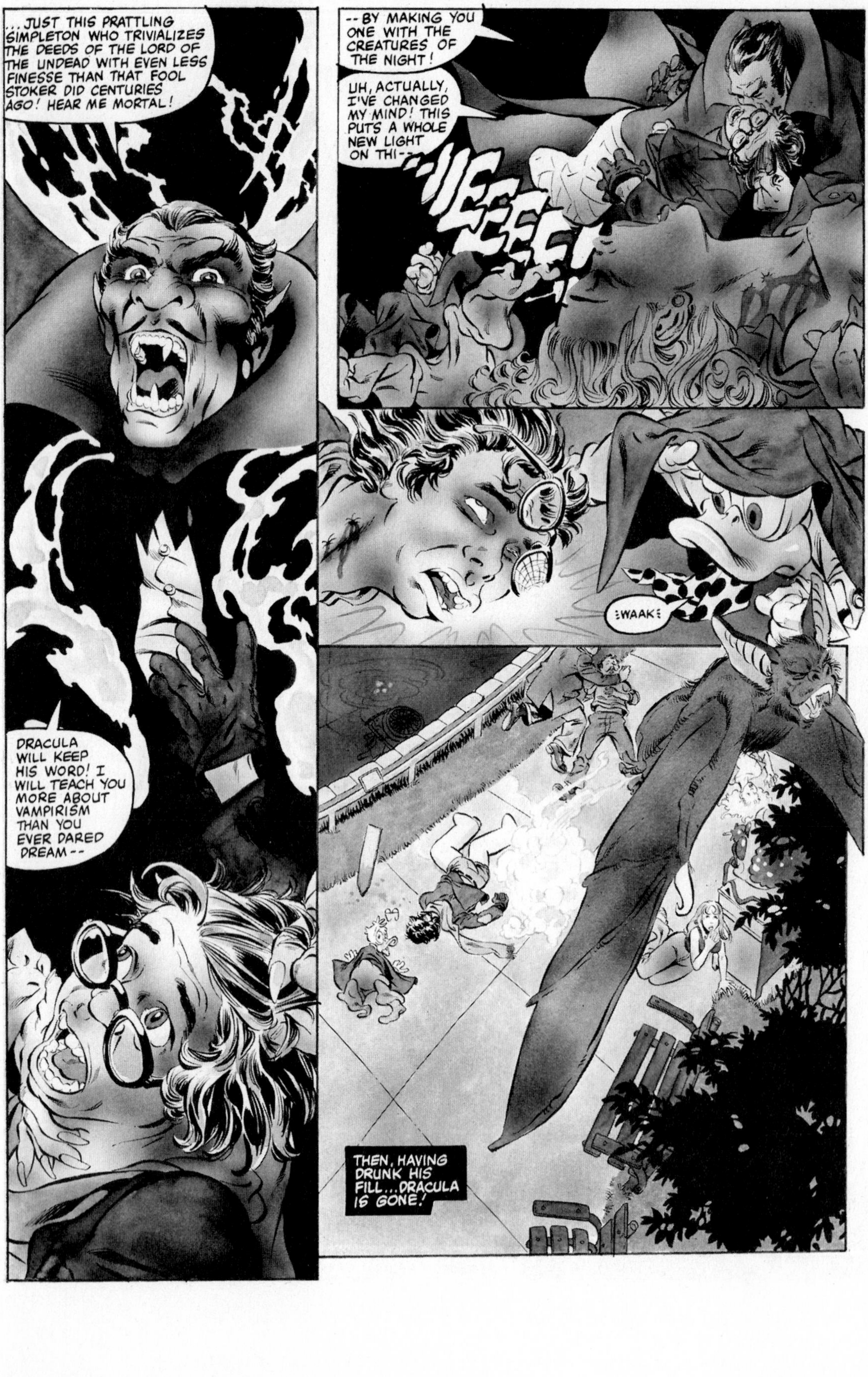
...JUST THIS PRATTLING SIMPLETON WHO TRIVIALIZES THE DEEDS OF THE LORD OF THE UNDEAD WITH EVEN LESS FINESSE THAN THAT FOOL STOKER DID CENTURIES AGO! HEAR ME MORTAL!
DRACULA WILL KEEP HIS WORD! I WILL TEACH YOU MORE ABOUT VAMPIRISM THAN YOU EVER DARED DREAM--
--BY MAKING YOU ONE WITH THE CREATURES OF THE NIGHT!
UH, ACTUALLY, I'VE CHANGED MY MIND! THIS PUTS A WHOLE NEW LIGHT ON THI--
WAAK
THEN, HAVING DRUNK HIS FILL...DRACULA IS GONE!

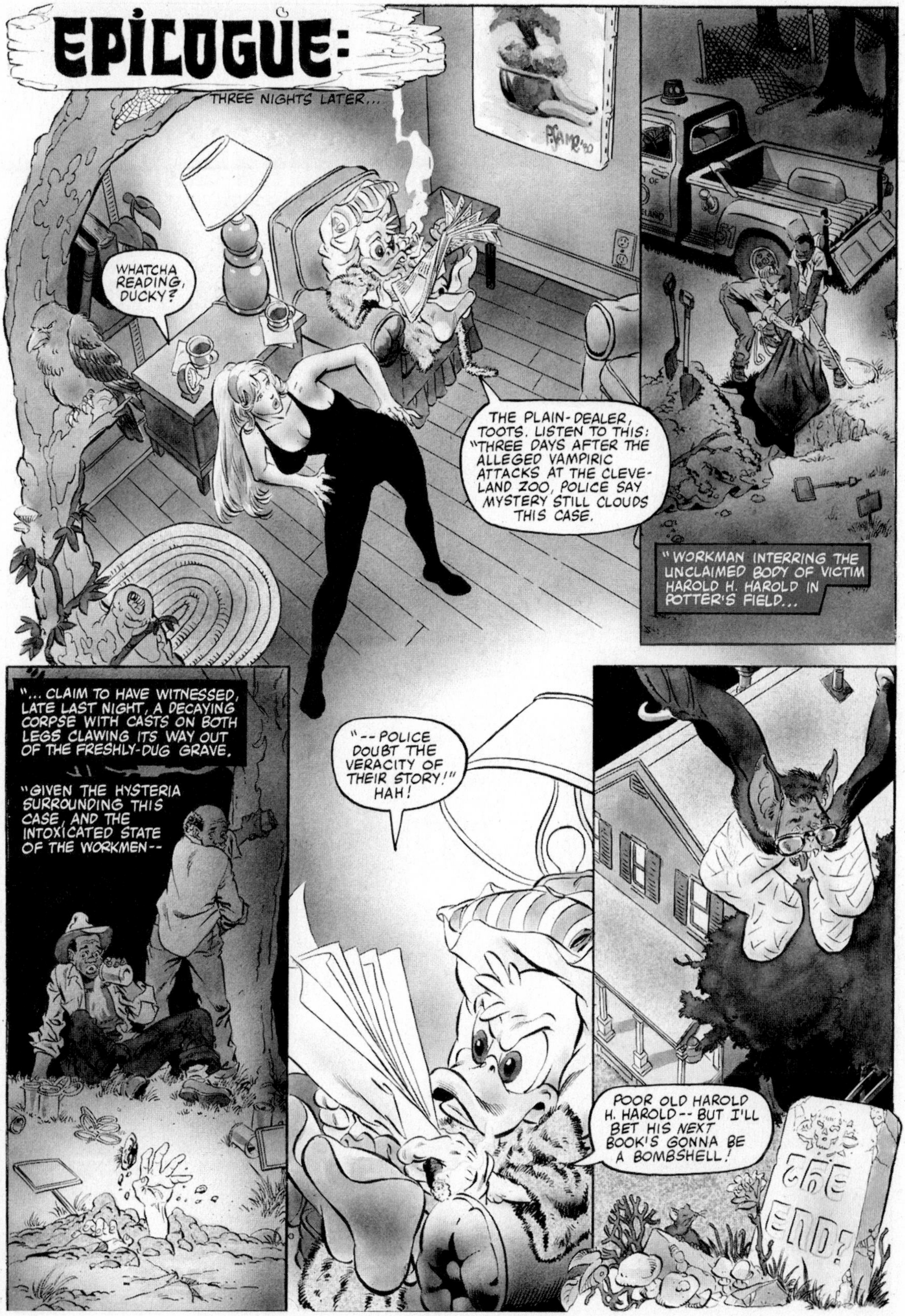
EPILOGUE:
THREE NIGHTS LATER...
WHATCHA READING, DUCKY?
THE PLAIN-DEALER, TOOTS. LISTEN TO THIS: "THREE DAYS AFTER THE ALLEGED VAMPIRIC ATTACKS AT THE CLEVELAND ZOO, POLICE SAY MYSTERY STILL CLOUDS THIS CASE.
"WORKMAN INTERRING THE UNCLAIMED BODY OF VICTIM HAROLD H. HAROLD IN POTTER'S FIELD...
"... CLAIM TO HAVE WITNESSED, LATE LAST NIGHT, A DECAYING CORPSE WITH CASTS ON BOTH LEGS CLAWING ITS WAY OUT OF THE FRESHLY-DUG GRAVE.
"GIVEN THE HYSTERIA SURROUNDING THIS CASE, AND THE INTOXICATED STATE OF THE WORKMEN--
"--POLICE DOUBT THE VERACITY OF THEIR STORY!" HAH!
POOR OLD HAROLD H. HAROLD-- BUT I'LL BET HIS NEXT BOOK'S GONNA BE A BOMBSHELL!
THE END?

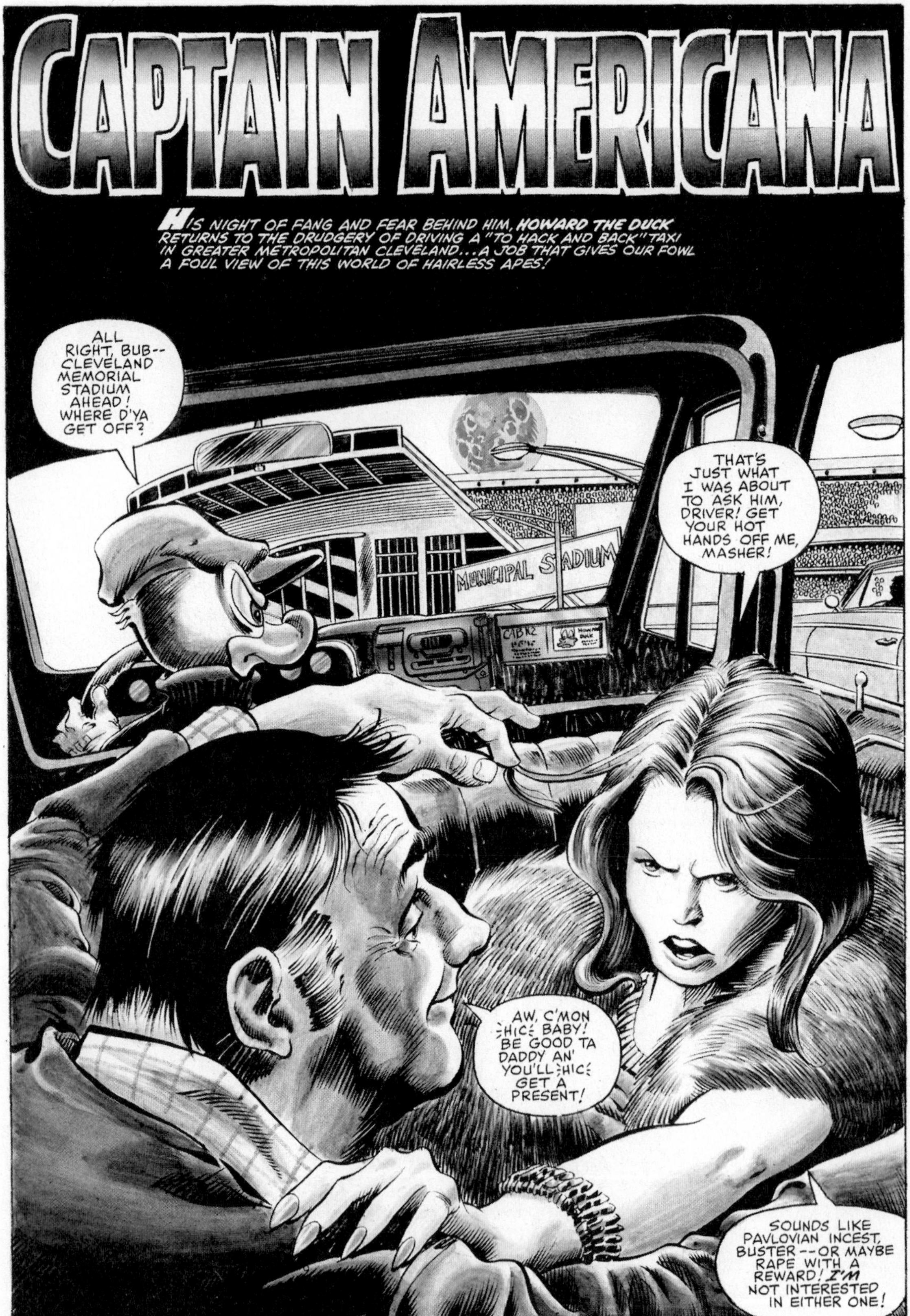
CAPTAIN AMERICANA
HIS NIGHT OF FANG AND FEAR BEHIND HIM, HOWARD THE DUCK RETURNS TO THE DRUDGERY OF DRIVING A "TO HACK AND BACK" TAXI IN GREATER METROPOLITAN CLEVELAND... A JOB THAT GIVES OUR FOWL A FOUL VIEW OF THIS WORLD OF HAIRLESS APES!
ALL RIGHT, BUB-- CLEVELAND MEMORIAL STADIUM AHEAD! WHERE D'YA GET OFF?
MUNICIPAL STADIUM
THAT'S JUST WHAT I WAS ABOUT TO ASK HIM, DRIVER! GET YOUR HOT HANDS OFF ME, MASHER!
AW, C'MON <HIC> BABY! BE GOOD TA DADDY AN' YOU'LL <HIC> GET A PRESENT!
SOUNDS LIKE PAVLOVIAN INCEST, BUSTER -- OR MAYBE RAPE WITH A REWARD! I'M NOT INTERESTED IN EITHER ONE!

Script: BILL MANTLO Art: GENE COLAN & DAVE SIMONS

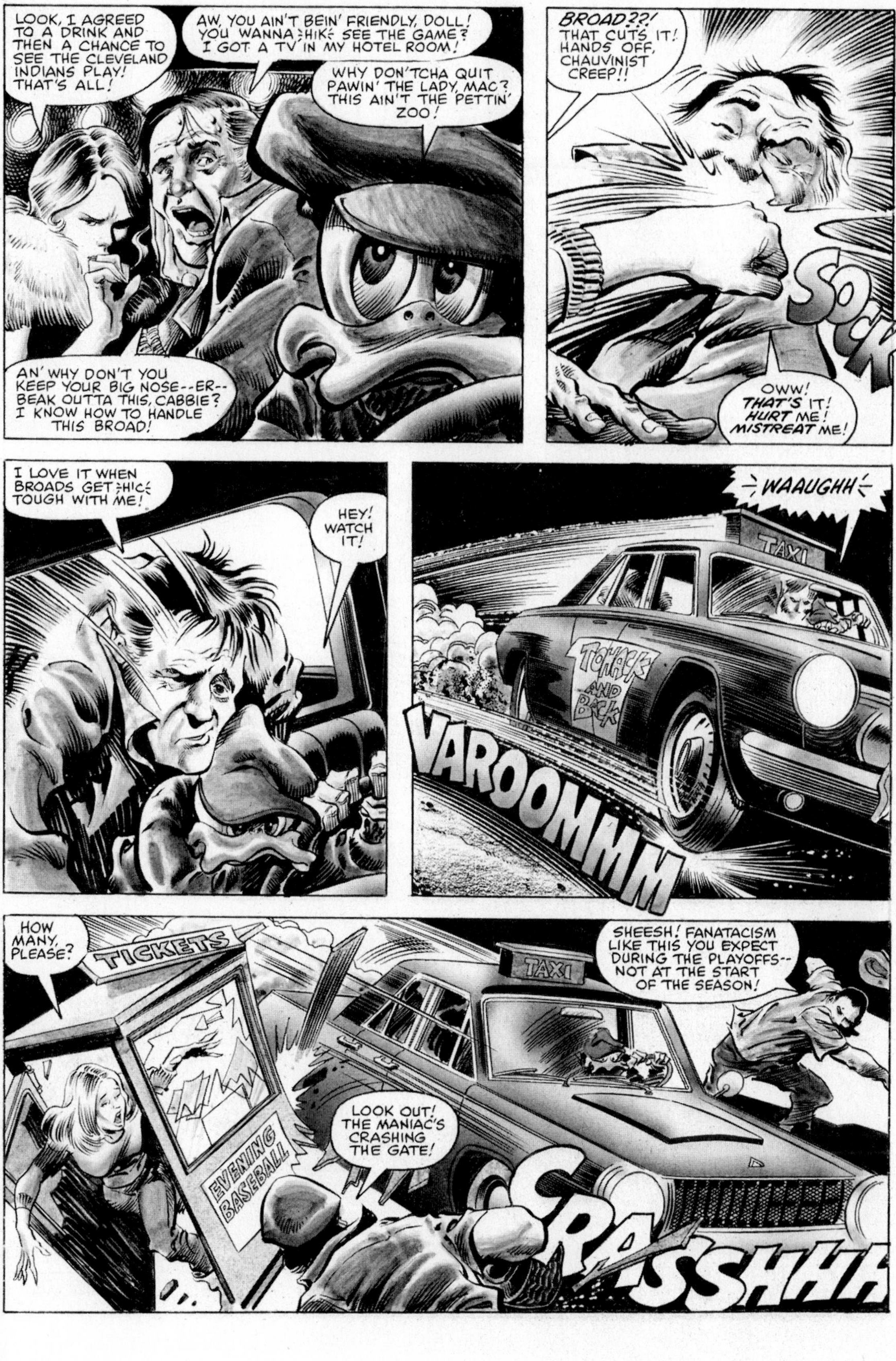

LOOK, I AGREED TO A DRINK AND THEN A CHANCE TO SEE THE CLEVELAND INDIANS PLAY! THAT'S ALL!
AW, YOU AIN'T BEIN' FRIENDLY, DOLL! YOU WANNA -HIK- SEE THE GAME? I GOT A TV IN MY HOTEL ROOM!
WHY DON'TCHA QUIT PAWIN' THE LADY, MAC? THIS AIN'T THE PETTIN' ZOO!
AN' WHY DON'T YOU KEEP YOUR BIG NOSE--ER--BEAK OUTTA THIS, CABBIE? I KNOW HOW TO HANDLE THIS BROAD!
BROAD??! THAT CUTS IT! HANDS OFF, CHAUVINIST CREEP!!
SOCK
OWW! THAT'S IT! HURT ME! MISTREAT ME!
I LOVE IT WHEN BROADS GET -HIC- TOUGH WITH ME!
HEY! WATCH IT!
WAAUGHH
TAXI
TO HACK AND BACK
VAROOMMMM
HOW MANY, PLEASE?
TICKETS
TAXI
SHEESH! FANATACISM LIKE THIS YOU EXPECT DURING THE PLAYOFFS--NOT AT THE START OF THE SEASON!
LOOK OUT! THE MANIAC'S CRASHING THE GATE!
EVENING BASEBALL
CRASSHHH

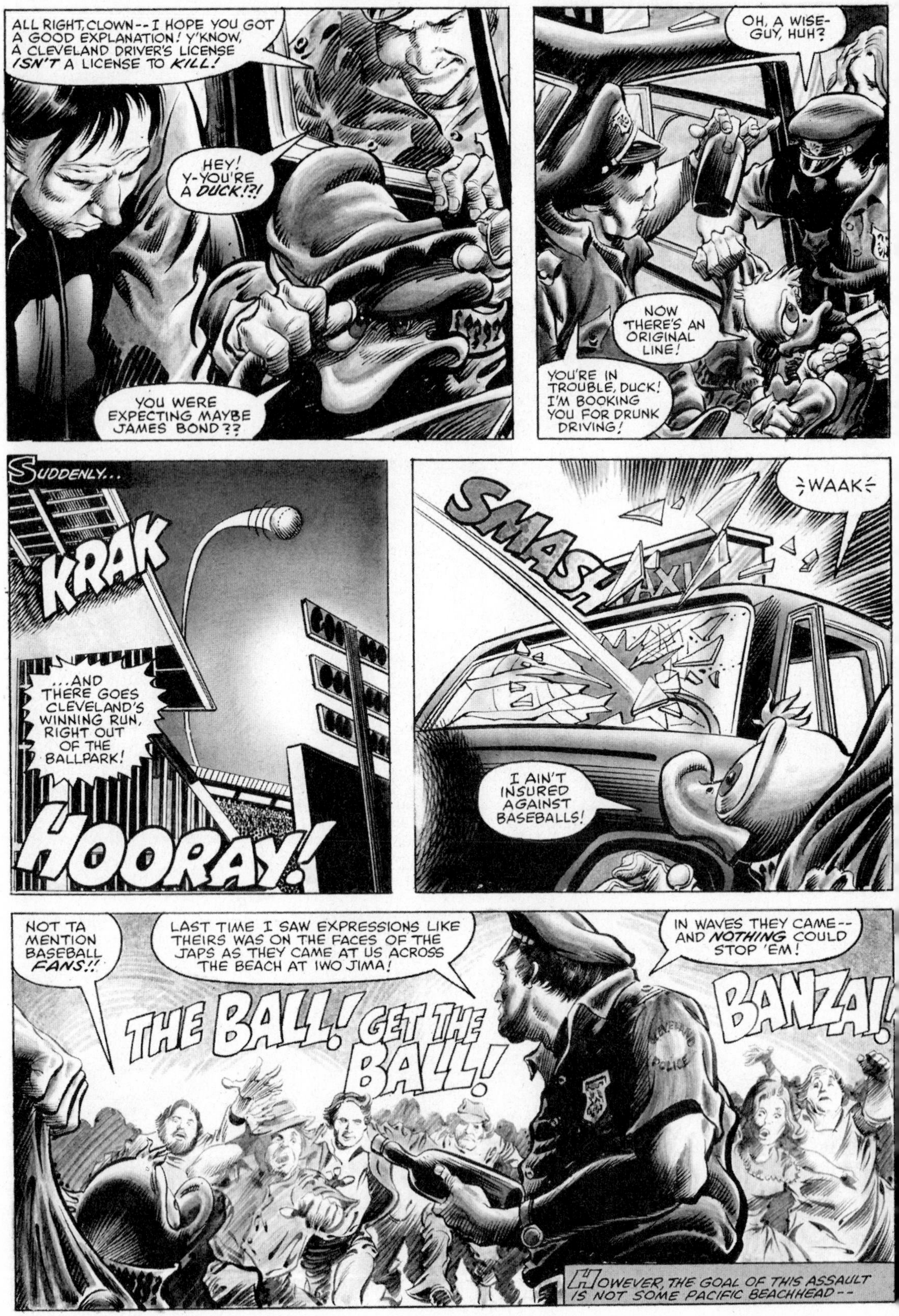
ALL RIGHT, CLOWN--I HOPE YOU GOT A GOOD EXPLANATION! Y'KNOW, A CLEVELAND DRIVER'S LICENSE ISN'T A LICENSE TO KILL!
HEY! Y-YOU'RE A DUCK!?!
YOU WERE EXPECTING MAYBE JAMES BOND??
OH, A WISE-GUY, HUH?
NOW THERE'S AN ORIGINAL LINE!
YOU'RE IN TROUBLE, DUCK! I'M BOOKING YOU FOR DRUNK DRIVING!
SUDDENLY...
KRAK
...AND THERE GOES CLEVELAND'S WINNING RUN, RIGHT OUT OF THE BALLPARK!
HOORAY!
SMASH
WAAK
I AIN'T INSURED AGAINST BASEBALLS!
NOT TA MENTION BASEBALL FANS!!
LAST TIME I SAW EXPRESSIONS LIKE THEIRS WAS ON THE FACES OF THE JAPS AS THEY CAME AT US ACROSS THE BEACH AT IWO JIMA!
IN WAVES THEY CAME--AND NOTHING COULD STOP 'EM!
THE BALL! GET THE BALL!
BANZAI!
HOWEVER, THE GOAL OF THIS ASSAULT IS NOT SOME PACIFIC BEACHHEAD--

...BUT A WINNING BASEBALL SMACKED OUT OF MEMORIAL STADIUM BY CLEVELAND INDIANS' SLUGGER, ANDRE THORNTON!

IT'S MINE!

MY ARMPIT IT IS, LADY!

IT'S *GOTTA* BE HERE SOMEWHERE!

GIMME, GIMME! I WANT HIM TO SIGN IT!

WHADDA YA THINK THE REST OF US WANT HIM TO DO-- *EAT* IT ??

I GOT IT! I GOT IT!

AW, POOT!

THE HORSEHIDE SPHEROID RECOVERED, THE CROWD DISPERSES.

*L*EAVING A HORRIFIED HOWARD TO SURVEY THE WRECKAGE

G-GEE, DUCK, THEY TORE YOUR TAXICAB APART LOOKING FOR THAT BALL! I-I WOULD HAVE STOPPED 'EM IF I COULD!

I FROZE AT IWO JIMA, TOO!

*T*HERE IS NO WAY HOWARD CAN RESPOND, FOR THERE IS NO SINGLE HAIRLESS APE AT WHICH TO POINT A FINGER IN BLAME.

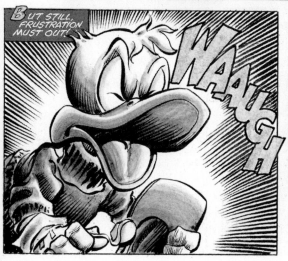

*B*UT STILL, FRUSTRATION MUST OUT!

WAAUGH

*L*ATER...

221

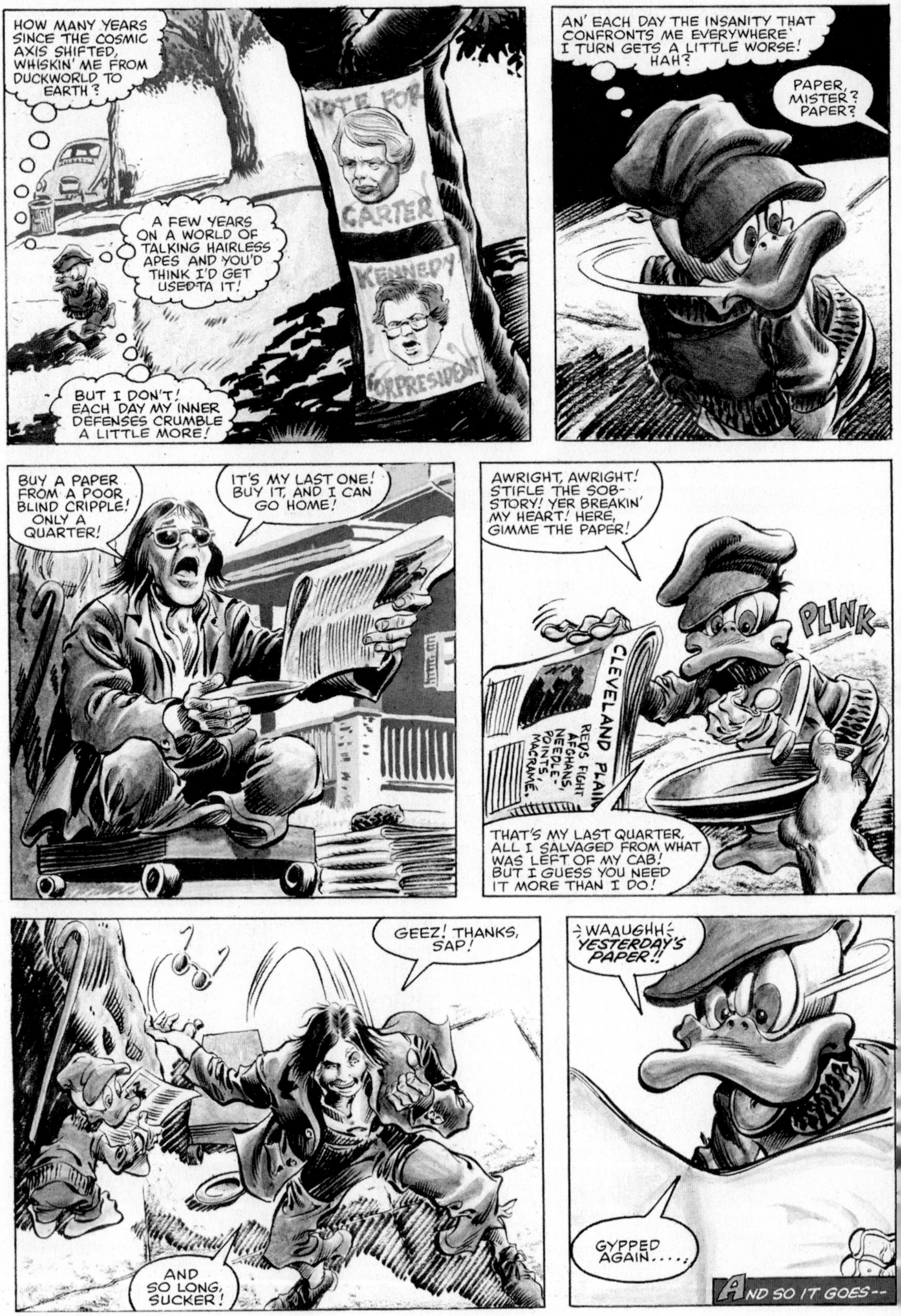
HOW MANY YEARS SINCE THE COSMIC AXIS SHIFTED, WHISKIN' ME FROM DUCKWORLD TO EARTH?
VOTE FOR CARTER
KENNEDY FOR PRESIDENT
A FEW YEARS ON A WORLD OF TALKING HAIRLESS APES AND YOU'D THINK I'D GET USED TA IT!
BUT I DON'T! EACH DAY MY INNER DEFENSES CRUMBLE A LITTLE MORE!
AN' EACH DAY THE INSANITY THAT CONFRONTS ME EVERYWHERE I TURN GETS A LITTLE WORSE! HAH?
PAPER, MISTER? PAPER?
BUY A PAPER FROM A POOR BLIND CRIPPLE! ONLY A QUARTER!
IT'S MY LAST ONE! BUY IT, AND I CAN GO HOME!
AWRIGHT, AWRIGHT! STIFLE THE SOB-STORY! YER BREAKIN' MY HEART! HERE, GIMME THE PAPER!
PLINK
CLEVELAND PLAIN
REDS FIGHT AFGHANS, NEEDLE-POINTS, MACRAMÉ
THAT'S MY LAST QUARTER, ALL I SALVAGED FROM WHAT WAS LEFT OF MY CAB! BUT I GUESS YOU NEED IT MORE THAN I DO!
GEEZ! THANKS, SAP!
AND SO LONG, SUCKER!
WAAUGHH YESTERDAY'S PAPER!!
GYPPED AGAIN....
AND SO IT GOES--

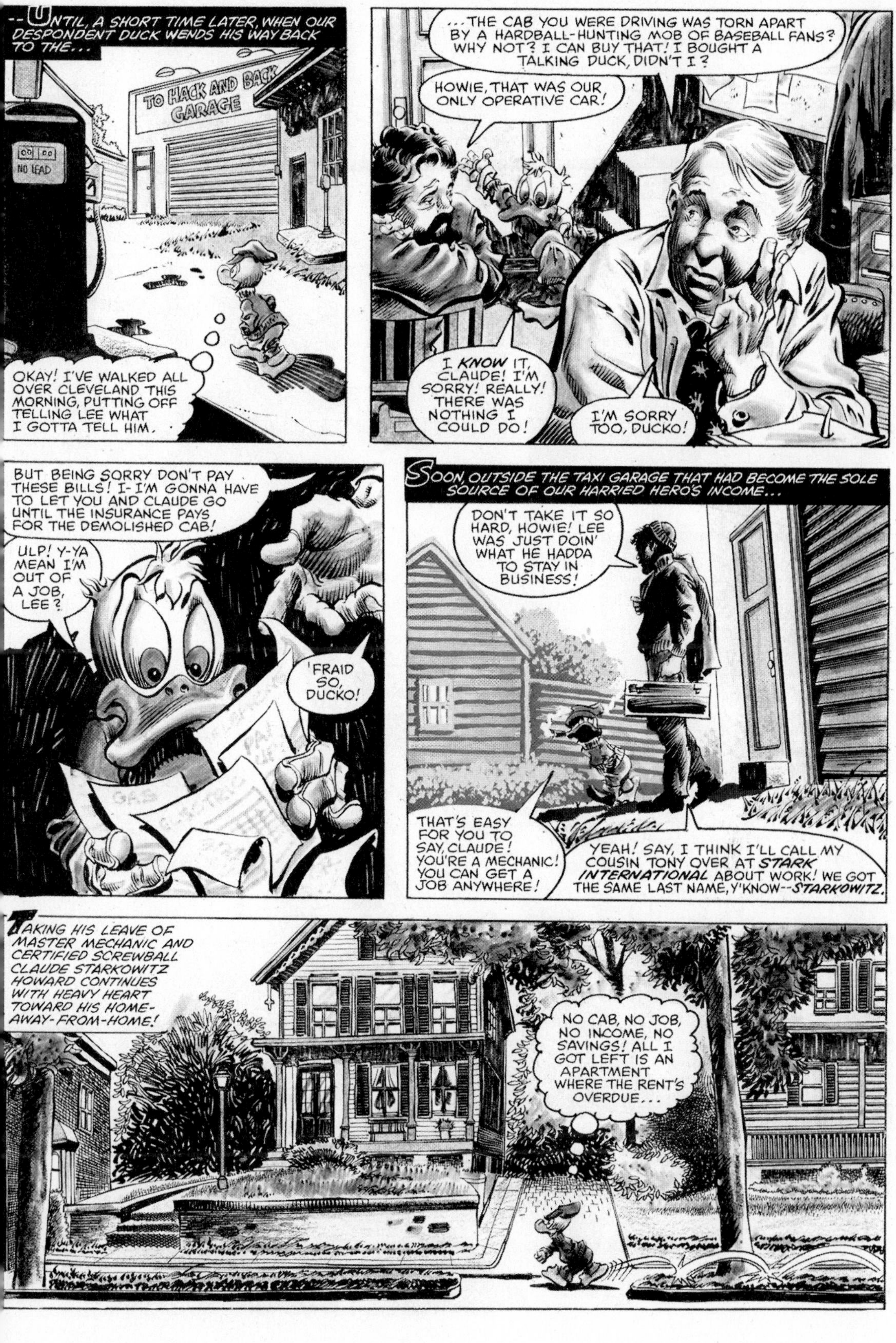
--UNTIL, A SHORT TIME LATER, WHEN OUR DESPONDENT DUCK WENDS HIS WAY BACK TO THE...
TO HACK AND BACK GARAGE
NO LEAD
OKAY! I'VE WALKED ALL OVER CLEVELAND THIS MORNING, PUTTING OFF TELLING LEE WHAT I GOTTA TELL HIM.
...THE CAB YOU WERE DRIVING WAS TORN APART BY A HARDBALL-HUNTING MOB OF BASEBALL FANS? WHY NOT? I CAN BUY THAT! I BOUGHT A TALKING DUCK, DIDN'T I?
HOWIE, THAT WAS OUR ONLY OPERATIVE CAR!
I KNOW IT, CLAUDE! I'M SORRY! REALLY! THERE WAS NOTHING I COULD DO!
I'M SORRY TOO, DUCKO!
BUT BEING SORRY DON'T PAY THESE BILLS! I- I'M GONNA HAVE TO LET YOU AND CLAUDE GO UNTIL THE INSURANCE PAYS FOR THE DEMOLISHED CAB!
ULP! Y-YA MEAN I'M OUT OF A JOB, LEE?
'FRAID SO, DUCKO!
SOON, OUTSIDE THE TAXI GARAGE THAT HAD BECOME THE SOLE SOURCE OF OUR HARRIED HERO'S INCOME...
DON'T TAKE IT SO HARD, HOWIE! LEE WAS JUST DOIN' WHAT HE HADDA TO STAY IN BUSINESS!
THAT'S EASY FOR YOU TO SAY, CLAUDE! YOU'RE A MECHANIC! YOU CAN GET A JOB ANYWHERE!
YEAH! SAY, I THINK I'LL CALL MY COUSIN TONY OVER AT STARK INTERNATIONAL ABOUT WORK! WE GOT THE SAME LAST NAME, Y'KNOW--STARKOWITZ.
TAKING HIS LEAVE OF MASTER MECHANIC AND CERTIFIED SCREWBALL CLAUDE STARKOWITZ HOWARD CONTINUES WITH HEAVY HEART TOWARD HIS HOME-AWAY-FROM-HOME!
NO CAB, NO JOB, NO INCOME, NO SAVINGS! ALL I GOT LEFT IS AN APARTMENT WHERE THE RENT'S OVERDUE...

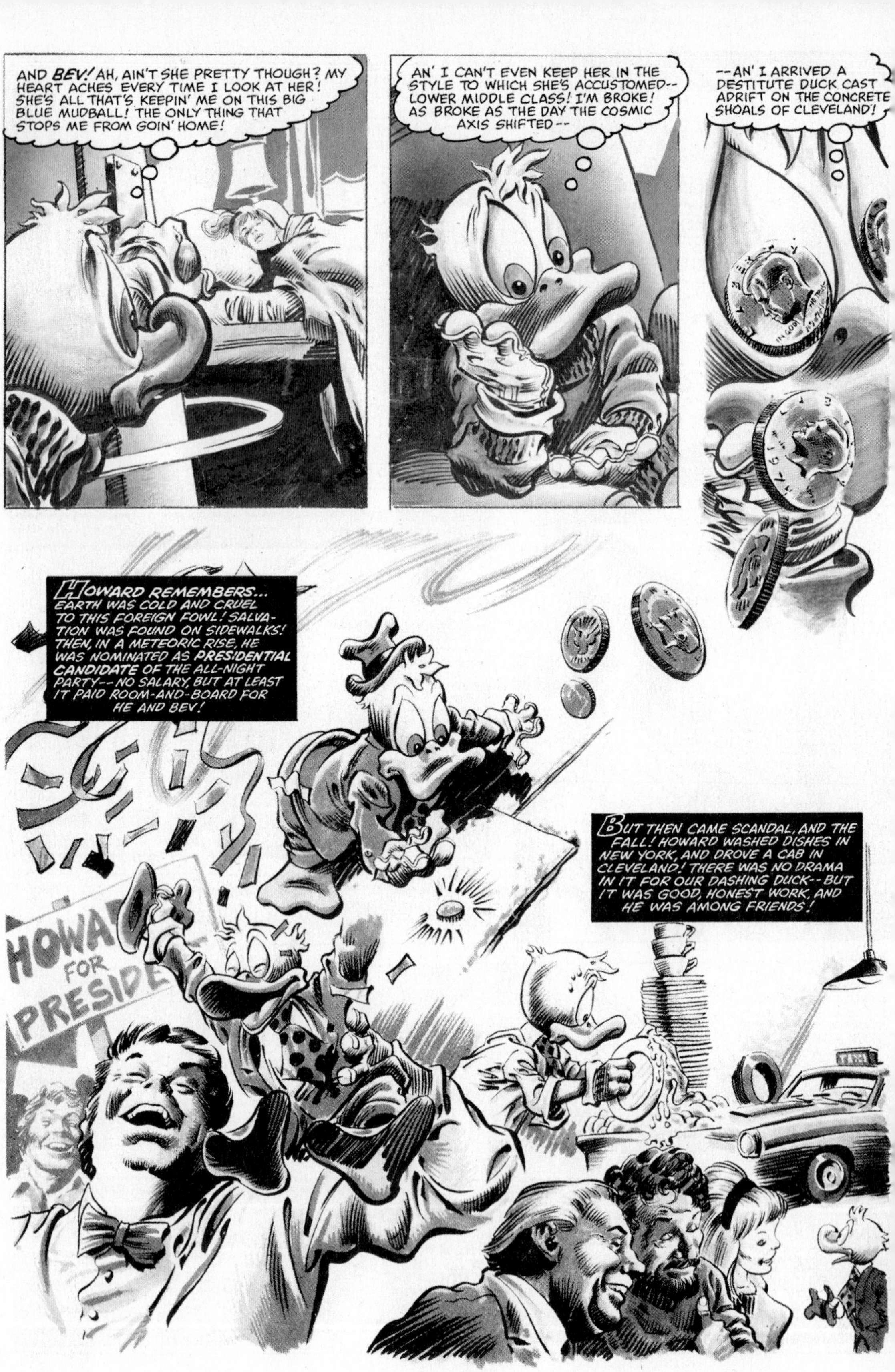
AND BEV! AH, AIN'T SHE PRETTY THOUGH? MY HEART ACHES EVERY TIME I LOOK AT HER! SHE'S ALL THAT'S KEEPIN' ME ON THIS BIG BLUE MUDBALL! THE ONLY THING THAT STOPS ME FROM GOIN' HOME!
AN' I CAN'T EVEN KEEP HER IN THE STYLE TO WHICH SHE'S ACCUSTOMED-- LOWER MIDDLE CLASS! I'M BROKE! AS BROKE AS THE DAY THE COSMIC AXIS SHIFTED--
--AN' I ARRIVED A DESTITUTE DUCK CAST ADRIFT ON THE CONCRETE SHOALS OF CLEVELAND!
HOWARD REMEMBERS... EARTH WAS COLD AND CRUEL TO THIS FOREIGN FOWL! SALVATION WAS FOUND ON SIDEWALKS! THEN, IN A METEORIC RISE, HE WAS NOMINATED AS PRESIDENTIAL CANDIDATE OF THE ALL-NIGHT PARTY-- NO SALARY, BUT AT LEAST IT PAID ROOM-AND-BOARD FOR HE AND BEV!
HOWA FOR PRESIDE
BUT THEN CAME SCANDAL, AND THE FALL! HOWARD WASHED DISHES IN NEW YORK, AND DROVE A CAB IN CLEVELAND! THERE WAS NO DRAMA IN IT FOR OUR DASHING DUCK-- BUT IT WAS GOOD, HONEST WORK, AND HE WAS AMONG FRIENDS!

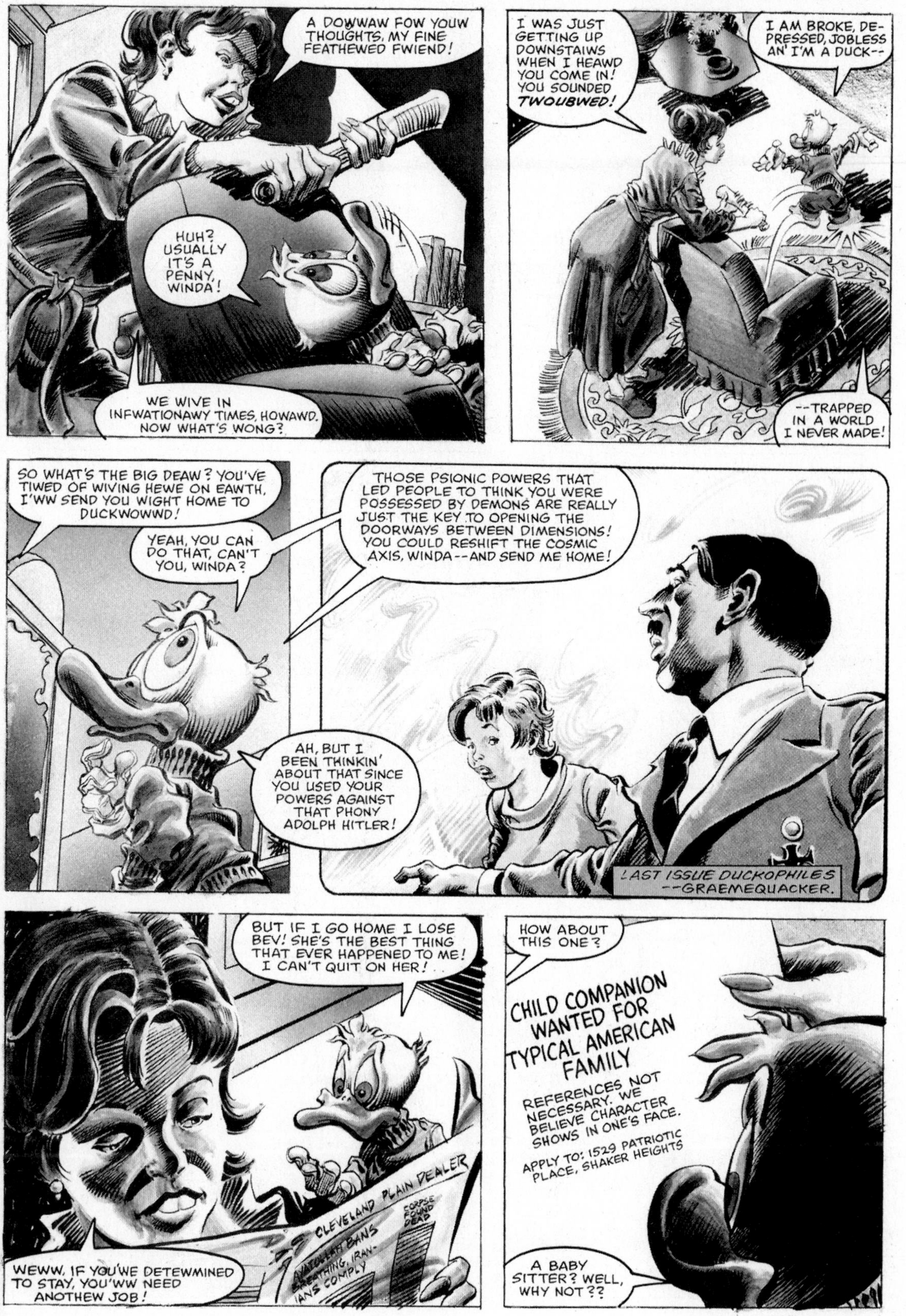

A DOWWAW FOW YOUW THOUGHTS, MY FINE FEATHEWED FWIEND!
HUH? USUALLY IT'S A PENNY, WINDA!
WE WIVE IN INFWATIONAWY TIMES, HOWAWD. NOW WHAT'S WONG?
I WAS JUST GETTING UP DOWNSTAIWS WHEN I HEAWD YOU COME IN! YOU SOUNDED **TWOUBWED**!
I AM BROKE, DE- PRESSED, JOBLESS AN' I'M A DUCK--
--TRAPPED IN A WORLD I NEVER MADE!
SO WHAT'S THE BIG DEAW? YOU'VE TIWED OF WIVING HEWE ON EAWTH, I'WW SEND YOU WIGHT HOME TO DUCKWOWWD!
YEAH, YOU CAN DO THAT, CAN'T YOU, WINDA?
AH, BUT I BEEN THINKIN' ABOUT THAT SINCE YOU USED YOUR POWERS AGAINST THAT PHONY ADOLPH HITLER!
THOSE PSIONIC POWERS THAT LED PEOPLE TO THINK YOU WERE POSSESSED BY DEMONS ARE REALLY JUST THE KEY TO OPENING THE DOORWAYS BETWEEN DIMENSIONS! YOU COULD RESHIFT THE COSMIC AXIS, WINDA--AND SEND ME HOME!
LAST ISSUE DUCKOPHILES --GRAEMEQUACKER.
BUT IF I GO HOME I LOSE BEV! SHE'S THE BEST THING THAT EVER HAPPENED TO ME! I CAN'T QUIT ON HER!
CLEVELAND PLAIN DEALER
AYATOLLAH BANS BREATHING, IRAN- IANS COMPLY
CORPSE FOUND DEAD
WEWW, IF YOU'WE DETEWMINED TO STAY, YOU'WW NEED ANOTHEW JOB!
HOW ABOUT THIS ONE?
CHILD COMPANION WANTED FOR TYPICAL AMERICAN FAMILY
REFERENCES NOT NECESSARY. WE BELIEVE CHARACTER SHOWS IN ONE'S FACE.
APPLY TO: 1529 PATRIOTIC PLACE, SHAKER HEIGHTS
A BABY SITTER? WELL, WHY NOT??

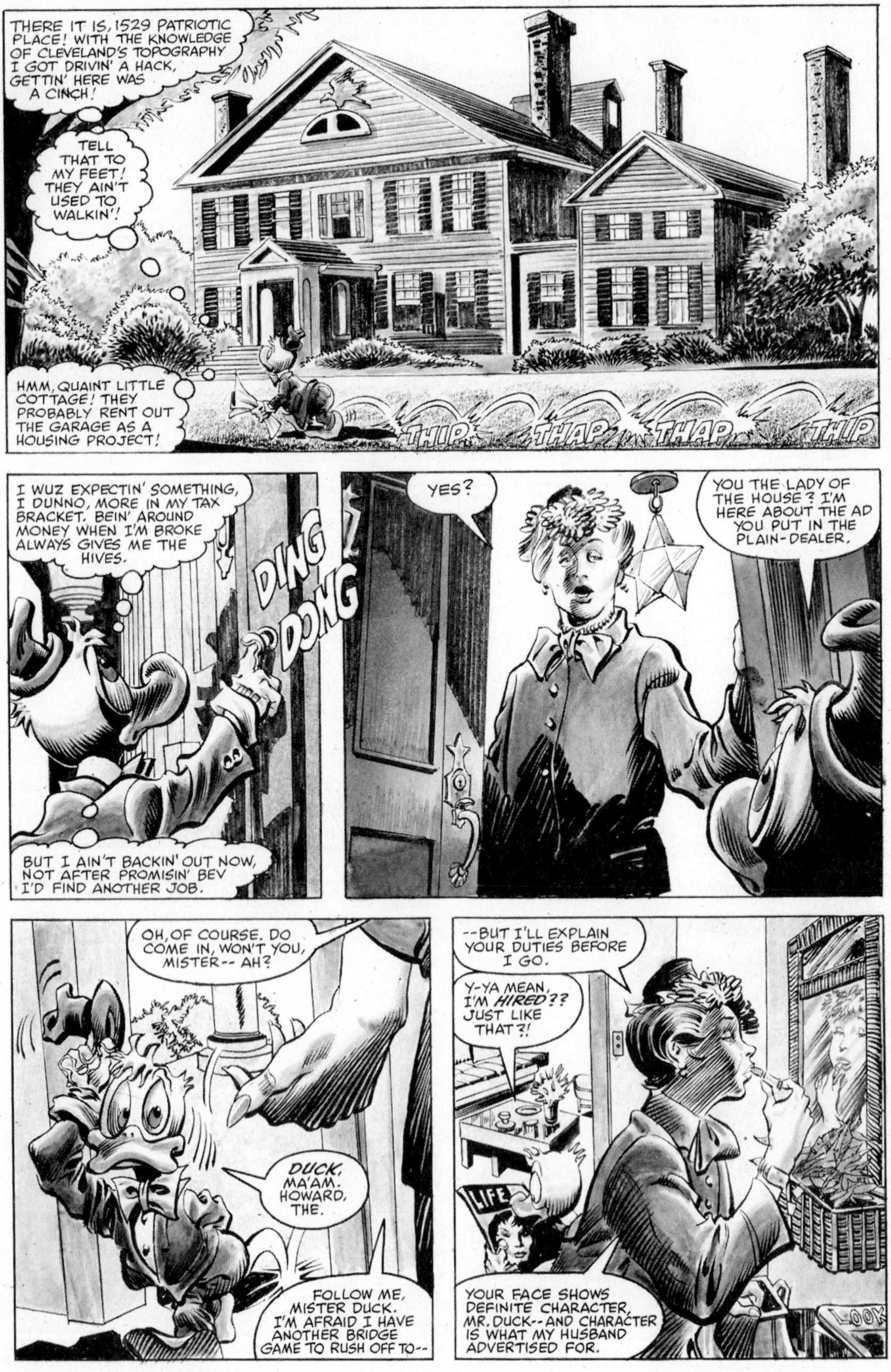
THERE IT IS, 1529 PATRIOTIC PLACE! WITH THE KNOWLEDGE OF CLEVELAND'S TOPOGRAPHY I GOT DRIVIN' A HACK, GETTIN' HERE WAS A CINCH!
TELL THAT TO MY FEET! THEY AIN'T USED TO WALKIN'!
HMM, QUAINT LITTLE COTTAGE! THEY PROBABLY RENT OUT THE GARAGE AS A HOUSING PROJECT!
THIP THAP THAP THIP
I WUZ EXPECTIN' SOMETHING, I DUNNO, MORE IN MY TAX BRACKET. BEIN' AROUND MONEY WHEN I'M BROKE ALWAYS GIVES ME THE HIVES.
DING DONG
BUT I AIN'T BACKIN' OUT NOW, NOT AFTER PROMISIN' BEV I'D FIND ANOTHER JOB.
YES?
YOU THE LADY OF THE HOUSE? I'M HERE ABOUT THE AD YOU PUT IN THE PLAIN-DEALER.
OH, OF COURSE. DO COME IN, WON'T YOU, MISTER-- AH?
DUCK, MA'AM. HOWARD, THE.
FOLLOW ME, MISTER DUCK. I'M AFRAID I HAVE ANOTHER BRIDGE GAME TO RUSH OFF TO--
--BUT I'LL EXPLAIN YOUR DUTIES BEFORE I GO.
Y-YA MEAN, I'M HIRED?? JUST LIKE THAT?!
LIFE
YOUR FACE SHOWS DEFINITE CHARACTER, MR. DUCK--AND CHARACTER IS WHAT MY HUSBAND ADVERTISED FOR.
LOOK

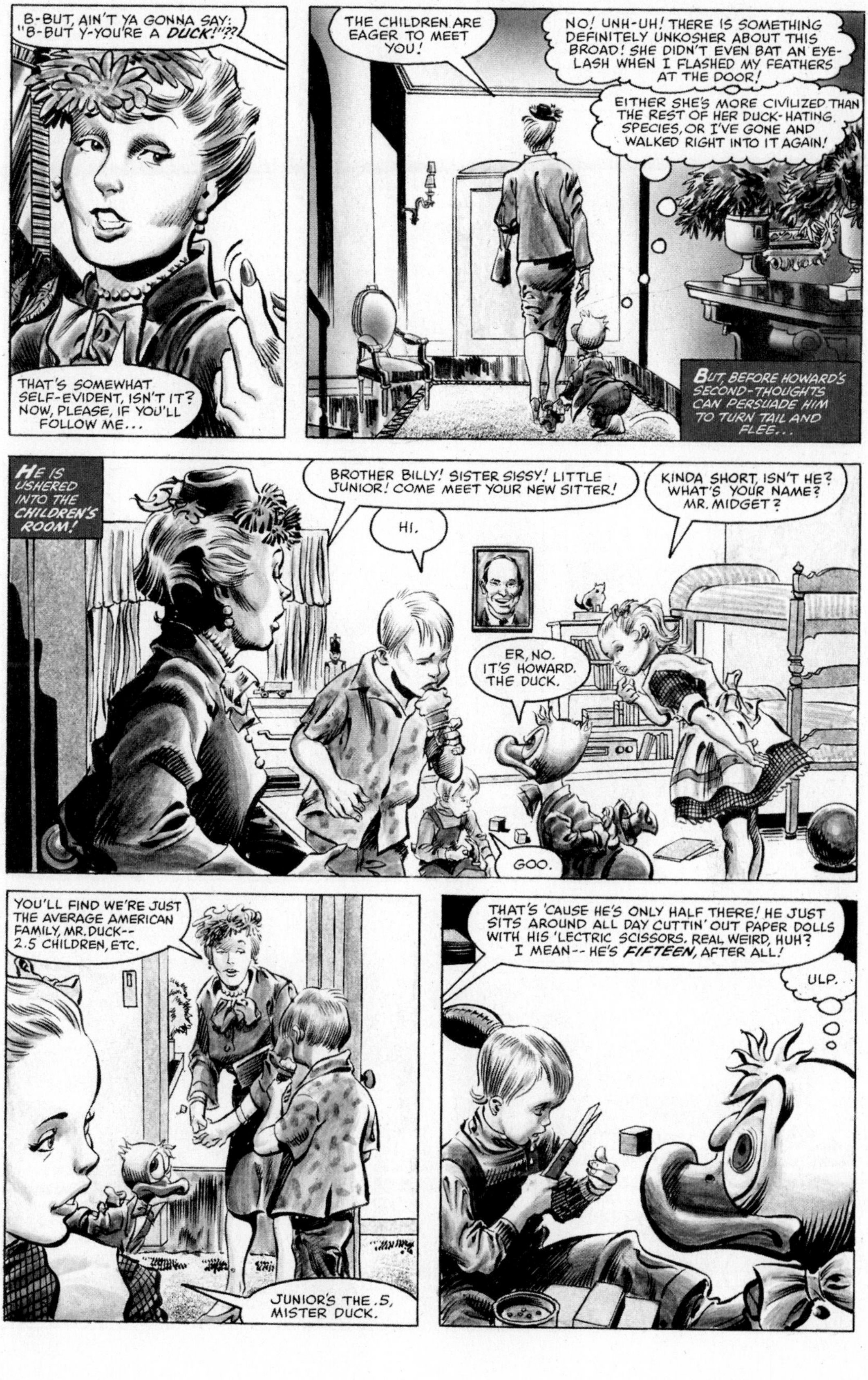

B-BUT, AIN'T YA GONNA SAY: "B-BUT Y-YOU'RE A DUCK!"??
THAT'S SOMEWHAT SELF-EVIDENT, ISN'T IT? NOW, PLEASE, IF YOU'LL FOLLOW ME...
THE CHILDREN ARE EAGER TO MEET YOU!
NO! UNH-UH! THERE IS SOMETHING DEFINITELY UNKOSHER ABOUT THIS BROAD! SHE DIDN'T EVEN BAT AN EYE-LASH WHEN I FLASHED MY FEATHERS AT THE DOOR!
EITHER SHE'S MORE CIVILIZED THAN THE REST OF HER DUCK-HATING SPECIES, OR I'VE GONE AND WALKED RIGHT INTO IT AGAIN!
BUT, BEFORE HOWARD'S SECOND-THOUGHTS CAN PERSUADE HIM TO TURN TAIL AND FLEE...
HE IS USHERED INTO THE CHILDREN'S ROOM!
BROTHER BILLY! SISTER SISSY! LITTLE JUNIOR! COME MEET YOUR NEW SITTER!
HI.
KINDA SHORT, ISN'T HE? WHAT'S YOUR NAME? MR. MIDGET?
ER, NO. IT'S HOWARD. THE DUCK.
GOO.
YOU'LL FIND WE'RE JUST THE AVERAGE AMERICAN FAMILY, MR. DUCK-- 2.5 CHILDREN, ETC.
JUNIOR'S THE .5, MISTER DUCK.
THAT'S 'CAUSE HE'S ONLY HALF THERE! HE JUST SITS AROUND ALL DAY CUTTIN' OUT PAPER DOLLS WITH HIS 'LECTRIC SCISSORS. REAL WEIRD, HUH? I MEAN-- HE'S FIFTEEN, AFTER ALL!
ULP.

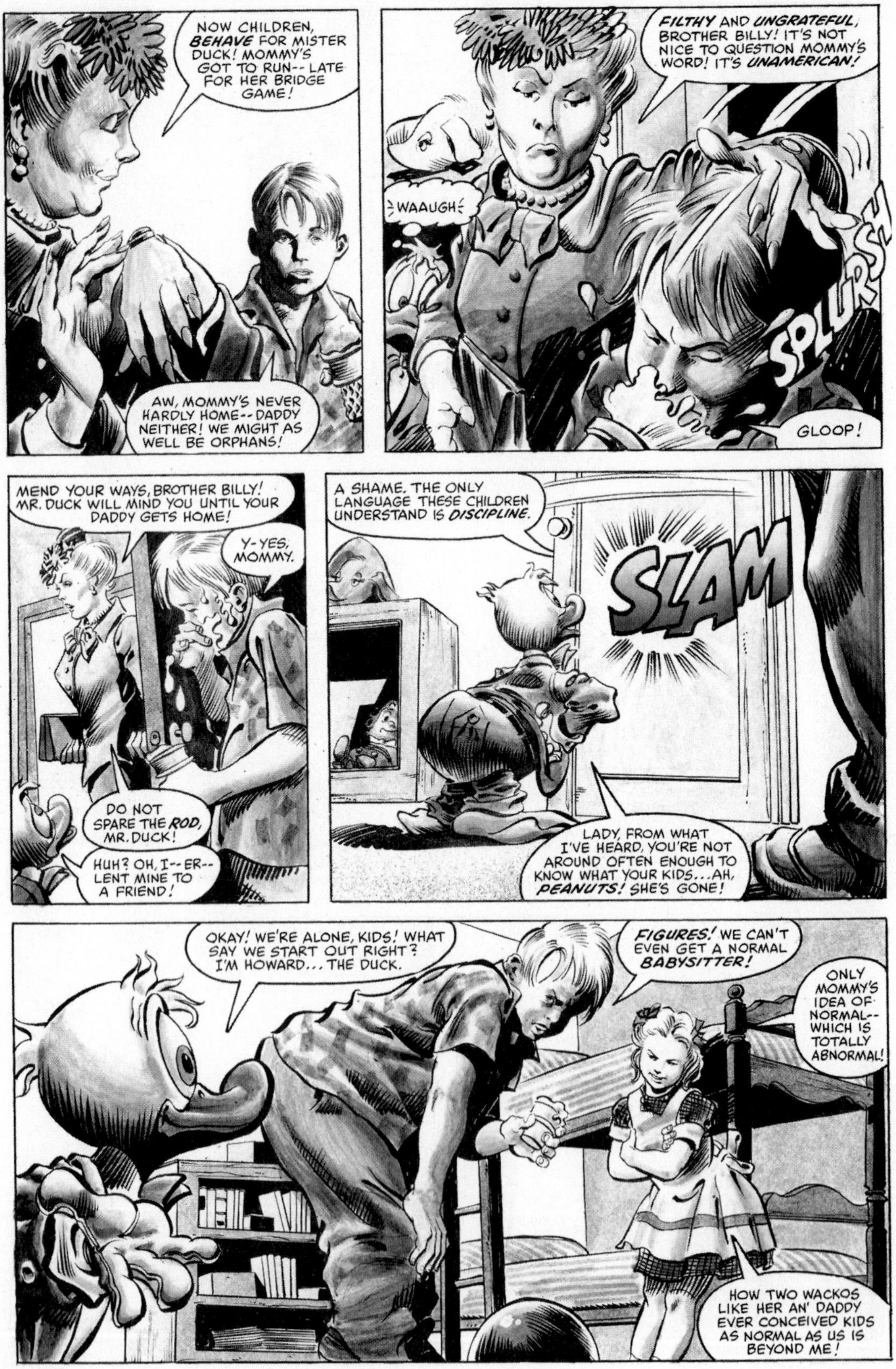
NOW CHILDREN, BEHAVE FOR MISTER DUCK! MOMMY'S GOT TO RUN-- LATE FOR HER BRIDGE GAME!
AW, MOMMY'S NEVER HARDLY HOME-- DADDY NEITHER! WE MIGHT AS WELL BE ORPHANS!
FILTHY AND UNGRATEFUL, BROTHER BILLY! IT'S NOT NICE TO QUESTION MOMMY'S WORD! IT'S UNAMERICAN!
WAAUGH
SPLURSH
GLOOP!
MEND YOUR WAYS, BROTHER BILLY! MR. DUCK WILL MIND YOU UNTIL YOUR DADDY GETS HOME!
Y-YES, MOMMY.
DO NOT SPARE THE ROD, MR. DUCK!
HUH? OH, I-- ER-- LENT MINE TO A FRIEND!
A SHAME. THE ONLY LANGUAGE THESE CHILDREN UNDERSTAND IS DISCIPLINE.
SLAM
LADY, FROM WHAT I'VE HEARD, YOU'RE NOT AROUND OFTEN ENOUGH TO KNOW WHAT YOUR KIDS... AH, PEANUTS! SHE'S GONE!
OKAY! WE'RE ALONE, KIDS! WHAT SAY WE START OUT RIGHT? I'M HOWARD... THE DUCK.
FIGURES! WE CAN'T EVEN GET A NORMAL BABYSITTER!
ONLY MOMMY'S IDEA OF NORMAL-- WHICH IS TOTALLY ABNORMAL!
HOW TWO WACKOS LIKE HER AN' DADDY EVER CONCEIVED KIDS AS NORMAL AS US IS BEYOND ME!

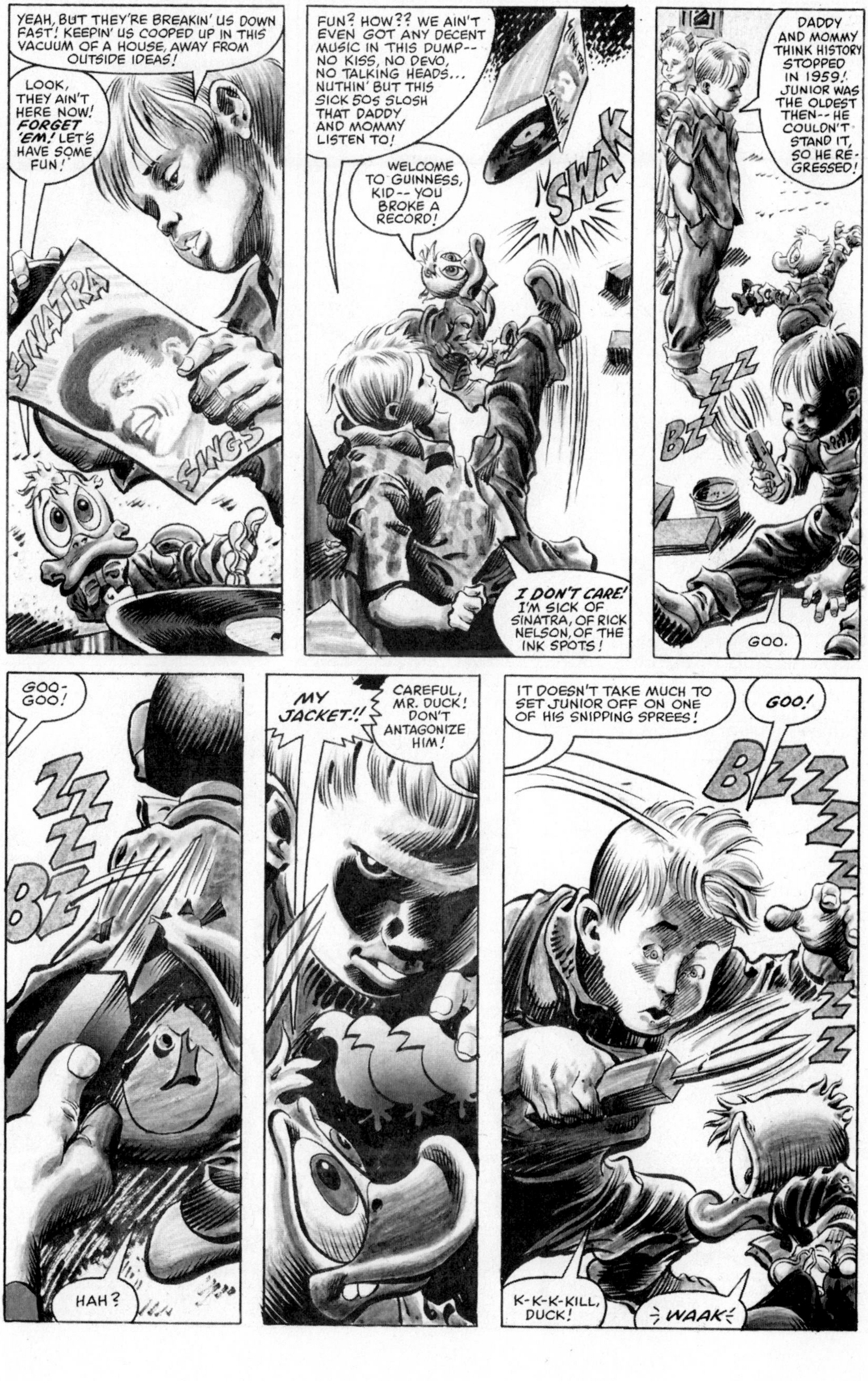

YEAH, BUT THEY'RE BREAKIN' US DOWN FAST! KEEPIN' US COOPED UP IN THIS VACUUM OF A HOUSE, AWAY FROM OUTSIDE IDEAS!
LOOK, THEY AIN'T HERE NOW! FORGET 'EM! LET'S HAVE SOME FUN!
SINATRA SINGS
FUN? HOW?? WE AIN'T EVEN GOT ANY DECENT MUSIC IN THIS DUMP-- NO KISS, NO DEVO, NO TALKING HEADS... NUTHIN' BUT THIS SICK 50s SLOSH THAT DADDY AND MOMMY LISTEN TO!
WELCOME TO GUINNESS, KID-- YOU BROKE A RECORD!
SWAK
I DON'T CARE! I'M SICK OF SINATRA, OF RICK NELSON, OF THE INK SPOTS!
DADDY AND MOMMY THINK HISTORY STOPPED IN 1959! JUNIOR WAS THE OLDEST THEN-- HE COULDN'T STAND IT, SO HE REGRESSED!
BZZZZ
GOO.
GOO-GOO!
BZZZZ
HAH?
MY JACKET!!
CAREFUL, MR. DUCK! DON'T ANTAGONIZE HIM!
IT DOESN'T TAKE MUCH TO SET JUNIOR OFF ON ONE OF HIS SNIPPING SPREES!
GOO!
BZZZZZZZ
K-K-K-KILL, DUCK!
WAAK

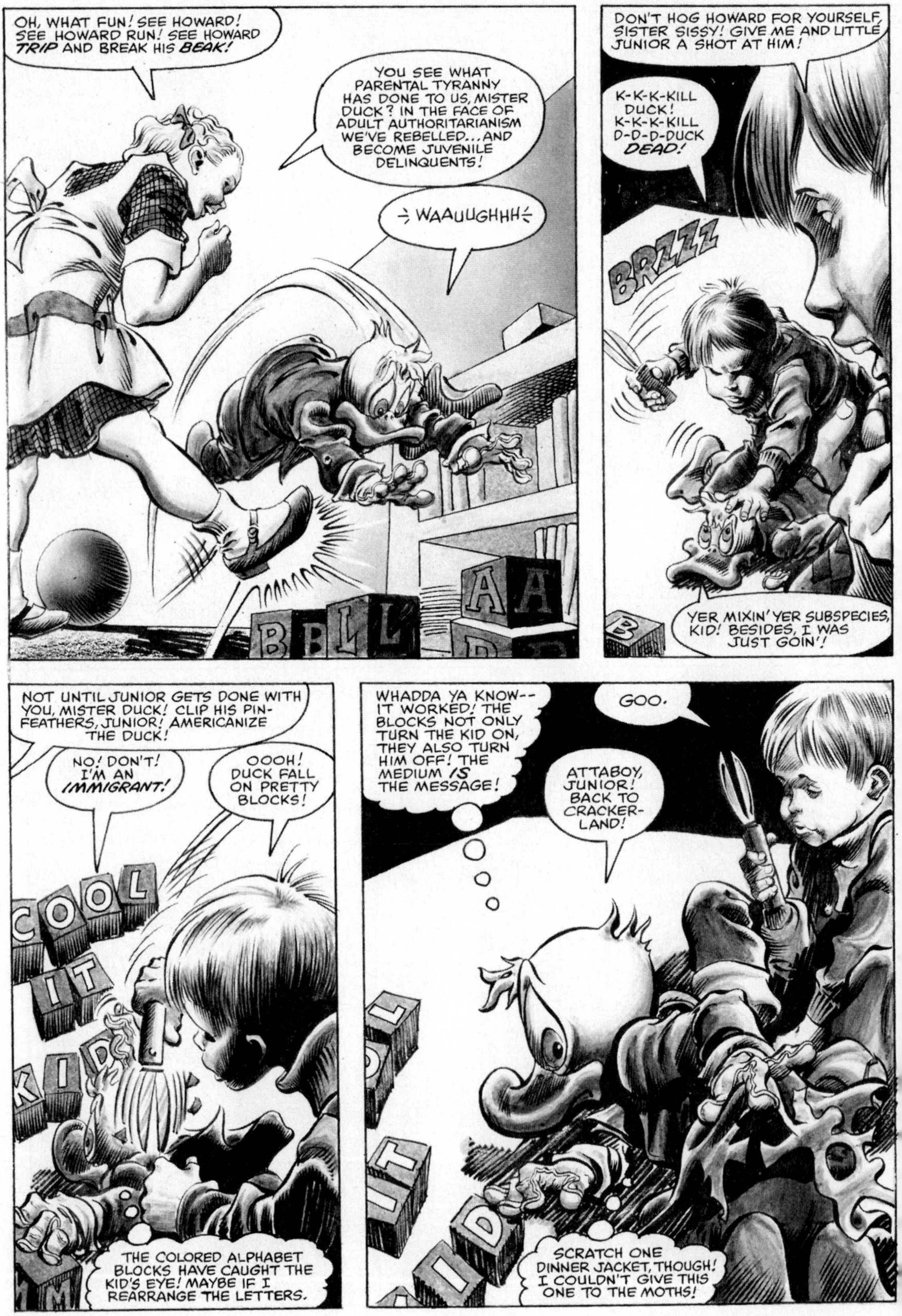
OH, WHAT FUN! SEE HOWARD! SEE HOWARD RUN! SEE HOWARD TRIP AND BREAK HIS BEAK!
YOU SEE WHAT PARENTAL TYRANNY HAS DONE TO US, MISTER DUCK? IN THE FACE OF ADULT AUTHORITARIANISM WE'VE REBELLED... AND BECOME JUVENILE DELINQUENTS!
WAAUUGHHH
DON'T HOG HOWARD FOR YOURSELF, SISTER SISSY! GIVE ME AND LITTLE JUNIOR A SHOT AT HIM!
K-K-K-KILL DUCK! K-K-K-KILL D-D-D-DUCK DEAD!
BRZZZ
YER MIXIN' YER SUBSPECIES, KID! BESIDES, I WAS JUST GOIN'!
NOT UNTIL JUNIOR GETS DONE WITH YOU, MISTER DUCK! CLIP HIS PIN-FEATHERS, JUNIOR! AMERICANIZE THE DUCK!
NO! DON'T! I'M AN IMMIGRANT!
OOOH! DUCK FALL ON PRETTY BLOCKS!
COOL IT KID
THE COLORED ALPHABET BLOCKS HAVE CAUGHT THE KID'S EYE! MAYBE IF I REARRANGE THE LETTERS.
WHADDA YA KNOW-- IT WORKED! THE BLOCKS NOT ONLY TURN THE KID ON, THEY ALSO TURN HIM OFF! THE MEDIUM IS THE MESSAGE!
GOO.
ATTABOY, JUNIOR! BACK TO CRACKER-LAND!
SCRATCH ONE DINNER JACKET, THOUGH! I COULDN'T GIVE THIS ONE TO THE MOTHS!

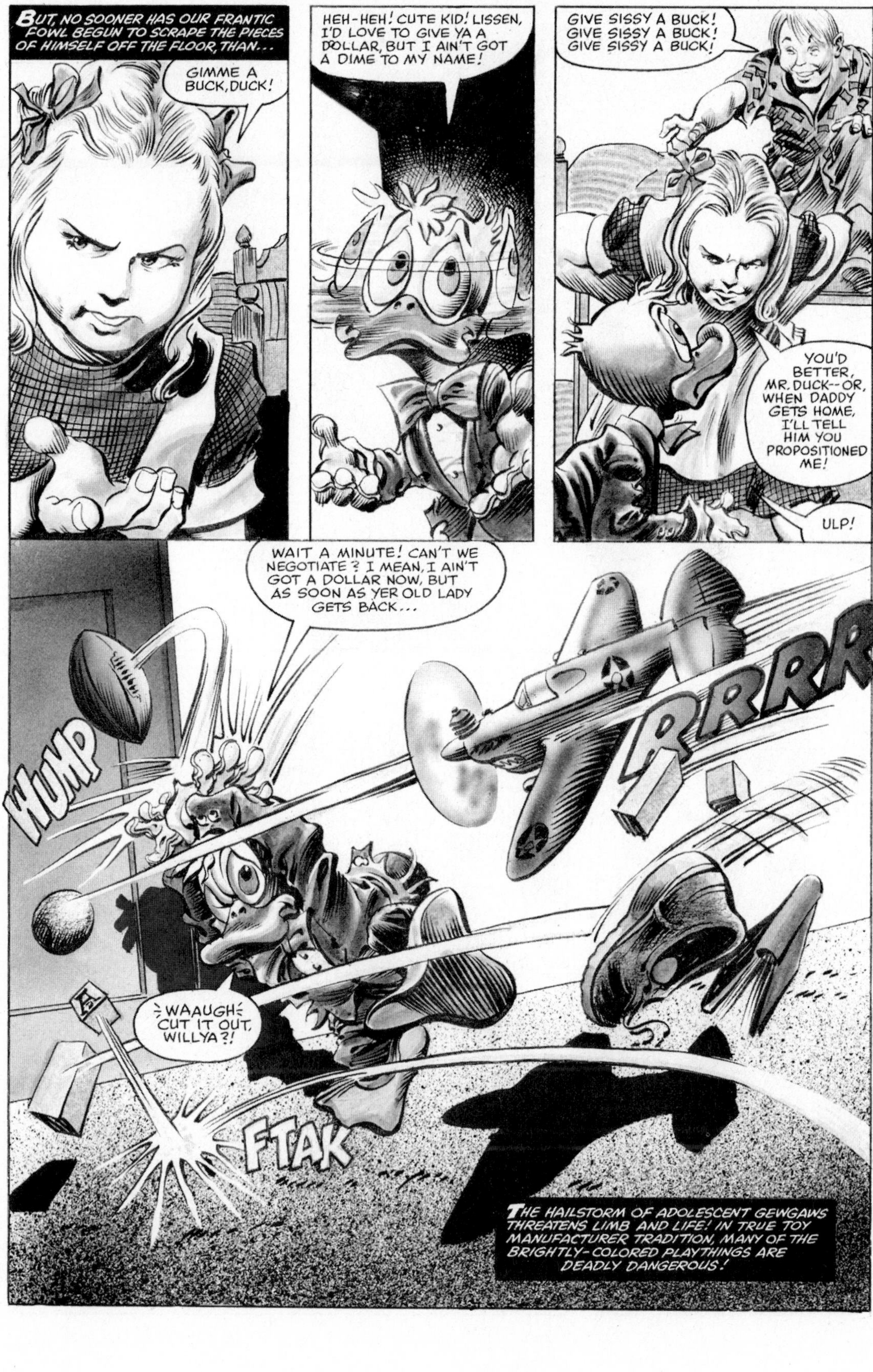
BUT, NO SOONER HAS OUR FRANTIC FOWL BEGUN TO SCRAPE THE PIECES OF HIMSELF OFF THE FLOOR, THAN...
GIMME A BUCK, DUCK!
HEH-HEH! CUTE KID! LISSEN, I'D LOVE TO GIVE YA A DOLLAR, BUT I AIN'T GOT A DIME TO MY NAME!
GIVE SISSY A BUCK! GIVE SISSY A BUCK! GIVE SISSY A BUCK!
YOU'D BETTER, MR. DUCK--OR, WHEN DADDY GETS HOME, I'LL TELL HIM YOU PROPOSITIONED ME!
ULP!
WAIT A MINUTE! CAN'T WE NEGOTIATE? I MEAN, I AIN'T GOT A DOLLAR NOW, BUT AS SOON AS YER OLD LADY GETS BACK...
WHUMP
RRRRR
WAAUGH CUT IT OUT, WILLYA?!
FTAK
THE HAILSTORM OF ADOLESCENT GEWGAWS THREATENS LIMB AND LIFE! IN TRUE TOY MANUFACTURER TRADITION, MANY OF THE BRIGHTLY-COLORED PLAYTHINGS ARE DEADLY DANGEROUS!

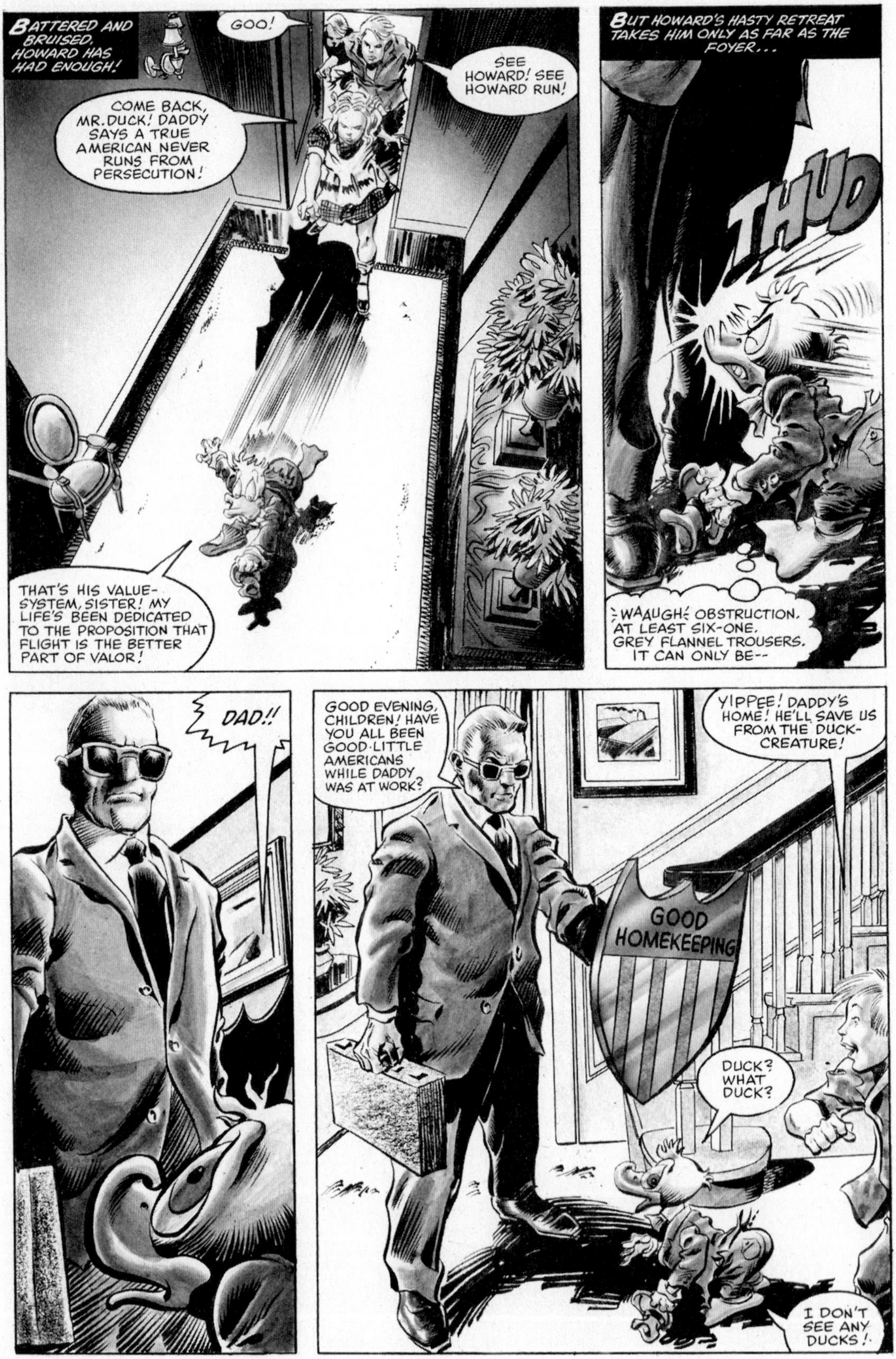
BATTERED AND BRUISED, HOWARD HAS HAD ENOUGH!
GOO!
SEE HOWARD! SEE HOWARD RUN!
COME BACK, MR. DUCK! DADDY SAYS A TRUE AMERICAN NEVER RUNS FROM PERSECUTION!
THAT'S HIS VALUE-SYSTEM, SISTER! MY LIFE'S BEEN DEDICATED TO THE PROPOSITION THAT FLIGHT IS THE BETTER PART OF VALOR!
BUT HOWARD'S HASTY RETREAT TAKES HIM ONLY AS FAR AS THE FOYER...
THUD
WAAUGH! OBSTRUCTION. AT LEAST SIX-ONE. GREY FLANNEL TROUSERS. IT CAN ONLY BE--
DAD!!
GOOD EVENING, CHILDREN! HAVE YOU ALL BEEN GOOD LITTLE AMERICANS WHILE DADDY WAS AT WORK?
YIPPEE! DADDY'S HOME! HE'LL SAVE US FROM THE DUCK-CREATURE!
GOOD HOMEKEEPING
DUCK? WHAT DUCK?
I DON'T SEE ANY DUCKS!

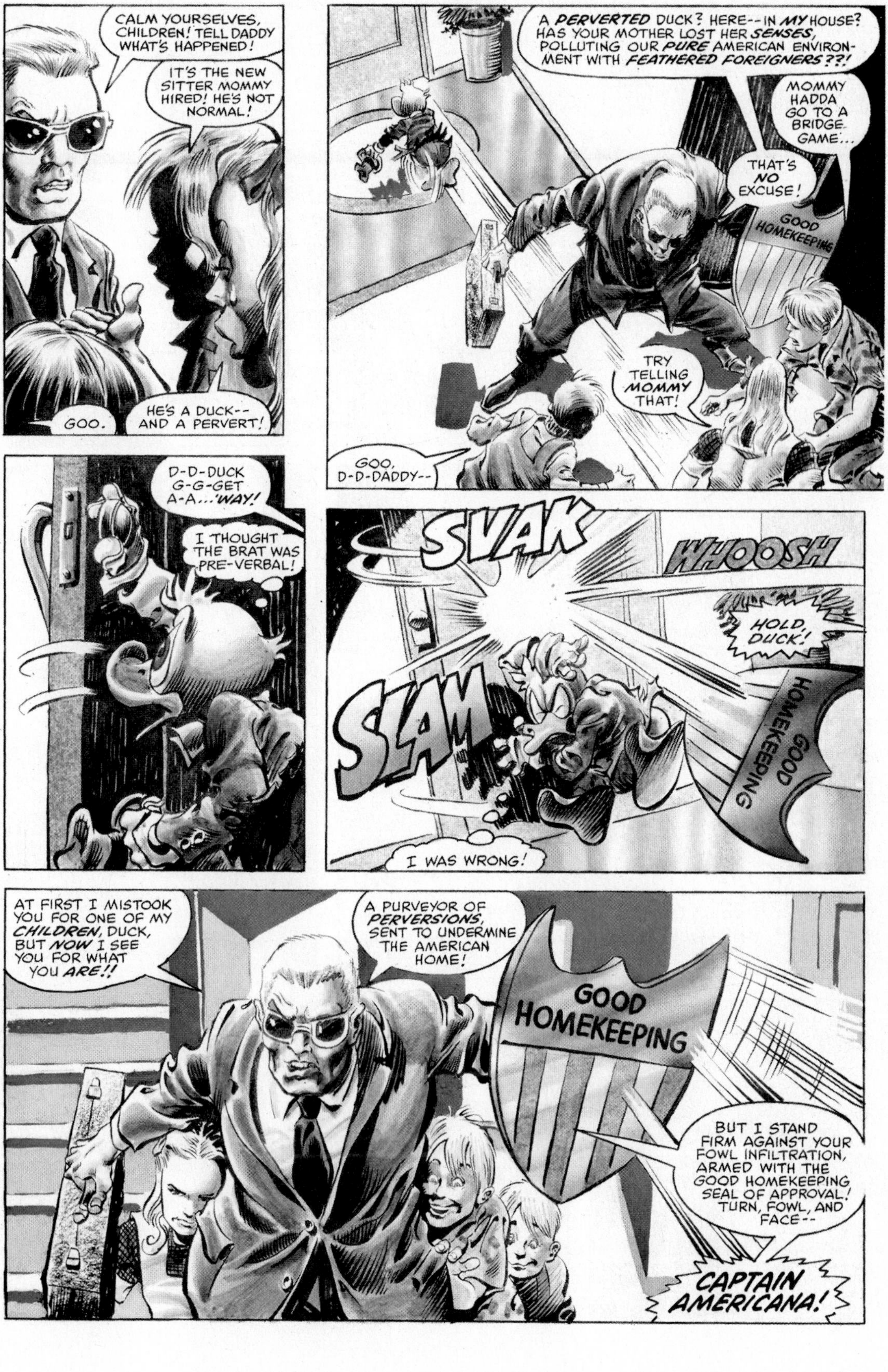
CALM YOURSELVES, CHILDREN! TELL DADDY WHAT'S HAPPENED!
IT'S THE NEW SITTER MOMMY HIRED! HE'S NOT NORMAL!
GOO.
HE'S A DUCK-- AND A PERVERT!
A PERVERTED DUCK? HERE--IN MY HOUSE? HAS YOUR MOTHER LOST HER SENSES, POLLUTING OUR PURE AMERICAN ENVIRONMENT WITH FEATHERED FOREIGNERS??!
MOMMY HADDA GO TO A BRIDGE GAME...
THAT'S NO EXCUSE!
GOOD HOMEKEEPING
TRY TELLING MOMMY THAT!
GOO, D-D-DADDY--
D-D-DUCK G-G-GET A-A...'WAY!
I THOUGHT THE BRAT WAS PRE-VERBAL!
SVAK
WHOOSH
HOLD, DUCK!
SLAM
GOOD HOMEKEEPING
I WAS WRONG!
AT FIRST I MISTOOK YOU FOR ONE OF MY CHILDREN, DUCK, BUT NOW I SEE YOU FOR WHAT YOU ARE!!
A PURVEYOR OF PERVERSIONS, SENT TO UNDERMINE THE AMERICAN HOME!
GOOD HOMEKEEPING
BUT I STAND FIRM AGAINST YOUR FOWL INFILTRATION, ARMED WITH THE GOOD HOMEKEEPING SEAL OF APPROVAL! TURN, FOWL, AND FACE--
CAPTAIN AMERICANA!

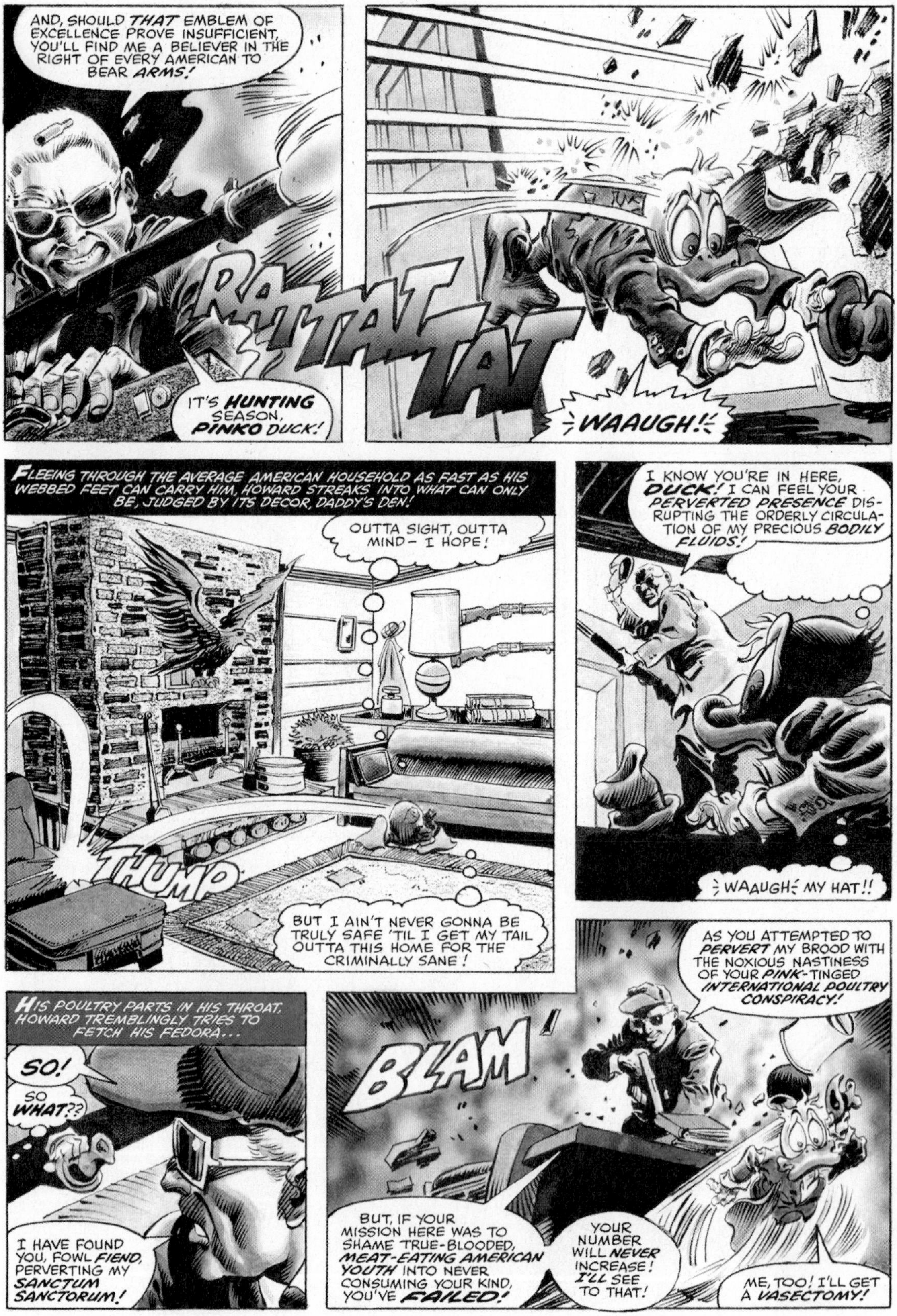
AND, SHOULD THAT EMBLEM OF EXCELLENCE PROVE INSUFFICIENT, YOU'LL FIND ME A BELIEVER IN THE RIGHT OF EVERY AMERICAN TO BEAR ARMS!
RATATAT TAT
IT'S HUNTING SEASON, PINKO DUCK!
WAAUGH!
FLEEING THROUGH THE AVERAGE AMERICAN HOUSEHOLD AS FAST AS HIS WEBBED FEET CAN CARRY HIM, HOWARD STREAKS INTO WHAT CAN ONLY BE, JUDGED BY ITS DECOR, DADDY'S DEN!
OUTTA SIGHT, OUTTA MIND– I HOPE!
THUMP
BUT I AIN'T NEVER GONNA BE TRULY SAFE 'TIL I GET MY TAIL OUTTA THIS HOME FOR THE CRIMINALLY SANE!
I KNOW YOU'RE IN HERE, DUCK! I CAN FEEL YOUR PERVERTED PRESENCE DISRUPTING THE ORDERLY CIRCULATION OF MY PRECIOUS BODILY FLUIDS!
WAAUGH– MY HAT!!
HIS POULTRY PARTS IN HIS THROAT, HOWARD TREMBLINGLY TRIES TO FETCH HIS FEDORA...
SO!
SO WHAT??
I HAVE FOUND YOU, FOWL FIEND, PERVERTING MY SANCTUM SANCTORUM!
AS YOU ATTEMPTED TO PERVERT MY BROOD WITH THE NOXIOUS NASTINESS OF YOUR PINK-TINGED INTERNATIONAL POULTRY CONSPIRACY!
BLAM
BUT, IF YOUR MISSION HERE WAS TO SHAME TRUE-BLOODED, MEAT-EATING AMERICAN YOUTH INTO NEVER CONSUMING YOUR KIND, YOU'VE FAILED!
YOUR NUMBER WILL NEVER INCREASE! I'LL SEE TO THAT!
ME, TOO! I'LL GET A VASECTOMY!

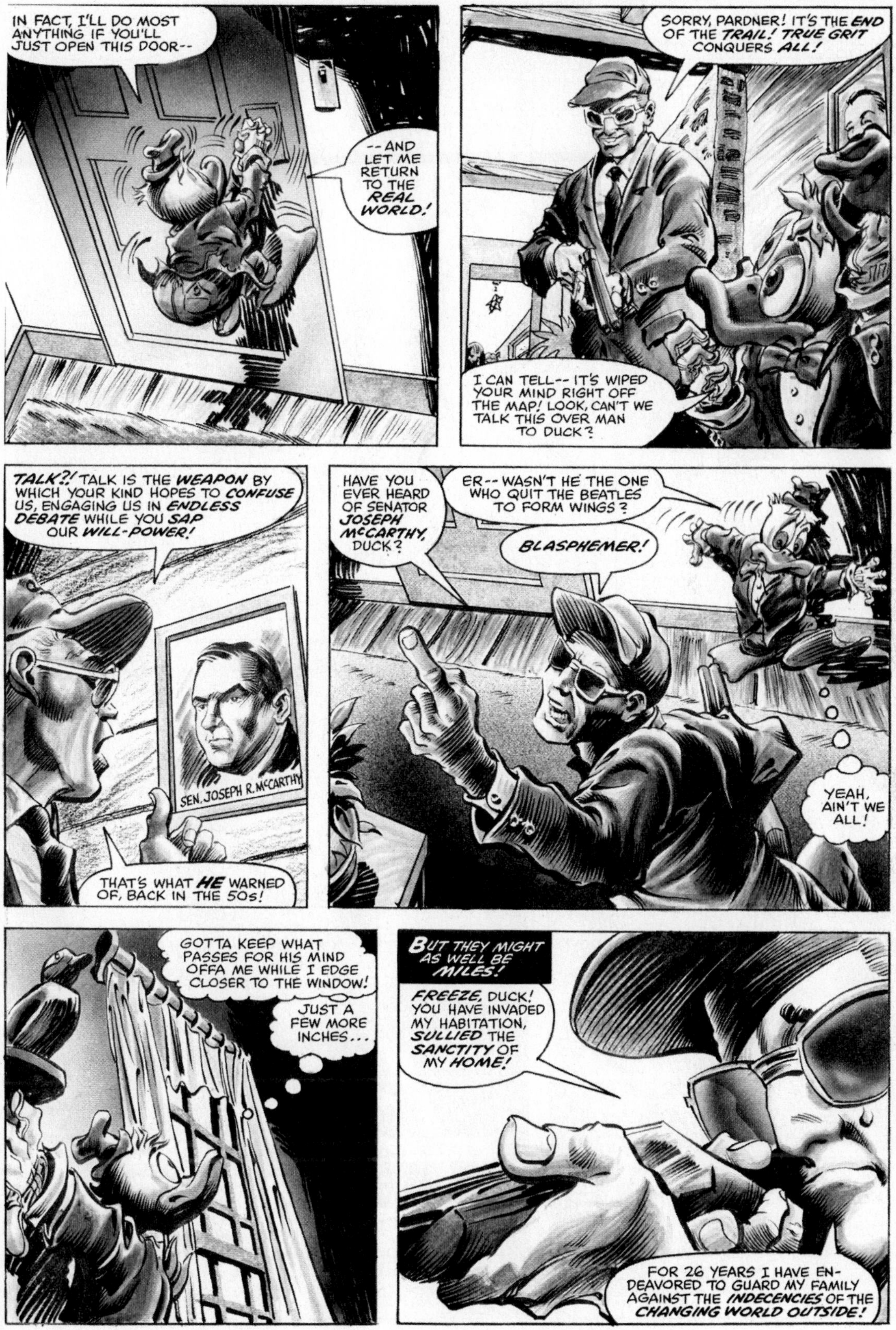

IN FACT, I'LL DO MOST ANYTHING IF YOU'LL JUST OPEN THIS DOOR--
--AND LET ME RETURN TO THE REAL WORLD!
SORRY, PARDNER! IT'S THE END OF THE TRAIL! TRUE GRIT CONQUERS ALL!
I CAN TELL-- IT'S WIPED YOUR MIND RIGHT OFF THE MAP! LOOK, CAN'T WE TALK THIS OVER MAN TO DUCK?
TALK?! TALK IS THE WEAPON BY WHICH YOUR KIND HOPES TO CONFUSE US, ENGAGING US IN ENDLESS DEBATE WHILE YOU SAP OUR WILL-POWER!
SEN. JOSEPH R. McCARTHY
THAT'S WHAT HE WARNED OF, BACK IN THE 50s!
HAVE YOU EVER HEARD OF SENATOR JOSEPH McCARTHY, DUCK?
ER-- WASN'T HE THE ONE WHO QUIT THE BEATLES TO FORM WINGS?
BLASPHEMER!
YEAH, AIN'T WE ALL!
GOTTA KEEP WHAT PASSES FOR HIS MIND OFFA ME WHILE I EDGE CLOSER TO THE WINDOW!
JUST A FEW MORE INCHES...
BUT THEY MIGHT AS WELL BE MILES!
FREEZE, DUCK! YOU HAVE INVADED MY HABITATION, SULLIED THE SANCTITY OF MY HOME!
FOR 26 YEARS I HAVE EN-DEAVORED TO GUARD MY FAMILY AGAINST THE INDECENCIES OF THE CHANGING WORLD OUTSIDE!

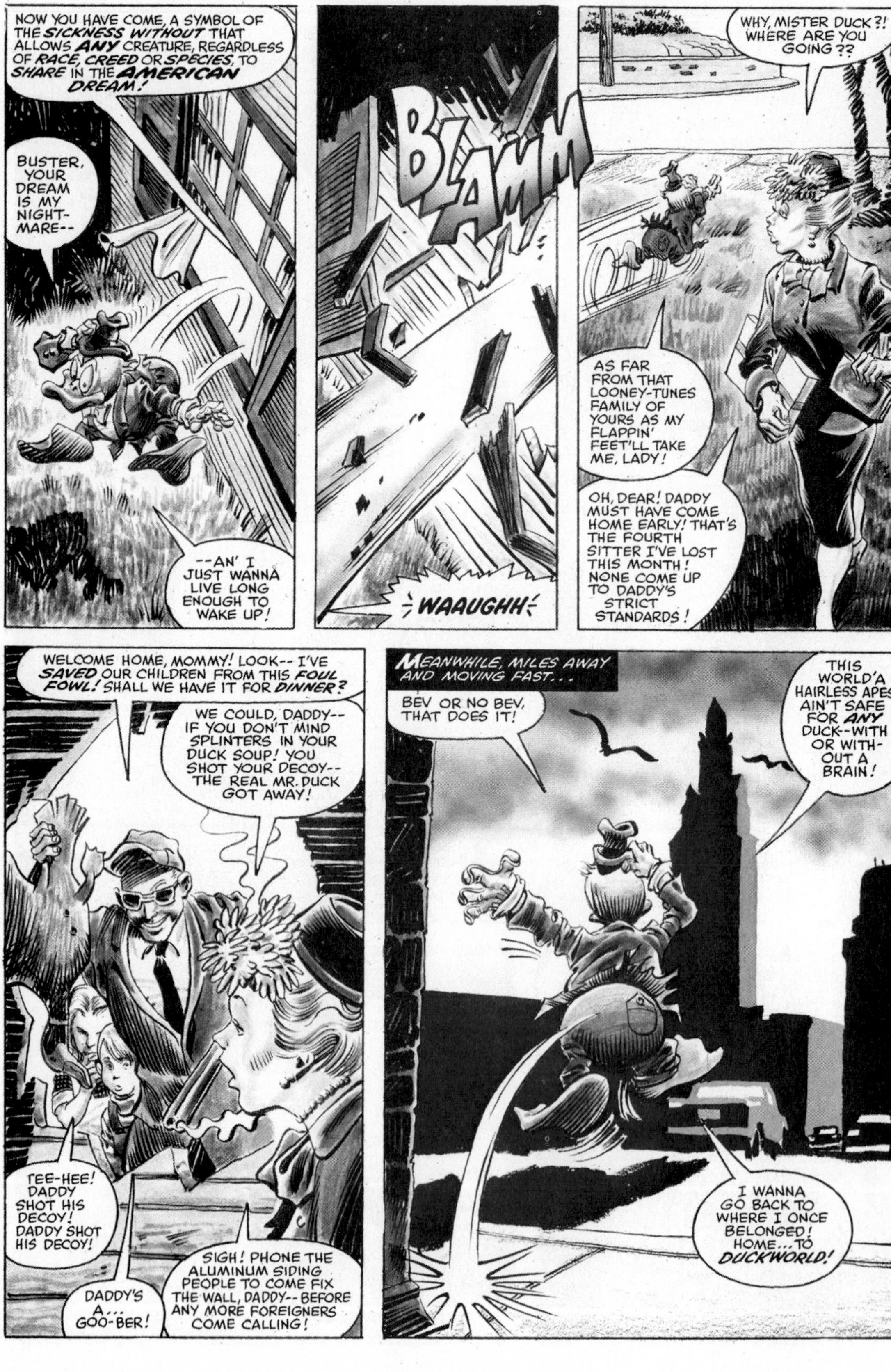
NOW YOU HAVE COME, A SYMBOL OF THE SICKNESS WITHOUT THAT ALLOWS ANY CREATURE, REGARDLESS OF RACE, CREED OR SPECIES, TO SHARE IN THE AMERICAN DREAM!
BUSTER, YOUR DREAM IS MY NIGHT-MARE--
--AN' I JUST WANNA LIVE LONG ENOUGH TO WAKE UP!
BLAMM
WAAUGHH
WHY, MISTER DUCK?! WHERE ARE YOU GOING??
AS FAR FROM THAT LOONEY-TUNES FAMILY OF YOURS AS MY FLAPPIN' FEET'LL TAKE ME, LADY!
OH, DEAR! DADDY MUST HAVE COME HOME EARLY! THAT'S THE FOURTH SITTER I'VE LOST THIS MONTH! NONE COME UP TO DADDY'S STRICT STANDARDS!
WELCOME HOME, MOMMY! LOOK-- I'VE SAVED OUR CHILDREN FROM THIS FOUL FOWL! SHALL WE HAVE IT FOR DINNER?
WE COULD, DADDY-- IF YOU DON'T MIND SPLINTERS IN YOUR DUCK SOUP! YOU SHOT YOUR DECOY-- THE REAL MR. DUCK GOT AWAY!
TEE-HEE! DADDY SHOT HIS DECOY! DADDY SHOT HIS DECOY!
DADDY'S A... GOO-BER!
SIGH! PHONE THE ALUMINUM SIDING PEOPLE TO COME FIX THE WALL, DADDY-- BEFORE ANY MORE FOREIGNERS COME CALLING!
MEANWHILE, MILES AWAY AND MOVING FAST...
BEV OR NO BEV, THAT DOES IT!
THIS WORLD'A HAIRLESS APES AIN'T SAFE FOR ANY DUCK--WITH OR WITH-OUT A BRAIN!
I WANNA GO BACK TO WHERE I ONCE BELONGED! HOME... TO DUCKWORLD!

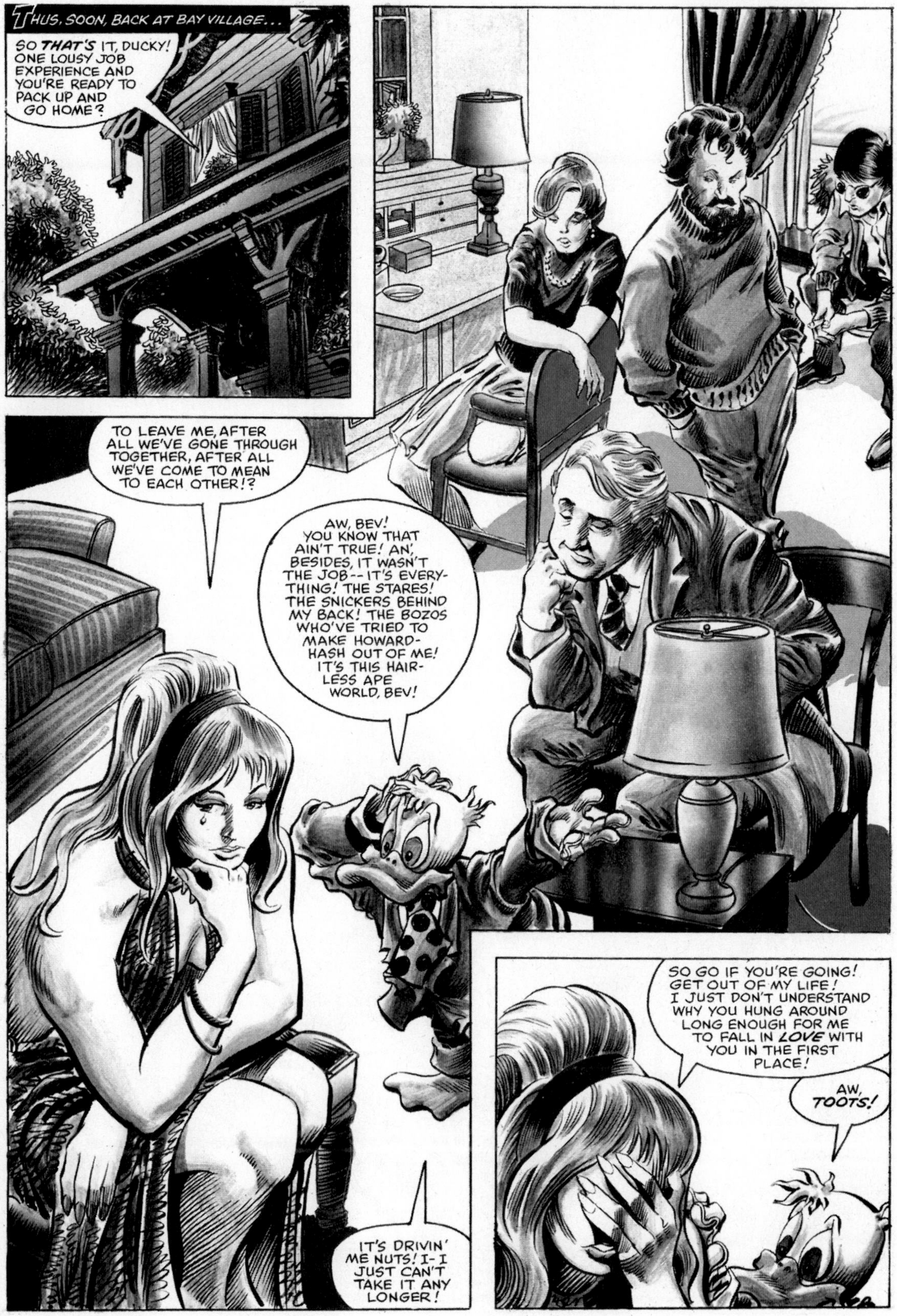
THUS, SOON, BACK AT BAY VILLAGE...
SO THAT'S IT, DUCKY! ONE LOUSY JOB EXPERIENCE AND YOU'RE READY TO PACK UP AND GO HOME?
TO LEAVE ME, AFTER ALL WE'VE GONE THROUGH TOGETHER, AFTER ALL WE'VE COME TO MEAN TO EACH OTHER!?
AW, BEV! YOU KNOW THAT AIN'T TRUE! AN', BESIDES, IT WASN'T THE JOB--IT'S EVERYTHING! THE STARES! THE SNICKERS BEHIND MY BACK! THE BOZOS WHO'VE TRIED TO MAKE HOWARD-HASH OUT OF ME! IT'S THIS HAIRLESS APE WORLD, BEV!
IT'S DRIVIN' ME NUTS! I-I JUST CAN'T TAKE IT ANY LONGER!
SO GO IF YOU'RE GOING! GET OUT OF MY LIFE! I JUST DON'T UNDERSTAND WHY YOU HUNG AROUND LONG ENOUGH FOR ME TO FALL IN LOVE WITH YOU IN THE FIRST PLACE!
AW, TOOTS!

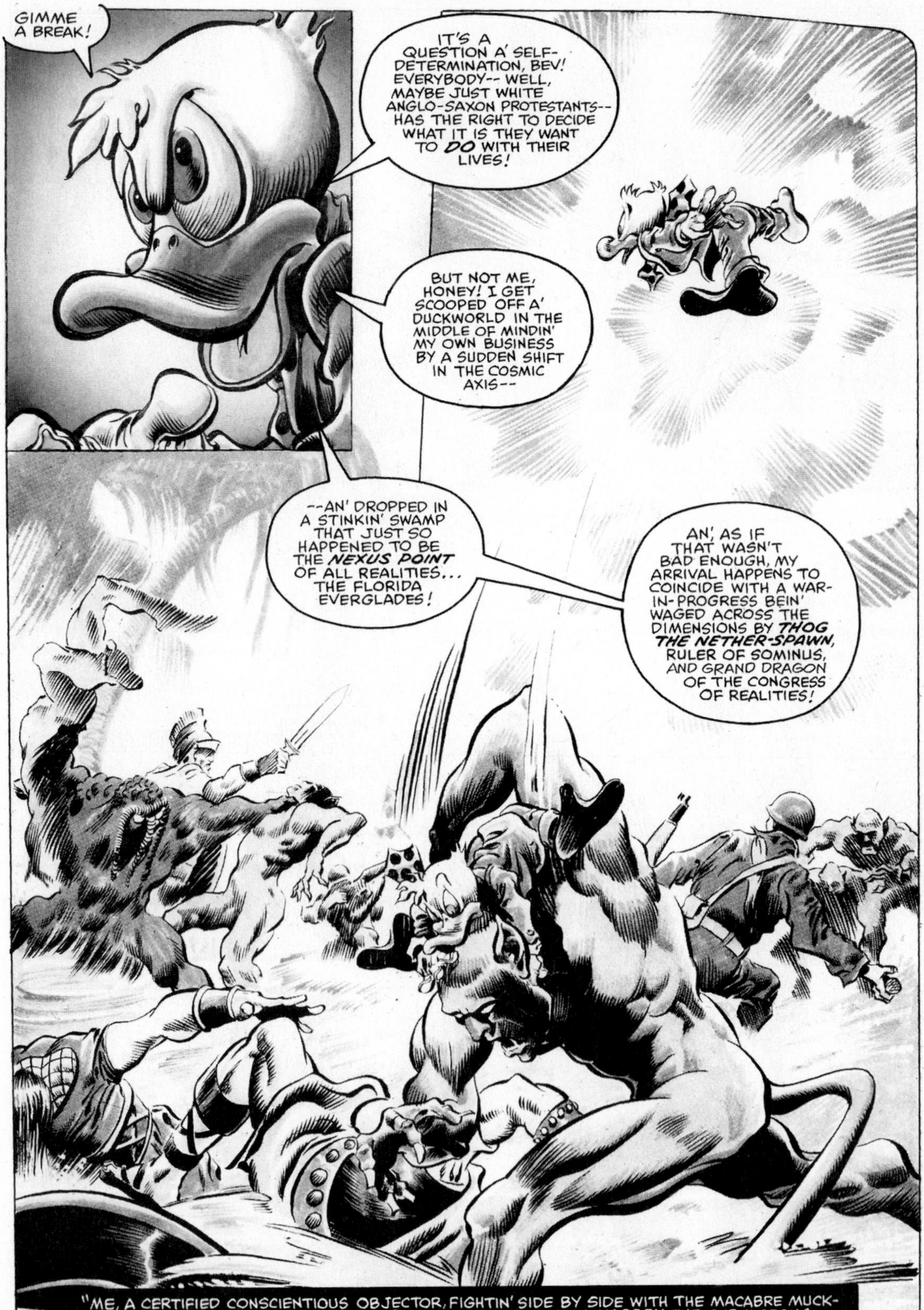
GIMME A BREAK!
IT'S A QUESTION A' SELF-DETERMINATION, BEV! EVERYBODY-- WELL, MAYBE JUST WHITE ANGLO-SAXON PROTESTANTS-- HAS THE RIGHT TO DECIDE WHAT IT IS THEY WANT TO DO WITH THEIR LIVES!
BUT NOT ME, HONEY! I GET SCOOPED OFF A' DUCKWORLD IN THE MIDDLE OF MINDIN' MY OWN BUSINESS BY A SUDDEN SHIFT IN THE COSMIC AXIS--
--AN' DROPPED IN A STINKIN' SWAMP THAT JUST SO HAPPENED TO BE THE NEXUS POINT OF ALL REALITIES... THE FLORIDA EVERGLADES!
AN', AS IF THAT WASN'T BAD ENOUGH, MY ARRIVAL HAPPENS TO COINCIDE WITH A WAR-IN-PROGRESS BEIN' WAGED ACROSS THE DIMENSIONS BY THOG THE NETHER-SPAWN, RULER OF SOMINUS, AND GRAND DRAGON OF THE CONGRESS OF REALITIES!
"ME, A CERTIFIED CONSCIENTIOUS OBJECTOR, FIGHTIN' SIDE BY SIDE WITH THE MACABRE MUCK-MONSTER KNOWN AS THE MAN-THING, THE BALMY BARBARIAN KORREK, THE CURVACEOUS SORCERESS JENNIFER KALE, AND THAT MUDDLED MYSTIC DAKIMH, AGAINST THOG'S DEMON-HORDE!"

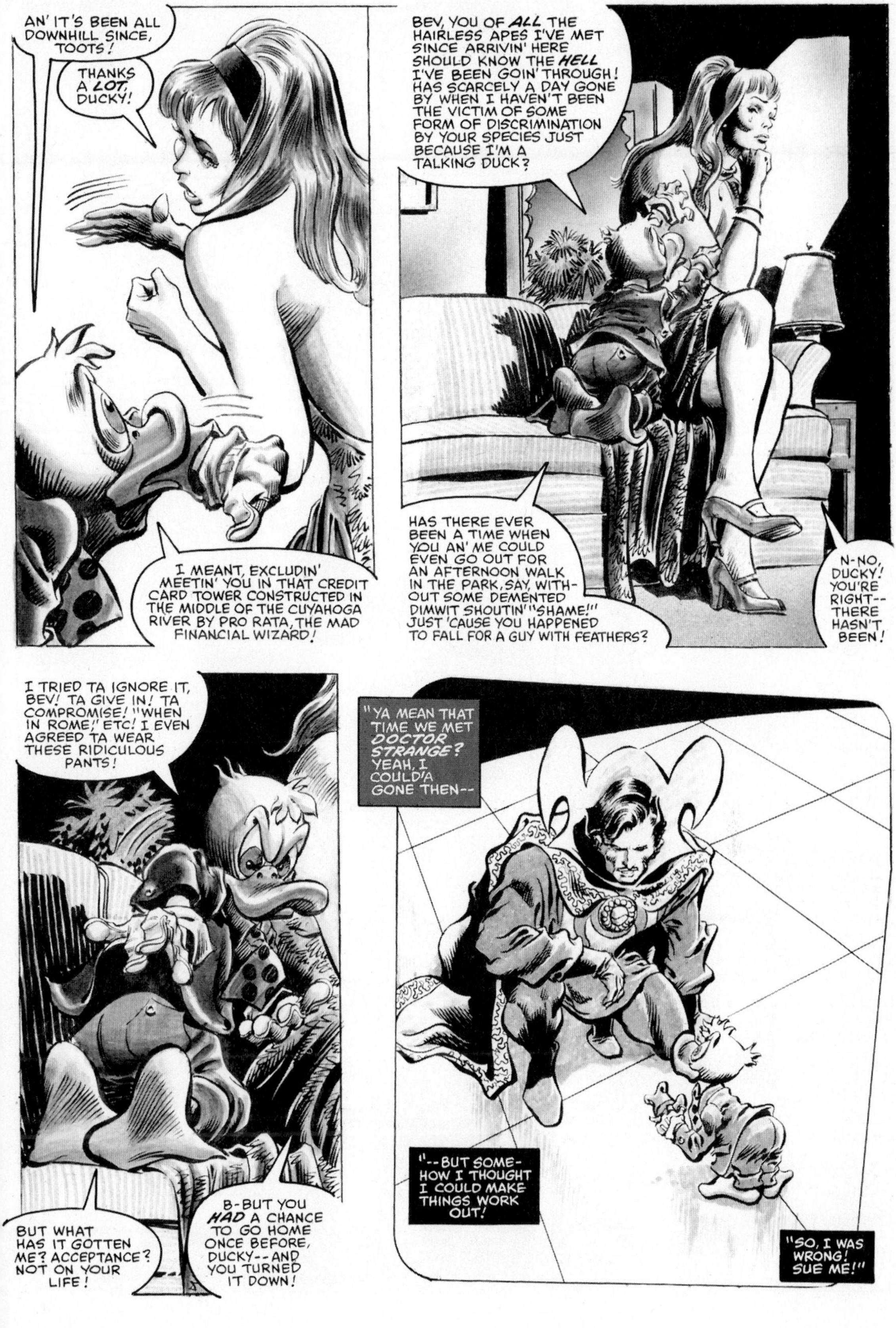
AN' IT'S BEEN ALL DOWNHILL SINCE, TOOTS!
THANKS A LOT, DUCKY!
I MEANT, EXCLUDIN' MEETIN' YOU IN THAT CREDIT CARD TOWER CONSTRUCTED IN THE MIDDLE OF THE CUYAHOGA RIVER BY PRO RATA, THE MAD FINANCIAL WIZARD!
BEV, YOU OF ALL THE HAIRLESS APES I'VE MET SINCE ARRIVIN' HERE SHOULD KNOW THE HELL I'VE BEEN GOIN' THROUGH! HAS SCARCELY A DAY GONE BY WHEN I HAVEN'T BEEN THE VICTIM OF SOME FORM OF DISCRIMINATION BY YOUR SPECIES JUST BECAUSE I'M A TALKING DUCK?
HAS THERE EVER BEEN A TIME WHEN YOU AN' ME COULD EVEN GO OUT FOR AN AFTERNOON WALK IN THE PARK, SAY, WITHOUT SOME DEMENTED DIMWIT SHOUTIN' "SHAME!!" JUST 'CAUSE YOU HAPPENED TO FALL FOR A GUY WITH FEATHERS?
N-NO, DUCKY! YOU'RE RIGHT-- THERE HASN'T BEEN!
I TRIED TA IGNORE IT, BEV! TA GIVE IN! TA COMPROMISE! "WHEN IN ROME," ETC! I EVEN AGREED TA WEAR THESE RIDICULOUS PANTS!
BUT WHAT HAS IT GOTTEN ME? ACCEPTANCE? NOT ON YOUR LIFE!
B-BUT YOU HAD A CHANCE TO GO HOME ONCE BEFORE, DUCKY-- AND YOU TURNED IT DOWN!
"YA MEAN THAT TIME WE MET DOCTOR STRANGE? YEAH, I COULD'A GONE THEN--
"--BUT SOMEHOW I THOUGHT I COULD MAKE THINGS WORK OUT!
"SO, I WAS WRONG! SUE ME!"

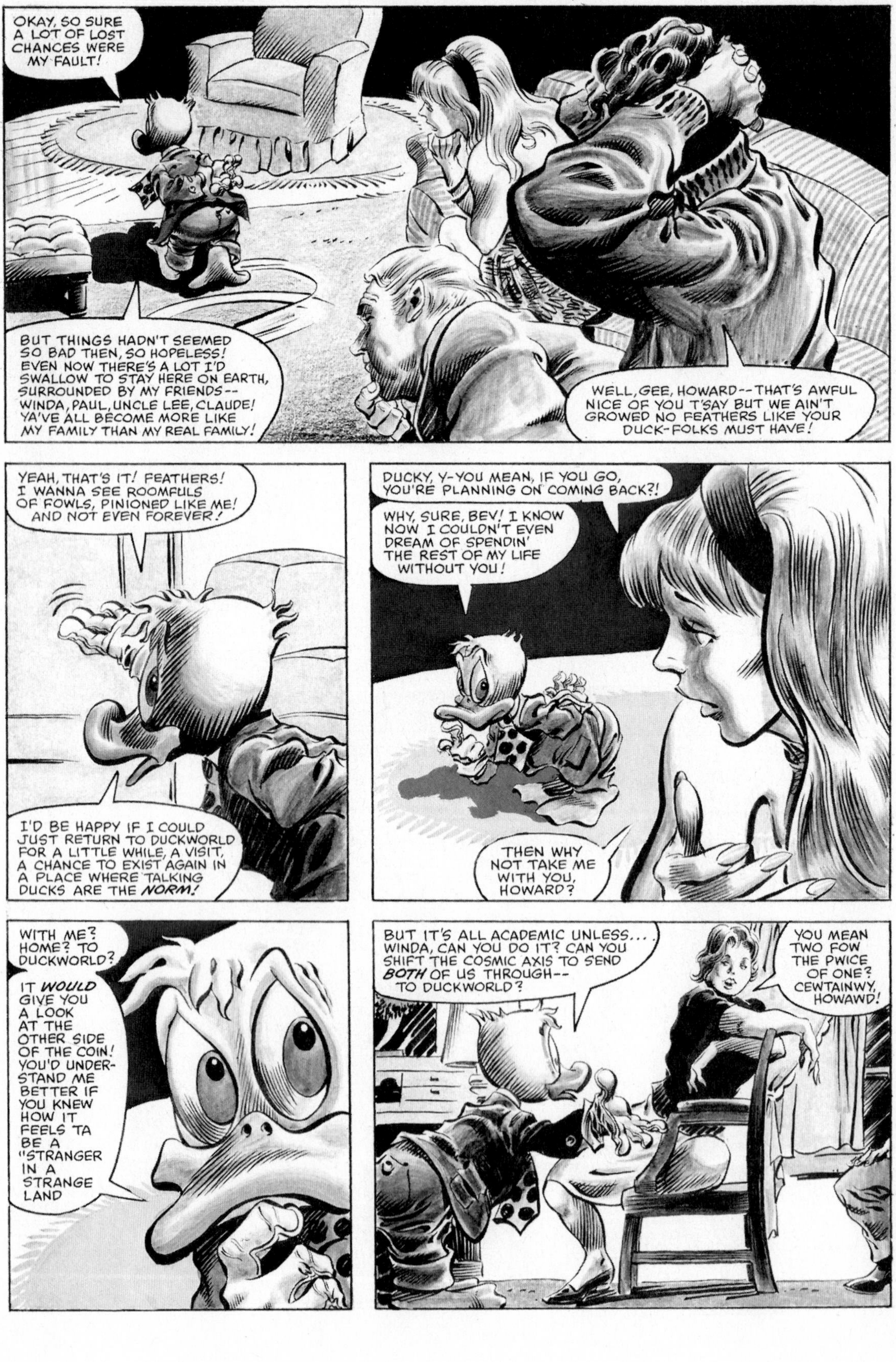
OKAY, SO SURE A LOT OF LOST CHANCES WERE MY FAULT!
BUT THINGS HADN'T SEEMED SO BAD THEN, SO HOPELESS! EVEN NOW THERE'S A LOT I'D SWALLOW TO STAY HERE ON EARTH, SURROUNDED BY MY FRIENDS-- WINDA, PAUL, UNCLE LEE, CLAUDE! YA'VE ALL BECOME MORE LIKE MY FAMILY THAN MY REAL FAMILY!
WELL, GEE, HOWARD--THAT'S AWFUL NICE OF YOU T'SAY BUT WE AIN'T GROWED NO FEATHERS LIKE YOUR DUCK-FOLKS MUST HAVE!
YEAH, THAT'S IT! FEATHERS! I WANNA SEE ROOMFULS OF FOWLS, PINIONED LIKE ME! AND NOT EVEN FOREVER!
I'D BE HAPPY IF I COULD JUST RETURN TO DUCKWORLD FOR A LITTLE WHILE, A VISIT, A CHANCE TO EXIST AGAIN IN A PLACE WHERE TALKING DUCKS ARE THE NORM!
DUCKY, Y-YOU MEAN, IF YOU GO, YOU'RE PLANNING ON COMING BACK?!
WHY, SURE, BEV! I KNOW NOW I COULDN'T EVEN DREAM OF SPENDIN' THE REST OF MY LIFE WITHOUT YOU!
THEN WHY NOT TAKE ME WITH YOU, HOWARD?
WITH ME? HOME? TO DUCKWORLD?
IT WOULD GIVE YOU A LOOK AT THE OTHER SIDE OF THE COIN! YOU'D UNDERSTAND ME BETTER IF YOU KNEW HOW IT FEELS TA BE A "STRANGER IN A STRANGE LAND
BUT IT'S ALL ACADEMIC UNLESS... WINDA, CAN YOU DO IT? CAN YOU SHIFT THE COSMIC AXIS TO SEND BOTH OF US THROUGH-- TO DUCKWORLD?
YOU MEAN TWO FOW THE PWICE OF ONE? CEWTAINWY, HOWAWD!

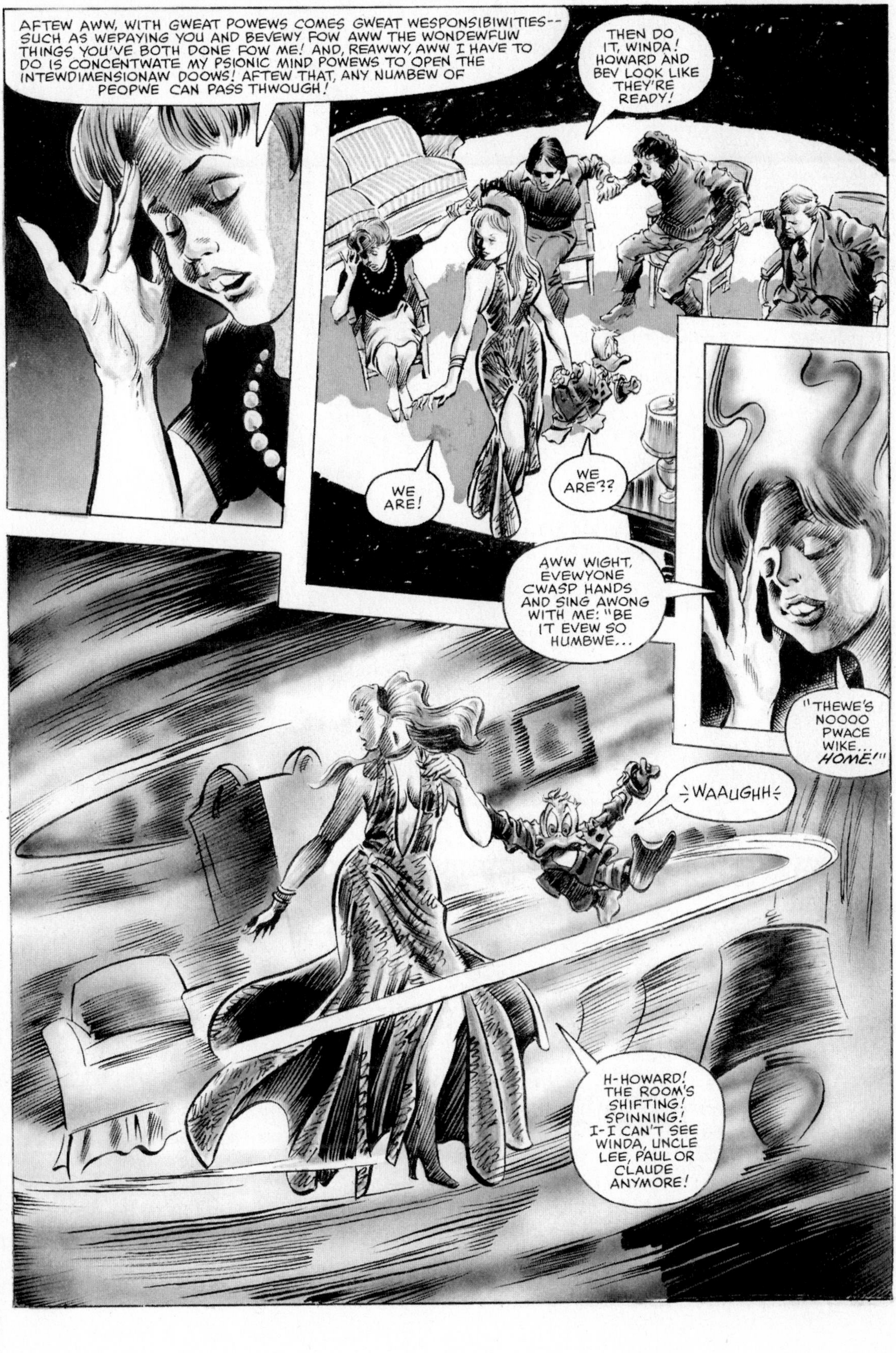
AFTEW AWW, WITH GWEAT POWEWS COMES GWEAT WESPONSIBIWITIES-- SUCH AS WEPAYING YOU AND BEVEWY FOW AWW THE WONDEWFUW THINGS YOU'VE BOTH DONE FOW ME! AND, REAWWY, AWW I HAVE TO DO IS CONCENTWATE MY PSIONIC MIND POWEWS TO OPEN THE INTEWDIMENSIONAW DOOWS! AFTEW THAT, ANY NUMBEW OF PEOPWE CAN PASS THWOUGH!
THEN DO IT, WINDA! HOWARD AND BEV LOOK LIKE THEY'RE READY!
WE ARE!
WE ARE??
AWW WIGHT, EVEWYONE CWASP HANDS AND SING AWONG WITH ME: "BE IT EVEW SO HUMBWE...
"THEWE'S NOOOO PWACE WIKE... HOME!"
WAAUGHH
H-HOWARD! THE ROOM'S SHIFTING! SPINNING! I-I CAN'T SEE WINDA, UNCLE LEE, PAUL OR CLAUDE ANYMORE!

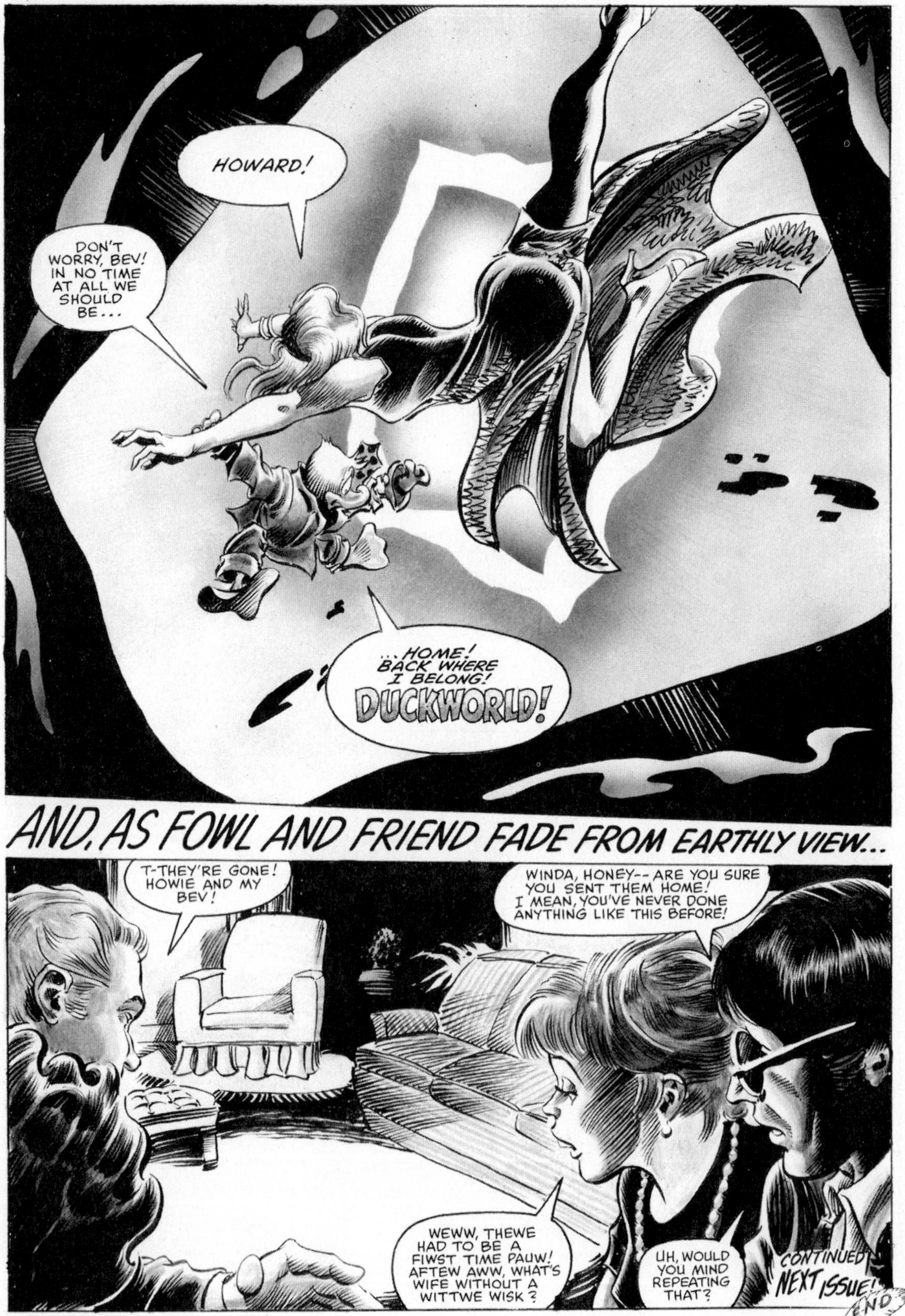
HOWARD!
DON'T WORRY, BEV! IN NO TIME AT ALL WE SHOULD BE...
...HOME! BACK WHERE I BELONG! DUCKWORLD!
AND, AS FOWL AND FRIEND FADE FROM EARTHLY VIEW...
T-THEY'RE GONE! HOWIE AND MY BEV!
WINDA, HONEY-- ARE YOU SURE YOU SENT THEM HOME! I MEAN, YOU'VE NEVER DONE ANYTHING LIKE THIS BEFORE!
WEWW, THEWE HAD TO BE A FIWST TIME PAUW! AFTEW AWW, WHAT'S WIFE WITHOUT A WITTWE WISK?
UH, WOULD YOU MIND REPEATING THAT?
CONTINUED NEXT ISSUE!
END

Fowl Fiends
And Felonious Fellows

WHO CAN YOU TRUST? This must be the primary question in our duck's mind as he remembers the various villains who've harrassed and tormented him in the past. For it isn't only the bad and the ugly who must be approached warily, but the *pretty*, the *innocuous* and the *banal!* Life, in Howard-land, is made miserable by those we least fear. Furthermore, you don't have to be a Freudian to understand the implications of the following villains, for it's obvious that they represent —

YOUR MOM?! What else would the Kidney Lady stand for, but a monster MOTHER, given to moralyzing speeches, insane polemics against impurity, and quick application of physical punishment? You can't win against her, because she's absolutely irrevocably and forever sure that she's right. This is the MOTHER MONSTER we all fear even if our real-life Mom is the greatest.

YOUR KIDS?! "I'm only baking cookies," says little Patsy. "Ah, but they're *godless* cookies, aren't they, little girl?" replies the Reverend Yuc, making the only accurate statement he's ever made. Listen, every parent knows that the time to worry is when the little monsters are *quiet,* that's when they're really up to mischief. And adult guilt comes in, too. There's probably no parent on earth without guilt toward his or her child. What if the kids should *turn* on us? Little Patsy does.

YOUR ACCOUNTANT?! Next to being injured by those close to your heart there's nothing worse than being manipulated and betrayed by those who are close to your wallet! Accountants and bankers can prove *anything*. No matter how right you feel, they'll produce miles of adding machine tape and reams of computer readout to prove you wrong.

WHO CAN YOU TRUST?
According to Howard the Duck, NO ONE!

At the bottom of these pages is a very small rogues gallery. It doesn't, of course, come close to listing the many and varied kinds of baddies our drake has come up against, but does further our point: in Howard's world it is those we least suspect of evil that are likely to do us in. Cute animals, vegetables, doctors, friends, and smiley buttons have all committed more than their share of villainy. Howard's original writer, Steve Gerber, took a turn as a villain of sorts with Howard the Duck comic #16 which, while a creative and audacious attempt to explain away missing a deadline, still let down the duck and his fans, who were looking forward to the conclusion of Howard's run-in with Dr. Bong. And, like the rest of us, Howard is sometimes his own worst enemy.

Howard lives in a paranoid's nightmare: not only does he **think** *they're all out to get him but they* **are.** *The only time he's being unrealistic is when he forgets this! But all these fiends and felonious fellows are only manifestations of the innate hostility of the universe.* **Reality,** *in Howard's case, is hostile in and of itself. He does his best to be dignified, noble, and caring. Yet invariably, at the point in which he stands clothed in good intentions, Life, with a hearty chuckle, jerks the rug from beneath his feet and he falls, dismayed, upon his oft-bruised posterior.*

Not a nice universe to live in. What does it do to your character when you find that no one and nothing can be trusted?

We decided to find out by having an

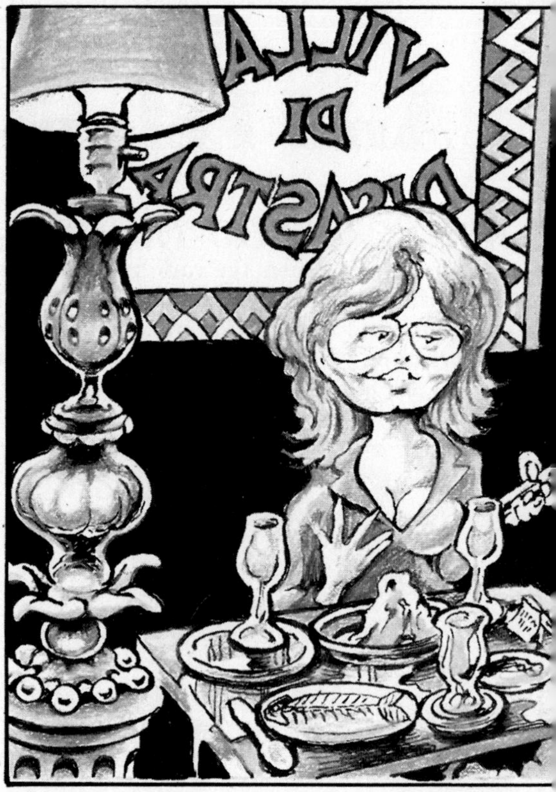

Interview with

It was a dark, rainy day — the kind of day which seems perfect for a meeting with a duck. Meet we did, by appointment, at an over-decorated and pretentious Italian restaurant on Manhattan's east side. He kept me waiting while armies of tuxedo-clad waiters whisked back and forth with trays that wafted delicious odors to this starving reporter.

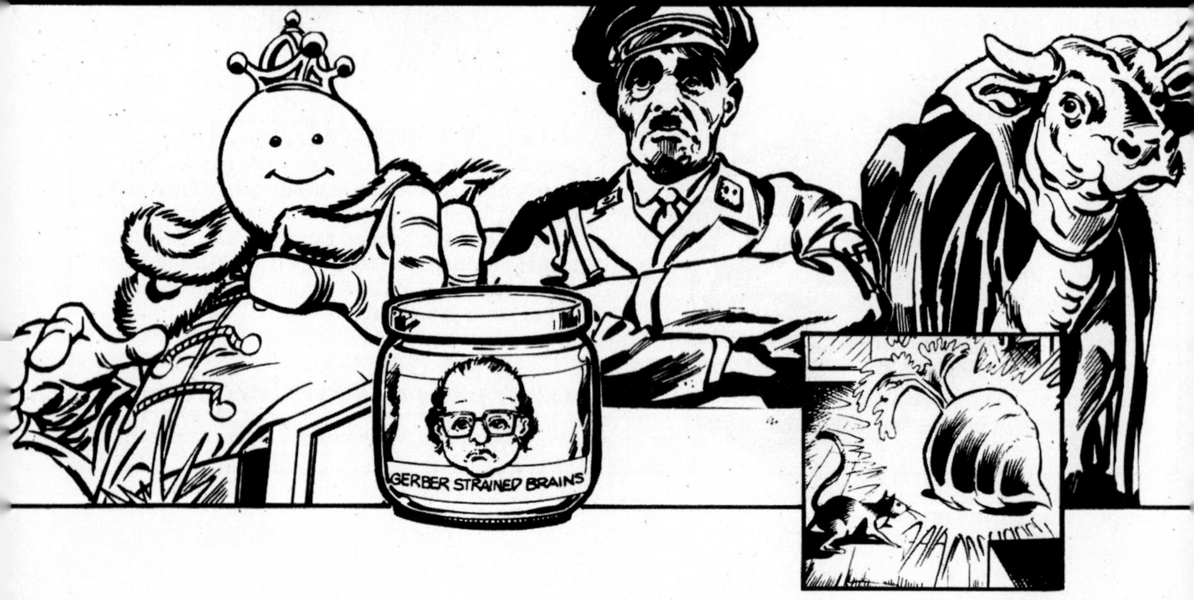
GERBER STRAINED BRAINS

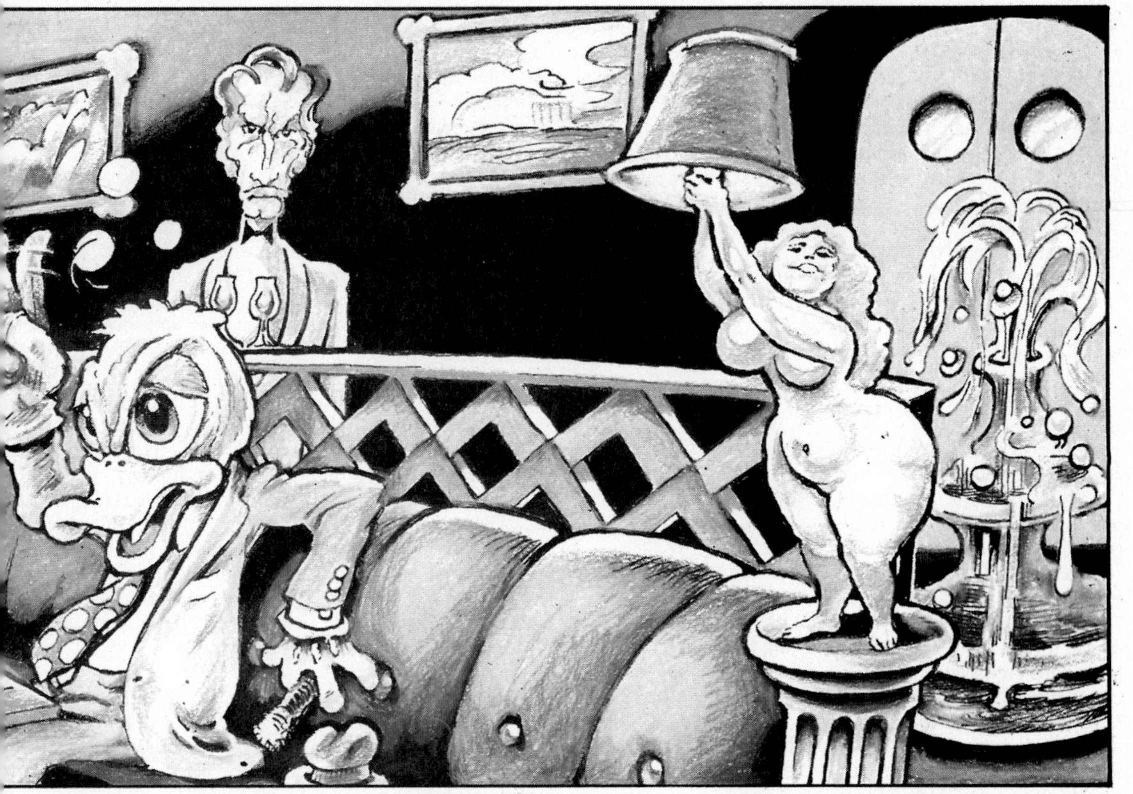

The Duck by Lynn Graeme

At last Howard arrived. He came in from the torrential rain remarkably dry, hat pulled down over his bill, tie skewed to the side, a jaunty little figure whose eyes flickered nervously from side to side as he took in his surroundings. Signs of paranoia? I wondered. The maitre d' — a tall, grand-looking fellow who looked remarkably like Cesare Romero — sniffed at Howard, standing there with droplets of water running off him and onto the carpet, and then deigned to show him to my table.

Face to beak the little guy seemed strangely imposing.

"Relax, toots," he said, hopping gracefully up onto the semi-circular booth, "I ain't as ugly as I look."

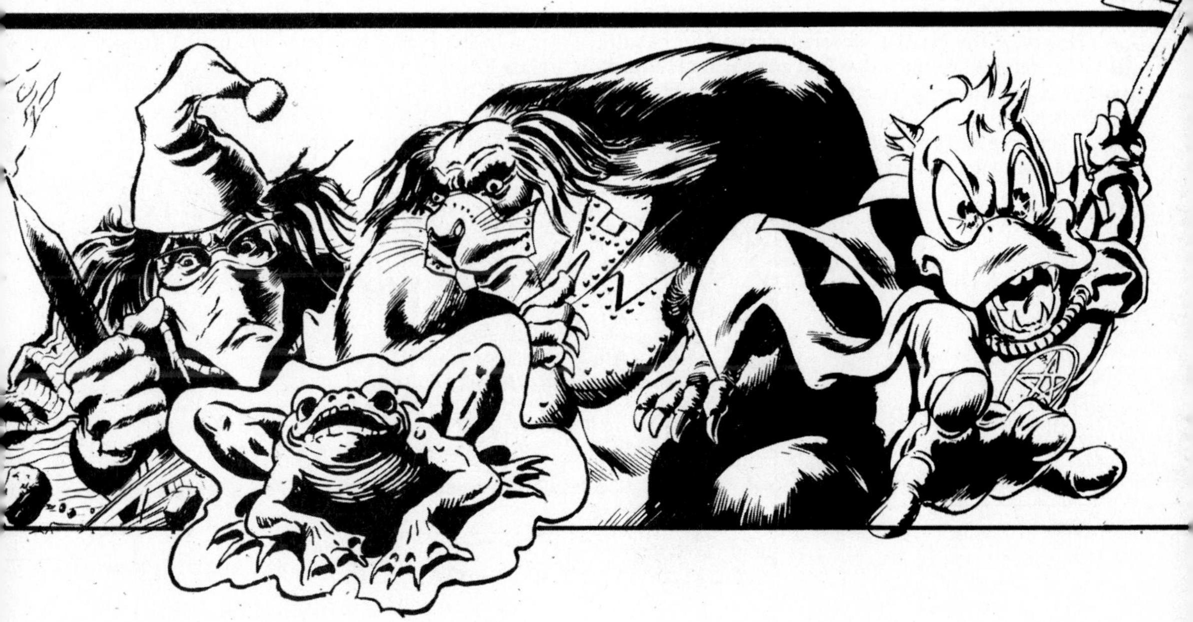

I agreed that wasn't possible, and told Howard to order whatever he wished — it was on the company.

While he studied the menu I studied him. It's always been a little hard for me to believe that a duck could pass as a man but, sitting next to Howard now, I understood. He just *acted* so self-assured and dignified that, unless I forced myself to look hard at him, I felt he was a person. Well, he *is* a person, of course, but I mean I felt he was a *people*-type person. He glanced up and caught me staring. I think I blushed.

"Take a picture, kid. It'll last longer."

"Sure!" I waved over at the bar where Ned Sonntag, scruffy photographer/artist, was waiting for just this moment. He shuffled shyly over and stared fixedly at Howard.

"I love ducks," Ned said softly, "ducks are a lotta fun."

Howard, in the midst of taking a drink of water, choked and sputtered.

"Just take the picture, Neddy, quick!" I hadn't known a duck could get red with anger, but Howard was definitely in a snit.

Ned snapped a few pictures and wandered back through the rivers of waiters to the bar.

We ordered while Howard kept darting bright, suspicious looks at Ned. Ned waved at him and Howard bit down hard on his cigar.

"Excuse me, Mr. Duck" — "Call me Howard," — "I'm sorry Ned got on your nerves, but there's nothing to worry about, well, not very much, anyway. I mean, just look at him — he's pretty innocent and harmless looking, don't you think?"

"Exactly!" Howard yelled; heads turned and he sank back into the booth. "Those're the ones ya can't trust, toots. Take it from me."

"That's exactly what I've been thinking about, Howard. It seems as though you have something about you — and I don't mean the fact that you're a duck, that seems almost irrelevant sometimes — but something about you that attracts some pretty strange villains.

"I mean, you get menaced by little girls, cookies, eggs-over-easy, alarm clocks, old ladies......"

"Ah, cut it out, will ya? I'm losin' my appetite!"

However, the meal he ordered showed he hadn't lost it entirely. When the waiter had gone again Howard sat alternately chewing his cigar and snapping bites of breadstick.

"The breadsticks are the best thing here," I said. Howard stared at me sharply, and then sighed.

"Okay. You want the truth, kid? That stuff about my bein' hounded by old ladies an' little kids an' soap bubbles an' all the rest — it's true, and it's *humiliatin'!* I already saved the universe a couple times, been a real *hero,* but what kinda stories d'you think I could ever tell my grandkids — if I ever have any, which I doubt — about my heroics? 'An' then there was the time I saved New York City from a big buncha bubbles, an' another time there was this giant roach that was gonna get control of the universe, but this caterpillar an' me....'. Ah, it just sounds dumb!" The waiter brought our shrimp cocktails and Howard ate them duck-style, tails and all, in little gulps. Ned snuck over and took another picture, then scuttled back to the bar when Howard glared at him.

"It must be tough, being a hero in such un-heroic ways," I said sympathetically.

"Life's just one big, slippery banana peel," Howard muttered gloomily. "Back home... Okay. I wasn't any kinda hero, ya know? I didn't really fit in anywhere, I was kinda on the fringes of life. But at least I wasn't being harrassed by nut cases" he glanced up just in time as the waiter leaned over to deliver our lunch, and for one moment Duck and Italian seemed in sympathy "an' reality didn't keep changin' on me. I don't hardly know what's real anymore."

"Fish."

"What?"

"Good fish," I repeated. "G'won, eat."

The half bottle of wine we'd ordered was almost empty and I ordered another as the duck quaffed deeply from his glass.

"It's because I don't belong here," the depressed drake muttered. "None of this stuff ever happened back on my own world. Back there I was nobody an' I *liked* it that way. Nobody stared at me and said —"

"W-Why, you're a duck!" the wine steward blurted as he spilled a good amount of the new bottle of wine on the table cloth. I winced, Howard scowled, and the shaken man went away, muttering and looking back.

"Howard, what's the thing you want most?"

"The old world, my world, the world of decent feathered folk. I wanna go home." Was that a tear I saw in his eye? I had tears in mine. Lifting my wine glass, I forced a smile.

"Then let's have a toast, Howard. To the day you go home."

The duck drank deep.

And that *was* a tear in his eye.

Claude Starkowitz

Son of Satan

You've heard the old saying: "With friends like these, who needs enemies?"

Well, not only has our harried hero *Howard the Duck* been accosted and assaulted by his fearsome foes time and again... he's also had to suffer because of those we would call his friends.

Take, for example, Howard's maiden voyage to Earth: If the Cosmic Axis had shifted for you or me we'd probably find ourselves in the Tape Boutique at the local shopping mall. Not our fowl! Y'see, snatched from Duckworld, Howard was dropped into the midst of the Florida Everglades... smack in the middle of a 'war of the worlds' between the forces of, what else?, good and evil.

A Fond Look At Fowl Friends

BY BILL MANTLO

Man-Thing

Good was represented by such luminaries as *Dakimh the Sorcerer*, the empath-opsychic *Jennifer Kale*, the klutzy *Korrek the Barbarian*, the macabre *Man-Thing* and, much to his distress, *Howard* himself! Evil, assembled under the banner of the *Overmaster*, was just too nasty to enumerate. Now, if you had friends like the abovementioned, you'd expect them to use their powers to get you the heck out of there, wouldn't you? Not Howard's newfound pals! They expected him to stay and, what's more, to fight!

So fight Howard did and, the fighting done, Dakimh then announced a further task for the comrades... to reshift the Cosmic Axis back to its proper position in time and space. Nice work if you can get it, but all Howard got was a fast fall from the Stepping Stones of Oblivion... a plunge that ended in a vacant lot in, of all places, Cleveland, USA!

So far, as you can see, having friends hadn't done a heckuva lot for our Howard. But friendless, having no one to turn to in a strange land inhabited by hairless apes who exhibited a marked intolerance toward talking ducks, didn't seem much better. Howard chose to deal

Santa Claus

forcefully with adversity... by commiting suicide.

Even that was not to be, however. Inside the tower from which Howard planned to hurl his body into space was one *Beverly Switzler*, a female hairless ape whose costume exposed as much of her hairlessness as possible under the Comics Code. Freeing her from the sinister sorcerer *Pro Rata*, Howard decided to keep company with the curvaceous damsel... a decision that began immediately to get him into trouble. After all, you don't place a duck beside a gal like Bev and expect people not to notice! Notice they did... starting with a

Dakimh the Sorcerer

foul-breathed old hag called the *Kidney Lady* whose torment of our dazed drake led directly to his encounter with Bev's boyfriend (sort of) *Arthur Winslow*, security guard and sometime author of unpublished science fiction who had the misfortune to come into contact with a tuber of unearthly origin — thus beginning his symbiotic relationship with the deadly *Space Turnip!*

Living with Bev, Howard also met *Paul Same*, an artist who roamed the night in a somnabulistic state, terrorizing critics and crooks alike as the wondrous *Winky-Man!* Then there was *Patty* and her *Cookie Monster*, a pastry pair sure to get a rise out of Howard, whom he would never have met unless

Jennifer Kale

Winda Wester

pressures — and when our canard's collapse came, it came big! A bus-ride to nightmare landed Howard in the Saurbraten County Mental Facility where a friendship with *Winda Wester* exposed Howard to demonic possession, exorcism, the *Son of Satan*, the cosmic *Kiss*, nasty *Nurse Barbara*, Rev. Yuc yet again... and *Adolph Hitler*. Yeah, things happened when Winda was around.

Reunited with Bev, Howard thought things might be normal for awhile. But Bev and Winda got themselves borne off on a flying carpet to the sunny arabian land of Bagmom and, determined to

Sunquist

he had regretted parting with Bev and gone to look for her... a search that also brought him into contact with the *Reverend Moon June Yuc* and his *Yuccies*, and *Heathcliff*, the world's weirdest real estate agent. And, tangentially, it was his association with Bev that got Howard involved in the 1976 Presidential race as a candidate for the All-Night Party — a position that saw him nearly assassinated, slandered, pilloried by the press, and attacked by the awesome *Le Beaver!*

Neither man nor mallard could long retain sanity in the face of such political

Korrek the Barbarian

help, Howard wound up supporting a palace revolution to free his ladyfriends.

Leaving Bagmom behind didn't prove to be any better. A melodic madman called *Doctor Bong* whisked our duo from the deck of the S.S. Damned to his island. There Bong proposed marriage to Bev and gave Howard "Neez"... a Preparation-H — for *H*uman — that transformed Howard into a member of that very species he so detested. Separated from Bev, Howard the Duck became Howard the hairless ape!

But, before long he was back to his harried self, employed by Bev's uncle

Lee Switzler as a dishwasher in a New York greasy spoon until a coworker accidentally combined a foaming cleanser with the rays of a microwave oven and became *Sudd, the Scrubbing Bubble that Walked Like a Man* — a one-man morality campaign that served to set the stage for the advent of the sinister *Soofi* and her odious organization, Save Our Offspring From Indecency.

Friends.

No sooner had Lee Switzler left for Cleveland than Dakimh, Korrek, Jennifer and the Man-Thing showed up again, this time to embroil Howard in a galactic war against the bestial *Bzzk' Joh* and his

Winky-Man

Imperium Emporium based aboard that deadliest of retail dealerships... the Death-Store!

Back on Earth, the universe saved, Howard found that life *without* friends could be just as depressing as life *with* them, so he met the incoming S.S. Damned and was reunited with Winda and Paul Same who had fallen head-over-heels for a sexy socialite named *Iris Raritan*. Iris was a friend in the pattern already laid down above. Her desire for excitement led her to invite the *Ringmaster* and his *Circus of Crime* to one of

Lee Switzler

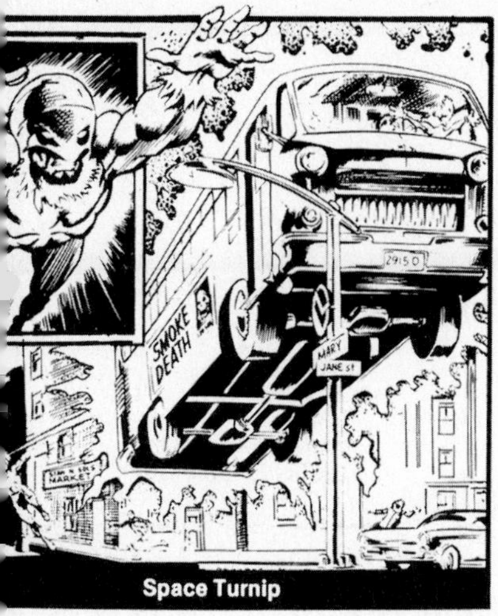
SMOKE DEATH
MARY JANE ST
Space Turnip

her parties — an invitation that, in turn, led to Howard's kidnapping as a major attraction and to the shooting of Paul Same and his subsequent lapse into a coma.

And, if that weren't enough, no sooner had Howard gotten Paul to a hospital when Dr. Bong reappeared to challenge Howard to a duel to the death, winner take all of Beverly's affections. It seems, despite her marriage to Bong, Bev still loved Howard. Armed as *Iron Duck* by Lee Switzler's mechanic friend *Claude Starkowitz,* a rattle-brained Vietnam vet who thought himself related to industrialist Tony Stark and chief armorer to Iron Man, Howard went into battle against Bong... and *won* — with help from Bev.

It was with a little help from his friends our Howard returned to Cleveland and took a job with Lee Switzler's To Hack and Back Taxi Company, driving around the "City of Light" into one case of insanity after another, becoming more and more enmeshed in this "World he never made," even to the point of being willing to befriend Claude Starkowitz's daughter *Carol* in order to save the world and Christmas from the ravages of that nuclear nutcase *Greedy Killerwatt.* What had come over our Howard? Was he giving up, accepting the status quo, losing his sarcasm and cynicism in the face of financial security and the concept of three square meals a day?

Not on your life!

Despite the love of his friends and the relative normalcy of the life he'd begun to forge for himself in Cleveland, Howard never lost sight of his roots. He longed to return to Duckworld.

And then, during their capture by the forces of B.E.S.T. —**B**ozoes **E**agerly **S**erving **T**yrants — when, Howard discovered that Winda Webster's mental powers could be employed to reshift the Cosmic Axis and send him home... well, all at once everything changed.

Howard once again had an alternative. It was no longer Earth or nothing. With Winda's help, he could escape this world he never made and revisit one he had helped to create. He would be free of both friends and foes at last!

But what about Bev? Sure, she'd gotten him into one perilous predicament after another. Sure she'd been married to Dr. Bong, leaving Howard to wander the world alone. Sure he'd had to lay his life on the line time and time again to win her back. But...

Well, it'd been worth it. Bev was still the best there was, as companion and lover. A bond had grown up between damsel and duck that just couldn't be forgotten or denied. Did Howard now have to choose between home and his love for Bev?

No, because Bev was a woman who truly loved her fowl. She knew what Howard had gone through on Earth, and she knew his delicate hold on sanity might go at any minute unless he could once again stand amidst those of his own kind on Duckworld.

Bev had to make a decision, and she decided on the basis of what was best for Howard. And best for her, too, because she was determined that their relationship last.

That's friendship.

That's love.

That's what it's all about. END

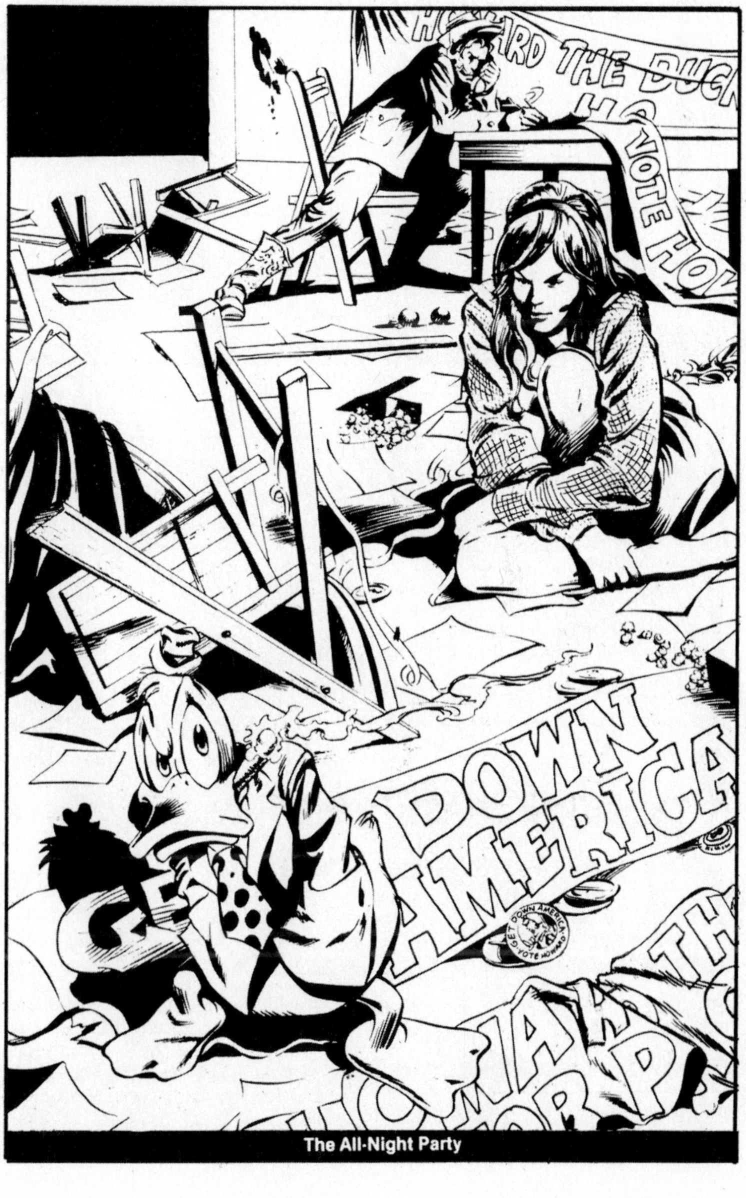
DOWN
AMERICA
The All-Night Party

ONCE IN A LIFETIME ISSUE!

DUCKWORLD!

or, BACK TO THE EGG!

BY Bill Mantlo, Michael Golden, Bob McLeod

PLUS! **A New Feature:**

STREET PEEPLE

It's San Francisco, mid 1960's and reality ain't ever *been* so real!

BY Lynn Graeme & Ned Sonntag

In **HOWARD THE DUCK**

#6

On Sale Late May

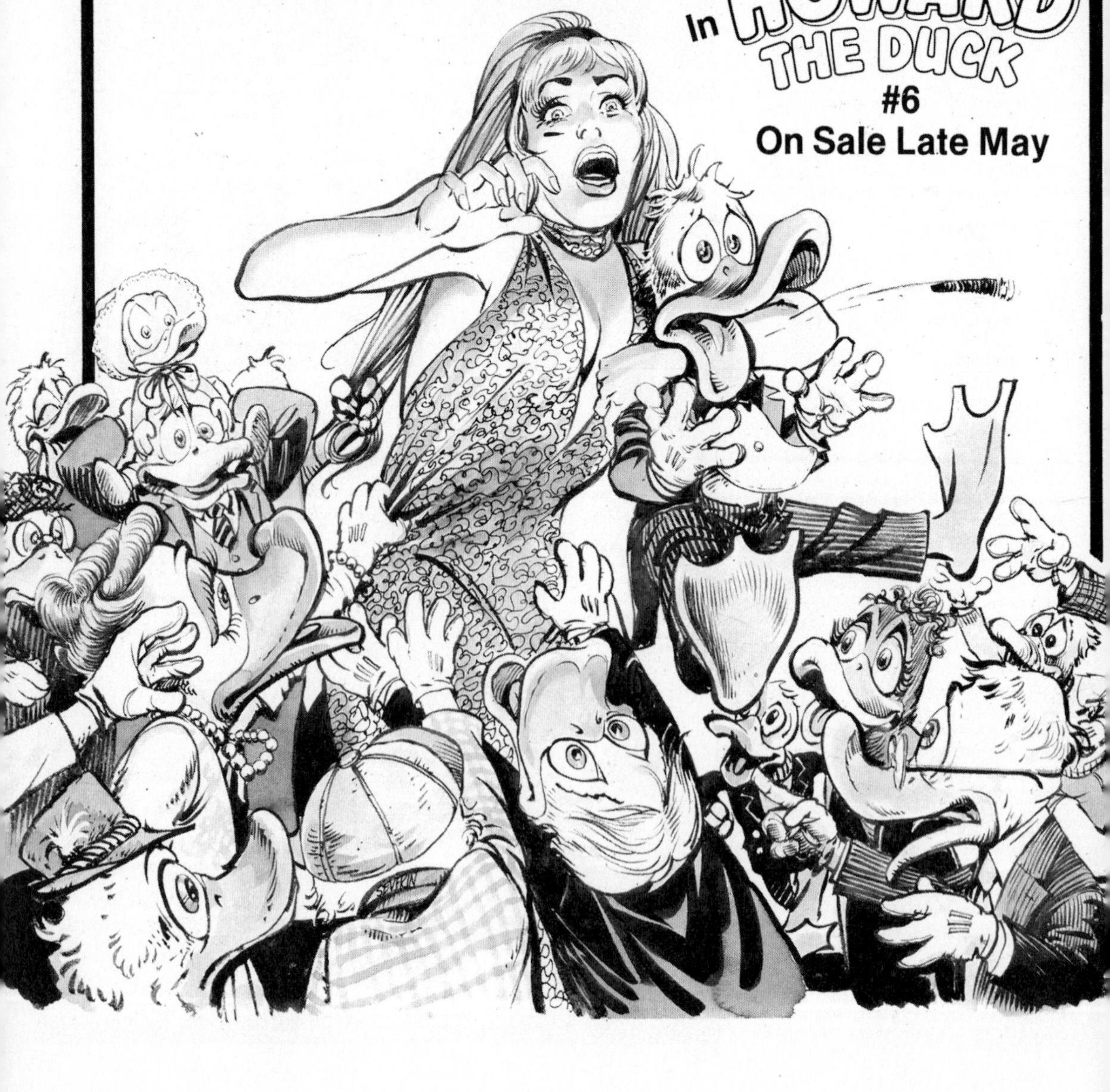

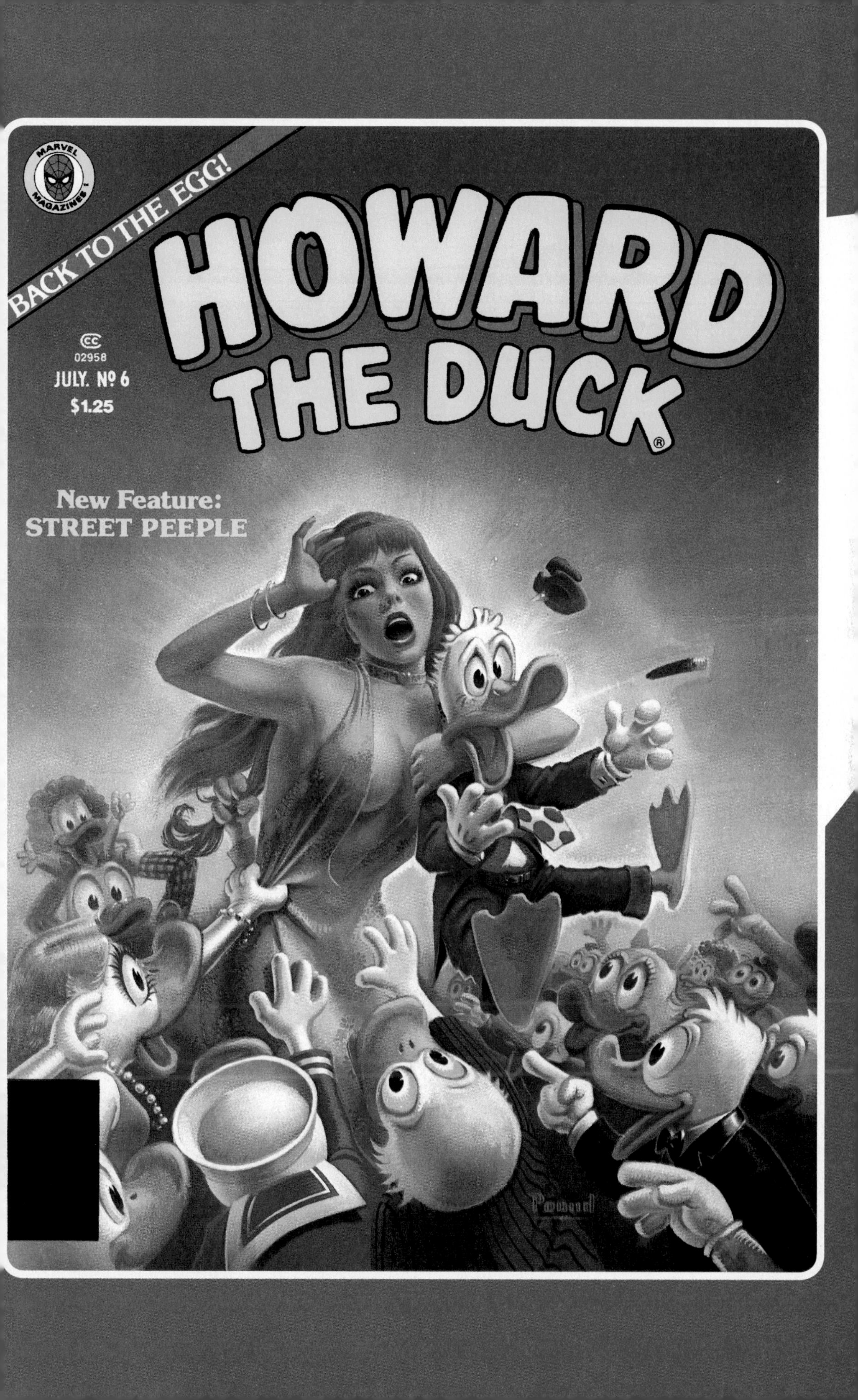
MARVEL MAGAZINES
BACK TO THE EGG!
HOWARD THE DUCK
02958
JULY. № 6
$1.25
New Feature:
STREET PEEPLE

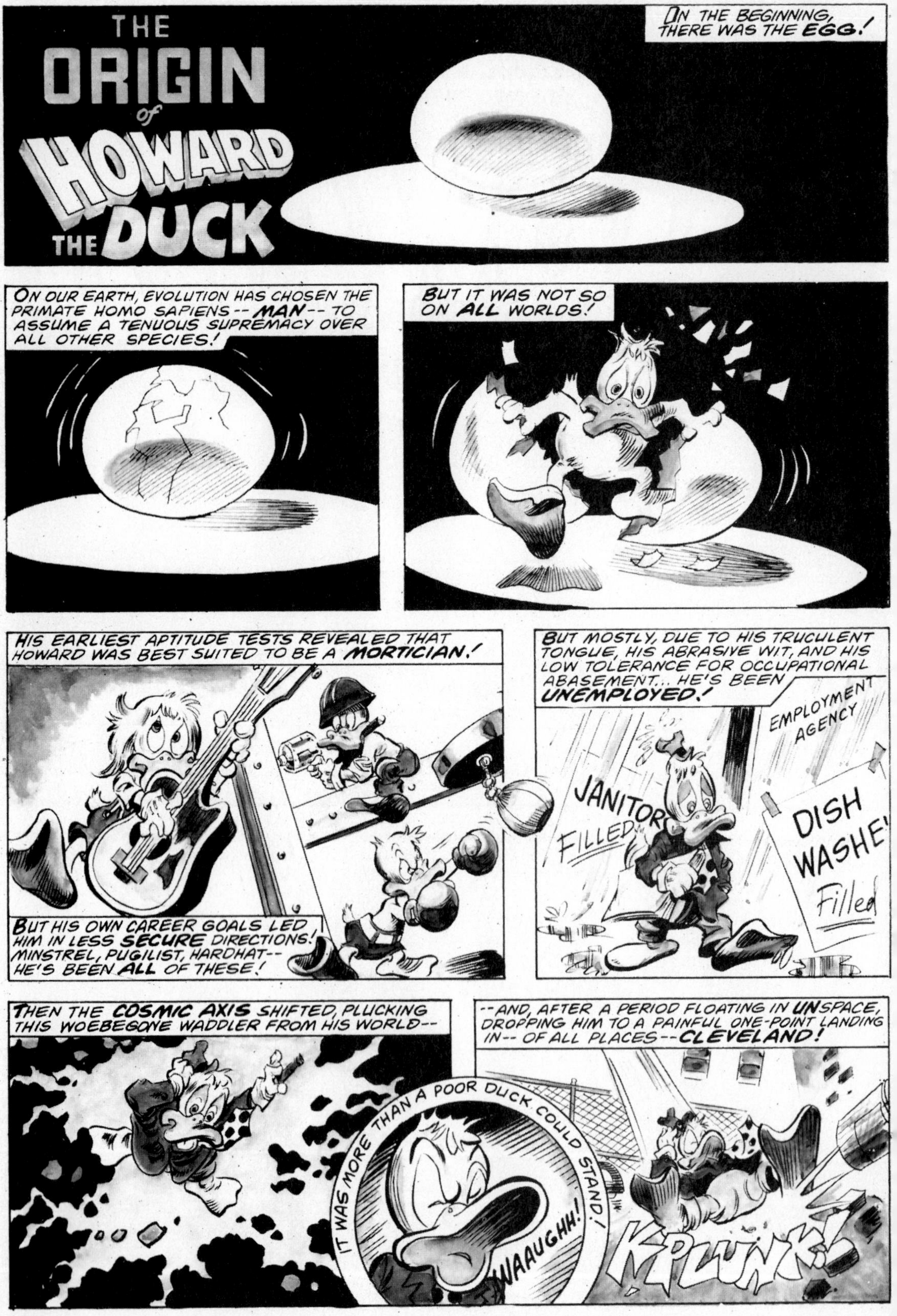
THE ORIGIN of HOWARD THE DUCK
IN THE BEGINNING, THERE WAS THE EGG!
ON OUR EARTH, EVOLUTION HAS CHOSEN THE PRIMATE HOMO SAPIENS -- MAN -- TO ASSUME A TENUOUS SUPREMACY OVER ALL OTHER SPECIES!
BUT IT WAS NOT SO ON ALL WORLDS!
HIS EARLIEST APTITUDE TESTS REVEALED THAT HOWARD WAS BEST SUITED TO BE A MORTICIAN!
BUT HIS OWN CAREER GOALS LED HIM IN LESS SECURE DIRECTIONS! MINSTREL, PUGILIST, HARDHAT-- HE'S BEEN ALL OF THESE!
BUT MOSTLY, DUE TO HIS TRUCULENT TONGUE, HIS ABRASIVE WIT, AND HIS LOW TOLERANCE FOR OCCUPATIONAL ABASEMENT... HE'S BEEN UNEMPLOYED!
EMPLOYMENT AGENCY
JANITOR
FILLED
DISH WASHE
Filled
THEN THE COSMIC AXIS SHIFTED, PLUCKING THIS WOEBEGONE WADDLER FROM HIS WORLD--
--AND, AFTER A PERIOD FLOATING IN UNSPACE, DROPPING HIM TO A PAINFUL ONE-POINT LANDING IN-- OF ALL PLACES--CLEVELAND!
IT WAS MORE THAN A POOR DUCK COULD STAND!
WAAUGHH!
K-PLUNK!

STAN LEE Presents:

HOWARD THE DUCK

Volume 1 No. 6   **July 1980**

JIM SHOOTER Editor-in-Chief • **LYNN GRAEME** Editor • **RALPH MACCIO** Associate Editor
MARK GRUENWALD Insulting Editor • **MILT SCHIFFMAN** V.P. Production
NORA MACLIN Design Director • **MICHAEL HIGGINS** Design Assistant • **JIM NOVAK, NED SONNTAG**
Letterers • **HELLEN KATZ, ELIOT BROWN, ROB CAROSELLA, LINDA FLORIO,**
DANNY CRESPI, ED NORTON, EDUARD LILINSHTEIN • Sensational Staff • **JOHN POUND** Cover

SPECIAL THANKS TO MARK GRUENWALD, WITHOUT WHOSE RESEARCHES INTO THE WORKS
OF TRUMAN CAPOULTRY, THIS STORY COULD NOT HAVE BEEN WRITTEN!

CONTENTS

EDITORIAL

*I despise the overuse of superlatives, adjectives, and adverbs. I once **ordered** my employer not to use those parts of speech for a month (we ran a theatre company, and meaningless hyperbole was the accepted style of communicating information about everything from a new play to the arrival of a new file clerk). So, **knowing** that I'm a softly spoken, modestly demeanored, **un**-exaggerating sort of person, you'll realize that I'm **really** enthusiastic when I say that this issue of HOWARD THE DUCK, this story, DUCKWORLD, is nothing short of SENSATIONAL, MOVING, EXCITING, SUPERLATIVE AND, BY GOLLY, A NEW HOWARD CLASSIC because I really don't like a lot of meaningless hype, and I wouldn't say it if I didn't believe it to be true, right?*

Lynn

NOTE: We are aware that Howard and Beverly are dressed differently when they land on Duckworld than when they left earth. No "No Prizes" will be awarded, no matter what! So back off, ye hungry masses yearning for glory! Tune in to next issue's editorial for the behind the scenes story.

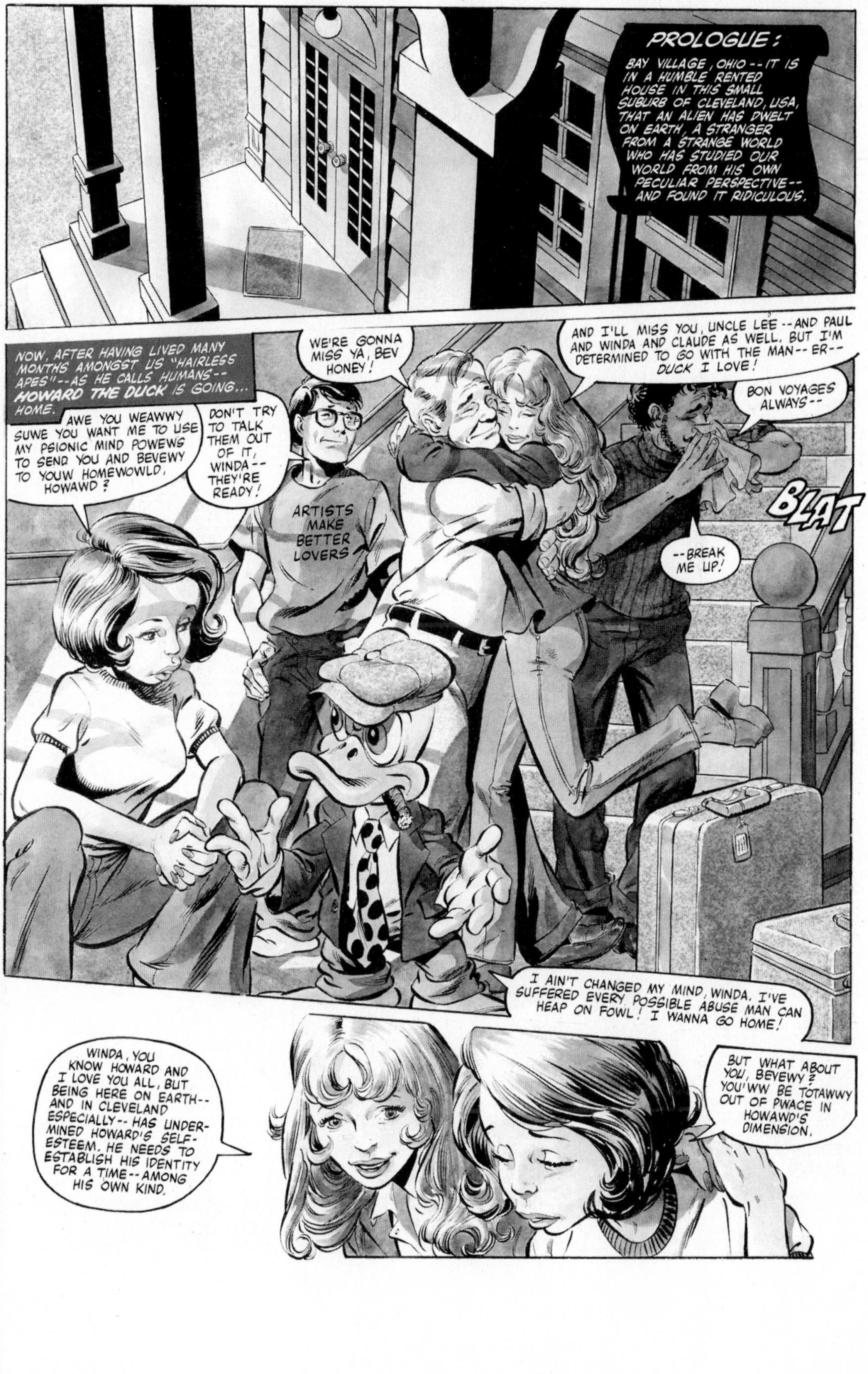
PROLOGUE:
BAY VILLAGE, OHIO -- IT IS IN A HUMBLE RENTED HOUSE IN THIS SMALL SUBURB OF CLEVELAND, USA, THAT AN ALIEN HAS DWELT ON EARTH, A STRANGER FROM A STRANGE WORLD WHO HAS STUDIED OUR WORLD FROM HIS OWN PECULIAR PERSPECTIVE -- AND FOUND IT RIDICULOUS.
NOW, AFTER HAVING LIVED MANY MONTHS AMONGST US "HAIRLESS APES" -- AS HE CALLS HUMANS -- HOWARD THE DUCK IS GOING... HOME.
AWE YOU WEAWWY SUWE YOU WANT ME TO USE MY PSIONIC MIND POWEWS TO SEND YOU AND BEVEWY TO YOUW HOMEWOWLD, HOWAWD?
DON'T TRY TO TALK THEM OUT OF IT, WINDA -- THEY'RE READY!
ARTISTS MAKE BETTER LOVERS
WE'RE GONNA MISS YA, BEV HONEY!
AND I'LL MISS YOU, UNCLE LEE -- AND PAUL AND WINDA AND CLAUDE AS WELL. BUT I'M DETERMINED TO GO WITH THE MAN -- ER -- DUCK I LOVE!
BON VOYAGES ALWAYS --
BLAT
-- BREAK ME UP!
I AIN'T CHANGED MY MIND, WINDA. I'VE SUFFERED EVERY POSSIBLE ABUSE MAN CAN HEAP ON FOWL! I WANNA GO HOME!
WINDA, YOU KNOW HOWARD AND I LOVE YOU ALL, BUT BEING HERE ON EARTH -- AND IN CLEVELAND ESPECIALLY -- HAS UNDERMINED HOWARD'S SELF-ESTEEM. HE NEEDS TO ESTABLISH HIS IDENTITY FOR A TIME -- AMONG HIS OWN KIND.
BUT WHAT ABOUT YOU, BEVEWY? YOU'WW BE TOTAWWY OUT OF PWACE IN HOWAWD'S DIMENSION.

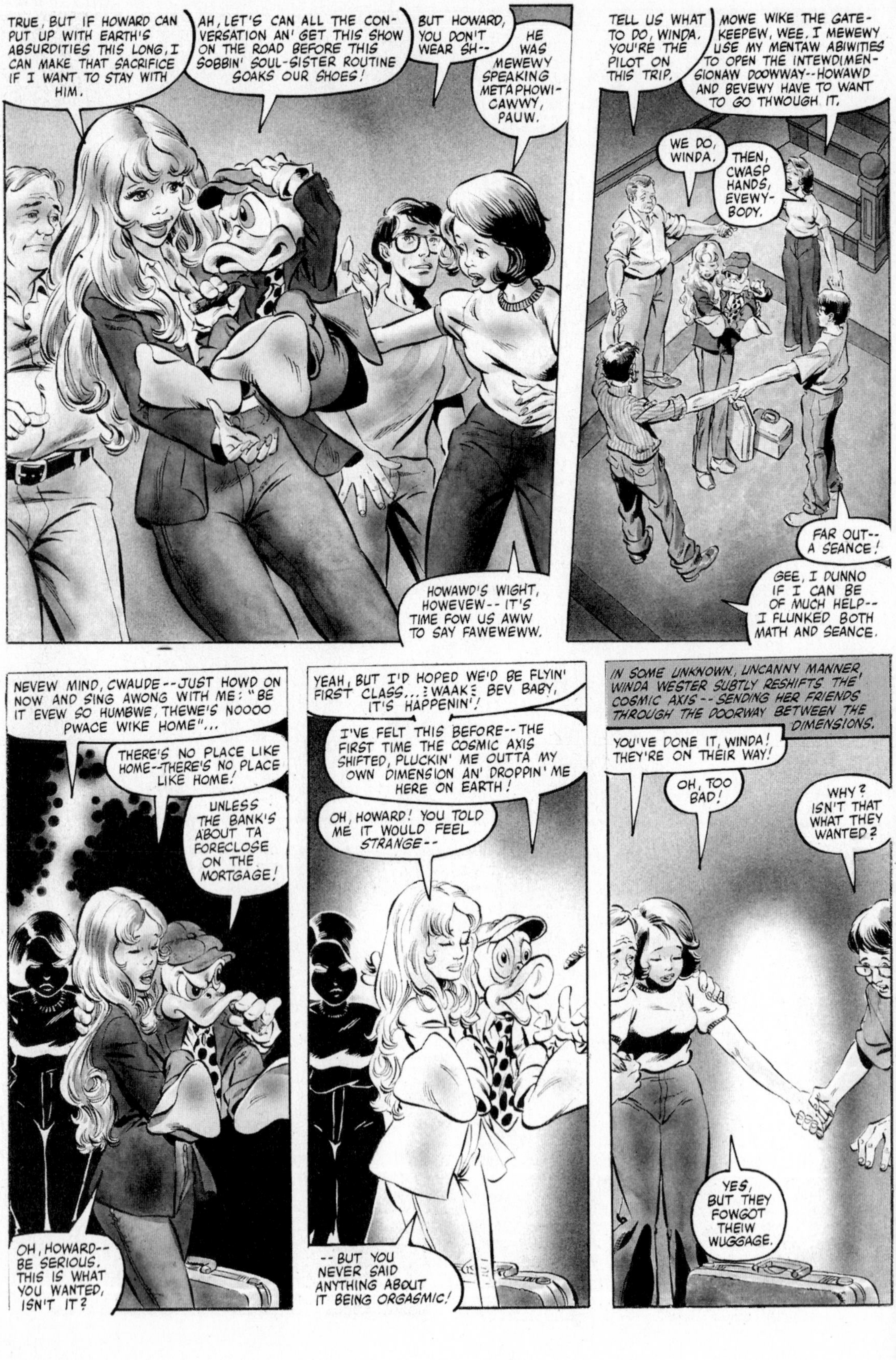

TRUE, BUT IF HOWARD CAN PUT UP WITH EARTH'S ABSURDITIES THIS LONG, I CAN MAKE THAT SACRIFICE IF I WANT TO STAY WITH HIM.
AH, LET'S CAN ALL THE CONVERSATION AN' GET THIS SHOW ON THE ROAD BEFORE THIS SOBBIN' SOUL-SISTER ROUTINE SOAKS OUR SHOES!
BUT HOWARD, YOU DON'T WEAR SH--
HE WAS MEWEWY SPEAKING METAPHOWICAWWY, PAUW.
HOWAWD'S WIGHT, HOWEVEW-- IT'S TIME FOW US AWW TO SAY FAWEWEWW.
TELL US WHAT TO DO, WINDA. YOU'RE THE PILOT ON THIS TRIP.
MOWE WIKE THE GATEKEEPEW, WEE. I MEWEWY USE MY MENTAW ABIWITIES TO OPEN THE INTEWDIMENSIONAW DOOWWAY--HOWAWD AND BEVEWY HAVE TO WANT TO GO THWOUGH IT.
WE DO, WINDA.
THEN, CWASP HANDS, EVEWYBODY.
FAR OUT-- A SEANCE!
GEE, I DUNNO IF I CAN BE OF MUCH HELP-- I FLUNKED BOTH MATH AND SEANCE.
NEVEW MIND, CWAUDE--JUST HOWD ON NOW AND SING AWONG WITH ME: "BE IT EVEW SO HUMBWE, THEWE'S NOOOO PWACE WIKE HOME"...
THERE'S NO PLACE LIKE HOME--THERE'S NO PLACE LIKE HOME!
UNLESS THE BANK'S ABOUT TA FORECLOSE ON THE MORTGAGE!
OH, HOWARD-- BE SERIOUS. THIS IS WHAT YOU WANTED, ISN'T IT?
YEAH, BUT I'D HOPED WE'D BE FLYIN' FIRST CLASS... WAAK! BEV BABY, IT'S HAPPENIN'!
I'VE FELT THIS BEFORE--THE FIRST TIME THE COSMIC AXIS SHIFTED, PLUCKIN' ME OUTTA MY OWN DIMENSION AN' DROPPIN' ME HERE ON EARTH!
OH, HOWARD! YOU TOLD ME IT WOULD FEEL STRANGE--
--BUT YOU NEVER SAID ANYTHING ABOUT IT BEING ORGASMIC!
IN SOME UNKNOWN, UNCANNY MANNER, WINDA WESTER SUBTLY RESHIFTS THE COSMIC AXIS--SENDING HER FRIENDS THROUGH THE DOORWAY BETWEEN THE DIMENSIONS.
YOU'VE DONE IT, WINDA! THEY'RE ON THEIR WAY!
OH, TOO BAD!
WHY? ISN'T THAT WHAT THEY WANTED?
YES, BUT THEY FOWGOT THEIW WUGGAGE.

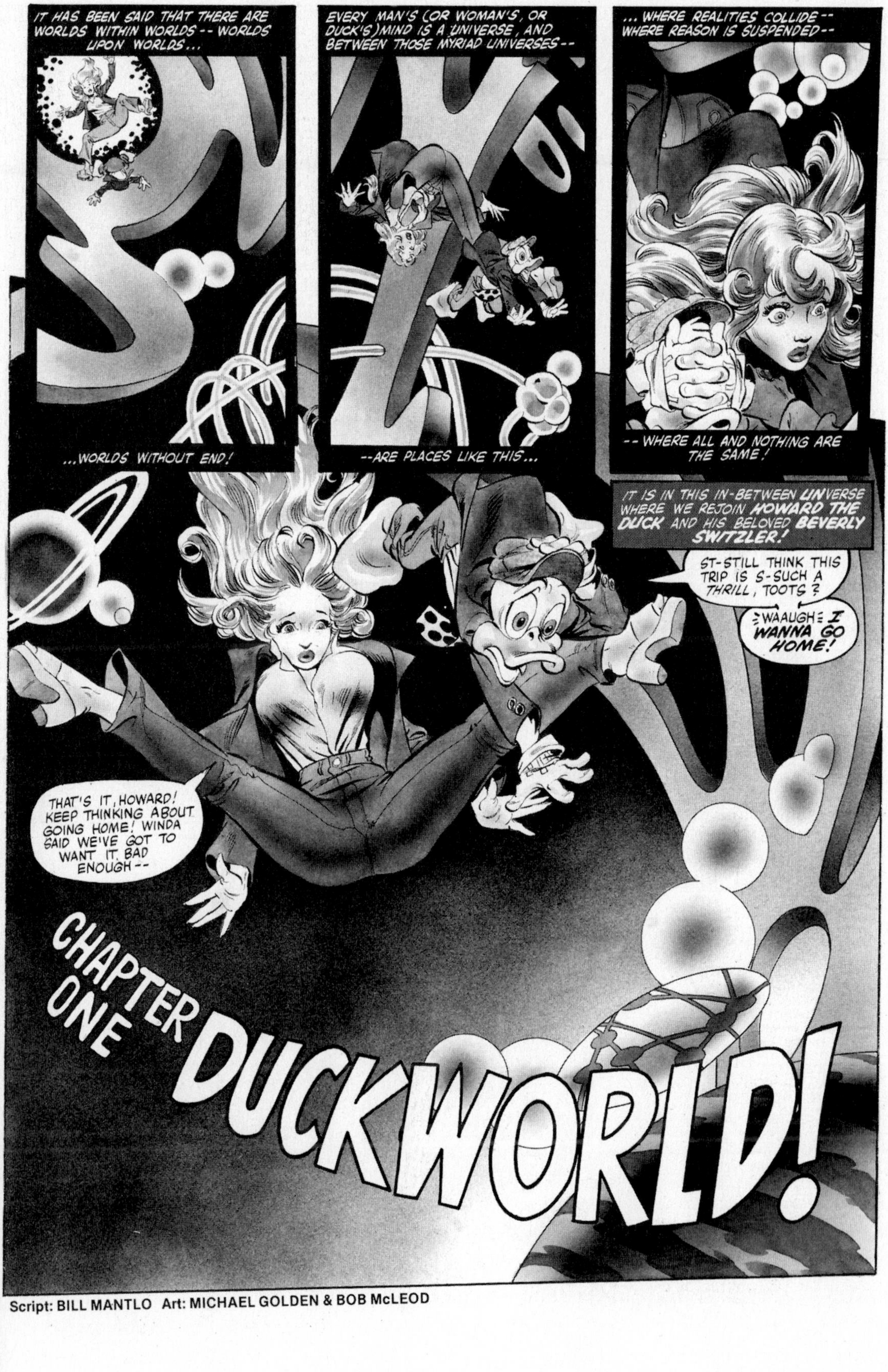

IT HAS BEEN SAID THAT THERE ARE WORLDS WITHIN WORLDS -- WORLDS UPON WORLDS...
...WORLDS WITHOUT END!
EVERY MAN'S (OR WOMAN'S, OR DUCK'S) MIND IS A UNIVERSE, AND BETWEEN THOSE MYRIAD UNIVERSES --
--ARE PLACES LIKE THIS...
... WHERE REALITIES COLLIDE -- WHERE REASON IS SUSPENDED --
-- WHERE ALL AND NOTHING ARE THE SAME!
IT IS IN THIS IN-BETWEEN UNVERSE WHERE WE REJOIN HOWARD THE DUCK AND HIS BELOVED BEVERLY SWITZLER!
ST-STILL THINK THIS TRIP IS S-SUCH A THRILL, TOOTS?
WAAUGH! I WANNA GO HOME!
THAT'S IT, HOWARD! KEEP THINKING ABOUT GOING HOME! WINDA SAID WE'VE GOT TO WANT IT BAD ENOUGH --
CHAPTER ONE
DUCKWORLD!

Script: BILL MANTLO Art: MICHAEL GOLDEN & BOB McLEOD

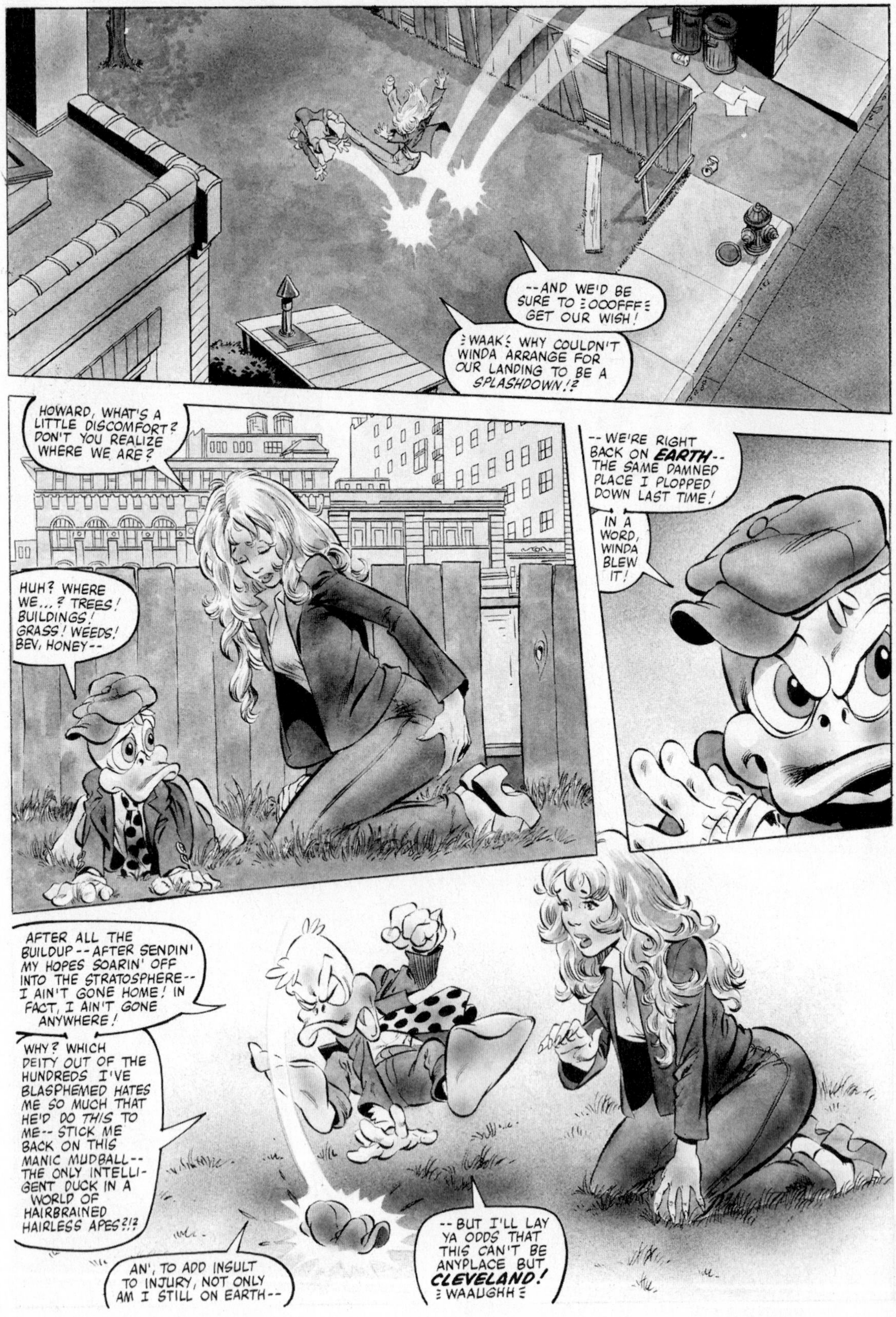
--AND WE'D BE SURE TO OOOFFF GET OUR WISH!
WAAK! WHY COULDN'T WINDA ARRANGE FOR OUR LANDING TO BE A SPLASHDOWN!?
HOWARD, WHAT'S A LITTLE DISCOMFORT? DON'T YOU REALIZE WHERE WE ARE?
HUH? WHERE WE...? TREES! BUILDINGS! GRASS! WEEDS! BEV, HONEY--
--WE'RE RIGHT BACK ON EARTH-- THE SAME DAMNED PLACE I PLOPPED DOWN LAST TIME!
IN A WORD, WINDA BLEW IT!
AFTER ALL THE BUILDUP--AFTER SENDIN' MY HOPES SOARIN' OFF INTO THE STRATOSPHERE--I AIN'T GONE HOME! IN FACT, I AIN'T GONE ANYWHERE!
WHY? WHICH DEITY OUT OF THE HUNDREDS I'VE BLASPHEMED HATES ME SO MUCH THAT HE'D DO THIS TO ME--STICK ME BACK ON THIS MANIC MUDBALL--THE ONLY INTELLIGENT DUCK IN A WORLD OF HAIRBRAINED HAIRLESS APES?!?
AN', TO ADD INSULT TO INJURY, NOT ONLY AM I STILL ON EARTH--
--BUT I'LL LAY YA ODDS THAT THIS CAN'T BE ANYPLACE BUT CLEVELAND! WAAUGHH

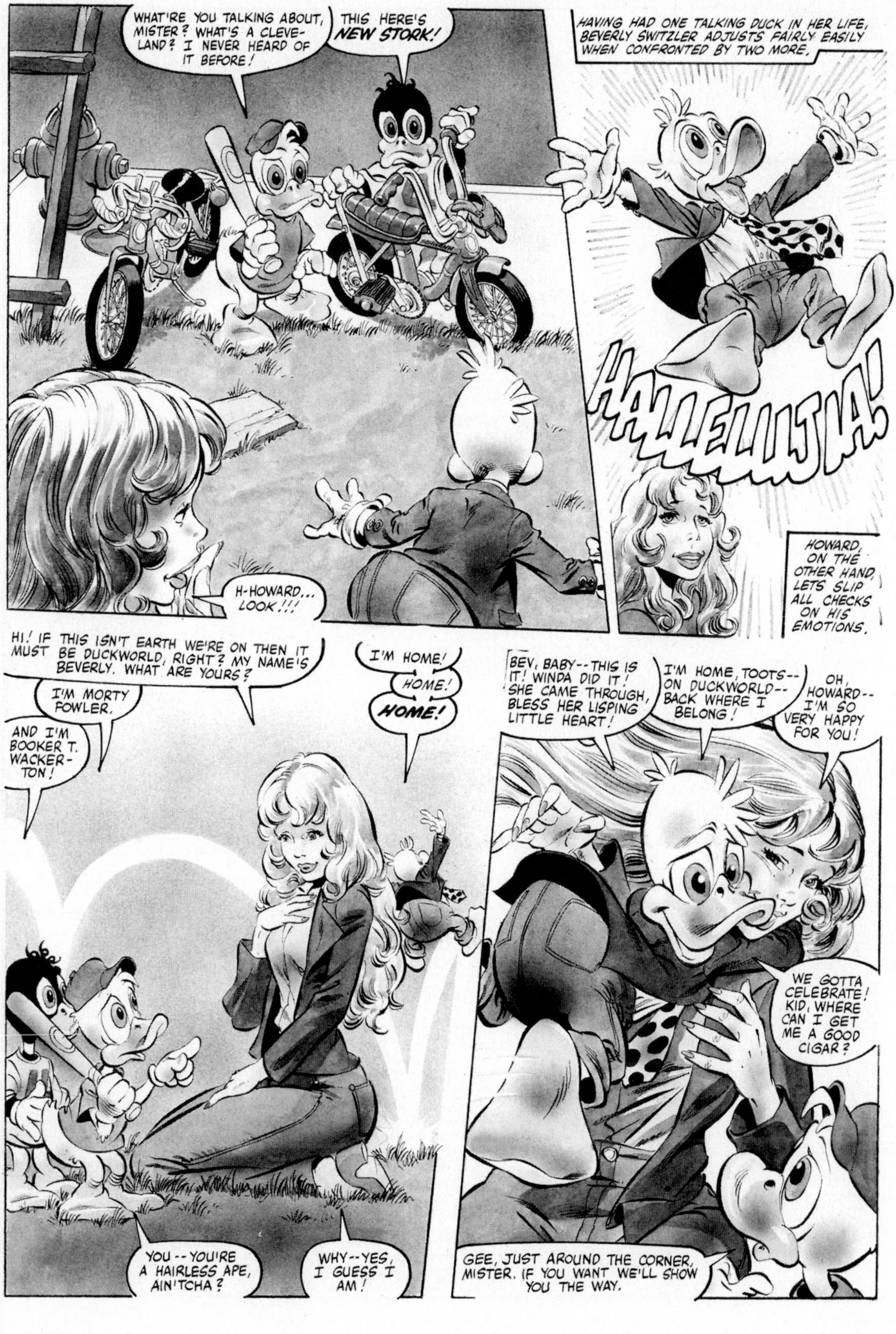

WHAT'RE YOU TALKING ABOUT, MISTER? WHAT'S A CLEVE-LAND? I NEVER HEARD OF IT BEFORE!
THIS HERE'S NEW STORK!
H-HOWARD... LOOK!!!
HAVING HAD ONE TALKING DUCK IN HER LIFE, BEVERLY SWITZLER ADJUSTS FAIRLY EASILY WHEN CONFRONTED BY TWO MORE.
HALLELUJAH!
HOWARD, ON THE OTHER HAND, LETS SLIP ALL CHECKS ON HIS EMOTIONS.
HI! IF THIS ISN'T EARTH WE'RE ON THEN IT MUST BE DUCKWORLD, RIGHT? MY NAME'S BEVERLY. WHAT ARE YOURS?
I'M MORTY FOWLER.
AND I'M BOOKER T. WACKER-TON!
I'M HOME!
HOME!
HOME!
YOU--YOU'RE A HAIRLESS APE, AIN'TCHA?
WHY--YES, I GUESS I AM!
BEV, BABY--THIS IS IT! WINDA DID IT! SHE CAME THROUGH, BLESS HER LISPING LITTLE HEART!
I'M HOME, TOOTS--ON DUCKWORLD--BACK WHERE I BELONG!
OH, HOWARD--I'M SO VERY HAPPY FOR YOU!
WE GOTTA CELEBRATE! KID, WHERE CAN I GET ME A GOOD CIGAR?
GEE, JUST AROUND THE CORNER, MISTER. IF YOU WANT WE'LL SHOW YOU THE WAY.

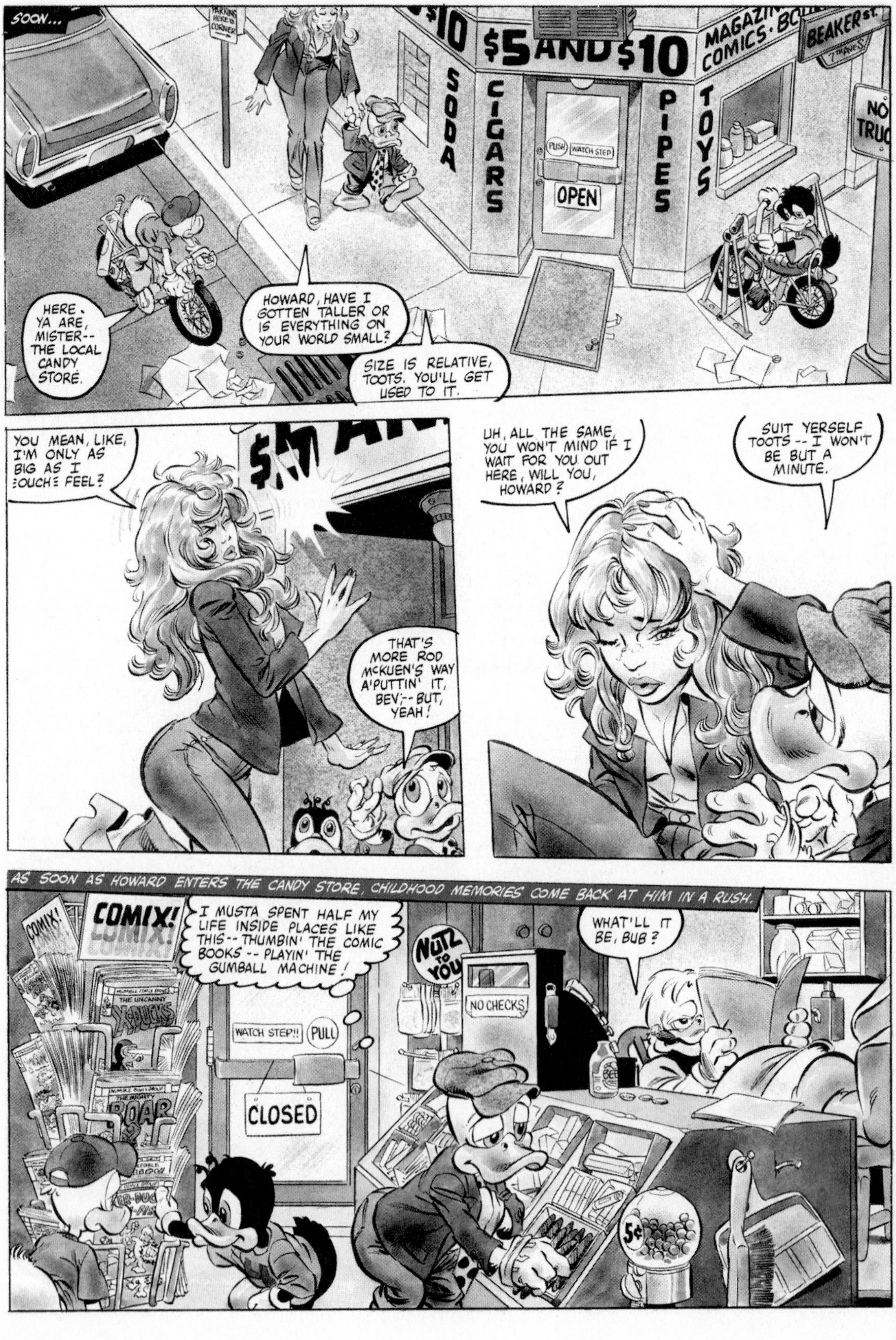
SOON...
$5 AND $10
SODA
CIGARS
PIPES
TOYS
MAGAZINES COMICS
BEAKER ST.
PUSH
WATCH STEP
OPEN
HERE, YA ARE, MISTER-- THE LOCAL CANDY STORE.
HOWARD, HAVE I GOTTEN TALLER OR IS EVERYTHING ON YOUR WORLD SMALL?
SIZE IS RELATIVE, TOOTS. YOU'LL GET USED TO IT.
YOU MEAN, LIKE, I'M ONLY AS BIG AS I ≡OUCH≡ FEEL?
THAT'S MORE ROD McKUEN'S WAY A'PUTTIN' IT, BEV;--BUT, YEAH!
UH, ALL THE SAME, YOU WON'T MIND IF I WAIT FOR YOU OUT HERE, WILL YOU, HOWARD?
SUIT YERSELF TOOTS -- I WON'T BE BUT A MINUTE.
AS SOON AS HOWARD ENTERS THE CANDY STORE, CHILDHOOD MEMORIES COME BACK AT HIM IN A RUSH.
COMIX!
I MUSTA SPENT HALF MY LIFE INSIDE PLACES LIKE THIS--THUMBIN' THE COMIC BOOKS--PLAYIN' THE GUMBALL MACHINE!
NUTZ TO YOU
WHAT'LL IT BE, BUB?
THE UNCANNY X-DUCKS
NO CHECKS
WATCH STEP!!
PULL
CLOSED
5¢

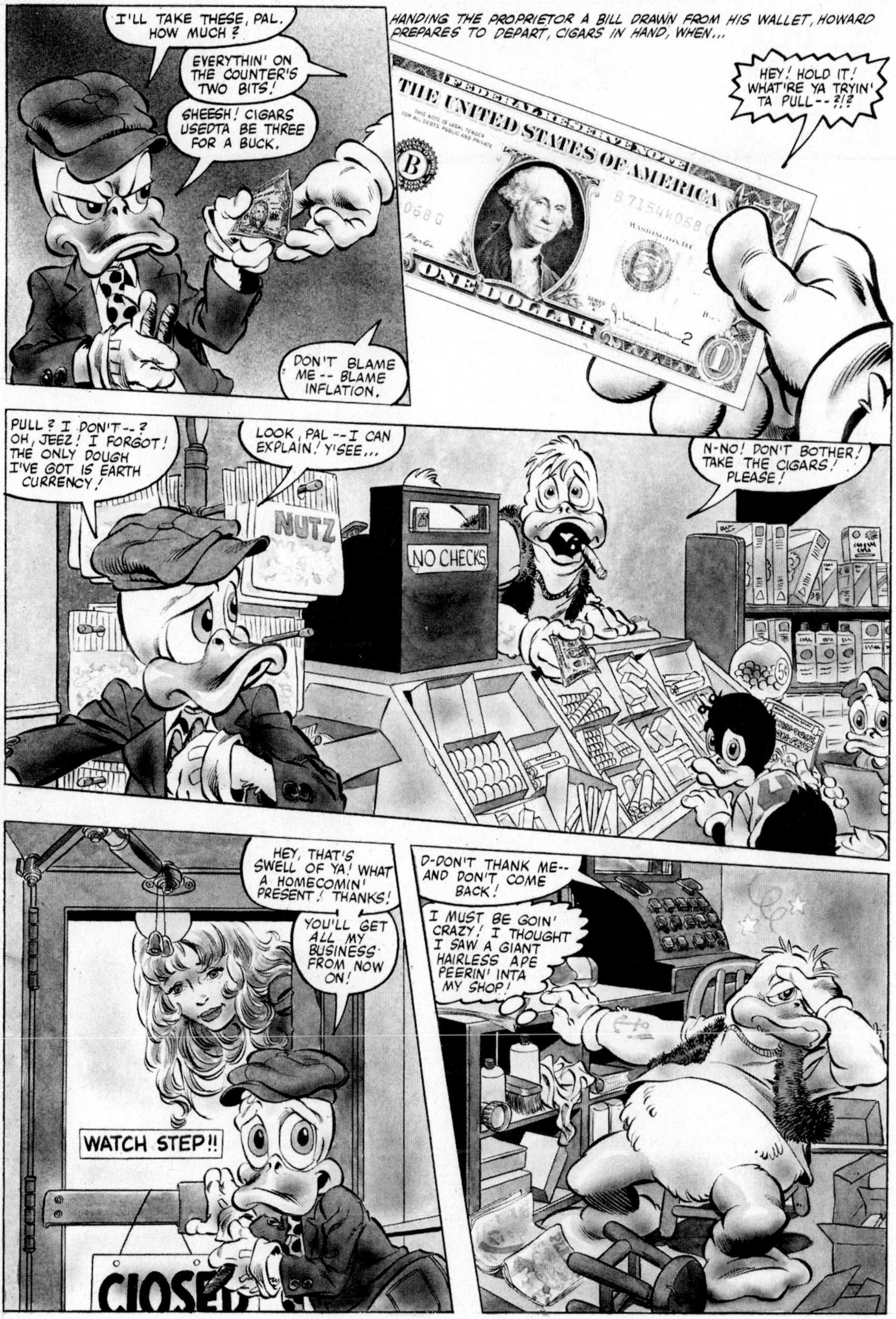
I'LL TAKE THESE, PAL. HOW MUCH?
EVERYTHIN' ON THE COUNTER'S TWO BITS!
SHEESH! CIGARS USEDTA BE THREE FOR A BUCK.
DON'T BLAME ME -- BLAME INFLATION.
HANDING THE PROPRIETOR A BILL DRAWN FROM HIS WALLET, HOWARD PREPARES TO DEPART, CIGARS IN HAND, WHEN...
FEDERAL RESERVE NOTE
THE UNITED STATES OF AMERICA
ONE DOLLAR
HEY! HOLD IT! WHAT'RE YA TRYIN' TA PULL-- ?!?
PULL? I DON'T--? OH, JEEZ! I FORGOT! THE ONLY DOUGH I'VE GOT IS EARTH CURRENCY!
LOOK, PAL--I CAN EXPLAIN! Y'SEE...
N-NO! DON'T BOTHER! TAKE THE CIGARS! PLEASE!
NUTZ
NO CHECKS
HEY, THAT'S SWELL OF YA! WHAT A HOMECOMIN' PRESENT! THANKS!
YOU'LL GET ALL MY BUSINESS FROM NOW ON!
WATCH STEP!!
CLOSED
D-DON'T THANK ME-- AND DON'T COME BACK!
I MUST BE GOIN' CRAZY! I THOUGHT I SAW A GIANT HAIRLESS APE PEERIN' INTA MY SHOP!

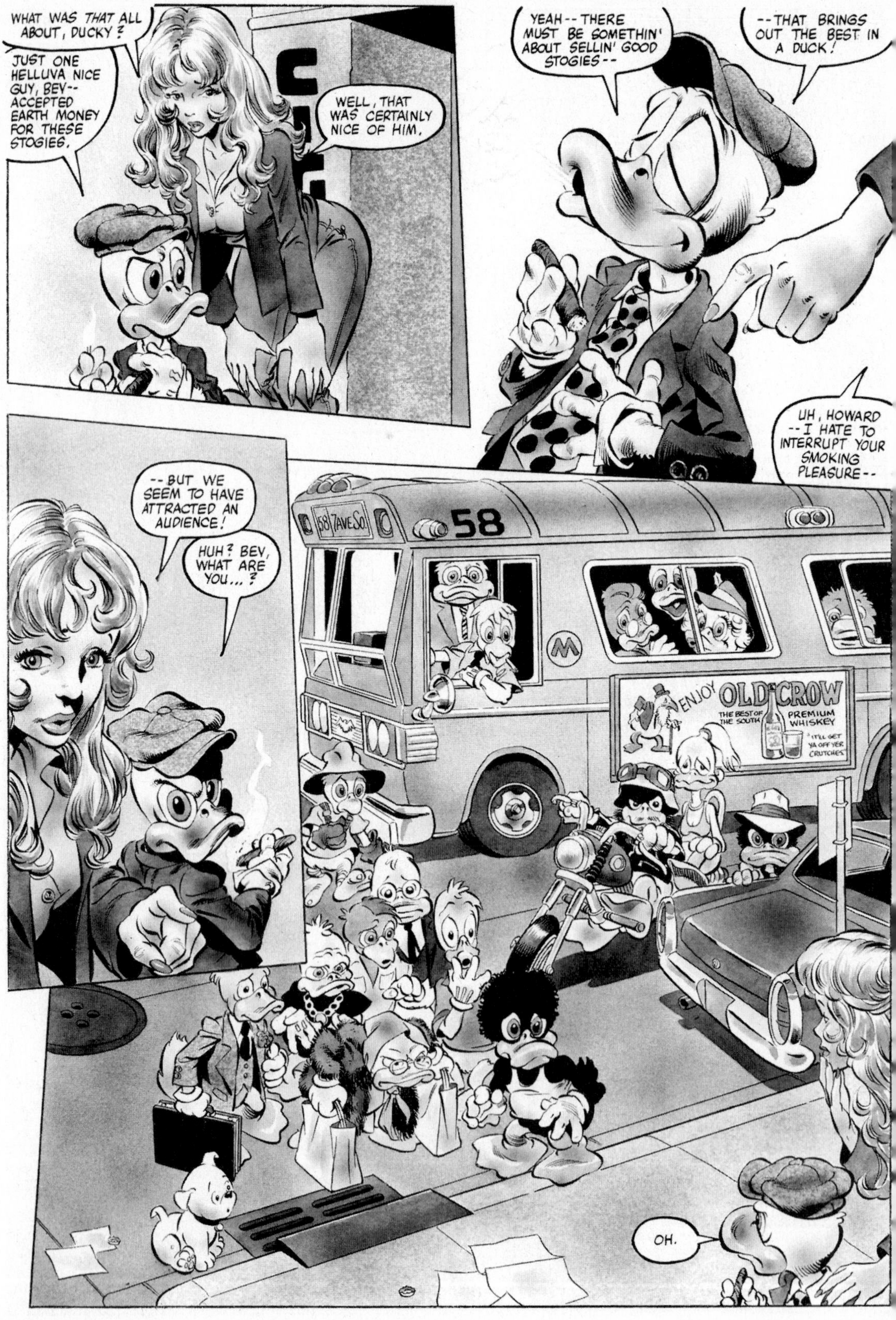
WHAT WAS THAT ALL ABOUT, DUCKY?
JUST ONE HELLUVA NICE GUY, BEV-- ACCEPTED EARTH MONEY FOR THESE STOGIES.
WELL, THAT WAS CERTAINLY NICE OF HIM.
YEAH--THERE MUST BE SOMETHIN' ABOUT SELLIN' GOOD STOGIES--
--THAT BRINGS OUT THE BEST IN A DUCK!
UH, HOWARD --I HATE TO INTERRUPT YOUR SMOKING PLEASURE--
--BUT WE SEEM TO HAVE ATTRACTED AN AUDIENCE!
HUH? BEV, WHAT ARE YOU...?
58 7AVE So.
58
ENJOY OLD CROW
THE BEST OF THE SOUTH
PREMIUM WHISKEY
IT'LL GET YA OFF YER CRUTCHES
OH.

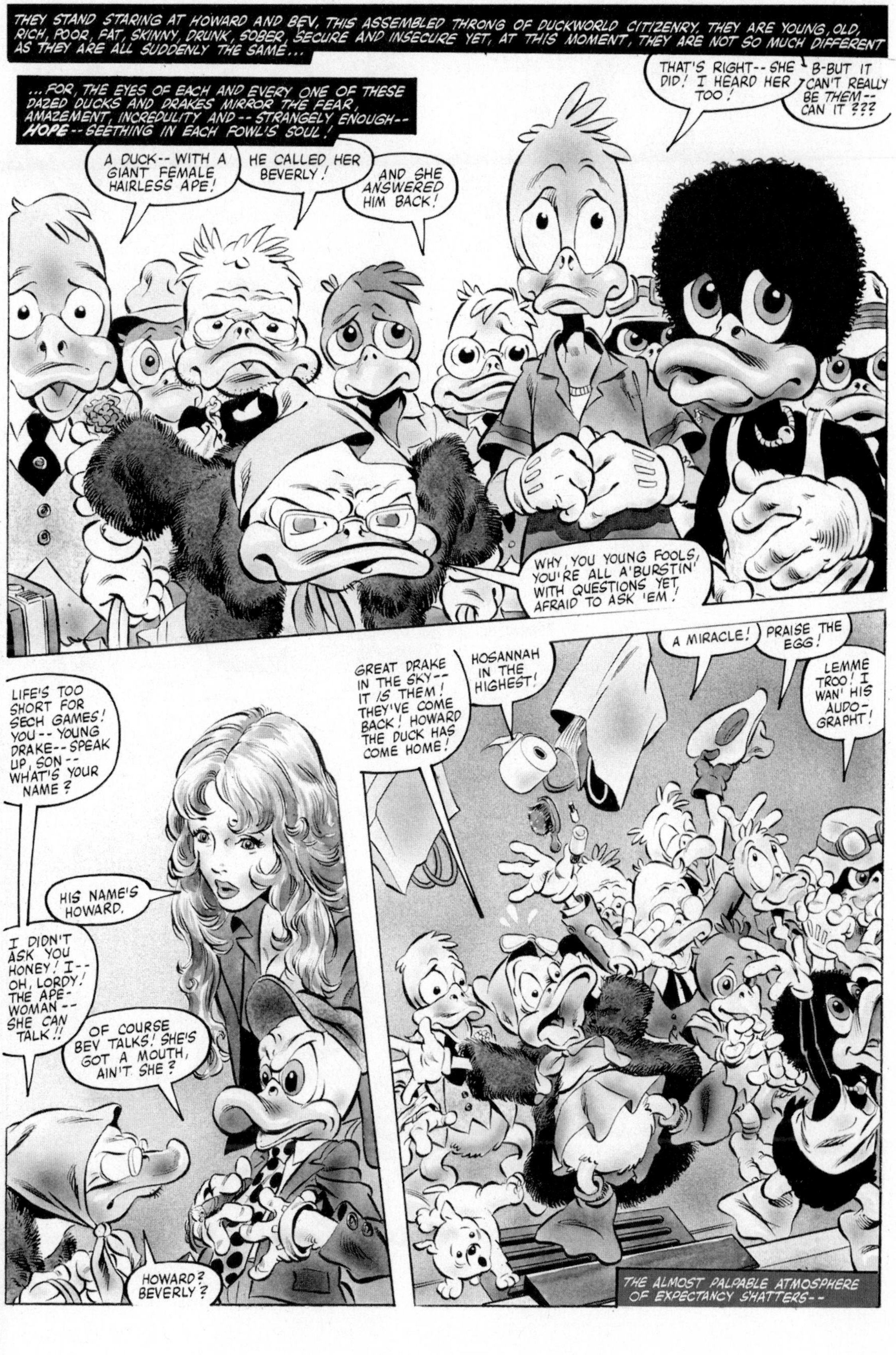
THEY STAND STARING AT HOWARD AND BEV, THIS ASSEMBLED THRONG OF DUCKWORLD CITIZENRY. THEY ARE YOUNG, OLD, RICH, POOR, FAT, SKINNY, DRUNK, SOBER, SECURE AND INSECURE YET, AT THIS MOMENT, THEY ARE NOT SO MUCH DIFFERENT AS THEY ARE ALL SUDDENLY THE SAME...
...FOR, THE EYES OF EACH AND EVERY ONE OF THESE DAZED DUCKS AND DRAKES MIRROR THE FEAR, AMAZEMENT, INCREDULITY AND--STRANGELY ENOUGH--HOPE--SEETHING IN EACH FOWL'S SOUL!
A DUCK--WITH A GIANT FEMALE HAIRLESS APE!
HE CALLED HER BEVERLY!
AND SHE ANSWERED HIM BACK!
THAT'S RIGHT--SHE DID! I HEARD HER TOO!
B-BUT IT CAN'T REALLY BE THEM--CAN IT???
WHY, YOU YOUNG FOOLS, YOU'RE ALL A'BURSTIN' WITH QUESTIONS YET AFRAID TO ASK 'EM!
LIFE'S TOO SHORT FOR SECH GAMES! YOU--YOUNG DRAKE--SPEAK UP, SON--WHAT'S YOUR NAME?
HIS NAME'S HOWARD.
I DIDN'T ASK YOU HONEY! I--OH, LORDY! THE APE-WOMAN--SHE CAN TALK!!
OF COURSE BEV TALKS! SHE'S GOT A MOUTH, AIN'T SHE?
HOWARD? BEVERLY?
GREAT DRAKE IN THE SKY--IT IS THEM! THEY'VE COME BACK! HOWARD THE DUCK HAS COME HOME!
HOSANNAH IN THE HIGHEST!
A MIRACLE!
PRAISE THE EGG!
LEMME TROO! I WAN' HIS AUDO-GRAPHT!
THE ALMOST PALPABLE ATMOSPHERE OF EXPECTANCY SHATTERS--

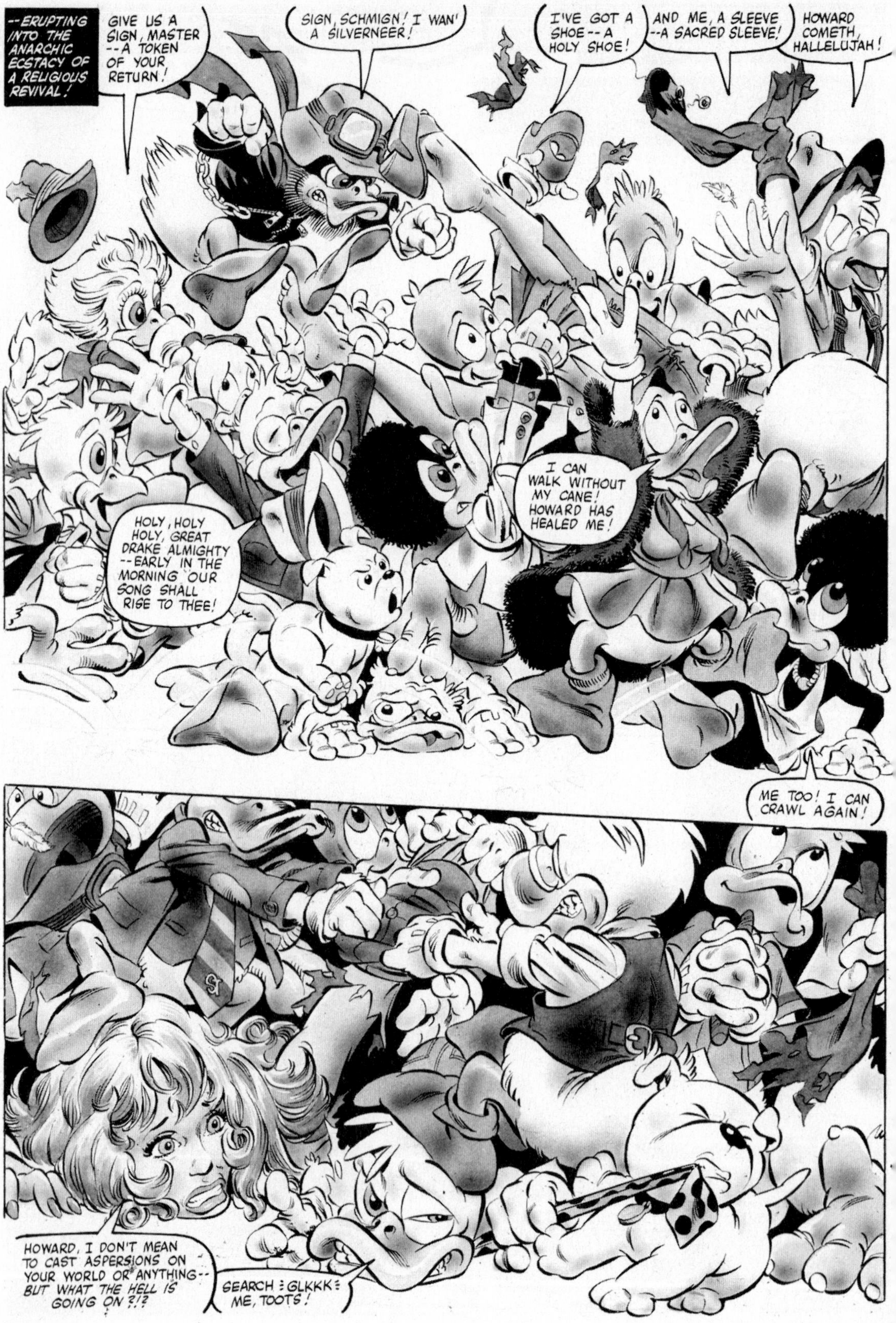
--ERUPTING INTO THE ANARCHIC ECSTACY OF A RELIGIOUS REVIVAL!
GIVE US A SIGN, MASTER --A TOKEN OF YOUR RETURN!
SIGN, SCHMIGN! I WAN' A SILVERNEER!
I'VE GOT A SHOE--A HOLY SHOE!
AND ME, A SLEEVE --A SACRED SLEEVE!
HOWARD COMETH, HALLELUJAH!
I CAN WALK WITHOUT MY CANE! HOWARD HAS HEALED ME!
HOLY, HOLY HOLY, GREAT DRAKE ALMIGHTY --EARLY IN THE MORNING OUR SONG SHALL RISE TO THEE!
ME TOO! I CAN CRAWL AGAIN!
HOWARD, I DON'T MEAN TO CAST ASPERSIONS ON YOUR WORLD OR ANYTHING-- BUT WHAT THE HELL IS GOING ON?!?
SEARCH : GLKKK : ME, TOOTS!

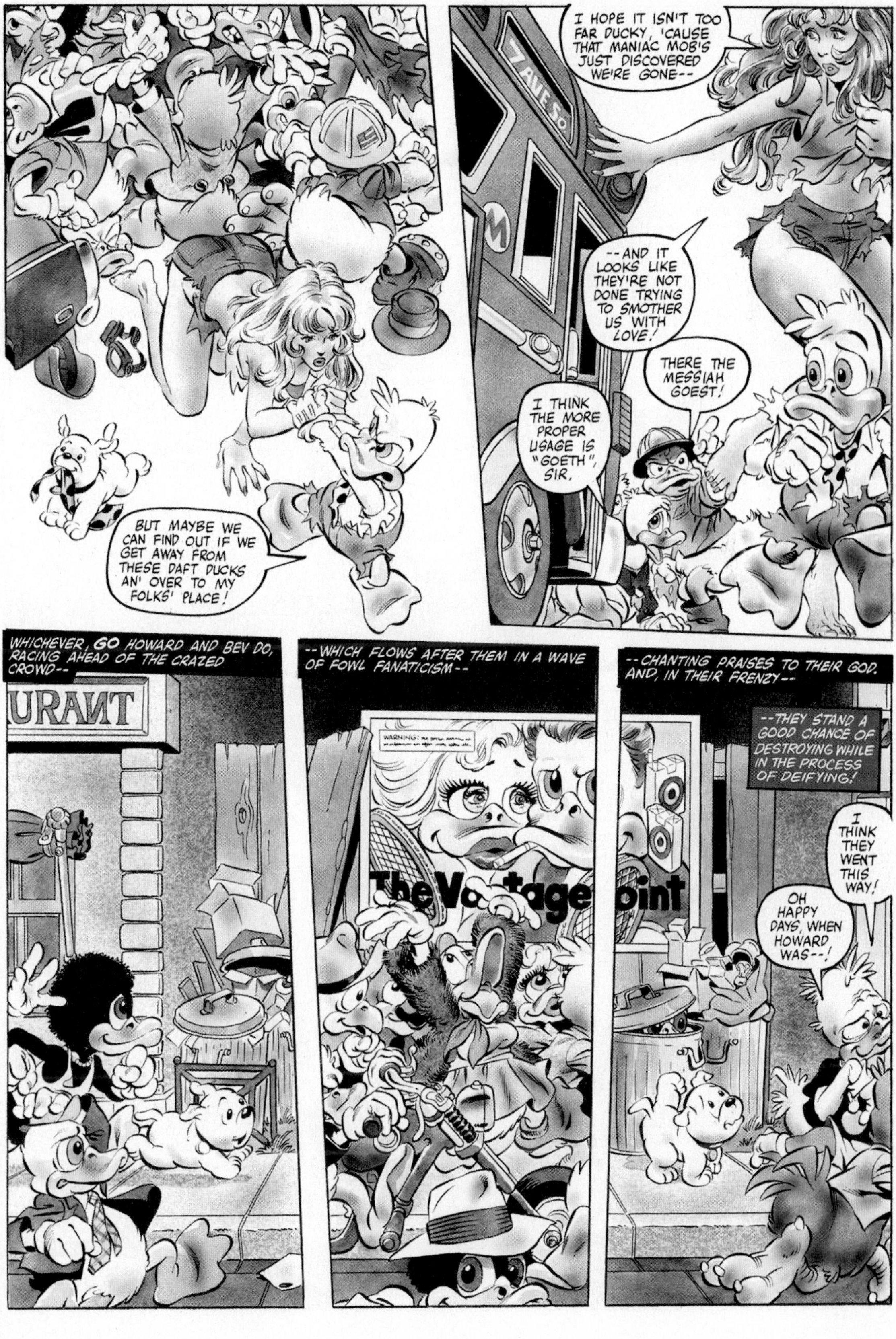
BUT MAYBE WE CAN FIND OUT IF WE GET AWAY FROM THESE DAFT DUCKS AN' OVER TO MY FOLKS' PLACE!
I HOPE IT ISN'T TOO FAR DUCKY, 'CAUSE THAT MANIAC MOB'S JUST DISCOVERED WE'RE GONE--
--AND IT LOOKS LIKE THEY'RE NOT DONE TRYING TO SMOTHER US WITH LOVE!
THERE THE MESSIAH GOEST!
I THINK THE MORE PROPER USAGE IS "GOETH", SIR.
WHICHEVER, GO HOWARD AND BEV DO, RACING AHEAD OF THE CRAZED CROWD--
--WHICH FLOWS AFTER THEM IN A WAVE OF FOWL FANATICISM--
--CHANTING PRAISES TO THEIR GOD. AND, IN THEIR FRENZY--
--THEY STAND A GOOD CHANCE OF DESTROYING WHILE IN THE PROCESS OF DEIFYING!
I THINK THEY WENT THIS WAY!
OH HAPPY DAYS, WHEN HOWARD WAS--!

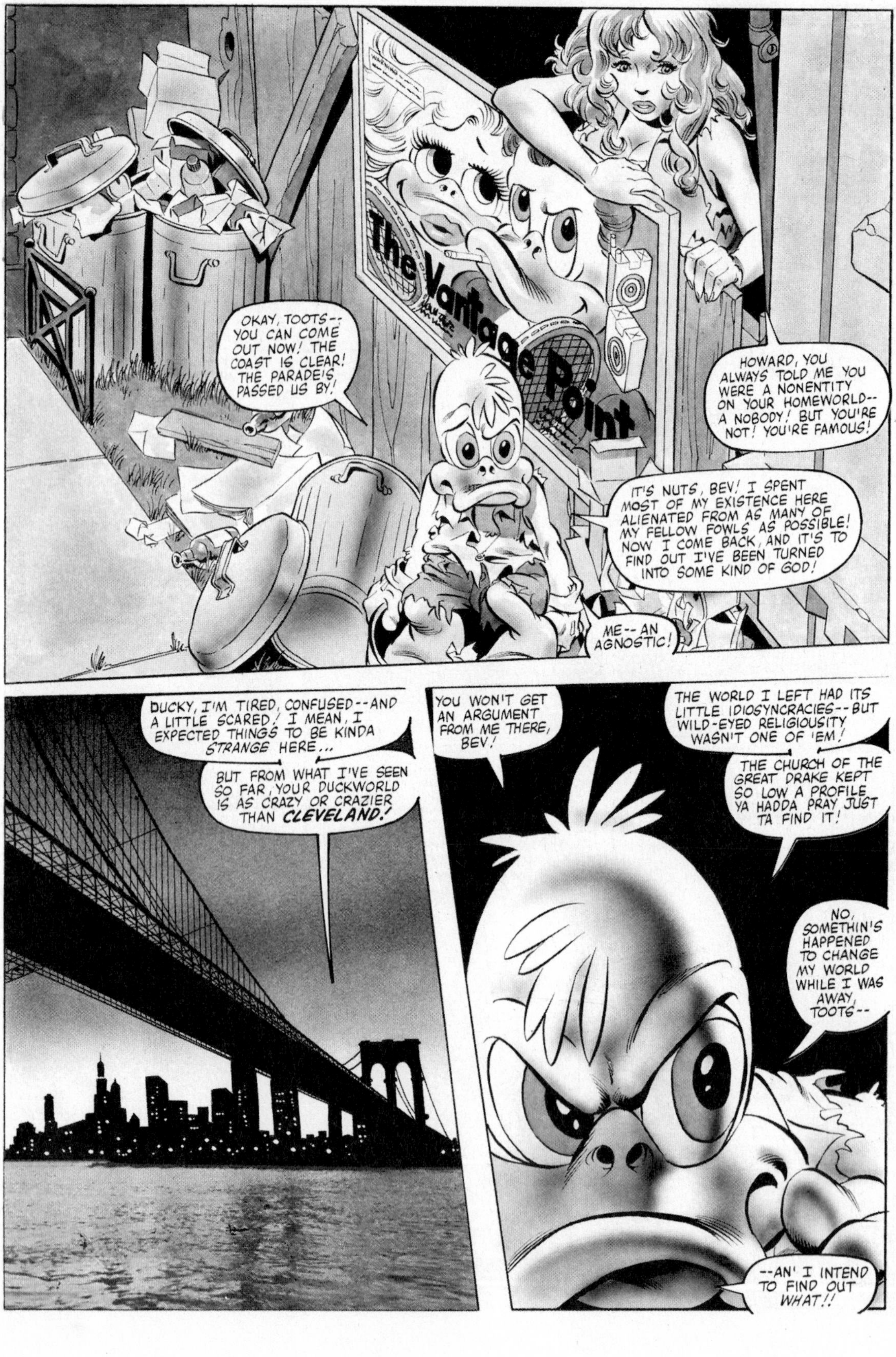
The Vantage Point
OKAY, TOOTS-- YOU CAN COME OUT NOW! THE COAST IS CLEAR! THE PARADE'S PASSED US BY!
HOWARD, YOU ALWAYS TOLD ME YOU WERE A NONENTITY ON YOUR HOMEWORLD-- A NOBODY! BUT YOU'RE NOT! YOU'RE FAMOUS!
IT'S NUTS, BEV! I SPENT MOST OF MY EXISTENCE HERE ALIENATED FROM AS MANY OF MY FELLOW FOWLS AS POSSIBLE! NOW I COME BACK, AND IT'S TO FIND OUT I'VE BEEN TURNED INTO SOME KIND OF GOD!
ME-- AN AGNOSTIC!
DUCKY, I'M TIRED, CONFUSED-- AND A LITTLE SCARED! I MEAN, I EXPECTED THINGS TO BE KINDA STRANGE HERE...
BUT FROM WHAT I'VE SEEN SO FAR, YOUR DUCKWORLD IS AS CRAZY OR CRAZIER THAN CLEVELAND!
YOU WON'T GET AN ARGUMENT FROM ME THERE, BEV!
THE WORLD I LEFT HAD ITS LITTLE IDIOSYNCRACIES-- BUT WILD-EYED RELIGIOUSITY WASN'T ONE OF 'EM!
THE CHURCH OF THE GREAT DRAKE KEPT SO LOW A PROFILE YA HADDA PRAY JUST TA FIND IT!
NO, SOMETHIN'S HAPPENED TO CHANGE MY WORLD WHILE I WAS AWAY, TOOTS--
--AN' I INTEND TO FIND OUT WHAT!!

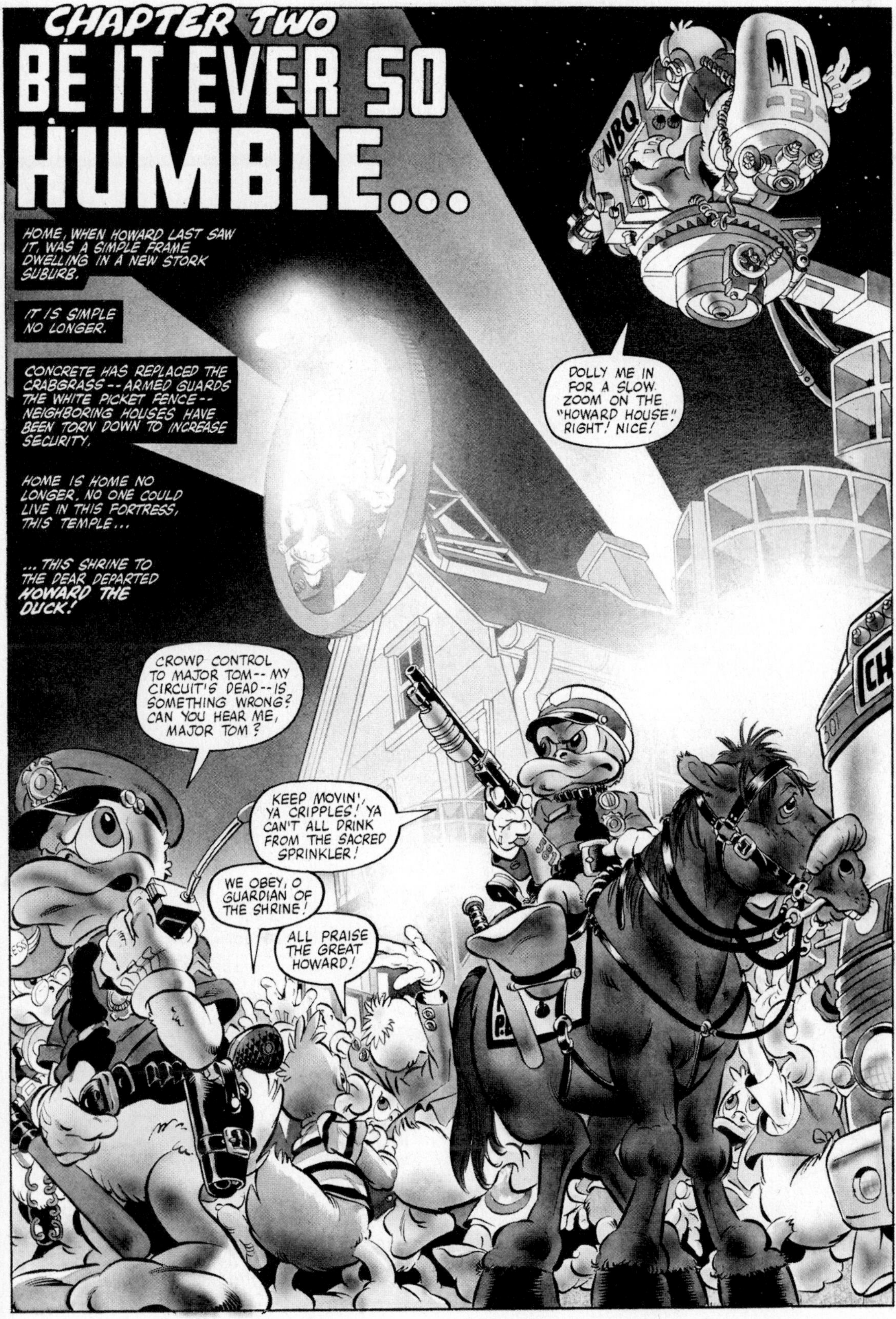

CHAPTER TWO
BE IT EVER SO HUMBLE...
HOME, WHEN HOWARD LAST SAW IT, WAS A SIMPLE FRAME DWELLING IN A NEW STORK SUBURB.
IT IS SIMPLE NO LONGER.
CONCRETE HAS REPLACED THE CRABGRASS--ARMED GUARDS THE WHITE PICKET FENCE--NEIGHBORING HOUSES HAVE BEEN TORN DOWN TO INCREASE SECURITY.
HOME IS HOME NO LONGER. NO ONE COULD LIVE IN THIS FORTRESS, THIS TEMPLE...
...THIS SHRINE TO THE DEAR DEPARTED HOWARD THE DUCK!
NBQ
3
DOLLY ME IN FOR A SLOW ZOOM ON THE "HOWARD HOUSE"! RIGHT! NICE!
CROWD CONTROL TO MAJOR TOM--MY CIRCUIT'S DEAD--IS SOMETHING WRONG? CAN YOU HEAR ME, MAJOR TOM?
KEEP MOVIN', YA CRIPPLES! YA CAN'T ALL DRINK FROM THE SACRED SPRINKLER!
WE OBEY, O GUARDIAN OF THE SHRINE!
ALL PRAISE THE GREAT HOWARD!

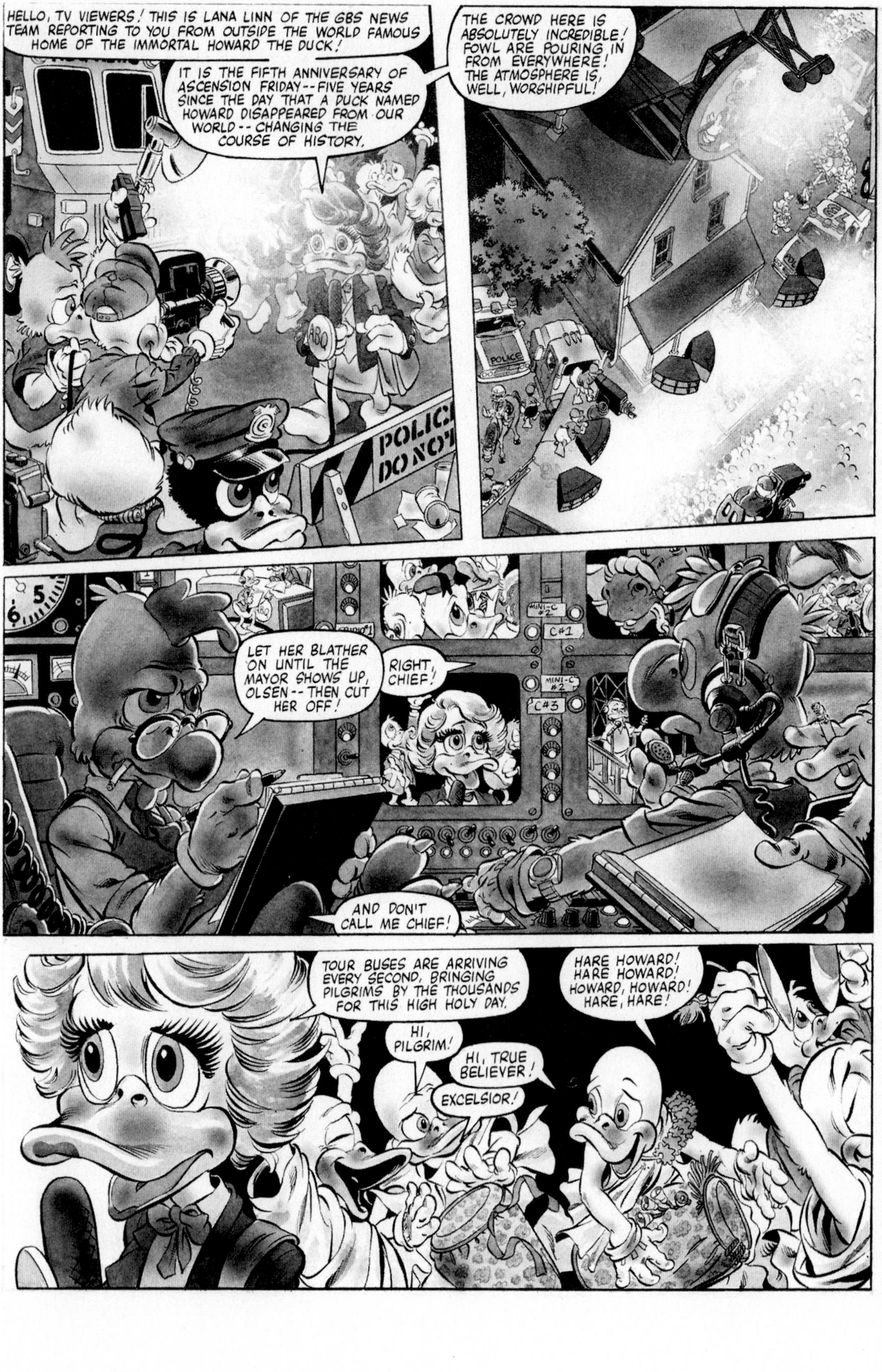
HELLO, TV VIEWERS! THIS IS LANA LINN OF THE GBS NEWS TEAM REPORTING TO YOU FROM OUTSIDE THE WORLD FAMOUS HOME OF THE IMMORTAL HOWARD THE DUCK!
IT IS THE FIFTH ANNIVERSARY OF ASCENSION FRIDAY--FIVE YEARS SINCE THE DAY THAT A DUCK NAMED HOWARD DISAPPEARED FROM OUR WORLD--CHANGING THE COURSE OF HISTORY.
ABQ
POLICE DO NOT
THE CROWD HERE IS ABSOLUTELY INCREDIBLE! FOWL ARE POURING IN FROM EVERYWHERE! THE ATMOSPHERE IS, WELL, WORSHIPFUL!
POLICE
MINI-C #2
C#1
MINI-C #2
C#3
LET HER BLATHER ON UNTIL THE MAYOR SHOWS UP, OLSEN--THEN CUT HER OFF!
RIGHT, CHIEF!
AND DON'T CALL ME CHIEF!
TOUR BUSES ARE ARRIVING EVERY SECOND, BRINGING PILGRIMS BY THE THOUSANDS FOR THIS HIGH HOLY DAY.
HARE HOWARD! HARE HOWARD! HOWARD, HOWARD! HARE, HARE!
HI, PILGRIM!
HI, TRUE BELIEVER!
EXCELSIOR!

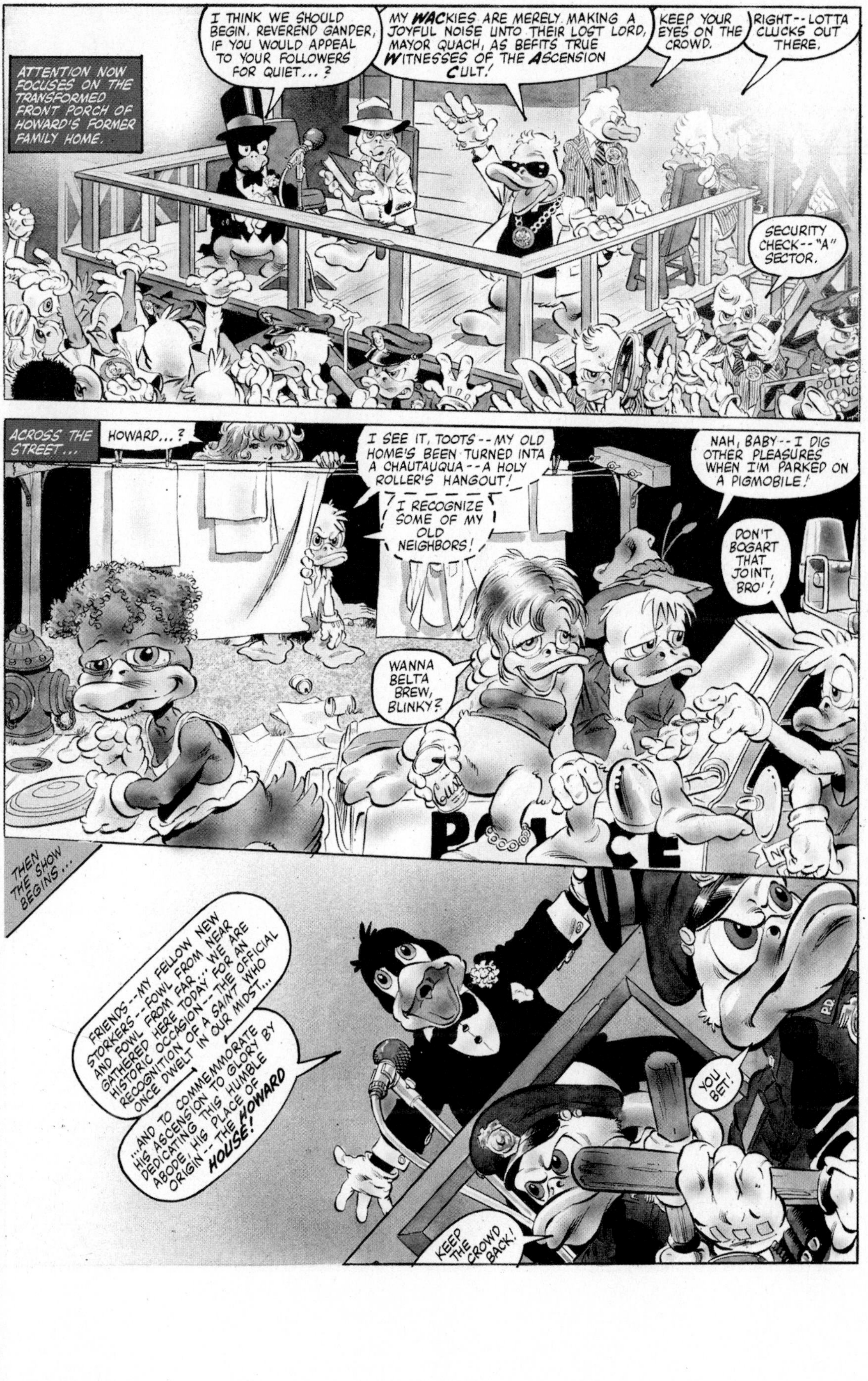

ATTENTION NOW FOCUSES ON THE TRANSFORMED FRONT PORCH OF HOWARD'S FORMER FAMILY HOME.
I THINK WE SHOULD BEGIN, REVEREND GANDER, IF YOU WOULD APPEAL TO YOUR FOLLOWERS FOR QUIET...?
MY WACKIES ARE MERELY MAKING A JOYFUL NOISE UNTO THEIR LOST LORD, MAYOR QUACH, AS BEFITS TRUE WITNESSES OF THE ASCENSION CULT!
KEEP YOUR EYES ON THE CROWD.
RIGHT--LOTTA CLUCKS OUT THERE.
SECURITY CHECK--"A" SECTOR.
ACROSS THE STREET...
HOWARD...?
I SEE IT, TOOTS--MY OLD HOME'S BEEN TURNED INTA A CHAUTAUQUA--A HOLY ROLLER'S HANGOUT!
I RECOGNIZE SOME OF MY OLD NEIGHBORS!
NAH, BABY--I DIG OTHER PLEASURES WHEN I'M PARKED ON A PIGMOBILE!
DON'T BOGART THAT JOINT, BRO'!
WANNA BELTA BREW, BLINKY?
POLICE
THEN THE SHOW BEGINS...
FRIENDS--MY FELLOW NEW STORKERS--FOWL FROM NEAR AND FOWL FROM FAR... WE ARE GATHERED HERE TODAY FOR AN HISTORIC OCCASION--THE OFFICIAL RECOGNITION OF A SAINT WHO ONCE DWELT IN OUR MIDST...
...AND TO COMMEMMORATE HIS ASCENSION TO GLORY BY DEDICATING THIS HUMBLE ABODE, HIS PLACE OF ORIGIN--THE HOWARD HOUSE!
YOU BET!
KEEP THE CROWD BACK!

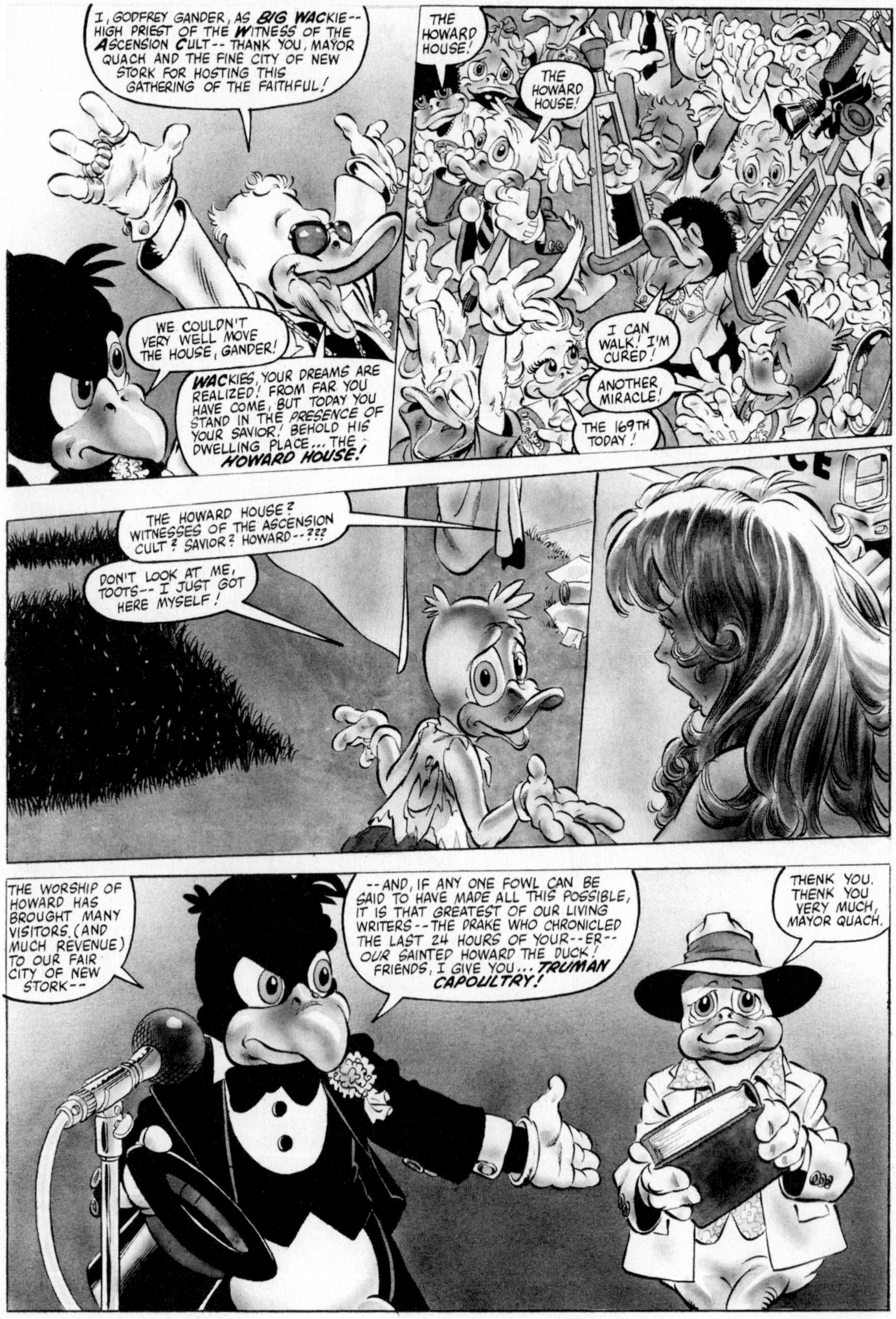

I, GODFREY GANDER, AS BIG WACKIE--HIGH PRIEST OF THE WITNESS OF THE ASCENSION CULT-- THANK YOU, MAYOR QUACH AND THE FINE CITY OF NEW STORK FOR HOSTING THIS GATHERING OF THE FAITHFUL!
WE COULDN'T VERY WELL MOVE THE HOUSE, GANDER!
WACKIES, YOUR DREAMS ARE REALIZED! FROM FAR YOU HAVE COME, BUT TODAY YOU STAND IN THE PRESENCE OF YOUR SAVIOR! BEHOLD HIS DWELLING PLACE... THE HOWARD HOUSE!
THE HOWARD HOUSE!
THE HOWARD HOUSE!
I CAN WALK! I'M CURED!
ANOTHER MIRACLE!
THE 169TH TODAY!
THE HOWARD HOUSE? WITNESSES OF THE ASCENSION CULT? SAVIOR? HOWARD--???
DON'T LOOK AT ME, TOOTS-- I JUST GOT HERE MYSELF!
THE WORSHIP OF HOWARD HAS BROUGHT MANY VISITORS (AND MUCH REVENUE) TO OUR FAIR CITY OF NEW STORK--
--AND, IF ANY ONE FOWL CAN BE SAID TO HAVE MADE ALL THIS POSSIBLE, IT IS THAT GREATEST OF OUR LIVING WRITERS--THE DRAKE WHO CHRONICLED THE LAST 24 HOURS OF YOUR--ER--OUR SAINTED HOWARD THE DUCK! FRIENDS, I GIVE YOU... TRUMAN CAPOULTRY!
THENK YOU. THENK YOU VERY MUCH, MAYOR QUACH.

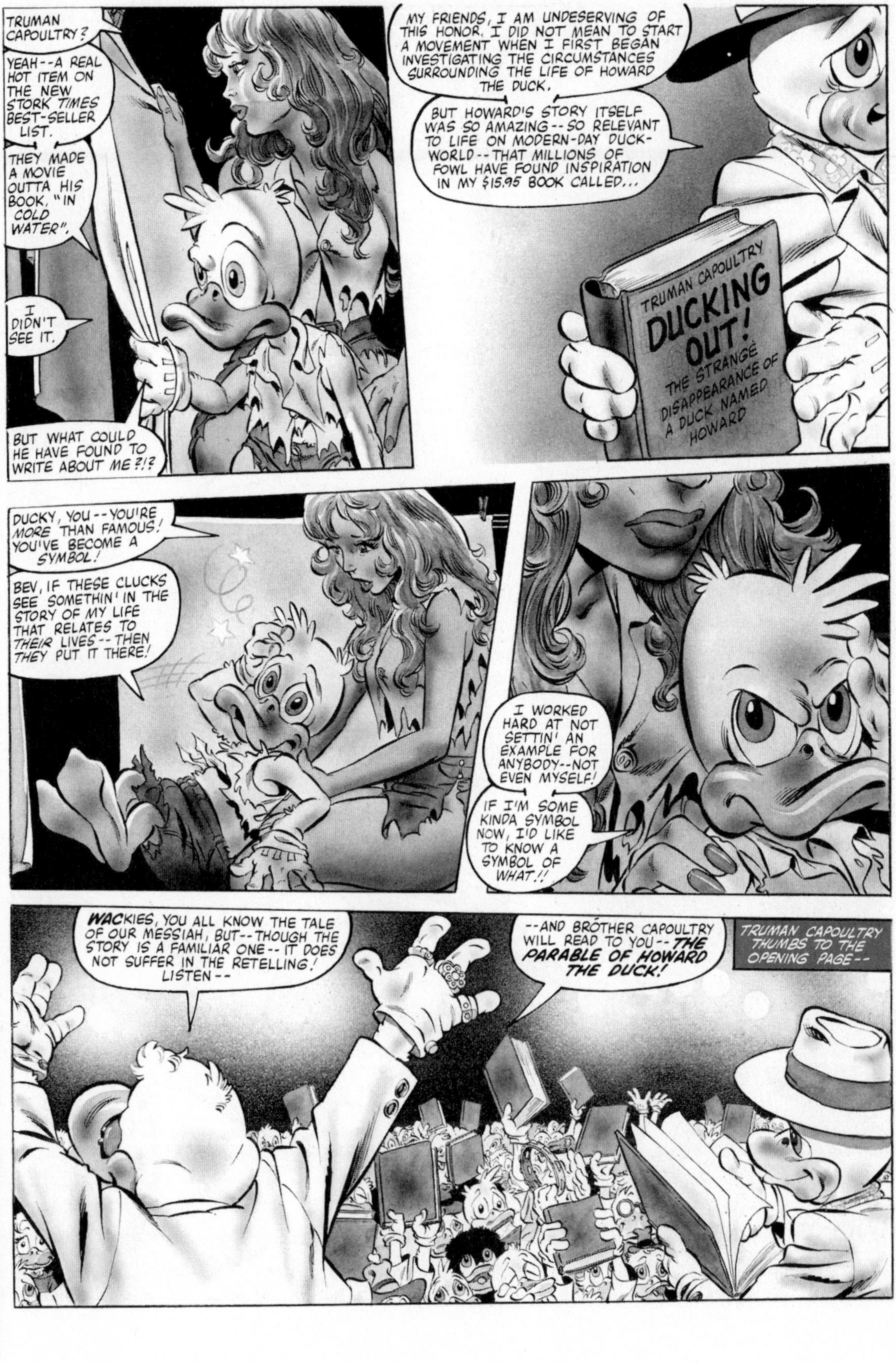
TRUMAN CAPOULTRY?
YEAH--A REAL HOT ITEM ON THE NEW STORK *TIMES* BEST-SELLER LIST.
THEY MADE A MOVIE OUTTA HIS BOOK, "IN COLD WATER".
I DIDN'T SEE IT.
BUT WHAT COULD HE HAVE FOUND TO WRITE ABOUT *ME*?!?
MY FRIENDS, I AM UNDESERVING OF THIS HONOR. I DID NOT MEAN TO START A MOVEMENT WHEN I FIRST BEGAN INVESTIGATING THE CIRCUMSTANCES SURROUNDING THE LIFE OF HOWARD THE DUCK.
BUT HOWARD'S STORY ITSELF WAS SO AMAZING--SO RELEVANT TO LIFE ON MODERN-DAY DUCK-WORLD--THAT MILLIONS OF FOWL HAVE FOUND INSPIRATION IN MY $15.95 BOOK CALLED...
TRUMAN CAPOULTRY
DUCKING OUT!
THE STRANGE DISAPPEARANCE OF A DUCK NAMED HOWARD
DUCKY, YOU--YOU'RE *MORE* THAN FAMOUS! YOU'VE BECOME A *SYMBOL*!
BEV, IF THESE CLUCKS SEE SOMETHIN' IN THE STORY OF MY LIFE THAT RELATES TO *THEIR* LIVES--THEN *THEY* PUT IT THERE!
I WORKED HARD AT NOT SETTIN' AN EXAMPLE FOR ANYBODY--NOT EVEN MYSELF!
IF I'M SOME KINDA SYMBOL NOW, I'D LIKE TO KNOW A SYMBOL OF *WHAT*!!
***WAC*KIES, YOU ALL KNOW THE TALE OF OUR MESSIAH, BUT--THOUGH THE STORY IS A FAMILIAR ONE--IT DOES NOT SUFFER IN THE RETELLING! LISTEN--
--AND BROTHER CAPOULTRY WILL READ TO YOU--***THE PARABLE OF HOWARD THE DUCK!***
TRUMAN CAPOULTRY THUMBS TO THE OPENING PAGE--

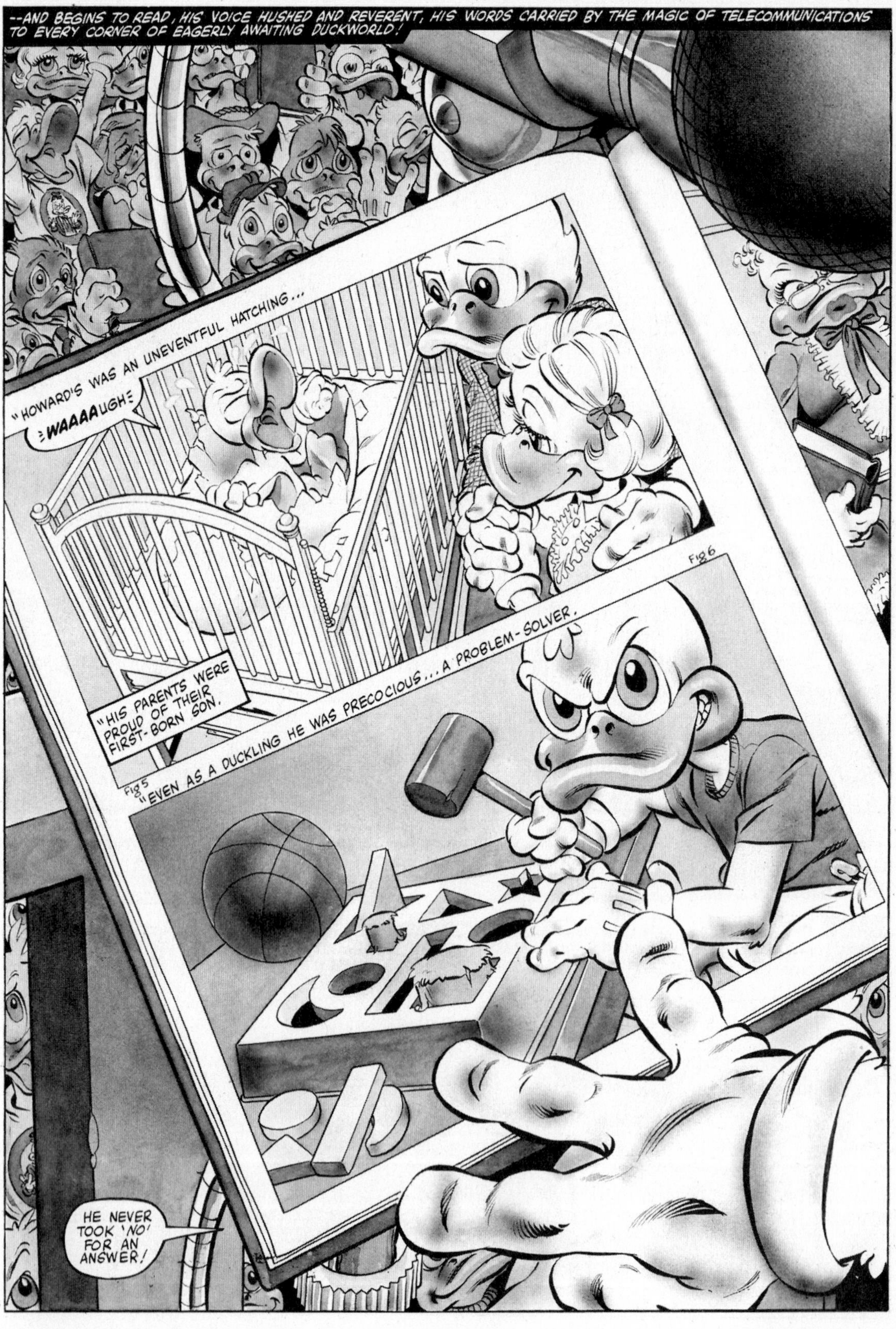
--AND BEGINS TO READ, HIS VOICE HUSHED AND REVERENT, HIS WORDS CARRIED BY THE MAGIC OF TELECOMMUNICATIONS TO EVERY CORNER OF EAGERLY AWAITING DUCKWORLD!
"HOWARD'S WAS AN UNEVENTFUL HATCHING...
WAAAAUGH
Fig 6
"HIS PARENTS WERE PROUD OF THEIR FIRST-BORN SON.
Fig 5
"EVEN AS A DUCKLING HE WAS PRECOCIOUS... A PROBLEM-SOLVER.
HE NEVER TOOK 'NO' FOR AN ANSWER!

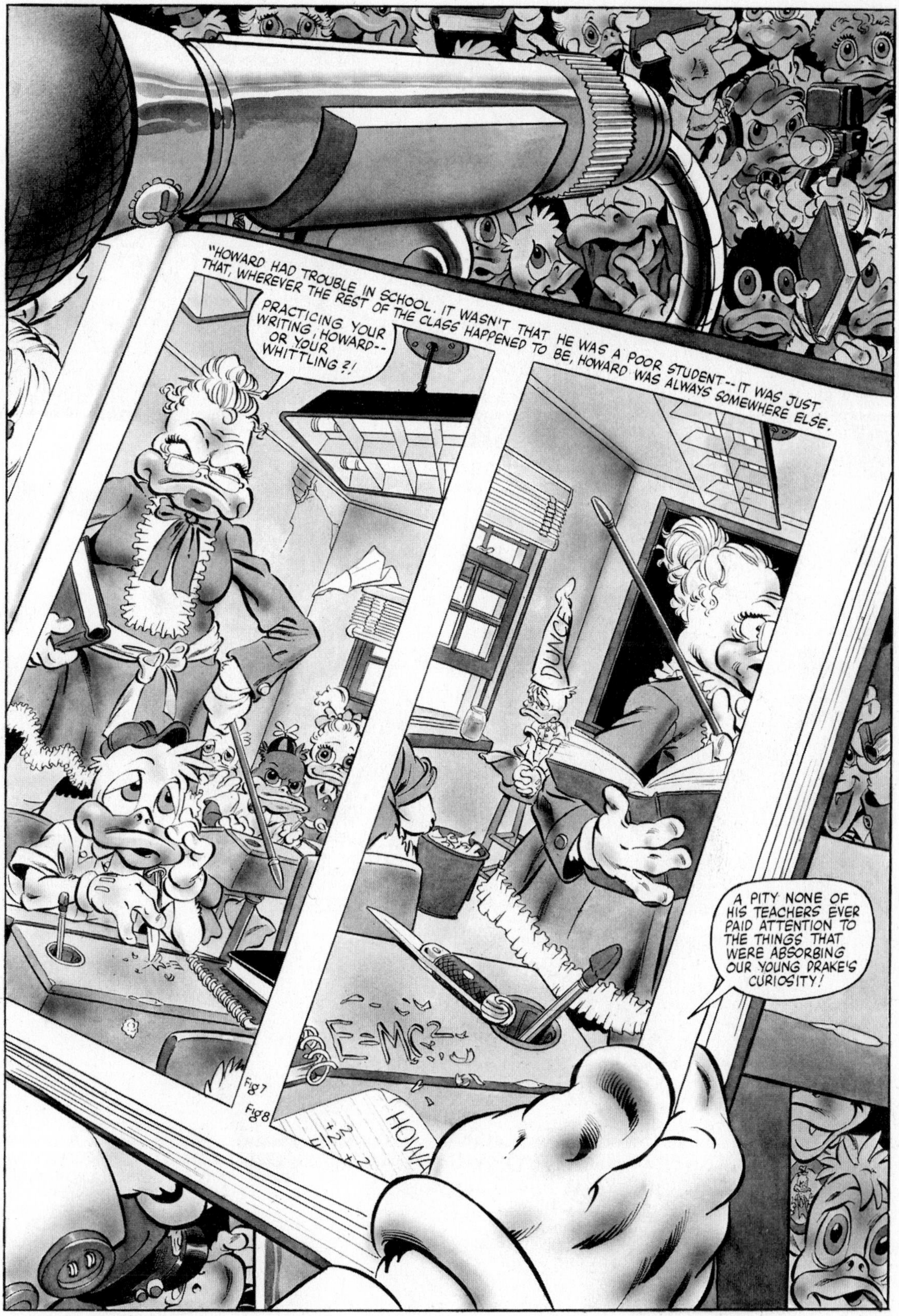
"HOWARD HAD TROUBLE IN SCHOOL. IT WASN'T THAT HE WAS A POOR STUDENT--IT WAS JUST THAT, WHEREVER THE REST OF THE CLASS HAPPENED TO BE, HOWARD WAS ALWAYS SOMEWHERE ELSE.
PRACTICING YOUR WRITING, HOWARD-- OR YOUR WHITTLING ?!
DUNCE
E=MC2
A PITY NONE OF HIS TEACHERS EVER PAID ATTENTION TO THE THINGS THAT WERE ABSORBING OUR YOUNG DRAKE'S CURIOSITY!
Fig 7
Fig 8

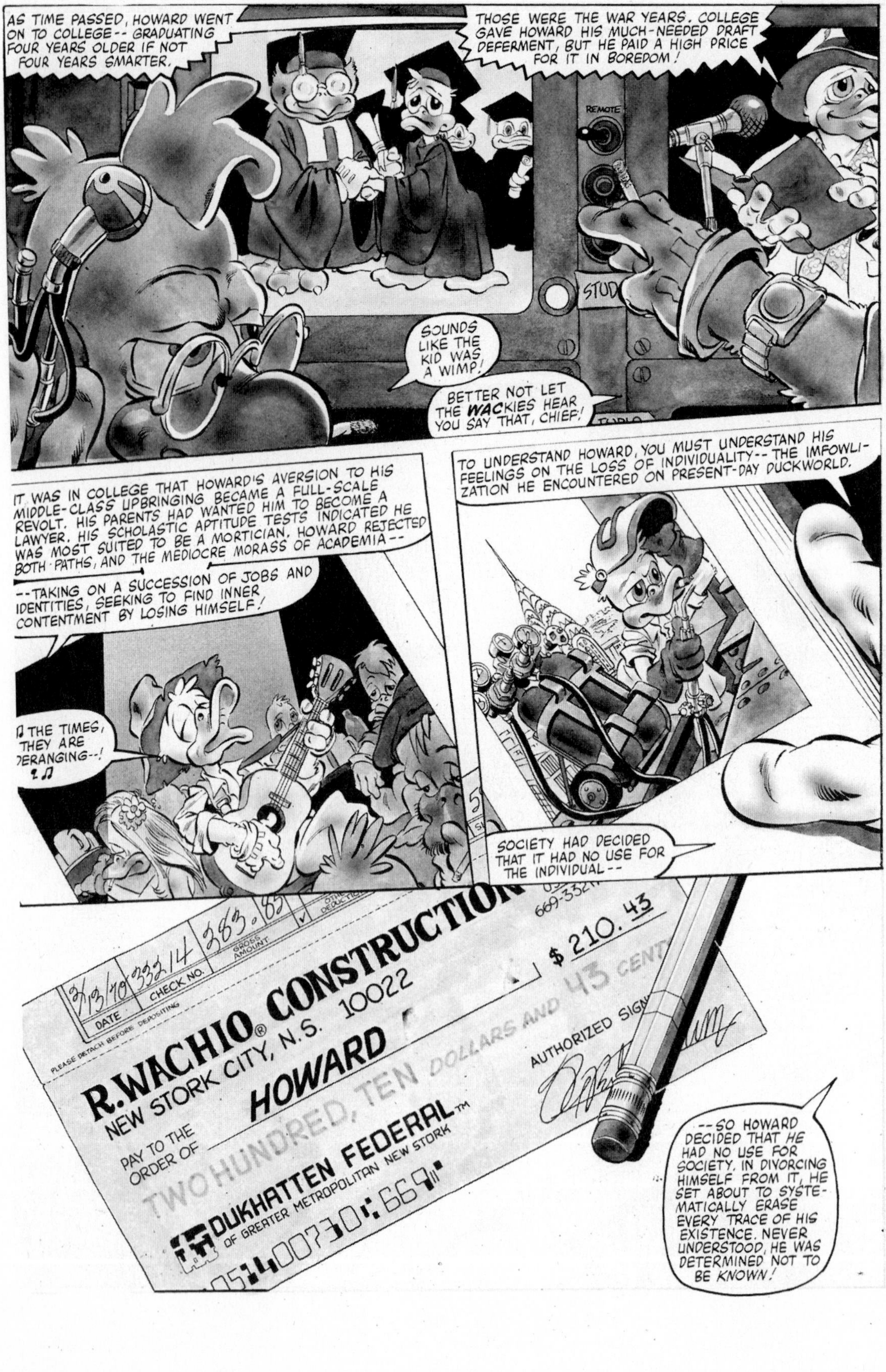

AS TIME PASSED, HOWARD WENT ON TO COLLEGE -- GRADUATING FOUR YEARS OLDER IF NOT FOUR YEARS SMARTER.
THOSE WERE THE WAR YEARS. COLLEGE GAVE HOWARD HIS MUCH-NEEDED DRAFT DEFERMENT, BUT HE PAID A HIGH PRICE FOR IT IN BOREDOM!
REMOTE
STUD
SOUNDS LIKE THE KID WAS A WIMP!
BETTER NOT LET THE WACKIES HEAR YOU SAY THAT, CHIEF!
IT WAS IN COLLEGE THAT HOWARD'S AVERSION TO HIS MIDDLE-CLASS UPBRINGING BECAME A FULL-SCALE REVOLT. HIS PARENTS HAD WANTED HIM TO BECOME A LAWYER. HIS SCHOLASTIC APTITUDE TESTS INDICATED HE WAS MOST SUITED TO BE A MORTICIAN. HOWARD REJECTED BOTH PATHS, AND THE MEDIOCRE MORASS OF ACADEMIA--
--TAKING ON A SUCCESSION OF JOBS AND IDENTITIES, SEEKING TO FIND INNER CONTENTMENT BY LOSING HIMSELF!
♫ THE TIMES, THEY ARE DERANGING--! ♫
TO UNDERSTAND HOWARD, YOU MUST UNDERSTAND HIS FEELINGS ON THE LOSS OF INDIVIDUALITY-- THE IMFOWLIZATION HE ENCOUNTERED ON PRESENT-DAY DUCKWORLD.
SOCIETY HAD DECIDED THAT IT HAD NO USE FOR THE INDIVIDUAL--
R.WACHIO® CONSTRUCTION
NEW STORK CITY, N.S. 10022
669-332
DATE
CHECK NO.
GROSS AMOUNT
3/13/70
332.14
383.85
PLEASE DETACH BEFORE DEPOSITING
$ 210.43
PAY TO THE ORDER OF
HOWARD
TWO HUNDRED, TEN DOLLARS AND 43 CENTS
AUTHORIZED SIGN
DUKHATTEN FEDERAL™
OF GREATER METROPOLITAN NEW STORK
--SO HOWARD DECIDED THAT HE HAD NO USE FOR SOCIETY. IN DIVORCING HIMSELF FROM IT, HE SET ABOUT TO SYSTEMATICALLY ERASE EVERY TRACE OF HIS EXISTENCE. NEVER UNDERSTOOD, HE WAS DETERMINED NOT TO BE KNOWN!

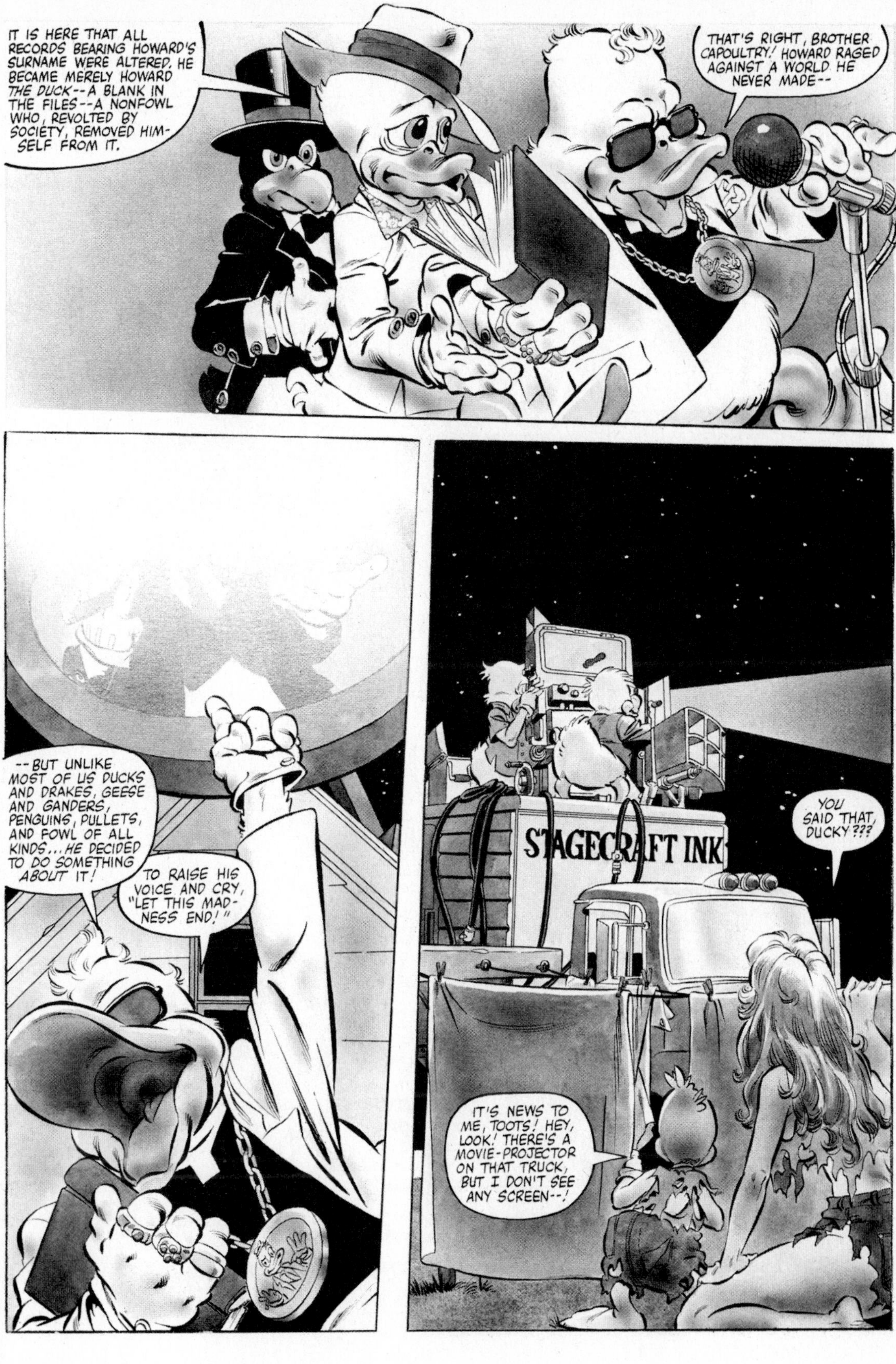
IT IS HERE THAT ALL RECORDS BEARING HOWARD'S SURNAME WERE ALTERED. HE BECAME MERELY HOWARD THE DUCK--A BLANK IN THE FILES--A NONFOWL WHO, REVOLTED BY SOCIETY, REMOVED HIMSELF FROM IT.
THAT'S RIGHT, BROTHER CAPOULTRY! HOWARD RAGED AGAINST A WORLD HE NEVER MADE--
--BUT UNLIKE MOST OF US DUCKS AND DRAKES, GEESE AND GANDERS, PENGUINS, PULLETS, AND FOWL OF ALL KINDS... HE DECIDED TO DO SOMETHING ABOUT IT!
TO RAISE HIS VOICE AND CRY, "LET THIS MADNESS END!"
STAGECRAFT INK
YOU SAID THAT, DUCKY???
IT'S NEWS TO ME, TOOTS! HEY, LOOK! THERE'S A MOVIE-PROJECTOR ON THAT TRUCK, BUT I DON'T SEE ANY SCREEN--!

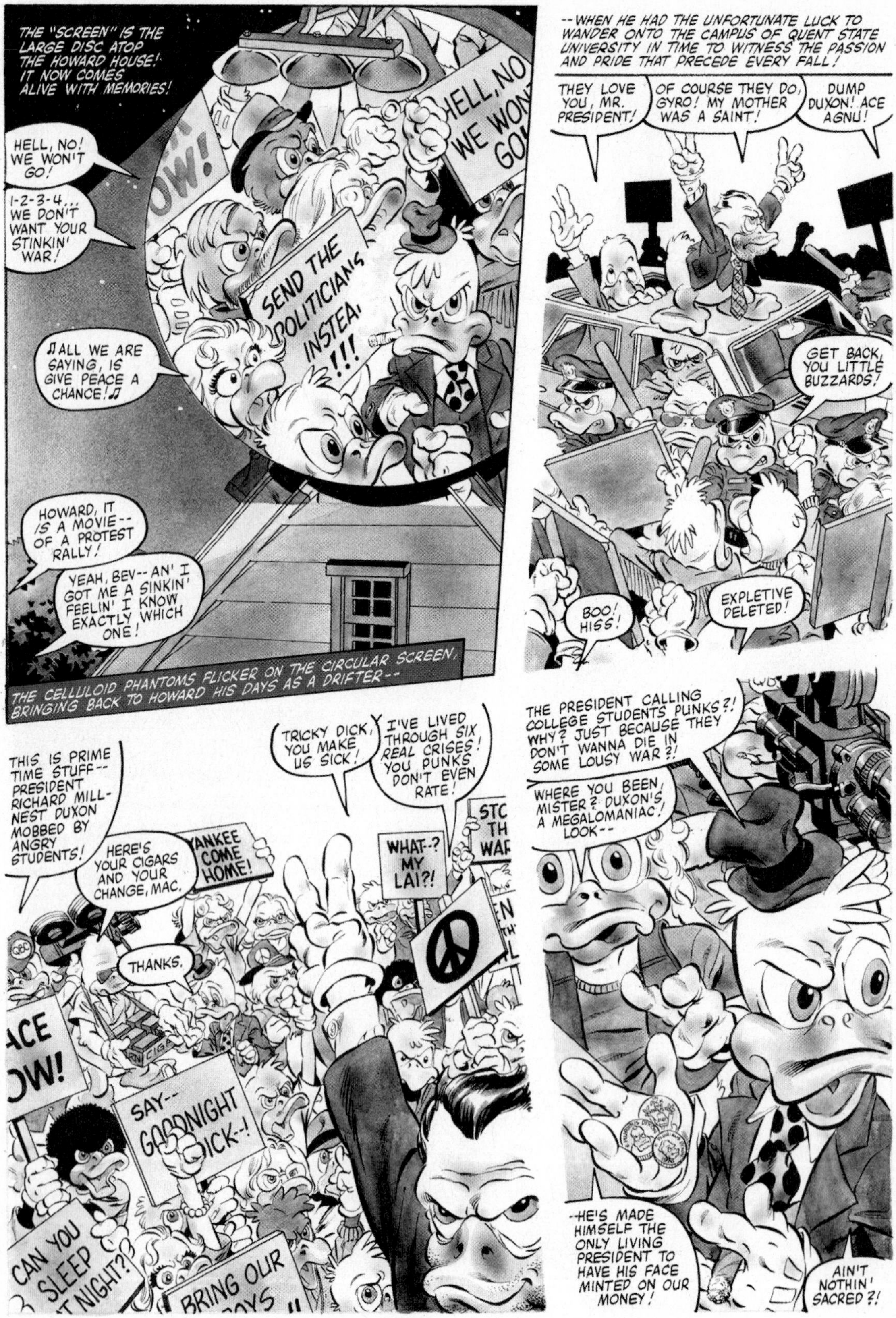
THE "SCREEN" IS THE LARGE DISC ATOP THE HOWARD HOUSE! IT NOW COMES ALIVE WITH MEMORIES!
HELL, NO! WE WON'T GO!
HELL, NO WE WON'T GO!
1-2-3-4... WE DON'T WANT YOUR STINKIN' WAR!
SEND THE POLITICIANS INSTEA !!!
♫ALL WE ARE SAYING, IS GIVE PEACE A CHANCE!♫
HOWARD, IT IS A MOVIE-- OF A PROTEST RALLY!
YEAH, BEV--AN' I GOT ME A SINKIN' FEELIN' I KNOW EXACTLY WHICH ONE!
THE CELLULOID PHANTOMS FLICKER ON THE CIRCULAR SCREEN, BRINGING BACK TO HOWARD HIS DAYS AS A DRIFTER--
--WHEN HE HAD THE UNFORTUNATE LUCK TO WANDER ONTO THE CAMPUS OF QUENT STATE UNIVERSITY IN TIME TO WITNESS THE PASSION AND PRIDE THAT PRECEDE EVERY FALL!
THEY LOVE YOU, MR. PRESIDENT!
OF COURSE THEY DO, GYRO! MY MOTHER WAS A SAINT!
DUMP DUXON! ACE AGNU!
GET BACK, YOU LITTLE BUZZARDS!
BOO! HISS!
EXPLETIVE DELETED!
THIS IS PRIME TIME STUFF-- PRESIDENT RICHARD MILL-NEST DUXON MOBBED BY ANGRY STUDENTS!
TRICKY DICK, YOU MAKE US SICK!
I'VE LIVED THROUGH SIX REAL CRISES! YOU PUNKS DON'T EVEN RATE!
YANKEE COME HOME!
WHAT--? MY LAI?!
HERE'S YOUR CIGARS AND YOUR CHANGE, MAC.
THANKS.
SAY-- GOODNIGHT DICK--!
CAN YOU SLEEP AT NIGHT?
BRING OUR BOYS
THE PRESIDENT CALLING COLLEGE STUDENTS PUNKS?! WHY? JUST BECAUSE THEY DON'T WANNA DIE IN SOME LOUSY WAR?!
WHERE YOU BEEN, MISTER? DUXON'S A MEGALOMANIAC! LOOK--
--HE'S MADE HIMSELF THE ONLY LIVING PRESIDENT TO HAVE HIS FACE MINTED ON OUR MONEY!
AIN'T NOTHIN' SACRED?!

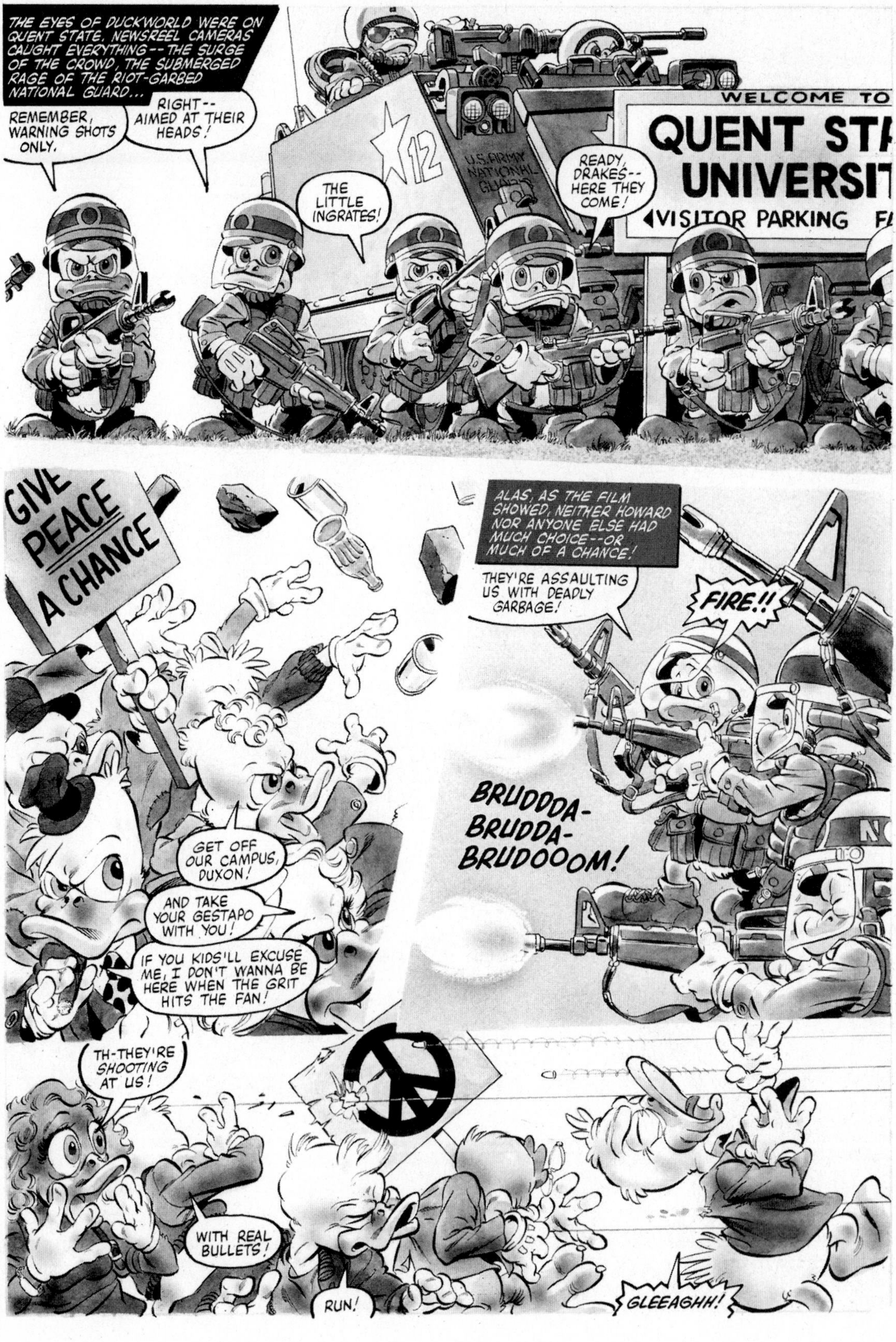
THE EYES OF DUCKWORLD WERE ON QUENT STATE. NEWSREEL CAMERAS CAUGHT EVERYTHING -- THE SURGE OF THE CROWD, THE SUBMERGED RAGE OF THE RIOT-GARBED NATIONAL GUARD...
REMEMBER, WARNING SHOTS ONLY.
RIGHT -- AIMED AT THEIR HEADS!
THE LITTLE INGRATES!
READY, DRAKES -- HERE THEY COME!
WELCOME TO
QUENT STA
UNIVERSIT
VISITOR PARKING
U.S. ARMY NATIONAL GUARD
12
GIVE PEACE A CHANCE
ALAS, AS THE FILM SHOWED, NEITHER HOWARD NOR ANYONE ELSE HAD MUCH CHOICE -- OR MUCH OF A CHANCE!
THEY'RE ASSAULTING US WITH DEADLY GARBAGE!
FIRE!!
BRUDDDA-BRUDDA-BRUDOOOM!
GET OFF OUR CAMPUS, DUXON!
AND TAKE YOUR GESTAPO WITH YOU!
IF YOU KIDS'LL EXCUSE ME, I DON'T WANNA BE HERE WHEN THE GRIT HITS THE FAN!
TH-THEY'RE SHOOTING AT US!
WITH REAL BULLETS!
RUN!
GLEEAGHH!

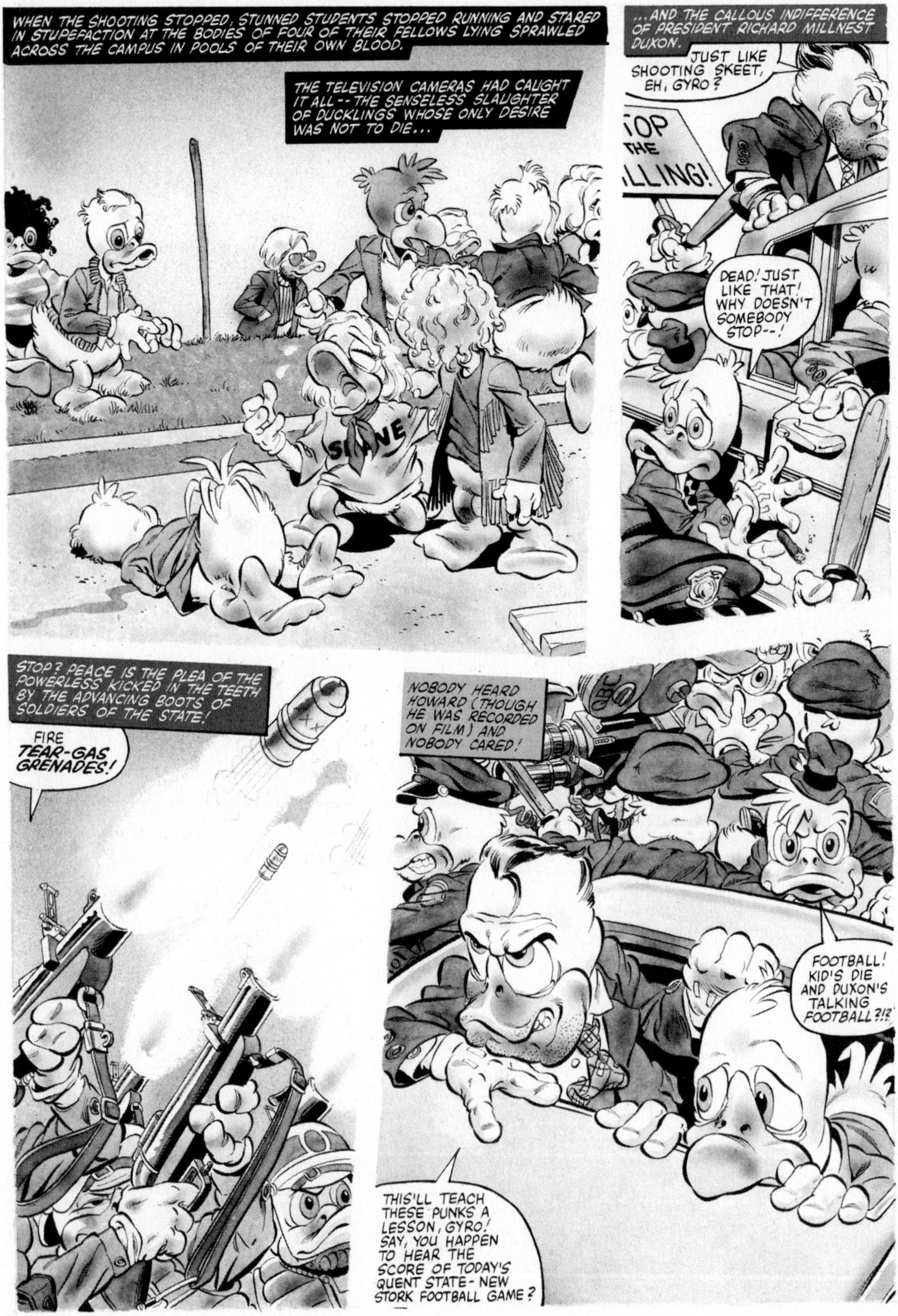
WHEN THE SHOOTING STOPPED, STUNNED STUDENTS STOPPED RUNNING AND STARED IN STUPEFACTION AT THE BODIES OF FOUR OF THEIR FELLOWS LYING SPRAWLED ACROSS THE CAMPUS IN POOLS OF THEIR OWN BLOOD.
THE TELEVISION CAMERAS HAD CAUGHT IT ALL--THE SENSELESS SLAUGHTER OF DUCKLINGS WHOSE ONLY DESIRE WAS NOT TO DIE...
...AND THE CALLOUS INDIFFERENCE OF PRESIDENT RICHARD MILLNEST DUXON.
JUST LIKE SHOOTING SKEET, EH, GYRO?
DEAD! JUST LIKE THAT! WHY DOESN'T SOMEBODY STOP--!
STOP? PEACE IS THE PLEA OF THE POWERLESS KICKED IN THE TEETH BY THE ADVANCING BOOTS OF SOLDIERS OF THE STATE!
FIRE TEAR-GAS GRENADES!
NOBODY HEARD HOWARD (THOUGH HE WAS RECORDED ON FILM) AND NOBODY CARED!
FOOTBALL! KID'S DIE AND DUXON'S TALKING FOOTBALL?!?
THIS'LL TEACH THESE PUNKS A LESSON, GYRO! SAY, YOU HAPPEN TO HEAR THE SCORE OF TODAY'S QUENT STATE-NEW STORK FOOTBALL GAME?

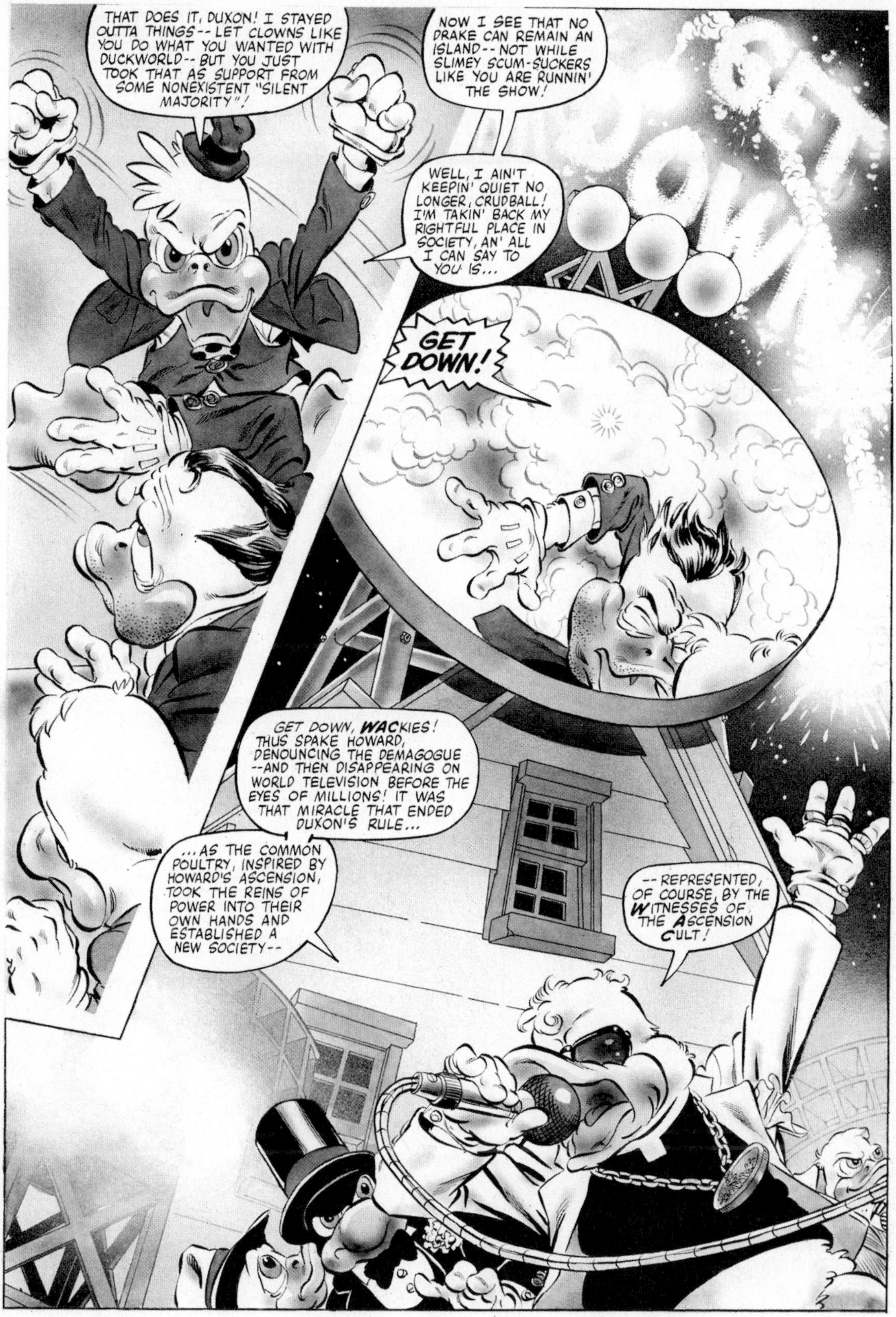
THAT DOES IT, DUXON! I STAYED OUTTA THINGS-- LET CLOWNS LIKE YOU DO WHAT YOU WANTED WITH DUCKWORLD-- BUT YOU JUST TOOK THAT AS SUPPORT FROM SOME NONEXISTENT "SILENT MAJORITY"!
NOW I SEE THAT NO DRAKE CAN REMAIN AN ISLAND-- NOT WHILE SLIMEY SCUM-SUCKERS LIKE YOU ARE RUNNIN' THE SHOW!
WELL, I AIN'T KEEPIN' QUIET NO LONGER, CRUDBALL! I'M TAKIN' BACK MY RIGHTFUL PLACE IN SOCIETY, AN' ALL I CAN SAY TO YOU IS...
GET DOWN!
GET DOWN!
GET DOWN, WACKIES! THUS SPAKE HOWARD, DENOUNCING THE DEMAGOGUE --AND THEN DISAPPEARING ON WORLD TELEVISION BEFORE THE EYES OF MILLIONS! IT WAS THAT MIRACLE THAT ENDED DUXON'S RULE...
...AS THE COMMON POULTRY, INSPIRED BY HOWARD'S ASCENSION, TOOK THE REINS OF POWER INTO THEIR OWN HANDS AND ESTABLISHED A NEW SOCIETY--
--REPRESENTED, OF COURSE, BY THE WITNESSES OF THE ASCENSION CULT!

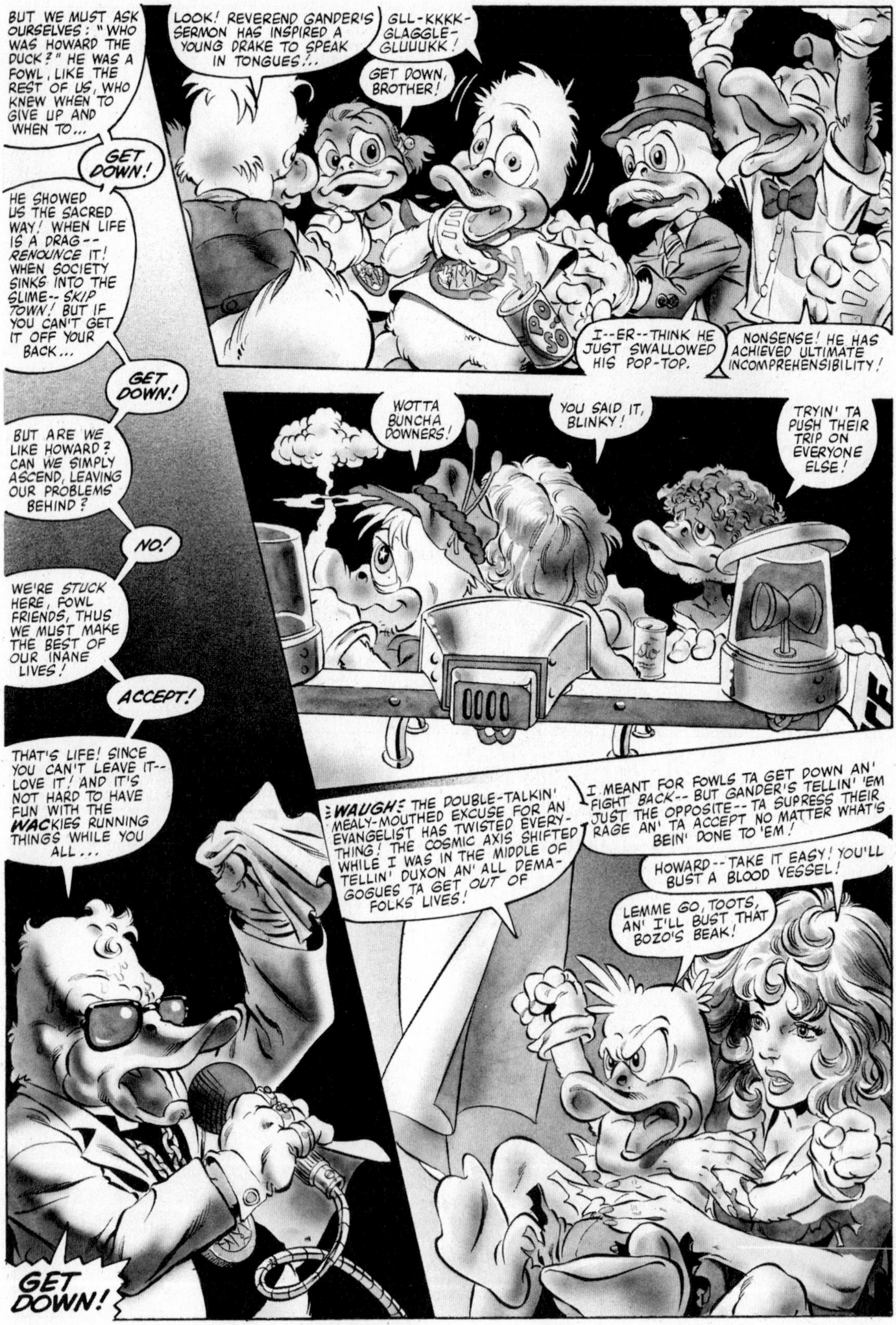
BUT WE MUST ASK OURSELVES: "WHO WAS HOWARD THE DUCK?" HE WAS A FOWL, LIKE THE REST OF US, WHO KNEW WHEN TO GIVE UP AND WHEN TO...
LOOK! REVEREND GANDER'S SERMON HAS INSPIRED A YOUNG DRAKE TO SPEAK IN TONGUES!..
GLL-KKKK-GLAGGLE-GLUUUKK!
GET DOWN, BROTHER!
GET DOWN!
HE SHOWED US THE SACRED WAY! WHEN LIFE IS A DRAG--RENOUNCE IT! WHEN SOCIETY SINKS INTO THE SLIME--SKIP TOWN! BUT IF YOU CAN'T GET IT OFF YOUR BACK...
I--ER--THINK HE JUST SWALLOWED HIS POP-TOP.
NONSENSE! HE HAS ACHIEVED ULTIMATE INCOMPREHENSIBILITY!
GET DOWN!
BUT ARE WE LIKE HOWARD? CAN WE SIMPLY ASCEND, LEAVING OUR PROBLEMS BEHIND?
NO!
WE'RE STUCK HERE, FOWL FRIENDS, THUS WE MUST MAKE THE BEST OF OUR INANE LIVES!
ACCEPT!
WOTTA BUNCHA DOWNERS!
YOU SAID IT, BLINKY!
TRYIN' TA PUSH THEIR TRIP ON EVERYONE ELSE!
THAT'S LIFE! SINCE YOU CAN'T LEAVE IT--LOVE IT! AND IT'S NOT HARD TO HAVE FUN WITH THE WACKIES RUNNING THINGS WHILE YOU ALL...
GET DOWN!
WAUGH! THE DOUBLE-TALKIN' MEALY-MOUTHED EXCUSE FOR AN EVANGELIST HAS TWISTED EVERY-THING! THE COSMIC AXIS SHIFTED WHILE I WAS IN THE MIDDLE OF TELLIN' DUXON AN' ALL DEMA-GOGUES TA GET OUT OF FOLKS LIVES!
I MEANT FOR FOWLS TA GET DOWN AN' FIGHT BACK--BUT GANDER'S TELLIN' 'EM JUST THE OPPOSITE--TA SUPRESS THEIR RAGE AN' TA ACCEPT NO MATTER WHAT'S BEIN' DONE TO 'EM!
HOWARD--TAKE IT EASY! YOU'LL BUST A BLOOD VESSEL!
LEMME GO, TOOTS, AN' I'LL BUST THAT BOZO'S BEAK!

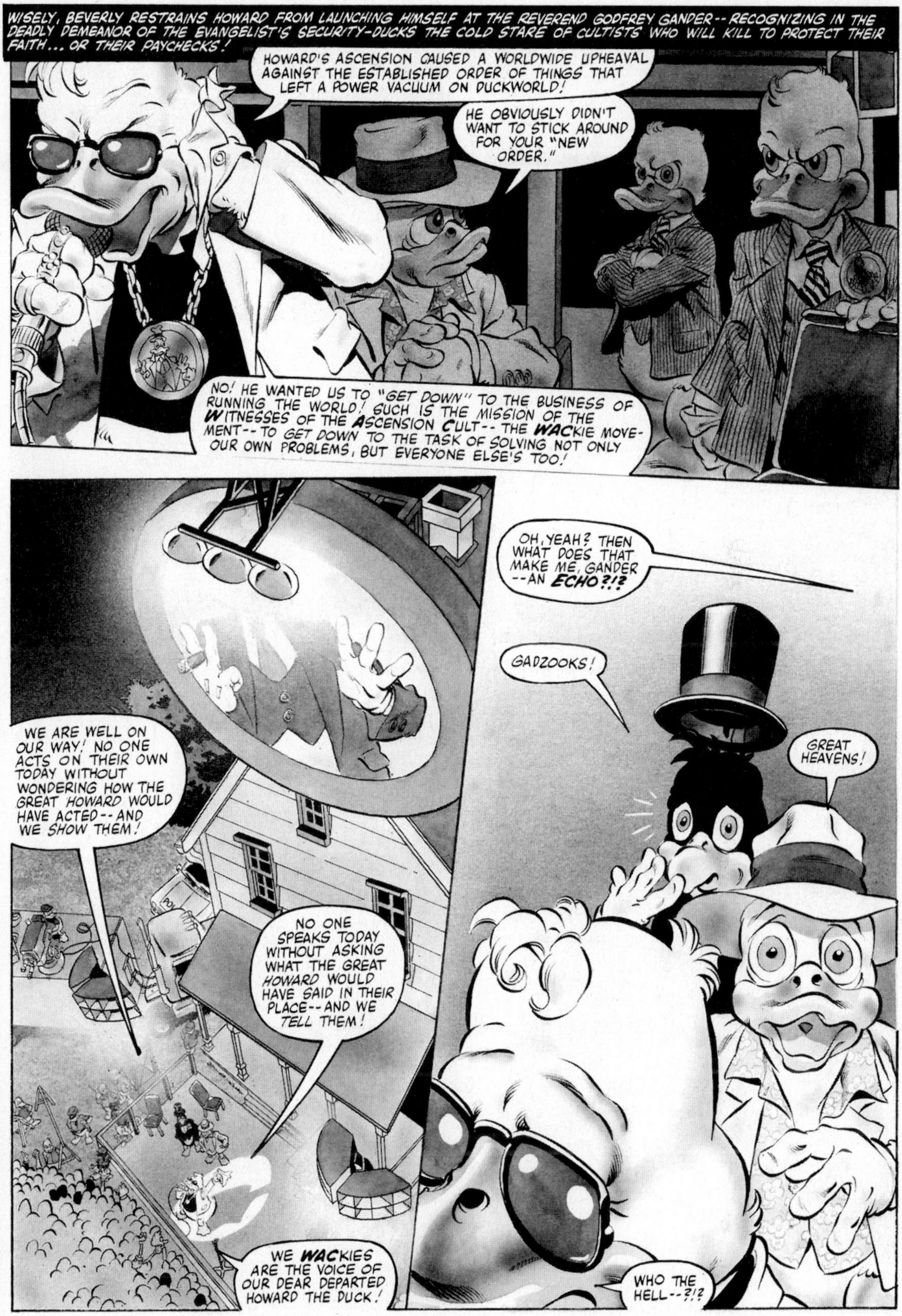
WISELY, BEVERLY RESTRAINS HOWARD FROM LAUNCHING HIMSELF AT THE REVEREND GODFREY GANDER--RECOGNIZING IN THE DEADLY DEMEANOR OF THE EVANGELIST'S SECURITY-DUCKS THE COLD STARE OF CULTISTS WHO WILL KILL TO PROTECT THEIR FAITH... OR THEIR PAYCHECKS!
HOWARD'S ASCENSION CAUSED A WORLDWIDE UPHEAVAL AGAINST THE ESTABLISHED ORDER OF THINGS THAT LEFT A POWER VACUUM ON DUCKWORLD!
HE OBVIOUSLY DIDN'T WANT TO STICK AROUND FOR YOUR "NEW ORDER."
NO! HE WANTED US TO "GET DOWN" TO THE BUSINESS OF RUNNING THE WORLD! SUCH IS THE MISSION OF THE WITNESSES OF THE ASCENSION CULT--THE WACKIE MOVEMENT--TO GET DOWN TO THE TASK OF SOLVING NOT ONLY OUR OWN PROBLEMS, BUT EVERYONE ELSE'S TOO!
WE ARE WELL ON OUR WAY! NO ONE ACTS ON THEIR OWN TODAY WITHOUT WONDERING HOW THE GREAT HOWARD WOULD HAVE ACTED--AND WE SHOW THEM!
NO ONE SPEAKS TODAY WITHOUT ASKING WHAT THE GREAT HOWARD WOULD HAVE SAID IN THEIR PLACE--AND WE TELL THEM!
WE WACKIES ARE THE VOICE OF OUR DEAR DEPARTED HOWARD THE DUCK!
OH, YEAH? THEN WHAT DOES THAT MAKE ME, GANDER--AN ECHO?!?
GADZOOKS!
GREAT HEAVENS!
WHO THE HELL--?!?

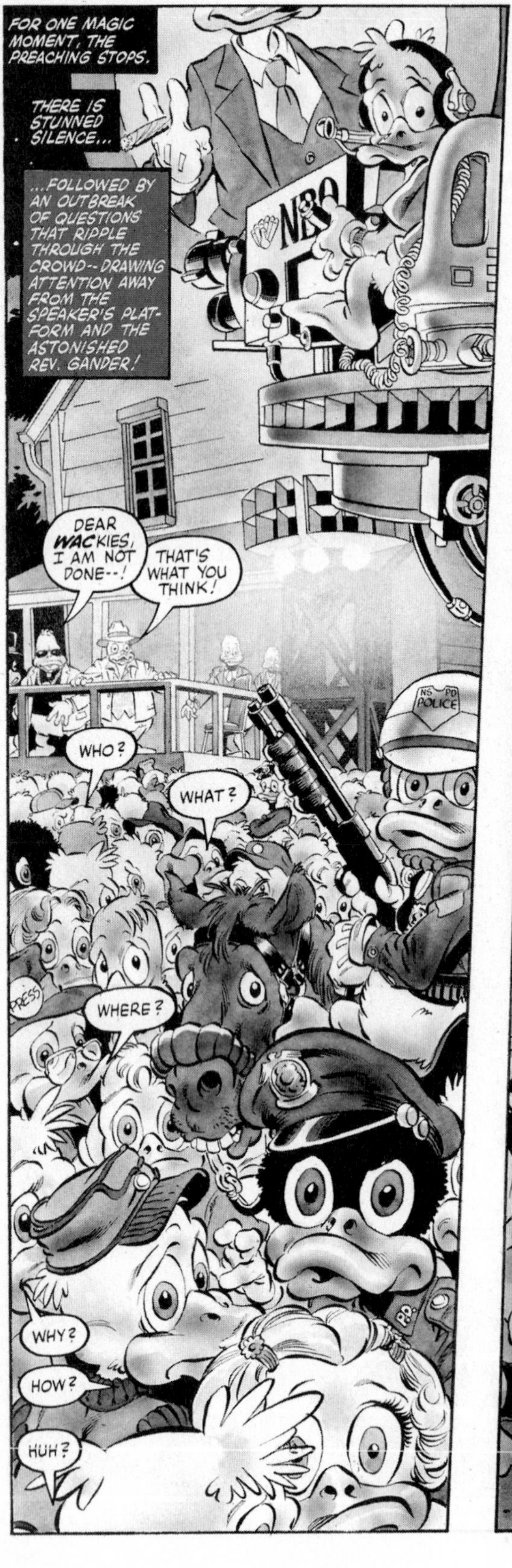

FOR ONE MAGIC MOMENT, THE PREACHING STOPS.
THERE IS STUNNED SILENCE...
...FOLLOWED BY AN OUTBREAK OF QUESTIONS THAT RIPPLE THROUGH THE CROWD--DRAWING ATTENTION AWAY FROM THE SPEAKER'S PLATFORM AND THE ASTONISHED REV. GANDER!
NBO
DEAR WACKIES, I AM NOT DONE--!
THAT'S WHAT YOU THINK!
POLICE
WHO?
WHAT?
PRESS
WHERE?
WHY?
HOW?
HUH?

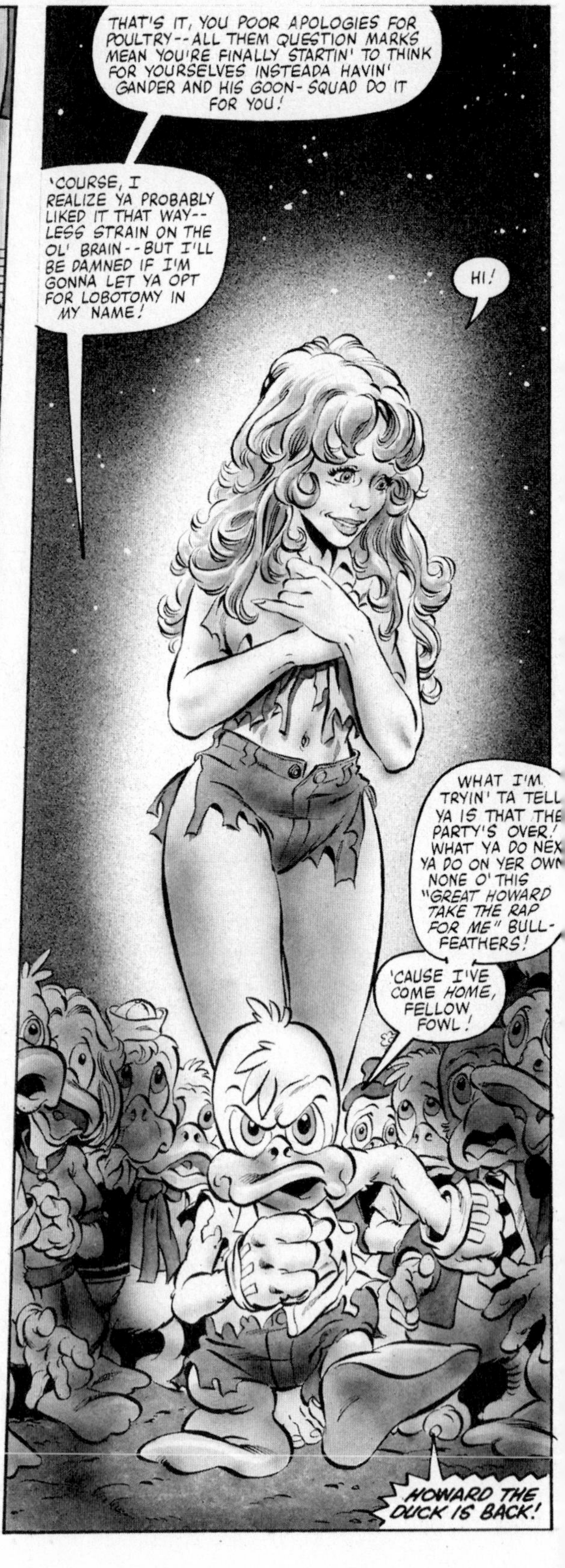

THAT'S IT, YOU POOR APOLOGIES FOR POULTRY--ALL THEM QUESTION MARKS MEAN YOU'RE FINALLY STARTIN' TO THINK FOR YOURSELVES INSTEADA HAVIN' GANDER AND HIS GOON-SQUAD DO IT FOR YOU!
'COURSE, I REALIZE YA PROBABLY LIKED IT THAT WAY--LESS STRAIN ON THE OL' BRAIN--BUT I'LL BE DAMNED IF I'M GONNA LET YA OPT FOR LOBOTOMY IN MY NAME!
HI!
WHAT I'M TRYIN' TA TELL YA IS THAT THE PARTY'S OVER! WHAT YA DO NEX YA DO ON YER OWN NONE O' THIS "GREAT HOWARD TAKE THE RAP FOR ME" BULL-FEATHERS!
'CAUSE I'VE COME HOME, FELLOW FOWL!
HOWARD THE DUCK IS BACK!

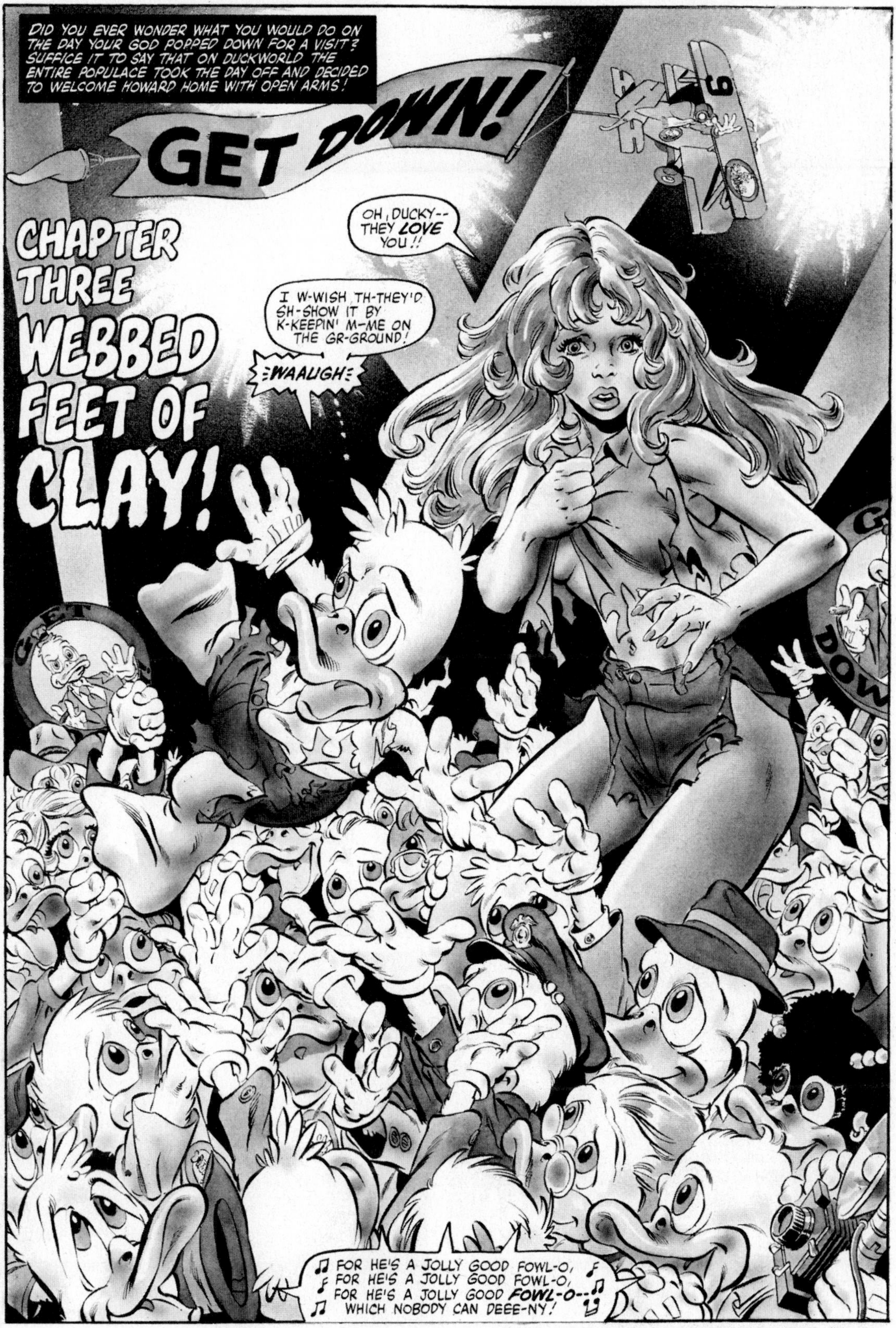
DID YOU EVER WONDER WHAT YOU WOULD DO ON THE DAY YOUR GOD POPPED DOWN FOR A VISIT? SUFFICE IT TO SAY THAT ON DUCKWORLD THE ENTIRE POPULACE TOOK THE DAY OFF AND DECIDED TO WELCOME HOWARD HOME WITH OPEN ARMS!
GET DOWN!
CHAPTER THREE
WEBBED FEET OF CLAY!
OH, DUCKY-- THEY LOVE YOU!!
I W-WISH TH-THEY'D SH-SHOW IT BY K-KEEPIN' M-ME ON THE GR-GROUND!
WAAUGH!
FOR HE'S A JOLLY GOOD FOWL-O, FOR HE'S A JOLLY GOOD FOWL-O, FOR HE'S A JOLLY GOOD FOWL-O-- WHICH NOBODY CAN DEEE-NY!

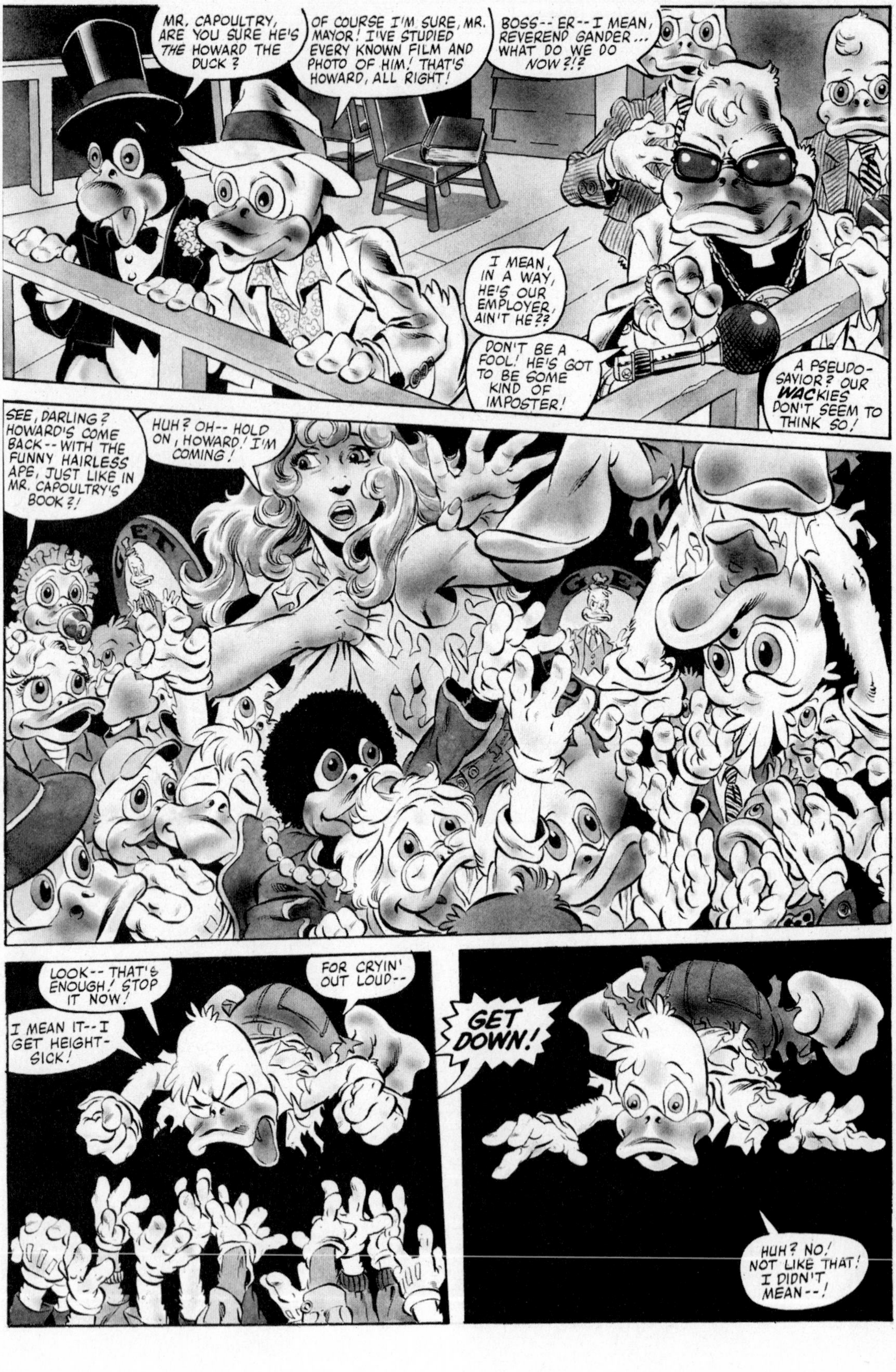
MR. CAPOULTRY, ARE YOU SURE HE'S THE HOWARD THE DUCK ?
OF COURSE I'M SURE, MR. MAYOR! I'VE STUDIED EVERY KNOWN FILM AND PHOTO OF HIM! THAT'S HOWARD, ALL RIGHT!
BOSS-- ER-- I MEAN, REVEREND GANDER... WHAT DO WE DO NOW?!?
I MEAN, IN A WAY, HE'S OUR EMPLOYER, AIN'T HE??
DON'T BE A FOOL! HE'S GOT TO BE SOME KIND OF IMPOSTER!
A PSEUDO-SAVIOR? OUR WACKIES DON'T SEEM TO THINK SO!
SEE, DARLING? HOWARD'S COME BACK-- WITH THE FUNNY HAIRLESS APE, JUST LIKE IN MR. CAPOULTRY'S BOOK?!
HUH? OH-- HOLD ON, HOWARD! I'M COMING!
LOOK-- THAT'S ENOUGH! STOP IT NOW!
I MEAN IT-- I GET HEIGHT-SICK!
FOR CRYIN' OUT LOUD--
GET DOWN!
HUH? NO! NOT LIKE THAT! I DIDN'T MEAN--!

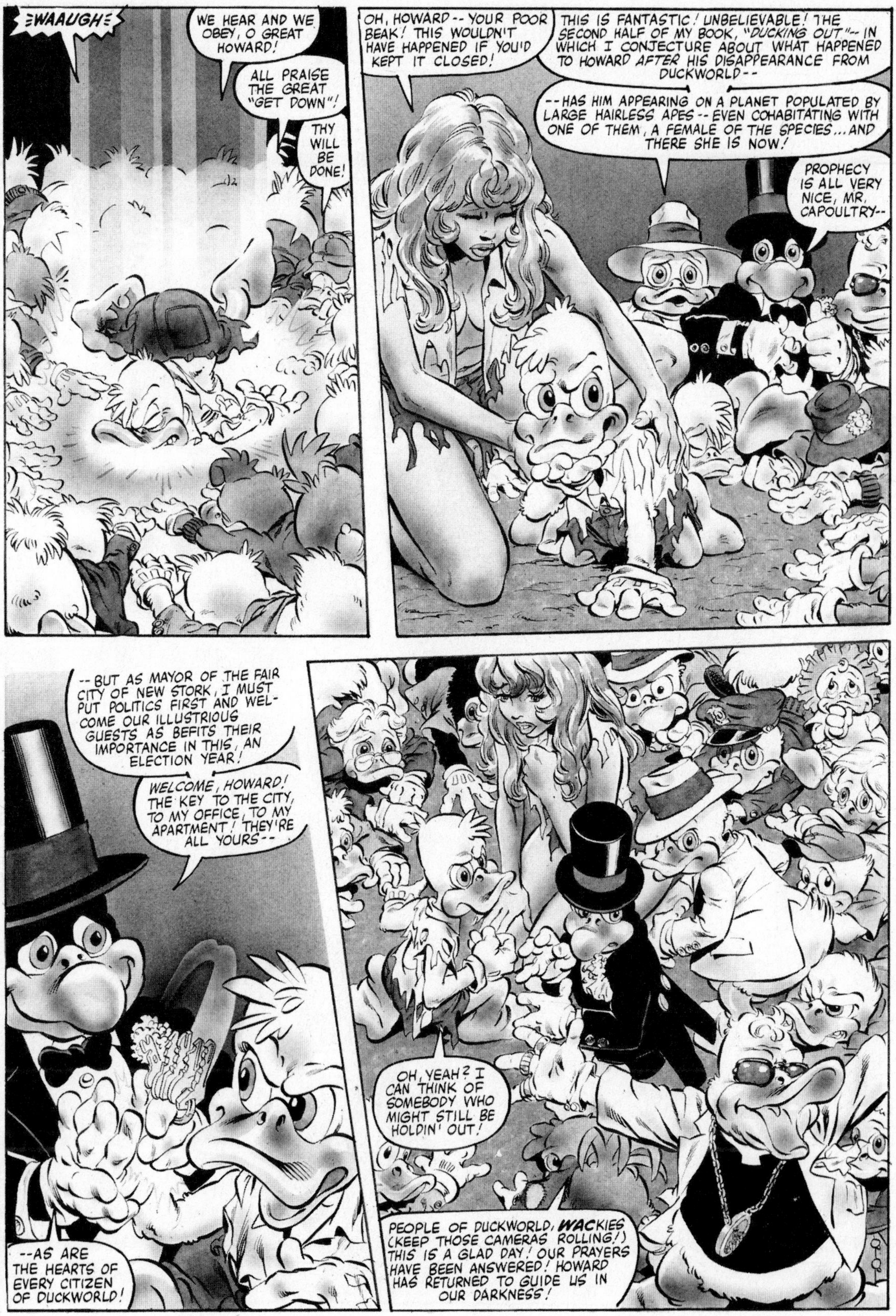
WAAUGH!
WE HEAR AND WE OBEY, O GREAT HOWARD!
ALL PRAISE THE GREAT "GET DOWN"!
THY WILL BE DONE!
OH, HOWARD -- YOUR POOR BEAK! THIS WOULDN'T HAVE HAPPENED IF YOU'D KEPT IT CLOSED!
THIS IS FANTASTIC! UNBELIEVABLE! THE SECOND HALF OF MY BOOK, "DUCKING OUT" -- IN WHICH I CONJECTURE ABOUT WHAT HAPPENED TO HOWARD AFTER HIS DISAPPEARANCE FROM DUCKWORLD --
-- HAS HIM APPEARING ON A PLANET POPULATED BY LARGE HAIRLESS APES -- EVEN COHABITATING WITH ONE OF THEM, A FEMALE OF THE SPECIES... AND THERE SHE IS NOW!
PROPHECY IS ALL VERY NICE, MR. CAPOULTRY--
-- BUT AS MAYOR OF THE FAIR CITY OF NEW STORK, I MUST PUT POLITICS FIRST AND WELCOME OUR ILLUSTRIOUS GUESTS AS BEFITS THEIR IMPORTANCE IN THIS, AN ELECTION YEAR!
WELCOME, HOWARD! THE KEY TO THE CITY, TO MY OFFICE, TO MY APARTMENT! THEY'RE ALL YOURS--
--AS ARE THE HEARTS OF EVERY CITIZEN OF DUCKWORLD!
OH, YEAH? I CAN THINK OF SOMEBODY WHO MIGHT STILL BE HOLDIN' OUT!
PEOPLE OF DUCKWORLD, WACKIES (KEEP THOSE CAMERAS ROLLING!) THIS IS A GLAD DAY! OUR PRAYERS HAVE BEEN ANSWERED! HOWARD HAS RETURNED TO GUIDE US IN OUR DARKNESS!

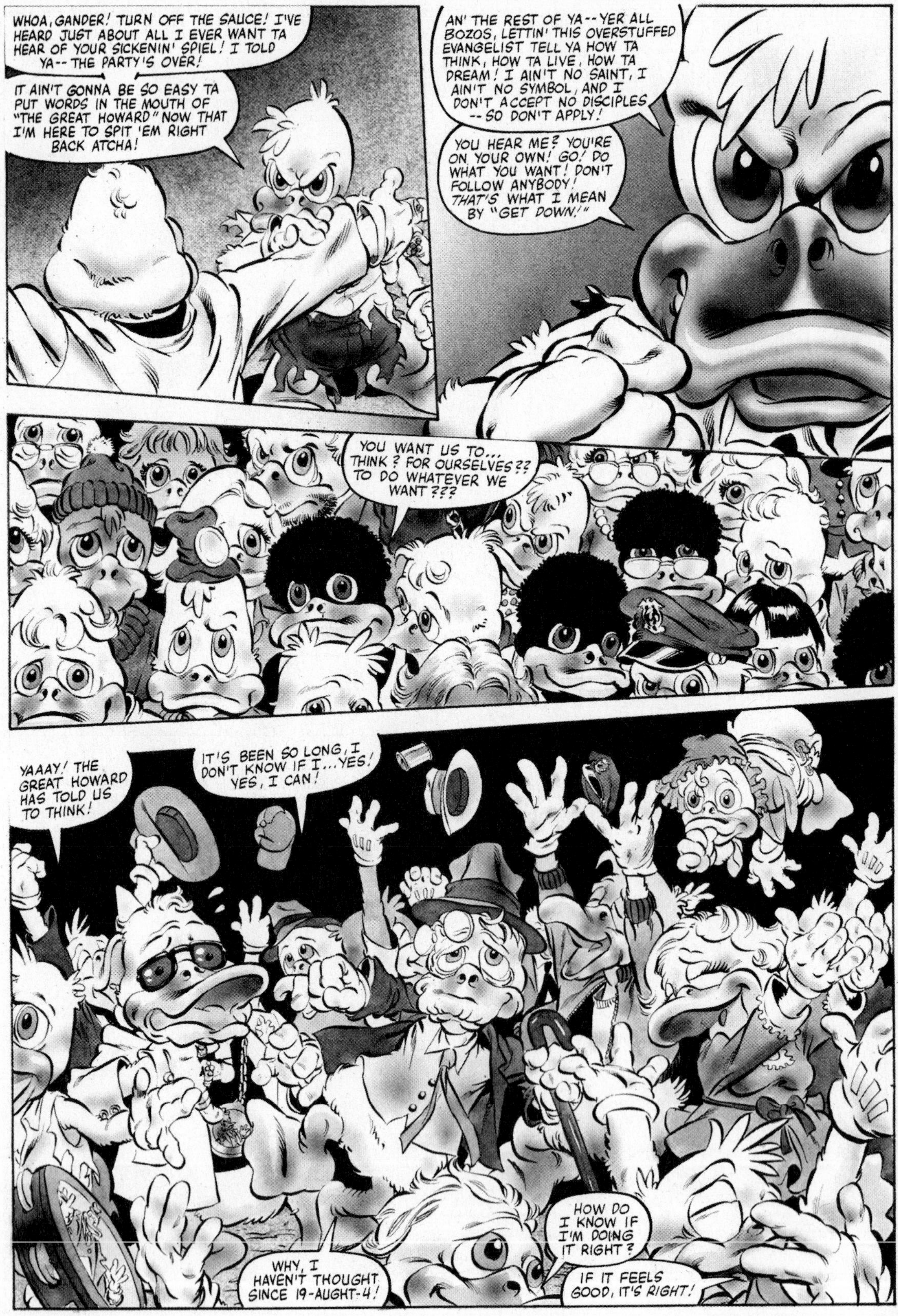
WHOA, GANDER! TURN OFF THE SAUCE! I'VE HEARD JUST ABOUT ALL I EVER WANT TA HEAR OF YOUR SICKENIN' SPIEL! I TOLD YA-- THE PARTY'S OVER!
IT AIN'T GONNA BE SO EASY TA PUT WORDS IN THE MOUTH OF "THE GREAT HOWARD" NOW THAT I'M HERE TO SPIT 'EM RIGHT BACK ATCHA!
AN' THE REST OF YA-- YER ALL BOZOS, LETTIN' THIS OVERSTUFFED EVANGELIST TELL YA HOW TA THINK, HOW TA LIVE, HOW TA DREAM! I AIN'T NO SAINT, I AIN'T NO SYMBOL, AND I DON'T ACCEPT NO DISCIPLES --SO DON'T APPLY!
YOU HEAR ME? YOU'RE ON YOUR OWN! GO! DO WHAT YOU WANT! DON'T FOLLOW ANYBODY! THAT'S WHAT I MEAN BY "GET DOWN!"
YOU WANT US TO... THINK? FOR OURSELVES?? TO DO WHATEVER WE WANT???
YAAAY! THE GREAT HOWARD HAS TOLD US TO THINK!
IT'S BEEN SO LONG, I DON'T KNOW IF I... YES! YES, I CAN!
HOW DO I KNOW IF I'M DOING IT RIGHT?
WHY, I HAVEN'T THOUGHT SINCE 19-AUGHT-4!
IF IT FEELS GOOD, IT'S RIGHT!

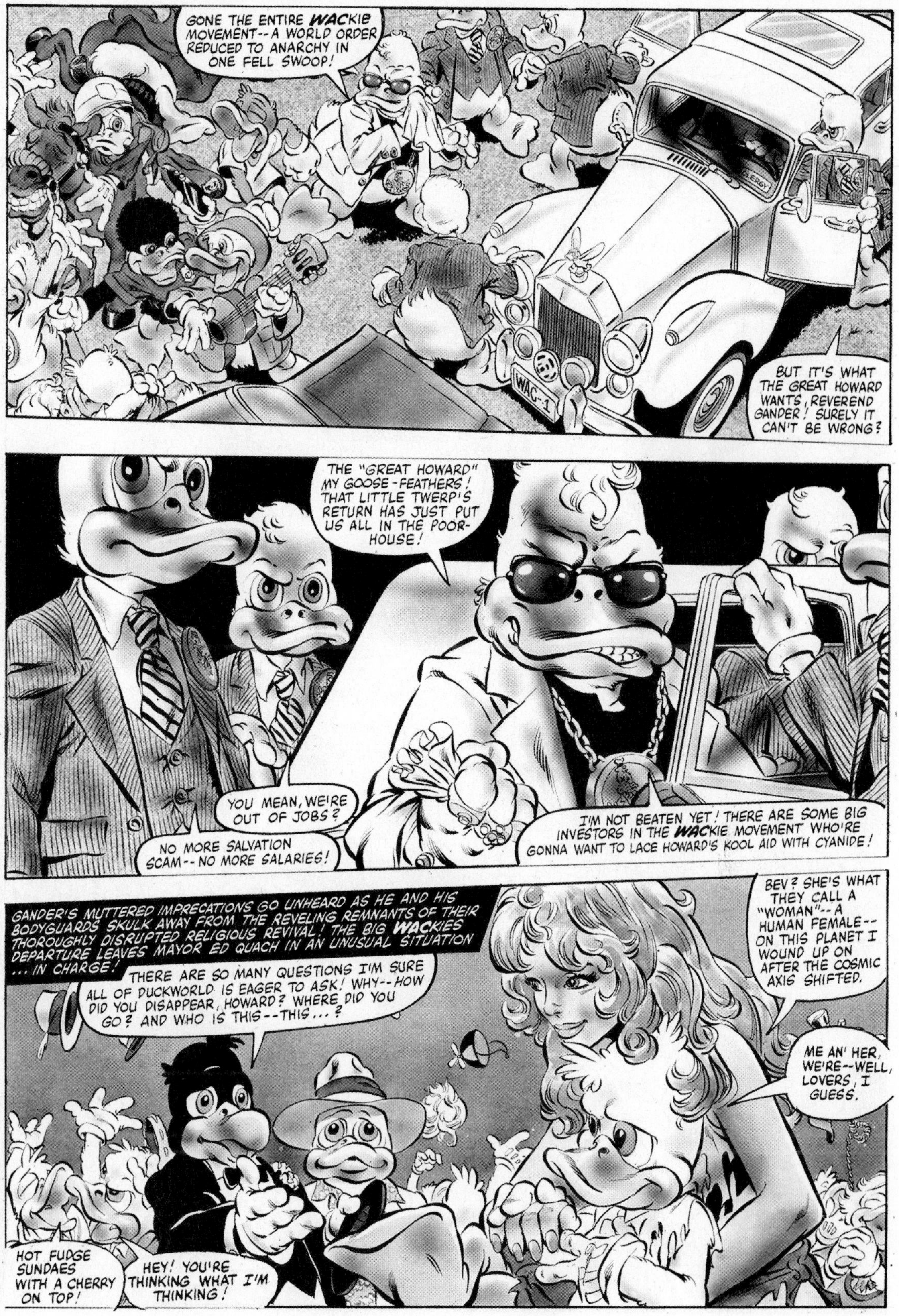
GONE THE ENTIRE WACKIE MOVEMENT--A WORLD ORDER REDUCED TO ANARCHY IN ONE FELL SWOOP!
BUT IT'S WHAT THE GREAT HOWARD WANTS, REVEREND GANDER! SURELY IT CAN'T BE WRONG?
WAC-1
THE "GREAT HOWARD" MY GOOSE-FEATHERS! THAT LITTLE TWERP'S RETURN HAS JUST PUT US ALL IN THE POOR-HOUSE!
YOU MEAN, WE'RE OUT OF JOBS?
NO MORE SALVATION SCAM--NO MORE SALARIES!
I'M NOT BEATEN YET! THERE ARE SOME BIG INVESTORS IN THE WACKIE MOVEMENT WHO'RE GONNA WANT TO LACE HOWARD'S KOOL AID WITH CYANIDE!
GANDER'S MUTTERED IMPRECATIONS GO UNHEARD AS HE AND HIS BODYGUARDS SKULK AWAY FROM THE REVELING REMNANTS OF THEIR THOROUGHLY DISRUPTED RELIGIOUS REVIVAL! THE BIG WACKIES DEPARTURE LEAVES MAYOR ED QUACH IN AN UNUSUAL SITUATION ... IN CHARGE!
THERE ARE SO MANY QUESTIONS I'M SURE ALL OF DUCKWORLD IS EAGER TO ASK! WHY--HOW DID YOU DISAPPEAR, HOWARD? WHERE DID YOU GO? AND WHO IS THIS--THIS...?
BEV? SHE'S WHAT THEY CALL A "WOMAN"--A HUMAN FEMALE--ON THIS PLANET I WOUND UP ON AFTER THE COSMIC AXIS SHIFTED.
ME AN' HER, WE'RE--WELL, LOVERS, I GUESS.
HOT FUDGE SUNDAES WITH A CHERRY ON TOP!
HEY! YOU'RE THINKING WHAT I'M THINKING!

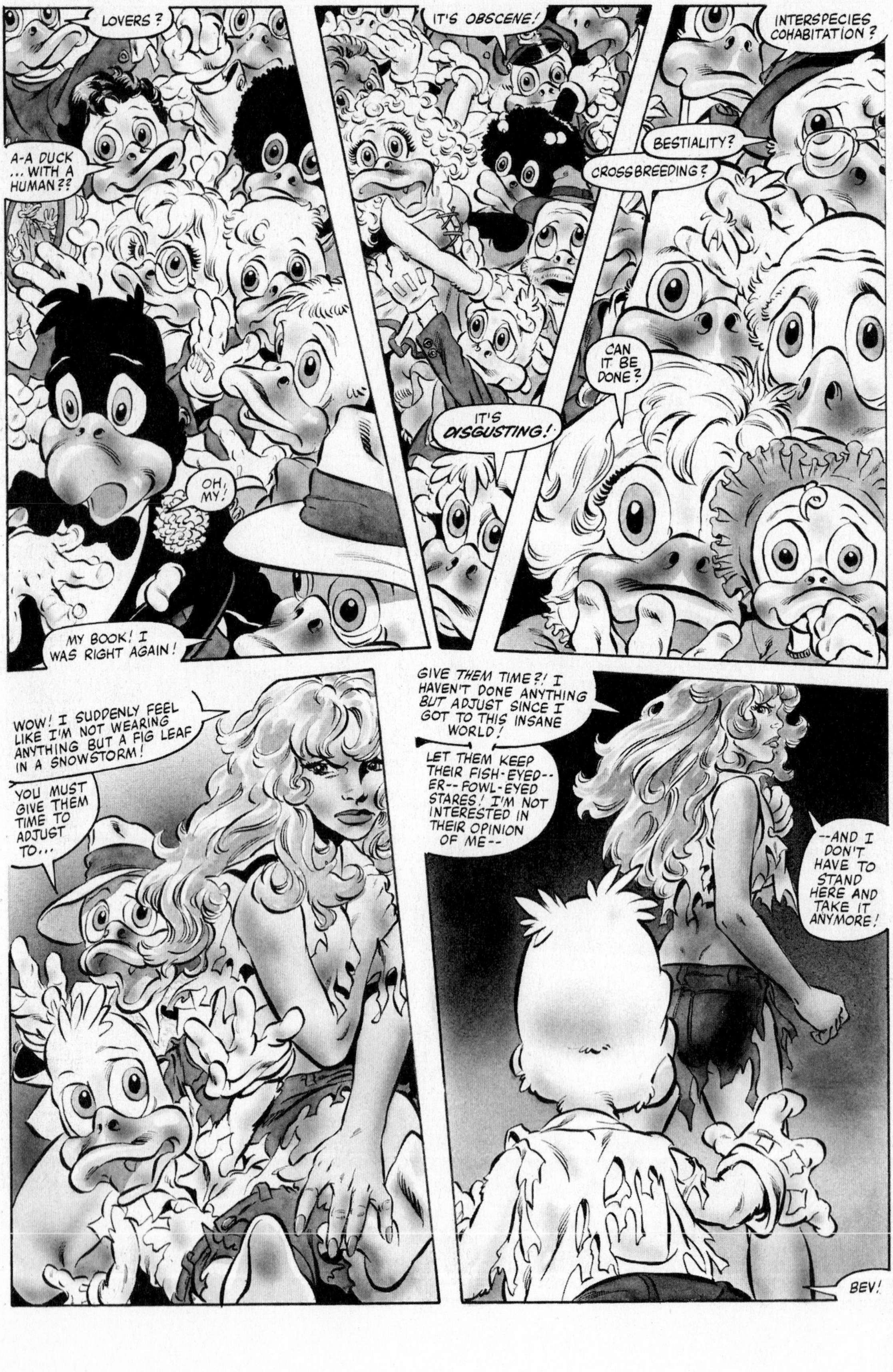
LOVERS?
A-A DUCK ...WITH A HUMAN??
OH, MY!
MY BOOK! I WAS RIGHT AGAIN!
IT'S OBSCENE!
IT'S DISGUSTING!
INTERSPECIES COHABITATION?
BESTIALITY?
CROSSBREEDING?
CAN IT BE DONE?
WOW! I SUDDENLY FEEL LIKE I'M NOT WEARING ANYTHING BUT A FIG LEAF IN A SNOWSTORM!
YOU MUST GIVE THEM TIME TO ADJUST TO...
GIVE THEM TIME?! I HAVEN'T DONE ANYTHING BUT ADJUST SINCE I GOT TO THIS INSANE WORLD!
LET THEM KEEP THEIR FISH-EYED-- ER-- FOWL-EYED STARES! I'M NOT INTERESTED IN THEIR OPINION OF ME--
--AND I DON'T HAVE TO STAND HERE AND TAKE IT ANYMORE!
BEV!

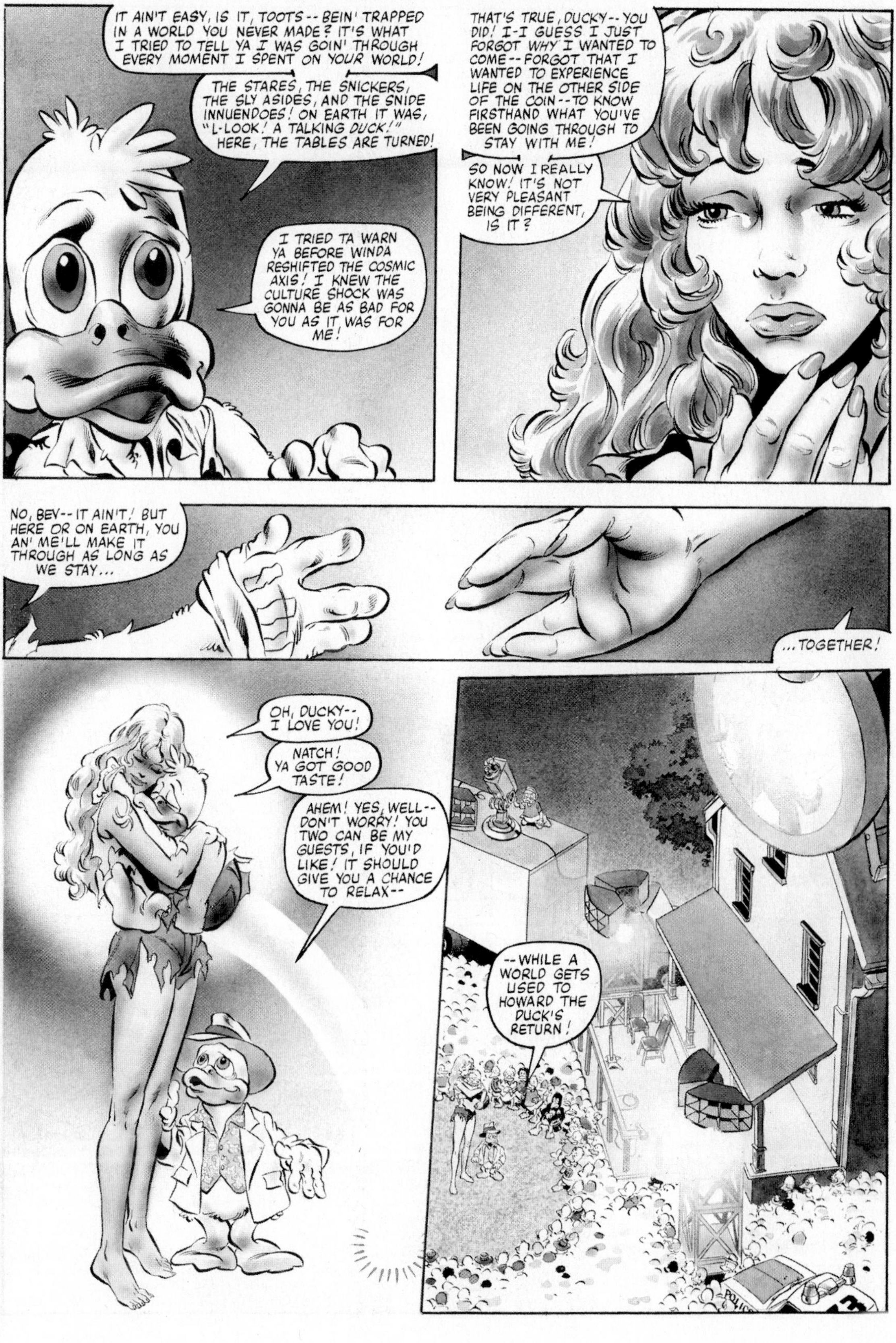
IT AIN'T EASY, IS IT, TOOTS -- BEIN' TRAPPED IN A WORLD YOU NEVER MADE? IT'S WHAT I TRIED TO TELL YA I WAS GOIN' THROUGH EVERY MOMENT I SPENT ON YOUR WORLD!
THE STARES, THE SNICKERS, THE SLY ASIDES, AND THE SNIDE INNUENDOES! ON EARTH IT WAS, "L-LOOK! A TALKING DUCK!" HERE, THE TABLES ARE TURNED!
I TRIED TA WARN YA BEFORE WINDA RESHIFTED THE COSMIC AXIS! I KNEW THE CULTURE SHOCK WAS GONNA BE AS BAD FOR YOU AS IT WAS FOR ME!
THAT'S TRUE, DUCKY -- YOU DID! I-I GUESS I JUST FORGOT WHY I WANTED TO COME -- FORGOT THAT I WANTED TO EXPERIENCE LIFE ON THE OTHER SIDE OF THE COIN -- TO KNOW FIRSTHAND WHAT YOU'VE BEEN GOING THROUGH TO STAY WITH ME!
SO NOW I REALLY KNOW! IT'S NOT VERY PLEASANT BEING DIFFERENT, IS IT?
NO, BEV -- IT AIN'T! BUT HERE OR ON EARTH, YOU AN' ME'LL MAKE IT THROUGH AS LONG AS WE STAY...
...TOGETHER!
OH, DUCKY -- I LOVE YOU!
NATCH! YA GOT GOOD TASTE!
AHEM! YES, WELL -- DON'T WORRY! YOU TWO CAN BE MY GUESTS, IF YOU'D LIKE! IT SHOULD GIVE YOU A CHANCE TO RELAX --
-- WHILE A WORLD GETS USED TO HOWARD THE DUCK'S RETURN!

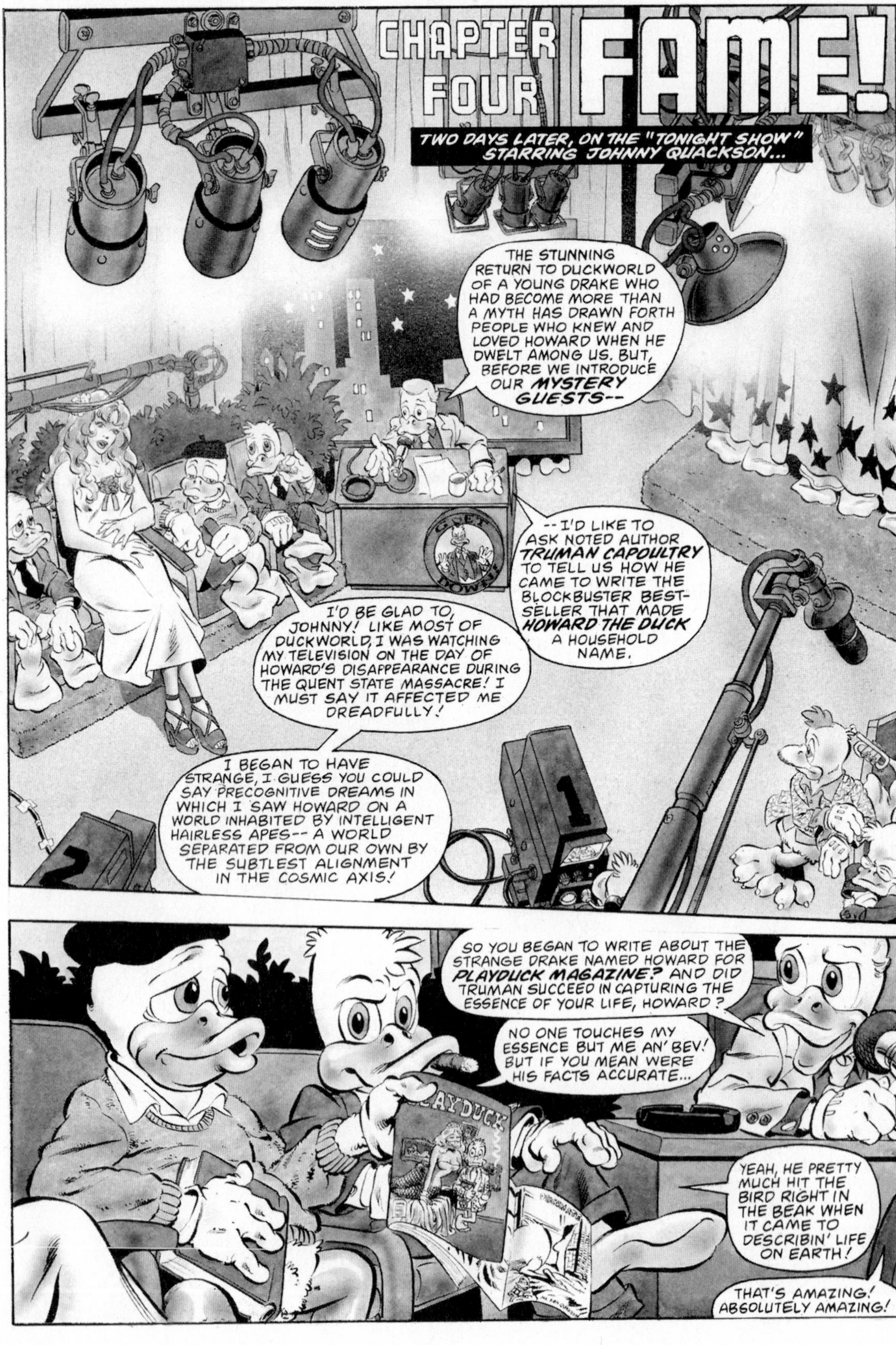
CHAPTER FOUR
FAME!
TWO DAYS LATER, ON THE "TONIGHT SHOW" STARRING JOHNNY QUACKSON...
THE STUNNING RETURN TO DUCKWORLD OF A YOUNG DRAKE WHO HAD BECOME MORE THAN A MYTH HAS DRAWN FORTH PEOPLE WHO KNEW AND LOVED HOWARD WHEN HE DWELT AMONG US. BUT, BEFORE WE INTRODUCE OUR MYSTERY GUESTS--
--I'D LIKE TO ASK NOTED AUTHOR TRUMAN CAPOULTRY TO TELL US HOW HE CAME TO WRITE THE BLOCKBUSTER BEST-SELLER THAT MADE HOWARD THE DUCK A HOUSEHOLD NAME.
I'D BE GLAD TO, JOHNNY! LIKE MOST OF DUCKWORLD, I WAS WATCHING MY TELEVISION ON THE DAY OF HOWARD'S DISAPPEARANCE DURING THE QUENT STATE MASSACRE! I MUST SAY IT AFFECTED ME DREADFULLY!
I BEGAN TO HAVE STRANGE, I GUESS YOU COULD SAY PRECOGNITIVE DREAMS IN WHICH I SAW HOWARD ON A WORLD INHABITED BY INTELLIGENT HAIRLESS APES-- A WORLD SEPARATED FROM OUR OWN BY THE SUBTLEST ALIGNMENT IN THE COSMIC AXIS!
SO YOU BEGAN TO WRITE ABOUT THE STRANGE DRAKE NAMED HOWARD FOR PLAYDUCK MAGAZINE? AND DID TRUMAN SUCCEED IN CAPTURING THE ESSENCE OF YOUR LIFE, HOWARD?
NO ONE TOUCHES MY ESSENCE BUT ME AN' BEV! BUT IF YOU MEAN WERE HIS FACTS ACCURATE...
YEAH, HE PRETTY MUCH HIT THE BIRD RIGHT IN THE BEAK WHEN IT CAME TO DESCRIBIN' LIFE ON EARTH!
THAT'S AMAZING! ABSOLUTELY AMAZING!

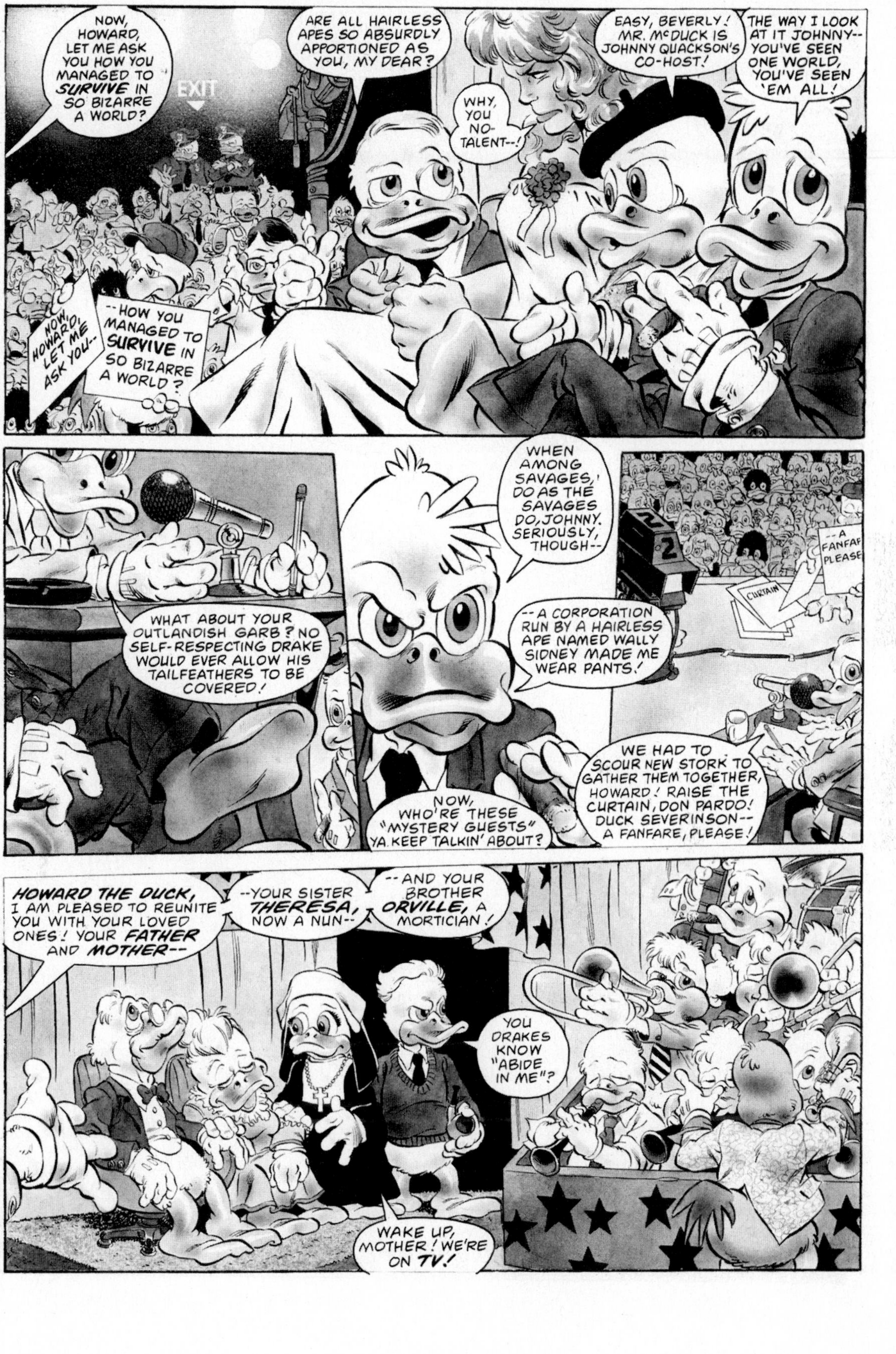
NOW, HOWARD, LET ME ASK YOU HOW YOU MANAGED TO SURVIVE IN SO BIZARRE A WORLD?
EXIT
ARE ALL HAIRLESS APES SO ABSURDLY APPORTIONED AS YOU, MY DEAR?
WHY, YOU NO-TALENT--!
EASY, BEVERLY! MR. McDUCK IS JOHNNY QUACKSON'S CO-HOST!
THE WAY I LOOK AT IT JOHNNY-- YOU'VE SEEN ONE WORLD, YOU'VE SEEN 'EM ALL!
NOW, HOWARD, LET ME ASK YOU--
--HOW YOU MANAGED TO SURVIVE IN SO BIZARRE A WORLD?
WHAT ABOUT YOUR OUTLANDISH GARB? NO SELF-RESPECTING DRAKE WOULD EVER ALLOW HIS TAILFEATHERS TO BE COVERED!
WHEN AMONG SAVAGES, DO AS THE SAVAGES DO, JOHNNY. SERIOUSLY, THOUGH--
--A CORPORATION RUN BY A HAIRLESS APE NAMED WALLY SIDNEY MADE ME WEAR PANTS!
NOW, WHO'RE THESE "MYSTERY GUESTS" YA KEEP TALKIN' ABOUT?
2
--A FANFARE PLEASE
CURTAIN
WE HAD TO SCOUR NEW STORK TO GATHER THEM TOGETHER, HOWARD! RAISE THE CURTAIN, DON PARDO! DUCK SEVERINSON-- A FANFARE, PLEASE!
HOWARD THE DUCK, I AM PLEASED TO REUNITE YOU WITH YOUR LOVED ONES! YOUR FATHER AND MOTHER--
--YOUR SISTER THERESA, NOW A NUN--
--AND YOUR BROTHER ORVILLE, A MORTICIAN!
YOU DRAKES KNOW "ABIDE IN ME"?
WAKE UP, MOTHER! WE'RE ON TV!

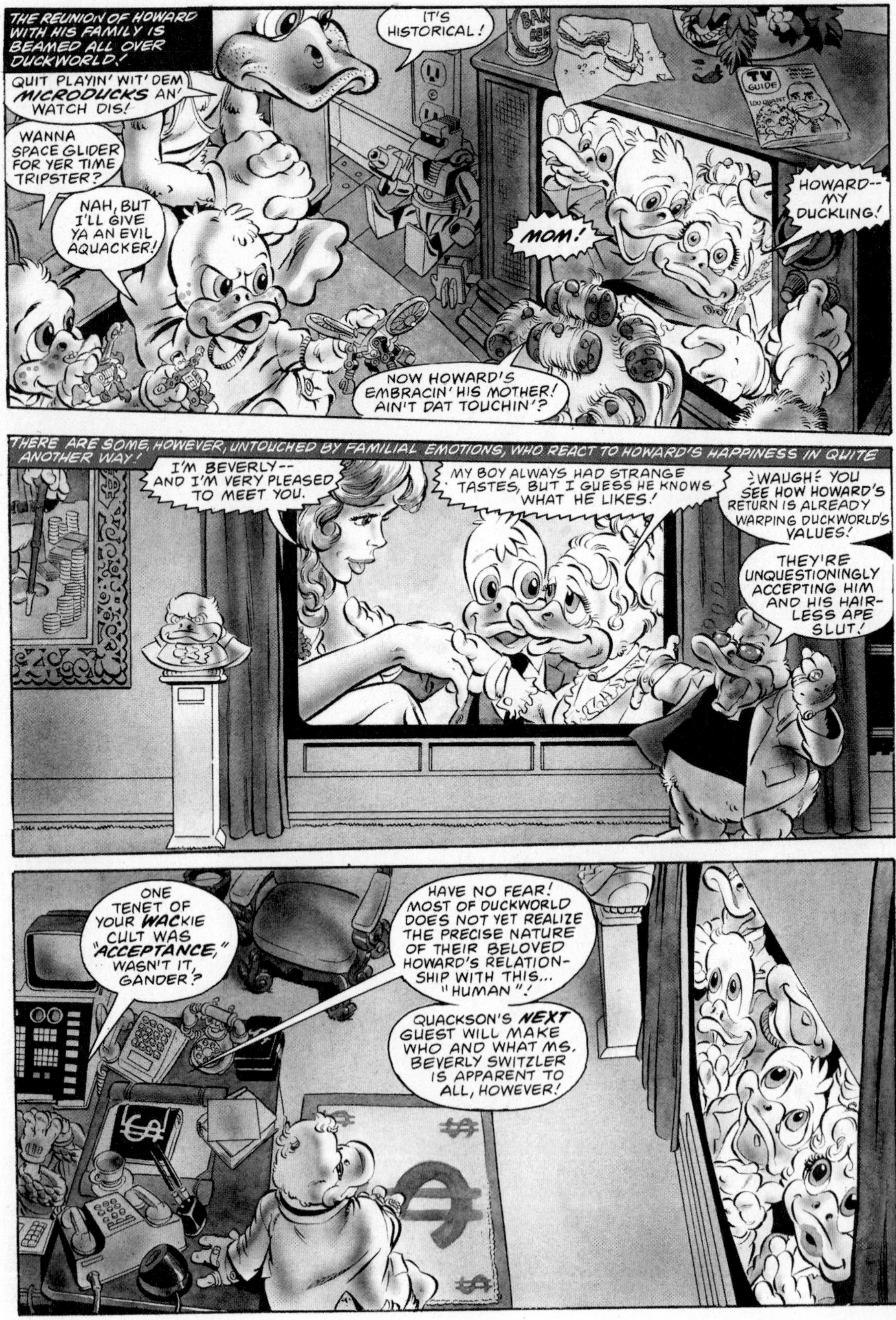
THE REUNION OF HOWARD WITH HIS FAMILY IS BEAMED ALL OVER DUCKWORLD!
IT'S HISTORICAL!
QUIT PLAYIN' WIT' DEM MICRODUCKS AN' WATCH DIS!
WANNA SPACE GLIDER FOR YER TIME TRIPSTER?
NAH, BUT I'LL GIVE YA AN EVIL AQUACKER!
MOM!
HOWARD-- MY DUCKLING!
NOW HOWARD'S EMBRACIN' HIS MOTHER! AIN'T DAT TOUCHIN'?
THERE ARE SOME, HOWEVER, UNTOUCHED BY FAMILIAL EMOTIONS, WHO REACT TO HOWARD'S HAPPINESS IN QUITE ANOTHER WAY!
I'M BEVERLY-- AND I'M VERY PLEASED TO MEET YOU.
MY BOY ALWAYS HAD STRANGE TASTES, BUT I GUESS HE KNOWS WHAT HE LIKES!
WAUGH! YOU SEE HOW HOWARD'S RETURN IS ALREADY WARPING DUCKWORLD'S VALUES!
THEY'RE UNQUESTIONINGLY ACCEPTING HIM AND HIS HAIRLESS APE SLUT!
ONE TENET OF YOUR WACKIE CULT WAS "ACCEPTANCE," WASN'T IT, GANDER?
HAVE NO FEAR! MOST OF DUCKWORLD DOES NOT YET REALIZE THE PRECISE NATURE OF THEIR BELOVED HOWARD'S RELATIONSHIP WITH THIS... "HUMAN"!
QUACKSON'S NEXT GUEST WILL MAKE WHO AND WHAT MS. BEVERLY SWITZLER IS APPARENT TO ALL, HOWEVER!

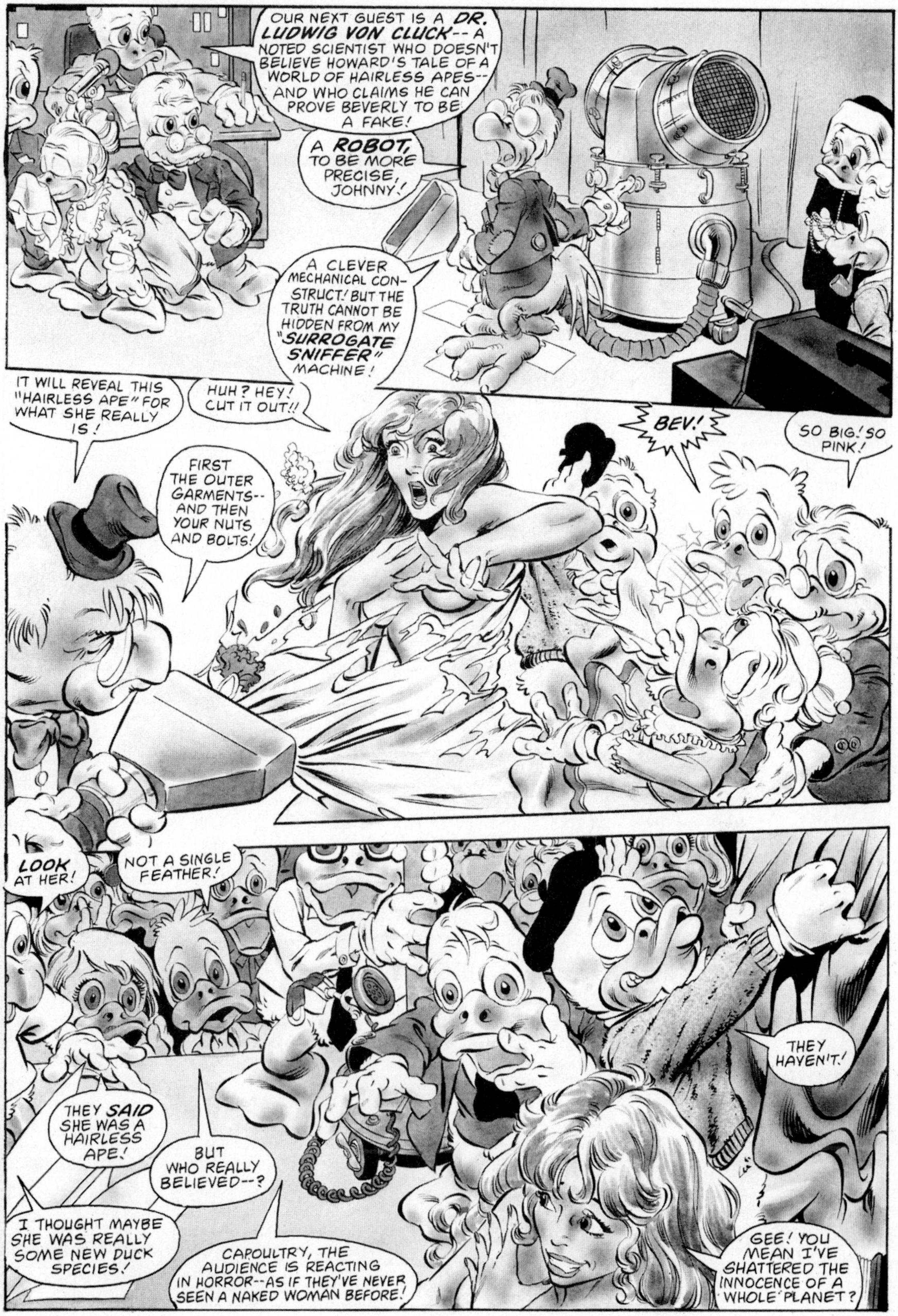

OUR NEXT GUEST IS A DR. LUDWIG VON CLUCK-- A NOTED SCIENTIST WHO DOESN'T BELIEVE HOWARD'S TALE OF A WORLD OF HAIRLESS APES-- AND WHO CLAIMS HE CAN PROVE BEVERLY TO BE A FAKE!
A ROBOT, TO BE MORE PRECISE, JOHNNY!
A CLEVER MECHANICAL CONSTRUCT! BUT THE TRUTH CANNOT BE HIDDEN FROM MY "SURROGATE SNIFFER" MACHINE!
IT WILL REVEAL THIS "HAIRLESS APE" FOR WHAT SHE REALLY IS!
HUH? HEY! CUT IT OUT!!
FIRST THE OUTER GARMENTS-- AND THEN YOUR NUTS AND BOLTS!
BEV!
SO BIG! SO PINK!
LOOK AT HER!
NOT A SINGLE FEATHER!
THEY SAID SHE WAS A HAIRLESS APE!
BUT WHO REALLY BELIEVED--?
THEY HAVEN'T!
I THOUGHT MAYBE SHE WAS REALLY SOME NEW DUCK SPECIES!
CAPOULTRY, THE AUDIENCE IS REACTING IN HORROR--AS IF THEY'VE NEVER SEEN A NAKED WOMAN BEFORE!
GEE! YOU MEAN I'VE SHATTERED THE INNOCENCE OF A WHOLE PLANET?

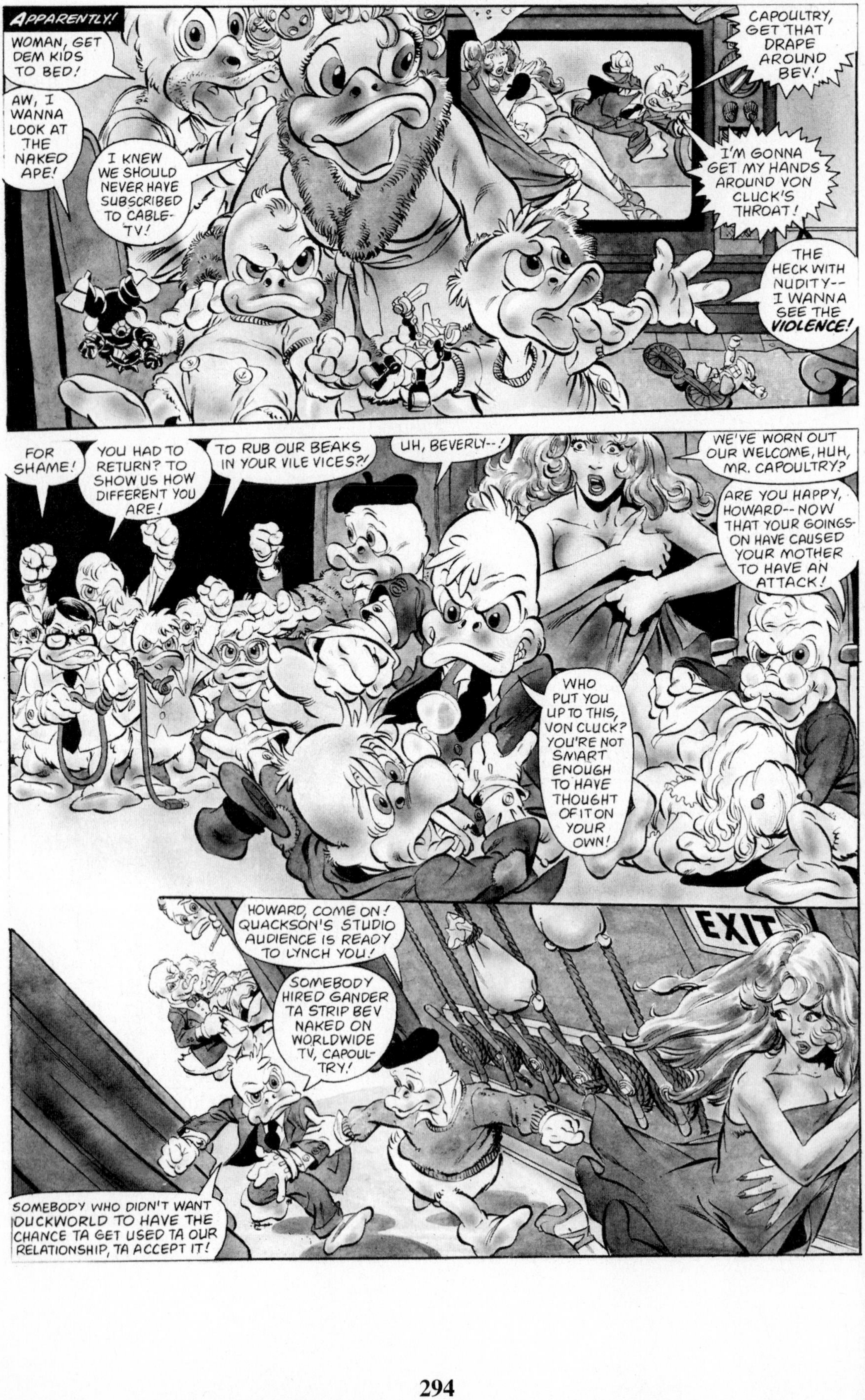
APPARENTLY!
WOMAN, GET DEM KIDS TO BED!
AW, I WANNA LOOK AT THE NAKED APE!
I KNEW WE SHOULD NEVER HAVE SUBSCRIBED TO CABLE-TV!
CAPOULTRY, GET THAT DRAPE AROUND BEV!
I'M GONNA GET MY HANDS AROUND VON CLUCK'S THROAT!
THE HECK WITH NUDITY-- I WANNA SEE THE VIOLENCE!
FOR SHAME!
YOU HAD TO RETURN? TO SHOW US HOW DIFFERENT YOU ARE!
TO RUB OUR BEAKS IN YOUR VILE VICES?!
UH, BEVERLY--!
WE'VE WORN OUT OUR WELCOME, HUH, MR. CAPOULTRY?
ARE YOU HAPPY, HOWARD-- NOW THAT YOUR GOINGS-ON HAVE CAUSED YOUR MOTHER TO HAVE AN ATTACK!
WHO PUT YOU UP TO THIS, VON CLUCK? YOU'RE NOT SMART ENOUGH TO HAVE THOUGHT OF IT ON YOUR OWN!
HOWARD, COME ON! QUACKSON'S STUDIO AUDIENCE IS READY TO LYNCH YOU!
EXIT
SOMEBODY HIRED GANDER TA STRIP BEV NAKED ON WORLDWIDE TV, CAPOULTRY!
SOMEBODY WHO DIDN'T WANT DUCKWORLD TO HAVE THE CHANCE TA GET USED TA OUR RELATIONSHIP, TA ACCEPT IT!

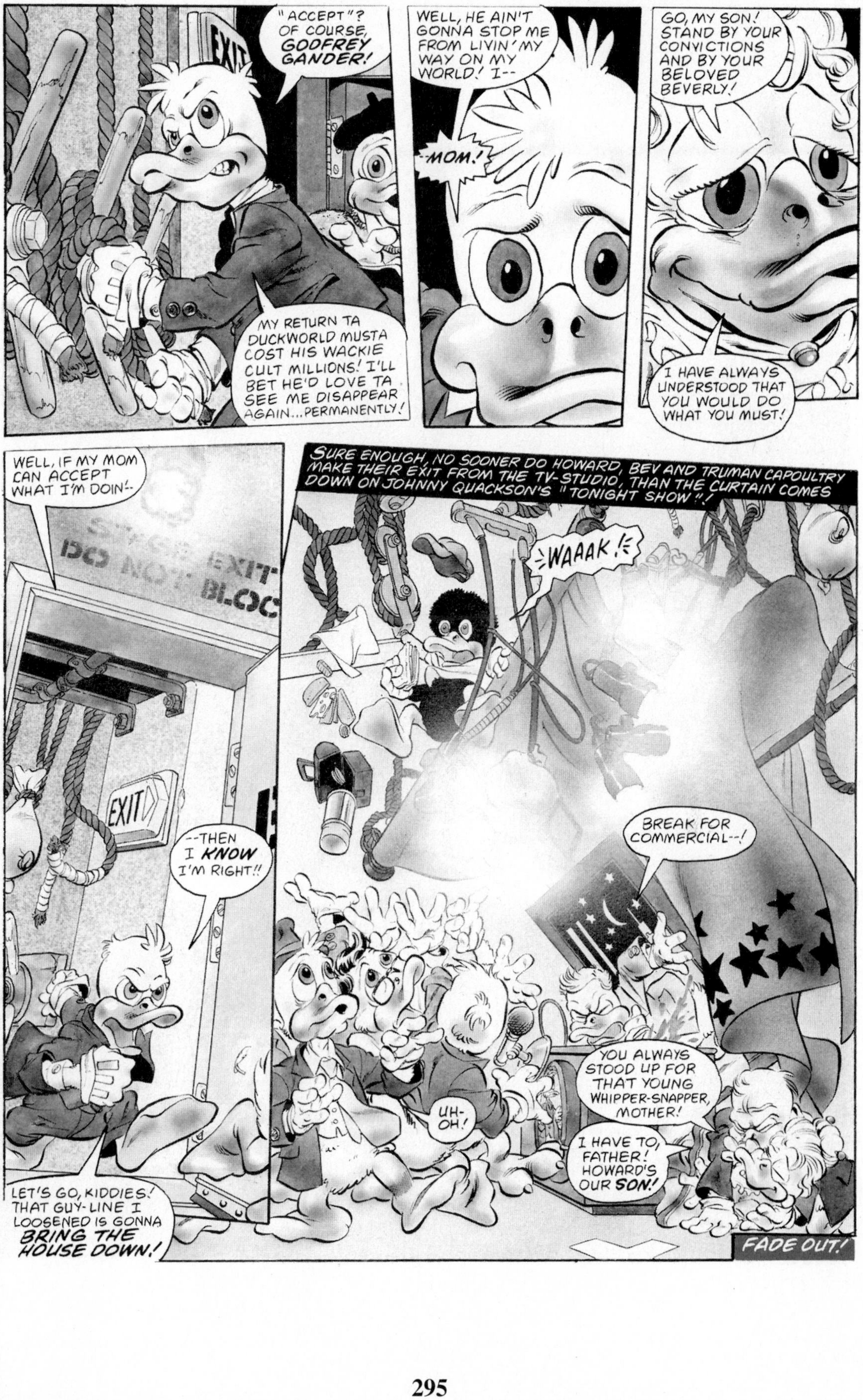
"ACCEPT"? OF COURSE, GODFREY GANDER!
MY RETURN TA DUCKWORLD MUSTA COST HIS WACKIE CULT MILLIONS! I'LL BET HE'D LOVE TA SEE ME DISAPPEAR AGAIN...PERMANENTLY!
EXIT
WELL, HE AIN'T GONNA STOP ME FROM LIVIN' MY WAY ON MY WORLD! I--
-MOM!
GO, MY SON! STAND BY YOUR CONVICTIONS AND BY YOUR BELOVED BEVERLY!
I HAVE ALWAYS UNDERSTOOD THAT YOU WOULD DO WHAT YOU MUST!
WELL, IF MY MOM CAN ACCEPT WHAT I'M DOIN'--
DO NOT BLOC
EXIT
--THEN I KNOW I'M RIGHT!!
LET'S GO, KIDDIES! THAT GUY-LINE I LOOSENED IS GONNA BRING THE HOUSE DOWN!
SURE ENOUGH, NO SOONER DO HOWARD, BEV AND TRUMAN CAPOULTRY MAKE THEIR EXIT FROM THE TV-STUDIO, THAN THE CURTAIN COMES DOWN ON JOHNNY QUACKSON'S "TONIGHT SHOW"!
WAAAK!
BREAK FOR COMMERCIAL--!
UH-OH!
YOU ALWAYS STOOD UP FOR THAT YOUNG WHIPPER-SNAPPER, MOTHER!
I HAVE TO, FATHER! HOWARD'S OUR SON!
FADE OUT!

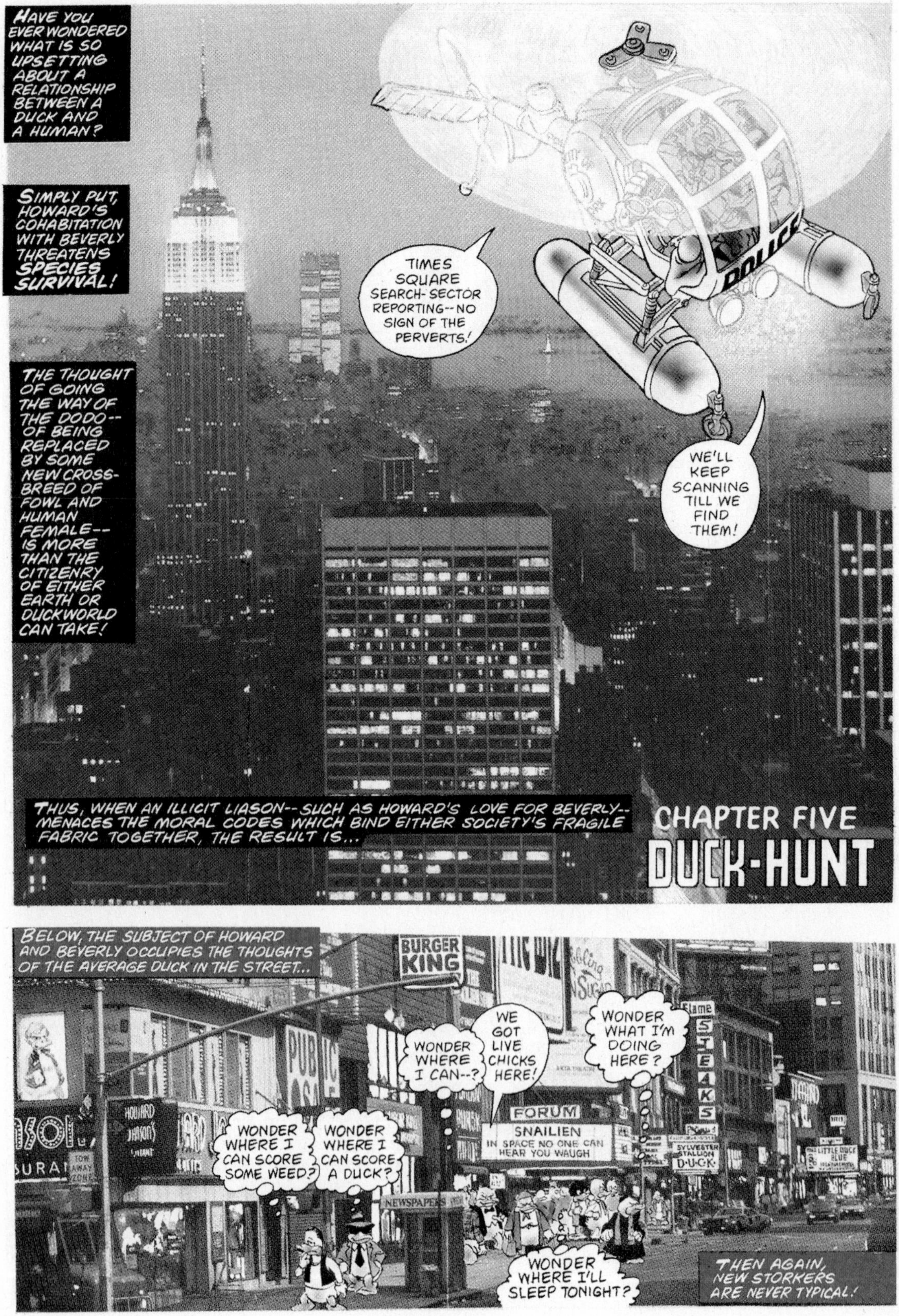

HAVE YOU EVER WONDERED WHAT IS SO UPSETTING ABOUT A RELATIONSHIP BETWEEN A DUCK AND A HUMAN?
SIMPLY PUT, HOWARD'S COHABITATION WITH BEVERLY THREATENS SPECIES SURVIVAL!
THE THOUGHT OF GOING THE WAY OF THE DODO-- OF BEING REPLACED BY SOME NEW CROSS-BREED OF FOWL AND HUMAN FEMALE-- IS MORE THAN THE CITIZENRY OF EITHER EARTH OR DUCKWORLD CAN TAKE!
TIMES SQUARE SEARCH-SECTOR REPORTING--NO SIGN OF THE PERVERTS!
WE'LL KEEP SCANNING TILL WE FIND THEM!
THUS, WHEN AN ILLICIT LIASON--SUCH AS HOWARD'S LOVE FOR BEVERLY--MENACES THE MORAL CODES WHICH BIND EITHER SOCIETY'S FRAGILE FABRIC TOGETHER, THE RESULT IS...
CHAPTER FIVE
DUCK-HUNT
BELOW, THE SUBJECT OF HOWARD AND BEVERLY OCCUPIES THE THOUGHTS OF THE AVERAGE DUCK IN THE STREET...
BURGER KING
WONDER WHERE I CAN--?
WE GOT LIVE CHICKS HERE!
WONDER WHAT I'M DOING HERE?
WONDER WHERE I CAN SCORE SOME WEED?
WONDER WHERE I CAN SCORE A DUCK?
FORUM
SNAILIEN
IN SPACE NO ONE CAN HEAR YOU WAUGH
STEAKS
SYLVESTER STALLION
D-U-C-K
NEWSPAPERS
WONDER WHERE I'LL SLEEP TONIGHT?
THEN AGAIN, NEW STORKERS ARE NEVER TYPICAL!

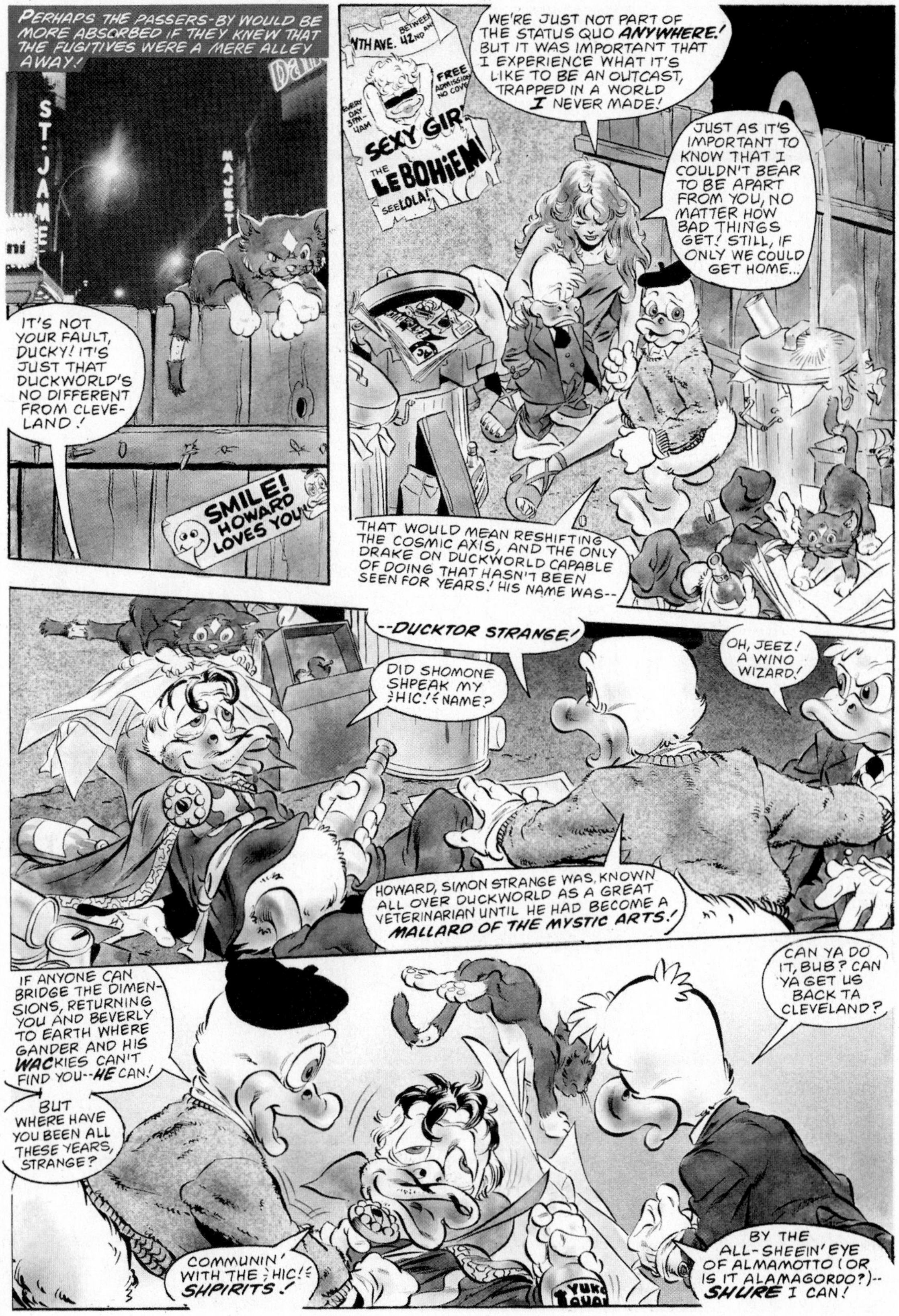
PERHAPS THE PASSERS-BY WOULD BE MORE ABSORBED IF THEY KNEW THAT THE FUGITIVES WERE A MERE ALLEY AWAY!
IT'S NOT YOUR FAULT, DUCKY! IT'S JUST THAT DUCKWORLD'S NO DIFFERENT FROM CLEVELAND!
SMILE! HOWARD LOVES YOU
WE'RE JUST NOT PART OF THE STATUS QUO ANYWHERE! BUT IT WAS IMPORTANT THAT I EXPERIENCE WHAT IT'S LIKE TO BE AN OUTCAST, TRAPPED IN A WORLD I NEVER MADE!
JUST AS IT'S IMPORTANT TO KNOW THAT I COULDN'T BEAR TO BE APART FROM YOU, NO MATTER HOW BAD THINGS GET! STILL, IF ONLY WE COULD GET HOME...
SEXY GIR
LE BOHIEM
SEE LOLA!
THAT WOULD MEAN RESHIFTING THE COSMIC AXIS, AND THE ONLY DRAKE ON DUCKWORLD CAPABLE OF DOING THAT HASN'T BEEN SEEN FOR YEARS! HIS NAME WAS--
--DUCKTOR STRANGE!
DID SHOMONE SHPEAK MY HIC! NAME?
OH, JEEZ! A WINO WIZARD!
HOWARD, SIMON STRANGE WAS KNOWN ALL OVER DUCKWORLD AS A GREAT VETERINARIAN UNTIL HE HAD BECOME A MALLARD OF THE MYSTIC ARTS!
IF ANYONE CAN BRIDGE THE DIMENSIONS, RETURNING YOU AND BEVERLY TO EARTH WHERE GANDER AND HIS WACKIES CAN'T FIND YOU--HE CAN!
BUT WHERE HAVE YOU BEEN ALL THESE YEARS, STRANGE?
COMMUNIN' WITH THE HIC! SHPIRITS!
CAN YA DO IT, BUB? CAN YA GET US BACK TA CLEVELAND?
BY THE ALL-SHEEIN' EYE OF ALMAMOTTO (OR IS IT ALAMAGORDO?)-- SHURE I CAN!

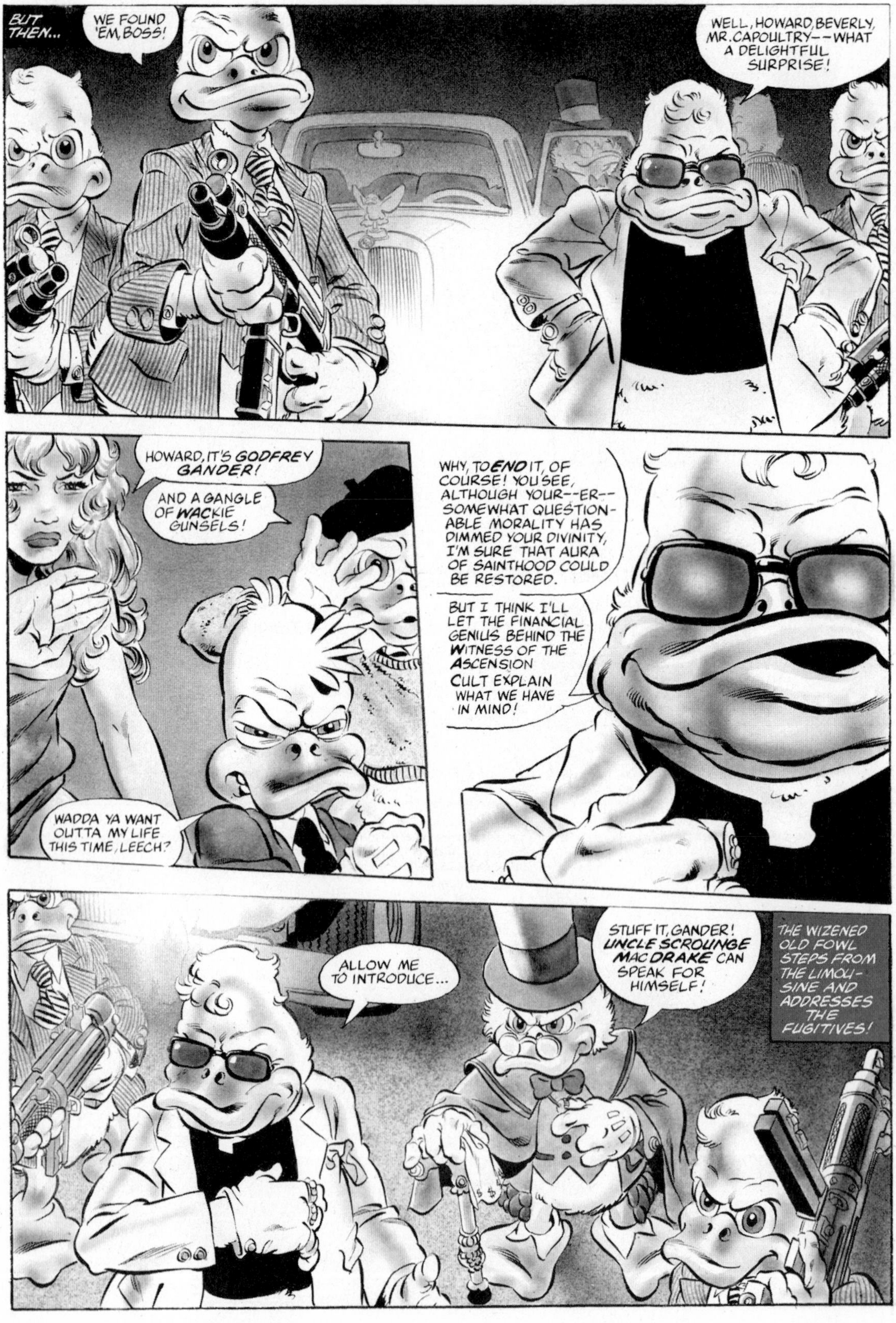
BUT THEN...
WE FOUND 'EM, BOSS!
WELL, HOWARD, BEVERLY, MR. CAPOULTRY--WHAT A DELIGHTFUL SURPRISE!
HOWARD, IT'S GODFREY GANDER!
AND A GANGLE OF WACKIE GUNSELS!
WADDA YA WANT OUTTA MY LIFE THIS TIME, LEECH?
WHY, TO END IT, OF COURSE! YOU SEE, ALTHOUGH YOUR--ER--SOMEWHAT QUESTIONABLE MORALITY HAS DIMMED YOUR DIVINITY, I'M SURE THAT AURA OF SAINTHOOD COULD BE RESTORED.
BUT I THINK I'LL LET THE FINANCIAL GENIUS BEHIND THE WITNESS OF THE ASCENSION CULT EXPLAIN WHAT WE HAVE IN MIND!
ALLOW ME TO INTRODUCE...
STUFF IT, GANDER! UNCLE SCROUNGE MACDRAKE CAN SPEAK FOR HIMSELF!
THE WIZENED OLD FOWL STEPS FROM THE LIMOUSINE AND ADDRESSES THE FUGITIVES!

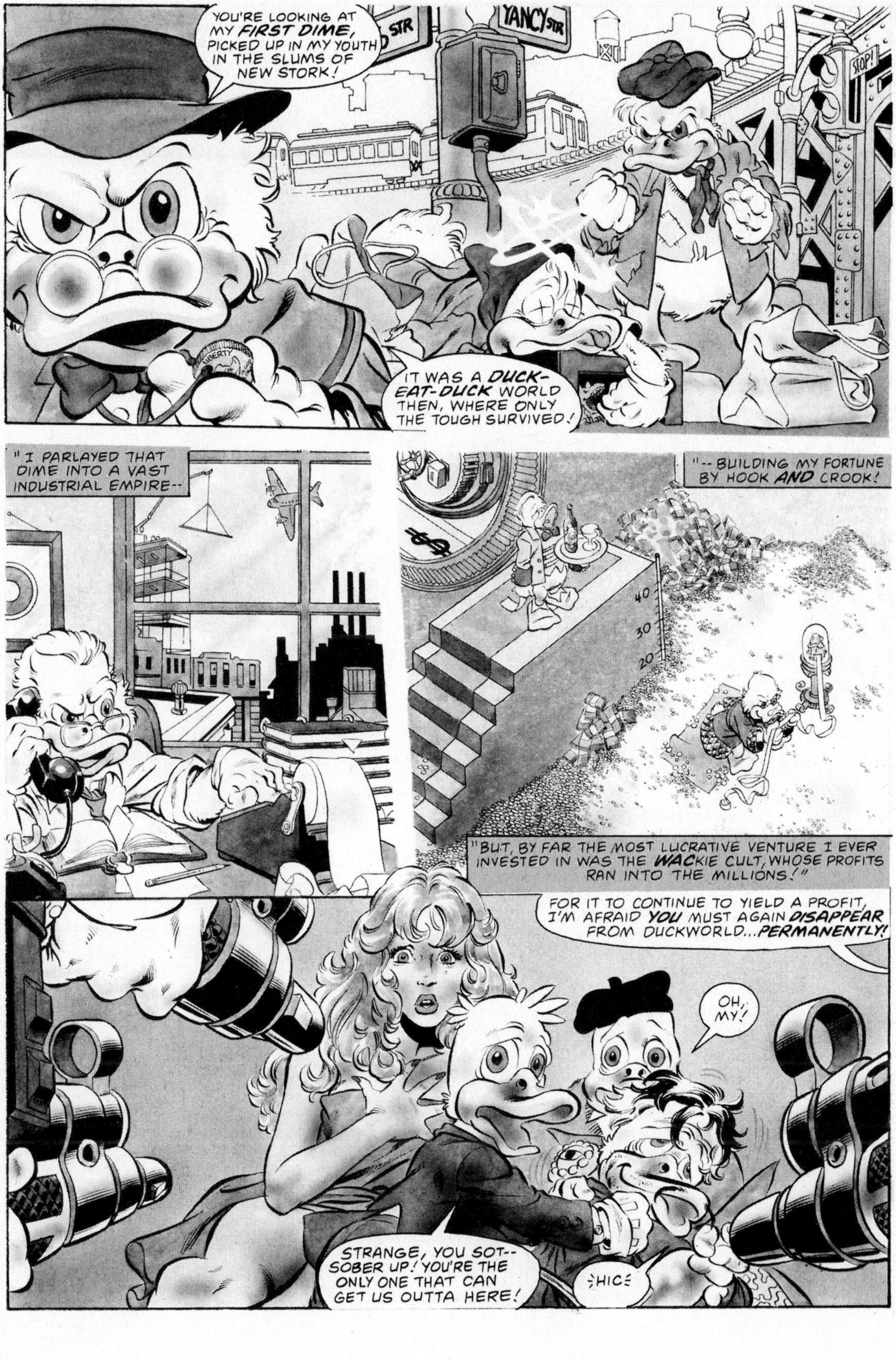
YOU'RE LOOKING AT MY FIRST DIME, PICKED UP IN MY YOUTH IN THE SLUMS OF NEW STORK!
YANCY STR
STOP!
IT WAS A DUCK-EAT-DUCK WORLD THEN, WHERE ONLY THE TOUGH SURVIVED!
"I PARLAYED THAT DIME INTO A VAST INDUSTRIAL EMPIRE--
"--BUILDING MY FORTUNE BY HOOK AND CROOK!
40
30
20
"BUT, BY FAR THE MOST LUCRATIVE VENTURE I EVER INVESTED IN WAS THE WACKIE CULT, WHOSE PROFITS RAN INTO THE MILLIONS!"
FOR IT TO CONTINUE TO YIELD A PROFIT, I'M AFRAID YOU MUST AGAIN DISAPPEAR FROM DUCKWORLD...PERMANENTLY!
OH, MY!
STRANGE, YOU SOT--SOBER UP! YOU'RE THE ONLY ONE THAT CAN GET US OUTTA HERE!
HIC

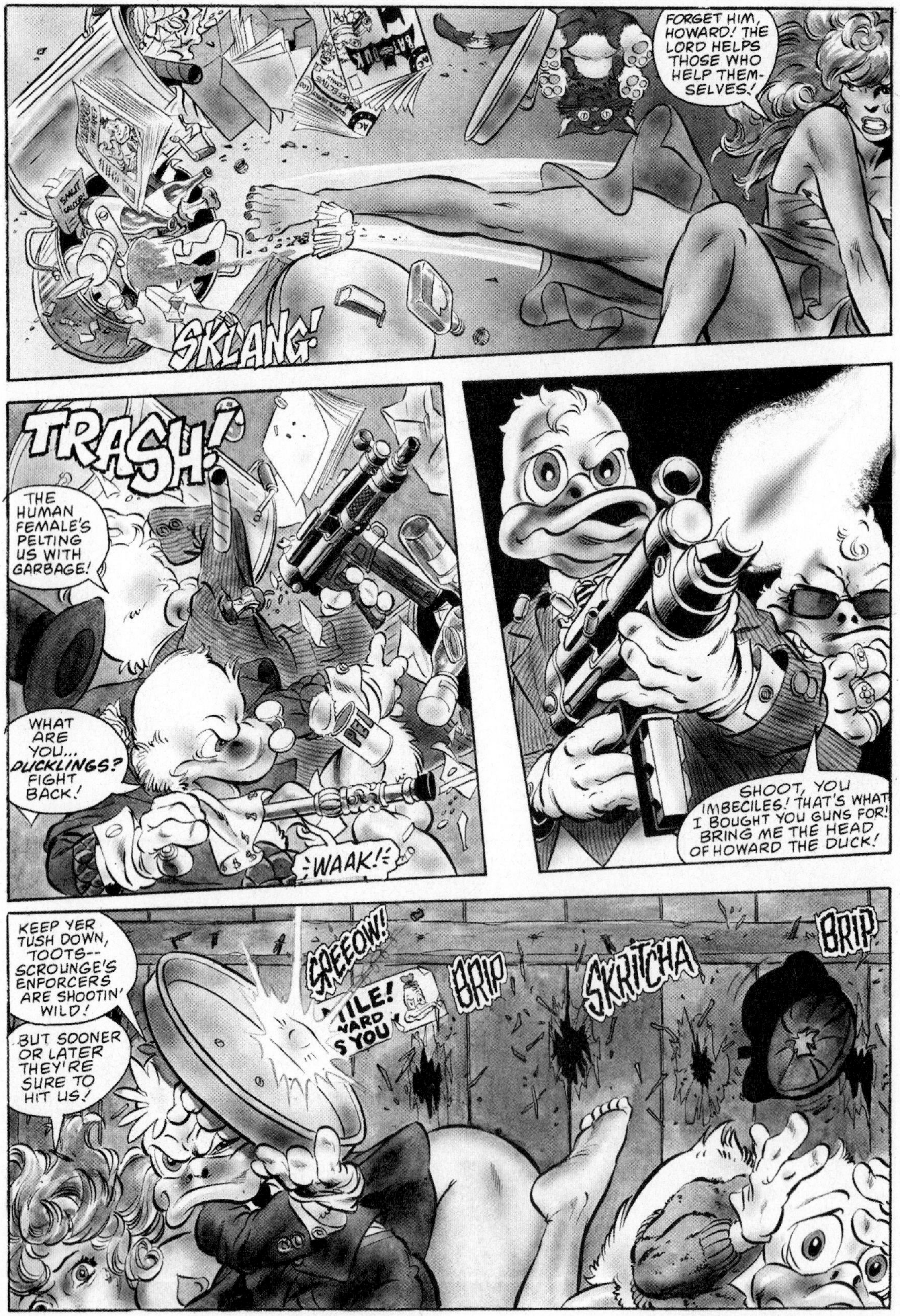
FORGET HIM, HOWARD! THE LORD HELPS THOSE WHO HELP THEM-SELVES!
SKLANG!
TRASH!
THE HUMAN FEMALE'S PELTING US WITH GARBAGE!
WHAT ARE YOU... DUCKLINGS? FIGHT BACK!
WAAK!
SHOOT, YOU IMBECILES! THAT'S WHAT I BOUGHT YOU GUNS FOR! BRING ME THE HEAD OF HOWARD THE DUCK!
KEEP YER TUSH DOWN, TOOTS-- SCROUNGE'S ENFORCERS ARE SHOOTIN' WILD!
BUT SOONER OR LATER THEY'RE SURE TO HIT US!
SPEEOW!
BRIP
SKRITCHA
BRIP

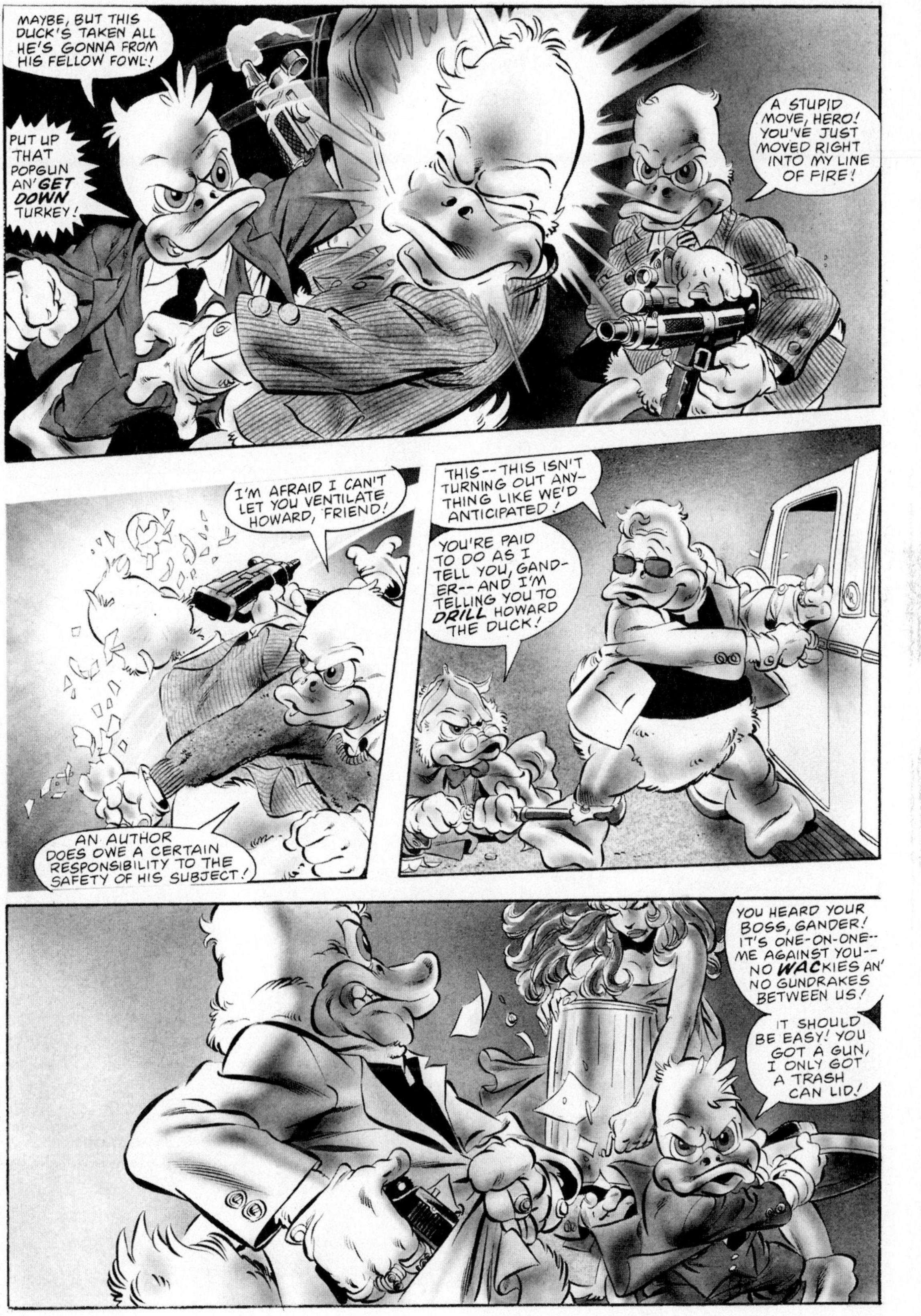
MAYBE, BUT THIS DUCK'S TAKEN ALL HE'S GONNA FROM HIS FELLOW FOWL!
PUT UP THAT POPGUN AN' GET DOWN TURKEY!
A STUPID MOVE, HERO! YOU'VE JUST MOVED RIGHT INTO MY LINE OF FIRE!
I'M AFRAID I CAN'T LET YOU VENTILATE HOWARD, FRIEND!
AN AUTHOR DOES OWE A CERTAIN RESPONSIBILITY TO THE SAFETY OF HIS SUBJECT!
THIS--THIS ISN'T TURNING OUT ANYTHING LIKE WE'D ANTICIPATED!
YOU'RE PAID TO DO AS I TELL YOU, GANDER--AND I'M TELLING YOU TO DRILL HOWARD THE DUCK!
YOU HEARD YOUR BOSS, GANDER! IT'S ONE-ON-ONE--ME AGAINST YOU--NO WACKIES AN' NO GUNDRAKES BETWEEN US!
IT SHOULD BE EASY! YOU GOT A GUN, I ONLY GOT A TRASH CAN LID!

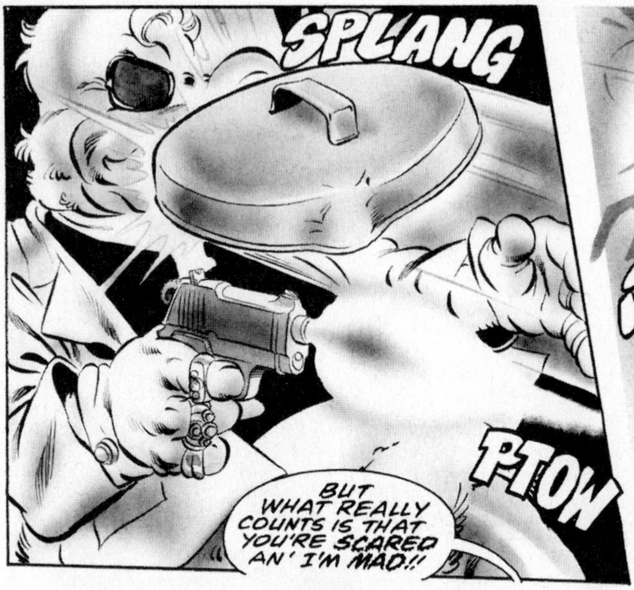
SPLANG
PTOW
BUT WHAT REALLY COUNTS IS THAT YOU'RE SCARED AN' I'M MAD!!
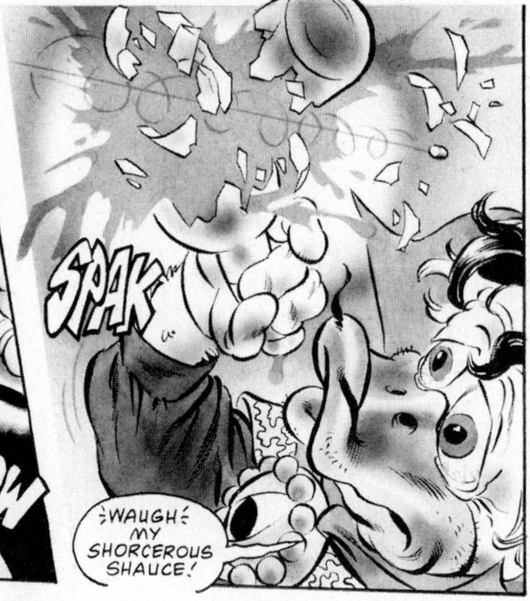
SPAK
WAUGH MY SHORCEROUS SHAUCE!
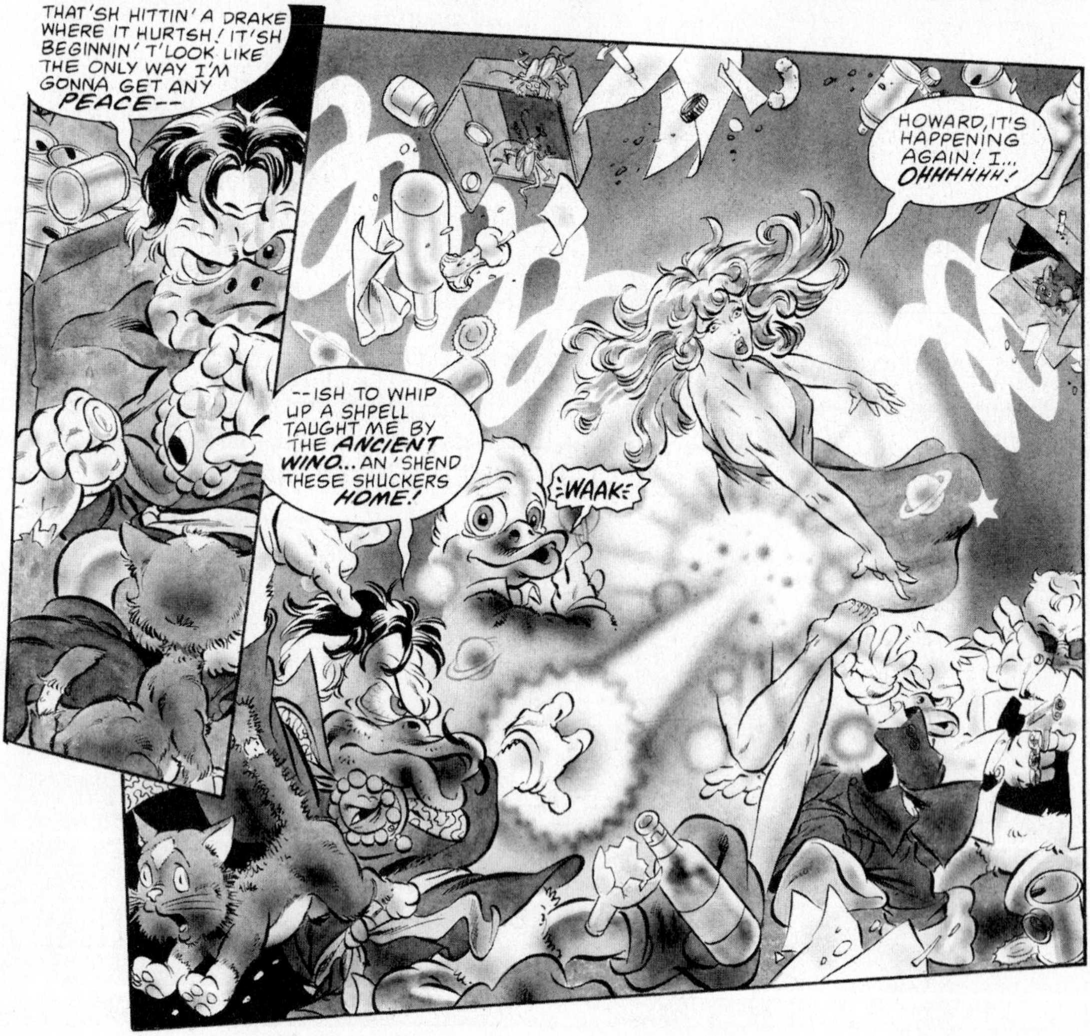
THAT'SH HITTIN' A DRAKE WHERE IT HURTSH! IT'SH BEGINNIN' T'LOOK LIKE THE ONLY WAY I'M GONNA GET ANY PEACE--
--ISH TO WHIP UP A SHPELL TAUGHT ME BY THE ANCIENT WINO... AN 'SHEND THESE SHUCKERS HOME!
HOWARD, IT'S HAPPENING AGAIN! I... OHHHHHH!
WAAK

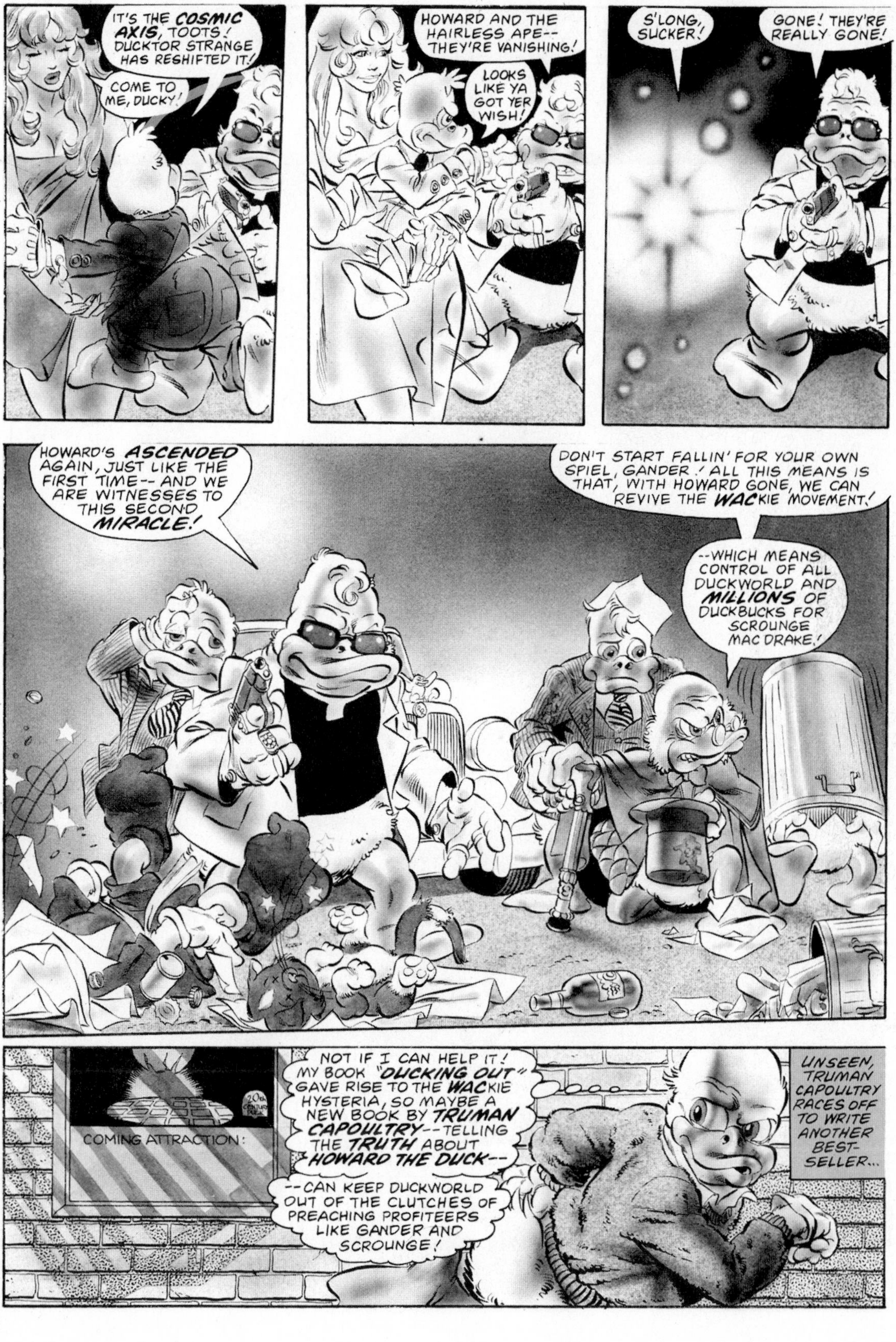
IT'S THE COSMIC AXIS, TOOTS! DUCKTOR STRANGE HAS RESHIFTED IT!
COME TO ME, DUCKY!
HOWARD AND THE HAIRLESS APE-- THEY'RE VANISHING!
LOOKS LIKE YA GOT YER WISH!
S'LONG, SUCKER!
GONE! THEY'RE REALLY GONE!
HOWARD'S ASCENDED AGAIN, JUST LIKE THE FIRST TIME-- AND WE ARE WITNESSES TO THIS SECOND MIRACLE!
DON'T START FALLIN' FOR YOUR OWN SPIEL, GANDER! ALL THIS MEANS IS THAT, WITH HOWARD GONE, WE CAN REVIVE THE WACKIE MOVEMENT!
--WHICH MEANS CONTROL OF ALL DUCKWORLD AND MILLIONS OF DUCKBUCKS FOR SCROUNGE MAC DRAKE!
COMING ATTRACTION:
NOT IF I CAN HELP IT! MY BOOK "DUCKING OUT" GAVE RISE TO THE WACKIE HYSTERIA, SO MAYBE A NEW BOOK BY TRUMAN CAPOULTRY--TELLING THE TRUTH ABOUT HOWARD THE DUCK--
--CAN KEEP DUCKWORLD OUT OF THE CLUTCHES OF PREACHING PROFITEERS LIKE GANDER AND SCROUNGE!
UNSEEN, TRUMAN CAPOULTRY RACES OFF TO WRITE ANOTHER BEST-SELLER...

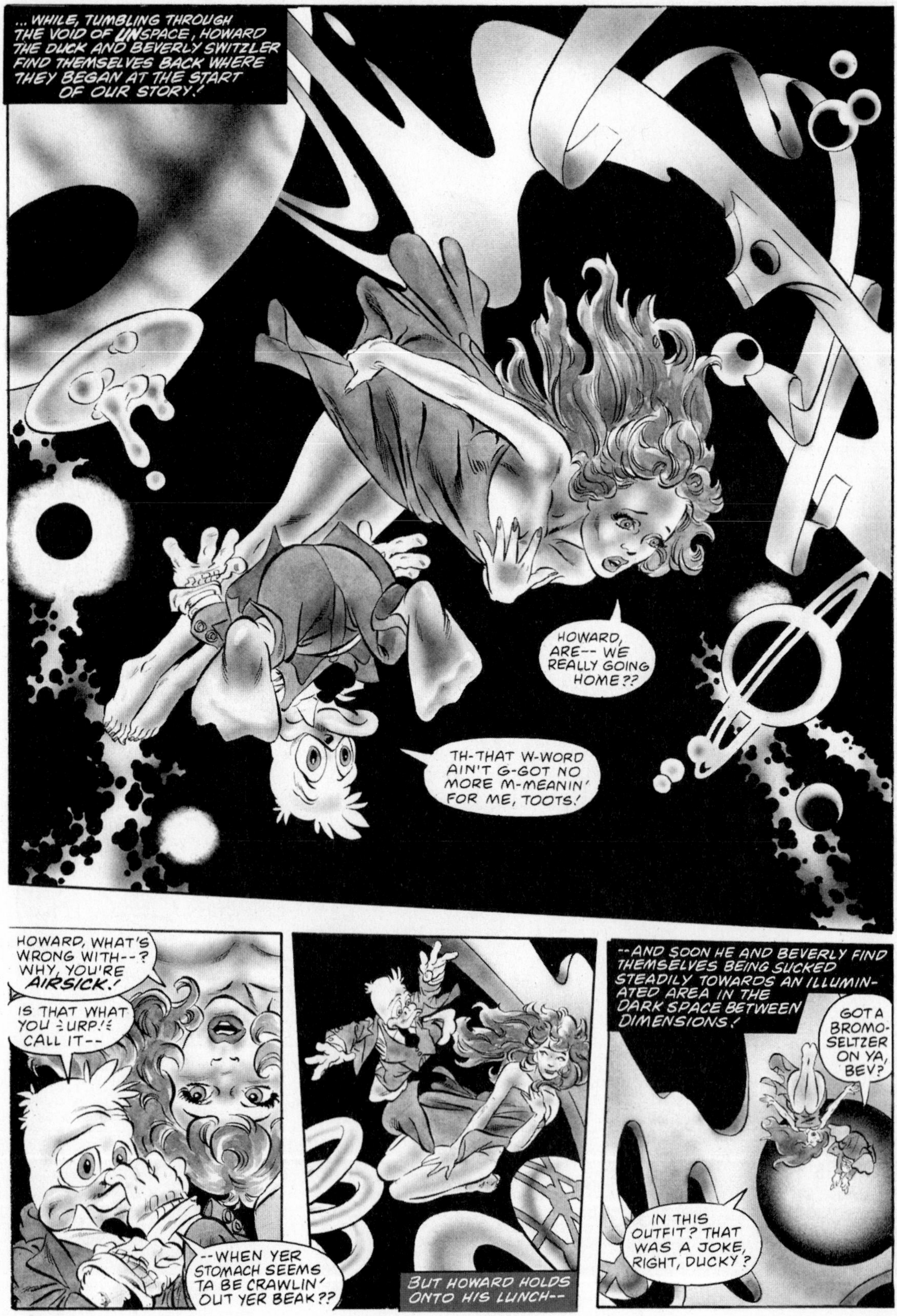

... WHILE, TUMBLING THROUGH THE VOID OF UNSPACE, HOWARD THE DUCK AND BEVERLY SWITZLER FIND THEMSELVES BACK WHERE THEY BEGAN AT THE START OF OUR STORY!
HOWARD, ARE-- WE REALLY GOING HOME??
TH-THAT W-WORD AIN'T G-GOT NO MORE M-MEANIN' FOR ME, TOOTS!
HOWARD, WHAT'S WRONG WITH--? WHY, YOU'RE AIRSICK!
IS THAT WHAT YOU -URP!- CALL IT--
--WHEN YER STOMACH SEEMS TA BE CRAWLIN' OUT YER BEAK??
BUT HOWARD HOLDS ONTO HIS LUNCH--
--AND SOON HE AND BEVERLY FIND THEMSELVES BEING SUCKED STEADILY TOWARDS AN ILLUMINATED AREA IN THE DARK SPACE BETWEEN DIMENSIONS!
GOT A BROMO-SELTZER ON YA, BEV?
IN THIS OUTFIT? THAT WAS A JOKE, RIGHT, DUCKY?

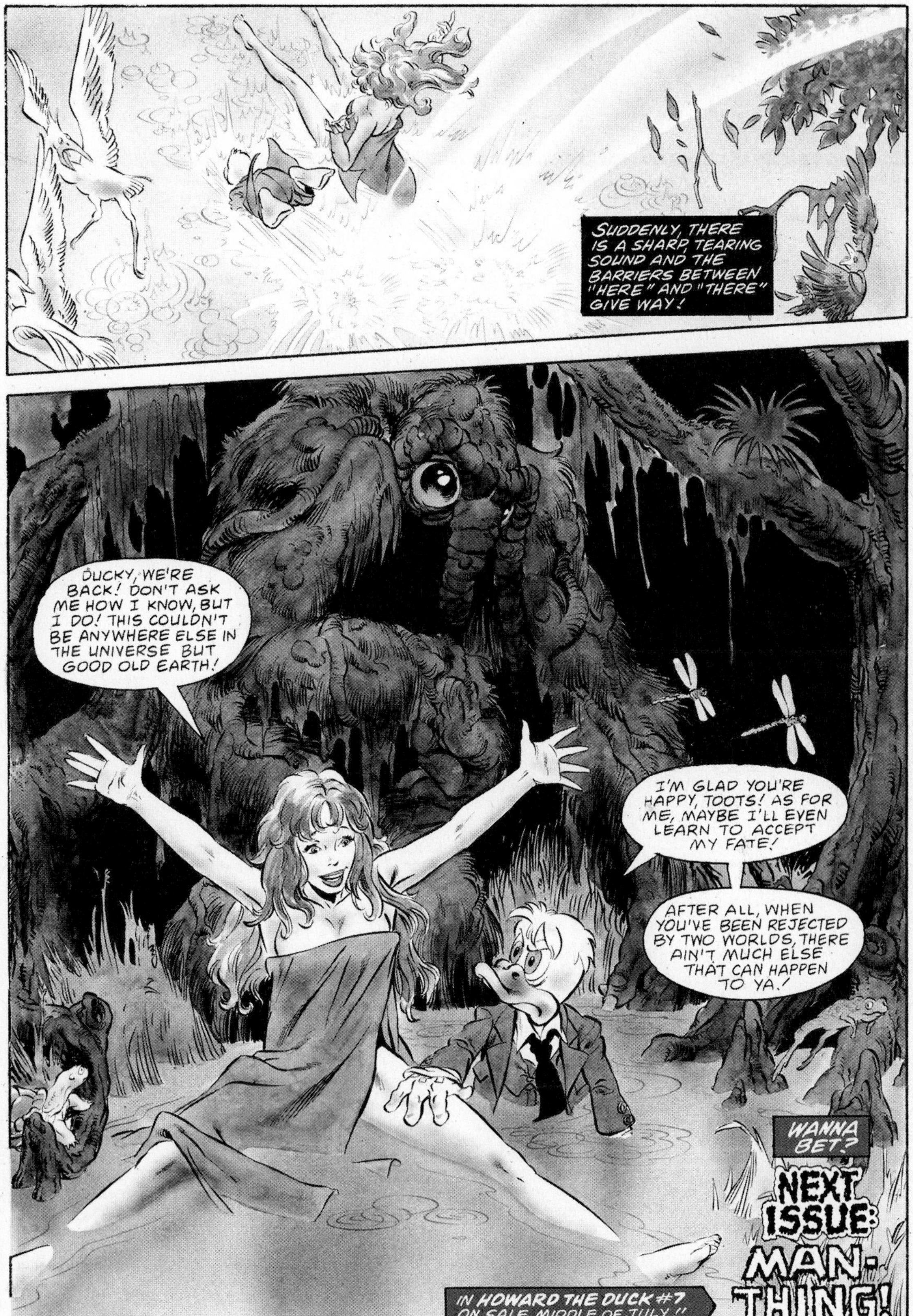
SUDDENLY, THERE IS A SHARP, TEARING SOUND AND THE BARRIERS BETWEEN "HERE" AND "THERE" GIVE WAY!
DUCKY, WE'RE BACK! DON'T ASK ME HOW I KNOW, BUT I DO! THIS COULDN'T BE ANYWHERE ELSE IN THE UNIVERSE BUT GOOD OLD EARTH!
I'M GLAD YOU'RE HAPPY, TOOTS! AS FOR ME, MAYBE I'LL EVEN LEARN TO ACCEPT MY FATE!
AFTER ALL, WHEN YOU'VE BEEN REJECTED BY TWO WORLDS, THERE AIN'T MUCH ELSE THAT CAN HAPPEN TO YA!
WANNA BET?
NEXT ISSUE: MAN-THING!
IN HOWARD THE DUCK #7 ON SALE MIDDLE OF JULY!!
END

THE FAR-OUT, OFF-THE-WALL STORY BEHIND

STREET PEEPLE

TRIP. SPEED. ACID ROCK. HIPPIE. YIPPIE. WEATHERMEN.

If these words mean something to you, you're either a survivor of the tumultuous sixties or a watcher of the Late-Late Show. Wow! It was like, far out, you know? Flower children — into yoga, natural foods, and drugs — thought that by just sending out "good vibes" they could make the world a better place. The Weathermen, on the other hand, thought that the only way to make a better world was to blow up the old one. And they gave it a serious try. The result? The seventies and now the eighties, with hippies and repressed idealists scrambling for a buck, looking in instead of out, looking out for "number 1" rather than trying to make a community of mankind.

It's all a little sad.

We were fortunate indeed that precognition is not a common talent, for if we'd seen what our dreams would end in, we wouldn't have enjoyed ourselves so much.

STREET PEEPLE is a look at the contrary, silly, violent, but — most of all — *innocent* sixties. All the characters are based on myself, my friends, and people I knew. There were real-life models for Qwami, Cheyanne, Riff, Moonchild, and even Horsemeat. Mr. Gloom lived in my apartment building on 14th street in New York City, and Officer Hip used to patrol Greenwich Village.

But this doesn't mean that STREET PEEPLE will be a realistic strip: to the contrary. Like memory, the background events will all flow together, with historical events jumbled. STREET PEEPLE, you see, is not so much about a time as it is about a feeling, a way of perceiving the world: the sixties as state-of-mind.

Another important point:

As you look at this story you'll notice immediately that it's a real departure from the representative sort of Marvel strip. Indeed, this, folks, is another high-wire act by yours truly. Why do I *do* these things to myself? Why can't I just play it comfortable and safe, not make waves, keep a low profile? Sigh.

Well, actually, I was hired to take chances and to try different kinds of things. For as vital, energetic and creative as Marvel is, it *must* keep growing and exploring new ideas in order to retain its dynamism. Still, as the risk-taker, I must say I occasionally look down at the dizzying fall and question my sanity.

STREET PEEPLE is a good example. I showed this episode to everyone in the Marvel offices: Jim, other editors, mailroom guys, statmen, secretaries — I missed the cleaning lady because I had an early dinner date — trying to get some idea of what *your* reaction would be. Result?

Some hated it. Some loved it. Somebody said it was "too sophisticated" for the HOWARD THE DUCK book, and someone else expressed doubt that anyone was interested in the sixties. Every single person had a completely individual reaction. What we have here, I've decided, is the world's first comic book Rorschach test!

So read it carefully, if only for therapeutic purposes, and let me know real quick what you think of it, because I'm having an anxiety attack. Also, I'd like your feedback in order to make Chapter Two, "Dynamite, Baby!" better than Chapter One.

Meanwhile, I'm going to take things a little easy for a while: get mellowed out, hang loose, keep my cool. Things get pretty tense up here on the tightwire!

Lynn

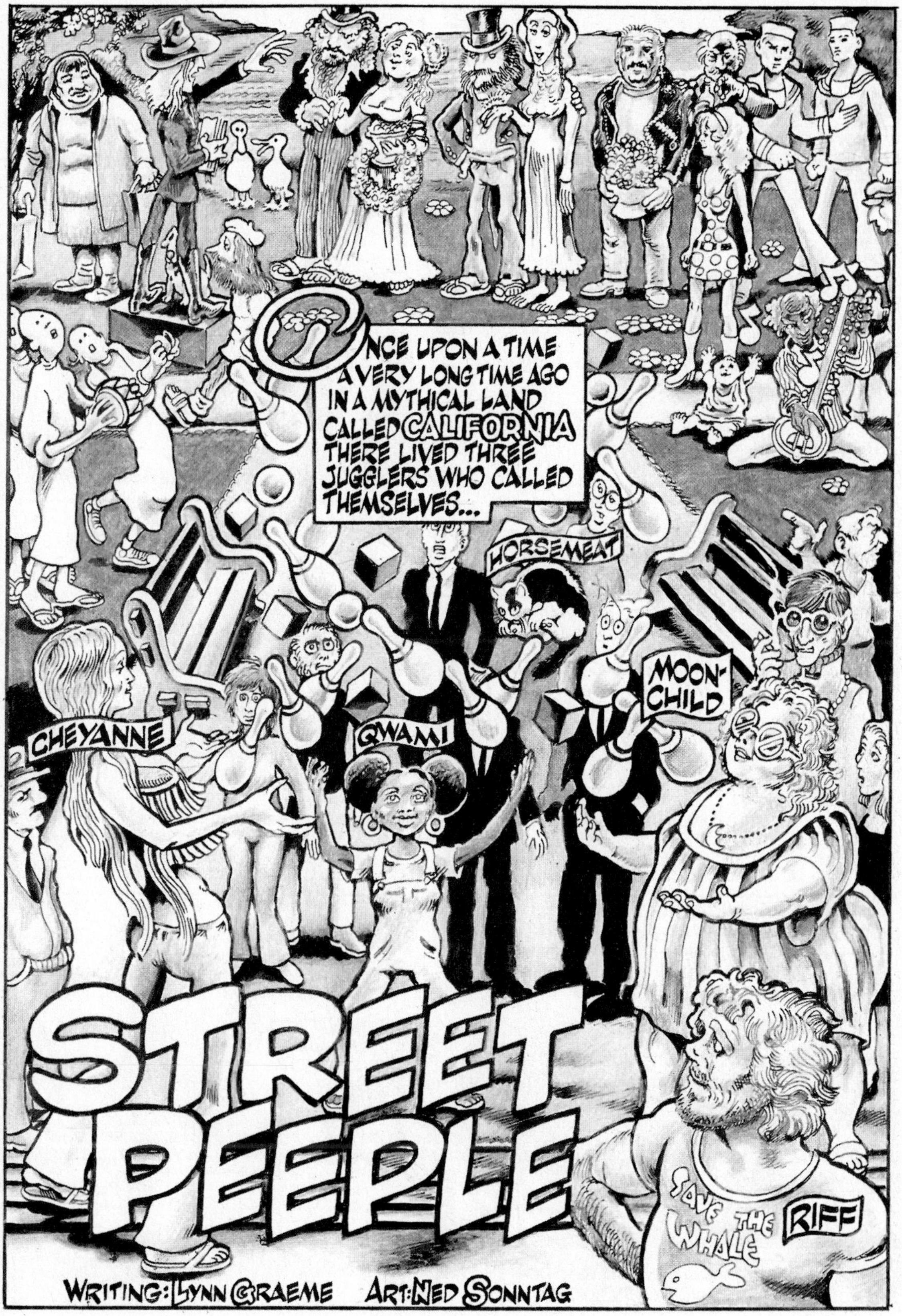
ONCE UPON A TIME
A VERY LONG TIME AGO
IN A MYTHICAL LAND
CALLED CALIFORNIA
THERE LIVED THREE
JUGGLERS WHO CALLED
THEMSELVES...
HORSEMEAT
MOON-CHILD
CHEYANNE
QWAMI
STREET PEEPLE
SAVE THE WHALE
RIFF
WRITING: LYNN GRAEME ART: NED SONNTAG

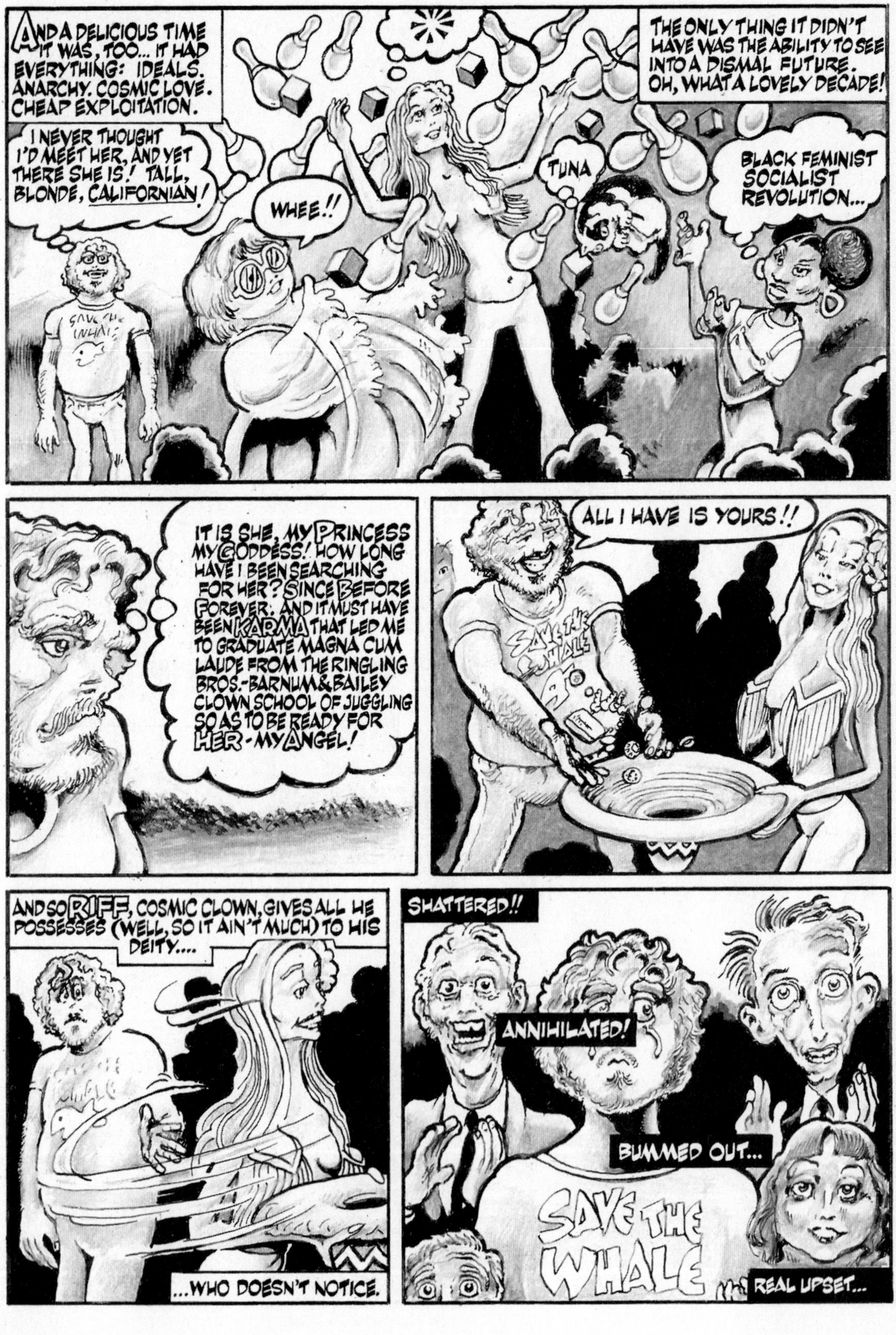

AND A DELICIOUS TIME IT WAS, TOO... IT HAD EVERYTHING: IDEALS. ANARCHY. COSMIC LOVE. CHEAP EXPLOITATION.
THE ONLY THING IT DIDN'T HAVE WAS THE ABILITY TO SEE INTO A DISMAL FUTURE. OH, WHAT A LOVELY DECADE!
I NEVER THOUGHT I'D MEET HER, AND YET THERE SHE IS! TALL, BLONDE, CALIFORNIAN!
WHEE!!
TUNA
BLACK FEMINIST SOCIALIST REVOLUTION...
SAVE THE WHALE
IT IS SHE, MY PRINCESS MY GODDESS! HOW LONG HAVE I BEEN SEARCHING FOR HER? SINCE BEFORE FOREVER. AND IT MUST HAVE BEEN KARMA THAT LED ME TO GRADUATE MAGNA CUM LAUDE FROM THE RINGLING BROS.-BARNUM & BAILEY CLOWN SCHOOL OF JUGGLING SO AS TO BE READY FOR HER - MY ANGEL!
ALL I HAVE IS YOURS!!
SAVE THE WHALE
AND SO RIFF, COSMIC CLOWN, GIVES ALL HE POSSESSES (WELL, SO IT AIN'T MUCH) TO HIS DEITY....
...WHO DOESN'T NOTICE.
SHATTERED!!
ANNIHILATED!
BUMMED OUT...
SAVE THE WHALE
REAL UPSET...

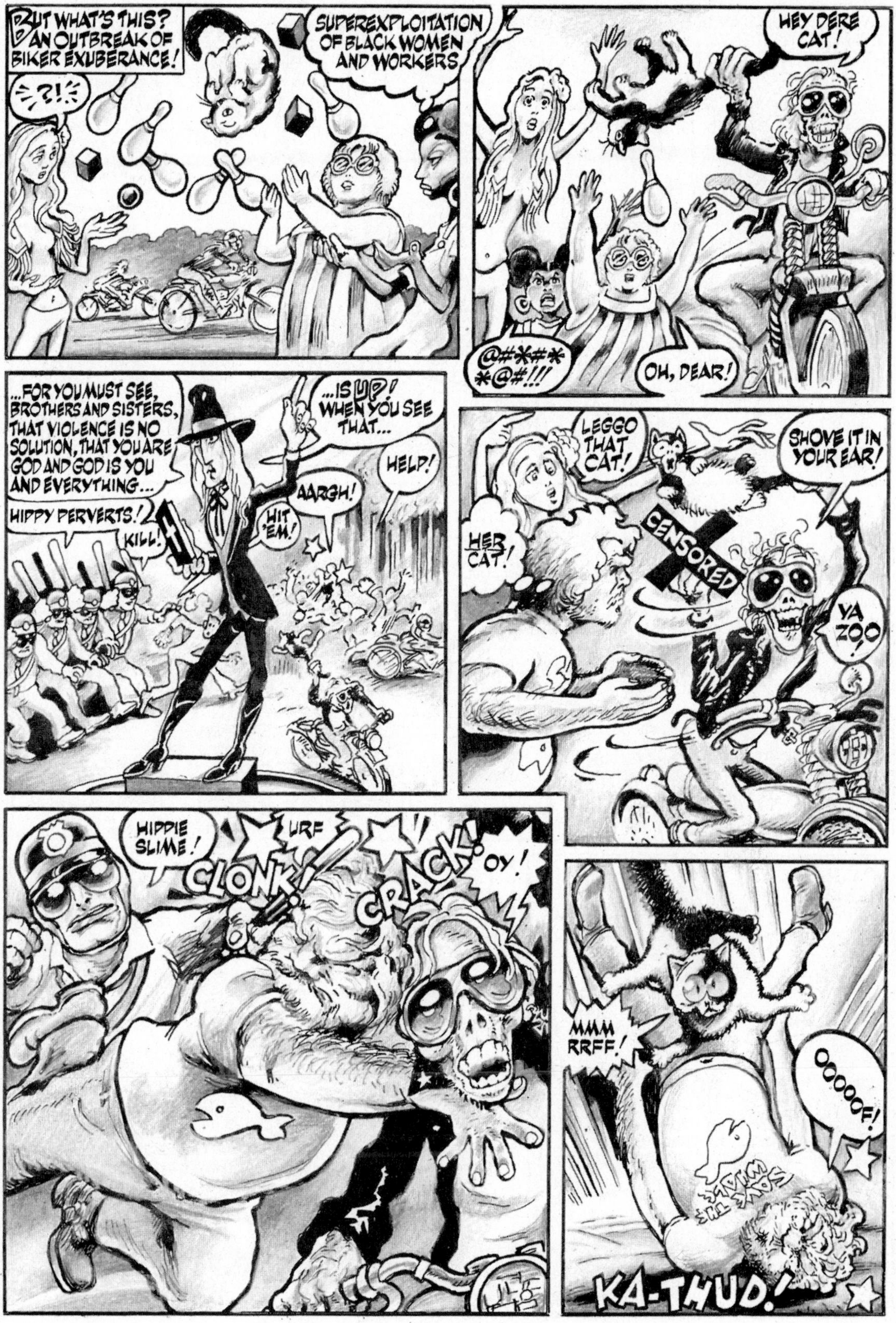
BUT WHAT'S THIS? AN OUTBREAK OF BIKER EXUBERANCE!
?!
SUPEREXPLOITATION OF BLACK WOMEN AND WORKERS
HEY DERE CAT!
@#*#* *@#!!!
OH, DEAR!
...FOR YOU MUST SEE, BROTHERS AND SISTERS, THAT VIOLENCE IS NO SOLUTION, THAT YOU ARE GOD AND GOD IS YOU AND EVERYTHING...
...IS UP! WHEN YOU SEE THAT...
HELP!
AARGH!
HIT 'EM!
HIPPY PERVERTS!
KILL!
LEGGO THAT CAT!
SHOVE IT IN YOUR EAR!
HER CAT!
CENSORED
YA ZOO!
HIPPIE SLIME!
URF
CLONK!
CRACK!
OY!
MMM RRFF!
OOOOOF!
KA-THUD!

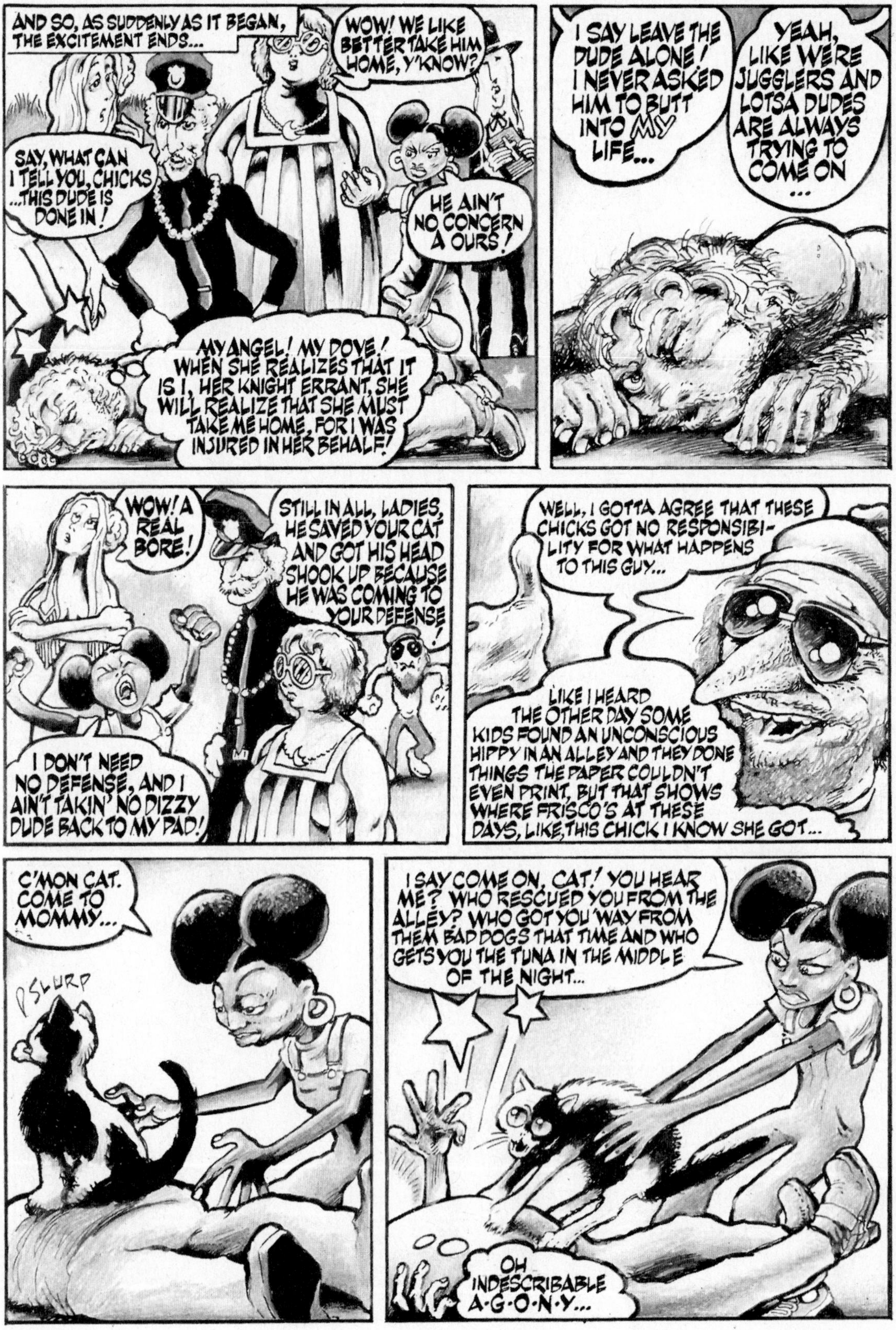
AND SO, AS SUDDENLY AS IT BEGAN, THE EXCITEMENT ENDS...
WOW! WE LIKE BETTER TAKE HIM HOME, Y'KNOW?
SAY, WHAT CAN I TELL YOU, CHICKS ...THIS DUDE IS DONE IN!
HE AIN'T NO CONCERN A OURS!
MY ANGEL! MY DOVE! WHEN SHE REALIZES THAT IT IS I, HER KNIGHT ERRANT, SHE WILL REALIZE THAT SHE MUST TAKE ME HOME, FOR I WAS INJURED IN HER BEHALF!
I SAY LEAVE THE DUDE ALONE! I NEVER ASKED HIM TO BUTT INTO MY LIFE...
YEAH, LIKE WE'RE JUGGLERS AND LOTSA DUDES ARE ALWAYS TRYING TO COME ON ...
WOW! A REAL BORE!
STILL IN ALL, LADIES, HE SAVED YOUR CAT AND GOT HIS HEAD SHOOK UP BECAUSE HE WAS COMING TO YOUR DEFENSE!
I DON'T NEED NO DEFENSE, AND I AIN'T TAKIN' NO DIZZY DUDE BACK TO MY PAD!
WELL, I GOTTA AGREE THAT THESE CHICKS GOT NO RESPONSIBILITY FOR WHAT HAPPENS TO THIS GUY...
LIKE I HEARD THE OTHER DAY SOME KIDS FOUND AN UNCONSCIOUS HIPPY IN AN ALLEY AND THEY DONE THINGS THE PAPER COULDN'T EVEN PRINT, BUT THAT SHOWS WHERE FRISCO'S AT THESE DAYS, LIKE, THIS CHICK I KNOW SHE GOT...
C'MON CAT. COME TO MOMMY...
SLURP
I SAY COME ON, CAT! YOU HEAR ME? WHO RESCUED YOU FROM THE ALLEY? WHO GOT YOU 'WAY FROM THEM BAD DOGS THAT TIME AND WHO GETS YOU THE TUNA IN THE MIDDLE OF THE NIGHT...
OH INDESCRIBABLE A-G-O-N-Y...

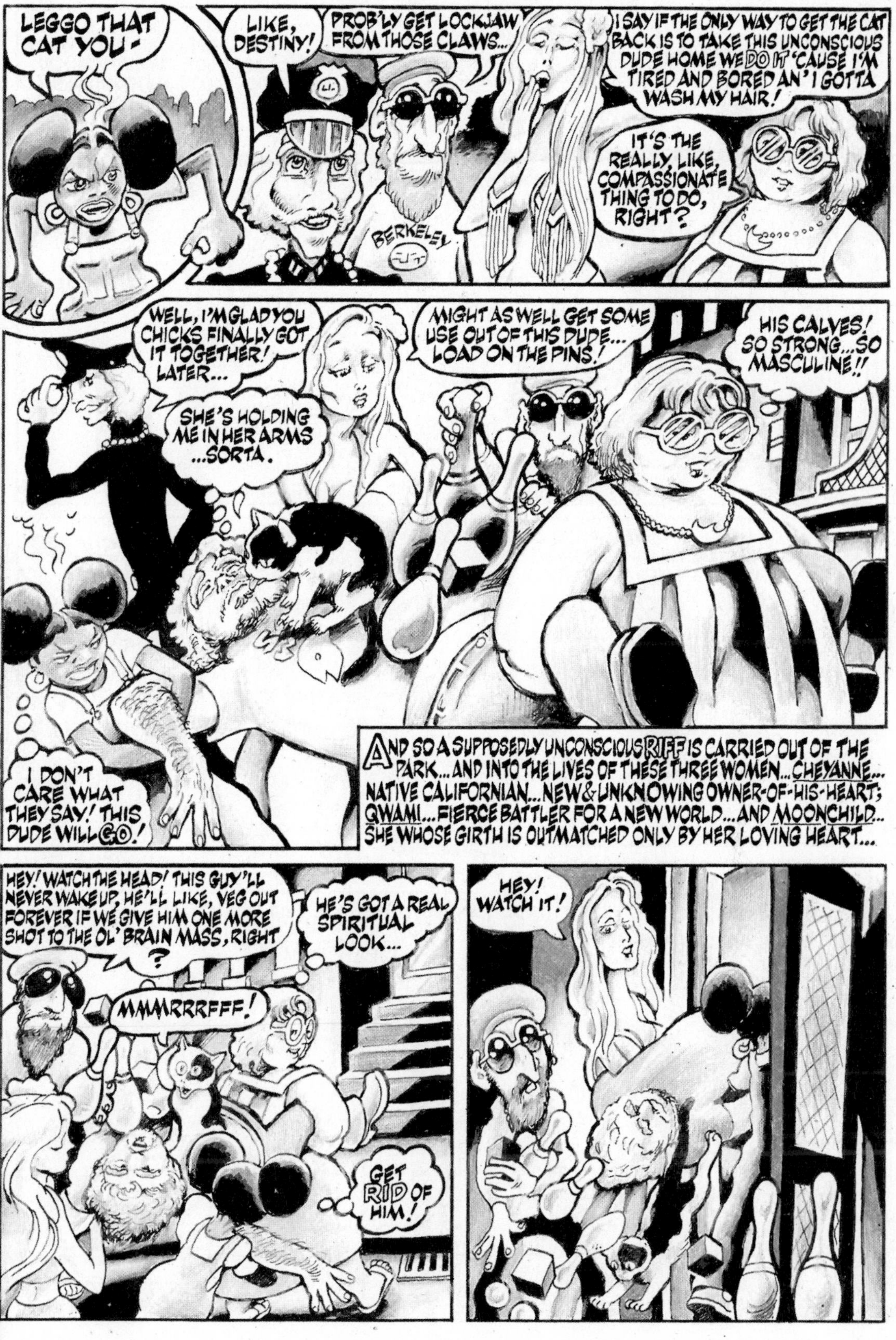
LEGGO THAT CAT YOU -
LIKE, DESTINY!
PROB'LY GET LOCKJAW FROM THOSE CLAWS...
I SAY IF THE ONLY WAY TO GET THE CAT BACK IS TO TAKE THIS UNCONSCIOUS DUDE HOME WE DO IT 'CAUSE I'M TIRED AND BORED AN' I GOTTA WASH MY HAIR!
IT'S THE REALLY, LIKE, COMPASSIONATE THING TO DO, RIGHT?
BERKELEY
WELL, I'M GLAD YOU CHICKS FINALLY GOT IT TOGETHER! LATER...
SHE'S HOLDING ME IN HER ARMS ...SORTA.
MIGHT AS WELL GET SOME USE OUT OF THIS DUDE... LOAD ON THE PINS!
HIS CALVES! SO STRONG...SO MASCULINE!!
I DON'T CARE WHAT THEY SAY! THIS DUDE WILL GO!
AND SO A SUPPOSEDLY UNCONSCIOUS RIFF IS CARRIED OUT OF THE PARK...AND INTO THE LIVES OF THESE THREE WOMEN...CHEYANNE... NATIVE CALIFORNIAN...NEW & UNKNOWING OWNER-OF-HIS-HEART; QWAMI...FIERCE BATTLER FOR A NEW WORLD...AND MOONCHILD... SHE WHOSE GIRTH IS OUTMATCHED ONLY BY HER LOVING HEART...
HEY! WATCH THE HEAD! THIS GUY'LL NEVER WAKE UP, HE'LL LIKE, VEG OUT FOREVER IF WE GIVE HIM ONE MORE SHOT TO THE OL' BRAIN MASS, RIGHT ?
HE'S GOT A REAL SPIRITUAL LOOK...
MMMRRRFFF!
GET RID OF HIM!
HEY! WATCH IT!

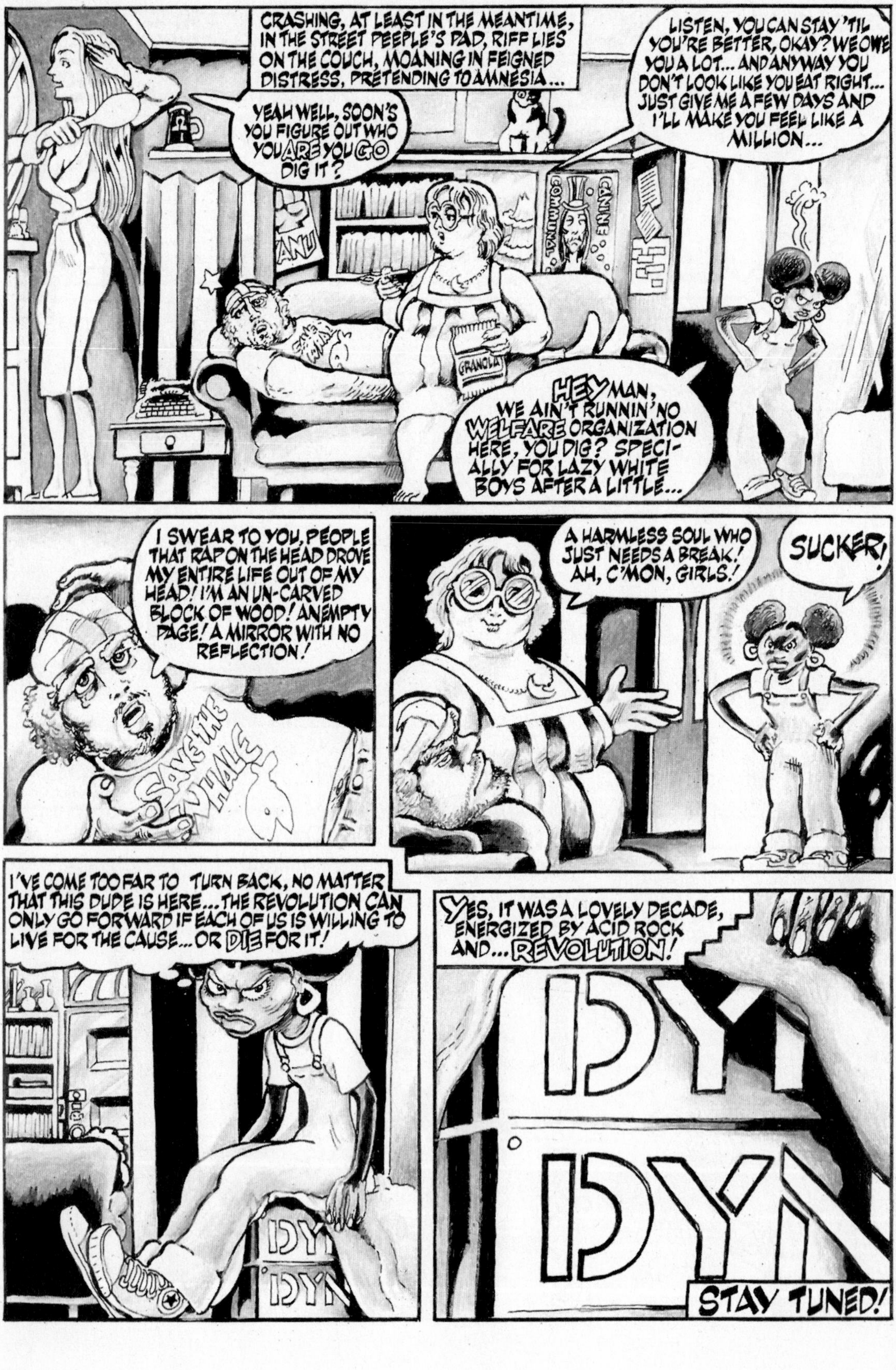
CRASHING, AT LEAST IN THE MEANTIME, IN THE STREET PEEPLE'S PAD, RIFF LIES ON THE COUCH, MOANING IN FEIGNED DISTRESS, PRETENDING TO AMNESIA...
YEAH WELL, SOON'S YOU FIGURE OUT WHO YOU ARE YOU GO DIG IT?
LISTEN, YOU CAN STAY 'TIL YOU'RE BETTER, OKAY? WE OWE YOU A LOT... AND ANYWAY YOU DON'T LOOK LIKE YOU EAT RIGHT... JUST GIVE ME A FEW DAYS AND I'LL MAKE YOU FEEL LIKE A MILLION...
HEY MAN, WE AIN'T RUNNIN' NO WELFARE ORGANIZATION HERE, YOU DIG? SPECI-ALLY FOR LAZY WHITE BOYS AFTER A LITTLE...
GRANOLA
I SWEAR TO YOU, PEOPLE THAT RAP ON THE HEAD DROVE MY ENTIRE LIFE OUT OF MY HEAD! I'M AN UN-CARVED BLOCK OF WOOD! AN EMPTY PAGE! A MIRROR WITH NO REFLECTION!
SAVE THE WHALE
A HARMLESS SOUL WHO JUST NEEDS A BREAK! AH, C'MON, GIRLS!
SUCKER!
I'VE COME TOO FAR TO TURN BACK, NO MATTER THAT THIS DUDE IS HERE... THE REVOLUTION CAN ONLY GO FORWARD IF EACH OF US IS WILLING TO LIVE FOR THE CAUSE... OR DIE FOR IT!
YES, IT WAS A LOVELY DECADE, ENERGIZED BY ACID ROCK AND... REVOLUTION!
DYN
DYN
STAY TUNED!

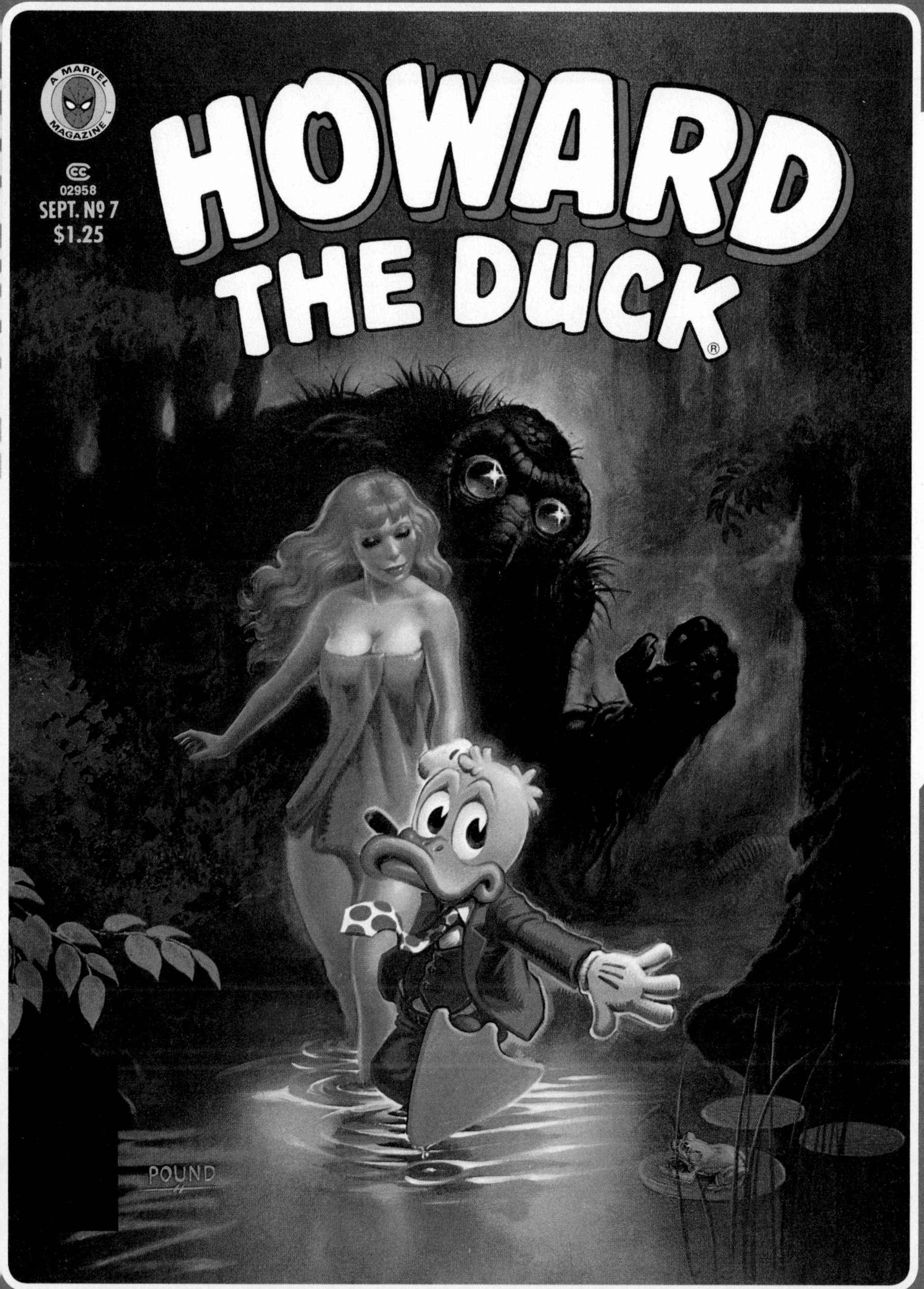
A MARVEL MAGAZINE
CC
02958
SEPT. Nº 7
$1.25
HOWARD THE DUCK
POUND

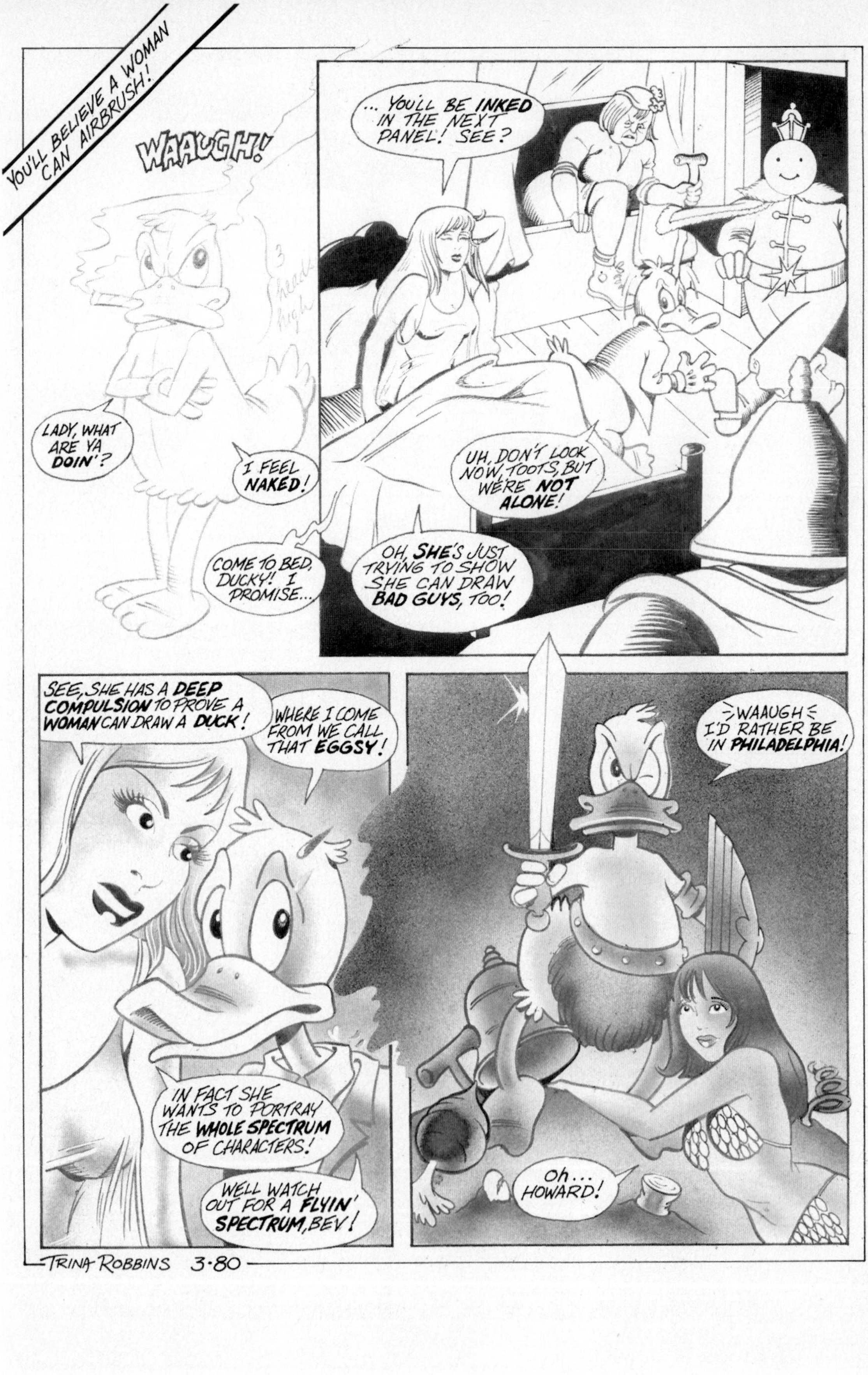
YOU'LL BELIEVE A WOMAN CAN AIRBRUSH!
WAAUGH!
3 heads high
LADY, WHAT ARE YA DOIN'?
I FEEL NAKED!
COME TO BED, DUCKY! I PROMISE...
... YOU'LL BE INKED IN THE NEXT PANEL! SEE?
UH, DON'T LOOK NOW, TOOTS, BUT WE'RE NOT ALONE!
OH, SHE'S JUST TRYING TO SHOW SHE CAN DRAW BAD GUYS, TOO!
SEE, SHE HAS A DEEP COMPULSION TO PROVE A WOMAN CAN DRAW A DUCK!
WHERE I COME FROM WE CALL THAT EGGSY!
IN FACT SHE WANTS TO PORTRAY THE WHOLE SPECTRUM OF CHARACTERS!
WELL WATCH OUT FOR A FLYIN' SPECTRUM, BEV!
WAAUGH I'D RATHER BE IN PHILADELPHIA!
Oh... HOWARD!
TRINA ROBBINS 3·80

STAN LEE Presents

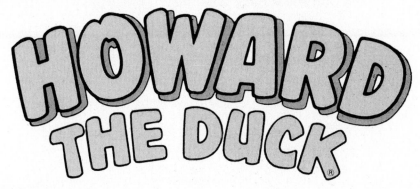

HOWARD THE DUCK®

September 1980 **Volume 1 No. 7**

JIM SHOOTER Editor-in-Chief • **LYNN GRAEME** Editor • **RALPH MACCHIO** Associate Editor
MARK GRUENWALD Insulting Editor • **MILT SCHIFFMAN** V.P. Production
NORA MACLIN Design Director • **MICHAEL HIGGINS** Design Assistant • **MARK ROGAN, NED SONNTAG** Letterers • **HELLEN KATZ, ELIOT BROWN, ROB CAROSELLA, LINDA FLORIO, CARL GAFFORD, VIRGINIA ROMITA, DANNY CRESPI, ED NORTON, EDUARD LILINSHTEIN** • Sensational Staff •
TRINA ROBBINS Frontispiece • **JOHN POUND** Cover

CONTENTS

HOWARD THE DUCK is published by MARVEL COMICS GROUP, OFFICE OF PUBLICATION 575 Madison Avenue, New York, N.Y. 10022. James E. Galton, President. Stan Lee, Publisher. Milton Schiffman, Vice-President, Production. Published bimonthly. Vol. 1, No. 7, September 1980 issue. Price $1.25 per copy in the U.S. and Canada. Subscription rate — $15.00 U.S.A., $16.00 Canada, $17.00 Foreign respectively for 12 issues including postage. All business inquiries should be addressed to Ed Shukin, Vice-President of Circulation, 9th floor.

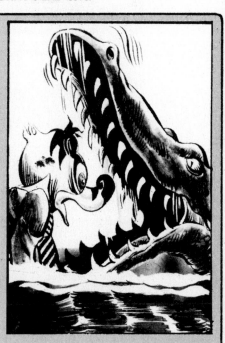

EDITORIAL

The Continued Saga of Those Scruffy Editors Who Bring You the Duck:

As you recall (maybe), last issue's semi-hysterical editorial promised to tell you the behind-the-scenes story of how the DUCK-WORLD issue came to be.

Like virtually all stories published here at Marvel, DUCKWORLD was hatched during an editorial conference. (This is a meeting between writer and editor — and sometimes artist — during which the spark of a story is gently fanned to full flame or rudely stamped out by those in charge: in this case, on this book, *me*.) There were those who, before this story appeared, thought such a story, in which Howard's world is depicted in detail, should never be told. But it *had* to be told!

Here's why:

Although fictional characters are created by people, it is a widely known phenomenon that said characters, if they're vividly and authentically formed, take on a life of their own. They begin to change and actualize themselves quite apart from what their creators sometimes intend. In Howard's case, he'd been making comparisons between his home — which Bill Mantlo dubbed Duckworld for the benefit of us humans (to ducks, it would just be *earth*, right?) — and our planet for some time, to our detriment.

And yet Howard's nostalgia for his lost home didn't quite jibe with known facts about him: that he'd been a rebel, a drop-out from his own society. Against *what* was he rebelling if it was all so lovely back home?

This, clearly, was a character living in a delusion, yearning for an Eden that had never existed.

And so it became imperative that Howard confront his delusions.

If you read the last issue you are well aware that Howard's return home left him free of his delusions, and yet also confused and... lost. How will he cope with his confusion and adjust to his loss?

Ahhhh! We have plans for this book that will knock your tail feathers off! If you thought returning Howard to Duckword was risky, wait'll ya see what we do in the future! From now on, consider this magazine a dangerous weapon, designed to blow up the status quo at any and every opportunity!

A Few Notes About the Personnel — Missing & Present — on the Duckworld Issue:

It was with real chagrin that, as we were planning the incredibly complicated DUCKWORLD story, I realized I'd overcommitted Gene Colan to such an extent that he would not be able to pencil the story. My excuse is inexperience in scheduling comicbook stories (This was ten months ago: I'm learnin'! I'm learnin'!). My relief is that Mr. Colan, one of the world's natural noblemen, has graciously forgiven me. I'm grateful beyond words for the incredible job Michael Golden and Bob McLeod turned out. Both were driven and over-worked to such a degree on this story that I'm amazed they're still with us — both in spirit and in the flesh!

Thanks also to the letterers and other production people, and to Design Director Nora Maclin, all of whom put forth time and effort far "beyond the call of duty." Ralph Macchio, as always, was the cool and efficient professional, keeping both me and the department from falling into total shambles.

LYNN

Being an acute observer and crafty reader you will have noticed that on the inside front cover, where we usually have a portrait of Howard and Bev, we have something different this time... **because** *(trumpets please!)* **We're Looking for People Who Want to Draw Howard the Duck!** *So we're inviting you to recommend artists you'd like to see in a second story (the first story belongs, of course, to Gene Colan). To artists we extend an invitation to "audition" — but only after contacting us first and getting the go-ahead, please. We will pay our usual rate for frontispieces. Now: take advantage of the opportunity to have an active part in the creation of future Howard the Duck issues by letting us know what you think of Trina Robbins' art re: Howard.*

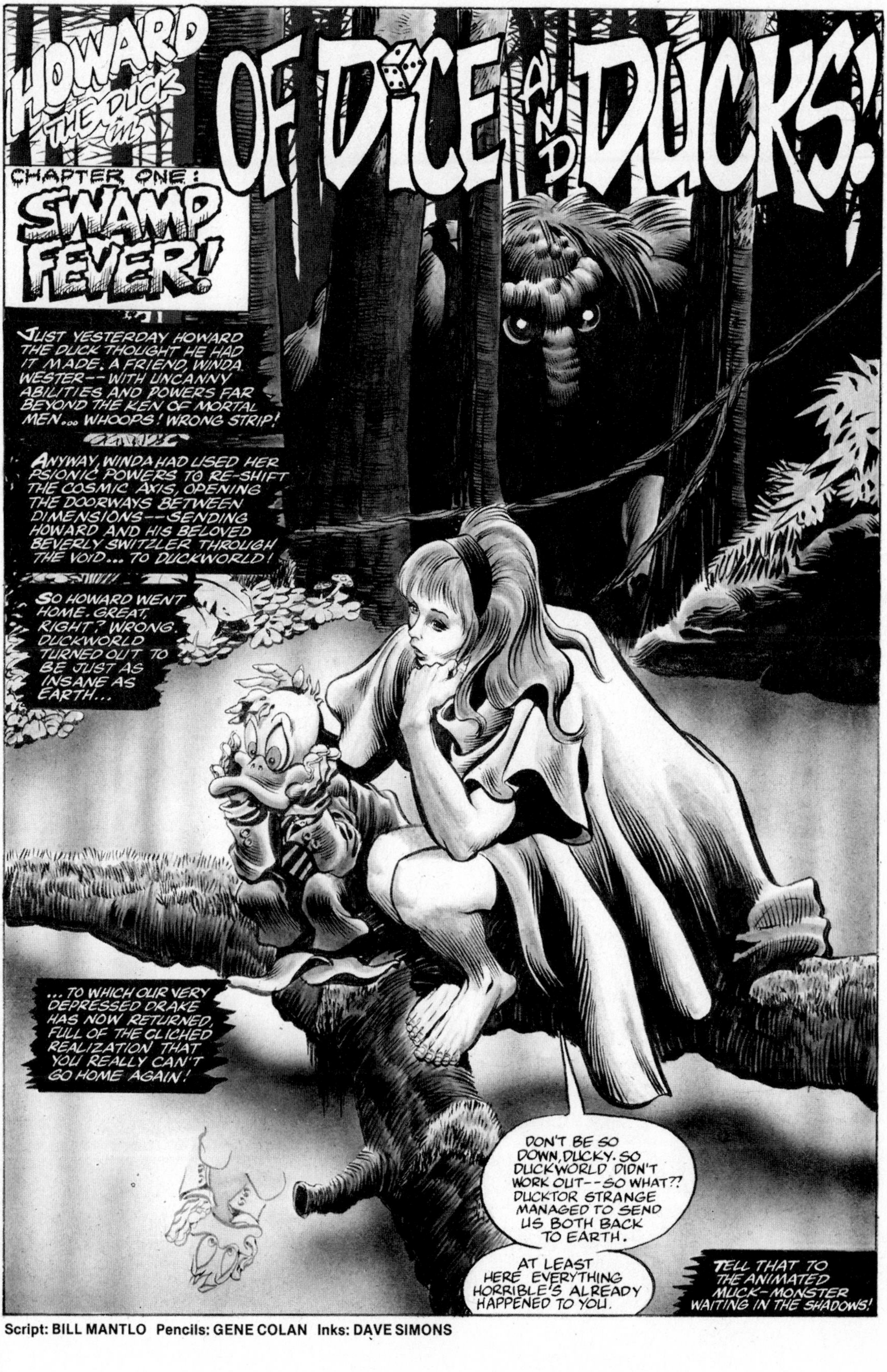
HOWARD THE DUCK in
OF DICE AND DUCKS!
CHAPTER ONE: SWAMP FEVER!
JUST YESTERDAY HOWARD THE DUCK THOUGHT HE HAD IT MADE. A FRIEND, WINDA WESTER-- WITH UNCANNY ABILITIES AND POWERS FAR BEYOND THE KEN OF MORTAL MEN... WHOOPS! WRONG STRIP!
ANYWAY, WINDA HAD USED HER PSIONIC POWERS TO RE-SHIFT THE COSMIC AXIS, OPENING THE DOORWAYS BETWEEN DIMENSIONS-- SENDING HOWARD AND HIS BELOVED BEVERLY SWITZLER THROUGH THE VOID... TO DUCKWORLD!
SO HOWARD WENT HOME. GREAT, RIGHT? WRONG. DUCKWORLD TURNED OUT TO BE JUST AS INSANE AS EARTH...
...TO WHICH OUR VERY DEPRESSED DRAKE HAS NOW RETURNED, FULL OF THE CLICHED REALIZATION THAT YOU REALLY CAN'T GO HOME AGAIN!
DON'T BE SO DOWN, DUCKY. SO DUCKWORLD DIDN'T WORK OUT--SO WHAT?? DUCKTOR STRANGE MANAGED TO SEND US BOTH BACK TO EARTH.
AT LEAST HERE EVERYTHING HORRIBLE'S ALREADY HAPPENED TO YOU.
TELL THAT TO THE ANIMATED MUCK-MONSTER WAITING IN THE SHADOWS!

Script: BILL MANTLO Pencils: GENE COLAN Inks: DAVE SIMONS

HIS EYES ARE RED ORBS-- WINDOWS TO NOTHING, FOR HE POSSESSES NO SOUL!

THINK OF THEM, RATHER, AS MIRRORS-- REFLECTING THE SOULS OF OTHERS.

UNABLE TO GENERATE NEEDS OR DESIRES OF HIS OWN, HIS EMPATHIC NATURE ALLOWS HIM TO FEEL ONLY WHAT OTHERS FEEL.

HOWARD, I DON'T MIND MOTHERING YOU THROUGH THE TOUGH PARTS--

--BUT *TALK* TO ME, HUH? GIVE ME SOME FEED-BACK. I NEED AFFECTION TOO!

I MEAN, GOING TO YOUR WORLD WITH YOU--THE SOLE HUMAN AMIDST MILLIONS OF TALKING DUCKS...

...THAT DIDN'T DO WONDERS FOR *MY* SELF-ESTEEM, EITHER!

PLUNK

YA DON'T HAVETA TELL ME, TOOTS-- I KNOW, WE BOTH LOST.

IT'S JUST THAT I HAVEN'T COME TA GRIPS WITH REALITY YET--WITH THE FACT THAT I'M DOOMED TA BE A STRANGER IN A STRANGE LAND WHEREVER I GO.

OR MAYBE I'M LOOKING AT THINGS WRONG? MAYBE LIKE *THE WACKIES,* THOSE DEMENTED DUCKS THAT FORMED A CULT IN MY NAME-- *

YEAH, MAYBE HOME IS WHEREVER I DECIDE TA HANG MY HAT--IF I HADN'T LOST IT ON DUCKWORLD, THAT IS.

--MAYBE I GOTTA *ACCEPT* BEIN' TRAPPED IN WORLDS I NEVER MADE?

* LAST ISH. --LYNN.

WE LEARNED SOMETHING ELSE, DUCKY. WE MAY NOT BELONG ON EARTH, *OR* ON DUCKWORLD--

--BUT WE DEFINITELY BELONG TOGETHER!

YEAH, THERE IS *THAT,* BEV. I ...BEV!!

WHAT IS IT, DUCKY? WHY ARE YOU STARING AT ME LIKE THAT?? WHAT'S WRONG??

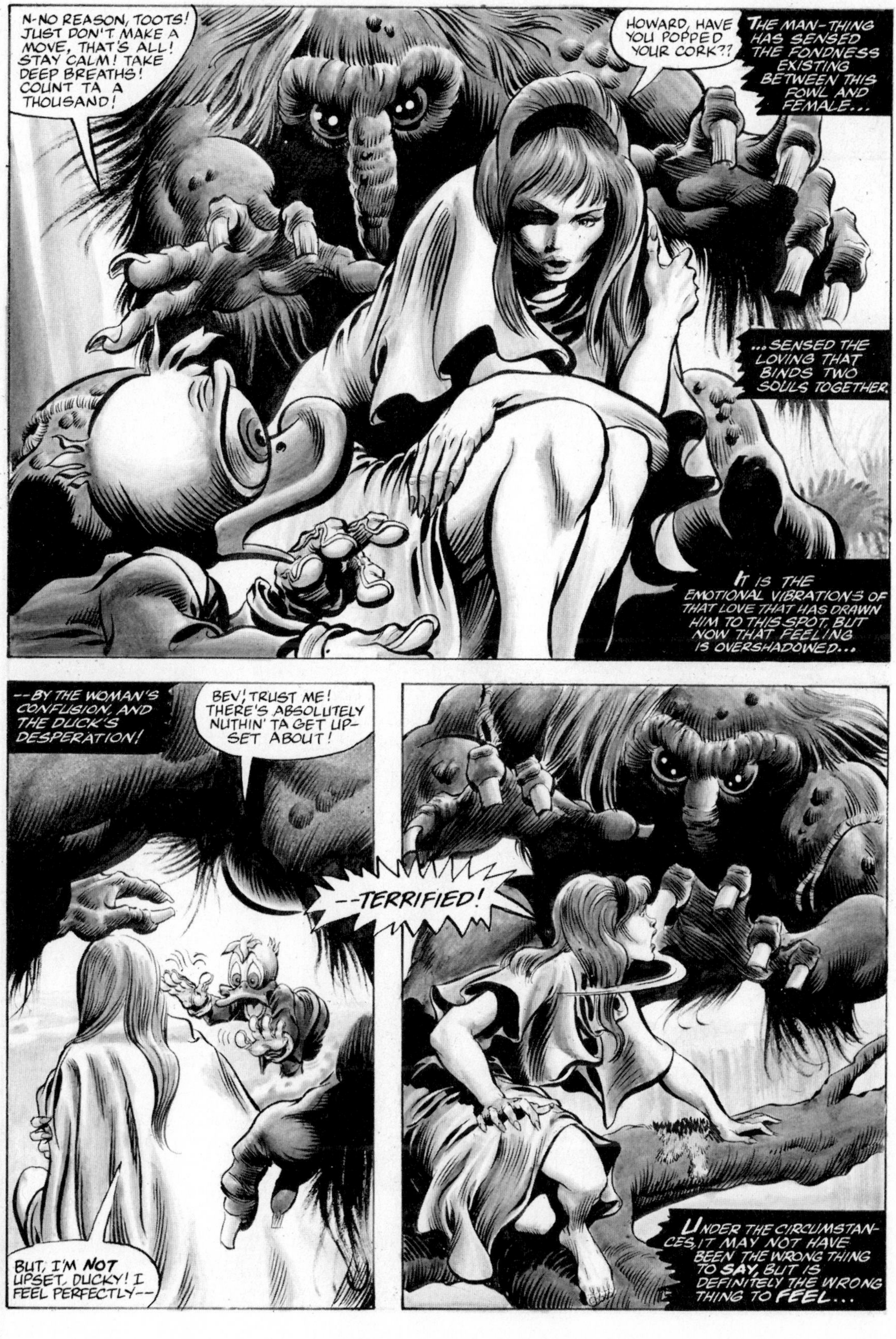
N-NO REASON, TOOTS! JUST DON'T MAKE A MOVE, THAT'S ALL! STAY CALM! TAKE DEEP BREATHS! COUNT TA A THOUSAND!
HOWARD, HAVE YOU POPPED YOUR CORK??
THE MAN-THING HAS SENSED THE FONDNESS EXISTING BETWEEN THIS FOWL AND FEMALE...
...SENSED THE LOVING THAT BINDS TWO SOULS TOGETHER.
IT IS THE EMOTIONAL VIBRATIONS OF THAT LOVE THAT HAS DRAWN HIM TO THIS SPOT, BUT NOW THAT FEELING IS OVERSHADOWED...
--BY THE WOMAN'S CONFUSION, AND THE DUCK'S DESPERATION!
BEV! TRUST ME! THERE'S ABSOLUTELY NUTHIN' TA GET UPSET ABOUT!
BUT, I'M NOT UPSET, DUCKY! I FEEL PERFECTLY--
--TERRIFIED!
UNDER THE CIRCUMSTANCES, IT MAY NOT HAVE BEEN THE WRONG THING TO SAY, BUT IS DEFINITELY THE WRONG THING TO FEEL...

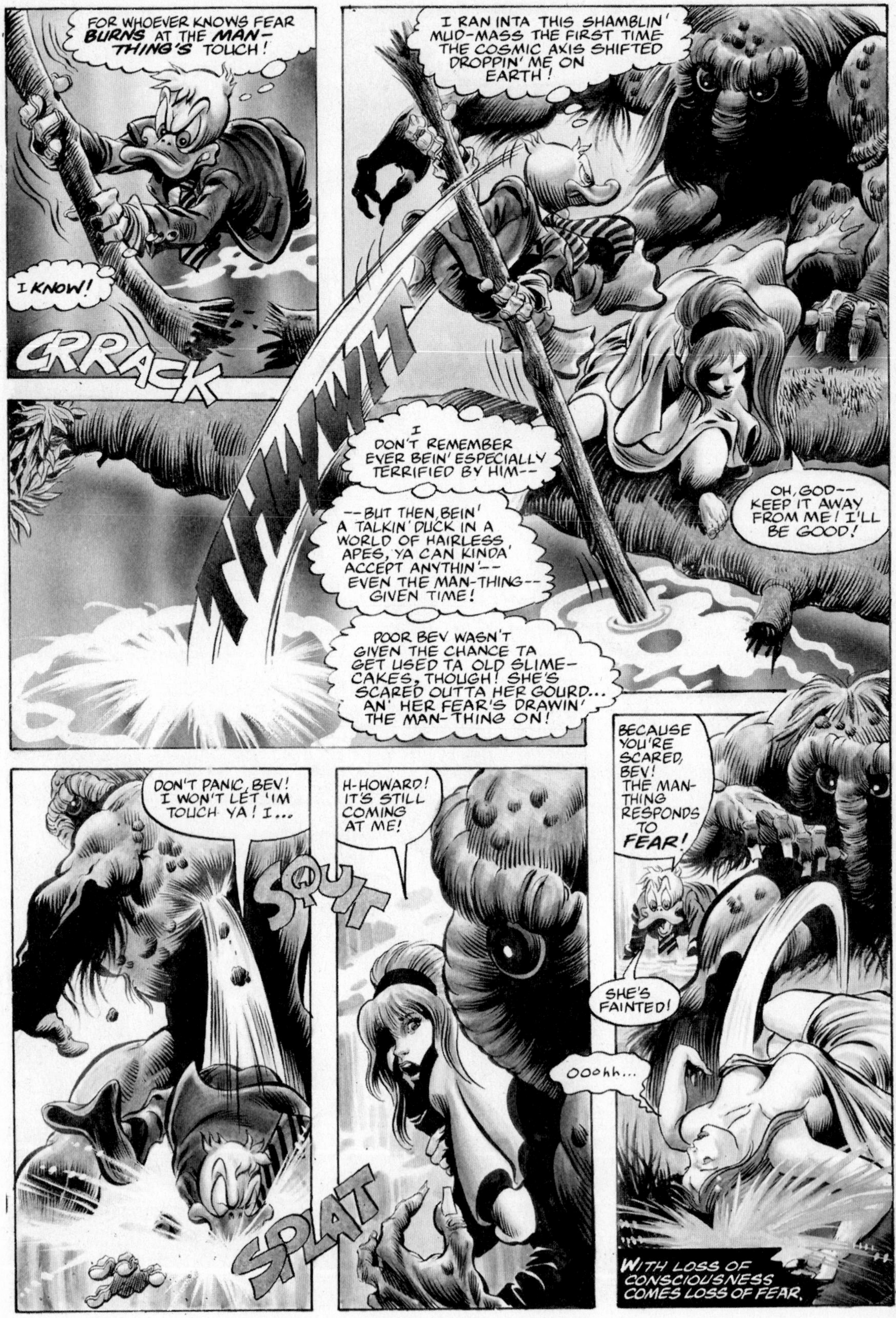
FOR WHOEVER KNOWS FEAR BURNS AT THE MAN-THING'S TOUCH!
I KNOW!
CRRACK
I RAN INTA THIS SHAMBLIN' MUD-MASS THE FIRST TIME THE COSMIC AXIS SHIFTED DROPPIN' ME ON EARTH!
I DON'T REMEMBER EVER BEIN' ESPECIALLY TERRIFIED BY HIM--
--BUT THEN BEIN' A TALKIN' DUCK IN A WORLD OF HAIRLESS APES, YA CAN KINDA' ACCEPT ANYTHIN'-- EVEN THE MAN-THING-- GIVEN TIME!
POOR BEV WASN'T GIVEN THE CHANCE TA GET USED TA OLD SLIME-CAKES, THOUGH! SHE'S SCARED OUTTA HER GOURD... AN' HER FEAR'S DRAWIN' THE MAN-THING ON!
OH, GOD-- KEEP IT AWAY FROM ME! I'LL BE GOOD!
DON'T PANIC, BEV! I WON'T LET 'IM TOUCH YA! I...
SQUIT
SPLAT
H-HOWARD! IT'S STILL COMING AT ME!
BECAUSE YOU'RE SCARED, BEV! THE MAN-THING RESPONDS TO FEAR!
SHE'S FAINTED!
OOohh...
WITH LOSS OF CONSCIOUSNESS COMES LOSS OF FEAR.

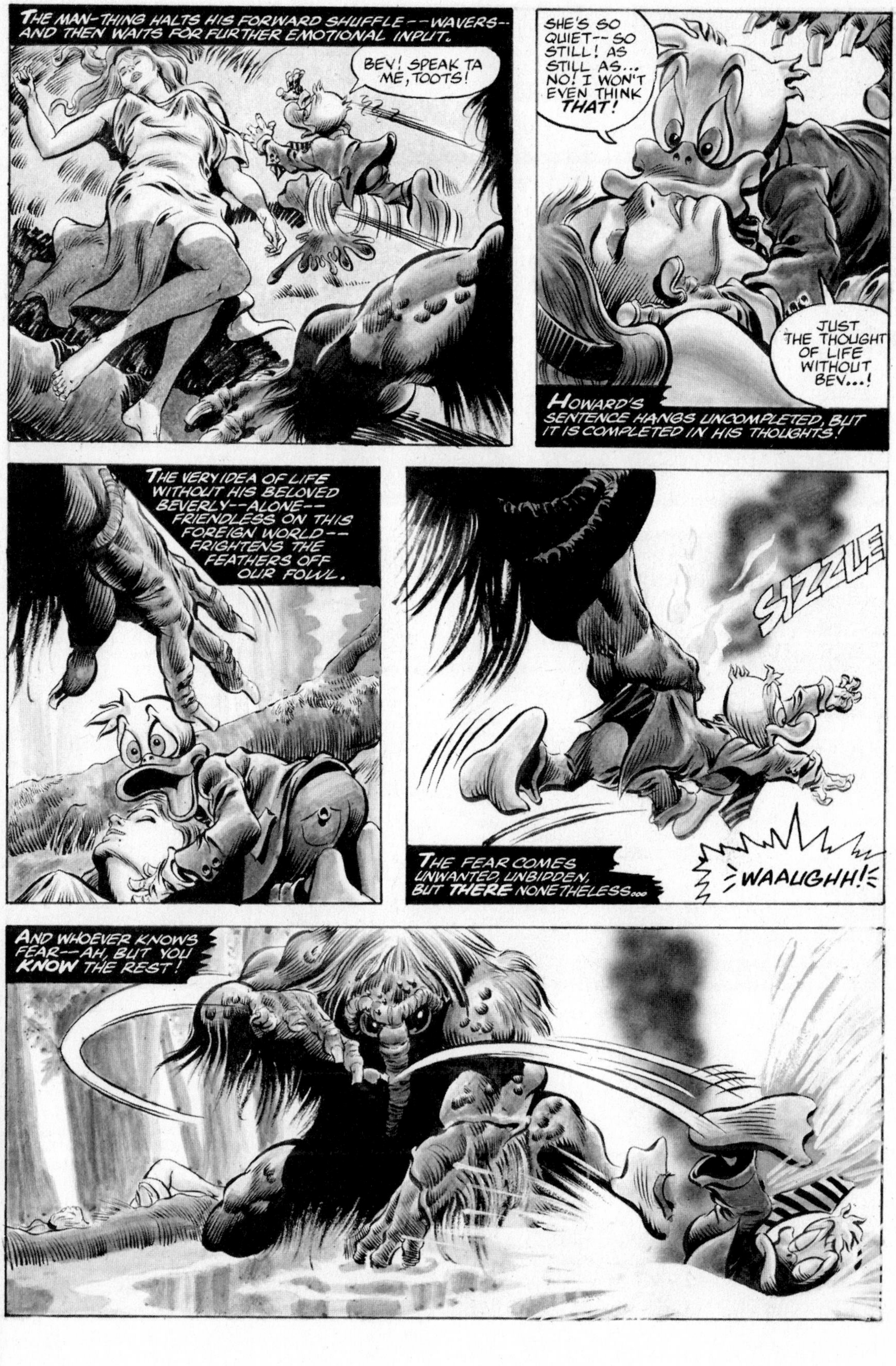
THE MAN-THING HALTS HIS FORWARD SHUFFLE--WAVERS--AND THEN WAITS FOR FURTHER EMOTIONAL INPUT.
BEV! SPEAK TA ME, TOOTS!
SHE'S SO QUIET--SO STILL! AS STILL AS... NO! I WON'T EVEN THINK THAT!
JUST THE THOUGHT OF LIFE WITHOUT BEV...!
HOWARD'S SENTENCE HANGS UNCOMPLETED, BUT IT IS COMPLETED IN HIS THOUGHTS!
THE VERY IDEA OF LIFE WITHOUT HIS BELOVED BEVERLY--ALONE--FRIENDLESS ON THIS FOREIGN WORLD--FRIGHTENS THE FEATHERS OFF OUR FOWL.
SIZZLE
THE FEAR COMES UNWANTED, UNBIDDEN, BUT THERE NONETHELESS...
WAAUGHH!
AND WHOEVER KNOWS FEAR--AH, BUT YOU KNOW THE REST!

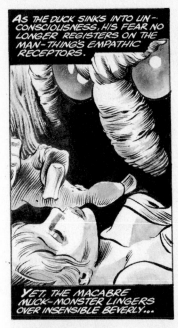

AS THE DUCK SINKS INTO UN-CONSCIOUSNESS, HIS FEAR NO LONGER REGISTERS ON THE MAN-THING'S EMPATHIC RECEPTORS.

YET, THE MACABRE MUCK-MONSTER LINGERS OVER INSENSIBLE BEVERLY...

...SENSING, ALTHOUGH SHE HERSELF IS SENSELESS, THE LOVE IN HER--

--THE MOTHERING INSTINCTS TO WHICH HE AT FIRST RESPONDED...

...AND IN SEARCH OF WHICH HE'D SCOURED THE SWAMP.

WHY? HE CANNOT SAY, FOR HE HAS NO MOUTH, NO MIND.

HE MERELY ACTS... FOR HE IS THE MAN-THING!

LATER. ESTABLISHING SHOT: THE SWAMP. HIGH NOON. BIRDS FLY. INSECTS BUZZ.

THE SUN FILTERS DOWN THROUGH THE PRIMORDIAL VEGETATION, HEATING THE FETID WATERS TO A STINKING STEW.

IT IS A HELL ON EARTH, AND IN IT SOME CREATURES ARE RIGHT AT HOME. THEY ARE PREDATORS...

...AND RARELY DO THEY FIND THEIR PREY SO SATISFYINGLY SERVED UP!

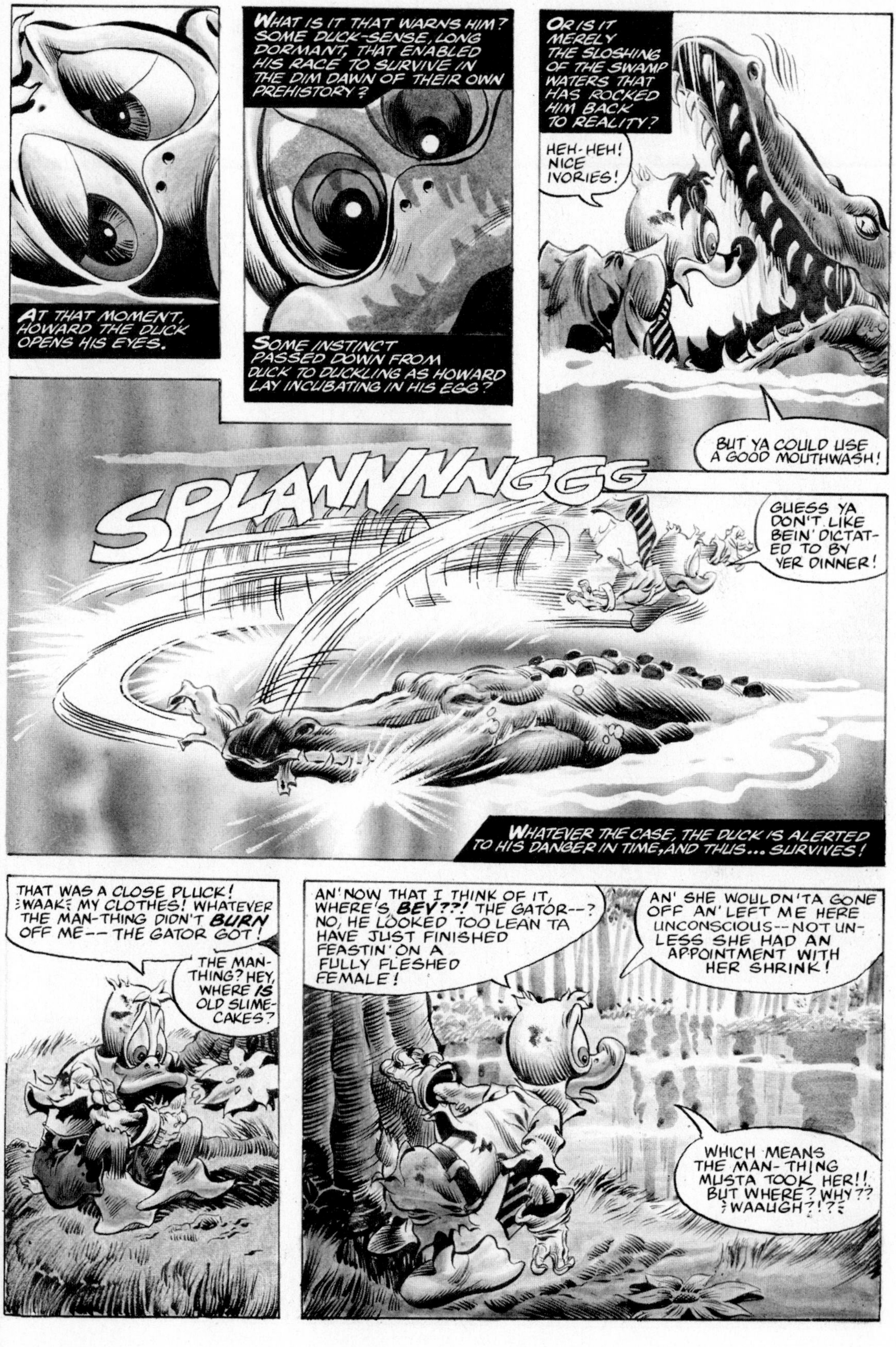

AT THAT MOMENT, HOWARD THE DUCK OPENS HIS EYES.
WHAT IS IT THAT WARNS HIM? SOME DUCK-SENSE, LONG DORMANT, THAT ENABLED HIS RACE TO SURVIVE IN THE DIM DAWN OF THEIR OWN PREHISTORY?
SOME INSTINCT PASSED DOWN FROM DUCK TO DUCKLING AS HOWARD LAY INCUBATING IN HIS EGG?
OR IS IT MERELY THE SLOSHING OF THE SWAMP WATERS THAT HAS ROCKED HIM BACK TO REALITY?
HEH-HEH! NICE IVORIES!
BUT YA COULD USE A GOOD MOUTHWASH!
SPLANNNNGGG
GUESS YA DON'T LIKE BEIN' DICTATED TO BY YER DINNER!
WHATEVER THE CASE, THE DUCK IS ALERTED TO HIS DANGER IN TIME, AND THUS... SURVIVES!
THAT WAS A CLOSE PLUCK! WAAK! MY CLOTHES! WHATEVER THE MAN-THING DIDN'T BURN OFF ME-- THE GATOR GOT!
THE MAN-THING? HEY, WHERE IS OLD SLIME-CAKES?
AN' NOW THAT I THINK OF IT, WHERE'S BEV??! THE GATOR--? NO, HE LOOKED TOO LEAN TA HAVE JUST FINISHED FEASTIN' ON A FULLY FLESHED FEMALE!
AN' SHE WOULDN'TA GONE OFF AN' LEFT ME HERE UNCONSCIOUS--NOT UNLESS SHE HAD AN APPOINTMENT WITH HER SHRINK!
WHICH MEANS THE MAN-THING MUSTA TOOK HER!! BUT WHERE? WHY?? WAAUGH?!?

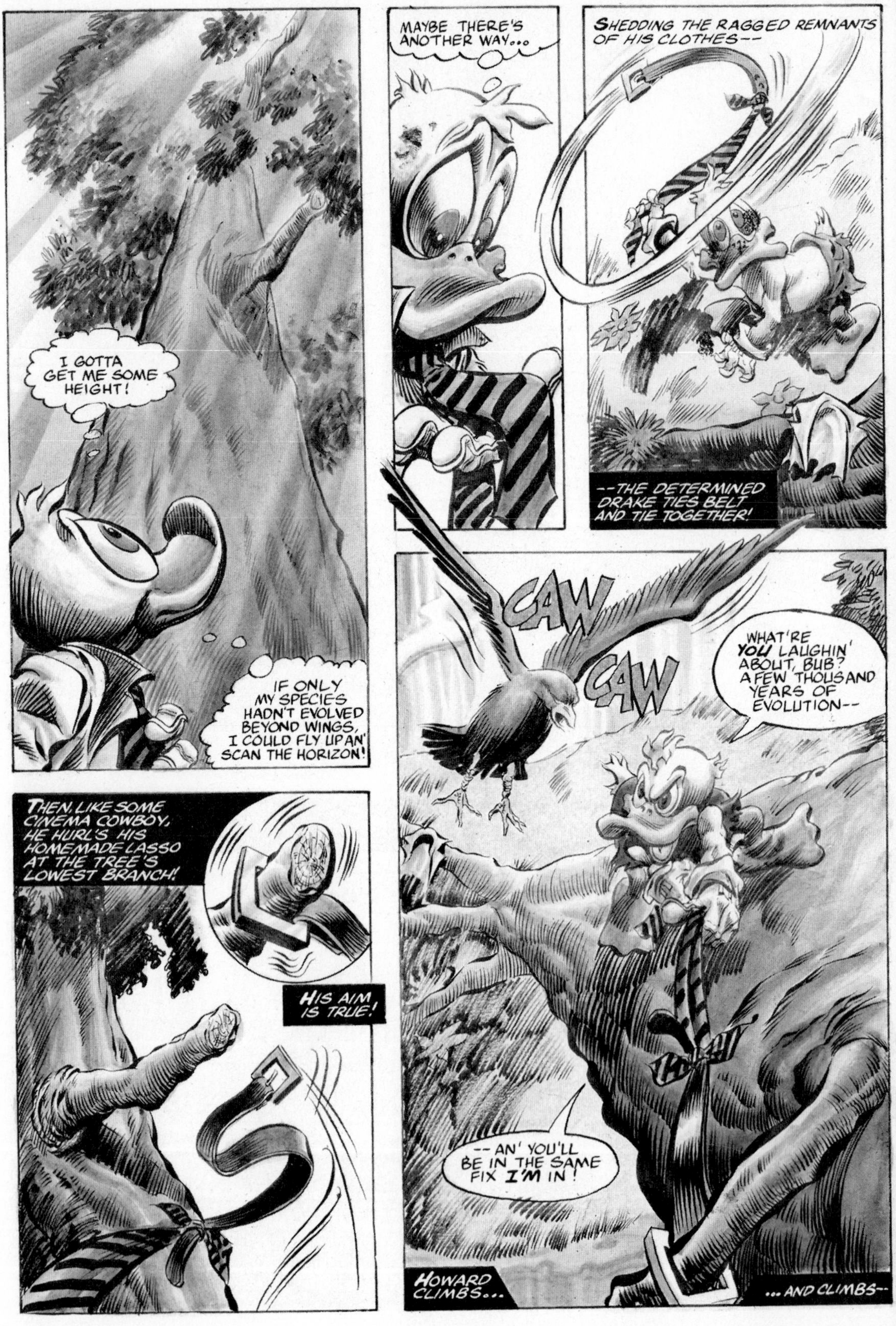
I GOTTA GET ME SOME HEIGHT!
IF ONLY MY SPECIES HADN'T EVOLVED BEYOND WINGS, I COULD FLY UP AN' SCAN THE HORIZON!
MAYBE THERE'S ANOTHER WAY...
SHEDDING THE RAGGED REMNANTS OF HIS CLOTHES--
--THE DETERMINED DRAKE TIES BELT AND TIE TOGETHER!
THEN, LIKE SOME CINEMA COWBOY, HE HURLS HIS HOMEMADE LASSO AT THE TREE'S LOWEST BRANCH!
HIS AIM IS TRUE!
CAW
CAW
WHAT'RE YOU LAUGHIN' ABOUT, BUB? A FEW THOUSAND YEARS OF EVOLUTION--
--AN' YOU'LL BE IN THE SAME FIX I'M IN!
HOWARD CLIMBS...
...AND CLIMBS--

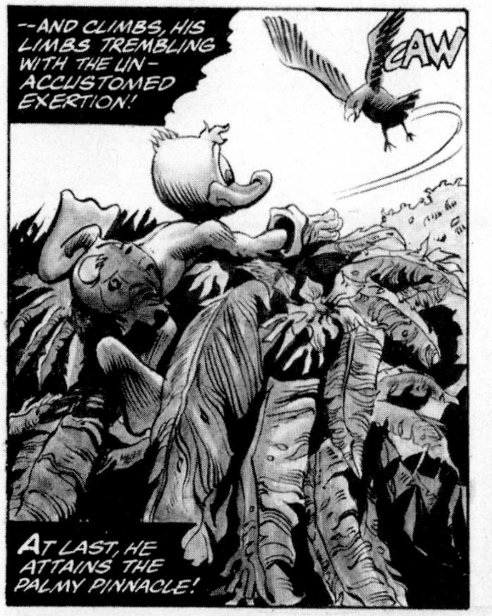
--AND CLIMBS, HIS LIMBS TREMBLING WITH THE UN-ACCUSTOMED EXERTION!
CAW
AT LAST, HE ATTAINS THE PALMY PINNACLE!

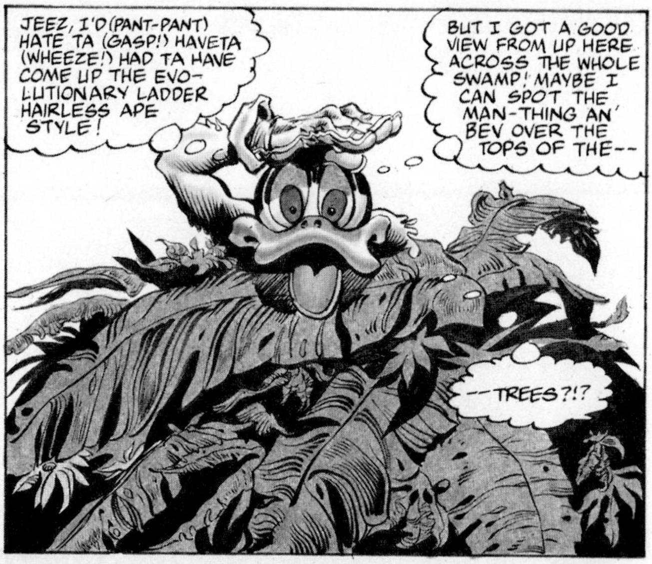
JEEZ, I'D (PANT-PANT) HATE TA (GASP!) HAVETA (WHEEZE!) HAD TA HAVE COME UP THE EVO-LUTIONARY LADDER HAIRLESS APE STYLE!
BUT I GOT A GOOD VIEW FROM UP HERE ACROSS THE WHOLE SWAMP! MAYBE I CAN SPOT THE MAN-THING AN' BEV OVER THE TOPS OF THE--
--TREES?!?

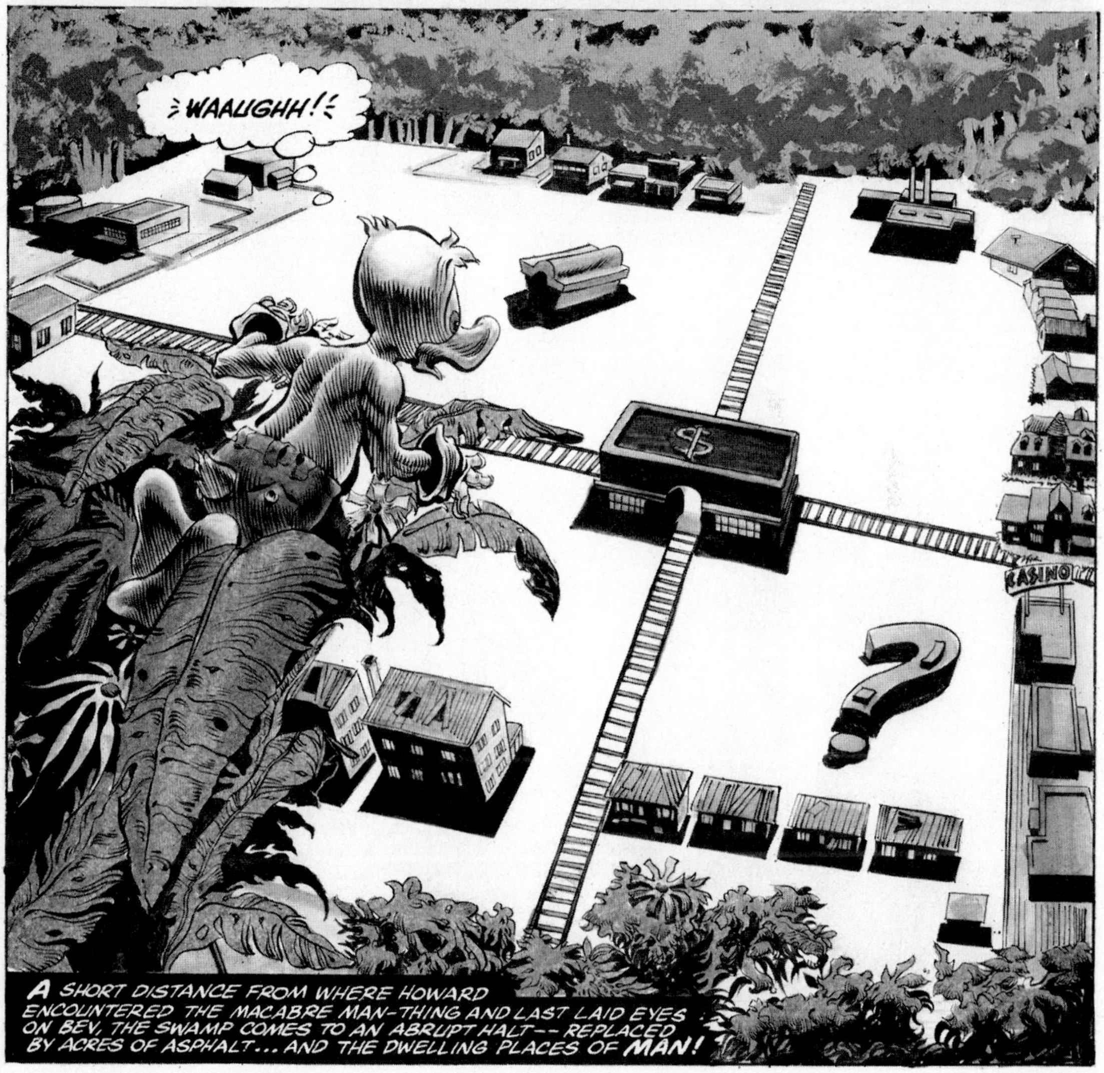
WAAUGHH!
CASINO
A SHORT DISTANCE FROM WHERE HOWARD ENCOUNTERED THE MACABRE MAN-THING AND LAST LAID EYES ON BEV, THE SWAMP COMES TO AN ABRUPT HALT-- REPLACED BY ACRES OF ASPHALT... AND THE DWELLING PLACES OF MAN!

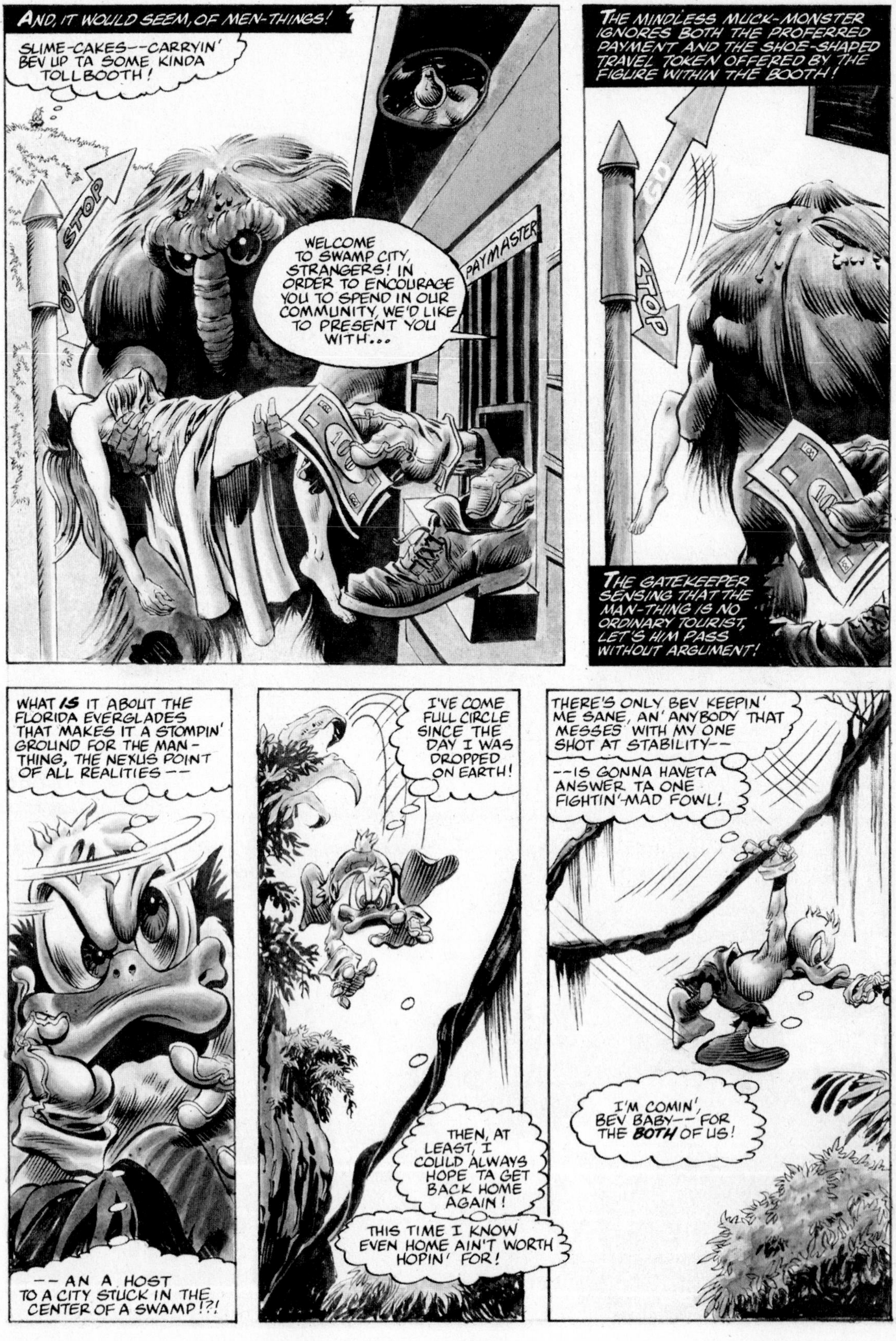
AND, IT WOULD SEEM, OF MEN-THINGS!
SLIME-CAKES--CARRYIN' BEV UP TA SOME KINDA TOLLBOOTH!
STOP
GO
PAYMASTER
WELCOME TO SWAMP CITY, STRANGERS! IN ORDER TO ENCOURAGE YOU TO SPEND IN OUR COMMUNITY, WE'D LIKE TO PRESENT YOU WITH...
THE MINDLESS MUCK-MONSTER IGNORES BOTH THE PROFERRED PAYMENT AND THE SHOE-SHAPED TRAVEL TOKEN OFFERED BY THE FIGURE WITHIN THE BOOTH!
GO
STOP
THE GATEKEEPER SENSING THAT THE MAN-THING IS NO ORDINARY TOURIST, LET'S HIM PASS WITHOUT ARGUMENT!
WHAT IS IT ABOUT THE FLORIDA EVERGLADES THAT MAKES IT A STOMPIN' GROUND FOR THE MAN-THING, THE NEXUS POINT OF ALL REALITIES--
--AN A HOST TO A CITY STUCK IN THE CENTER OF A SWAMP!?!
I'VE COME FULL CIRCLE SINCE THE DAY I WAS DROPPED ON EARTH!
THEN, AT LEAST, I COULD ALWAYS HOPE TA GET BACK HOME AGAIN!
THIS TIME I KNOW EVEN HOME AIN'T WORTH HOPIN' FOR!
THERE'S ONLY BEV KEEPIN' ME SANE, AN' ANYBODY THAT MESSES WITH MY ONE SHOT AT STABILITY--
--IS GONNA HAVETA ANSWER TA ONE FIGHTIN'-MAD FOWL!
I'M COMIN', BEV BABY--FOR THE BOTH OF US!

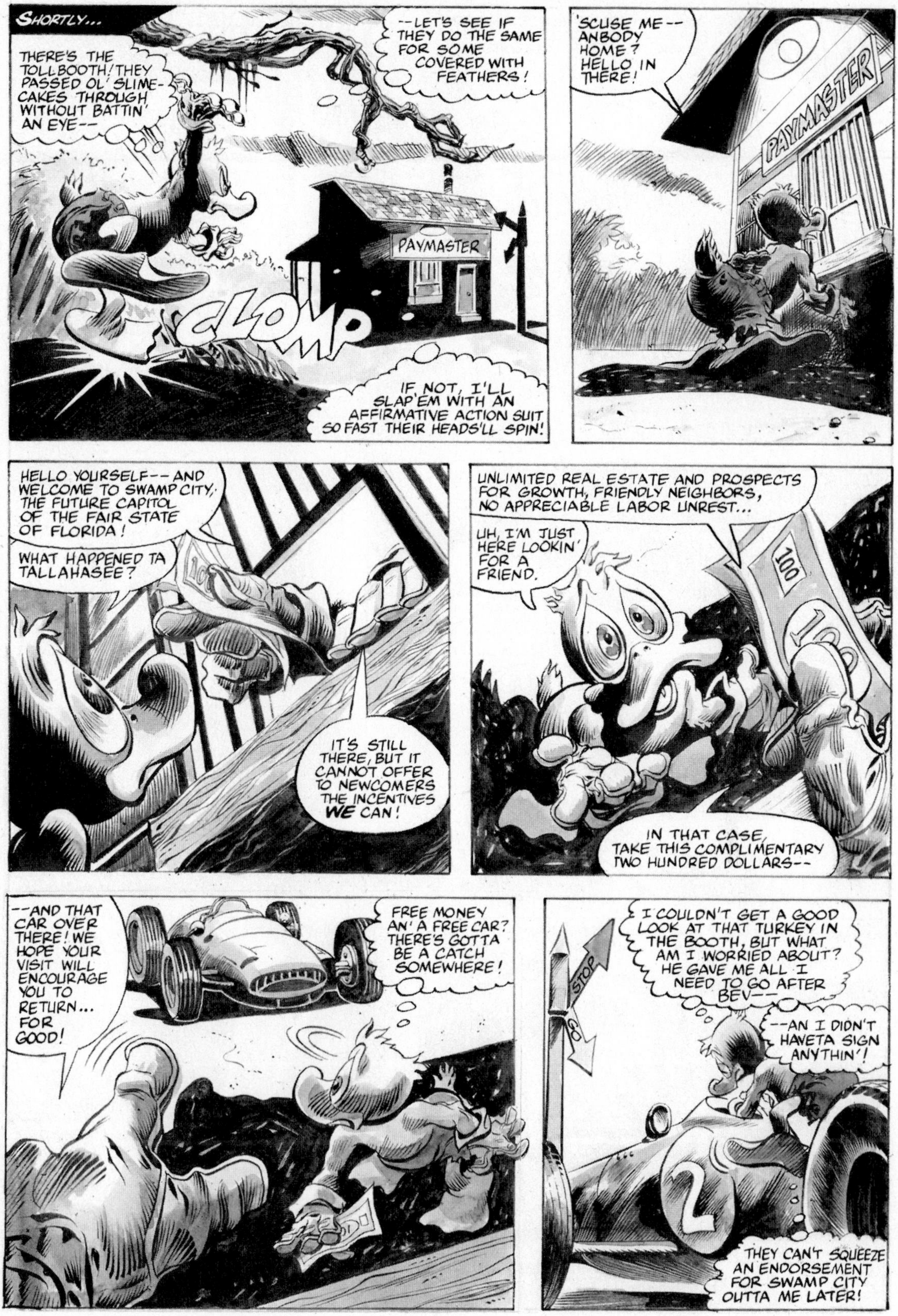
SHORTLY...
THERE'S THE TOLLBOOTH! THEY PASSED OL' SLIME-CAKES THROUGH WITHOUT BATTIN' AN EYE--
--LET'S SEE IF THEY DO THE SAME FOR SOME COVERED WITH FEATHERS!
PAYMASTER
CLOMP
IF NOT, I'LL SLAP'EM WITH AN AFFIRMATIVE ACTION SUIT SO FAST THEIR HEADS'LL SPIN!
'SCUSE ME-- ANBODY HOME? HELLO IN THERE!
PAYMASTER
HELLO YOURSELF-- AND WELCOME TO SWAMP CITY, THE FUTURE CAPITOL OF THE FAIR STATE OF FLORIDA!
WHAT HAPPENED TA TALLAHASEE?
IT'S STILL THERE, BUT IT CANNOT OFFER TO NEWCOMERS THE INCENTIVES WE CAN!
UNLIMITED REAL ESTATE AND PROSPECTS FOR GROWTH, FRIENDLY NEIGHBORS, NO APPRECIABLE LABOR UNREST...
UH, I'M JUST HERE LOOKIN' FOR A FRIEND.
IN THAT CASE, TAKE THIS COMPLIMENTARY TWO HUNDRED DOLLARS--
--AND THAT CAR OVER THERE! WE HOPE YOUR VISIT WILL ENCOURAGE YOU TO RETURN... FOR GOOD!
FREE MONEY AN' A FREE CAR? THERE'S GOTTA BE A CATCH SOMEWHERE!
STOP
GO
I COULDN'T GET A GOOD LOOK AT THAT TURKEY IN THE BOOTH, BUT WHAT AM I WORRIED ABOUT? HE GAVE ME ALL I NEED TO GO AFTER BEV--
--AN I DIDN'T HAVETA SIGN ANYTHIN'!
THEY CAN'T SQUEEZE AN ENDORSEMENT FOR SWAMP CITY OUTTA ME LATER!

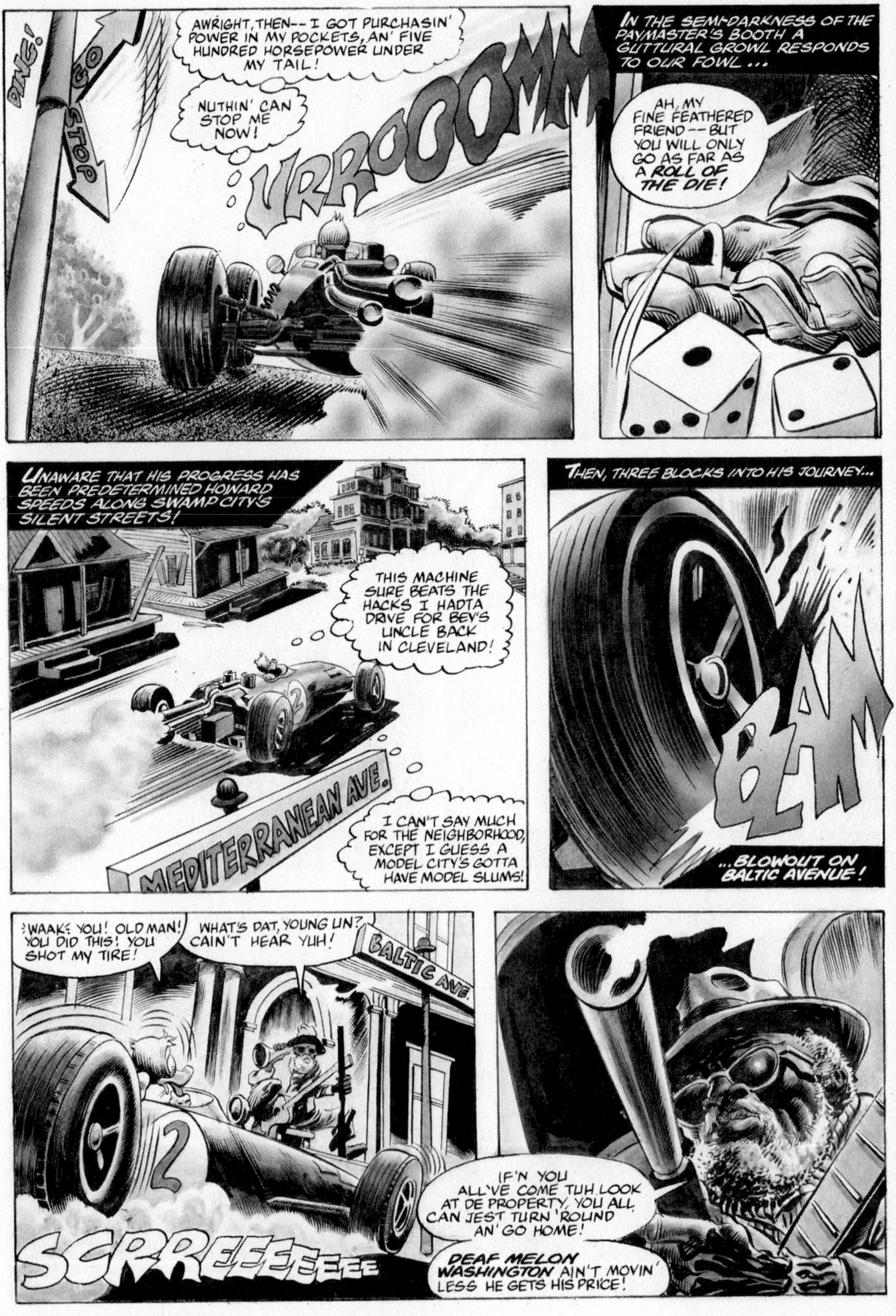
DING!
GO
STOP
AWRIGHT, THEN-- I GOT PURCHASIN' POWER IN MY POCKETS, AN' FIVE HUNDRED HORSEPOWER UNDER MY TAIL!
NUTHIN' CAN STOP ME NOW!
URROOOOMMM
IN THE SEMI-DARKNESS OF THE PAYMASTER'S BOOTH A GUTTURAL GROWL RESPONDS TO OUR FOWL...
AH, MY FINE FEATHERED FRIEND -- BUT YOU WILL ONLY GO AS FAR AS A ROLL OF THE DIE!
UNAWARE THAT HIS PROGRESS HAS BEEN PREDETERMINED HOWARD SPEEDS ALONG SWAMP CITY'S SILENT STREETS!
THIS MACHINE SURE BEATS THE HACKS I HADTA DRIVE FOR BEV'S UNCLE BACK IN CLEVELAND!
MEDITERRANEAN AVE.
I CAN'T SAY MUCH FOR THE NEIGHBORHOOD, EXCEPT I GUESS A MODEL CITY'S GOTTA HAVE MODEL SLUMS!
THEN, THREE BLOCKS INTO HIS JOURNEY...
BLAM
...BLOWOUT ON BALTIC AVENUE!
WAAK! YOU! OLD MAN! YOU DID THIS! YOU SHOT MY TIRE!
WHAT'S DAT, YOUNG UN? CAIN'T HEAR YUH!
BALTIC AVE.
SCRREEEEEEEE
IF'N YOU ALL'VE COME TUH LOOK AT DE PROPERTY, YOU ALL CAN JEST TURN 'ROUND AN' GO HOME!
DEAF MELON WASHINGTON AIN'T MOVIN' LESS HE GETS HIS PRICE!

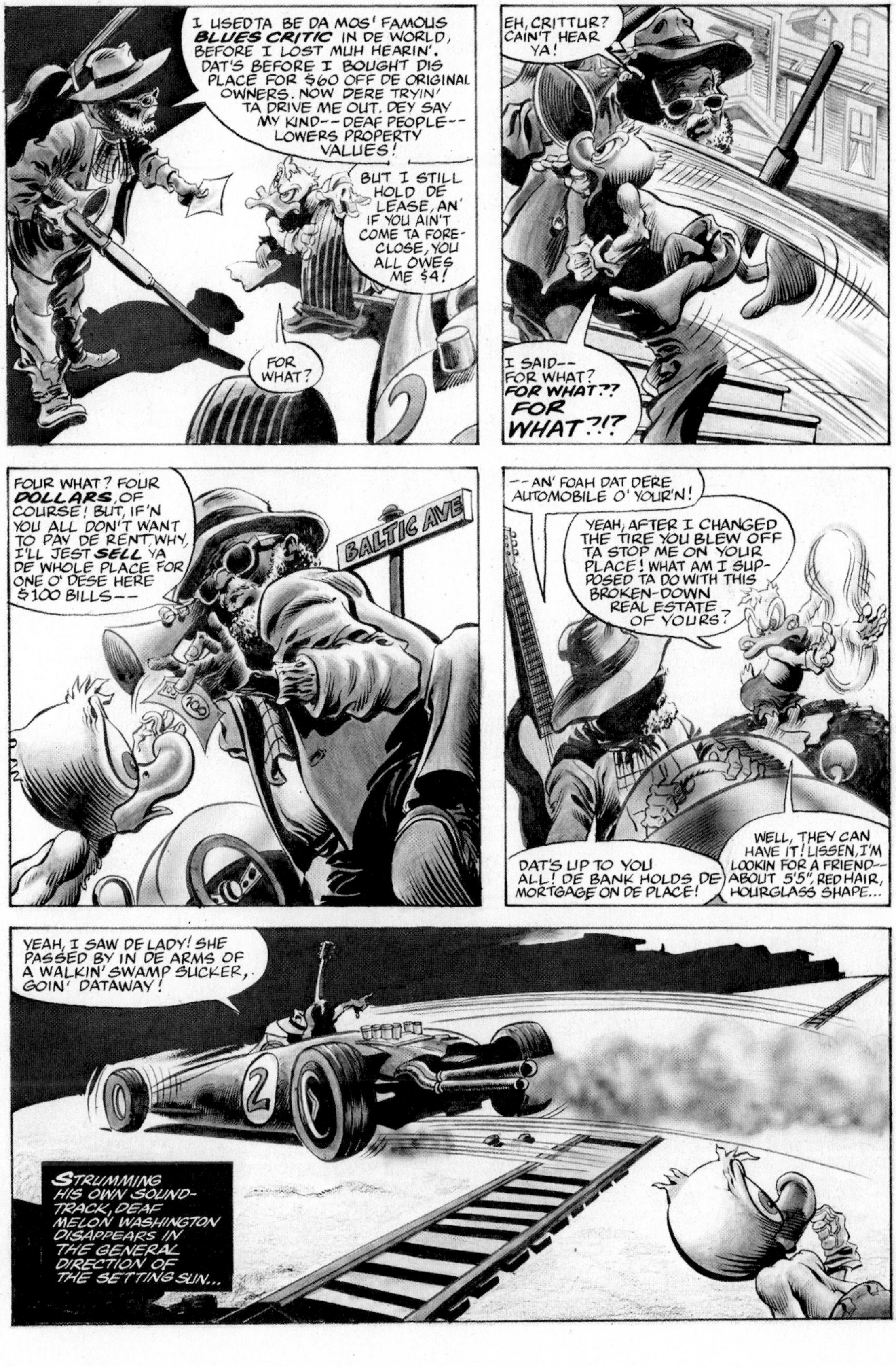
I USEDTA BE DA MOS' FAMOUS BLUES CRITIC IN DE WORLD, BEFORE I LOST MUH HEARIN'. DAT'S BEFORE I BOUGHT DIS PLACE FOR $60 OFF DE ORIGINAL OWNERS. NOW DERE TRYIN' TA DRIVE ME OUT. DEY SAY MY KIND--DEAF PEOPLE--LOWERS PROPERTY VALUES!
BUT I STILL HOLD DE LEASE, AN' IF YOU AIN'T COME TA FORECLOSE, YOU ALL OWES ME $4!
FOR WHAT?
EH, CRITTUR? CAIN'T HEAR YA!
I SAID--FOR WHAT? FOR WHAT?!? FOR WHAT?!?
FOUR WHAT? FOUR DOLLARS, OF COURSE! BUT, IF'N YOU ALL DON'T WANT TO PAY DE RENT, WHY, I'LL JEST SELL YA DE WHOLE PLACE FOR ONE O' DESE HERE $100 BILLS--
BALTIC AVE
--AN' FOAH DAT DERE AUTOMOBILE O' YOUR'N!
YEAH, AFTER I CHANGED THE TIRE YOU BLEW OFF TA STOP ME ON YOUR PLACE! WHAT AM I SUPPOSED TA DO WITH THIS BROKEN-DOWN REAL ESTATE OF YOURS?
DAT'S UP TO YOU ALL! DE BANK HOLDS DE MORTGAGE ON DE PLACE!
WELL, THEY CAN HAVE IT! LISSEN, I'M LOOKIN FOR A FRIEND--ABOUT 5'5", RED HAIR, HOURGLASS SHAPE...
YEAH, I SAW DE LADY! SHE PASSED BY IN DE ARMS OF A WALKIN' SWAMP SUCKER, GOIN' DATAWAY!
STRUMMING HIS OWN SOUNDTRACK, DEAF MELON WASHINGTON DISAPPEARS IN THE GENERAL DIRECTION OF THE SETTING SUN...

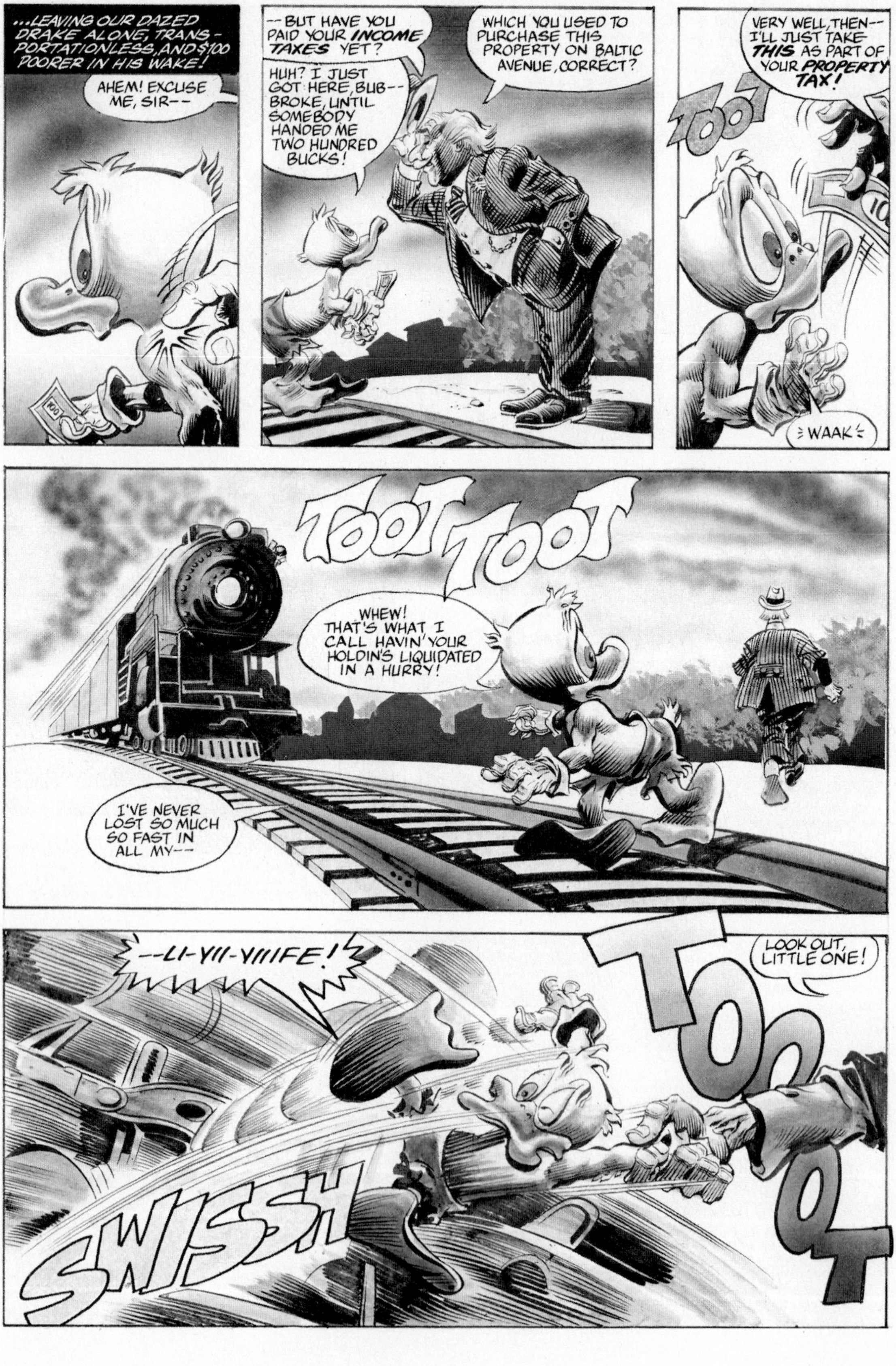
...LEAVING OUR DAZED DRAKE ALONE, TRANSPORTATIONLESS, AND $100 POORER IN HIS WAKE!
AHEM! EXCUSE ME, SIR--
--BUT HAVE YOU PAID YOUR INCOME TAXES YET?
HUH? I JUST GOT HERE, BUB--BROKE, UNTIL SOMEBODY HANDED ME TWO HUNDRED BUCKS!
WHICH YOU USED TO PURCHASE THIS PROPERTY ON BALTIC AVENUE, CORRECT?
VERY WELL, THEN--I'LL JUST TAKE THIS AS PART OF YOUR PROPERTY TAX!
TOOT
WAAK
TOOT TOOT
WHEW! THAT'S WHAT I CALL HAVIN' YOUR HOLDIN'S LIQUIDATED IN A HURRY!
I'VE NEVER LOST SO MUCH SO FAST IN ALL MY--
--LI-YII-YIIIFE!
TOOOOT
LOOK OUT, LITTLE ONE!
SWISSH

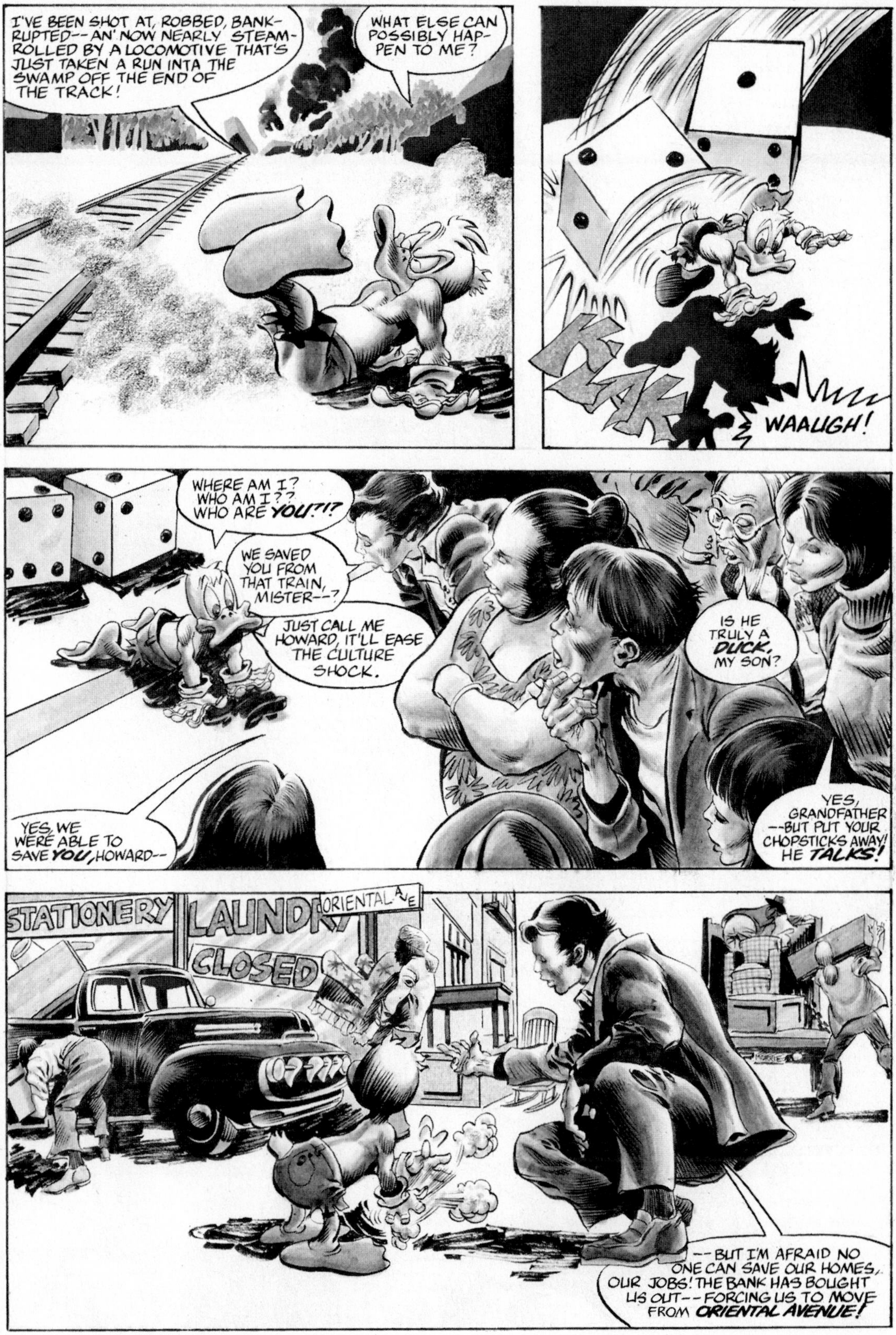

I'VE BEEN SHOT AT, ROBBED, BANKRUPTED-- AN' NOW NEARLY STEAMROLLED BY A LOCOMOTIVE THAT'S JUST TAKEN A RUN INTA THE SWAMP OFF THE END OF THE TRACK!
WHAT ELSE CAN POSSIBLY HAPPEN TO ME?
KLAK
WAAUGH!
WHERE AM I? WHO AM I?? WHO ARE YOU?!?
WE SAVED YOU FROM THAT TRAIN, MISTER--?
JUST CALL ME HOWARD, IT'LL EASE THE CULTURE SHOCK.
IS HE TRULY A DUCK, MY SON?
YES, WE WERE ABLE TO SAVE YOU, HOWARD--
YES, GRANDFATHER --BUT PUT YOUR CHOPSTICKS AWAY! HE TALKS!
STATIONERY
LAUNDRY
ORIENTAL AVE
CLOSED
--BUT I'M AFRAID NO ONE CAN SAVE OUR HOMES, OUR JOBS! THE BANK HAS BOUGHT US OUT--FORCING US TO MOVE FROM ORIENTAL AVENUE!

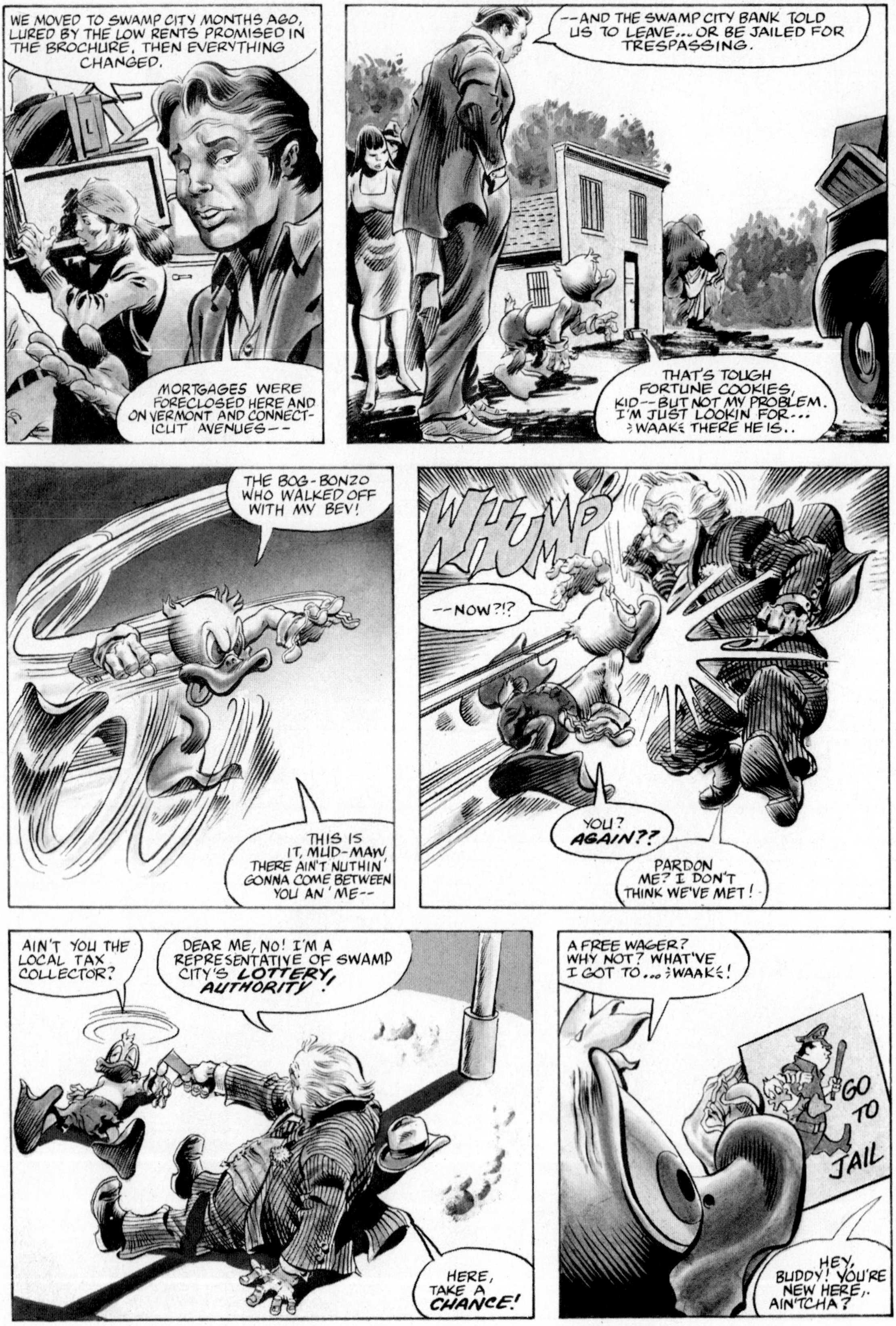
WE MOVED TO SWAMP CITY MONTHS AGO, LURED BY THE LOW RENTS PROMISED IN THE BROCHURE. THEN EVERYTHING CHANGED.
MORTGAGES WERE FORECLOSED HERE AND ON VERMONT AND CONNECTICUT AVENUES--
--AND THE SWAMP CITY BANK TOLD US TO LEAVE... OR BE JAILED FOR TRESPASSING.
THAT'S TOUGH FORTUNE COOKIES, KID--BUT NOT MY PROBLEM. I'M JUST LOOKIN FOR--- WAAK THERE HE IS..
THE BOG-BONZO WHO WALKED OFF WITH MY BEV!
THIS IS IT, MUD-MAW THERE AIN'T NUTHIN' GONNA COME BETWEEN YOU AN' ME--
WHUMP
--NOW?!?
YOU? AGAIN??
PARDON ME? I DON'T THINK WE'VE MET!
AIN'T YOU THE LOCAL TAX COLLECTOR?
DEAR ME, NO! I'M A REPRESENTATIVE OF SWAMP CITY'S LOTTERY AUTHORITY!
HERE, TAKE A CHANCE!
A FREE WAGER? WHY NOT? WHAT'VE I GOT TO... WAAK!
GO TO JAIL
HEY, BUDDY! YOU'RE NEW HERE, AIN'TCHA?

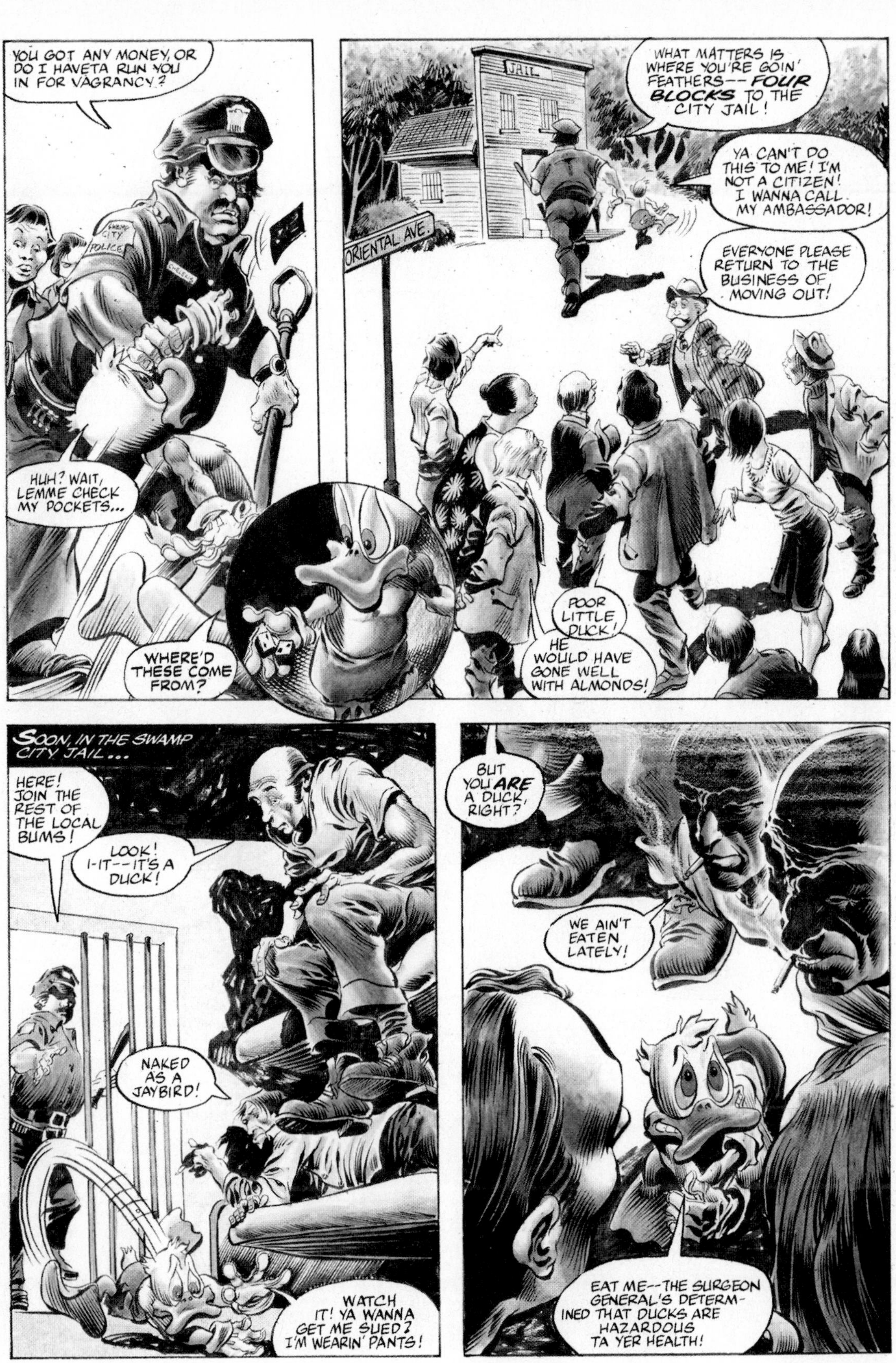
YOU GOT ANY MONEY, OR DO I HAVETA RUN YOU IN FOR VAGRANCY?
HUH? WAIT, LEMME CHECK MY POCKETS...
WHERE'D THESE COME FROM?
ORIENTAL AVE.
JAIL
WHAT MATTERS IS WHERE YOU'RE GOIN' FEATHERS-- FOUR BLOCKS TO THE CITY JAIL!
YA CAN'T DO THIS TO ME! I'M NOT A CITIZEN! I WANNA CALL MY AMBASSADOR!
EVERYONE PLEASE RETURN TO THE BUSINESS OF MOVING OUT!
POOR LITTLE DUCK!
HE WOULD HAVE GONE WELL WITH ALMONDS!
SOON, IN THE SWAMP CITY JAIL...
HERE! JOIN THE REST OF THE LOCAL BUMS!
LOOK! I-IT--IT'S A DUCK!
NAKED AS A JAYBIRD!
WATCH IT! YA WANNA GET ME SUED? I'M WEARIN' PANTS!
BUT YOU ARE A DUCK, RIGHT?
WE AIN'T EATEN LATELY!
EAT ME--THE SURGEON GENERAL'S DETERMINED THAT DUCKS ARE HAZARDOUS TA YER HEALTH!

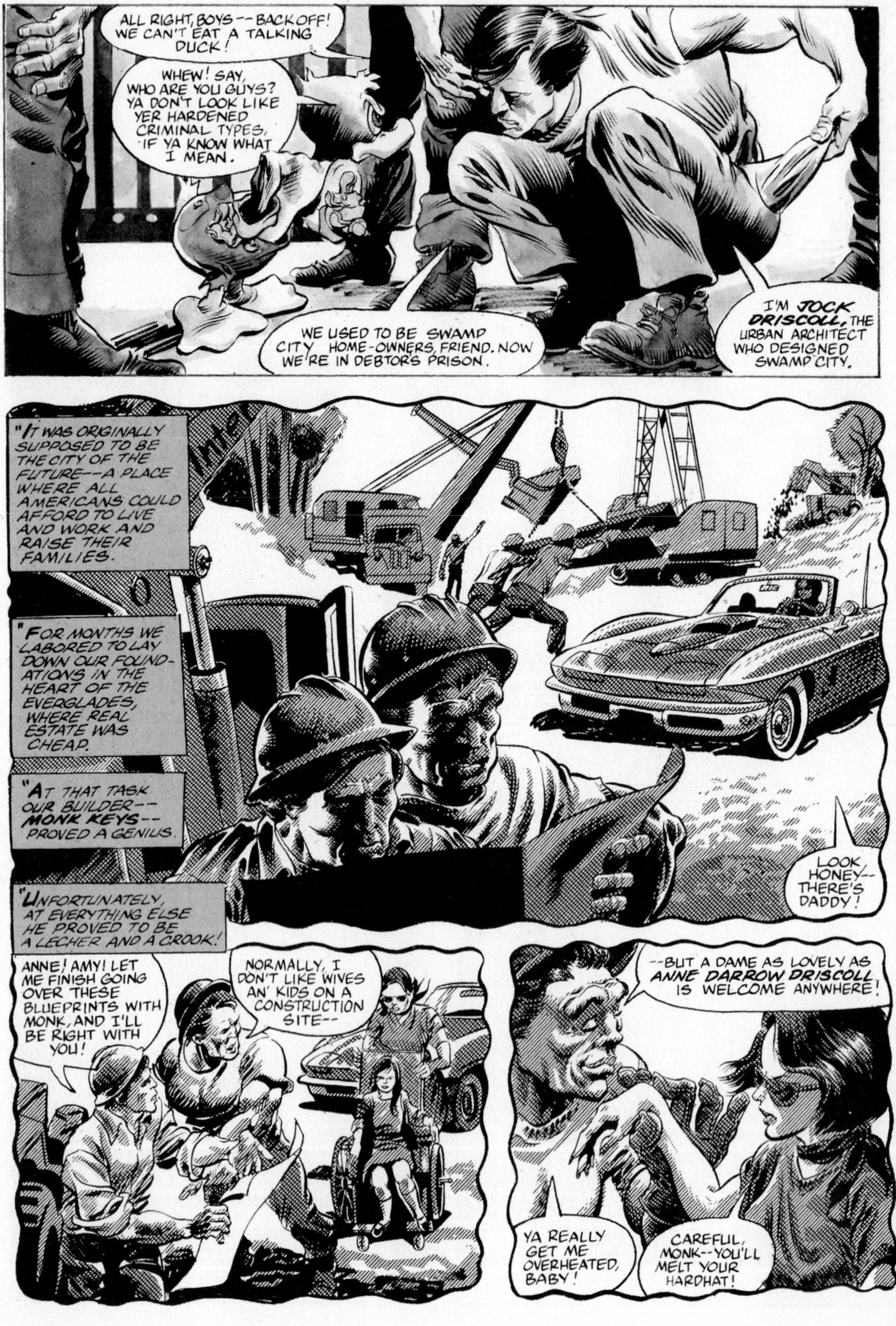
ALL RIGHT, BOYS--BACK OFF! WE CAN'T EAT A TALKING DUCK!
WHEW! SAY, WHO ARE YOU GUYS? YA DON'T LOOK LIKE YER HARDENED CRIMINAL TYPES, IF YA KNOW WHAT I MEAN.
WE USED TO BE SWAMP CITY HOME-OWNERS, FRIEND. NOW WE'RE IN DEBTOR'S PRISON.
I'M JOCK DRISCOLL, THE URBAN ARCHITECT WHO DESIGNED SWAMP CITY.
"IT WAS ORIGINALLY SUPPOSED TO BE THE CITY OF THE FUTURE--A PLACE WHERE ALL AMERICANS COULD AFFORD TO LIVE AND WORK AND RAISE THEIR FAMILIES.
"FOR MONTHS WE LABORED TO LAY DOWN OUR FOUNDATIONS IN THE HEART OF THE EVERGLADES, WHERE REAL ESTATE WAS CHEAP.
"AT THAT TASK OUR BUILDER--MONK KEYS--PROVED A GENIUS.
"UNFORTUNATELY, AT EVERYTHING ELSE HE PROVED TO BE A LECHER AND A CROOK!
LOOK HONEY--THERE'S DADDY!
ANNE! AMY! LET ME FINISH GOING OVER THESE BLUEPRINTS WITH MONK, AND I'LL BE RIGHT WITH YOU!
NORMALLY, I DON'T LIKE WIVES AN' KIDS ON A CONSTRUCTION SITE--
--BUT A DAME AS LOVELY AS ANNE DARROW DRISCOLL IS WELCOME ANYWHERE!
YA REALLY GET ME OVERHEATED, BABY!
CAREFUL, MONK--YOU'LL MELT YOUR HARDHAT!

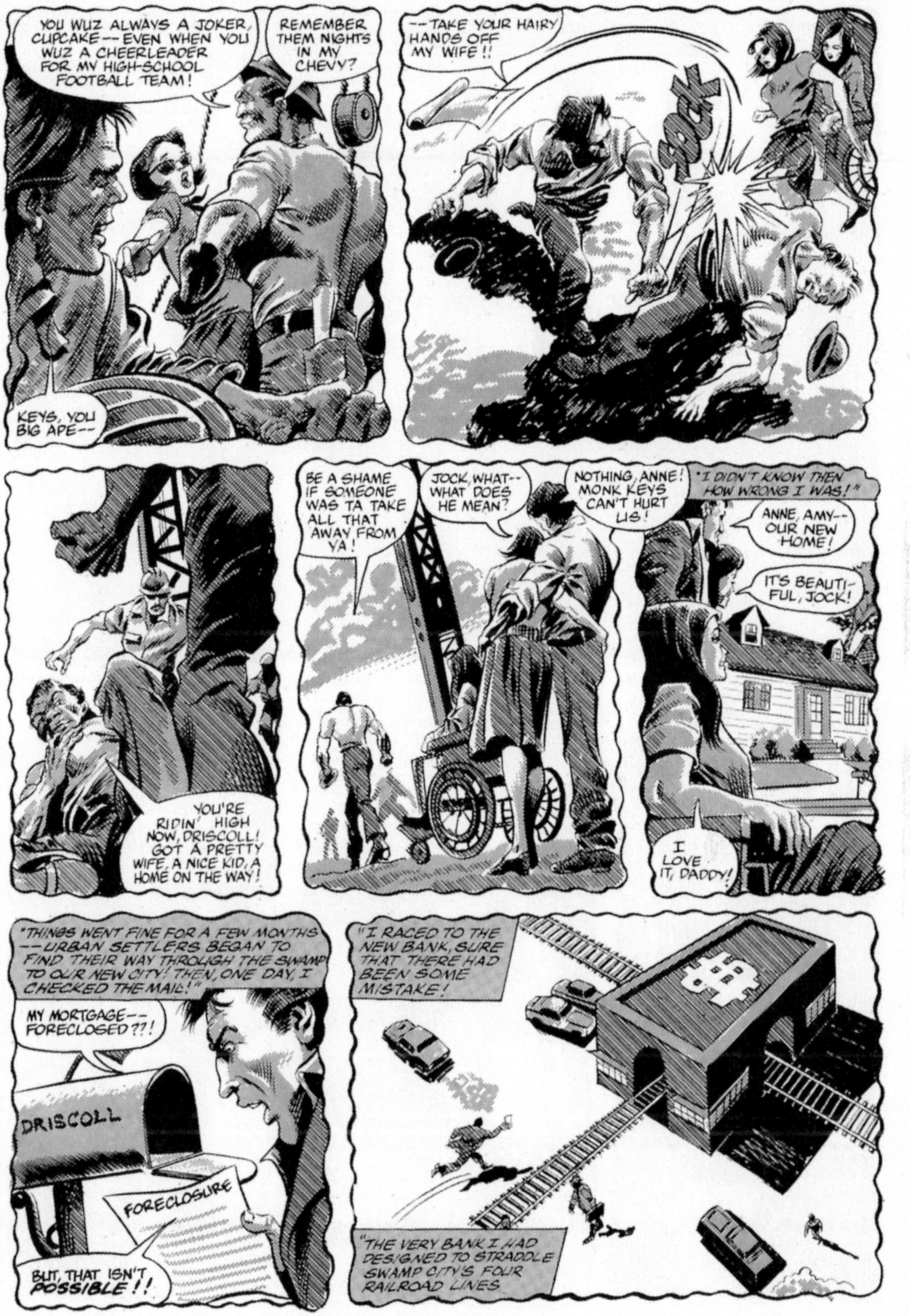
YOU WUZ ALWAYS A JOKER, CUPCAKE -- EVEN WHEN YOU WUZ A CHEERLEADER FOR MY HIGH-SCHOOL FOOTBALL TEAM!
REMEMBER THEM NIGHTS IN MY CHEVY?
KEYS, YOU BIG APE--
--TAKE YOUR HAIRY HANDS OFF MY WIFE!!
SOCK
YOU'RE RIDIN' HIGH NOW, DRISCOLL! GOT A PRETTY WIFE, A NICE KID, A HOME ON THE WAY!
BE A SHAME IF SOMEONE WAS TA TAKE ALL THAT AWAY FROM YA!
JOCK, WHAT-- WHAT DOES HE MEAN?
NOTHING, ANNE! MONK KEYS CAN'T HURT US!
"I DIDN'T KNOW THEN HOW WRONG I WAS!"
ANNE, AMY-- OUR NEW HOME!
IT'S BEAUTIFUL, JOCK!
I LOVE IT, DADDY!
"THINGS WENT FINE FOR A FEW MONTHS -- URBAN SETTLERS BEGAN TO FIND THEIR WAY THROUGH THE SWAMP TO OUR NEW CITY! THEN, ONE DAY, I CHECKED THE MAIL!"
MY MORTGAGE-- FORECLOSED??!
DRISCOLL
FORECLOSURE
BUT, THAT ISN'T POSSIBLE!!
"I RACED TO THE NEW BANK, SURE THAT THERE HAD BEEN SOME MISTAKE!
"THE VERY BANK I HAD DESIGNED TO STRADDLE SWAMP CITY'S FOUR RAILROAD LINES

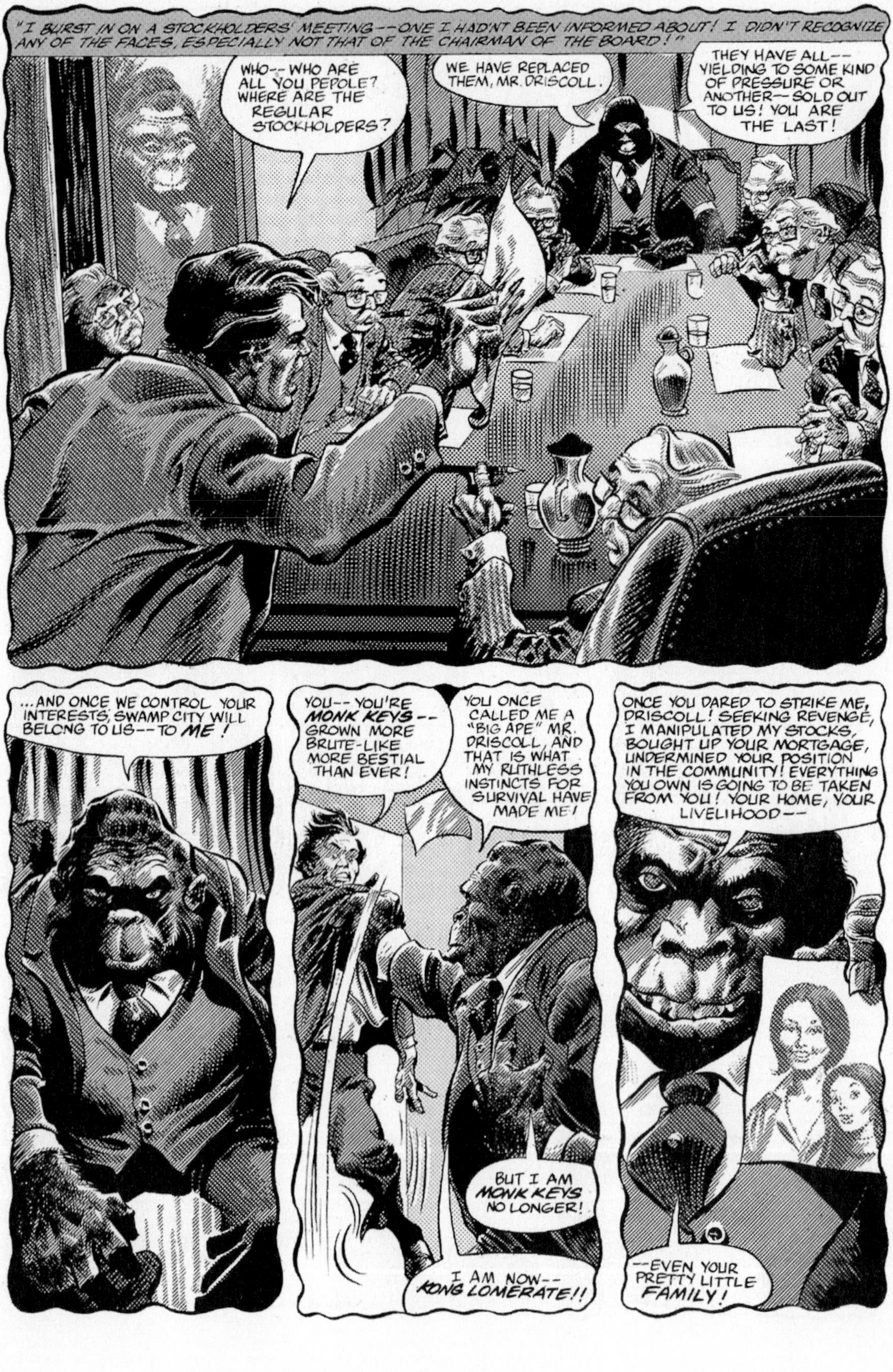
"I BURST IN ON A STOCKHOLDERS' MEETING--ONE I HADN'T BEEN INFORMED ABOUT! I DIDN'T RECOGNIZE ANY OF THE FACES, ESPECIALLY NOT THAT OF THE CHAIRMAN OF THE BOARD!"
WHO-- WHO ARE ALL YOU PEPOLE? WHERE ARE THE REGULAR STOCKHOLDERS?
WE HAVE REPLACED THEM, MR. DRISCOLL.
THEY HAVE ALL-- YIELDING TO SOME KIND OF PRESSURE OR ANOTHER-- SOLD OUT TO US! YOU ARE THE LAST!
...AND ONCE WE CONTROL YOUR INTERESTS, SWAMP CITY WILL BELONG TO US-- TO ME!
YOU-- YOU'RE MONK KEYS-- GROWN MORE BRUTE-LIKE MORE BESTIAL THAN EVER!
YOU ONCE CALLED ME A "BIG APE" MR. DRISCOLL, AND THAT IS WHAT MY RUTHLESS INSTINCTS FOR SURVIVAL HAVE MADE ME!
BUT I AM MONK KEYS NO LONGER!
I AM NOW-- KONG LOMERATE!!
ONCE YOU DARED TO STRIKE ME, DRISCOLL! SEEKING REVENGE, I MANIPULATED MY STOCKS, BOUGHT UP YOUR MORTGAGE, UNDERMINED YOUR POSITION IN THE COMMUNITY! EVERYTHING YOU OWN IS GOING TO BE TAKEN FROM YOU! YOUR HOME, YOUR LIVELIHOOD--
--EVEN YOUR PRETTY LITTLE FAMILY!

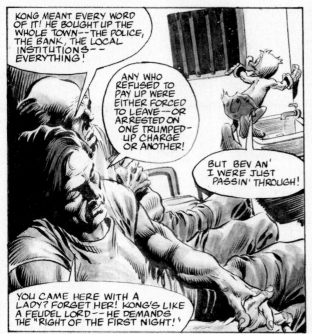

KONG MEANT EVERY WORD OF IT! HE BOUGHT UP THE WHOLE TOWN--THE POLICE, THE BANK, THE LOCAL INSTITUTIONS-- EVERYTHING!

ANY WHO REFUSED TO PAY UP WERE EITHER FORCED TO LEAVE--OR ARRESTED ON ONE TRUMPED-UP CHARGE OR ANOTHER!

BUT BEV AN' I WERE JUST PASSIN' THROUGH!

YOU CAME HERE WITH A LADY? FORGET HER! KONG'S LIKE A FEUDEL LORD--HE DEMANDS THE "RIGHT OF THE FIRST NIGHT!"

IF THAT'S WHAT HE'S GOT IN MIND FOR BEV, HE'S A LITTLE LATE! WAAK!

THERE SHE IS NOW--

ELECTRIC C

--STILL UNCONSCIOUS AN' STILL IN THE ARMS OF THAT SHUFFLIN' SLAB O' SWAMP!

BEV! WAKE UP, TOOTS!

NUTS! IT'S USELESS! SHE CAN'T HEAR ME!

AND YOU CAN'T GET OUT TO HELP HER, LIKE WE CAN'T HELP OUR FAMILIES! SORRY, SHORT-STUFF!

DON'T BE SORRY--BE USEFUL! I GOT A PLAN TA BUST OUTTA THIS JOINT!

IMPOSSIBLE! I DESIGNED IT-- I KNOW!

NUTHIN'S IMPOSSIBLE FOR ME PAL! LISSEN...

337

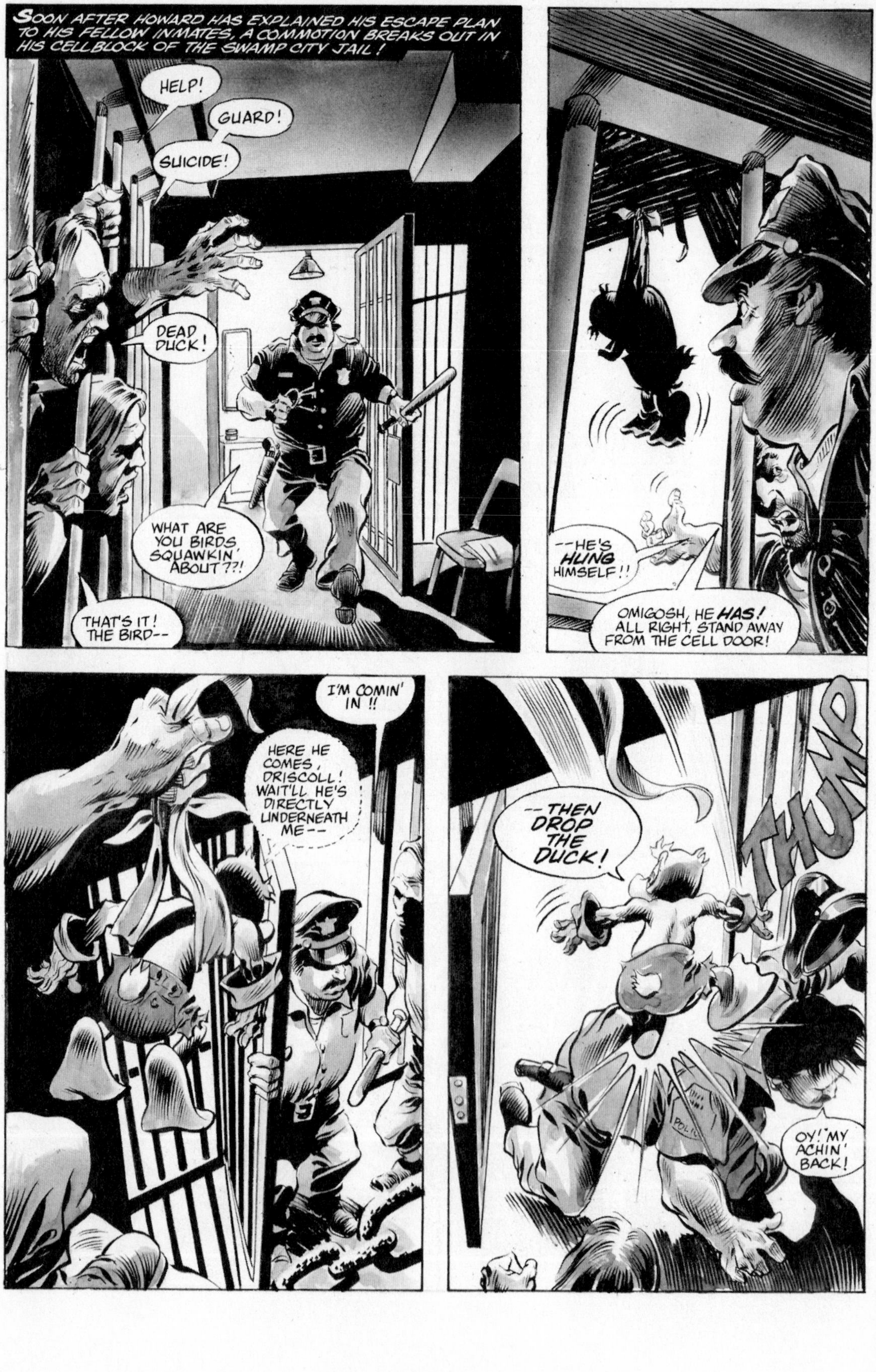
SOON AFTER HOWARD HAS EXPLAINED HIS ESCAPE PLAN TO HIS FELLOW INMATES, A COMMOTION BREAKS OUT IN HIS CELLBLOCK OF THE SWAMP CITY JAIL!
HELP!
GUARD!
SUICIDE!
DEAD DUCK!
WHAT ARE YOU BIRDS SQUAWKIN' ABOUT??!
THAT'S IT! THE BIRD--
--HE'S HUNG HIMSELF!!
OMIGOSH, HE HAS! ALL RIGHT, STAND AWAY FROM THE CELL DOOR!
I'M COMIN' IN!!
HERE HE COMES, DRISCOLL! WAIT'LL HE'S DIRECTLY UNDERNEATH ME--
--THEN DROP THE DUCK!
THUMP
OY! MY ACHIN' BACK!

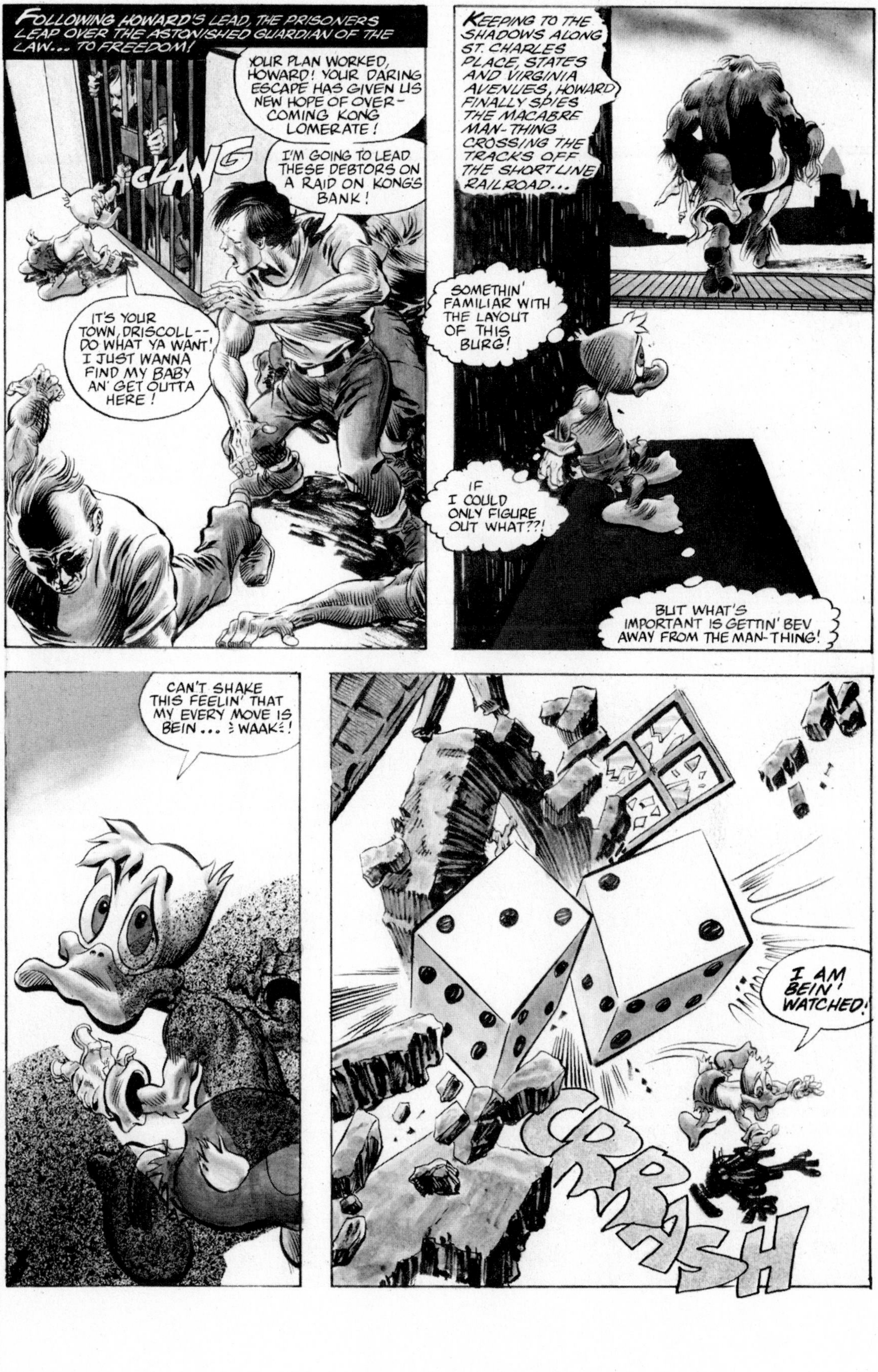
FOLLOWING HOWARD'S LEAD, THE PRISONERS LEAP OVER THE ASTONISHED GUARDIAN OF THE LAW... TO FREEDOM!
YOUR PLAN WORKED, HOWARD! YOUR DARING ESCAPE HAS GIVEN US NEW HOPE OF OVER-COMING KONG LOMERATE!
CLANG
I'M GOING TO LEAD THESE DEBTORS ON A RAID ON KONG'S BANK!
IT'S YOUR TOWN, DRISCOLL--DO WHAT YA WANT! I JUST WANNA FIND MY BABY AN' GET OUTTA HERE!
KEEPING TO THE SHADOWS ALONG ST. CHARLES PLACE, STATES AND VIRGINIA AVENUES, HOWARD FINALLY SPIES THE MACABRE MAN-THING CROSSING THE TRACKS OFF THE SHORT LINE RAILROAD...
SOMETHIN' FAMILIAR WITH THE LAYOUT OF THIS BURG!
IF I COULD ONLY FIGURE OUT WHAT??!
BUT WHAT'S IMPORTANT IS GETTIN' BEV AWAY FROM THE MAN-THING!
CAN'T SHAKE THIS FEELIN' THAT MY EVERY MOVE IS BEIN... ≥WAAK≤!
I AM BEIN' WATCHED!
CRASH

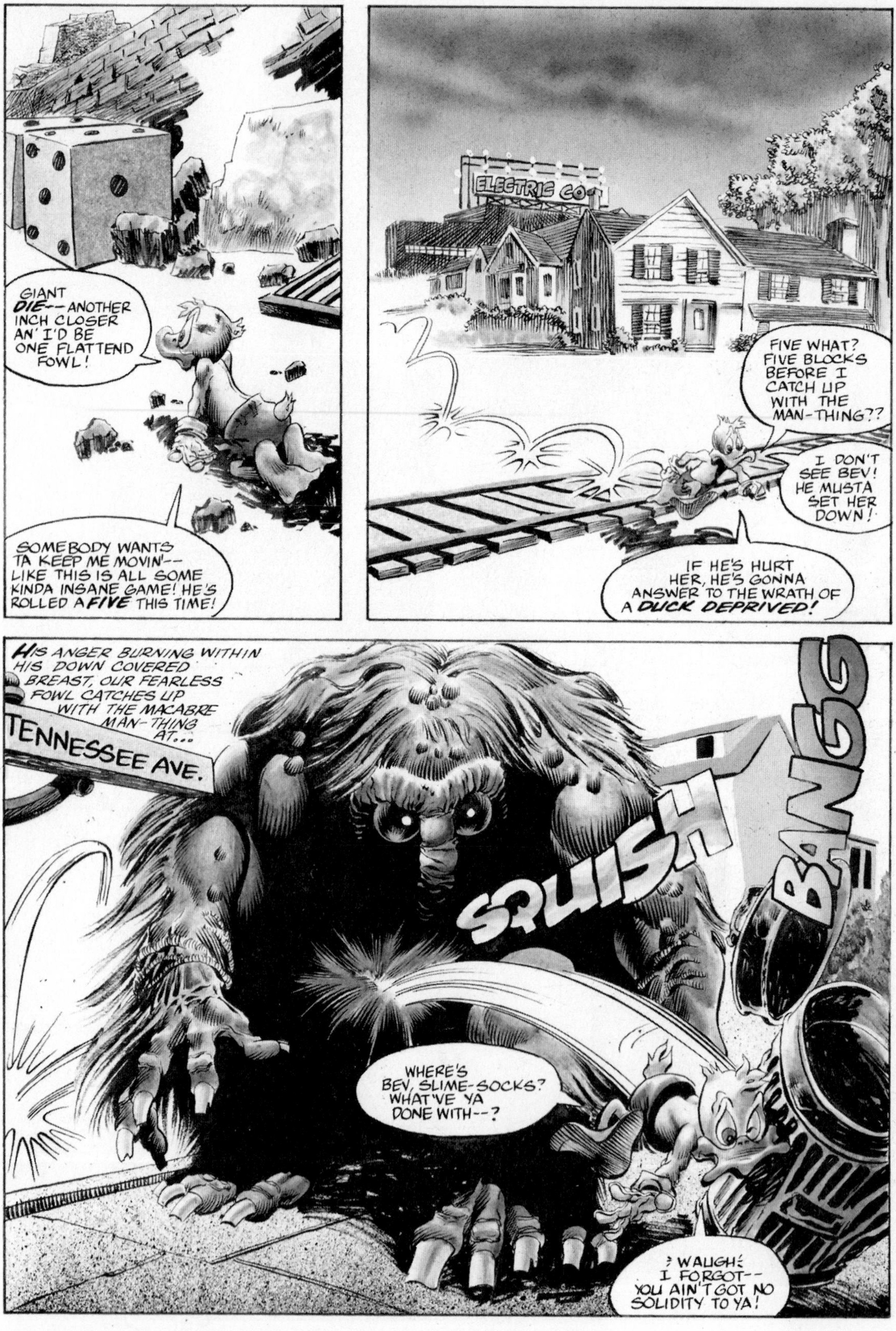
GIANT DIE--ANOTHER INCH CLOSER AN' I'D BE ONE FLATTEND FOWL!
SOMEBODY WANTS TA KEEP ME MOVIN'--LIKE THIS IS ALL SOME KINDA INSANE GAME! HE'S ROLLED A FIVE THIS TIME!
ELECTRIC CO.
FIVE WHAT? FIVE BLOCKS BEFORE I CATCH UP WITH THE MAN-THING??
I DON'T SEE BEV! HE MUSTA SET HER DOWN!
IF HE'S HURT HER, HE'S GONNA ANSWER TO THE WRATH OF A DUCK DEPRIVED!
HIS ANGER BURNING WITHIN HIS DOWN COVERED BREAST, OUR FEARLESS FOWL CATCHES UP WITH THE MACABRE MAN-THING AT...
TENNESSEE AVE.
SQUISH
BANG
WHERE'S BEV, SLIME-SOCKS? WHAT'VE YA DONE WITH--?
WAUGH! I FORGOT--YOU AIN'T GOT NO SOLIDITY TO YA!

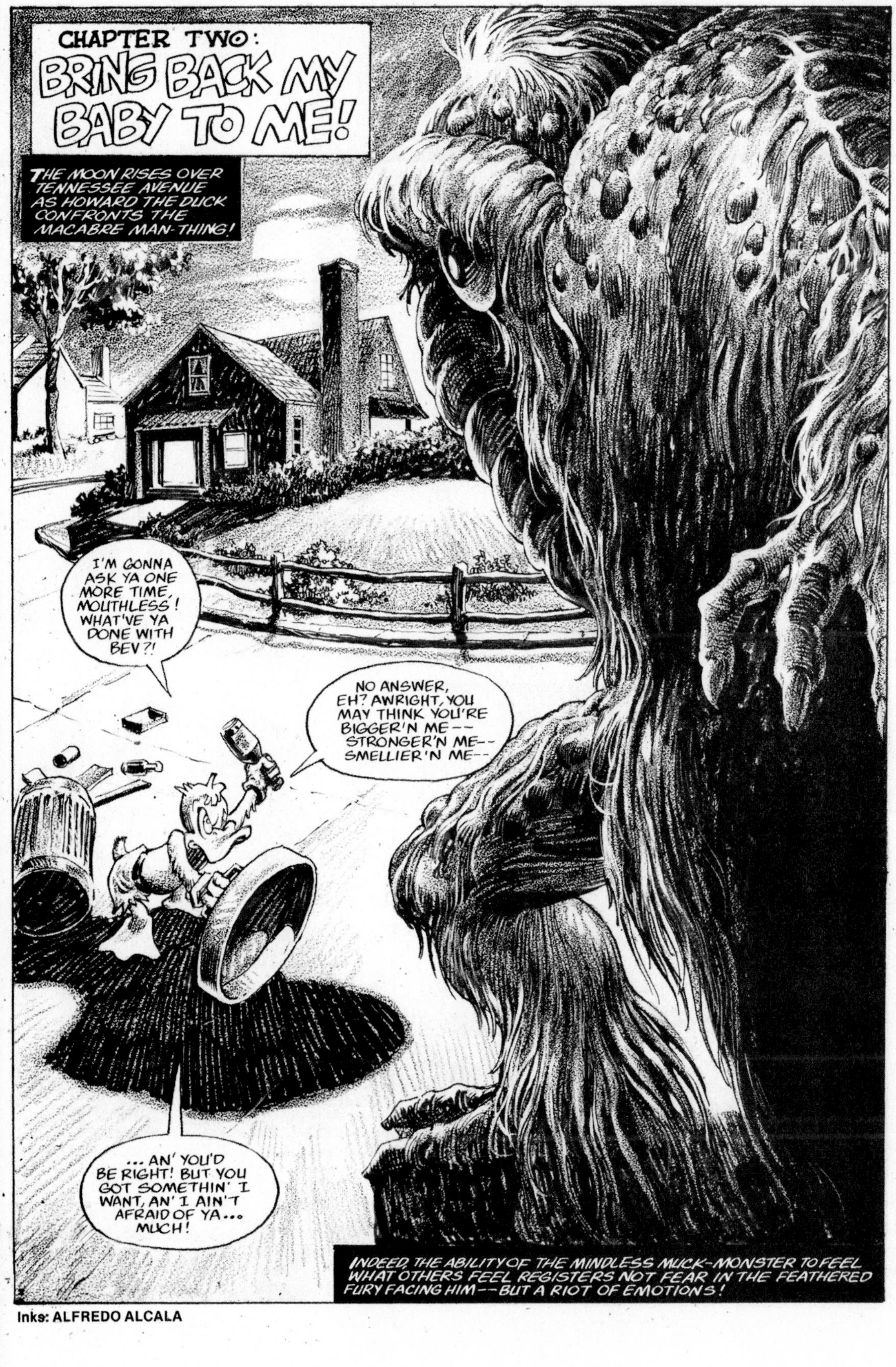
CHAPTER TWO:
BRING BACK MY BABY TO ME!
THE MOON RISES OVER TENNESSEE AVENUE AS HOWARD THE DUCK CONFRONTS THE MACABRE MAN-THING!
I'M GONNA ASK YA ONE MORE TIME, MOUTHLESS! WHAT'VE YA DONE WITH BEV?!
NO ANSWER, EH? AWRIGHT, YOU MAY THINK YOU'RE BIGGER'N ME-- STRONGER'N ME-- SMELLIER'N ME--
...AN' YOU'D BE RIGHT! BUT YOU GOT SOMETHIN' I WANT, AN' I AIN'T AFRAID OF YA... MUCH!
INDEED, THE ABILITY OF THE MINDLESS MUCK-MONSTER TO FEEL WHAT OTHERS FEEL REGISTERS NOT FEAR IN THE FEATHERED FURY FACING HIM--BUT A RIOT OF EMOTIONS!

Inks: ALFREDO ALCALA

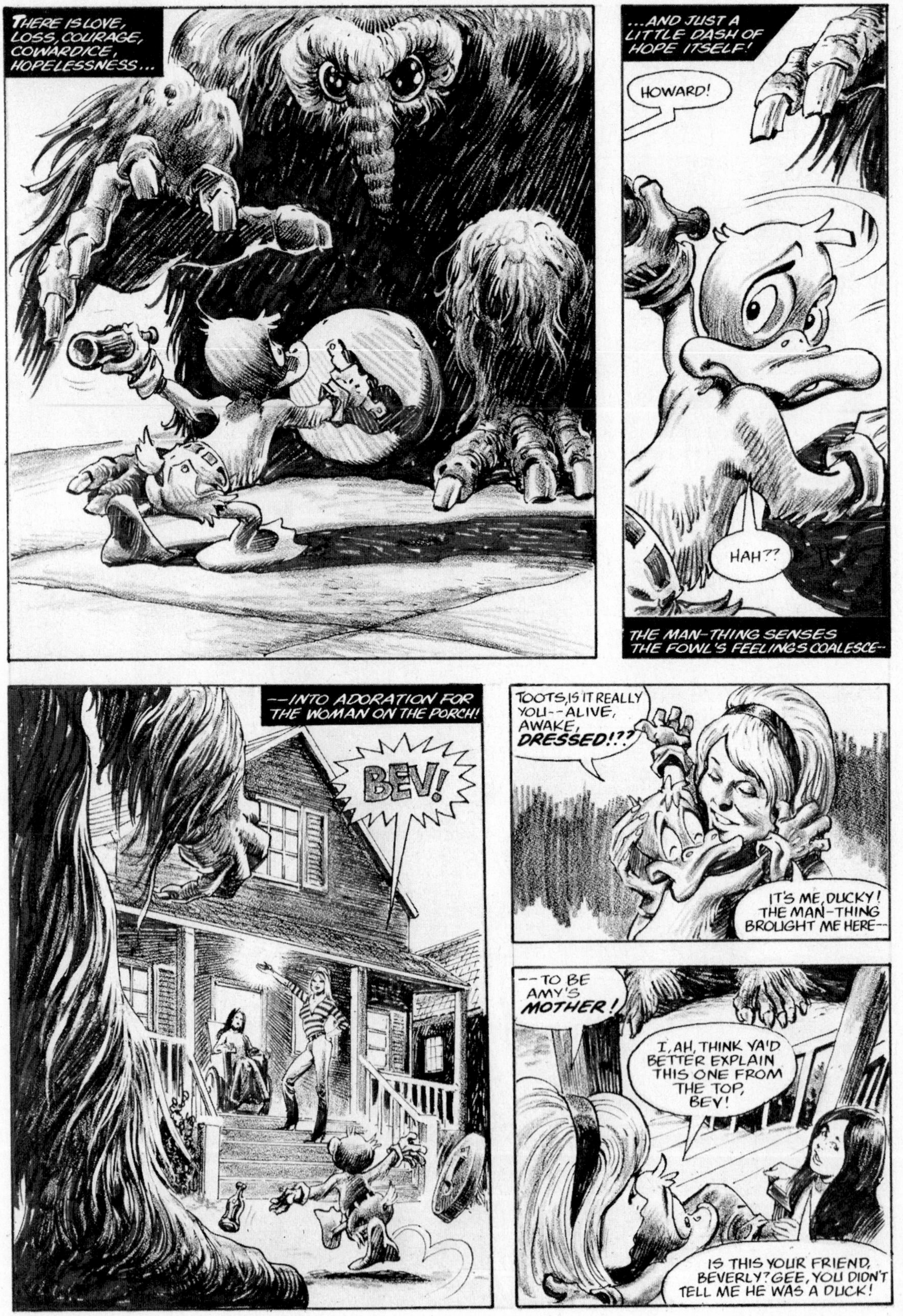
THERE IS LOVE, LOSS, COURAGE, COWARDICE, HOPELESSNESS...
...AND JUST A LITTLE DASH OF HOPE ITSELF!
HOWARD!
HAH??
THE MAN-THING SENSES THE FOWL'S FEELINGS COALESCE--
--INTO ADORATION FOR THE WOMAN ON THE PORCH!
BEV!
TOOTS, IS IT REALLY YOU--ALIVE, AWAKE, DRESSED!??
IT'S ME, DUCKY! THE MAN-THING BROUGHT ME HERE--
--TO BE AMY'S MOTHER!
I, AH, THINK YA'D BETTER EXPLAIN THIS ONE FROM THE TOP, BEV!
IS THIS YOUR FRIEND, BEVERLY? GEE, YOU DIDN'T TELL ME HE WAS A DUCK!

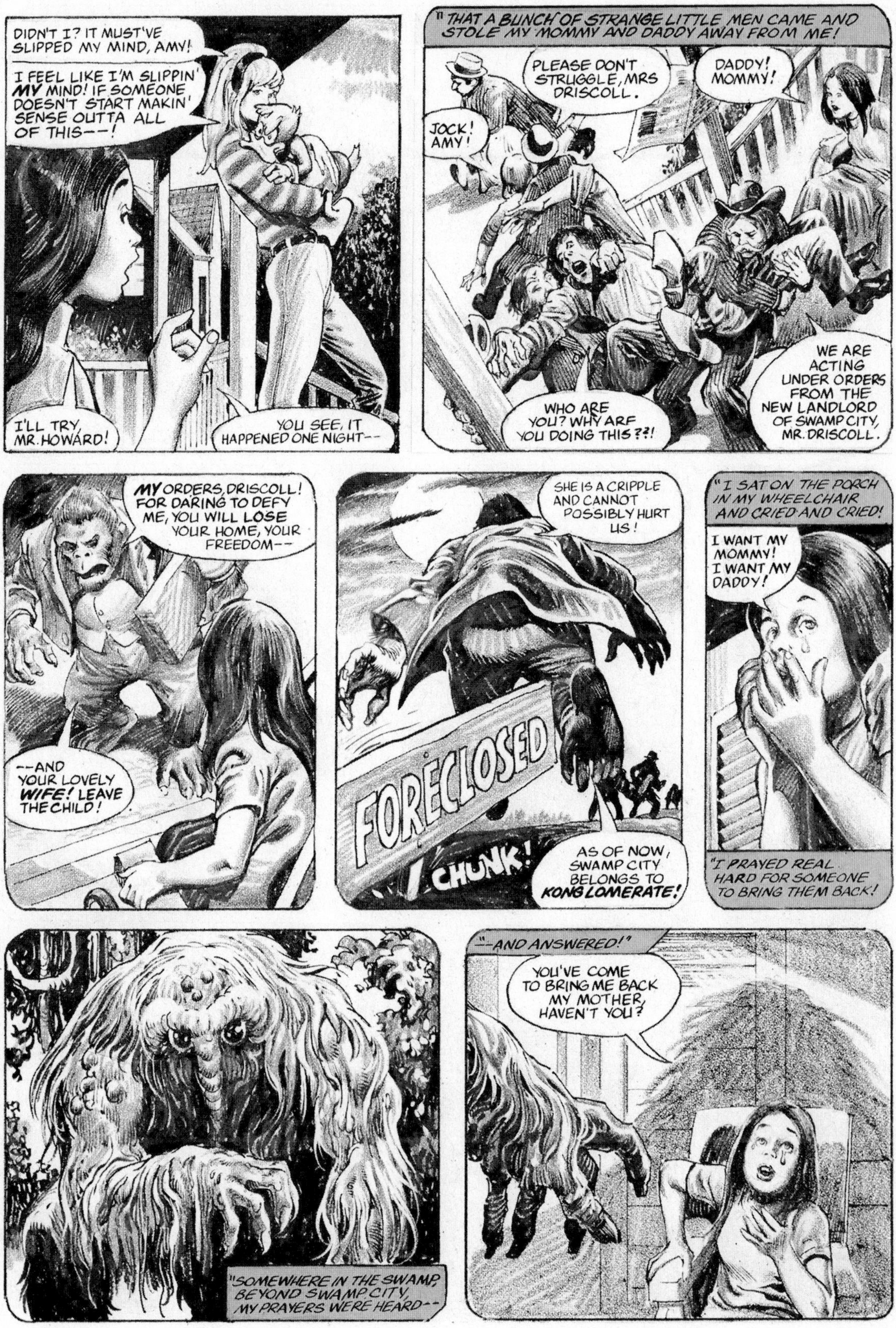
DIDN'T I? IT MUST'VE SLIPPED MY MIND, AMY!
I FEEL LIKE I'M SLIPPIN' MY MIND! IF SOMEONE DOESN'T START MAKIN' SENSE OUTTA ALL OF THIS--!
I'LL TRY, MR. HOWARD!
YOU SEE, IT HAPPENED ONE NIGHT--
"THAT A BUNCH OF STRANGE LITTLE MEN CAME AND STOLE MY MOMMY AND DADDY AWAY FROM ME!
PLEASE DON'T STRUGGLE, MRS DRISCOLL.
DADDY! MOMMY!
JOCK! AMY!
WHO ARE YOU? WHY ARF YOU DOING THIS??!
WE ARE ACTING UNDER ORDERS FROM THE NEW LANDLORD OF SWAMP CITY, MR. DRISCOLL.
MY ORDERS, DRISCOLL! FOR DARING TO DEFY ME, YOU WILL LOSE YOUR HOME, YOUR FREEDOM--
--AND YOUR LOVELY WIFE! LEAVE THE CHILD!
SHE IS A CRIPPLE AND CANNOT POSSIBLY HURT US!
FORECLOSED
CHUNK!
AS OF NOW, SWAMP CITY BELONGS TO KONGLOMERATE!
"I SAT ON THE PORCH IN MY WHEELCHAIR AND CRIED AND CRIED!
I WANT MY MOMMY! I WANT MY DADDY!
"I PRAYED REAL HARD FOR SOMEONE TO BRING THEM BACK!
"SOMEWHERE IN THE SWAMP, BEYOND SWAMP CITY, MY PRAYERS WERE HEARD--
"--AND ANSWERED!"
YOU'VE COME TO BRING ME BACK MY MOTHER, HAVEN'T YOU?

AMY EMOTIONALLY COMMUNICATED HER LOSS TO THE MAN-THING, DUCKY.

IT'S A GOOD THING YA WEREN'T SCARED, KID! OL' SLIME-CAKES WOULDA FRENCH-FRIED YA!

SHE WAS TOO UPSET TO BE SCARED--

"--AND THE MAN-THING'S EMPATHIC NATURE BECAME SO AGITATED BY HER PROJECTED FEELINGS...

"...THAT HE SHAMBLED OFF IN SEARCH OF SOME WAY TO SATISFY AMY'S LONGINGS."

THAT'S WHEN HE FOUND ME MAKING MATERNAL WITH YOU IN THE SWAMP, DUCKY.

PSYCHICALLY, I GUESS I SEEMED AN EMOTIONAL ANALOG TO THE EMPATHIC PICTURE THE MAN-THING FORMED OF AMY'S MOM.

WAAK

"SO MANNY DELIVERED ME TO AMY IN AN EFFORT TO CANCEL OUT HER DESPAIR WHICH WAS DISTURBING HIS PSYCHE."

WELL, SHE'S NOT MOMMY-- BUT I GUESS SHE'LL DO!

I AWOKE TO FIND MYSELF ADORNED... AND ADOPTED.

I DON'T KNOW WHY I'M FINDING THIS SO HARD TO SWALLOW!

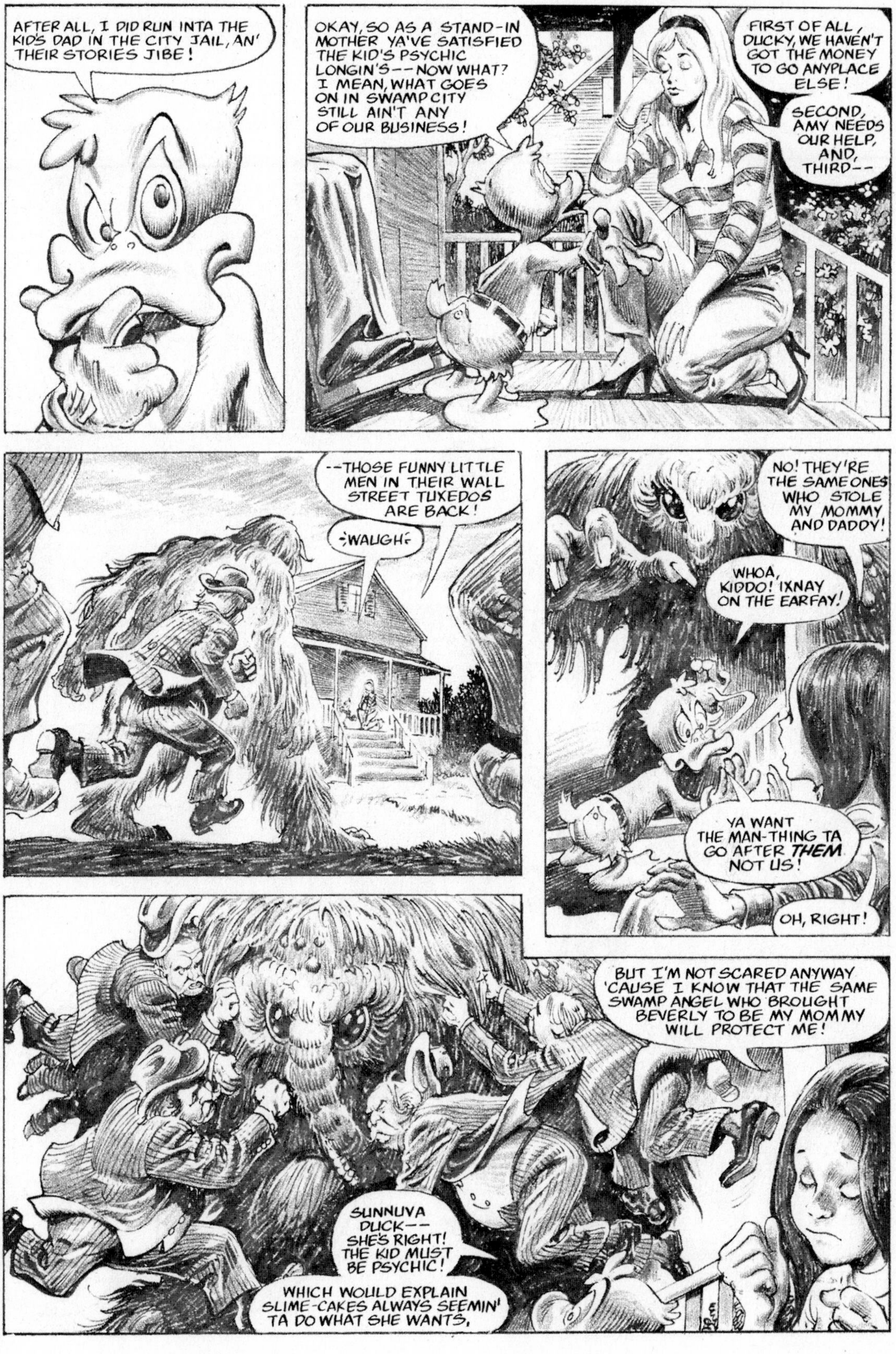
AFTER ALL, I DID RUN INTA THE KID'S DAD IN THE CITY JAIL, AN' THEIR STORIES JIBE!
OKAY, SO AS A STAND-IN MOTHER YA'VE SATISFIED THE KID'S PSYCHIC LONGIN'S-- NOW WHAT? I MEAN, WHAT GOES ON IN SWAMP CITY STILL AIN'T ANY OF OUR BUSINESS!
FIRST OF ALL, DUCKY, WE HAVEN'T GOT THE MONEY TO GO ANYPLACE ELSE!
SECOND, AMY NEEDS OUR HELP, AND, THIRD--
--THOSE FUNNY LITTLE MEN IN THEIR WALL STREET TUXEDOS ARE BACK!
WAUGH
NO! THEY'RE THE SAME ONES WHO STOLE MY MOMMY AND DADDY!
WHOA, KIDDO! IXNAY ON THE EARFAY!
YA WANT THE MAN-THING TA GO AFTER THEM NOT US!
OH, RIGHT!
BUT I'M NOT SCARED ANYWAY 'CAUSE I KNOW THAT THE SAME SWAMP ANGEL WHO BROUGHT BEVERLY TO BE MY MOMMY WILL PROTECT ME!
SUNNUVA DUCK-- SHE'S RIGHT! THE KID MUST BE PSYCHIC!
WHICH WOULD EXPLAIN SLIME-CAKES ALWAYS SEEMIN' TA DO WHAT SHE WANTS.

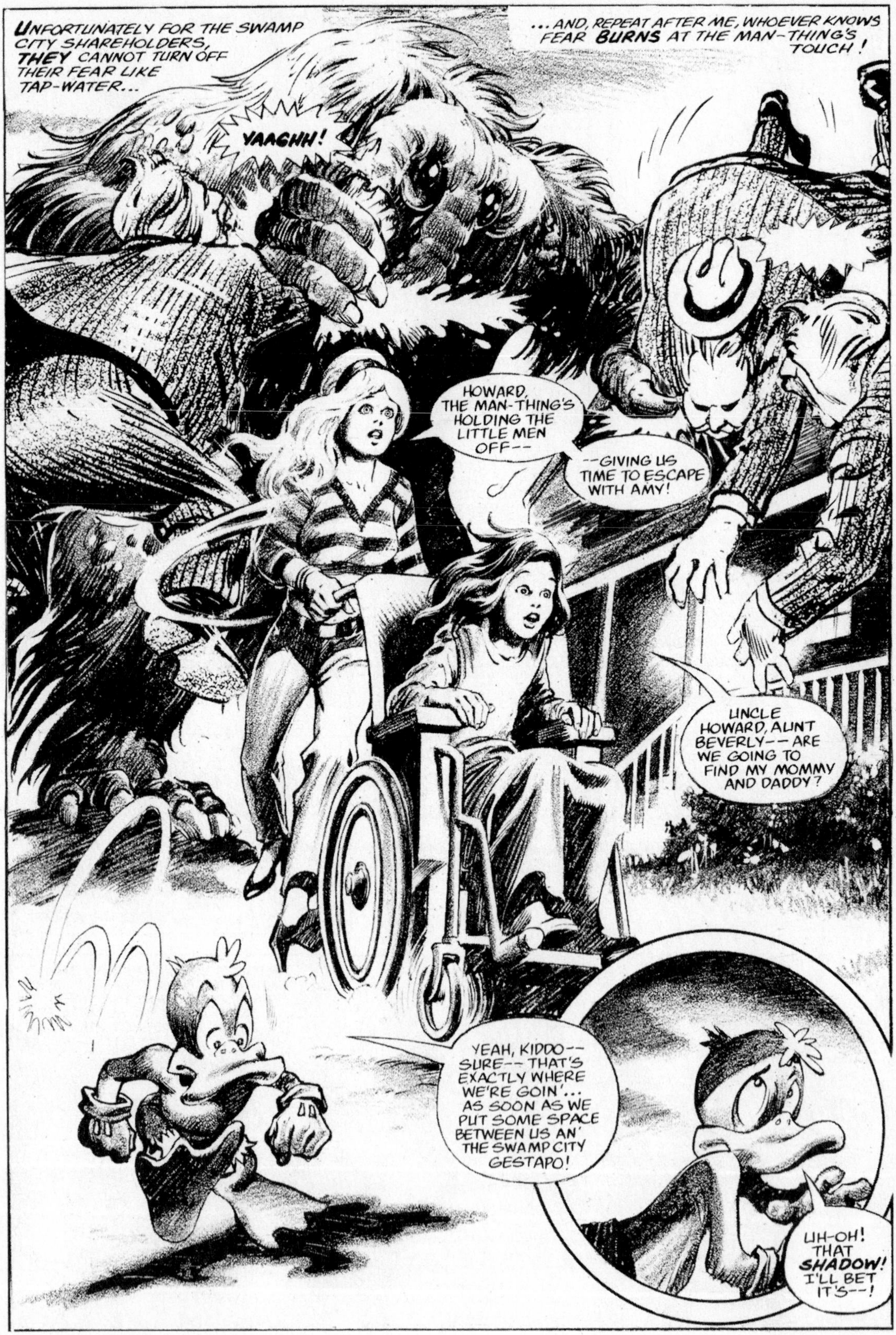
UNFORTUNATELY FOR THE SWAMP CITY SHAREHOLDERS, THEY CANNOT TURN OFF THEIR FEAR LIKE TAP-WATER...
...AND, REPEAT AFTER ME, WHOEVER KNOWS FEAR BURNS AT THE MAN-THING'S TOUCH!
YAAGHH!
HOWARD, THE MAN-THING'S HOLDING THE LITTLE MEN OFF--
--GIVING US TIME TO ESCAPE WITH AMY!
UNCLE HOWARD, AUNT BEVERLY-- ARE WE GOING TO FIND MY MOMMY AND DADDY?
YEAH, KIDDO-- SURE-- THAT'S EXACTLY WHERE WE'RE GOIN'... AS SOON AS WE PUT SOME SPACE BETWEEN US AN' THE SWAMP CITY GESTAPO!
UH-OH! THAT SHADOW! I'LL BET IT'S--!

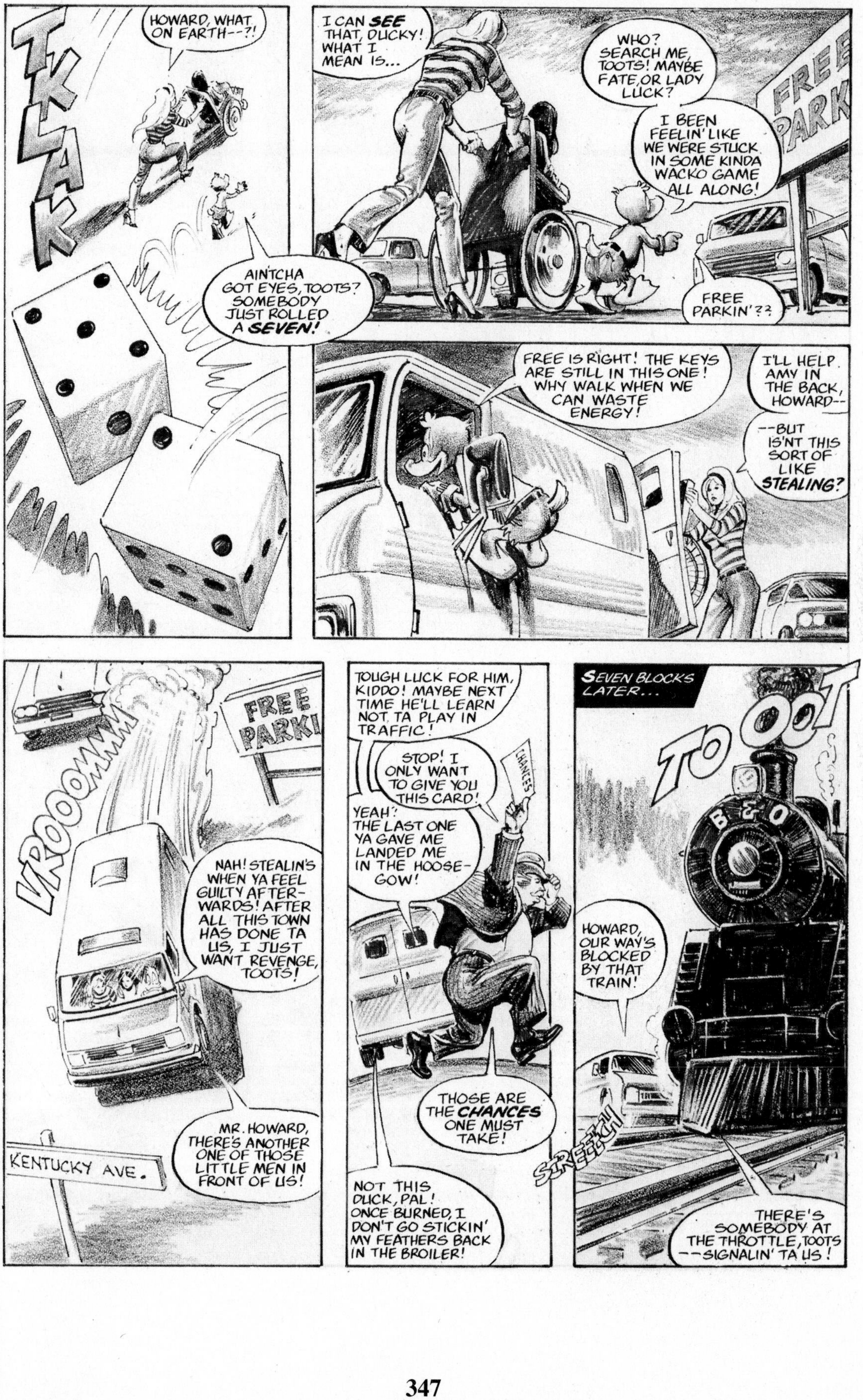
HOWARD, WHAT ON EARTH--?!
TKLAK
AIN'TCHA GOT EYES, TOOTS? SOMEBODY JUST ROLLED A SEVEN!
I CAN SEE THAT, DUCKY! WHAT I MEAN IS...
WHO? SEARCH ME, TOOTS! MAYBE FATE, OR LADY LUCK?
I BEEN FEELIN' LIKE WE WERE STUCK IN SOME KINDA WACKO GAME ALL ALONG!
FREE PARK
FREE PARKIN'??
FREE IS RIGHT! THE KEYS ARE STILL IN THIS ONE! WHY WALK WHEN WE CAN WASTE ENERGY!
I'LL HELP AMY IN THE BACK, HOWARD--
--BUT ISN'T THIS SORT OF LIKE STEALING?
FREE PARKI
VROOOMMM
NAH! STEALIN'S WHEN YA FEEL GUILTY AFTER-WARDS! AFTER ALL THIS TOWN HAS DONE TA US, I JUST WANT REVENGE, TOOTS!
KENTUCKY AVE.
MR. HOWARD, THERE'S ANOTHER ONE OF THOSE LITTLE MEN IN FRONT OF US!
TOUGH LUCK FOR HIM, KIDDO! MAYBE NEXT TIME HE'LL LEARN NOT TA PLAY IN TRAFFIC!
STOP! I ONLY WANT TO GIVE YOU THIS CARD!
CHANCES
YEAH! THE LAST ONE YA GAVE ME LANDED ME IN THE HOOSE-GOW!
THOSE ARE THE CHANCES ONE MUST TAKE!
NOT THIS DUCK, PAL! ONCE BURNED, I DON'T GO STICKIN' MY FEATHERS BACK IN THE BROILER!
SEVEN BLOCKS LATER...
TOOOT
B&O
HOWARD, OUR WAY'S BLOCKED BY THAT TRAIN!
SKREEEE
THERE'S SOMEBODY AT THE THROTTLE, TOOTS --SIGNALIN' TA US!

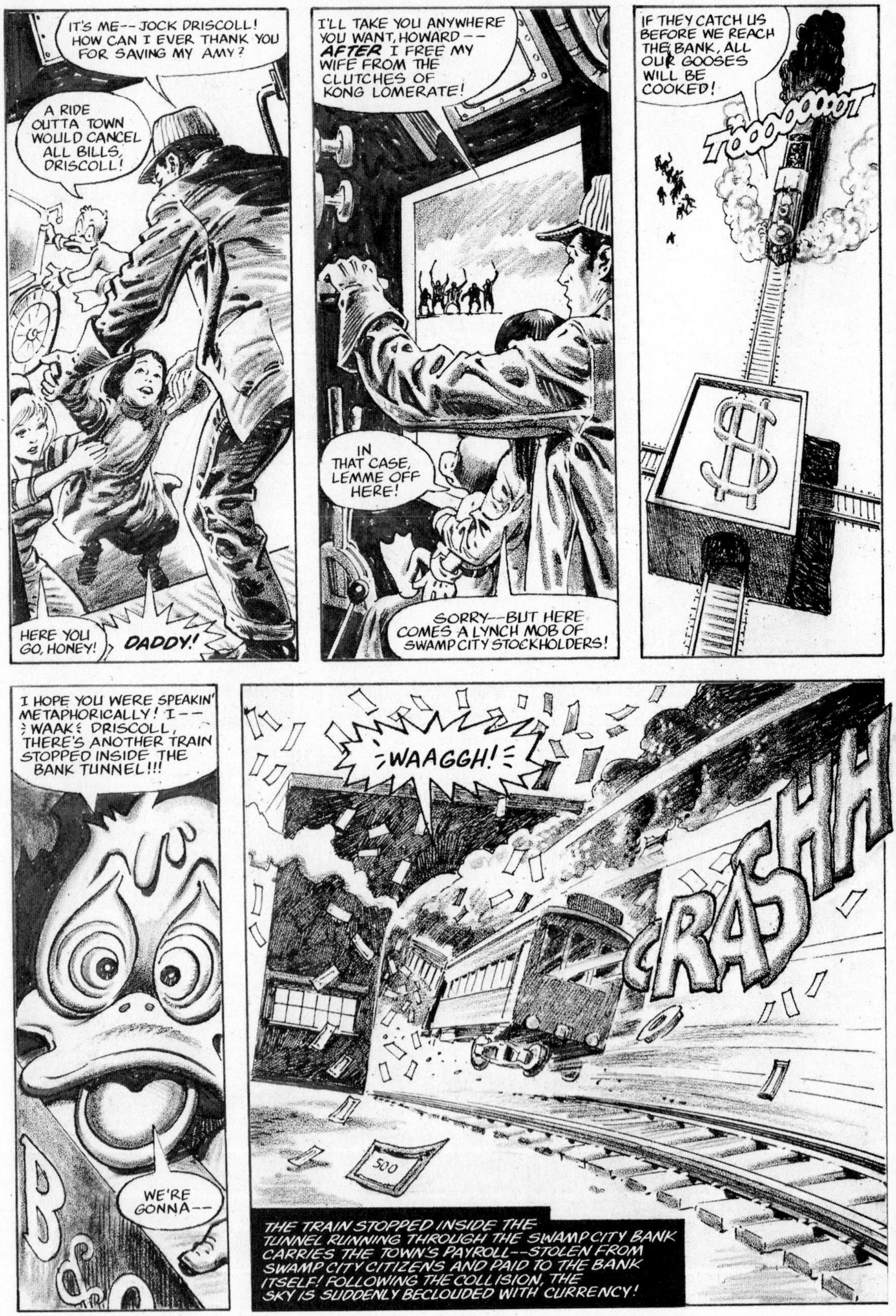
IT'S ME-- JOCK DRISCOLL! HOW CAN I EVER THANK YOU FOR SAVING MY AMY?
A RIDE OUTTA TOWN WOULD CANCEL ALL BILLS, DRISCOLL!
HERE YOU GO, HONEY!
DADDY!
I'LL TAKE YOU ANYWHERE YOU WANT, HOWARD -- AFTER I FREE MY WIFE FROM THE CLUTCHES OF KONG LOMERATE!
IN THAT CASE, LEMME OFF HERE!
SORRY--BUT HERE COMES A LYNCH MOB OF SWAMP CITY STOCKHOLDERS!
IF THEY CATCH US BEFORE WE REACH THE BANK, ALL OUR GOOSES WILL BE COOKED!
TOOOOOOOOT
I HOPE YOU WERE SPEAKIN' METAPHORICALLY! I-- WAAK! DRISCOLL, THERE'S ANOTHER TRAIN STOPPED INSIDE THE BANK TUNNEL!!!
WE'RE GONNA--
WAAGGH!
CRASHH
500
THE TRAIN STOPPED INSIDE THE TUNNEL RUNNING THROUGH THE SWAMP CITY BANK CARRIES THE TOWN'S PAYROLL--STOLEN FROM SWAMP CITY CITIZENS AND PAID TO THE BANK ITSELF! FOLLOWING THE COLLISION, THE SKY IS SUDDENLY BECLOUDED WITH CURRENCY!

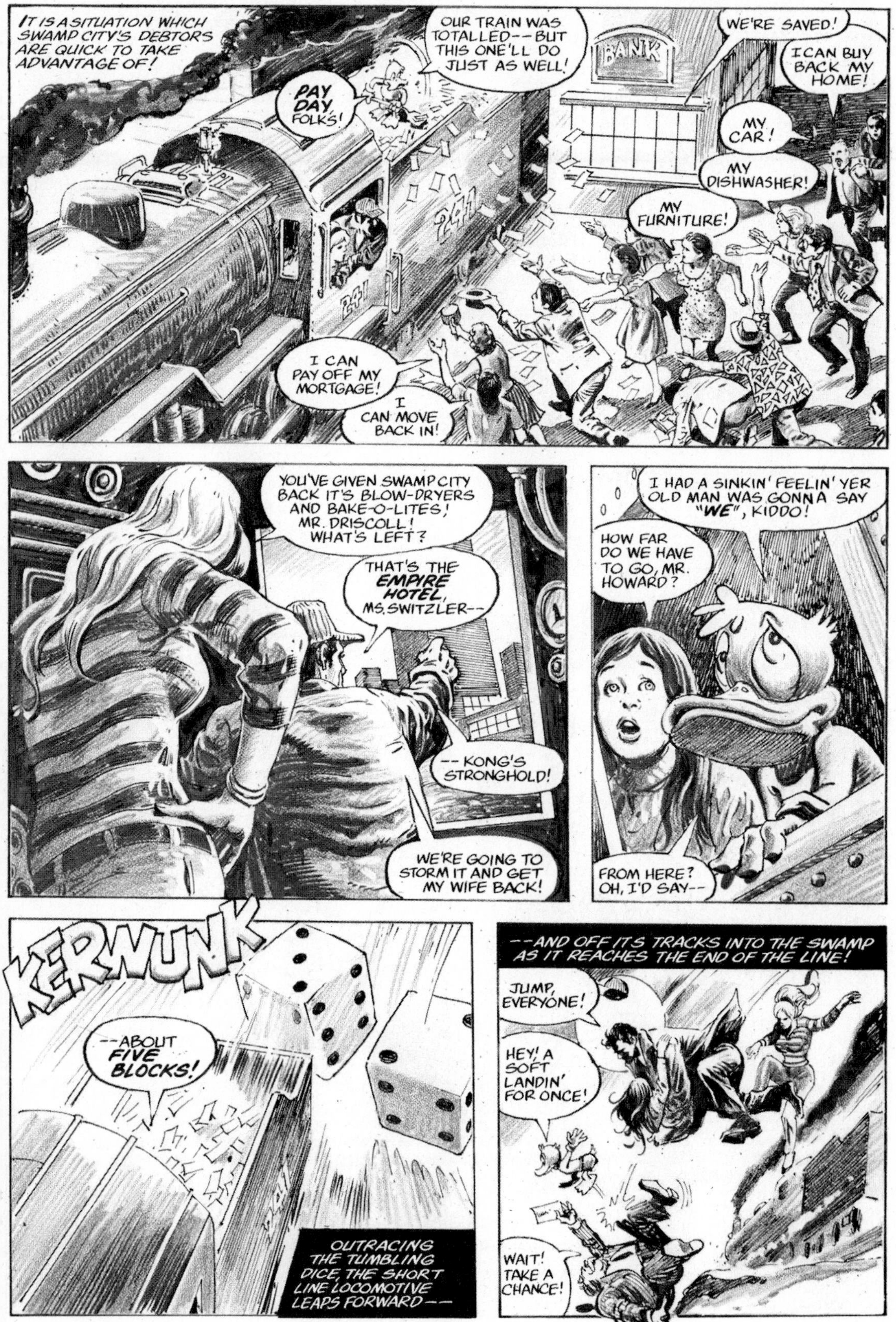

IT IS A SITUATION WHICH SWAMP CITY'S DEBTORS ARE QUICK TO TAKE ADVANTAGE OF!
OUR TRAIN WAS TOTALLED--BUT THIS ONE'LL DO JUST AS WELL!
PAY DAY, FOLKS!
BANK
WE'RE SAVED!
I CAN BUY BACK MY HOME!
MY CAR!
MY DISHWASHER!
MY FURNITURE!
I CAN PAY OFF MY MORTGAGE!
I CAN MOVE BACK IN!
YOU'VE GIVEN SWAMP CITY BACK IT'S BLOW-DRYERS AND BAKE-O-LITES, MR. DRISCOLL! WHAT'S LEFT?
THAT'S THE EMPIRE HOTEL, MS. SWITZLER--
--KONG'S STRONGHOLD!
WE'RE GOING TO STORM IT AND GET MY WIFE BACK!
I HAD A SINKIN' FEELIN' YER OLD MAN WAS GONNA SAY "WE", KIDDO!
HOW FAR DO WE HAVE TO GO, MR. HOWARD?
FROM HERE? OH, I'D SAY--
KERWUNK
--ABOUT FIVE BLOCKS!
OUTRACING THE TUMBLING DICE, THE SHORT LINE LOCOMOTIVE LEAPS FORWARD--
--AND OFF ITS TRACKS INTO THE SWAMP AS IT REACHES THE END OF THE LINE!
JUMP, EVERYONE!
HEY! A SOFT LANDIN' FOR ONCE!
WAIT! TAKE A CHANCE!

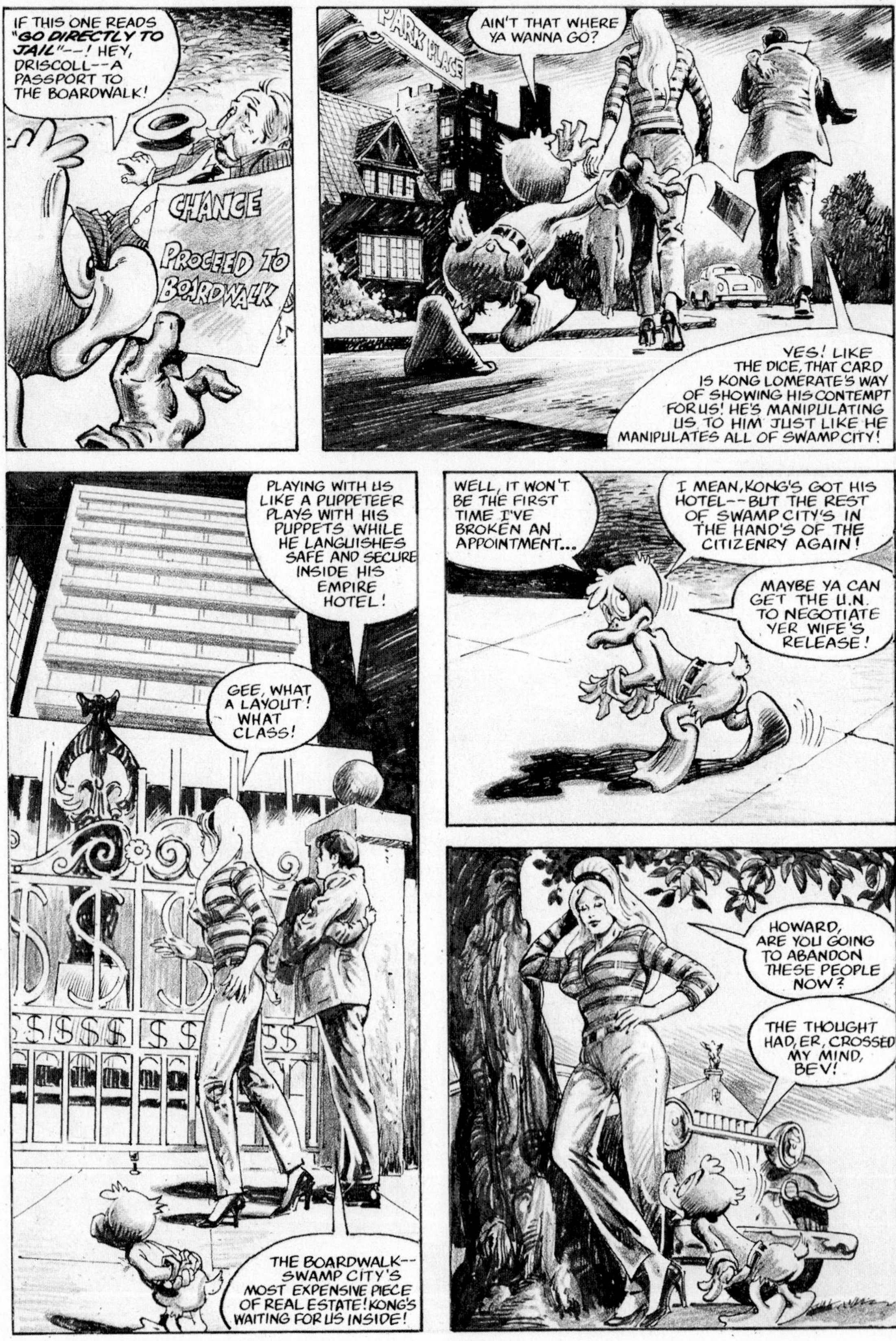

IF THIS ONE READS "GO DIRECTLY TO JAIL"--! HEY, DRISCOLL--A PASSPORT TO THE BOARDWALK!
CHANCE
PROCEED TO BOARDWALK
PARK PLACE
AIN'T THAT WHERE YA WANNA GO?
YES! LIKE THE DICE, THAT CARD IS KONG LOMERATE'S WAY OF SHOWING HIS CONTEMPT FOR US! HE'S MANIPULATING US TO HIM JUST LIKE HE MANIPULATES ALL OF SWAMP CITY!
PLAYING WITH US LIKE A PUPPETEER PLAYS WITH HIS PUPPETS WHILE HE LANGUISHES SAFE AND SECURE INSIDE HIS EMPIRE HOTEL!
GEE, WHAT A LAYOUT! WHAT CLASS!
THE BOARDWALK-- SWAMP CITY'S MOST EXPENSIVE PIECE OF REAL ESTATE! KONG'S WAITING FOR US INSIDE!
WELL, IT WON'T BE THE FIRST TIME I'VE BROKEN AN APPOINTMENT...
I MEAN, KONG'S GOT HIS HOTEL--BUT THE REST OF SWAMP CITY'S IN THE HAND'S OF THE CITIZENRY AGAIN!
MAYBE YA CAN GET THE U.N. TO NEGOTIATE YER WIFE'S RELEASE!
HOWARD, ARE YOU GOING TO ABANDON THESE PEOPLE NOW?
THE THOUGHT HAD, ER, CROSSED MY MIND, BEV!

BOARDWALK

WELL, I'M NOT GOING TO RUN OUT ON THEM!

AW, TOOTS, YA KNOW I CAN'T LET YA GO IN THERE ALONE!

I'D RATHER DIE A COWARD THAN FACE THE THOUGHT OF LIFE WITHOUT YA!

SOON, OUR FRIGHTENED FOURSOME, ENTERS THE EXOTIC LOBBY OF THE EMPIRE HOTEL!

IF ONLY I'D KNOWN WHEN I'D DESIGNED THIS EDIFICE THAT MY CONTRACTOR WOULD TURN IT INTO A DEN OF INIQUITY!

DON'T BE SCARED, AMY! DADDY'S HERE-- AND SOON WE'RE GOING TO FIND MOMMY!

UNLESS SHE CHECKED OUT! THE JOINT SEEMS DESERT--

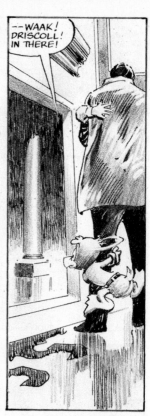

--WAAK! DRISCOLL! IN THERE!

IT'S HIM-- KONG LOMERATE! ALL RIGHT, APE, I'VE COME FOR MY WIFE!... A-ANNE!?!

TH- THAT'S YOUR WIFE??!

MOMMY??!

WHY DON'T YOU ANSWER YOUR FAWNING FAMILY, ANNE, DEAREST?

SURELY YOU'RE JOKING, KONG DARLING? WHO IS THIS DESTITUTE AND DIRTY PAIR? NO ONE I KNOW!

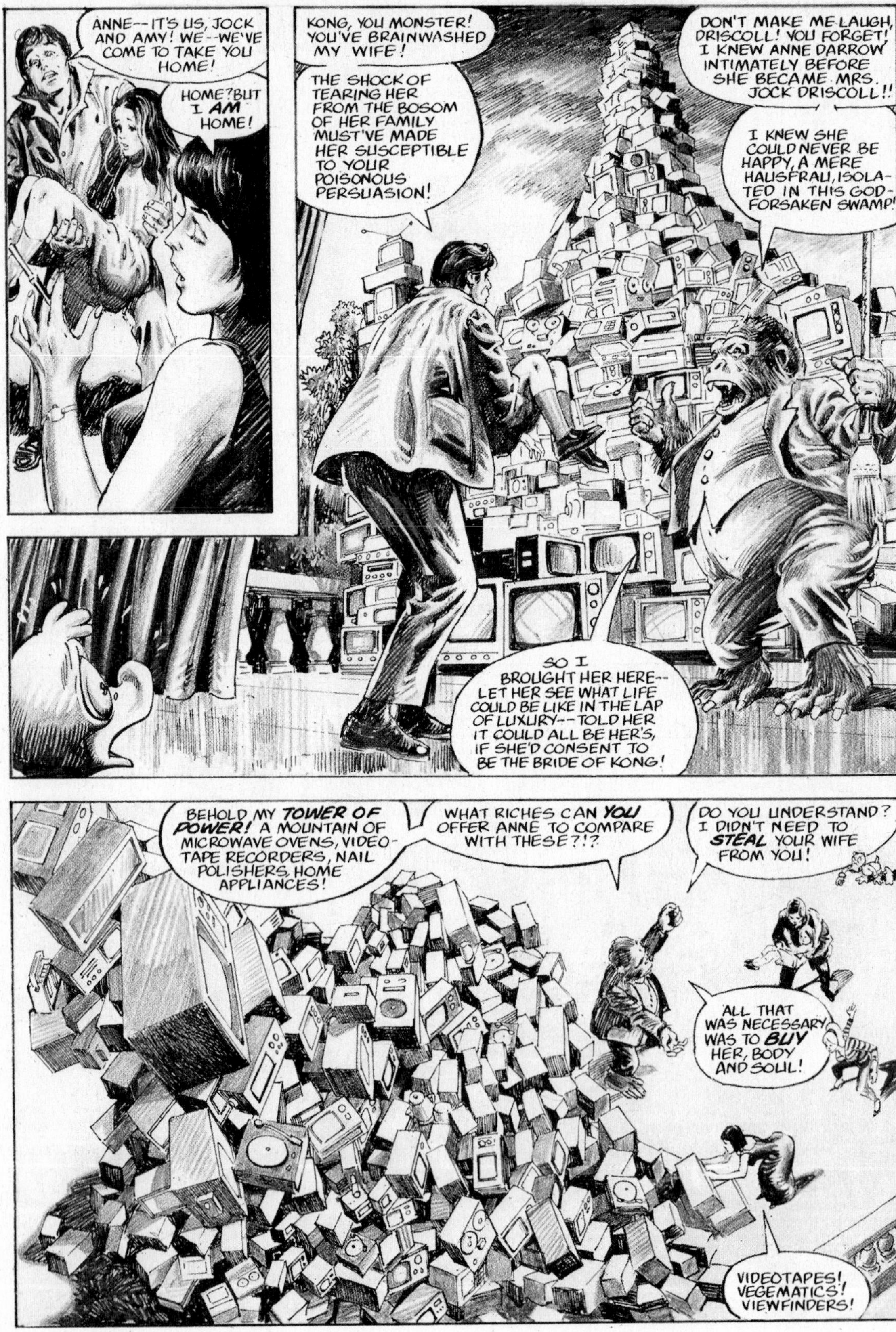
ANNE--IT'S US, JOCK AND AMY! WE--WE'VE COME TO TAKE YOU HOME!
HOME? BUT I AM HOME!
KONG, YOU MONSTER! YOU'VE BRAINWASHED MY WIFE!
THE SHOCK OF TEARING HER FROM THE BOSOM OF HER FAMILY MUST'VE MADE HER SUSCEPTIBLE TO YOUR POISONOUS PERSUASION!
DON'T MAKE ME LAUGH, DRISCOLL! YOU FORGET! I KNEW ANNE DARROW INTIMATELY BEFORE SHE BECAME MRS. JOCK DRISCOLL!!
I KNEW SHE COULD NEVER BE HAPPY, A MERE HAUSFRAU, ISOLATED IN THIS GOD-FORSAKEN SWAMP!
SO I BROUGHT HER HERE-- LET HER SEE WHAT LIFE COULD BE LIKE IN THE LAP OF LUXURY--TOLD HER IT COULD ALL BE HER'S, IF SHE'D CONSENT TO BE THE BRIDE OF KONG!
BEHOLD MY TOWER OF POWER! A MOUNTAIN OF MICROWAVE OVENS, VIDEO-TAPE RECORDERS, NAIL POLISHERS, HOME APPLIANCES!
WHAT RICHES CAN YOU OFFER ANNE TO COMPARE WITH THESE?!?
DO YOU UNDERSTAND? I DIDN'T NEED TO STEAL YOUR WIFE FROM YOU!
ALL THAT WAS NECESSARY WAS TO BUY HER, BODY AND SOUL!
VIDEOTAPES! VEGEMATICS! VIEWFINDERS!

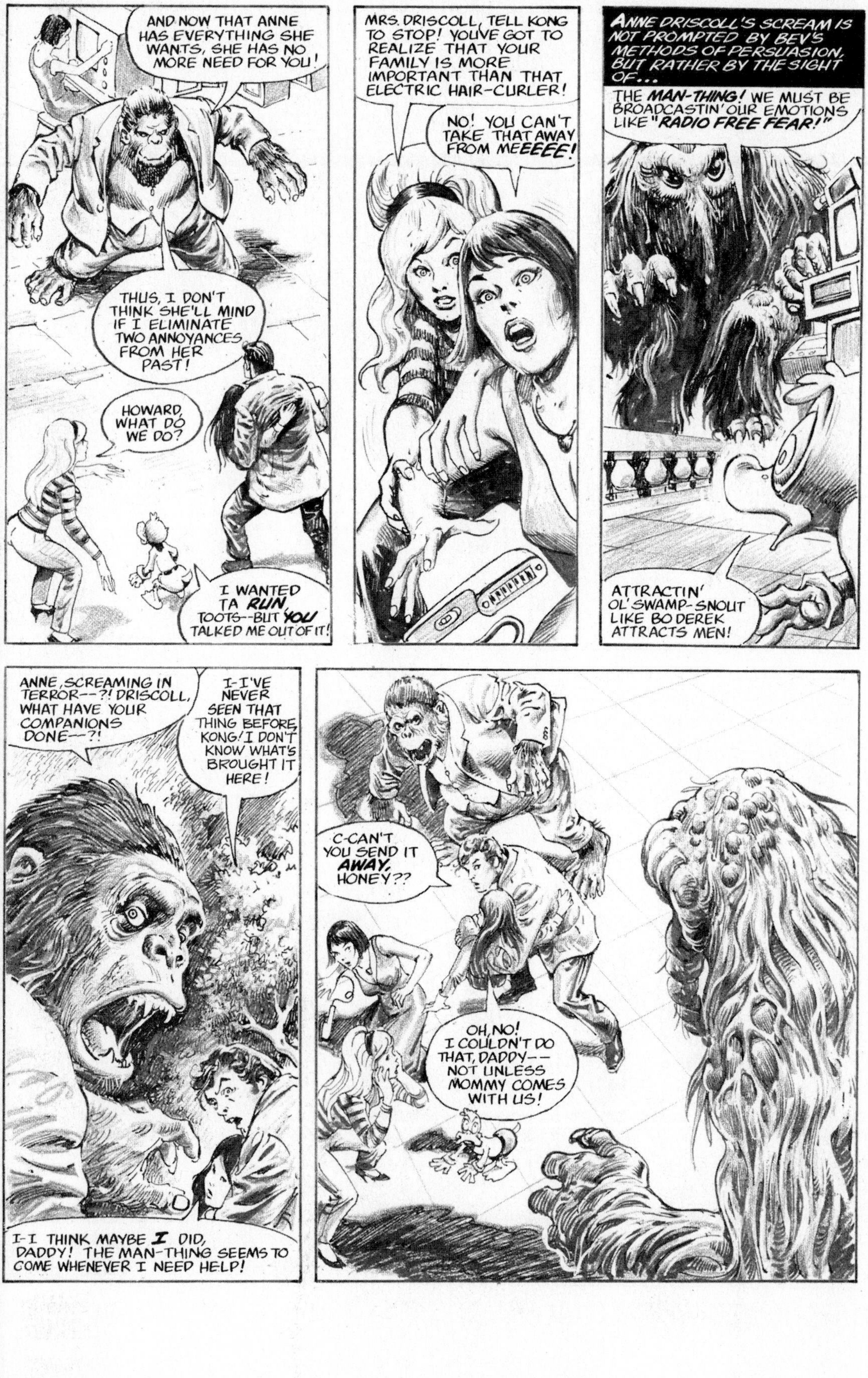
AND NOW THAT ANNE HAS EVERYTHING SHE WANTS, SHE HAS NO MORE NEED FOR YOU!
THUS, I DON'T THINK SHE'LL MIND IF I ELIMINATE TWO ANNOYANCES FROM HER PAST!
HOWARD, WHAT DO WE DO?
I WANTED TA RUN, TOOTS--BUT YOU TALKED ME OUT OF IT!
MRS. DRISCOLL, TELL KONG TO STOP! YOU'VE GOT TO REALIZE THAT YOUR FAMILY IS MORE IMPORTANT THAN THAT ELECTRIC HAIR-CURLER!
NO! YOU CAN'T TAKE THAT AWAY FROM MEEEEE!
ANNE DRISCOLL'S SCREAM IS NOT PROMPTED BY BEV'S METHODS OF PERSUASION, BUT RATHER BY THE SIGHT OF...
THE MAN-THING! WE MUST BE BROADCASTIN' OUR EMOTIONS LIKE "RADIO FREE FEAR!"
ATTRACTIN' OL' SWAMP-SNOUT LIKE BO DEREK ATTRACTS MEN!
ANNE, SCREAMING IN TERROR--?! DRISCOLL, WHAT HAVE YOUR COMPANIONS DONE--?!
I-I'VE NEVER SEEN THAT THING BEFORE, KONG! I DON'T KNOW WHAT'S BROUGHT IT HERE!
I-I THINK MAYBE I DID, DADDY! THE MAN-THING SEEMS TO COME WHENEVER I NEED HELP!
C-CAN'T YOU SEND IT AWAY, HONEY??
OH, NO! I COULDN'T DO THAT, DADDY-- NOT UNLESS MOMMY COMES WITH US!

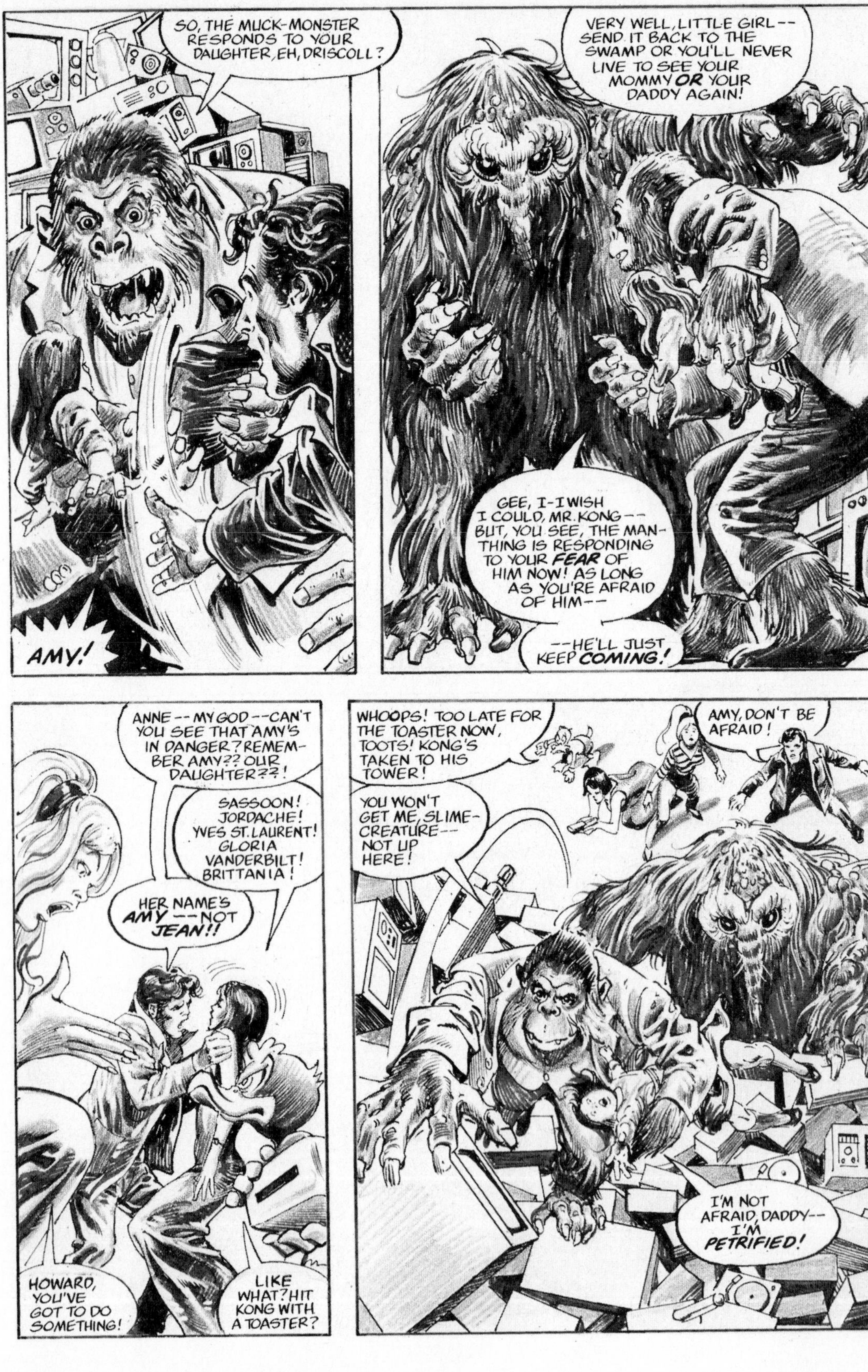
SO, THE MUCK-MONSTER RESPONDS TO YOUR DAUGHTER, EH, DRISCOLL?
AMY!
VERY WELL, LITTLE GIRL-- SEND IT BACK TO THE SWAMP OR YOU'LL NEVER LIVE TO SEE YOUR MOMMY OR YOUR DADDY AGAIN!
GEE, I-I WISH I COULD, MR. KONG-- BUT, YOU SEE, THE MAN-THING IS RESPONDING TO YOUR FEAR OF HIM NOW! AS LONG AS YOU'RE AFRAID OF HIM--
--HE'LL JUST KEEP COMING!
ANNE--MY GOD--CAN'T YOU SEE THAT AMY'S IN DANGER? REMEMBER AMY?? OUR DAUGHTER??!
SASSOON! JORDACHE! YVES ST. LAURENT! GLORIA VANDERBILT! BRITTANIA!
HER NAME'S AMY--NOT JEAN!!
HOWARD, YOU'VE GOT TO DO SOMETHING!
LIKE WHAT? HIT KONG WITH A TOASTER?
WHOOPS! TOO LATE FOR THE TOASTER NOW, TOOTS! KONG'S TAKEN TO HIS TOWER!
AMY, DON'T BE AFRAID!
YOU WON'T GET ME, SLIME-CREATURE-- NOT UP HERE!
I'M NOT AFRAID, DADDY-- I'M PETRIFIED!

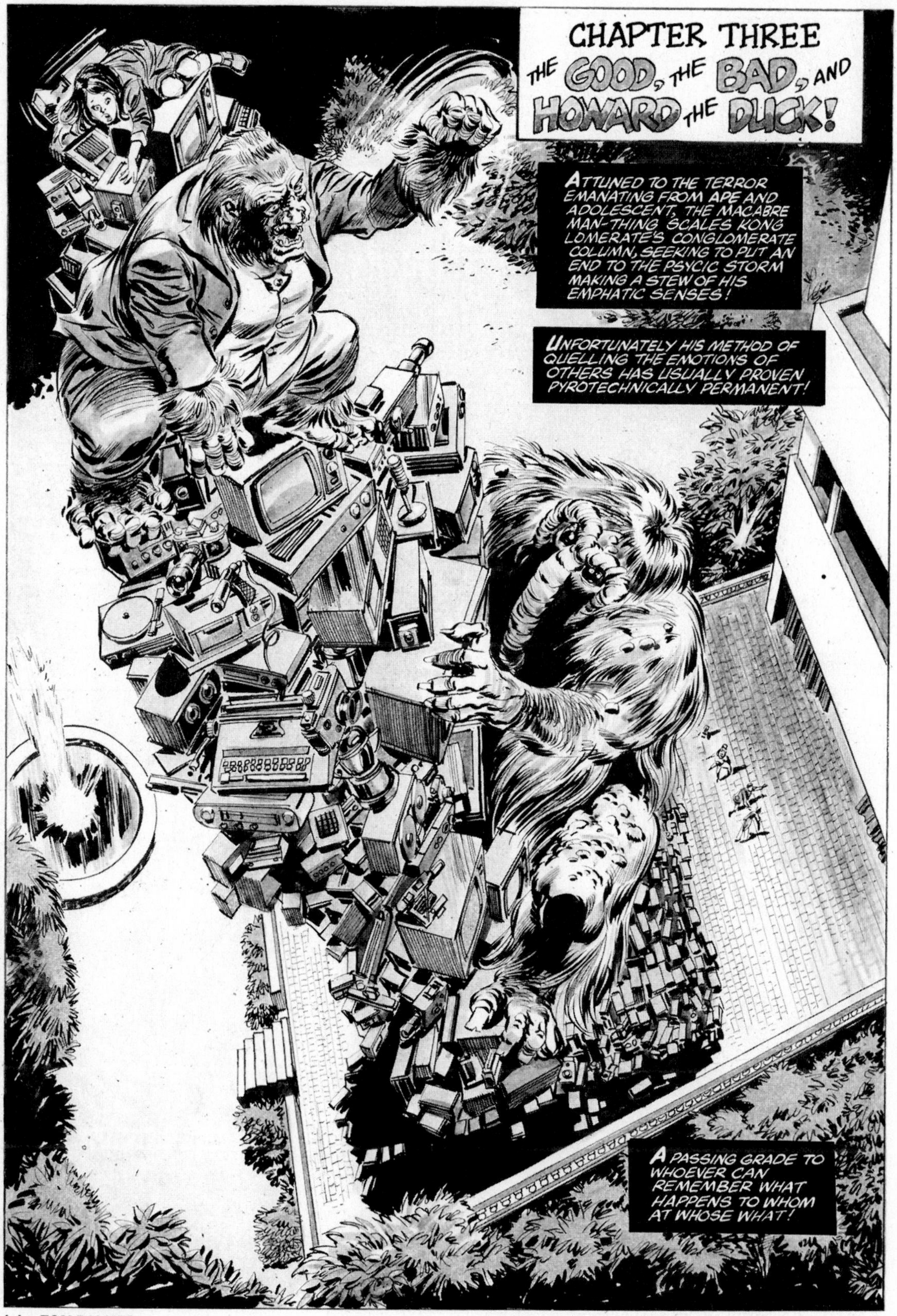
CHAPTER THREE
THE GOOD, THE BAD, AND HOWARD THE DUCK!
ATTUNED TO THE TERROR EMANATING FROM APE AND ADOLESCENT, THE MACABRE MAN-THING SCALES KONG LOMERATE'S CONGLOMERATE COLUMN, SEEKING TO PUT AN END TO THE PSYCIC STORM MAKING A STEW OF HIS EMPHATIC SENSES!
UNFORTUNATELY HIS METHOD OF QUELLING THE EMOTIONS OF OTHERS HAS USUALLY PROVEN PYROTECHNICALLY PERMANENT!
A PASSING GRADE TO WHOEVER CAN REMEMBER WHAT HAPPENS TO WHOM AT WHOSE WHAT!

Inks: TOM PALMER

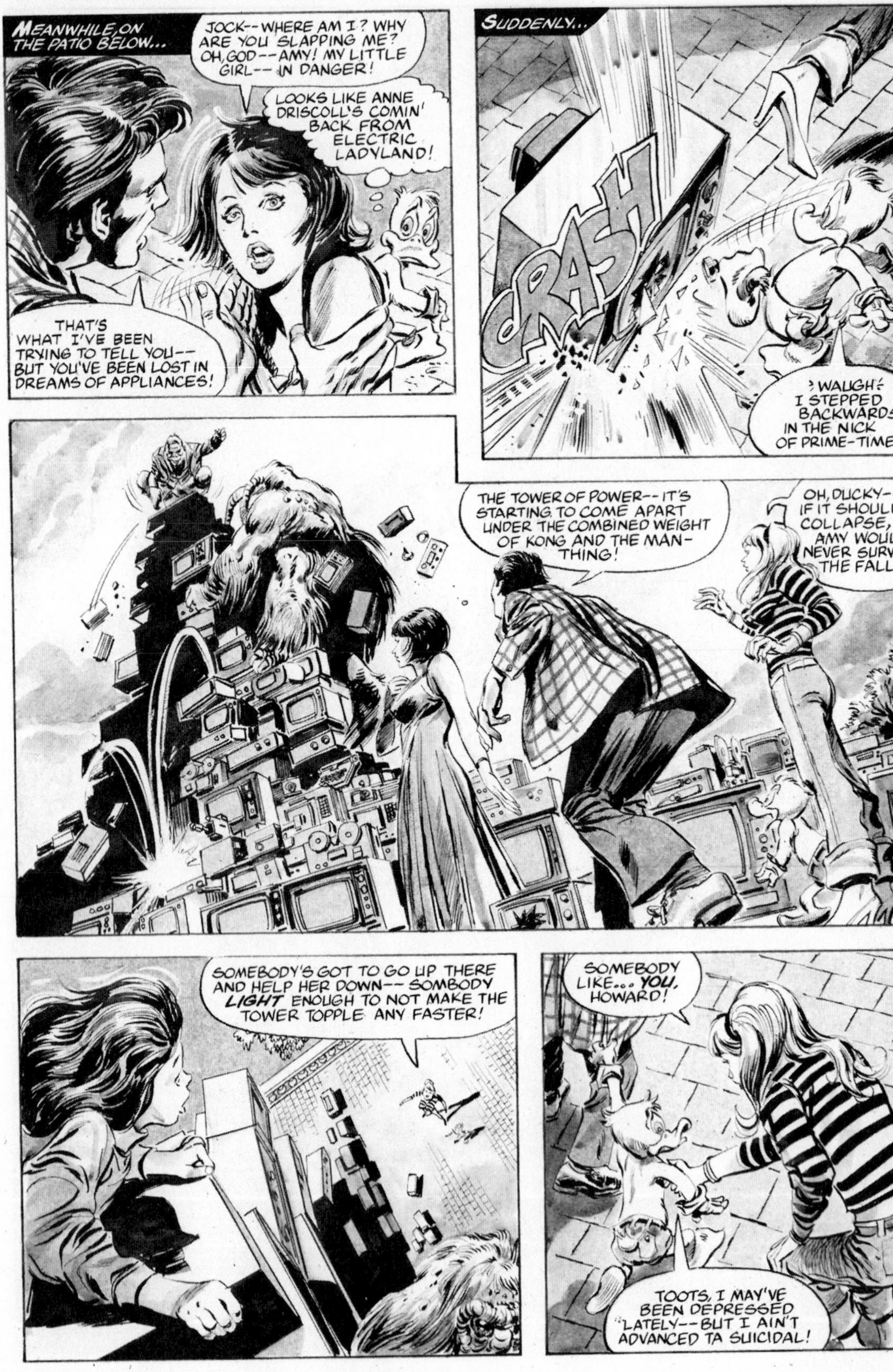
MEANWHILE, ON THE PATIO BELOW...
JOCK--WHERE AM I? WHY ARE YOU SLAPPING ME? OH, GOD--AMY! MY LITTLE GIRL--IN DANGER!
LOOKS LIKE ANNE DRISCOLL'S COMIN' BACK FROM ELECTRIC LADYLAND!
THAT'S WHAT I'VE BEEN TRYING TO TELL YOU--BUT YOU'VE BEEN LOST IN DREAMS OF APPLIANCES!
SUDDENLY...
CRASH
WAUGH! I STEPPED BACKWARDS IN THE NICK OF PRIME-TIME!
THE TOWER OF POWER--IT'S STARTING TO COME APART UNDER THE COMBINED WEIGHT OF KONG AND THE MAN-THING!
OH, DUCKY--IF IT SHOULD COLLAPSE, AMY WOULD NEVER SURVIVE THE FALL!
SOMEBODY'S GOT TO GO UP THERE AND HELP HER DOWN--SOMBODY LIGHT ENOUGH TO NOT MAKE THE TOWER TOPPLE ANY FASTER!
SOMEBODY LIKE... YOU, HOWARD!
TOOTS, I MAY'VE BEEN DEPRESSED LATELY--BUT I AIN'T ADVANCED TA SUICIDAL!

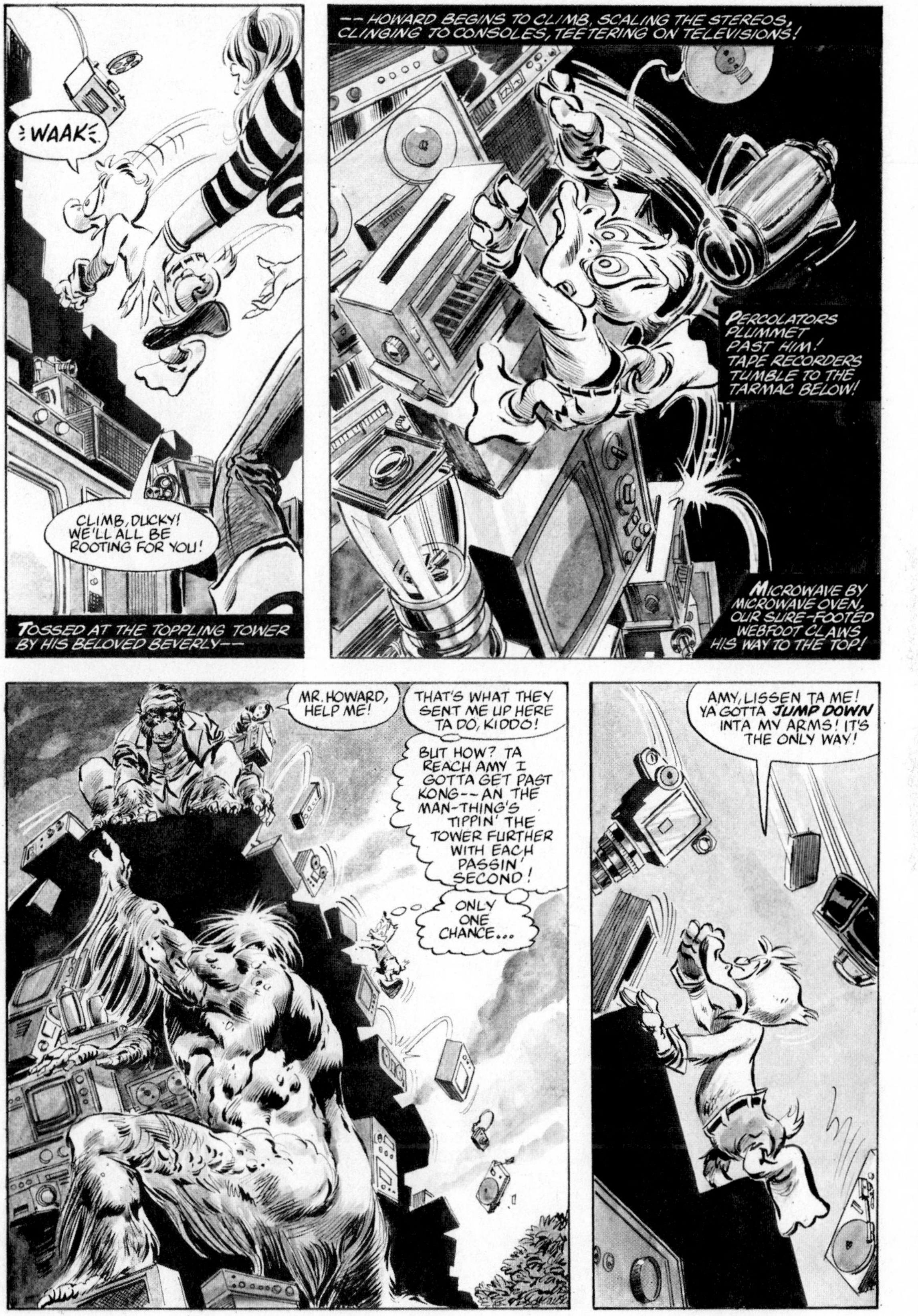

WAAK
CLIMB, DUCKY! WE'LL ALL BE ROOTING FOR YOU!
TOSSED AT THE TOPPLING TOWER BY HIS BELOVED BEVERLY--
--HOWARD BEGINS TO CLIMB, SCALING THE STEREOS, CLINGING TO CONSOLES, TEETERING ON TELEVISIONS!
PERCOLATORS PLUMMET PAST HIM! TAPE RECORDERS TUMBLE TO THE TARMAC BELOW!
MICROWAVE BY MICROWAVE OVEN, OUR SURE-FOOTED WEBFOOT CLAWS HIS WAY TO THE TOP!
MR. HOWARD, HELP ME!
THAT'S WHAT THEY SENT ME UP HERE TA DO, KIDDO!
BUT HOW? TA REACH AMY I GOTTA GET PAST KONG--AN THE MAN-THING'S TIPPIN' THE TOWER FURTHER WITH EACH PASSIN' SECOND!
ONLY ONE CHANCE...
AMY, LISSEN TA ME! YA GOTTA JUMP DOWN INTA MY ARMS! IT'S THE ONLY WAY!

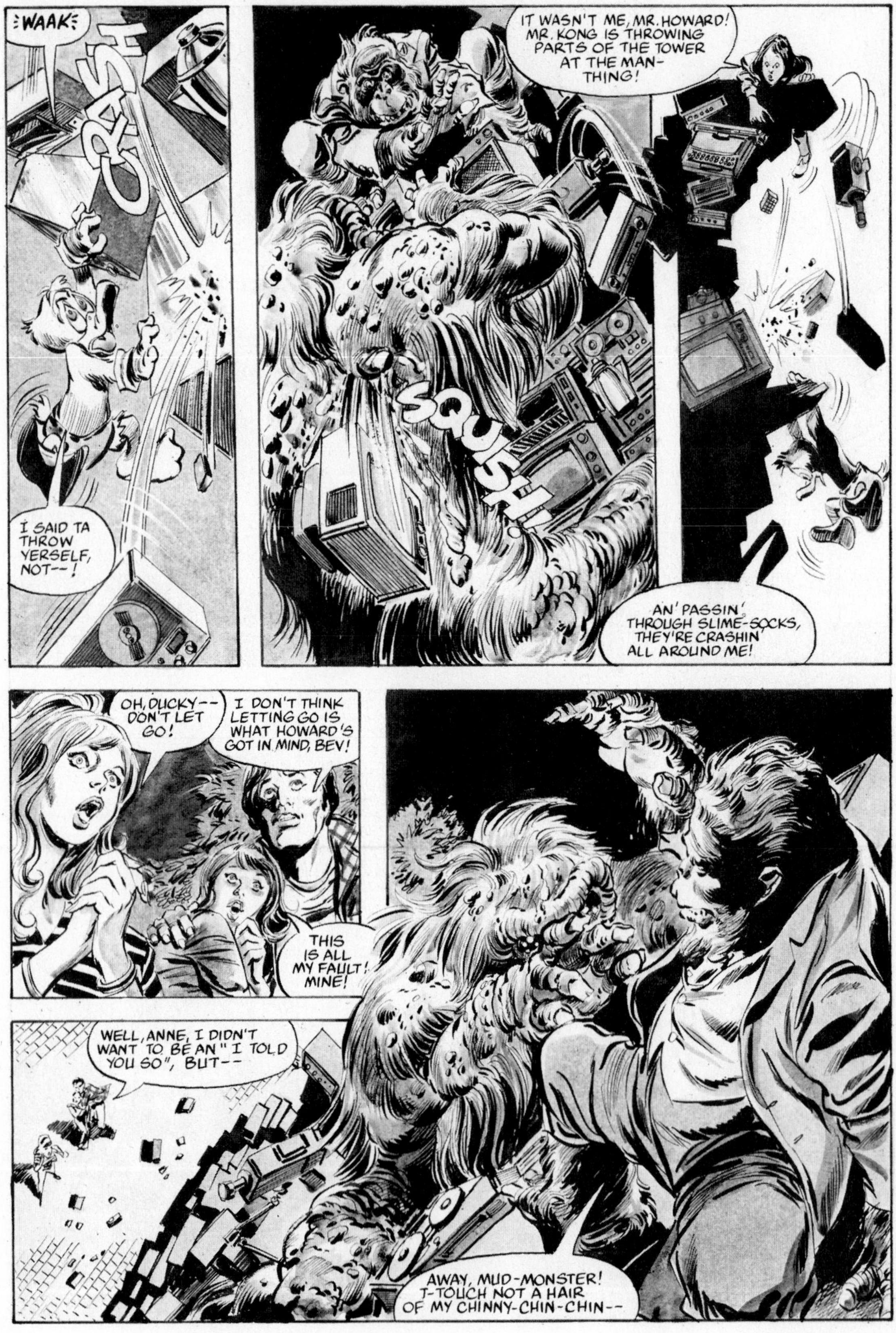
WAAK!
CRASH
IT WASN'T ME, MR. HOWARD! MR. KONG IS THROWING PARTS OF THE TOWER AT THE MAN-THING!
SQUISH!
I SAID TA THROW YERSELF, NOT--!
AN' PASSIN' THROUGH SLIME-SOCKS, THEY'RE CRASHIN' ALL AROUND ME!
OH, DUCKY-- DON'T LET GO!
I DON'T THINK LETTING GO IS WHAT HOWARD'S GOT IN MIND, BEV!
THIS IS ALL MY FAULT! MINE!
WELL, ANNE, I DIDN'T WANT TO BE AN "I TOLD YOU SO", BUT--
AWAY, MUD-MONSTER! T-TOUCH NOT A HAIR OF MY CHINNY-CHIN-CHIN--

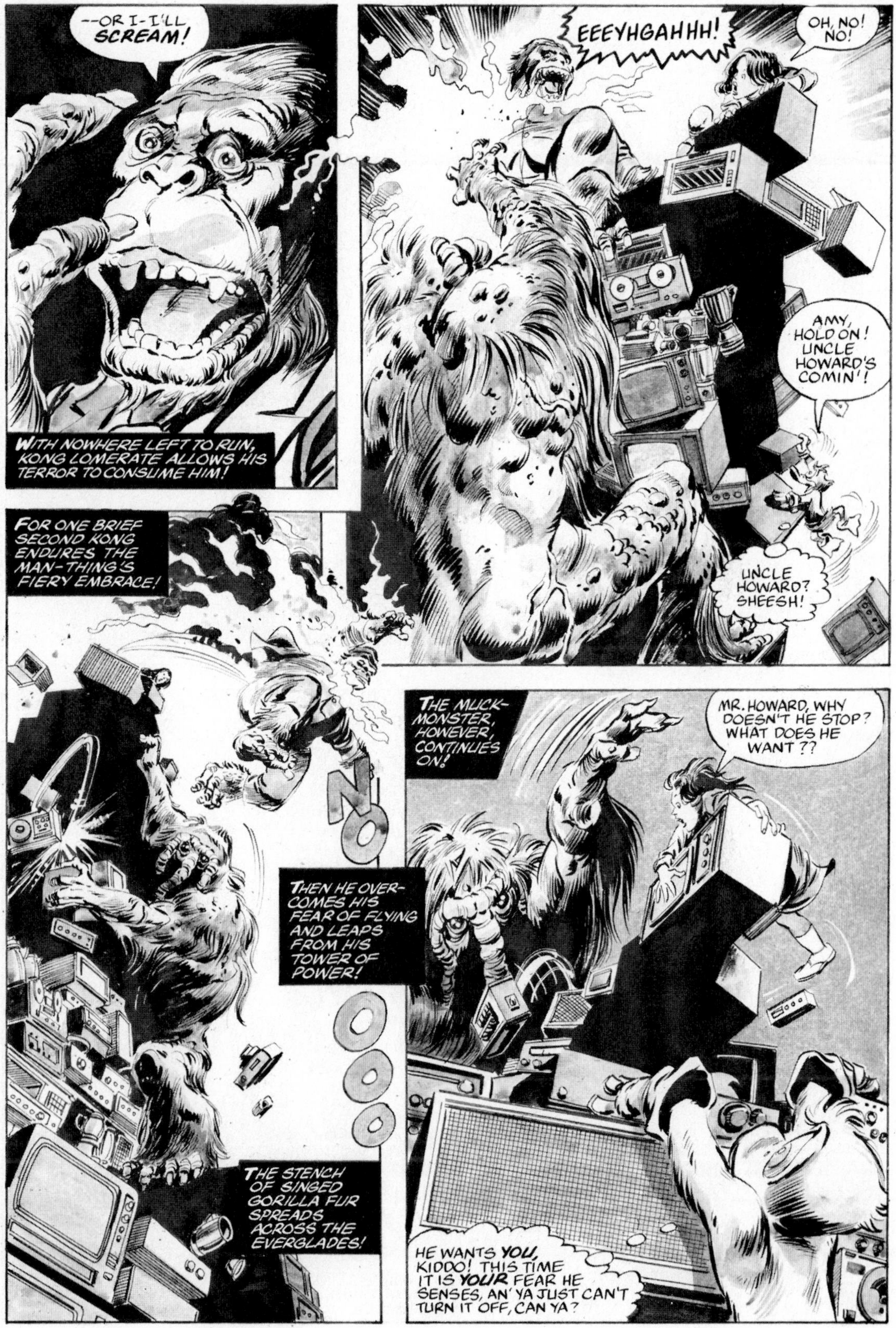
--OR I-I'LL SCREAM!
WITH NOWHERE LEFT TO RUN, KONG LOMERATE ALLOWS HIS TERROR TO CONSUME HIM!
EEEYHGAHHH!
OH, NO! NO!
AMY, HOLD ON! UNCLE HOWARD'S COMIN'!
UNCLE HOWARD? SHEESH!
FOR ONE BRIEF SECOND KONG ENDURES THE MAN-THING'S FIERY EMBRACE!
NOOOO
THEN HE OVER-COMES HIS FEAR OF FLYING AND LEAPS FROM HIS TOWER OF POWER!
THE STENCH OF SINGED GORILLA FUR SPREADS ACROSS THE EVERGLADES!
THE MUCK-MONSTER, HOWEVER, CONTINUES ON!
MR. HOWARD, WHY DOESN'T HE STOP? WHAT DOES HE WANT??
HE WANTS YOU, KIDDO! THIS TIME IT IS YOUR FEAR HE SENSES, AN' YA JUST CAN'T TURN IT OFF, CAN YA?

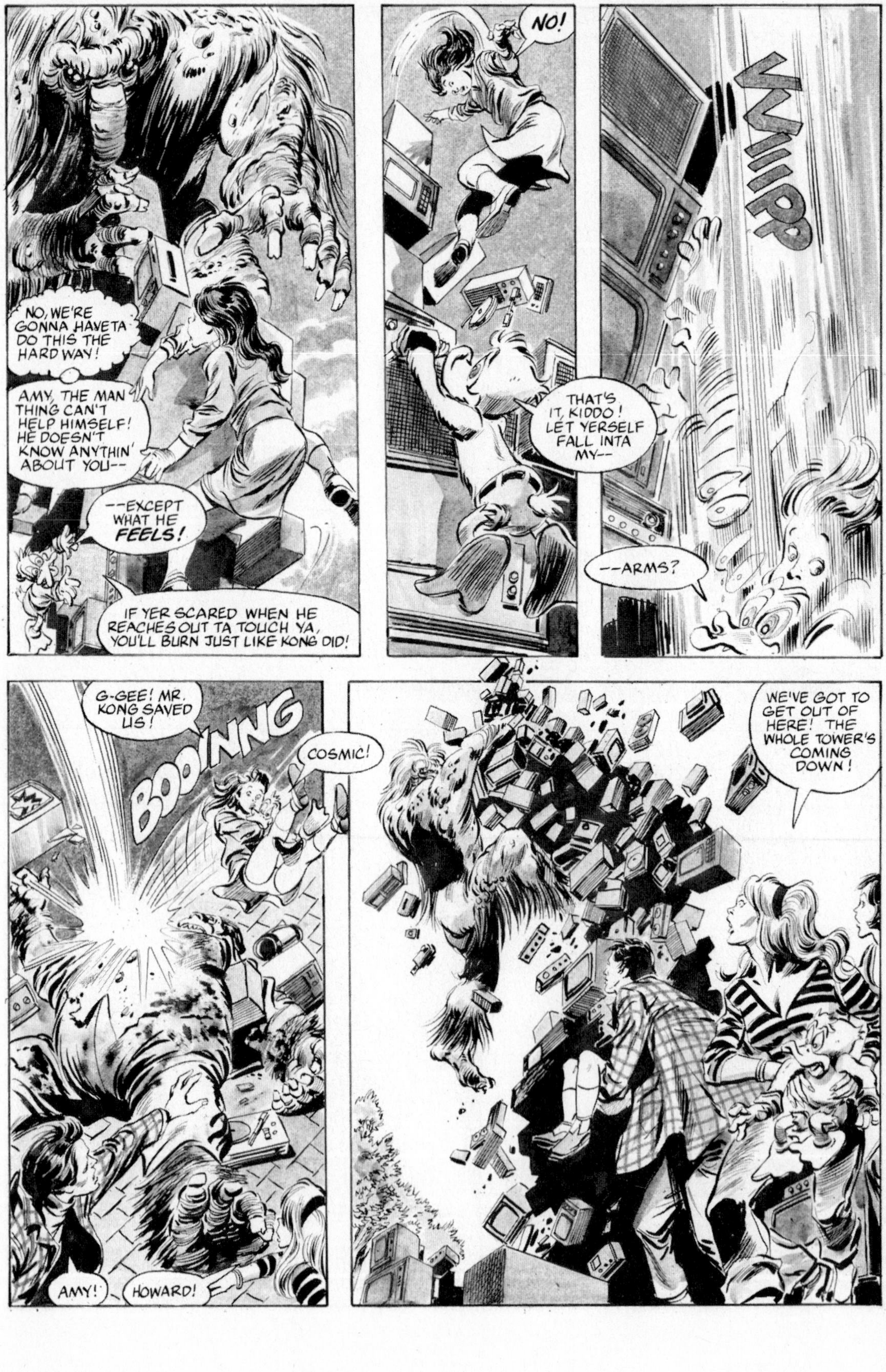
NO, WE'RE GONNA HAVETA DO THIS THE HARD WAY!
AMY, THE MAN THING CAN'T HELP HIMSELF! HE DOESN'T KNOW ANYTHIN' ABOUT YOU--
--EXCEPT WHAT HE FEELS!
IF YER SCARED WHEN HE REACHES OUT TA TOUCH YA, YOU'LL BURN JUST LIKE KONG DID!
NO!
THAT'S IT, KIDDO! LET YERSELF FALL INTA MY--
VVIIPP
--ARMS?
G-GEE! MR. KONG SAVED US!
BOOINNG
COSMIC!
AMY!
HOWARD!
WE'VE GOT TO GET OUT OF HERE! THE WHOLE TOWER'S COMING DOWN!

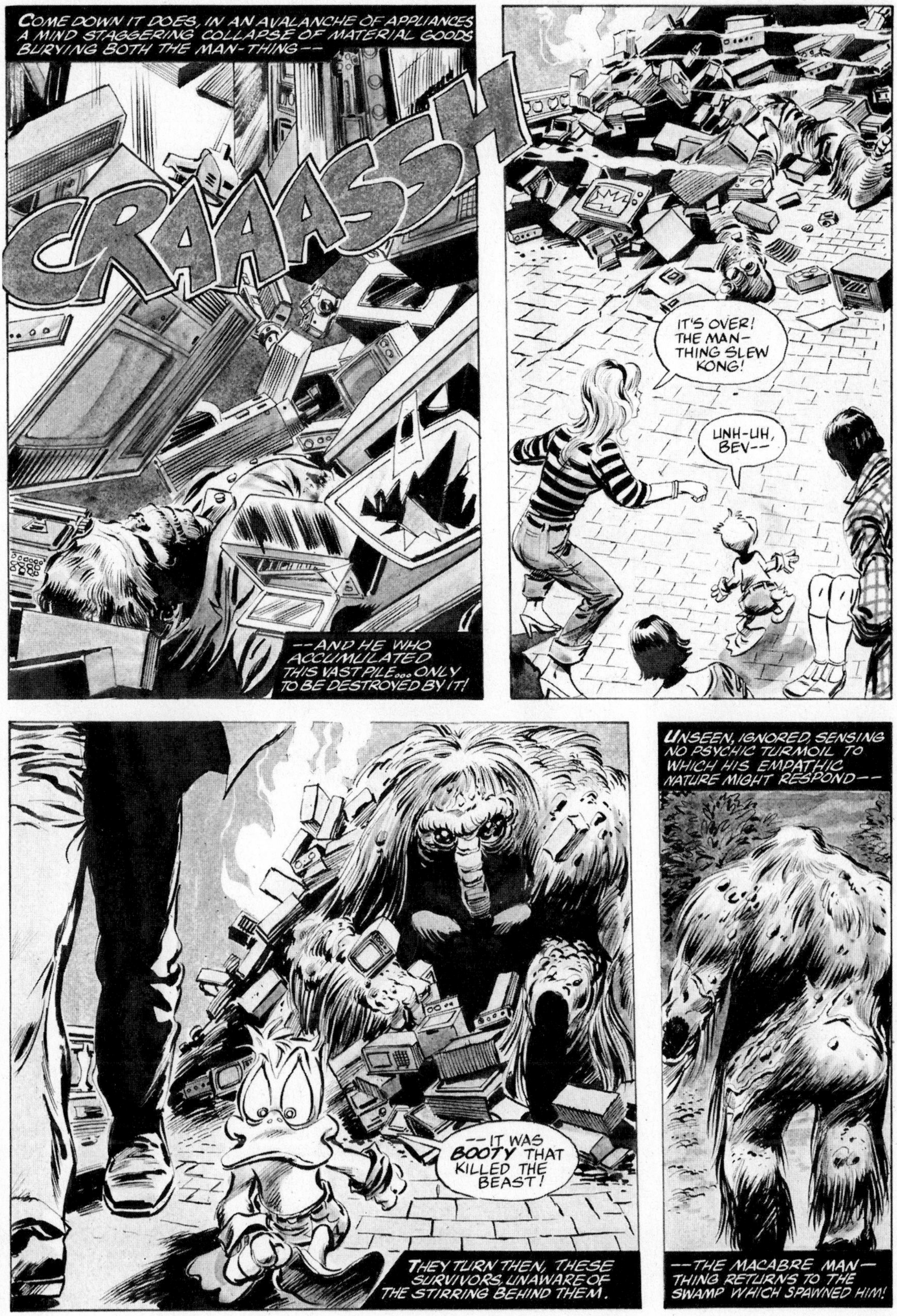
COME DOWN IT DOES, IN AN AVALANCHE OF APPLIANCES A MIND STAGGERING COLLAPSE OF MATERIAL GOODS BURYING BOTH THE MAN-THING--
CRAAASSH
--AND HE WHO ACCUMULATED THIS VAST PILE... ONLY TO BE DESTROYED BY IT!
IT'S OVER! THE MAN-THING SLEW KONG!
UNH-UH, BEV--
--IT WAS BOOTY THAT KILLED THE BEAST!
THEY TURN THEN, THESE SURVIVORS, UNAWARE OF THE STIRRING BEHIND THEM.
UNSEEN, IGNORED, SENSING NO PSYCHIC TURMOIL TO WHICH HIS EMPATHIC NATURE MIGHT RESPOND--
--THE MACABRE MAN-THING RETURNS TO THE SWAMP WHICH SPAWNED HIM!

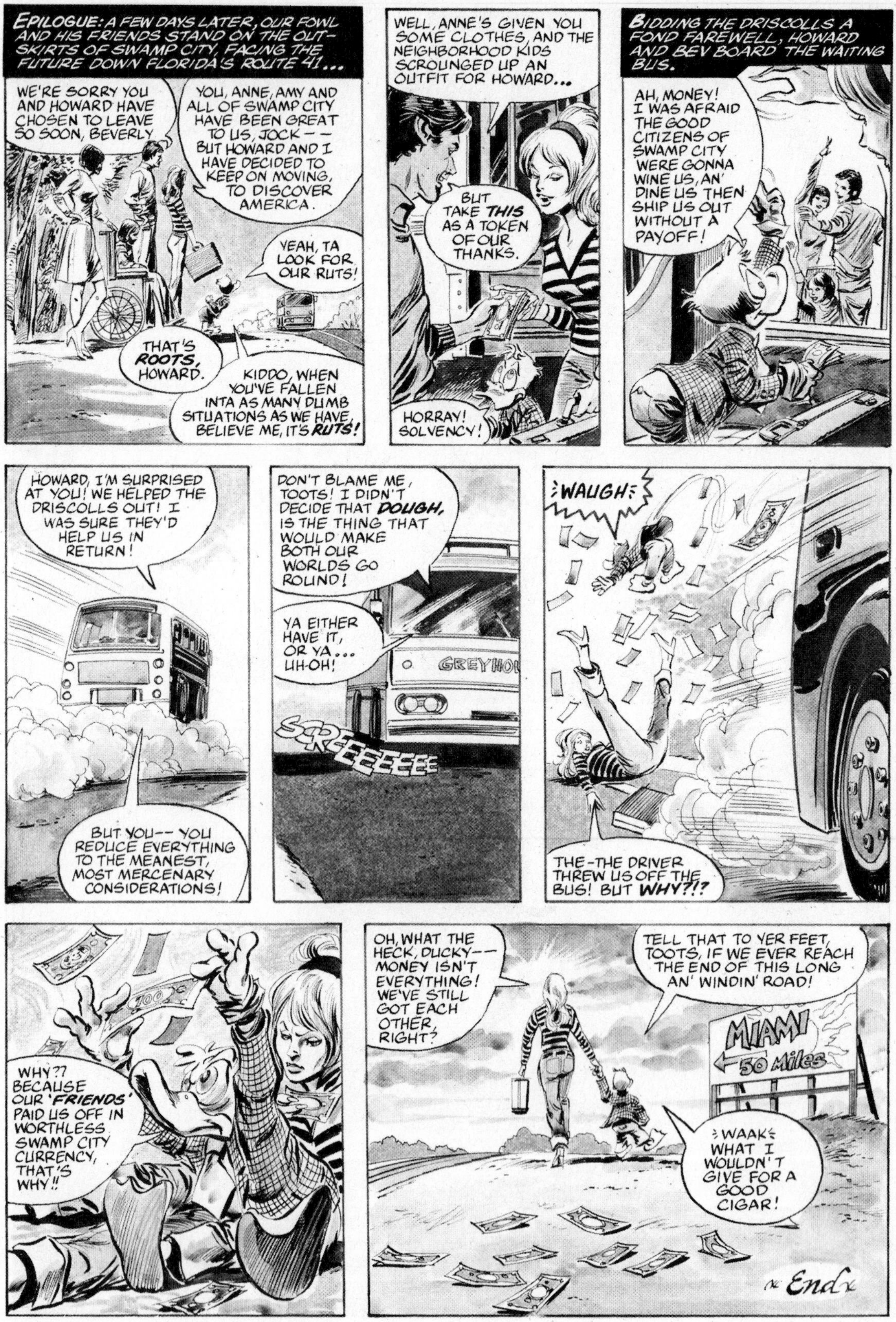
EPILOGUE: A FEW DAYS LATER, OUR FOWL AND HIS FRIENDS STAND ON THE OUT-SKIRTS OF SWAMP CITY, FACING THE FUTURE DOWN FLORIDA'S ROUTE 41...
WE'RE SORRY YOU AND HOWARD HAVE CHOSEN TO LEAVE SO SOON, BEVERLY.
YOU, ANNE, AMY AND ALL OF SWAMP CITY HAVE BEEN GREAT TO US, JOCK -- BUT HOWARD AND I HAVE DECIDED TO KEEP ON MOVING, TO DISCOVER AMERICA.
YEAH, TA LOOK FOR OUR RUTS!
THAT'S ROOTS, HOWARD.
KIDDO, WHEN YOU'VE FALLEN INTA AS MANY DUMB SITUATIONS AS WE HAVE, BELIEVE ME, IT'S RUTS!
WELL, ANNE'S GIVEN YOU SOME CLOTHES, AND THE NEIGHBORHOOD KIDS SCROUNGED UP AN OUTFIT FOR HOWARD...
BUT TAKE THIS AS A TOKEN OF OUR THANKS.
HORRAY! SOLVENCY!
BIDDING THE DRISCOLLS A FOND FAREWELL, HOWARD AND BEV BOARD THE WAITING BUS.
AH, MONEY! I WAS AFRAID THE GOOD CITIZENS OF SWAMP CITY WERE GONNA WINE US, AN' DINE US THEN SHIP US OUT WITHOUT A PAYOFF!
HOWARD, I'M SURPRISED AT YOU! WE HELPED THE DRISCOLLS OUT! I WAS SURE THEY'D HELP US IN RETURN!
BUT YOU-- YOU REDUCE EVERYTHING TO THE MEANEST, MOST MERCENARY CONSIDERATIONS!
DON'T BLAME ME, TOOTS! I DIDN'T DECIDE THAT DOUGH, IS THE THING THAT WOULD MAKE BOTH OUR WORLDS GO ROUND!
YA EITHER HAVE IT, OR YA... UH-OH!
GREYHOU
SCREEEEEEEE
WAUGH!
THE-THE DRIVER THREW US OFF THE BUS! BUT WHY?!?
WHY?? BECAUSE OUR 'FRIENDS' PAID US OFF IN WORTHLESS SWAMP CITY CURRENCY, THAT'S WHY!!
OH, WHAT THE HECK, DUCKY-- MONEY ISN'T EVERYTHING! WE'VE STILL GOT EACH OTHER, RIGHT?
TELL THAT TO YER FEET, TOOTS, IF WE EVER REACH THE END OF THIS LONG AN' WINDIN' ROAD!
MIAMI
50 Miles
WAAK! WHAT I WOULDN'T GIVE FOR A GOOD CIGAR!
End

Duck Of Many Faces

By Bill Mantlo

There must be something about HOWARD THE DUCK that brings out the best in artists. When we asked several of the leading illustrators in the comic mag business to contribute to our FAMOUS ARTISTS' PORTFOLIO, the response was both immediate and inspired. In fact, so much interest was generated that we may publish another portfolio in the future for those whose work didn't make it in this time.

For this ish, words just aren't adequate to describe MARIE SEVERIN's Dashiell Hammetesque CHEAP DUCKTECTIVE, with BEV as Mary Astor and HOWARD as the brash and brazen Bogart. (And is that Peter Lorre with the rabbit ears framed outside the door?)

Then there's Wondrous WALT SIMONSON doing a reprise of his "Alien" adaptation with SNAILIAN — a super-slug menacing our mallard and maid aboard a freighter to the stars.

What can we say about MARSHALL ROGERS' parody of our Distinguished Competitor's Darknight Detective? All the elements of a successful parody are there — the sky-stabbing Duck Signal, the marvelous Duckmobile — as HOWARD and BEV adopt the habits of DUCK-MAN and DUCK-GIRL to strike fowl fear into the hardened arteries of those whose hearts are too atrophied to care. DUCK-MAN is also the basis of next issue's hilarious festcapade.

JOHN BYRNE, whose work on Marvel's X-MEN, FANTASTIC FOUR, and CAPTAIN AMERICA has established a new criteria of excellence tries his hand at illustrating and embellishing with HOWARD (not Carter) breaking the curse of King Tut's tomb. Well, Tut *was* a boy-king, and, at the sight of BEV after all those years, even Mummy's boys will be boys (Ouch!).

HOWARD ("Fast Hands") CHAYKIN finishes off this edition of the FAMOUS ARTISTS' PORTFOLIO with a scene out of a Fred Astaire-Ginger Rogers musical, casting HOWARD and BEV as those light-on-their feet lovers of Hollywood's Golden Age. Actually, we had wanted Howie to do a Busby Berkeley routine, replete with hundreds of frenzied fowl in various stages of undress, but he calmly slicked back his brilliantined locks and, fixing an eye on Editor Lynn Graeme, said, "Okay, baby, but I charge a buck a duck." Even Marvel, unfortunately, has budgetary limits.

That's it for this installment. We've got some ideas for which artists to feature next time, but we'd also like to hear suggestions from you Duckophiles. Is there any Famous Artist whose rendition of HOWARD THE DUCK would simply blow you away? If so, drop a line to WISE QUACKS--FAMOUS ARTISTS PORTFOLIO and we'll contact those ladies or gents whose work you clamor for.

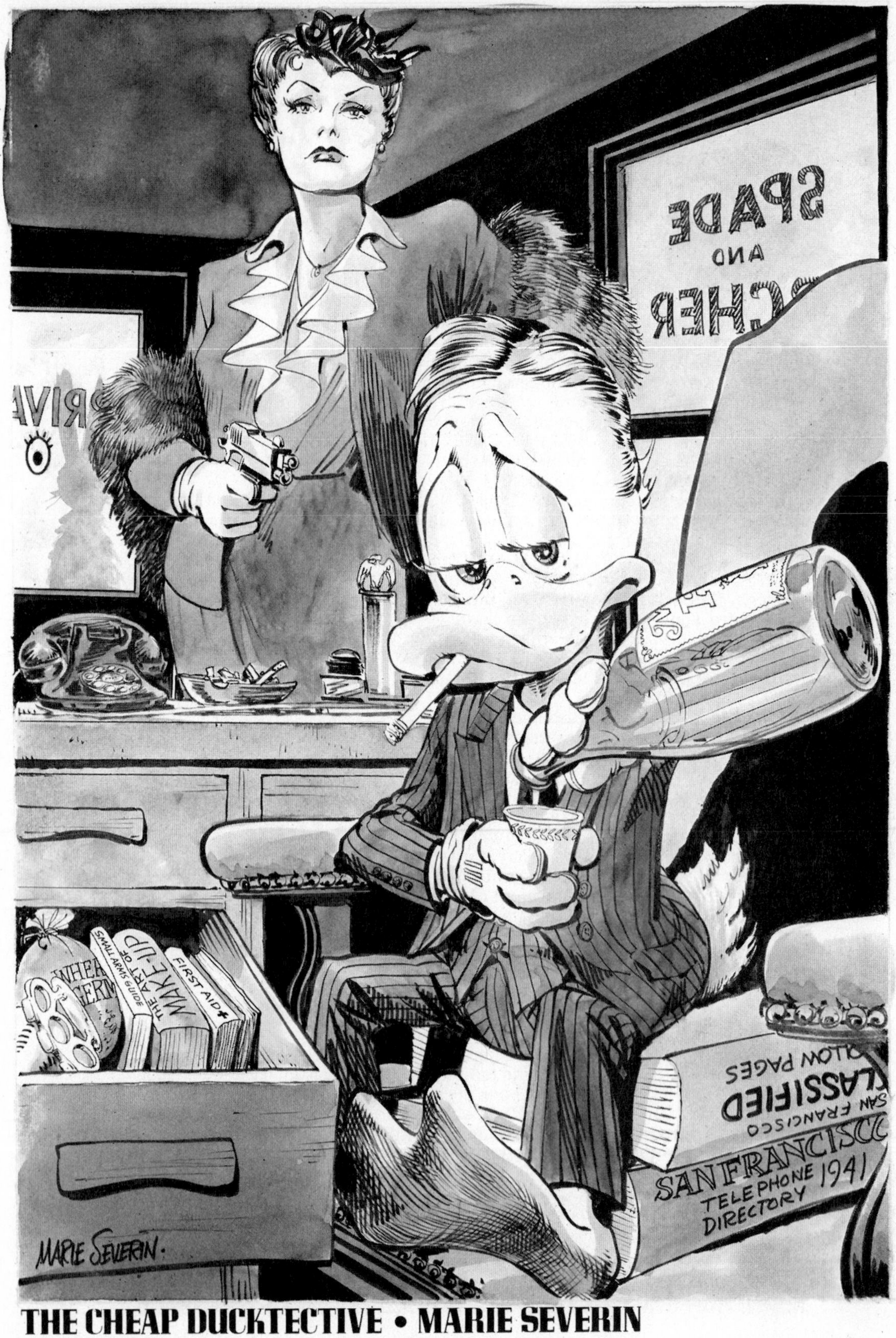
SPADE
AND
SMALL ARMS GUIDE
THE ART OF MAKE-UP
FIRST AID
SAN FRANCISCO
TELEPHONE
DIRECTORY 1941
MARIE SEVERIN

THE CHEAP DUCKTECTIVE • MARIE SEVERIN

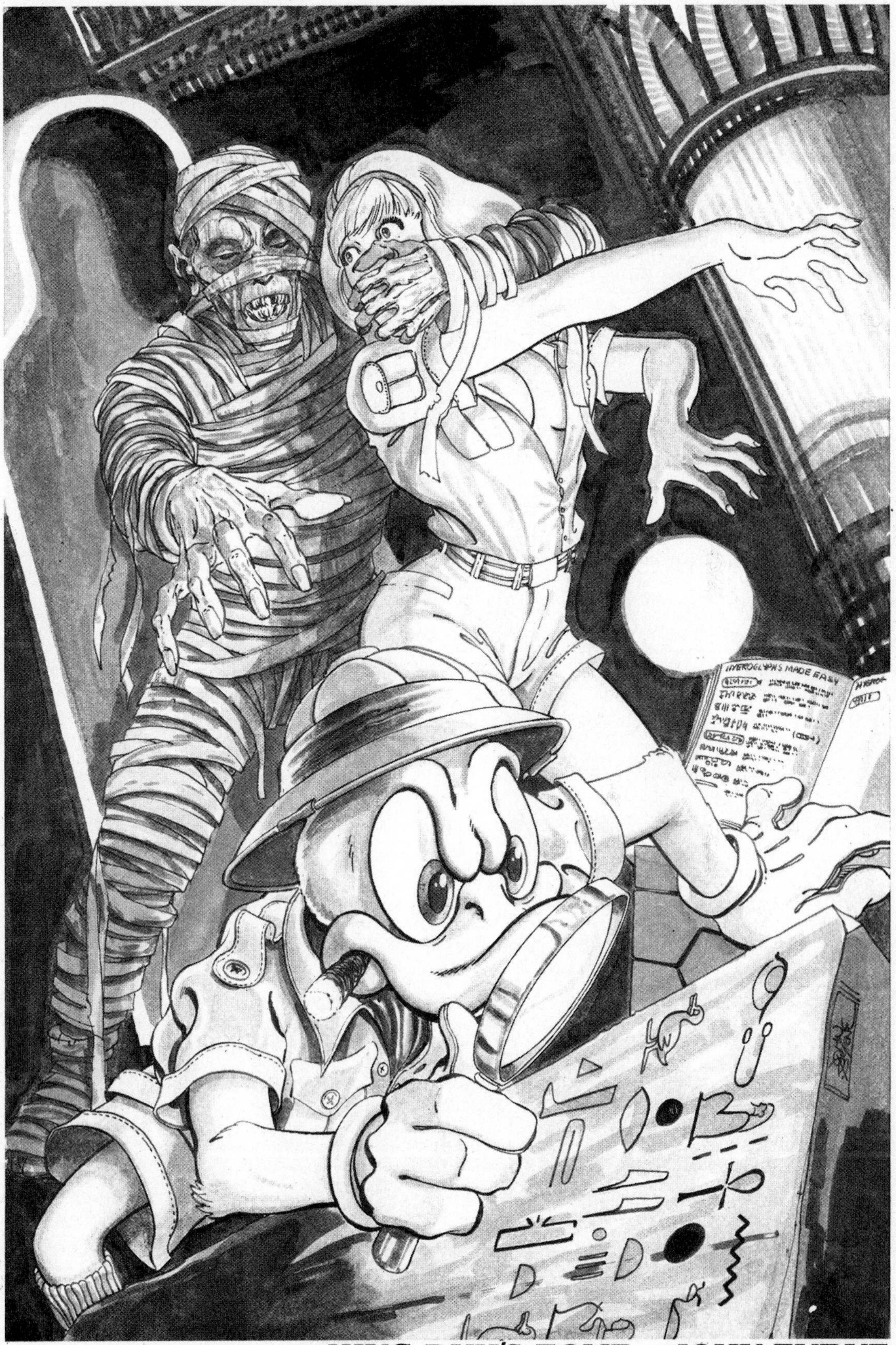
HIEROGLYPHS MADE EASY

KING DUK'S TOMB • JOHN BYRNE

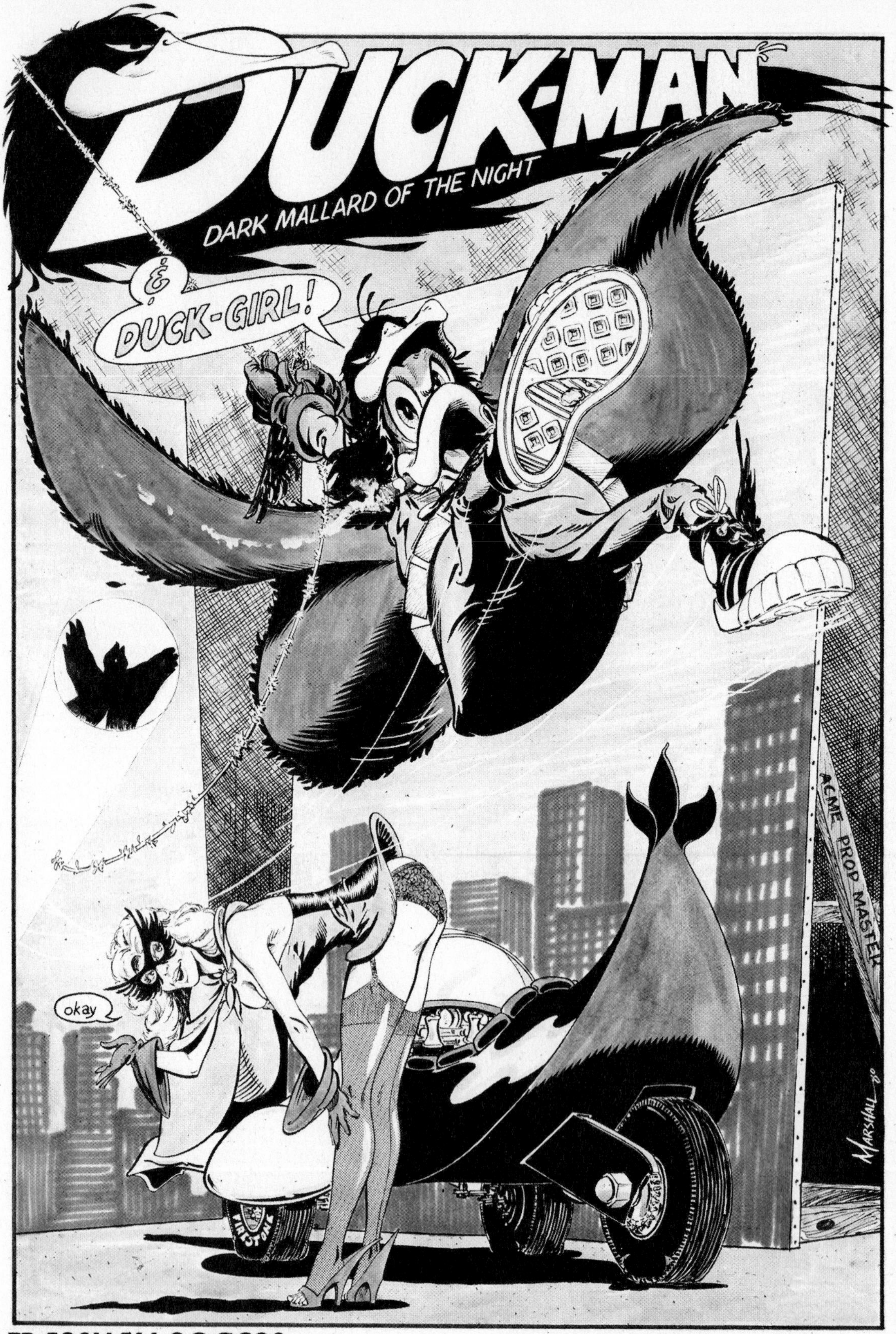
DUCK-MAN
DARK MALLARD OF THE NIGHT
& DUCK-GIRL!
okay
ACME PROP MASTER
MARSHALL '80

MARSHALL ROGERS

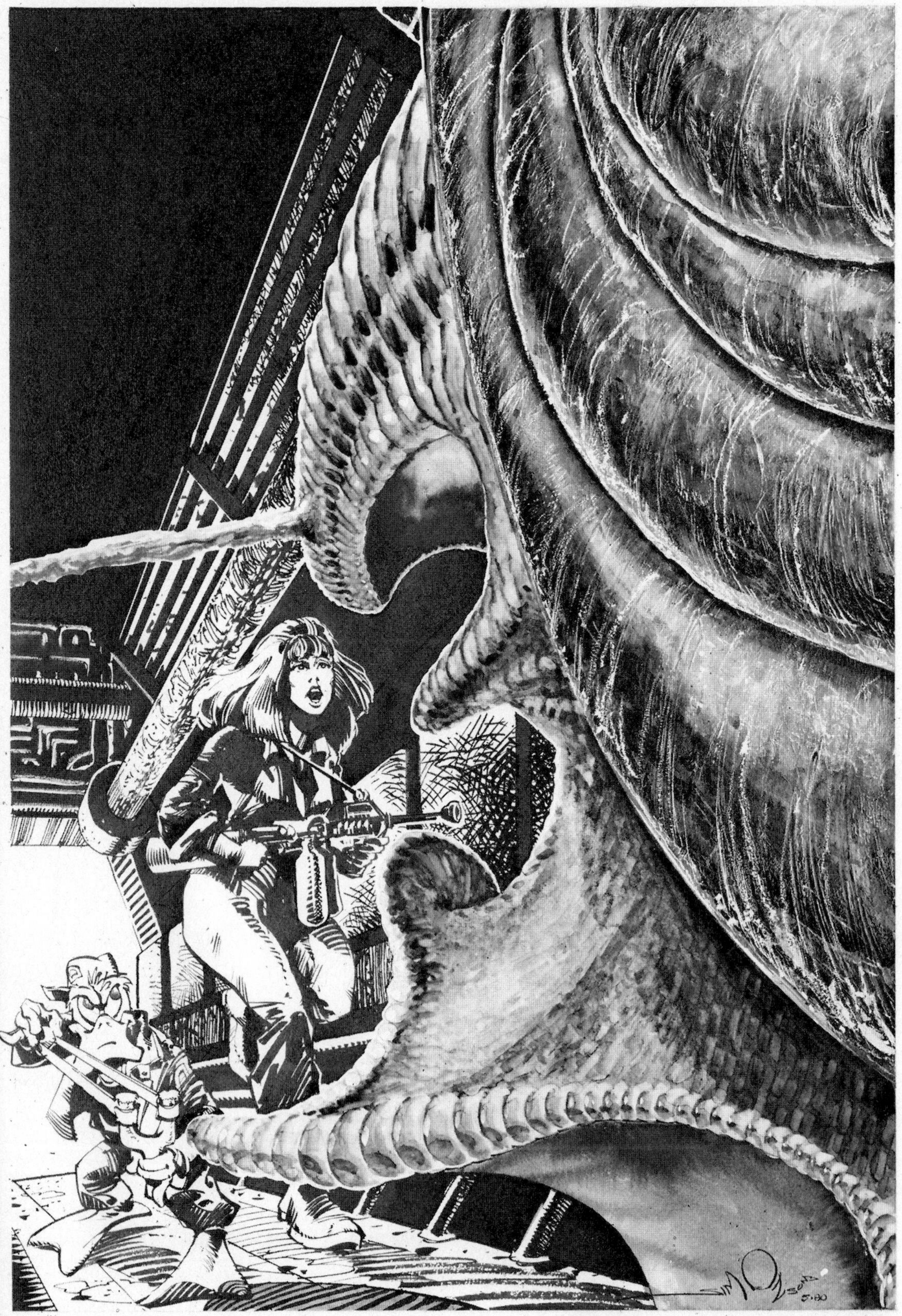

SNAILIAN • WALT SIMONSON

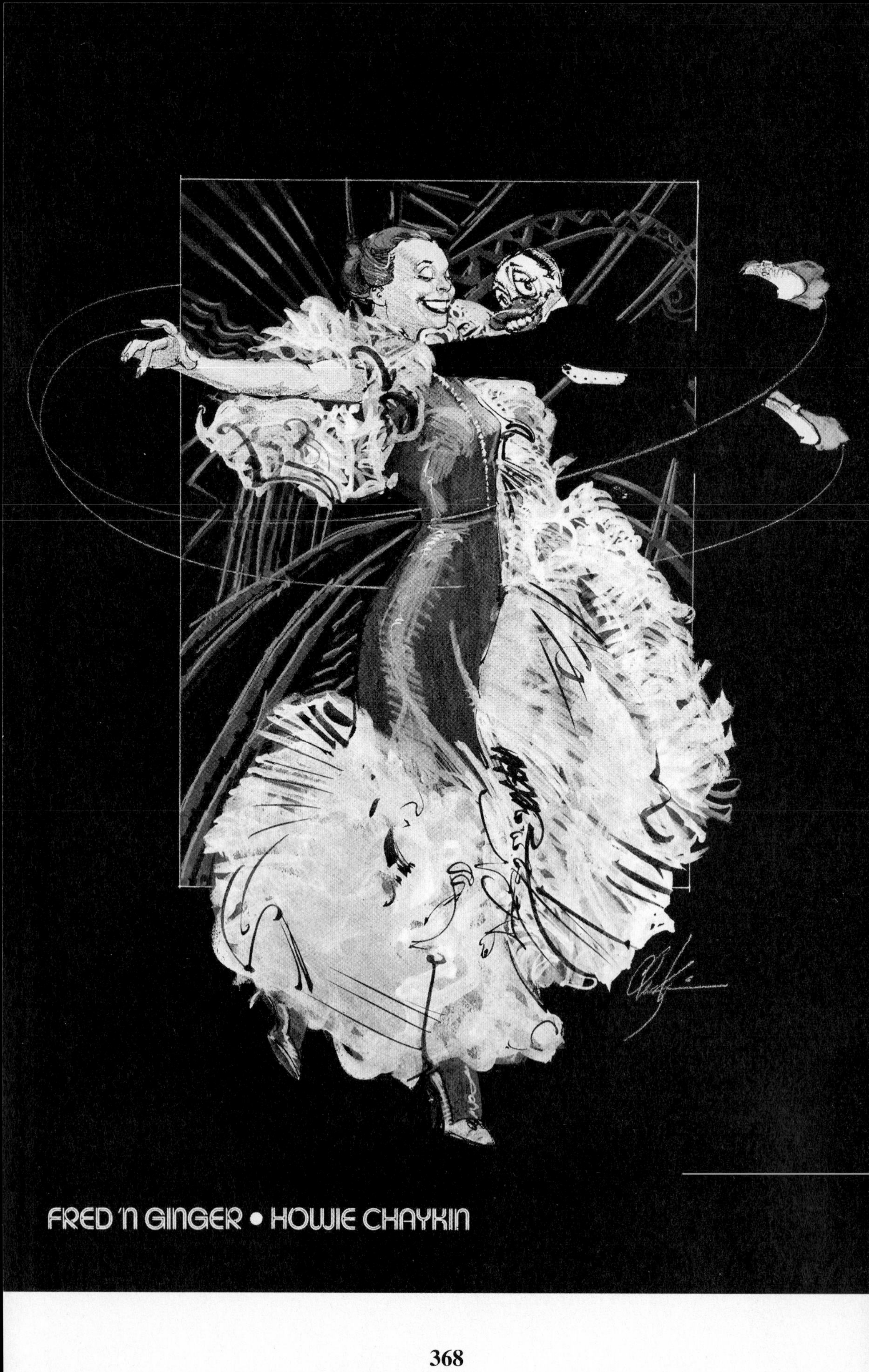

FRED 'N GINGER • HOWIE CHAYKIN

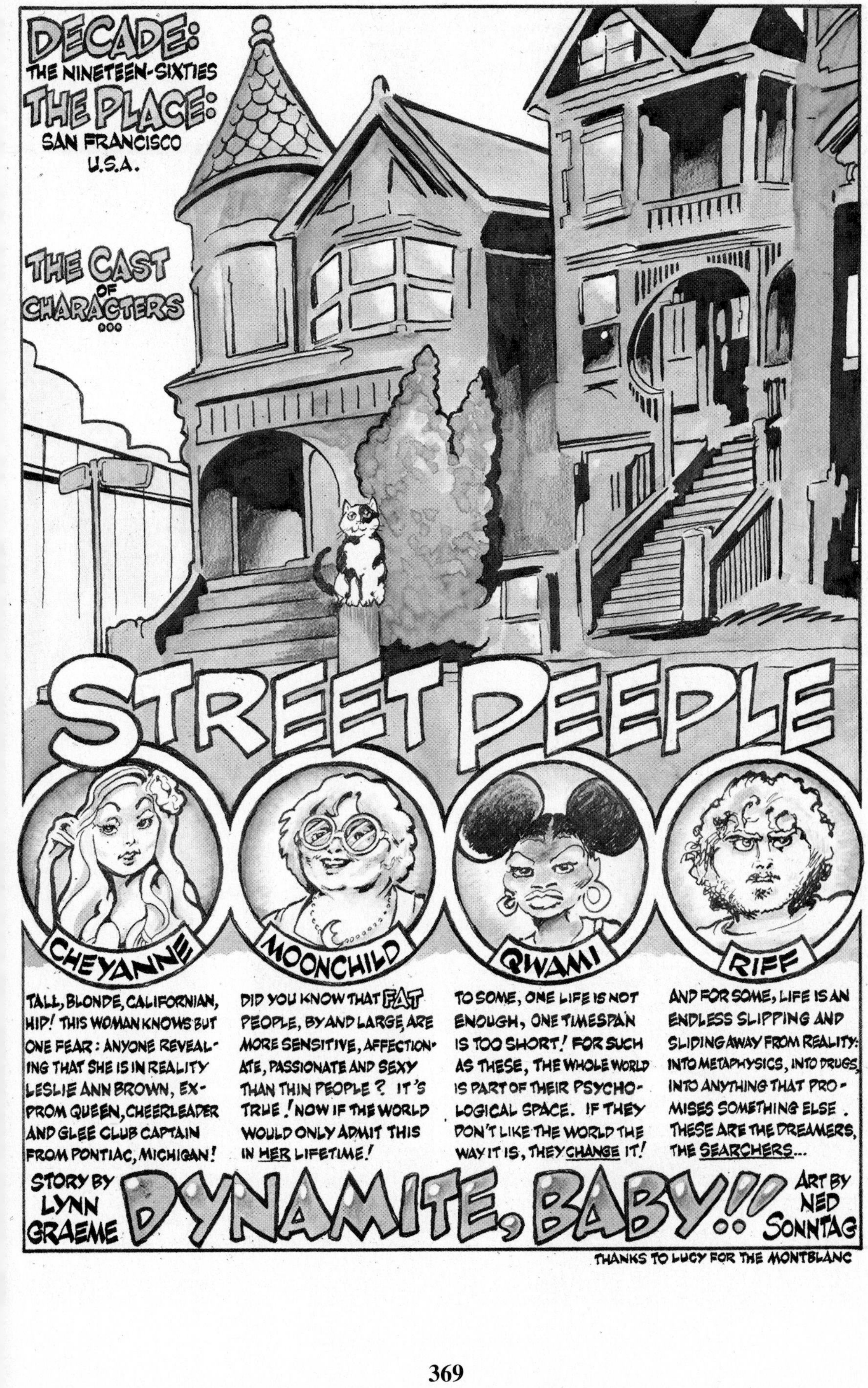
DECADE:
THE NINETEEN-SIXTIES
THE PLACE:
SAN FRANCISCO
U.S.A.
THE CAST OF CHARACTERS...
STREET PEEPLE
CHEYANNE
MOONCHILD
QWAMI
RIFF
TALL, BLONDE, CALIFORNIAN, HIP! THIS WOMAN KNOWS BUT ONE FEAR: ANYONE REVEALING THAT SHE IS IN REALITY LESLIE ANN BROWN, EX-PROM QUEEN, CHEERLEADER AND GLEE CLUB CAPTAIN FROM PONTIAC, MICHIGAN!
DID YOU KNOW THAT FAT PEOPLE, BY AND LARGE, ARE MORE SENSITIVE, AFFECTIONATE, PASSIONATE AND SEXY THAN THIN PEOPLE? IT'S TRUE! NOW IF THE WORLD WOULD ONLY ADMIT THIS IN HER LIFETIME!
TO SOME, ONE LIFE IS NOT ENOUGH, ONE TIMESPAN IS TOO SHORT! FOR SUCH AS THESE, THE WHOLE WORLD IS PART OF THEIR PSYCHOLOGICAL SPACE. IF THEY DON'T LIKE THE WORLD THE WAY IT IS, THEY CHANGE IT!
AND FOR SOME, LIFE IS AN ENDLESS SLIPPING AND SLIDING AWAY FROM REALITY: INTO METAPHYSICS, INTO DRUGS, INTO ANYTHING THAT PROMISES SOMETHING ELSE. THESE ARE THE DREAMERS, THE SEARCHERS...
STORY BY LYNN GRAEME
DYNAMITE, BABY!!
ART BY NED SONNTAG
THANKS TO LUCY FOR THE MONTBLANC

SATURDAY MORNING IN THE STREET PEEPLE'S PAD AND ALL IS WELL—WHICH IS PRETTY UNUSUAL! RIFF, CHEYANNE AND MOONCHILD ARE TAKEN BY SURPRISE AS AN OMINOUSLY CHEERFUL QWAMI ARISES AT THE FIENDISH HOUR OF TEN A.M.!

HI, YOU GUYS!

SHE'S FIGURED A WAY TO GET RID OF ME!

WOW, I'M GLAD YOU'RE UP 'CAUSE I GOT FRESH GROATS FOR YA!

SAVE THE WHALE

STRIKE MISSION, OPERATION BREAK-FAST, COMMENCE!

YOU STILL HERE WHITE TOAST?!

PANIC

SOME OF IT'S STARTING TO COME BACK! THERE WAS A CRIB, I REMEMBER THAT! AND ...AND A BLUE RATTLE! WITH A LITTLE HELP, A LITTLE COMPASSIONATE REFUGE, I KNOW MY MEMORY WILL RETURN!

BULL COOKIES!

GEE, I'M GLAD YOU'RE OKAY, LIKE YOU WERE ACTIN' SO STRANGE, Y'KNOW? CHEERFUL!

SO I WAS A LITTLE CHEERFUL, BIG DEAL! AIN'T I GOT A RIGHT TO BE IN A GOOD MOOD ONCE IN A WHILE?

FOOD?

MRRRRF?

CHORE CHART

DAWN BLITZ TEA

MY CHANCE TO STRIKE BACK AT THE IMPERIALIST PATRIARCHY IS NEAR!

I KNOW SHE'S FIGURED OUT HOW TO GET RID OF ME...

WELL, WE CAN GET AN EARLY START TODAY. OUGHTA BE A GOOD CROWD IN FRONT OF THE UNITED STATES BANK, DON'TCHA THINK...?

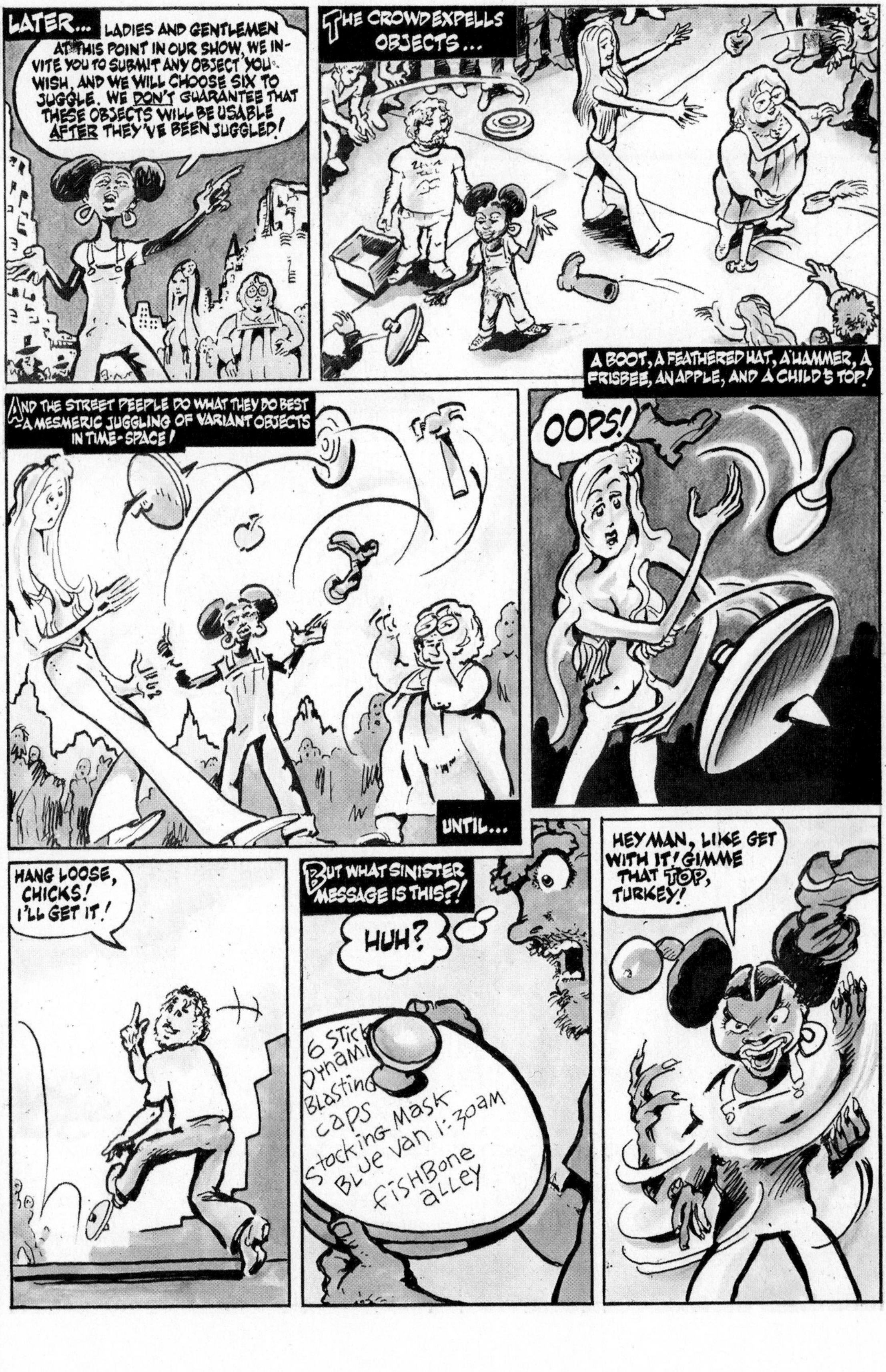
LATER...
LADIES AND GENTLEMEN AT THIS POINT IN OUR SHOW, WE INVITE YOU TO SUBMIT ANY OBJECT YOU WISH, AND WE WILL CHOOSE SIX TO JUGGLE. WE DON'T GUARANTEE THAT THESE OBJECTS WILL BE USABLE AFTER THEY'VE BEEN JUGGLED!
THE CROWD EXPELLS OBJECTS...
A BOOT, A FEATHERED HAT, A HAMMER, A FRISBEE, AN APPLE, AND A CHILD'S TOP!
AND THE STREET PEEPLE DO WHAT THEY DO BEST -A MESMERIC JUGGLING OF VARIANT OBJECTS IN TIME-SPACE!
UNTIL...
OOPS!
HANG LOOSE, CHICKS! I'LL GET IT!
BUT WHAT SINISTER MESSAGE IS THIS?!
HUH?
6 Stick
Dynami
Blasting
caps
Stocking Mask
Blue van 1:30AM
fishBone
alley
HEY MAN, LIKE GET WITH IT! GIMME THAT TOP, TURKEY!

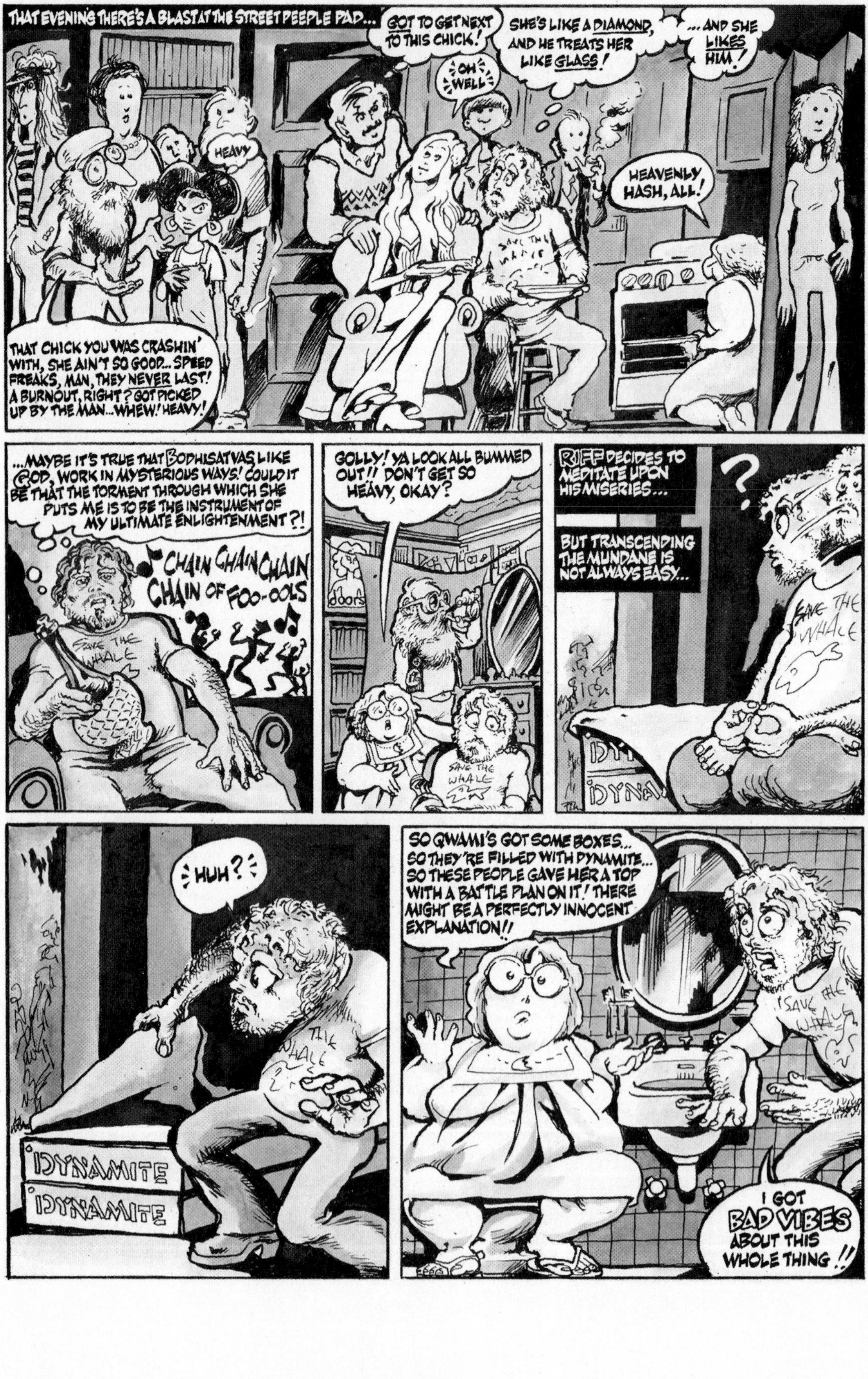
THAT EVENING THERE'S A BLAST AT THE STREET PEEPLE PAD...
GOT TO GET NEXT TO THIS CHICK!
OH WELL
SHE'S LIKE A DIAMOND, AND HE TREATS HER LIKE GLASS!
...AND SHE LIKES HIM!
HEAVY
HEAVENLY HASH, ALL!
SAVE THE WHALE
THAT CHICK YOU WAS CRASHIN' WITH, SHE AIN'T SO GOOD... SPEED FREAKS, MAN, THEY NEVER LAST! A BURNOUT, RIGHT? GOT PICKED UP BY THE MAN... WHEW! HEAVY!
...MAYBE IT'S TRUE THAT BODHISATVAS, LIKE GOD, WORK IN MYSTERIOUS WAYS! COULD IT BE THAT THE TORMENT THROUGH WHICH SHE PUTS ME IS TO BE THE INSTRUMENT OF MY ULTIMATE ENLIGHTENMENT?!
CHAIN CHAIN CHAIN CHAIN OF FOO-OOLS
SAVE THE WHALE
GOLLY! YA LOOK ALL BUMMED OUT!! DON'T GET SO HEÄVY, OKAY?
doors
SAVE THE WHALE
RIFF DECIDES TO MEDITATE UPON HIS MISERIES...
BUT TRANSCENDING THE MUNDANE IS NOT ALWAYS EASY...
?
SAVE THE WHALE
HUH?
IDYNAMITE
IDYNAMITE
SO QWAMI'S GOT SOME BOXES... SO THEY'RE FILLED WITH DYNAMITE... SO THESE PEOPLE GAVE HER A TOP WITH A BATTLE PLAN ON IT! THERE MIGHT BE A PERFECTLY INNOCENT EXPLANATION!!
SAVE THE WHALE
I GOT BAD VIBES ABOUT THIS WHOLE THING!!

BY ONE A.M. ALL IS SILENT AND DARK IN THE STREET PEEPLE-PAD. IN FOUR BEDS LIE FOUR HUDDLED SHAPES...BUT ONLY ONE OF THEM ...CHEYANNE...IS REAL! THE OLD PILLOW TRICK!

OUTSIDE

THERE IT IS...THE BLUE VAN!

OH WOW! YOU WERE RIGHT!!

YES THE BLUE VAN, THE MEANS OF DESTRUCTION FOR THE UNITED STATES BANK, FOR QWAMI AND HER FELLOW REVOLUTIONARIES INTEND TO BLOW IT UP!

FISHBONE ALLEY

BUT....!

GET OUTTA HERE MAN! THE FEDS ARE ONTO US ...THEY'RE WATCHING THE VAN !

≈PARANOIA≈

SAVE THE WHA

FEDS !! INTERNATIONAL FASCIST CONSPIRACY!

IT'S MY KARMA TO SAVE QWAMI FROM HERSELF!

SAVE THE WHALE

I COULD GET INTO THIS WHOLE THING AND BE KOOL... BUT THIS STOCKING BELONGS TO HER...MY DEITY! OH, EXCRUCIATING BLISS!!

THE WHALE

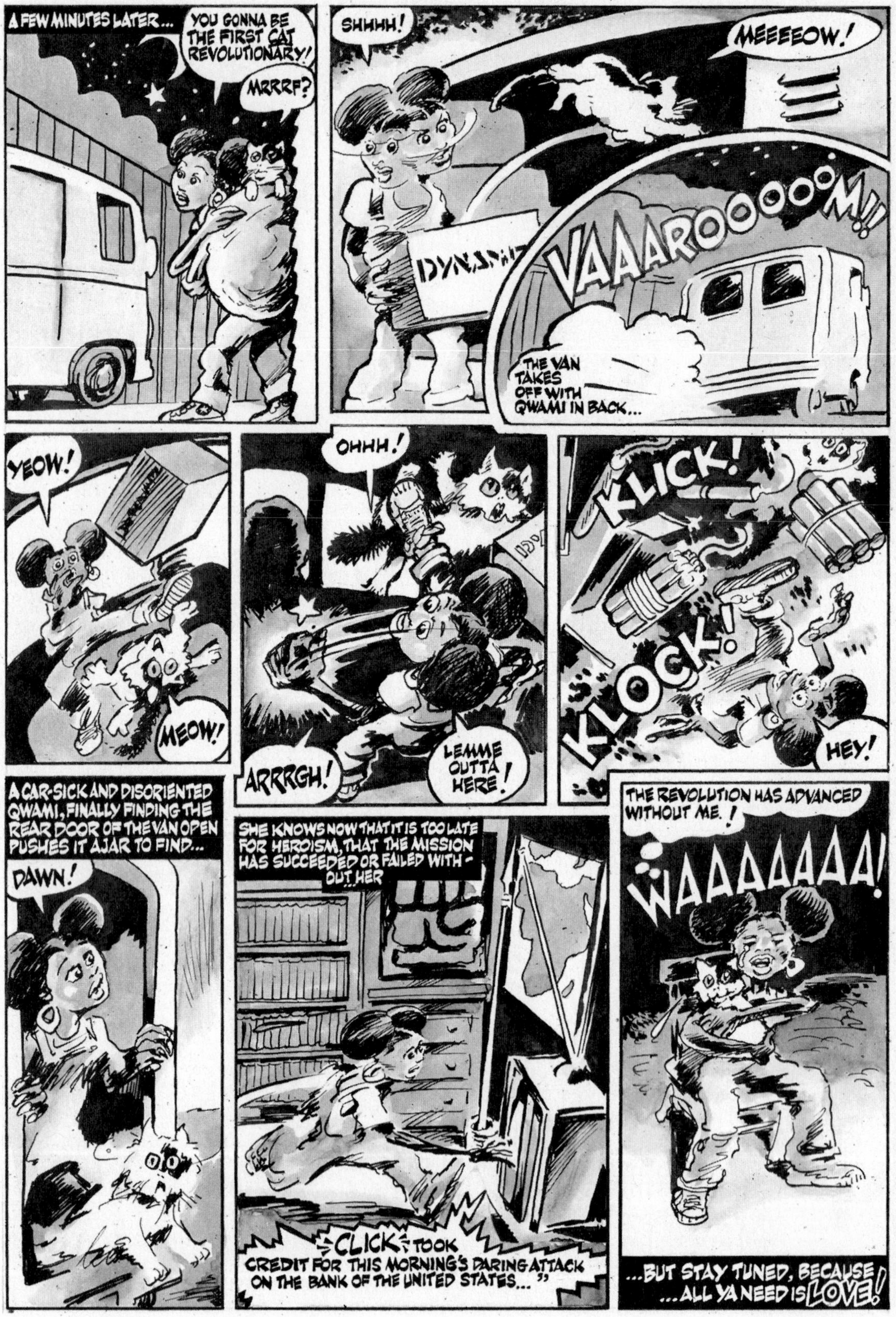

A FEW MINUTES LATER...
YOU GONNA BE THE FIRST CAT REVOLUTIONARY!
MRRRF?
SHHHH!
MEEEEOW!
VAAAROOOOOM!!
THE VAN TAKES OFF WITH QWAMI IN BACK...
YEOW!
MEOW!
OHHH!
ARRRGH!
LEMME OUTTA HERE!
KLICK!
KLOCK!
HEY!
A CAR-SICK AND DISORIENTED QWAMI, FINALLY FINDING THE REAR DOOR OF THE VAN OPEN PUSHES IT AJAR TO FIND...
DAWN!
SHE KNOWS NOW THAT IT IS TOO LATE FOR HEROISM, THAT THE MISSION HAS SUCCEEDED OR FAILED WITH-OUT HER...
CLICK TOOK CREDIT FOR THIS MORNING'S DARING ATTACK ON THE BANK OF THE UNITED STATES..."
THE REVOLUTION HAS ADVANCED WITHOUT ME. !
WAAAAAAA!
...BUT STAY TUNED, BECAUSE ...ALL YA NEED IS LOVE!

FIRST THERE WAS THE CAPED CRUSADER
NOW THERE IS
DUCKMAN!

DUCKMAN: DARK MALLARD OF THE NIGHT Strikes Terror Into the Hearts of Evil-Doers and Love Into the Heart of His Faithful **DUCKGIRL!** Even the **MAULER** Cannot Bring Doom to this Duck! This Incredible Tale is Brought to You by **BILL MANTLO & MARSHALL ROGERS.**

PLUS!

THE GREY PANTHER is Loosed Upon An Unsuspecting Sunshine State by **BILL MANTLO & GENE COLAN.**

AND!

STREET PEEPLE (a story about *humans!*)

All This Excitement is Lovingly Wrapped in the Beautiful Art of **JOHN POUND,** and contains the usual blathering, complaining, and overwrought editorial as well as an "audition" by **Dave Sim,** the witty creator of **CEREBUS.**

HOWARD THE DUCK #8, On Sale in September!

Crazy Magazine #59, February 1980

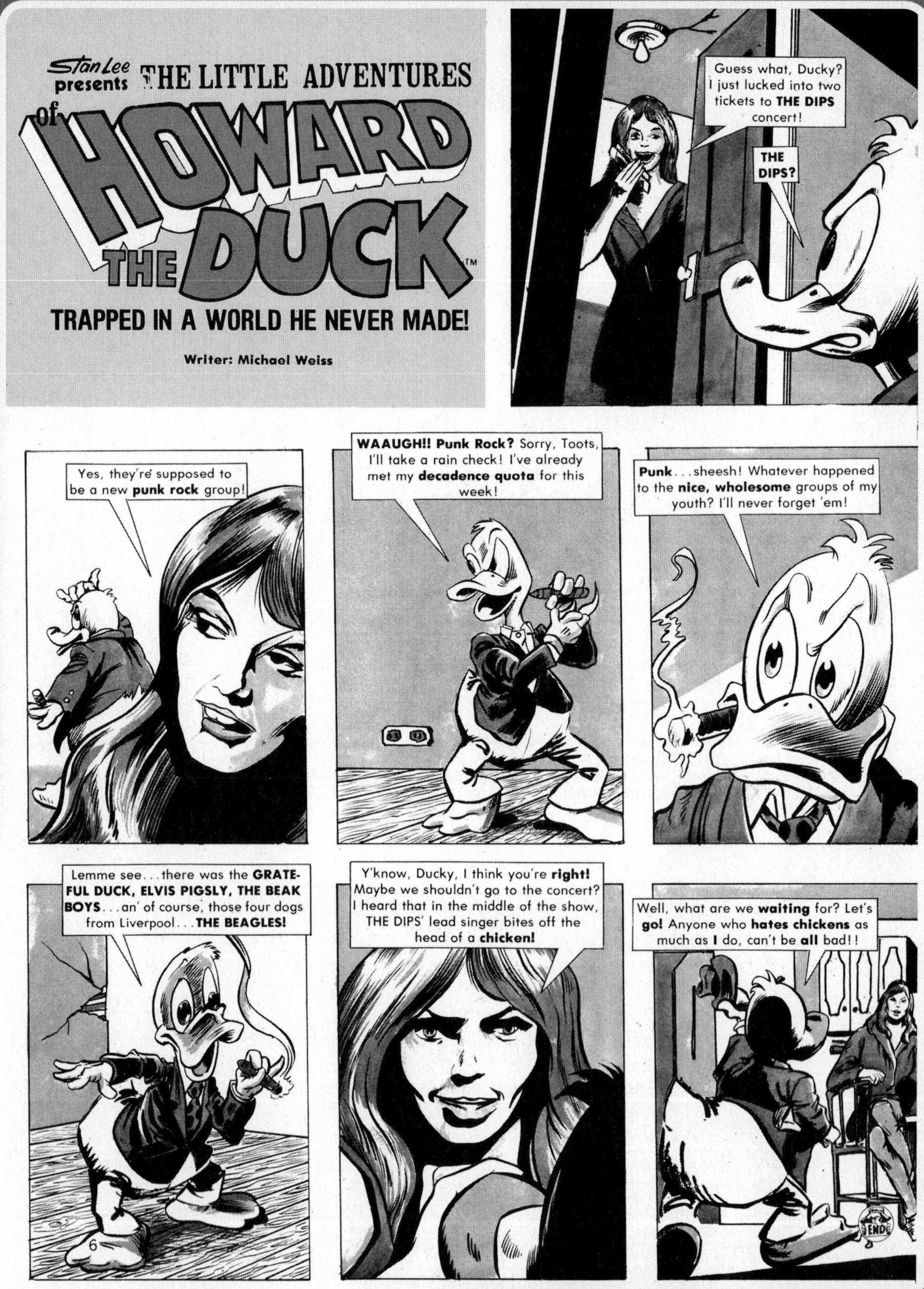
Stan Lee presents THE LITTLE ADVENTURES of HOWARD THE DUCK™
TRAPPED IN A WORLD HE NEVER MADE!
Writer: Michael Weiss
Guess what, Ducky? I just lucked into two tickets to THE DIPS concert!
THE DIPS?
Yes, they're supposed to be a new punk rock group!
WAAUGH!! Punk Rock? Sorry, Toots, I'll take a rain check! I've already met my decadence quota for this week!
Punk...sheesh! Whatever happened to the nice, wholesome groups of my youth? I'll never forget 'em!
Lemme see...there was the GRATEFUL DUCK, ELVIS PIGSLY, THE BEAK BOYS...an' of course, those four dogs from Liverpool...THE BEAGLES!
Y'know, Ducky, I think you're right! Maybe we shouldn't go to the concert? I heard that in the middle of the show, THE DIPS' lead singer bites off the head of a chicken!
Well, what are we waiting for? Let's go! Anyone who hates chickens as much as I do, can't be all bad!!
6
THE END

Crazy Magazine
Editors: Paul Laikin & Larry Hama
Art Directors: Eden Norah & Marie Severin
Associate Editor: Jim Owsley
Assistant Editor: Aron Mayer

Crazy Magazine #63, June 1980

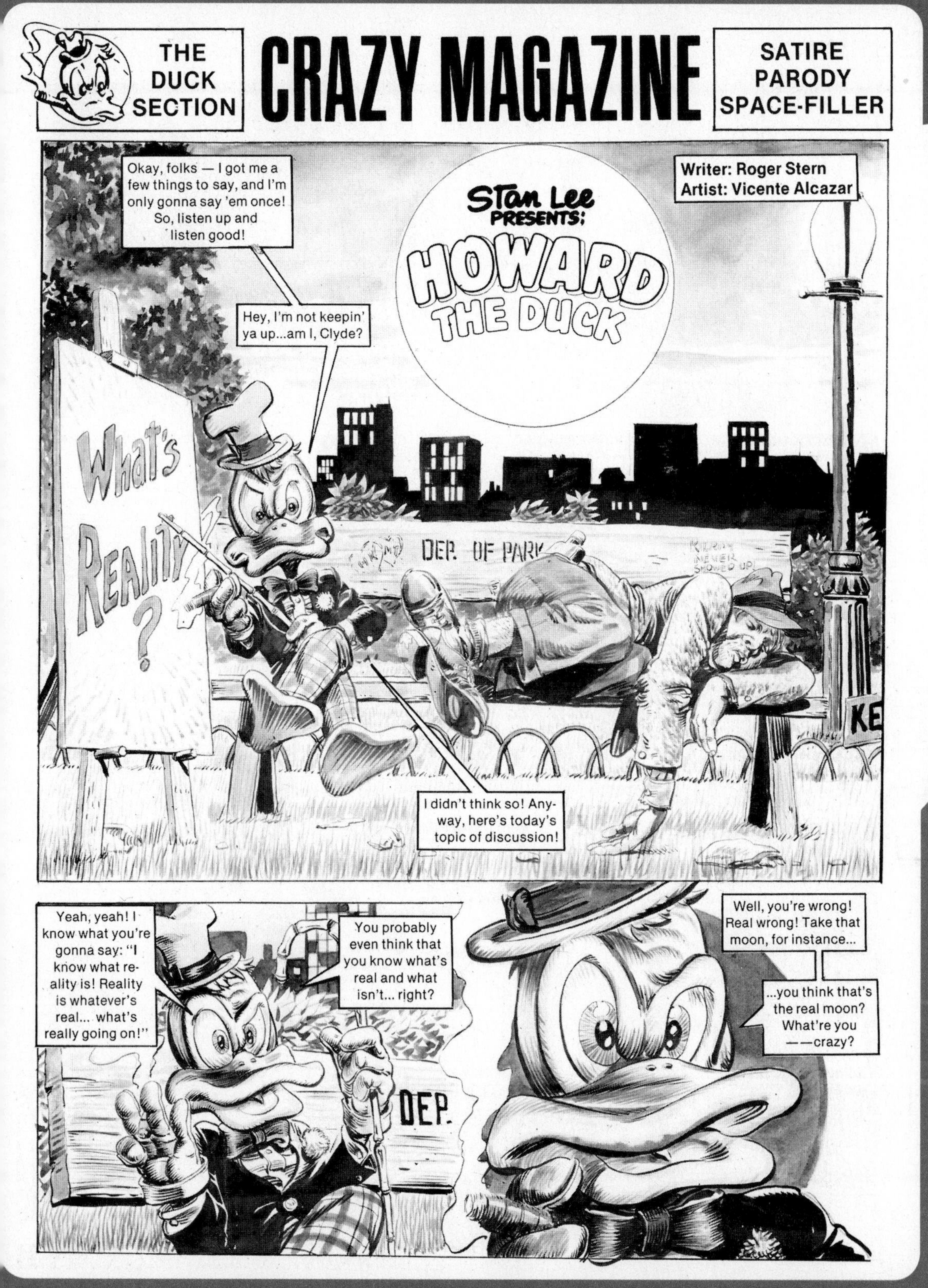

THE DUCK SECTION
CRAZY MAGAZINE
SATIRE PARODY SPACE-FILLER
Okay, folks — I got me a few things to say, and I'm only gonna say 'em once! So, listen up and listen good!
Writer: Roger Stern
Artist: Vicente Alcazar
STan Lee PRESENTS:
HOWARD THE DUCK
Hey, I'm not keepin' ya up...am I, Clyde?
What's Reality?
DEP. OF PARK
I didn't think so! Any-way, here's today's topic of discussion!
Yeah, yeah! I know what you're gonna say: "I know what re-ality is! Reality is whatever's real... what's really going on!"
You probably even think that you know what's real and what isn't... right?
DEP.
Well, you're wrong! Real wrong! Take that moon, for instance...
...you think that's the real moon? What're you ——crazy?

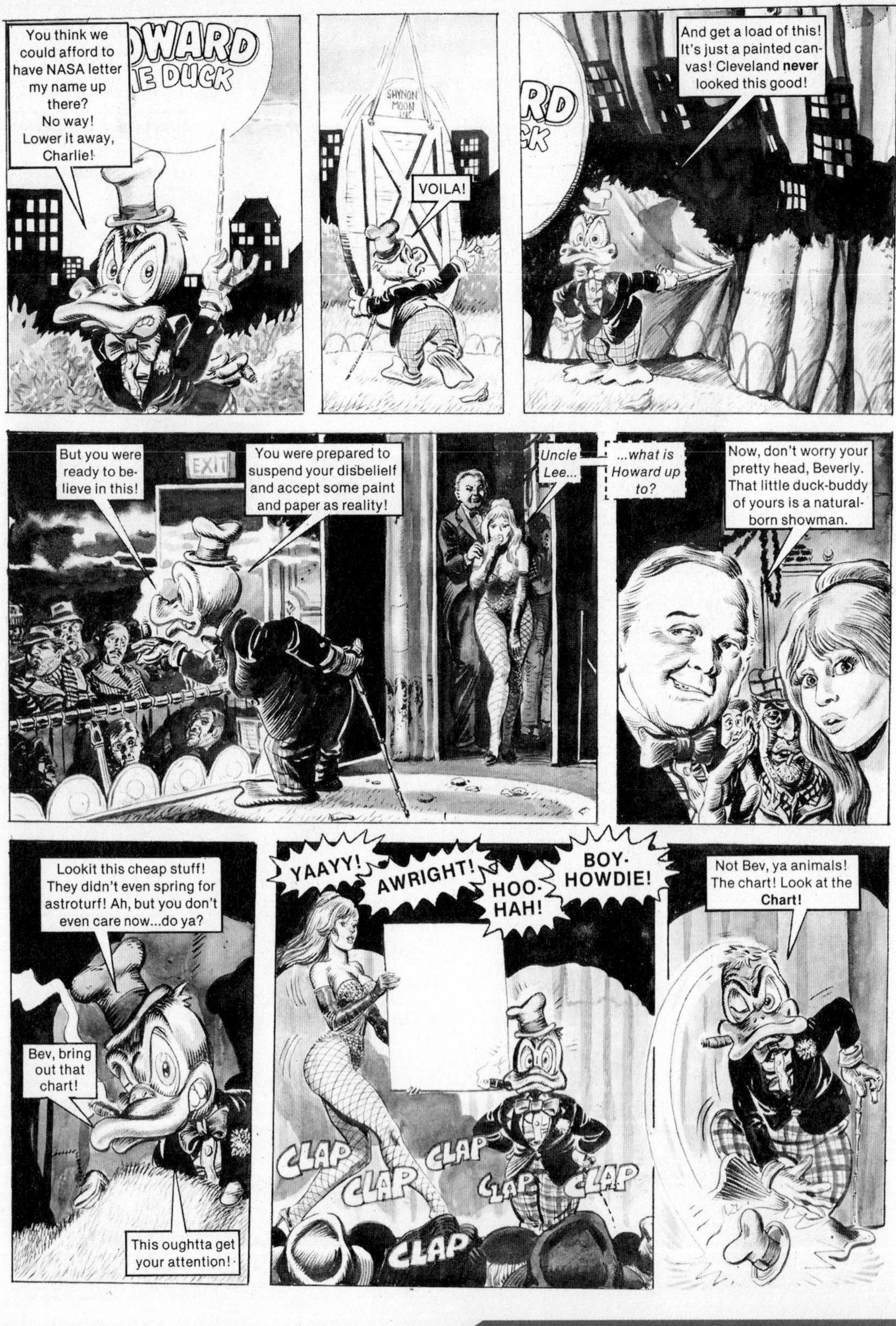

You think we could afford to have NASA letter my name up there? No way! Lower it away, Charlie!
HOWARD THE DUCK
SHYNON MOON INC.
VOILA!
And get a load of this! It's just a painted canvas! Cleveland **never** looked this good!
EXIT
But you were ready to believe in this!
You were prepared to suspend your disbelief and accept some paint and paper as reality!
Uncle Lee...
...what is Howard up to?
Now, don't worry your pretty head, Beverly. That little duck-buddy of yours is a natural-born showman.
Lookit this cheap stuff! They didn't even spring for astroturf! Ah, but you don't even care now...do ya?
Bev, bring out that chart!
This oughtta get your attention!
YAAYY!
AWRIGHT!
HOO-HAH!
BOY-HOWDIE!
CLAP CLAP CLAP CLAP CLAP CLAP
Not Bev, ya animals! The chart! Look at the **Chart!**

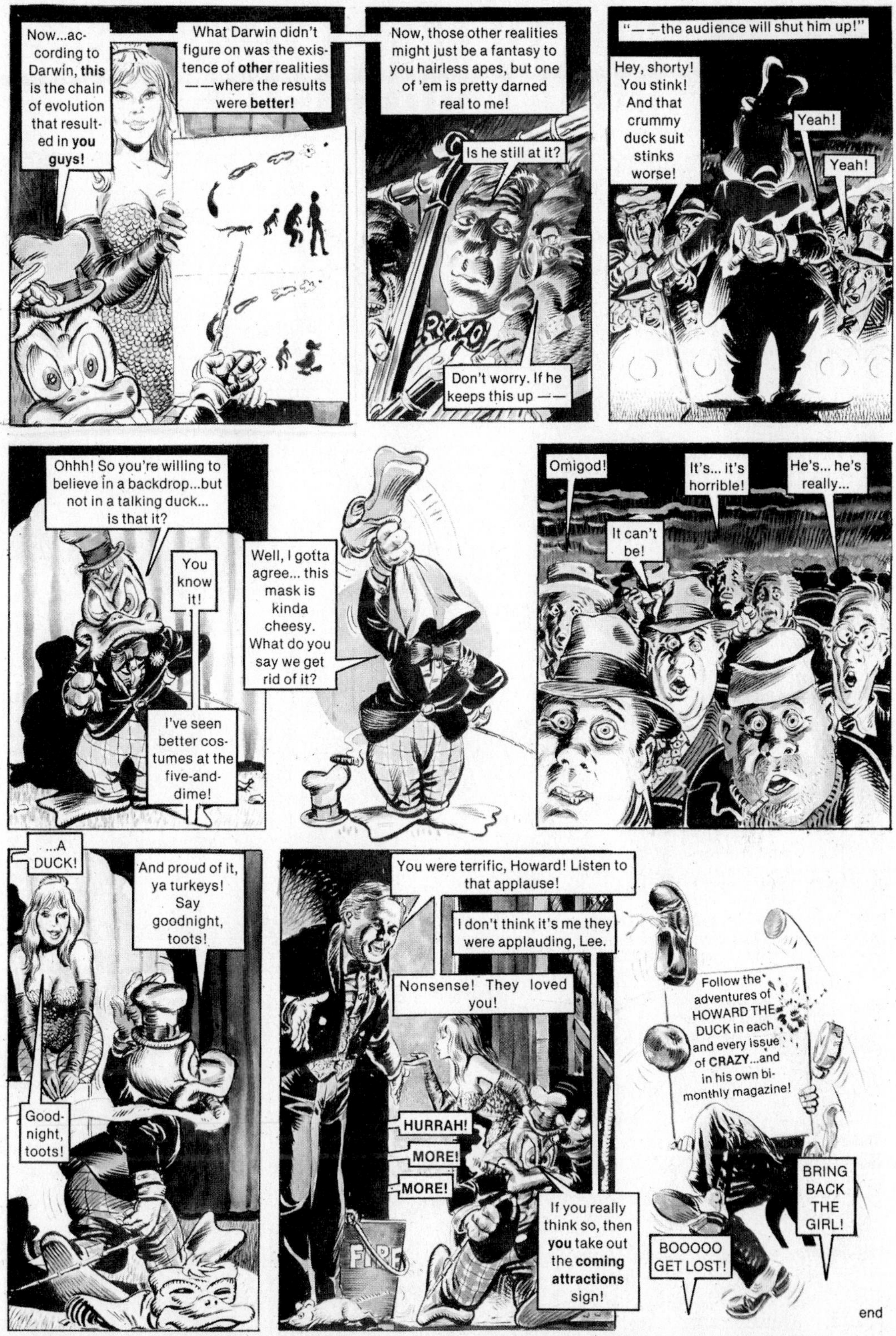

Now...according to Darwin, **this** is the chain of evolution that resulted in **you guys!**
What Darwin didn't figure on was the existence of **other** realities ——where the results were **better!**
Now, those other realities might just be a fantasy to you hairless apes, but one of 'em is pretty darned real to me!
Is he still at it?
Don't worry. If he keeps this up ——
"——the audience will shut him up!"
Hey, shorty! You stink! And that crummy duck suit stinks worse!
Yeah!
Yeah!
Ohhh! So you're willing to believe in a backdrop...but not in a talking duck... is that it?
You know it!
I've seen better costumes at the five-and-dime!
Well, I gotta agree... this mask is kinda cheesy. What do you say we get rid of it?
Omigod!
It's... it's horrible!
He's... he's really...
It can't be!
...A DUCK!
And proud of it, ya turkeys! Say goodnight, toots!
Good-night, toots!
You were terrific, Howard! Listen to that applause!
I don't think it's me they were applauding, Lee.
Nonsense! They loved you!
HURRAH!
MORE!
MORE!
If you really think so, then **you** take out the **coming attractions** sign!
FIRE
Follow the adventures of HOWARD THE DUCK in each and every issue of **CRAZY**...and in his own bi-monthly magazine!
BRING BACK THE GIRL!
BOOOOO GET LOST!
end

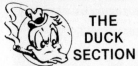

Crazy Magazine #65, August 1980

THE DUCK SECTION

CRAZY MAGAZINE

SATIRE
PARODY
SPACE-FILLER

Writer: Roger Stern Artists: Pat Broderick and Armando Gil

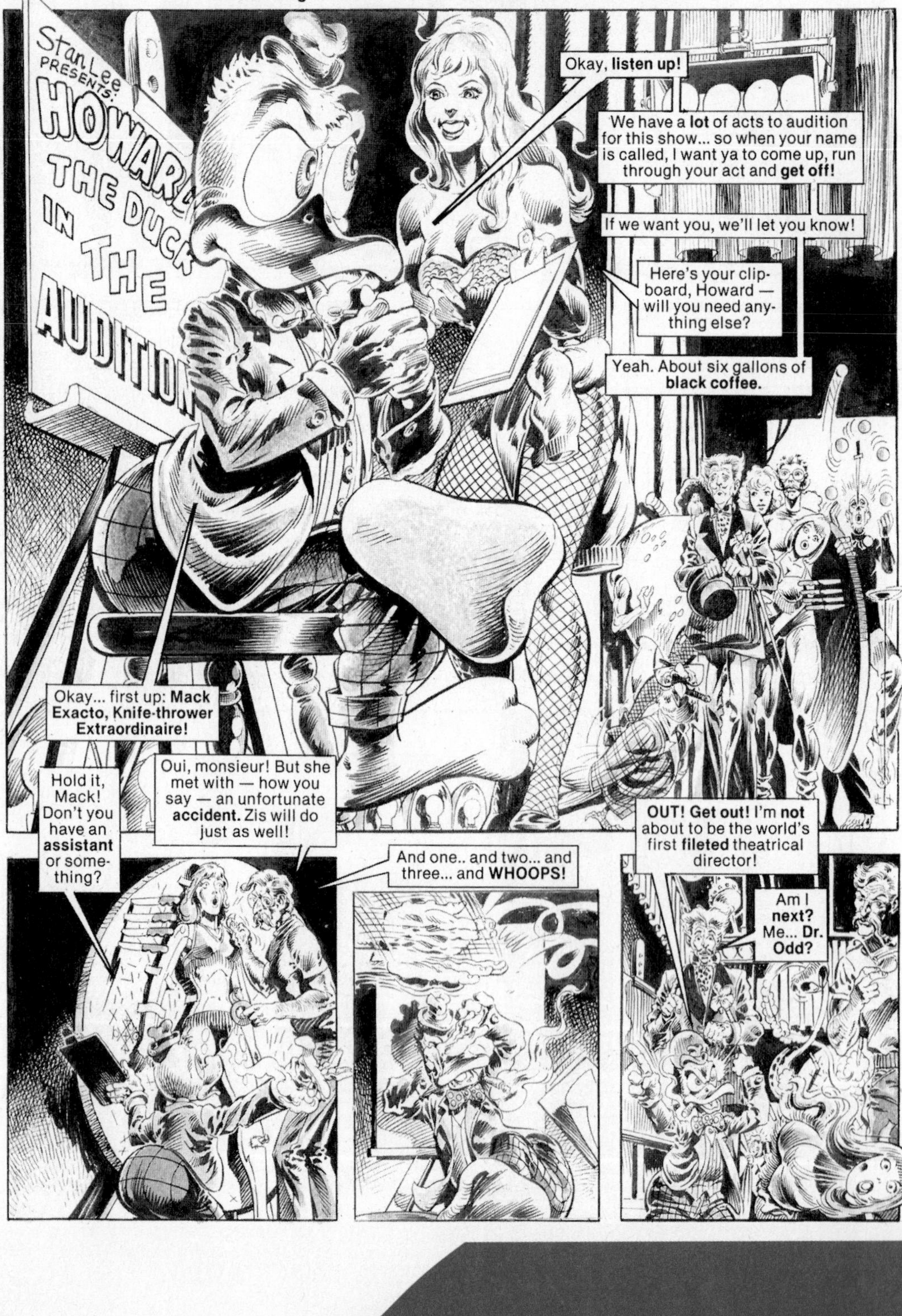

Stan Lee PRESENTS:
HOWARD THE DUCK IN THE AUDITION
Okay, listen up!
We have a lot of acts to audition for this show... so when your name is called, I want ya to come up, run through your act and get off!
If we want you, we'll let you know!
Here's your clip-board, Howard — will you need any-thing else?
Yeah. About six gallons of black coffee.
Okay... first up: Mack Exacto, Knife-thrower Extraordinaire!
Hold it, Mack! Don't you have an assistant or some-thing?
Oui, monsieur! But she met with — how you say — an unfortunate accident. Zis will do just as well!
And one.. and two... and three... and WHOOPS!
OUT! Get out! I'm not about to be the world's first fileted theatrical director!
Am I next? Me... Dr. Odd?

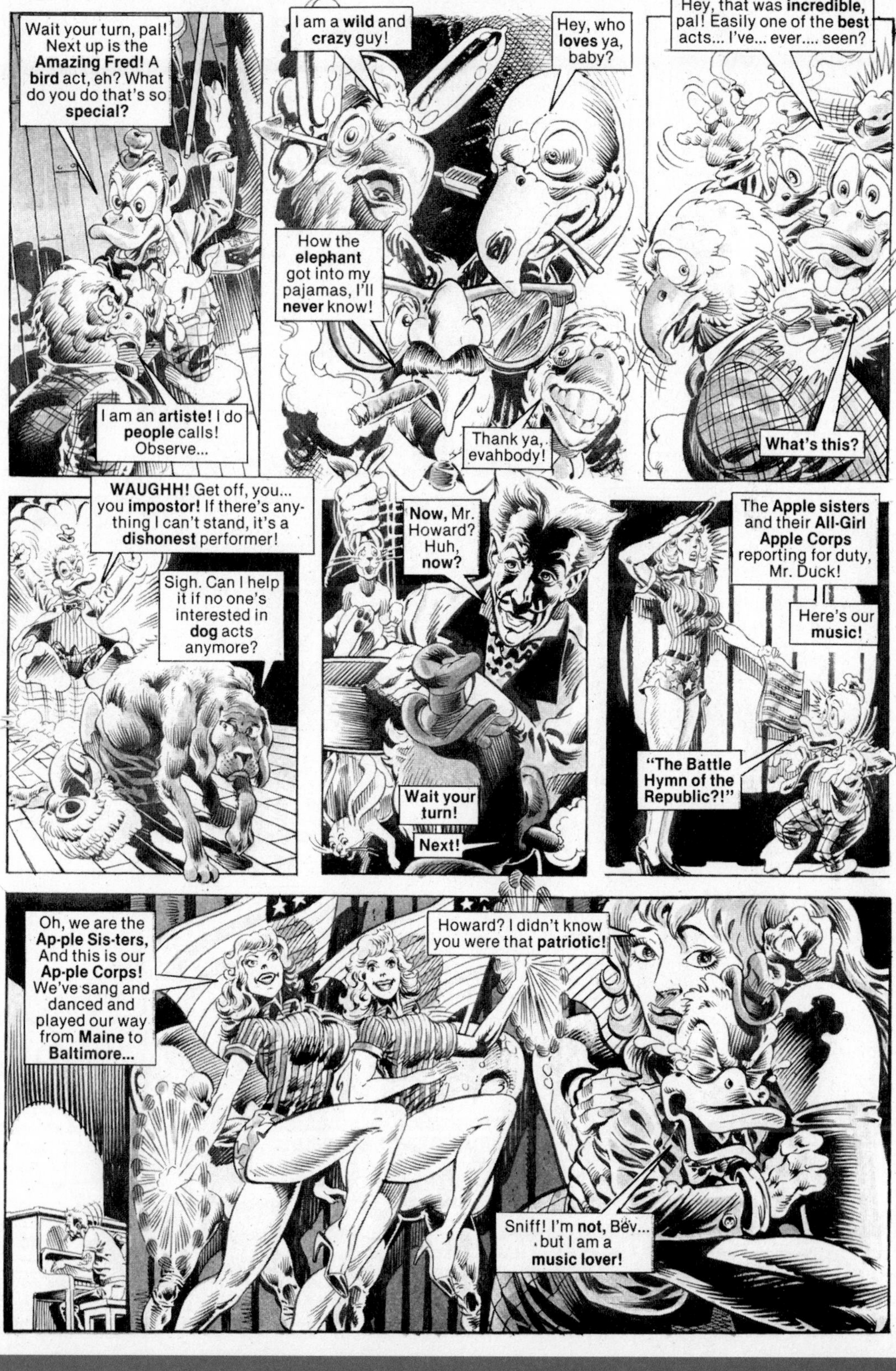
Wait your turn, pal! Next up is the Amazing Fred! A bird act, eh? What do you do that's so special?
I am an artiste! I do people calls! Observe...
I am a wild and crazy guy!
Hey, who loves ya, baby?
How the elephant got into my pajamas, I'll never know!
Thank ya, evahbody!
Hey, that was incredible, pal! Easily one of the best acts... I've... ever.... seen?
What's this?
WAUGHH! Get off, you... you impostor! If there's anything I can't stand, it's a dishonest performer!
Sigh. Can I help it if no one's interested in dog acts anymore?
Now, Mr. Howard? Huh, now?
Wait your turn!
Next!
The Apple sisters and their All-Girl Apple Corps reporting for duty, Mr. Duck!
Here's our music!
"The Battle Hymn of the Republic?!"
Oh, we are the Ap-ple Sis-ters, And this is our Ap-ple Corps! We've sang and danced and played our way from Maine to Baltimore...
Howard? I didn't know you were that patriotic!
Sniff! I'm not, Bev... but I am a music lover!

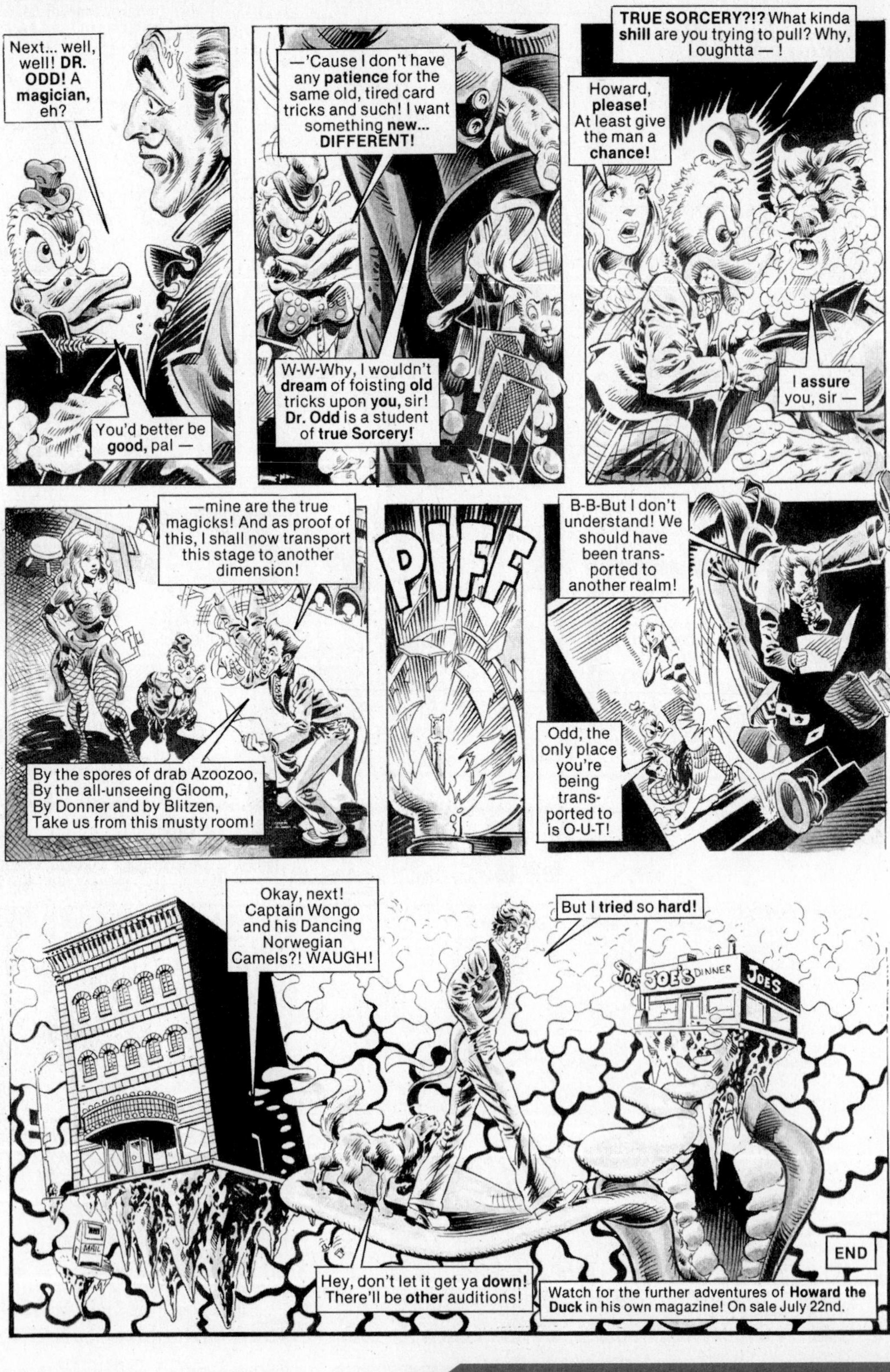

Next... well, well! DR. ODD! A magician, eh?
You'd better be good, pal —
—'Cause I don't have any patience for the same old, tired card tricks and such! I want something new... DIFFERENT!
W-W-Why, I wouldn't dream of foisting old tricks upon you, sir! Dr. Odd is a student of true Sorcery!
TRUE SORCERY?!? What kinda shill are you trying to pull? Why, I oughtta — !
Howard, please! At least give the man a chance!
I assure you, sir —
—mine are the true magicks! And as proof of this, I shall now transport this stage to another dimension!
By the spores of drab Azoozoo,
By the all-unseeing Gloom,
By Donner and by Blitzen,
Take us from this musty room!
PIFF
B-B-But I don't understand! We should have been transported to another realm!
Odd, the only place you're being transported to is O-U-T!
Okay, next! Captain Wongo and his Dancing Norwegian Camels?! WAUGH!
But I tried so hard!
JOE'S
JOE'S DINNER
JOE'S
MAIL
Hey, don't let it get ya down! There'll be other auditions!
END
Watch for the further adventures of Howard the Duck in his own magazine! On sale July 22nd.

WANTED! FOR EXCITEMENT, ACTION, THRILLS AND LAUGHS!

SPECIAL OFFER TO ALL WHO JOIN US FOR THE FIRST TIME IN 1980!

Subscribe before December 31, 1980, and save up to 36% on your yearly subscription! It's *practically a steal!*

Title	#of Issues	Special Rate	Regular Sub Rate	Savings
☐ Crazy	12	$6.99	$11.00	36%
☐ Howard the Duck	12	$9.75	$15.00	35%
☐ Marvel Preview	4	$3.50	$4.50	22%
☐ Savage Sword of Conan	12	$9.75	$15.00	35%
☐ The Hulk	6	$6.95	$9.50	27%
☐ Tomb of Dracula	12	$9.75	$15.00	35%

The more you order, the more you SAVE!

Check your selection on the Left: **BW-380**

Name________________ **Age**_____
(Please Print)

Address________________

City__________ State__________ Zip_____

Allow 10 weeks for delivery

Please send checks payable to Marvel Comics

Canada: Add $1.00 per year per title.
Foreign: Add $2.00 per year per title.

I enclose a total of $________________
Offer ends Dec. 31st, 1980.

Spring 1980 subscription ads

MARVEL MAGAZINES'LL GRAB YA!

YES! I WANT TO BE GRABBED!

MARVEL MAGAZINE GROUP, Subscription Dept.
575 MADISON AVENUE, NEW YORK, N.Y. 10022

SPECIAL OFFER TO ALL WHO JOIN US FOR THE 1st TIME IN 1980!

Subscribe to titles listed below before Dec. 31, 1980 and save up to 36% on your yearly subscription.

TITLE	# OF ISSUES	SPECIAL RATE	REGULAR SUB RATE	SAVINGS
☐ CRAZY	12	$6.99	$11.00	36%
☐ HOWARD THE DUCK	12	9.75	15.00	35%
☐ MARVEL PREVIEW	4	3.50	4.50	22%
☐ SAVAGE SWORD OF CONAN	12	9.75	15.00	35%
☐ THE HULK	6	6.95	9.50	27%
☐ TOMB OF DRACULA	12	9.75	15.00	35%

The more you order, the more you SAVE!

Check your selection above:

Name ________________
(Please Print)

Address________________

City__________ State__________ Zip__________

Allow 10 weeks for delivery. Please send checks payable to Marvel Comics.

Canada: Add $1.00 per year, per title.
Foreign: Add $2.00 per year, per title.

I enclose a total of $__________ Offer ends Dec. 31st, 1980.

30

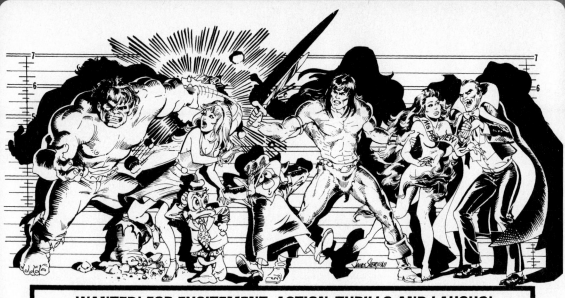

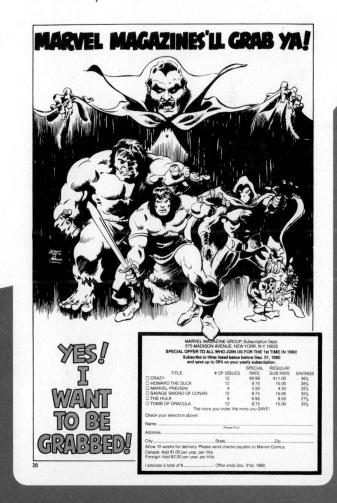

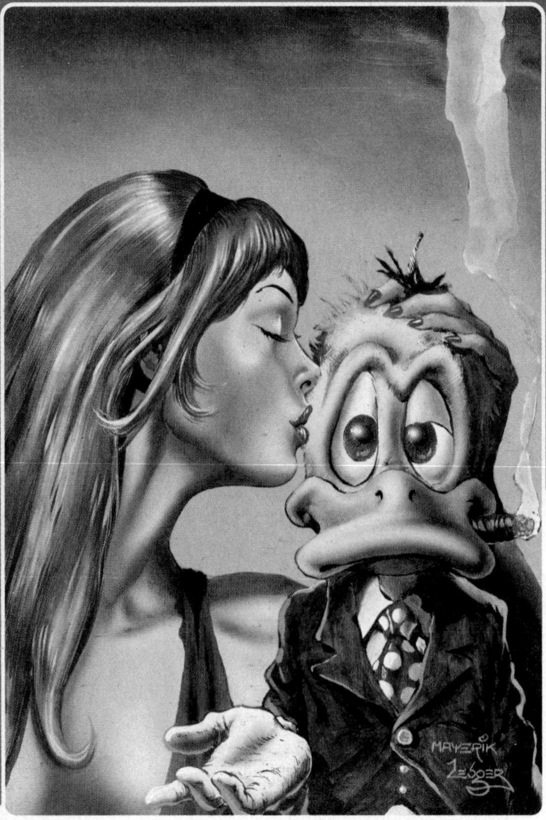
MAYERIK
LEDGER

Howard the Duck Magazine #2 cover art by Val Mayerik & Peter Ledger

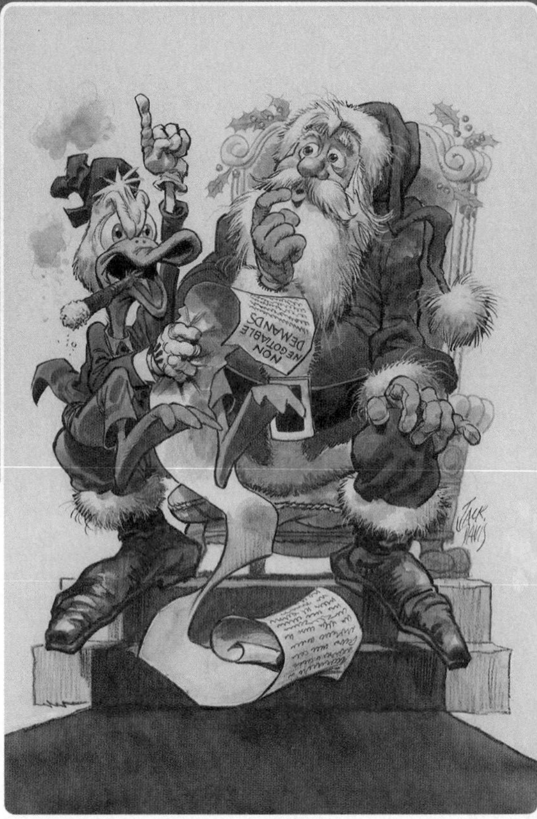
NON NEGOTIABLE DEMANDS
JACK DAVIS

Howard the Duck Magazine #3 cover art by Jack Davis

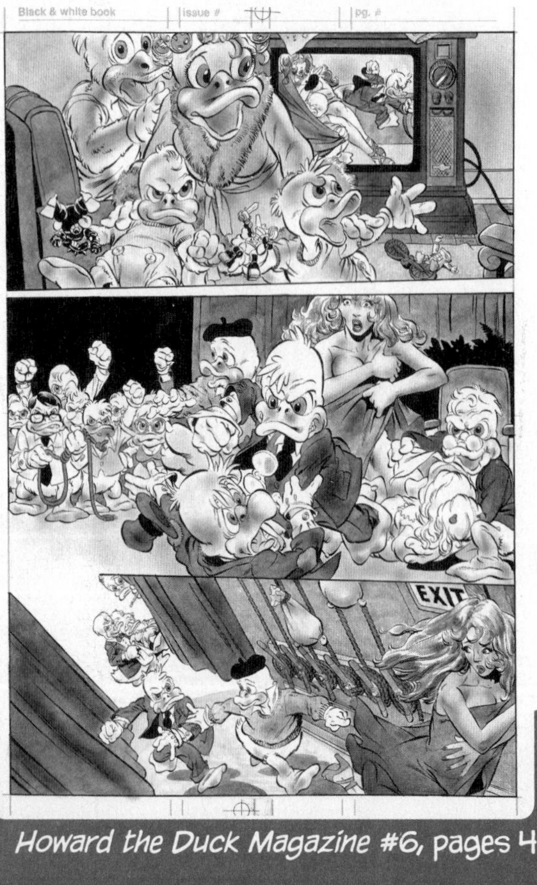
Black & white book
issue #
pg. #
EXIT

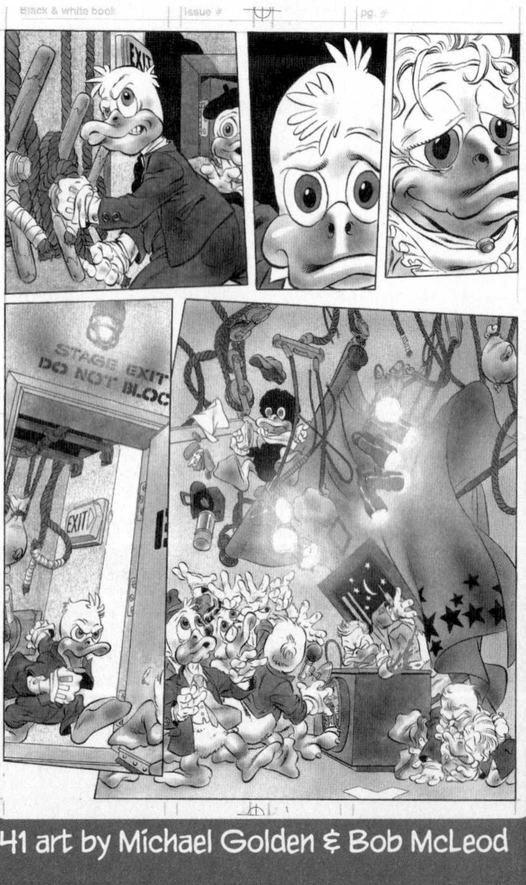
Black & white book
issue #
pg. #
EXIT
STAGE EXIT
DO NOT BLOC
EXIT

Howard the Duck Magazine #6, pages 40-41 art by Michael Golden & Bob McLeod

Images courtesy of HeritageAuctions.com